Financial Aid
for African Americans
2017-2019

Gail Ann Schlachter
R. David Weber

A Listing of Scholarships, Fellowships, Grants, Awards, and
Other Sources of Free Money Available Primarily or
Exclusively to African Americans, Plus a Set of Six Indexes
(Program Title, Sponsoring Organization, Residency,
Tenability, Subject, and Deadline Date)

R

AdmitHub
Boston, Massachusetts

AdmitHub
Harvard Innovation Launch Lab
114 Western Ave.
Boston, MA 02134
 (617) 575-9369
  E-mail: rsp@admithub.com
Visit our web site: www.admithub.com

Manufactured in the United States of America

Contents

Foreword

About Dr. Gail Schlachter and Reference Service Press

Dr. Gail Ann Schlachter (1943-2015), original founder of Reference Service Press, was working as a librarian in the mid-1970s when she recognized that women applying for college faced significant obstacles finding information about financial aid resources designed to help them. This challenge inspired her to publish her ground-breaking book, Directory of Financial Aids for Women, in 1977. The book's success prompted additional financial aid directories for other underserved communities, including the present volume for African Americans.

By 1985, the business had become so successful that she left her job as a publishing company executive to run her company, Reference Service Press, full-time. Over the years, the company's offerings expanded to over two dozen financial aid titles covering many different types of students—law students, business students, students studying abroad, and many more. The company's success was driven by its database of tens of thousands of financial aid programs, laboriously hand-built over the decades and kept current to exacting specifications. In 1995, Reference Service Press once again broke new ground by launching one of the first-ever searchable electronic databases of financial aid resources (initially through America Online). For more background about the founding and success of Reference Service Press, see Katina Strauch's 1997 "Against the Grain" interview with Dr. Schlachter, available at http://docs.lib.purdue.edu/cgi/viewcontent.cgi?article=2216&context=atg.

Dr. Schlachter was also a major figure in the library community for nearly five decades. She served: as reference book review editor for RQ (now Reference and User Services Quarterly) for 10 years; as president of the American Library Association's Reference and User Services Association; as editor of the Reference and User Services Association Quarterly; seven terms on the American Library Association's governing council; and as a member of the association's Executive Board at the time of her death. She was posthumously inducted into the California Library Association Hall of Fame. The University of Wisconsin School of Library and Information Studies named Dr. Schlachter an "Alumna of the Year," and she was recognized with both the Isadore Gilbert Mudge Citation and the Louis Shores/Oryx Press Award.

Dr. Schlachter will be remembered for how her financial aid directories helped thousands of students achieve their educational and professional dreams. She also will be remembered for her countless contributions to the library profession. And, as an American Library Association Executive Board resolution from June 2015 says, she will be remembered, "most importantly, for her mentorship, friendship, and infectious smile." Yet, despite her impressive lifetime of professional accomplishments, Dr. Schlachter always was most proud of her family, including her husband Stuart Hauser, her daughter Dr. Sandy Hirsh (and Jay Hirsh) and son Eric Goldman (and Lisa Goldman), and her grandchildren Hayley, Leah, Jacob, and Dina.

Introduction

WHY THIS DIRECTORY IS NEEDED

Despite our country's ongoing economic problems and increased college costs, the financial aid picture for minorities has never looked brighter. Currently, billions of dollars are set aside each year specifically for African Americans, Asian Americans, Hispanic Americans, and Native Americans. This funding is open to minorities at any level (high school through postdoctoral and professional) for a variety of activities, including study, research, travel, training, career development, and creative projects.

While numerous print and online listings have been prepared to identify and describe general financial aid opportunities (those open to all segments of society), those resources have never covered more than a small portion of the programs designed primarily or exclusively for minorities. As a result, many advisors, librarians, scholars, researchers, and students often have been unaware of the extensive funding available to African Americans and other minorities. But, with the ongoing publication of *Financial Aid for African Americans,* that has all changed. Here, in just one place, African American students, professionals, and postdoctorates now have current and detailed information about the special resources set aside specifically for them.

Financial Aid for African Americans is prepared biennially as part of Reference Service Press' four-volume *Minority Funding Set* (the other volumes in the set cover funding for Asian Americans, Hispanic Americans, and Native Americans). Each of the volumes in this set is sold separately, or the complete set can be purchased at a discounted price.

No other source, in print or online, comes anywhere close to matching the extensive coverage of funding for minorities provided by these titles. That's why the Grantsmanship Center labeled the set "a must for every organization serving minorities," *Reference Sources for Small and Medium-Sized Libraries* called the titles "the absolute best guides for finding funding," and *Reference Books Bulletin* selected each of the volumes in the *Minority Funding Set* as their "Editor's Choice." *Financial Aid for African Americans,* itself, has also received rave reviews. *Off to College* rated it as "the top of all books of this sort," About.com selected it as one of the seven "Top Financial Aid and Scholarship Guides," and *EMIE Bulletin* called it "the only comprehensive and current listing of programs for this group." Perhaps *Multicultural Review* sums up the critical reaction best: "nothing short of superb."

WHAT'S UPDATED?

The preparation of each new edition of *Financial Aid for African Americans* involves extensive updating and revision. To make sure that the information included here is both reliable and current, the editors at Reference Service Press 1) reviewed and updated all relevant programs covered in the previous edition of the directory, 2) collected information on all programs open to African Americans that were added to Reference Service Press' funding database since the last edition of the directory, and then 3) searched extensively for new program leads in a variety of sources, including printed directories, news reports, journals, newsletters, house organs, annual reports, and sites on the Internet. We only include program descriptions that are written directly from information supplied by the sponsoring organization in print or online (no information is ever taken from secondary sources). When that information could not be found, we sent up to four data collection letters (followed by up to three telephone or e-mail inquiries, if necessary) to those sponsors. Despite our best efforts, however, some sponsoring organizations still failed to respond and, as a result, their programs are not included in this edition of the directory.

The 2017-2019 edition of *Financial Aid for African Americans* completely revises and updates the previous (eighth) edition. Programs that have ceased operations have been dropped from the listing. Similarly, programs that have broadened their scope and no longer focus on African Americans have also been removed from the directory. Profiles of continuing programs have been rewritten to reflect current requirements; nearly 80 percent of the continuing programs reported substantive changes in their locations, requirements (particularly application deadline), benefits, or eligibility requirements since the 2014-2016 edition. In addition, hundreds of new entries have been added to the program section of the directory. The resulting listing describes the more than 1,300 biggest and best sources of free money available to African Americans, including scholarships, fellowships, grants, awards, and other funding opportunities.

WHAT MAKES THIS DIRECTORY UNIQUE?

The 2017-2019 edition of *Financial Aid for African Americans* identifies billions of dollars available for study, research, creative activities, past accomplishments, future projects, professional development, and many other activities. The listings cover every major subject area, are sponsored by more than 900 different private and public agencies and organizations, and are open to African Americans at any level, from college-bound high school students through professionals and postdoctorates.

Not only does *Financial Aid for African Americans* provide the most comprehensive coverage of available funding (1,377 entries), but it also displays the most informative program descriptions (on the average, more than twice the detail found in any other listing). In addition to this extensive and focused coverage, *Financial Aid for African Americans* also offers several other unique features. First of all, hundreds of funding opportunities listed here have never been covered in any other source. So, even if you have checked elsewhere, you will want to look at *Financial Aid for African Americans* for additional leads. And, here's another plus: all of the funding programs in this edition of the directory offer "free" money; not one of the programs will ever require you to pay anything back (provided, of course, that you meet the program requirements).

Further, unlike other funding directories, which generally follow a straight alphabetical arrangement, *Financial Aid for African Americans* groups entries by intended recipients (undergraduates, graduate students, or professionals/postdoctorates), to make it easy for you to search for appropriate programs. This same convenience is offered in the indexes, where title, sponsoring organization, geographic, subject, and deadline date entries are each subdivided by recipient group.

Finally, we have tried to anticipate all the ways you might wish to search for funding. The volume is organized so you can identify programs not only by intended recipient, but by subject focus, sponsoring organization, program title, residency requirements, where the money can be spent, and even deadline date. Plus, we've included all the information you'll need to decide if a program is right for you: purpose, eligibility requirements, financial data, duration, special features, limitations, number awarded, and application date. You even get fax numbers, toll-free numbers, e-mail addresses, and web sites (when available), along with complete contact information.

WHAT'S EXCLUDED?

While this book is intended to be the most comprehensive source of information on funding available to African Americans, there are some programs we've specifically excluded from the directory:

- *Programs that do not accept applications from U.S. citizens or residents.* If a program is open only to foreign nationals or excludes Americans from applying, it is not covered.

- *Programs that are open equally to all segments of the population.* Only funding opportunities set aside primarily or exclusively for African Americans are included here.

- *Money for study or research outside the United States.* Since there are comprehensive and up-to-date directories that describe the available funding for study, research, and other activities abroad, only programs that fund activities in the United States are covered here.

- *Very restrictive programs.* In general, programs are excluded if they are open only to a limited geographic area (less than a state) or offer limited financial support (less than $1,000). Note, however, that the vast majority of programs included here go way beyond that, paying up to full tuition or stipends that exceed $25,000 a year!

- *Programs administered by individual academic institutions solely for their own students.* The directory identifies "portable" programs—ones that can be used at any number of schools. Financial aid administered by individual schools specifically for their own students is not covered. Write directly to the schools you are considering to get information on their offerings.

- *Scholarships offered by individual law firms.* Many law firms attempt to promote diversity by offering scholarships to African American and other underrepresented students, but usually tie the stipend to employment at the firm.

- *Money that must be repaid.* Only "free money" is identified here. If a program requires repayment or charges interest, it's not listed. Now you can find out about billions of dollars in aid and know (if you meet the program requirements) that not one dollar of that will ever need to be repaid.

HOW THE DIRECTORY IS ORGANIZED

Financial Aid for African Americans is divided into two sections: 1) a detailed list of funding opportunities open to African Americans and 2) a set of six indexes to help you pinpoint appropriate funding programs.

Financial Aid Programs Open to African Americans. The first section of the directory describes 1,377 sources of free money available to African Americans. The focus is on financial aid aimed at American citizens or residents to support study, research, or other activities in the United States. The programs listed here are sponsored by more than 900 different government agencies, professional organizations, corporations, sororities and fraternities, foundations, religious groups, educational associations, and military/veterans organizations. All areas of the sciences, social sciences, and humanities are covered.

To help you focus your search, the entries in this section are grouped into the following three chapters:

- **Undergraduates:** Included here are more than 700 scholarships, grants, awards, and other sources of free money that support undergraduate study, research, or creative activities. These programs are open to high school seniors, high school graduates, currently-enrolled college students, and students returning to college after an absence. Money is available to support these students in any type of public or private postsecondary institution, ranging from technical schools and community colleges to major universities in the United States.

- **Graduate Students:** Described here are nearly more than 500 fellowships, grants, awards, and other sources of free money that support post-baccalaureate study, training, research, and creative activities. These programs are open to students applying to, currently enrolled in, or returning to a master's, doctoral, professional, or specialist program in public or private graduate schools in the United States.

- **Professionals/Postdoctorates:** Included here are more than 150 funding programs for U.S. citizens or residents who 1) are in professional positions (e.g., artists, writers), whether or not they have an advanced degree; 2) are master's or professional degree recipients; 3) have earned a doctoral degree or its equivalent (e.g., Ph.D., Ed.D., M.D.); or 4) have recognized stature as established scientists, scholars, academicians, or researchers.

Within each of these three chapters, entries appear alphabetically by program title. Since some of the programs supply assistance to more than one specific group, those are listed in all relevant chapters. For example, the Agnes Jones Jackson Scholarships support both undergraduate or graduate study, so the program is described in both the Undergraduates *and* Graduate Students chapters.

Each program entry has been designed to give you a concise profile that, as the sample on page 7 illustrates, includes information (when available) on organization address and telephone numbers (including toll-free and fax numbers), e-mail address and web site, purpose, eligibility, money awarded, duration, special features, limitations, number of awards, and application deadline.

The information reported for each of the programs in this section was gathered from research conducted through the middle of 2017. While the listing is intended to cover as comprehensively as possible the biggest and best sources of free money available to African Americans, some sponsoring organizations did not post information online or respond to our research inquiries and, consequently, are not included in this edition of the directory.

Indexes. To help you find the aid you need, we have constructed six indexes; these will let you access the listings by program title, sponsoring organization, residency, tenability, subject focus, and deadline date. These indexes use a word-by-word alphabetical arrangement. Note: numbers in the index refer to entry numbers, not to page numbers in the book.

Program Title Index. If you know the name of a particular funding program and want to find out where it is covered in the directory, use the Program Title Index. To assist you in your search, every program is listed by all its known names, former names, and abbreviations. Since one program can be included in more than one place (e.g., a program providing assistance to both undergraduate and graduate students is described in both the first and second chapters), each entry number in the index has been coded to indicate the intended recipient group (for example, "U" = Undergraduates; "G" = Graduate Students). By using this coding system, you can avoid duplicate entries and turn directly to the programs that match your eligibility characteristics.

Sponsoring Organization Index. This index makes it easy to identify agencies that offer funding primarily or exclusively to African Americans. More than 900 organizations are indexed here. As in the Program Title Index, we've used a code to help you determine which organizations sponsor programs that match your educational level.

Residency Index. Some programs listed in this book are restricted to African Americans in a particular state or region. Others are open to African Americans wherever they live. This index helps you identify programs available only to residents in your area as well as programs that have no residency requirements. Further, to assist you in your search, we've also indicated the recipient level for the funding offered to residents in each of the areas listed in the index.

Tenability Index. This index identifies the geographic locations where the funding described in *Financial Aid for African Americans* may be used. Index entries (city, county, state, region) are arranged alphabetically (word by word) and subdivided by recipient group. Use this index when you are looking for money to support your activities in a particular geographic area.

Subject Index. This index allows you to identify the subject focus of each of the financial aid opportunities described in *Financial Aid for African Americans*. More than 250 different subject terms are listed. Extensive "see" and "see also" references, as well as recipient group subdivisions, will help you locate appropriate funding opportunities.

Calendar Index. Since most financial aid programs have specific deadline dates, some may have closed by the time you begin to look for funding. You can use the Calendar Index to determine which programs are still open. This index is arranged by recipient group (Undergraduates, Graduate

Students, and Professionals/Postdoctorates) and subdivided by the month during which the deadline falls. Filing dates can and quite often do vary from year to year; consequently, this index should be used only as a guide for deadlines beyond 2016.

HOW TO USE THE DIRECTORY

Here are some tips to help you get the most out of the funding opportunities listed in *Financial Aid for African Americans.*

To Locate Funding by Recipient Group.   To bring together programs with a similar educational focus, this directory is divided into three chapters: Undergraduates, Graduate Students, and Professionals/Postdoctorates. If you want to get an overall picture of the sources of free money available to African Americans in any of these categories, turn to the appropriate chapter and then review the entries there. Since each of these chapters functions as a self-contained entity, you can browse through any of them without having to first consulting an index.

To Find Information on a Particular Financial Aid Program.   If you know the name of a particular financial aid program, and the group eligible for that award, then go directly to the appropriate chapter in the directory (e.g., Undergraduates, Graduate Students), where you will find the program profiles arranged alphabetically by title. To save time, though, you should always check the Program Title Index first if you know the name of a specific award but are not sure in which chapter it has been listed. Plus, since we index each program by all its known names and abbreviations, you'll also be able to track down a program there when you may not know its exact official title.

To Locate Programs Sponsored by a Particular Organization.   The Sponsoring Organization Index makes it easy to identify agencies that provide financial assistance to African Americans or to identify specific financial aid programs offered by a particular organization. Each entry number in the index is coded to identify recipient group (Undergraduates, Graduate Students, Professionals/Postdoctorates), so that you can quickly target appropriate entries.

To Browse Quickly Through the Listings.   Look at the listings in the chapter that covers the educational level of interest to you (Undergraduates, Graduate Students, or Professionals/Postdoctorates) and read the "Summary" paragraph in each entry. In seconds, you'll know if this is an opportunity that you might want to pursue. If it is, be sure to read the rest of the information in the entry, to make sure you meet all of the program requirements before writing or going online for an application form. Please, save your time and energy. Don't apply if you don't qualify!

To Locate Funding Available to African Americans from or Tenable in a Particular City, County, or State.   The Residency Index identifies financial aid programs open to African Americans in a specific state, region, etc. The Tenability Index shows where the money can be spent. In both indexes, "see" and "see also" references are used liberally, and index entries for a particular geographic area are subdivided by recipient group (Undergraduates, Graduate Students, and Professional/Postdoctorates) to help you identify the funding that's right for you. When using these indexes, always check the listings under the term "United States," since the programs indexed there have no geographic restrictions and can be used in any area.

To Locate Financial Aid Programs Open to African Americans in a Particular Subject Area.   Turn to the Subject Index first if you are interested in identifying funding programs for African Americans that are focused on a particular subject area. To make your search easier, the intended recipient groups (Undergraduates, Graduate Students, Professionals/Postdoctorates) are clearly labeled in the more than 250 subject listings. Extensive cross-references are also provided. Since a large number of programs are not restricted by subject, be sure to check the references listed under the "General programs" heading in the index, in addition to the specific terms that directly relate to your interest areas. The listings under "General programs" can be used to fund activities in any subject area (although the programs may be restricted in other ways).

To Locate Financial Aid Programs for African Americans by Deadline Date.   If you are working with specific time constraints and want to weed out the financial aid programs whose filing dates you won't be able to meet, turn first to the Calendar Index and check the program references listed under the appropriate recipient group and month. Note: not all sponsoring organizations supplied deadline information; those programs are listed under the "Deadline not specified" entries in the index. To identify every relevant financial aid program, regardless of filing date, go the appropriate chapter and read through all the entries there that match your educational level.

To Locate Financial Aid Programs Open to All Segments of the Population. Only programs available to African Americans are listed in this publication. However, there are thousands of other programs that are open equally to all segments of the population. To identify these programs, talk to your local librarian, check with your financial aid office on campus, look at the list of RSP print resources on the page opposite the title page in this directory, or see if your library subscribes to Reference Service Press' interactive online funding database: *RSP FundingFinder.* For more information on that award-winning resource, go online to: www.rspfunding.com/esubscriptions.html.

PLANS TO UPDATE THE DIRECTORY

This volume, covering 2017-2019, is the ninth edition of *Financial Aid for African Americans.* The next biennial edition will cover the years 2019-2021 and will be issued by the beginning of 2019.

ACKNOWLEDGEMENTS

A debt of gratitude is owed all the organizations that contributed information to the 2017-2017 edition of *Financial Aid for African Americans.* Their generous cooperation has helped to make this publication a current and comprehensive survey of awards.

SAMPLE ENTRY

(1) **[490]**

(2) **AFRICAN AMERICAN FUTURE ACHIEVERS SCHOLARSHIP PROGRAM**

(3) Ronald McDonald House Charities
Attn: U.S. Scholarship Program
One Kroc Drive
Oak Brook, IL 60523
(630) 623-7048
Fax: (630) 623-7488
E-mail: info@rmhc.org
Web: www.rmhc.org/rmhc-us-scholarships

(4) **Summary** To provide financial assistance for college to African American high school seniors in specified geographic areas.

(5) **Eligibility** This program is open to high school seniors in designated McDonald's market areas who are legal residents of the United States and have at least 1 parent of African American or Black Caribbean heritage. Applicants must be planning to enroll full time at an accredited 2- or 4-year college, university, or vocational/technical school. They must have a GPA of 2.7 or higher. Along with their application, they must submit a personal statement, up to 2 pages in length, on their African American or Black Caribbean background, career goals, and desire to contribute to their community; information about unique, personal, or financial circumstances may be added. Selection is based on that statement, high school transcripts with GPA and standardized test scores, a letter of recommendation, and financial need.

(6) **Financial data** Stipends are determined by participating McDonald's areas, but most are $1,000 per year. Funds are paid directly to the recipient's school.

(7) **Duration** 1 year; nonrenewable.

(8) **Additional Information** This program is a component of the Ronald McDonald House Charities U.S. Scholarship Program, which began in 1985. It is administered by International Scholarship and Tuition Services, Inc. For a list of participating McDonald's market areas, contact Ronald McDonald House Charities (RMHC).

(9) **Number awarded** Varies each year; since RMHC began this program, it has awarded more than $60 million in scholarships

(10) **Deadline** January of each year.

DEFINITION

(1) **Entry number:** The consecutive number that is given to each entry and used to identify the entry in the index.

(2) **Program title:** Title of scholarship, fellowship, grant, award, or other source of free money described in the directory.

(3) **Sponsoring organization:** Name, address, and telephone number, toll-free number, fax number, e-mail address, and/or web site (when information was available) for organization sponsoring the program.

(4) **Summary:** Identifies the major program requirements; read the rest of the entry for additional detail.

(5) **Eligibility:** Qualifications required of applicants, plus information on application procedure and selection process.

(6) **Financial data:** Financial details of the program, including fixed sum, average amount, or range of funds offered, expenses for which funds may and may not be applied, and cash-related benefits supplied (e.g., room and board).

(7) **Duration:** Period for which support is provided; renewal prospects.

(8) **Additional information:** Any unusual (generally nonmonetary) benefits, features, restrictions, or limitations associated with the program.

(9) **Number awarded:** Total number of recipients each year or other specified period.

(10) **Deadline:** The month by which applications must be submitted.

ABOUT THE AUTHORS

Dr. Gail Ann Schlachter (1943-2015) worked for more than three decades as a library manager, a library educator, and an administrator of library-related publishing companies. Among the reference books to her credit are the biennially-issued *Directory of Financial Aids for Women* and two award-winning bibliographic guides: *Minorities and Women: A Guide to Reference Literature in the Social Sciences* (which was chosen as an "outstanding reference book of the year" by *Choice)* and *Reference Sources in Library and Information Services* (which won the first Knowledge Industry Publications "Award for Library Literature"). She was the reference book review editor for *RQ* (now *Reference and User Services Quarterly)* for 10 years, was a past president of the American Library Association's Reference and User Services Association, was the editor-in-chief of the *Reference and User Services Association Quarterly,* and was serving her sixth term on the American Library Association's governing council at the time of her death. In recognition of her outstanding contributions to reference service, Dr. Schlachter was named the University of Wisconsin School of Library and Information Studies "Alumna of the Year" and was awarded both the Isadore Gilbert Mudge Citation and the Louis Shores/Oryx Press Award.

Dr. R. David Weber taught history and economics at Los Angeles Harbor College (in Wilmington, California) for many years and continues to teach history there as an emeritus professor. During his years at Harbor College, and earlier at East Los College, he directed the Honors Program and was frequently chosen the "Teacher of the Year." He has written a number of critically-acclaimed reference works, including *Dissertations in Urban History* and the three-volume *Energy Information Guide.* With Gail Schlachter, he is the author of Reference Service Press' *Financial Aid for the Disabled and Their Families,* which was selected by *Library Journal* as one of the "best reference books of the year," and a number of other financial aid titles, including the *College Student's Guide to Merit and Other No-Need Funding,* which was chosen as one of the "outstanding reference books of the year" by *Choice.*

Financial Aid Programs Open to African Americans

Undergraduates ●

Graduate Students ●

Professionals/Postdoctorates ●

Undergraduates

Listed alphabetically by program title and described in detail here are 703 scholarships, forgivable loans, grants, awards, and other sources of "free money" set aside for African Americans who are college-bound high school seniors or continuing and returning undergraduate students. This funding is available to support study, training, research, and/or creative activities in the United States.

[1]
100 BLACK MEN OF AMERICA NATIONAL SCHOLARSHIP PROGRAM

100 Black Men of America, Inc.
Attn: National Scholarship Administrator
141 Auburn Avenue N.E.
Atlanta, GA 30303
(404) 688-5100   Toll Free: (800) 598-3411
Fax: (404) 688-1028   E-mail: scholarship@100bmoa.org
Web: survey.constantcontact.com

Summary To provide financial assistance for college to high school seniors and current undergraduates who are affiliated with a local chapter of 100 Black Men of America.

Eligibility This program is open to high school seniors and undergraduates who are attending or planning to attend an accredited postsecondary institution as a full-time student. Applicants must be a mentee or affiliate of a chapter of 100 Black Men of America. They must have a GPA of 2.5 or higher and be able to demonstrate financial need. Along with their application, they must submit a 500-word essay on why they are applying for a needs-abased scholarship. U.S. citizenship or permanent resident status is required.

Financial data Stipends range from $500 to $5,000. Funds are disbursed directly to the student's institution.

Duration 1 year.

Number awarded Varies each year.

Deadline March of each year.

[2]
AAF-LOUISVILLE EDUCATION FOUNDATION DIVERSITY SCHOLARSHIP

American Advertising Federation-Louisville
Attn: AAF-Louisville Education Foundation
130 St. Matthews Avenue, Suite 302
Louisville, KY 40207
(502) 895-2500   Fax: (502) 895-2555
E-mail: mary@louisvilleadfed.org
Web: www.louisvilleadfed.org

Summary To provide financial assistance to residents of Kentucky and southeastern Indiana who are African Americans or members of a diverse ethnic background and are working on an undergraduate degree in a field related to advertising.

Eligibility This program is open to residents of Kentucky and the Indiana counties of Clark, Floyd, and Harrison who are U.S. citizens of African, Hispanic, Native American, Asian, Middle Eastern, or Pacific Island descent. Applicants must be 1) entering their junior or senior year at a 4-year college or university in any state; or 2) enrolled in their last year of an associate degree or technical certificate program. They must be enrolled full time and have a GPA of 3.0 or higher. Their major may involve any field related to advertising or marketing communications, including communications, mass communications, journalism, public relations, marketing, business communications, graphic arts, computer design, multi-media, or English. Along with their application, they must submit a 500-word essay on their understanding of and need for a more diverse and inclusive workforce for the benefit of the community and the Louisville advertising and communications industry.

Financial data The stipend is $2,500.

Duration 1 year.

Number awarded 1 each year.

Deadline April of each year.

[3]
AAPT-ALPHA AWARD

American Association of Physics Teachers
Attn: Awards Committee
One Physics Ellipse
College Park, MD 20740-3845
(301) 209-3311   Fax: (301) 209-0845
E-mail: awards@aapt.org
Web: www.aapt.org

Summary To recognize and reward undergraduate students, especially African Americans and members of other underrepresented groups, who build and develop an advanced laboratory experiment for their school's advanced laboratory program.

Eligibility This award is available to undergraduate students, acting individually or in a group, who have built (and possibly developed) an advanced laboratory experiment that will become a new part of their school's program. The experiment must be new to the home department, either based on the literature or being used at other institutions. It may have been carried out as a senior project, senior thesis, or equivalent. Nominations of women and members of underrepresented minority groups are especially encouraged.

Financial data The award includes an honorarium of $4,000, a citation, reimbursement of travel expenses to the meeting of the American Association of Physics Teachers (AAPT) at which the award is presented, and the opportunity to present a talk at that meeting. The faculty supervisor receives a citation and travel expenses to the same AAPT meeting. For groups of students, the honorarium is shared among all those involved.

Duration The award is presented annually.

Additional information This program began in 2014 with support from TeachSpin, Inc. It is jointly administered by AAPT and the Advanced Laboratory Physics Association (ALPhA).

Number awarded 1 each year.

Deadline August of each year.

[4]
ACADEMIC MAJOR-BASED SCHOLARSHIPS OF THE UNITED NEGRO COLLEGE FUND

United Negro College Fund
Attn: Scholarships and Grants Department
1805 Seventh Street, N.W.
Washington, DC 20001
(202) 810-0258   Toll Free: (800) 331-2244
E-mail: scholarships@uncf.org
Web: www.scholarships.uncf.org

Summary To provide financial assistance to students who are interested in majoring in specified fields at academic institutions affiliated with the United Negro College Fund (UNCF).

Eligibility These programs are open to students planning to pursue designated majors at UNCF-member institutions. Applicants must be high school seniors or graduates with strong academic backgrounds (minimum GPA of 2.5). Students who have completed their junior year in high school with a record of distinction may also be considered. Financial need must be demonstrated. Applications should be submitted directly to the UNCF-member institution the student plans to attend.

Financial data The general stipend is $5,000 per year.

Duration 1 year; may be renewed.

Additional information Recipients must attend a UNCF-member institution of higher learning. These are: Miles College, Oakwood College, Stillman College, Talladega College, and Tuskegee University in Alabama; Philander Smith College in Arkansas; Bethune-Cookman University, Edward Waters College, and Florida Memorial College in Florida; Clark Atlanta University, Interdenominational Theological Center, Morehouse College, Paine College, and Spelman College in Georgia; Dillard University and Xavier University in Louisiana; Rust College and Tougaloo College in Mississippi; Bennett College, Johnson C. Smith University, Livingstone College, Saint Augustine's University, and Shaw University in North Carolina; Wilberforce University in Ohio; Allen University, Benedict College, Claflin University, Morris College, and Voorhees College in South Carolina; Fisk University, Lane College, and LeMoyne-Owen College in Tennessee; Huston-Tillotson College, Jarvis Christian College, Texas College, and Wiley College in Texas; and Virginia Union University in Virginia.

Number awarded A total of nearly 1,200 UNCF scholarships is awarded each year.

Deadline March of each year.

[5]
ACADEMY OF NUTRITION AND DIETETICS BACCALAUREATE (DIDACTIC OR COORDINATED PROGRAM) SCHOLARSHIPS

Academy of Nutrition and Dietetics
Attn: Foundation
120 South Riverside Plaza, Suite 2000
Chicago, IL 60606-6995
(312) 899-4821   Toll Free: (800) 877-1600, ext. 4821
Fax: (312) 899-4796   E-mail: scholarship@eatright.org
Web: www.eatrightacend.org

Summary To provide financial assistance to undergraduate student members of the Academy of Nutrition and Dietetics, including African Americans and members of othr underrepresented groups.

Eligibility This program is open to ADA members enrolled at a CADE-accredited/approved college or university program for at least junior status in the dietetics program. Applicants must be U.S. citizens or permanent residents and show promise of being a valuable, contributing member of the profession. Some scholarships require membership in a specific dietetic practice group, residency in a specific state, or underrepresented minority group status. The same application form can be used for all categories.

Financial data Stipends range from $500 to $10,000 but most are for $1,000.

Duration 1 year.

Additional information The Academy of Nutrition and Dietetics was formerly the American Dietetic Association.

Number awarded Between 30 and 35 each year.

Deadline February of each year.

[6]
ACCELERATOR APPLICATIONS DIVISION SCHOLARSHIP

American Nuclear Society
Attn: Scholarship Coordinator
555 North Kensington Avenue
La Grange Park, IL 60526-5535
(708) 352-6611   Toll Free: (800) 323-3044
Fax: (708) 352-0499   E-mail: outreach@ans.org
Web: www.ans.org/honors/scholarships/aad

Summary To provide financial assistance to undergraduate students, espeically African American and members of other underrepresented groups, who are interested in preparing for a career dealing with accelerator applications aspects of nuclear science or nuclear engineering.

Eligibility This program is open to students entering their junior year in physics, engineering, or materials science at an accredited institution in the United States. Applicants must submit a description of their long- and short-term professional objectives, including their research interests related to accelerator aspects of nuclear science and engineering. Selection is based on that statement, faculty recommendations, and academic performance. Special consideration is given to members of underrepresented groups (women and minorities), students who can demonstrate financial need, and applicants who have a record of service to the American Nuclear Society (ANS).

Financial data The stipend is $1,000 per year.

Duration 1 year (the junior year); may be renewed for the senior year.

Additional information This program is offered by the Accelerator Applications Division (AAD) of the ANS.

Number awarded 1 each year.

Deadline January of each year.

[7]
ACCESS PATH TO PSYCHOLOGY AND LAW EXPERIENCE (APPLE) PROGRAM

American Psychological Association
Attn: Division 41 (American Psychology-Law Society)
c/o Jennifer Hunt, Minority Affairs Committee Chair
Buffalo State University of New York, Psychology
   Department
Classroom Building C308
1300 Elmwood Avenue
Buffalo, NY 14222
(716) 878-3421   E-mail: huntjs@buffalostate.edu
Web: www.apadivisions.org

Summary To provide an opportunity for undergraduate students from African American and other underrepresented groups to gain research and other experience to prepare them for graduate work in psychology and law.

Eligibility This program is open to undergraduate students who are members of underrepresented groups, including, but are not limited to, racial and ethnic minorities; first-generation college students; lesbian, gay, bisexual, and transgender students; and physically disabled students. Applicants must be interested in participating in a program in which they work on research for approximately 10 hours per week; participate in GRE classes and/or other development opportunities; attend a conference of the American Psychology-Law Society (AP-

LS); submit a proposal to present their research at an AP-LS conference or in the Division 41 program of an American Psychological Association (APA) conference; submit a summary of their research experience to the AP-LS Minority Affairs Committee chair within 1 month of its completion; and correspond with a secondary mentor from the Minority Affairs Committee to participate in the ongoing assessment of this program. Selection is based on the quality of the proposed research and mentoring experience and the potential for the student to become a successful graduate student.

Financial data Grants range up to $3,000, including a stipend of $1,200 per semester or $800 per quarter or summer, $100 for research expenses, and up to $500 to attend the AP-LS conference.

Duration Up to 1 year.

Number awarded 6 each year.

Deadline November of each year.

[8]
ACCOUNTANCY BOARD OF OHIO EDUCATION ASSISTANCE PROGRAM

Accountancy Board of Ohio
Attn: Executive Director
77 South High Street, Suite 1802
Columbus, OH 43215-6128
(614) 466-4135   Fax: (614) 466-2628
E-mail: john.e.patterson@acc.ohio.gov
Web: www.acc.ohio.gov

Summary To provide financial assistance to African American and other financially disadvantaged students enrolled in an accounting education program at Ohio academic institutions approved by the Accountancy Board of Ohio.

Eligibility This program is open to minority and financially disadvantaged Ohio residents who apply as full-time juniors or seniors in an accounting program at an accredited college or university in the state. Students who remain in good standing at their institutions and who enter a qualified fifth-year program are then eligible to receive these funds. Minority is defined as Blacks, Native Americans, Hispanics, and Asian. Financial disadvantage is defined according to information provided on the Free Application for Federal Student Aid (FAFSA). U.S. citizenship or permanent resident status is required.

Financial data The amount of the stipend is determined annually but does not exceed the in-state tuition at Ohio public universities (currently, $13,067).

Duration 1 year (the fifth year of an accounting program). Funds committed to students who apply as juniors must be used within 4 years and funds committed to students who apply as seniors must be used within 3 years. The award is nonrenewable and may only be used when the student enrolls in the fifth year of a program.

Number awarded Several each year.

Deadline Applications may be submitted at any time.

[9]
ACT SIX SCHOLARSHIPS

Act Six
c/o Degrees of Change
1109 A Street, Suite 101
P.O. Box 1573
Tacoma, WA 98401
(253) 642-6712   E-mail: tim.herron@actsix.org
Web: www.actsix.org

Summary To provide financial assistance to residents of Washington and Oregon who are African Americans or members of other diverse backgrounds and are interested in attending designated private faith-based universities in those states.

Eligibility This program is open to high school seniors or recent graduates and planning to enter college as freshmen who come from diverse, multicultural backgrounds. Applicants must be residents of the following regions and interested in attending designated colleges for that region: Portland: George Fox University or Warner Pacific College; Spokane: Gonzaga University or Whitworth University; Tacoma-Seattle: Gonzaga University, Northwest University, Pacific Lutheran University, or Whitworth University; or Yakima Valley: Heritage University. Students are not required to make a faith commitment, but they must be willing to explore Christian spirituality as it relates to service and leadership. Ethnicity and family income are considered as factors in selecting an intentionally diverse group of scholars, but there are no income restrictions and students from all ethnic backgrounds are encouraged to apply.

Financial data The program makes up the difference between any other assistance the student receives and full tuition. For recipients who demonstrate financial need in excess of tuition, awards cover some or all of the cost of room and board, books, travel, and personal expenses.

Duration 1 year; may be renewed.

Number awarded Varies each year; recently, 56 were awarded.

Deadline November of each year.

[10]
ACTUARIAL DIVERSITY SCHOLARSHIPS

Actuarial Foundation
Attn: Actuarial Education and Research Fund Committee
475 North Martingale Road, Suite 600
Schaumburg, IL 60173-2226
(847) 706-3535   Fax: (847) 706-3599
E-mail: scholarships@actfnd.org
Web: www.actuarialfoundation.org

Summary To provide financial assistance to African American and other minority undergraduate students who are preparing for a career in actuarial science.

Eligibility This program is open to members of minority groups, defined as having at least 1 birth parent who is Black/African American, Hispanic, Native North American, or Pacific Islander. Applicants must be graduating high school seniors or current full-time undergraduate students working on or planning to work on a degree at an accredited 2- or 4-year college or university that may lead to a career in the actuarial profession. They must have a GPA of 3.0 or higher; high school seniors must also have a minimum score of 28 on the ACT mathematics examination or 600 on the SAT mathematics examination. Along with their application, they must submit a 1- or 2-page personal statement that covers why they are interested in becoming an actuary, the steps they are taking to enter the actuarial profession, participation in actuarial internships, and participation in extracurricular activities. Financial need is not considered in the selection process.

Financial data Annual stipends are $1,000 for high school seniors applying for freshman year, $2,000 for college freshmen applying for sophomore year, $3,000 for college sophomores applying for junior year, or $4,000 for college juniors applying for senior year.

Duration 1 year; may be renewed, provided the recipient remains enrolled full time, in good academic standing, in a course of study that may lead to a career in the actuarial profession, and (for college juniors and higher) passes actuarial examinations.

Additional information This program began in 1977 by the Casualty Actuarial Society and the Society of Actuaries. In 2008, it was transferred to the Actuarial Foundation.

Number awarded Varies each year; recently, 40 were awarded.

Deadline April of each year.

[11]
ACXIOM DIVERSITY SCHOLARSHIP PROGRAM

Acxiom Corporation
601 East Third Street
P.O. Box 8190
Little Rock, AR 72203-8190
(501) 342-1000   Toll Free: (877) 314-2049
E-mail: Candice.Davis@acxiom.com
Web: www.acxiom.com/about-acxiom/careers

Summary To provide financial assistance and possible work experience to upper-division and graduate students who are Africans or members of other diverse populations that historically have been underrepresented in the information technology work force.

Eligibility This program is open to juniors, seniors, and graduate students who are working full time on a degree in a field of information technology, including computer science, computer information systems, management information systems, information quality, information systems, engineering, mathematics, statistics, or related areas of study. Women, veterans, minorities, and individuals with disabilities are encouraged to apply. Applicants must have a GPA of 3.0 or higher. Along with their application, they must submit a 500-word essay describing how the scholarship will help them achieve their academic, professional, and personal goals. Selection is based on academic achievement, relationship of field of study to information technology, and relationship of areas of professional interest to the sponsor's business needs.

Financial data The stipend is $5,000 per year.

Duration 1 year; may be renewed 1 additional year, provided the recipient remains enrolled full time, maintains a GPA of 3.0 or higher, and (if offered an internship) continues to meet internship expectations.

Additional information Recipients may be offered an internship (fall, spring, summer, year-round) at 1 of the sponsor's offices in Austin (Texas), Conway (Arkansas), Downers Grove (Illinois), Little Rock (Arkansas), Nashville (Tennessee), New York (New York), or Redwood City (California).

Number awarded Up to 5 each year.

Deadline December of each year.

[12]
A.D. OSHERMAN SCHOLARSHIP FUND

Greater Houston Community Foundation
Attn: Scholarships Assistant
5120 Woodway Drive, Suite 6000
Houston, TX 77056
(713) 333-2236   Fax: (713) 333-2220
E-mail: jlauver@ghcf.org
Web: www.ghcfscholar.org

Summary To provide financial assistance to residents of Texas who are African Americans or members of other designated groups and are interested in attending college in any state.

Eligibility This program is open to Texas residents who are graduating high school seniors or full-time freshmen, sophomores, or juniors at an accredited public 2- or 4-year college or university in any state. Applicants must qualify as a member of a recognized minority group, the first in their family to attend college, or a veteran with active service, particularly service in Iraq or Afghanistan. They must have a GPA of 2.75 or higher and a history of community service. Financial need is considered in the selection process.

Financial data The stipend is $2,500 per year for students at 4-year universities or $1,500 per year for students at 2-year colleges.

Duration 1 year; recipients may reapply.

Number awarded 2 each year.

Deadline March of each year.

[13]
ADDIE B. MORRIS SCHOLARSHIP

American Association of Railroad Superintendents
P.O. Box 200
La Fox, IL 60147
(331) 643-3369   E-mail: aars@supt.org
Web: www.railroadsuperintendents.org/Scholarships

Summary To provide financial assistance to undergraduate and graduate students, especially African Americans and other minorities working on a degree in transportation.

Eligibility This program is open to full-time undergraduate and graduate students enrolled at accredited colleges and universities in Canada or the United States. Applicants must have completed enough credits to have standing as a sophomore and must have a GPA of 2.75 or higher. Preference is given to minority students enrolled in the transportation field who can demonstrate financial need.

Financial data The stipend is $1,000. Funds are sent directly to the recipient's institution.

Duration 1 year.

Number awarded 1 or more each year.

Deadline June of each year.

[14]
AFRICAN AMERICAN COMMUNITY COLLEGE SCHOLARSHIP

Scholarship Administrative Services, Inc.
Attn: MEFUSA Program
13730 Loumont Street
Whittier, CA 90601

Summary To provide financial assistance to African American high school seniors who are interested in attending a community college.

Eligibility This program is open to African Americans graduating from high schools anywhere in the United States. Applicants must be planning to attend a community college on a full-time basis. Along with their application, they must submit a 1,000-word essay on their educational and career goals, how a community college education will help them to achieve those goals, and how they plan to serve the African American community after completing their education. Selection is based on the essay, high school GPA (2.5 or higher), SAT or ACT scores, involvement in the African American community, and financial need.

Financial data The stipend is $5,000 per year.

Duration 1 year; may be renewed 1 additional year if the recipient maintains full-time enrollment and a GPA of 2.5 or higher.

Additional information This program is sponsored by the Minority Educational Foundation of the United States of America (MEFUSA) and administered by Scholarship Administrative Services, Inc. MEFUSA was established in 2001 to meet the needs of minority students who "show a determination to get a college degree," but who, for financial or other personal reasons, are not able to attend a 4-year college or university. Requests for applications should be accompanied by a self-addressed stamped envelope, the student's e-mail address, and the name of the source where they found the scholarship information.

Number awarded Up to 100 each year.

Deadline April of each year.

[15]
AFRICAN AMERICAN FUTURE ACHIEVERS SCHOLARSHIP PROGRAM

Ronald McDonald House Charities
Attn: U.S. Scholarship Program
One Kroc Drive
Oak Brook, IL 60523
(630) 623-7048   Fax: (630) 623-7488
E-mail: info@rmhc.org
Web: www.rmhc.org/rmhc-us-scholarships

Summary To provide financial assistance for college to African American high school seniors in specified geographic areas.

Eligibility This program is open to high school seniors in designated McDonald's market areas who are legal residents of the United States and have at least 1 parent of African American or Black Caribbean heritage. Applicants must be planning to enroll full time at an accredited 2- or 4-year college, university, or vocational/technical school. They must have a GPA of 2.7 or higher. Along with their application, they must submit a personal statement, up to 2 pages in length, on their African American or Black Caribbean background, career goals, and desire to contribute to their community; information about unique, personal, or financial circumstances may be added. Selection is based on that statement, high school transcripts with GPA and standardized test scores, a letter of recommendation, and financial need.

Financial data Stipends are determined by participating McDonald's areas, but most are $1,000 per year. Funds are paid directly to the recipient's school.

Duration 1 year; nonrenewable.

Additional information This program is a component of the Ronald McDonald House Charities U.S. Scholarship Program, which began in 1985. It is administered by International Scholarship and Tuition Services, Inc. For a list of participating McDonald's market areas, contact Ronald McDonald House Charities (RMHC).

Number awarded Varies each year; since RMHC began this program, it has awarded more than $60 million in scholarships.

Deadline January of each year.

[16]
AFRICAN AMERICAN NETWORK-CAROLINAS SCHOLARSHIP FUND

Foundation for the Carolinas
Attn: Vice President, Scholarships
220 North Tryon Street
Charlotte, NC 28202
(704) 973-4535   Toll Free: (800) 973-7244
Fax: (704) 973-4935   E-mail: qaustin@fftc.org
Web: fftcscholarships.communityforce.com

Summary To provide financial assistance to African American and other high school seniors from North and South Carolina who are interested in studying designated fields in college.

Eligibility This program is open to seniors graduating from high schools in North and South Carolina. Applicants must be planning to attend a 4-year college or university in those states to major in accounting, business administration, computer science, engineering, finance, or the sciences. Selection is based on GPA, residence, leadership skills, and financial need.

Financial data A stipend is awarded (amount not specified).

Duration 1 year; recipients may reapply, provided they remain enrolled full time and meet all qualifying requirements.

Additional information This program is sponsored by the African American Network, a resource group of African American employees of Duke Energy. Recipients are selected by colleges, universities, and community service organizations according to criteria established by the Network. Interested students must contact their college, university, or community service organization to apply for this scholarship.

Number awarded 3 each year: 2 selected by colleges and universities and 1 selected by a community service organization.

Deadline February of each year.

[17]
AFRICAN HERITAGE CAUCUS SCHOLARSHIPS

African Heritage Caucus
Attn: Scholarship Chair
2318 Mill Road, Suite 1300
Alexandria, VA 22314-6868
(281) 660-4721   E-mail: aapaahc@gmail.com
Web: www.africanheritagecaucusofaapa.org/190368345

Summary   To provide financial assistance to members of the African Heritage Caucus within the American Academy of Physician Assistants (AAPA).

Eligibility   This program is open to physician assistant students who are entering their clinical phase of training and are members of both the AAPA and its African Heritage Caucus. Applicants must submit an essay of 500 to 750 words on 1 of the following topics: 1) their opinion on the impact of universal health care in addressing the issues of racial health care disparities in our country; or 2) the major health care disparities facing the African American community and how they will address those as a practicing physician assistant. Selection is based on academic progress, financial need, community and/or professional activities, and knowledge of health care issues and the physician assistant's role.

Financial data   Stipends range from $500 to $1,000.

Duration   1 year.

Number awarded   Up to 2 each year.

Deadline   May of each year.

[18]
AFRICAN WOMEN'S EDUCATION FUND OF UTAH

Community Foundation of Utah
423 West 800 South, Suite A101
Salt Lake City, UT 84101
(801) 559-3005   Fax: (866) 935-2353
E-mail: scholarships@utahcf.org
Web: www.utahcf.org

Summary   To provide financial assistance for higher education in Utah to women refugees or asylees from Africa.

Eligibility   This program is open to women refugees or asylees from Africa who wish to enroll in educational or technical training or certification through qualified schools or programs in Utah. The institution must be an accredited public nonprofit 2- or 4-year college or university or a vocational/technical school or training program. Students at academic institutions should have a GPA of 2.0 or higher; students at vocational institutions should be able to demonstrate progress as reported by teachers and administrators. Selection is based on academic progress and achievement, desire and intent to achieve education or training, and financial need.

Financial data   A stipend is awarded (amount not specified).

Duration   1 year.

Additional information   This program began in 2013.

Number awarded   Varies each year.

Deadline   April of each year.

[19]
AFRICAN-AMERICAN CHURCH PLANTERS SCHOLARSHIPS

Louisiana Baptist Convention
Attn: Woman's Missionary Union
1250 MacArthur Drive
P.O. Box 311
Alexandria, LA 71309-0311
(318) 448-3402   Toll Free: (800) 622-6549
E-mail: WMM@louisianabaptists.org
Web: www.louisianabaptists.org

Summary   To provide financial assistance to African American Southern Baptists from Louisiana who are enrolled at a seminary in any state to prepare for a career as a missions pastor.

Eligibility   This program is open to African Americans who are endorsed by the director of missions and the pastor of a sponsoring Southern Baptist church in Louisiana. Applicants must be enrolled full time at a Southern Baptist seminary or a satellite campus and working on a master's degree or a Christian education diploma. They must be participating in a missions education organization of the church or on campus and must contribute to offerings of the church and other programs. Along with their application, they must submit evidence of their "devotion to the Lord and their call to ministry."

Financial data   The stipend is $1,200 per year.

Duration   Up to 3 years.

Number awarded   1 or more each year.

Deadline   June of each year.

[20]
AFRO-ACADEMIC, CULTURAL, TECHNOLOGICAL AND SCIENTIFIC OLYMPICS (ACT-SO)

National Association for the Advancement of Colored
   People
Attn: ACT-SO Director
4805 Mt. Hope Drive
Baltimore, MD 21215
(410) 580-5650   Toll Free: (877) NAACP-98
E-mail: ACTSO@naacpnet.org
Web: www.naacp.org/act-so/about

Summary   To recognize and reward (with college scholarships) outstanding African American high school students who distinguish themselves in the Afro-Academic, Cultural, Technological and Scientific Olympics (ACT-SO) program.

Eligibility   This competition is open to high school students (grades 9-12) of African descent who are U.S. citizens and amateurs in the category in which they wish to participate. Competitions are held in 32 categories in 6 general areas: humanities (music composition, original essay, playwriting, poetry, and short story); STEM (biology and microbiology, chemistry and biochemistry, computer science, earth and space science, engineering, mathematics, medicine and health, and physics); performing arts (dance: ballet, dance: contemporary, dance: modern, dance: traditional, dramatics, music instrumental/classical, music instrumental/contemporary, music vocal/classical, music vocal/contemporary, oratory, and poetry performance); visual arts (architecture, drawing, filmmaking, painting, photography, and sculpture); business (entrepreneurship); and culinary arts. Competition is first conducted by local chapters of the NAACP; winners in each event at the local level then compete at the national level.

Financial data In each category, the first-prize winner receives a gold medal and a $2,000 scholarship, the second-prize winner receives a silver medal and a $1,500 scholarship, and the third-prize winner receives a bronze medal and a $1,000 scholarship.

Duration The competition is held annually.

Additional information This competition began in 1977.

Number awarded 78 each year: 3 in each of 26 categories.

Deadline Local letters of intent must be submitted by November of each year.

[21]
AFSCME UNION SCHOLARSHIPS OF THE THURGOOD MARSHALL COLLEGE FUND

Thurgood Marshall College Fund
Attn: Senior Manager of Scholarship Programs
901 F Street, N.W., Suite 300
Washington, DC 20004
(202) 507-4851   Fax: (202) 652-2934
E-mail: deshuandra.walker@tmcfund.org
Web: www.tmcf.org

Summary To provide financial assistance and work experience with the American Federation of State, County and Municipal Employees (AFSCME) to African American and other students of color interested in preparing for a career in the labor union movement.

Eligibility This program is open to students of color (African American, American Indian/Alaskan Native, Asian Pacific Islander American, Latino American) who are currently enrolled as sophomores or juniors at a college or university in any state. Applicants must be interested in participating in a summer field placement in a union organizing campaign at 1 of several locations across the country followed by a year of academic study at their college or university. They must have a current GPA of 2.5 or higher and a demonstrated interest in working through the union labor movement. Along with their application, they must submit a personal statement on an assigned topic, a letter of recommendation, and their current academic transcript.

Financial data The program provides 1) a stipend of up to $4,000 (provided by AFSCME) and on-site housing for the summer field placement; and 2) an academic scholarship of up to $6,300 for the school year, based on successful completion of the summer program and financial need.

Duration 10 weeks for the summer field placement; students who enter the program as sophomores are eligible for a second placement at AFSCME headquarters in Washington, D.C.; 1 year for the academic scholarship.

Additional information This program is sponsored by AFSCME.

Number awarded Varies each year.

Deadline February of each year.

[22]
AGA INVESTING IN THE FUTURE STUDENT RESEARCH FELLOWSHIPS

American Gastroenterological Association
Attn: AGA Research Foundation
Research Awards Manager
4930 Del Ray Avenue
Bethesda, MD 20814-2512
(301) 222-4012   Fax: (301) 654-5920
E-mail: awards@gastro.org
Web: www.gastro.org

Summary To provide funding for research on digestive diseases or nutrition to African American and undergraduate and medical students from other underrepresented minority groups.

Eligibility This program is open to undergraduate and medical students at accredited U.S. institutions who are African Americans, Hispanic/Latino Americans, Alaska Natives, American Indians, or Natives of the U.S. Pacific Islands. Applicants must be interested in conducting research on digestive diseases or nutrition. They may not hold similar salary support awards from other agencies (e.g., American Liver Foundation, Crohn's and Colitis Foundation). Research must be conducted under the supervision of a preceptor who is a full-time faculty member at an institution in a state other than the student's, directing a research project in a gastroenterology-related area, and a member of the American Gastroenterological Association (AGA).

Financial data Fellowships provide payment of housing, travel, and a stipend of $5,000.

Duration 8 to 10 weeks. The work may take place at any time during the year.

Additional information This program is supported by the National Institute of Diabetes and Digestive and Kidney Diseases (NIDDKD) of the U.S. National Institutes of Health (NIH).

Number awarded 12 each year.

Deadline February of each year.

[23]
AGNES JONES JACKSON SCHOLARSHIPS

POISE Foundation
Two Gateway Center, Suite 1700
603 Stanwix Street
Pittsburgh, PA 15222
(412) 281-4967   Fax: (412) 562-0292
Web: www.poisefoundation.org

Summary To provide financial assistance to members of the National Association for the Advancement of Colored People (NAACP) who are attending or planning to attend college or graduate school.

Eligibility This program is open to members of the NAACP who are younger than 25 years of age and full-time undergraduates or full- or part-time graduate students. The minimum GPA is 2.5 for graduating high school seniors and undergraduate students or 3.0 for graduate students. All applicants must be able to demonstrate financial need (family income must be less than $16,755 for a family of 1, ranging up to $58,335 for a family of 8) and U.S. citizenship. Along with their application, they must submit a 1-page essay on their interest in their major and a career, their life's ambition, what they hope to accomplish in their lifetime, and what position they hope to attain.

Financial data   The stipend ranges up to $2,000 per year.

Duration   1 year; recipients may apply for renewal.

Additional information   This program is managed by POISE Foundation on behalf of the NAACP.

Number awarded   Approximately 20 to 40 each year.

Deadline   March of each year.

[24]
AHIMA FOUNDATION DIVERSITY SCHOLARSHIPS

American Health Information Management Association
Attn: AHIMA Foundation
233 North Michigan Avenue, 21st Floor
Chicago, IL 60601-5809
(312) 233-1137   Fax: (312) 233-1537
E-mail: info@ahimafoundation.org
Web: www.ahimafoundation.org

Summary   To provide financial assistance to African American and other members of the American Health Information Management Association (AHIMA) who are interested in working on an undergraduate or graduate degree in health information management (HIM) or health information technology (HIT) and who will contribute to diversity in the profession.

Eligibility   This program is open to AHIMA members who are enrolled at least half time in an accredited program. Applicants must be working on a degree in HIM or HIT at the associate, bachelor's, post-baccalaureate, master's, or doctoral level. They must have a GPA of 3.5 or higher and at least 6 credit hours remaining after the date of the award. To qualify for this support, applicants must demonstrate how they will contribute to diversity in the health information management profession; diversity is defined as differences in race, ethnicity, nationality, gender, sexual orientation, socioeconomic status, age, physical capabilities, or religious beliefs. Along with their application, they must submit essays on assigned topics related to their involvement in the HIM profession. Selection is based on the clarity and completeness of thought in the essays; cumulative GPA; volunteer, work, and/or leadership experience; honors, awards, or recognitions; commitment to the HIM profession; and references.

Financial data   Stipends are $1,000 for associate degree students, $1,500 for bachelor's degree or post-baccalaureate certificate students, $2,000 for master's degree students, or $2,500 for doctoral degree students.

Duration   1 year.

Number awarded   1 or more each year.

Deadline   September of each year.

[25]
AIA/F DIVERSITY ADVANCEMENT SCHOLARSHIP

American Institute of Architects
Attn: AIA Foundation
1799 New York Avenue, N.W.
Washington, DC 20006-5292
(202) 626-7511   Fax: (202) 626-7420
E-mail: divscholarship@aia.org
Web: www.aia.org/about/initiatives/AIAB101856

Summary   To provide financial assistance to high school and college students who are African Americans or from other diverse backgrounds and interested in studying architecture in college.

Eligibility   This program is open to students from minority and/or financially disadvantaged backgrounds who are high school seniors, students in a community college or technical school transferring to an accredited architectural program, or college freshmen entering a professional degree program at an accredited program of architecture. Students who have completed 1 or more years of a 4-year college curriculum are not eligible. Applicants must submit 2 or 3 drawings, including 1 freehand sketch of any real life object (e.g., buildings, people, objects, self-portrait) and 1 or 2 additional images of drawings or drafted floor plans or drawings using computer-aided design (CAD). Selection is based on those drawings and financial need.

Financial data   Stipends range from $3,000 to $4,000 per year, depending upon individual need. Students must apply for supplementary funds from other sources.

Duration   1 year; may be renewed for up to 4 additional years or until completion of a degree.

Additional information   This program was established in 1970 as the AIA/AAF Minority Disadvantaged Scholarship Program.

Number awarded   2 each year.

Deadline   April of each year.

[26]
AICPA SCHOLARSHIPS FOR MINORITY ACCOUNTING STUDENTS

American Institute of Certified Public Accountants
Attn: Academic and Career Development Division
220 Leigh Farm Road
Durham, NC 27707-8110
(919) 402-4500   Fax: (919) 402-4505
E-mail: scholarships@aicpa.org
Web: www.aicpa.org

Summary   To provide financial assistance to African and other minorities interested in studying accounting at the undergraduate or graduate school level.

Eligibility   This program is open to minority undergraduate and graduate students, enrolled full time, who have a GPA of 3.3 or higher (both cumulatively and in their major) and intend to pursue a C.P.A. credential. The program defines minority students as those whose heritage is Black or African American, Hispanic or Latino, Native American, or Asian American. Undergraduates must have completed at least 30 semester hours, including at least 6 semester hours of a major in accounting. Graduate students must be working on a master's degree in accounting, finance, taxation, or a related program. Applicants must be U.S. citizens or permanent residents and student affiliate members of the American Institute of Certified Public Accountants (AICPA). Along with their application, they must submit 500-word essays on 1) why they want to become a C.P.A. and how attaining that licensure will contribute to their goals; and 2) how they would spread the message about accounting and the C.P.A. profession in their community and school. In the selection process, some consideration is given to financial need.

Financial data   Stipends range up to $5,000 per year. Funds are disbursed directly to the recipient's school.

Duration 1 year; may be renewed up to 3 additional years or until completion of a bachelor's or master's degree, whichever is earlier.

Additional information This program began in 1969. Additional support is provided by the Accounting Education Foundation of the Texas Society of Certified Public Accountants, the New Jersey Society of Certified Public Accountants, Robert Half International, and the Virgin Islands Society of Certified Public Accountants.

Number awarded Varies each year; recently, 94 students received funding through this program.

Deadline March of each year.

[27]
AIET MINORITIES AND WOMEN EDUCATIONAL SCHOLARSHIP PROGRAM

Appraisal Institute
Attn: Appraisal Institute Education Trust
200 West Madison Street, Suite 1500
Chicago, IL 60606
(312) 335-4133   Fax: (312) 335-4134
E-mail: educationtrust@appraisalinstitute.org
Web: www.appraisalinstitute.org

Summary To provide financial assistance to African American and other minority undergraduate students majoring in real estate or allied fields.

Eligibility This program is open to members of groups underrepresented in the real estate appraisal profession. Those groups include women, Blacks or African Americans, American Indians, Alaska Natives, Asians and Pacific Islanders, and Hispanics. Applicants must be full- or part-time students enrolled in real estate courses within a degree-granting college, university, or junior college. They must have a GPA of 2.5 or higher and be able to demonstrate financial need. U.S. citizenship is required.

Financial data The stipend is $1,000. Funds are paid directly to the recipient's institution to be used for tuition and fees.

Duration 1 year.

Number awarded At least 1 each year.

Deadline April of each year.

[28]
ALAN COMPTON AND BOB STANLEY MINORITY AND INTERNATIONAL SCHOLARSHIP

Baptist Communicators Association
Attn: Scholarship Committee
4519 Lashley Court
Marietta, GA 30068
(678) 641-4457   E-mail: margaretcolson@bellsouth.net
Web: www.baptistcommunicators.org/about/scholarship.cfm

Summary To provide financial assistance to African American and other minority and international students who are working on an undergraduate degree to prepare for a career in Baptist communications.

Eligibility This program is open to undergraduate students of minority or international origin. Applicants must be majoring in communications, English, journalism, or public relations and have a GPA of 2.5 or higher. Their vocational objective must be in Baptist communications. Along with their application, they must submit a statement explaining why they want to receive this scholarship.

Financial data The stipend is $1,000.

Duration 1 year; recipients may reapply.

Additional information This program began in 1996.

Number awarded 1 each year.

Deadline March of each year.

[29]
ALICE S. MARRIOTT SCHOLARSHIP FUND

Alpha Kappa Alpha Sorority, Inc.
Attn: Educational Advancement Foundation
5656 South Stony Island Avenue
Chicago, IL 60637
(773) 947-0026   Toll Free: (800) 653-6528
Fax: (773) 947-0277   E-mail: akaeaf@akaeaf.net
Web: www.akaeaf.org/alice_s_marriott.htm

Summary To provide financial assistance to African Americans and members of other underrepresented groups who are attending college to prepare for a career in the hospitality industry.

Eligibility This program is open to members of groups traditionally underrepresented in the hospitality industry who are working on a bachelor's degree in the field. Applicants must submit an essay explaining their understanding of what the hospitality industry entails, the specific careers that interest them in the industry, and their career goals upon graduation. Financial need is not considered in the selection process.

Financial data The stipend is $1,000.

Duration 1 year.

Additional information Marriott International established this program in 2012 in partnership with the Educational Advancement Foundation of Alpha Kappa Alpha, a traditionally African American sorority.

Number awarded 2 each year.

Deadline April of each year.

[30]
ALIENE CARRINGTON EWELL SCHOLARSHIP

Chi Eta Phi Sorority, Inc.
3029 13th Street, N.W.
Washington, DC 20009
(202) 232-3858   Fax: (202) 232-3460
E-mail: chietaphi@verizon.net
Web: www.chietaphi.com

Summary To provide financial assistance to members of Chi Eta Phi who are working on an undergraduate degree in nursing.

Eligibility This program is open to current members of Chi Eta Phi and the American Nurses Association who are working on an undergraduate degree in nursing. Selection is based on financial need, scholastic ability, interest in nursing, and leadership potential.

Financial data The stipend is $1,500.

Duration 1 year.

Additional information This program is named in honor of Aliene Carrington Ewell, who founded Chi Eta Phi in 1932 as an organization for African American nurses.

Number awarded 1 or more each year.

Deadline January of each year.

[31]
ALLISON E. FISHER SCHOLARSHIP

National Association of Black Journalists
Attn: Program Manager
University of Maryland
1100 Knight Hall, Suite 3100
College Park, MD 20742
(301) 405-7520   Fax: (301) 314-1714
E-mail: Sberry@nabj.org
Web: www.nabj.org/?page=ScholarshipsFisher

Summary   To provide financial assistance to undergraduate or graduate student members of the National Association of Black Journalists (NABJ) who are majoring in journalism.

Eligibility   This program is open to African American undergraduate or graduate student members of NABJ who are currently enrolled full time at an accredited 4-year college or university. Applicants must be working on a degree in journalism or another communications-related discipline and have a GPA of 3.0 or higher. They must be able to demonstrate financial need. Along with their application, they must submit 5 samples of their work, an official college transcript, 3 letters of recommendation, a resume, and an essay of 1,000 to 2,000 words on the reasons why they are preparing for a career in journalism and what they hope their legacy as a journalist will be.

Financial data   The stipend is $2,500. Funds are paid directly to the recipient's college or university.

Duration   1 year; nonrenewable.

Number awarded   1 each year.

Deadline   February of each year.

[32]
ALMA EXLEY SCHOLARSHIP

Community Foundation of Greater New Britain
Attn: Scholarship Manager
74A Vine Street
New Britain, CT 06052-1431
(860) 229-6018, ext. 305   Fax: (860) 225-2666
E-mail: cfarmer@cfgnb.org
Web: www.cfgnb.org

Summary   To provide financial assistance to African American and other minority college students in Connecticut who are interested in preparing for a teaching career.

Eligibility   This program is open to students of color (African Americans, Asian Americans, Hispanic Americans, and Native Americans) enrolled in a teacher preparation program in Connecticut. Applicant must 1) have been admitted to a traditional teacher preparation program at an accredited 4-year college or university in the state; or 2) be participating in the Alternate Route to Certification (ARC) program sponsored by the Connecticut Department of Higher Education.

Financial data   The stipend is $1,500 per year for students at a 4-year college or university or $500 for a student in the ARC program.

Duration   2 years for students at 4-year colleges or universities; 1 year for students in the ARC program.

Number awarded   2 each year: 1 to a 4-year student and 1 to an ARC student.

Deadline   October of each year.

[33]
ALPHA KAPPA ALPHA ENDOWMENT AWARDS

Alpha Kappa Alpha Sorority, Inc.
Attn: Educational Advancement Foundation
5656 South Stony Island Avenue
Chicago, IL 60637
(773) 947-0026   Toll Free: (800) 653-6528
Fax: (773) 947-0277   E-mail: akaeaf@akaeaf.net
Web: www.akaeaf.org/fellowships_endowments.htm

Summary   To provide financial assistance to undergraduate and graduate students (especially African American women) who meet designated requirements.

Eligibility   This program is open to undergraduate and graduate students who are enrolled full time as sophomores or higher in an accredited degree-granting institution and are planning to continue their program of education. Applicants may apply for scholarships that include specific requirements established by the donor of the endowment that supports it. Along with their application, they must submit 1) a list of honors, awards, and scholarships received; 2) a list of organizations in which they have memberships, especially minority organizations; and 3) a statement of their personal and career goals, including how this scholarship will enhance their ability to attain those goals. The sponsor is a traditionally African American women's sorority.

Financial data   Award amounts are determined by the availability of funds from the particular endowment. Recently, stipends averaged more than $1,700 per year.

Duration   1 year or longer.

Additional information   Each endowment establishes its own requirements. Examples of requirements include residence of the applicant, major field of study, minimum GPA, attendance at an Historically Black College or University (HBCU) or member institution of the United Negro College Fund (UNCF), or other personal feature. For further information on all endowments, contact the sponsor.

Number awarded   Varies each year; recently, 49 were awarded.

Deadline   April of each year.

[34]
ALPHA KAPPA ALPHA UNDERGRADUATE SCHOLARSHIPS

Alpha Kappa Alpha Sorority, Inc.
Attn: Educational Advancement Foundation
5656 South Stony Island Avenue
Chicago, IL 60637
(773) 947-0026   Toll Free: (800) 653-6528
Fax: (773) 947-0277   E-mail: akaeaf@akaeaf.net
Web: www.akaeaf.org/undergraduate_scholarships.htm

Summary   To provide financial assistance to students (especially African American women) who are working on an undergraduate degree in any field.

Eligibility   This program is open to undergraduate students who are enrolled full time as sophomores or higher in an accredited degree-granting institution and are planning to continue their program of education. Applicants may apply either for a scholarship based on merit (requires a GPA of 3.0 or higher) or on financial need (requires a GPA of 2.5 or higher). Along with their application, they must submit 1) a list of honors, awards, and scholarships received; 2) a list of organizations in which they have memberships, especially minority organizations; and 3) a statement of their personal and career goals, including how this scholarship will enhance their ability to attain those goals. The sponsor is a traditionally African American women's sorority.

Financial data Stipends range up to $2,500.

Duration 1 year; nonrenewable.

Number awarded Varies each year; recently, 133 were awarded.

Deadline April of each year.

[35]
ALPHONSO DEAL SCHOLARSHIP AWARD

National Black Police Association
320 South RL Thornton Freeway, Suite 230
Dallas, TX 75226
Toll Free: (855) 879-6272   Fax: (855) 879-6272
E-mail: nationaloffice@blackpolice.org
Web: www.blackpolice.org/scholarships.html

Summary To provide financial assistance to African American high school seniors interested in preparing for a career in criminal justice.

Eligibility This program is open to African American high school seniors who are planning to attend an accredited 2- or 4-year college or university to prepare for a career in criminal justice. Applicants must be U.S. citizens and of good character. Along with their application, they must submit a 500-word essay describing the course of study they plan to pursue and their general outlook as to future endeavors. Selection is based on academic record, extracurricular activities, and recommendations; financial need is not considered.

Financial data A stipend is awarded (amount not specified).

Duration 1 year.

Number awarded 1 or more each year.

Deadline May of each year.

[36]
ALTRIA SCHOLARSHIPS OF THE THURGOOD MARSHALL COLLEGE FUND

Thurgood Marshall College Fund
Attn: Senior Manager of Scholarship Programs
901 F Street, N.W., Suite 300
Washington, DC 20004
(202) 507-4851   Fax: (202) 652-2934
E-mail: deshuandra.walker@tmcfund.org
Web: www.tmcf.org

Summary To provide financial assistance to African American students working on a degree in designated fields at public Historically Black Colleges and Universities (HBCUs) that are members of the Thurgood Marshall College Fund (TMCF).

Eligibility This program is open to students currently enrolled as sophomores or juniors at any of the 47 TMCF member institutions. Applicants must be majoring in accounting, business administration, computer science, economics, engineering (chemical, electrical, industrial, or mechanical), finance, human resources, management information systems, marketing, or supply chain management. They must have a GPA of 3.0 or higher and be able to demonstrate financial need. Along with their application, they must submit a

500-word essay on the solutions they would propose to improve or resolve a current issue, such as health care, the economy, or discrimination. U.S. citizenship is required.

Financial data The stipend is $3,100 per semester ($6,200 per year). Funds are awarded through the institution to be used for tuition, on-campus room and board, and required textbooks.

Duration 1 year; nonrenewable.

Additional information This program is sponsored by Altria Group (parent company of Philip Morris USA). Recipients also have an opportunity to apply for paid summer internships at the company between their junior and senior year.

Number awarded 17 each year.

Deadline April of each year.

[37]
ALVAN T. AND VIOLA D. FULLER JUNIOR RESEARCH FELLOWSHIP

American Cancer Society-New England Division
30 Speen Street
Framingham, MA 01701
(508) 270-4645   Toll Free: (800) 952-7664, ext. 4645
Fax: (508) 393-8607 E-mail: maureen.morse@cancer.org
Web: www.cancer.org

Summary To provide funding for summer cancer research to undergraduate students in New England, especially African Americans and other minorities.

Eligibility This program is open to residents of New England currently enrolled as juniors or seniors at a college or university in any state. Applicants must be interested in working on a summer research project at a teaching hospital, university, or medical school in New England. They must be interested in working under the supervision of an accomplished cancer investigator. Preference is given to student with advanced science course work, laboratory skills, and an interest in research. Minority students and those with American Cancer Society volunteer experience are especially encouraged to apply.

Financial data The grant is $4,500.

Duration 10 weeks during the summer.

Number awarded 1 or more each year.

Deadline January of each year.

[38]
ALVARO L. MARTINS SCHOLARSHIP

Executive Leadership Council
Attn: Executive Leadership Foundation
1001 North Fairfax Street, Suite 300
Alexandria, VA 22314
(703) 706-5200   Fax: (703) 535-6830
E-mail: elcinfo@elcinfo.com
Web: www.elcinfo.com

Summary To provide financial assistance to male students at Historically Black Colleges and Universities (HBCUs).

Eligibility This program is open to African American male undergraduate students enrolled in good academic standing at an accredited HBCU. Applicants must be U.S. citizens and have a GPA of 3.0 or higher. Along with their application, they must submit an essay between 800 and 1,000 words on a topic that changes each year; recently, applicants were invited to write on the topic, "How is your passion and/or purpose influencing the career path you have chosen to pursue?" Selection is based on that essay and financial need.

Financial data The stipend is $7,000. All recipients receive a trip to New York City and Washington D.C. to participate in the foundation's Student Honors Symposium.

Duration 1 year; nonrenewable.

Additional information The Executive Leadership Foundation was founded in 1989 as an affiliate of the Executive Leadership Council, the association of African American senior executives of Fortune 500 companies.

Number awarded 13 each year.

Deadline March of each year.

[39]
AMAC MEMBER AWARD

Airport Minority Advisory Council
Attn: AMAC Foundation
2001 Jefferson Davis Highway, Suite 500
Arlington, VA 22202
(703) 414-2622   Fax: (703) 414-2686
E-mail: terrifrierson@palladiumholdingsco.com
Web: amac-org.com/amac-foundation/scholarships

Summary To provide financial assistance to African American and other minority high school seniors and undergraduates who are preparing for a career in the aviation industry and are connected to Airport Minority Advisory Council (AMAC).

Eligibility This program is open to minority and female high school seniors and current undergraduates who have a GPA of 2.5 or higher and a record of involvement in community and extracurricular activities. Applicants must be interested in working on a bachelor's degree in accounting, architecture, aviation, business administration, engineering, or finance as preparation for a career in the aviation or airport industry. They must be AMAC members, family of members, or mentees of member. Along with their application, they must submit a 750-word essay on how they have overcome barriers in life to achieve their academic and/or career goals; their dedication to succeed in the aviation industry and how AMAC can help them achieve their goal; and the most important issues that the aviation industry is facing today and how they see themselves changing those. Financial need is not considered in the selection process. U.S. citizenship is required.

Financial data The stipend is $2,000 per year.

Duration 1 year; recipients may reapply.

Number awarded 4 each year.

Deadline May of each year.

[40]
AME CHURCH PREACHER'S KID SCHOLARSHIP

African Methodist Episcopal Church
Connectional Ministers' Spouses, Widows and Widowers
   Organization
c/o Yuolanda Murray, Scholarship Committee Chair
12701 Larchmere Boulevard, Unit 4D
Cleveland, OH 44120
E-mail: ConnMSWAWOPk@aol.com
Web: www.ameconnmswawopk.com/#!pk-scholarship/c1lfp

Summary To provide financial assistance for college to children of ministers in the African Methodist Episcopal (AME) Church.

Eligibility This program is open to dependent children under 21 years of age who are entering college freshmen and whose parent or legal guardian is an AME minister. Applicants must be a member of the AME Church, have a score on the SAT of 850 or higher or on the ACT of 20 or higher, rank in the top 50% of their high school class, and have a cumulative GPA of 2.5 or higher. Along with their application, they must submit an essay of 300 to 350 words on how the AME Church has made a difference in their life and what they will do to support their church. Their minister parent must have been a member of the Connectional AME Ministers' Spouses, Widows and Widowers Organization for at least 1 year.

Financial data The scholarship stipend is $2,500. Book awards are $500.

Duration 1 year.

Number awarded Varies each year; recently, the program awarded 1 scholarship and 4 book awards.

Deadline April of each year.

[41]
AMELIA KEMP MEMORIAL SCHOLARSHIP

Women of the Evangelical Lutheran Church in America
Attn: Scholarships
8765 West Higgins Road
Chicago, IL 60631-4101
(773) 380-2741   Toll Free: (800) 638-3522, ext. 2741
Fax: (773) 380-2419   E-mail: valora.starr@elca.org
Web: www.womenoftheelca.org

Summary To provide financial assistance to African American and other lay women of color who are members of Evangelical Lutheran Church of America (ELCA) congregations and who wish to study on the undergraduate, graduate, professional, or vocational school level.

Eligibility This program is open to ELCA lay women of color who are at least 21 years of age and have experienced an interruption of at least 2 years in their education since high school. Applicants must have been admitted to an educational institution to prepare for a career in other than ordained ministry. U.S. citizenship is required.

Financial data The maximum stipend is $1,000 per year.

Duration 1 year; recipients may reapply for 1 additional year.

Number awarded 1 or more each year.

Deadline February of each year.

[42]
AMERICAN AIRLINES AND OBAP EDUCATIONAL FUND SCHOLARSHIP

Organization of Black Aerospace Professionals, Inc.
Attn: Scholarship Coordinator
One Westbrook Corporate Center, Suite 300
Westchester, IL 60154
(708) 449-7755   Toll Free: (800) JET-OBAP
Fax: (708) 449-7754 E-mail: obapscholarships@obap.org
Web: www.obap.org

Summary To provide financial assistance to members of the Organization of Black Aerospace Professionals (OBAP) who are interested in further training as a pilot to advance their career in the aviation industry.

Eligibility This program is open to OBAP members who are enrolled at a 4-year college or university aviation program and working on an advanced pilot rating. Applicants must have a private and instrument pilot certificate. Along with their application, they must submit a 500-word essay that includes why they should be awarded this scholarship, their achievements in and out of the classroom, their career and professional development to date, their future goals, and how this scholarship will help them achieve those goals.

Financial data The stipend is $4,000. Funds are paid directly to the recipient's college.

Duration 1 year.

Additional information The OBAP was originally established in 1976 as the Organization of Black Airline Pilots to make certain Blacks and other minorities had a group that would keep them informed about opportunities for advancement within commercial aviation. This program is sponsored by American Airlines.

Number awarded 1 each year.

Deadline May of each year.

[43]
AMERICAN ASSOCIATION OF BLACKS IN ENERGY NATIONAL SCHOLARSHIPS

American Association of Blacks in Energy
Attn: Scholarship Committee
1625 K Street, N.W., Suite 405
Washington, DC 20006
(202) 371-9530   Fax: (202) 371-9218
E-mail: info@aabe.org
Web: www.aabe.org/index.php?component=pages&id=4

Summary To provide financial assistance to African American and other underrepresented minority high school seniors who are interested in preparing for a career in a field related to energy in college.

Eligibility This program is open to members of minority groups underrepresented in energy-related fields (African Americans, Hispanics, and Native Americans) who are graduating high school seniors. Applicants must have a GPA of 3.0 or higher and have taken the SAT and/or ACT test. They must be planning to attend an accredited college or university to major in business, engineering, mathematics, technology, or the physical sciences. Along with their application, they must submit a 350-word essay that includes 1) when they discovered their interest in the field of energy and what sparked their interest; and 2) either what excites them about the field of energy or how they expect their education to prepare them for the field of energy. Financial need is not considered in the selection process. All applications must be submitted to the local office of the sponsoring organization in the student's state. For a list of local offices, contact the scholarship committee at the national office. The highest-ranked applicant receives the Rufus D. Gladney Premier Award.

Financial data The stipends are $3,000. The Rufus D. Gladney Premier Award is $5,000. All funds are paid directly to the students upon proof of enrollment at an accredited college or university.

Duration 1 year; nonrenewable.

Number awarded 6 each year (1 in each of the organization's regions); of those 6 winners, 1 is chosen to receive the Rufus D. Gladney Premier Award.

Deadline March of each year.

[44]
AMERICAN ASSOCIATION OF PHYSICISTS IN MEDICINE DIVERSITY RECRUITMENT THROUGH EDUCATION AND MENTORING (DREAM) PROGRAM

American Association of Physicists in Medicine
Attn: AAPM Education and Research Fund
One Physics Ellipse
College Park, MD 20740
(301) 209-3350   Fax: (301) 209-0862
E-mail: jackie@aapm.org
Web: www.aapm.org/education/GrantsFellowships.asp

Summary To provide an opportunity for African American and other minority upper-division students to gain summer work experience performing research in a medical physics laboratory or assisting with clinical service at a clinical facility.

Eligibility This program is open to minority undergraduates who are entering their junior or senior year at an Historically Black College or University (HBCU), Minority Serving Institution (MSI), or non-Minority Serving Institution. Applicants must be interested in gaining experience in medical physics by performing research in a laboratory or assisting with clinical service at a clinical facility. Preference is given to those who have declared a major in physics, engineering, or other science that requires mathematics at least through differential equations and junior-level courses in modern physics or quantum mechanics and electricity and magnetism or equivalent courses in engineering sciences. They must be U.S. citizens, U.S. permanent residents, or Canadian citizens. Work must be conducted under the supervision of a mentor who is a member of the American Association of Physicists in Medicine (AAPM) employed by a university, hospital, clinical facility, or radiological industry within the United States.

Financial data The stipend is $5,000.

Duration 10 weeks during the summer.

Additional information This program was formerly known as the American Association of Physicists in Medicine Minority Undergraduate Experience Program.

Number awarded Varies each year; recently, 9 were awarded.

Deadline February of each year.

[45]
AMERICAN BUS ASSOCIATION DIVERSITY SCHOLARSHIPS

American Bus Association
Attn: ABA Foundation
111 K Street, N.E., Ninth Floor
Washington, DC 20002
(202) 842-1645   Toll Free: (800) 283-2877
Fax: (202) 842-0850   E-mail: abainfo@buses.org
Web: www.buses.org/aba-foundation/scholarships/diversity

Summary To provide financial assistance for college to African Amricans and members of other traditionally underrepresented groups who are preparing for a career in the transportation, travel, hospitality, and tourism industry.

Eligibility This program is open to members of traditionally underrepresented groups who have completed at least 1 year of study at a 2- or 4-year college or university. Applicants must be working on a degree in a course of study related to the transportation, travel, hospitality, and tourism industry. They must have a GPA of 3.0 or higher. Along with their application, they must submit a 500-word essay on the role they hope to play in advancing the future of the transportation, travel, hospitality, and tourism industry. Selection is based on academic achievement, character, leadership, financial need, and commitment to advancing the transportation, travel, hospitality, and tourism industry. Additional consideration is given to applicants who are affiliated with a company that is a member of the American Bus Association (ABA).

Financial data The stipend is $2,500.

Duration 1 or more each year.

Deadline April of each year.

[46]
AMERICAN CHEMICAL SOCIETY SCHOLARS PROGRAM

American Chemical Society
Attn: Scholars Program
1155 16th Street, N.W.
Washington, DC 20036
(202) 872-6250   Toll Free: (800) 227-5558, ext. 6250
Fax: (202) 872-4361   E-mail: scholars@acs.org
Web: www.acs.org

Summary To provide financial assistance to African American and other underrepresented minority students who have a strong interest in chemistry and a desire to prepare for a career in a chemically-related science.

Eligibility This program is open to 1) college-bound high school seniors; 2) freshmen, sophomores, and juniors enrolled full time at an accredited college or university; 3) community college students planning to transfer to a 4-year school; and 4) community college students working on a 2-year degree. Applicants must be African American, Hispanic/Latino, or Native American. They must be majoring or planning to major in chemistry, biochemistry, chemical engineering, or other chemically-related fields, such as environmental science, materials science, or toxicology, in preparation for a career in the chemical sciences or chemical technology. Students planning careers in medicine or pharmacy are not eligible. U.S. citizenship or permanent resident status is required. Selection is based on academic record (GPA of 3.0 or higher), career objective, leadership ability, participation in school activities, community service, and financial need.

Financial data Stipends range up to $5,000 per year, depending on the availability of funding, the number of scholarships awarded, and the need of the recipient. Funds are sent directly to the recipient's college or university.

Duration 1 year; may be renewed.

Additional information This program began in 1994.

Number awarded Varies each year; recently, 309 students received these awards.

Deadline February of each year.

[47]
AMERICAN METEOROLOGICAL SOCIETY NAMED SCHOLARSHIPS

American Meteorological Society
Attn: Development and Student Program Manager
45 Beacon Street
Boston, MA 02108-3693
(617) 227-2426, ext. 3907   Fax: (617) 742-8718
E-mail: dFernandez@ametsoc.org
Web: www2.ametsoc.org

Summary To provide financial assistance to undergraduates majoring in meteorology or an aspect of atmospheric sciences, especially African Americans and members of other underrepresented groups.

Eligibility This program is open to full-time students entering their final year of undergraduate study and majoring in meteorology or an aspect of the atmospheric or related oceanic and hydrologic sciences. Applicants must intend to make atmospheric or related sciences their career. They must be U.S. citizens or permanent residents enrolled at a U.S. institution and have a cumulative GPA of 3.25 or higher. Along with their application, they must submit 200-word essays on 1) their most important attributes and achievements that qualify them for this scholarship; and 2) their career goals in the atmospheric or related sciences. Financial need is considered in the selection process. The sponsor specifically encourages applications from women, minorities, and students with disabilities who are traditionally underrepresented in the atmospheric and related sciences.

Financial data Stipend amounts vary each year.

Duration 1 year.

Additional information All scholarships awarded through this program are named after individuals who have assisted the sponsor in various ways.

Number awarded Varies each year; recently, 22 were awarded.

Deadline February of each year.

[48]
AMGEN SCHOLARS PROGRAM AT NIH

National Institutes of Health
Attn: Office of Intramural Training and Education
2 Center Drive
Building 2, Second Floor
Bethesda, MD 20892-0230
(301) 594-2053   Fax: (301) 594-9606
TDD: (888) 352-3001   E-mail: NIH-Amgen@od.nih.gov
Web: www.training.nih.gov/amgenscholars

Summary To provide an opportunity for undergraduates, especially African Americans and members of other diverse groups, to participate in summer research projects in intramural biomedical science laboratories of the National Institutes of Health (NIH).

Eligibility This program is open to rising juniors and seniors at 4-year colleges and universities in the United States, Puerto Rico, and other U.S. territories. Applicants must be U.S. citizens or permanent residents who have a cumulative GPA of 3.2 or higher and an interest in continuing on for a Ph.D. or other combined degree program in the sciences.

Financial data The stipend is $2,140 per month for rising juniors or $2,240 per month for rising seniors. Students with experience in health disparities and a keen interest in learning more about the biological, environmental, social, and genetic causes of health disparities are especially encouraged to apply. Preference is given to students who lack opportunities to perform independent research during the school year. NIH welcomes applications from students in all science disciplines and encourages students from diverse backgrounds to apply.

Duration 10 weeks during the summer.

Additional information This program serves as the NIH component of the Amgen Scholars Program, which also operates at 9 U.S. universities and is funded by the Amgen Foundation.

Number awarded Approximately 20 each year.

Deadline January of each year.

[49]
AMS FRESHMAN UNDERGRADUATE SCHOLARSHIPS

American Meteorological Society
Attn: Development and Student Program Manager
45 Beacon Street
Boston, MA 02108-3693
(617) 227-2426, ext. 3907　　　Fax: (617) 742-8718
E-mail: dFernandez@ametsoc.org
Web: www2.ametsoc.org

Summary To provide financial assistance to high school seniors, especially African Americans and members of other underrepresented groups, who are planning to attend college to prepare for a career in the atmospheric or related oceanic or hydrologic sciences.

Eligibility This program is open to high school seniors entering their freshman year of college to work on a bachelor's degree in the atmospheric or related oceanic or hydrologic sciences. Applicants must be U.S. citizens or permanent residents planning to enroll full time. Along with their application, they must submit a 500-word essay on how they believe their college education, and what they learn in the atmospheric and related sciences, will help them to serve society during their professional career. Selection is based on performance in high school, including academic records, recommendations, scores from a national examination, and the essay. Financial need is not considered. The sponsor specifically encourages applications from women, minorities, and students with disabilities who are traditionally underrepresented in the atmospheric and related oceanic sciences.

Financial data The stipend is $2,500 per academic year.

Duration 1 year; may be renewed for the second year of college study.

Number awarded Varies each year; recently, 13 were awarded.

Deadline February of each year.

[50]
AMS MINORITY SCHOLARSHIPS

American Meteorological Society
Attn: Development and Student Program Manager
45 Beacon Street
Boston, MA 02108-3693
(617) 227-2426, ext. 3907　　　Fax: (617) 742-8718
E-mail: dFernandez@ametsoc.org
Web: www2.ametsoc.org

Summary To provide financial assistance to African American and other underrepresented minority students entering college and planning to major in meteorology or an aspect of atmospheric sciences.

Eligibility This program is open to members of minority groups traditionally underrepresented in the sciences (especially Blacks/African Americans, Hispanics, and Native Americans) who are entering their freshman year at a college or university and planning to work on a degree in the atmospheric or related oceanic and hydrologic sciences. Applicants must submit an official high school transcript showing grades from the past 3 years, a letter of recommendation from a high school teacher or guidance counselor, a copy of scores from an SAT or similar national entrance exam, and a 500-word essay on a topic that changes annually; recently, applicants were invited to write on global change and how they would use their college education in atmospheric science (or a closely-related field) to make their community a better place in which to live. Selection is based on the essay and academic performance in high school.

Financial data The stipend is $3,000 per year.

Duration 1 year; may be renewed for the second year of college study.

Additional information This program is funded by grants from industry and by donations to the American Meteorological Society (AMS) 21st Century Campaign. Requests for an application must be accompanied by a self-addressed stamped envelope.

Number awarded Varies each year; recently, 3 were awarded.

Deadline February of each year.

[51]
ANA MULTICULTURAL EXCELLENCE SCHOLARSHIP

American Association of Advertising Agencies
Attn: AAAA Foundation
1065 Avenue of the Americas, 16th Floor
New York, NY 10018
(212) 262-2500　　　E-mail: ameadows@aaaa.org
Web: www.aaaa.org

Summary To provide financial assistance to African American and other multicultural students who are working on an undergraduate degree in advertising.

Eligibility This program is open to undergraduate students who are U.S. citizens of proven multicultural heritage and have at least 1 grandparent of multicultural heritage. Applicants must be participating in the Multicultural Advertising Intern Program (MAIP). They must be entering their senior year at an accredited college or university in the United States and have a GPA of 3.0 or higher. Selection is based on academic ability.

Financial data The stipend is $2,500.

Duration 1 year.

Additional information This program was established by the Association of National Advertisers (ANA) in 2001. The American Association of Advertising Agencies (AAAA) assumed administration in 2003.

Number awarded 2 each year.

Deadline Deadline not specified.

[52]
ANAC STUDENT DIVERSITY MENTORSHIP SCHOLARSHIP

Association of Nurses in AIDS Care
Attn: Awards Committee
3538 Ridgewood Road
Akron, OH 44333-3122
(330) 670-0101   Toll Free: (800) 260-6780
Fax: (330) 670-0109   E-mail: anac@anacnet.org
Web: www.nursesinaidscare.org

Summary To provide financial assistance to student nurses from African American and other minority groups who are interested in HIV/AIDS nursing and in attending the national conference of the Association of Nurses in AIDS Care (ANAC).

Eligibility This program is open to student nurses from a diverse racial or ethnic background, defined to include African Americans, Hispanics/Latinos, Asians/Pacific Islanders, and American Indians/Alaskan Natives. Candidates must have a genuine interest in HIV/AIDS nursing, be interested in attending the ANAC national conference, and desire to develop a mentorship relationship with a member of the ANAC Diversity Specialty Committee. They may be 1) pre-licensure students enrolled in an initial R.N. or L.P.N./L.V.N. program (i.e. L.P.N./L.V.N., A.D.N., diploma, B.S./B.S.N.); or 2) current licensed R.N. students with an associate or diploma degree who are enrolled in a bachelor's degree program. Nominees may be recommended by themselves, nursing faculty members, or ANAC members, but their nomination must be supported by an ANAC member. Along with their nomination form, they must submit a 2,000-character essay describing their interest or experience in HIV/AIDS care and why they want to attend the ANAC conference.

Financial data Recipients are awarded a $1,000 scholarship (paid directly to the school), up to $599 in reimbursement of travel expenses to attend the ANAC annual conference, free conference registration, an award plaque, a free ticket to the awards ceremony at the conference, and a 2-year ANAC membership.

Duration 1 year.

Additional information The mentor will be assigned at the conference and will maintain contact during the period of study.

Number awarded 1 each year.

Deadline August of each year.

[53]
ANGELA DUCKER RICHARDSON MEMORIAL SCHOLARSHIP

Alpha Kappa Alpha Sorority, Inc.-Rho Mu Omega Chapter
Attn: DC Pearls III Foundation
Scholarship Committee
P.O. Box 91191
Washington, DC 20090-1198
(202) 277-8946   E-mail: scholarship@rhomuomega.org
Web: www.rhomuomega.org/scholarship.htm

Summary To provide financial assistance to high school seniors in Washington, D.C. who plan to attend an Historically Black College or University (HBCU) and major in health or science.

Eligibility This program is open to seniors graduating from high schools in Washington, D.C. and planning to enroll full time at an HBCU. Applicants must intend to major in health or science. They must have a GPA of 2.5 or higher and have taken the ACT or SAT test. Along with their application, they must submit a 2-page personal statement on the greatest challenge they have faced in their academic life and how it has motivated them to prepare for a career in a health or science field. Selection is based on academic record, school and community activities, leadership, and financial need. U.S. citizenship or permanent resident status is required.

Financial data The stipend is $1,000.

Duration 1 year.

Number awarded 1 each year.

Deadline April of each year.

[54]
ANN FUDGE SCHOLARSHIP

Executive Leadership Council
Attn: Executive Leadership Foundation
1001 North Fairfax Street, Suite 300
Alexandria, VA 22314
(703) 706-5200   Fax: (703) 535-6830
E-mail: elcinfo@elcinfo.com
Web: www.elcinfo.com

Summary To provide financial assistance to female students at Historically Black Colleges and Universities (HBCUs).

Eligibility This program is open to African American female undergraduate students enrolled in good academic standing at an accredited HBCU. Applicants must be U.S. citizens and have a GPA of 3.0 or higher. Along with their application, they must submit an essay between 800 and 1,000 words on a topic that changes each year; recently, applicants were invited to write on their leadership style and how they have been able to exhibit their specific leadership behavior in their current environment. Selection is based on that essay and financial need.

Financial data The stipend is $7,000. All recipients receive a trip to New York City and Washington D.C. to participate in the foundation's Student Honors Symposium.

Duration 1 year; nonrenewable.

Additional information The Executive Leadership Foundation was founded in 1989 as an affiliate of the Executive Leadership Council, the association of African American senior executives of Fortune 500 companies.

Number awarded 13 each year.

Deadline March of each year.

[55]
ANN MCALLISTER HUGHES FOUNDATION FELLOWSHIP

Alpha Kappa Alpha Sorority, Inc.
Attn: Educational Advancement Foundation
5656 South Stony Island Avenue
Chicago, IL 60637
(773) 947-0026   Toll Free: (800) 653-6528
Fax: (773) 947-0277   E-mail: akaeaf@akaeaf.net
Web: www.akaeaf.org/fellowships_endowments.htm

Summary To provide financial assistance to members of Alpha Kappa Alpha Sorority from Maryland who are working on a degree in art.

Eligibility This program is open to members of Alpha Kappa Alpha, a traditionally African American sorority, who are residents of Maryland and enrolled as sophomores or higher at an accredited degree-granting institution in any state. Applicants must be majoring in art. Along with their application, they must submit 1) a list of honors, awards, and scholarships received; 2) a list of organizations in which they have memberships, especially minority organizations; and 3) a statement of their personal and career goals, including how this scholarship will enhance their ability to attain those goals. The sponsor is.

Financial data A stipend is awarded (amount not specified).

Duration 1 year.

Number awarded 1 or more each even-numbered year.

Deadline April of each even-numbered year.

[56]
ANNE SHEN SMITH ENDOWED SCHOLARSHIP

Society of Women Engineers
Attn: Scholarship Selection Committee
203 North LaSalle Street, Suite 1675
Chicago, IL 60601-1269
(312) 596-5223   Toll Free: (877) SWE-INFO
Fax: (312) 644-8557   E-mail: scholarships@swe.org
Web: societyofwomenengineers.swe.org

Summary To provide financial assistance to women, especially African Americans and members of other underrepresented groups, working on an undergraduate degree in engineering at colleges in California.

Eligibility This program is open to women who are entering their sophomore, junior, or senior year at a 4-year ABET-accredited college or university in California. Applicants must be working full time on a degree in computer science or any field of engineering. Preference is given to members of groups underrepresented in engineering. U.S. citizenship is required. Selection is based on merit.

Financial data The stipend is $1,000.

Duration 1 year.

Additional information This program began in 2015.

Number awarded 1 each year.

Deadline February of each year.

[57]
ANTHEM BLUE CROSS BLUE SHIELD OF WISCONSIN NURSING SCHOLARSHIPS

Wisconsin League for Nursing
Attn: Scholarship Chair
P.O. Box 653
Germantown, WI 53022
(414) 454-9561   E-mail: info@wisconsinwln.org
Web: www.wisconsinwln.org/t/Scholarships

Summary To provide financial assistance to residents of Wisconsin, especially African Americans and other minorities, attending a school of nursing in the state.

Eligibility This program is open to residents of Wisconsin who are enrolled at an accredited school of nursing in the state in an L.P.N., A.D.N., B.S.N., M.S.N., D.N.P., or Ph.D. program. Applicants must have completed at least half the credits needed for graduation. Ethnic minority students are especially encouraged to apply. Students must submit their applications to their school, not directly to the sponsor. Each school may nominate 4 graduate students, 6 students in an R.N. program, and 2 L.P.N. students. Selection is based on scholastic ability, professional abilities and/or community service, understanding of the nursing profession, goals upon graduation, and financial need.

Financial data Stipends are $500 for L.P.N. students or $1,000 for all other students.

Duration 1 year.

Additional information This program is sponsored by Anthem Blue Cross Blue Shield of Wisconsin.

Number awarded Varies each year; recently, the program awarded 31 scholarships, including 2 L.P.N. awards, 10 associate degree awards, 16 B.S.N. awards, and 3 graduate awards.

Deadline April of each year.

[58]
APPLE HBCU SCHOLARS PROGRAM

Thurgood Marshall College Fund
Attn: Senior Manager of Scholarship Programs
901 F Street, N.W., Suite 300
Washington, DC 20004
(202) 507-4851   Fax: (202) 652-2934
E-mail: deshuandra.walker@tmcfund.org
Web: www.tmcf.org

Summary To provide financial assistance and work experience to students majoring in designated fields at a Historically Black College or University (HBCU) or Predominantly Black Institution (PBI).

Eligibility This program is open to students who are currently enrolled full time in their second-to-last year (i.e., juniors or seniors in a 5-year program) at a 4-year HBCU or PBI. The program targets students majoring in fields of science, technology, engineering, and mathematics (STEM), but opportunities exist in other fields as well. They must have a current GPA of 3.25 or higher and be available for a summer internship in Cupertino, California. Selection is based on both a technical fit (analytical ability, verbal and written communication skills, ability to articulate ideas, ability to learn new concepts) and cultural fit (highly motivated, persuasive and candid, focused on results, team player, sound judgment, and critical thinking skills).

Financial data The stipend is $25,000.

Duration 1 year (the final year of study).

Additional information This program was established in 2015 by Apple.

Number awarded Varies each year; recently, 33 were awarded.

Deadline April of each year.

[59]
APS/IBM RESEARCH INTERNSHIP FOR UNDERREPRESENTED MINORITY STUDENTS

American Physical Society
Attn: Committee on Minorities
One Physics Ellipse
College Park, MD 20740-3844
(301) 209-3232   Fax: (301) 209-0865
E-mail: apsibmin@us.ibm.com
Web: www.aps.org

Summary To provide an opportunity for African American and other underrepresented minority students to participate in a summer research internship in science or engineering at facilities of IBM.

Eligibility This program is open to members of underrepresented minority groups currently enrolled as sophomores or juniors and majoring in biology, chemistry, chemical engineering, computer science or engineering, electrical engineering, materials science or engineering, mechanical engineering, or physics. Applicants are not required to be U.S. citizens, but they must be enrolled at a college or university in the United States. They must be interested in working as a research intern at a participating IBM laboratory. A GPA of at least 3.0 is required. Selection is based on commitment to and interest in their major field of study.

Financial data Interns receive a competitive salary of approximately $8,000 for the summer.

Duration 10 weeks during the summer.

Additional information Participating IBM laboratories are the Almaden Research Center in San Jose, California, the Watson Research Center in Yorktown Heights, New York, or the Austin Research Laboratory in Austin, Texas.

Number awarded 1 each year.

Deadline February of each year.

[60]
ARCELORMITTAL EMERGING LEADER SCHOLARSHIPS

Society of Women Engineers
Attn: Scholarship Selection Committee
203 North LaSalle Street, Suite 1675
Chicago, IL 60601-1269
(312) 596-5223   Toll Free: (877) SWE-INFO
Fax: (312) 644-8557   E-mail: scholarships@swe.org
Web: societyofwomenengineers.swe.org

Summary To provide financial assistance to members of the Society of Women Engineers (SWE), especially African Americans and members of other underrepresented groups, who are interested in studying specified fields of engineering at designated universities.

Eligibility This program is open to SWE members who are entering their junior year at Ohio State University, Indiana University, Purdue University, Michigan State University,

Michigan Technological University, Pennsylvania State University, Rose-Hulman Institute of Technology, Purdue University Northwest (formerly Purdue University-Calumet), Missouri University of Science and Technology, Iowa State University, or University of Illinois at Urbana-Champaign. Applicants must be enrolled full time and majoring in computer science or computer, electrical, or materials engineering. They must be U.S. citizens. Preference is given to members of underrepresented groups, including veterans. Selection is based on merit and financial need.

Financial data The stipend is $1,000.

Duration 1 year.

Additional information This program is sponsored by ArcelorMittal.

Number awarded 1 each year.

Deadline February of each year.

[61]
ARKANSAS CONFERENCE ETHNIC AND LANGUAGE CONCERNS COMMITTEE SCHOLARSHIPS

United Methodist Church-Arkansas Conference
Attn: Committee on Ethnic and Language Concerns
800 Daisy Bates Drive
Little Rock, AR 72202
(501) 324-8045   Toll Free: (877) 646-1816
Fax: (501) 324-8018   E-mail: mallen@arumc.org
Web: www.arumc.org/docs-and-forms

Summary To provide financial assistance to African American and other ethnic minority Methodist students from Arkansas who are interested in attending college or graduate school in any state.

Eligibility This program is open to ethnic minority undergraduate and graduate students who are active members of local congregations affiliated with the Arkansas Conference of the United Methodist Church (UMC). Applicants must be currently enrolled in an accredited institution of higher education in any state. Along with their application, they must submit an essay explaining how this scholarship will make them a leader in the UMC. Preference is given to students attending a UMC-affiliated college or university.

Financial data The stipend is $500 per semester ($1,000 per year) for undergraduates or $1,000 per semester ($2,000 per year) for graduate students.

Duration 1 year; may be renewed.

Number awarded 5 each year: 1 in each UMC Arkansas district.

Deadline February or September of each year.

[62]
ARTHUR H. GOODMAN MEMORIAL SCHOLARSHIP

San Diego Foundation
Attn: Community Scholarships
2508 Historic Decatur Road, Suite 200
San Diego, CA 92106
(619) 814-1343   Fax: (619) 239-1710
E-mail: scholarships@sdfoundation.org
Web: www.sdfoundation.org

Summary To provide financial assistance to African American and other minority community college students in California or Arizona planning to transfer to a 4-year school in any state to prepare for a career in economic development.

Eligibility This program is open to women and minorities currently enrolled at a community college in California or Arizona and planning to transfer as a full- or part-time student at a 4-year school in any state. Applicants must submit information on their long-term career goal, a list of volunteer and extracurricular activities, documentation of financial need, and a 3-page personal statement on their commitment to community involvement and desire to prepare for a career in the field of economic development.

Financial data Stipends range from $1,500 to $3,000.

Duration 1 year.

Additional information This program was established in 1998 by the CDC Small Business Finance Corporation.

Number awarded Varies each year; recently, 5 were awarded.

Deadline April of each year.

[63]
ARTTABLE MENTORED INTERNSHIPS FOR DIVERSITY IN THE VISUAL ARTS PROFESSIONS

ArtTable Inc.
1 East 53rd Street, Fifth Floor
New York, NY 10022
(212) 343-1735   Fax: (866) 363-4188
E-mail: info@arttable.org
Web: www.arttable.org/summermentoredinternship

Summary To provide an opportunity for African American and other women from diverse backgrounds to gain mentored work experience during the summer and to prepare for a career as an art professional.

Eligibility This program is open to women who are college seniors, recent graduates, or graduate students and interested in preparing for a career as a visual arts professional (including administrative director, art adviser, art appraiser, art critic, art dealer, art librarian, arts funder, arts lawyer, conservator, curator, editor, educator, fundraiser, management consultant, public relations consultant, writer). Applicants must be from a cultural or ethnic background that is underrepresented in the field. They must be interested in working during the summer with a mentor at an art museum or similar facility. U.S. citizenship or permanent resident status is required.

Financial data The stipend is $3,000. The hosting institution or mentor receives $500 for administrative and other costs.

Duration 8 weeks during the summer.

Additional information This program began in 2000. Support is provided by the Samuel H. Kress Foundation.

Number awarded Varies each year; recently, 5 of these internships were awarded.

Deadline February of each year.

[64]
ASCPA EDUCATIONAL FOUNDATION DIVERSITY SCHOLARSHIPS

Alabama Society of Certified Public Accountants
Attn: ASCPA Educational Foundation
1041 Longfield Court
P.O. Box 242987
Montgomery, AL 36124-2987
(334) 834-7650   Toll Free: (800) 227-1711 (within AL)
Fax: (334) 834-7603
Web: www.ascpa.org

Summary To provide financial assistance to African American and other minority accounting students at colleges and universities in Alabama.

Eligibility This program is open to minority (Black or African American, Hispanic or Latino, Native American, or Asian) residents of any state enrolled at least half time at colleges and universities in Alabama with at least 1 full year of school remaining. Applicants must have declared a major in accounting and have completed intermediate accounting courses. They must have a GPA of 3.0 or higher overall and in all accounting classes. Along with their application, they must submit a 25-word essay on why the scholarship is important to them. Financial need is not considered in the selection process. Preference is given to students who have a strong interest in a career as a C.P.A. in Alabama. U.S. citizenship or permanent resident status is required.

Financial data The stipend is $2,500.

Duration 1 year.

Additional information This program began in 2012.

Number awarded 5 each year.

Deadline March of each year.

[65]
ASLA COUNCIL OF FELLOWS SCHOLARSHIPS

Landscape Architecture Foundation
Attn: Leadership in Landscape Scholarship Program
1129 20th Street, N.W., Suite 202
Washington, DC 20036
(202) 331-7070   Fax: (202) 331-7079
E-mail: scholarships@lafoundation.org
Web: www.lafoundation.org

Summary To provide financial assistance to upper-division students, especially African Americans and members of other disadvantaged and underrepresented groups, working on a degree in landscape architecture.

Eligibility This program is open to landscape architecture students in the third, fourth, or fifth year of undergraduate work. Preference is given to, and 1 scholarship is reserved for, members of underrepresented ethnic or cultural groups. Applicants must submit a 500-word essay on how they envision themselves contributing to the profession of landscape architecture, 2 letters of recommendation, documentation of financial need, and (for students applying for the scholarship reserved for underrepresented groups) a statement identifying their association with a specific ethnic or cultural group. U.S. citizenship or permanent resident status is required.

Financial data The stipend is $4,000. Students also receive a 1-year membership in the American Society of Landscape Architects (ASLA), general registration fees for the ASLA annual meeting, and a travel stipend to attend the meeting.

Duration   1 year.

Additional information   This program is sponsored by ASLA and administered by the Landscape Architecture Foundation.

Number awarded   3 each year, of which 1 is reserved for a member of an underrepresented group.

Deadline   February of each year.

[66]
ASSE DIVERSITY COMMITTEE UNDERGRADUATE SCHOLARSHIP

American Society of Safety Engineers
Attn: ASSE Foundation
Scholarship Award Program
520 North Northwest Highway
Park Ridge, IL 60068-2538
(847) 699-2929   Fax: (847) 296-3769
E-mail: assefoundation@asse.org
Web: foundation.asse.org/scholarships-and-grants

Summary   To provide financial assistance to upper-division students who are African Americans or members of other diverse groups and working on a degree related to occupational safety.

Eligibility   This program is open to students who are working on an undergraduate degree in occupational safety, health, environment, industrial hygiene, occupational health nursing, or a closely-related field (e.g., industrial or environmental engineering). Applicants must be full-time students who have completed at least 60 semester hours and have a GPA of 3.0 or higher. A goal of this program is to support individuals regardless of race, ethnicity, gender, religion, personal beliefs, age, sexual orientation, physical challenges, geographic location, university, or specific area of study. U.S. citizenship is not required. Membership in the American Society of Safety Engineers (ASSE) is not required, but preference is given to members.

Financial data   The stipend is $1,000 per year.

Duration   1 year; recipients may reapply.

Number awarded   1 each year.

Deadline   November of each year.

[67]
ASSOCIATED FOOD AND PETROLEUM DEALERS MINORITY SCHOLARSHIPS

Associated Food and Petroleum Dealers
Attn: AFPD Foundation
5779 West Maple Road
West Bloomfield, MI 48322
(248) 671-9600   Toll Free: (800) 666-6233
Fax: (866) 601-9610   E-mail: info@afpdonline.org
Web: www.afpdonline.org/michigan-scholarship.php

Summary   To provide financial assistance to minority high school seniors and current college students from Michigan who are enrolled or planning to enroll at a college in any state.

Eligibility   This program is open to Michigan residents who are high school seniors or college freshmen, sophomores, or juniors. Applicants must be members of 1 of the following minority groups: African American, Hispanic, Asian, Native

American, or Arab/Chaldean. They must be enrolled or planning to enroll full time at a college or university in any state. Preferential consideration is given to applicants with a membership affiliation in the Associated Food and Petroleum Dealers (AFPD), although membership is not required. Selection is based on academic performance, leadership, and participation in school and community activities; college grades are considered if the applicant is already enrolled in college.

Financial data   The stipend is $1,500 per year.

Duration   1 year; may be renewed 1 additional year.

Additional information   This program is administered by International Scholarship and Tuition Services, Inc. The AFPD was formed in 2006 by a merger of the Associated Food Dealers of Michigan and the Great Lakes Petroleum Retailers and Allied Trades Association.

Number awarded   At least 10 each year, of which at least 3 must be awarded to member customers.

Deadline   March of each year.

[68]
ASSOCIATION FOR WOMEN GEOSCIENTISTS MINORITY SCHOLARSHIP

Association for Women Geoscientists
Attn: AWG Foundation
12000 North Washington Street, Suite 285
Thornton, CO 80241
(303) 412-6219   Fax: (303) 253-9220
E-mail: office@awg.org
Web: www.awg.org/eas/minority.htm

Summary   To provide financial assistance to African American and other underrepresented minority women who are interested in working on an undergraduate degree in the geosciences.

Eligibility   This program is open to women who are African American, Hispanic, or Native American (including Eskimo, Hawaiian, Samoan, or American Indian). Applicants must be full-time students working on, or planning to work on, an undergraduate degree in the geosciences (including geology, geophysics, geochemistry, hydrology, meteorology, physical oceanography, planetary geology, or earth science education). They must submit a 500-word essay on their academic and career goals, 2 letters of recommendation, high school and/or college transcripts, and SAT or ACT scores. Financial need is not considered in the selection process. U.S. citizenship is required.

Financial data   A total of $6,000 is available for this program each year.

Duration   1 year; may be renewed.

Additional information   This program, first offered in 2004, is supported by ExxonMobil Foundation.

Number awarded   1 or more each year.

Deadline   June of each year.

[69]
ATKINS NORTH AMERICA ACHIEVEMENT COLLEGE SCHOLARSHIP

Conference of Minority Transportation Officials
Attn: National Scholarship Program
100 M Street, S.E., Suite 917
Washington, DC 20003
(202) 506-2917   E-mail: info@comto.org
Web: www.comto.org/page/scholarships

Summary To provide financial assistance to African American and other minority undergraduates interested in working on a degree in transportation or a related field.

Eligibility This program is open to minority students who have completed at least 12 semester hours as full-time undergraduates. Applicants must be studying transportation, engineering, planning, or a related discipline. Along with their application they must submit a cover letter on their transportation-related career goals and life aspirations. Financial need is not considered in the selection process.

Financial data The stipend is $2,000. Funds are paid directly to the recipient's college or university.

Duration 1 year.

Additional information This program is sponsored by Atkins North America.

Number awarded 1 each year.

Deadline April of each year.

[70]
ATKINS NORTH AMERICA ACHIEVEMENT HIGH SCHOOL SCHOLARSHIP

Conference of Minority Transportation Officials
Attn: National Scholarship Program
100 M Street, S.E., Suite 917
Washington, DC 20003
(202) 506-2917   E-mail: info@comto.org
Web: www.comto.org/page/scholarships

Summary To provide financial assistance to African American and other minority high school seniors interested in working on a degree in transportation or a related field.

Eligibility This program is open to minority seniors graduating from high school with a GPA of 3.0 or higher. Applicants must be planning to study aspects of transportation, including technology, engineering, planning, or management. Along with their application they must submit a cover letter on their transportation-related career goals and life aspirations. Financial need is not considered in the selection process.

Financial data The stipend is $2,000. Funds are paid directly to the recipient's college or university.

Duration 1 year.

Additional information This program is sponsored by Atkins North America.

Number awarded 1 each year.

Deadline April of each year.

[71]
ATKINS NORTH AMERICA LEADERSHIP SCHOLARSHIP

Conference of Minority Transportation Officials
Attn: National Scholarship Program
100 M Street, S.E., Suite 917
Washington, DC 20003
(202) 506-2917   E-mail: info@comto.org
Web: www.comto.org/page/scholarships

Summary To provide financial assistance to African American and other minority undergraduate and graduate students interested in working on a degree in transportation or a related field.

Eligibility This program is open to minority 1) undergraduates who have completed at least 12 semester hours of study; and 2) graduate students. Applicants must be studying transportation, engineering, planning, or a related discipline. Along with their application they must submit a cover letter on their transportation-related career goals and life aspirations. Financial need is not considered in the selection process.

Financial data The stipend is $3,000. Funds are paid directly to the recipient's college or university.

Duration 1 year.

Additional information This program is sponsored by Atkins North America.

Number awarded 1 each year.

Deadline April of each year.

[72]
ATLANTA CHAPTER AABE SCHOLARSHIPS

American Association of Blacks in Energy-Atlanta
  Chapter
Attn: Scholarship Committee
P.O. Box 55216
Atlanta, GA 30308-5216
(404) 506-6756
E-mail: G2AABEATCHAP@southernco.com
Web: www.aabe.org/atlanta

Summary To provide financial assistance to African Americans and members of other underrepresented minority groups who are high school seniors in Georgia and planning to major in an energy-related field at a college in any state.

Eligibility This program is open to seniors graduating from high schools in Georgia and planning to attend a college or university in any state. Applicants must be African Americans, Hispanics, or Native Americans who have a GPA of 3.0 or higher and who have taken the ACT and/or SAT test. Their intended major must be business, engineering, technology, mathematics, the physical sciences, or other energy-related field. Along with their application, they must submit a 350-word essay that includes 1) when they discovered their interest in the field of energy and what sparked their interest; and 2) either what excites them about the field of energy or how they expect their education to prepare them for the field of energy. Financial need is not considered in the selection process.

Financial data Stipends of varying amounts are awarded.

Duration 1 year; may be renewed at the rate of $500 per year, provided the recipient remains enrolled full time and maintains a GPA of 3.0 or higher.

Additional information The winners are eligible to compete for regional and national scholarships.

Number awarded 1 or more each year.

Deadline March of each year.

[73]
ATLANTA CHAPTER NBMBAA UNDERGRADUATE SCHOLARSHIPS

National Black MBA Association-Atlanta Chapter
Attn: Director, Student Affairs
P.O. Box 54656
Atlanta, GA 30308-0656
(404) 572-8001   E-mail: scholarship@atlbmba.org
Web: www.atlbmba.org/student-affairs/scholarships

Summary To provide financial assistance to members of the National Black MBA Association (NBMBAA) from any state who are high school seniors or undergraduates working on a degree in business at a college in the metropolitan Atlanta area of Georgia.

Eligibility This program is open to African American residents of any state who are NBMBAA members and currently enrolled or planning to enroll full time at a designated college or university in the Atlanta metropolitan area of Georgia. Applicants must be interested in working on a bachelor's degree in accounting, business, finance, or management. They must have a GPA of 3.0 or higher. Along with their application, they must submit a 500-word essay on a specified topic that changes annually but relates to African Americans and business. Financial need is not considered in the selection process. U.S. citizenship is required.

Financial data The stipend is $1,500.

Duration 1 year.

Additional information The eligible institutions are Clark Atlanta University, Clayton State University, Emory University, Georgia Institute of Technology, Georgia State University, Kennesaw State University, Mercer University, Morehouse College, and the University of Georgia. Recipients must agree to attend the annual scholarship awards luncheon and engage in limited public relations activities of the sponsoring organization.

Number awarded 1 or more each year; normally, this sponsor awards $20,000 in scholarships annually.

Deadline September of each year.

[74]
ATLANTA JAMAICAN ASSOCIATION SCHOLARSHIP

Atlanta Jamaican Association
Attn: Education Committee
P.O. Box 2207
Lithonia, GA 30058
(678) 549-4876   E-mail: secretary@ajaatlanta.org
Web: www.ajaatlanta.org/Scholarship.aspx

Summary To provide financial assistance for college to high school seniors and current undergraduates who are of Jamaican heritage.

Eligibility This program is open to high school seniors and currently-enrolled undergraduates who live in any state and are of Jamaican parentage (at least 1 parent must be Jamaican). Applicants must be attending or planning to attend a 2- or 4-year college or university. They must have a GPA of 3.0

or higher. Along with their application, they must submit a 500-word essay on a topic that changes annually but relates to Jamaica; recently, students were invited to write on how Jamaica's educational system has evolved over the past 50 years. Finalists are interviewed.

Financial data A stipend is awarded (amount not specified).

Duration 1 year.

Additional information This program began in 1995.

Number awarded 1 or more each year.

Deadline May of each year.

[75]
AUDRE LORDE SCHOLARSHIP AWARD

ZAMI NOBLA
Attn: Audre Lorde Scholarship Fund
P.O. Box 90986
Atlanta, GA 30364
(404) 647-4754   E-mail: zami@zami.org
Web: www.zami.org/audrelordescholar.html

Summary To provide financial assistance to mature out Black lesbians who are interested in entering or continuing in college or graduate school.

Eligibility This program is open to Black lesbians who are at least 40 years of age and out to themselves and their family, friends, and community. Applicants must be enrolled or planning to enroll full or part time at a technical, undergraduate, or graduate school in any state. They must have a cumulative GPA in high school, college, or technical school of 3.0 or higher. Along with their application, they must submit an essay of 2 to 3 pages on their choice of 2 of 5 assigned topics that relate to their experience as a Black lesbian.

Financial data The stipend is $1,000.

Duration 1 year.

Additional information From 1995 to 2008, the Audre Lorde Scholarship Fund was maintained by an organization named ZAMI: Atlanta's Premiere Organization for Lesbians of African Descent. The fund was reestablished in 2013 by the current sponsor, which stands for ZAMI National Organization of Black Lesbians on Aging.

Number awarded 1 each year.

Deadline April of each year.

[76]
AVIATION AND PROFESSIONAL DEVELOPMENT SCHOLARSHIP

Airport Minority Advisory Council
Attn: AMAC Foundation
2001 Jefferson Davis Highway, Suite 500
Arlington, VA 22202
(703) 414-2622   Fax: (703) 414-2686
E-mail: terrifrierson@palladiumholdingsco.com
Web: amac-org.com/amac-foundation/scholarships

Summary To provide financial assistance to African American and other minority high school seniors and undergraduates who are preparing for a career in the aviation industry and interested in participating in activities of the Airport Minority Advisory Council (AMAC).

Eligibility This program is open to minority and female high school seniors and current undergraduates who have a GPA of 2.5 or higher and a record of involvement in community and extracurricular activities. Applicants must be interested in working on a bachelor's degree in accounting, architecture, aviation, business administration, engineering, or finance as preparation for a career in the aviation or airport industry. They must be interested in participating in the AMAC program, including becoming a member if they are awarded a scholarship, and communicating with AMAC once each semester during the term of the scholarship. Along with their application, they must submit a 750-word essay on how they have overcome barriers in life to achieve their academic and/ or career goals; their dedication to succeed in the aviation industry and how AMAC can help them achieve their goal; and the most important issues that the aviation industry is facing today and how they see themselves changing those. Financial need is not considered in the selection process. U.S. citizenship is required.

Financial data The stipend is $2,000 per year.

Duration 1 year; recipients may reapply.

Number awarded 4 each year.

Deadline May of each year.

[77]
AVIS DAISY ELLISON FELLOWSHIP

Alpha Kappa Alpha Sorority, Inc.
Attn: Educational Advancement Foundation
5656 South Stony Island Avenue
Chicago, IL 60637
(773) 947-0026   Toll Free: (800) 653-6528
Fax: (773) 947-0277   E-mail: akaeaf@akaeaf.net
Web: www.akaeaf.org/fellowships_endowments.htm

Summary To provide financial assistance to undergraduates from Maryland (especially African American women) who are working on a degree in mathematics.

Eligibility This program is open to residents of Maryland who are enrolled as sophomores or juniors at an accredited degree-granting institution in any state. Applicants must be majoring in mathematics and have a GPA of 2.75 or higher. Along with their application, they must submit 1) a list of honors, awards, and scholarships received; 2) a list of organizations in which they have memberships, especially minority organizations; and 3) a statement of their personal and career goals, including how this scholarship will enhance their ability to attain those goals. The sponsor is a traditionally African American women's sorority.

Financial data A stipend is awarded (amount not specified).

Duration 1 year.

Number awarded 1 or more each even-numbered year.

Deadline April of each even-numbered year.

[78]
AWARD FOR EXCELLENCE IN BUSINESS COMMENTARY

Executive Leadership Council
Attn: Executive Leadership Foundation
1001 North Fairfax Street, Suite 300
Alexandria, VA 22314
(703) 706-5200   Fax: (703) 535-6830
E-mail: elcinfo@elcinfo.com
Web: www.elcinfo.com

Summary To recognize and reward, with college scholarships, outstanding essays written by African American students on selected business topics.

Eligibility This competition is open to African American undergraduate students in good academic standing enrolled full time at an accredited college or university. Applicants must be U.S. citizens and have a GPA of 3.0 or higher. They must write an essay between 800 and 1,000 words on a topic that changes each year; recently, applicants were invited to write on what they believe attracts the best candidates to employers.

Financial data The top 5 winners receive scholarships ranging from $8,000 to $15,000. Honorable mention winners receive $4,000 scholarships. All contest winners receive a trip to New York City and Washington D.C. to participate in the foundation's Student Honors Symposium.

Duration The competition is held annually.

Additional information The Executive Leadership Foundation was founded in 1989 as an affiliate of the Executive Leadership Council, the association of African American senior executives of Fortune 500 companies. This competition is sponsored by the Coca-Cola Company.

Number awarded 13 each year: 1 for each of the first 5 places and 8 honorable mention winners.

Deadline March of each year.

[79]
AWS FOX VALLEY SECTION SCHOLARSHIP

American Welding Society-Fox Valley Section
c/o AWS Foundation, Inc.
8669 N.W. 36th Street, Suite 130
Doral, FL 33166-6672
(305) 443-9353   Toll Free: (800) 443-9353, ext. 250
Fax: (305) 443-7559   E-mail: nprado-pulido@aws.org
Web: www.awssection.org/foxvalley/scholarship

Summary To provide financial assistance to residents of Wisconsin and the Upper Peninsula of Michigan, especially African Americans and members of other underrepresented groups, who are interested in working on a certificate or degree in a welding-related field at a school in any state.

Eligibility This program is open to residents of Wisconsin and the Upper Peninsula of Michigan who are U.S. citizens and either high school seniors or current undergraduate students. Applicants must be working or planning to work full or part time (preferable full time) on a welding program certificate or college degree focused on welding at a school in any state. They must have a GPA of 2.5 or higher. Financial need is not considered in the selection process. Preference is given to members of groups underrepresented in the welding industry.

Financial data The stipend is $1,500 per year; funds are paid directly to the educational institution.

Duration 1 year; may be renewed for 1 additional year.

Number awarded 1 each year.

Deadline February of each year.

[80]
AWS TIDEWATER VIRGINIA SECTION SCHOLARSHIP

American Welding Society-Tidewater Section
c/o Jackie Phillips, Section Chair
Newport News Shipbuilding
4101 Washington Avenue
Newport News, VA 23607
(757) 688-4469 E-mail: jacqueline.a.phillips@hii-nns.com
Web: www.awssection.org/tidewater/scholarship

Summary To provide financial assistance to residents of Virginia, especially African Americans and members of other underrepresented groups, who are interested in working on an undergraduate degree in designated fields related to welding.

Eligibility This program is open to students working on an associated or bachelor's degree in welding engineering, materials joining engineering, welding engineering technology, or materials joining engineering technology. Priority is given in the following order: first to residents of the Tidewater region of Virginia; second to residents of Virginia; and third to students at LeTourneau University. High school seniors must have a GPA of 2.4 or higher; students already enrolled in college must have a GPA of at least 2.1 overall and 2.3 in their major. Preference is given to full-time students, but part-time students are encouraged to apply if they are also working at a job or have other circumstances that prevent them from enrolling full time. U.S. citizenship is required. Financial need is considered in the selection process. Special consideration is given to applicants who are enrolled in an ABET-accredited program, have a documented working history that includes hands-on welding experience, have successfully completed a high school welding curriculum, or are from a group underrepresented in the welding industry.

Financial data The stipend is $1,000 per year.

Duration 1 year; may be renewed up to 2 additional years upon reapplication.

Number awarded 1 or more each year.

Deadline April of each year.

[81]
BALTIMORE CHAPTER AABE SCHOLARSHIPS

American Association of Blacks in Energy-Baltimore
  Chapter
Attn: Scholarship Committee
P.O. Box 1903
Baltimore, MD 21203
E-mail: aabe.baltimore@gmail.com
Web: www.aabe.org

Summary To provide financial assistance to members of African American and other underrepresented minority groups who are high school seniors in Maryland and planning to major in an energy-related field at a college in any state.

Eligibility This program is open to seniors graduating from high schools in Maryland and planning to attend a college or university in any state. Applicants must be African Americans, Hispanics, or Native Americans who have a GPA of 3.0 or higher and who have taken the ACT and/or SAT test. Their intended major must be business, engineering, technology, mathematics, the physical sciences, or other energy-related field. Along with their application, they must submit a 350-word essay that includes 1) when they discovered their interest in the field of energy and what sparked their interest; and 2) either what excites them about the field of energy or how they expect their education to prepare them for the field of energy. Financial need is not considered in the selection process.

Financial data The stipend is $1,000.

Duration 1 year.

Additional information The winners are eligible to compete for regional and national scholarships.

Number awarded 2 each year.

Deadline March of each year.

[82]
BARBARA TOBE SCHOLARSHIPS

Blacks in Government-National Oceanic and Atmospheric
  Administration Chapter
Attn: Scholarship Committee Chair
P.O. Box 14361
Silver Spring, MD 20911-0361
(301) 713-9667   Fax: (301) 713-0372
Web: www.noaabig.org/calendar/scholarships

Summary To provide financial assistance to African Americans who are either high school seniors in the Washington, D.C. metropolitan area or the family of employees of the U.S. National Oceanic and Atmospheric Administration (NOAA) and planning to major in selected fields in college.

Eligibility This program is open to African American high school seniors who are either attending a selected high school in the Washington, D.C. area or the family member of NOAA employees and living in that area. Applicants must be planning to attend college in any state to major or minor in a field that relates to the oceans or the atmosphere or that supports the NOAA administrative or managerial infrastructure; eligible academic disciplines include the sciences (biology, physics, chemistry, oceanography, atmospheric sciences, or meteorology), mathematics, computer science, engineering, information or management technology, business, management, administration, contracts, law, aviation, geography, medicine, or related fields. They must have a GPA of 3.0 or higher, a record of participation in school activities, demonstrated leadership abilities, involvement in community outreach activities, special talents and awards, and good moral character. Eligible graduating seniors include those at the 2 high schools in the area selected by the sponsor each year. Eligible family members include children, grandchildren, nieces, nephews, foster children, and custodial children.

Financial data The stipend is $1,000.

Duration 1 year.

Additional information This program began in 1996.

Number awarded 1 or more each year.

Deadline June of each year.

[83]
BAYER SCHOLARSHIPS

Society of Women Engineers
Attn: Scholarship Selection Committee
203 North LaSalle Street, Suite 1675
Chicago, IL 60601-1269
(312) 596-5223   Toll Free: (877) SWE-INFO
Fax: (312) 644-8557   E-mail: scholarships@swe.org
Web: societyofwomenengineers.swe.org

Summary To provide financial assistance to women, especially African Americans and members of other underrepresented groups, working on an undergraduate degree in designated fields of engineering at colleges in Pennsylvania and Texas.

Eligibility This program is open to women who are entering their sophomore, junior, or senior year at a 4-year ABET-accredited college or university in Pennsylvania or Texas. Applicants must be working full time on a degree in computer science or chemical, electrical, materials, or mechanical engineering. Preference is given to members of groups underrepresented in engineering, including veterans. Selection is based on financial need and merit.

Financial data The stipend is $2,500.

Duration 1 year.

Additional information This program, which began in 2015, is sponsored by Bayer.

Number awarded 2 each year.

Deadline February of each year.

[84]
BDPA JOHNSON & JOHNSON SCHOLARSHIP

Black Data Processing Associates
Attn: Scholarship
9500 Arena Drive, Suite 106
Largo, MD 20774
(301) 584-3135　　　　　　　　Fax: (301) 560-8300
E-mail: scholarships@bdpa.org
Web: www.bdpa.org/?page=Scholarships

Summary To provide financial assistance to members of Black Data Processing Associates (BDPA) who are working on an undergraduate degree in a field of science, technology, engineering, or mathematics (STEM).

Eligibility This program is open to BDPA members who are enrolled full time at a 4-year college or university as rising sophomores or higher. Applicants must be majoring in a field of STEM and have a GPA of 3.0 or higher. Selection is based on 1) civic, community, volunteer, and extracurricular activities in which they participated in the last year; 2) a list of scholastic, academic, civic, volunteer, and other awards and honors that they have received; 3) a brief statement on how being a member of BDPA will have an impact on their career development; and 4) a 500-word essay on the impact of their involvement in the community.

Financial data The stipend is $2,500.

Duration 1 year; nonrenewable.

Additional information This scholarship is sponsored by Johnson & Johnson.

Number awarded Up to 4 each year.

Deadline October of each year.

[85]
BDPA ORACLE SCHOLARSHIP

Black Data Processing Associates
Attn: Scholarship
9500 Arena Drive, Suite 106
Largo, MD 20774
(301) 584-3135　　　　　　　　Fax: (301) 560-8300
E-mail: scholarships@bdpa.org
Web: www.bdpa.org/?page=Scholarships

Summary To provide financial assistance to members of Black Data Processing Associates (BDPA) who are working on an undergraduate degree in a field related to computer technology.

Eligibility This program is open to graduating high school seniors and current undergraduates who are BDPA members. Applicants must be enrolled or planning to enroll full time at an accredited college or university and major in engineering, computer and information science, computer engineering, or mathematics. They must have a GPA of 3.0 or higher. Along with their application, they must submit a personal statement that includes information on their family background, involvement in school and community activities, involvement in BDPA, and financial need.

Financial data Stipends are $4,000 or $5,000.

Duration 1 year.

Additional information This scholarship, first awarded in 2009, is sponsored by Oracle.

Number awarded Varies each year; recently, 11 were awarded.

Deadline July of each year.

[86]
BEAUTIFUL MINDS SCHOLARSHIP

RentDeals.com
Attn: Scholarships
14173 Northwest Freeway, Suite 190
Houston, TX 77040
Toll Free: (800) 644-5012
Web: www.rentdeals.com/scholarship.php

Summary To provide financial assistance to African American and other minority high school seniors who submit outstanding essays on finding their purpose and plan to attend college.

Eligibility This program is open to graduating high school seniors who are members of minority groups and have a GPA of 3.0 or higher. Applicants must be planning to enroll at an accredited postsecondary institution and major in any field. Selection is based primarily on an essay on the topic, "Finding My Purpose."

Financial data The stipend is $1,000.

Duration 1 year.

Number awarded 1 each year.

Deadline March of each year.

[87]
BECHTEL UNDERGRADUATE FELLOWSHIP AWARD

National Action Council for Minorities in Engineering
Attn: Director, Scholarships and University Relations
440 Hamilton Avenue, Suite 302
White Plains, NY 10601-1813
(914) 539-4316　　　　　　　　Fax: (914) 539-4032
E-mail: scholars@nacme.org
Web: www.nacme.org/scholarships

Summary To provide financial assistance to African American and other underrepresented minority college juniors majoring in construction engineering.

Eligibility This program is open to African American, Latino, and American Indian college juniors who have a GPA of 3.0 or higher and have demonstrated academic excellence, leadership skills, and a commitment to science and engineering as a career. Applicants must be enrolled full time at an ABET-accredited engineering program and preparing for a career in a construction-related engineering discipline.

Financial data   The stipend is $2,500 per year. Funds are sent directly to the recipient's university.

Duration   Up to 2 years.

Additional information   This program was established by the Bechtel Group Foundation.

Number awarded   2 each year.

Deadline   April of each year.

[88]
BERNARD AND SYLVIA DAVIS THOMPSON SCHOLARSHIP

National Organization of Black Law Enforcement
Executives
Attn: NOBLE Scholarships
4609 Pinecrest Office Park Drive, Suite F
Alexandria, VA 22312-1442
(703) 658-1529   Fax: (703) 658-9479
E-mail: wleach@noblenatl.org
Web: www.noblenational.org

Summary   To provide financial assistance for college to high school seniors, especially African Americans, who are interested in preparing for a criminal justice career.

Eligibility   This program is open to high school seniors who have a GPA of 3.7 or higher and are interested in preparing for a career in criminal justice. Applicants must be planning to attend an accredited academic institution in the United States to major in a social science (e.g. technology, forensic investigations, or other criminal investigative studies) related to a career in law enforcement or criminal justice. They must be U.S. citizens and able to demonstrate financial need. Along with their application, they must submit a 1-page essay on their career goals and interests and why they feel they should receive this scholarship.

Financial data   The stipend is $1,500.

Duration   1 year; nonrenewable.

Additional information   The sponsor is an organization of African American law enforcement officers.

Number awarded   1 each year.

Deadline   April of each year.

[89]
BERTHA PITTS CAMPBELL SCHOLARSHIP PROGRAM

Delta Sigma Theta Sorority, Inc.
Attn: Scholarship and Standards Committee Chair
1707 New Hampshire Avenue, N.W.
Washington, DC 20009
(202) 986-2400   Fax: (202) 986-2513
E-mail: dstemail@deltasigmatheta.org
Web: www.deltasigmatheta.org

Summary   To provide financial assistance to members of Delta Sigma Theta who are working on an undergraduate or graduate degree in education.

Eligibility   This program is open to current undergraduate and graduate students who are working on a degree in education. Applicants must be active, dues-paying members of

Delta Sigma Theta. Selection is based on meritorious achievement.

Financial data   The stipends range from $1,000 to $2,000. The funds may be used to cover tuition, fees, and living expenses.

Duration   1 year; may be renewed for 1 additional year.

Additional information   This sponsor is a traditionally-African American social sorority. The application fee is $20.

Number awarded   1 or more each year.

Deadline   March of each year.

[90]
BILL BERNBACH DIVERSITY SCHOLARSHIPS

American Association of Advertising Agencies
Attn: AAAA Foundation
1065 Avenue of the Americas, 16th Floor
New York, NY 10018
(212) 262-2500   E-mail: bbscholarship@ddb.com
Web: www.aaaa.org

Summary   To provide financial assistance to African American and other multicultural students interested in working on an undergraduate or graduate degree in advertising at designated schools.

Eligibility   This program is open to African Americans, Asian Americans, Hispanic Americans, and Native Americans (including American Indians, Alaska Natives, Native Hawaiians, and other Pacific Islanders) who are interested in studying the advertising creative arts at designated institutions as a full-time student. Applicants must be working on or have already received an undergraduate degree and be able to demonstrate creative talent and promise. They must be U.S. citizens, nationals, or permanent residents. Along with their application, they must submit 10 samples of creative work in their respective field of expertise.

Financial data   The stipend is $5,000.

Duration   1 year.

Additional information   This program, which began in 1998, is currently sponsored by DDB Worldwide. The participating schools are the Art Center College of Design (Pasadena, California), Creative Circus (Atlanta, Georgia), Miami Ad School (Miami Beach, Florida), University of Oklahoma (Norman, Oklahoma), University of Texas at Austin, VCU Brandcenter (Richmond, Virginia), Savannah College of Art and Design (Savannah, Georgia), University of Oregon (Eugene), City College of New York, School of Visual Arts (New York, New York), Fashion Institute of Technology (New York, New York), and Howard University (Washington, D.C.).

Number awarded   3 each year.

Deadline   May of each year.

[91]
BILL DICKEY GOLF SCHOLARSHIPS

Bill Dickey Scholarship Association
Attn: Scholarship Committee
1241 East Washington Street, Suite 101
Phoenix, AZ 85034
(602) 258-7851   Fax: (602) 258-3412
E-mail: andrea@bdscholar.org
Web: www.nmjgsa.org/scholarships.php

Summary To provide financial assistance to African American and other minority high school seniors and undergraduate students who excel at golf.

Eligibility This program is open to graduating high school seniors and current undergraduate students who are members of minority groups (African American, Asian/Pacific Islander, Hispanic, or American Indian/Alaskan Native). Applicants must submit a 500-word essay on a topic that changes annually but relates to minorities and golf. Selection is based on academic achievement, leadership, evidence of community service, golfing ability, and financial need.

Financial data Stipends range from 1-time awards of $1,000 to 4-year awards of $3,500 per year. Funds are paid directly to the recipient's college.

Duration 1 year or longer.

Additional information This sponsor was established in 1984 as the National Minority Junior Golf Association and given its current name in 2006. Support is provided by the Jackie Robinson Foundation, PGA of America, Anheuser-Busch, the Tiger Woods Foundation, and other cooperating organizations.

Number awarded Varies; generally 80 or more each year.

Deadline May of each year.

[92]
BIRMINGHAM CHAPTER AABE SCHOLARSHIPS

American Association of Blacks in Energy-Birmingham
  Chapter
Attn: Scholarship Committee
P.O. Box 3035
Birmingham, AL 35202
(205) 325-3578   E-mail: larringt@southernco.com
Web: www.aabe.org/index.php?component=pages&id=161

Summary To provide financial assistance to African Americans and members of other underrepresented minority groups who are high school seniors in Alabama and planning to major in an energy-related field at a college in any state.

Eligibility This program is open to seniors graduating from high schools in Alabama and planning to attend a college or university in any state. Applicants must be African Americans, Hispanics, or Native Americans who have a GPA of 3.0 or higher and who have taken the ACT and/or SAT test. Their intended major must be business, engineering, technology, mathematics, the physical sciences, or other energy-related field. Along with their application, they must submit a 350-word essay that includes 1) when they discovered their interest in the field of energy and what sparked their interest; and 2) either what excites them about the field of energy or how they expect their education to prepare them for the field of energy. Financial need is not considered in the selection process.

Financial data The stipend is $5,000.

Duration 1 year.

Additional information The winner is eligible to compete for regional and national scholarships.

Number awarded 1 each year.

Deadline March of each year.

[93]
BISHOP T. LARRY KIRKLAND SCHOLARSHIP OF EXCELLENCE

African Methodist Episcopal Church
Fifth Episcopal District Lay Organization
c/o Anita West-Ware, Scholarship Committee Chair
4027 East 30th Avenue
Denver, CO 80207
(303) 377-2731 E-mail: KirklandScholarship@yahoo.com
Web: www.fifthdistrictlay.org/5th-district-scholarships

Summary To provide financial assistance to members of African Methodist Episcopal (AME) churches in its Fifth Episcopal District who are students currently attending college in any state.

Eligibility This program is open to residents of the AME Fifth Episcopal District (Alaska, Arizona, California, Colorado, Idaho, Kansas, Missouri, Montana, Nebraska, Nevada, New Mexico, North Dakota, Oregon, South Dakota, Utah, Washington, and Wyoming) who are currently enrolled at an accredited institution of higher learning in any state. Applicants must have been a member of an AME church for at least 12 months and have been an active member of its Lay Organization or other church ministry. They must have a GPA of 2.5 or higher. Along with their application, they must submit a personal essay of 300 to 500 words that describes their long-range plans, community and church involvement, accomplishments or special awards, challenges they have faced, and how they responded. Selection is based on that essay (30%), academic record (30%), letters of recommendation (15%), participation in school and community extracurricular activities (15%), and quality of application (10%).

Financial data The stipend is $1,500.

Duration 1 year.

Number awarded 1 each year.

Deadline May of each year.

[94]
BLACK NURSES' ASSOCIATION OF GREATER WASHINGTON FOUNDERS SCHOLARSHIP

Black Nurses' Association of Greater Washington, D.C.
  Area, Inc.
Attn: Scholarship Committee Chair
P.O. Box 55285
Washington, DC 20040
(202) 291-8866
Web: www.bnaofgwdca.org/scholarships.html

Summary To provide financial assistance to African American high school seniors in the Washington, D.C. area who are interested in enrolling in a nursing program at a school in any state.

Eligibility This program is open to African American seniors graduating from high schools in the District of Columbia or adjoining counties in Maryland (Anne Arundel, Calvert, Charles, Howard, Montgomery, and Prince George's). Applicants must be U.S. citizens or permanent residents and have a GPA of 2.8 or higher. They must have been accepted at a college or university in the United States that offers an NLN-accredited A.D.N., B.S.N., or L.P.N. nursing program. Along with their application, they must submit a 300-word statement that describes their personal and academic accomplishments, community service, future goals for a career in nursing, and financial need.

Financial data A stipend is awarded (amount not specified).

Duration 1 year.

Additional information This program began in 2011.

Number awarded 2 each year.

Deadline April of each year.

[95]
BLACKS AT MICROSOFT SCHOLARSHIPS

Seattle Foundation
Attn: Scholarship Administrator
1200 Fifth Avenue, Suite 1300
Seattle, WA 98101-3151
(206) 515-2119   Fax: (206) 622-7673
E-mail: scholarships@seattlefoundation.org
Web: www.microsoft.com

Summary To provide financial assistance to African American high school seniors from any state who plan to major in engineering, computer science, or a business-related field in college.

Eligibility This program is open to seniors of African descent graduating from high school in any state and planning to attend a 4-year college or university. Applicants must be planning to work on a bachelor's degree in engineering, computer science, computer information systems, or selected business fields (such as finance, business administration, or marketing). They must be able to demonstrate a "passion for technology," leadership at school or in the community, a need for financial assistance to attend college, and a GPA of 3.3 or higher. Along with their application, they must submit a 500-word essay on how they plan to engage in the technology industry in their future career and a 250-word essay on their financial need for this scholarship.

Financial data The stipend is $5,000 per year.

Duration 1 year; may be renewed up to 3 additional years.

Additional information Blacks at Microsoft is an organization of African American employees of Microsoft.

Number awarded 2 each year.

Deadline February of each year.

[96]
BLACKS IN SAFETY ENGINEERING SCHOLARSHIP

American Society of Safety Engineers
Attn: ASSE Foundation
Scholarship Award Program
520 North Northwest Highway
Park Ridge, IL 60068-2538
(847) 699-2929   Fax: (847) 296-3769
E-mail: assefoundation@asse.org
Web: foundation.asse.org/scholarships-and-grants

Summary To provide financial assistance to upper-division students, especially Blacks, who are working on a degree related to occupational safety.

Eligibility This program is open to students who are majoring in occupational safety, health, environment, industrial hygiene, occupational health nursing, or a closely-related field (e.g., industrial or environmental engineering). Priority is given to students who are Black. Applicants must be full-time

students who have completed at least 60 semester hours and have a GPA of 3.0 or higher. U.S. citizenship is not required. Membership in the American Society of Safety Engineers (ASSE) is not required, but preference is given to members.

Financial data The stipend is $1,000 per year.

Duration 1 year; recipients may reapply.

Number awarded 1 each year.

Deadline November of each year.

[97]
BLANDY EXPERIMENTAL FARM RESEARCH EXPERIENCES FOR UNDERGRADUATES PROGRAM

University of Virginia
Attn: Blandy Experimental Farm
400 Blandy Farm Lane
Boyce, VA 22620
(540) 837-1758, ext. 292   Fax: (540) 837-1523
E-mail: blandy@virginia.edu
Web: sites.google.com/site/blandyreu

Summary To provide an opportunity for undergraduates, especially African Americans and other minorities, to conduct ecological and evolutionary research during the summer at the Blandy Experimental Farm in Clarke County, Virginia.

Eligibility This program is open to undergraduate students interested in ecological and evolutionary biology. Applicants must submit a proposal for a research project at the farm under the mentorship of a professional staff member. Current research interests of the staff include plant reproductive ecology, aquatic community ecology, biological invasions, plant population biology, conservation biology, pollination, and plant succession. Interested students should submit, along with their application, a current transcript, 2 letters of recommendation, a statement describing how this program would contribute to their education and career goals, and the names of the mentors whose research areas interest them. They must be U.S. citizens or permanent residents. Applications are especially encouraged from underrepresented minorities, persons with disabilities, and women.

Financial data Students receive a $5,775 stipend, an additional meal budget, free housing, and a modest budget for supplies and travel.

Duration 11 weeks, from late May through mid-August.

Additional information This program, established in 1993, receives funding support from the Research Experiences for Undergraduates (REU) program of the National Science Foundation.

Number awarded 10 each year.

Deadline February of each year.

[98]
BLUECROSS BLUESHIELD CIO SCHOLARSHIP FOR BDPA STUDENTS

Black Data Processing Associates
Attn: BDPA Education Technology Foundation
4423 Lehigh Road, Number 277
College Park, MD 20740
(513) 284-4968   Fax: (202) 318-2194
E-mail: scholarships@betf.org
Web: www.betf.org/scholarships/bluecross-blueshield.shtml

Summary To provide financial assistance to high school seniors in designated states who are members of the Black Data Processing Associates (BDPA) and interested in studying information technology at a college in those states.

Eligibility This program is open to seniors graduating from high schools in Illinois, Montana, New Mexico, Oklahoma, or Texas and planning to enroll at an accredited 4-year college or university in any state. Applicants must be planning to work on a degree in information technology. They must have a GPA of 3.3 or higher. Along with their application, they must submit a 500-word essay on a topic that changes annually; recently, students were asked to write on the topic, "2020 Innovation in Health Care." Selection is based on that essay, academic achievement, leadership ability through academic or civic involvement, and participation in community service activities. U.S. citizenship or permanent resident status is required.

Financial data The stipend is $2,500. Funds may be used to pay for tuition, fees, books, room and board, or other college-related expenses.

Duration 1 year; nonrenewable.

Additional information The BDPA established its Education and Technology Foundation (BETF) in 1992 to advance the skill sets needed by African American and other minority adults and young people to compete in the information technology industry. This program is sponsored by Blue Cross and Blue Shield of Illinois, of Montana, of New Mexico, of Oklahoma, and of Texas.

Number awarded 2 each year.

Deadline July of each year.

[99]
BLUECROSS BLUESHIELD OF TENNESSEE COMMUNITY TRUST DIVERSITY SCHOLARSHIP

National Association of Health Services Executives-
  Memphis Chapter
Attn: Selection Committee
P.O. Box 40051
Memphis, TN 38174-0051
E-mail: nahsememphis@gmail.com
Web: www.bcbst.com

Summary This program is open to African American and other minority students who are residents of Tennessee working on an undergraduate degree in a field of health care at a college in the state.

Eligibility This program is open to minority residents of Tennessee who are currently enrolled as full-time sophomores or juniors at an accredited college or university in the state. Applicants must be working on a degree in a field of health care and have a GPA of 2.5 or higher. They must be U.S. citizens between 18 and 23 years of age. Along with their application, they must submit a 500-word essay on their particular field of study, why they chose to prepare for a career in health care, and how they plan to use their skills or knowledge to help raise awareness of health issues in their community.

Financial data The stipend is $10,000. Funds are paid directly to the recipient's university.

Duration 1 year.

Additional information This program is sponsored by BlueCross BlueShield of Tennessee in collaboration with the Memphis Chapter of the National Association of Health Services Executives (NAHSE).

Number awarded 3 each year: 1 each for the west, middle, and east region of Tennessee.

Deadline March of each year.

[100]
BOX ENGINEERING DIVERSITY SCHOLARSHIP

Box, Inc.
Attn: Scholarship
4440 El Camino Real
Los Altos, CA 94022
Toll Free: (877) 729-4269   E-mail: scholarship@box.com
Web: www.boxdiversityscholarship.com

Summary To provide financial assistance to college students majoring in designated fields of technology who are African Americans or members of other groups underrepresented in those fields.

Eligibility This program is open to U.S. citizens currently enrolled as sophomores or juniors at a 4-year college or university who are majoring in science, engineering, information technology, mathematics, or a related field. Applicants must identify with an underrepresented minority (e.g., female, LGBT, Hispanic, African American, or Native American). Finalists are invited to the sponsor's headquarters in Los Altos, California.

Financial data Stipends are $20,000 or $4,000.

Duration 1 year.

Number awarded 1 at $20,000 and 4 at $4,000 each year.

Deadline October of each year.

[101]
BRANDON C. FRANCISCO ACHIEVEMENT SCHOLARSHIP

Organization of Black Aerospace Professionals, Inc.
Attn: Scholarship Coordinator
One Westbrook Corporate Center, Suite 300
Westchester, IL 60154
(708) 449-7755   Toll Free: (800) JET-OBAP
Fax: (708) 449-7754 E-mail: obapscholarships@obap.org
Web: www.obap.org/brandon-francisco-scholarship

Summary To provide financial assistance to members of the Organization of Black Aerospace Professionals (OBAP) who plan to work on an aerospace degree at a school in any state.

Eligibility This program is open to OBAP members who are high school seniors or students currently enrolled in an accredited collegiate aerospace program. Applicants must be interested in preparing for a career in aviation, including, but not limited to, airlines, military, or corporate aviation. They must have a GPA of 2.5 or higher. Along with their application, they must submit a 300-word essay where they see themselves in 5 years and how they will accomplish their goals.

Financial data The stipend is $2,500.

Duration 1 year.

Additional information The OBAP was originally established in 1976 as the Organization of Black Airline Pilots to make certain Blacks and other minorities had a group that would keep them informed about opportunities for advancement within commercial aviation.

Number awarded   2 each year.

Deadline   May of each year.

[102]
BREAKTHROUGH TO NURSING SCHOLARSHIPS

National Student Nurses' Association
Attn: Foundation
45 Main Street, Suite 606
Brooklyn, NY 11201
(718) 210-0705   Fax: (718) 210-0710
E-mail: nsna@nsna.org
Web: www.nsna.org

Summary   To provide financial assistance to African American and other minority undergraduate and graduate students who wish to prepare for careers in nursing.

Eligibility   This program is open to students currently enrolled in state-approved schools of nursing or pre-nursing associate degree, baccalaureate, diploma, generic master's, generic doctoral, R.N. to B.S.N., R.N. to M.S.N., or L.P.N./L.V.N. to R.N. programs. Graduating high school seniors are not eligible. Support for graduate education is provided only for a first degree in nursing. Applicants must be members of a racial or ethnic minority underrepresented among registered nurses (Black or African American, American Indian or Alaska Native, Hispanic or Latino, Native Hawaiian or other Pacific Islander, or Asian). They must be committed to providing quality health care services to underserved populations. Along with their application, they must submit a 200-word description of their professional and educational goals and how this scholarship will help them achieve those goals. Selection is based on academic achievement, financial need, and involvement in student nursing organizations and community health activities. U.S. citizenship or permanent resident status is required.

Financial data   Stipends range from $1,000 to $2,000.

Duration   1 year.

Additional information   Applications must be accompanied by a $10 processing fee.

Number awarded   Varies each year; recently, 13 were awarded: 10 sponsored by the American Association of Critical-Care Nurses and 3 sponsored by the Mayo Clinic.

Deadline   January of each year.

[103]
BRIGADIER GENERAL ROSCOE C. CARTWRIGHT AWARDS

The ROCKS, Inc.
c/o WSC Associates, LLP
P.O. Box 47435
Forestville, MD 20753
(301) 856-9319   Toll Free: (888) 762-5747
Fax: (301) 856-5220
E-mail: rocksnationalboard@gmail.com
Web: natlrocks.clubexpress.com

Summary   To provide financial assistance to students enrolled in ROTC programs at Historically Black Colleges and Universities (HBCUs).

Eligibility   This program is open to Army and Air Force Cadets and Navy Midshipmen at HBCUs. Applicants must be planning to enter military service as officers following graduation from college. They must submit 1) a 1-page paper on a

topic related to leadership or mentorship; and 2) a letter of recommendation from their professor of military science evaluating their appearance, attitude, APFT score, dedication, initiative, integrity, judgment, leadership potential, and written and oral communication ability. Financial need is not considered in the selection process.

Financial data   The stipend is $1,500.

Duration   1 year.

Additional information   This program began in 1974.

Number awarded   Varies each year; recently, 12 were awarded.

Deadline   December of each year.

[104]
BRONSON T.J. TREMBLAY MEMORIAL SCHOLARSHIP

Colorado Nurses Foundation
Attn: Scholarships
P.O. Box 3406
Englewood, CO 80155
(303) 694-4728   Toll Free: (800) 205-6655
Fax: (303) 200-7099   E-mail: mail@cnfound.org
Web: www.coloradonursesfoundation.com/?page_id=1087

Summary   To provide financial assistance to African American and other non-white male undergraduate and graduate nursing students in Colorado.

Eligibility   This program is open to non-white male Colorado residents who have been accepted as a student in an approved nursing program in the state. Applicants may be 1) second-year students in an associate degree program; 2) junior or senior level B.S.N. undergraduate students; 3) R.N.s enrolled in a baccalaureate or higher degree program in a school of nursing; 4) R.N.s with a master's degree in nursing, currently practicing in Colorado and enrolled in a doctoral program; or 5) students in the second or third year of a Doctorate Nursing Practice (D.N.P.) or Ph.D. program. Undergraduates must have a GPA of 3.25 or higher and graduate students must have a GPA of 3.5 or higher. Selection is based on professional philosophy and goals, dedication to the improvement of patient care in Colorado, demonstrated commitment to nursing, potential for leadership, involvement in community and professional organizations, recommendations, GPA, and financial need.

Financial data   The stipend is $1,000.

Duration   1 year.

Number awarded   1 each year.

Deadline   October of each year.

[105]
BROWN AND CALDWELL MINORITY SCHOLARSHIP

Brown and Caldwell
Attn: HR/Scholarship Program
1527 Cole Boulevard, Suite 300
Lakewood, CO 80401
(303) 239-5400   Fax: (303) 239-5454
E-mail: scholarships@brwncald.com
Web: www.brownandcaldwell.com/Scholarships.asp?id=1

Summary   To provide financial assistance to African American and other minority students working on an undergraduate or graduate degree in an environmental or engineering field.

Eligibility This program is open to members of minority groups (African Americans, Hispanics, Asians, Pacific Islanders, Native Americans, or Alaska Natives) who are full-time juniors, seniors, or graduate students at an accredited 4-year college or university. Applicants must have a GPA of 3.0 or higher and a declared major in civil, chemical, or environmental engineering or an environmental science (e.g., biology, ecology, geology, hydrogeology). They must be U.S. citizens or permanent residents. Along with their application, they must submit an essay (up to 250 words) on a topic that changes annually but relates to their personal development. Financial need is not considered in the selection process.

Financial data The stipend is $5,000.

Duration 1 year.

Number awarded 1 each year.

Deadline May of each year.

[106]
BYRON KENNETH ARMSTRONG SCHOLARS AWARD

Kappa Alpha Psi Fraternity
Attn: Grand Chapter
2322-24 North Broad Street
Philadelphia, PA 19132-4590
(215) 228-7184   Fax: (215) 228-7181
Web: www.kappaalphapsi1911.com

Summary To recognize and reward members of Kappa Alpha Psi Fraternity, a traditionally African American men's organization, who demonstrate outstanding achievement.

Eligibility This program is open to undergraduate members of the fraternity who are eligible for graduation in the term immediately preceding or during the period that the Province Council is being held. Candidates must have a GPA of 3.0 or higher. Selection is based on involvement in fraternity, college or university, and community activities.

Financial data Awards are $1,000 for first place, $750 for second place, and $500 for third place.

Duration Awards are presented annually.

Number awarded 3 each year.

Deadline Applications must be received within 14 days following the candidate's Province Council.

[107]
CABJ COLLEGE JOURNALISM SCHOLARSHIPS

Colorado Association of Black Journalists
c/o Gabrielle Bryant, President
Colorado Public Television
2900 Welton Street, First Floor
Denver, CO 80205
(303) 296-1212   Toll Free: (800) 727-8812
Fax: (303) 296-6650
E-mail: gabriellebryantnews@gmail.com
Web: www.cabj-denver.org/scholarships

Summary To provide financial assistance to African American high school and college students from Colorado who are interested in majoring in a field related to journalism.

Eligibility This program is open to African American students currently attending a high school or college in Colorado. Applicants must be majoring or planning to major in

journalism or mass communications. They must have a GPA of 3.0 or higher. Along with their application, they must submit a transcript, a letter of recommendation, and 3 samples of their media work (such as school newspaper clips, broadcast news stories, photographs, documentaries and radio excepts, or class work).

Financial data Stipends are $2,500 or $1,000. Winning students are also given a 1-year membership in the Colorado Association of Black Journalists (CABJ).

Duration 1 year.

Number awarded 3 each year: 1 at $2,500 (designated the Reynelda Muse Journalism Scholarship) and 2 at $1,000.

Deadline June of each year.

[108]
CALDER SUMMER UNDERGRADUATE RESEARCH PROGRAM

Fordham University
Attn: Louis Calder Center Biological Field Station
53 Whippoorwill Road
P.O. Box 887
Armonk, NY 10504
(914) 273-3078, ext. 10   Fax: (914) 273-2167
E-mail: REUatCalder@fordham.edu
Web: www.fordham.edu

Summary To provide an opportunity for undergraduates, especially African Americans and other underrepresented students, to pursue summer research activities in biology at Fordham University's Louis Calder Center Biological Field Station.

Eligibility This program is open to undergraduates interested in conducting a summer research project of their own design at the center. Applicants must be U.S. citizens, nationals, or permanent residents. Fields of interest must relate to the activities of staff who will serve as mentors on the projects; those include forest ecology, limnology, wildlife ecology, microbial ecology, Lyme disease, insect-plant interactions, evolutionary ecology, and the effects of urbanization on ecosystem processes. Applications from underrepresented minorities and women are especially encouraged.

Financial data The program provides a stipend of $5,000, housing on the site, and support for research supplies and local travel.

Duration 10 weeks during the summer.

Additional information This program has operated since 1967 with support from the Research Experiences for Undergraduates (REU) program of the National Science Foundation.

Number awarded Up to 10 each year.

Deadline January of each year.

[109]
CALIFORNIA BLACK CHAMBER OF COMMERCE FOUNDATION YOUTH SCHOLARSHIP

California Black Chamber of Commerce Foundation
Attn: Scholarship Committee
1600 Sacramento Inn Way, Suite 232
Sacramento, CA 95815
(916) 463-0178   Fax: (916) 463-0190
E-mail: cbcc@calbcc.org
Web: www.calbcc.org

Summary   To provide financial assistance to high school seniors and college freshmen in California who are interested in entrepreneurial activity.

Eligibility   This program is open to graduating high school seniors and current college freshmen between 17 and 25 years of age in California. Applicants do not need to be interested in becoming an entrepreneur, but they must know and understand what it means to be one. They must have a GPA between 2.0 and 3.5. Along with their application, they must submit a 500-word essay on what it means to be an entrepreneur. Selection is based on that essay, entrepreneurial goals, community service, and academic achievement.

Financial data   The stipend is $1,000; funds are sent directly to the recipient's college.

Duration   1 year.

Number awarded   Varies each year.

Deadline   July of each year.

[110]
CALIFORNIA PLANNING FOUNDATION DIVERSITY IN PLANNING SCHOLARSHIP

American Planning Association-California Chapter
Attn: California Planning Foundation
c/o Kelly Main
California Polytechnic State University at San Luis Obispo
City and Regional Planning Department
Office 21-116B
San Luis Obispo, CA 93407-0283
(805) 756-2285   Fax: (805) 756-1340
E-mail: cpfapplications@gmail.com
Web: www.californiaplanningfoundation.org

Summary   To provide financial assistance to African American and other undergraduate and graduate students in accredited planning programs at California universities who will increase diversity in the profession.

Eligibility   This program is open to students entering their final year for an undergraduate or master's degree in an accredited planning program at a university in California. Applicants must be students who will increase diversity in the planning profession. Along with their application, they must submit 1) a 500-word personal statement explaining why planning is important to them, their potential contribution to the profession of planning in California, and how this scholarship would help them to complete their degree; 2) a 500-word description of their experience in planning (e.g., internships, volunteer experiences, employment); and 3) a 500-word essay on what they consider to be 1 of the greatest planning challenges in California today. Selection is based on academic performance, increasing diversity in the planning profession, commitment to serve the planning profession in California, and financial need.

Financial data   The stipend is $3,000. The award includes a 1-year student membership in the American Planning Association (APA) and payment of registration for the APA California Conference.

Duration   1 year.

Additional information   The accredited planning programs are at 3 campuses of the California State University system (California State Polytechnic University at Pomona, California Polytechnic State University at San Luis Obispo, and San Jose State University), 3 campuses of the University of California (Berkeley, Irvine, and Los Angeles), and the University of Southern California.

Number awarded   1 each year.

Deadline   March of each year.

[111]
CALTECH AMGEN SCHOLARS PROGRAM

California Institute of Technology
Attn: Student-Faculty Programs
1200 East California Boulevard
MailCode 330-87
Pasadena, CA 91125
(626) 395-2885   Fax: (626) 389-5467
E-mail: sfp@clatech.edu
Web: sfp.caltech.edu/programs/amgen_scholars

Summary   To provide an opportunity for undergraduate students, especially African Americans and members of other diverse populations, to participate in biological and chemical summer research at the California Institute of Technology (Caltech).

Eligibility   This program is open to sophomores, juniors, and non-graduating seniors at 4-year colleges and universities in the United States, Puerto Rico, and other U.S. territories. Applicants must be U.S. citizens or permanent residents who have a cumulative GPA of 3.2 or higher and an interest in preparing for a Ph.D. or M.D./Ph.D. They must be interested in working on a summer research project at Caltech in biology, chemistry, or biotechnical-related fields. Applications are encouraged from, but not limited to, underrepresented minorities, women, first-generation college students, geographically underrepresented students, educationally and financially disadvantaged students, and students with disabilities.

Financial data   Scholars receive a stipend of $6,000, campus housing, a modest board allowance, and travel to and from Pasadena.

Duration   10 weeks during the summer.

Additional information   This program serves as the Cal Tech component of the Amgen Scholars Program, which operates at 8 other U.S. universities (and the National Institutes of Health) and is funded by the Amgen Foundation.

Number awarded   Varies each year.

Deadline   February of each year.

[112]
CAMMER-HILL GRANT

Wisconsin Women of Color Network, Inc.
c/o P.E. Kiram
756 North 35th Street, Suite 101
Milwaukee, WI 53208
(414) 899-2329   E-mail: pekiram64@gmail.com

Summary   To provide financial assistance for vocation/ technical school or community college to African American and other adult women of color from Wisconsin.

Eligibility   This program is open to residents of Wisconsin who are adult women of color planning to continue their education at a vocational/technical school or community college in any state. Applicants must be a member of 1 of the following groups: African American, Asian, American Indian, or Hispanic. They must be able to demonstrate financial need. Along with their application, they must submit a 1-page essay on how this scholarship will help them accomplish their educational goal. U.S. citizenship is required.

Financial data A stipend is awarded (amount not specified).

Duration 1 year.

Additional information This program began in 1994.

Number awarded 1 each year.

Deadline May of each year.

[113]
CANCER RESEARCH SUMMER FELLOWSHIP

University of Colorado Cancer Center
Attn: Cancer Research Summer Fellowship
13001 East 17th Place
Building 500, Sixth Floor
Mailstop F434
Aurora, CO 80045
(303) 724-3174   Fax: (303) 724-3163
E-mail: jill.penafiel@ucdenver.edu
Web: www.ucdenver.edu

Summary To provide an opportunity for high school seniors and college undergraduates, especially African Americans and other minorities, to work during the summer on a cancer research project In Colorado.

Eligibility This program is open to high school seniors and college undergraduates who are interested in working on a cancer research project at the University of Colorado Anschutz Medical Center, the Boulder campus of the University of Colorado, or other institutions in the Denver area. Along with their application, they must submit a 2-page essay explaining why they wish to apply for this fellowship, school transcripts, and 2 letters of recommendation. Minority students are particularly encouraged to apply.

Financial data The stipend is $2,000 for high school seniors or $3,000 for college undergraduates.

Duration 10 weeks during the summer.

Additional information Funding for this program is provided by a grant from the National Cancer Institute.

Number awarded Varies each year; recently, 41 students participated in this project.

Deadline January of each year.

[114]
CANFIT PROGRAM CULINARY ARTS SCHOLARSHIPS

Communities-Adolescents-Nutrition-Fitness
Attn: Scholarship Program
P.O. Box 3989
Berkeley, CA 94703
(510) 644-1533, ext. 112   Toll Free: (800) 200-3131
Fax: (510) 843-9705   E-mail: info@canfit.org
Web: www.canfit.org/scholarships

Summary To provide financial assistance to African American and other minority culinary arts students in California.

Eligibility This program is open to African Americans, American Indians, Alaska Natives, Asian Americans, Pacific Islanders, and Latinos/Hispanics from California who are enrolled at a culinary arts college in the state. Applicants are not required to have completed any college units. Along with their application, they must submit 1) documentation of financial need; 2) letters of recommendation from 2 individuals; 3)

a 1-to 2-page letter describing their academic goals and involvement in community nutrition and/or physical education activities; and 4) an essay of 500 to 1,000 words on a topic related to healthy foods for youth from low-income communities of color.

Financial data A stipend is awarded (amount not specified).

Number awarded 1 or more each year.

Deadline March of each year.

[115]
CANFIT PROGRAM UNDERGRADUATE SCHOLARSHIPS

Communities-Adolescents-Nutrition-Fitness
Attn: Scholarship Program
P.O. Box 3989
Berkeley, CA 94703
(510) 644-1533, ext. 112   Toll Free: (800) 200-3131
Fax: (510) 843-9705   E-mail: info@canfit.org
Web: www.canfit.org/scholarships

Summary To provide financial assistance to African American and other minority undergraduate students who are working on a degree in nutrition, culinary arts, or physical education in California.

Eligibility This program is open to African Americans, American Indians, Alaska Natives, Asian Americans, Pacific Islanders, and Latinos/Hispanics from California who are enrolled in an approved bachelor's degree program in nutrition, culinary arts, or physical education in the state. Applicants must have completed at least 50 semester units and have a GPA of 2.5 or higher. Along with their application, they must submit 1) documentation of financial need; 2) letters of recommendation from 2 individuals; 3) a 1-to 2-page letter describing their academic goals and involvement in community nutrition and/or physical education activities; and 4) an essay of 500 to 1,000 words on a topic related to healthy foods for youth from low-income communities of color.

Financial data A stipend is awarded (amount not specified).

Number awarded 1 or more each year.

Deadline March of each year.

[116]
CAPT CYNTHIA I. MACRI SCHOLARSHIP

National Naval Officers Association-Washington, D.C.
   Chapter
c/o LCDR Stephen Williams
P.O. Box 30784
Alexandria, VA 22310
(703) 644-2605   Fax: (703) 644-8503
E-mail: Stephen.Williams@navy.mil
Web: www.dcnnoa.org/dcnnoa-scholarship

Summary To provide financial assistance to African American and other minority high school seniors from the Washington, D.C. area who are interested in majoring in a field of science, technology, engineering, or mathematics (STEM) at a college in any state.

Eligibility This program is open to minority seniors graduating from high schools in the Washington, D.C. metropolitan area who plan to enroll full time and major in a STEM discipline at an accredited 2- or 4-year college or university in any state. Applicants must have a GPA of 3.0 or higher and be U.S. citizens or permanent residents. Selection is based on academic achievement, community involvement, and financial need.

Financial data　The stipend is $1,000.

Duration　1 year; nonrenewable.

Additional information　This program is sponsored by the Washington D.C. Chapter of the National Naval Officers Association (DCNNOA), an organization of African American naval officers, but all minorities are eligible and recipients are not required to join or affiliate with the military in any way.

Number awarded　1 each year.

Deadline　February of each year.

[117]
CAPTAIN FARIAH PETERSON SCHOLARSHIP

Organization of Black Aerospace Professionals, Inc.
Attn: Scholarship Coordinator
One Westbrook Corporate Center, Suite 300
Westchester, IL 60154
(708) 449-7755　　　　　　　Toll Free: (800) JET-OBAP
Fax: (708) 449-7754　E-mail: obapscholarships@obap.org
Web: www.obap.org/fariah-peterson-scholarship

Summary　To provide financial assistance to female members of the Organization of Black Aerospace Professionals (OBAP) who are enrolled in a flight training program.

Eligibility　This program is open to African American females who are OBAP members enrolled or entering a flight program to advance a rating, certificate, or degree. Applicants must have a GPA of 2.5 or higher. Along with their application, they must submit a 500-word essay on how this scholarship will help them achieve their goals.

Financial data　The stipend is $7,000. Funds are paid directly to the recipient's college.

Duration　1 year.

Additional information　The OBAP was originally established in 1976 as the Organization of Black Airline Pilots to make certain Blacks and other minorities had a group that would keep them informed about opportunities for advancement within commercial aviation.

Number awarded　1 each year.

Deadline　May of each year.

[118]
CAREERS IN TRANSPORTATION FOR YOUTH (CITY) INTERNSHIP PROGRAM

Conference of Minority Transportation Officials
Attn: Internship Program
100 M Street, S.E., Suite 917
Washington, DC 20003
(202) 506-2917　　　　　E-mail: bwilliams@comto.org
Web: www.comto.org/page/internship

Summary　To provide summer work experience in transportation-related fields to African American and ohter underrepresented upper-division students.

Eligibility　This program is open to full-time minority or underrepresented students entering their junior or senior year with a GPA of 2.5 or higher. Applicants must be working on a degree related to public transportation. They must be interested in a summer internship with transit firms or agencies in Chicago, Dallas, Detroit, Jacksonville, New York, Oakland,

Philadelphia, San Antonio, Seattle, southern California, Tampa, or Washington, D.C. Along with their application, they must submit a 1-page essay on their transportation interests, including how participation in this internship will enhance their educational plan, their mid- and long-term professional goals, their specific transportation-related goal, the issues of interest to them, their plans to further their education and assist in making future contributions to their field of study, and their expectations for this internship experience. U.S. citizenship is required.

Financial data　The stipend recently was $15 per hour.

Duration　10 weeks during the summer.

Additional information　This program is managed by the Conference of Minority Transportation Officials (COMTO), with funding provided by the Federal Transit Administration. Interns work at transit agencies, private transit-related consulting firms, transportation service providers, manufacturers, and suppliers.

Number awarded　Varies each year; recently, internships were awarded to 30 students.

Deadline　April of each year.

[119]
CARMEN E. TURNER SCHOLARSHIPS

Conference of Minority Transportation Officials
Attn: National Scholarship Program
100 M Street, S.E., Suite 917
Washington, DC 20003
(202) 506-2917　　　　　　E-mail: info@comto.org
Web: www.comto.org/page/scholarships

Summary　To provide financial assistance for college or graduate school to African American and other members of the Conference of Minority Transportation Officials (COMTO) and their families.

Eligibility　This program is open to undergraduate and graduate students who have been members or whose parents, guardians, or grandparents have been members of COMTO for at least 1 year. Applicants must be working on a degree in a field related to transportation and have a GPA of 2.5 or higher. Along with their application they must submit a cover letter on their transportation-related career goals and life aspirations. Financial need is not considered in the selection process.

Financial data　The stipend is $3,500. Funds are paid directly to the recipient's college or university.

Duration　1 year.

Number awarded　1 each year.

Deadline　April of each year.

[120]
CARMEN MERCER SCHOLARSHIP

National Sorority of Phi Delta Kappa, Inc.-Delta Beta
　Chapter
c/o Christella Cain, Chapter Scholarship Chair
1422 Salem Meadow Circle
Austin, TX 78745
(512) 971-6866

Summary　To provide financial assistance to African American high school seniors who plan to study education in college.

Eligibility This program is open to African American graduating high school seniors who are planning to attend a 4-year college and major in the field of education. Along with their application, they must submit documentation of financial need, high school transcripts, 2 letters of recommendation, SAT and/or ACT scores, a list of honors and awards received in high school, and a list of extracurricular, community, and volunteer activities.

Financial data The stipend is $2,000.

Duration 1 year.

Number awarded 1 each year.

Deadline January of each year.

[121]
CAROLE SIMPSON NABJ SCHOLARSHIP

National Association of Black Journalists
Attn: Program Manager
University of Maryland
1100 Knight Hall, Suite 3100
College Park, MD 20742
(301) 405-7520   Fax: (301) 314-1714
E-mail: Sberry@nabj.org
Web: www.nabj.org/?page=ScholarshipsSimpson

Summary To provide financial assistance to undergraduate or graduate student members of the National Association of Black Journalists (NABJ) who are working on a degree in broadcast journalism.

Eligibility This program is open to African American undergraduate or graduate student members of NABJ who are currently enrolled full time at an accredited 4-year college or university. Applicants must be studying broadcast journalism as preparation for a career in television news and have a GPA of 2.5 or higher. They must be able to demonstrate financial need. Along with their application, they must submit 5 samples of their work, an official college transcript, 3 letters of recommendation, a resume, and an essay of 1,000 to 2,000 words on how the career of this program's namesake inspired them to prepare for a career in broadcast journalism and what they hope their legacy will be.

Financial data The stipend is $2,500. Funds are paid directly to the recipient's college or university.

Duration 1 year; nonrenewable.

Number awarded 1 each year.

Deadline February of each year.

[122]
CAROLE SIMPSON RTDNF SCHOLARSHIP

Radio Television Digital News Foundation
Attn: Membership and Programs Manager
529 14th Street, N.W., Suite 1240
Washington, DC 20045
(202) 662-7257   Fax: (202) 223-4007
E-mail: karenh@rtdna.org
Web: www.rtdna.org/content/carole_simpson_scholarship

Summary To provide financial assistance to African American and other minority undergraduate students who are interested in preparing for a career in electronic journalism.

Eligibility This program is open to sophomore or more advanced minority undergraduate students enrolled in a radio, television, or digital journalism sequence at an accredited or nationally-recognized college or university. Applicants

must submit a cover letter that discusses their current and past journalism experience, describes how they would use the funds if they were to receive the scholarship, discusses their reasons for preparing for a career in electronic journalism, and includes 3 to 5 links to their best and most relevant work samples.

Financial data The stipend is $2,000, paid in semiannual installments of $1,000 each.

Duration 1 year.

Additional information The Radio Television Digital News Foundation (RTDNF) also provides an all-expense paid trip to the Excellence in Journalism conference held that year. The RTDNF was formerly the Radio and Television News Directors Foundation (RTNDF).

Number awarded 1 each year.

Deadline May of each year.

[123]
CARROLL R. GIBSON SCHOLARSHIP AWARD

National Association of Black Narcotic Agents
c/o April Whitesell, Scholarship Award Committee Co-Chair
P.O. Box 277928
Miramar, FL 33027
E-mail: nabna1@verizon.net
Web: www.nabna.org/content/carroll-r-gibson

Summary To provide financial assistance to undergraduates working on a degree in criminal justice at an Historically Black College or University (HBCU).

Eligibility This program is open to full-time students currently enrolled at an HBCU and working on an undergraduate degree in criminal justice. Applicants must have a GPA of 2.5 or higher and a record of school and community involvement. A personal interview is required. Selection is based on merit; financial need is not considered.

Financial data Stipends range from $500 to $5,000.

Duration 1 year.

Additional information This program began in 1988.

Number awarded 1 or more each year.

Deadline Deadline not specified.

[124]
CARY INSTITUTE OF ECOSYSTEM STUDIES RESEARCH EXPERIENCES FOR UNDERGRADUATES PROGRAM

Cary Institute of Ecosystem Studies
Attn: Undergraduate Research Program
2801 Sharon Turnpike
P.O. Box AB
Millbrook, NY 12545
(845) 677-7600, ext. 326   Fax: (845) 677-5976
E-mail: caryreu@caryinstitute.org
Web: www.caryinstitute.org/students/reu-program

Summary To provide undergraduate students, especially African Americans and other diverse students, with an opportunity to conduct research on translational ecology during the summer at the Cary Institute of Ecosystem Studies (IES) at Millbrook, New York.

Eligibility This program is open to undergraduate freshmen, sophomores, juniors, and first semester seniors. Applicants must be interested in conducting an independent research project of their own design under the guidance of a mentor scientist. They must identify their interest in ecological research, their current career plans, and how participating in this program could help them in their degree program and their future pursuits. Recently, research topics focused on translational ecology. The program welcomes applications from students of diverse backgrounds at schools in all parts of the country. U.S. citizenship or permanent resident status is required.

Financial data The stipend is $6,300. Housing and a $900 allowance for food are also provided.

Duration 12 weeks during the summer.

Additional information This program is supported by the National Science Foundation as part of its Research Experiences for Undergraduates (REU) program.

Number awarded 8 to 12 each year.

Deadline February of each year.

[125]
CBC SPOUSES HEINEKEN USA PERFORMING ARTS SCHOLARSHIP

Congressional Black Caucus Foundation, Inc.
Attn: Director, Educational Programs
1720 Massachusetts Avenue, N.W.
Washington, DC 20036
(202) 263-2800   Toll Free: (800) 784-2577
Fax: (202) 775-0773   E-mail: scholarships@cbcfinc.org
Web: www.cbcfinc.org/cbcs-pa

Summary To provide financial assistance to African American and other undergraduate students who are interested in studying the performing arts.

Eligibility This program is open to graduating high school seniors and current undergraduates enrolled or planning to enroll full time at an accredited college or university. Applicants must be interested in preparing for a career in the performing arts, including theater, motion pictures, drama, comedy, music, dance, opera, marching bands, and other musical ensembles. They must have a GPA of 2.5 or higher. Along with their application, they must submit a 2-minute recorded sample of their performance; a 1-page resume listing their extracurricular activities, honors, employment, community service, and special skills; and a personal statement of 500 to 1,000 words on themselves and their interests. They must also be able to demonstrate financial need, leadership ability, and participation in community service activities.

Financial data The stipend is $3,000.

Duration 1 year.

Additional information This program, established in 2000, is sponsored by Heineken USA and administered by the Congressional Black Caucus (CBC) Foundation.

Number awarded Up to 10 each year.

Deadline April of each year.

[126]
CBC SPOUSES VISUAL ARTS SCHOLARSHIP

Congressional Black Caucus Foundation, Inc.
Attn: Director, Educational Programs
1720 Massachusetts Avenue, N.W.
Washington, DC 20036
(202) 263-2800   Toll Free: (800) 784-2577
Fax: (202) 775-0773   E-mail: scholarships@cbcfinc.org
Web: www.cbcfinc.org/cbcs-va

Summary To provide financial assistance to African American and other undergraduate students who are interested in studying the visual arts.

Eligibility This program is open to graduating high school seniors and current undergraduates enrolled or planning to enroll full time at an accredited college or university. Applicants must be interested in preparing for a career in the visual arts, including architecture, ceramics, drawing, fashion, graphic design, illustration, interior design, painting, photography, sketching, video production, or other decorative arts. They must have a GPA of 2.5 or higher. Along with their application, they must submit 5 samples of their work in the art genre for which they are applying; a 1-page resume listing their extracurricular activities, honors, employment, community service, and special skills; and a personal statement of 500 to 1,000 words on themselves and their interests. They must also be able to demonstrate financial need, leadership ability, and participation in community service activities.

Financial data The stipend is $3,000.

Duration 1 year.

Additional information This program began in 2006. It is administered by the Congressional Black Caucus (CBC) Foundation, the organization of African American members of the U.S. Congress.

Number awarded Up to 10 each year.

Deadline April of each year.

[127]
CBCF GENERAL MILLS HEALTH SCHOLARSHIP

Congressional Black Caucus Foundation, Inc.
Attn: Director, Educational Programs
1720 Massachusetts Avenue, N.W.
Washington, DC 20036
(202) 263-2800   Toll Free: (800) 784-2577
Fax: (202) 775-0773   E-mail: scholarships@cbcfinc.org
Web: www.cbcfinc.org/cbcs-cheerios

Summary To provide financial assistance to undergraduate and graduate students who are interested in preparing for a health-related career and who reside in a Congressional district represented by a member of the Congressional Black Caucus (CBC).

Eligibility This program is open to students attending or planning to attend an accredited institution of higher education as a full-time undergraduate or graduate student. Applicants must reside or attend school in a Congressional district represented by a member of the CBC. Preference is given to African Americans. Applicants must be interested in preparing for a career in a medical or other health-related field, including medicine, technology, nutrition, engineering, or other health-related field. They must have a GPA of 2.75 or higher. Along with their application, they must submit transcripts; a 1-page resume listing their extracurricular activities, honors, employment, community service, and special skills; and a personal statement of 500 to 1,000 words on themselves and their interests. They must also be able to demonstrate financial need, leadership ability, and participation in community service activities.

Financial data The stipend is $2,500.

Duration 1 year.

Additional information The program was established in 1998 with support from General Mills, Inc.

Number awarded Up to 46 each year.

Deadline February of each year.

[128]
CENIE "JOMO" WILLIAMS TUITION SCHOLARSHIP

National Association of Black Social Workers
Attn: NABSW Scholarships
2305 Martin Luther King Avenue, S.E.
Washington, DC 20020
(202) 678-4570   Fax: (202) 678-4572
E-mail: office-manager@nabsw.org
Web: www.nabsw.org/?page=ScholarshipsRecipien

Summary To provide financial assistance for college or graduate school to members of the National Association of Black Social Workers (NABSW).

Eligibility This program is open to African American members of NABSW enrolled full time at an accredited social work or social welfare program with a GPA of 2.5 or higher. Applicants must be able to demonstrate community service and a research interest in the Black community. Along with their application, they must submit an essay of 2 to 3 pages on their professional interests, future social work aspirations, previous social work experiences (volunteer and professional), honors and achievements (academic and community service), and research interests within the Black community (for master's and doctoral students). Financial need is considered in the selection process.

Financial data The stipend is $2,000. Funds are sent directly to the recipient's school.

Duration 1 year.

Number awarded 2 each year.

Deadline December of each year.

[129]
CESDA DIVERSITY SCHOLARSHIPS

Colorado Educational Services and Development
  Association
P.O. Box 40214
Denver, CO 80204
(303) 492-2178   E-mail: Maria.Barajas@colorado.edu
Web: www.cesda.org/#!scholarships/crq5

Summary To provide financial assistance to high school seniors in Colorado who are planning to attend college in the state and are either first-generation college students or African Americans or members of other underrepresented ethnic or racial minorities.

Eligibility This program is open to seniors graduating from high schools in Colorado who are 1) the first member of their family to attend college; 2) a member of an underrepresented ethnic or racial minority (African American, Asian/Pacific Islander, American Indian, Hispanic/Chicano/Latino); and/or

3) able to demonstrate financial need. Applicants must have a GPA of 2.8 or higher and be planning to enroll at a 2- or 4-year college or university in Colorado. U.S. citizenship or permanent resident status is required. Selection is based on leadership and community service (particularly within minority communities), past academic performance, personal and professional accomplishments, personal attributes, special abilities, academic goals, and financial need.

Financial data The stipend is $1,000.

Duration 1 year; nonrenewable.

Number awarded Varies each year.

Deadline March of each year.

[130]
CFA HEA/SSP SOLAR SUMMER INTERN PROGRAM

Harvard-Smithsonian Center for Astrophysics
Attn: Solar REU Program
60 Garden Street, Mail Stop 58
Cambridge, MA 02138
(617) 496-7703   E-mail: sdaly@cfa.harvard.edu
Web: www.cfa.harvard.edu

Summary To enable undergraduates, especially African Americans and other underrepresented students, to participate in a summer research program at the Harvard-Smithsonian Center for Astrophysics (CfA).

Eligibility This program is open to U.S. citizens, nationals, and permanent residents who are full-time undergraduates, preferably those entering their junior or senior year. Applicants must be interested in working during the summer on a project in either of 2 CfA divisions: high energy astrophysics (HEA), which focuses on X-ray astronomy, or solar, stellar, and planetary (SSP) group, which focuses on understanding star and planet formation and the physical processes in the Sun, stars, and stellar systems. Applications from underrepresented minorities, persons with disabilities, and women are encouraged.

Financial data The stipend is $5,000. Housing and travel expenses are also covered.

Duration 10 weeks during the summer.

Additional information This program is supported by the National Science Foundation as part of its Research Experiences for Undergraduates (REU) Program and by the U.S. National Aeronautics and Space Administration (NASA).

Number awarded 8 each year.

Deadline February of each year.

[131]
CH2M HILL INDUSTRY PARTNER SCHOLARSHIP

Conference of Minority Transportation Officials
Attn: National Scholarship Program
100 M Street, S.E., Suite 917
Washington, DC 20003
(202) 506-2917   E-mail: info@comto.org
Web: www.comto.org/page/scholarships

Summary To provide financial assistance to African American and other minority high school and college students interested in working on a degree in a field related to transportation.

Eligibility This program is open to minority high school seniors and current undergraduates who have a GPA of 3.0

or higher. Applicants must be working on or planning to work on a degree in engineering with a focus on the field of transportation. Along with their application they must submit a cover letter on their transportation-related career goals and life aspirations. Financial need is not considered in the selection process.

Financial data   The stipend is $3,000. Funds are paid directly to the recipient's college or university.

Duration   1 year.

Additional information   This program is sponsored by CH2M Hill.

Number awarded   1 each year.

Deadline   April of each year.

[132]
CH2M HILL/WILLIE T. LOUD SCHOLARSHIP

National Forum for Black Public Administrators
Attn: Scholarship Program
777 North Capitol Street, N.E., Suite 807
Washington, DC 20002
(202) 408-9300   Fax: (202) 408-8558
E-mail: vharris@nfbpa.org
Web: www.nfbpa.org/i4a/pages/index.cfm?pageid=4047

Summary   To provide financial assistance to African Americans working on a bachelor's or master's degree in public administration.

Eligibility   This program is open to African American graduate students preparing for a career in public service. Applicants must be working full time on a bachelor's or master's degree in public administration, urban affairs, or a related field. They must have a GPA of 3.0 or higher, strong interpersonal skills, and excellent writing, analytical, and oral communication abilities. Along with their application, they must submit a 3-page autobiographical essay that includes their academic and career goals and objectives. Selection is based on academic record, leadership ability, participation in school activities, community service, and financial need.

Financial data   The stipend is $5,000.

Duration   1 year.

Additional information   This program, established in 1997, is sponsored by CH2M Hill. Recipients are required to attend the sponsor's annual conference to receive their scholarship; limited hotel and air accommodations are arranged and provided.

Number awarded   1 each year.

Deadline   March of each year.

[133]
CHARLES FONSECA SCHOLARSHIP AWARD

National Organization of Black Law Enforcement
  Executives
Attn: NOBLE Scholarships
4609 Pinecrest Office Park Drive, Suite F
Alexandria, VA 22312-1442
(703) 658-1529   Fax: (703) 658-9479
E-mail: wleach@noblenatl.org
Web: www.noblenational.org

Summary   To provide financial assistance for college to high school seniors, especially African Americans, who are interested in preparing for a criminal justice career.

Eligibility   This program is open to high school seniors who have a GPA of 3.7 or higher and are interested in preparing for a career in criminal justice. Applicants must be planning to attend an accredited academic institution in the United States to major in a social science (e.g. technology, forensic investigations, or other criminal investigative studies) related to a career in law enforcement or criminal justice. They must be U.S. citizens and able to demonstrate financial need. Along with their application, they must submit a 1-page essay on their career goals and interests and why they feel they should receive this scholarship.

Financial data   The stipend is $2,000.

Duration   1 year; nonrenewable.

Additional information   The sponsor is an organization of African American law enforcement officers.

Number awarded   1 each year.

Deadline   April of each year.

[134]
CHARLES L. WARREN MEMORIAL HERITAGE SCHOLARSHIP

Ohio Association for College Admission Counseling
Attn: Inclusion, Access and Success Committee
P.O. Box 959
Marysville, OH 43040
(937) 642-1234   E-mail: execadmin@oacac.org
Web: www.oacac.org/student-scholarships

Summary   To provide financial assistance for college in Ohio to seniors at high schools that are members of the Ohio Association for College Admission Counseling (OACAC), especially African Americans and members of other underrepresented groups.

Eligibility   This program is open to seniors graduating from high schools that are members of OACAC and planning to attend a college or university in the state. Members of underrepresented populations are encouraged to apply. Applicants must have a GPA of 3.0 or higher and be able to show a continued commitment to cultural and intellectual diversity. Along with their application, they must submit a 500-word essay that includes a description of the environment (family, community, or school) from which they came and how it has influenced what they value most about their heritage, how they have contributed to the intellectual and cultural diversity of their high school or community and how they plan to continue their commitment at their college or university, and why they are deserving of this scholarship.

Financial data   The stipend is $1,000.

Duration   1 year; nonrenewable.

Number awarded   Several each year.

Deadline   January of each year.

[135]
CHELLE WILSON 2013 NOLA SCHOLARS FELLOWSHIP

Alpha Kappa Alpha Sorority, Inc.
Attn: Educational Advancement Foundation
5656 South Stony Island Avenue
Chicago, IL 60637
(773) 947-0026   Toll Free: (800) 653-6528
Fax: (773) 947-0277   E-mail: akaeaf@akaeaf.net
Web: www.akaeaf.org/fellowships_endowments.htm

Summary To provide financial assistance to undergraduates from Louisiana (especially African American women) who are working on a degree in any field.

Eligibility This program is open to residents of Louisiana who are enrolled as sophomores or higher at an accredited degree-granting institution in any state. Applicants may be majoring in any field, but they must have a GPA of 3.0 or higher. Along with their application, they must submit 1) a list of honors, awards, and scholarships received; 2) a list of organizations in which they have memberships, especially minority organizations; and 3) a statement of their personal and career goals, including how this scholarship will enhance their ability to attain those goals. The sponsor is a traditionally African American women's sorority.

Financial data A stipend is awarded (amount not specified).

Duration 1 year.

Number awarded 1 or more each even-numbered year.

Deadline April of each even-numbered year.

[136]
CHEVRON/NSBE CORPORATE SCHOLARSHIP

National Society of Black Engineers
Attn: Programs Department
205 Daingerfield Road
Alexandria, VA 22314
(703) 549-2207   Fax: (703) 683-5312
E-mail: scholarships@nsbe.org
Web: connect.nsbe.org/Scholarships/ScholarshipList.aspx

Summary To provide financial assistance to high school seniors and current undergraduates who are members of the National Society of Black Engineers (NSBE) and interested in studying engineering or a related field.

Eligibility This program is open to members of the society who are either high school seniors or current college freshmen, sophomores, juniors, or seniors. Applicants must be majoring or planning to major in engineering or a related field. They must have a GPA of 3.0 or higher and be U.S. citizens. Selection is based on academic standing, leadership skills, focus on the applications of engineering in the work world, and financial need.

Financial data The stipend is $5,000.

Duration 1 year.

Additional information This program is sponsored by Chevron.

Number awarded 20 each year.

Deadline March of each year.

[137]
CHIPS QUINN SCHOLARS PROGRAM

Newseum Institute
Attn: Chips Quinn Scholars Program
555 Pennsylvania Avenue, N.W.
Washington, DC 20001
(202) 292-6271   Fax: (202) 292-6275
E-mail: kcatone@freedomforum.org
Web: www.newseuminstitute.org

Summary To provide work experience to African American and other minority college students and recent graduates who are majoring in journalism.

Eligibility This program is open to students of color who are college juniors, seniors, graduate students, or recent graduates with journalism majors or career goals in newspapers. Candidates must be nominated or endorsed by journalism faculty, campus media advisers, editors of newspapers, or leaders of minority journalism associations. Along with their application, they must submit a resume, transcripts, 2 letters of recommendation, and an essay of 200 to 400 words on why they want to be a Chips Quinn Scholar. Reporters and copy editors must also submit 6 samples of published articles they have written; photographers must submit 15 to 25 photographs on a DVD; multimedia journalists and graphic designers should submit 6 to 10 samples of their work on a DVD. Applicants must have a car and be available to work as a full-time intern during the spring or summer. U.S. citizenship or permanent resident status is required. Campus newspaper experience is strongly encouraged.

Financial data Students chosen for this program receive a travel stipend to attend a Multimedia training program in Nashville, Tennessee prior to reporting for their internship, a $500 housing allowance from the Freedom Forum, and a competitive salary during their internship.

Duration Internships are for 10 to 12 weeks, in spring or summer.

Additional information This program began in 1991 in memory of the late John D. Quinn Jr., managing editor of the *Poughkeepsie Journal*. Funding is provided by the Freedom Forum, formerly the Gannett Foundation. After graduating from college and obtaining employment with a newspaper, alumni of this program are eligible to apply for fellowship support to attend professional journalism development activities.

Number awarded Approximately 70 each year. Since the program began, more than 1,300 scholars have been selected.

Deadline September of each year.

[138]
CHRISTIAN COLLEGE LEADERS SCHOLARSHIPS

Foundation for College Christian Leaders
2658 Del Mar Heights Road
PMB 266
Del Mar, CA 92014
(858) 481-0848   E-mail: LMHays@aol.com
Web: www.collegechristianleader.com

Summary To provide financial assistance for college to Christian students from California, Oregon, and Washington, especially African Americans and other minority students.

Eligibility This program is open to entering or continuing undergraduate students who reside or attend college in California, Oregon, or Washington. Applicants must have a GPA of 3.0 or higher, be able to document financial need (parents must have a combined income of less than $75,000), and be able to demonstrate Christian testimony and Christian leadership. Selection is based on identified leadership history, academic achievement, financial need, and demonstrated academic, vocational, and ministry training to further the Kingdom of Jesus Christ. Special consideration is given to minority students.

Financial data A stipend is awarded (amount not specified).

Duration 1 year; may be renewed.

Additional information The foundation, formerly known as the Eckmann Foundation, was founded in 1988.

Number awarded Varies each year.

Deadline May of each year.

[139]
CIGNA HEALTHCARE UNDERGRADUATE SCHOLARSHIP

National Forum for Black Public Administrators
Attn: Scholarship Program
777 North Capitol Street, N.E., Suite 807
Washington, DC 20002
(202) 408-9300   Fax: (202) 408-8558
E-mail: vharris@nfbpa.org
Web: www.nfbpa.org/i4a/pages/index.cfm?pageid=4047

Summary To provide financial assistance to African Americans working on an undergraduate degree in public administration or a related field at an Historically Black College or University (HBCU).

Eligibility This program is open to African American undergraduate students preparing for a career in public administration. Applicants must be working full time on a degree in public administration, political science, urban affairs, public policy, or a related field at an HBCU. They must have a GPA of 3.5 or higher, excellent interpersonal and analytical abilities, and strong oral and written communication skills. Along with their application, they must submit a 3-page autobiographical essay that includes their academic and career goals and objectives, their SAT or ACT scores, and documentation of financial need. Selection is based on academic record, leadership ability, participation in school activities, community service, and financial need.

Financial data The stipend is $10,000.

Duration 1 year.

Additional information This program is sponsored by CIGNA Healthcare. Recipients are required to attend the sponsor's annual conference to receive their scholarship; limited hotel and air accommodations are arranged and provided.

Number awarded 1 each year.

Deadline March of each year.

[140]
CIRCLE CITY CLASSIC SCHOLARSHIPS

Indiana Black Expo, Inc.
Attn: Circle City Classic
3145 North Meridian
Indianapolis, IN 46208
(317) 925-2702   Fax: (317) 237-5223
E-mail: communications@indianablackexpo.com
Web: www.circlecityclassic.com/scholarships

Summary To provide financial assistance to high school seniors and current college students in Indiana who are interested in enrolling at a college or university in any state, especially at an Historically Black College or University (HBCU).

Eligibility This program is open to residents of Indiana who are graduating high school seniors or undergraduates currently enrolled full time at a college, university, community college, or vocational/technical program in any state. Applicants must have a GPA of 2.5 or higher and be U.S. citizens or permanent residents. Special consideration is given to students who 1) are the first in their family to attend college; or 2) can demonstrate financial need. Along with their application, they must submit an essay on any personal life challenges they have overcome that developed their character and contributed to their desire to attain their goal of pursuing higher education. All Indiana residents are eligible, but some scholarships are reserved for students who attend an HBCU.

Financial data A stipend is awarded (amount not specified).

Duration 1 year.

Additional information Indiana Black Expo (IBE) was established in 1984 to promote the social and economic advancement of African Americans in Indiana. Support for this program is provided by proceeds from the Circle City Classic (CCC) football game.

Number awarded Varies each year; recently, 58 were awarded, including at least 2 scholarships reserved for students attending an HBCU. Since its establishment, this program has awarded more than $4.1 million in scholarships.

Deadline February of each year.

[141]
CIRILO MCSWEEN (NEW YORK LIFE) SCHOLARSHIP

PUSH Excel
Attn: General Offices
930 East 50th Street
Chicago, IL 60615
(773) 373-3366   E-mail: pushexcel@rainbowpush.org
Web: www.pushexcel.org/pages/scholarships

Summary To provide financial assistance to African American and other college students who are majoring in business and willing to help promote the scholarship program of PUSH-Excel.

Eligibility This program is open to entering freshmen, sophomores, juniors, and seniors at an accredited 4-year college or university who are majoring in business. Applicants must be U.S. citizens and have a GPA of 3.0 or higher. Along with their application, they must submit a 500-word essay that identifies 5 prerequisites for success, explains their personal philosophy for the pursuit of excellence, and explains how they will use their college education to achieve this pursuit of excellence. They must also agree to cooperate with the scholarship committee of PUSH-Excel by promoting its program, participating in its public relations activities, and attending its Annual National Conference luncheon and Education Leadership Conference. Selection is based on the essay, academic preparation to attend college and succeed, and ability to overcome obstacles to achieve academic and personal goals.

Financial data The stipend is $5,000 per year.

Duration 1 year; may be renewed up to 3 additional years if the recipient maintains a GPA of 3.0 or higher and fulfills the obligations to PUSH-Excel.

Additional information PUSH-Excel was founded in 1975 by the Rev. Jesse Jackson. This program is named for Cirilo McSween, the first African American agent for New York Life (which sponsors this program).

Number awarded 1 or more each year.

Deadline April of each year.

[142]
CITE TRADITIONAL SCHOLARSHIPS

Consortium of Information and Telecommunications
Executives, Inc.
c/o Monica Felton, Scholarship Committee Chair
P.O. Box 280233
Northridge, CA 91328
(818) 365-2787

Summary To provide financial assistance to African American high school seniors who plan to major in any field in college.

Eligibility This program is open to African American high school seniors who have been accepted by an accredited 4-year college or university in any state as a full-time student. Applicants must have a GPA of 3.0 or higher and a family income of $75,000 per year or less. They may be planning to major in any field. Along with their application, they must submit a 1-page essay on their educational and career goals. Employees of Verizon Communications or affiliated subsidiaries and their family members are ineligible. U.S. citizenship is required.

Financial data Stipends are $2,000 or $1,000.

Duration 1 year; nonrenewable.

Additional information The Consortium of Information and Telecommunications Executives (CITE) is an organization of African American employees of Verizon, founded in 1984 after the dissolution of the former Bell systems.

Number awarded 2 each year: 1 at $2,000 and 1 at $1,000. Awards are presented in each CITE Region: South East (Florida, Georgia, and North Carolina), Mid-Atlantic (Delaware, New Jersey, and Pennsylvania), Maryland, New England, New York, Virginia, and West (California, Illinois, and Texas).

Deadline May of each year.

[143]
CLANSEER AND ANNA JOHNSON SCHOLARSHIPS

Community Foundation of New Jersey
Attn: Chief Operating Officer
35 Knox Hill Road
P.O. Box 338
Morristown, NJ 07963-0338
(973) 267-5533, ext. 227   Toll Free: (800) 659-5533
Fax: (973) 267-2903   E-mail: fkrueger@cfnj.org
Web: www.cfnj.org/current-funds/student-scholarships

Summary To provide financial assistance to African American high school seniors in New Jersey who plan to attend college in any state.

Eligibility This program is open to African American seniors graduating from high schools in New Jersey who have been accepted to attend an educational institution in the United States. Applicants must have earned a grade of "A" or "B" in classes related to the sciences or mathematics and have maintained above average grades in all course work. They must have been born in the United States. Selection is based primarily on financial need, but academic performance, extracurricular activities, and work experience are also considered.

Financial data The stipend is $1,500 per year. Funds are made payable jointly to the recipients and their educational institution.

Duration 4 years, provided the recipient maintains a GPA of 2.5 or higher.

Additional information Recipients must agree to donate at least 10 hours of community service per week within New Jersey for 1 year following graduation.

Number awarded 4 each year.

Deadline March of each year.

[144]
CLARKE WATSON SCHOLARSHIPS

American Association of Blacks in Energy-Denver Area
Chapter
Attn: Scholarship Committee
18601 Green Valley Ranch Boulevard, 108-264
Denver, CO 80249
E-mail: Denver@aabe.org
Web: www.aabe.org/index.php?component=pages&id=270

Summary To provide financial assistance to African Americans and members of other underrepresented minority groups who are high school seniors in Colorado and planning to major in an energy-related field at a college in any state.

Eligibility This program is open to seniors graduating from high schools in Colorado who are planning to work on a bachelor's degree at a college or university in any state. Applicants must be African Americans, Hispanics, or Native Americans who have a GPA of 3.0 or higher and have taken the ACT and/or SAT test. They must be planning to major in a field of business, engineering, technology, physical science, or mathematics related to energy. Along with their application, they must submit a 350-word essay that includes 1) when they discovered their interest in the field of energy and what sparked their interest; and 2) either what excites them about the field of energy or how they expect their education to prepare them for the field of energy. Financial need is not considered in the selection process.

Financial data The stipend is $1,000. Funds are disbursed directly to the recipient's college or university.

Duration 1 year; may be renewed.

Additional information Winners are eligible to compete for regional and national scholarships.

Number awarded 1 or more each year.

Deadline February of each year.

[145]
CLAY FORD MINORITY SCHOLARSHIPS

Florida Board of Accountancy
Florida Department of Business and Professional
Regulation
Attn: Division of Certified Public Accounting
240 N.W. 76th Drive, Suite A
Gainesville, FL 32607-6656
(352) 333-2505   Fax: (352) 333-2508
E-mail: CPA.Applications@dbpr.state.fl.us
Web: www.myfloridalicense.com

Summary To provide financial assistance to African American and other minority residents of Florida who are entering the fifth year of an accounting program.

Eligibility This program is open to Florida residents who have completed at least 120 credit hours at a college or university in the state and have a GPA of 2.5 or higher. Applicants must be planning to remain in school as a full-time student for the fifth year required to sit for the C.P.A. examination. They must be members of a minority group, defined to include African Americans, Hispanic Americans, Asian Americans, Native Americans, or women. Selection is based on scholastic ability and performance and financial need.

Financial data Stipends range from $3,000 to $6,000 per semester.

Duration 1 semester; may be renewed 1 additional semester.

Number awarded Varies each year; a total of $200,000 is available for this program annually.

Deadline May of each year.

[146]
CLBC CALIFORNIA SCHOLARS

California Legislative Black Caucus
Attn: Alana Troutt
State Capitol, Room 4126
Sacramento, CA 95814
(916) 319-2059   Fax: (916) 319-2159
Web: blackcaucus.legislature.ca.gov/clbccaliforniascholars

Summary To provide financial assistance to residents of California who live in a state legislative district represented by a member of the California Legislative Black Caucus and are interested in attending college in any state.

Eligibility This program is open to graduating high school seniors and college freshmen currently enrolled full time at an accredited institution of higher learning in any state. Applicants must reside in a district whose member of the State Senate or General Assembly is a member of the California Legislative Black Caucus. They must have a GPA of 2.5 or higher. Along with their application, they must submit an essay on the experiences that have influenced their decision to pursue higher education and who those experiences will help them with their career goals and a short paragraph on how the scholarship will benefit them.

Financial data The stipend is $2,500.

Duration 1 year.

Additional information Recently, 2 state senators and 10 state assembly members constituted the California Legislative Black Caucus. Applications must be submitted directly to them. For their names and addresses, consult the caucus.

Number awarded 1 or more each year.

Deadline June of each year.

[147]
COALITION OF BLACK TRADE UNIONISTS UNDERGRADUATE SCHOLARSHIPS

Coalition of Black Trade Unionists
Attn: Scholarship Awards Committee
1150 17th Street, N.W., Suite 300
P.O. Box 66268
Washington, DC 20035-6268
(202) 778-3318   Fax: (202) 293-5308
E-mail: cbtu1@hotmail.com
Web: www.cbtu.org/bell%20ball.html

Summary To provide financial assistance to undergraduates who are members or sponsored by members of the Coalition of Black Trade Unionists (CBTU).

Eligibility This program is open to students who are enrolled or planning to enroll at a college or university. Applicants must be a CBTU member or sponsored by a member and must specify their relationship to their sponsor. Along with their application, they must submit SAT or ACT scores and a 300-word essay on assigned topics that differ, depending on the applicant's year in school. Students already enrolled in college must have a GPA of 2.5 or higher. Financial need is not considered in the selection process.

Financial data The stipend is $2,000.

Duration 1 year.

Additional information This program includes the James H. Bell Scholarship and the Leonard C. Ball Scholarship.

Number awarded 10 each year.

Deadline April of each year.

[148]
COKER/DAVIS SCHOLARSHIP

National Naval Officers Association-Washington, D.C. Chapter
c/o LCDR Stephen Williams
P.O. Box 30784
Alexandria, VA 22310
(703) 644-2605   Fax: (703) 644-8503
E-mail: Stephen.Williams@navy.mil
Web: www.dcnnoa.org/dcnnoa-scholarship

Summary To provide financial assistance to male African American high school seniors from the Washington, D.C. area who are interested in attending college in any state.

Eligibility This program is open to male African American seniors graduating from high schools in the Washington, D.C. metropolitan area who plan to enroll full time at an accredited 2- or 4-year college or university in any state. Applicants must have a GPA of 2.5 or higher and be U.S. citizens or permanent residents. Selection is based on academic achievement, community involvement, and financial need.

Financial data The stipend is $1,000.

Duration 1 year; nonrenewable.

Additional information Recipients are not required to join or affiliate with the military in any way.

Number awarded 1 each year.

Deadline February of each year.

[149]
COLGATE "BRIGHT SMILES, BRIGHT FUTURES" MINORITY SCHOLARSHIPS

American Dental Hygienists' Association
Attn: Institute for Oral Health
444 North Michigan Avenue, Suite 3400
Chicago, IL 60611-3980
(312) 440-8900, ext. 244   Fax: (312) 440-6726
E-mail: institute@adha.net
Web: www.adha.org/ioh-associate-certificate-scholarships

Summary To provide financial assistance to African American and other minority students and males of any race who are members of the American Dental Hygienists' Association (ADHA) and enrolled in certificate programs in dental hygiene.

Eligibility This program is open to members of groups currently underrepresented in the dental hygiene profession (African Americans, Native Americans, Hispanics, Asians, and males) who are student or active members of the ADHA. Applicants must have a GPA of 3.5 or higher and have completed at least 1 year of full-time enrollment in an accredited dental hygiene certificate or associate degree program in the United States.

Financial data The stipend is $1,250.

Duration 1 year; nonrenewable.

Additional information These scholarships are sponsored by the Colgate-Palmolive Company.

Number awarded 2 each year.

Deadline January of each year.

[150]
COLLABORATIVE RESEARCH EXPERIENCES FOR UNDERGRADUATES

Computing Research Association
1828 L Street, N.W., Suite 800
Washington, DC 20036-4632
(202) 234-2111   Fax: (202) 667-1066
E-mail: creu@cra.org
Web: www.cra.org/cra-w/creu

Summary To provide funding to African Americans and other underrepresented undergraduate students who are interested in conducting a research project in computer science or engineering.

Eligibility This program is open to teams of 2 or 4 undergraduates who have completed 2 years of study, including at least 4 courses in computer science or computer engineering, at a college or university in the United States. Applicants must be interested in conducting a research project directly related to computer science or computer engineering. They must apply jointly with 1 or 2 sponsoring faculty members. Teams consisting of underrepresented groups (women, African Americans, Mexican-Americans, American Indians, Alaska Natives, Native Hawaiians, Pacific Islanders, mainland Puerto Ricans, individuals who identify as part of the LGBTQI community, and persons with disabilities) are especially encouraged to apply; teams may also include students from non-underrepresented groups, but financial support is available only to underrepresented students. U.S. citizenship or permanent resident status is required.

Financial data The program provides a stipend of $3,000 for the academic year. Students who wish to participate in an optional summer extension receive an additional stipend of $4,000. Additional funding up to $1,500 per team may be available for purchase of supporting materials and/or travel to conferences to present the work.

Duration 1 academic year plus an optional summer extension.

Additional information This program is sponsored by the Computing Research Association's Committee on the Status of Women in Computing Research (CRA-W) and the Coalition to Diversify Computing (CDC) in cooperation with the National Science Foundation.

Number awarded Varies each year; recently, 14 teams of students received support from this program.

Deadline May of each year.

[151]
COLLEGE STUDENT PRE-COMMISSIONING INITIATIVE

U.S. Coast Guard
Attn: Recruiting Command
2703 Martin Luther King, Jr. Avenue, S.E., Stop 7419
Washington, DC 20593-7200
(202) 795-6864
Web: www.gocoastguard.com

Summary To provide financial assistance to college students at minority or other designated institutions who are willing to serve in the Coast Guard following graduation.

Eligibility This program is open to students entering their junior or senior year at a college or university designated as an Historically Black College or University (HBCU), Predominantly Black Institution (PBI), Hispanic Serving Institution (HSI), Asian American and Native American Pacific Islander-Serving Institution, American Indian Tribally Controlled College or University (TCU), Alaska Native Serving Institution (ANSI), or Native American Serving, Non-Tribal Institution. Applicants must be U.S. citizens; have a GPA of 2.5 or higher; have scores of 1100 or higher on the critical reading and mathematics SAT, 23 or higher on the ACT, or 109 or higher technical score on the ASVAB; be between 19 and 27 years of age; and meet all physical requirements for a Coast Guard commission. They must agree to attend the Coast Guard Officer Candidate School following graduation and serve on active duty as an officer for at least 3 years.

Financial data Those selected to participate receive full payment of tuition, books, and fees; monthly housing and food allowances; medical and life insurance; special training in leadership, management, law enforcement, navigation, and marine science; 30 days of paid vacation per year; and a Coast Guard monthly salary of approximately $1,800.

Duration Up to 2 years.

Number awarded Varies each year; recently, 38 were awarded.

Deadline September or January of each year.

[152]
COLORADO EDUCATION ASSOCIATION MINORITY STUDENT SCHOLARSHIPS

Colorado Education Association
Attn: Ethnic Minority Advisory Council
1500 Grant Street
Denver, CO 80203
(303) 837-1500   Toll Free: (800) 332-5939
Web: www.coloradoea.org

Summary To provide financial assistance to African Americans and other minority high school seniors in Colorado who are children of members of the Colorado Education Association (CEA) and planning to attend college in any state.

Eligibility This program is open to seniors graduating from high schools in Colorado who are members of a minority ethnic group, defined to include Blacks, American Indians/Alaska Natives, Asians, Hispanics, Native Hawaiians/Pacific Islanders, and multi-ethnic. Applicants must be the dependent child of an active, retired, or deceased CEA member. They must be planning to attend an accredited institution of higher education in any state. Along with their application, they must submit brief statements on 1) their need for this scholarship; and 2) why they plan to pursue a college education.

Financial data The stipend is $1,000.

Duration 1 year; nonrenewable.

Number awarded 4 each year.

Deadline April of each year.

[153]
COLUMBIA UNIVERSITY/BARNARD COLLEGE AMGEN SCHOLARS SUMMER RESEARCH PROGRAM

Columbia University
Attn: Biological Sciences
1212 Amsterdam Avenue
MC2454
New York, NY 10027
(212) 854-2262   E-mail: amgen@biology.columbia.edu
Web: www.columbia.edu/cu/biology/ug/amgen

Summary To provide an opportunity for undergraduates, especially African Americans and other underrepresented minorities, to participate in summer research projects in the biological sciences at Columbia University.

Eligibility This program is open to sophomores, juniors, and non-graduating seniors at 4-year colleges and universities in the United States, Puerto Rico, and other U.S. territories. Applicants must be U.S. citizens or permanent residents who have a cumulative GPA of 3.2 or higher. They must be interested in working on a summer research project at Columbia University in the following laboratory programs: biochemistry and molecular biophysics, biological sciences, biomedical engineering, genetics and development, microbiology and immunology, pathology and cell biology, physiology and cell biophysics, or psychiatry. The Amgen Scholars Program encourages applications from students who are members of groups underrepresented in the biological sciences.

Financial data Scholars receive a stipend of $4,000, a flex meal plan of $500, transportation to and from New York, and housing on the Morningside campus of Columbia.

Duration 10 weeks during the summer.

Additional information This program serves as the Columbia component of the Amgen Scholars Program, which operates at 8 other U.S. universities (and the National Institutes of Health) and is funded by the Amgen Foundation.

Number awarded Up to 30 each year, of whom half are from Columbia or Barnard and half from other universities.

Deadline January of each year.

[154]
COMMISSION ON DIETETIC REGISTRATION DIVERSITY SCHOLARSHIPS

Academy of Nutrition and Dietetics
Attn: Foundation
120 South Riverside Plaza, Suite 2000
Chicago, IL 60606-6995
(312) 899-4821   Toll Free: (800) 877-1600, ext. 4821
Fax: (312) 899-4796   E-mail: blabrador@eatright.org
Web: www.eatrightfoundation.org/foundation/scholarships

Summary To provide financial assistance to African Americans and members of other underrepresented minority groups who are enrolled in an undergraduate or graduate program in dietetics.

Eligibility This program is open to students enrolled at a CADE-accredited/approved college or university in the undergraduate coordinated dietetics program, the undergraduate didactic program in dietetics, a dietetic internship program, a dietetic technician program, or a dietetic graduate program. Applicants must be members of underrepresented minority groups (African American, Hispanic, Native American). They must be U.S. citizens or permanent residents and show promise of being a valuable, contributing member of the profession. Membership in the Academy of Nutrition and Dietetics is encouraged but not required.

Financial data The stipend is $5,000.

Duration 1 year.

Number awarded 20 each year.

Deadline March of each year.

[155]
COMMUNICATIONS INTERNSHIP AWARD FOR STUDENTS OF COLOR

College and University Public Relations and Allied
  Professionals
237 South Fraser Street
P.O. Box 10034
State College, PA 16805-0034
Fax: (814) 863-3428   E-mail: ehanson@cuprap.org
Web: www.cuprap.org/awards/communications-internships

Summary To provide an opportunity for African Americans and other students of color at institutions that are members of the College and University Public Relations and Allied Professionals (CUPRAP) to complete an internship in communications.

Eligibility This program is open to students of color (i.e., African Americans, Asian/Pacific Islanders, Hispanics/Latinos, and Native Americans) who have completed the first year of college and are enrolled as a degree candidate in the second year or higher. Applicants must obtain and complete a verifiable internship of at least 150 hours in a communications-related field (e.g., print media, radio, television, public relations, advertising, graphic/web design). They must be enrolled full time at an accredited 2- or 4-year college or university that is a member of CUPRAP. Selection is based on financial need, academic ability, communication skills, and creativity as demonstrated through work samples.

Financial data The stipend is $2,000, paid upon confirmation of employment in an internship position.

Duration The internship award is presented annually; recipients may reapply.

Additional information This internship award was first presented in 1983.

Number awarded 1 each year.

Deadline January of each year.

[156]
COMMUNICATIONS INTERNSHIP PROGRAM SPONSORED BY STATE FARM

Congressional Black Caucus Foundation, Inc.
Attn: Leadership Institute for Public Service
1720 Massachusetts Avenue, N.W.
Washington, DC 20036
(202) 263-2800   Toll Free: (800) 784-2577
Fax: (202) 775-0773   E-mail: internships@cbcfinc.org
Web: www.cbcfinc.org

Summary To provide African American and other undergraduate students with an opportunity to work during the fall with the press secretary or communications director in the office of a member of the Congressional Black Caucus (CBC).

Eligibility This program is open to African American and other full-time undergraduate students majoring in public relations, journalism, or other media-related field. Applicants must be interested in working with the press secretary or communications director of a CBC member. They should have a demonstrated professional familiarity with public relations, journalism, or other media-related field. Selection is based on GPA (at least 2.5), strength of a faculty nomination, evidence of leadership skills, writing skills, and work experience in communications fields. U.S. citizenship or permission to work in the United States are required.

Financial data Interns receive housing accommodations and a $4,000 stipend to cover expenses related to travel, meals, and personal expenses.

Duration 13 weeks during the fall.

Additional information This program is sponsored by State Farm. Interns research legislation, prepare press releases, write op-editorials, write arguments for a position, organize and help to prepare for briefings and forums, and perform various office tasks.

Number awarded Varies each year.

Deadline June of each year.

[157]
COMTO COLORADO SCHOLARSHIPS

Conference of Minority Transportation Officials-Colorado
  Chapter
Attn: Scholarship Committee
1114 West Seventh Avenue
P.O. Box 13582
Denver, CO 80201
E-mail: DrMaryDavis@aol.com
Web: www.comtocolorado.org/scholarship-program

Summary To provide financial assistance to African American and other minority high school seniors in Colorado who are interested in studying a transportation-related field at a college or university in any state.

Eligibility This program is open to minority seniors graduating from high schools in Colorado with a GPA of 2.5 or higher. Applicants must be planning to attend an accredited college, university, or trade school in any state. They must be planning to major in archaeology and/or cultural resources, architecture, aviation, engineering (chemical, civil, electrical, mechanical, or structural), computer aided design, computer science, construction engineering technology, construction and/or construction management, diesel mechanics, electrical, electronics, environmental science and related fields, geology and/or geotechnical engineering, heating and air conditioning, hydraulic and/or elevator mechanics, public information and outreach programs, security systems, urban planning, or vehicle design and maintenance. Along with their application, they must submit an essay of 500 to 700 words on why they chose their planned field of study, how they think their course work and life experiences have helped them prepare for their college studies and the future, and why they are an excellent candidate for this scholarship. Selection is based on that essay (20%), GPA (15%), participation in career-related activities (10%), letters of recommendation (15%), high school citizenship (15%), and an interview (25%).

Financial data A stipend is awarded (amount not specified). Funds may be used for tuition, books, and/or room and board expenses.

Duration 1 year.

Number awarded Up to 10 each year.

Deadline March of each year.

[158]
CONGRESSIONAL BLACK CAUCUS FOUNDATION CONGRESSIONAL INTERNSHIP PROGRAM

Congressional Black Caucus Foundation, Inc.
Attn: Leadership Institute for Public Service
1720 Massachusetts Avenue, N.W.
Washington, DC 20036
(202) 263-2800   Toll Free: (800) 784-2577
Fax: (202) 775-0773   E-mail: internships@cbcfinc.org
Web: www.cbcfinc.org/congressional-internship-program

Summary To provide African American and other undergraduate students with an opportunity to work during the summer in a Congressional office and to participate in the legislative process.

Eligibility This program is open to African American and other full-time undergraduate students in good academic standing. Applicants must be interested in a legislative internship on the staff of an African American member of Congress. They should have a demonstrated interest in public service, governance, and the policy-making process. Selection is based on scholastic achievement, evidence of leadership skills, writing skills, and community service contributions. U.S. citizenship or permission to work in the United States are required.

Financial data Interns receive housing accommodations and a stipend of $3,000 to cover expenses related to travel, meals, and personal expenses.

Duration 9 weeks during the summer.

Additional information This program began in 1986.

Number awarded Varies each year; recently, 42 interns served in this program.

Deadline February of each year.

[159]
CONGRESSIONAL BLACK CAUCUS SPOUSES EDUCATION SCHOLARSHIP

Congressional Black Caucus Foundation, Inc.
Attn: Director, Educational Programs
1720 Massachusetts Avenue, N.W.
Washington, DC 20036
(202) 263-2800   Toll Free: (800) 784-2577
Fax: (202) 775-0773   E-mail: scholarships@cbcfinc.org
Web: www.cbcfinc.org/scholarships.html

Summary To provide financial assistance to African American and other undergraduate and graduate students, especially those who reside or attend college in a Congressional district represented by a member of the Congressional Black Caucus (CBC).

Eligibility This program is open to 1) minority and other graduating high school seniors planning to attend an accredited institution of higher education; and 2) currently-enrolled full-time undergraduate, graduate, and doctoral students in good academic standing with a GPA of 2.5 or higher. Preference is given to African Americans who reside or attend school in a Congressional district represented by a member of the CBC. Along with their application, they must a personal statement of 500 to 1,000 words on 1) their future goals, major field of study, and how that field of study will help them to achieve their future career goals; 2) involvement in school activities, community and public service, hobbies, and sports; 3) how receiving this award will affect their current and future plans; and 4) other experiences, skills, or qualifications. They must also be able to demonstrate financial need, leadership ability, and participation in community service activities.

Financial data A stipend is awarded (amount not specified).

Duration 1 year.

Additional information The program began in 1988.

Number awarded Varies each year.

Deadline May of each year.

[160]
CONNECTICUT CHAPTER AABE SCHOLARSHIPS

American Association of Blacks in Energy-Connecticut
  Chapter
Attn: Scholarship Committee
P.O. Box 1898
Hartford, CT 06144
(203) 499-2418   E-mail: presctchapter@gmail.com
Web: www.aabe.org/index.php?component=pages&id=827

Summary To provide financial assistance to African Americans and members of other underrepresented minority groups who are high school seniors in Connecticut and western Massachusetts and planning to major in an energy-related field at a college in any state.

Eligibility This program is open to seniors graduating from high schools in Connecticut or western Massachusetts and planning to work on a bachelor's degree at a college or university in any state. Applicants must be African Americans, Hispanics, or Native Americans who have a GPA of 3.0 or higher and have taken the SAT and/or ACT test. Their intended major must be a field of business, engineering, mathematics, or science (e.g., chemistry, geology, meteorol-

ogy, physics) related to energy. Along with their application, they must submit a 350-word essay that includes 1) when they discovered their interest in the field of energy and what sparked their interest; and 2) either what excites them about the field of energy or how they expect their education to prepare them for the field of energy. Financial need is not considered in the selection process.

Financial data The stipend is $2,500. Funds are disbursed directly to the students.

Duration 1 year; nonrenewable.

Additional information Winners are eligible to compete for regional and national scholarships. This program began in 2003.

Number awarded 4 or 5 each year. Since this program began, it has awarded 45 scholarships with a total value of $109,000.

Deadline April of each year.

[161]
CONNECTICUT EDUCATION FOUNDATION SCHOLARSHIPS FOR MINORITY HIGH SCHOOL STUDENTS

Connecticut Education Association
Attn: Connecticut Education Foundation, Inc.
21 Oak Street, Suite 500
Hartford, CT 06106-8001
(860) 525-5641   Toll Free: (800) 842-4316
Fax: (860) 725-6323   E-mail: jeffl@cea.org
Web: www.cea.org/cef/ethnic-minority-scholarship-fund

Summary To provide financial assistance to African Americans and other minority high school seniors in Connecticut who are interested in attending college in the state to prepare for a teaching career.

Eligibility This program is open to minority seniors (Blacks, Native Americans or Alaskan Natives, Asian or Pacific Islanders, and Hispanics or Latinos) graduating from high schools in Connecticut. Applicants have been accepted at an accredited 2- or 4-year college or university in the state and be planning to enter the teaching profession. They must have a GPA of 2.75 or higher. Finalists may be interviewed. Financial need is considered in the selection process.

Financial data The stipend is $2,000 per year.

Duration 1 year; may be renewed.

Number awarded At least 1 each year.

Deadline April of each year.

[162]
CONNECTICUT MINORITY TEACHER INCENTIVE GRANTS

Connecticut Office of Higher Education
Attn: Minority Teacher Incentive Grant Program
450 Columbus Boulevard, Suite 510
Hartford, CT 06103-1841
(860) 947-1855   Toll Free: (800) 842-0229 (within CT)
Fax: (860) 947-1311   E-mail: mtip@ctohe.org
Web: www.ctohe.org/sfa/sfa.shtml

Summary To provide financial assistance and loan repayment to minority upper-division college students in Connecticut who are interested in teaching at public schools in the state.

Eligibility This program is open to juniors and seniors enrolled full time in Connecticut college and university teacher preparation programs. Applicants must be members of a minority group, defined as African American, Hispanic/ Latino, Asian American, or Native American. They must be nominated by the education dean at their institution.

Financial data The maximum stipend is $5,000 per year. In addition, if recipients complete a credential and begin teaching at a public school in Connecticut within 16 months of graduation, they may receive up to $2,500 per year, for up to 4 years, to help pay off college loans.

Duration Up to 2 years.

Number awarded Varies each year.

Deadline October of each year.

[163]
CORNELL UNIVERSITY SUMMER PROGRAM IN ASTRONOMY AND ASTROPHYSICS

Cornell University
Department of Astronomy
Attn: REU Astronomy Coordinator
510 Space Sciences Building
Ithaca, NY 14853-6801
(607) 255-0288   Fax: (607) 255-1767
E-mail: reu@astro.cornell.edu
Web: astro.cornell.edu/specialprograms/reu

Summary To provide an opportunity for undergraduate students, especially African Americans and other underrepresented minorities, to work as student assistants on astronomy research projects at Cornell University during the summer.

Eligibility This program is open to undergraduate students who have completed 1 to 3 years of academic training. Applicants must be interested in working with Cornell University faculty and research staff on projects covering a wide range of disciplines in planetary science, astronomical instrumentation, astrophysics, general relativity, and cosmology. They must be U.S. citizens or permanent residents. Applications are especially encouraged from underrepresented minorities, persons with disabilities, and women.

Financial data The stipend is $6,800. Other support includes $1,000 for relocation and housing and up to $1,000 for travel to a scientific meeting to present the results of the research.

Duration 10 weeks during the summer.

Additional information This program is funded by the National Science Foundation as part of its Research Experiences for Undergraduates (REU) Program.

Number awarded 8 each year.

Deadline February of each year.

[164]
CORPORATE PARTNER SCHOLARSHIPS OF THE NATIONAL ASSOCIATION OF BLACK ACCOUNTANTS

National Association of Black Accountants
Attn: National Scholarship Program
7474 Greenway Center Drive, Suite 1120
Greenbelt, MD 20770
(301) 474-NABA   Fax: (301) 474-3114
E-mail: scholarships@nabainc.org
Web: www.nabainc.org/scholarship

Summary To provide financial assistance to student members of the National Association of Black Accountants (NABA) who are working on an undergraduate or graduate degree in a field related to accounting.

Eligibility This program is open to minorities who are NABA members and enrolled full time as 1) an undergraduate freshman, sophomore, junior, or first-semester senior majoring in accounting, business, or finance at a 4-year college or university; or 2) a graduate student working on a master's degree in accounting. High school seniors are not eligible. Applicants must have a GPA of 3.5 or higher in their major and 3.3 or higher overall. Along with their application, they must submit a 500-word personal statement on their involvement in NABA, career objectives, leadership abilities, and community activities. Financial need is not considered in the selection process.

Financial data Stipends range from $1,000 to $10,000.

Duration 1 year.

Number awarded Varies each year.

Deadline January of each year.

[165]
COSTCO SCHOLARSHIP PROGRAM OF THE THURGOOD MARSHALL COLLEGE FUND

Thurgood Marshall College Fund
Attn: Senior Manager of Scholarship Programs
901 F Street, N.W., Suite 300
Washington, DC 20004
(202) 507-4851   Fax: (202) 652-2934
E-mail: deshuandra.walker@tmcfund.org
Web: www.tmcf.org

Summary To provide financial assistance to African American students at public Historically Black Colleges and Universities (HBCUs) that are members of the Thurgood Marshall College Fund (TMCF).

Eligibility This program is open to full-time students at any of the 47 TMCF member institutions. Applicants may be majoring in any field. They must have a GPA of 3.0 or higher. Selection is based on merit, but students must submit their Student Aid Report from their FAFSA. Along with their application, they must submit a 500-word essay on their most meaningful achievements and how those relate to their field of study and their future goals. U.S. citizenship or permanent resident status is required.

Financial data The stipend is $6,200.

Duration 1 year.

Additional information This program is sponsored by Costco Wholesale.

Number awarded 1 or more each year.

Deadline April of each year.

[166]
COY AND MAE DELL YOUNG SCHOLARSHIP

National Naval Officers Association-Washington, D.C.
   Chapter
c/o LCDR Stephen Williams
P.O. Box 30784
Alexandria, VA 22310
(703) 644-2605   Fax: (703) 644-8503
E-mail: Stephen.Williams@navy.mil
Web: www.dcnnoa.org/dcnnoa-scholarship

Summary   To provide financial assistance to African American and other minority high school seniors from the Washington, D.C. area who are interested in attending college in any state.

Eligibility   This program is open to minority seniors graduating from high schools in the Washington, D.C. metropolitan area who plan to enroll full time at an accredited 2- or 4-year college or university in any state. Applicants must have a GPA of 2.7 or higher and be U.S. citizens or permanent residents. Selection is based on academic achievement, community involvement, and financial need.

Financial data   The stipend is $1,000.

Duration   1 year; nonrenewable.

Additional information   This program is sponsored by the Washington D.C. Chapter of the National Naval Officers Association (DCNNOA), an organization of African American naval officers, but all minorities are eligible and recipients are not required to join or affiliate with the military in any way.

Number awarded   1 each year.

Deadline   February of each year.

[167]
CPS-HR/WALTER VAUGHN EXCELLENCE IN HUMAN RESOURCES SCHOLARSHIP

National Forum for Black Public Administrators
Attn: Scholarship Program
777 North Capitol Street, N.E., Suite 807
Washington, DC 20002
(202) 408-9300   Fax: (202) 408-8558
E-mail: vharris@nfbpa.org
Web: www.nfbpa.org/i4a/pages/index.cfm?pageid=4047

Summary   To provide financial assistance to African Americans working on an undergraduate or graduate degree in public administration with an emphasis on human resource management.

Eligibility   This program is open to African American undergraduate and graduate students preparing for a career in public service. Applicants must be working full time on a degree in public administration, human resource management, or a related field. They must have a GPA of 3.0 or higher, a record of involvement in extracurricular activities (excluding athletics), excellent interpersonal and leadership abilities, and strong oral and written communication skills. Along with their application, they must submit a 3-page autobiographical essay that includes their academic and career goals and objectives. Selection is based on academic record, leadership ability, participation in school activities, community service, and financial need.

Financial data   The stipend is $2,500.

Duration   1 year.

Additional information   This program is sponsored by CPS Human Resource Services. Recipients are required to attend the sponsor's annual conference to receive their scholarship; limited hotel and air accommodations are arranged and provided.

Number awarded   1 each year.

Deadline   March of each year.

[168]
CUBA WADLINGTON, JR. AND MICHAEL P. JOHNSON SCHOLARSHIP

Tulsa Community Foundation
Attn: Scholarships
7030 South Yale Avenue, Suite 600
Tulsa, OK 74136
(918) 494-8823   Fax: (918) 494-9826
E-mail: scholarships@tulsacf.org
Web: www.tulsacf.org/whatwedo/education/scholarships

Summary   To provide financial assistance to upper-division students at colleges in any state who are African Americans and members of other underrepresented groups in the energy industry.

Eligibility   This program is open to students entering their junior or senior year at a college or university in any state and preparing for a career in the energy industry with a major in accounting, engineering, finance, or technology. Applicants must be members of a group underrepresented in the energy industry (women and ethnic minorities). They must have a GPA of 3.0 or higher. Along with their application, they must submit a 2-page personal essay that includes their future or academic career goals, any adversity or challenge they have overcome or anticipate in pursuit of their educational goals, and the importance of diversity in the workplace and how dealing with diversity in their own life has shaped them. Financial need is not considered in the selection process.

Financial data   The stipend is $2,000. Funds are paid directly to the university.

Duration   1 year; nonrenewable.

Additional information   This program is supported by the Williams Companies of Tulsa, Oklahoma.

Number awarded   Varies each year.

Deadline   June of each year.

[169]
CUMMINS SCHOLARSHIPS

Society of Women Engineers
Attn: Scholarship Selection Committee
203 North LaSalle Street, Suite 1675
Chicago, IL 60601-1269
(312) 596-5223   Toll Free: (877) SWE-INFO
Fax: (312) 644-8557   E-mail: scholarships@swe.org
Web: societyofwomenengineers.swe.org

Summary   To provide financial assistance to women, especially African Americans and others of other underrepresented groups, who are working on an undergraduate degree in computer science or designated engineering specialties.

Eligibility   This program is open to women who are sophomores, re-entry, or nontraditional students at 4-year ABET-accredited colleges and universities. Applicants must be working full time on a degree in computer science, industrial systems, metrology, metallurgy, or automotive, chemical, computer, electrical, industrial, manufacturing, materials, or mechanical engineering and have a GPA of 3.0 or higher. Preference is given to members of groups underrepresented in engineering or computer science and to students interested in an internship with the sponsor. Selection is based on merit.

Financial data The stipend is $2,500.

Duration 1 year.

Additional information This program is sponsored by Cummins, Inc.

Number awarded 2 each year.

Deadline February of each year.

[170]
DAMON P. MOORE SCHOLARSHIP

Indiana State Teachers Association
Attn: ISTA Foundation for the Improvement of Education
150 West Market Street, Suite 900
Indianapolis, IN 46204-2814
(317) 263-3306   Toll Free: (800) 382-4037, ext. 3306
Fax: (800) 777-6128   E-mail: ccherry@ista-in.org
Web: www.ista-in.org/our-profession/scholarships-awards

Summary To provide financial assistance to African American and other ethnic minority high school seniors in Indiana who are interested in studying education at a college in any state.

Eligibility This program is open to ethnic minority public high school seniors in Indiana who are interested in studying education in college. Selection is based on academic achievement, leadership ability as expressed through co-curricular activities and community involvement, recommendations, and a 300-word essay on their educational goals and how they plan to use this scholarship.

Financial data The stipend is $1,000.

Duration 1 year; may be renewed for 3 additional years if the recipient maintains at least a "C+" average and continues to pursue a teaching credential.

Additional information This program began in 1987.

Number awarded 1 each year.

Deadline February of each year.

[171]
DAVID J. STERN SPORTS SCHOLARSHIP PROGRAM

Thurgood Marshall College Fund
Attn: Senior Manager of Scholarship Programs
901 F Street, N.W., Suite 300
Washington, DC 20004
(202) 507-4851   Fax: (202) 652-2934
E-mail: deshuandra.walker@tmcfund.org
Web: www.tmcf.org

Summary To provide financial assistance to students currently enrolled at a Historically Black College or University (HBCU) and interested in preparing for a career in sports.

Eligibility This program is open to students who are currently enrolled full time as sophomores at a 4-year HBCU. Applicants may be majoring in any field but they must have an interest in sports. They must have a current GPA of 3.0 or higher and be able to demonstrate financial need. Along with their application, they must submit 1) a resume that includes community service, leadership activities, and employment/

internship experience; 2) their Student Aid report from their FAFSA; 3) their most recent transcript; 4) a recommendation from a current school faculty member; and 5) a 500-word essay on how they have embodied the lessons taught by sports (such as teamwork, leadership, and discipline) in their academic work, their team, and their community, and the impact this scholarship will have on their education.

Financial data The stipend is $10,000 per year.

Duration 1 year; may be renewed up to 2 additional years.

Additional information This program was established in 2015 by the National Basketball Association.

Number awarded 1 each year.

Deadline April of each year.

[172]
DAVID SANKEY MINORITY SCHOLARSHIP IN METEOROLOGY

National Weather Association
Attn: Executive Director
3100 Monitor Avenue, Suite 123
Norman, OK 73072
(405) 701-5167   Fax: (405) 701-5227
E-mail: exdir@nwas.org
Web: www.nwas.org

Summary To provide financial assistance to African Americans and members of other underrepresented groups working on an undergraduate or graduate degree in meteorology.

Eligibility This program is open to members of underrepresented ethnic groups who are either entering their sophomore or higher year of undergraduate study or enrolled as graduate students. Applicants must be working on a degree in meteorology. Along with their application, they must submit a 1-page statement explaining why they are applying for this scholarship. Selection is based on that statement, academic achievement, and 2 letters of recommendation.

Financial data The stipend is $1,000.

Duration 1 year.

Additional information This program began in 2002.

Number awarded 1 each year.

Deadline April of each year.

[173]
DAVIS & DAVIS SCHOLARSHIP

National Naval Officers Association-Washington, D.C.
  Chapter
c/o LCDR Stephen Williams
P.O. Box 30784
Alexandria, VA 22310
(703) 644-2605   Fax: (703) 644-8503
E-mail: Stephen.Williams@navy.mil
Web: www.dcnnoa.org/dcnnoa-scholarship

Summary To provide financial assistance to female African American high school seniors from the Washington, D.C. area who are interested in attending college in any state.

Eligibility This program is open to female African American seniors graduating from high schools in the Washington, D.C. metropolitan area who plan to enroll full time at an accredited 2- or 4-year college or university in any state. Applicants must have a GPA of 2.5 or higher and be U.S. citizens or permanent residents. Selection is based on academic achievement, community involvement, and financial need.

Financial data   The stipend is $1,000.

Duration   1 year; nonrenewable.

Additional information   Recipients are not required to join or affiliate with the military in any way.

Number awarded   Varies each year; recently, 2 were awarded.

Deadline   February of each year.

[174]
DCBMBAA CHAPTER UNDERGRADUATE SCHOLARSHIP PROGRAM

National Black MBA Association-Washington, DC Chapter
Attn: Scholarship Program
455 Massachusetts Avenue, N.W., Suite 150-331
Washington, DC 20001
(202) 628-0138   E-mail: outreach@dcbmbaa.org
Web: www.dcbmbaa.org/scholarships

Summary   To provide financial assistance to African American and other minority students from Washington, D.C., Maryland, or Virginia who are working on an undergraduate degree in business or management at a school in any state.

Eligibility   This program is open to minority residents of Washington, D.C., Maryland, or Virginia who are graduating high school seniors or current full-time undergraduates at a college or university in any state. Applicants must be working on or planning to work on a bachelor's degree in business or management. Along with their application, they must submit an essay (from 500 to 600 words) on a topic that changes annually but focuses on minorities in business. Selection is based the essay, GPA, extracurricular activity, and community involvement.

Financial data   The stipend is $1,500 or $1,000.

Duration   1 year.

Additional information   This program began in 2000.

Number awarded   2 each year: 1 at $1,500 and 1 at $1,000.

Deadline   June of each year.

[175]
DELAWARE ATHLETIC TRAINERS' ASSOCIATION ETHNIC DIVERSITY ADVISORY COMMITTEE SCHOLARSHIP

Delaware Athletic Trainers' Association
c/o Education Committee Chair
University of Delaware
159 Fred Rust Ice Arena
Newark, DE 19716
(302) 831-6402   E-mail: kaminski@udel.edu
Web: www.delata.org/scholarship-applications.html

Summary   To provide financial assistance to American American and other ethnic minority members of the National Athletic Trainers' Association (NATA) from Delaware who are working on an undergraduate or graduate degree in the field.

Eligibility   This program is open to NATA members who are members of ethnic diversity groups and residents of Delaware or attending college in that state. Applicants must be enrolled full time in an undergraduate athletic training education program or a graduate athletic training program and have a GPA of 2.5 or higher. They must intend to prepare for the profession of athletic training. Along with their application, they must submit an 800-word statement on their athletic training background, experience, philosophy, and goals. Selection is based equally on academic performance and athletic training clinical achievement.

Financial data   A stipend is awarded (amount not specified).

Duration   1 year.

Number awarded   1 or more each year.

Deadline   February of each year.

[176]
DELLA H. RANEY NURSING SCHOLARSHIP

Tuskegee Army Nurses
P.O. Box 99
Tuskegee Institute, AL 36087-0099
Toll Free: (855) TAFS-ANC
E-mail: TuskegeeArmyNurses@gmail.com
Web: www.tuskegeearmynurses.info

Summary   To provide financial assistance to African American and other nursing students who apply through the Tuskegee Airmen.

Eligibility   This program is open to students enrolled in at least the sophomore year of an accredited B.S.N. degree program. They must submit their application to a local chapter of the Tuskegee Airmen, a group of African Americans who served as pilots in World War II. Along with their application, they must submit a 2-page essay 1) describing their extracurricular activities and community involvement (including local chapter activities, community-based projects, school level projects, organizational efforts, state-level student nurse activities, and other activities impacting on the health and social condition of African Americans and other culturally diverse groups); 2) presenting their ideas of what they can do as an individual nurse to improve the health status and/or social condition of African Americans; and 3) stating their future goals in nursing.

Financial data   The stipend ranges from $500 to $2,000 per year.

Duration   1 year; may be renewed.

Additional information   This program began in 2012 as a joint activity of the National Black Nurses Association (NBNA) and the Tuskegee Airmen Scholarship Foundation.

Number awarded   1 each year.

Deadline   April of each year.

[177]
DELTA SIGMA THETA SORORITY GENERAL SCHOLARSHIPS

Delta Sigma Theta Sorority, Inc.
Attn: Scholarship and Standards Committee Chair
1707 New Hampshire Avenue, N.W.
Washington, DC 20009
(202) 986-2400   Fax: (202) 986-2513
E-mail: dstemail@deltasigmatheta.org
Web: www.deltasigmatheta.org

Summary   To provide financial assistance to members of Delta Sigma Theta who are working on an undergraduate or graduate degree in any field.

Eligibility This program is open to active, dues-paying members of Delta Sigma Theta who are currently enrolled in college or graduate school. Applicants must submit an essay on their major goals and educational objectives, including realistic steps they foresee as necessary for the fulfillment of their plans. Financial need is considered in the selection process.

Financial data The stipends range from $1,000 to $2,000. The funds may be used to cover tuition, fees, and living expenses.

Duration 1 year; may be renewed for 1 additional year.

Additional information This sponsor is a traditionally-African American social sorority. The application fee is $20.

Number awarded Varies each year.

Deadline March of each year.

[178]
DEPARTMENT OF DEFENSE (DOD) SCHOLARSHIPS OF THE THURGOOD MARSHALL COLLEGE FUND

Thurgood Marshall College Fund
Attn: Senior Manager of Scholarship Programs
901 F Street, N.W., Suite 300
Washington, DC 20004
(202) 507-4851   Fax: (202) 652-2934
E-mail: deshuandra.walker@tmcfund.org
Web: www.tmcf.org

Summary To provide financial assistance to African American high school seniors interested in working on a degree in designated fields of science, technology, engineering, or mathematics (STEM) at Historically Black Colleges and Universities (HBCUs).

Eligibility This program is open to high school seniors planning to enroll full time at an HBCU, especially public institutions. Applicants must major in a field of STEM, especially biosciences, chemical engineering, chemistry, civil engineering, computer engineering, computer science or technology, environmental science, geosciences, mathematics, mechanical engineering, nuclear engineering, or physics. They must have a GPA of 3.25 or higher (including a grade of "B" or better in pre-calculus or higher mathematics) and be able to demonstrate financial need. Along with their application, they must submit a 750-word essay on their interest in STEM studies, their commitment to achieving a degree in that area, and their long-term professional goals. U.S. citizenship or permanent resident status is required.

Financial data The stipend is $15,000 per year.

Duration 1 year; may be renewed up to 3 additional years, provided the recipient meets certain GPA, conduct, and STEM persistence goals each year.

Additional information This program is sponsored by the U.S. Department of Defense.

Number awarded 25 each year.

Deadline April of each year.

[179]
DETROIT CHAPTER NBMBAA HIGH SCHOOL SCHOLARSHIP

National Black MBA Association-Detroit Chapter
Attn: Scholarship Awards
P.O. Box 32960
Detroit, MI 48232-0960
(313) 237-0089   Fax: (313) 237-0093
E-mail: scholarships@detroitblackmba.org
Web: www.detroitblackmba.org

Summary To provide financial assistance to African American and other minority high school seniors in Michigan and Toledo, Ohio who are planning to attend a college or university in any state and major in business administration.

Eligibility This program is open to minority seniors graduating from high schools in Michigan or Toledo, Ohio who are planning to enroll at a college or university in any state and major in business administration. Applicants must have a GPA of 3.0 or higher. Along with their application, they must submit a 500-word essay on a topic that changes annually; recently, students were asked to describe what they want to accomplish with their life within the next 10 years and why. Selection is based on that essay, transcripts, and a biography.

Financial data The stipend is $1,000.

Duration 1 year.

Number awarded 1 or more each year.

Deadline February of each year.

[180]
DETROIT CHAPTER NBMBAA UNDERGRADUATE SCHOLARSHIP

National Black MBA Association-Detroit Chapter
Attn: Scholarship Awards
P.O. Box 32960
Detroit, MI 48232-0960
(313) 237-0089   Fax: (313) 237-0093
E-mail: scholarships@detroitblackmba.org
Web: www.detroitblackmba.org

Summary To provide financial assistance to residents of Michigan and Toledo, Ohio who are members of the Detroit Chapter of the National Black MBA Association (NBMBAA) and working on a bachelor's degree in business at a university in any state.

Eligibility This program is open to members of the NBMBAA Detroit Chapter who live in Michigan or Toledo, Ohio and are enrolled as juniors or seniors at a college or university in any state. Applicants must be working on a bachelor's degree in business or management. They must have a GPA of 3.0 or higher. Along with their application, they must submit a 500-word essay on a topic that changes annually but relates to African Americans and business. Selection is based on that essay, transcripts, and a biography.

Financial data The stipend is $1,500.

Duration 1 year.

Number awarded 1 or more each year.

Deadline February of each year.

[181]
DEVELOPMENT FUND FOR BLACK STUDENTS IN SCIENCE AND TECHNOLOGY SCHOLARSHIPS

Development Fund for Black Students in Science and
Technology
2705 Bladensburg Road, N.E.
Washington, DC 20018
(202) 635-3604   E-mail: DLHinson@earthlink.net
Web: www.dfbsstscholarship.org/dfb_sch.html

Summary   To provide scholarships to African American students who enroll in scientific or technical fields of study at designated Historically Black Colleges and Universities (HBCUs).

Eligibility   Deans and faculty members of engineering and science departments at selected HBCUs are invited to identify students to be considered for these scholarships. Nominees must be enrolled or planning to enroll at a predominantly Black college or university or already be enrolled at the school and planning to major in a technical field (e.g., engineering, mathematics, science). U.S. citizenship or permanent resident status is required. Selection is based on academic achievement (grades and SAT scores, especially in science and mathematics), a personal essay describing career goals and relevant extracurricular activities, recommendations, and financial need.

Financial data   Stipends range up to $2,000 per year.

Duration   1 year; may be renewed for up to 4 years, as long as the recipient remains in good academic standing and enrolled full time in a science or engineering curriculum.

Additional information   Prior to 1995, these scholarships were awarded solely or primarily through the National Merit Scholarship Corporation's National Achievement Scholarship Program. Scholarship applications are available only through the financial aid offices of prequalified schools. Currently, those are: Bennett College, Clark Atlanta University, Elizabeth City State University, Fisk University, Florida A&M University, Fort Valley State College, Hampton University, Howard University, Langston University, Lincoln University of Pennsylvania, Morehouse University, Morgan State University, North Carolina A&T State University, Prairie View A&M University, Southern University and A&M College, Spelman College, Tennessee State University, Tuskegee University, Wilberforce University, and Xavier University of Louisiana.

Number awarded   Several each year.

Deadline   June of each year.

[182]
DEVERNE CALLOWAY UNDERGRADUATE SCHOLARSHIP

Missouri Legislative Black Caucus Foundation
c/o Representative Gail McCann Beatty
4609 Paseo Boulevard, Suite 102
Kansas City, MO 64110
(573) 761-4166   Toll Free: (877) 63-MLBCF
Fax: (816) 861-2845   E-mail: mail@mlbcf.org
Web: www.mlbcf.org/scholarships/undergraduate

Summary   To provide financial assistance to African American residents of Missouri who are historically underrepresented in higher education and are interested in working on an undergraduate degree in any field at a school in any state.

Eligibility   This program is open to African American residents of Missouri who are enrolled full time in an under graduate program at a college or university in any state. Applicants must have a GPA of 2.5 or higher. Along with their application, they must submit a 200-word personal statement on how their education will assist them in achieving their goals. Selection is based on academic performance, community service, leadership skills, and financial need.

Financial data   A stipend is awarded (amount not specified).

Duration   1 year; recipients may reapply for up to 3 additional years of support.

Number awarded   1 or more each year.

Deadline   May of each year.

[183]
DEWAYNE WICKHAM FOUNDER'S HIGH SCHOOL SCHOLARSHIP

National Association of Black Journalists
Attn: Program Manager
University of Maryland
1100 Knight Hall, Suite 3100
College Park, MD 20742
(301) 405-7520   Fax: (301) 314-1714
E-mail: Sberry@nabj.org
Web: www.nabj.org/?page=ScholarshipsWickham

Summary   To provide financial assistance to African American high school seniors who are planning to major in journalism in college.

Eligibility   This program is open to African American high school seniors who are planning to attend an accredited 4-year college or university and major in journalism or other communications-related discipline. Applicants must have a GPA of 2.5 to 3.0 and be able to demonstrate financial need and community involvement. Along with their application, they must submit 3 samples of their work, an official college transcript, 3 letters of recommendation, a resume, and an essay of 800 to 1,000 words describing their biggest challenge to their career goal of being a journalist.

Financial data   The stipend is $2,500.

Duration   1 year.

Number awarded   1 each year.

Deadline   February of each year.

[184]
DIETETIC TECHNICIAN PROGRAM SCHOLARSHIPS

Academy of Nutrition and Dietetics
Attn: Foundation
120 South Riverside Plaza, Suite 2000
Chicago, IL 60606-6995
(312) 899-4821   Toll Free: (800) 877-1600, ext. 4821
Fax: (312) 899-4796   E-mail: scholarship@eatright.org
Web: www.eatrightacend.org

Summary   To provide financial assistance to student members of the Academy of Nutrition and Dietetics, especially African Americans and members of other underrepresented groups, who are in the second year of a dietetic technician program.

Eligibility   This program is open to ADA student members entering the second year of study in an accredited dietetic technician program. Applicants must be U.S. citizens or permanent residents and show evidence of leadership and academic ability. Some scholarships require membership in a specific dietetic practice group, residency in a specific state, or underrepresented minority group status. The same application form can be used for all categories.

Financial data Stipends range from $500 to $10,000 but most are for $1,000.

Duration 1 year.

Additional information The Academy of Nutrition and Dietetics was formerly the American Dietetic Association.

Number awarded Varies each year.

Deadline February of each year.

[185]
DIGITASLBI MULTICULTURAL SCHOLARSHIP

American Association of Advertising Agencies
Attn: AAAA Foundation
1065 Avenue of the Americas, 16th Floor
New York, NY 10018
(212) 262-2500   E-mail: ameadows@aaaa.org
Web: www.aaaa.org

Summary To provide financial assistance to African American and other multicultural students who are working on an undergraduate degree in advertising.

Eligibility This program is open to undergraduate students of proven multicultural heritage. Applicants must be participating in the Multicultural Advertising Intern Program (MAIP). They must be enrolled at an accredited college or university in the United States and be able to demonstrate financial need.

Financial data The stipend is $5,000.

Duration 1 year.

Additional information This program is funded by DigitasLBi.

Number awarded 1 each year.

Deadline July of each year.

[186]
DISTRIBUTED RESEARCH EXPERIENCES FOR UNDERGRADUATES

Computing Research Association
1828 L Street, N.W., Suite 800
Washington, DC 20036-4632
(202) 234-2111   Fax: (202) 667-1066
E-mail: dreu@cra.org
Web: www.cra.org/cra-w/dreu

Summary To provide an opportunity for African American and other underrepresented undergraduate students to work on a summer research project in computer science or engineering.

Eligibility This program is open to members of underrepresented groups (African Americans, Hispanics, American Indians, women, students with disabilities) who are entering their junior or senior year of college. Applicants must be interested in conducting a summer research project directly related to computer science or computer engineering under the mentorship of a faculty member at the mentor's home university. They must be U.S. citizens or permanent residents. Selection is based on the student's potential for success in graduate school, the extent of the student's experience and skills, the student's potential gain from the experience, and the potential that the student's participation will advance the goals of the program.

Financial data Students receive a stipend of $7,000 plus relocation travel assistance up to $500 if appropriate.

Duration 10 weeks during the summer.

Additional information This program began in 1994 as the Distributed Mentor Project (DMP) by the Computing Research Association's Committee on the Status of Women in Computing Research (CRA-W). In 2007, the Coalition to Diversify Computing (CDC) became a cosponsor of the program and in 2009 it was given its current name. From the beginning, funding has been provided by the National Science Foundation.

Number awarded Varies each year; recently, 46 students were selected to participate in this program.

Deadline February of each year.

[187]
DIVERSITY SCHOLARSHIP FOR ENTRY-LEVEL ATHLETIC TRAINING STUDENTS

Indiana Athletic Trainers' Association
Attn: Scholarship Committee
125 West Market Street, Suite 300
Indianapolis, IN 46204
(317) 396-0002, ext. 2   Fax: (317) 634-5964
E-mail: jillewing@thecorydongroup.com
Web: www.iata-usa.org/page-1462928

Summary To provide financial assistance to undergraduate and graduate student members of the Indiana Athletic Trainers' Association (IATA) who are African Americans or from another ethnic or social diverse background.

Eligibility This program is open to members of IATA who are from an ethnic or social diverse background and enrolled as full-time juniors, seniors, or graduate students at a college or university in Indiana. Undergraduates must have been an athletic training student for at least 1 year in a CAATE-accredited program; graduate students must be in the second semester of such a program. All applicants must have a GPA of 3.0 or higher and a sponsor who is a full-time member of the athletic training education program faculty or a full-time member of the athletic training staff. Along with their application, they must submit a brief personal statement on why they chose athletic training as a career and their future plans in the field. Financial need is not considered in the selection process.

Financial data The stipend is $1,000.

Duration 1 year.

Number awarded 1 each year.

Deadline September of each year.

[188]
DIVERSITY SUMMER HEALTH-RELATED RESEARCH EDUCATION PROGRAM

Medical College of Wisconsin
Attn: Office of Student Diversity Affairs
8701 Watertown Plank Road
Milwaukee, WI 53226
(414) 955-8735   Fax: (414) 955-0129
E-mail: studentdiversity@mcw.edu
Web: www.mcw.edu/Diversity-Programs.htm

Summary To provide an opportunity for African American and other undergraduate residents of any state who come from diverse backgrounds to participate in a summer research training experience at the Medical College of Wisconsin.

Eligibility This program is open to U.S. citizens and permanent residents who come from an ethnically, economically, and/or educationally disadvantaged backgrounds. The program targets African Americans, Mexican-Americans, Native Americans (American Indians, Alaska Natives, and Native Hawaiians), Pacific Islanders, Hmong, mainland Puerto Ricans, and individuals with disabilities. Applicants must be interested in participating in a summer research training program at the Medical College of Wisconsin. They must have completed at least 1 year of undergraduate study at an accredited college or university (or be a community college student enrolled in at least 3 courses per academic term) and have a GPA of 3.4 or higher.

Financial data The stipend is $10 per hour for a 40-hour week. Housing is provided for students who live outside Milwaukee County and travel expenses are paid for those who live outside Wisconsin.

Duration 10 weeks during the summer.

Additional information Students are "matched" with a full-time faculty investigator to participate in a research project addressing the causes, prevention, and treatment of cardiovascular, pulmonary, or hematological diseases. This program is funded by the National Heart, Lung, and Blood Institute (NHLBI) of the National Institutes of Health (NIH). Participants are required to prepare an abstract of their research and make a brief oral presentation of their project at the conclusion of the summer.

Number awarded Approximately 12 each year.

Deadline January of each year.

[189]
DIVISION OF PHYSICAL SCIENCES RESEARCH EXPERIENCE FOR UNDERGRADUATES

American Museum of Natural History
Attn: Division of Physical Sciences
Central Park West at 79th Street
New York, NY 10024-5192
(212) 769-5055   E-mail: Fellowships-rggs@amnh.org
Web: www.amnh.org

Summary To provide an opportunity for undergraduate students, especially those who attend a minority-serving institution, to gain research experience in designated physical sciences during the summer at the American Museum of Natural History in New York City.

Eligibility This program is open to U.S. citizens and permanent residents who are currently working on a bachelor's degree. Applicants must be interested in participating in a research project at the American Museum of Natural History in the fields of earth and planetary sciences or astrophysics. Applications are especially encouraged from students who attend minority-serving institutions.

Financial data Participants receive a stipend of approximately $5,100, dormitory housing on a nearby university campus or an equivalent housing stipend, a subsistence allowance, and (depending on need) reimbursement of travel costs to and from New York.

Duration Approximately 10 weeks during the summer.

Additional information This program is sponsored by the National Science Foundation as part of its Research Experiences for Undergraduates (REU) program.

Number awarded Approximately 8 each year.

Deadline January of each year.

[190]
DOMINION DIVERSITY SCHOLARSHIP PROGRAM

Dominion Resources Inc.
Attn: Diversity Team
701 East Cary Street, 13th Floor
Richmond, VA 23219
(804) 819-2000   E-mail: diversity@dom.com
Web: www.dom.com

Summary To provide financial assistance and work experience to high school seniors and college students who are African Americans or will contribute to the diversity of the sponsor in other ways.

Eligibility This program is open to high school seniors and current college students who will not graduate for at least 2 years. Community college students must be enrolled in a program that will prepare them to transfer to a 4-year institution. Applicants must commit to a paid intern work session during the summer following their first year of scholarship support. Along with their application, they must submit an essay of 1,000 to 1,250 words that 1) describes the experiences or ideas they would bring to the diversity of the sponsor; 2) includes the new perspectives or new talents they will contribute to the sponsor; and 3) describes how this diversity scholarship program will help them achieve their career goals. The sponsor defines diversity to include minorities, women, protected veterans, and individuals with disabilities.

Financial data The scholarship stipend is $5,000. A competitive salary is paid for the internship.

Duration 1 year for the scholarship; 10 to 12 weeks during the summer for the internship.

Additional information The sponsor operates electric distribution and transmission companies in North Carolina and Virginia and natural gas distribution companies in Ohio and West Virginia.

Number awarded 30 each year.

Deadline May of each year.

[191]
DON SAHLI–KATHY WOODALL MINORITY STUDENT SCHOLARSHIP

Tennessee Education Association
Attn: Sahli-Woodall Scholarship Fund
801 Second Avenue North
Nashville, TN 37201-1099
(615) 242-8392   Toll Free: (800) 342-8367
Fax: (615) 259-4581   E-mail: jdemain@tea.nea.org
Web: www.teateachers.org

Summary To provide financial assistance to African American and other minority high school seniors in Tennessee who are interested in majoring in education at a college or university in the state.

Eligibility This program is open to minority high school seniors in Tennessee who are planning to attend a college or university in the state and major in education. Application must be made either by a Future Teachers of America chapter affiliated with the Tennessee Education Association (TEA) or by the student with the recommendation of an active TEA member. Selection is based on academic record, leadership ability, financial need, and demonstrated interest in becoming a teacher.

Financial data The stipend is $1,000.

Duration 1 year.

Number awarded 1 each year.

Deadline February of each year.

[192]
DONALD AND ITASKER THORNTON MEMORIAL SCHOLARSHIP

Thornton Sisters Foundation
P.O. Box 21
Atlantic Highlands, NJ 07716-0021
(732) 872-1353   E-mail: tsfoundation2001@yahoo.com
Web: www.thornton-sisters.com/ttsf.htm

Summary To provide financial assistance for college to African American and other women of color in New Jersey.

Eligibility This program is open to women of color (defined as African Americans, Latino Americans, Caribbean Americans, and Native Americans) who are graduating from high schools in New Jersey. Applicants must have a grade average of "C+" or higher and be able to document financial need. They must be planning to attend an accredited 4-year college or university. Along with their application, they must submit a 500-word essay describing their family background, personal and financial hardships, honors or academic distinctions, and community involvement and activities.

Financial data A stipend is awarded (amount not specified). Funds are to be used for tuition and/or books.

Duration 1 year; nonrenewable.

Number awarded 1 or more each year.

Deadline May of each year.

[193]
DR. ALICE MCNEELY SWAIN ENDOWED SCHOLARSHIP

Sigma Gamma Rho Sorority, Inc.
Attn: National Education Fund
1000 Southhill Drive, Suite 200
Cary, NC 27513
(919) 678-9720   Toll Free: (888) SGR-1922
Fax: (919) 678-9721
E-mail: customerservice@sgrho1922.org
Web: www.sgrho1922.org/nef

Summary To provide financial assistance to undergraduate students, especially African Americans, working on a degree in English or journalism.

Eligibility This program is open to undergraduates working on a degree in English or print journalism. The sponsor is a traditionally African American sorority, but support is available to males and females of all races. Applicants must have a GPA of "C" or higher and be able to demonstrate financial need.

Financial data A stipend is awarded (amount not specified).

Duration 1 year.

Additional information A processing fee of $20 is required.

Number awarded 1 each year.

Deadline April of each year.

[194]
DR. ARNITA YOUNG BOSWELL SCHOLARSHIP

National Hook-Up of Black Women, Inc.
Attn: Scholarship Committee
1809 East 71st Street, Suite 205
Chicago, IL 60649-2000
(773) 667-7061   Fax: (773) 667-7064
E-mail: info@nhbwinc.com
Web: www.nhbwinc.com/scholarship.html

Summary To provide financial assistance to African American high school and college students who are interested in earning an undergraduate degree.

Eligibility This program is open to African American high school seniors or currently-enrolled college students. They must be attending or preparing to attend an accredited school and have a GPA of 2.75 or higher. They must demonstrate written communication skills by preparing an essay of 300 to 500 words on a topic that changes annually but relates to current events of national interest. Selection is based on academic record, financial need, community service, concern for the African American family, and a desire to complete a college degree.

Financial data The stipend is $1,000. Funds are paid directly to the college or university of the recipient's choice.

Duration 1 year.

Number awarded Varies each year; recently, 3 were awarded.

Deadline February of each year.

[195]
DR. BLANCA MOORE-VELEZ WOMAN OF SUBSTANCE SCHOLARSHIP

National Association of Negro Business and Professional
  Women's Clubs
Attn: Scholarship Committee
1806 New Hampshire Avenue, N.W.
Washington, DC 20009-3206
(202) 483-4206   Fax: (202) 462-7253
E-mail: arlucas48@gmail.com
Web: www.nanbpwc.org/index-11.html

Summary To provide financial assistance to mature African American women who are interested in working on an undergraduate degree at a college in any state.

Eligibility This program is open to African American women over 35 years of age who are working on an undergraduate degree at an accredited college or university in any state. They must have a GPA of 3.0 or higher. Along with their application, they must submit a 500-word essay on "Challenges to the Mature Student and How I Overcame Them." Financial need is not considered in the selection process. U.S. citizenship is required.

Financial data A stipend is awarded (amount not specified).

Duration 1 year.

Number awarded 1 each year.

Deadline February of each year.

[196]
DR. JESSE BEMLEY SCHOLARSHIP

Black Data Processing Associates
Attn: BDPA Education Technology Foundation
4423 Lehigh Road, Number 277
College Park, MD 20740
(513) 284-4968   Fax: (202) 318-2194
E-mail: scholarships@betf.org
Web: www.betf.org/scholarships/jesse-bemley.shtml

Summary   To recognize and reward, with college scholarships, high school students who participate in the annual national computer competition of the Black Data Processing Associates (BDPA).

Eligibility   This competition is open to students who are members of a team that participates in the High School Computer Competition at the BDPA annual conference. Each team consists of 5 students. At the end of the competition, the sponsor sends award letters to all of the eligible team members who have graduated from high school, have been accepted to a 4-year degree program, and plan to major in an information technology field. Letter recipients are invited to apply for these scholarships. Selection is based on performance at the computer competition.

Financial data   Awards for each member of the top teams are $2,000 for first place, $1,500 for second place, $1,000 for third place, and $500 for fourth place. Funds are paid directly to the student's college or university to be used for tuition or other school expenses.

Duration   The competition is held annually.

Additional information   The BDPA established its Education and Technology Foundation (BETF) in 1992 to advance the skill sets needed by African American and other minority adults and young people to compete in the information technology industry. Previously, this program was known as the Student Information Technology Education & Scholarship.

Number awarded   20 each year: 5 members of each of the top 4 teams win awards.

Deadline   Deadline not specified.

[197]
DR. JO ANN OTA FUJIOKA SCHOLARSHIP

Phi Delta Kappa International
Attn: PDK Educational Foundation
320 West Eighth Street, Suite 216
P.O. Box 7888
Bloomington, IN 47407-7888
(812) 339-1156   Toll Free: (800) 766-1156
Fax: (812) 339-0018   E-mail: scholarships@pdkintl.org
Web: www.pdkintl.org

Summary   To provide financial assistance to African American and other high school seniors and undergraduates of color who plan to study education at a college in any state and have a connection to Phi Delta Kappa (PDK).

Eligibility   This program is open to high school seniors and undergraduates of color who are majoring or planning to major in education and can meet 1 of the following criteria: 1) is a member of Educators Rising (formerly the Future Educators Association); 2) is the child or grandchild of a PDK member; or 3) has a reference letter written by a PDK member. Also eligible are undergraduate members of PDK or Educators Rising who are enrolled in a college education program.

Applicants must submit a 500-word essay on a topic related to education that changes annually. Selection is based on the essay, academic standing, letters of recommendation, service activities, educational activities, and leadership activities; financial need is not considered.

Financial data   The stipend is $2,000.

Duration   1 year.

Additional information   This program began in 2006.

Number awarded   1 each year.

Deadline   March of each year.

[198]
DR. JOHNELLA BANKS SCHOLARSHIP FUND

Black Nurses' Association of Greater Washington, D.C. Area, Inc.
Attn: Scholarship Committee Chair
P.O. Box 55285
Washington, DC 20040
(202) 291-8866
Web: www.bnaofgwdca.org/scholarships.html

Summary   To provide financial assistance to nursing students from the Washington, D.C. area who have been active in the African American community.

Eligibility   This program is open to students currently enrolled as sophomores, juniors, or first-semester seniors in an NLN-accredited registered nursing or practical nursing program. Applicants must be residents of Washington, D.C. or adjoining counties in Maryland (Anne Arundel, Calvert, Charles, Howard, Montgomery, and Prince George's). They must be U.S. citizens or permanent residents and have a GPA of 2.8 or higher. Along with their application, they must submit an essay that describes their personal nursing goals and objectives, their financial need, and how Black nurses can address specific needs of the African American community. Selection is based on that essay, participation in student nurses activities and organizations, community service in the greater Washington, D.C. metropolitan area, and financial need.

Financial data   A stipend is awarded (amount not specified).

Duration   1 year.

Number awarded   1 or more each year.

Deadline   January of each year.

[199]
DR. JULIANNE MALVEAUX SCHOLARSHIP

National Association of Negro Business and Professional Women's Clubs
Attn: Scholarship Committee
1806 New Hampshire Avenue, N.W.
Washington, DC 20009-3206
(202) 483-4206   Fax: (202) 462-7253
E-mail: arlucas48@gmail.com
Web: www.nanbpwc.org/index-11.html

Summary   To provide financial assistance to African American women studying journalism, economics, or a related field in college.

Eligibility   This program is open to African American women enrolled at an accredited college or university as a sophomore or junior. Applicants must have a GPA of 3.0 or higher and be majoring in journalism, economics, or a related field. Along with their application, they must submit an essay, up to 1,000 words in length, on their career plans and their relevance to the theme of the program: "Black Women's Hands Can Rock the World." U.S. citizenship is required.

Financial data The stipend is $1,000.

Duration 1 year.

Number awarded 1 or more each year.

Deadline February of each year.

[200]
DR. MARTIN LUTHER KING, JR. DRUM MAJOR FOR JUSTICE ADVOCACY COMPETITION

National Bar Institute
1225 11th Street, N.W.
Washington, DC 20001-4217
(202) 842-3900   Fax: (202) 315-3051
E-mail: nbischolarship@outlook.com
Web: www.nationalbar.org

Summary To recognize and reward, with college scholarships, African American and other high school students of color who make outstanding written and oral presentations.

Eligibility This competition is open to high school juniors and seniors of color who enter in 1 of 12 regions of the National Bar Association (NBA). Applicants first submit an essay, up to 1,000 words in length, on an assigned topic that changes annually but relate to the views of Dr. Martin Luther King, Jr. Recently, students were asked whether Dr. King, if he were alive, would encourage Blacks to focus on Black Lives Matter or to reach more globally and generally on the All Lives Matter movement. Based on their essays, selected students are invited to make oral presentations from 3 to 7 minutes on the same topic. Selection of essays and oral presentations is based on quality, content, persuasiveness, style, organization, and creativity. Winners of regional competitions are invited to the NBA annual convention, where the national competition is held.

Financial data Awards are a $5,000 scholarship for the national first place winner, $3,000 for second, $2,000 for third, and $500 for the other finalists. Prizes are awarded when winners enter college.

Duration The competition is held annually.

Additional information This program, which began in 2000, is supported by MetLife.

Number awarded 12 finalists, 1 from each region, receive awards each year.

Deadline Deadlines for regional competitions are usually in March of each year.

[201]
DR. MARTIN LUTHER KING, JR. SCHOLARSHIP

North Carolina Association of Educators, Inc.
Attn: Human and Civil Rights Commission
700 South Salisbury Street
P.O. Box 27347
Raleigh, NC 27611-7347
(919) 832-3000, ext. 203
Toll Free: (800) 662-7924, ext. 203
Fax: (919) 839-8229   E-mail: derevana.leach@ncae.org
Web: www.ncae.org/get-involved/awards

Summary To provide financial assistance to African American and other high school seniors in North Carolina who plan to attend college in any state.

Eligibility This program is open to seniors graduating from high schools in North Carolina who plan to attend a college or university in any state. They must have a GPA of 2.5 or higher. Along with their application, they must submit 1-page essays on 1) how the philosophies and ideals of Dr. Martin Luther King influenced their life; and 2) why they feel they deserve this scholarship and their need for financial assistance. Selection is based on those essays; academic record; a resume of accomplishments, extracurricular activities, scholarships, affiliations, and organizations; and 2 letters of recommendation.

Financial data A stipend is awarded (amount not specified).

Duration 1 year.

Additional information This program was established in 1992 by the Minority Affairs Commission of the North Carolina Association of Educators (NCAE). It currently operates in partnership with the North Carolina Foundation for Public School Children.

Number awarded 1 or more each year.

Deadline January of each year.

[202]
DR. SANTANA AND KAREN WILLIAMS SCHOLARSHIP

Sigma Gamma Rho Sorority, Inc.
Attn: National Education Fund
1000 Southhill Drive, Suite 200
Cary, NC 27513
(919) 678-9720   Toll Free: (888) SGR-1922
Fax: (919) 678-9721
E-mail: customerservice@sgrho1922.org
Web: www.sgrho1922.org/nef

Summary To provide financial assistance to undergraduate students working on a degree in any field at an Historically Black College or University (HBCU).

Eligibility This program is open to undergraduates working on a degree in any field at an HBCU. The sponsor is a traditionally African American sorority, but support is available to males and females of all races. Applicants must have a GPA of 3.0 or higher, a record of community service, and demonstrated financial need.

Financial data A stipend is awarded (amount not specified).

Duration 1 year.

Additional information A processing fee of $20 is required.

Number awarded 1 each year.

Deadline April of each year.

[203]
DRS. KATIE K. WHITE AND JOSEPH C. WHITE ENDOWED SCHOLARSHIP

Sigma Gamma Rho Sorority, Inc.
Attn: National Education Fund
1000 Southhill Drive, Suite 200
Cary, NC 27513
(919) 678-9720   Toll Free: (888) SGR-1922
Fax: (919) 678-9721
E-mail: customerservice@sgrho1922.org
Web: www.sgrho1922.org/nef

Summary   To provide financial assistance to African American and other undergraduate students working on a degree in a medical or scientific field.

Eligibility   This program is open to undergraduates working on a degree in a medical or scientific field. The sponsor is a traditionally African American sorority, but support is available to males and females of all races. Applicants must have a GPA of "C" or higher and be able to demonstrate financial need.

Financial data   A stipend is awarded (amount not specified).

Duration   1 year.

Additional information   A processing fee of $20 is required.

Number awarded   1 each year.

Deadline   April of each year.

[204]
DUANE MOORER SCHOLARSHIP

Organization of Black Aerospace Professionals, Inc.
Attn: Scholarship Coordinator
One Westbrook Corporate Center, Suite 300
Westchester, IL 60154
(708) 449-7755   Toll Free: (800) JET-OBAP
Fax: (708) 449-7754 E-mail: obapscholarships@obap.org
Web: www.obap.org/duane-moorer-scholarship

Summary   To provide financial assistance to members of the Organization of Black Aerospace Professionals (OBAP) who plan to work on an aerospace degree at a school in any state.

Eligibility   This program is open to OBAP members who are high school seniors or students currently enrolled in an accredited collegiate aerospace program. Applicants must be interested in preparing for a career in aviation. They must have a GPA of 2.5 or higher. Along with their application, they must submit a 250-word essay on the importance of giving back.

Financial data   The stipend is $2,000.

Duration   1 year.

Additional information   The OBAP was originally established in 1976 as the Organization of Black Airline Pilots to make certain Blacks and other minorities had a group that would keep them informed about opportunities for advancement within commercial aviation.

Number awarded   1 each year.

Deadline   May of each year.

[205]
DWIGHT DAVID EISENHOWER HISTORICALLY BLACK COLLEGES AND UNIVERSITIES TRANSPORTATION FELLOWSHIP PROGRAM

Department of Transportation
Federal Highway Administration
Attn: Universities and Grants Programs
4600 North Fairfax Drive, Suite 800
Arlington, VA 22203-1553
(703) 235-0538   Toll Free: (877) 558-6873
Fax: (703) 235-0593   E-mail: transportationedu@dot.gov
Web: www.fhwa.dot.gov/tpp/ddetfp.htm

Summary   To provide financial assistance to undergraduate and graduate students working on a degree in a transportation-related field at a designated Historically Black College or University (HBCU).

Eligibility   This program is open to students working on a bachelor's, master's, or doctoral degree at 1 of 18 federally-designated 4-year HBCUs. Applicants must be working on a degree in a transportation-related field (e.g., engineering, business, aviation, architecture, public policy and analysis, urban and regional planning). They must be U.S. citizens or have an I-20 (foreign student) or I-551 (permanent resident) identification card. Undergraduates must be entering at least their junior year and have a GPA of 3.0 or higher. Graduate students must have a GPA of at least 3.25. Selection is based on their proposed plan of study, academic achievement (based on class standing, GPA, and transcripts), transportation work experience, and letters of recommendation.

Financial data   Fellows receive payment of full tuition and fees (to a maximum of $10,000) and a monthly stipend of $1,450 for undergraduates, $1,700 for master's students, or $2,000 for doctoral students. They are also provided with a 1-time allowance of up to $1,500 to attend the annual Transportation Research Board (TRB) meeting.

Duration   1 year.

Additional information   This program is administered by the participating HBCUs: Alabama A&M University, Benedict College, Florida A&M University, Hampton University, Howard University, Jackson State University, Lincoln University of Pennsylvania, Morgan State University, North Carolina A&T University, Prairie View A&M University. South Carolina State University, Southern University and A&M College, Tuskegee University, Texas Southern University, University of Maryland Eastern Shore, and Virginia State University.

Number awarded   Varies each year; recently, 47 were awarded.

Deadline   January of each year.

[206]
DWIGHT MOSLEY SCHOLARSHIPS

United States Tennis Association
Attn: USTA Foundation
70 West Red Oak Lane
White Plains, NY 10604
(914) 696-7223   Fax: (914) 697-2307
E-mail: foundation@usta.com
Web: www.ustafoundation.com

Summary   To provide financial assistance to female and male high school seniors (judged separately) who are African Americans or members of other diverse ethnic groups, have participated in an organized community tennis program, and plan to attend college in any state.

Eligibility This program is open to high school seniors from diverse ethnic backgrounds who have excelled academically, demonstrated achievements in leadership, and participated extensively in an organized community tennis program. Applicants must be planning to enroll as a full-time undergraduate student at a 4-year college or university. They must have a GPA of 3.0 or higher and be able to demonstrate financial need and sportsmanship. Along with their application, they must submit an essay of 1 to 2 pages about how their participation in a tennis and education program has influenced their life, including examples of special mentors, volunteer service, and future goals. Females and males are considered separately.

Financial data The stipend is $2,500 per year. Funds are paid directly to the recipient's college or university.

Duration 4 years.

Number awarded 2 each year: 1 female and 1 male.

Deadline February of each year.

[207]
EARLINE S. ROGERS STUDENT TEACHING STIPEND FOR MINORITIES

Indiana Commission for Higher Education
Attn: Financial Aid and Student Support Services
101 West Ohio Street, Suite 300
Indianapolis, IN 46204-4206
(317) 232-1023   Toll Free: (888) 528-4719 (within IN)
Fax: (317) 232-3260   E-mail: Scholars@che.in.gov
Web: www.in.gov/che/4511.htm

Summary To provide scholarship/loans to Black and Hispanic undergraduate students in Indiana interested in participating in student teaching at a college in the state.

Eligibility This program is open to Black and Hispanic students seeking certification in order to teach at an accredited elementary or secondary school in Indiana. Applicants must be Indiana residents and U.S. citizens or permanent residents who are enrolled as full-time students at an academic institution in Indiana. They must be entering a student teaching program or a school administration internship. Their GPA must qualify them for admission to their college's school of education.

Financial data For students whose GPA is greater than 3.5, the stipend is $5,000. For students whose GPA is greater than 3.0 but less than 3.5, the stipend is $4,000. Recipients must agree in writing to apply for a teaching or administration position at an accredited school in Indiana following certification and, if hired, to teach or work as an administrator for at least 3 years.

Duration 1 year.

Additional information This program began in 2013 and was given its current name in 2016. Participating colleges in Indiana select the recipients. Students must submit their application to the financial aid office of the college they attend.

Number awarded Varies each year.

Deadline October of each year for students who begin student teaching in the fall; January of each year for students who begin student teaching in the spring.

[208]
EAST TENNESSEE CHAPTER AABE SCHOLARSHIPS

American Association of Blacks in Energy-East
  Tennessee Chapter
Attn: Chair of Scholarship and Fundraising Committee
P.O. Box 11446
Chattanooga, TN 37401
E-mail: irvinjo@epb.net
Web: www.aabe.org

Summary To provide financial assistance to African Americans and members of other underrepresented minority groups who are high school seniors in Tennessee and planning to major in an energy-related field at a college in any state.

Eligibility This program is open to seniors graduating from high schools in Tennessee and planning to attend a college or university in any state. Applicants must be African Americans, Hispanics, or Native Americans who have a GPA of 3.0 or higher and can demonstrate financial need. Their intended major must be business, engineering, technology, mathematics, the physical sciences, or other energy-related field. Along with their application, they must submit a description of why they need this scholarship and how the money will aid them in reaching their educational and/or career goals. U.S. citizenship is required.

Financial data The stipend is $1,500.

Duration 1 year.

Additional information Winners are eligible to compete for regional and national scholarships. This program is supported by the Tennessee Valley Authority (TVA).

Number awarded 2 each year.

Deadline April of each year.

[209]
ED BRADLEY SCHOLARSHIP

Radio Television Digital News Foundation
Attn: Membership and Programs Manager
529 14th Street, N.W., Suite 1240
Washington, DC 20045
(202) 662-7257   Fax: (202) 223-4007
E-mail: karenh@rtdna.org
Web: www.rtdna.org/content/ed_bradley_scholarship

Summary To provide financial assistance to African American and other minority undergraduate students who are preparing for a career in electronic journalism.

Eligibility This program is open to sophomore or more advanced minority undergraduate students enrolled in an electronic journalism sequence at an accredited or nationally-recognized college or university. Applicants must submit a cover letter that discusses their current and past journalism experience, describes how they would use the funds if they were to receive the scholarship, discusses their reasons for preparing for a career in electronic journalism, and includes 3 to 5 links to their best and most relevant work samples.

Financial data The stipend is $10,000, paid in semiannual installments of $5,000 each.

Duration 1 year.

Additional information The Radio Television Digital News Foundation (RTDNF) was formerly the Radio and Television News Directors Foundation (RTNDF).

Number awarded 1 each year.

Deadline May of each year.

[210]
EDDIE PHILLIPS SCHOLARSHIP PROGRAM FOR AFRICAN-AMERICAN MEN

Minnesota Private College Council
Attn: Minnesota Private College Fund
445 Minnesota Street, Suite 500
St. Paul, MN 55101-2903
(651) 228-9061   Toll Free: (888) PRI-FUND
Fax: (651) 228-0379
E-mail: cjones@mnprivatecolleges.org
Web: www.mnprivatecolleges.org

Summary To provide financial assistance to African American male students at designated private colleges and universities in Minnesota.

Eligibility This program is open to African-American male students currently enrolled as full-time sophomores at any of 16 private colleges and universities in Minnesota. Applicants must have a GPA of 2.5 or higher and be on track to graduate within 4 years.

Financial data Scholars receive "significant" scholarships (amount not specified).

Duration 2 years.

Additional information This program was established by The Jay and Rose Phillips Family Foundation in 2015. The member institutions of the Minnesota Private College Council are Augsburg College, Bethany Lutheran College, Carleton College, College of St. Benedict, College of St. Scholastica, Concordia College (Moorhead), Concordia College (St. Paul), Gustavus Adolphus College, Hamline University, Macalester College, Minneapolis College of Art and Design, St. John's University, St. Mary's University of Minnesota, St. Catherine University, St. Olaf College, and University of St. Thomas.

Number awarded Varies each year; recently, 3 of these scholarships were awarded.

Deadline January of each year.

[211]
EDNA R. ANTHONY MEMORIAL SCHOLARSHIP

BECA, Incorporated
Attn: Women of BECA
P.O. Box 42039
Charlotte, NC 28215
(704) 236-6067   Fax: (704) 231-0647
E-mail: info@womenofbeca.com
Web: www.womenofbeca.com/scholarship-application

Summary To provide financial assistance to high school seniors who plan to attend an Historically Black College or University (HBCU) and major in a designated field.

Eligibility This program is open to graduating high school seniors who have a GPA of 2.5 or higher. Applicants must be planning to attend an HBCU and major in nursing/health care, criminal justice/political science, or journalism/communication. Along with their application, they must submit a 1,000-word essay on why they want to prepare for a career in their field of choice.

Financial data The stipend is $1,000.

Duration 1 year; nonrenewable.

Additional information The sponsor's name stands for Believe, Excel, and Commit to Achieve.

Number awarded Up to 3 each year.

Deadline April of each year.

[212]
EDSA MINORITY SCHOLARSHIP

Landscape Architecture Foundation
Attn: Leadership in Landscape Scholarship Program
1129 20th Street, N.W., Suite 202
Washington, DC 20036
(202) 331-7070   Fax: (202) 331-7079
E-mail: scholarships@lafoundation.org
Web: www.lafoundation.org

Summary To provide financial assistance to African American and other minority college students who are interested in studying landscape architecture.

Eligibility This program is open to African American, Hispanic, Native American, and minority college students of other cultural and ethnic backgrounds. Applicants must be entering their final 2 years of undergraduate study in landscape architecture or working on a graduate degree in that field. Along with their application, they must submit a 500-word essay on a design or research effort they plan to pursue (explaining how it will contribute to the advancement of the profession and to their ethnic heritage), 3 work samples, and 2 letters of recommendation. Selection is based on professional experience, community involvement, extracurricular activities, and financial need.

Financial data The stipend is $5,000.

Additional information This scholarship was formerly designated the Edward D. Stone, Jr. and Associates Minority Scholarship.

Number awarded 1 each year.

Deadline February of each year.

[213]
EDUCATIONAL FOUNDATION OF THE COLORADO SOCIETY OF CERTIFIED PUBLIC ACCOUNTANTS MINORITY SCHOLARSHIPS

Colorado Society of Certified Public Accountants
Attn: Educational Foundation
7887 East Belleview Avenue, Suite 200
Englewood, CO 80111
(303) 773-2877   Toll Free: (800) 523-9082 (within CO)
Fax: (303) 773-6344
Web: www.cocpa.org

Summary To provide financial assistance to African American and other minority upper-division and graduate students in Colorado who are majoring in accounting.

Eligibility This program is open to Colorado minority residents (Black or African American, Hispanic or Latino, Native American, Asian American) who are upper-division or graduate students at colleges and universities in the state and have completed at least 6 semester hours of accounting courses. Applicants must have a GPA of at least 3.0 overall and 3.25 in accounting classes. They must be U.S. citizens or noncitizens legally living and studying in Colorado with a valid visa that enables them to become employed. Financial need is not considered in the selection process.

Financial data The stipend is $2,500. Funds are paid directly to the recipient's school to be used for books, C.P.A. review materials, tuition, fees, and dormitory room and board.

Duration 1 year; recipients may reapply.

Number awarded 1 or more each year.

Deadline May of each year for fall semester or quarter; November of each year for winter quarter or spring semester.

[214]
EDWARD S. ROTH SCHOLARSHIP

Society of Manufacturing Engineers
Attn: SME Education Foundation
One SME Drive
P.O. Box 930
Dearborn, MI 48121-0930
(313) 425-3300   Toll Free: (866) 547-6333
Fax: (313) 425-3411   E-mail: foundation@sme.org
Web: www.smeef.org

Summary To provide financial assistance to students, especially African Americans and other minorities, who are enrolled or planning to work on a bachelor's or master's degree in manufacturing engineering at selected universities.

Eligibility This program is open to U.S. citizens who are graduating high school seniors or currently-enrolled undergraduate or graduate students. Applicants must be enrolled or planning to enroll as a full-time student at 1 of 13 selected 4-year universities to work on a bachelor's or master's degree in manufacturing engineering. They must have a GPA of 3.0 or higher. Preference is given to 1) students demonstrating financial need; 2) minority students; and 3) students participating in a co-op program. Along with their application, they must submit a brief statement about why they chose their major, their career and educational objectives, and how this scholarship will help them attain those objectives.

Financial data Stipends range from $1,000 to $6,000 and recently averaged approximately $2,000.

Duration 1 year; may be renewed.

Additional information The eligible institutions are California Polytechnic State University at San Luis Obispo, California State Polytechnic State University at Pomona, University of Miami (Florida), Bradley University (Illinois), Central State University (Ohio), Miami University (Ohio), Boston University, Worcester Polytechnic Institute (Massachusetts), University of Massachusetts, St. Cloud State University (Minnesota), University of Texas at Rio Grande Valley, Brigham Young University (Utah), and Utah State University.

Number awarded 2 each year.

Deadline January of each year.

[215]
ELAINE REIKO AKAGI SCHOLARSHIP

Japanese American Citizens League-Seattle Chapter
P.O. Box 18558
Seattle, WA 98118
(253) 256-2204   E-mail: bcaldwell44@yahoo.com
Web: www.jaclseattle.org

Summary To provide financial assistance to African Americans and other people of color who are working on a degree in special education at a school in any state.

Eligibility This program is open to people of color who are enrolled at a college or university in any state. Applicants must have a declared major in special education and a GPA of 2.5 or higher. Along with their application, they must submit a list of extracurricular and community activities, 2 letters of recommendation, a list of awards or recognitions they have earned, and a 500-word essay on the importance of increasing the number of teachers of color in special education classrooms. In the selection process, consideration is given to how the applicants plan to give back to the education community, the reasons they wish to prepare for the field of education, their experiences in working with children with disabilities, their experience working with children of color, and the teaching field in which they are specializing; financial need is not considered.

Financial data The stipend is $3,000.

Duration 1 year.

Additional information This program began in 2011.

Number awarded 1 each year.

Deadline March of each year.

[216]
ELI LILLY AND COMPANY SCHOLARSHIP FOR BDPA STUDENTS

Black Data Processing Associates
Attn: BDPA Education Technology Foundation
4423 Lehigh Road, Number 277
College Park, MD 20740
(513) 284-4968   Fax: (202) 318-2194
E-mail: scholarships@betf.org
Web: www.betf.org/scholarships/eli-lilly.shtml

Summary To provide financial assistance to minority high school seniors and current college students who are members of Black Data Processing Associates (BDPA) and interested in studying information technology at a college in any state.

Eligibility This program is open to graduating high school seniors and current college undergraduates who are minority students (African American, Hispanic, Asian, or Native American) and members of BDPA. Applicants must be enrolled or planning to enroll at an accredited 4-year college or university and work on a degree in information technology. They must have a GPA of 3.0 or higher. Along with their application, they must submit a 500-word essay on why information technology is important. Selection is based on that essay, academic achievement, leadership ability through academic or civic involvement, and participation in community service activities. U.S. citizenship or permanent resident status is required.

Financial data The stipend is $5,000. Funds may be used to pay for tuition, fees, books, room and board, or other college-related expenses.

Duration 1 year; nonrenewable.

Additional information The BDPA established its Education and Technology Foundation (BETF) in 1992 to advance the skill sets needed by African American and other minority adults and young people to compete in the information technology industry. This program, which began in 2007, is sponsored by Eli Lilly and Company.

Number awarded 2 each year.

Deadline July of each year.

[217]
ELLIS INJURY LAW DIVERSITY SCHOLARSHIPS

Ellis Law Corporation
Attn: Scholarship
883 North Douglas Street
El Segundo, CA 90245
Toll Free: (888) 559-7672
E-mail: scholarships@alelaw.com
Web: www.ellisinjurylaw.com/scholarships

Summary To provide financial assistance to pre-law and law students who either are African Americans or members of another ethnic minority group or have been involved in diversity issues.

Eligibility This program is open to students accepted or enrolled at 1) a 4-year college or university with the intention of working on a law degree; and 2) an ABA-accredited law school. Applicants must be either members of an ethnic/racial minority or individuals who have made a demonstrative commitment to diversity within their school and/or community. They must have a GPA of 3.0 or higher. Along with their application, they must submit an essay of 1,500 to 2,000 words answering 3 questions about recent Supreme Court decisions regarding affirmative action. Selection is based on that essay and transcripts.

Financial data The stipend is $1,000.

Duration 1 year.

Additional information This program began in 2014.

Number awarded 3 each year.

Deadline December of each year.

[218]
ELSIE MAE WHITE MEMORIAL SCHOLARSHIP FUND

Columbus Foundation
Attn: Scholarship Manager
1234 East Broad Street
Columbus, OH 43205-1453
(614) 251-4000   Fax: (614) 251-4009
E-mail: aszempruch@columbusfoundation.org
Web: tcfapp.org

Summary To provide financial assistance for college or graduate school to African American high school seniors and college students from any state.

Eligibility This program is open to African American high school seniors and college students. High school seniors must rank in the top third of their class; college students must have a GPA of 2.8 or higher. Applicants must be attending or planning to attend an accredited college or university in the United States as a full- or part-time undergraduate or graduate student. Preference is given to students at land grant colleges and universities. Along with their application, they must submit 300-word essays on 1) their educational and career plans and goals, why they have chosen their particular field, and why they think they will be a success; 2) why they feel they need this scholarship, especially as related to financial need; and 3) any other information that will assist the selection committee in making its decision.

Financial data The stipend is $1,000.

Duration 1 year.

Number awarded Varies each year.

Deadline May of each year.

[219]
EMERGING ARCHIVAL SCHOLARS PROGRAM

Archival Education and Research Institute
Center for Information as Evidence
c/o UCLA Graduate School of Education and Information Studies
Office of External Relations
2043 Moore Hall
Los Angeles, CA 90095-1521
(310) 206-0375   Fax: (310) 794-5324
Web: aeri.gseis.ucla.edu/fellowships.htm

Summary To provide an opportunity for African American and other minority undergraduate and graduate students to learn more about the field of archival studies and to be exposed to research in the field.

Eligibility This program is open to undergraduates who have completed their junior year and to students who have completed the first year of a master's degree program. Applicants must be African American, Hispanic/Latino, Asian/Pacific Islander, Native American, Puerto Rican, or any other person who will add diversity to the field of archival studies. They must have a GPA of 3.0 or higher, but they may be working on a degree in any field and are not required to have prior knowledge of or experience in archival studies. U.S. citizenship or permanent resident status is required. Applicants must be interested in attending the week-long Archival Education and Research Institute (AERI), held at a different university each summer, where they are assigned both a faculty research mentor and a Ph.D. student mentor who introduce them to doctoral research and careers in archival studies.

Financial data Grants provide payment of round-trip travel, accommodation, and most meals.

Duration These grants are offered annually.

Additional information This program, first offered in 2009, is supported by the Institute of Museum and Library Services. Scholars who indicate an interest in continuing on to a doctoral program in archival studies after completing the AERI may be invited to participate in a supervised research project that will last up to 1 year and to present results of their research in a poster session at the AERI of the following year.

Number awarded Up to 7 each year.

Deadline April of each year.

[220]
EMERGING LEADERS INTERNSHIP PROGRAM SPONSORED BY WALMART

Congressional Black Caucus Foundation, Inc.
Attn: Leadership Institute for Public Service
1720 Massachusetts Avenue, N.W.
Washington, DC 20036
(202) 263-2800   Toll Free: (800) 784-2577
Fax: (202) 775-0773   E-mail: internships@cbcfinc.org
Web: www.cbcfinc.org

Summary To provide African American and other undergraduate students with an opportunity to work during the fall in a Congressional office or federal government agency.

Eligibility This program is open to African American and other full-time undergraduate students who have a GPA of 2.5 or higher. Applicants must be interested in a legislative internship on the staff of an African American member of Congress or an assignment with a federal government agency. They should have a demonstrated interest in public service, governance, and the policy-making process. Selection is based on scholastic achievement, evidence of leadership skills, writing skills, and community service contributions. U.S. citizenship or permission to work in the United States are required.

Financial data Interns receive housing accommodations and a $4,000 stipend to cover expenses related to travel, meals, and personal expenses.

Duration 13 weeks during the fall.

Additional information This program, established in 2007, is sponsored by Walmart. In addition to their work assignments, interns attend educational seminars that focus on domestic and international issues, participate in leadership training sessions, and visit cultural and historical sites in the Washington, D.C. area. As a team, they participate in a community service project.

Number awarded Varies each year; recently, 9 interns served in this program.

Deadline June of each year.

[221]
EMMA AND MELOID ALGOOD TUITION SCHOLARSHIP

National Association of Black Social Workers
Attn: NABSW Scholarships
2305 Martin Luther King Avenue, S.E.
Washington, DC 20020
(202) 678-4570   Fax: (202) 678-4572
E-mail: office-manager@nabsw.org
Web: www.nabsw.org/?page=ScholarshipsRecipien

Summary To provide financial assistance to members of the National Association of Black Social Workers (NABSW) who are working on a bachelor's degree.

Eligibility This program is open to African American members of NABSW working full time on a bachelor's degree at an accredited U.S. social work or social welfare program with a GPA of 2.5 or higher. Applicants must be able to demonstrate community service. Along with their application, they must submit an essay of 2 to 3 pages on their professional interests, future social work aspirations, previous social work experiences (volunteer and professional), and honors and achievements (academic and community service). Financial need is considered in the selection process.

Financial data The stipend is $1,000. Funds are sent directly to the recipient's school.

Duration 1 year.

Number awarded 1 each year.

Deadline December of each year.

[222]
EMMA L. BOWEN FOUNDATION INTERNSHIPS

Emma L. Bowen Foundation
Attn: Senior Vice President, Eastern Region and National Recruitment
30 Rockefeller Plaza
(Campus 1221 Avenue of the Americas #28A41)
New York, NY 10112
(212) 975-2545   E-mail: sdrice@cbs.com
Web: www.emmabowenfoundation.com

Summary To provide financial assistance and work experience to African American and other minority students interested in preparing for a career in the media industry.

Eligibility This program is open to minority students who are rising high school seniors, graduating high school seniors, or college freshmen. Applicants must be interested in working at a media company during the summer and school breaks until they graduate from college. They must have a GPA of 3.0 or higher, plans to attend an accredited 4-year college or university, and an interest in the media industry as a career. Along with their application, they must submit an essay of 500 to 1,000 words on how the media industry helps to create the images that influence our decisions and perceptions on a daily basis. U.S. citizenship or permanent resident status is required.

Financial data Interns receive a stipend of $2,500 to $3,000 and matching compensation of $2,500 to $3,000 to help pay for college tuition and other expenses.

Duration 1 summer for the internship; 1 academic year for the educational support; may be renewed until the intern graduates from college if he or she maintains a GPA of 3.0 or higher.

Additional information This program began in 1989. The sponsoring companies have included Broadcast Music Inc., CBS Incorporated, Charter Communications, Comcast NBC Universal, C-SPAN, Cox Communications, Fox Television Stations, Inc., Gannett Television, National Association of Broadcasters Educational Foundation, Turner Entertainment Networks.

Number awarded Approximately 60 to 70 new interns are selected each year.

Deadline Applications may be submitted at any time.

[223]
EMPIRE STATE DIVERSITY HONORS SCHOLARSHIP PROGRAM

State University of New York
Attn: Office of Diversity, Equity and Inclusion
State University Plaza, T1000A
353 Broadway
Albany, NY 12246
(518) 320-1189   E-mail: carlos.medina@suny.edu
Web: system.suny.edu/odei/diversity-programs

Summary To provide financial assistance to residents of New York who are attending campuses of the State University of New York (SUNY) and are African Americans or will contribute to the diversity of the student body in other ways.

Eligibility This program is open to U.S. citizens and permanent residents who are New York residents and enrolled as undergraduate students at any of the participating SUNY colleges. Applicants must be able to demonstrate 1) how they will contribute to the diversity of the student body, primarily by having overcome a disadvantage or other impediment to success in higher education; and 2) high academic achievement. Economic disadvantage, although not a requirement, may be the basis for eligibility. Membership in a racial or ethnic group that is underrepresented at the applicant's school or program may serve as a plus factor in making awards, but may not form the sole basis of selection.

Financial data The maximum stipend provided by the SUNY system is half the student's cost of attendance or

$3,000, whichever is less. The individual campus must match the SUNY award in an equal amount.

Duration 1 year; renewable.

Number awarded Varies each year; recently, 929 students at 41 SUNY institutions received support from this program.

Deadline Deadline not specified.

[224]
EMPOWER BOOK SCHOLARSHIPS

Greater Washington Urban League
Attn: Thursday Network
Kristin Shymoniak
P.O. Box 73203
Washington, DC 20056-3202
E-mail: scholarship@thursdaynetwork.org
Web: www.thursdaynetwork.org/signature-programs

Summary To provide financial assistance to African American and Hispanic high school seniors in the service area of the Greater Washington Urban League (GWUL) who plan to attend college in any state.

Eligibility This program is open to African American and Hispanic/Latino seniors graduating from high schools in Washington, D.C., Prince George's County (Maryland), or Montgomery County (Maryland) and planning to enroll at a 4-year college or university in any state. Applicants must have a GPA of 2.5 or higher. Along with their application, they must submit copies of their SAT or ACT scores, documentation of financial need, and 2 essays of up to 500 words each on topics that change annually but relate to their community service. U.S. citizenship is required.

Financial data Stipends are $500 or $1,000. Funds are paid directly to the recipient's institution to assist in the purchase of books.

Duration 1 year.

Additional information This program is operated by the Thursday Network, the young professionals' auxiliary of the GWUL, as part of its Young Blacks Give Back (YBGB) Month.

Number awarded Varies each year; recently, 3 at $1,000 and 4 at $500 were awarded.

Deadline January of each year.

[225]
ENC ROBERT E. CATO USCG (RET.) SCHOLARSHIP

National Naval Officers Association-Washington, D.C.
   Chapter
c/o LCDR Stephen Williams
P.O. Box 30784
Alexandria, VA 22310
(703) 566-3840   Fax: (703) 566-3813
E-mail: Stephen.Williams@Navy.mil
Web: dcnnoa.memberlodge.com/page-309002

Summary To provide financial assistance to African American high school seniors from the Washington, D.C. area who are interested in attending college in any state.

Eligibility This program is open to African American seniors graduating from high schools in the Washington, D.C. metropolitan area who plan to enroll full time at an accredited 2- or 4-year college or university in any state. Applicants must have a GPA of 2.5 or higher and be U.S. citizens or perma-

nent residents. Selection is based on academic achievement, community involvement, and financial need.

Financial data The stipend is $1,500.

Duration 1 year; nonrenewable.

Additional information Recipients are not required to join or affiliate with the military in any way.

Number awarded 1 each year.

Deadline February of each year.

[226]
ENCOURAGE MINORITY PARTICIPATION IN OCCUPATIONS WITH EMPHASIS ON REHABILITATION

Allina Health System
Courage Kenny Rehabilitation Institute-Volunteer
   Services
Attn: EMPOWER Scholarship Committee
3915 Golden Valley Road
Minneapolis, MN 55422
(612) 775-2728   E-mail: ckriempower@allina.com
Web: www.allinahealth.org

Summary To provide financial assistance to African American and other students of color from Minnesota and western Wisconsin interested in attending college in any state to prepare for a career in the medical rehabilitation field.

Eligibility This program is open to ethnically diverse students accepted at or enrolled in an institution of higher learning in any state. Applicants must be residents of Minnesota or western Wisconsin (Burnett, Pierce, Polk, and St. Croix counties). They must be able to demonstrate a career interest in the medical rehabilitation field by a record of volunteer involvement related to health care and must have a GPA of 2.0 or higher. Along with their application, they must submit a 1-page essay that covers their medical/rehabilitation career-related volunteer service, including detailed information about patients or clients with whom they worked, what they did, what they think they accomplished and gained from their experience and how it will assist them in your future endeavors. Financial need is considered in the selection process.

Financial data The stipend is $1,500.

Duration 1 year.

Additional information This program, established in 1995 by the Courage Center, is also identified by its acronym as the EMPOWER Scholarship Award. The Courage Kenny Rehabilitation Institute was established in 2013 when Courage Center merged with the Sister Kenny Rehabilitation Institute and became part of Allina Health.

Number awarded 2 each year.

Deadline May of each year.

[227]
ESA FOUNDATION SCHOLARSHIP PROGRAM

Entertainment Software Association
Attn: ESA Foundation
317 Madison Avenue, 22nd Floor
New York, NY 10017
(917) 522-3250
Web: www.esafoundation.org/scholarship.asp

Summary To provide financial assistance to African Americans and members of other minority groups who are interested in attending college to prepare for a career in computer and video game arts.

Eligibility This program is open to women and members of minority groups who are high school seniors or undergraduates currently enrolled full time at an accredited 4-year college or university. Applicants must be interested in working on a degree leading to a career in computer and video game arts. They must be U.S. citizens and have a GPA of 2.75 or higher.

Financial data The stipend is $3,000.

Duration 1 year; nonrenewable.

Additional information This program began in 2007.

Number awarded Up to 30 each year: 15 to graduating high school seniors and 15 to current undergraduates.

Deadline March of each year.

[228]
ETHEL LEE HOOVER ELLIS SCHOLARSHIP

National Association of Negro Business and Professional Women's Clubs
Attn: Scholarship Committee
1806 New Hampshire Avenue, N.W.
Washington, DC 20009-3206
(202) 483-4206   Fax: (202) 462-7253
E-mail: arlucas48@gmail.com
Web: www.nanbpwc.org/index-11.html

Summary To provide financial assistance to African American women from designated southern states studying business at a college in any state.

Eligibility This program is open to African Americans women who are residents of Alabama, Florida, Georgia, Mississippi, North Carolina, South Carolina, Tennessee, or West Virginia. Applicants must be enrolled at an accredited college or university in any state as a sophomore or junior. They must have a GPA of 3.0 or higher and be majoring in business. Along with their application, they must submit an essay, up to 750 words in length, on the topic, "Business and Community United." U.S. citizenship is required.

Financial data A stipend is awarded (amount not specified).

Duration 1 year.

Number awarded 1 or more each year.

Deadline February of each year.

[229]
ETHIOPIAN HERITAGE COLLEGE SCHOLARSHIP FUND

Chaikin, Sherman, Cammarata & Siegel, P.C.
1232 17th Street, N.W.
Washington, DC 20036
(202) 644-8303
Web: www.chaikinandsherman.com

Summary To provide financial assistance to high school seniors in the Washington, D.C. metropolitan area whose families are recent immigrants from Ethiopia and who plan to attend college in any state.

Eligibility This program is open to seniors graduating from high schools in the Greater Metropolitan Washington D.C. area and planning to enroll full time at a 2- or 4-year college or university in any state. Applicants must be from newly immigrant families from Ethiopia and have few economic

resources. Along with their application, they must submit a 400-word essay on their choice of 4 assigned topics about themselves. Selection is based on that essay, transcripts, and a list of community service contributions.

Financial data The stipend is $1,000.

Duration 1 year.

Additional information This program began in 2008.

Number awarded 1 or more each year.

Deadline June of each year.

[230]
EUGENE CAMPBELL SCHOLARSHIP

Southern New England Association of Technical Professionals
Attn: Scholarships
P.O. Box 280303
East Hartford, CT 06128-0115
E-mail: sneatp@gmail.com
Web: www.sneatp.org

Summary To provide financial assistance to members of the National Society of Black Engineers (NSBE) at colleges in Connecticut, Boston, or western Massachusetts who are studying a field of science, technology, engineering, or mathematics (STEM).

Eligibility This program is open to residents of any state enrolled at ABET-accredited colleges and universities in Connecticut, Boston, and western Massachusetts who are active members of their collegiate NSBE Chapter. Applicants must be working on a degree in a STEM field of study. They must have a GPA of 2.8 or higher. Along with their application, they must submit a 500-word essay on how obtaining a degree in a STEM field will help them to impact their community positively.

Financial data The stipend is $2,000.

Duration 1 year.

Number awarded 1 each year.

Deadline June of each year.

[231]
EXELON SCHOLARSHIPS

Society of Women Engineers
Attn: Scholarship Selection Committee
203 North LaSalle Street, Suite 1675
Chicago, IL 60601-1269
(312) 596-5223   Toll Free: (877) SWE-INFO
Fax: (312) 644-8557   E-mail: scholarships@swe.org
Web: societyofwomenengineers.swe.org

Summary To provide financial assistance to women, especially African Americans and members of other underrepresented groups, who will be entering their freshman, sophomore, or junior year and are interested in studying engineering or computer science.

Eligibility This program is open to women who are enrolling full time in their freshman, sophomore, or junior year at an ABET-accredited 4-year college or university. Preference is given to students at Bradley University, Illinois Institute of Technology, University of Illinois at Chicago, University of Illinois at Urbana-Champaign, University of Maryland-Baltimore County, University of Maryland at College Park, Morgan State University, Pennsylvania State University, or Purdue University. Applicants must be planning to major in computer science or computer, electrical, or mechanical engineering. U.S. citizenship is required. Preference is given to members of groups underrepresented in engineering and computer science, including ethnic and racial minorities, persons with disabilities, and veterans. Selection is based on merit.

Financial data   The stipend is $1,000.

Duration   1 year.

Additional information   This program is sponsored by Exelon Corporation, parent of ComEd and PECO, the electric utilities for northern Illinois and southeastern Pennsylvania, respectively.

Number awarded   5 each year.

Deadline   May of each year for entering freshmen; February of each year for continuing sophomores and juniors.

[232]
EXXONMOBIL BERNARD HARRIS MATH AND SCIENCE SCHOLARSHIPS

Council of the Great City Schools
1301 Pennsylvania Avenue, N.W., Suite 702
Washington, DC 20004
(202) 393-2427   Fax: (202) 393-2400
Web: www.cgcs.org/Page/47

Summary   To provide financial assistance to African American and Hispanic high school seniors interested in studying science, technology, engineering, or mathematics (STEM) in college.

Eligibility   This program is open to African American and Hispanic seniors graduating from high schools in a district that is a member of the Council of the Great City Schools, a coalition of 67 of the nation's largest urban public school systems. Applicants must be planning to enroll full time at a 4-year college or university and major in a STEM field of study. They must have a GPA of 3.0 or higher. Along with their application, they must submit 1-page essays on 1) how mathematics and science education has impacted their lives so far; and 2) why they have chosen to prepare for a career in a STEM field. Selection is based on those essays; academic achievement; extracurricular activities, community service, or other experiences that demonstrate commitment to a career in a STEM field; and 3 letters of recommendation. Financial need is not considered. Males and females are judged separately.

Financial data   The stipend is $5,000.

Duration   1 year; nonrenewable.

Additional information   This program, which began in 2010, is sponsored by the ExxonMobil Corporation and The Harris Foundation.

Number awarded   4 each year: an African American male and female and an Hispanic male and female.

Deadline   May of each year.

[233]
EXXONMOBIL NSBE CORPORATE SCHOLARSHIPS

National Society of Black Engineers
Attn: Programs Department
205 Daingerfield Road
Alexandria, VA 22314
(703) 549-2207   Fax: (703) 683-5312
E-mail: scholarships@nsbe.org
Web: connect.nsbe.org/Scholarships/ScholarshipList.aspx

Summary   To provide financial assistance to members of the National Society of Black Engineers (NSBE) who are majoring in designated engineering fields.

Eligibility   This program is open to members of the society who are college sophomores or juniors majoring in chemical, civil, electrical, or mechanical engineering. Applicants must have a GPA of 3.5 or higher. Along with their application, they must submit essays of 300 words on 1) the advice they would offer fellow engineering students to motivate them to make academic excellence a priority in their college career; and 2) why academic excellence has been a priority in their college career. U.S. citizenship or permanent resident status is required.

Financial data   The stipend is $2,000.

Duration   1 year.

Additional information   This program is sponsored by ExxonMobil Corporation.

Number awarded   Up to 10 each year.

Deadline   May of each year.

[234]
FARM CREDIT EAST SCHOLARSHIPS

Farm Credit East
Attn: Scholarship Program
240 South Road
Enfield, CT 06082
(860) 741-4380   Toll Free: (800) 562-2235
Fax: (860) 741-4389
E-mail: specialoffers@famcrediteast.com
Web: www.farmcrediteast.com

Summary   To provide financial assistance to residents of designated northeastern states, including African Americans and other minorities, who plan to attend school in any state to work on an undergraduate or graduate degree in a field related to agriculture, forestry, or fishing.

Eligibility   This program is open to residents of Connecticut, Maine, Massachusetts, New Jersey, Rhode Island, and portions of New York and New Hampshire. Applicants must be working on or planning to work on an associate, bachelor's, or graduate degree in production agriculture, agribusiness, the forest products industry, or commercial fishing at a college or university in any state. They must submit a 200-word essay on why they wish to prepare for a career in agriculture, forestry, or fishing. Selection is based on the essay, extracurricular activities (especially farm work experience and activities indicative of an interest in preparing for a career in agriculture or agribusiness), and interest in agriculture. The program includes diversity scholarships reserved for members of minority groups (Black or African American, American Indian or Alaska Native, Asian, Native Hawaiian or other Pacific Islander, or Hispanic or Latino).

Financial data   The stipend is $1,500. Funds are paid directly to the student to be used for tuition, room and board, books, and other academic charges.

Duration   1 year; nonrenewable.

Additional information   Recipients are given priority for an internship with the sponsor in the summer following their junior year. Farm Credit East was formerly named First Pioneer Farm Credit.

Number awarded Varies each year; recently, 32, including several diversity scholarships, were awarded.

Deadline April of each year.

[235]
FAYE AND ROBERT LETT SCHOLARSHIP

American Baptist Churches of Ohio
Attn: Ohio Baptist Education Society
136 Galway Drive North
Granville, OH 43023-9577
(740) 587-0804   Fax: (740) 587-0807
Web: www.abc-ohio.org/index.php/menu-obes

Summary To provide funding to African American upper-division and graduate students from Ohio who are interested in preparing for the Baptist ministry at a college or seminary in any state.

Eligibility This program is open to African American residents of Ohio who have completed at least 2 years of study at an accredited college or university in any state and are interested in continuing their education as an upper-division or seminary student. Applicants must 1) hold active membership in a church affiliated with the American Baptist Churches of Ohio or a church dually-aligned with the American Baptist Churches of Ohio; 2) be in the process of preparing for a professional career in Christian ministry (such as a local church pastor, church education, youth or young adult ministries, church music, specialized ministry, chaplaincy, ministry in higher education, or missionary service); 3) be committed to working professionally within the framework of the American Baptist Churches USA; and 4) acknowledge a personal commitment to the Gospel of Jesus Christ, an understanding of the Christian faith, and a definite call to professional Christian ministry as a life work. Financial need must be demonstrated.

Financial data Stipends generally range from $1,000 to $1,500 a year.

Duration 1 year.

Additional information This program began in 1990.

Number awarded 1 or more each year.

Deadline March of each year.

[236]
FEDERAL CITY ALUMNAE CHAPTER HBCU SCHOLARSHIPS

Delta Sigma Theta Sorority, Inc.-Federal City Alumnae
   Chapter
Attn: Educational Development Committee
P.O. Box 1605
Washington, DC 20013
(202) 545-1913   E-mail: education@thefcacdst.org
Web: www.thefcacdst.org/#!educational-development/c12rb

Summary To provide financial assistance to high school seniors in Washington, D.C. who plan to attend a 4-year Historically Black College or University (HBCU) in any state.

Eligibility This program is open to seniors graduating from public or charter high schools in the District of Columbia and planning to enroll full time at an accredited 4-year HBCU in any state. Applicants must have a GPA of 2.5 or higher. Along with their application, they must submit transcripts that include SAT/ACT scores, a 1-page essay on their involvement in community service, and an essay of 450 to 500 words on either how they plan to use their education to make the world

a better place or why they should be selected to receive this scholarship.

Financial data The stipend ranges from $500 to $4,000.

Duration 1 year.

Additional information The sponsor is the local alumnae chapter of a traditionally African American social sorority.

Number awarded 1 or more each year.

Deadline March of each year.

[237]
FEDERAL EMPLOYEE EDUCATION AND ASSISTANCE (FEEA)-BLACKS IN GOVERNMENT (BIG) SCHOLARSHIP PROGRAM

Blacks in Government
Attn: National Program and Planning Chair
3005 Georgia Avenue, N.W.
Washington, DC 20001-5015
(202) 667-3280   Fax: (202) 667-3705
E-mail: BIGprograms@bignet.org
Web: www.bignet.org

Summary To provide financial assistance for college or graduate school to dependents of members of Blacks in Government (BIG).

Eligibility This program is open to the children, stepchildren, and grandchildren of BIG members. The sponsoring BIG member must have at least 3 years of federal, state, or local government employment and 2 years of membership in BIG. Applicants must be entering or enrolled full time in an accredited 2- or 4-year postsecondary, graduate, or postgraduate program and have a GPA of 3.0 or higher. Along with their application, they must submit a 2-page essay on a topic related to a career in public service with the government, a letter of recommendation, a transcript, a list of extracurricular and community service activities, and verification of government employment; high school seniors must also submit a copy of their ACT, SAT, or other examination scores. Financial need is not considered in the selection process.

Financial data The stipend is $1,000 per year.

Duration 1 year; may be renewed.

Additional information This program, established in 2007, is jointly administered by BIG and the Federal Employee Education and Assistance Fund (FEEA).

Number awarded Up to 11 each year: 1 in each BIG region.

Deadline March of each year.

[238]
FELICIA C. BRADY SCHOLARSHIP FUND

Black Nurses' Association of Greater Washington, D.C.
   Area, Inc.
Attn: Scholarship Committee Chair
P.O. Box 55285
Washington, DC 20040
(202) 291-8866
Web: www.bnaofgwdca.org/scholarships.html

Summary To provide financial assistance to registered nurses from the Washington, D.C. area who are members of the National Black Nurses' Association and its local affiliate, and are interested in working on an advanced degree.

Eligibility This program is open to registered nurses who are currently enrolled in an associate, bachelor's, master's, or doctoral program and have a GPA of 3.0 or higher. Applicants must be residents of Washington, D.C. or adjoining counties in Maryland (Anne Arundel, Calvert, Charles, Howard, Montgomery, and Prince George's). They must be U.S. citizens, members of the National Black Nurses' Association, and members of the Black Nurses' Association of Greater Washington, D.C. Area. Along with their application, they must submit a copy of their nursing license, an official transcript from their nursing program, 2 letters of recommendation, and a written essay that describes their personal goals and objectives, financial need, and contributions to nursing and community service involvement in the greater Washington, D.C. area.

Financial data   A stipend is awarded (amount not specified).

Duration   1 year.

Number awarded   1 each year.

Deadline   January of each year.

[239]
FIRST TRANSIT SCHOLARSHIP

Conference of Minority Transportation Officials
Attn: National Scholarship Program
100 M Street, S.E., Suite 917
Washington, DC 20003
(202) 506-2917   E-mail: info@comto.org
Web: www.comto.org/page/scholarships

Summary   To provide financial assistance to African American and other minority upper-division and graduate students in engineering or other field related to transportation.

Eligibility   This program is open to minority juniors, seniors, and graduate students in transporation, planning, engineering or other technical transportation-related disciplines. Applicants must submit a cover letter on their transportation-related career goals and life aspirations. Financial need is not considered in the selection process.

Financial data   The stipend is $6,000. Funds are paid directly to the recipient's college or university.

Duration   1 year.

Additional information   This program is sponsored by First Transit Inc.

Number awarded   1 each year.

Deadline   April of each year.

[240]
FLORIDA CHAPTER AABE SCHOLARSHIPS

American Association of Blacks in Energy-Florida
   Chapter
c/o Atanya Lewis, Scholarship Committee
700 Universe Boulevard, JNE/JB
Juno Beach, FL 33408
E-mail: Atanya.Lewis@fpl.com
Web: www.aabe.org/index.php?component=pages&id=811

Summary   To provide financial assistance to African Americans and members of other underrepresented minority groups who are high school seniors in Florida and planning to major in an energy-related field at a college in the state.

Eligibility   This program is open to seniors graduating from high schools in Florida and planning to attend an accredited college or university in Florida. Applicants must be African Americans, Hispanics, or Native Americans who have a GPA of 3.0 or higher and have taken the SAT and/or ACT test. Their intended major must be business (business administration, accounting, finance); engineering (agricultural/biological, chemical, civil, computer, electrical, environmental, industrial, materials, mechanical, nuclear); technology (computer science); mathematics (applied or any other branch); the physical sciences (astronomy, chemistry, physics, or energy-related non-medical biology); or other energy-related field. Along with their application, they must submit a 350-word essay that includes 1) when they discovered their interest in the field of energy and what sparked their interest; and 2) either what excites them about the field of energy or how they expect their education to prepare them for the field of energy. The program includes both need-based and no-need scholarships.

Financial data   A stipend is awarded (amount not specified).

Duration   1 year.

Additional information   Winners are eligible to compete for regional and national scholarships.

Number awarded   Varies each year.

Deadline   March of each year.

[241]
FORD BLUE OVAL SCHOLARSHIP OF THE THURGOOD MARSHALL COLLEGE FUND

Thurgood Marshall College Fund
Attn: Senior Manager of Scholarship Programs
901 F Street, N.W., Suite 300
Washington, DC 20004
(202) 507-4851   Fax: (202) 652-2934
E-mail: deshuandra.walker@tmcfund.org
Web: www.tmcf.org

Summary   To provide financial assistance to male African American high school seniors planning to attend public Historically Black Colleges and Universities (HBCUs) that are members of the Thurgood Marshall College Fund (TMCF).

Eligibility   This program is open to African American males who are high school seniors planning to enroll full time at any of the 47 TMCF member institutions. Applicants may major in any field. They must have a GPA of 3.0 or higher and be able to demonstrate financial need. Along with their application, they must submit a 500-word essay on what they think will be the most challenging aspect of transitioning from high school to college, how they will overcome that challenge, and their motivation to do so. U.S. citizenship or permanent resident status is required.

Financial data   The stipend is $6,200.

Duration   1 year.

Additional information   This program is sponsored by the Ford Motor Company Fund.

Number awarded   1 or more each year.

Deadline   April of each year.

[242]
FORUM FOR CONCERNS OF MINORITIES SCHOLARSHIPS

American Society for Clinical Laboratory Science
Attn: Forum for Concerns of Minorities
1861 International Drive, Suite 200
McLean, VA 22102
(571) 748-3770   E-mail: ascls@ascls.org
Web: www.ascls.org/forum-for-concerns-of-minorities

Summary To provide financial assistance to African American and other minority students in clinical laboratory scientist and clinical laboratory technician programs.

Eligibility This program is open to minority students who are enrolled in a program in clinical laboratory science, including clinical laboratory science/medical technology (CLS/MT) and clinical laboratory technician/medical laboratory technician (CLT/MLT). Applicants must be able to demonstrate financial need. Membership in the American Society for Clinical Laboratory Science is encouraged but not required.

Financial data Stipends depend on the need of the recipients and the availability of funds.

Duration 1 year.

Number awarded 2 each year: 1 to a CLS/MT student and 1 to a CLT/MLT student.

Deadline March of each year.

[243]
FRANCES W. HARRIS SCHOLARSHIP

New England Regional Black Nurses Association, Inc.
P.O. Box 190690
Roxbury, MA 02119
(617) 524-1951   E-mail: nerbascholarships@gmail.com
Web: nerbna.nursingnetwork.com

Summary To provide financial assistance to nursing students from New England who are of African descent and interested in working on a degree at a school in any state.

Eligibility The program is open to African American residents of the New England states who are enrolled full time in a NLN-accredited associate or bachelor's nursing program in any state. Applicants must have a GPA of 3.0 or higher and at least 1 full year of school remaining. They must be members of the New England Regional Black Nurses Association (NERBNA). Along with their application, they must submit a 3-page essay that covers their reasons for furthering their career in nursing; why minority nursing leadership is important; how minority nursing leadership can assist them in furthering their career; why they chose to prepare for a career in nursing; and any financial hardships that may hinder them from completing their education.

Financial data A stipend is awarded (amount not specified).

Duration 1 year.

Number awarded 1 or more each year.

Deadline February of each year.

[244]
FRANCIS M. KEVILLE MEMORIAL SCHOLARSHIP

Construction Management Association of America
Attn: CMAA Foundation
7926 Jones Branch Drive, Suite 800
McLean, VA 22101-3303
(703) 677-3361   E-mail: foundation@cmaanet.org
Web: www.cmaafoundation.org

Summary To provide financial assistance to African American and other minority undergraduate and graduate students working on a degree in construction management.

Eligibility This program is open to women and members of minority groups who are enrolled as full-time undergraduate or graduate students. Applicants must have completed at least 1 year of study and have at least 1 full year remaining for a bachelor's or master's degree in construction management or a related field. Along with their application, they must submit essays on why they are interested in a career in construction management and why they should be awarded this scholarship. Selection is based on that essay (20%), academic performance (40%), recommendation of the faculty adviser (15%), and extracurricular activities (25%); a bonus of 5% is given to student members of the Construction Management Association of America (CMAA).

Financial data The stipend is $5,000. Funds are disbursed directly to the student's university.

Duration 1 year.

Number awarded 1 each year.

Deadline April of each year.

[245]
FRANK GILBERT MEMORIAL SCHOLARSHIP

South Carolina Professional Association for Access and Equity
Attn: Financial Secretary
P.O. Box 71297
North Charleston, SC 29415
(843) 670-4890   E-mail: anderson4569@bellsouth.net
Web: www.scpaae.org/#!scholarships/c11tv

Summary To provide financial assistance to undergraduate students at colleges and universities in South Carolina who are African Americans or other underrepresented minorities on their campus and have been involved in public service.

Eligibility This program is open to residents of any state who have completed at least 12 semester hours at a college or university in South Carolina. Applicants must be recognized as an underrepresented ethnic minority on their campus. They must have a GPA of 3.5 or higher. Along with their application, they must submit 1) a personal letter on their public service, academic and career goals, honors and awards, leadership skills and organization participation, community service, and a statement of why they would like to receive this scholarship; and 2) a paragraph defining access and equity and describing how they can assist in achieving access and equity within South Carolina. Financial need is not considered in the selection process.

Financial data The stipend is $1,500.

Duration 1 year.

Number awarded   1 or more each year.

Deadline   February of each year.

[246]
FRANK WATTS SCHOLARSHIP

Watts Charity Association, Inc.
6245 Bristol Parkway, Suite 224
Culver City, CA 90230
(310) 671-0394   Fax: (323) 778-2613
E-mail: wattscharity@yahoo.com
Web: 4watts.tripod.com/id5.html

Summary   To provide financial assistance to upper-division African Americans interested in preparing for a career as a minister.

Eligibility   This program is open to U.S. citizens of African American descent who are enrolled full time as a college or university junior. Applicants must be studying to become a minister. They must have a GPA of 3.0 or higher, be between 17 and 24 years of age, and be able to demonstrate that they intend to continue their education for at least 2 years. Along with their application, they must submit 1) a 1-paragraph statement on why they should be awarded a Watts Charity Association scholarship; and 2) a 1- to 2-page essay on a specific type of cancer, based either on how it has impacted their life or on researched information.

Financial data   A stipend is awarded (amount not specified).

Duration   1 year.

Additional information   Royce R. Watts, Sr. established the Watts Charity Association after he learned he had cancer in 2001.

Number awarded   1 each year.

Deadline   May of each year.

[247]
FRED J. STUART SCHOLARSHIP OF ACHIEVEMENT

African Methodist Episcopal Church
Fifth Episcopal District Lay Organization
c/o Anita West-Ware, Scholarship Committee Chair
4027 East 30th Avenue
Denver, CO 80207
(303) 377-2731   E-mail: StuartScholarship@yahoo.com
Web: www.fifthdistrictlay.org/5th-district-scholarships

Summary   To provide financial assistance to members of African Methodist Episcopal (AME) churches in its Fifth Episcopal District who are high school seniors interested in attending college in any state.

Eligibility   This program is open to residents of the AME Fifth Episcopal District (Alaska, Arizona, California, Colorado, Idaho, Kansas, Missouri, Montana, Nebraska, Nevada, New Mexico, North Dakota, Oregon, South Dakota, Utah, Washington, and Wyoming) who are graduating high school seniors and planning to attend an accredited institution of higher learning in any state. Applicants must have been a member of an AME church for at least 12 months and have been an active member of its Lay Organization or other church ministry. They must have a GPA of 3.0 or higher. Along with their application, they must submit a personal essay of 250 to 300 words that describes their long-range plans, community and church involvement, accomplishments or special

awards, challenges they have faced, and how they responded. Selection is based on that essay (30%), academic record (30%), letters of recommendation (15%), participation in school and community extracurricular activities (15%), and quality of application (10%).

Financial data   The stipend is $1,000.

Duration   1 year.

Number awarded   1 each year.

Deadline   May of each year.

[248]
FREDDY MIRANDA ACCESS SCHOLARSHIP

Iowa Association for College Admission Counseling
c/o Lauren Garcia, Inclusion, Access and Success Chair
University of Iowa
Center for Diversity and Enrichment
24 Philips Hall
16 North Clinton Street
Iowa City, IA 52242-1323
(319) 335-3555   Fax: (319) 353-2537
E-mail: info@iowaacac.org
Web: www.iowaacac.com/resources-schol-

Summary   To provide financial assistance to seniors, especially African Americans and members of other underrepresented groups, at high schools that are members of the Iowa Association for College Admission Counseling (ACAC) and planning to attend college in Iowa or nearby states.

Eligibility   This program is open to seniors graduating from Iowa ACAC member high schools and planning to enroll full time at a postsecondary Iowa ACAC member institution (including those in Illinois, Kansas, Minnesota, Missouri, Nebraska, Ohio, South Dakota, and Wisconsin). Special consideration is given to those who are from underrepresented populations, first generation, or able to demonstrate financial need. Students must be nominated by a high school counselor, teaching, administrator, or board member. They must exhibit a commitment to learning and have demonstrated involvement and leadership in their schools, the community, and or service to others with a desire to complete their educational program. Letters of nomination must include a 300-word statement on why the student should receive the scholarship.

Financial data   The stipend is $1,000.

Duration   1 year.

Additional information   Contact Iowa ACAC for a list of its high school and college members.

Number awarded   2 each year.

Deadline   March of each year.

[249]
FREDERICK C. BRANCH MARINE CORPS LEADERSHIP SCHOLARSHIPS

U.S. Navy
Attn: Naval Service Training Command Officer
  Development
NAS Pensacola
250 Dallas Street
Pensacola, FL 32508-5220
(850) 452-4941, ext. 29395
Toll Free: (800) NAV-ROTC, ext. 29395
Fax: (850) 452-2486
E-mail: pnsc_nrotc.scholarship@navy.mil
Web: www.marines.com

Summary To provide financial assistance to students who are entering or enrolled at specified Historically Black Colleges or Universities (HBCUs) and interested in joining Navy ROTC to prepare for service as an officer in the U.S. Marine Corps.

Eligibility This program is open to students attending or planning to attend 1 of 17 specified HBCUs with a Navy ROTC unit on campus. Applicants may either apply through their local Marine recruiter for a 4-year scholarship or be nominated by the professor of naval science at their institution and meet academic requirements set by each school for 2- or 3-year scholarships. They must be U.S. citizens between 17 and 23 years of age who are willing to serve for 4 years as active-duty Marine Corps officers following graduation from college. They must not have reached their 27th birthday by the time of college graduation and commissioning; applicants who have prior active-duty military service may be eligible for age adjustments for the amount of time equal to their prior service, up to a maximum of 36 months. The qualifying scores are 1000 composite on the SAT or 22 composite on the ACT. Current enlisted and former military personnel are also eligible if they will complete the program by the age of 30.

Financial data These scholarships provide payment of full tuition and required educational fees, as well as a specified amount for textbooks, supplies, and equipment. The program also provides a stipend for 10 months of the year that is $250 per month as a freshman, $300 per month as a sophomore, $350 per month as a junior, and $400 per month as a senior.

Duration Scholarships are available for 2-, 3-, or 4-year terms.

Additional information Recipients must complete 4 years of study in naval science classes as students at 1 of the following HBCUs: Allen University, Clark Atlanta University, Dillard University, Florida A&M University, Hampton University, Howard University, Huston-Tillotson University, Morehouse College, Norfolk State University, Prairie View A&M University, Savannah State University, Southern University and A&M College, Spelman College, Tennessee State University, Texas Southern University, Tuskegee University, or Xavier University. After completing the program, all participants are commissioned as second lieutenants in the Marine Corps Reserve with an 8-year service obligation, including 4 years of active duty. Current military personnel who are accepted into this program are released from active duty and are not eligible for active-duty pay and allowances, medical benefits, or other active-duty entitlements.

Number awarded Varies each year.

Deadline January of each year for students applying for a 4-year scholarship through their local Marine recruiter; July of each year if applying for a 2- or 3-year scholarship through the Navy ROTC unit at their institution.

[250]
FREEMONT FOUNDATION SCHOLARSHIP PROGRAM

James M. and Emma T. Freemont Foundation
Attn: Scholarship Committee
P.O. Box 82563
Hapeville, GA 30344
E-mail: info@freemontfoundation.com
Web: www.freemontfoundation.com/scholarships.html

Summary To provide financial assistance to high school seniors planning to attend an Historically Black College or University (HBCU).

Eligibility This program is open to U.S. citizens who are seniors graduating from high schools in any state and planning to attend an HBCU. Applicants must have a GPA of 3.0 or higher and scores of at least 1800 on the SAT or 28 on the ACT. They must have a record of leadership and volunteerism in the community in non-school sponsored activities and participation in extracurricular school activities.

Financial data A stipend is awarded (amount not specified); funds are paid directly to the recipient's school.

Duration 1 year.

Number awarded Varies each year; recently, 8 were awarded.

Deadline January of each year.

[251]
FULL CIRCLE COMMUNICATIONS/MAYNARD JACKSON SCHOLARSHIP

National Forum for Black Public Administrators
Attn: Scholarship Program
777 North Capitol Street, N.E., Suite 807
Washington, DC 20002
(202) 408-9300   Fax: (202) 408-8558
E-mail: vharris@nfbpa.org
Web: www.nfbpa.org/i4a/pages/index.cfm?pageid=4047

Summary To provide financial assistance to African American undergraduate and graduate students preparing for a career in public service or a business field that supports the administration of public service.

Eligibility This program is open to African American undergraduate and graduate students preparing for a career in public service or a business field that supports the administration of public service. Applicants must be working full time on a degree in public administration, political science, urban affairs, public policy, business administration, or a related field. They must have a GPA of 3.0 or higher, a well-balanced focus of academic excellence and volunteerism/community involvement, and strong leadership and communication (oral and written) skills. Along with their application, they must submit a 3-page autobiographical essay that includes their academic and career goals and objectives. Selection is based on academic record, leadership ability, participation in school activities, community service, and financial need.

Financial data The stipend is $2,000.

Duration 1 year.

Additional information This program is sponsored by Full Circle Communications, a media management consulting firm based in Puerto Rico. Recipients are required to attend the sponsor's annual conference to receive their scholarship; limited hotel and air accommodations are arranged and provided.

Number awarded 1 each year.

Deadline March of each year.

[252]
GARRETT A. MORGAN TRANSPORTATION ACHIEVEMENT SCHOLARSHIP

Conference of Minority Transportation Officials-Michigan
　Chapter
Attn: President
P.O. Box 32439
Detroit, MI 48232
(269) 491-7279　　　　　E-mail: averyk@michigan.gov
Web: www.comtomichigan.org/scholarships.html

Summary To provide financial assistance to African American and other minority high school seniors in Michigan who plan to attend college in any state to major in a transportation-related field.

Eligibility This program is open to seniors graduating from high schools in Michigan who are members of minority groups. Applicants must be planning to attend an accredited college, university, or vocational/technical institute and major in the field of transportation or a transportation-related discipline. They must have a GPA of 2.5 or higher. U.S. citizenship or legal resident status is required.

Financial data The stipend ranges from $500 to $3,000. Funds are paid directly to the student.

Duration 1 year.

Number awarded 1 or more each year.

Deadline April of each year.

[253]
GATES MILLENNIUM SCHOLARS PROGRAM

Bill and Melinda Gates Foundation
P.O. Box 10500
Fairfax, VA 22031-8044
Toll Free: (877) 690-GMSP　　　Fax: (703) 205-2079
Web: www.gmsp.org

Summary To provide financial assistance to outstanding low-income African American and other minority students, particularly those interested in majoring in specific fields in college.

Eligibility This program is open to African Americans, Alaska Natives, American Indians, Hispanic Americans, and Asian Pacific Islander Americans who are graduating high school seniors with a GPA of 3.3 or higher. Principals, teachers, guidance counselors, tribal higher education representatives, and other professional educators are invited to nominate students with outstanding academic qualifications, particularly those likely to succeed in the fields of computer science, education, engineering, library science, mathematics, public health, or science. Nominees should have significant financial need and have demonstrated leadership abilities through participation in community service, extracurricular, or other activities. U.S. citizenship, nationality, or permanent res-

ident status is required. Nominees must be planning to enter an accredited college or university as a full-time, degree-seeking freshman in the following fall.

Financial data The program covers the cost of tuition, fees, books, and living expenses not paid for by grants and scholarships already committed as part of the recipient's financial aid package.

Duration 4 years or the completion of the undergraduate degree, if the recipient maintains at least a 3.0 GPA.

Additional information This program, established in 1999, is funded by the Bill and Melinda Gates Foundation and administered by the United Negro College Fund with support from the American Indian Graduate Center, the Hispanic Scholarship Fund, and the Asian & Pacific Islander American Scholarship Fund.

Number awarded 1,000 new scholarships are awarded each year.

Deadline January of each year.

[254]
GATEWAYS TO THE LABORATORY PROGRAM

Cornell University
Attn: Weill Cornell/Rockefeller/Sloan-Kettering Tri-
　Institutional MD-PhD Program
Gateways to the Laboratory Program
1300 York Avenue, Room C-103
New York, NY 10065-4805
(212) 746-6023　　　　　Fax: (212) 746-8678
E-mail: mdphd@med.cornell.edu
Web: weill.cornell.edu/mdphd/summerprogram

Summary To provide African American and other under-represented minority or disadvantaged college freshmen and sophomores with an opportunity to participate in a summer research internship in New York City through the Tri-Institutional MD-PhD Program of Weill Cornell Medical College, Rockefeller University, and Sloan-Kettering Institute.

Eligibility This program is open to college freshmen and sophomores who are defined by the National Institutes of Health (NIH) as in need of special recruitment and retention, i.e., members of racial and ethnic groups underrepresented in health-related sciences (Blacks or African Americans, American Indians or Alaska Natives, Hispanics or Latinos, and Native Hawaiians or Other Pacific Islanders), persons with disabilities, and individuals from disadvantaged backgrounds (low-income or from a rural or inner-city environment). Applicants must be interested in continuing on to a combined M.D./Ph.D. program following completion of their undergraduate degree. They should have a GPA of 3.0 or higher and have completed a college level calculus class. Along with their application, they must submit an essay summarizing their laboratory experience, research interests, and goals. U.S. citizenship or permanent resident status is required.

Financial data Students receive a stipend of $4,300 and reimbursement of travel expenses. At the end of the summer, 1 family member receives airfare and hotel accommodations to come to New York for the final presentations.

Duration 10 weeks, during the summer.

Additional information Interns work independently on a research project at Weill Cornell Medical College, Rockefeller University, or Memorial Sloan-Kettering Cancer Center, all located across the street from each other on the Upper East Side of New York City.

Number awarded 15 each year.

Deadline January of each year.

[255]
GAUFF/TYRANCE SCHOLARSHIP

National Naval Officers Association-Washington, D.C.
  Chapter
c/o LCDR Stephen Williams
P.O. Box 30784
Alexandria, VA 22310
(703) 644-2605   Fax: (703) 644-8503
E-mail: Stephen.Williams@navy.mil
Web: www.dcnnoa.org/dcnnoa-scholarship

Summary To provide financial assistance to African American high school seniors from the Washington, D.C. area who are interested in attending an Historically Black College or University (HBCU) in any state.

Eligibility This program is open to African American seniors graduating from high schools in the Washington, D.C. metropolitan area who plan to enroll full time at an HBCU in any state. Applicants must have a GPA of 3.0 or higher and be U.S. citizens or permanent residents. Selection is based on academic achievement, community involvement, and financial need.

Financial data The stipend is $1,000.

Duration 1 year; nonrenewable.

Additional information Recipients are not required to join or affiliate with the military in any way.

Number awarded 1 each year.

Deadline February of each year.

[256]
GENERATION GOOGLE SCHOLARSHIPS FOR CURRENT UNIVERSITY STUDENTS

Google Inc.
Attn: Scholarships
1600 Amphitheatre Parkway
Mountain View, CA 94043-8303
(650) 253-0000   Fax: (650) 253-0001
E-mail: generationgoogle@google.com
Web: www.google.com

Summary To provide financial assistance to members of African American and other underrepresented groups enrolled as undergraduate or graduate students in a computer-related field.

Eligibility This program is open to students enrolled as full-time undergraduate or graduate students at a college or university in the United States or Canada. Applicants must be members of a group underrepresented in computer science: African Americans, Hispanics, American Indians, or Filipinos/ Native Hawaiians/Pacific Islanders. They must be working on a degree in computer science, computer engineering, or a closely-related field. Selection is based on academic achievement, leadership, and passion for computer science and technology.

Financial data The stipend is $10,000 per year for U.S. students or $C5,000 for Canadian students.

Duration 1 year; may be renewed.

Additional information Recipients are also invited to attend Google's Computer Science Summer Institute at Mountain View, California, Seattle, Washington, or Cambridge, Massachusetts in the summer.

Number awarded Varies each year.

Deadline February of each year.

[257]
GENERATION GOOGLE SCHOLARSHIPS FOR HIGH SCHOOL SENIORS

Google Inc.
Attn: Scholarships
1600 Amphitheatre Parkway
Mountain View, CA 94043-8303
(650) 253-0000   Fax: (650) 253-0001
E-mail: generationgoogle@google.com
Web: www.google.com

Summary To provide financial assistance to African Americans and members of other underrepresented groups planning to work on a bachelor's degree in a computer-related field.

Eligibility This program is open to high school seniors planning to enroll full time at a college or university in the United States or Canada. Applicants must be members of a group underrepresented in computer science: African Americans, Hispanics, American Indians, Filipinos/Native Hawaiians/Pacific Islanders, women, or people with a disability. They must be interested in working on a bachelor's degree in computer science, computer engineering, or a closely-related field. Selection is based on academic achievement, leadership, and passion for computer science and technology.

Financial data The stipend is $10,000 per year for U.S. students or $C5,000 for Canadian students.

Duration 1 year; may be renewed for up to 3 additional years or until graduation, whichever comes first.

Additional information Recipients are required to attend Google's Computer Science Summer Institute at Mountain View, California, Seattle, Washington, or Cambridge, Massachusetts in the summer.

Number awarded Varies each year.

Deadline February of each year.

[258]
GENSLER DIVERSITY SCHOLARSHIP

Gensler
Attn: Donna Taliercio
2020 K Street, N.W.
Washington, DC 20006
(202) 263-5433   Fax: (202) 872-8587
E-mail: diversity@gensler.com
Web: www.gensler.com/scholarships

Summary To provide financial assistance to African American students completing a degree in architecture.

Eligibility This program is open to African American students beginning their final year of study in an accredited architecture program. They must be nominated by their institution, each of which may nominate up to 2 students. Nominees must submit an advanced-level commercial architecture project with a written description (up to 500 words and 10 pages). Selection is based on academic excellence, design ability, and presentation creativity.

Financial data A stipend is awarded (amount not specified).

Duration 1 year.

Additional information This program began in 2009.

Number awarded 3 each year.

Deadline December of each year.

[259]
GEOCORPS AMERICA DIVERSITY INTERNSHIPS

Geological Society of America
Attn: Program Officer, GeoCorps America
3300 Penrose Place
P.O. Box 9140
Boulder, CO 80301-9140
(303) 357-1025   Toll Free: (800) 472-1988, ext. 1025
Fax: (303) 357-1070   E-mail: mdawson@geosociety.org
Web: rock.geosociety.org

Summary To provide work experience at national parks to student members of the Geological Society of America (GSA) who are African Americans or members of other underrepresented groups.

Eligibility This program is open to all GSA members, but applications are especially encouraged from groups historically underrepresented in the sciences (African Americans, American Indians, Alaska Natives, Hispanics, Native Hawaiians, other Pacific Islanders, and persons with disabilities). Applicants must be interested in a short-term work experience in facilities of the U.S. government. Geoscience knowledge and skills are a significant requirement for most positions, but students from diverse disciplines (e.g., chemistry, physics, engineering, mathematics, computer science, ecology, hydrology, meteorology, the social sciences, and the humanities) are also invited to apply. Activities involve research; interpretation and education; inventory and monitoring; or mapping, surveying, and GIS. Prior interns are not eligible. U.S. citizenship or possession of a proper visa is required.

Financial data Each internship provides a $2,750 stipend. Also provided are free housing or a housing allowance of $1,500 to $2,000.

Duration 3 months during the spring, summer, fall, or winter.

Additional information This program is offered by the GSA in partnership with the National Park Service, the U.S. Forest Service, and the Bureau of Land Management.

Number awarded Varies each year.

Deadline March of each year for spring or summer positions; June of each year for fall or winter positions.

[260]
GEOLOGICAL SOCIETY OF AMERICA MINORITY STUDENT SCHOLARSHIP PROGRAM

Geological Society of America
Attn: Program Officer-Grants, Awards and Recognition
3300 Penrose Place
P.O. Box 9140
Boulder, CO 80301-9140
(303) 357-1060   Toll Free: (888) 443-4472, ext. 1060
Fax: (303) 357-1070   E-mail: awards@geosociety.org
Web: www.geosociety.org

Summary To provide financial assistance to African American and other minority undergraduate student members of the Geological Society of America (GSA) working on a degree in geoscience.

Eligibility This program is open to GSA members who are U.S. citizens and members of a minority group working on an undergraduate degree. Applicants must have taken at least 2 introductory geoscience courses and be enrolled in additional geoscience courses for the upcoming academic year. Selection is based on the scientific merits of the proposal, the capability of the investigator, and the reasonableness of the budget.

Financial data The stipend is $1,500. Funds may be used to pay college fees, purchase text books, or attend GSA field courses or conferences. Winners also receive meeting registration for the GSA annual meeting where the awards are presented and a complimentary GSA membership for the following year.

Duration 1 year.

Additional information This program is sponsored by ExxonMobil.

Number awarded 6 each year: 1 in each GSA geographic section.

Deadline January of each year.

[261]
GEORGE A. LOTTIER GOLF FOUNDATION INTERNSHIP AND SCHOLARSHIP AWARD

Atlanta Tribune: The Magazine
Attn: Editor
875 Old Roswell Road, Suite C-100
Roswell, GA 30076-1660
(770) 587-0501, ext. 202   Fax: (770) 642-6501
E-mail: internship@atlantatribune.com
Web: www.atlantatribune.com/extras

Summary To provide financial assistance and summer work experience at the *Atlanta Tribune: The Magazine* to African American and other minority upper-division and graduate students from any state interested in a career in print journalism.

Eligibility This program is open to minority college students from any state entering their junior or senior year of college or enrolled in a graduate program with a GPA of 3.0 or higher. Applicants must be majoring in a field related to print media, including communications, English, graphic design (with an emphasis on publication layout and design), journalism, marketing, or sales. Along with their application, they must submit a 500-word personal essay.

Financial data The program provides a paid internship and a scholarship stipend of $1,500.

Duration 1 year, including 10 weeks during the summer for the internship.

Number awarded Varies each year; recently, 4 of these scholarships and internships were awarded.

Deadline November of each year.

[262]
GEORGE AND PEARL STRICKLAND SCHOLARSHIP FUND

Community Foundation for Greater Atlanta, Inc.
191 Peachtree Street N.E., Suite 1000
Atlanta, GA 30303
(404) 688-5525   Fax: (404) 688-3060
E-mail: scholarships@cfgreateratlanta.org
Web: www.cfgreateratlanta.org

Summary To provide financial assistance to Georgia residents attending or planning to attend designated Historically Black Colleges and Universities in the Atlanta area.

Eligibility This program is open to residents of Georgia enrolled or accepted for enrollment as undergraduate or graduate students at Clark Atlanta University, Morehouse College, Morehouse School of Medicine, or Spelman College. Applicants must have a GPA of 2.0 or higher and be able to demonstrate financial need, potential for success in their chosen field, and commitment to community service.

Financial data The stipend ranges from $1,000 to $2,000 per year.

Duration 1 year; may be renewed.

Number awarded 20 to 30 each year.

Deadline February of each year.

[263]
GEORGE CAMPBELL, JR. FELLOWSHIP IN ENGINEERING

National Action Council for Minorities in Engineering
Attn: Director, Scholarships and University Relations
440 Hamilton Avenue, Suite 302
White Plains, NY 10601-1813
(914) 539-4316   Fax: (914) 539-4032
E-mail: scholars@nacme.org
Web: www.nacme.org/scholarships

Summary To provide financial assistance to African American and other underrepresented minority college sophomores majoring in engineering or related fields.

Eligibility This program is open to African American, Latino, and American Indian college sophomores who have a GPA of 3.0 or higher and have demonstrated academic excellence, leadership skills, and a commitment to science and engineering as a career. Applicants must be enrolled full time at an ABET-accredited engineering program. Fields of study include all areas of engineering as well as computer science, materials science, mathematics, operations research, or physics.

Financial data The stipend is $5,000 per year. Funds are sent directly to the recipient's university.

Duration Up to 3 years.

Number awarded 1 each year.

Deadline April of each year.

[264]
GEORGIA FUNERAL SERVICE PRACTITIONERS ASSOCIATION SCHOLARSHIPS

Georgia Funeral Service Practitioners Association
Attn: Scholarship Committee
55 South Alexander Street
P.O. Box 422
Toccoa, GA 30577
(404) 617-9585
Web: www.gfspa.net/education—-scholarships.html

Summary To provide financial assistance to students at mortuary schools in any state who are recommended by a member of the Georgia Funeral Service Practitioners Association, successor to the Georgia Colored Funeral Directors and Embalmers Association.

Eligibility This program is open to full-time students who have completed at least 1 of the last 3 quarters of an accredited program of mortuary science or funeral service at a school in any state. Applicants must have a GPA of 3.0 or higher and demonstrated qualities of professionalism that are needed for success in funeral service. Along with their application, they must submit an essay on their interest in funeral service, 2 letters of recommendation (including 1 from an active member of the Georgia Funeral Service Practitioners Association), transcripts, and information on their financial situation. U.S. citizenship is required.

Financial data A stipend is awarded (amount not specified).

Duration 1 year.

Additional information The Georgia Funeral Service Practitioners Association was established in 1925 as the Georgia Colored Funeral Directors and Embalmers Association, the Georgia affiliate of the National Negro Funeral Directors Association.

Number awarded 1 or more each year.

Deadline April of each year.

[265]
GLENN A. CASSIS SCHOLARSHIP

Southern New England Association of Technical Professionals
Attn: Scholarships
P.O. Box 280303
East Hartford, CT 06128-0115
E-mail: sneatp@gmail.com
Web: www.sneatp.org

Summary To provide financial assistance to high school seniors who are members of the National Society of Black Engineers (NSBE) in Connecticut or western Massachusetts and interested in studying a field of science, technology, engineering, or mathematics (STEM) at a college in any state.

Eligibility This program is open to seniors graduating from high schools in Connecticut and western Massachusetts who are active members of an NSBE Jr./NSBE PCI Chapter. Applicants must have been accepted into an ABET-accredited college or university in any state to work on a degree in a STEM field of study. They must have a GPA of 3.0 or higher. Along with their application, they must submit a 750-word essay on what has inspired them to enter the STEM field as a college major.

Financial data The stipend is $2,000.

Duration 1 year.
Number awarded 1 each year.
Deadline June of each year.

[266]
GLOSTER B. CURRENT, SR. SCHOLARSHIP

United Methodist Church-New York Annual Conference
Attn: Gloster B. Current Scholarship Committee
c/o Rev. Andrew Peck-McClain
Cornwall United Methodist Church
196 Main Street
Cornwall, NY 12518
(845) 534-2794   Fax: (914) 235-7313
E-mail: Andrew.Peck-McClain@nyac-umc.com
Web: www.nyac.com/highereducationcampusministries

Summary To provide financial assistance to Methodist undergraduate students of African descent from any state who are preparing for a career in public service.

Eligibility This program is open to members of United Methodist Church (UMC) congregations in any state who are of African descent. Applicants must be enrolled or planning to enroll at an accredited institution of higher education in any state to work on an undergraduate degree in a field of public service (e.g., the ministry, social work, health care, or government service). They must be between 16 and 25 years of age and have a GPA of at least "C" in high school and/or 2.75 or higher in college. Along with their application, they must submit a 1-page essay on their interest in a career of public service. Selection is based on academic record, leadership potential, a letter of recommendation from a UMC local pastor, and financial need.

Financial data The stipend is $1,000.
Duration 1 year; nonrenewable.
Additional information This program began in 2003.
Number awarded 1 or more each year.
Deadline April of each year.

[267]
GO ON GIRL ASPIRING WRITER SCHOLARSHIP

Go On Girl! Book Club, Inc.
P.O. Box 3368
New York, NY 10185
E-mail: writingawards@goongirl.org
Web: www.goongirl.org/scholarships/index.php

Summary To provide financial assistance to women majoring in a field related to writing at an Historically Black College or University (HBCU).

Eligibility This program is open to female U.S. citizens of African descent who are full-time freshmen, sophomores, or juniors at HBCUs majoring in a writing-related field (e.g., English, literature, journalism). Applicants must have a GPA of 2.5 or higher. Along with their application, they must submit an 800-word essay on "The Power of the Written Word."

Financial data The stipend is $1,000.
Duration 1 year.
Additional information Go On Girl! Book Club was founded in 1991 and is currently the largest reading group for Black women in the country. It first awarded this scholarship in 2001.

Number awarded 1 each year.
Deadline March of each year.

[268]
GO RED MULTICULTURAL SCHOLARSHIP FUND

American Heart Association
Attn: Go Red for Women
7272 Greenville Avenue
Dallas, TX 75231-4596
Toll Free: (800) AHA-USA1
E-mail: GoRedScholarship@heart.org
Web: www.goredforwomen.org

Summary To provide financial assistance to women who are African Americans or members of other multicultural groups who are preparing for a career in a field of health care.

Eligibility This program is open to women who are currently enrolled at an accredited college, university, health care institution, or program and have a GPA of 3.0 or higher. Applicants must be U.S. citizens or permanent residents of African American, Hispanic, Asian/Pacific Islander, or other minority origin. They must be working on an undergraduate or graduate degree as preparation for a career as a nurse, physician, or allied health care worker. Selection is based on community involvement, a personal essay, transcripts, and 2 letters of recommendation.

Financial data The stipend is $2,500.
Duration 1 year.
Additional information This program, which began in 2012, is supported by Macy's.
Number awarded 16 each year.
Deadline December of each year.

[269]
GOLDMAN SACHS SCHOLARSHIP FOR EXCELLENCE

Goldman Sachs
Attn: Human Capital Management
200 West Street, 25th Floor
New York, NY 10282
E-mail: Iris.Birungi@gs.com
Web: www.goldmansachs.com

Summary To provide financial assistance and work experience to African American and other underrepresented minority students preparing for a career in the financial services industry.

Eligibility This program is open to undergraduate students of Black, Latino, or Native American heritage. Applicants must be entering their sophomore or junior year and have a GPA of 3.4 or higher. Students with all majors and disciplines are encouraged to apply, but they must be able to demonstrate an interest in the financial services industry. Along with their application, they must submit 2 essays on the following topics: 1) the business principle of the sponsoring firm that resonates most with them personally, professionally or academically, and how they have exemplified this principle through their experiences; and 2) how they will embody the business principle they selected throughout their summer internship and as a campus ambassador of the firm. Selection is based on academic achievement, interest in the financial services industry, community involvement, and demonstrated leadership and teamwork capabilities.

Financial data Sophomores receive a stipend of $10,000, a summer internship at Goldman Sachs, an opportunity to receive a second award upon successful completion of the internship, and an offer to return for a second summer internship. Juniors receive a stipend of $15,000 and a summer internship at Goldman Sachs.

Duration Up to 2 years.

Additional information This program was initiated in 1994 when it served only students at 4 designated Historically Black Colleges and Universities: Florida A&M University, Howard University, Morehouse College, and Spelman College. It has since been expanded to serve underrepresented minority students in all states.

Number awarded 1 or more each year.

Deadline December of each year.

[270]
GORDON STAFFORD SCHOLARSHIP IN ARCHITECTURE

Stafford King Wiese Architects
Attn: Scholarship Selection Committee
622 20th Street
Sacramento, CA 95811
(916) 930-5900   Fax: (916) 290-0100
E-mail: info@skwaia.com
Web: www.skwarchitects.com/about/scholarship

Summary To provide financial assistance to African Americans and members of other minority groups from California interested in studying architecture at a college in any state.

Eligibility This program is open to California residents currently enrolled at accredited schools of architecture in any state as first-year new or first-year transfer students and working on a bachelor's or 5-year master's degree. Applicants must be able to demonstrate minority status (defined as Black, Hispanic, Native American, Pacific Asian, or Asian Indian). They must submit a 500-word statement expressing their desire to prepare for a career in architecture. Finalists are interviewed and must travel to Sacramento, California at their own expense for the interview.

Financial data The stipend is $3,000 per year. That includes $1,500 deposited in the recipient's school account and $1,500 paid to the recipient directly.

Duration 1 year; may be renewed up to 4 additional years.

Additional information This program began in 1995.

Number awarded Up to 5 each year.

Deadline June of each year.

[271]
GREAT LAKES SECTION IFT DIVERSITY SCHOLARSHIP

Institute of Food Technologists-Great Lakes Section
c/o Andrea Kirk, Scholarship Chair
Post Foods, LLC
275 Cliff Street
Battle Creek, MI 49014
E-mail: greatlakesift@gmail.com
Web: www.greatlakesift.org/student-scholarships

Summary To provide financial assistance to African American and other minority members of the Great Lakes Section of the Institute of Food Technologists (IFT) from any state

who are working on an undergraduate or graduate degree related to food technology at a college in Michigan.

Eligibility This program is open to minority residents of any state who are members of the IFT Great Lakes Section (GLS) and working full time on an undergraduate or graduate degree in food science, nutrition, food engineering, food packaging, or related fields at a college or university in Michigan. Applicants must have a GPA of 3.0 or higher and plans for a career in the food industry. Along with their application, they must submit a 1-page personal statement that covers their academic program, future plans and career goals, extracurricular activities (including involvement in community, university, GLS, or national IFT activities), and work experience. Financial need is not considered in the selection process.

Financial data The stipend is $1,000.

Duration 1 year; nonrenewable.

Number awarded 1 each year.

Deadline February of each year.

[272]
GREATER HARTFORD CHAPTER NABA SCHOLARSHIP ESSAY CONTEST

National Association of Black Accountants-Greater
  Hartford Chapter
Attn: Ronita Fisher, Scholarship Committee
P.O. Box 0242
Hartford, CT 06141
E-mail: nabaghc@gmail.com
Web: www.nabahartford.org/scholarships.php

Summary To recognize and reward, with scholarships for additional study, undergraduate and graduate accounting students, especially African Americans and other minorities, at colleges and universities in southern and western New England who submit outstanding essays.

Eligibility This competition is open to undergraduate and graduate accounting students enrolled full time at 2- and 4-year colleges and universities in southern and western New England. Graduate students must have entered graduate school immediately after receiving their undergraduate degree. Applicants must submit an essay of 500 to 700 words on their choice of 3 assigned topics that change annually but relate to minorities in accounting. They must also submit a 100-word personal statement describing their involvement in the National Association of Black Accountants (NABA), career objectives, leadership ability, and community activities. In the selection process, consideration is also given to academic excellence, civic responsibility in the community, and need. All students are eligible to apply, but a goal of the sponsoring organization is to address the concerns of minorities entering the accounting profession.

Financial data The award is a $1,000 scholarship.

Duration The competition is held annually.

Additional information This program began in 2008.

Number awarded Up to 10 each year.

Deadline March of each year.

[273]
HALLIE Q. BROWN SCHOLARSHIPS

National Association of Colored Women's Clubs
1601 R Street, N.W.
Washington, DC 20009
(202) 667-4080   Fax: (202) 667-2574
E-mail: cearly@nacwcya.org
Web: www.nacwc.org/programs/scholarships.html

Summary To provide financial assistance for college to students who are nominated by a member of the National Association of Colored Women's Clubs.

Eligibility This program is open to students who have completed at least 1 semester of postsecondary education. Candidates must be nominated by a member of the National Association of Colored Women's Clubs; the nomination must be endorsed by the member's club and the club's region. Nominees must have a GPA of 2.0 or higher and be able to demonstrate financial need.

Financial data The amount awarded varies, according to financial need, and has ranged from $1,000 to $2,000 per year.

Duration The award is presented biennially, in even-numbered years.

Additional information In the past, recipients were to attend 1 of the United Negro College Fund universities or colleges; now, recipients may enroll in any accredited postsecondary institution of their choice.

Number awarded Approximately 20 every other year.

Deadline March of even-numbered years.

[274]
HAMPTON ROADS BLACK MEDIA PROFESSIONALS COLLEGE SCHOLARSHIPS

Hampton Roads Black Media Professionals
Attn: Education/Scholarship Chair
P.O. Box 2622
Norfolk, VA 23501-2622
(757) 446-2273 E-mail: larry.rubama@pilotonline.com
Web: www.hrbmp.org

Summary To provide financial assistance to outstanding African American undergraduate students in the Hampton Roads area of Virginia who are preparing for a career in journalism.

Eligibility This program is open to 1) African American undergraduate students from any state working on media-related degrees at a college or university in the Hampton Roads area of Virginia; and 2) African American students who are residents of Hampton Roads and pursuing media-related degrees at a college or university anywhere in Virginia. Applicants must have a GPA of 3.0 or higher in their major and 2.5 or higher overall. Along with their application, they must submit a college transcript, a list of extracurricular activities, 2 letters of recommendation, an essay of 500 to 1,200 words on an assigned topic related to current issues in journalism, another essay of 500 to 1,200 words on their commitment to a career in journalism or other media-related fields, and samples of their work in their student newspaper or broadcast program.

Financial data Stipends are $1,000 or $500.

Duration 1 year; may be renewed.

Number awarded Varies each year; recently, 1 at $1,000 and 4 at $500 were awarded.

Deadline April of each year.

[275]
HANDY SIMMONS SCHOLARSHIP

African Methodist Episcopal Church
Women's Missionary Society
c/o Loretta Howell-Lillard
3270 Walton Riverwood Lane, Number 1039
Atlanta, GA 30339
(404) 771-5713   Fax: (404) 254-1171
E-mail: lorettahowell@yahoo.com
Web: www.wmsscholarship.org/application_information

Summary To provide financial assistance to members of African Methodist Episcopal (AME) churches who are attending college.

Eligibility This program is open to active members of AME churches and its Young People's Department (YPD). Applicants must be currently enrolled as college freshmen, sophomores, or juniors and working on an associate, technical, or bachelor's degree in any field. They must have a GPA of 2.5 or higher. Along with their application, they must submit an essay of 500 to 1,000 words on a topic that changes annually but relates to Christian themes. Selection is based on that essay, academic performance, quality and level of church participation, leadership and extracurricular activities, letters of reference, and financial need.

Financial data Stipends range from $300 to $1,000.

Duration 1 year.

Number awarded 1 or more each year.

Deadline March of each year.

[276]
HAROLD HAYDEN MEMORIAL SCHOLARSHIP

National Organization of Black County Officials
1425 K Street, N.W., Suite 350
Washington, DC 20005
(202) 350-6696   Fax: (202) 350-6699
E-mail: nobco@nocboinc.org
Web: www.nobcoinc.org/scholarship.html

Summary To provide financial assistance for college to high school and currently-enrolled college students nominated by members of the National Association of Black County Officials (NABCO).

Eligibility This program is open to high school seniors and currently-enrolled college students. Applicants must submit an endorsement from a NABCO member and a brief (up to 3 pages) autobiographical essay. Selection is based on academic record, leadership record, character and personality, personal achievement, interest in government and politics, and commitment to human and civil rights. Financial need is not considered in the selection process.

Financial data A stipend is awarded (amount not specified).

Duration 1 year.

Additional information This fund was established in 1984 to honor a co-founder of the NABCO.

Number awarded Varies each year; recently, 5 were awarded.

Deadline June of each year.

[277]
HARRY R. KENDALL LEADERSHIP DEVELOPMENT SCHOLARSHIPS

United Methodist Church
General Board of Global Ministries
Attn: United Methodist Committee on Relief
Health and Welfare Ministries
475 Riverside Drive, Room 330
New York, NY 10115
(212) 870-3871   Toll Free: (800) UMC-GBGM
E-mail: jyoung@gbgm-umc.org
Web: umc-gbcs.org/conference-connections/grants

Summary To provide financial assistance to African Americans who are Methodists or other Christians and preparing for a career in a health-related field.

Eligibility This program is open to undergraduate and graduate students who are U.S. citizens or permanent residents of African American descent. Applicants must be professed Christians, preferably United Methodists. They must be planning to enter a health care field or already be a practitioner in such a field. Financial need is considered in the selection process.

Financial data The stipend is $2,000.

Duration 1 year.

Additional information This program began in 1980.

Number awarded Varies each year.

Deadline June of each year.

[278]
HARVARD AMGEN SCHOLARS PROGRAM

Harvard College
Attn: Office of Undergraduate Research and Fellowships
77 Dunster Street, Second Floor
Cambridge, MA 02138
(617) 496-6220   E-mail: amgenscholars@harvard.edu
Web: uraf.harvard.edu/amgen-scholars

Summary To provide an opportunity for undergraduates, especially African Americans and members of other underrepresented groups, to participate in summer research projects in the biological sciences at Harvard University.

Eligibility This program is open to sophomores, juniors, and non-graduating seniors at 4-year colleges and universities in the United States, Puerto Rico, and other U.S. territories. Applicants must be U.S. citizens or permanent residents who have a cumulative GPA of 3.2 or higher and an interest in preparing for a Ph.D. or M.D./Ph.D. They must be interested in working on a summer research project at Harvard in fields of biotechnology. Applications are encouraged from members of groups traditionally underrepresented in fields of biotechnology: African American/Black, Chicano/Latino/Hispanic, Puerto Rican, American Indian/Alaskan Native, Pacific Islander, women, and those with disabilities, as well as students who come from rural or inner-city areas and individuals whose backgrounds and experiences would bring diversity to the biotechnology fields.

Financial data Scholars receive a stipend of $4,000, a meal allowance of $500, housing in a residential River House of Harvard, and, for non-Harvard students, travel to and from Boston.

Duration 10 weeks during the summer.

Additional information This program serves as the Harvard component of the Amgen Scholars Program, which operates at 8 other U.S. universities (and the National Institutes of Health) and is funded by the Amgen Foundation.

Number awarded Approximately 20 each year.

Deadline January of each year.

[279]
HARVARD SCHOOL OF PUBLIC HEALTH SUMMER INTERNSHIPS IN BIOLOGICAL SCIENCES IN PUBLIC HEALTH

Harvard T.H. Chan School of Public Health
Attn: Summer Program Coordinator
677 Huntington Avenue, SPH2-119
Boston, MA 02115
(617) 432-4397   Fax: (617) 432-0433
E-mail: BPH@hsph.harvard.edu
Web: www.hsph.harvard.edu

Summary To enable African American and other minority or disadvantaged college science students to participate in a summer research internship in biological sciences at Harvard School of Public Health.

Eligibility This program is open to U.S. citizens, nationals, and permanent residents who are 1) members of ethnic groups underrepresented in graduate education (African Americans, Hispanics/Latinos, American Indians, Alaskan Natives, Pacific Islanders, and Native Hawaiians); 2) first-generation college students; and 3) students from an economically disadvantaged background. Applicants must be entering their junior or senior year with a GPA of 3.0 or higher and be interested in preparing for a research career in the biological sciences. They must be interested in participating in a summer research project related to biological science questions that are important to the prevention of disease, especially such public health questions as cancer, infections (malaria, tuberculosis, parasites), lung diseases, common diseases of aging, diabetes, and obesity.

Financial data The program provides a stipend of at least $3,600, a travel allowance of up to $500, and free dormitory housing.

Duration 8 weeks, beginning in mid-June.

Additional information Interns conduct research under the mentorship of Harvard faculty members who are specialists in cancer cell biology, immunology and infectious diseases, molecular and cellular toxicology, environmental health sciences, nutrition, and cardiovascular research. Funding for this program is provided by the National Institutes of Health.

Number awarded Up to 10 each year.

Deadline January of each year.

[280]
HATTIE J. HILLIARD SCHOLARSHIP

Wisconsin Women of Color Network, Inc.
c/o P.E. Kiram
756 North 35th Street, Suite 101
Milwaukee, WI 53208
(414) 899-2329   E-mail: pekiram64@gmail.com

Summary To provide financial assistance to African Americans and other women of color from Wisconsin who are interested in studying art at a school in any state.

Eligibility This program is open to residents of Wisconsin who are women of color enrolled or planning to enroll at a college, university, or vocational/technical school in any state. Applicants must be a member of 1 of the following groups: African American, Asian, American Indian, or Hispanic. Their field of study must be art, graphic art, commercial art, or a related area. They must be able to demonstrate financial need. Along with their application, they must submit a 1-page essay on how this scholarship will help them accomplish their educational goal. U.S. citizenship is required.

Financial data A stipend is awarded (amount not specified).

Duration 1 year.

Additional information This program began in 1995.

Number awarded 1 each year.

Deadline May of each year.

[281]
HAYNES/HETTING AWARD

Philanthrofund Foundation
Attn: Scholarship Committee
1409 Willow Street, Suite 109
Minneapolis, MN 55403-2241
(612) 870-1806   Toll Free: (800) 435-1402
Fax: (612) 871-6587   E-mail: info@PfundOnline.org
Web: www.pfundonline.org/scholarships.html

Summary To provide funds to African American and Native American Minnesota students who have supported gay, lesbian, bisexual, and transgender (GLBT) activities.

Eligibility This program is open to residents of Minnesota and students attending a Minnesota educational institution who are African American or Native American. Applicants must be self-identified as GLBT or from a GLBT family. They may be attending or planning to attend a trade school, technical college, college, or university (as an undergraduate or graduate student). Selection is based on the applicant's 1) affirmation of GLBT or allied identity; 2) evidence of experience and skills in service and leadership; and 3) evidence of service, leading, and working for change in GLBT communities, including serving as a role model, mentor, and/or adviser.

Financial data The stipend is $5,000. Funds must be used for tuition, books, fees, or dissertation expenses.

Duration 1 year.

Number awarded 1 each year.

Deadline January of each year.

[282]
HEALTH RESEARCH AND EDUCATIONAL TRUST SCHOLARSHIPS

New Jersey Hospital Association
Attn: Health Research and Educational Trust
760 Alexander Road
P.O. Box 1
Princeton, NJ 08543-0001
(609) 275-4224   Fax: (609) 452-8097
E-mail: jhritz@njha.com
Web: www.njha.com/education/scholarships

Summary To provide financial assistance to New Jersey residents, especially African Americans and other minorities, who are working on an undergraduate or graduate degree in a field related to health care administration at a school in any state.

Eligibility This program is open to residents of New Jersey enrolled in an upper-division or graduate program in hospital or health care administration, public administration, nursing, or other allied health profession at a school in any state. Graduate students working on an advanced degree to prepare to teach nursing are also eligible. Applicants must have a GPA of 3.0 or higher and be able to demonstrate financial need. Along with their application, they must submit a 2-page essay (on which 50% of the selection is based) describing their academic plans for the future. Minorities and women are especially encouraged to apply.

Financial data The stipend is $2,000.

Duration 1 year.

Additional information This program began in 1983.

Number awarded Varies each year; recently, 3 were awarded.

Deadline June of each year.

[283]
HERMAN J. NEAL ACCOUNTING TUITION SCHOLARSHIPS

Illinois CPA Society
Attn: CPA Endowment Fund of Illinois
550 West Jackson, Suite 900
Chicago, Il 60661-5716
(312) 993-0407   Toll Free: (800) 993-0407 (within IL)
Fax: (312) 993-9432
Web: www.icpas.org

Summary To provide financial assistance to African American residents of Illinois enrolled as upper-division or graduate students in accounting at a college or university in the state.

Eligibility This program is open to African American residents of Illinois enrolled as juniors, seniors, or graduate student at a college or university in the state. Applicants must be studying accounting and have a GPA of 3.0 or higher. They must be able to demonstrate a commitment to becoming a C.P.A. and financial need. U.S. citizenship or permanent resident status is required.

Financial data The maximum stipend is $4,000 for payment of tuition and fees.

Duration 1 year.

Additional information The scholarship does not cover the cost of C.P.A. examination review courses. Recipients may not receive a full graduate assistantship, fellowship, or scholarship from a college or university, participate in a full-tuition reimbursement cooperative education or internship program, or participate in an employee full-tuition reimbursement program during the scholarship period.

Number awarded Varies each year; recently, 4 were awarded.

Deadline March of each year.

[284]
HERMAN S. DREER SCHOLARSHIP/ LEADERSHIP AWARD

Omega Psi Phi Fraternity
Attn: Charles R. Drew Memorial Scholarship Commission
3951 Snapfinger Parkway
Decatur, GA 30035-3203
(404) 284-5533   Fax: (404) 284-0333
E-mail: scholarshipchairman@oppf.org
Web: www.oppf.org/scholarship

Summary   To provide financial assistance to undergraduate Omega Psi Phi Fraternity men who can demonstrate leadership and humanitarian accomplishments.

Eligibility   This program is open to members of Omega Psi Phi at 4-year colleges and universities who are full-time sophomores or higher and have a GPA of 3.0 or higher. Each of the fraternity's 12 district representatives may nominate 1 member. Candidates must submit 1) a statement of 200 to 250 words on their purpose for applying for this scholarship, how they believe funds from the fraternity can assist them in achieving their career goals, and other circumstances (including financial need) that make it important for them to receive financial assistance; and 2) a 500-word essay detailing their leadership and humanitarian accomplishments. The award is given to the undergraduate student best exemplifying the fraternity's principles of manhood, scholarship, perseverance, and uplift.

Financial data   The stipend is $5,000.

Duration   1 year.

Additional information   The winner is required to attend the Omega Psi Phi Grand Conclave or Leadership Conference. Up to $1,000 in travel expenses for attendance is provided.

Number awarded   1 each year.

Deadline   April of each year.

[285]
HERSHEY SCHOLARSHIPS OF THE THURGOOD MARSHALL COLLEGE FUND

Thurgood Marshall College Fund
Attn: Senior Manager of Scholarship Programs
901 F Street, N.W., Suite 300
Washington, DC 20004
(202) 507-4851   Fax: (202) 652-2934
E-mail: deshuandra.walker@tmcfund.org
Web: www.tmcf.org

Summary   To provide financial assistance to African American upper-division students working on a degree in designated fields at public Historically Black Colleges and Universities (HBCUs) that are members of the Thurgood Marshall College Fund (TMCF).

Eligibility   This program is open to students currently enrolled as juniors or seniors at any of the 47 TMCF member institutions. Applicants must be majoring in a field of STEM (science, technology, engineering, or mathematics), finance, sales, or supply chain management. They must have a GPA of 3.0 or higher and be able to demonstrate financial need. Along with their application, they must submit a 500-word essay on their interest in their major, their commitment to achieving a degree in that area, and their long-term profes-

sional goals. U.S. citizenship or permanent resident status is required.

Financial data   The stipend is $3,100 per semester ($6,200 per year). Funds are awarded through the institution to be used for tuition, on-campus room and board, and required textbooks.

Duration   1 year; nonrenewable.

Additional information   This program is sponsored by the Hershey Company.

Number awarded   1 or more each year.

Deadline   April of each year.

[286]
HHS/COLLEGE PARK COMPLEX CHAPTER BIG SCHOLARSHIP AWARDS

Blacks in Government-Department of Health and Human
   Services/College Park Complex Chapter
c/o Rhona Johnson, Scholarship Committee Chair
U.S. Food and Drug Administration/HFS-317
5100 Paint Branch Parkway
College Park, MD 20740
(240) 402-2066   E-mail: Rhona.Johnson@fda.hhs.gov
Web: www.bignet.org

Summary   To provide financial assistance to high school seniors in the Washington, D.C. area who submit outstanding essays on Black History Month and plan to attend college in any state.

Eligibility   This program is open to seniors graduating from high schools in the Washington D.C. area (including the counties of Charles, Montgomery, and Prince George's in Maryland, the counties of Arlington, Fairfax, Loudoun, and Prince William in Virginia, and the cities of Alexandria, Fairfax, and Falls Church in Virginia). Applicants must be planning to enroll full time at a 4-year college or university in any state. They must have a GPA of 2.75 or higher. Along with their application, they must submit a 1- to 3-page essay on a topic that changes annually but relates to the theme of Black History Month for that year. Relatives of members of the sponsoring organization are not eligible. The program includes Reginald Bennett and Garnett Wood Book Awards.

Financial data   Academic stipends are $1,000 and book awards are $500.

Duration   1 year.

Additional information   The sponsoring organization is comprised of African American civil service employees of the Department of Health and Human Services and its Food and Drug Administration who work in Washington, D.C. and College Park, Maryland.

Number awarded   3 academic scholarships and 2 book awards are presented each year.

Deadline   March of each year.

[287]
HILIARY H. HOLLOWAY PROVINCE SCHOLARSHIPS

Kappa Alpha Psi Fraternity
Attn: Foundation
2322 North Broad Street
Philadelphia, PA 19132
(215) 225-6566   Fax: (215) 225-2205
E-mail: info@thekappafoundation.org
Web: www.thekappafoundation.org/scholarships

Summary   To provide financial assistance to members of Kappa Alpha Psi Fraternity, a traditionally African American men's organization, who demonstrate outstanding achievement.

Eligibility   This program is open to undergraduate members of the fraternity who apply to their regional Province. Each Province determines its own criteria for selection, but they normally consider academic performance, extracurricular activities, and fraternity and community involvement.

Financial data   A stipend is awarded (amount not specified).

Duration   1 year.

Number awarded   Up to 12 each year: 1 for each of the fraternity's provinces.

Deadline   Each Province establishes its own deadline.

[288]
HNTB SCHOLARSHIP

Conference of Minority Transportation Officials
Attn: National Scholarship Program
100 M Street, S.E., Suite 917
Washington, DC 20003
(202) 506-2917   E-mail: info@comto.org
Web: www.comto.org/page/scholarships

Summary   To provide financial assistance to African American and other minority high school seniors interested in working on a degree in transportation or a related field.

Eligibility   This program is open to minority seniors graduating from high school with a GPA of 3.0 or higher. Applicants must have been accepted at an accredited university or technical college with the intent to study transportation or a transportation-related discipline. They must be able to demonstrate leadership skills and activities. Along with their application they must submit a cover letter on their transportation-related career goals and life aspirations. Financial need is not considered in the selection process.

Financial data   The stipend is $5,000. Funds are paid directly to the recipient's college or university.

Duration   1 year.

Additional information   This program is sponsored by HNTB Corporation.

Number awarded   1 each year.

Deadline   April of each year.

[289]
HOB SCHOLARSHIP PROGRAM

House of Blahnik
2939 Turner Street
Philadelphia, PA 19121
(215) 431-1790   E-mail: info@houseofblahnik.org
Web: houseofblahnik.org

Summary   To provide financial assistance for college to lesbian, gay, bisexual, and transgender (LBGT) people of color who are members of the house/ballroom community.

Eligibility   This program is open to members of the house/ballroom community who are enrolled or applying to a college, university, or vocational program. Applicants must submit a personal statement regarding their work and aspirations, unofficial transcripts or a letter of acceptance to the institution they are planning to attend, and 2 letters of reference. The program includes scholarships for formal members of the House of Blahnik and for non-members who have demonstrated outstanding contributions to their local community and to their own personal and professional development.

Financial data   The stipend normally is $1,000.

Duration   1 year.

Additional information   The House of Blahnik was founded in 2000 by African American and Latino gay and transgender persons to provide support to the ballroom community. This program began in 2008.

Number awarded   2 each year: 1 to a formal member of the House of Blahnik and 1 to a non-member.

Deadline   December of each year.

[290]
HONDA SWE SCHOLARSHIPS

Society of Women Engineers
Attn: Scholarship Selection Committee
203 North LaSalle Street, Suite 1675
Chicago, IL 60601-1269
(312) 596-5223   Toll Free: (877) SWE-INFO
Fax: (312) 644-8557   E-mail: scholarships@swe.org
Web: societyofwomenengineers.swe.org

Summary   To provide financial assistance to undergraduate women from designated states, especially African Americans and members of other underrepresented groups, who are majoring in designated engineering specialties.

Eligibility   This program is open to SWE members who are entering their junior or senior year at a 4-year ABET-accredited college or university. Preference is given to members of underrepresented ethnic or racial groups, candidates with disabilities, and veterans. Applicants must be U.S. citizens working full time on a degree in automotive engineering, chemical engineering, computer science, electrical engineering, engineering technology, manufacturing engineering, materials science and engineering, or mechanical engineering. They must be residents of or attending college in Illinois, Indiana, Michigan, Ohio, Pennsylvania, or Wisconsin. Financial need is considered in the selection process.

Financial data   The stipend is $1,000.

Duration   1 year.

Additional information   This program is sponsored by American Honda Motor Company.

Number awarded   5 each year.

Deadline   February of each year.

[291]
HONEYWELL SCHOLARSHIPS

Society of Women Engineers
Attn: Scholarship Selection Committee
203 North LaSalle Street, Suite 1675
Chicago, IL 60601-1269
(312) 596-5223   Toll Free: (877) SWE-INFO
Fax: (312) 644-8557   E-mail: scholarships@swe.org
Web: societyofwomenengineers.swe.org

Summary To provide financial assistance to members of the Society of Women Engineers (SWE) from designated states, especially African Americans and members of other underrepresented groups, interested in studying specified fields of engineering in college.

Eligibility This program is open to SWE members who are rising college sophomores, juniors, or seniors and have a GPA of 3.5 or higher. Applicants must be enrolled full time at an ABET-accredited 4-year college or university and major in computer science or aerospace, automotive, chemical, computer, electrical, industrial, manufacturing, materials, mechanical, or petroleum engineering. They must reside or attend college in Arizona, California, Florida, Indiana, Kansas, Minnesota, New Mexico, Puerto Rico, Texas, or Washington. Preference is given to members of groups underrepresented in computer science and engineering who can demonstrate financial need. U.S. citizenship is required.

Financial data The stipend is $5,000.

Duration 1 year.

Additional information This program is sponsored by Honeywell International Inc.

Number awarded 3 each year.

Deadline February of each year for current college students; May of each year for high school seniors.

[292]
HONORABLE ERNESTINE WASHINGTON LIBRARY SCIENCE/ENGLISH LANGUAGE ARTS SCHOLARSHIP

African-American/Caribbean Education Association, Inc.
P.O. Box 1224
Valley Stream, NY 11582-1224
(718) 949-6733   E-mail: aaceainc@yahoo.com
Web: www.aaceainc.com/Scholarships.html

Summary To provide financial assistance to high school seniors of African American or Caribbean heritage who plan to study a field related to library science or English language arts in college.

Eligibility This program is open to graduating high school seniors who are U.S. citizens of African American or Caribbean heritage. Applicants must be planning to attend a college or university and major in a field related to library science or English language arts. They must have completed 4 years of specified college preparatory courses with a grade of 90 or higher and have an SAT score of at least 1790. They must also have completed at least 200 hours of community service during their 4 years of high school, preferably in the field that they plan to study in college. Financial need is not considered in the selection process. New York residency is not required, but applicants must be available for an interviews in the Queens, New York area.

Financial data The stipend ranges from $1,000 to $1,500. Funds are paid directly to the recipient.

Duration 1 year.

Number awarded 1 each year.

Deadline April of each year.

[293]
HORACE AND SUSIE REVELS CAYTON SCHOLARSHIP

Public Relations Society of America-Puget Sound Chapter
Attn: Diane Bevins
1006 Industry Drive
P.O. Box 58530
Seattle, WA 98138-1530
(206) 623-8632   Fax: (206) 575-9255
E-mail: prsascholarship@asi-seattle.net
Web: www.prsapugetsound.org/Page.aspx?nid=73

Summary To provide financial assistance to African American and other minority upperclassmen from Washington who are interested in preparing for a career in public relations.

Eligibility This program is open to U.S. citizens who are members of minority groups, defined as African Americans, Asian Americans, Hispanic/Latino Americans, Native Americans, and Pacific Islanders. Applicants must be full-time juniors or seniors attending a college in Washington or Washington students (who graduated from a Washington high school or whose parents live in the state year-round) attending college elsewhere. They must have overcome barriers in pursuit of personal or academic goals. Selection is based on academic achievement, financial need, and demonstrated aptitude in public relations and related courses, activities, and/or internships.

Financial data The stipend is $3,500.

Duration 1 year.

Additional information This program began in 1992.

Number awarded 1 each year.

Deadline May of each year.

[294]
HOUSTON CHAPTER AABE SCHOLARSHIPS

American Association of Blacks in Energy-Houston Chapter
Attn: Scholarship Committee
P.O. Box 132723
Spring, TX 77393-2723
E-mail: scholarships@aabehouston.org
Web: www.aabe.org/index.php?component=pages&id=335

Summary To provide financial assistance to African Americans and members of other underrepresented minority groups who are high school seniors in Texas and planning to major in an energy-related field at a college in any state.

Eligibility This program is open to seniors graduating from high schools in Texas and planning to attend a college or university in any state. Applicants must be African Americans, Hispanics, or Native Americans who have a GPA of 3.0 or higher and who have taken the ACT and/or SAT test. Their intended major must be business, engineering, technology, mathematics, the physical sciences, or other energy-related field. Along with their application, they must submit a 350-word essay that includes 1) when they discovered their interest in the field of energy and what sparked their interest; and 2) either what excites them about the field of energy or how they expect their education to prepare them for the field of energy. Financial need is not considered in the selection process.

Financial data   Stipend amounts vary; a total of $10,000 is available for this program each year.

Duration   1 year.

Additional information   Winners are eligible to compete for regional and national scholarships.

Number awarded   3 or more each year.

Deadline   March of each year.

[295]
HOUSTON CHAPTER NBMBAA SCHOLARSHIP PROGRAM

National Black MBA Association-Houston Chapter
Attn: Scholarship Program
P.O. Box 56509
Houston, TX 77256
(713) 899-8657
E-mail: scholarships@houstonblackmba.net
Web: nbmbaa.pgmsolutions.com

Summary   To provide financial assistance to African American business and management students who have a connection to Houston and are working on an undergraduate or master's degree.

Eligibility   This program is open to African American students who are either enrolled at a college or university in the Houston area or natives of Houston enrolled at a college or university in the continental United States. Applicants must be sophomores, juniors, seniors, or master's degree students in a business or management program. Along with their application, they must submit an essay of 650 to 1,000 words identifying 5 critical skills they must obtain while they are completing their degree that will make them the most attractive candidate for internships and full-time employment upon graduation. Financial need is not considered in the selection process.

Financial data   A stipend is awarded (amount not specified).

Duration   1 year.

Number awarded   Varies each year.

Deadline   November of each year.

[296]
HOUSTON SUN SCHOLARSHIP

National Association of Negro Business and Professional Women's Clubs
Attn: Scholarship Committee
1806 New Hampshire Avenue, N.W.
Washington, DC 20009-3206
(202) 483-4206   Fax: (202) 462-7253
E-mail: arlucas48@gmail.com
Web: www.nanbpwc.org/index-11.html

Summary   To provide financial assistance to African Americans from designated states studying journalism at a college in any state.

Eligibility   This program is open to African Americans (men or women) who are residents of Arkansas, Kansas, Louisiana, Missouri, New Mexico, Oklahoma, or Texas. Applicants

must be enrolled at an accredited college or university in any state as a sophomore or junior. They must have a GPA of 3.0 or higher and be majoring in journalism. Along with their application, they must submit an essay, up to 750 words in length, on the topic, "Credo of the Black Press." U.S. citizenship is required.

Financial data   The stipend is $1,000.

Duration   1 year.

Number awarded   1 or more each year.

Deadline   February of each year.

[297]
HUBERTUS W.V. WILLEMS SCHOLARSHIP FOR MALE STUDENTS

POISE Foundation
Two Gateway Center, Suite 1700
603 Stanwix Street
Pittsburgh, PA 15222
(412) 281-4967   Fax: (412) 562-0292
Web: www.poisefoundation.org

Summary   To provide funding to males, particularly male members of the National Association for the Advancement of Colored People (NAACP), who are interested in undergraduate or graduate education in selected scientific fields.

Eligibility   This program is open to males who are high school seniors, college students, or graduate students. Applicants must be majoring (or planning to major) in 1 of the following fields: engineering, chemistry, physics, or mathematics. Preference is given to members of the NAACP. The required minimum GPA is 2.5 for graduating high school seniors and undergraduate students or 3.0 for graduate students. Undergraduates must be enrolled full time but graduate students may be full- or part-time students. Applicants must be able to demonstrate financial need, defined as a family income of less than $16,755 for a family of 1 ranging to less than $58,335 for a family of 7. Along with their application, they must submit a 1-page essay on their interest in their major and a career, their life's ambition, what they hope to accomplish in their lifetime, and what position they hope to attain. Full-time enrollment is required for undergraduate students, although graduate students may be enrolled full or part time. U.S. citizenship is required.

Financial data   The stipend ranges up to $3,000 per year.

Duration   1 year; may be renewed.

Additional information   This program is managed by POISE Foundation on behalf of the NAACP.

Number awarded   Approximately 20 to 40 each year.

Deadline   March of each year.

[298]
HURSTON/WRIGHT AWARD FOR COLLEGE WRITERS

Zora Neale Hurston/Richard Wright Foundation
Attn: Hurston/Wright Awards
840 First Street, N.E., Third Floor
Washington, DC 20002
(202) 248-5051   E-mail: info@hurstonwright.org
Web: www.hurstonwright.org/programs/college-awards

Summary   To recognize and reward the best fiction and poetry written by undergraduate or graduate students of African descent.

Eligibility This program is open to students of African descent who are enrolled full time as undergraduate or graduate students at a college or university in the United States. Applicants should submit a manuscript of fiction (up to 20 pages) or poetry (up to 3 poems). Only 1 entry may be submitted per applicant. Writers who have already published a book (in any genre) are ineligible.

Financial data Cash prizes are awarded (amount not specified).

Duration The prizes are awarded annually.

Additional information There is a $25 processing fee.

Number awarded Varies each year; recently, 3 fiction writers and 1 poet received these awards.

Deadline January of each year.

[299]
HYATT HOTELS FUND FOR MINORITY LODGING MANAGEMENT STUDENTS

American Hotel & Lodging Educational Foundation
Attn: Manager of Foundation Programs
1250 I Street, N.W., Suite 1100
Washington, DC 20005-5904
(202) 289-3180   Fax: (202) 289-3199
E-mail: foundation@ahlef.org
Web: www.ahlef.org

Summary To provide financial assistance to African American and other minority college students working on a degree in hotel management.

Eligibility This program is open to students majoring in hospitality management at a 4-year college or university as at least a junior. Applicants must be members of a minority group (African American, Hispanic, American Indian, Alaskan Native, Asian, or Pacific Islander). They must be enrolled full time. Along with their application, they must submit a 500-word essay on their personal background, including when they became interested in the hospitality field, the traits they possess or will need to succeed in the industry, and their plans as related to their educational and career objectives and future goals. Selection is based on industry-related work experience; financial need; academic record and educational qualifications; professional, community, and extracurricular activities; personal attributes, including career goals; the essay; and neatness and completeness of the application. U.S. citizenship or permanent resident status is required.

Financial data The stipend is $2,000.

Duration 1 year.

Additional information Funding for this program, established in 1988, is provided by Hyatt Hotels & Resorts.

Number awarded Varies each year; recently, 18 were awarded. Since this program was established, it has awarded scholarships worth $702,000 to 351 minority students.

Deadline April of each year.

[300]
I EMPOWER SCHOLARSHIP

Greater Washington Urban League
Attn: Thursday Network
Kristin Shymoniak
P.O. Box 73203
Washington, DC 20056-3202
E-mail: scholarship@thursdaynetwork.org
Web: www.thursdaynetwork.org/signature-programs

Summary To provide financial assistance to African American and Hispanic high school seniors in the service area of the Greater Washington Urban League (GWUL) who plan to attend college in any state.

Eligibility This program is open to African American and Hispanic/Latino seniors graduating from high schools in Washington, D.C., Prince George's County (Maryland), or Montgomery County (Maryland) and planning to enroll at a 4-year college or university in any state. Applicants must have a GPA of 2.5 or higher. Along with their application, they must submit copies of their SAT or ACT scores, documentation of financial need, and 2 essays of up to 500 words each on topics that change annually but relate to their community service. U.S. citizenship is required.

Financial data Stipends range from $500 to $3,000. Funds are paid directly to the recipient's institution.

Duration 1 year.

Additional information This program, which began in 1992, is operated by the Thursday Network, the young professionals' auxiliary of the GWUL, as part of its Young Blacks Give Back (YBGB) Month.

Number awarded 2 each year. Since the program began, it has awarded more than $158,000 in scholarships.

Deadline January of each year.

[301]
IDAHO STATE BROADCASTERS ASSOCIATION SCHOLARSHIPS

Idaho State Broadcasters Association
1674 Hill Road, Suite 3
Boise, ID 83702
(208) 345-3072   Fax: (208) 343-8046
E-mail: isba@qwestoffice.net
Web: www.idahobroadcasters.org/index.php/scholarships

Summary To provide financial assistance to African Americans and other diverse students at Idaho colleges and universities who are preparing for a career in the broadcasting field.

Eligibility This program is open to full-time students at Idaho schools who are preparing for a career in broadcasting, including business administration, sales, journalism, or engineering. Applicants must have a GPA of at least 2.0 for the first 2 years of school or 2.5 for the last 2 years. Along with their application, they must submit a letter of recommendation from the general manager of a broadcasting station that is a member of the Idaho State Broadcasters Association and a 1-page essay describing their career plans and why they want the scholarship. Applications are encouraged from a broad and diverse student population. Financial need is not considered in the selection process.

Financial data The stipend is $1,000.

Duration 1 year.

Number awarded At least 2 each year.

Deadline March of each year.

[302]
ILLINOIS BROADCASTERS ASSOCIATION MULTICULTURAL INTERNSHIPS

Illinois Broadcasters Association
Attn: MIP Coordinator
200 Missouri Avenue
Carterville, IL 62918
(618) 985-5555   Fax: (618) 985-6070
E-mail: iba@ilba.org
Web: www.ilba.org/careers/internship-program

Summary To provide funding to African American and other minority college students in Illinois who are majoring in broadcasting and interested in interning at a radio or television station in the state.

Eligibility This program is open to currently-enrolled minority students majoring in broadcasting at a college or university in Illinois. Applicants must be interested in a fall, spring, or summer internship at a radio or television station that is a member of the Illinois Broadcasters Association. Along with their application, they must submit 1) a 250-word essay on how they expect to benefit from a grant through this program; and 2) at least 2 letters of recommendation from a broadcasting faculty member or professional familiar with their career potential and 1 other letter. The internship coordinator of the sponsoring organization selects those students nominated by their schools who have the best opportunity to make it in the world of broadcasting and matches them with internship opportunities that would otherwise be unpaid.

Financial data This program provides a grant to pay the living expenses for the interns in the Illinois communities where they are assigned. The amount of the grant depends on the length of the internship.

Duration 16 weeks in the fall and spring terms or 12 weeks in the summer.

Number awarded 12 each year: 4 in each of the 3 terms.

Deadline Deadline not specified.

[303]
ILLINOIS NURSES FOUNDATION CENTENNIAL SCHOLARSHIP

Illinois Nurses Association
Attn: Illinois Nurses Foundation
P.O. Box 636
Manteno, IL 60950
(815) 468-8804   Fax: (773) 304-1419
E-mail: info@ana-illinois.org
Web: www.ana-illinois.org

Summary To provide financial assistance to nursing undergraduate and graduate students who are African American or members of other underrepresented groups.

Eligibility This program is open to students working on an associate, bachelor's, or master's degree at an accredited NLNAC or CCNE school of nursing. Applicants must be members of a group underrepresented in nursing (African Americans, Hispanics, American Indians, Asians, and males). Undergraduates must have earned a passing grade in all nursing courses taken to date and have a GPA of 2.85 or higher. Graduate students must have completed at least 12 semester hours of graduate work and have a GPA of 3.0 or higher. All applicants must be willing to 1) act as a spokesperson to other student groups on the value of the scholarship to continuing their nursing education; and 2) be profiled in any media or marketing materials developed by the Illinois Nurses Foundation. Along with their application, they must submit a narrative of 250 to 500 words on how they, as nurses, plan to affect policy at either the state or national level that impacts on nursing or health care generally, or how they believe they will impact the nursing profession in general.

Financial data A stipend is awarded (amount not specified).

Duration 1 year.

Number awarded 1 or more each year.

Deadline March of each year.

[304]
INDIANA CHAPTER AABE SCHOLARSHIPS

American Association of Blacks in Energy-Indiana
    Chapter
c/o Tawana Tucker, Scholarship Committee Chair
801 East 86th Avenue
Merrillville, IN 46410
E-mail: tawanatucker@nisource.com
Web: www.aabe.org/index.php?component=pages&id=348

Summary To provide financial assistance to African Americans or members of other underrepresented minority groups who are high school seniors in Indiana and planning to major in an energy-related field at a college in any state.

Eligibility This program is open to seniors graduating from high schools in Indiana and planning to work on a bachelor's degree at a college or university in any state. Applicants must be African Americans, Hispanics, or Native Americans who have a GPA of 3.0 or higher and have taken the ACT and/or SAT test. Their intended major must be a field of business, engineering, physical science, mathematics, or technology related to energy. Along with their application, they must submit a 350-word essay that includes 1) when they discovered their interest in the field of energy and what sparked their interest; and 2) either what excites them about the field of energy or how they expect their education to prepare them for the field of energy. Financial need is not considered in the selection process.

Financial data The stipend is $2,000 or $1,000.

Duration 1 year; nonrenewable.

Additional information Winners are eligible to compete for regional and national scholarships.

Number awarded 3 each year: 1 at $2,000 and 2 at $1,000.

Deadline March of each year.

[305]
INDIANA INDUSTRY LIAISON GROUP SCHOLARSHIP

Indiana Industry Liaison Group
c/o Candee Chambers, Vice Chair
DirectEmployers Association
9002 North Purdue Road, Suite 100
Indianapolis, IN 46268
(317) 874-9000   Toll Free: (866) 268-6202
E-mail: vchair@indianailg.org
Web: www.indianailg.org

Summary To provide financial assistance to African American and other students from any state enrolled at colleges and universities in Indiana who have been involved in activities to promote diversity.

Eligibility This program is open to residents of any state currently enrolled at an accredited college or university in Indiana. Applicants must either 1) be enrolled in programs or classes related to diversity/Affirmative Action (AA)/Equal Employment Opportunity (EEO); or 2) have work or volunteer experience with diversity/AA/EEO organizations. Along with their application, they must submit an essay of 400 to 500 words on 1 of the following topics: 1) their personal commitment to diversity/AA/EEO within their community or business; 2) a time or situation in which they were able to establish and/or sustain a commitment to diversity; 3) a time when they have taken a position in favor of affirmative action and/or diversity; or 4) activities in which they have participated within their community that demonstrate their personal commitment to moving the community's diversity agenda forward. Financial need is not considered in the selection process.

Financial data The stipend is $1,000.

Duration 1 year.

Number awarded 1 each year.

Deadline January of each year.

[306]
INDIANAPOLIS CHAPTER NBMBAA UNDERGRADUATE SCHOLARSHIP PROGRAM

National Black MBA Association-Indianapolis Chapter
Attn: Scholarship Program
P.O. Box 2325
Indianapolis, IN 46206-2325
(317) 308-6447   E-mail: scholarship@nbmbaa-indy.org
Web: www.nbmbaa-indy.org/nbmbaa_education.htm

Summary To provide financial assistance to African American students from Indiana working on an undergraduate degree in business or management.

Eligibility This program is open to African American students enrolled full time in an undergraduate business or management program and working on a bachelor's degree at a college or university. Applicants must be residents of Indiana or attending school in that state. Along with their application, they must submit a 2-page essay on a current events topic that changes annually; recently, students were invited to write on how social networking has influenced the way companies conduct business in today's market. Selection is based on the essay, transcripts, and a list of extracurricular activities; financial need is not considered.

Financial data The stipend is $1,000.

Duration 1 year.

Number awarded 1 each year.

Deadline October of each year.

[307]
INFRASTRUCTURE ENGINEERING SCHOLARSHIP

Conference of Minority Transportation Officials
Attn: National Scholarship Program
100 M Street, S.E., Suite 917
Washington, DC 20003
(202) 506-2917   E-mail: info@comto.org
Web: www.comto.org/page/scholarships

Summary To provide financial assistance to African American and other minority upper-division and graduate students interested in working on a degree in transportation or a related field.

Eligibility This program is open to minority juniors, seniors, and graduate student at an accredited college, university, or vocational/technical school. Applicants must be studying transportation, engineering, planning, or a related discipline. They must have a GPA of 2.5 or higher. Along with their application they must submit a cover letter on their transportation-related career goals and life aspirations. Financial need is not considered in the selection process. Membership in the Conference of Minority Transportation Officials is considered a plus but is not required.

Financial data The stipend is $2,500. Funds are paid directly to the recipient's college or university.

Duration 1 year.

Additional information This program is sponsored by Infrastructure Engineering Inc.

Number awarded 1 each year.

Deadline April of each year.

[308]
INROADS NATIONAL COLLEGE INTERNSHIPS

INROADS, Inc.
10 South Broadway, Suite 300
St. Louis, MO 63102
(314) 241-7488   Fax: (314) 241-9325
E-mail: info@inroads.org
Web: www.inroads.org

Summary To provide an opportunity for African Americans and other young people of color to gain work experience in business or industry.

Eligibility This program is open to African Americans, Hispanics, and Native Americans who reside in the areas served by INROADS. Applicants must be interested in preparing for a career in accounting, business, computer sciences, economics. engineering, finance, health care, management information systems, retail store management, or supply chain management. They must be high school seniors or freshmen or sophomores in 4-year colleges and universities and have a GPA of 3.0 or higher. International students may apply if they have appropriate visas.

Financial data Salaries vary, depending upon the specific internship assigned; recently, the range was from $170 to $750 per week.

Duration Up to 4 years.

Additional information INROADS places interns in Fortune 1000 companies, where training focuses on preparing them for corporate and community leadership. The INROADS organization offers internship opportunities through 35 local affiliates in 26 states, Canada, and Mexico.

Number awarded Approximately 2,000 high school and college students are currently working for more than 200 corporate sponsors nationwide.

Deadline March of each year.

[309]
INTERMOUNTAIN SECTION AWWA DIVERSITY SCHOLARSHIP

American Water Works Association-Intermountain
  Section
Attn: Member Services Coordinator
3430 East Danish Road
Sandy, UT 84093
(801) 712-1619, ext. 2   Fax: (801) 487-6699
E-mail: nicoleb@ims-awwa.org
Web: ims-awwa.site-ym.com/group/StudentPO

Summary To provide financial assistance to African American and other minority undergraduate and graduate students working on a degree in the field of water quality, supply, and treatment at a university in the Intermountain West.

Eligibility This program is open to 1) women; and 2) students who identify as Black or African American, Hispanic or Latino, Native Hawaiian or other Pacific Islander, Asian, or American Indian or Alaska Native. Applicants must be entering or enrolled in an undergraduate or graduate program at a college or university in the Intermountain West (defined to include all or portions of Arizona, Colorado, Idaho, Montana, Nevada, New Mexico, Utah, or Wyoming) that relates to water quality, supply, or treatment. Along with their application, they must submit a 2-page essay on their academic interests and career goals and how those relate to water quality, supply, or treatment. Selection is based on that essay, letters of recommendation, and potential to contribute to the field of water quality, supply, and treatment in the Intermountain West.

Financial data The stipend is $1,000. The winner also receives a 1-year student membership in the Intermountain Section of the American Water Works Association (AWWA).

Duration 1 year; nonrenewable.

Number awarded 1 each year.

Deadline November of each year.

[310]
INTERNATIONAL ASSOCIATION OF BLACK ACTUARIES SCHOLARSHIPS

International Association of Black Actuaries
Attn: IABA Foundation Scholarship Committee
P.O. Box 270701
West Hartford, CT 06127
(860) 906-1286   Fax: (860) 906-1369
E-mail: iaba@blackactuaries.org
Web: www.blackactuaries.org/page/Scholarship

Summary To provide financial assistance to Black upper-division and graduate students preparing for an actuarial career.

Eligibility This program is open to full-time juniors, seniors, and graduate students who are of African descent, originating from the United States, Canada, the Caribbean, or African nations. Applicants must have been admitted to a college or

university offering either a program in actuarial science or courses that will prepare them for an actuarial career. They must be citizens or permanent residents of the United States or Canada or eligible to study in those countries under a U.S. student visa or Canadian student authorization. Other requirements include a GPA of 3.0 or higher, a mathematics SAT score of at least 600 or a mathematics ACT score of at least 28, completion of probability and calculus courses, attempting or passing an actuarial examination, completion of Validation by Educational Experience (VEE) requirements, and familiarity with actuarial profession demands. Selection is based on merit and financial need.

Financial data Stipends range from $3,000 to $5,000 per year.

Duration 1 year; may be renewed.

Additional information Support for this program is provided by Allstate, DW Simpson, Ernst & Young, Liberty Mutual, New York Life, Prudential, Travelers, and Willis Towers Watson.

Number awarded Varies each year; recently, 25 of these scholarships, with a total value of $81,000, were awarded.

Deadline May of each year.

[311]
INTERPUBLIC GROUP SCHOLARSHIP AND INTERNSHIP

New York Women in Communications, Inc.
Attn: NYWICI Foundation
355 Lexington Avenue, 15th Floor
New York, NY 10017-6603
(212) 297-2133   Fax: (212) 370-9047
E-mail: nywicipr@nywici.org
Web: www.nywici.org/foundation/scholarships

Summary To provide financial assistance and work experience to women who are African Americans or members of other ethnically diverse groups and residents of designated eastern states enrolled as juniors at a college in any state to prepare for a career in advertising or public relations.

Eligibility This program is open to female residents of New York, New Jersey, Connecticut, or Pennsylvania who are from ethnically diverse groups and currently enrolled as juniors at a college or university in any state. Also eligible are women who reside outside the 4 states but are currently enrolled at a college or university within 1 of the 5 boroughs of New York City. Applicants must be preparing for a career in advertising or public relations and have a GPA of 3.2 or higher. They must be available for a summer internship with Interpublic Group (IPG) in New York City. Along with their application, they must submit a 2-page resume; a personal essay of 300 words on an assigned topic that changes annually; 2 letters of recommendation; and an official transcript. Selection is based on academic record, need, demonstrated leadership, participation in school and community activities, honors and other awards or recognition, work experience, goals and aspirations, and unusual personal and/or family circumstances. U.S. citizenship or permanent status is required.

Financial data The scholarship stipend ranges up to $10,000; the internship is salaried (amount not specified).

Duration 1 year.

Additional information This program is sponsored by IPG, a holding company for a large number of firms in the advertising industry.

Number awarded 2 each year.

Deadline January of each year.

[312]
IRA DORSEY SCHOLARSHIP ENDOWMENT FUND

Alpha Phi Alpha Fraternity, Inc.-Xi Alpha Lambda Chapter
Attn: Director of Education
P.O. Box 10371
Alexandria, VA 22310
(540) 657-6523   E-mail: idsef1@gmail.com
Web: idsef.apaxal.com

Summary To provide financial assistance to African American and other male high school seniors in the Washington, D.C. metropolitan area who plan to attend college in any state.

Eligibility This program is open to male seniors graduating from high schools in the metropolitan Washington area of Virginia, Maryland, and the District of Columbia. Applicants must have a GPA of 2.5 or higher and be planning to attend a 4-year college or university in any state. Along with their application, they must submit a 500-word essay on a topic that changes annually; recently, they were invited to comment on whether affirmative action programs are still needed in this country. Selection is based on the quality of that essay, academic achievement, participation in school and community clubs and organizations, honors and awards, and financial need.

Financial data The stipend is $1,500.

Duration 1 year; nonrenewable.

Additional information Alpha Phi Alpha is the first collegiate fraternity established primarily for African American men. Xi Alpha Lambda is the alumni chapter for northern Virginia.

Number awarded Varies each year; recently, 8 were awarded.

Deadline April of each year.

[313]
IRLET ANDERSON SCHOLARSHIP AWARD

National Organization of Black Law Enforcement
  Executives
Attn: NOBLE Scholarships
4609 Pinecrest Office Park Drive, Suite F
Alexandria, VA 22312-1442
(703) 658-1529   Fax: (703) 658-9479
E-mail: wleach@noblenatl.org
Web: www.noblenational.org

Summary To provide financial assistance for college to high school seniors, especially African Americans, who are interested in preparing for a criminal justice career.

Eligibility This program is open to high school seniors who have a GPA of 3.7 or higher and are interested in preparing for a career in criminal justice. Applicants must be planning to attend an accredited academic institution in the United States to major in a social science (e.g. technology, forensic investigations, or other criminal investigative studies) related to a career in law enforcement or criminal justice. They must be

U.S. citizens and able to demonstrate financial need. Along with their application, they must submit a 1-page essay on their career goals and interests and why they feel they should receive this scholarship.

Financial data The stipend is $2,500.

Duration 1 year; nonrenewable.

Additional information The sponsor is an organization of African American law enforcement officers.

Number awarded 1 each year.

Deadline April of each year.

[314]
IRTS SUMMER FELLOWSHIP PROGRAM

International Radio and Television Society Foundation
Attn: Director, Special Projects
420 Lexington Avenue, Suite 1601
New York, NY 10170-0101
(212) 867-6650   Toll Free: (888) 627-1266
Fax: (212) 867-6653   E-mail: apply@irts.org
Web: irtsfoundation.org/summer-fellowship-program

Summary To provide summer work experience to upper-division and graduate students, especially African Americans and other minorities, who are interested in working during the summer in broadcasting and related fields in the New York City area.

Eligibility This program is open to juniors, seniors, and graduate students at 4-year colleges and universities. Applicants must either be a communications major or have demonstrated a strong interest in the field through extracurricular activities or other practical experience. Minority (African American, Hispanic/Latino, Asian/Pacific Islander, American Indian/Alaskan Native) students are especially encouraged to apply.

Financial data Travel, housing, and a living allowance are provided.

Duration 9 weeks during the summer.

Additional information The first week consists of a comprehensive orientation to broadcasting, cable, advertising, and new media. Then, the participants are assigned an 8-week fellowship. This full-time "real world" experience in a New York-based corporation allows them to reinforce or redefine specific career goals before settling into a permanent job. Fellows have worked at all 4 major networks, at local New York City radio and television stations, and at national rep firms, advertising agencies, and cable operations. This program includes fellowships reserved for students at designated universities (University of Pennsylvania, Brooklyn College, City College of New York, College of the Holy Cross) and the following named awards: the Thomas S. Murphy Fellowship (sponsored by ABC National Television Sales), the Helen Karas Memorial Fellowship, the Mel Karmazin Fellowship, the Neil Postman Memorial Summer Fellowship, the Ari Bluman Memorial Summer Fellowship (sponsored by Group M), the Thom Casadonte Memorial Fellowship (sponsored by Bloomberg), the Joanne Mercado Memorial Fellowship (sponsored by Nielsen), the Donald V. West Fellowship (sponsored by the Library of American Broadcasting Foundation), the Leslie Moonves Fellowship (sponsored by CBS Television Station Sales), and the Sumner M. Redstone Fellowship (sponsored by CBS Television Station Sales). Other sponsors include the National Academy of Television Arts & Sciences, Fox Networks, NBCUniversal, and Unilever.

Number awarded   Varies; recently, 30 were awarded.

Deadline   November of each year.

[315]
ISABEL M. HERSON SCHOLARSHIP IN EDUCATION

Zeta Phi Beta Sorority, Inc.
Attn: National Educational Foundation
1734 New Hampshire Avenue, N.W.
Washington, DC 20009
(202) 387-3103   Fax: (202) 232-4593
E-mail: info@zetaphibetasororityhq.org
Web: www.zpbnef1975.org/scholarships-and-descriptions

Summary   To provide financial assistance to undergraduate and graduate students, especiall African American women, interested in preparing for a career in education.

Eligibility   This program is open to students enrolled full time in an undergraduate or graduate program leading to a degree in either elementary or secondary education. Proof of enrollment is required. Along with their application, they must submit a 150-word essay on their educational goals and professional aspirations, how this award will help them to achieve those goals, and why they should receive the award. Financial need is not considered in the selection process.

Financial data   The stipend ranges from $500 to $1,000.

Duration   1 academic year.

Additional information   Zeta Phi Beta is a traditionally African American sorority.

Number awarded   1 or more each year.

Deadline   January of each year.

[316]
ITW SCHOLARSHIPS

Society of Women Engineers
Attn: Scholarship Selection Committee
203 North LaSalle Street, Suite 1675
Chicago, IL 60601-1269
(312) 596-5223   Toll Free: (877) SWE-INFO
Fax: (312) 644-8557   E-mail: scholarships@swe.org
Web: societyofwomenengineers.swe.org

Summary   To provide financial assistance to undergraduate women, especially African Americans and other underrepresented minorities, who are majoring in designated engineering specialties.

Eligibility   This program is open to women who are entering their junior year at a 4-year ABET-accredited college or university. Applicants must be working full time on a degree in computer science, electrical or mechanical engineering, or polymer science. Preference is given to 1) members of groups underrepresented in engineering or computer science; 2) students interested in an internship with the sponsor; 3) residents of Illinois, Ohio, Texas, or Wisconsin; and 4) students attending the University of Illinois at Chicago, Georgia Institute of Technology, Ohio State University, Northwestern University, or Pennsylvania State University. Selection is based on merit. U.S. citizenship is required.

Financial data   The stipend is $2,500 per year.

Duration   1 year; may be renewed 1 additional year.

Additional information   This program is sponsored by Illinois Tool Works, Inc.

Number awarded   2 each year.

Deadline   February of each year.

[317]
IVORY MOORE COMMUNITY COLLEGE, UNDERGRADUATE AND GRADUATE SCHOLARSHIPS

Texas Association of Black Personnel in Higher Education
c/o Allison Joubert, Scholarship Committee Chair
St. Philip's College
1801 Martin Luther King Drive
San Antonio, TX 78203
(210) 486-2420   E-mail: ajoubert@mail.accd.edu
Web: www.tabphe.org/Scholarships

Summary   To provide financial assistance to African Americans enrolled as community college students, undergraduates, or graduate students at colleges in Texas.

Eligibility   This program is open to African American students currently enrolled full time at an accredited community college, 4-year university, or graduate school in Texas. Applicants must have a GPA of 3.0 or higher. Along with their application, they must submit a 500-word essay on the topic, "As an African American student pursuing a degree in the 21st century, how will the Ivory Moore Scholarship assist me in my future career endeavors?"

Financial data   Stipends are $500 for community college students or $1,000 for undergraduate and graduate students.

Duration   1 year.

Number awarded   3 each year: 1 each to a community college student, undergraduate, and graduate student.

Deadline   January of each year.

[318]
IVY VINE CHARITIES SCHOLARSHIPS

Alpha Kappa Alpha Sorority, Inc.-Theta Omega Omega Chapter
Attn: Ivy Vine Charities, Inc.
43 Randolph Road
PMB 102
Silver Spring, MD 20904
(301) 368-2105   E-mail: ivcscholarship@gmail.com
Web: www.ivyvinecharities.org/scholarship.html

Summary   To provide financial assistance to high school seniors from the Washington, D.C. metropolitan area who plan to attend college, especially an Historically Black College or University (HBCU), in any state.

Eligibility   This program is open to seniors graduating from high schools in Washington, D.C. or the Maryland counties of Montgomery or Prince George's. Applicants must have a GPA of 2.7 or higher and a record of participation in school and community activities. They must have been accepted by a 4-year college or university in any state; for some of the awards, that must be an HBCU. Along with their application, they must submit transcripts that include SAT and/or ACT scores; documentation of their school activities and/or community involvement; 2 letters of recommendation; and an essay, up to 3 pages in length, on what they would give back to their community as a result of their education and why.

Financial data   Scholarship stipends are $2,000; book awards are $500.

Duration   1 year.

Additional information Alpha Kappa Alpha was founded in 1908 at Howard University and is currently 1 of the largest social sororities whose membership is predominantly African American women. The Theta Omega Omega chapter serves alumnae members in the Washington, D.C. metropolitan area.

Number awarded 3 scholarships (2 for students attending an HBCU and 1 for a student at another college or university) are awarded each year. The number of book awards varies; recently, 4 were presented.

Deadline February of each year.

[319]
JACK KORALESKI SCHOLARSHIP

Union Pacific Railroad Black Employee Network
c/o Michele Brown
Streamline Company
222 South 15th Street, Suite 402-S
Omaha, NE 68102
Toll Free: (800) 262-2549
Web: www.up.com

Summary To provide financial assistance to African Americans from Nebraska who are attending college or graduate school in that state.

Eligibility This program is open to U.S. citizens who are African American residents of Nebraska. Applicants must be attending a college or university in that state and have completed at least 60 semester credit hours as an undergraduate or 15 semester credit hours of work on a master's degree. They must have a GPA of 3.0 or higher, a record of active involvement in school and community activities, and demonstrated social awareness and involvement. Along with their application, they must submit 5 essays of 200words each on assigned topics. Selection is based on academic ability, leadership, and community involvement; personal or family financial need may also be considered. Preference is given to applicants majoring in a transportation-related field.

Financial data The stipend is $5,000.

Duration 1 year.

Number awarded 1 or more each year.

Deadline October of each year.

[320]
JACKIE ROBINSON SCHOLARSHIPS

Jackie Robinson Foundation
Attn: Education and Leadership Development Program
75 Varick Street, Second Floor
New York, NY 10013-1917
(212) 290-8600   Fax: (212) 290-8081
E-mail: general@jackierobinson.org
Web: www.jackierobinson.org

Summary To provide financial assistance for college to African American and other minority high school seniors.

Eligibility This program is open to members of an ethnic minority group who are high school seniors accepted at a 4-year college or university. Applicants must have a mathematics and critical reading SAT score of 1000 or higher or ACT score of 21 or higher. Selection is based on academic achievement, financial need, dedication towards community service, and leadership potential. U.S. citizenship is required.

Financial data The maximum stipend is $7,000 per year.

Duration 4 years.

Additional information The program also offers personal and career counseling on a year-round basis, a week of interaction with other scholarship students from around the country, and assistance in obtaining summer jobs and permanent employment after graduation. It was established in 1973 by a grant from Chesebrough-Pond.

Number awarded Approximately 60 each year.

Deadline February of each year.

[321]
JACOBS ENGINEERING SCHOLARSHIP

Conference of Minority Transportation Officials
Attn: National Scholarship Program
100 M Street, S.E., Suite 917
Washington, DC 20003
(202) 506-2917   E-mail: info@comto.org
Web: www.comto.org/page/scholarships

Summary To provide financial assistance to African American and other minority upper-division and graduate student members of the Conference of Minority Transportation Officials (COMTO) working on a degree in transportation or a related field.

Eligibility This program is open to minority juniors, seniors, and graduate student who are COMTO members. Applicants must be studying transportation, engineering (civil, construction, or environmental), safety, urban planning, or a related discipline. They must have a GPA of 3.0 or higher. Along with their application they must submit a cover letter on their transportation-related career goals and life aspirations. Financial need is not considered in the selection process. Membership in the Conference of Minority Transportation Officials is considered a plus but is not required.

Financial data The stipend is $2,500. Funds are paid directly to the recipient's college or university.

Duration 1 year.

Additional information This program is sponsored by Jacobs Engineering Group.

Number awarded 1 or more each year.

Deadline April of each year.

[322]
JACOBS ENGINEERING TRANSPORTATION SCHOLARSHIP

Conference of Minority Transportation Officials
Attn: National Scholarship Program
100 M Street, S.E., Suite 917
Washington, DC 20003
(202) 506-2917   E-mail: info@comto.org
Web: www.comto.org/page/scholarships

Summary To provide financial assistance to African American and other minority upper-division and graduate student members of the Conference of Minority Transportation Officials (COMTO) and family of members working on a degree in transportation or a related field.

Eligibility This program is open to minority juniors, seniors, and graduate student who are COMTO members or whose parents, guardians, or grandparents are members. Applicants must be studying transportation, engineering (civil, construction, or environmental), safety, urban planning, or a related discipline. They must have a GPA of 3.0 or higher.

Along with their application they must submit a cover letter on their transportation-related career goals and life aspirations. Financial need is not considered in the selection process.

Financial data   The stipend is $2,500. Funds are paid directly to the recipient's college or university.

Duration   1 year.

Additional information   This program is sponsored by Jacobs Engineering Group.

Number awarded   1 or more each year.

Deadline   April of each year.

[323]
JACQUES AVENT SCHOLARSHIP

Arizona Community Foundation
Attn: Director of Scholarships
2201 East Camelback Road, Suite 405B
Phoenix, AZ 85016
(602) 381-1400   Toll Free: (800) 222-8221
Fax: (602) 381-1575
E-mail: scholarship@azfoundation.org
Web: azfoundation.academicworks.com/opportunities/2468

Summary   To provide financial assistance to African American upper-division and graduate students who are preparing for a career in public administration at a college in Arizona.

Eligibility   This program is open to African American undergraduates who have completed at least 48 credit hours and full-time graduate students at colleges and universities in Arizona. Applicants must be preparing for a career in public administration by working on a degree in public administration, public affairs, public policy, political science, or urban and metropolitan studies; students in business, criminal justice, education, health care, information technology, and nursing are eligible and encouraged to apply. They must have a GPA of 3.0 or higher. Along with their application, they must submit an essay that covers 1) their educational and career goals; 2) their civic and community involvement; and 3) the challenges facing African American in the field of public administration and how they plan to help strengthen the role of African Americans in public administration.

Financial data   The stipend is $5,000.

Duration   1 year.

Additional information   This program is supported by the Central Arizona Chapter of the National Forum for Black Public Administrators.

Number awarded   1 or more each year.

Deadline   March of each year.

[324]
JAMES B. MORRIS SCHOLARSHIPS

James B. Morris Scholarship Fund
Attn: Scholarship Selection Committee
P.O. Box 12145
Des Moines, IA 50312
(515) 864-0922
Web: www.morrisscholarship.org

Summary   To provide financial assistance to African American and other minority undergraduate, graduate, and law students from Iowa.

Eligibility   This program is open to minority students (African Americans, Asian/Pacific Islanders, Hispanics, or Native Americans) who are interested in working on an undergradu-

ate or graduate degree. Applicants must be either Iowa residents attending a college or university anywhere in the United States or non-Iowa residents who are attending a college or university in Iowa. Along with their application, they must submit an essay of 250 to 500 words on why they are applying for this scholarship, activities or organizations in which they are involved, and their future plans. Selection is based on the essay, academic achievement (GPA of 2.5 or higher), community service, and financial need. U.S. citizenship is required.

Financial data   The stipend ranges from $1,000 to $2,500 per year.

Duration   1 year; may be renewed.

Additional information   This fund was established in 1978 in honor of the J.B. Morris family, who founded the Iowa branch of the National Association for the Advancement of Colored People and published the *Iowa Bystander* newspaper. The program includes the Ann Chapman Scholarships, the Vincent Chapman, Sr. Scholarships, the Catherine Williams Scholarships, and the Brittany Hall Memorial Scholarships. Support for additional scholarships is provided by EMC Insurance Group and Wells Fargo Bank.

Number awarded   Varies each year; recently, 22 were awarded.

Deadline   February of each year.

[325]
JAMES CARLSON MEMORIAL SCHOLARSHIP

Oregon Office of Student Access and Completion
Attn: Scholarship Processing Coordinator
1500 Valley River Drive, Suite 100
Eugene, OR 97401-2146
(541) 687-7422   Toll Free: (800) 452-8807, ext. 7422
Fax: (541) 687-7414   TDD: (800) 735-2900
E-mail: cheryl.a.connolly@state.or.us
Web: app.oregonstudentaid.gov/Catalog/Default.aspx

Summary   To provide financial assistance to Oregon residents who are African American or other diverse students majoring in education on the undergraduate or graduate school level at a school in any state.

Eligibility   This program is open to residents of Oregon who are U.S. citizens or permanent residents and enrolled at a college or university in any state. Applicants must be either 1) college seniors or fifth-year students majoring in elementary or secondary education; or 2) graduate students working on an elementary or secondary certificate. Full-time enrollment and financial need are required. Priority is given to 1) students who come from diverse environments and submit an essay of 250 to 350 words on their experience living or working in diverse environments; 2) dependents of members of the Oregon Education Association; and 3) applicants committed to teaching autistic children.

Financial data   Stipends for scholarships offered by the Oregon Office of Student Access and Completion (OSAC) range from $1,000 to $10,000 but recently averaged $4,368.

Duration   1 year; nonrenewable.

Additional information   This program is administered by the OSAC with funds provided by the Oregon Community Foundation.

Number awarded Varies each year; recently, 3 were awarded.

Deadline February of each year.

[326]
JAMES E. WEBB INTERNSHIPS

Smithsonian Institution
Attn: Office of Fellowships and Internships
470 L'Enfant Plaza, Suite 7102
P.O. Box 37012, MRC 902
Washington, DC 20013-7012
(202) 633-7070　　　　　　　Fax: (202) 633-7069
E-mail: siofi@si.edu
Web: www.smithsonianofi.com

Summary To provide internship opportunities throughout the Smithsonian Institution to African American and other minority upper-division and graduate students in business or public administration.

Eligibility This program is open to minorities who are juniors, seniors, or graduate students majoring in areas of business or public administration (finance, human resource management, accounting, or general business administration). Applicants must have a GPA of 3.0 or higher. They must seek placement in offices, museums, and research institutes within the Smithsonian Institution.

Financial data Interns receive a stipend of $600 per week and a travel allowance.

Duration 10 weeks during the summer, fall, or spring.

Number awarded Varies each year; recently, 8 of these internships were awarded.

Deadline January of each year for summer or fall; September of each year for spring.

[327]
JAMES ECHOLS SCHOLARSHIP

California Association for Health, Physical Education,
　　Recreation and Dance
Attn: Chair, Scholarship Committee
1501 El Camino Avenue, Suite 3
Sacramento, CA 95815-2748
(916) 922-3596　　　Toll Free: (800) 499-3596 (within CA)
Fax: (916) 922-0133　　　E-mail: reception@cahperd.org
Web: www.cahperd.org

Summary To provide financial assistance to African American and other minority student members of the California Association for Health, Physical Education, Recreation and Dance.

Eligibility This program is open to California residents who have been members of the association for at least 60 days and are attending a 2- or 4-year college or university in the state. Applicants must be undergraduate or graduate students working on a degree in health education, physical education, recreation, or dance and have completed at least 60 semester hours of college work. Selection is based on scholastic proficiency (a GPA of 3.0 or higher); leadership ability in school, community, and professional activities; and personal qualities of enthusiasm, cooperativeness, responsibility, initiative, and ability to work with others. This scholarship is awarded to the highest-ranked minority (Asian, African American, Latino, or Native American) applicant.

Financial data The stipend is $1,000.

Duration 1 year.

Number awarded 1 each year.

Deadline November of each year.

[328]
JAMES J. WYCHOR SCHOLARSHIPS

Minnesota Broadcasters Association
Attn: Scholarship Program
3033 Excelsior Boulevard, Suite 440
Minneapolis, MN 55416
(612) 926-8123　　　　　　　Toll Free: (800) 245-5838
Fax: (612) 926-9761
E-mail: llasere@minnesotabroadcasters.com
Web: www.minnesotabroadcasters.com/career-prep

Summary To provide financial assistance to Minnesota residents, especially African Americans and other minorities, who are interested in studying broadcasting at a college in any state.

Eligibility This program is open to residents of Minnesota who are accepted or enrolled at an accredited postsecondary institution in any state offering a broadcast-related curriculum. Applicants must have a high school or college GPA of 2.5 or higher and must submit a 500-word essay on why they wish to prepare for a career in broadcasting or electronic media. Employment in the broadcasting industry is not required, but students who are employed must include a letter from their general manager describing the duties they have performed as a radio or television station employee and evaluating their potential for success in the industry. Financial need is not considered in the selection process. Some of the scholarships are awarded only to minority or women candidates.

Financial data The stipend is $1,500.

Duration 1 year; recipients who are college seniors may reapply for an additional 1-year renewal as a graduate student.

Number awarded 10 each year, distributed as follows: 3 within the 7-county metro area, 5 allocated geographically throughout the state (northeast, northwest, central, southeast, southwest), and 2 reserved specifically for women and minority applicants.

Deadline June of each year.

[329]
JAMES WILCOX ENDOWED SCHOLARSHIPS

Florida Institute of CPAs
Attn: FICPA Educational Foundation
325 West College Avenue
P.O. Box 5437
Tallahassee, FL 32314
(850) 224-2727　　　Toll Free: (800) 342-3197 (within FL)
Fax: (850) 222-8190　　　E-mail: wilsonb@ficpa.org
Web: www.ficpa.org

Summary To provide financial assistance to African American residents of Florida who are members of the Florida Institute of CPAs (FICPA) and completing a program of accounting study at a school in the state.

Eligibility This program is open to African American residents of Florida who are FICPA members and fourth- or fifth-year accounting students enrolled full time in an accounting program at a college or university in the state. A faculty member in the accounting department of their college must nominate them. The program is intended for full-time students, but part-time students may be considered. Applicants should be planning to sit for the C.P.A. exam and indicate a desire to work in Florida. Selection is based on financial need, educational achievement, and demonstrated involvement with FICPA and other professional, social, and charitable activities. U.S. citizenship or permanent resident status is required.

Financial data   The stipend is $5,000 for full-time students or $2,500 for part-time students.

Duration   1 year.

Number awarded   4 each year.

Deadline   March of each year.

[330]
JAMYE COLEMAN WILLIAMS SCHOLARSHIP

African Methodist Episcopal Church
Connectional Lay Organization
Attn: Scholarship Chair
P.O. Box 42224
Philadelphia, PA 19101
(215) 941-0344   Fax: (360) 343-0344
Web: www.connectionallay-amec.org

Summary   To provide financial assistance to members of the African Methodist Episcopal (AME) Church who are interested in attending a college or university, especially those interested preparing for leadership in the denomination.

Eligibility   This program is open to members of AME churches who are working on or planning to work on a bachelor's degree in any field at a college or university. Applicants must submit a 500-word essay on the importance of a college education in the 21st century. Preference is given to students who desire to serve the AME Church in a leadership capacity. Selection is based on academic record, qualities of leadership, extracurricular activities and accomplishments, reference letters, and financial need.

Financial data   The stipend is $5,000. Funds are sent directly to the student.

Duration   1 year.

Number awarded   1 each year.

Deadline   March of each year.

[331]
JANE C. WALDBAUM ARCHAEOLOGICAL FIELD SCHOOL SCHOLARSHIP

Archaeological Institute of America
c/o Boston University
656 Beacon Street, Sixth Floor
Boston, MA 02215-2006
(617) 358-4184   Fax: (617) 353-6550
E-mail: fellowships@aia.bu.edu
Web: www.archaeological.org/grants/708

Summary   To provide funding to African American and other minority upper-division and graduate students who are interested in participating in an archaeological field project in the United States or any other country.

Eligibility   This program is open to junior and senior undergraduates and first-year graduate students who are currently enrolled at a college or university in the United States or Canada. Minority and disadvantaged students are encouraged to apply. Applicants must be interested in participating in an

archaeological excavation or survey project in any country. They may not have previously participated in an archaeological excavation. Students majoring in archaeology or related disciplines are especially encouraged to apply.

Financial data   The grant is $1,000.

Duration   At least 1 month during the summer.

Additional information   These scholarships were first awarded in 2007.

Number awarded   Varies each year; recently, 15 were awarded.

Deadline   February of each year.

[332]
J.D. WILLIAMS SCHOLARSHIP

African Methodist Episcopal Church
Connectional Lay Organization
Attn: Scholarship Chair
P.O. Box 42224
Philadelphia, PA 19101
(215) 941-0344   Fax: (360) 343-0344
Web: www.connectionallay-amec.org

Summary   To provide financial assistance to members of the African Methodist Episcopal (AME) Church who are interested in working on an undergraduate or graduate degree at a college or university affiliated with the denomination.

Eligibility   This program is open to members of AME churches who are working on or planning to work on a bachelor's, M.Div., or D.Min. degree at an AME college, university, or seminary. Applicants must submit a 500-word essay on the importance of a college education in the 21st century. Selection is based on academic record, qualities of leadership, extracurricular activities and accomplishments, reference letters, and financial need.

Financial data   The stipend is $5,000. Funds are sent directly to the student.

Duration   1 year.

Number awarded   1 or more each year.

Deadline   March of each year.

[333]
JDOS-INTERNATIONAL SCHOLARSHIP

National Forum for Black Public Administrators
Attn: Scholarship Program
777 North Capitol Street, N.E., Suite 807
Washington, DC 20002
(202) 408-9300   Fax: (202) 408-8558
E-mail: vharris@nfbpa.org
Web: www.nfbpa.org/i4a/pages/index.cfm?pageid=4047

Summary   To provide financial assistance to African Americans working on an undergraduate or graduate degree in public administration or a related field.

Eligibility   This program is open to African American undergraduate and graduate students preparing for a career in public service. Applicants must be working full time on a degree in public administration, political science, urban affairs, public policy, or a related field. They must have excellent interpersonal and analytical abilities and strong oral and written communication skills. Along with their application, they must submit a 3-page autobiographical essay that includes their academic and career goals and objectives. Selection is based on academic record, leadership ability, participation in school activities, community service, and financial need.

Financial data The stipend is $2,000.

Duration 1 year.

Additional information This program is sponsored by the construction management firm JDOS-International of Washington, D.C. Recipients are required to attend the sponsor's annual conference to receive their scholarship; limited hotel and air accommodations are arranged and provided.

Number awarded 1 each year.

Deadline March of each year.

[334]
JERRY MORRIS AND SUMMER HOUSTON MEMORIAL SCHOLARSHIP

Union Pacific Railroad Black Employee Network
c/o Michele Brown
Streamline Company
222 South 15th Street, Suite 402-S
Omaha, NE 68102
Toll Free: (800) 262-2549
Web: www.up.com

Summary To provide financial assistance to African Americans from designated states who plan to attend college in their state.

Eligibility This program is open to U.S. citizens who are African American residents of Arkansas, California, Illinois, Louisiana, Missouri, Nebraska, or Texas. Applicants must be seniors in high school or full-time freshmen or sophomores at a college or university in those states. They must have a GPA of 3.0 or higher, a record of active involvement in school and community activities, and demonstrated social awareness and involvement. Along with their application, they must submit a 500-word essay on a topic that changes annually but relates to leadership. Selection is based on that essay, GPA, SAT/ACT scores, letters of recommendation, and financial need.

Financial data The stipend is $2,000 per year.

Duration 1 year; may be renewed 1 additional year.

Number awarded 1 or more each year.

Deadline March of each year.

[335]
JESSICA M. BLANDING MEMORIAL SCHOLARSHIP

New England Regional Black Nurses Association, Inc.
P.O. Box 190690
Roxbury, MA 02119
(617) 524-1951   E-mail: nerbascholarships@gmail.com
Web: nerbna.nursingnetwork.com

Summary To provide financial assistance to licensed practical nurses from New England who are of African descent and interested in working on a degree.

Eligibility The program is open to African American residents of the New England states who are licensed practical nurses working on an associate or bachelor's degree in nursing at a school in any state. Applicants must have a GPA of 3.0 or higher and at least 1 full year of school remaining. They must be members of the New England Regional Black Nurses Association (NERBNA). Along with their application, they must submit a 3-page essay that covers their reasons for

furthering their career in nursing; why minority nursing leadership is important; how minority nursing leadership can assist them in furthering their career; why they chose to prepare for a career in nursing; and any financial hardships that may hinder them from completing their education.

Financial data A stipend is awarded (amount not specified).

Duration 1 year.

Number awarded 1 or more each year.

Deadline February of each year.

[336]
JIMMY A. YOUNG MEMORIAL EDUCATION RECOGNITION AWARD

American Association for Respiratory Care
Attn: American Respiratory Care Foundation
9425 North MacArthur Boulevard, Suite 100
Irving, TX 75063-4706
(972) 243-2272   Fax: (972) 484-2720
E-mail: info@arcfoundation.org
Web: www.arcfoundation.org

Summary To provide financial assistance to college students, especially African Americans and other minorities, who are interested in becoming respiratory therapists.

Eligibility Candidates must be enrolled in an accredited respiratory therapy program, have completed at least 1 semester/quarter of the program, and have a GPA of 3.0 or higher. Preference is given to nominees of minority origin. Applications must include 6 copies of an original referenced paper on some aspect of respiratory care and letters of recommendation. The foundation prefers that the candidates be nominated by a school or program, but any student may initiate a request for sponsorship by a school (in order that a deserving candidate is not denied the opportunity to compete simply because the school does not initiate the application).

Financial data The stipend is $1,000. The award also provides airfare, 1 night's lodging, and registration for the association's international congress.

Duration 1 year.

Number awarded 1 each year.

Deadline June of each year.

[337]
JOANN JETER MEMORIAL DIVERSITY SCHOLARSHIP

Associates Foundation
Attn: Claudia Perot, Scholarship Committee Chair
JCD 6
P.O. Box 3621
Portland, OR 97208-3621
(503) 230-3754
Web: www.theassociatesonline.org

Summary To provide financial assistance to African Americans and other students who reflect elements of diversity and are interested in working on an undergraduate or graduate degree in any field.

Eligibility This program is open to students who are enrolled or planning to enroll as a full-time undergraduate or graduate student at an accredited 4-year college or university or a full-time student at a 2-year college enrolled in a program leading to an academic degree. Applicants must be from a diverse background, including first-generation college student, cultural and/or ethnic minority background, low-income, or other clearly articulated aspects of diversity as presented in an essay.

Financial data The stipend ranges from $500 to $1,000.

Duration 1 year.

Number awarded Varies each year; recently, 3 were awarded.

Deadline April of each year.

[338]
JOANNE ROBINSON MEMORIAL SCHOLARSHIP

JoAnne Robinson Memorial Scholarship Fund
c/o WEWS
3001 Euclid Avenue
Cleveland, OH 44115
(216) 431-5555

Summary To provide financial assistance to African American undergraduates who are majoring in broadcast journalism.

Eligibility This program is open to full-time college students who are African American and majoring in broadcast journalism. Applicants must exemplify the following characteristics: hard working, detail oriented, outstanding communication and interpersonal skills, and dedication to excellence (personally and professionally). Along with their application, they must submit a statement on the goals, values, and characteristics that make them worthy of this scholarship. Financial need is not considered in the selection process.

Financial data The stipend is $1,000. Funds may be used for tuition, books, and other educational expenses.

Duration 1 year; nonrenewable.

Additional information This scholarship is administered by the Scripps Howard Foundation, which forwards the stipend to the recipient's institution.

Number awarded 1 each year.

Deadline February of each year.

[339]
JOHN AND MURIEL LANDIS SCHOLARSHIPS

American Nuclear Society
Attn: Scholarship Coordinator
555 North Kensington Avenue
La Grange Park, IL 60526-5535
(708) 352-6611　　　Toll Free: (800) 323-3044
Fax: (708) 352-0499　　　E-mail: outreach@ans.org
Web: committees.ans.org/need/apply.html

Summary To provide financial assistance to African American and other minority undergraduate or graduate students who are interested in preparing for a career in nuclear-related fields and can demonstrate financial need.

Eligibility This program is open to undergraduate and graduate students at colleges or universities located in the United States who are preparing for, or planning to prepare for, a career in nuclear science, nuclear engineering, or a nuclear-related field. Qualified high school seniors are also eligible. Applicants must have greater than average financial need and have experienced circumstances that render them disadvantaged. Along with their application, they must submit an essay on their academic and professional goals, experiences that have affected those goals, etc. Selection is based

on that essay, academic achievement, letters of recommendation, and financial need. Women and members of minority groups are especially urged to apply. U.S. citizenship is not required.

Financial data The stipend is $5,000, to be used to cover tuition, books, fees, room, and board.

Duration 1 year; nonrenewable.

Number awarded Up to 9 each year.

Deadline January of each year.

[340]
JOHN D. O'BRYANT MERIT SCHOLARSHIP

John D. O'Bryant National Think Tank for Black
　Professionals in Higher Education on Predominantly
　White Campuses
Attn: Tekeia Howard
Xavier University
3800 Victory Parkway
Cincinnati, OH 45207
(513) 745-1029　　　E-mail: howardt@xavier.edu
Web: www.johndobryant.org/index.php/scholarships

Summary To provide financial assistance to Black undergraduate students attending predominantly white colleges and universities.

Eligibility This program is open to Black students who are enrolled full time at a predominantly white 2- or 4-year college or university in the United States. Applicants must be undergraduates who have completed at least 30 credit hours and have a GPA of 3.0 or higher. Along with their application, they must submit a 150-word statement explaining why they deserve and/or need the scholarship, transcripts, letters of recommendation, and a 300-word essay on a topic that changes annually but relates to a current issue involving civil rights for Black Americans.

Financial data Stipends are $1,000 or $500.

Duration 1 year.

Number awarded 2 each year: 1 at $1,000 and 1 at $500.

Deadline October of each year.

[341]
JOHN DEERE SCHOLARSHIP FOR FEMALE AND MINORITY STUDENTS

American Welding Society
Attn: AWS Foundation, Inc.
8669 N.W. 36th Street, Suite 130
Doral, FL 33166-6672
(305) 443-9353　　　Toll Free: (800) 443-9353, ext. 250
Fax: (305) 443-7559　　　E-mail: nprado-pulido@aws.org
Web: www.aws.org/foundation/page/john-deere-scholarship

Summary To provide financial assistance to African American and other minority undergraduate students, especially those from designated states, who are working on a degree in welding engineering or welding engineering technology at a university in any state.

Eligibility This award is available to U.S. citizens who are women or members of minority groups. Preference is given to residents of Illinois, Iowa, Kansas Minnesota, Missouri, Nebraska, North Dakota, South Dakota, or Wisconsin. Applicants must have completed at least 1 semester of full-time study in a 4-year undergraduate program of welding engineering, welding engineering technology, or mechanical or manufacturing engineering with a welding emphasis. They must have a GPA of 3.0 or higher. Along with their application, they must submit a statement of unmet financial need (although financial need is not required to apply), transcripts, 2 letters of recommendation, and a personal statement that provides their personal objectives and values, their career objectives with a statement of why they want to prepare for a career in welding, participation and leadership in campus and outside organizations, participation in American Welding Society (AWS) student and section activities, and general background information.

Financial data The stipend is $2,500.

Duration 1 year; nonrenewable.

Additional information This program is sponsored by John Deere.

Number awarded 1 each year.

Deadline February of each year.

[342]
JOHN T. SMITH SCHOLARSHIPS

Kentucky Community and Technical College System
Attn: Financial Aid
300 North Main Street
Versailles, KY 40383
(859) 256-3100   Toll Free: (877) 528-2748 (within KY)
Web: www.kctcs.edu

Summary To provide financial assistance to African American and other minority students attending or planning to attend participating institutions within the Kentucky Community and Technical College System (KCTCS).

Eligibility This program is open to minority residents of Kentucky who are attending or planning to attend a participating KCTCS institution. Applicants must be enrolled or planning to enroll in a transfer program to a 4-year institution. They must be able to demonstrate unmet financial need and a GPA of 2.5 or higher. Most colleges require full-time enrollment. Selection is based on academic record, extracurricular activities, racial status, and financial need.

Financial data Stipends vary at each participating college, but they are intended to provide full payment of tuition and required fees.

Duration 1 year; may be renewed 1 additional year.

Additional information This program is named after the first African American to receive a doctoral degree from the University of Kentucky.

Number awarded Varies each year.

Deadline Each college sets its own deadline.

[343]
JOHN W. WORK III MEMORIAL FOUNDATION SCHOLARSHIP

Community Foundation of Middle Tennessee
Attn: Scholarship Coordinator
3833 Cleghorn Avenue, Suite 400
Nashville, TN 37215-2519
(615) 321-4939, ext. 116   Toll Free: (888) 540-5200
Fax: (615) 327-2746   E-mail: pcole@cfmt.org
Web: www.cfmt.org/request/scholarships/allscholarships

Summary To provide financial assistance to upper-division and graduate students from Tennessee, especially African Americans, who are working on a degree in music at a school in any state.

Eligibility This program is open to residents of Tennessee, especially African Americans, enrolled as juniors, seniors, or graduate students at an accredited college, university, or institute in any state. Applicants must be working on a degree in music and have a GPA of 3.0 or higher. Selection is based on demonstrated potential for excellence in music, academic record, standardized test scores, extracurricular activities, work experience, community involvement, recommendations, and financial need.

Financial data Stipends range from $500 to $2,500 per year. Funds are paid to the recipient's school and must be used for tuition, fees, books, supplies, room, board, or miscellaneous expenses.

Duration 1 year.

Additional information This program began in 2002.

Number awarded 1 or more each year.

Deadline March of each year.

[344]
JOSEPH C. MCKINNEY SCHOLARSHIP

African Methodist Episcopal Church
Connectional Lay Organization
Attn: Scholarship Chair
P.O. Box 42224
Philadelphia, PA 19101
(215) 941-0344   Fax: (360) 343-0344
Web: www.connectionallay-amec.org

Summary To provide financial assistance to members of the African Methodist Episcopal (AME) Church who are interested in attending a college or university, especially those interested preparing for leadership in the denomination.

Eligibility This program is open to members of AME churches who are working on or planning to work on a bachelor's degree in any field at a college or university. Applicants must submit a 500-word essay on the importance of a college education in the 21st century. Preference is given to students who desire to serve the AME Church in a leadership capacity. Selection is based on academic record, qualities of leadership, extracurricular activities and accomplishments, reference letters, and financial need.

Financial data The stipend is $5,000. Funds are sent directly to the student.

Duration 1 year.

Number awarded 1 each year.

Deadline March of each year.

[345]
JOSHUA DAVID GARDNER MEMORIAL SCHOLARSHIP

Joshua David Gardner Memorial Scholarship
  Endowment, Inc.
3955 Wess Park Drive
Cincinnati, OH 45217
(703) 373-7172
E-mail: gardner@joshgardnerendowment.org
Web: www.joshgardnerendowment.org

Summary To provide financial assistance to undergraduates enrolled or planning to enroll at an Historically Black College or University (HBCU).

Eligibility This program is open to U.S. citizens between 17 and 25 years of age who are enrolled or planning to enroll at an accredited 4-year HBCU. Applicants must have a GPA of 2.8 or higher and scores of at least 1200 on the SAT or 21 on the ACT. Along with their application, they must submit a 500-word essay on the importance of participating in the political and social change processes. Financial need is considered in the selection process.

Financial data The stipend is $2,000.

Duration 1 year; nonrenewable.

Additional information This program began in 2006.

Number awarded At least 2 each year.

Deadline April of each year.

[346]
JOSIE K. CLAIBORNE MEMORIAL SCHOLARSHIPS

American Association of Blacks in Energy-South Carolina Chapter
Attn: Scholarship Committee
P.O. Box 7696
Columbia, SC 29202
(803) 933-7252   E-mail: mpriester-clarke@scana.com
Web: www.aabe.org/index.php?component=pages&id=920

Summary To provide financial assistance to African Americans and members of other underrepresented minority groups who are high school seniors in South Carolina and planning to major in an energy-related field at a college in any state.

Eligibility This program is open to seniors graduating from high schools in South Carolina and planning to work on a bachelor's degree at a college or university in any state. Applicants must be African Americans, Hispanics, or Native Americans who have a GPA of 3.0 or higher and have taken the ACT and/or SAT test. Their intended major must be a field of business, engineering, physical sciences, mathematics, or technology related to energy. Along with their application, they must submit a 350-word essay that includes 1) when they discovered their interest in the field of energy and what sparked their interest; and 2) either what excites them about the field of energy or how they expect their education to prepare them for the field of energy. Financial need is not considered in the selection process.

Financial data The stipend is $1,000.

Duration 1 year; nonrenewable.

Additional information Winners are eligible to compete for regional and national scholarships.

Number awarded Up to 2 each year.

Deadline March of each year.

[347]
JOYCE WASHINGTON SCHOLARSHIP

Watts Charity Association, Inc.
6245 Bristol Parkway, Suite 224
Culver City, CA 90230
(310) 671-0394   Fax: (323) 778-2613
E-mail: wattscharity@yahoo.com
Web: 4watts.tripod.com/id5.html

Summary To provide financial assistance to upper-division African Americans majoring in child development, teaching, or social services.

Eligibility This program is open to U.S. citizens of African American descent who are enrolled full time as a college or university junior. Applicants must be majoring in child development, teaching, or social services. They must have a GPA of 3.0 or higher, be between 17 and 24 years of age, and be able to demonstrate that they intend to continue their education for at least 2 years. Along with their application, they must submit 1) a 1-paragraph statement on why they should be awarded a Watts Charity Association scholarship; and 2) a 1- to 2-page essay on a specific type of cancer, based either on how it has impacted their life or on researched information.

Financial data A stipend is awarded (amount not specified).

Duration 1 year.

Additional information Royce R. Watts, Sr. established the Watts Charity Association after he learned he had cancer in 2001.

Number awarded 1 each year.

Deadline May of each year.

[348]
JUANITA A. WILKINSON FELLOWSHIP

Alpha Kappa Alpha Sorority, Inc.
Attn: Educational Advancement Foundation
5656 South Stony Island Avenue
Chicago, IL 60637
(773) 947-0026   Toll Free: (800) 653-6528
Fax: (773) 947-0277   E-mail: akaeaf@akaeaf.net
Web: www.akaeaf.org/fellowships_endowments.htm

Summary To provide financial assistance to undergraduates from New York City or the U.S. Virgin Islands (especially African American women) who are working on a degree in any field.

Eligibility This program is open to residents of New York City or the U.S. Virgin Islands who are enrolled as sophomores or higher at an accredited degree-granting institution in any state. Applicants may be majoring in any field. Along with their application, they must submit 1) a list of honors, awards, and scholarships received; 2) a list of organizations in which they have memberships, especially minority organizations; and 3) a statement of their personal and career goals, including how this scholarship will enhance their ability to attain those goals. Selection is based on academic merit and financial need. The sponsor is a traditionally African American women's sorority.

Financial data A stipend is awarded (amount not specified).

Duration 1 year.

Number awarded 1 or more each even-numbered year.

Deadline April of each even-numbered year.

[349]
JUDITH MCMANUS PRICE SCHOLARSHIPS

American Planning Association
Attn: Leadership Affairs Associate
205 North Michigan Avenue, Suite 1200
Chicago, IL 60601
(312) 431-9100   Fax: (312) 786-6700
E-mail: mgroh@planning.org
Web: www.planning.org/scholarships/apa

Summary To provide financial assistance to African American and other underrepresented minority students enrolled in undergraduate or graduate degree programs at recognized planning schools.

Eligibility This program is open to undergraduate and graduate students in urban and regional planning who are women or members of the following minority groups: African American, Hispanic American, or Native American. Applicants must be citizens of the United States and able to document financial need. They must intend to work as practicing planners in the public sector. Along with their application, they must submit a 2-page personal and background statement describing how their education will be applied to career goals and why they chose planning as a career path. Selection is based (in order of importance), on: 1) commitment to planning as reflected in their personal statement and on their resume; 2) academic achievement and/or improvement during the past 2 years; 3) letters of recommendation; 4) financial need; and 5) professional presentation.

Financial data Stipends range from $2,000 to $4,000 per year. The money may be applied to tuition and living expenses only. Payment is made to the recipient's university and divided by terms in the school year.

Duration 1 year; recipients may reapply.

Additional information This program began in 2002.

Number awarded Varies each year; recently, 3 were awarded.

Deadline April of each year.

[350]
JUSTINE E. GRANNER MEMORIAL SCHOLARSHIP

Iowa United Methodist Foundation
2301 Rittenhouse Street
Des Moines, IA 50321
(515) 974-8927
Web: www.iumf.org/scholarships/general

Summary To provide financial assistance to African American and other ethnic minority members of United Methodist churches in Iowa who are interested in majoring in a health-related field.

Eligibility This program is open to ethnic minority students who are members of United Methodist churches and preparing for a career in nursing, public health, or a related field at a college or school of nursing in Iowa. Preference is given to graduates of Iowa high schools. Applicants must have a GPA of 3.0 or higher. They must submit transcripts, 3 letters of recommendation, ACT and/or SAT scores, and documentation of financial need.

Financial data The stipend is $1,000.

Duration 1 year.

Number awarded 1 each year.

Deadline February of each year.

[351]
K. LEROY IRVIS UNDERGRADUATE SCHOLARSHIPS

Pennsylvania Black Conference on Higher Education
c/o Brenda Sanders Dédé, Scholarship Committee Chair
Clarion University of Pennsylvania
Academic Affairs
115 Carrier
840 Wood Street
Clarion, PA 16214
(814) 393-2223　　　　　E-mail: bdede@clarion.edu
Web: www.pbcohe.com/scholarships.html

Summary To provide financial assistance to African American residents of any state who are enrolled as undergraduates at colleges in Pennsylvania.

Eligibility This program is open to African Americans from any state who have completed at least the first semester as an undergraduate at a college or university in Pennsylvania. Applicants must have a GPA of 3.0 or higher. Along with their application, they must submit an essay, up to 5 pages in length, on why they should receive this scholarship. Selection is based on that essay, academics, extracurricular activity participation, leadership qualities, and interpersonal qualities.

Financial data The stipend is $1,000.

Duration 1 year.

Number awarded 3 each year: 1 in each of 3 regions (eastern, central, and western) in Pennsylvania.

Deadline January of each year.

[352]
KAISER PERMANENTE COLORADO DIVERSITY SCHOLARSHIP PROGRAM

Kaiser Permanente
Attn: Diversity Development Department
10065 East Harvard Avenue, Suite 400
Denver, CO 80231
Toll Free: (877) 457-4772
E-mail: co-diversitydevelopment@kp.org

Summary To provide financial assistance to Colorado residents who are African Americans or members of other diverse groups and are interested in working on an undergraduate or graduate degree in a health care field at a public college in the state.

Eligibility This program is open to all residents of Colorado, including those who identify as 1 or more of the following: African American, Asian Pacific, Latino, lesbian, gay, bisexual, transgender, intersex, Native American, U.S. veteran, and/or a person with a disability. Applicants must be enrolled or planning to enroll full time at a publicly-funded college, university, or technical school in Colorado as 1) a graduating high school senior with a GPA of 2.7 or higher; 2) a GED recipient with a GED score of 520 or higher; 3) an undergraduate student; or 4) a graduate or doctoral student. They must be preparing for a career in health care (e.g., athletic training, audiology, cardiovascular perfusion technology, clinical medical assisting, cytotechnology, dental assisting, dental hygiene, diagnostic medicine, dietetics, emergency medical technology, medicine, nursing, occupational therapy, pharmacy, phlebotomy, physical therapy, physician assistant, radiology, respiratory therapy, social work, sports medicine, surgical technology). Selection is based on academic achievement, character qualities, community outreach and volunteering, and financial need.

Financial data   Stipends range from $1,400 to $2,600 per year.

Duration   1 year; may be renewed.

Number awarded   Varies each year; recently, 17 were awarded.

Deadline   March of each year.

[353]
KAISER PERMANENTE NORTHWEST HEALTH CARE CAREER SCHOLARSHIPS

Kaiser Permanente Northwest
Attn: Community Health Careers Coordinator
500 N.E. Multnomah Street, Suite 100
Portland, OR 97232
(503) 813-4478   E-mail: kpnwscholarship@gmail.com
Web: www.kpnwscholarship.scholarsapply.org/Awards

Summary   To provide financial assistance to seniors at designated high schools in Oregon and southwestern Washington, especially African Americans and members of other diverse groups, who plan to attend college in any state to prepare for a career as a health care professional.

Eligibility   This program is open to seniors graduating from 106 approved high schools in Oregon and 26 in southwestern Washington. Applicants must be planning to enroll full time at a college or university in any state to prepare for a career as a medical or dental health care professional. They must have a GPA of 2.5 or higher. Proof of U.S. citizenship or permanent resident status is not required; undocumented students and those with Deferred Action for Childhood Arrival (DACA) status are eligible. Preference is given to students who 1) can demonstrate financial need; 2) are the first member of their family to attend college; 3) speak English plus a second language fluently; 4) are a member of a diverse population, including an ethnic or racial group underrepresented in the health professions (Black or African American, Hispanic or Latino, Native American, Asian or Pacific Islander), LGBTQ, and those with a disability; 5) engage in organized health and wellness activities at school and/or school-based health center activities; or 6) regularly volunteer or work in a public health setting such as a free clinic or health education organization.

Financial data   Most stipends are $2,000 per year. Some awards are for $10,000 or $5,000 ($5,000 or $2,500 per year).

Duration   1 year (the freshman year of college) for the $2,000 awards or 2 years (the freshmen and sophomore years) for the $10,000 and $5,000 students; recipients may apply for 1 additional year (the junior year of college) of funding at $2,000.

Additional information   This program began in 2008.

Number awarded   At least 1 at each of the 132 approved high schools plus 24 to former recipients entering their junior year of college.

Deadline   January of each year.

[354]
KANSAS ETHNIC MINORITY SCHOLARSHIP PROGRAM

Kansas Board of Regents
Attn: Student Financial Assistance
1000 S.W. Jackson Street, Suite 520
Topeka, KS 66612-1368
(785) 296-3518   Fax: (785) 296-0983
E-mail: loldhamburns@ksbor.org
Web: www.kansasregents.org/scholarships_and_grants

Summary   To provide financial assistance to African Americans and other minority students in Kansas who are interested in attending college in the state.

Eligibility   Eligible to apply are Kansas residents who fall into 1 of these minority groups: African American, Asian, American Indian, Alaskan Native, Pacific Islander, or Hispanic. Applicants may be current college students (enrolled in community colleges, colleges, or universities in Kansas), but high school seniors graduating in the current year receive priority consideration. Minimum academic requirements include 1 of the following: 1) ACT score of 21 or higher or combined mathematics and critical reading SAT score of 990 or higher; 2) cumulative GPA of 3.0 or higher; 3) high school rank in upper 33%; 4) completion of the Kansas Scholars Curriculum (4 years of English, 4 years of mathematics, 3 years of science, 3 years of social studies, and 2 years of foreign language); 5) selection by the National Merit Corporation in any category; or 6) selection by the College Board as a Hispanic Scholar. Selection is based primarily on financial need.

Financial data   A stipend of up to $1,850 is provided, depending on financial need and availability of state funds.

Duration   1 year; may be renewed for up to 3 additional years (4 additional years for designated 5-year programs), provided the recipient maintains a 2.0 cumulative GPA and has financial need.

Number awarded   Approximately 200 each year.

Deadline   April of each year.

[355]
KANSAS SPJ MINORITY STUDENT SCHOLARSHIP

Society of Professional Journalists-Kansas Professional
  Chapter
c/o Denise Neil, Scholarship Committee
Wichita Eagle
825 East Douglas Avenue
P.O. Box 820
Wichita, KS 67201-0820
(316) 268-6327   E-mail: dneil@wichitaeagle.com

Summary   To provide financial assistance to residents of any state enrolled at colleges and universities in Kansas who are African Americans or members of other racial or ethnic minority groups and interested in a career in journalism.

Eligibility   This program is open to residents of any state who are members of a racial or ethnic minority group and entering their junior or senior year at colleges and universities in Kansas. Applicants must be seriously considering a career in journalism. They must be enrolled at least half time and have a GPA of 2.5 or higher. Along with their application, they must submit a professional resume, 4 to 6 examples of their best work (clips or stories, copies of photographs, tapes or transcripts of broadcasts, printouts of web pages) and a 1-page cover letter about themselves, how they came to be interested in journalism, their professional goals, and (if appropriate) their financial need for this scholarship.

Financial data The stipend is $1,000.

Duration 1 year.

Number awarded 1 each year.

Deadline March of each year.

[356]
KAPPA SCHOLARSHIP ENDOWMENT FUND AWARDS

Kappa Alpha Psi Fraternity-Washington (DC) Alumni
 Chapter
Attn: Kappa Scholarship Endowment Fund, Inc.
P.O. Box 29331
Washington, DC 20017-0331
Toll Free: (866) 671-5295   E-mail: info@ksef-inc.com
Web: www.ksef-inc.com

Summary To provide financial assistance to African American and other high school seniors in Washington, D.C. who plan to attend college in any state.

Eligibility This program is open to seniors graduating from public or charter high schools in Washington, D.C. with a GPA of 2.5 or higher. Applicants must be planning to enroll full time at an accredited 4-year institution of higher learning in any state. They must be able to demonstrate involvement in school and community activities and financial need.

Financial data Stipend amounts vary; recently, they averaged $4,000.

Duration 1 year.

Additional information The sponsor is an historically African American social fraternity, but both women and men are eligible for these scholarships.

Number awarded Varies each year; recently, 28 were awarded.

Deadline March of each year.

[357]
KATHY MANN MEMORIAL SCHOLARSHIP

Wisconsin Education Association Council
Attn: Scholarship Committee
33 Nob Hill Drive
P.O. Box 8003
Madison, WI 53708-8003
(608) 276-7711   Toll Free: (800) 362-8034, ext. 278
Fax: (608) 276-8203   E-mail: BrisackM@weac.org
Web: www.weac.org

Summary To provide financial assistance to African American and other minority high school seniors whose parent is a member of the Wisconsin Education Association Council (WEAC) and who plan to study education at a college in any state.

Eligibility This program is open to high school seniors whose parent is an active WEAC member, an active retired member, or a person who died while holding a WEAC membership. Applicants must be members of a minority group (Black, American Indian, Eskimo or Aleut, Hispanic, Asian, or Pacific Islander). They must rank in the top 25% of their graduating class or have a GPA of 3.0 or higher, plan to major or minor in education at a college in any state, and intend to

teach in Wisconsin. Selection is based on an essay on why they want to enter the education profession and what they hope to accomplish, GPA, letters of recommendation, school and community activities, and financial need.

Financial data The stipend is $1,450 per year.

Duration 4 years, provided the recipient maintains a GPA of 3.0 or higher.

Number awarded 1 each year.

Deadline February of each year.

[358]
KAY MADRY SULLIVAN FELLOWSHIP

Alpha Kappa Alpha Sorority, Inc.
Attn: Educational Advancement Foundation
5656 South Stony Island Avenue
Chicago, IL 60637
(773) 947-0026   Toll Free: (800) 653-6528
Fax: (773) 947-0277   E-mail: akaeaf@akaeaf.net
Web: www.akaeaf.org/fellowships_endowments.htm

Summary To provide financial assistance to residents of designated states (especially African American women) who have been involved in foster care and are interested in attending college in any state.

Eligibility This program is open to undergraduate students who are enrolled full time as sophomores or higher in an accredited 4-year degree-granting institution in any state. Applicants must have a GPA of 2.5 or higher. They must have been involved in the foster care system and be residents of Florida; if no residents of Florida apply, the scholarship may be awarded to a resident of Georgia or South Carolina. Along with their application, they must submit 1) a list of honors, awards, and scholarships received; 2) a list of organizations in which they have memberships, especially minority organizations; and 3) a statement of their personal and career goals, including how this scholarship will enhance their ability to attain those goals. The sponsor is a traditionally African American women's sorority.

Financial data A stipend is awarded (amount not specified).

Duration 1 year.

Number awarded 1 or more each even-numbered year.

Deadline April of each even-numbered year.

[359]
KENTUCKY LIBRARY ASSOCIATION SCHOLARSHIP FOR MINORITY STUDENTS

Kentucky Library Association
c/o Executive Director
5932 Timber Ridge Drive, Suite 101
Prospect, KY 40059
(502) 223-5322   Fax: (502) 223-4937
E-mail: info@kylibasn.org
Web: www.klaonline.org/scholarships965.cfm

Summary To provide financial assistance to African Americans and members of other minority groups who are residents of Kentucky or attending school there and are working on an undergraduate or graduate degree in library science.

Eligibility This program is open to members of minority groups (defined as Black, American Indian, Alaskan Native, Hispanic, Pacific Islander, or other ethnic group) who are entering or continuing at a graduate library school accredited by the American Library Association (ALA) or an undergraduate library program accredited by the National Council for Teacher Education (NCATE). Applicants must be residents of Kentucky or a student in a library program in the state. Along with their application, they must submit a statement of their career objectives, why they have chosen librarianship as a career, and their reasons for applying for this scholarship. Selection is based on that statement, cumulative undergraduate and graduate GPA (if applicable), academic merit and potential, and letters of recommendation. U.S. citizenship or permanent resident status is required.

Financial data　The stipend is $1,000.

Duration　1 year; nonrenewable.

Number awarded　1 or more each year.

Deadline　June of each year.

[360]
KENTUCKY MINORITY EDUCATOR RECRUITMENT AND RETENTION SCHOLARSHIPS

Kentucky Department of Education
Attn: Office of Next-Generation Learners
500 Mero Street, 19th Floor
Frankfort, KY 40601
(502) 564-1479　　　　　　　Fax: (502) 564-4007
TDD: (502) 564-4970
E-mail: jennifer.baker@education.ky.gov
Web: www.education.ky.gov

Summary　To provide forgivable loans to African American and other minority undergraduate and graduate students enrolled in Kentucky public institutions who want to become teachers.

Eligibility　This program is open to residents of Kentucky who are undergraduate or graduate students pursuing initial teacher certification at a public university or community college in the state. Applicants must have a GPA of 2.75 or higher and either maintain full-time enrollment or be a part-time student within 18 semester hours of receiving a teacher education degree. They must be U.S. citizens and meet the Kentucky definition of a minority student.

Financial data　Stipends are $5,000 per year at the 8 state universities in Kentucky or $2,000 per year at community and technical colleges. This is a scholarship/loan program. Recipients are required to teach 1 semester in Kentucky for each semester or summer term the scholarship is received. If they fail to fulfill that requirement, the scholarship converts to a loan payable at 6% annually.

Duration　1 year; may be renewed up to 3 additional years.

Additional information　The Kentucky General Assembly established this program in 1992.

Number awarded　Varies each year.

Deadline　Each state college of teacher education sets its own deadline.

[361]
KILBY FAMILY ENDOWED SCHOLARSHIP FUND

POISE Foundation
Two Gateway Center, Suite 1700
603 Stanwix Street
Pittsburgh, PA 15222
(412) 281-4967　　　　　　　Fax: (412) 562-0292
Web: www.poisefoundation.org

Summary　To provide financial assistance for college to descendants of persons enslaved prior to the Civil War in Culpeper and Rappahannock counties in Virginia.

Eligibility　This program is open to descendants of persons held as slaves in Culpeper and Rappahannock counties in Virginia, especially those enslaved by John Kilby of Culpeper County (1715-1752). Applicants must be enrolled or planning to enroll at a 2- or 4-year college, university, or vocational school in any state to work on an associate, bachelor's, or technical degree. They must be able to document proof of lineal descent from a slave in the designated counties.

Financial data　The stipend ranges from $1,250 to $2,500.

Duration　1 year.

Additional information　This program began in 1998.

Number awarded　Up to 2 each year.

Deadline　April of each year.

[362]
KITTRELL-ALLEN-ADAMS SCHOLARSHIP

African Methodist Episcopal Church
Second Episcopal District
c/o Gail P. Radcliff, District Coordinator
9285 Berry Road
Waldorf, MD 20603
(301) 870-8492

Summary　To provide financial assistance to members of the African Methodist Episcopal (AME) Church in its Second Episcopal District who are interested in attending college in any state.

Eligibility　This program is open to AME members in the Second Episcopal District, which includes the Conferences of Baltimore, Washington, Virginia, North Carolina, and Western North Carolina. Applicants must be graduating high school seniors or students already working on an undergraduate degree at a college or university in any state. Along with their application, they must submit an autobiographical essay of 1 to 2 pages that includes information about their future goals and family, school, church, and community involvements. Selection is based on that essay, high school grades and SAT scores, letters of recommendation, and financial need.

Financial data　A stipend is awarded (amount not specified).

Duration　1 year.

Number awarded　1 or more each year.

Deadline　July of each year.

[363]
LAGRANT FOUNDATION UNDERGRADUATE SCHOLARSHIPS

Lagrant Foundation
Attn: Senior Talent Acquisition and Fundraising Manager
633 West Fifth Street, 48th Floor
Los Angeles, CA 90071
(323) 469-8680, ext. 223   Fax: (323) 469-8683
E-mail: erickainiguez@lagrant.com
Web: www.lagrantfoundation.org/Scholarship%20Program

Summary To provide financial assistance to African American and other minority college students who are interested in majoring in advertising, public relations, or marketing.

Eligibility This program is open to African Americans, Asian Americans/Pacific Islanders, Hispanics/Latinos, and Native Americans/American Indians who are full-time students at a 4-year accredited institution. Applicants must have a GPA of 2.75 or higher and be either majoring in advertising, marketing, or public relations or minoring in communications with plans to prepare for a career in advertising, marketing, or public relations. Along with their application, they must submit 1) a 1- to 2-page essay outlining their career goals; what steps they will take to increase ethnic representation in the fields of advertising, marketing, and public relations; and the role of an advertising, marketing, or public relations practitioner; 2) a paragraph describing the college and/or community activities in which they are involved; 3) a brief paragraph describing any honors and awards they have received; 4) a letter of reference; 5) a resume; and 6) an official transcript. U.S. citizenship or permanent resident status is required.

Financial data The stipend is $2,500.

Duration 1 year.

Number awarded Varies each year; recently, 22 were awarded.

Deadline February of each year.

[364]
LARRY AND CAROLYN SUAREZ FELLOWSHIP

Alpha Kappa Alpha Sorority, Inc.
Attn: Educational Advancement Foundation
5656 South Stony Island Avenue
Chicago, IL 60637
(773) 947-0026   Toll Free: (800) 653-6528
Fax: (773) 947-0277   E-mail: akaeaf@akaeaf.net
Web: www.akaeaf.org/fellowships_endowments.htm

Summary To provide financial assistance to members of Alpha Kappa Alpha Sorority who are working on an undergraduate degree in business and entrepreneurship.

Eligibility This program is open to undergraduate members of Alpha Kappa Alpha, a traditionally African American sorority, who are enrolled full time as sophomores or higher in an accredited degree-granting institution in any state. Applicants must be majoring in business and/or entrepreneurship and have a GPA of 3.0 or higher. Along with their application, they must submit 1) a list of honors, awards, and scholarships received; 2) a list of organizations in which they have memberships, especially minority organizations; and 3) a statement of their personal and career goals, including how this scholarship will enhance their ability to attain those goals.

Financial data A stipend is awarded (amount not specified).

Duration 1 year.

Number awarded 1 or more each even-numbered year.

Deadline April of each even-numbered year.

[365]
LARRY W. CARTER SCHOLARSHIP

Greater Des Moines Community Foundation
Finkbine Mansion
1915 Grand Avenue
Des Moines, IA 50309
(515) 883-2626   Fax: (515) 309-0704
E-mail: trettin@desmoinesfoundation.org
Web:
   www.communityfoundationofgreaterdesmoines.wordpress.com

Summary To provide financial assistance to African American undergraduate and graduate students in Iowa.

Eligibility Eligible to apply are African Americans who reside in Iowa and are enrolled in college or graduate school on a full- or part-time basis. Applicants must submit a personal statement that explains why they feel they should be selected to receive this scholarship and describes their personal and educational goals, motivations, and reasons for pursuing higher education. Financial need is considered in the selection process.

Financial data The stipend is $3,000.

Duration 1 year.

Number awarded Varies each year; recently, 3 were awarded.

Deadline May of each year.

[366]
LARRY WHITESIDE SCHOLARSHIP

National Association of Black Journalists
Attn: Program Manager
University of Maryland
1100 Knight Hall, Suite 3100
College Park, MD 20742
(301) 405-7520   Fax: (301) 314-1714
E-mail: Sberry@nabj.org
Web: www.nabj.org/?page=ScholarshipWhiteside

Summary To provide financial assistance to undergraduate or graduate student members of the National Association of Black Journalists (NABJ) who are preparing for a career in sports journalism.

Eligibility This program is open to African American undergraduate or graduate student members of NABJ who are currently enrolled full time at an accredited 4-year college or university. Applicants must be studying journalism as preparing for a career in sports journalism and have a GPA of 2.5 or higher in their major and 2.0 overall. They must be able to demonstrate financial need. Along with their application, they must submit 5 samples of their work, an official college transcript, 3 letters of recommendation, a resume, and an essay of 1,000 to 2,000 words on a sports journalist (living or deceased) whom they admire and why that person has inspired them to prepare for a career in sports journalism.

Financial data The stipend is $3,000. Funds are paid directly to the recipient's college or university.

Duration 1 year; nonrenewable.

Number awarded 1 each year.
Deadline February of each year.

[367]
LAUNCHING LEADERS UNDERGRADUATE SCHOLARSHIP

JPMorgan Chase
Campus Recruiting
Attn: Launching Leaders
277 Park Avenue, Second Floor
New York, NY 10172
(212) 270-6000
E-mail: bronwen.x.baumgardner@jpmorgan.com
Web: careers.jpmorgan.com

Summary To provide financial assistance and work experience to Black and other underrepresented minority undergraduate students interested in a career in financial services.

Eligibility This program is open to Black, Hispanic, and Native American students enrolled as sophomores or juniors and interested in financial services. Applicants must have a GPA of 3.5 or higher. Along with their application, they must submit 500-word essays on 1) why they should be considered potential candidates for CEO of the sponsoring bank in 2020; and 2) the special background and attributes they would contribute to the sponsor's diversity agenda. They must be interested in a summer associate position in the sponsor's investment banking, sales and trading, or research divisions.

Financial data The stipend is $5,000 for recipients accepted as sophomores or $10,000 for recipients accepted as juniors. For students accepted as sophomores and whose scholarship is renewed for a second year, the stipend is $15,000. The summer internship is a paid position.

Duration 1 year; may be renewed 1 additional year if the recipient successfully completes the 10-week summer intern program and maintains a GPA of 3.5 or higher.

Number awarded Approximately 12 each year.
Deadline October of each year.

[368]
LAURENCE R. FOSTER MEMORIAL SCHOLARSHIPS

Oregon Office of Student Access and Completion
Attn: Scholarship Processing Coordinator
1500 Valley River Drive, Suite 100
Eugene, OR 97401-2146
(541) 687-7422   Toll Free: (800) 452-8807, ext. 7422
Fax: (541) 687-7414   TDD: (800) 735-2900
E-mail: cheryl.a.connolly@state.or.us
Web: app.oregonstudentaid.gov/Catalog/Default.aspx

Summary To provide financial assistance to African American and other residents of Oregon from diverse environments who are enrolled at a college or graduate school in any state to prepare for a public health career.

Eligibility This program is open to residents of Oregon who are enrolled at least half time at a 4-year college or university in any state to prepare for a career in public health (not private practice). Preference is given first to applicants from diverse environments; second to persons employed in, or graduate students working on a degree in, public health; and third to juniors and seniors majoring in a health program (e.g., nursing, medical technology, physician assistant). Applicants

must be able to demonstrate financial need. Along with their application, they must submit essays of 250 to 350 words on 1) what public health means to them; 2) the public health aspect they intend to practice and the health and population issues impacted by that aspect; and 3) their experience living or working in diverse environments.

Financial data Stipends for scholarships offered by the Oregon Office of Student Access and Completion (OSAC) range from $1,000 to $10,000 but recently averaged $4,368.

Duration 1 year.

Additional information This program is administered by the OSAC with funds provided by the Oregon Community Foundation.

Number awarded Varies each year; recently, 6 were awarded.

Deadline February of each year.

[369]
LCDR EIFFERT FOSTER STUDENT SCHOLARSHIP

National Naval Officers Association-Washington, D.C.
  Chapter
c/o LCDR Stephen Williams
P.O. Box 30784
Alexandria, VA 22310
(703) 644-2605   Fax: (703) 644-8503
E-mail: Stephen.Williams@navy.mil
Web: www.dcnnoa.org/dcnnoa-scholarship

Summary To provide financial assistance to female African American high school seniors from the Washington, D.C. area who have been in foster care and are interested in attending college in any state.

Eligibility This program is open to female African American seniors graduating from high schools in the Washington, D.C. metropolitan area who plan to enroll full time at an accredited 2- or 4-year college or university in any state. Applicants must have lived in a foster home. They must have a GPA of 2.5 or higher and be U.S. citizens or permanent residents. Selection is based on academic achievement, community involvement, and financial need.

Financial data The stipend is $1,000.

Duration 1 year; nonrenewable.

Additional information Recipients are not required to join or affiliate with the military in any way.

Number awarded 1 each year.

Deadline February of each year.

[370]
LCDR JANET COCHRAN AND CDR CONNIE GREENE SCHOLARSHIP

National Naval Officers Association-Washington, D.C.
  Chapter
c/o LCDR Stephen Williams
P.O. Box 30784
Alexandria, VA 22310
(703) 644-2605   Fax: (703) 644-8503
E-mail: Stephen.Williams@navy.mil
Web: www.dcnnoa.org/dcnnoa-scholarship

Summary To provide financial assistance to female African American and other minority high school seniors from the

Washington, D.C. area who are interested in attending college in any state.

Eligibility This program is open to female minority seniors graduating from high schools in the Washington, D.C. metropolitan area who plan to enroll full time at an accredited 2- or 4-year college or university in any state. Applicants must have a GPA of 2.5 or higher and be U.S. citizens or permanent residents. Selection is based on academic achievement, community involvement, and financial need.

Financial data The stipend is $1,500.

Duration 1 year; nonrenewable.

Additional information This program is sponsored by the Washington D.C. Chapter of the National Naval Officers Association (DCNNOA), an organization of African American naval officers, but all minorities are eligible and recipients are not required to join or affiliate with the military in any way.

Number awarded 1 each year.

Deadline February of each year.

[371]
LCDR MICHAEL FILES EAGLE SCOUT LEADERSHIP SCHOLARSHIP

National Naval Officers Association-Washington, D.C.
Chapter
c/o LCDR Stephen Williams
P.O. Box 30784
Alexandria, VA 22310
(703) 644-2605   Fax: (703) 644-8503
E-mail: Stephen.Williams@navy.mil
Web: www.dcnnoa.org/dcnnoa-scholarship

Summary To provide financial assistance to male African American high school seniors from the Washington, D.C. area who are Eagle Scouts and interested in attending college in any state.

Eligibility This program is open to male African American seniors graduating from high schools in the Washington, D.C. metropolitan area who plan to enroll full time at an accredited 2- or 4-year college or university in any state. Applicants must be Eagle Scouts. They must have a GPA of 3.0 or higher and be U.S. citizens or permanent residents. Selection is based on academic achievement, community involvement, and financial need.

Financial data The stipend is $1,000.

Duration 1 year; nonrenewable.

Additional information Recipients are not required to join or affiliate with the military in any way.

Number awarded 1 each year.

Deadline February of each year.

[372]
LEADERSHIP FOR DIVERSITY SCHOLARSHIP

California School Library Association
Attn: CSL Foundation
6444 East Spring Street, Number 237
Long Beach, CA 90815-1553
Toll Free: (888) 655-8480   Fax: (888) 655-8480
E-mail: info@csla.net
Web: www.csla.net/awards-2/scholarships

Summary To provide financial assistance to African American and other students who reflect the diversity of California's population and are interested in earning a credential as a library media teacher in the state.

Eligibility This program is open to students who are members of a traditionally underrepresented group enrolled in a college or university library media teacher credential program in California. Applicants must intend to work as a library media teacher in a California school library media center for a minimum of 3 years. Along with their application, they must submit a 250-word statement on what they can contribute to the profession, their commitment to serving the needs of multicultural and multilingual students, and their financial need.

Financial data The stipend is $1,500.

Duration 1 year.

Number awarded 1 each year.

Deadline September of each year.

[373]
LEDGENT DIVERSITY UNDERGRADUATE SCHOLARSHIPS

Accounting and Financial Women's Alliance
Attn: Educational Foundation
2365 Harrodsburg Road, A325
Lexington, KY 40504
(859) 219-3532   Toll Free: (800) 326-2163
Fax: (859) 219-3577   E-mail: foundation@afwa.org
Web: www.afwa.org/foundation/scholarships

Summary To provide financial assistance to African American and other minority undergraduates interested in preparing for a career in accounting or finance.

Eligibility This program is open to members of minority groups (African Americans, Hispanic Americans, Native Americans, or Asian Americans) who are entering their third, fourth, or fifth year of undergraduate study at a college, university, or professional school of accounting. Applicants must have completed at least 60 semester hours with a declared major in accounting or finance and a GPA of 3.0 or higher. Along with their application, they must submit an essay of 150 to 250 words on their career goals and objectives, the impact they want to have on the accounting world, community involvement, and leadership examples. Selection is based on leadership, character, communication skills, scholastic average, and financial need. Membership in the Accounting and Financial Women's Alliance (AFWA) is not required. Applications must be submitted to a local ASWA chapter.

Financial data A stipend is awarded (amount not specified).

Duration 1 year; recipients may reapply.

Additional information This program is sponsored by Ledgent.

Number awarded 1 each year.

Deadline Local chapters must submit their candidates to the national office by September of each year.

[374]
LELA DUFFEL MORRIS NATIONAL SCHOLARSHIP

Auxiliary to the National Medical Association
8403 Colesville Road, Suite 820
Silver Spring, MD 20910
(301) 495-3779   Fax: (301) 495-0037
E-mail: anmanationaloffice@earthlink.net
Web: www.anmanet.org

Summary   To provide financial assistance to African American nursing or public health students.

Eligibility   This program is open to African Americans who are currently enrolled in an accredited nursing or public health program. Applicants must have a GPA of 3.0 or higher and a record of participation in school and/or community activities. Along with their application, they must submit a 500-word essay that covers their highest achievement, community service participation, what they see themselves doing in 5 years, and how this scholarship would affect their plans.

Financial data   The stipend is $2,000.

Duration   1 year.

Additional information   This program began in 2012.

Number awarded   1 each year.

Deadline   May of each year.

[375]
LEON BRADLEY SCHOLARSHIPS

American Association of School Personnel Administrators
Attn: Scholarship Program
11863 West 112th Street, Suite 100
Overland Park, KS 66210
(913) 327-1222   Fax: (913) 327-1223
E-mail: aaspa@aaspa.org
Web: www.aaspa.org/leon-bradley-scholarship

Summary   To provide financial assistance to African American and other minority undergraduates, paraprofessionals, and graduate students preparing for a career in teaching and school leadership at colleges in designated southeastern states.

Eligibility   This program is open to members of minority groups (Black, American Indian, Alaskan Native, Asian, Pacific Islander, Hispanic, Middle Easterner) currently enrolled full time at a college or university in Alabama, Florida, Georgia, Kentucky, North Carolina, South Carolina, Tennessee, or Virginia. Applicants must be 1) undergraduates in their final year (including student teaching) of an initial teaching certification program; 2) paraprofessional career-changers in their final year (including student teaching) of an initial teaching certification program; or 3) graduate students who have served as a licensed teacher and are working on a school administrator credential. They must have an overall GPA of 3.0 or higher. Priority is given to applicants who 1) can demonstrate work experience that has been applied to college expenses; 2) have received other scholarship or financial aid support; or 3) are seeking initial certification and/or endorsement in a state-identified critical area.

Financial data   Stipends are $2,500 for undergraduates in their final year, $1,500 for paraprofessionals in their final year, and $1,500 for graduate students.

Duration   1 year.

Number awarded   4 each year: 1 undergraduate, 1 paraprofessional, and 2 graduate students.

Deadline   May of each year.

[376]
LEONARD M. PERRYMAN COMMUNICATIONS SCHOLARSHIP FOR ETHNIC MINORITY STUDENTS

United Methodist Communications
Attn: Communications Ministry Team
810 12th Avenue South
P.O. Box 320
Nashville, TN 37202-0320
(615) 742-5481   Toll Free: (888) CRT-4UMC
Fax: (615) 742-5485   E-mail: scholarships@umcom.org
Web: www.umcom.org

Summary   To provide financial assistance to African American and other minority United Methodist college students who are interested in careers in religious communications.

Eligibility   This program is open to United Methodist ethnic minority students enrolled in accredited institutions of higher education as juniors or seniors. Applicants must be interested in preparing for a career in religious communications. For the purposes of this program, "communications" is meant to cover audiovisual, electronic, and print journalism. Selection is based on Christian commitment and involvement in the life of the United Methodist church, academic achievement, journalistic experience, clarity of purpose, and professional potential as a religion communicator.

Financial data   The stipend is $2,500 per year.

Duration   1 year.

Additional information   The scholarship may be used at any accredited institution of higher education.

Number awarded   1 each year.

Deadline   March of each year.

[377]
LEONARDO WATTS SCHOLARSHIP

Watts Charity Association, Inc.
6245 Bristol Parkway, Suite 224
Culver City, CA 90230
(310) 671-0394   Fax: (323) 778-2613
E-mail: wattscharity@yahoo.com
Web: 4watts.tripod.com/id5.html

Summary   To provide financial assistance to upper-division African Americans working on a degree in classical music.

Eligibility   This program is open to U.S. citizens of African American descent who are enrolled full time as a college or university junior. Applicants must be studying classical music, including voice and/or instrumental. They must have a GPA of 3.0 or higher, be between 17 and 24 years of age, and be able to demonstrate that they intend to continue their education for at least 2 years. Along with their application, they must submit 1) a 1-paragraph statement on why they should be awarded a Watts Charity Association scholarship; and 2) a 1- to 2-page essay on a specific type of cancer, based either on how it has impacted their life or on researched information.

Financial data   A stipend is awarded (amount not specified).

Duration   1 year.

Additional information Royce R. Watts, Sr. established the Watts Charity Association after he learned he had cancer in 2001.

Number awarded 1 each year.

Deadline May of each year.

[378]
LEROY APKER AWARD

American Physical Society
Attn: Honors Program
One Physics Ellipse
College Park, MD 20740-3844
(301) 209-3268   Fax: (301) 209-0865
E-mail: honors@aps.org
Web: www.aps.org/programs/honors/awards/apker.cfm

Summary To recognize and reward African American and other underrepresented undergraduate students for outstanding work in physics.

Eligibility This program is open to undergraduate students at colleges and universities in the United States. Nominees should have completed or be completing the requirements for an undergraduate degree with an excellent academic record and should have demonstrated exceptional potential for scientific research by making an original contribution to physics. Each department of physics in the United States may nominate only 1 student. Each nomination packet should include the student's academic transcript, a description of the original contribution written by the student (such as a manuscript or reprint of a research publication or senior thesis), a 1,000-word summary, and 2 letters of recommendation. Nominations of qualified women and members of underrepresented minority groups are especially encouraged.

Financial data The award consists of a $5,000 honorarium for the student, a certificate citing the work and school of the recipient, and an allowance for travel expenses to the meeting of the American Physical Society (APS) at which the prize is presented. Each of the finalists receives an honorarium of $2,000 and a certificate. Each of the physics departments whose nominees are selected as recipients and finalists receives a certificate and an award; the departmental award is $5,000 for recipients and $1,000 for finalists.

Duration The award is presented annually.

Additional information This award was established in 1978.

Number awarded 6 finalists are selected each year, of whom 2 receive awards: 1 to a student at a Ph.D. granting institution and 1 at a non-Ph.D. granting institution.

Deadline June of each year.

[379]
LEROY C. SCHMIDT, CPA MINORITY 150-HOUR ACCOUNTING SCHOLARSHIPS

Wisconsin Institute of Certified Public Accountants
Attn: WICPA Educational Foundation
W233N2080 Ridgeview Parkway, Suite 201
Waukesha, WI 53188
(262) 785-0445, ext. 3025
Toll Free: (800) 772-6939 (within WI)
Fax: (262) 785-0838   E-mail: jessica@wicpa.org
Web: www.wicpa.org

Summary To provide financial assistance to African American and other underrepresented minority residents of Wisconsin enrolled at a college or university in the state and working to meet the requirements to sit for the Certified Public Accountant (C.P.A.) examination.

Eligibility This program is open to minority residents of Wisconsin (African American, Native American/Alaska Native, Pacific Islander, or Hispanic) who have completed 120 credit hours at a college or university in the state in a degree program that qualifies them to sit for the Uniform C.P.A. Examination. Applicants must be entering their fifth-year requirement and eligible to receive a master's degree in business, a double major/minor, or additional courses for credit to satisfy the 150-hour requirement. They must be enrolled full time, have a GPA of 3.0 or higher, and be U.S. citizens.

Financial data The stipend is $5,000 or $2,500.

Duration 1 year.

Number awarded Varies each year; recently, 2 were awarded: 1 at $5,000 and 1 at $2,500.

Deadline February of each year.

[380]
LES PAYNE FOUNDER'S SCHOLARSHIP

National Association of Black Journalists
Attn: Program Manager
University of Maryland
1100 Knight Hall, Suite 3100
College Park, MD 20742
(301) 405-7520   Fax: (301) 314-1714
E-mail: Sberry@nabj.org
Web: www.nabj.org/?page=ScholarshipsPayne

Summary To provide financial assistance to undergraduate and graduate student members of the National Association of Black Journalists (NABJ) who are working on a degree in print journalism.

Eligibility This program is open to African American undergraduate or graduate student members of NABJ who are currently enrolled full time at an accredited 4-year college or university. Applicants must be working on a degree in print journalism and have a GPA of 3.0 or higher. They must be able to demonstrate financial need. Along with their application, they must submit 5 samples of their work, an official college transcript, 3 letters of recommendation, a resume, and an essay of 1,000 to 2,000 words describing 3 issues about which they are passionate and which they hope to cover as a professional journalist.

Financial data The stipend is $2,500.

Duration 1 year.

Number awarded 1 each year.

Deadline February of each year.

[381]
LORRAINE HANSBERRY PLAYWRITING AWARD

John F. Kennedy Center for the Performing Arts
Education Department
Attn: Kennedy Center American College Theater Festival
2700 F Street, N.W.
Washington, DC 20566
(202) 416-8864   Fax: (202) 416-8860
E-mail: ghenry@kennedy-center.org
Web: web.kennedy-center.org

Summary To recognize and reward student authors of plays on the African American experience in America.

Eligibility Students at any accredited junior or senior college in the United States are eligible to compete, provided their college agrees to participate in the Kennedy Center American College Theater Festival (KCACTF). Undergraduate students must be carrying at least 6 semester hours, graduate students must be enrolled in at least 3 semester hours, and continuing part-time students must be enrolled in a regular degree or certificate program. These awards are presented to the best plays written by students of African or Diasporan descent on the subject of the African American experience.

Financial data The first-place award is $1,000 and the second-place award is $500. Other benefits include appropriate membership in the Dramatists Guild and an all-expense paid professional development opportunity.

Duration The awards are presented annually.

Additional information This program is supported by the Kennedy Center and Dramatic Publishing Company. It honors the first African American playwright to win the New York Drama Critics Award who died in 1965 at the age of 34. First presented in 1977, it is part of the Michael Kanin Playwriting Awards Program. The sponsoring college or university must pay a registration fee of $275 for each production.

Number awarded 2 each year.

Deadline November of each year.

[382]
LOUIS B. RUSSELL, JR. MEMORIAL SCHOLARSHIP

Indiana State Teachers Association
Attn: ISTA Foundation for the Improvement of Education
150 West Market Street, Suite 900
Indianapolis, IN 46204-2814
(317) 263-3306   Toll Free: (800) 382-4037, ext. 3306
Fax: (800) 777-6128   E-mail: ccherry@ista-in.org
Web: www.ista-in.org/our-profession/scholarships-awards

Summary To provide financial assistance to African American and other ethnic minority high school seniors in Indiana who are interested in attending vocational school in any state.

Eligibility This program is open to ethnic minority high school seniors in Indiana who are interested in continuing their education in the area of industrial arts, vocational education, or technical preparation at an accredited postsecondary institution in any state. Selection is based on academic achievement, leadership ability as expressed through co-curricular activities and community involvement, recommendations, and a 300-word essay on their educational goals and how they plan to achieve those goals.

Financial data The stipend is $1,000.

Duration 1 year; may be renewed for 1 additional year, provided the recipient maintains a GPA of "C+" or higher.

Number awarded 1 each year.

Deadline February of each year.

[383]
LOUISE JANE MOSES/AGNES DAVIS MEMORIAL SCHOLARSHIP

California Librarians Black Caucus-Greater Los Angeles Chapter
Attn: Scholarship Committee
P.O. Box 882276
Los Angeles, CA 90009
E-mail: scholarship@clbc.org
Web: www.clbc.org/scholar.html

Summary To provide financial assistance to African Americans in California who are interested in becoming librarians or library paraprofessionals.

Eligibility This program is open to African American residents of California who are working on a degree from an accredited library/information science program or an accredited library/information science paraprofessional program in the state. Applicants must submit an essay of 300 to 500 words on their professional goals and their interest in a library or information-related career. Selection is based on demonstrated financial need, scholastic achievement, and commitment to the goals of encouraging and supporting African American library professionals and improving library service to the African American community. Interviews are required.

Financial data Stipends range from $750 to $1,500.

Duration 1 year.

Number awarded 2 to 3 each year.

Deadline October of each year.

[384]
LOUISE MORITZ MOLITORIS LEADERSHIP AWARD

Women's Transportation Seminar
Attn: WTS Foundation
1701 K Street, N.W., Suite 800
Washington, DC 20006
(202) 955-5085   Fax: (202) 955-5088
E-mail: wts@wtsinternational.org
Web: www.wtsinternational.org/education/scholarships

Summary To provide financial assistance to undergraduate women, especially African Americans and other minorities, who are interested in a career in transportation.

Eligibility This program is open to women who are working on an undergraduate degree in transportation or a transportation-related field (e.g., transportation engineering, planning, finance, or logistics). Applicants must have a GPA of 3.0 or higher. Along with their application, they must submit a 500-word statement about their career goals after graduation and why they think they should receive the scholarship award; their statement should specifically address the issue of leadership. Applications must be submitted first to a local chapter; the chapters forward selected applications for consideration on the national level. Minority women are especially encouraged to apply. Selection is based on transportation involvement and goals, job skills, academic record, and leadership potential; financial need is not considered.

Financial data The stipend is $5,000.

Duration 1 year.

Additional information Local chapters may also award additional funding to winners for their area.

Number awarded 1 each year.

Deadline Applications must be submitted by November to a local WTS chapter.

[385]
LOVE SCHOLARSHIP FOR DIVERSITY

International Council of Shopping Centers
Attn: ICSC Foundation
1221 Avenue of the Americas, 41st Floor
New York, NY 10020-1099
(646) 728-3628   Fax: (732) 694-1690
E-mail: foundation@icsc.org
Web: www.icsc.org

Summary To provide financial assistance to African American and other minority undergraduate students who are preparing for a career as a retail real estate professional.

Eligibility This program is open to U.S. citizens who are full-time juniors or seniors working on a degree related to the retail real estate profession. Applicants must be a member of an underrepresented ethnic minority group (African American, American Indian or Alaskan Native, Asian or Pacific Islander, Hispanic, Caribbean). They must have a GPA of 3.0 or higher.

Financial data The stipend is $1,000.

Duration 1 year.

Number awarded 1 or more each year.

Deadline January of each year.

[386]
LOVETTE HOOD JR. SCHOLARSHIP

Sigma Gamma Rho Sorority, Inc.
Attn: National Education Fund
1000 Southhill Drive, Suite 200
Cary, NC 27513
(919) 678-9720   Toll Free: (888) SGR-1922
Fax: (919) 678-9721
E-mail: customerservice@sgrho1922.org
Web: www.sgrho1922.org/nef

Summary To provide financial assistance to African American and other undergraduate students working on a degree in theology.

Eligibility This program is open to undergraduates working on a degree in theology. The sponsor is a traditionally African American sorority, but support is available to males and females of all races. Applicants must have a GPA of "C" or higher and be able to demonstrate financial need.

Financial data A stipend is awarded (amount not specified).

Duration 1 year.

Additional information A processing fee of $20 is required.

Number awarded 1 each year.

Deadline April of each year.

[387]
LOWE'S GAP SCHOLARSHIPS OF THE THURGOOD MARSHALL COLLEGE FUND

Thurgood Marshall College Fund
Attn: Senior Manager of Scholarship Programs
901 F Street, N.W., Suite 300
Washington, DC 20004
(202) 507-4851   Fax: (202) 652-2934
E-mail: deshuandra.walker@tmcfund.org
Web: www.tmcf.org

Summary To provide financial assistance to African American students currently completing a degree at a college or university that is a member of the Thurgood Marshall College Fund (TMCF) and facing a gap of an unmet financial need.

Eligibility This program is open to students who are entering their final semester at 1 of 47 TMCF member institutions, which are public Historically Black Colleges and Universities (HBCUs). Applicants must have an unmet financial need of $500 to $3,100 to complete their education. They must have a current GPA of 2.0 or higher and be U.S. citizens or permanent residents. Along with their application, they must submit 1) a resume that includes community service and leadership abilities; 2) their Student Aid report from their FAFSA; 3) their most recent transcript; and 4) documentation of their current need gap.

Financial data The stipend ranges from $500 to $3,100 depending on the gap documented by the student.

Duration 1 year.

Additional information This program is sponsored by Lowe's.

Number awarded Varies each year.

Deadline December of each year.

[388]
LSAMP UNDERGRADUATE SUMMER RESEARCH PROGRAM

Cornell University
College of Engineering
Attn: Diversity Programs in Engineering
146 Olin Hall
Ithaca, NY 14853-5201
(607) 255-6403   Fax: (607) 255-2834
E-mail: dpeng@cornell.edu
Web: www.engineering.cornell.edu

Summary To provide an opportunity for African American and other traditionally underrepresented minority groups in the sciences and engineering to participate in a summer research program in a field of science, technology, engineering, or mathematics (STEM) at Cornell University.

Eligibility This program is open to members of minority groups traditionally underrepresented in the sciences and engineering who are entering their sophomore, junior, or senior year at a college or university anywhere in the country. Applicants must be interested in working on a research project in a field of STEM under the guidance of a faculty or research mentor at Cornell University. They must have a GPA of 3.0 or higher and be U.S. citizens or permanent residents.

Financial data Participating students receive a stipend of $4,000, a round-trip travel stipend of up to $300, a double room in a campus residential hall, and access to laboratories, libraries, computer facilities, and study lounges.

Duration 10 weeks during the summer.

Additional information This program is part of the Louis Stokes Alliance for Minority Participation (LSAMP), supported by the National Science Foundation as part of its Research Experiences for Undergraduates (REU) program. Students are encouraged to enter and present their research at their affiliated National Society of Black Engineers (NSBE), Society of Hispanic Professional Engineers (SHPE), or American Indian Science and Engineering Society (AISES) or professional conference.

Number awarded Varies each year; recently, 9 were accepted.

Deadline February of each year.

[389]
LTG EDWARD HONOR SCHOLARSHIP AWARD

The ROCKS, Inc.
c/o WSC Associates, LLP
P.O. Box 47435
District Heights, MD 20753
(301) 856-9319   Toll Free: (888) 762-5747
Fax: (301) 856-5220
E-mail: rocksnationalboard@gmail.com
Web: natlrocks.clubexpress.com

Summary To recognize and reward college seniors who have participated in ROTC programs at Historically Black Colleges and Universities (HBCUs).

Eligibility This award is available to graduating seniors who are Army or Air Force Cadets or Navy Midshipmen at HBCUs. Applicants must submit 1) a 2-page paper on a topic related to leadership or mentorship; and 2) a letter of recommendation from their professor of military science evaluating their appearance, attitude, APFT score, dedication, initiative, integrity, judgment, leadership potential, and written and oral communication ability.

Financial data The award is $2,000.

Duration The award is presented annually.

Number awarded Varies each year; recently, 3 were awarded.

Deadline December of each year.

[390]
LTK ENGINEERING SCHOLARSHIP

Conference of Minority Transportation Officials
Attn: National Scholarship Program
100 M Street, S.E., Suite 917
Washington, DC 20003
(202) 506-2917   E-mail: info@comto.org
Web: www.comto.org/page/scholarships

Summary To provide financial assistance to African American and other minority upper-division and graduate students in engineering or other field related to transportation.

Eligibility This program is open to full-time minority juniors, seniors, and graduate students in engineering or other technical transportation-related disciplines. Applicants must have a GPA of 3.0 or higher. Along with their application they must submit a cover letter on their transportation-related career goals and life aspirations. Financial need is not considered in the selection process.

Financial data The stipend is $6,000. Funds are paid directly to the recipient's college or university.

Duration 1 year.

Additional information This program is sponsored by LTK Engineering Services.

Number awarded 1 each year.

Deadline April of each year.

[391]
LTK ENGINEERING TRANSPORTATION PLANNING SCHOLARSHIP

Conference of Minority Transportation Officials
Attn: National Scholarship Program
100 M Street, S.E., Suite 917
Washington, DC 20003
(202) 506-2917   E-mail: info@comto.org
Web: www.comto.org/page/scholarships

Summary To provide financial assistance to African American and other minority upper-division and graduate students in planning or other field related to transportation.

Eligibility This program is open to full-time minority juniors, seniors, and graduate students in planning of other technical transportation-related disciplines. Applicants must have a GPA of 3.0 or higher. Along with their application they must submit a cover letter on their transportation-related career goals and life aspirations. Financial need is not considered in the selection process.

Financial data The stipend is $5,000. Funds are paid directly to the recipient's college or university.

Duration 1 year.

Additional information This program is sponsored by LTK Engineering Services.

Number awarded 1 each year.

Deadline April of each year.

[392]
LUCILLE BLUFORD JOURNALISM SCHOLARSHIP

Missouri Legislative Black Caucus Foundation
c/o Representative Gail McCann Beatty
4609 Paseo Boulevard, Suite 102
Kansas City, MO 64110
(573) 761-4166   Toll Free: (877) 63-MLBCF
Fax: (816) 861-2845   E-mail: mail@mlbcf.org
Web: www.mlbcf.org/scholarships/journalism

Summary To provide financial assistance to African American residents of Missouri who are interested in working on an undergraduate or graduate degree in journalism at a school in any state.

Eligibility This program is open to African American residents of Missouri who are enrolled full time in an undergraduate or graduate program in journalism at a college or university in any state. Applicants must have a GPA of 3.0 or higher. Along with their application, they must submit a writing sample and a 200-word personal statement on how their education will assist them in achieving their goals. Selection is based on academic performance, community service, leadership skills, and financial need.

Financial data A stipend is awarded (amount not specified).

Duration 1 year; recipients may reapply for up to 3 additional years of support.

Number awarded 1 or more each year.

Deadline May of each year.

[393]
LULLELIA W. HARRISON COUNSELING SCHOLARSHIP

Zeta Phi Beta Sorority, Inc.
Attn: National Educational Foundation
1734 New Hampshire Avenue, N.W.
Washington, DC 20009
(202) 387-3103   Fax: (202) 232-4593
E-mail: info@zetaphibetasororityhq.org
Web: www.zpbnef1975.org/scholarships-and-descriptions

Summary To provide financial assistance to undergraduate and graduate students interested in preparing for a career in counseling.

Eligibility This program is open to students enrolled full time in an undergraduate or graduate program leading to a degree in counseling. Proof of enrollment is required. Along with their application, they must submit a 150-word essay on their educational goals and professional aspirations, how this award will help them to achieve those goals, and why they should receive the award. Financial need is not considered in the selection process.

Financial data The stipend ranges from $500 to $1,000.

Duration 1 academic year.

Additional information Zeta Phi Beta is a traditionally African American sorority.

Number awarded 3 or more each year.

Deadline January of each year.

[394]
LUTHER AND MARY IDA VANDROSS SCHOLARSHIPS

Philadelphia Foundation
1234 Market Street, Suite 1800
Philadelphia, PA 19107-3794
(215) 563-6417   Fax: (215) 563-6882
E-mail: scholarships@philafound.org
Web: app.smarterselect.com

Summary To provide financial assistance to residents of Delaware, New Jersey, New York, and Pennsylvania who are upper-division students at Historically Black Colleges and Universities (HBCUs).

Eligibility This program is open to students entering their third, fourth, or fifth year of undergraduate study at a 4-year HBCU in any state. Applicants must be residents of Delaware, New Jersey, New York, or Pennsylvania. They must have a GPA of 2.5 or higher and be able to demonstrate financial need. Along with their application, they must submit an essay on what makes them stand out from other students and any talents, skills, or hobbies of which they are particularly proud.

Financial data The stipend is $10,000.

Duration 1 year.

Number awarded 5 each year.

Deadline April of each year.

[395]
LYDIA BARASHANGO SCHOLARSHIP

National Naval Officers Association-Washington, D.C. Chapter
c/o LCDR Stephen Williams
P.O. Box 30784
Alexandria, VA 22310
(703) 644-2605   Fax: (703) 644-8503
E-mail: Stephen.Williams@navy.mil
Web: www.dcnnoa.org/dcnnoa-scholarship

Summary To provide financial assistance to African American high school seniors from the Washington, D.C. area who are interested in majoring in a field of education, social work, or medicine at a college in any state.

Eligibility This program is open to African American seniors graduating from high schools in the Washington, D.C. metropolitan area who plan to enroll full time and major in education, social work, or a medical field at a college or university in any state. Applicants must have a GPA of 2.5 or higher and be U.S. citizens or permanent residents. Selection is based on academic achievement, community involvement, and financial need.

Financial data The stipend is $1,000.

Duration 1 year; nonrenewable.

Additional information Recipients are not required to join or affiliate with the military in any way.

Number awarded 1 each year.

Deadline February of each year.

[396]
MABEL SMITH MEMORIAL SCHOLARSHIP

Wisconsin Women of Color Network, Inc.
c/o P.E. Kiram
756 North 35th Street, Suite 101
Milwaukee, WI 53208
(414) 899-2329   E-mail: pekiram64@gmail.com

Summary To provide financial assistance for vocation/technical school or community college to African American and other minority residents of Wisconsin.

Eligibility This program is open to residents of Wisconsin who are high school or GED-equivalent graduating seniors planning to continue their education at a vocational/technical school or community college in any state. Applicants must be a member of 1 of the following groups: African American, Asian, American Indian, Latina, or biracial. They must have a GPA of 2.0 or higher and be able to demonstrate financial need. Along with their application, they must submit a 1-page essay on how this scholarship will help them accomplish their educational goal. U.S. citizenship is required.

Financial data A stipend is awarded (amount not specified).

Duration 1 year.

Additional information This program began in 1990.

Number awarded 1 each year.

Deadline May of each year.

[397]
MAHLON MARTIN FELLOWSHIPS

Arkansas Department of Higher Education
Attn: Financial Aid Division
423 Main Street, Suite 400
Little Rock, AR 72201-3801
(501) 371-2050   Toll Free: (800) 54-STUDY
Fax: (501) 371-2001   E-mail: finaid@adhe.edu
Web: scholarships.adhe.edu

Summary To provide funding to African American undergraduate students in Arkansas interested in conducting a research project.

Eligibility This program is open to African American undergraduate students at Arkansas colleges and universities who are interested in conducting a research project in their field of study under the mentorship of a faculty member. Applicants must have completed at least 30 semester credit hours toward their degree and have a GPA of 3.25 or higher. Their institution may be a public or private institution of higher education in Arkansas that offers 2 or more years of college study. The faculty member must be tenured or tenure-track; temporary instructors and adjunct faculty are not eligible. Students must be U.S. citizens or permanent residents.

Financial data The maximum grant is $1,250 for spring and fall semesters, spring and summer, or spring, summer, and fall. The institution must match the SURF grant up to an additional $1,250, so the total budget may be up to $2,500. Spring semester only grants of $625, matched by the institution for an additional $625, are also available. Students are also eligible for a travel grant up to $750 to attend a meeting of experts in their research area. Faculty mentors are eligible for grants up to $750.

Duration Grants are available for 2 semesters, spring and summer, 2 semesters and summer, or spring only; students may compete for up to 2 years of additional funding.

Number awarded 2 to 4 each year.

Deadline October of each year.

[398]
MAHOGANY AND BLUES BABE FOUNDATION SCHOLARSHIP PROGRAM

Blues Babe Foundation
2233 North Broad Street, Second Floor
Philadelphia, PA 19132
(267) 324-5600   E-mail: info@bluesbabefoundation.org
Web: bluesbabefoundation.org

Summary To provide financial assistance to African American college students working on a degree in the writing arts.

Eligibility This program is open to African American students enrolled full time at a 4-year college or university. Applicants must be preparing for a career in the writing arts. Selection is based on transcripts, a 2- to 4-page writing sample, a letter of recommendation, and information on financial need.

Financial data The stipend is $10,000.

Duration 1 year.

Additional information This program was established in 2015 by the Mahogany Brands of Hallmark Cards and the Blues Babe Foundation.

Number awarded Up to 2 each year.

Deadline October of each year.

[399]
MAINE SECTION ASCE HIGH SCHOOL SCHOLARSHIP

American Society of Civil Engineers-Maine Section
c/o Leslie L. Corrow, Scholarship Chair
Kleinschmidt Associates
141 Main Street
P.O. Box 650
Pittsfield, ME 04967
(207) 487-3328   Fax: (207) 487-3124
E-mail: scholarships@maineasce.org
Web: www.facebook.com/maineasce

Summary To provide financial assistance to high school seniors in Maine, especially African Americans and other minorities, who are interested in studying civil engineering in college.

Eligibility This program is open to graduating high school seniors who are Maine residents and who intend to study civil engineering in college. Women and minorities are especially encouraged to apply. Applicants must submit a 200-word statement describing why they have chosen civil engineering as a career and what they hope to accomplish by being a civil engineer. Selection is based on the statement, academic performance, extracurricular activities, and letters of recommendation.

Financial data A total of $4,000 is available for this program each year.

Duration 1 year; nonrenewable.

Number awarded Several each year.

Deadline January of each year.

[400]
MARCIA SILVERMAN MINORITY STUDENT AWARD

Public Relations Student Society of America
Attn: Vice President of Member Services
33 Maiden Lane, 11th Floor
New York, NY 10038-5150
(212) 460-1474   Fax: (212) 995-0757
E-mail: prssa@prsa.org
Web: www.prssa.prsa.org

Summary To provide financial assistance to African American and other minority college seniors who are interested in preparing for a career in public relations.

Eligibility This program is open to minority (African American/Black, Hispanic/Latino, Asian, Native American, Alaskan Native, or Pacific Islander) students who are entering their senior year at an accredited 4-year college or university. Applicants must have a GPA of 3.0 or higher and be working on a degree in public relations, journalism, or other field to prepare for a career in public relations. Along with their application, they must submit an essay on their view of the public relations profession and their public relations career goals. Selection is based on academic achievement, demonstrated leadership, practical experience, commitment to public relations, writing skills, and letters of recommendation.

Financial data The stipend is $5,000.

Duration 1 year.

Additional information This program began in 2010.

Number awarded 1 each year.

Deadline June of each year.

[401]
MARGARET A. PEMBERTON SCHOLARSHIP FUND

Black Nurses' Association of Greater Washington, D.C. Area, Inc.
Attn: Scholarship Committee Chair
P.O. Box 55285
Washington, DC 20040
(202) 291-8866
Web: www.bnaofgwdca.org/scholarships.html

Summary To provide financial assistance to African American high school seniors in the Washington, D.C. area who are interested in working on a baccalaureate degree in nursing at a school in any state.

Eligibility This program is open to African American seniors graduating from high schools in the District of Columbia or adjoining counties in Maryland (Anne Arundel, Calvert, Charles, Howard, Montgomery, and Prince George's). Applicants must be U.S. citizens or permanent residents and have a GPA of 2.8 or higher. They must have been accepted into a baccalaureate nursing program at a college or university in the United States. Along with their application, they must submit a 1-page essay that describes their personal and educational goals, reasons why they should be selected (including evidence of financial need), and current and projected contributions to the community (including high school service and/or volunteer activities).

Financial data A stipend is awarded (amount not specified).

Duration 1 year.

Additional information This program began in 2002.

Number awarded 1 each year.

Deadline April of each year.

[402]
MARJORIE BOWENS-WHEATLEY SCHOLARSHIPS

Unitarian Universalist Association
Attn: UU Women's Federation
258 Harvard Street
Brookline, MA 02446
(617) 838-6989   E-mail: uuwf@uua.org
Web: www.uuwf.org

Summary To provide financial assistance to African American and other women of color who are working on an undergraduate or graduate degree to prepare for Unitarian Universalist ministry or service.

Eligibility This program is open to women of color who are either 1) aspirants or candidates for the Unitarian Universalist ministry; or 2) candidates in the Unitarian Universalist Association's professional religious education or music leadership credentialing programs. Applicants must submit a 1- to 2-page narrative that covers their call to UU ministry, religious education, or music leadership; their passions; how their racial/ethnic/cultural background influences their goals for their calling; and how the work of the program's namesake relates to their dreams and plans for their UU service.

Financial data The stipend is $1,500.

Duration 1 year.

Additional information This program began in 2009.

Number awarded Varies each year; recently, 2 were awarded.

Deadline March of each year.

[403]
MARTIN LUTHER KING, JR. MEMORIAL SCHOLARSHIP FUND

California Teachers Association
Attn: CTA Foundation for Teaching and Learning
1705 Murchison Drive
P.O. Box 921
Burlingame, CA 94011-0921
(650) 697-1400   E-mail: scholarships@cta.org
Web: www.cta.org

Summary To provide financial assistance for college or graduate school to African Americans and other racial and ethnic minorities who are members of the California Teachers Association (CTA), children of members, or members of the Student CTA.

Eligibility This program is open to members of racial or ethnic minority groups (African Americans, American Indians/Alaska Natives, Asians/Pacific Islanders, and Hispanics) who are 1) active CTA members; 2) dependent children of active, retired, or deceased CTA members; or 3) members of Student CTA. Applicants must be interested in preparing for a teaching career in public education or already engaged in such a career.

Financial data Stipends vary each year; recently, they ranged up to $6,000.

Duration 1 year.

Number awarded Varies each year; recently, 24 were awarded: 1 to a CTA member, 10 to children of CTA members, and 13 to Student CTA members.

Deadline February of each year.

[404]
MARTIN LUTHER KING JR. SCHOLARSHIP AWARDS

American Correctional Association
Attn: Scholarship Award Committee
206 North Washington Street, Suite 200
Alexandria, VA 22314
(703) 224-0000   Toll Free: (800) ACA-JOIN
Fax: (703) 224-0179   E-mail: execoffice@aca.org
Web: www.aca.org

Summary To provide financial assistance for undergraduate or graduate study to African Americans and other minorities interested in a career in the criminal justice field.

Eligibility Members of the American Correctional Association (ACA) may nominate a minority person for these awards. Nominees do not need to be ACA members, but they must have been accepted to or be enrolled in an undergraduate or graduate program in criminal justice at a 4-year college or university. Along with the nomination package, they must submit a 250-word essay describing their reflections on the ideals and philosophies of Dr. Martin Luther King and how they have attempted to emulate those qualities in their lives. They must provide documentation of financial need, academic achievement, and commitment to the principles of Dr. King.

Financial data A stipend is awarded (amount not specified). Funds are paid directly to the recipient's college or university.

Duration 1 year.

Number awarded 1 each year.

Deadline May of each year.

[405]
MARY A. MCDOWELL FELLOWSHIP

Alpha Kappa Alpha Sorority, Inc.
Attn: Educational Advancement Foundation
5656 South Stony Island Avenue
Chicago, IL 60637
(773) 947-0026   Toll Free: (800) 653-6528
Fax: (773) 947-0277   E-mail: akaeaf@akaeaf.net
Web: www.akaeaf.org/fellowships_endowments.htm

Summary To provide financial assistance to undergraduates (especially African American women) who are working on a degree in special needs education.

Eligibility This program is open to undergraduate students who are enrolled full time as sophomores or higher in an accredited degree-granting institution in any state. Applicants must be majoring in special needs education. Along with their application, they must submit 1) a list of honors, awards, and scholarships received; 2) a list of organizations in which they have memberships, especially minority organizations; and 3) a statement of their personal and career goals, including how this scholarship will enhance their ability to attain those goals. The sponsor is a traditionally African American women's sorority.

Financial data A stipend is awarded (amount not specified).

Duration 1 year.

Number awarded 1 or more each even-numbered year.

Deadline April of each even-numbered year.

[406]
MARY E. BORDER SCHOLARSHIP

Kansas 4-H
c/o K-State Research and Extension
201 Umberger Hall
Manhattan, KS 66506-3404
(785) 532-5800   Fax: (785) 532-5981
Web: www.kansas4-h.org/p.aspx?tabid=479

Summary To provide financial assistance to members of Kansas 4-H who are African American or other minority or economically-disadvantaged high school seniors or returning adults planning to enroll at a college in any state and major in any field.

Eligibility This program is open to residents of Kansas who have completed at least 1 year of 4-H work and are planning to enroll at a college in any state and major in any field. Applicants may be 1) economically-disadvantaged high school seniors; 2) high school seniors who are members of minority groups (African American, Asian/Pacific Islander, American Indian/Alaska Native, Hispanic/Latino); or 3) adults returning to college. Along with their application, they must submit a 1-page summary of 4-H leadership, community service, participation, and recognition; a 1-page essay on how 4-H has impacted them; and a 1-page summary of non-4-H leadership, community service, participation, and recognition

in school and community. Selection is based on 4-H leadership (40%), 4-H citizenship and community service (30%), 4-H participation and recognition (20%), and non-4-H leadership, citizenship, and recognition (10%).

Financial data The stipend is $1,500.

Duration 1 year.

Number awarded 1 each year.

Deadline January of each year.

[407]
MARY E. WOOD SCHOLARSHIP

Greater Des Moines Community Foundation
Finkbine Mansion
1915 Grand Avenue
Des Moines, IA 50309
(515) 883-2626   Fax: (515) 309-0704
E-mail: trettin@desmoinesfoundation.org
Web: www.communityfoundationmarywood.wordpress.com

Summary To provide financial assistance to African American residents of Iowa working on an undergraduate degree at a school in any state.

Eligibility Eligible to apply are African Americans who reside in Iowa and have received either a high school diploma or a GED diploma. Applicants must be attending a college, university, or trade school in any state. Along with their application, they must submit a personal statement that explains why they feel they should be selected to receive this scholarship and describes their personal and educational goals, motivations, and reasons for pursuing higher education. Financial need is considered in the selection process.

Financial data A stipend is awarded (amount not specified).

Duration 1 year.

Number awarded 1 or more each year.

Deadline May of each year.

[408]
MARY ELIZA MAHONEY SCHOLARSHIP

New England Regional Black Nurses Association, Inc.
P.O. Box 190690
Roxbury, MA 02119
(617) 524-1951   E-mail: nerbascholarships@gmail.com
Web: nerbna.nursingnetwork.com

Summary To provide financial assistance to high school seniors in New England who are of African descent and interested in studying nursing at a school in any state.

Eligibility The program is open to African American seniors graduating from high schools in New England who are planning to enroll full time in an NLN-accredited baccalaureate program in nursing in any state. Applicants must have a GPA of 3.0 or higher. Along with their application, they must submit a 3-page essay that covers their reasons for furthering their career in nursing; why minority nursing leadership is important; how minority nursing leadership can assist them in furthering their career; why they chose to prepare for a career in nursing; and any financial hardships that may hinder them from completing their education.

Financial data A stipend is awarded (amount not specified).

Duration 1 year.

Number awarded 1 or more each year.

Deadline February of each year.

[409]
MARY HILL DAVIS ETHNIC/MINORITY SCHOLARSHIP PROGRAM

Baptist General Convention of Texas
Attn: Theological Education
7557 Rambler Road, Suite 1200
Dallas, TX 75231-2388
(214) 828-5252   Toll Free: (888) 244-9400
Fax: (214) 828-5261   E-mail: institutions@bgct.org
Web: www.texasbaptists.org

Summary To provide financial assistance for college to African American and other ethnic minority residents of Texas who are members of Texas Baptist congregations.

Eligibility This program is open to members of Texas Baptist congregations who are of African American, Hispanic, Native American, or other intercultural heritage. Applicants must be attending or planning to attend a university affiliated with the Baptist General Convention of Texas to work on a bachelor's degree as preparation for service as a future lay or vocational ministry leader in a Texas Baptist ethnic/minority church. They must have been active in their respective ethnic/minority community. Along with their application, they must submit a letter of recommendation from their pastor and transcripts. Students still in high school must have a GPA of at least 3.0; students previously enrolled in a college must have at least a 2.0 GPA. U.S. citizenship or permanent resident status is required.

Financial data Stipends are $800 per semester ($1,600 per year) for full-time students or $400 per semester ($800 per year) for part-time students.

Duration 1 semester; may be renewed up to 7 additional semesters.

Additional information The scholarships are funded through the Week of Prayer and the Mary Hill Davis Offering for state missions sponsored annually by Women's Missionary Union of Texas. The eligible institutions are Baptist University of The Americas, Baylor University, Dallas Baptist University, East Texas Baptist University, Hardin Simmons University, Houston Baptist University, Howard Payne University, University of Mary Hardin Baylor, and Wayland Baptist University.

Number awarded Varies each year.

Deadline April of each year.

[410]
MARY MCLEOD BETHUNE SCHOLARSHIPS

Florida Department of Education
Attn: Office of Student Financial Assistance
State Scholarship and Grant Programs
325 West Gaines Street, Suite 1314
Tallahassee, FL 32399-0400
(850) 410-5160   Toll Free: (888) 827-2004
Fax: (850) 487-1809   E-mail: osfa@fldoe.org
Web: www.floridastudentfinancialaid.org

Summary To provide financial assistance to high school seniors interested in attending Historically Black Colleges and Universities (HBCUs) in Florida.

Eligibility Eligible are high school seniors who wish to attend Florida A&M University, Bethune-Cookman University, Edward Waters College, or Florida Memorial University for a minimum of 12 credit hours per term. Applicants must be Florida residents, be U.S. citizens or eligible noncitizens, have a GPA of 3.0 or higher, be able to demonstrate financial need, and not be in default or owe repayment on any federal or state grant, scholarship, or loan program. Priority may be given to students with the lowest total family resources.

Financial data The stipend is $3,000 per year.

Duration 1 year; may be renewed up to 3 additional years if the student maintains full-time enrollment and a GPA of 3.0 or higher and continues to demonstrate financial need.

Number awarded Varies each year; recently, this program awarded 88 new and 50 renewal grants.

Deadline Deadlines are established by the participating institutions.

[411]
MARYLAND SEA GRANT RESEARCH EXPERIENCES FOR UNDERGRADUATES PROGRAM

Maryland Sea Grant
Attn: Associate Director for Research and Administration
University of Maryland
4321 Hartwick Road, Suite 300
College Park, MD 20740
(301) 405-7500   Fax: (301) 405-5780
E-mail: mallen@mdsg.umd.edu
Web: www.mdsg.umd.edu/reu

Summary To provide an opportunity for African American and other underrepresented undergraduates to conduct summer research related to the mission of Maryland Sea Grant.

Eligibility This program is open to U.S. citizens and permanent residents who have completed at least 2 years of undergraduate work on a bachelor's degree but have not yet completed that degree; preference is given to rising seniors. Students from underrepresented groups and institutions with limited research opportunities are especially encouraged to apply. Applicants must be majoring in marine science, ecology, environmental science, biology, chemistry, engineering, physics, or mathematics. They must be interested in working on a summer research project at either of the research laboratories of the University of Maryland Center for Environmental Sciences on Chesapeake Bay: the Chesapeake Biological Laboratory in Solomons, Maryland or the Horn Point Laboratory in Cambridge, Maryland.

Financial data Fellows receive a stipend of $6,000, housing costs, and round-trip travel expenses.

Duration 12 weeks during the summer.

Additional information This program is supported by the National Science Foundation through its Research Experiences for Undergraduates program.

Number awarded 15 each year.

Deadline February of each year.

[412]
MASSMUTUAL SCHOLARS PROGRAM

Massachusetts Mutual Life Insurance Company
1295 State Street
Springfield, MA 01111-0001
Toll Free: (800) 542-6767
Web: www.massmutual.scholarsapply.org

Summary To provide financial assistance to African American and other undergraduates who reflect the diversity of the country and are preparing for a career in the insurance and financial services industry.

Eligibility This program is open to full-time students from diverse backgrounds who are entering their sophomore, junior, senior, or fifth-year senior year at an accredited college or university in the United States, Puerto Rico, U.S. Virgin Islands, or Guam. Applicants must be U.S. citizens or permanent residents and have a GPA of 3.0 or higher. They may be majoring in any field, but preference is given to students who demonstrate 1) an interest in preparing for a career in the insurance and financial services industry; and 2) leadership and participation in extracurricular activities. Financial need is considered in the selection process.

Financial data The stipend is $2,500 for students at 2-year colleges or $5,000 for students at 4-year institutions.

Duration 1 year.

Number awarded 30 each year.

Deadline March of each year.

[413]
MAUDE DAVIS/JOSEPH C. MCKINNEY SCHOLARSHIP

African Methodist Episcopal Church
Second Episcopal District Lay Organization
c/o Dr. V. Susie Oliphant, District Coordinator
910 Luray Place
Hyattsville, MD 20783
(301) 559-9488   E-mail: vsfo@verizon.net

Summary To provide financial assistance to members of the African Methodist Episcopal (AME) Church in its Second Episcopal District who are interested in attending college in any state.

Eligibility This program is open to AME members in the Second Episcopal District, which includes the Conferences of Baltimore, Washington, Virginia, North Carolina, and Western North Carolina. Applicants must be graduating high school seniors or college freshmen who are attending or planning to attend a college or university in any state to work on an undergraduate degree or certification. Along with their application, they must submit a high school transcript and SAT scores, 3 letters of recommendation, a 1-page biographical statement that includes career goals, and documentation of financial need.

Financial data A stipend is awarded (amount not specified).

Duration 1 year.

Number awarded Each of the 5 Conferences may award 1 or more of these scholarships each year.

Deadline June of each year.

[414]
MAUREEN L. AND HOWARD N. BLITMAN, P.E. SCHOLARSHIP TO PROMOTE DIVERSITY IN ENGINEERING

National Society of Professional Engineers
Attn: NSPE Educational Foundation
1420 King Street
Alexandria, VA 22314-2794
(703) 684-2833   Toll Free: (888) 285-NSPE
Fax: (703) 684-2821   E-mail: education@nspe.org
Web: www.nspe.org

Summary To provide financial assistance for college to African Americans and members of other underrepresented ethnic minority groups interested in preparing for a career in engineering.

Eligibility This program is open to members of underrepresented ethnic minorities (African Americans, Hispanics, or Native Americans) who are high school seniors accepted into an ABET-accredited engineering program at a 4-year college or university. Applicants must have a GPA of 3.5 or higher, verbal SAT score of 600 or higher, and math SAT score of 700 or higher (or English ACT score of 29 or higher and math ACT score of 29 or higher). They must submit brief essays on 4 assigned topics. Selection is based on those essays, GPA, internship/co-op experience and community involvement, 2 faculty recommendations, and honors/scholarships/awards. U.S. citizenship is required.

Financial data The stipend is $5,000 per year; funds are paid directly to the recipient's institution.

Duration 1 year; nonrenewable.

Number awarded 1 each year.

Deadline February of each year.

[415]
MAX OLIGARIO VISIONARY SCHOLARSHIP

National Black MBA Association-Tampa Bay Chapter
Attn: Scholarship Committee
P.O. Box 173367
Tampa Bay, FL 33672
(813) 476-0242
E-mail: Membership@TampaBayBMBAA.org
Web: www.tampabaybmbaa.org/programs

Summary To provide financial assistance to African American and other minority undergraduate and graduate students at colleges in the Tampa Bay area of Florida working on a degree in business.

Eligibility This program is open to minority students enrolled full time at AACSB-accredited colleges and universities in the Tampa Bay area of Florida. Applicants must be working on an undergraduate or graduate degree in business. Undergraduates must have a GPA of 2.5 or higher. U.S. citizenship is required.

Financial data The stipend is $1,000.

Duration 1 year.

Number awarded 1 each year.

Deadline October of each year.

[416]
MAXINE V. FENNELL/ROBIN GAINES MEMORIAL SCHOLARSHIP

New England Regional Black Nurses Association, Inc.
P.O. Box 190690
Roxbury, MA 02119
(617) 524-1951   E-mail: nerbascholarships@gmail.com
Web: nerbna.nursingnetwork.com

Summary To provide financial assistance to registered nurses (R.N.s) from New England who are of African descent and interested in working on a degree in nursing or public health at a school in any state.

Eligibility The program is open to African American residents of the New England states who are R.N.s and currently enrolled in an NLN-accredited bachelor's, master's, or doctoral degree program in nursing or public health at a school in any state. Applicants must have a GPA of 3.0 or higher and at least 1 full year of school remaining. They must be members of the New England Regional Black Nurses Association (NERBNA). Along with their application, they must submit a 3-page essay that covers their reasons for furthering their career in nursing; why minority nursing leadership is important; how minority nursing leadership can assist them in furthering their career; why they chose to prepare for a career in nursing; and any financial hardships that may hinder them from completing their education.

Financial data A stipend is awarded (amount not specified).

Duration 1 year.

Number awarded 1 or more each year.

Deadline February of each year.

[417]
MCKINNEY FAMILY FUND SCHOLARSHIP

Cleveland Foundation
Attn: Scholarship Processing
1422 Euclid Avenue, Suite 1300
Cleveland, OH 44115-2001
(216) 861-3810   Fax: (216) 861-1729
E-mail: mbaker@clevefdn.org
Web: www.clevelandfoundation.org

Summary To provide financial assistance to residents of Ohio, especially African Americans and members of other minority groups, who are interested in attending college or graduate school in any state.

Eligibility This program is open to U.S. citizens who have been residents of Ohio for at least 2 years. Applicants must be high school seniors or graduate students and interested in working full or part time on an associate, bachelor's, master's, or doctoral degree at an accredited college or university in any state. They must have a GPA of 2.5 or higher. Preference is given to applicants of minority descent. Selection is based on evidence of sincerity toward obtaining an academic credential. Financial need may be used as a tiebreaker.

Financial data The stipend is $2,000 per year. Funds are paid directly to the school and must be applied to tuition, fees, books, supplies, and equipment required for course work.

Duration 1 year; may be renewed up to 3 additional.

Number awarded 1 or more each year.

Deadline March of each year.

[418]
MEDIA GENERAL MINORITY SCHOLARSHIP AND TRAINING PROGRAM

Media General
Attn: Angie Cartwright, Human Resources
9101 Burnet Road
Austin, TX 78758
(512) 380-4400
Web: www.mediageneral.com/careers/scholarship.html

Summary To provide scholarship/loans to African American and other minority undergraduates interested in earning a degree in a field related to broadcast journalism and working at a station owned by LIN Television Corporation.

Eligibility This program is open to U.S. citizens and permanent residents of non-white origin who are enrolled as a sophomore or junior at a college or university. Applicants must have a declared major in broadcast journalism, digital multimedia, mass/speech/digital communication, television production, or marketing and a GPA of 3.0 or higher. Along with their application, they must submit a list of organizations and activities in which they have held leadership positions, 3 references, a 50-word description of their career goals, a list of personal achievements and honors, and a 500-word essay about themselves. Financial need is not considered in the selection process.

Financial data The program pays for tuition and fees, books, and room and board, to a maximum of $10,000 per year. Recipients must sign an employment agreement that guarantees them part-time employment as an intern during school and a 2-year regular position at a television station owned by Media General following graduation. If they fail to honor the employment agreement, they must repay all scholarship funds received.

Duration 2 years.

Additional information This program began in 1998 under LIN Television Corporation, which was acquired by Media General in 2014. Media General owns 71 television stations in 48 media markets in the United States. Recipients of these scholarships must work at a station selected by Media General management.

Number awarded 2 each year: 1 for a student in broadcast television and 1 for a student in digital media.

Deadline January of each year.

[419]
MELLON UNDERGRADUATE CURATORIAL FELLOWSHIP PROGRAM

Art Institute of Chicago
Attn: Coordinator, Andrew W. Mellon Academic Programs
111 South Michigan Avenue
Chicago, IL 60603
(312) 443-3581   E-mail: fmings@artic.edu
Web: www.artic.edu/mellon

Summary To provide an opportunity for undergraduates who are African Americans or members of other groups historically underrepresented in the curatorial field to gain academic training and work experience to prepare for a career as an art curator.

Eligibility This program is open to undergraduates (typically freshmen or sophomores) who can commit 2 years to a program of preparation for a career as an art curator. Applicants must be studying art history, art, or the museum field at a college or university in the vicinity of 5 designated art museums. They must be members of groups historically underrepresented in the curatorial field and interested in continuing on to graduate school for advanced study in a relevant academic discipline. They must also be available to work with a mentor at the museum during the academic year to gain experience with curators and staff on exhibitions, collections, and programs and to participate in a summer internship. Interested students first apply to participate in a Summer Academy at the museum in their area. Selection for the Academy is based on academic record, extracurricular activities, background or other experiences, and expected contribution to the program. Based on performance during the Academy and personal interviews, Curatorial Fellows are selected at each of the 5 museums.

Financial data   Students selected for the Summer Academies receive a per diem allowance. Students selected as fellows receive an academic stipend of $4,000 per year and a grant of $6,000 for the summer internship.

Duration   The Summer Academy lasts 1 week. The fellowship is 2 years, including 10-week summer internships.

Additional information   The Andrew W. Mellon Foundation established this program in 2013. In addition to the Art Institute of Chicago, it also operates at the High Museum of Art in Atlanta, the Los Angeles County Museum of Art, the Museum of Fine Arts, Houston, and the Nelson-Atkins Museum of Art in Kansas City. Students who attend college in the vicinity of those museums should contact them about this program.

Number awarded   15 students at each of the 5 museums are selected each year to participate in the Summer Academy. Of those, 2 are selected at each museum to receive the Curatorial Fellowship.

Deadline   February of each year.

[420]
MERCHANT EXCELLENCE AND LEADERSHIP AND EXCELLENCE HBCU SCHOLARSHIP

National Naval Officers Association-Washington, D.C.
  Chapter
c/o LCDR Stephen Williams
P.O. Box 30784
Alexandria, VA 22310
(703) 644-2605   Fax: (703) 644-8503
E-mail: Stephen.Williams@navy.mil
Web: www.dcnnoa.org/dcnnoa-scholarship

Summary   To provide financial assistance to female African American high school seniors from the Washington, D.C. area who are interested in majoring in a field of science, technology, engineering, or mathematics (STEM) at an Historically Black College or University (HBCU) in any state.

Eligibility   This program is open to female African American seniors graduating from high schools in the Washington, D.C. metropolitan area who plan to enroll full time and major in a STEM discipline at an HBCU in any state. Applicants must have a GPA of 3.0 or higher and be U.S. citizens or permanent residents. Selection is based on academic achievement, community involvement, and financial need.

Financial data   The stipend is $1,000.

Duration   1 year; nonrenewable.

Additional information   Recipients are not required to join or affiliate with the military in any way.

Number awarded   1 each year.

Deadline   February of each year.

[421]
METRO DC CHAPTER NABA SCHOLARSHIP

National Association of Black Accountants-Metro
  Washington DC Chapter
Attn: Student Member Services Directors
P.O. Box 18602
Washington, DC 20036-8602
(202) 455-LIFT
E-mail: studentservices@nabametrodc.org
Web: www.nabametrodc.org

Summary   To provide financial assistance to members of the Metro Washington DC chapter of the National Association of Black Accountants (NABA) who are working on an undergraduate or graduate degree in accounting, business, or finance.

Eligibility   This program is open to NABA members who live or attend school in the Metropolitan Washington D.C. area (Maryland, northern Virginia, and the District of Columbia). Applicants must be 1) full-time freshmen, sophomores, juniors, or first-year seniors majoring in accounting, business, or finance; or 2) graduate students enrolled in a C.P.A. review program. They must have an overall GPA of 3.0 or higher. Along with their application, they must submit an essay of 500 to 750 words on a topic that changes annually but relates to minorities in finance. Financial need is not considered in the selection process.

Financial data   A stipend is awarded (amount not specified).

Duration   1 year.

Number awarded   1 or more each year.

Deadline   February of each year.

[422]
METRO NEW YORK CHAPTER NBMBAA SCHOLARSHIPS

National Black MBA Association-Metro New York Chapter
Attn: Scholarship Committee
P.O. Box 8135
New York, NY 10116
(212) 202-7544
E-mail: studentrelations@nyblackmba.org
Web: www.nyblackmba.org/learn/scholarship-application-2

Summary   To provide financial assistance to African American and other minority students from any state working on an undergraduate or graduate degree at a school in the New York metropolitan area.

Eligibility   This program is open to minority students who may be residents of any state but must be enrolled full or part time in an accredited New York metropolitan area graduate business or management program working toward an undergraduate or graduate degree. Applicants must have a record of at least 5 hours of community service or extracurricular activities each semester. Along with their application, they must submit 1,000-word essays on 1) how they are involved in improving the African American or minority community; and

2) their leadership style. Financial need is not considered in the selection process.

Financial data A stipend is awarded (amount not specified).

Duration 1 year.

Number awarded Varies each year.

Deadline November of each year.

[423]
MIAMI CHAPTER BLACK NURSES' ASSOCIATION GRADUATE SCHOLARSHIP

Black Nurses' Association, Inc.-Miami Chapter
Attn: Scholarship Committee
P.O. Box 472826
Miami, FL 33147-2826
(305) 754-2280   E-mail: miamibna@gmail.com
Web: www.bna-miami.org/annual-scholarship—1.html

Summary To provide financial assistance to members of the National Black Nurses' Association (NBNA) from Florida who are working on a degree in nursing at a school in any state.

Eligibility This program is open to residents of Florida who are NBNA members and enrolled in a nursing program (doctoral, M.S.N., B.S.N., A.S.N., L.P.N.) at a school in any state. Applicants must have a GPA of 2.5 or higher and be able to demonstrate financial need. Along with their application, they must submit a brief statement about themselves, their future goals in nursing, and how they will be an asset to the sponsor and its community. U.S. citizenship or permanent resident status is required.

Financial data The stipend is $1,000.

Duration 1 year.

Number awarded 3 to 4 each year.

Deadline April of each year.

[424]
MIAMI CHAPTER BLACK NURSES' ASSOCIATION UNDERGRADUATE SCHOLARSHIPS

Black Nurses' Association, Inc.-Miami Chapter
Attn: Scholarship Committee
P.O. Box 472826
Miami, FL 33147-2826
(305) 754-2280   E-mail: miamibna@gmail.com
Web: www.bna-miami.org/annual-scholarship—1.html

Summary To provide financial assistance to members of the National Black Nurses' Association (NBNA) from Florida who are enrolled in an undergraduate program in nursing at a school in any state.

Eligibility This program is open to NBNA members who are residents of Florida and have completed at least 1 semester of an R.N. or L.P.N. program in any state. Applicants must have a GPA of 2.5 or higher and be able to demonstrate financial need. Along with their application, they must submit a brief statement about themselves, their future goals in nursing, and how they will be an asset to the sponsor and its community. U.S. citizenship or permanent resident status is required.

Financial data The stipend is $1,000 per year.

Duration 1 year; may be renewed 1 additional, provided the recipient maintains a GPA of 2.5 or higher.

Additional information This program includes the Lessie Pryor Scholarship and the Ruby Murphy Scholarship.

Number awarded 1 to 3 each year.

Deadline April of each year.

[425]
MICHAEL BAKER SCHOLARSHIP FOR DIVERSITY IN ENGINEERING

Association of Independent Colleges and Universities of Pennsylvania
101 North Front Street
Harrisburg, PA 17101-1404
(717) 232-8649   Fax: (717) 233-8574
E-mail: info@aicup.org
Web: www.aicup.org/Foundation-Scholarships

Summary To provide financial assistance to African American and other minority students from any state enrolled at member institutions of the Association of Independent Colleges and Universities of Pennsylvania (AICUP) who are majoring in designated fields of engineering.

Eligibility This program is open to full-time undergraduate students from any state enrolled at designated AICUP colleges and universities who are women and/or members of the following minority groups: Blacks/African Americans, American Indians, Alaska Natives, Asians, Hispanics/Latinos, Native Hawaiians, or Pacific Islanders. Applicants must be juniors majoring in architectural, civil, or environmental engineering with a GPA of 3.0 or higher. Along with their application, they must submit a 2-page essay on what they believe will be the greatest challenge facing the engineering profession over the next decade, and why.

Financial data The stipend is $2,500 per year.

Duration 1 year; may be renewed 1 additional year if the recipient maintains appropriate academic standards.

Additional information This program, sponsored by the Michael Baker Corporation, is available at the 88 private colleges and universities in Pennsylvania that comprise the AICUP.

Number awarded 1 each year.

Deadline April of each year.

[426]
MICHIGAN CHAPTER AABE SCHOLARSHIPS

American Association of Blacks in Energy-Michigan Chapter
Attn: Scholarship Committee
37637 Five Mile Road, Suite 405
Livonia, MI 48154
(810) 760-3465   E-mail: aaron.parket@cmsenergy.com
Web: www.aabe.org/index.php?component=pages&id=582

Summary To provide financial assistance to African Americans and members of other underrepresented minority groups who are high school seniors in Michigan and planning to major in an energy-related field at a college in any state.

Eligibility This program is open to seniors graduating from high schools in Michigan and planning to work on a bachelor's degree at a college or university in any state. Applicants must be African Americans, Hispanics, or Native Americans who have a GPA of 3.0 or higher and have taken the ACT and/

or SAT test. Their intended major must be a field of business, engineering, physical science, mathematics, or technology related to energy. Along with their application, they must submit a 350-word essay that includes 1) when they discovered their interest in the field of energy and what sparked their interest; and 2) either what excites them about the field of energy or how they expect their education to prepare them for the field of energy. Financial need is not considered in the selection process.

Financial data A stipend is awarded (amount not specified).

Duration 1 year; nonrenewable.

Additional information Winners are eligible to compete for regional and national scholarships.

Number awarded At least 1 each year.

Deadline March of each year.

[427]
MICHIGAN CHAPTER COMTO SCHOLARSHIPS

Conference of Minority Transportation Officials-Michigan
  Chapter
Attn: President
P.O. Box 32439
Detroit, MI 48232
(269) 491-7279   E-mail: averyk@michigan.gov
Web: www.comtomichigan.org/scholarships.html

Summary To provide financial assistance to African American and other minority undergraduate and graduate students in Michigan who are working on a degree in a transportation-related field.

Eligibility This program is open to members of minority groups enrolled full time as sophomores, juniors, seniors, or graduate students at colleges or universities in Michigan. Applicants must be working on a degree in engineering, planning, or other transportation-related discipline. Graduate students must be members of the Conference of Minority Transportation Officials (COMTO); if undergraduates are not already members, they must become a member within 30 days of the scholarship award. U.S. citizenship or legal resident status is required.

Financial data The stipend ranges from $500 to $3,000. Funds are paid directly to the student.

Duration 1 year.

Number awarded Varies each year; recently, 7 were awarded: 1 at $3,000, 1 at $2,000, 2 at $1,000, and 3 at $500.

Deadline April of each year.

[428]
MICKEY LELAND ENERGY FELLOWSHIPS

Oak Ridge Institute for Science and Education
Attn: MLEF Fellowship Program
1299 Bethel Valley Road, Building SC-200
P.O. Box 117, MS 36
Oak Ridge, TN 37831-0117
(865) 574-6440   Fax: (865) 576-0734
E-mail: barbara.dunkin@orau.org
Web: orise.orau.gov/mlef/index.html

Summary To provide summer work experience at fossil energy sites of the Department of Energy (DOE) to African American and other underrepresented minority students or postdoctorates.

Eligibility This program is open to U.S. citizens currently enrolled full time at an accredited college or university. Applicants must be undergraduate, graduate, or postdoctoral students in fields of science, technology (IT), engineering, or mathematics (STEM) and have a GPA of 3.0 or higher. They must be interested in a summer work experience at a DOE fossil energy research facility. Along with their application, they must submit a 100-word statement on why they want to participate in this program. A goal of the program is to recruit women and underrepresented minorities into careers related to fossil energy, although all qualified students are encouraged to apply.

Financial data Weekly stipends are $600 for undergraduates, $750 for master's degree students, or $850 for doctoral and postdoctoral students. Travel costs for a round trip to and from the site and for a trip to a designated place for technical presentations are also paid.

Duration 10 weeks during the summer.

Additional information This program began as 3 separate activities: the Historically Black Colleges and Universities Internship Program established in 1995, the Hispanic Internship Program established in 1998, and the Tribal Colleges and Universities Internship Program, established in 2000. Those 3 programs were merged into the Fossil Energy Minority Education Initiative, renamed the Mickey Leland Energy Fellowship Program in 2000. Sites to which interns may be assigned include the National Energy Technology Laboratory (Morgantown, West Virginia, Albany, Oregon and Pittsburgh, Pennsylvania), Pacific Northwest National Laboratory (Richland, Washington), Sandia National Laboratory (Livermore, California), Lawrence Berkeley National Laboratory (Berkeley, California), Los Alamos National Laboratory (Los Alamos, New Mexico), Strategic Petroleum Reserve Project Management Office (New Orleans, Louisiana), or U.S. Department of Energy Headquarters (Washington, D.C.).

Number awarded Varies each year; recently, 30 students participated in this program.

Deadline December of each year.

[429]
MIDWIVES OF COLOR-WATSON MIDWIFERY STUDENT SCHOLARSHIP

American College of Nurse-Midwives
Attn: ACNM Foundation, Inc.
8403 Colesville Road, Suite 1550
Silver Spring, MD 20910-6374
(240) 485-1850   Fax: (240) 485-1818
E-mail: foundation@acnmf.org
Web: www.midwife.org

Summary To provide financial assistance for midwifery education to African American and other students of color who belong to the American College of Nurse-Midwives (ACNM).

Eligibility This program is open to ACNM members of color who are currently enrolled in an accredited basic midwife education program and have successfully completed 1 academic or clinical semester/quarter or clinical module. Applicants must submit they must submit a 150-word essay on their 5-year midwifery career plans; a 150-word essay on their intended future participation in the local, regional, and/or national activities of the ACNM; a 150-word essay on their need for financial assistance; and a 100-word statement on how they would use the funds if they receive the scholarship. Selection is based on academic excellence, leadership potential, and financial need.

Financial data The stipend is $3,000.

Duration 1 year.

Number awarded Varies each year; recently, 3 were awarded.

Deadline February of each year.

[430]
MILDRED COLLINS NURSING/HEALTH SCIENCE/MEDICINE SCHOLARSHIP

African-American/Caribbean Education Association, Inc.
P.O. Box 1224
Valley Stream, NY 11582-1224
(718) 949-6733   E-mail: aaceainc@yahoo.com
Web: www.aaceainc.com/Scholarships.html

Summary To provide financial assistance to high school seniors of African American or Caribbean heritage who plan to study a field related to nursing, health science, or medicine in college.

Eligibility This program is open to graduating high school seniors who are U.S. citizens of African American or Caribbean heritage. Applicants must be planning to attend a college or university and major in a field related to nursing, health science, or medicine. They must have completed 4 years of specified college preparatory courses with a grade of 90 or higher and have an SAT score of at least 1790. They must also have completed at least 200 hours of community service during their 4 years of high school, preferably in the field that they plan to study in college. Financial need is not considered in the selection process. New York residency is not required, but applicants must be available for an interviews in the Queens, New York area.

Financial data The stipend ranges from $1,000 to $1,500. Funds are paid directly to the recipient.

Duration 1 year.

Number awarded 1 each year.

Deadline April of each year.

[431]
MILLERCOORS SCHOLARSHIPS OF THE THURGOOD MARSHALL COLLEGE FUND

Thurgood Marshall College Fund
Attn: Senior Manager of Scholarship Programs
901 F Street, N.W., Suite 300
Washington, DC 20004
(202) 507-4851   Fax: (202) 652-2934
E-mail: deshuandra.walker@tmcfund.org
Web: www.tmcf.org

Summary To provide financial assistance to African American and other students currently working on a degree at a college or university that is a member of the Thurgood Marshall College Fund (TMCF).

Eligibility This program is open to students who are 21 years of age or older and enrolled at 1 of 47 TMCF member institutions, which are public Historically Black Colleges and Universities (HBCUs). Applicants must be U.S. citizens or permanent residents. They must have a current GPA of 3.0 or higher and be able to demonstrate financial need. Along with their application, they must submit 1) a resume that includes

community service, leadership activities, and employment/internship experience; 2) their Student Aid report from their FAFSA; 3) their most recent transcript; 4) a recommendation from a current school faculty member; and 5) a 500-word essay on a significant setback, risk they have taken, or ethical dilemma they have faced, the impact it has had on them, and how that experience enhanced their leadership ability.

Financial data The stipend is $3,100 per semester ($6,200 per year). Funds are awarded through the institution to be used for tuition, on-campus room and board, and required textbooks.

Duration 1 year.

Additional information This program was established in 1987 by the Miller Brewing Company (now MillerCoors).

Number awarded Varies each year.

Deadline April of each year.

[432]
MINNESOTA SOCIAL SERVICE ASSOCIATION DIVERSITY SCHOLARSHIP

Minnesota Social Service Association
Attn: Membership and Diversity Committee
125 Charles Avenue
St. Paul, MN 55103
(651) 644-0556   Fax: (651) 224-6540
E-mail: ajorgensen@mnssa.org
Web: www.mnssa.org

Summary To provide financial assistance to African Americans and other students from a diverse background who are enrolled in an undergraduate program in the health and human services field at a college in the upper Midwest.

Eligibility This program is open to residents of any state entering their junior or senior year at a college or university in Iowa, Minnesota, North Dakota, South Dakota, or Wisconsin. Applicants must be working full time on a degree in the health and human services field and have a GPA of 3.0 or higher. They must be from a diverse background, which may be along the dimensions of race, ethnicity, gender, sexual orientation, socioeconomic status, age, physical ability, religion, or other ideology. Financial need is considered in the selection process.

Financial data The stipend is $1,000.

Duration 1 year.

Number awarded 1 each year.

Deadline May of each year.

[433]
MINORITIES IN GOVERNMENT FINANCE SCHOLARSHIP

Government Finance Officers Association
Attn: Scholarship Committee
203 North LaSalle Street, Suite 2700
Chicago, IL 60601-1210
(312) 977-9700   Fax: (312) 977-4806
Web: www.gfoa.org

Summary To provide financial assistance to African American and other minority upper-division and graduate students who are preparing for a career in state and local government finance.

Eligibility This program is open to upper-division and graduate students who are preparing for a career in public finance by working on a degree in public administration, accounting, finance, political science, economics, or business administration (with a specific focus on government or nonprofit management). Applicants must be members of a minority group, citizens or permanent residents of the United States or Canada, and able to provide a letter of recommendation from a representative of their school. Selection is based on career plans, academic record, plan of study, letters of recommendation, and GPA. Financial need is not considered.

Financial data The stipend is $6,000.

Duration 1 year.

Additional information This program defines minorities as Blacks or African Americans, American Indians or Alaskan Natives, Hispanics or Latinos, Native Hawaiians or other Pacific Islanders, or Asians.

Number awarded 1 each year.

Deadline February of each year.

[434]
MINORITY AFFAIRS COMMITTEE'S AWARD FOR OUTSTANDING SCHOLASTIC ACHIEVEMENT

American Institute of Chemical Engineers
Attn: Minority Affairs Committee
120 Wall Street, FL 23
New York, NY 10005-4020
Toll Free: (800) 242-4363   Fax: (203) 775-5177
E-mail: awards@aiche.org
Web: www.aiche.org

Summary To recognize and reward African American and other underrepresented minority students majoring in chemical engineering who serve as role models for other minority students.

Eligibility Members of the American Institute of Chemical Engineers (AIChE) may nominate any chemical engineering student who serves as a role model for minority students in that field. Nominees must be members of a minority group that is underrepresented in chemical engineering (i.e., African American, Hispanic, Native American, Alaskan Native). They must have a GPA of 3.0 or higher. Along with their application, they must submit a 300-word essay on their immediate plans after graduation, areas of chemical engineering of most interest, and long-range career plans. Selection is based on that essay, academic record, participation in AIChE student chapter and professional or civic activities, and financial need.

Financial data The award consists of a plaque and a $1,500 honorarium.

Duration The award is presented annually.

Additional information This award was first presented in 1996.

Number awarded 1 each year.

Deadline Nominations must be submitted by May of each year.

[435]
MINORITY AND UNDERREPRESENTED ENVIRONMENTAL LITERACY PROGRAM

Missouri Department of Higher Education
Attn: Student Financial Assistance
205 Jefferson Street
P.O. Box 1469
Jefferson City, MO 65102-1469
(573) 751-2361   Toll Free: (800) 473-6757
Fax: (573) 751-6635   E-mail: info@dhe.mo.gov
Web: www.dhe.mo.gov/ppc/grants/muelp_0310_final.php

Summary To provide financial assistance to African American and other underrepresented students from Missouri who are or will be working on a bachelor's or master's degree in an environmental field.

Eligibility This program is open to residents of Missouri who are high school seniors or current undergraduate or graduate students enrolled or planning to enroll full time at a college or university in the state. Priority is given to members of the following underrepresented minority ethnic groups: African Americans, Hispanic or Latino Americans, Native Americans and Alaska Natives, and Native Hawaiians and Pacific Islanders. Applicants must be working on or planning to work on a bachelor's or master's degree in 1) engineering (civil, chemical, environmental, mechanical, or agricultural); 2) environmental studies (geology, biology, wildlife management, natural resource planning, natural resources, or a closely-related course of study); 3) environmental chemistry; or 4) environmental law enforcement. They must be U.S. citizens or permanent residents or otherwise lawfully present in the United States. Graduating high school seniors must have a GPA of 3.0 or higher; students currently enrolled in college or graduate school must have a GPA of 2.5 or higher. Along with their application, they must submit a 1-page essay on why they are applying for this scholarship, 3 letters of recommendation, a resume of school and community activities, and transcripts that include SAT or ACT scores. Financial need is not considered in the selection process.

Financial data Stipends vary each year; recently, they averaged approximately $3,045 per year.

Duration 1 year; may be renewed if the recipient maintains a GPA of 2.5 or higher and full-time enrollment.

Additional information This program was established by the Missouri Department of Natural Resources but transferred to the Department of Higher Education in 2009.

Number awarded Varies each year.

Deadline May of each year.

[436]
MINORITY SCHOLARSHIP AWARD FOR ACADEMIC EXCELLENCE IN PHYSICAL THERAPY

American Physical Therapy Association
Attn: Honors and Awards Program
1111 North Fairfax Street
Alexandria, VA 22314-1488
(703) 684-APTA   Toll Free: (800) 999-APTA, ext. 8082
Fax: (703) 684-7343   TDD: (703) 683-6748
E-mail: honorsandawards@apta.org
Web: www.apta.org

Summary To provide financial assistance to African American and other minority students who are interested in becoming a physical therapist or physical therapy assistant.

Eligibility This program is open to U.S. citizens and permanent residents who are members of the following minority groups: African American or Black, Asian, Native Hawaiian or other Pacific Islander, American Indian or Alaska Native, or Hispanic/Latino. Applicants must be in the final year of a professional physical therapy or physical therapy assistant education program. They must submit a personal essay outlining their professional goals and minority service. U.S. citizenship or permanent resident status is required. Selection is based on 1) demonstrated evidence of contributions in the area of minority affairs and services with an emphasis on contributions made while enrolled in a physical therapy program; 2) potential to contribute to the profession of physical therapy; and 3) scholastic achievement. Preference is given to members of the American Physical Therapy Association (APTA).

Financial data The stipend varies; recently, stipends were $5,000 for physical therapy professional education students or $2,000 for physical therapy assistant students.

Duration 1 year.

Number awarded Varies each year; recently, 7 professional education students and 1 physical therapy assistant student received awards.

Deadline November of each year.

[437]
MINORITY SCHOLARSHIP AWARDS FOR COLLEGE STUDENTS IN CHEMICAL ENGINEERING

American Institute of Chemical Engineers
Attn: Minority Affairs Committee
120 Wall Street, FL 23
New York, NY 10005-4020
Toll Free: (800) 242-4363   Fax: (203) 775-5177
E-mail: awards@aiche.org
Web: www.aiche.org

Summary To provide financial assistance for the undergraduate study of chemical engineering to African American and other underrepresented minority college student members of the American Institute of Chemical Engineers (AIChE).

Eligibility This program is open to undergraduate student AIChE members who are also members of a minority group that is underrepresented in chemical engineering (African Americans, Hispanics, Native Americans, Alaskan Natives, and Pacific Islanders). They must have a GPA of 3.0 or higher. Along with their application, they must submit a 300-word essay on their immediate plans after graduation, areas of chemical engineering of most interest, and long-range career plans. Selection is based on that essay, academic record, participation in AIChE student chapter and professional or civic activities, and financial need.

Financial data The stipend is $1,000.

Duration 1 year; nonrenewable.

Number awarded Varies each year; recently, 16 were awarded.

Deadline June of each year.

[438]
MINORITY SCHOLARSHIP AWARDS FOR INCOMING COLLEGE FRESHMEN IN CHEMICAL ENGINEERING

American Institute of Chemical Engineers
Attn: Minority Affairs Committee
120 Wall Street, FL 23
New York, NY 10005-4020
Toll Free: (800) 242-4363   Fax: (203) 775-5177
E-mail: awards@aiche.org
Web: www.aiche.org

Summary To provide financial assistance to incoming African American and other minority freshmen interested in studying science or engineering in college.

Eligibility Eligible are members of a minority group that is underrepresented in chemical engineering (African Americans, Hispanics, Native Americans, Alaskan Natives, and Pacific Islanders). Applicants must be graduating high school seniors planning to enroll at a 4-year university with a major in science or engineering. They must be nominated by an American Institute of Chemical Engineers (AIChE) local section. Selection is based on academic record (including a GPA of 3.0 or higher), participation in school and work activities, a 300-word letter outlining the reasons for choosing science or engineering, and financial need.

Financial data The stipend is $1,000.

Duration 1 year; nonrenewable.

Number awarded Approximately 10 each year.

Deadline Nominations must be submitted by June of each year.

[439]
MINORITY SCHOLARSHIP IN CLASSICS AND CLASSICAL ARCHAEOLOGY

Society for Classical Studies
Attn: Executive Director
New York University
20 Cooper Square
New York, NY 10003
(212) 992-7828   Fax: (212) 995-3531
E-mail: xd@classicalstudies.org
Web: www.classicalstudies.org

Summary To provide African American and other minority undergraduates with summer training as preparation for advanced work in the classics or classical archaeology.

Eligibility Eligible to apply are minority (African American, Hispanic American, Asian American, and Native American) undergraduate students who wish to engage in summer study as preparation for graduate work in the classics or classical archaeology. Applicants may propose participation in summer programs in Italy, Greece, Egypt, or other classical centers; language training at institutions in the United States, Canada, or Europe; or other relevant courses of study. Selection is based on academic qualifications, especially in classics; demonstrated ability in at least 1 classical language; quality of the proposal for study with respect to preparation for a career in classics; and financial need.

Financial data The maximum award is $4,500.

Duration 1 summer.

Additional information This program includes 1 scholarship supported by the Gladys Krieble Delmas Foundation.

Number awarded   2 each year.

Deadline   December of each year.

[440]
MINORITY SERVING INSTITUTION SCHOLARSHIP PROGRAM

U.S. Navy
Attn: Naval Service Training Command Officer
  Development
NAS Pensacola
250 Dallas Street
Pensacola, FL 32508-5220
(850) 452-4941, ext. 29395
Toll Free: (800) NAV-ROTC, ext. 29395
Fax: (850) 452-2486
E-mail: pnsc_nrotc.scholarship@navy.mil
Web: www.nrotc.navy.mil/MSI.html

Summary   To provide financial assistance to students at specified minority institutions who are interested in joining Navy ROTC to prepare for service as an officer in the U.S. Navy.

Eligibility   This program is open to students attending or planning to attend 1 of 17 specified Historically Black Colleges or Universities (HBCUs), 1 of 3 High Hispanic Enrollment (HHE) schools, or 1 other minority institution, all of which have a Navy ROTC unit on campus. Applicants must be nominated by the professor of naval science at their institution and meet academic requirements set by each school. They must be U.S. citizens between 17 and 23 years of age who are willing to serve for 4 years as active-duty Navy officers following graduation from college. They must not have reached their 27th birthday by the time of college graduation and commissioning; applicants who have prior active-duty military service may be eligible for age adjustments for the amount of time equal to their prior service, up to a maximum of 36 months. The qualifying scores are 550 critical reading and 540 mathematics on the SAT or 22 on English and 21 on mathematics on the ACT. Current enlisted and former military personnel are also eligible if they will complete the program by the age of 30.

Financial data   These scholarships provide payment of full tuition and required educational fees, as well as a specified amount for textbooks, supplies, and equipment. The program also provides a stipend for 10 months of the year that is $250 per month as a freshman, $300 per month as a sophomore, $350 per month as a junior, and $400 per month as a senior.

Duration   Up to 4 years.

Additional information   The eligible HBCUs are Allen University, Clark Atlanta University, Dillard University, Florida A&M University, Hampton University, Howard University, Huston-Tillotson University, Morehouse College, Norfolk State University, Prairie View A&M University, Savannah State University, Southern University and A&M College, Spelman College, Tennessee State University, Texas Southern University, Tuskegee University, and Xavier University. The eligible HHEs are Central New Mexico Community College, Pima Community College, and the University of New Mexico. The other minority institution is Kennedy King College. After completing the program, all participants are commissioned as ensigns in the Naval Reserve with an 8-year service obligation, including 4 years of active duty. Current military personnel who are accepted into this program are released from active duty and

are not eligible for active-duty pay and allowances, medical benefits, or other active-duty entitlements.

Number awarded   Varies each year.

Deadline   January of each year.

[441]
MINORITY TEACHER EDUCATION SCHOLARSHIPS

Florida Fund for Minority Teachers, Inc.
Attn: Executive Director
G415 Norman Hall
618 S.W. 12th Street
P.O. Box 117045
Gainesville, FL 32611-7045
(352) 392-9196   Fax: (352) 846-3011
E-mail: info@ffmt.org
Web: www.ffmt.org/mtes-application-active

Summary   To provide scholarship/loans to Florida residents who are African Americans or members of other minority groups preparing for a career as a teacher.

Eligibility   This program is open to Florida residents who are African American/Black, Hispanic/Latino, Asian American/Pacific Islander, or American Indian/Alaskan Native. Applicants must be entering their junior year in a teacher education program at a participating college or university in Florida. Along with their application, they must submit an essay of 100 to 300 words on how their life experiences have impacted them to go into the field of education. Special consideration is given to community college graduates. Selection is based on writing ability, communication skills, overall academic performance, and evidence of commitment to the youth of America (preferably demonstrated through volunteer activities).

Financial data   The stipend is $4,000 per year. Recipients are required to teach 1 year in a Florida public school for each year they receive the scholarship. If they fail to teach in a public school, they are required to repay the total amount of support received at an annual interest rate of 8%.

Duration   Up to 2 consecutive years, provided the recipient remains enrolled full time with a GPA of 2.5 or higher.

Additional information   For a list of the 22 participating public institutions and the 16 participating private institutions, contact the Florida Fund for Minority Teachers (FFMT). Recipients are also required to attend the annual (FFMT) recruitment and retention conference.

Number awarded   Varies each year.

Deadline   June of each year for fall semester; October of each year for spring semester.

[442]
MINORITY TEACHERS OF ILLINOIS SCHOLARSHIP PROGRAM

Illinois Student Assistance Commission
Attn: Scholarship and Grant Services
1755 Lake Cook Road
Deerfield, IL 60015-5209
(847) 948-8550   Toll Free: (800) 899-ISAC
Fax: (847) 831-8549   TDD: (800) 526-0844
E-mail: isac.studentservices@isac.illinois.gov
Web: www.isac.org

Summary   To provide scholarship/loans to African Americans and other minority students in Illinois who plan to become teachers at the preschool, elementary, or secondary level.

Eligibility Applicants must be Illinois residents, U.S. citizens or eligible noncitizens, members of a minority group (African American/Black, Hispanic American, Asian American, or Native American), and high school graduates or holders of a General Educational Development (GED) certificate. They must be enrolled at least half time as an undergraduate or graduate student, have a GPA of 2.5 or higher, not be in default on any student loan, and be enrolled or accepted for enrollment in a teacher education program.

Financial data Grants up to $5,000 per year are awarded. This is a scholarship/loan program. Recipients must agree to teach full time 1 year for each year of support received. The teaching agreement may be fulfilled at a public, private, or parochial preschool, elementary school, or secondary school in Illinois; at least 30% of the student body at those schools must be minority. It must be fulfilled within the 5-year period following the completion of the undergraduate program for which the scholarship was awarded. The time period may be extended if the recipient serves in the U.S. armed forces, enrolls full time in a graduate program related to teaching, becomes temporarily disabled, is unable to find employment as a teacher at a qualifying school, or takes additional courses on at least a half-time basis to obtain certification as a teacher in Illinois. Recipients who fail to honor this work obligation must repay the award with 5% interest.

Duration 1 year; may be renewed for a total of 8 semesters or 12 quarters.

Number awarded Varies each year.

Deadline Priority consideration is given to applications received by February of each year.

[443]
MINORITY TEACHING FELLOWS PROGRAM OF TENNESSEE

Tennessee Student Assistance Corporation
Parkway Towers
404 James Robertson Parkway, Suite 1510
Nashville, TN 37243-0820
(615) 741-1346   Toll Free: (800) 342-1663
Fax: (615) 741-6101   E-mail: TSAC.Aidinfo@tn.gov
Web: www.tn.gov

Summary To provide scholarship/loans to African American and other minority residents of Tennessee who wish to attend college in the state to prepare for a career in the teaching field.

Eligibility This program is open to minority residents of Tennessee who are either high school seniors planning to enroll full time at a college or university in the state or continuing college students at a Tennessee college or university. High school seniors must have a GPA of 2.75 or higher and an ACT score of at least 18 or an equivalent SAT score. Continuing college students must have a college GPA of 2.5 or higher. All applicants must agree to teach at the K-12 level in a Tennessee public school following graduation from college. Along with their application, they must submit a 250-word essay on why they chose teaching as a profession. U.S. citizenship is required.

Financial data The scholarship/loan is $5,000 per year. Recipients incur an obligation to teach at the preK-12 level in

a Tennessee public school 1 year for each year the award is received.

Duration 1 year; may be renewed for up to 3 additional years, provided the recipient maintains full-time enrollment and a cumulative GPA of 2.5 or higher.

Additional information This program began in 1989.

Number awarded Varies each year; recently, 62 fellows received $287,000 in support through this program.

Deadline April of each year.

[444]
MISSISSIPPI CHAPTER AABE SCHOLARSHIPS

American Association of Blacks in Energy-Mississippi Chapter
Attn: Scholarship Committee Chair
P.O. Box 986
Jackson, MS 39205
(601) 969-2326   E-mail: aabems1990@yahoo.com
Web: www.aabe.org/index.php?component=pages&id=387

Summary To provide financial assistance to African Americans and members of other underrepresented minority groups who are high school seniors in Mississippi and planning to major in an energy-related field at a college in any state.

Eligibility This program is open to seniors graduating from high schools in Mississippi and planning to attend a 4-year college or university in any state. Applicants must be African Americans, Hispanics, or Native Americans who have a GPA of 3.0 or higher and have taken the ACT and/or SAT test. Their intended major must be a field of business, engineering, physical science, mathematics, or technology related to energy. Along with their application, they must submit a 350-word essay that includes 1) when they discovered their interest in the field of energy and what sparked their interest; and 2) either what excites them about the field of energy or how they expect their education to prepare them for the field of energy. Financial need is not considered in the selection process.

Financial data Stipends are $2,000 or $1,000.

Duration 1 year.

Additional information Winners are eligible to compete for regional and national scholarships.

Number awarded Varies each year; recently, 5 were awarded.

Deadline March of each year.

[445]
MISSOURI MINORITY TEACHING SCHOLARSHIP PROGRAM

Missouri Department of Higher Education
Attn: Student Financial Assistance
205 Jefferson Street
P.O. Box 1469
Jefferson City, MO 65102-1469
(573) 751-2361   Toll Free: (800) 473-6757
Fax: (573) 751-6635   E-mail: info@dhe.mo.gov
Web: www.dhe.mo.gov/ppc/grants/minorityteaching.php

Summary To provide scholarships and forgivable loans to African American and other minority high school seniors, high school graduates, and college students in Missouri who are interested in preparing for a teaching career in mathematics or science.

Eligibility   This program is open to Missouri residents who are African American, Asian American, Hispanic American, or Native American. Applicants must be 1) high school seniors, college students, or returning adults (without a degree) who rank in the top 25% of their high school class and have scores in the top 25% of the ACT or SAT examination (recently, that meant a composite score of 24 or higher on the ACT or 1360 or higher on the composite critical reading and mathematics SAT); or 2) baccalaureate degree-holders who are returning to an approved mathematics or science teacher education program. They must be a U.S. citizen or permanent resident or otherwise lawfully present in the United States. All applicants must be enrolled full time in an approved teacher education program at a community college, 4-year college, or university in Missouri. Selection is based on high school class rank, ACT or SAT scores, school and community activities, career interest in teaching, leadership skills, employment experience, and recommendations.

Financial data   The stipend is $3,000 per year, of which $2,000 is provided by the state as a forgivable loan and $1,000 is provided by the school as a scholarship. Recipients must commit to teaching in a Missouri public elementary or secondary school for 5 years following graduation. If they fail to fulfill that obligation, they must repay the state portion of the scholarship with interest at 9.5%.

Duration   Up to 4 years.

Number awarded   Up to 100 each year.

Deadline   May of each year.

[446]
MIT AMGEN-UROP SCHOLARS PROGRAM

Massachusetts Institute of Technology
Attn: Undergraduate Research Opportunities Program
Office of Undergraduate Advising and Academic
   Programming
77 Massachusetts Avenue, Room 7-104
Cambridge, MA 02139
(617) 253-7306   E-mail: mit-amgenscholars@mit.edu
Web: web.mit.edu/urop/amgenscholars

Summary   To provide an opportunity for undergraduates, especially African Americans and other minorities, to participate in summer research projects in biotechnology at Massachusetts Institute of Technology (MIT).

Eligibility   This program is open to sophomores, juniors, and non-graduating seniors at 4-year colleges and universities in the United States, Puerto Rico, and other U.S. territories. Applicants must be U.S. citizens or permanent residents who have a cumulative GPA of 3.2 or higher and an interest in preparing for a Ph.D. or M.D./Ph.D. They must be interested in working on a summer research project at MIT in the following laboratory programs: biological engineering; biology, brain, and cognitive sciences; environmental health; chemistry; chemical engineering; health sciences and technology; or mechanical engineering (for bioengineering or biotechnology only). The Amgen Scholars Program encourages applications from students who are members of groups underrepresented in fields of biotechnology.

Financial data   Scholars receive a stipend of $4,320, a meal allowance of $800, housing in a designated MIT resi-

dence hall, and, for non-MIT students, travel to and from Boston.

Duration   9 weeks during the summer.

Additional information   This program serves as the MIT component of the Amgen Scholars Program, which operates at 8 other U.S. universities (and the National Institutes of Health) and is funded by the Amgen Foundation.

Number awarded   Up to 20 each year.

Deadline   January of each year.

[447]
MNACC STUDENT OF COLOR SCHOLARSHIP

Minnesota Association of Counselors of Color
c/o Cristina Montañez, Scholarship Committee
University of Minnesota at Morris
600 East Fourth Street
Morris, MN 56267
E-mail: scholarships@mnacc.org
Web: www.mnacc.org

Summary   To provide financial assistance to high school seniors of color in Minnesota who plan to attend college in the area.

Eligibility   This program is open to seniors graduating from public and private high schools in Minnesota who are students of color. Applicants must be planning to enroll full time at a 4-year college or university, a 2-year college, or a trade or technical college that is a member of the Minnesota Association of Counselors of Color (MnACC). Along with their application, they must submit an essay, up to 500 words in length, on their choice of assigned topics.

Financial data   Stipends are $1,000 or $500.

Duration   1 year; nonrenewable.

Additional information   These scholarships may be used at approximately 67 MnACC member institutions, including colleges, universities, and technical schools in Minnesota as well as selected schools in Iowa, Michigan, North Dakota, South Dakota, and Wisconsin.

Number awarded   Varies each year; recently, 26 were awarded.

Deadline   March of each year.

[448]
MONSANTO BDPA NATIONAL SCHOLARSHIPS

Black Data Processing Associates
Attn: BDPA Education Technology Foundation
4423 Lehigh Road, Number 277
College Park, MD 20740
(513) 284-4968   Fax: (202) 318-2194
E-mail: scholarships@betf.org
Web: www.betf.org/scholarships/monsanto.shtml

Summary   To provide financial assistance to members of the Black Data Processing Associates (BDPA) who are interested in studying information technology at a college in any state.

Eligibility   This program is open to BDPA members who are either graduating high school seniors or college students with at least 1 year remaining in a 4-year degree program. Applicants must be working on or planning to work on a degree in information technology. They must have a GPA of 3.0 or higher. Along with their application, they must submit a 500-word essay on how information technology is impacting agriculture. Selection is based on that essay, academic achievement, leadership ability through academic or civic involvement, and participation in community service activities. U.S. citizenship or permanent resident status is required.

Financial data The stipend is $2,500 per year. Funds may be used to pay for tuition, fees, books, room and board, or other college-related expenses.

Duration 4 years.

Additional information The BDPA established its Education and Technology Foundation (BETF) in 1992 to advance the skill sets needed by African American and other minority adults and young people to compete in the information technology industry. This program is sponsored by the Monsanto Company.

Number awarded 4 each year.

Deadline July of each year.

[449]
MONTFORD POINT MARINE ASSOCIATION SCHOLARSHIP

Montford Point Marine Association
c/o James Maillard, National Scholarship Director
7714 113th Street, Number 2G
Forest Hills, NY 11375-7119
(718) 261-9640   Fax: (718) 261-3021
E-mail: Scholarships@montfordpointmarines.com
Web: www.montfordpointmarines.com

Summary To provide financial assistance to African American and other high school seniors, high school graduates, and current undergraduates who have a connection to the Montford Point Marine Association (MPMA).

Eligibility This program is open to high school seniors, high school graduates, or current college students who have a connection to the MPMA. Along with their application, they must submit academic transcripts, information on their connection to MPMA, and a 500-word essay on a topic that changes periodically. Only undergraduate study is supported. The family income of applicants must be less than $90,000 per year.

Financial data Stipends depend on the need of the recipient and the availability of funds, but generally range from $500 to $2,500 per year.

Duration 1 year.

Additional information Membership in the MPMA is restricted to former Marines and the families of Marines who served at Camp Montford Point, North Carolina where African Americans trained during the days of segregation from 1942 to 1949. This scholarship program, which began in 2003, operates in coordination with the Marine Corps Scholarship Foundation.

Number awarded 1 or more each year.

Deadline Deadline not specified.

[450]
MONTGOMERY SUMMER RESEARCH DIVERSITY FELLOWSHIPS

American Bar Foundation
Attn: Summer Research Diversity Fellowship
750 North Lake Shore Drive
Chicago, IL 60611-4403
(312) 988-6515   Fax: (312) 988-6579
E-mail: fellowships@abfn.org
Web: www.americanbarfoundation.org

Summary To provide an opportunity for undergraduate students who are African Americans or members of other diverse backgrounds to work on a summer research project in the field of law and social science.

Eligibility This program is open to U.S. citizens and permanent residents who are African Americans, Hispanic/Latinos, Asians, Puerto Ricans, Native Americans, or other individuals who will add diversity to the field of law and social science such as persons with disabilities and LGBTQ individuals. Applicants must be sophomores or juniors in college, have a GPA of 3.0 or higher, be majoring in the social sciences or humanities, and be willing to consider an academic or research career. Along with their application, they must submit a 200-word essay on their future plans and why this fellowship would contribute to them, another essay on an assigned topic, official transcripts, and a letter of recommendation from a faculty member familiar with their work.

Financial data Participants receive a stipend of $3,600.

Duration 35 hours per week for 8 weeks during the summer.

Additional information Students are assigned to an American Bar Foundation Research Professor who involves the student in the design and conduct of the professor's research project and who acts as mentor during the student's tenure.

Number awarded 4 each year.

Deadline February of each year.

[451]
MOORE LIFE LEARNING FELLOWSHIP

Alpha Kappa Alpha Sorority, Inc.
Attn: Educational Advancement Foundation
5656 South Stony Island Avenue
Chicago, IL 60637
(773) 947-0026   Toll Free: (800) 653-6528
Fax: (773) 947-0277   E-mail: akaeaf@akaeaf.net
Web: www.akaeaf.org/fellowships_endowments.htm

Summary To provide financial assistance to members of Alpha Kappa Alpha (a traditionally African American women's sorority) who are engaged in a program of life-long learning.

Eligibility This program is open to sorority members who are enrolled full time as sophomores or higher in an accredited degree-granting institution and are planning to continue their program of education. Applicants must be enrolled in a program of life-long learning at a college or university in any state. Along with their application, they must submit 1) a list of honors, awards, and scholarships received; 2) a list of organizations in which they have memberships, especially minority organizations; and 3) a statement of their personal and career goals, including how this scholarship will enhance their ability to attain those goals. The sponsor is a traditionally African American women's sorority.

Financial data A stipend is awarded (amount not specified).

Duration 1 year.

Number awarded 1 each even-numbered year.

Deadline April of each even-numbered year.

[452]
MOSS ADAMS FOUNDATION SCHOLARSHIP

Educational Foundation for Women in Accounting
Attn: Foundation Administrator
136 South Keowee Street
Dayton, OH 45402
(937) 424-3391   Fax: (937) 222-5749
E-mail: info@efwa.org
Web: www.efwa.org/scholarships_graduate.php

Summary To provide financial support to women, including African American and other minority women, who are working on an accounting degree.

Eligibility This program is open to women who are enrolled in an accounting degree program at an accredited college or university. Applicants must meet 1 of the following criteria: 1) women pursuing a fifth-year requirement either through general studies or within a graduate program; 2) women returning to school as current or reentry juniors or seniors; or 3) minority women. Selection is based on aptitude for accounting and business, commitment to the goal of working on a degree in accounting (including evidence of continued commitment after receiving this award), clear evidence that the candidate has established goals and a plan for achieving those goals (both personal and professional), financial need, and a demonstration of how the scholarship will impact her life. U.S. citizenship is required.

Financial data The stipend is $1,000.

Duration 1 year.

Additional information This program was established by Rowling, Dold & Associates LLP, a woman-owned C.P.A. firm based in San Diego. It was renamed when that firm merged with Moss Adams LLP.

Number awarded 2 each year: 1 to an undergraduate and 1 to a graduate student.

Deadline April of each year.

[453]
MR. CHARLIE TOMPKINS SCHOLARSHIP

National Naval Officers Association-Washington, D.C.
   Chapter
c/o LCDR Stephen Williams
P.O. Box 30784
Alexandria, VA 22310
(703) 566-3840   Fax: (703) 566-3813
E-mail: Stephen.Williams@navy.mil
Web: dcnnoa.memberlodge.com/page-309002

Summary To provide financial assistance to African American and other minority high school seniors from the Washington, D.C. area who are interested in attending college in any state.

Eligibility This program is open to minority seniors graduating from high schools in the Washington, D.C. metropolitan area who plan to enroll full time at an accredited 2- or 4-year

college or university in any state. Applicants must have a GPA of 2.5 or higher and be U.S. citizens or permanent residents. Selection is based on academic achievement, community involvement, and financial need.

Financial data The stipend is $2,000.

Duration 1 year; nonrenewable.

Additional information This program is sponsored by the Washington D.C. Chapter of the National Naval Officers Association (DCNNOA), an organization of African American naval officers, but all minorities are eligible and recipients are not required to join or affiliate with the military in any way.

Number awarded 1 each year.

Deadline February of each year.

[454]
MR. COLLEGIATE AFRICAN AMERICAN SCHOLARSHIP PROGRAM

Mr. Collegiate African American Scholarship Pageant
P.O. Box 5433
Prairie View, TX 77446
(979) 221-8430
E-mail: mrcollegiateafricanamerican@gmail.com
Web: mrcollegiatepageant.blogspot.com

Summary To recognize and reward, with college scholarships, outstanding African American men who participate in a pageant.

Eligibility This competition is open to African American men between 18 and 30 years of age attending 4-year colleges and universities, especially Historically Black Colleges and Universities. Applicants must be interested in participating in a pageant where they are judged on a personal and private interview (20%), platform expression (25%), talent (35%), evening wear (10%), and on-stage interview (10%).

Financial data A total of $5,000 in scholarships and prizes is awarded.

Duration The pageant is held annually.

Additional information This program began in 1990. The pageant is held in Prairie View, Texas.

Number awarded Varies each year.

Deadline September of each year.

[455]
MR. JAMES E. TATUM SCHOLARSHIP PROGRAM

National Organization of Professional Black Natural
   Resources Conservation Service Employees
c/o Jacqueline Thibodeaux Horne Scholarship Committee
   Chair
919 Azalea Court
Burleson, TX 76028
E-mail: Jacqueline.horne@ftw.usda.gov www.nopbnrcse.
   memberlodge.org/scholarships

Summary To provide financial assistance to students working on a bachelor's degree in agriculture, natural resource sciences, or a related field at an 1890 Historically Black Land-Grant Institution.

Eligibility This program is open to students enrolled or planning to enroll at 1 of the 19 universities designated as an 1890 Historically Black Land-Grant Institution. Applicants must be interested in working on a bachelor's degree in 1 of the following fields: agriculture, agricultural business/management, agricultural economics, agricultural engineering/ mechanics, agricultural production and technology, agronomy or crop science, animal science, botany, environmental sciences, farm and range management, food science and technology, forestry, horticulture, natural resource management, nutritional science, soil conservation and science, or wildlife management. They must have a GPA of 2.8 or higher. Along with their application, they must submit 250-word essays on 1) the reason they are majoring in their selected field; 2) their short- and long-term career goals and objectives; and 3) why they need financial assistance to continue their education. U.S. citizenship is required.

Financial data The stipend is $1,000.

Duration 1 year; nonrenewable.

Additional information The eligible 1890 Historically Black Land-Grant Institutions are Alabama A&M University, Alcorn State University (Mississippi), Central State University (Ohio), Delaware State University, Florida A&M University, Fort Valley State University (Georgia), Kentucky State University, Langston University (Oklahoma), Lincoln University (Missouri), North Carolina A&T State University, Prairie View A&M University (Texas), South Carolina State University, Southern University (Louisiana), Tennessee State University, Tuskegee University (Alabama), University of Arkansas at Pine Bluff, University of Maryland Eastern Shore, Virginia State University, and West Virginia State University.

Number awarded 10 each year.

Deadline October of each year.

[456]
MRS. PATRICIA THOMPSON SCHOLARSHIP

National Naval Officers Association-Washington, D.C.
  Chapter
c/o LCDR Stephen Williams
P.O. Box 30784
Alexandria, VA 22310
(703) 644-2605   Fax: (703) 644-8503
E-mail: Stephen.Williams@navy.mil
Web: www.dcnnoa.org/dcnnoa-scholarship

Summary To provide financial assistance to male African American high school seniors from the Washington, D.C. area who are interested in attending college in any state.

Eligibility This program is open to male African American seniors graduating from high schools in the Washington, D.C. metropolitan area who plan to enroll full time at an accredited 2- or 4-year college or university in any state. Applicants must have a GPA of 2.5 or higher and be U.S. citizens or permanent residents. Selection is based on academic achievement, community involvement, and financial need.

Financial data The stipend is $1,000.

Duration 1 year; nonrenewable.

Additional information Recipients are not required to join or affiliate with the military in any way.

Number awarded 1 each year.

Deadline February of each year.

[457]
MSCPA MINORITY SCHOLARSHIPS

Missouri Society of Certified Public Accountants
Attn: MSCPA Educational Foundation
540 Maryville Centre Drive, Suite 200
P.O. Box 958868
St. Louis, MO 63195-8868
(314) 997-7966   Toll Free: (800) 264-7966 (within MO)
Fax: (314) 997-2592   E-mail: dhull@mocpa.org
Web: www.mocpa.org/students/scholarships

Summary To provide financial assistance to African American and other minority residents of Missouri who are working on an undergraduate or graduate degree in accounting at a university in the state.

Eligibility This program is open to members of minority groups underrepresented in the accounting profession (Black/African American, Hispanic/Latino, Native American, Asian American) who are currently working full time on an undergraduate or graduate degree in accounting at a college or university in Missouri. Applicants must either be residents of Missouri or the children of members of the Missouri Society of Certified Public Accountants (MSCPA). They must be U.S. citizens, have completed at least 30 semester hours of college work, have a GPA of 3.3 or higher, and be student members of the MSCPA. Selection is based on the GPA, involvement in MSCPA, educator recommendations, and leadership potential. Financial need is not considered.

Financial data The stipend is $1,250 per year.

Duration 1 year; may be renewed.

Number awarded Varies each year; recently, 3 were awarded.

Deadline February of each year.

[458]
MSCPA/NABA SCHOLARSHIPS

Massachusetts Society of Certified Public Accountants
Attn: MSCPA Educational Foundation
105 Chauncy Street, Tenth Floor
Boston, MA 02111
(617) 556-4000   Toll Free: (800) 392-6145
Fax: (617) 556-4126   E-mail: info@mscpaonline.org
Web: www.cpatrack.com/scholarships

Summary To provide financial assistance to members of the National Association of Black Accountants (NABA) from Massachusetts working on an undergraduate or graduate degree in accounting at a college or university in the state.

Eligibility This program is open to African American students from Massachusetts who are members of the Boston Metropolitan Chapter of NABA and enrolled at a college or university in the state. Applicants must be undergraduates who have completed at least the first semester of their sophomore year or graduate students. They must be able to demonstrate financial need, academic excellence, and an intention to prepare for a career as a Certified Public Accountant (C.P.A.) at a firm in Massachusetts.

Financial data The stipend is $2,500.

Duration 1 year.

Additional information This program is sponsored by the Boston Metropolitan Chapter of NABA and the Massachusetts Society of Certified Public Accountants (MSCPA).

Number awarded   2 each year.

Deadline   March of each year.

[459]
MSIPP INTERNSHIPS

Department of Energy
Office of Environmental Management
Savannah River National Laboratory
Attn: MSIPP Program Manager
Building 773-41A, 232
Aiken, SC 29808
(803) 725-9032   E-mail: connie.yung@srnl.doe.gov
Web: srnl.doe.gov/msipp/internships.htm

Summary   To provide an opportunity for undergraduate and graduate students at Minority Serving Institutions (MSIs) to work on a summer research project at designated National Laboratories of the U.S. Department of Energy (DOE).

Eligibility   This program is open to full-time undergraduate and graduate students enrolled at an accredited MSI. Applicants must be interested in working during the summer on a research project at a participating DOE National Laboratory. They must be working on a degree in a field of science, technology, engineering, or mathematics (STEM); the specific field depends on the particular project on which they wish to work. Their GPA must be 3.0 or higher. U.S. citizenship is required.

Financial data   The stipend depends on the cost of living at the location of the host laboratory.

Duration   10 weeks during the summer.

Additional information   This program is administered at the Savannah River National Laboratory (SRNL) in Aiken, South Carolina, which serves as the National Laboratory for the DOE Office of Environmental Management. The other participating National Laboratories are Argonne National Laboratory (ANL) in Argonne, Illinois, Idaho National Laboratory (INL) in Idaho Falls, Idaho, Los Alamos National Laboratory (LANL) in Los Alamos, New Mexico, Oak Ridge National Laboratory (ORNL) in Oak Ridge, Tennessee, and Pacific Northwest National Laboratory (PNNL) in Richland, Washington. The program began in 2016.

Number awarded   Varies each year. Recently, the program offered 11 research projects at SRNL, 12 at ANL, 1 at INL, 7 at LANL, 4 at ORNL, and 7 at PNNL.

Deadline   March of each year.

[460]
MULTICULTURAL AUDIENCE DEVELOPMENT INITIATIVE INTERNSHIPS

Metropolitan Museum of Art
Attn: Internship Programs
1000 Fifth Avenue
New York, NY 10028-0198
(212) 570-3710   Fax: (212) 570-3782
E-mail: mmainterns@metmuseum.org
Web: www.metmuseum.org

Summary   To provide summer work experience at the Metropolitan Museum of Art to college undergraduates, graduate students, and recent graduates who are African Americans or members of diverse groups.

Eligibility   This program is open to members of diverse groups who are undergraduate juniors and seniors, students currently working on a master's degree, or individuals who completed a bachelor's or master's degree within the past year. Ph.D. students may be eligible to apply during the first 12 months of their program, provided they have not yet achieved candidacy. Students from various academic backgrounds are encouraged to apply, but they must be interested in preparing for a career in the arts and museum fields. Freshmen and sophomores are not eligible.

Financial data   The stipend is $3,750.

Duration   10 weeks, beginning in June.

Additional information   Interns are assigned to departmental projects (curatorial, administration, or education) at the Metropolitan Museum of Art; other assignments may include giving gallery talks and working at the Visitor Information Center. The assignment is for 35 hours a week. The internships are funded by the Multicultural Audience Initiative at the museum.

Number awarded   1 or more each year.

Deadline   January of each year.

[461]
MUSIC AND CHRISTIAN ARTS MINISTRY SCHOLARSHIP

African Methodist Episcopal Church
Attn: Christian Education Department
Music and Christian Arts Ministry
500 Eighth Avenue South
Nashville, TN 37203
Toll Free: (800) 525-7282   Fax: (615) 726-1866
E-mail: cedoffice@ameced.com
Web: www.ameced.com/music.shtml

Summary   To provide financial assistance to members of African Methodist Episcopal (AME) churches who are interested in working on an undergraduate degree in music at a Black-related college in any state.

Eligibility   This program is open to graduating high school seniors who are members of an AME congregation. Applicants must be planning to attend an AME-supported college or university or an Historically Black College or University (HBCU) in any state to study music. They must be planning to assume a music leadership position in a local AME church. Along with their application, they must submit a current high school transcript, 3 letters of recommendation (including 1 from their music teacher or director and 1 from their pastor), a 1-page essay on why they should be awarded this scholarship, and a CD or cassette recording of a musical performance. Selection is based on academic achievement, school involvement, music involvement and performance genre, community involvement, and other honors and awards.

Financial data   The stipend is $2,000 per year. Funds are sent directly to the student upon proof of enrollment.

Duration   1 year; recipients may apply for 1 additional year if they earn a GPA of 3.3 or higher in their first year.

Number awarded   1 or more each year.

Deadline   May of each year.

[462]
MUTUAL OF OMAHA ACTUARIAL SCHOLARSHIP FOR MINORITY STUDENTS

Mutual of Omaha
Attn: Strategic Staffing-Actuarial Recruitment
3300 Mutual of Omaha Plaza
Omaha, NE 68175
Toll Free: (800) 365-1405
E-mail: diversity@mutualofomaha.com
Web: www.mutualofomaha.com

Summary To provide financial assistance and work experience to African American and other minority undergraduate students who are preparing for an actuarial career.

Eligibility This program is open to members of minority groups (African American, Hispanic, Native American, Asian or Pacific Islander, or Alaskan Eskimo) who have completed at least 24 semester hours of full-time study. Applicants must be working on an actuarial or mathematics-related degree with the goal of preparing for an actuarial career. They must have a GPA of 3.4 or higher and have passed at least 1 actuarial examination. Prior to accepting the award, they must be available to complete a summer internship at the sponsor's home office in Omaha, Nebraska. Along with their application, they must submit a 1-page personal statement on why they are interested in becoming an actuary and how they are preparing themselves for an actuarial career. Status as a U.S. citizen, permanent resident, asylee, or refugee must be established.

Financial data The scholarship stipend is $5,000 per year. Funds are paid directly to the student. For the internship, students receive an hourly rate of pay, subsidized housing, and financial incentives for successful examination results received during the internship period.

Duration 1 year. Recipients may reapply if they maintain a cumulative GPA of 3.4 or higher.

Number awarded Varies each year.

Deadline October of each year.

[463]
MV TRANSIT COLLEGE SCHOLARSHIP

Conference of Minority Transportation Officials
Attn: National Scholarship Program
100 M Street, S.E., Suite 917
Washington, DC 20003
(202) 506-2917   E-mail: info@comto.org
Web: www.comto.org/page/scholarships

Summary To provide financial assistance to African American and other minority college student members of the Conference of Minority Transportation Officials (COMTO) and family of members working on a degree in transportation or a related field.

Eligibility This program is open to minority undergraduate students who have been COMTO members or whose parents, guardians, or grandparents have been members for at least 1 year. Applicants must be majoring in transportation, engineering, planning, or a related discipline. They must have a GPA of 2.0 or higher. Along with their application they must submit a cover letter on their transportation-related career goals and life aspirations. Financial need is not considered in the selection process.

Financial data The stipend is $4,000. Funds are paid directly to the recipient's college or university.

Duration 1 year.

Additional information This program is sponsored by MV Transportation, Inc.

Number awarded 1 or more each year.

Deadline April of each year.

[464]
MV TRANSIT HIGH SCHOOL SENIOR SCHOLARSHIP

Conference of Minority Transportation Officials
Attn: National Scholarship Program
100 M Street, S.E., Suite 917
Washington, DC 20003
(202) 506-2917   E-mail: info@comto.org
Web: www.comto.org/page/scholarships

Summary To provide financial assistance to African American and other minority high school seniors who are members of the Conference of Minority Transportation Officials (COMTO) or family of members and interested in working on a degree in transportation or a related field.

Eligibility This program is open to minority high school seniors who have been COMTO members or whose parents, guardians, or grandparents have been members for at least 1 year. Applicants must be planning to enroll at an accredited college, university, or vocational/technical institute and major in a transportation-related field. They must have a GPA of 2.0 or higher. Along with their application they must submit a cover letter on their transportation-related career goals and life aspirations. Financial need is not considered in the selection process.

Financial data The stipend is $3,500. Funds are paid directly to the recipient's college or university.

Duration 1 year.

Additional information This program is sponsored by MV Transportation, Inc.

Number awarded 1 or more each year.

Deadline April of each year.

[465]
NABA ATLANTA CHAPTER SCHOLARSHIPS

National Association of Black Accountants-Atlanta
  Chapter
Attn: Student Member Services
P.O. Box 92811
Atlanta, GA 30314
E-mail: students@nabaatl.org
Web: thiswaytocpa.com

Summary To provide financial assistance to members of the National Association of Black Accountants (NABA) from Georgia who are working on an undergraduate or master's degree in an accounting-related field.

Eligibility This program is open to NABA members who are working full time on an undergraduate or master's degree in accounting, business, or finance. Applicants must be residents of Georgia or residents of other states attending a college or university in that state. They must have completed at least 3 hours of accounting classes but have at least 1 semester remaining before completion of their degree. Selection is based on academic excellence and extracurricular involvement.

Financial data   Stipends range from $500 to $5,000.

Duration   1 year.

Number awarded   8 each year.

Deadline   March of each year.

[466]
NABA MEMBER SCHOLARSHIP AWARDS

National Association of Black Accountants
Attn: National Scholarship Program
7474 Greenway Center Drive, Suite 1120
Greenbelt, MD 20770
(301) 474-NABA   Fax: (301) 474-3114
E-mail: scholarships@nabainc.org
Web: www.nabainc.org/scholarship

Summary   To provide financial assistance to student members of the National Association of Black Accountants (NABA) who are working on an undergraduate or graduate degree in a field related to accounting.

Eligibility   This program is open to minorities who are NABA members and enrolled full time as 1) an undergraduate freshman, sophomore, junior, or first-semester senior majoring in accounting, business, or finance at a 4-year college or university; or 2) a graduate student working on a master's degree in accounting. High school seniors are not eligible. Applicants must have a GPA of 3.5 or higher in their major and 3.3 or higher overall. Along with their application, they must submit a 500-word personal statement on their involvement in NABA, career objectives, leadership abilities, and community activities. Financial need is not considered in the selection process.

Financial data   The stipend ranges from $1,000 to $3,000.

Duration   1 year.

Additional information   This program includes named scholarships that vary from time to time. Recently, those included the Ralph and Valerie Thomas Scholarship, the TDC Scholarship, the Crimson and Cream Scholarship (sponsored by Delta Sigma Theta Sorority), the Lloyd Trotter/GEAAF Scholarship, the Chuck Burch Scholarship, the Eddie Nesby Memorial Scholarship, the Les Netter Scholarship, the William L. Jackson, Jr. Memorial Scholarship, and the Claudette Griffin Memorial Scholarship.

Number awarded   Varies each year.

Deadline   January of each year.

[467]
NABA NATIONAL SCHOLARSHIP

National Association of Black Accountants
Attn: National Scholarship Program
7474 Greenway Center Drive, Suite 1120
Greenbelt, MD 20770
(301) 474-NABA   Fax: (301) 474-3114
E-mail: scholarships@nabainc.org
Web: www.nabainc.org

Summary   To provide financial assistance to student members of the National Association of Black Accountants (NABA) who are working on an undergraduate or graduate degree in a field related to accounting.

Eligibility   This program is open to minorities who are NABA members and enrolled full time as 1) an undergradu-

ate freshman, sophomore, junior, or first-semester senior majoring in accounting, business, or finance at a 4-year college or university; or 2) a graduate student working on a master's degree in accounting. High school seniors are not eligible. Applicants must have a GPA of 3.5 or higher in their major and 3.3 or higher overall. Along with their application, they must submit a 500-word personal statement on their involvement in NABA, career objectives, leadership abilities, and community activities. Financial need is not considered in the selection process.

Financial data   The stipend is $1,500.

Duration   1 year.

Number awarded   1 each year.

Deadline   January of each year.

[468]
NABANY SCHOLARSHIP PROGRAM

National Association of Black Accountants-New York
    Chapter
Attn: Scholarship Program
Grand Central Station
P.O. Box 2791
New York, NY 10163
(212) 969-0560   E-mail: scholarship@nabany.org
Web: www.nabany.org

Summary   To provide financial assistance to members of the National Association of Black Accountants New York (NABANY) chapter who are working on an undergraduate degree in a business-related field at a school in any state.

Eligibility   This program is open to NABANY members who are full-time freshmen, sophomores, juniors, or non-graduating seniors. Applicants must be working on a bachelor's or master's degree in accounting, business, economics, finance, or other business-related field at an accredited college or university. They must have a GPA of 3.0 or higher.

Financial data   A stipend is awarded (amount not specified).

Duration   1 year.

Number awarded   1 or more each year.

Deadline   February of each year.

[469]
NABJ SCHOLARSHIP

National Association of Black Journalists
Attn: Program Manager
University of Maryland
1100 Knight Hall, Suite 3100
College Park, MD 20742
(301) 405-7520   Fax: (301) 314-1714
E-mail: Sberry@nabj.org
Web: www.nabj.org/?page=ScholarshipsNABJ

Summary   To provide financial assistance to undergraduate or graduate student members of the National Association of Black Journalists (NABJ) who are working on a degree in a field related to journalism.

Eligibility   This program is open to African American undergraduate or graduate student members of NABJ who are currently enrolled full time at an accredited 4-year college or university. Applicants must be working on a degree in journalism or other communications-related field and have a GPA of 2.5 or higher. They must be able to demonstrate financial need and a record of community service. Along with their application, they must submit 5 samples of their work, an official college transcript, 3 letters of recommendation, a resume, and an essay of 1,000 to 2,000 words on how they see themselves as a journalist and what they would improve about the media business.

Financial data The stipend is $2,500. Funds are paid directly to the recipient's college or university.

Duration 1 year; nonrenewable.

Number awarded 1 each year.

Deadline February of each year.

[470]
NABNA-FEEA SCHOLARSHIP PROGRAM

National Association of Black Narcotic Agents
c/o Federal Employee Education and Assistance Fund
Attn: Scholarship Program
3333 South Wadsworth Boulevard, Suite 300
Lakewood, CO 80227
(303) 933-7580   Toll Free: (800) 323-4140
Fax: (303) 933-7587   E-mail: admin@feea.org
Web: www.feea.org

Summary To provide financial assistance for college or graduate school to members of the National Association of Black Narcotic Agents (NABNA) and their dependents.

Eligibility This program is open to federal employees who are NABNA members and their dependent spouses and children entering or enrolled in an accredited 2- or 4-year undergraduate, graduate, or postgraduate program. Dependents must be full-time students; federal employees may be part-time students. Applicants or their sponsoring federal employee must have at least 3 years of civilian federal service. Along with their application, they must submit a 2-page essay on a topic related to a career in public service with the federal government, a letter of recommendation, a transcript with a GPA of 3.0 or higher, and a copy of their federal "Notice of Personnel Action;" high school seniors must also submit a copy of their ACT, SAT, or other examination scores. Financial need is not considered in the selection process.

Financial data The stipend is $1,000 per year.

Duration 1 year; may be renewed.

Additional information This program is jointly administered by NABNA and the Federal Employee Education and Assistance Fund (FEEA).

Number awarded 1 or more each year.

Deadline March of each year.

[471]
NASA SCHOLARSHIP AND RESEARCH OPPORTUNITIES (SRO) MINORITY UNIVERSITY RESEARCH AND EDUCATION PROJECT (MUREP) SCHOLARSHIPS

National Aeronautics and Space Administration
Attn: National Scholarship Deputy Program Manager
Office of Education and Public Outreach
Ames Research Center
Moffett Field, CA 94035
(650) 604-6958   E-mail: elizabeth.a.cartier@nasa.gov
Web: intern.nasa.gov

Summary To provide financial assistance and summer research experience at National Aeronautics and Space

Administration (NASA) facilities to undergraduate students majoring in designated fields of science, technology, engineering, or mathematics (STEM) at a Minority Serving Institution (MSI).

Eligibility This program is open to U.S. citizens and nationals who are working on an undergraduate degree at an MSI and have a GPA of 3.0 or higher with at least 2 years of full-time study remaining. Applicants must be majoring in chemistry, computer and information science and engineering, engineering (aeronautical and aerospace, biomedical, chemical, civil, computer, electrical and electronic, environmental, industrial and operations research, materials, mechanical, nuclear, ocean, optical, polymer, or systems) geosciences (including geophysics, hydrology, physical and dynamic meteorology, physical oceanography, planetary science), life sciences (including biochemistry, cell biology, developmental biology, evolutionary biology, genetics, physiology), materials research, mathematical sciences, or physics and astronomy. They must be available for an internship at a NASA center performing aeronautical research during the summer between their junior and senior years. Along with their application, they must submit a 1,000-word essay on 1) their professional goals and what attracted them to their intended STEM field of study; 2) the events and individuals that have been critical in influencing their academic and career decisions; and 3) how receiving the MUREP scholarship would help them accomplish their professional goals. Financial need is not considered in the selection process.

Financial data Students receive 75% of their tuition and education-related costs, up to $9,000 per academic year. The stipend for the summer internship is $6,000.

Duration 2 years.

Number awarded Up to 20 each year.

Deadline March of each year.

[472]
NATHAN L. ANDERSON MEMORIAL SCHOLARSHIPS

Nathan L. Anderson Memorial Scholarship Foundation, Inc.
Attn: Application Review Committee
4403 Knott Street
Beltsville, MD 20705
(301) 931-0867
Web: www.rememberingnathananderson.com

Summary To provide financial assistance to African American and other minority students interested in working on a bachelor's degree in specified fields.

Eligibility This program is open to minority students who are U.S. citizens. Applicants must be working on or planning to work on a bachelor's degree in aviation, computer science, music, or nursing. Along with their application, they must submit a 1,200-word essay about themselves, their goals, their ambitions, and how those are compatible with the Foundation's focus and purpose. Financial need is not considered in the selection process.

Financial data Stipends vary; recently, they averaged approximately $1,800.

Duration 1 year.

Number awarded Varies each year; recently, 17 were awarded.

Deadline January or August of each year.

[473]
NATIONAL ASSOCIATION OF NEGRO BUSINESS AND PROFESSIONAL WOMEN'S CLUBS NATIONAL SCHOLARSHIPS

National Association of Negro Business and Professional
  Women's Clubs
Attn: Scholarship Committee
1806 New Hampshire Avenue, N.W.
Washington, DC 20009-3206
(202) 483-4206   Fax: (202) 462-7253
E-mail: arlucas48@gmail.com
Web: www.nanbpwc.org/index-11.html

Summary To provide financial assistance for college to African American high school seniors.

Eligibility This program is open to African American high school seniors planning to enroll in an accredited college or university. Applicants must have a GPA of 3.0 or higher. Along with their application, they must submit an essay (at least 300 words) on a topic that changes annually but relates to persons of African descent in the United States. Financial need is not considered in the selection process. U.S. citizenship is required.

Financial data The stipend is $1,000.

Duration 1 year.

Number awarded 10 each year.

Deadline February of each year.

[474]
NATIONAL ASSOCIATION OF NEGRO MUSICIANS SCHOLARSHIP CONTEST

National Association of Negro Musicians, Inc.
Attn: Treasurer
P.O. Box 51669
Durham, NC 27717
E-mail: nanm@nanm.org
Web: www.nanm.org/scholar-main

Summary To recognize and reward (with scholarships for additional study) young musicians who are sponsored by a branch of the National Association of Negro Musicians.

Eligibility This competition is open to musicians between 18 and 30 years of age. Contestants must be sponsored by a branch in good standing, although they do not need to be a member of a local branch or the national organization. For each category of the competition, they must select 2 compositions from assigned lists to perform, of which 1 list consists of works by African American composers. People ineligible to compete include former first-place winners of this competition; full-time public school teachers and college faculty (although graduate students holding teaching assistantships are still eligible if they receive less than 50% of their employment from that appointment); vocalists who have contracts as full-time solo performers in operatic, oratorio, or other types of professional singing organizations; instrumentalists with contractual full-time orchestral or ensemble jobs; and professional performers under management. Local branches nominate competitors for regional competitions. Regional winners advance to the national competition. The category of the competition rotates on a 5-year schedule as follows: 2018: organ; 2019: winds and percussion; 2020: piano; 2021: voice; 2022: strings.

Financial data In the national competition, awards are at least $3,000 for first place, $2,000 for second, $1,000 for third, and $250 for each honorable mention. All funds are paid directly to the winner's teacher/coach or institution.

Duration The competition is held annually.

Additional information The application fee is $50.

Number awarded 5 each year.

Deadline February of each year.

[475]
NATIONAL BLACK ASSOCIATION FOR SPEECH-LANGUAGE AND HEARING STUDENT RESEARCH AWARD

National Black Association for Speech-Language and
  Hearing
Attn: Awards and Scholarship Committee
700 McKnight Park Drive, Suite 708
Pittsburgh, PA 15237
(855) 727-2836   Fax: (888) 729-3489
E-mail: nbaslh@nbaslh.org
Web: www.nbaslh.org/scholarships/scholarship-main.html

Summary To recognize and reward outstanding research papers on communication sciences or disorders written by undergraduate or graduate student members of the National Black Association for Speech-Language and Hearing (NBASLH).

Eligibility This competition is open to African American students who are NBASLH members and enrolled full time in an ASHA-accredited undergraduate, master's, or doctoral degree program in speech-language pathology, audiology, or the speech-language-hearing sciences. Applicants must submit a paper of scientific or scholarly merit that deals with issues relevant to communication sciences and disorders. The research should focus on culturally and linguistically diverse populations. It may address 1 of the following: 1) an empirical investigation that requires data gathering and analysis; 2) an issue paper that aims to redefine, evaluate, and synthesize existing knowledge in ways that offer a new conceptual framework or approach for conducting research or engaging in clinical practice; or 3) a description of a clinical case study that has implications for future research and/or clinical practice. The manuscript should not exceed 8 typed pages (2,000 words). Selection is based on completeness, appropriateness, manuscript quality, and significance.

Financial data The award is $1,000. In addition, the winner receives a $100 travel allowance to attend the association's convention (and read the paper there).

Duration The award is presented annually.

Number awarded 2 each year.

Deadline February of each year.

[476]
NATIONAL BLACK MBA ASSOCIATION UNDERGRADUATE SCHOLARSHIP PROGRAM

National Black MBA Association
Attn: Scholarship Program
400 West Peachtree Street N.W., Suite 203
Atlanta, GA 30308
(404) 260-5444   E-mail: scholarship@nbmbaa.org
Web: www.nbmbaa.org

Summary To provide financial assistance to members of the National Black MBA Association (NBMBAA) interested in working on a bachelor's degree in a field related to business.

Eligibility This program is open to minority students who are currently enrolled full time in the first, second, third, or fourth year of a bachelor's degree program in business, management, or related field in the United States or Canada. Applicants must submit a 300-word essay on an assigned topic that relates to minorities in business. They must have a GPA of 3.0 or higher. Selection is based on the quality of the paper, academic excellence, leadership potential, communication skills, and involvement in local communities through service to others. U.S. or Canadian citizenship is required.

Financial data Stipends range up to $5,000.

Duration 1 year.

Number awarded Varies each year; recently, the sponsor awarded 18 undergraduate and graduate scholarships.

Deadline June of each year.

[477]
NATIONAL INSTITUTES OF HEALTH UNDERGRADUATE SCHOLARSHIP PROGRAM

National Institutes of Health
Attn: Office of Intramural Training and Education
2 Center Drive
Building 2, Room 2E24
Bethesda, MD 20892-0230
(301) 594-2222   Fax: (301) 594-9606
TDD: (888) 352-3001   E-mail: ugsp@nih.gov
Web: www.training.nih.gov/programs/ugsp

Summary To provide loans-for-service for undergraduate education in the life sciences to African Americans and other students from disadvantaged backgrounds.

Eligibility This program is open to U.S. citizens, nationals, and permanent residents who are enrolled or accepted for enrollment as full-time students at accredited 4-year institutions of higher education and committed to careers in biomedical, behavioral, and social science health-related research. Applicants must come from a family that meets federal standards of low income, currently defined as a family with an annual income below $23,540 for a 1-person family, ranging to below $81,780 for families of 8 or more. They must have a GPA of 3.3 or higher or be in the top 5% of their class. Selection is based on commitment to a career in biomedical, behavioral, or social science health-related research as an employee of the National Institutes of Health (NIH); academic achievements; recommendations and evaluations of skills, abilities, and goals; and relevant extracurricular activities. Applicants are ranked according to the following priorities: first, juniors and seniors who have completed 2 years of undergraduate course work including 4 core science courses in biology, chemistry, physics, and calculus; second, other undergraduates who have completed those 4 core science courses; third, freshmen and sophomores at accredited undergraduate institutions; and fourth, high school seniors who have been accepted for enrollment as full-time students at accredited undergraduate institutions. The sponsor especially encourages applications from underrepresented minorities, women, and individuals with disabilities.

Financial data Stipends are available up to $20,000 per year, to be used for tuition, educational expenses (such as books and lab fees), and qualified living expenses while attending a college or university. Recipients incur a service obligation to work as an employee of the NIH in Bethesda, Maryland for 10 consecutive weeks (during the summer) during the sponsored year and, upon graduation, for 52 weeks for each academic year of scholarship support. The NIH 52-week employment obligation may be deferred if the recipient goes to graduate or medical school.

Duration 1 year; may be renewed for up to 3 additional years.

Number awarded 15 each year.

Deadline March of each year.

[478]
NATIONAL OCEANIC AND ATMOSPHERIC ADMINISTRATION EDUCATIONAL PARTNERSHIP PROGRAM WITH MINORITY SERVING INSTITUTIONS UNDERGRADUATE SCHOLARSHIPS

National Oceanic and Atmospheric Administration
Attn: Office of Education
1315 East-West Highway
SSMC3, Room 10600
Silver Spring, MD 20910-6233
(301) 628-2900   E-mail: EPP.USP@noaa.gov
Web: www.noaa.gov

Summary To provide financial assistance and research experience to undergraduate students at Minority Serving Institutions who are majoring in scientific fields of interest to the National Oceanic and Atmospheric Administration (NOAA).

Eligibility This program is open to full-time juniors at Minority Serving Institutions, including Hispanic Serving Institutions (HSIs), Historically Black Colleges and Universities (HBCUs), Tribal Colleges and Universities (TCUs), Alaskan Native Serving Institutions, and Native Hawaiian Serving Institutions. Applicants must have a GPA of 3.2 or higher and a major in atmospheric science, biology, computer science, engineering, environmental science, geography, hydrology, mathematics, oceanography, physical science, physics, remote sensing, social science, or other field that supports NOAA's programs and mission. They must also be interested in participating in a research internship at an NOAA site. Selection is based on relevant course work (30%), education plan and statement of career interest (40%), recommendations (20%), and additional experience related to diversity of education, extracurricular activities, honors and awards, non-academic and volunteer work, and communication skills (10%). U.S. citizenship is required.

Financial data Total support for 2 academic years and 2 summer internships is $45,000.

Duration 2 academic years and 2 summer internships.

Number awarded   Up to 15 each year.

Deadline   February of each year.

[479]
NATIONAL PRESS CLUB SCHOLARSHIP FOR JOURNALISM DIVERSITY

National Press Club
Attn: Executive Director's Office
529 14th Street, N.W., 13th Floor
Washington, DC 20045
(202) 662-7599
Web: www.press.org/about/scholarships/diversity

Summary   To provide funding to high school seniors who are planning to major in journalism in college and are African Americans or other students who will bring diversity to the field.

Eligibility   This program is open to high school seniors who have been accepted to college and plan to prepare for a career in journalism. Applicants must submit 1) a 500-word essay explaining how they would add diversity to U.S. journalism; 2) up to 5 work samples demonstrating an ongoing interest in journalism through work on a high school newspaper or other media; 3) letters of recommendation from 3 people; 4) a copy of their high school transcript; 5) documentation of financial need; 6) a letter of acceptance from the college or university of their choice; and 7) a brief description of how they have pursued journalism in high school.

Financial data   The stipend is $2,000 for the first year and $2,500 for each subsequent year. The program also provides an additional $500 book stipend, designated the Ellen Masin Persina Scholarship, for the first year.

Duration   4 years.

Additional information   The program began in 1990.

Number awarded   1 each year.

Deadline   February of each year.

[480]
NATIONAL SORORITY OF PHI DELTA KAPPA SCHOLARSHIPS

National Sorority of Phi Delta Kappa, Inc.
Attn: Perpetual Scholarship Foundation
8233 South King Drive
Chicago, IL 60619
(773) 783-7379   Fax: (773) 783-7354
E-mail: nspdkhq@aol.com

Summary   To provide financial assistance to African American high school seniors interested in studying education in college.

Eligibility   This program is open to African American high school seniors who are interested in working on a 4-year college degree in education. Men and women compete separately. Financial need is considered in the selection process.

Financial data   The stipend is $1,500 per year.

Duration   4 years, provided the recipient maintains a GPA of 2.5 or higher and a major in education.

Additional information   The sponsor was founded in 1923 as an organization of female African American educators.

Number awarded   10 each year: 1 male and 1 female in each of the organization's 5 regions.

Deadline   Applications must be submitted to a local chapter of the organization by January of each year.

[481]
NATIONAL SPACE GRANT COLLEGE AND FELLOWSHIP PROGRAM

National Aeronautics and Space Administration
Attn: Office of Education
300 E Street, S.W.
Mail Suite 6M35
Washington, DC 20546-0001
(202) 358-1069   Fax: (202) 358-7097
E-mail: aleksandra.korobov@nasa.gov
Web: www.nasa.gov

Summary   To provide financial assistance to undergraduate and graduate students, especially African Americans and other underrepresented minorities, interested in preparing for a career in a space-related field.

Eligibility   This program is open to undergraduate and graduate students at colleges and universities that participate in the National Space Grant program of the U.S. National Aeronautics and Space Administration (NASA) through their state consortium. Applicants must be interested in a program of study and/or research in a field of science, technology, engineering, or mathematics (STEM) related to space. A specific goal of the program is to recruit and train U.S. citizens, especially underrepresented minorities, women, and persons with disabilities, for careers in aerospace science and technology. Financial need is not considered in the selection process.

Financial data   Each consortium establishes the terms of the fellowship program in its state.

Additional information   NASA established the Space Grant program in 1989. It operates through 52 consortia in each state, the District of Columbia, and Puerto Rico. Each consortium includes selected colleges and universities in that state as well as other affiliates from industry, museums, science centers, and state and local agencies.

Number awarded   Varies each year.

Deadline   Each consortium sets its own deadlines.

[482]
NAVAL RESEARCH LABORATORY SUMMER RESEARCH PROGRAM FOR HBCU/MI UNDERGRADUATES AND GRADUATES

Naval Research Laboratory
Attn: Personnel Operations Branch
4555 Overlook Avenue, S.W.
Washington, DC 20375-5320
(202) 767-8313
Web: www.nrl.navy.mil/hbcu/description

Summary   To provide research experience at the Naval Research Laboratory (NRL) to undergraduate and graduate students in fields of science, technology, engineering, and mathematics (STEM) at minority institutions.

Eligibility   This program is open to undergraduate and graduate students who have completed at least 1 year of study at an Historically Black College or University (HBCU), Minority Institution (MI), or Tribal College or University (TCU).

Applicants must be working on a degree in a field of STEM and have a cumulative GPA of 3.0 or higher. They must be interested in participating in a research program at NRL under the mentorship of a senior staff scientist. U.S. citizenship or permanent resident status is required.

Financial data The stipend is $810 per week for undergraduates or $1,050 per week for graduate students. Subsidized housing is provided at a motel in the area.

Duration 10 weeks during the summer.

Additional information This program is conducted in accordance with a planned schedule and a working agreement between NRL, the educational institution, and the student.

Number awarded Varies each year.

Deadline February of each year.

[483]
NBCFAE NATIONAL SCHOLARSHIP PROGRAM

National Black Coalition of Federal Aviation Employees
c/o Phyllis Seaward, National Education, Recruitment,
  and Training Chair
FAA Employee Relations Division
800 Independence Avenue, S.W.
Washington, DC 20591
(202) 276-4891
E-mail: nationalnbcfaescholarship@nbcfaeinfo.org
Web: nbcfae.clubexpress.com

Summary To provide financial assistance to undergraduate students, especially African Americans and member of other underrepresented groups, who are interested in preparing for a career in a field related to aviation.

Eligibility This program is open to entering and continuing full-time undergraduate students preparing for a career in aviation, science, or technology. Applicants must be U.S. citizens and have a GPA of 2.5 or higher. The program encourages applications from women, minorities, and people with disabilities. Selection is based on academic achievement, leadership, community involvement, and financial need.

Financial data The stipend is $1,000.

Duration 1 year.

Additional information This program began in 2005.

Number awarded Up to 8 each year: 8 in each of the sponsor's regions.

Deadline May of each year.

[484]
NBNA SCHOLARSHIP PROGRAM

National Black Nurses Association, Inc.
Attn: Scholarship Committee
8630 Fenton Street, Suite 330
Silver Spring, MD 20910-3803
(301) 589-3200   Fax: (301) 589-3223
E-mail: gbelizaire@nbna.org
Web: www.nbna.org/content.asp?contentid=82

Summary To provide financial assistance for undergraduate or graduate nursing education to members of the National Black Nurses Association (NBNA).

Eligibility This program is open to members of the association who are currently enrolled in a B.S.N., A.D., diploma, L.P.N./L.V.N., master's, or doctoral program with at least 1 full year of school remaining. Along with their application, they must submit a 2-page essay 1) describing their extracurricular activities and community involvement (including local chapter activities, community-based projects, school level projects, organizational efforts, state-level student nurse activities, and other activities impacting on the health and social condition of African Americans and other culturally diverse groups); 2) presenting their ideas of what they can do as an individual nurse to improve the health status and/or social condition of African Americans; and 3) stating their future goals in nursing.

Financial data The stipend ranges from $1,000 to $6,000 per year.

Duration 1 year; may be renewed.

Additional information This program includes the following named scholarships: the Dr. Lauranne Sams Scholarship, the Martha R. Dudley Scholarship, the Maria Dudley Advanced Scholarship, the NBNA Board of Directors Scholarship, the Rita E. Miller Scholarship, the Dr. Martha A. Dawson Genesis Scholarship, the Margaret Pemberton Scholarship, the Lynne Edwards Research Scholarship, the Dr. Hilda Richards Scholarship, the Children's Mercy Hospitals and Clinics Scholarship, and the George Freeman Memorial Scholarship.

Number awarded Varies each year.

Deadline April of each year.

[485]
NELLIE STONE JOHNSON SCHOLARSHIP

Nellie Stone Johnson Scholarship Program
P.O. Box 40309
St. Paul, MN 55104
(651) 738-1404   Toll Free: (866) 738-5238
E-mail: info@nelliestone.org
Web: www.nelliestone.org/scholarship-program

Summary To provide financial assistance to African American and other racial minority union members and their families who are interested in working on an undergraduate or graduate degree in any field at a Minnesota state college or university.

Eligibility This program is open to students in undergraduate and graduate programs at a 2- or 4-year institution that is a component of Minnesota State Colleges and Universities (MnSCU). Applicants must be a minority (Asian, American Indian, Alaska Native, Black/African American, Chicano(a) or Latino(a), Native Hawaiian, or Pacific Islander) and a union member or the child, grandchild, or spouse of a minority union member. They must submit a 2-page essay about their background, educational goals, career goals, and commitment to the causes of human or civil rights. Undergraduates must have a GPA of 2.0 or higher; graduate students must have a GPA of 3.0 or higher. Preference is given to Minnesota residents. Selection is based on the essay, commitment to human or civil rights, extracurricular activities, volunteer activities, community involvement, academic standing, and union verification.

Financial data Stipends are $1,200 per year for full-time students or $500 per year for part-time students.

Duration 1 year; may be renewed up to 3 additional years for students working on a bachelor's degree, 1 additional year for students working on a master's degree, or 1 additional year for students in a community or technical college program.

Number awarded Varies each year; recently, 18 were awarded.

Deadline May of each year.

[486]
NEW JERSEY CHAPTER AABE SCHOLARSHIPS

American Association of Blacks in Energy-New Jersey Chapter
Attn: Scholarship Committee
P.O. Box 32578
Newark, NJ 07102
E-mail: NewJersey@aabe.org
Web: www.aabe.org/index.php?component=pages&id=692

Summary To provide financial assistance to Africans and members of other underrepresented minority groups who are high school seniors in New Jersey and planning to major in an energy-related field at a college in any state.

Eligibility This program is open to seniors graduating from high schools in New Jersey and planning to attend a college or university in any state. Applicants must be African Americans, Hispanics, or Native Americans who have a GPA of 3.0 or higher and who have taken the ACT and/or SAT test. Their intended major must be business, engineering, technology, mathematics, the physical sciences, or other energy-related field. Along with their application, they must submit a 350-word essay that includes 1) when they discovered their interest in the field of energy and what sparked their interest; and 2) either what excites them about the field of energy or how they expect their education to prepare them for the field of energy. Financial need is not considered in the selection process.

Financial data The stipend is $1,000.

Duration 1 year.

Additional information The winner is eligible to compete for regional and national scholarships.

Number awarded 1 each year.

Deadline March of each year.

[487]
NEW JERSEY CHAPTER NBMBAA UNDERGRADUATE SCHOLARSHIPS

National Black MBA Association-New Jersey Chapter
Attn: Scholarship Program
P.O. Box 28023
Newark, NJ 07101
(732) 246-2878
E-mail: bmba-info@nbmbaa-newjersey.org
Web: www.nbmbaa-newjersey.org/program

Summary To provide financial assistance to African American students from New Jersey interested in working on an undergraduate degree in business or management at a school in any state.

Eligibility This program is open to African American residents of New Jersey who are graduating high school seniors or full-time undergraduates enrolled in their first, second, or third year at an accredited college or university in any state. Applicants must be working on or planning to work on a bachelor's degree in business or management. Along with their application, they must submit a 2-page essay on a topic that changes annually but relates to African Americans in business. Selection is based on that essay, transcripts, a resume of work experience and extracurricular or volunteer activities, and 2 letters of recommendation.

Financial data A stipend is awarded (amount not specified).

Duration 1 year.

Number awarded Varies each year.

Deadline July of each year.

[488]
NEW MEDIA INTERNSHIP SPONSORED BY STATE FARM

Congressional Black Caucus Foundation, Inc.
Attn: Leadership Institute for Public Service
1720 Massachusetts Avenue, N.W.
Washington, DC 20036
(202) 263-2800   Toll Free: (800) 784-2577
Fax: (202) 775-0773   E-mail: internships@cbcfinc.org
Web: www.cbcfinc.org

Summary To provide African American and other undergraduate students with an opportunity to work on digital media activities of the Congressional Black Caucus (CBC).

Eligibility This program is open to African Americans who are at least college juniors and have a demonstrated interest in communications, journalism, press, and social media. Applicants must be interested in working at CBC in marketing, graphic design, and public and media relations. Selection is based on academic achievement (at least 2.5 GPA), editing and writing skills, ability to work independently, ability to manage several projects and meet critical deadlines, and quality of paper application and interview performance. U.S. citizenship or permission to work in the United States are required.

Financial data Interns receive a stipend of $15 per hour, or a maximum of $31,200 per year.

Duration 20 to 30 hours per week for at least 9 months.

Additional information This program, which began in 2013, is sponsored by State Farm. Intern responsibilities include executing digital media strategies for the CBC and its programs and initiatives, providing editorial support, developing weekly content for social media promoters, and introducing creative ideas and opportunities to expand the CBC reach using digital media.

Number awarded 1 or more each year.

Deadline April of each year.

[489]
NEW YORK EXCEPTIONAL UNDERGRADUATE/ GRADUATE STUDENT SCHOLARSHIP

Conference of Minority Transportation Officials
Attn: National Scholarship Program
100 M Street, S.E., Suite 917
Washington, DC 20003
(202) 506-2917   E-mail: info@comto.org
Web: www.comto.org/page/scholarships

Summary To provide financial assistance to African American and other minority students who are members or relatives of members of the Conference of Minority Transportation Officials (COMTO) in New York and working on an undergraduate or graduate degree in transportation.

Eligibility This program is open to minorities who have been members or relatives of members of COMTO in New York for at least 1 year. Applicants must be enrolled full time at an accredited college, university, or vocational/technical institute and working on an undergraduate or graduate degree in a transportation-related discipline. They must have a GPA of 3.5 or higher. Along with their application they must submit a cover letter on their transportation-related career goals and life aspirations. Financial need is not considered in the selection process.

Financial data The stipend is $5,000. Funds are paid directly to the recipient's college or university.

Duration 1 year.

Number awarded 1 each year.

Deadline April of each year.

[490]
NIDDK DIVERSITY SUMMER RESEARCH TRAINING PROGRAM (DSRTP) FOR UNDERGRADUATE STUDENTS

National Institute of Diabetes and Digestive and Kidney Diseases
Attn: Office of Minority Health Research Coordination
6707 Democracy Boulevard, Room 906A
Bethesda, MD 20892-5454
(301) 435-2988   Fax: (301) 594-9358
E-mail: MartinezW@mail.nih.gov
Web: www.niddk.nih.gov

Summary To provide African American and other underrepresented minority undergraduate students with an opportunity to conduct research in the laboratory of a National Institute of Diabetes and Digestive and Kidney Diseases (NIDDK) intramural scientist during the summer.

Eligibility This program is open to undergraduate students who come from backgrounds underrepresented in biomedical research, including individuals from disadvantaged backgrounds and those from of underrepresented racial and ethnic groups. Applicants must be interested in participating in a research project conducted at an intramural research laboratory of NIDDK in Bethesda, Maryland or Phoenix, Arizona. They must have completed at least 1 year at an accredited institution and have a GPA of 3.0 or higher. Along with their application, they must submit a 2-page personal statement of their research interest, career goals, and reasons for applying for training at NIDDK. U.S. citizenship or permanent resident status is required.

Financial data Students receive a stipend of $2,600, housing, and (for those who live outside the Washington metropolitan area or the state of Arizona) a travel allowance of $700.

Duration 10 weeks during the summer.

Number awarded Varies each year.

Deadline February of each year.

[491]
NJUA EXCELLENCE IN DIVERSITY SCHOLARSHIP

New Jersey Utilities Association
50 West State Street, Suite 1117
Trenton, NJ 08608
(609) 392-1000   Fax: (609) 396-4231
E-mail: info@njua.com
Web: www.njua.com/excellence_in_diversity_scholarship

Summary To provide financial assistance to African American and other underrepresented disabled high school seniors in New Jersey interested in attending college in any state.

Eligibility This program is open to seniors graduating from high schools in New Jersey who are women, minorities (Black or African American, Hispanic or Latino, American Indian or Alaska Native, Asian, Native Hawaiian or Pacific Islander, or 2 or more races), and persons with disabilities. Applicants must be planning to work on a bachelor's degree at a college or university in any state. Along with their application, they must submit a 500-word essay explaining their career ambition and why they have chosen that career. Children of employees of any New Jersey Utilities Association-member company are ineligible. Selection is based on overall academic excellence and demonstrated financial need. U.S. citizenship or permanent resident status is required.

Financial data The stipend is $1,500 per year. Funds are paid to the recipient's college or university.

Duration 4 years.

Number awarded 1 each year.

Deadline April of each year.

[492]
NOKIA BELL LABORATORIES INTERN PROGRAM

Nokia Bell Laboratories
Attn: Special Programs Manager
600-700 Mountain Avenue
Murray Hill, NJ 07974
(908) 582-3000   E-mail: info@bell-labs.com
Web: www.bell-labs.com/connect/internships

Summary To provide technical work experience at facilities of Nokia Bell Laboratories during the summer to African American and other underrepresented minority undergraduate students.

Eligibility This program is open to women and members of minority groups (African Americans, Hispanics, and Native American Indians) who are underrepresented in the sciences. Applicants must be interested in pursuing technical employment experience in research and development facilities of Nokia Bell Laboratories. The program is primarily directed at undergraduate students who have completed their second or third year of college. Emphasis is placed on the following disciplines: business modeling, chemical engineering, chemistry, computer science and engineering, economics, electrical engineering, engineering mechanics, industrial engineering, manufacturing engineering, mathematics, mechanical engineering, operations research, physics, statistics, systems engineering, and telecommunications. U.S. citizenship or permanent resident status is required. Selection is based on academic achievement, personal motivation, and compatibility of student interests with current Nokia Bell Laboratories activities.

Financial data Salaries are commensurate with those of regular Nokia Bell Laboratories employees with comparable education. Interns are reimbursed for travel expenses up to the cost of round-trip economy-class airfare.

Duration 10 weeks during the summer.

Additional information Nokia Bell Laboratories facilities are located in central and northern New Jersey and in Naperville, Illinois.

Number awarded Varies each year.

Deadline November of each year.

[493]
NORMA KORNEGAY CLARKE SCHOLARSHIP

Northeast Human Resources Association
Attn: Director of Professional Development
490 Virginia Road, Suite 32
Concord, MA 01742-2747
(781) 239-8718   Fax: (781) 237-8745
E-mail: nreiser@nehra.com
Web: www.nehra.com/?page=DIScholarshipApp

Summary To provide financial assistance for college to African American and other high school seniors from the New England states who have promoted diversity.

Eligibility This program is open to seniors who are graduating from high schools in New England and planning to attend a college or university. Applicants should have demonstrated academic responsibility, performed community service, offered a helping hand to fellow students, and promoted harmony among diverse groups. They must have a GPA of 3.0 or higher and be able to demonstrate financial need. Along with their application, they must submit a 750-word personal statement explaining what diversity means to them, how they promote diversity in their community or school, and how they propose to promote diversity in the future.

Financial data The stipend is $5,000.

Duration 1 year.

Additional information The sponsor is an affiliate of the Society for Human Resource Management (SHRM). Its Diversity and Inclusion Committee focuses on veterans, the GLBT community, people with disabilities, gender equity, and race/ethnicity. The Back Bay Staffing Group established this program in 1998.

Number awarded 1 each year.

Deadline February of each year.

[494]
NORTH CAROLINA CHAPTER AABE SCHOLARSHIPS

American Association of Blacks in Energy-North Carolina
  Chapter
Attn: Scholarship Committee
P.O. Box 207
Raleigh, NC 27602-0207
E-mail: northcarolina@aabe.org
Web: www.aabe.org

Summary To provide financial assistance to African Americans and members of other underrepresented minority groups who are high school seniors in North Carolina and planning to major in an energy-related field at a college in any state.

Eligibility This program is open to seniors graduating from high schools in North Carolina and planning to work on a bachelor's degree at a college or university in any state. Applicants must be African Americans, Hispanics, or Native Americans who have a GPA of 3.0 or higher and have taken the ACT and/or SAT test. Their intended major must be a field of business, engineering, physical science, mathematics, or technology related to energy. Along with their application, they must submit a 350-word essay that includes 1) when they discovered their interest in the field of energy and what sparked their interest; and 2) either what excites them about the field of energy or how they expect their education to prepare them for the field of energy. Financial need is not considered in the selection process.

Financial data The stipend is $1,000.

Duration 1 year; nonrenewable.

Additional information Winners are eligible to compete for regional and national scholarships.

Number awarded 1 or more each year.

Deadline March of each year.

[495]
NORTH CAROLINA CPA FOUNDATION OUTSTANDING MINORITY ACCOUNTING STUDENT SCHOLARSHIPS

North Carolina Association of Certified Public
  Accountants
Attn: North Carolina CPA Foundation, Inc.
P.O. Box 80188
Raleigh, NC 27623-0188
(919) 469-1040, ext. 130   Toll Free: (800) 722-2836
Fax: (919) 378-2000   E-mail: nccpafound@ncacpa.org
Web: www.ncacpa.org/scholarship-recipients

Summary To provide financial assistance to African American and other minority undergraduate students working on a degree in accounting at colleges and universities in North Carolina.

Eligibility This program is open to North Carolina residents who are members of a minority group, defined as Black, Native American/Alaskan Native, Middle-Eastern, Asian or Pacific Islander, or Hispanic, and enrolled full time in an accounting program at a college or university in the state. Applicants must have completed at least 36 semester hours, including at least 1 college or university-level accounting course, and have a GPA of 3.0 or higher. They must be sponsored by an accounting faculty member. Selection is based on the content of an essay on a topic related to the public accounting profession (35%), essay grammar (35%), and extracurricular activities (30%).

Financial data Stipends are $2,000 or $1,000.

Duration 1 year; may be renewed up to 2 additional years.

Number awarded 2 each year: 1 at $2,000 and 1 at $1,000.

Deadline February of each year.

[496]
NORTH TEXAS EXCEPTIONAL HIGH SCHOOL STUDENT SCHOLARSHIP

Conference of Minority Transportation Officials
Attn: National Scholarship Program
100 M Street, S.E., Suite 917
Washington, DC 20003
(202) 506-2917   E-mail: info@comto.org
Web: www.comto.org/page/scholarships

Summary To provide financial assistance to African American and other minority high school seniors who are members or family of members of the Conference of Minority Transportation Officials (COMTO) in Texas and planning to work on a degree in transportation.

Eligibility   This program is open to minority residents of Texas who have been members or whose parents, guardians, or grandparents have been members of COMTO for at least 1 year. Applicants must be high school seniors who have been accepted at an accredited college, university, or vocational/ technical institute and planning to work on a degree in a transportation-related discipline. They must have a GPA of 2.0 or higher. Along with their application they must submit a cover letter on their transportation-related career goals and life aspirations. Financial need is not considered in the selection process.

Financial data   The stipend is $3,000. Funds are paid directly to the recipient's college or university.

Duration   1 year.

Number awarded   1 each year.

Deadline   April of each year.

[497]
NORTH TEXAS EXCEPTIONAL UNDERGRADUATE/GRADUATE STUDENT SCHOLARSHIP

Conference of Minority Transportation Officials
Attn: National Scholarship Program
100 M Street, S.E., Suite 917
Washington, DC 20003
(202) 506-2917   E-mail: info@comto.org
Web: www.comto.org/page/scholarships

Summary   To provide financial assistance to African American and other minority residents of Texas who are working on an undergraduate or graduate degree in transportation.

Eligibility   This program is open to minorities who are residents of Texas enrolled at an accredited college, university, or vocational/technical institute and working on an undergraduate or graduate degree in a transportation-related discipline. Applicants must have a GPA of 2.5 or higher. Along with their application they must submit a cover letter on their transportation-related career goals and life aspirations. Financial need is not considered in the selection process. Membership in the Conference of Minority Transportation Officials (COMTO) is considered a plus but is not required.

Financial data   The stipend is $4,500. Funds are paid directly to the recipient's college or university.

Duration   1 year.

Number awarded   1 each year.

Deadline   April of each year.

[498]
NORTHERN NEW JERSEY CHAPTER NABA COLLEGE SCHOLARSHIPS

National Association of Black Accountants-Northern New
   Jersey Chapter
Attn: Scholarship Committee
P.O. Box 1091
Newark, NJ 07101
E-mail: Scholarships@nabannj.org
Web: www.nabannj.org/students

Summary   To provide financial assistance to residents of New Jersey who are members of the National Association of Black Accountants (NABA) and studying a field related to accounting at a college in any state.

Eligibility   This program is open to residents of New Jersey who are of African descent (including African Americans, Caribbean Americans, Afro-Americans, and other subgroups considered "Black") and NABA members. Applicants must have completed at least 6 hours of credits related to a major in accounting, business, or finance at an accredited college or university in any state. They must have a GPA of 3.0 or higher. Along with their application, they must submit a 700-word essay on a topic that changes annually; recently, students were asked to explain if building relationships is important to their academic and/or career success. Selection is based on that essay, academic record, extracurricular activities, and recommendations.

Financial data   The stipend is $1,000.

Duration   1 year.

Number awarded   Approximately 3 each year.

Deadline   February of each year.

[499]
NORTHERN NEW JERSEY CHAPTER NABA HIGH SCHOOL SCHOLARSHIPS

National Association of Black Accountants-Northern New
   Jersey Chapter
Attn: Scholarship Committee
P.O. Box 1091
Newark, NJ 07101
E-mail: Scholarships@nabannj.org
Web: www.nabannj.org/students

Summary   To provide financial assistance to high school seniors in New Jersey who are of African descent and planning to attend college in any state.

Eligibility   This program is open to seniors graduating from high schools in New Jersey who are of African descent (including African Americans, Caribbean Americans, Afro-Americans, and other subgroups considered "Black"). Applicants must be planning to attend an accredited college or university in any state. They must have a GPA of 3.0 or higher. Along with their application, they must submit a 500-word essay on a topic that changes annually; recently, students were asked to explain what success means to them and their top 3 steps to success. Selection is based on that essay, academic record, extracurricular activities, and recommendations. U.S. citizenship is required.

Financial data   The stipend is $1,000.

Duration   1 year.

Number awarded   Approximately 3 each year.

Deadline   March of each year.

[500]
NORTHWEST FARM CREDIT SERVICES MINORITY SCHOLARSHIPS

Northwest Farm Credit Services
Attn: Public Relations and Events Manager
P.O. Box 2515
Spokane, WA 99220-2515
(509) 340-5467   Toll Free: (800) 743-2125
Fax: (800) 255-1789
E-mail: heidi.whitman@northwestfcs.com
Web: www.northwestfcs.com

Summary To provide financial assistance to African American and other minority students who are majoring in a field related to agricultural business at universities in designated northwestern states.

Eligibility This program is open to members of minority ethnic groups (African American or Black, American Indian or Alaska Native, Asian, Latino/Hispanic, or Pacific Islander) currently enrolled as full-time sophomores or higher at 4-year universities in Alaska, Idaho, Montana, Oregon, Utah, or Washington. Applicants must be studying accounting, business, finance, agricultural business, or economics. They must have a GPA of 3.0 or higher and be U.S. citizens or legal residents. Along with their application, they must submit a 1-page essay on how they will use their education and degree to make a positive impact. Selection is based on that essay (20%), academic achievement (20%), leadership (25%), participation in extracurricular activities (25%), and letters of recommendation (10%).

Financial data The stipend is $2,000.

Duration 1 year; nonrenewable.

Number awarded 4 each year.

Deadline February of each year.

[501]
NORTHWEST JOURNALISTS OF COLOR SCHOLARSHIP AWARDS

Northwest Journalists of Color
c/o Anika Anand
The Evergrey
P.O. Box 30854
Seattle, WA 98113
E-mail: anikaanand00@gmail.com
Web: www.aajaseattle.org/scholarships

Summary To provide financial assistance to students from Washington state who demonstrate a commitment to the importance of diverse cultural backgrounds and are interested in careers in journalism.

Eligibility This program is open to students who are 1) current high school juniors or seniors in Washington; 2) residents of any state attending a 2- or 4-year college, university, or vocational school in Washington; or 3) seniors graduating from Washington high schools and planning to attend a 2- or 4-year college, university, or vocational school in any state. Applicants must be preparing for a career in broadcast, photo, or print journalism. They do not need to identify as a student of color, but strong preference is given to applicants who demonstrate an understanding of and commitment to the importance of diverse cultural backgrounds and experiences in newsrooms. Along with their application, they must submit 1) a 500-word essay about their interest in a career as a journalist; 2) link to a resume; 3) up to 3 work samples; and 4) a 250-word statement of financial need.

Financial data Stipends range up to $2,500 per year.

Duration 1 year; may be renewed.

Additional information This program, established in 1986, is sponsored by local chapters of the Asian American Journalists Association, the Native American Journalists Association, the Black Journalists Association of Seattle, and the National Association of Hispanic Journalists.

Number awarded Varies each year.

Deadline April of each year.

[502]
NSBE JUNIOR SUMMER BRIDGE SCHOLARSHIP

National Society of Black Engineers
Attn: Programs Department
205 Daingerfield Road
Alexandria, VA 22314
(703) 549-2207   Fax: (703) 683-5312
E-mail: scholarships@nsbe.org
Web: www.nsbe.org/Programs/Scholarships.aspx

Summary To provide funding to junior members of the National Society of Black Engineers (NSBE) who are graduating from high school and wish to attend a summer enrichment conducted by the university they plan to attend.

Eligibility This program is open to junior members of the society who are graduating from high school during the current school year and have been accepted to an ABET-accredited engineering program for the fall. Applicants must wish to enroll in a summer enrichment program that is run by the university they plan to attend and that is focused on science, technology, engineering, or mathematics (STEM). They must be able to demonstrate financial need.

Financial data A stipend is awarded (amount not specified).

Duration 1 summer.

Number awarded Varies each year.

Deadline Applications are accepted through the end of June of each year.

[503]
NSCA MINORITY SCHOLARSHIPS

National Strength and Conditioning Association
Attn: NSCA Foundation
1885 Bob Johnson Drive
Colorado Springs, CO 80906-4000
(719) 632-6722, ext. 152   Toll Free: (800) 815-6826
Fax: (719) 632-6367   E-mail: foundation@nsca.org
Web: www.nsca.com/foundation/nsca-scholarships

Summary To provide financial assistance to African American and other minorities who are interested in working on an undergraduate or graduate degree in strength training and conditioning.

Eligibility This program is open to Blacks, Hispanics, Asian Americans, and Native Americans who are 17 years of age and older. Applicants must have been accepted into an accredited postsecondary institution to work on an undergraduate or graduate degree in the strength and conditioning field. Along with their application, they must submit a 500-word essay on their personal and professional goals and how receiving this scholarship will assist them in achieving those goals. Selection is based on that essay, academic achievement, strength and conditioning experience, honors and awards, community involvement, letters of recommendation, and involvement in the National Strength and Conditioning Association (NSCA).

Financial data The stipend is $1,500.

Duration 1 year.

Additional information The NSCA is a nonprofit organization of strength and conditioning professionals, including coaches, athletic trainers, physical therapists, educators, researchers, and physicians. This program was first offered in 2003.

Number awarded Varies each year; recently, 5 were awarded.

Deadline March of each year.

[504]
NYSACAC SCHOLARSHIP

New York State Association for College Admission
  Counseling
Attn: Scholarship Committee
P.O. Box 28
Red Hook, NY 12571
(845) 389-1300   Fax: (866) 370-1008
E-mail: Scholarship@nysacad.org
Web: www.nysacac.org/nysacac-scholarship

Summary To provide financial assistance to residents of New York, especially African Americans and members of other underrepresented groups, who are nominated by a member of the New York State Association for College Admission Counseling (NYSACAC) and plan to attend a NYSACAC member college.

Eligibility This program is open to residents of New York who are graduating from a public or private secondary school in the state, are completing a home school program in the state, or obtained a GED. Applicants must have overcome barriers, have succeeded with limited resources; or be a member of an underrepresented group. They must be entering freshmen at a 2- or 4-year college or university that is a NYSACAC member. A NYSACAC individual member must nominate them. Along with their application, they must submit a 500-word essay on 1 of the following topics: 1) how they have overcome barriers; 2) how they have applied the sponsor's motto of Leading the Way; or 3) the person who has influenced them the most through the college admission process.

Financial data The stipend is $1,000.

Duration 1 year.

Number awarded 4 each year.

Deadline May of each year.

[505]
OHIO HIGH SCHOOL ATHLETIC ASSOCIATION MINORITY SCHOLAR ATHLETE SCHOLARSHIPS

Ohio High School Athletic Association
Attn: Foundation
4080 Roselea Place
Columbus, OH 43214
(614) 267-2502   Fax: (614) 267-1677
Web: www.ohsaa.org/School-Resources

Summary To provide financial assistance to African American and othr minority high school seniors in Ohio who have participated in athletics and plan to attend college in any state.

Eligibility This program is open to minority seniors graduating from high schools in Ohio that are members of the Ohio High School Athletic Association (OHSAA). Applicants must have received at least 3 varsity letters in 1 sport or 4 letters in 2 sports and have a GPA of 3.25 or higher. They must be planning to attend a college or university in any state. Along with their application, they must submit a 1-page essay on the role that interscholastic athletics has played in their life and how such participation will benefit them in the future. Selec-

tion is based on that essay, GPA, ACT and SAT scores, varsity letters earned, and athletic honors.

Financial data The stipend is $1,000.

Duration 1 year.

Number awarded 6 each year: 1 in each OHSSA District.

Deadline April of each year.

[506]
OHIO NEWSPAPERS FOUNDATION MINORITY SCHOLARSHIPS

Ohio Newspaper Association
Attn: Foundation
1335 Dublin Road, Suite 216-B
Columbus, OH 43215-7038
(614) 486-6677, ext. 1010   Fax: (614) 486-6373
E-mail: ariggs@ohionews.org
Web: www.ohionews.org/aws/ONA/pt/sp/scholarships

Summary To provide financial assistance to African American and other minority high school seniors in Ohio planning to attend college in any state to prepare for a career in the newspaper industry.

Eligibility This program is open to high school seniors in Ohio who are members of minority groups (African American, Hispanic, Asian American, or American Indian) and planning to prepare for a career in the newspaper industry, especially advertising, communications, journalism, or marketing. Applicants must have a high school GPA of 2.5 or higher and demonstrate writing ability in an autobiography of 750 to 1,000 words that describes their academic and career interests, awards, extracurricular activities, and journalism-related activities. They must be planning to attend a college or university in Ohio.

Financial data The stipend is $1,500.

Duration 1 year; nonrenewable.

Additional information This program began in 1990.

Number awarded 1 each year.

Deadline March of each year.

[507]
OHIO NURSES FOUNDATION MINORITY STUDENT SCHOLARSHIP

Ohio Nurses Association
Attn: Ohio Nurses Foundation
4000 East Main Street
Columbus, OH 43213-2983
(614) 237-5414   Fax: (614) 237-6081
E-mail: info@ohionursesfoundation.org
Web: www.ohionursesfoundation.org

Summary To provide financial assistance to African American and other minority residents of Ohio who are interested in working on a degree in nursing at a school in any state.

Eligibility This program is open to residents of Ohio who are members of a minority group and interested in attending college in any state to prepare for a career as a nurse. Applicants must be attending or have attended a high school in the state. If still in high school, they must have a cumulative GPA of 3.5 or higher at the end of their junior year. If out of high school, they may not have had a break of more than 2 years between high school and enrollment in a nursing program. Selection is based on a personal statement, high school or college academic records, school activities, and community services.

Financial data   The stipend is $1,000.

Duration   1 year; recipients may reapply for 1 additional year if they remain enrolled full time and maintain a cumulative GPA of 2.5 or higher.

Number awarded   1 or more each year.

Deadline   January of each year.

[508]
OHIO SOCIETY OF CPAS COLLEGE SCHOLARSHIP PROGRAM

Ohio Society of CPAs
Attn: Ohio CPA Foundation
535 Metro Place South
P.O. Box 1810
Dublin, OH 43017-7810
(614) 764-2727, ext. 344
Toll Free: (800) 686-2727, ext. 344
Fax: (614) 764-5880   E-mail: oscpa@ohio-cpa.com
Web: www.ohiocpa.com

Summary   To provide financial assistance to undergraduate and graduate student members of the Ohio Society of CPAs, especially African Americans and members of other underrepresented groups, who are working on a degree in accounting at colleges and universities in the state.

Eligibility   This program is open to U.S. citizens who are Ohio residents working on undergraduate or graduate degrees in accounting at colleges and universities in the state in order to complete the 150 hours required for the C.P.A. examination. Applicants must have completed at least 30 hours of college credit and have a GPA of 3.0 or higher. Awards are available to 3 categories of students: 1) 2-year awards, for students at community colleges or other 2-year institutions; 2) 4-year awards, for students at 4-year colleges and universities; and 3) diversity awards, for students from underrepresented ethnic, racial, or cultural groups.

Financial data   The stipend is $2,000.

Duration   1 year; nonrenewable.

Number awarded   Varies each year; recently, 20 were awarded.

Deadline   November of each year.

[509]
OKLAHOMA CAREERTECH FOUNDATION TEACHER RECRUITMENT/RETENTION SCHOLARSHIP FOR STUDENTS

Oklahoma CareerTech Foundation
Attn: Administrator
1500 West Seventh Avenue
Stillwater, OK 74074-4364
(405) 743-5453   Fax: (405) 743-5541
E-mail: leden@careertech.ok.gov
Web: www.okcareertech.org

Summary   To provide financial assistance to African American residents of Oklahoma and other students reflecting the diversity of the state who are attending a college or university in the state to prepare for a career in the Oklahoma CareerTech system.

Eligibility   This program is open to residents of Oklahoma who are juniors or seniors at an institution of higher education

in the state. Applicants must be working on a bachelor's degree and teacher certification in Oklahoma's CareerTech system. They must reflect the ethnic diversity of the state. Along with their application, they must submit brief statements on their interest and commitment to the CareerTech teaching profession and their financial need.

Financial data   The stipend ranges from $500 per semester to $1,500 per year.

Duration   1 semester; may be renewed, provided the recipient maintains a GPA of 2.5 or higher.

Number awarded   1 or more each year.

Deadline   May of each year.

[510]
OLFIELD DUKES MULTICULTURAL STUDENT AWARD

Public Relations Student Society of America
Attn: Vice President of Member Services
33 Maiden Lane, 11th Floor
New York, NY 10038-5150
(212) 460-1474   Fax: (212) 995-0757
E-mail: DukesScholarship@prsa.org
Web: www.prssa.prsa.org

Summary   To provide financial assistance to African American and other multicultural college seniors who are interested in preparing for a career in public relations.

Eligibility   This program is open to multicultural (African American/Black, Hispanic/Latino, Asian, Native American, Alaskan Native, or Pacific Islander) students who are entering their junior year at an accredited 4-year college or university. Applicants must have a GPA of 3.0 or higher and be working on a degree in public relations, journalism, or other field to prepare for a career in public relations. Selection is based on academic achievement, specific examples of commitment to service and social responsibility, awards and honors received for academic or extracurricular achievements, writing skills, and letters of recommendation.

Financial data   The stipend is $1,000.

Duration   1 year.

Additional information   This program began in 2013 with support from Prudential Financial and Weber Shandwick.

Number awarded   1 each year.

Deadline   June of each year.

[511]
OMEGA MASON/MAUDE BISSON SCHOLARSHIP

Auxiliary to the National Medical Association
8403 Colesville Road, Suite 820
Silver Spring, MD 20910
(301) 495-3779   Fax: (301) 495-0037
E-mail: anmanationaloffice@earthlink.net
Web: www.anmanet.org

Summary   To provide financial assistance to African American nursing or allied health students.

Eligibility   Applicants must be African American, be currently enrolled in an accredited nursing or allied health school, have earned a GPA of 3.2 or higher, be able to demonstrate financial need, and have a record of community involvement. For 2-year nursing programs, applicants must be second-year students; for 4-year programs, applicants must be entering their third year. In addition to completing a formal application, students must submit a 1-page essay detailing their educational goals and reasons for requesting this scholarship. The scholarship is awarded to student nurses and allied health students in the city where the national convention of the Auxiliary to the National Medical Association (ANMA) is held each year.

Financial data A stipend is awarded (amount not specified).

Duration 1 year.

Number awarded 2 each year.

Deadline April of each year.

[512]
OMEGA PSI PHI DISTRICT AND INTERNATIONAL SCHOLAR OF THE YEAR AWARDS

Omega Psi Phi Fraternity
Attn: Charles R. Drew Memorial Scholarship Commission
3951 Snapfinger Parkway
Decatur, GA 30035-3203
(404) 284-5533   Fax: (404) 284-0333
E-mail: scholarshipchairman@oppf.org
Web: www.oppf.org/scholarship

Summary To recognize and reward members of Omega Psi Phi fraternity who demonstrate outstanding academic achievement and involvement in extracurricular and community activities.

Eligibility This program is open to members of the fraternity who are enrolled as a full-time sophomore or higher at a 4-year college or university. Applicants must have a GPA of 3.3 or higher. Chapters nominate their most outstanding member to the district. Each of the 13 districts selects a District Scholar of the Year winner. Those winners become candidates for the International Scholar of the Year Award. Candidates must submit a statement of 200 to 250 words on their purpose for applying for this scholarship, how they believe funds from the fraternity can assist them in achieving their career goals, and other circumstances (including financial need) that make it important for them to receive financial assistance. Selection is based on academic excellence, participation in extracurricular activities, and campus and community involvement.

Financial data District Scholars win a certificate and $6,500. The International Scholar of the Year wins an additional $10,000.

Duration The awards are presented annually.

Additional information Omega Psi Phi is a traditionally Black college fraternity. The winners are required to attend the Omega Psi Phi Grand Conclave or Leadership Conference. Up to $1,000 in travel expenses for attendance is provided.

Number awarded Up to 13 district winners are selected each year; 1 of those is designated International Scholar of the Year.

Deadline Applications must be submitted to the district scholarship committee chair by February of each year.

[513]
OMEGA PSI PHI FOUNDERS' MEMORIAL SCHOLARSHIPS

Omega Psi Phi Fraternity
Attn: Charles R. Drew Memorial Scholarship Commission
3951 Snapfinger Parkway
Decatur, GA 30035-3203
(404) 284-5533   Fax: (404) 284-0333
E-mail: scholarshipchairman@oppf.org
Web: www.oppf.org/scholarship

Summary To provide financial assistance to outstanding undergraduate and graduate members of Omega Psi Phi fraternity.

Eligibility This program is open to members of the fraternity who are enrolled full time as sophomores, juniors, or graduate students and have a GPA of 3.0 or higher. Each chapter may nominate 1 undergraduate and 1 graduate member to the district. Candidates must submit a statement of 200 to 250 words on their purpose for applying for this scholarship, how they believe funds from the fraternity can assist them in achieving their career goals, and other circumstances (including financial need) that make it important for them to receive financial assistance. Selection is based on academic achievement, extracurricular activities, and community and campus involvement.

Financial data The stipend is $5,000.

Duration The scholarships are offered annually.

Additional information Omega Psi Phi is a traditionally Black college fraternity. The winners are required to attend the Omega Psi Phi Grand Conclave or Leadership Conference. Up to $1,000 in travel expenses for attendance is provided.

Number awarded 4 each year: 3 to undergraduates and 1 to a graduate student.

Deadline Applications must be submitted to the district scholarship committee chair by January of each year.

[514]
OMEGA PSI PHI UNDERGRADUATE AND GRADUATE SCHOLARSHIPS

Omega Psi Phi Fraternity
Attn: Charles R. Drew Memorial Scholarship Commission
3951 Snapfinger Parkway
Decatur, GA 30035-3203
(404) 284-5533   Fax: (404) 284-0333
E-mail: scholarshipchairman@oppf.org
Web: www.oppf.org/scholarship

Summary To provide financial assistance for undergraduate, graduate, or professional education to members of Omega Psi Phi who have an outstanding academic record.

Eligibility This program is open to members of the fraternity who are either 1) a sophomore, junior, or senior planning to continue on to graduate or professional school; or 2) currently attending graduate or professional school. Applicants must be enrolled full time at a 4-year college or university and have a GPA of 3.0 or higher. Along with their application, they must submit a statement of 200 to 250 words on their purpose for applying for this scholarship, how they believe funds from the fraternity can assist them in achieving their career goals, and other circumstances (including financial need) that make it important for them to receive financial assistance.

Financial data   The stipend is $4,000.

Duration   1 year.

Additional information   Omega Psi Phi is a traditionally Black college fraternity. The winners are required to attend the Omega Psi Phi Grand Conclave or Leadership Conference. Up to $1,000 in travel expenses for attendance is provided.

Number awarded   2 each year: 1 to an undergraduate and 1 to a graduate student.

Deadline   April of each year.

[515]
OPERATION JUMP START III SCHOLARSHIPS

American Association of Advertising Agencies
Attn: AAAA Foundation
1065 Avenue of the Americas, 16th Floor
New York, NY 10018
(212) 262-2500   E-mail: ameadows@aaaa.org
Web: www.aaaa.org

Summary   To provide financial assistance to African American andother multicultural art directors and copywriters interested in working on an undergraduate or graduate degree in advertising.

Eligibility   This program is open to African Americans, Asian Americans, Hispanic Americans, and Native Americans who are U.S. citizens or permanent residents. Applicants must be incoming graduate students at 1 of 6 designated portfolio schools or full-time juniors at 1 of 2 designated colleges. They must be able to demonstrate extreme financial need, creative talent, and promise. Along with their application, they must submit 10 samples of creative work in their respective field of expertise.

Financial data   The stipend is $5,000 per year.

Duration   Most awards are for 2 years.

Additional information   Operation Jump Start began in 1997 and was followed by Operation Jump Start II in 2002. The current program began in 2006. The 6 designated portfolio schools are the AdCenter at Virginia Commonwealth University, the Creative Circus in Atlanta, the Portfolio Center in Atlanta, the Miami Ad School, the University of Texas at Austin, and Pratt Institute. The 2 designated colleges are the Minneapolis College of Art and Design and the Art Center College of Design at Pasadena, California.

Number awarded   20 each year.

Deadline   Deadline not specified.

[516]
ORA LEE SANDERS SCHOLARSHIP

PUSH Excel
Attn: General Offices
930 East 50th Street
Chicago, IL 60615
(773) 373-3366   E-mail: pushexcel@rainbowpush.org
Web: www.pushexcel.org/pages/scholarships

Summary   To provide financial assistance to African American and other college students who are willing to help promote the scholarship program of PUSH-Excel.

Eligibility   This program is open to entering freshmen, sophomores, juniors, and seniors at an accredited 4-year college or university. Applicants must be U.S. citizens and have a GPA of 2.5 or higher. Along with their application, they must submit a 500-word essay that identifies 5 prerequisites for success, explains their personal philosophy for the pursuit of excellence, and explains how they will use their college education to achieve this pursuit of excellence. They must also agree to cooperate with the scholarship committee of PUSH-Excel by promoting its program, participating in its public relations activities, and attending its Annual National Conference luncheon and Education Leadership Conference. Selection is based on the essay, academic preparation to attend college and succeed, ability to overcome obstacles to achieve academic and personal goals, and financial need.

Financial data   The stipend is $2,500 per year.

Duration   1 year; may be renewed up to 3 additional years if the recipient maintains a GPA of 2.5 or higher and fulfills the obligations to PUSH-Excel.

Additional information   PUSH-Excel was founded in 1975 by the Rev. Jesse Jackson.

Number awarded   Varies each year; recently, 50 were awarded.

Deadline   April of each year.

[517]
OREGON ALLIANCE OF INDEPENDENT COLLEGES AND UNIVERSITIES NAMED SCHOLARSHIP FOR UNDERREPRESENTED POPULATIONS

Oregon Alliance of Independent Colleges and Universities
Attn: Vice President
16101 S.W. 72nd Avenue, Suite 100
Portland, OR 97224
(503) 639-4541   Fax: (503) 639-4851
E-mail: brent@oaicu.org
Web: www.oaicu.org

Summary   To provide financial assistance to residents of Oregon who are African Americans or members of other underrepresented populations and interested in studying at an independent college in the state.

Eligibility   This program is open to Oregon residents who are members of underrepresented populations and are enrolled or planning to enroll full time at a college or university that is a member of the Oregon Alliance of Independent Colleges and Universities (OAICU). Applicants must be planning to major in a field related to the business focus of designated sponsors. Selection is based on academic record in high school, achievements in school or community activities, financial need, and a written statement, up to 500 words, on the meaning of good citizenship and how the fulfillment of their personal goals will help applicants live up to that definition.

Financial data   Stipends awarded by OAICU normally average approximately $2,500.

Duration   1 year.

Additional information   The OAICU member institutions are Concordia University, Corban University, George Fox University, Lewis and Clark College, Linfield College, Marylhurst University, Northwest Christian University, Pacific University, Reed College, University of Portland, Warner Pacific College, and Willamette University. Recent sponsors included the BNSF Railway Foundation, Costco Wholesale, KeyBank, NW Natural, UPS Foundation, and Wells Fargo Bank.

Number awarded Varies each year.

Deadline March of each year.

[518]
OSA LEADERSHIP TUITION SCHOLARSHIP

National Association of Black Social Workers
Attn: NABSW Scholarships
2305 Martin Luther King Avenue, S.E.
Washington, DC 20020
(202) 678-4570   Fax: (202) 678-4572
E-mail: office-manager@nabsw.org
Web: www.nabsw.org/?page=ScholarshipsRecipien

Summary To provide financial assistance to members of the National Association of Black Social Workers (NABSW) who have provided outstanding community service and are working on an undergraduate or graduate degree.

Eligibility This program is open to African American members of NABSW who are enrolled at least half time at an accredited U.S. institution. Applicants must be working on an associate, bachelor's, master's, or Ph.D. degree in social work, sociology, or other field of human services. They must have a GPA of 3.0 or higher and a record of volunteer service to the African American community. Along with their application, they must submit a letter of recommendation from a prestigious community leader that highlights their volunteer work and leadership efforts within the African American community. Financial need is considered in the selection process.

Financial data The stipend is $1,000. Funds are sent directly to the recipient's school.

Duration 1 year.

Number awarded 1 each year.

Deadline December of each year.

[519]
PA STUDENT SCHOLARSHIPS

American Academy of Physician Assistants
Attn: Physician Assistant Foundation
2318 Mill Road, Suite 1300
Alexandria, VA 22314-6868
(703) 836-2272   Fax: (703) 684-1924
E-mail: pafoundation@aapa.org
Web: www.pa-foundation.org

Summary To provide financial assistance to student members of the American Academy of Physician Assistants (AAPA) who are African Americans, otherunderrepresented minorities, or economically and/or educationally disadvantaged.

Eligibility This program is open to AAPA student members attending a physician assistant program accredited by the Commission on Accreditation of Allied Health Education Programs. Applicants must qualify as 1) an underrepresented minority (Black or African American, Alaska Native, American Indian, Hispanic or Latino, Native Hawaiian or other Pacific Islander, or Asian other than Chinese, Filipino, Japanese, Korean, Asian Indian, or Thai); 2) economically disadvantaged (with income below a specified level); or 3) educationally disadvantaged (from a high school with low SAT scores, from a school district in which less than half of graduates go on to college, has a diagnosed physical or mental impairment, English is not their primary language, the first member

of their family to attend college). They must have completed at least 1 semester of PA studies.

Financial data Stipends are $2,500, $2,000, or $1,000.

Duration 1 year; nonrenewable.

Additional information This program includes the AAPA Past Presidents Scholarship, the Bristol-Myers Squibb Endowed Scholarship, the National Commission on Certification of Physician Assistants Endowed Scholarships, the Procter & Gamble Endowed Scholarship, and the PA Foundation Scholarships.

Number awarded Varies each year; recently, 32 were awarded: 3 at $2,500, 27 at $2,000, and 2 at $1,000.

Deadline January of each year.

[520]
PAGE EDUCATION FOUNDATION GRANTS

Page Education Foundation
901 North Third Street, Suite 355
P.O. Box 581254
Minneapolis, MN 55458-1254
(612) 332-0406   Fax: (612) 332-0403
E-mail: info@page-ed.org
Web: www.page-ed.org

Summary To provide funding to African American and other high school seniors of color in Minnesota who plan to attend college in the state.

Eligibility This program is open to students of color who are graduating from high schools in Minnesota and planning to enroll full time at a postsecondary school in the state. Applicants must submit a 500-word essay that deals with why they believe education is important, their plans for the future, and the service-to-children project they would like to complete in the coming school year. Selection is based on the essay, 3 letters of recommendation, and financial need.

Financial data Stipends range from $1,000 to $2,500 per year.

Duration 1 year; may be renewed up to 3 additional years.

Additional information This program was founded in 1988 by Alan Page, a former football player for the Minnesota Vikings. While attending college, the Page Scholars fulfill a 50-hour service-to-children contract that brings them into contact with K-8 students of color.

Number awarded Varies each year; recently, 503 Page Scholars (210 new recipients and 293 renewals) were enrolled, of whom 260 were African American, 141 Asian American, 70 Chicano/Latino, 13 American Indian, and 19 biracial or multiracial.

Deadline April of each year.

[521]
PCMA EDUCATION FOUNDATION DIVERSITY SCHOLARSHIP

Professional Convention Management Association
Attn: PCMA Education Foundation
35 East Wacker Drive, Suite 500
Chicago, IL 60601
(312) 423-7262   Toll Free: (877) 827-7262
Fax: (312) 423-7222   E-mail: foundation@pcma.org
Web: www.pcma.org

Summary To provide financial assistance to student members of the Professional Convention Management Association (PCMA) who are African Americans or members of other underrepresented groups and majoring in a field related to the meetings or hospitality industry.

Eligibility This program is open to PCMA members who are currently enrolled in at least 6 credit hours with a major directly related to the meetings or hospitality industry. Applicants must be students traditionally underrepresented in the industry, including (but not limited to) those identifying by a certain race, sex, color, religion, creed, sexual orientation, gender identity or expression, or disability, as well as those with a history of overcoming adversity. They must have a GPA of 2.75 or higher. Along with their application, they must submit a 750-word essay that details how they became interested in the meetings and events industry and a short paragraph describing the potential impact receiving this scholarship would have for them. Selection is based on that essay, academic record, meetings industry experience, and a letter of recommendation.

Financial data The stipend is $2,500.

Duration 1 year.

Number awarded 1 each year.

Deadline March of each year.

[522]
PDEF MICKEY WILLIAMS MINORITY SCHOLARSHIPS

Society of Nuclear Medicine and Molecular Imaging
Attn: Grants and Awards
1850 Samuel Morse Drive
Reston, VA 20190-5316
(703) 708-9000, ext. 1255   Fax: (703) 708-9015
E-mail: grantinfo@snm.org
Web: www.snmmi.org

Summary To provide financial support to African American and other minority students working on an associate or bachelor's degree in nuclear medicine technology.

Eligibility This program is open to members of the Technologist Section of the Society of Nuclear Medicine and Molecular Imaging (SNMMI-TS) who are accepted or enrolled in a baccalaureate or associate degree program in nuclear medicine technology. Applicants must be members of a minority group: African American, Native American (including American Indian, Eskimo, Hawaiian, and Samoan), Hispanic American, Asian American, or Pacific Islander. They must have a cumulative GPA of 2.5 or higher and be able to demonstrate financial need. Along with their application, they must submit an essay on their reasons for entering the nuclear medicine technology field, their career goals, and their financial need. U.S. citizenship or permanent resident status is required.

Financial data The stipend is $2,500.

Duration 1 year; may be renewed for 1 additional year.

Additional information This program is supported by corporate sponsors of the Professional Development and Education Fund (PDEF) of the SNMMI-TS.

Number awarded Varies each year; recently, 2 were awarded.

Deadline December of each year.

[523]
PEGGY PETERMAN SCHOLARSHIP

Tampa Bay Times
Attn: Director of Corporate Giving
490 First Avenue South
St. Petersburg, FL 33701
(727) 893-8780   Toll Free: (800) 333-7505, ext. 8780
Fax: (727) 892-2257   E-mail: waclawek@tampabay.com
Web: www.tampabay.com

Summary To provide financial assistance to African American and other minority undergraduate and graduate students who are interested in preparing for a career in the newspaper industry and who accept an internship at the *Tampa Bay Times*.

Eligibility This program is open to minority college sophomores, juniors, seniors, and graduate students from any state who are interested in preparing for a career in the newspaper industry. Applicants must be interested in an internship at the *Tampa Bay Times* and must apply for that at the same time as they apply for this scholarship. They should have experience working on a college publication and at least 1 professional internship.

Financial data The stipend is $5,000.

Duration Internships are for 12 weeks during the summer. Scholarships are for 1 year.

Number awarded 1 each year.

Deadline October of each year.

[524]
PENNSYLVANIA ACADEMY OF NUTRITION AND DIETETICS FOUNDATION DIVERSITY SCHOLARSHIP

Pennsylvania Academy of Nutrition and Dietetics
Attn: Foundation
96 Northwoods Boulevard, Suite B2
Columbus, OH 43235
(614) 436-6136   Fax: (614) 436-6181
E-mail: padafoundation@eatrightpa.org
Web: www.eatrightpa.org/scholarshipapp.cfm

Summary To provide financial assistance to members of the Pennsylvania Academy of Nutrition and Dietetics who are African Americans or members of other minority groups and working on an associate or bachelor's degree in dietetics.

Eligibility This program is open to academy members who are Black, Hispanic, Asian or Pacific Islander, or Native American (Alaskan Native, American Indian, or Hawaiian Native). Applicants must be 1) enrolled in the first year of study in an accredited dietetic technology program; or 2) enrolled in the third year of study in an accredited undergraduate or coordinated program in dietetics. They must have a GPA of 2.5 or higher. Along with their application, they must submit a letter indicating their intent and the reason they are applying for the scholarship, including a description of their personal financial situation. Selection is based on academic achievement (20%), commitment to the dietetic profession (30%), leadership ability (30%), and financial need (20%).

Financial data The stipend is $1,000.

Duration 1 year.

Additional information The Pennsylvania Academy of Nutrition and Dietetics is the Pennsylvania affiliate of the Academy of Nutrition and Dietetics.

Number awarded   1 or more each year.
Deadline   April of each year.

[525]
PFATS-NFL CHARITIES MINORITY SCHOLARSHIPS

Professional Football Athletic Trainers Society
c/o Britt Brown, ATC, Associate Athletic Trainer
Dallas Cowboys
One Cowboys Parkway
Irving, TX 75063
(972) 497-4992   E-mail: bbrown@dallascowboys.net
Web: www.pfats.com/about/scholarships

Summary   To provide financial assistance to African American and other ethnic minority undergraduate and graduate students working on a degree in athletic training.

Eligibility   This program is open to ethnic minority students who are working on an undergraduate or graduate degree in athletic training. Applicants must have a GPA of 2.5 or higher. Along with their application, they must submit a cover letter, a curriculum vitae, and a letter of recommendation from their supervising athletic trainer. Female athletic training students are encouraged to apply.

Financial data   A stipend is awarded (amount not specified).

Duration   1 year.

Additional information   Recipients also have an opportunity to work at summer training camp of a National Football League (NFL) team. Support for this program, which began in 1993, is provided by NFL Charities.

Number awarded   1 or more each year.

Deadline   March of each year.

[526]
PGA OF AMERICA DIVERSITY SCHOLARSHIP PROGRAM

Professional Golfers' Association of America
Attn: PGA Foundation
100 Avenue of the Champions
Palm Beach Gardens, FL 33418
Toll Free: (888) 532-6662   E-mail: sjubb@pgahq.com
Web: www.pgafoundation.com

Summary   To provide financial assistance to African American and other minorities interested in attending a designated college or university to prepare for a career as a golf professional.

Eligibility   This program is open to women and minorities interested in becoming a licensed PGA Professional. Applicants must be interested in attending 1 of 20 colleges and universities that offer the Professional Golf Management (PGM) curriculum sanctioned by the PGA.

Financial data   The stipend is $3,000 per year.

Duration   1 year; may be renewed.

Additional information   This program began in 1993. Programs are offered at the following universities: Arizona State University (Tempe), Campbell University (Buies Creek, North Carolina), Clemson University (Clemson, South Carolina), Coastal Carolina University (Conway, South Carolina), Eastern Kentucky University (Richmond), Ferris State University (Big Rapids, Michigan), Florida State University (Tallahassee), Florida Gulf Coast University (Fort Myers), Methodist University (Fayetteville, North Carolina), Mississippi State University (Mississippi State), New Mexico State University (Las Cruces), North Carolina State University (Raleigh), Pennsylvania State University (University Park), Sam Houston State University (Huntsville), University of Central Oklahoma (Edmond), University of Colorado at Colorado Springs, University of Idaho (Moscow), University of Maryland Eastern Shore (Princess Anne), University of Nebraska at Lincoln, and University of Nevada at Las Vegas.

Number awarded   Varies each year; recently, 20 were awarded.

Deadline   Deadline not specified.

[527]
PHILADELPHIA ASSOCIATION OF BLACK JOURNALISTS COLLEGE SCHOLARSHIPS

Philadelphia Association of Black Journalists
Attn: Scholarship Chair
P.O. Box 8232
Philadelphia, PA 19101
(215) 977-5353   E-mail: char.pabj@aol.com
Web: www.phillyabj.org

Summary   To provide financial assistance to African American residents of any state who are attending college in the Philadelphia region to prepare for a career in journalism.

Eligibility   This program is open to African American residents of any state currently enrolled full or part time at an accredited 4-year college or university in the Philadelphia region (the Pennsylvania counties of Bucks, Chester, Delaware, Montgomery, and Philadelphia; southern New Jersey; and Delaware). Applicants must be working on a degree in journalism or communications (broadcast, print, new media). They must have a GPA of 3.0 or higher. Along with their application, they must submit an essay of 1,200 words on a topic that changes annually but relates to careers in journalism and a 2-minute demo reel that represents their current work.

Financial data   The stipend is $1,000 for full-time students or $500 for part-time students.

Duration   1 year.

Number awarded   3 each year: 2 for full-time students and 1 for a part-time student.

Deadline   April of each year.

[528]
PHILADELPHIA ASSOCIATION OF BLACK JOURNALISTS FUTURE JOURNALIST SCHOLARSHIP

Philadelphia Association of Black Journalists
Attn: Scholarship Chair
P.O. Box 8232
Philadelphia, PA 19101
(215) 977-5353   E-mail: char.pabj@aol.com
Web: www.phillyabj.org

Summary   To provide financial assistance to African American high school seniors in the Philadelphia region who are planning to attend college in the region and prepare for a career in journalism.

Eligibility   This program is open to African American high school seniors in the Philadelphia region (the Pennsylvania counties of Bucks, Chester, Delaware, Montgomery, and Philadelphia; southern New Jersey; and Delaware) who are planning to attend an accredited 4-year college or university in the region. Applicants must be planning to work on a college degree in journalism or multimedia arts. They must have a GPA of 3.0 or higher. Along with their application, they must submit 1) an essay of 1,200 words on their journalism aspirations, who or what has been their biggest inspiration, and the piece of equipment they would select to help them practice journalism; and 2) a 2-minute demo reel that represents their current work.

Financial data   The stipend is $1,000; a portion of the funds must be used to purchase equipment of their choice to assist them in fulfilling their journalism ambitions.

Duration   1 year.

Number awarded   1 each year.

Deadline   April of each year.

[529]
PHILADELPHIA CHAPTER AABE SCHOLARSHIPS

American Association of Blacks in Energy-Philadelphia
   Chapter
Attn: Scholarship Committee
P.O. Box 34282
Philadelphia, PA 19104
(267) 882-7385 E-mail: Sherri.Pennington@pgworks.com
Web: www.aabe.org/index.php?component=pages&id=706

Summary   To provide financial assistance to African Americans and members of other underrepresented minority groups who are high school seniors in Delaware and Pennsylvania and planning to major in an energy-related field at a college in any state.

Eligibility   This program is open to seniors graduating from high schools in Delaware or Pennsylvania and planning to work on a bachelor's degree at a college or university in any state. Applicants must be African Americans, Hispanics, or Native Americans who have a GPA of 3.0 or higher and have taken the ACT and/or SAT test. Their intended major must be a field of business, engineering, physical sciences, mathematics, or technology related to energy. Along with their application, they must submit a 350-word essay that includes 1) when they discovered their interest in the field of energy and what sparked their interest; and 2) either what excites them about the field of energy or how they expect their education to prepare them for the field of energy. Financial need is not considered in the selection process.

Financial data   The stipend is $2,000.

Duration   1 year; nonrenewable.

Additional information   Winners are eligible to compete for regional and national scholarships.

Number awarded   6 each year.

Deadline   March of each year.

[530]
PHILADELPHIA CHAPTER NBMBAA UNDERGRADUATE SCHOLARSHIP

National Black MBA Association-Philadelphia Chapter
Attn: Scholarship Ad Hoc Committee
P.O. Box 1384
Philadelphia, PA 19105
(215) 472-BMBA
E-mail: studentaffairs@nbmbaa-philly.org
Web: www.nbmbaa-philly.org/scholarships.html

Summary   To provide financial assistance to African American residents of the greater Philadelphia metropolitan area working on an undergraduate degree in business in any state.

Eligibility   This program is open to African American residents of the greater Philadelphia metropolitan area (Delaware, southern New Jersey, and the Pennsylvania counties of Berks, Bucks, Chester, Delaware, Lehigh, Montgomery, and Philadelphia). Applicants must be entering or currently enrolled full time at an AACSB-accredited college or university in any state and working on an undergraduate degree in a business-related or management field. Along with their application, they must submit a 2-page essay on a topic that changes annually but relates to African Americans and business. Selection is based on that essay, academic achievement, community service and involvement, verbal communication skills, a resume, and reference letters.

Financial data   The stipend ranges from $500 to $1,500. Funds are disbursed directly to the college or university.

Duration   1 year; nonrenewable.

Number awarded   Varies each year.

Deadline   September of each year.

[531]
PHILLIP D. REED UNDERGRADUATE ENDOWMENT FELLOWSHIP

National Action Council for Minorities in Engineering
Attn: Director, Scholarships and University Relations
440 Hamilton Avenue, Suite 302
White Plains, NY 10601-1813
(914) 539-4316   Fax: (914) 539-4032
E-mail: scholars@nacme.org
Web: www.nacme.org/scholarships

Summary   To provide financial assistance to African American and other underrepresented minority college sophomores majoring in engineering or related fields.

Eligibility   This program is open to African American, Latino, and American Indian college sophomores who have a GPA of 3.0 or higher and have demonstrated academic excellence, leadership skills, and a commitment to science and engineering as a career. Applicants must be enrolled full time at an ABET-accredited engineering program. Fields of study include all areas of engineering as well as computer science, materials science, mathematics, operations research, or physics.

Financial data   The stipend is $5,000 per year. Funds are sent directly to the recipient's university.

Duration   Up to 3 years.

Number awarded   1 each year.

Deadline   April of each year.

[532]
PHYLLIS G. MEEKINS SCHOLARSHIP

Ladies Professional Golf Association
Attn: LPGA Foundation
100 International Golf Drive
Daytona Beach, FL 32124-1082
(386) 274-6200   Fax: (386) 274-1099
E-mail: foundation.scholarships@lpga.com
Web: www.lpga.com

Summary To provide financial assistance to African American and other minority female graduating high school seniors who played golf in high school and plan to continue to play in college.

Eligibility This program is open to female high school seniors who are members of a recognized minority group. Applicants must have a GPA of 3.0 or higher and a background in golf. They must be planning to enroll full time at a college or university in the United States and play competitive golf. Along with their application, they must submit a letter that describes how golf has been an integral part of their lives and includes their personal, academic, and professional goals; their chosen discipline of study; and how this scholarship will be of assistance. Financial need is considered in the selection process. U.S. citizenship or legal resident status is required.

Financial data The stipend is $1,250.

Duration 1 year.

Additional information This program began in 2006.

Number awarded 1 each year.

Deadline May of each year.

[533]
P.O. PISTILLI SCHOLARSHIPS

Design Automation Conference
c/o Andrew B. Kahng, Scholarship Director
University of California at San Diego-Jacobs School of
  Engineering
Jacobs Hall, EBU3B, Rpp, 2134
9500 Gilman Drive
La Jolla, CA 92093-0404
(858) 822-4884   Fax: (858) 534-7029
E-mail: abk@cs.ucsd.edu
Web: www.dac.com

Summary To provide financial assistance to African American and other underrepresented high school seniors who are interested in preparing for a career in computer science or electrical engineering.

Eligibility This program is open to graduating high school seniors who are members of underrepresented groups: women, African Americans, Hispanics, Native Americans, and students with disabilities. Applicants must be interested in preparing for a career in electrical engineering, computer engineering, or computer science. They must have at least a 3.0 GPA, have demonstrated high achievements in math and science courses, have demonstrated involvement in activities associated with the underrepresented group they represent, and be able to demonstrate significant financial need. U.S. citizenship is not required, but applicants must be U.S. residents when they apply and must plan to attend an accredited U.S. college or university. Along with their application, they must submit 3 letters of recommendation, official transcripts, ACT/SAT and/or PSAT scores, a personal statement outlining future goals and why they think they should receive this scholarship, and documentation of financial need.

Financial data Stipends are $4,000 per year. Awards are paid each year in 2 equal installments.

Duration 1 year; may be renewed up to 4 additional years.

Additional information This program is funded by the Design Automation Conference of the Association for Computing Machinery's Special Interest Group on Design Automation.

Number awarded 2 to 7 each year.

Deadline January of each year.

[534]
PRAXAIR ENGINEERS OF TOMORROW
SCHOLARSHIP

Executive Leadership Council
Attn: Executive Leadership Foundation
1001 North Fairfax Street, Suite 300
Alexandria, VA 22314
(703) 706-5200   Fax: (703) 535-6830
E-mail: elcinfo@elcinfo.com
Web: www.elcinfo.com

Summary To provide financial assistance to African American and other minority students working on an undergraduate degree in chemical or mechanical engineering.

Eligibility This program is open to minority students enrolled full time in a chemical or mechanical engineering program at a 4-year college or university. Applicants must be U.S. citizens and have a GPA of 3.0 or higher. Along with their application, they must submit an essay between 800 and 1,000 words on a topic that changes each year; recently, applicants were invited to write on the challenges they have overcome in achieving their education, who or what influenced them to prepare for a career in engineering, their short- and long-term goals, and the types of leadership roles they have experienced. Selection is based on that essay and financial need.

Financial data The stipend is $12,000. All recipients receive a trip to New York City and Washington D.C. to participate in the foundation's Student Honors Symposium.

Duration 1 year; nonrenewable.

Additional information The Executive Leadership Foundation was founded in 1989 as an affiliate of the Executive Leadership Council, the association of African American senior executives of Fortune 500 companies. This program is sponsored by Praxair, Inc.

Number awarded 3 each year.

Deadline March of each year.

[535]
PRINCETON SUMMER UNDERGRADUATE
RESEARCH EXPERIENCE

Princeton University
Attn: Graduate School
Office of Academic Affairs and Diversity
Clio Hall
Princeton, NJ 08544-0255
(609) 258-2066   E-mail: diverse@princeton.edu
Web: gradschool.princeton.edu

Summary To provide an opportunity for African American or other minority or disadvantaged students to assist Princeton faculty in any area during the summer.

Eligibility This program is open to full-time sophomores and juniors at all colleges and universities in the United States who are majoring in any academic discipline and have a GPA of 3.5 or higher in their major. Current college freshmen and graduating seniors are not eligible. Applicants must be interested in working during the summer with a Princeton faculty member. They should have a goal of continuing on for a Ph.D. and preparing for a career in college or university teaching and research. Students in the sciences and engineering normally work in a laboratory group on an aspect of the faculty member's current research. Students in the humanities and social sciences might assist a faculty member engaged in a particular research, editing, bibliographical, or course-preparation project; alternatively, they may work on a research paper under faculty supervision. Members of racial and ethnic minority groups underrepresented in doctoral research programs, students from socioeconomically disadvantaged backgrounds, and students at small liberal arts colleges are especially encouraged to apply.

Financial data Participants receive a stipend of $3,750, housing in a campus dormitory, a $150 meal card, and up to $500 in reimbursement of travel costs.

Duration 8 weeks during the summer.

Number awarded Up to 20 each year.

Deadline January of each year.

[536]
PRINGLE AND PRINGLE HIGHER EDUCATION SCHOLARSHIP

National Naval Officers Association-Washington, D.C.
  Chapter
c/o LCDR Stephen Williams
P.O. Box 30784
Alexandria, VA 22310
(703) 644-2605   Fax: (703) 644-8503
E-mail: Stephen.Williams@navy.mil
Web: www.dcnnoa.org/dcnnoa-scholarship

Summary To provide financial assistance to African American high school seniors from the Washington, D.C. area who are interested in attending college in any state.

Eligibility This program is open to African American seniors graduating from high schools in the Washington, D.C. metropolitan area who plan to enroll full time at an accredited 2- or 4-year college or university in any state. Applicants must have a GPA of 2.5 or higher and be U.S. citizens or permanent residents. Selection is based on academic achievement, community involvement, and financial need.

Financial data The stipend is $1,000.

Duration 1 year; nonrenewable.

Additional information Recipients are not required to join or affiliate with the military in any way. In addition to a number of scholarships with additional requirements, this program includes the following named general scholarships: the David and Sheila Garnett Leadership Scholarship, the Pringle & Pringle Higher Education Scholarship, the Rear Admiral Mack and Nancy Gaston Leadership Scholarship, the Rear Admiral Michelle Howard Excellence in Leadership Scholarship, and the William A. Borders Jr. Justice Scholarship.

Number awarded 1 each year.

Deadline February of each year.

[537]
PROFESSIONAL STAFFING GROUP SCHOLARSHIP

Northeast Human Resources Association
Attn: Director of Professional Development
490 Virginia Road, Suite 32
Concord, MA 01742-2747
(781) 239-8718   Fax: (781) 237-8745
E-mail: nreiser@nehra.com
Web: www.nehra.com/?page=DIScholarshipApp

Summary To provide financial assistance for college to high school seniors from the New England states who are African Americans or have promoted diversity in other ways.

Eligibility This program is open to seniors who are graduating from high schools in New England and planning to attend a college or university. Applicants should have exemplified living an inclusive life and promoting diversity through education. They must have a GPA of 3.0 or higher and be able to demonstrate financial need. Along with their application, they must submit a 750-word personal statement explaining what diversity means to them, how they promote diversity in their community or school, and how they propose to promote diversity in the future.

Financial data The stipend is $5,000.

Duration 1 year.

Additional information The sponsor is an affiliate of the Society for Human Resource Management (SHRM). Its Diversity and Inclusion Committee focuses on veterans, the GLBT community, people with disabilities, gender equity, and race/ethnicity. The Professional Staffing Group established this program in 2004.

Number awarded 1 each year.

Deadline February of each year.

[538]
PROMISING SCHOLARS FUND EDWARD A. BOUCHET SCHOLARSHIPS

Community Foundation for Greater New Haven
Attn: Scholarships
70 Audubon Street
New Haven, CT 06510-9755
(203) 777-7076   Fax: (203) 777-6584
E-mail: dcanning@cfgnh.org
Web: www.sms.scholarshipamerica.org

Summary To provide financial assistance to African American high school seniors and graduates in Connecticut who plan to attend college in any state.

Eligibility This program is open to African American high school seniors and recent graduates from 20 designated high schools in Connecticut who are planning to enter an accredited 2- or 4-year college or university in any state as a full-time undergraduate. Applicants must be U.S. citizens and have a GPA of 2.5 or higher. Selection is based on academic record, demonstrated leadership, and participation in school and community activities. Some consideration is given to honors, work experience, a statement of goals and aspirations, and unusual personal or family circumstances. First preference is given to males and secondary to residents of New Haven County.

Financial data Stipends depend on financial need of the recipient, ranging up to $6,000 per year.

Duration 1 year; recipients may reapply.

Additional information This program, established in 2007, is funded by the Beta Tau Boulé (the New Haven chapter) of Sigma Pi Phi and administered by the Scholarship Management Services division of Scholarship America.

Number awarded Up to 20 each year.

Deadline March of each year.

[539]
PROVIDENCE ALUMNAE CHAPTER SCHOLASTIC ACHIEVEMENT AWARD

Delta Sigma Theta Sorority, Inc.-Providence Alumnae
  Chapter
Attn: Scholarship Committee
P.O. Box 40175
Providence, RI 02940-0175
E-mail: PACScholarship@hotmail.com
Web: www.dstprovidencealumnae.org/scholarship.html

Summary To provide financial assistance to female African American residents of Rhode Island who are attending college in any state.

Eligibility This program is open to African American women who are residents of Rhode Island. Applicants must be attending a 4-year college or university in any state and have a GPA of 3.0 or higher. Along with their application, they must submit a current official transcript that includes ACT and/or SAT scores; documentation of financial need; a description of their career goals, community service activities, educational accomplishments, and personal interests and talents; and a 650-word essay on a topic that changes annually but relates to their personal development.

Financial data The stipend is $1,000.

Duration 1 year.

Number awarded 1 or more each year.

Deadline February of each year.

[540]
PROVIDENCE ALUMNAE IN MEMORIUM AWARD

Delta Sigma Theta Sorority, Inc.-Providence Alumnae
  Chapter
Attn: Scholarship Committee
P.O. Box 40175
Providence, RI 02940-0175
E-mail: PACScholarship@hotmail.com
Web: www.dstprovidencealumnae.org/scholarship.html

Summary To provide financial assistance to African American female high school seniors from Rhode Island who are planning to attend college in any state.

Eligibility This program is open to African American women who are seniors graduating from high schools in Rhode Island. Applicants must be planning to enroll at a college in any state. Along with their application, they must submit a current official transcript that includes ACT and/or SAT scores; documentation of financial need; a description of their career goals, community service activities, educational accomplishments, and personal interests and talents; and a 650-word essay on a topic that changes annually but relates to their personal development.

Financial data The stipend is $1,250.

Duration 1 year.

Number awarded 1 or more each year.

Deadline February of each year.

[541]
PRSA DIVERSITY MULTICULTURAL SCHOLARSHIPS

Public Relations Student Society of America
Attn: Vice President of Member Services
33 Maiden Lane, 11th Floor
New York, NY 10038-5150
(212) 460-1474   Fax: (212) 995-0757
E-mail: prssa@prsa.org
Web: www.prssa.prsa.org

Summary To provide financial assistance to African American and other minority college students who are interested in preparing for a career in public relations.

Eligibility This program is open to minority (African American/Black, Hispanic/Latino, Asian, Native American, Alaskan Native, or Pacific Islander) students who are at least juniors at an accredited 4-year college or university. Applicants must be enrolled full time, be able to demonstrate financial need, and have a GPA of 3.0 or higher. Membership in the Public Relations Student Society of America is preferred but not required. A major or minor in public relations is preferred; students who attend a school that does not offer a public relations degree or program must be enrolled in a communications degree program (e.g., journalism, mass communications).

Financial data The stipend is $1,500.

Duration 1 year.

Additional information This program began in 1989.

Number awarded 2 each year.

Deadline May of each year.

[542]
PUGET SOUND CHAPTER SHARON D. BANKS MEMORIAL UNDERGRADUATE SCHOLARSHIP

Women's Transportation Seminar-Puget Sound Chapter
c/o Laurie Thomsen, Scholarship Co-Chair
Osborn Consulting, Inc.
1800 112th Avenue N.E.
Bellevue, WA 98004
(425) 451-4009   Fax: (888) 391-8517
E-mail: laurie@osbornconsulting.com
Web: www.wtsinternational.org

Summary To provide financial assistance to women undergraduate students from Washington, especially African Americans and other minorities, who are working on a degree related to transportation.

Eligibility This program is open to women who are residents of Washington, studying at a college in the state, or working as an intern in the state. Applicants must be currently enrolled in an undergraduate degree program in a transportation-related field, such as engineering, planning, finance, or logistics. They must have a GPA of 3.0 or higher and plans to prepare for a career in a transportation-related field. Minority women are especially encouraged to apply. Along with their application, they must submit a 500-word statement about their career goals after graduation and why they think they should receive this scholarship award. Selection is based on that statement, academic record, and transportation-related activities or job skills. Financial need is not considered.

Financial data   The stipend is $4,000.

Duration   1 year.

Additional information   The winner is also nominated for scholarships offered by the national organization of the Women's Transportation Seminar.

Number awarded   1 each year.

Deadline   November of each year.

[543]
RACE RELATIONS MULTIRACIAL STUDENT SCHOLARSHIP

Christian Reformed Church
Attn: Office of Race Relations
1700 28th Street, S.E.
Grand Rapids, MI 49508
(616) 224-5883   Toll Free: (877) 864-3977
Fax: (616) 224-0834   E-mail: elugo@crcna.org
Web: www.crcna.org/race/scholarships

Summary   To provide financial assistance to undergraduate and graduate African Americans and other minority students interested in attending colleges related to the Christian Reformed Church in North America (CRCNA).

Eligibility   This program is open to students of color in the United States and Canada. Normally, applicants are expected to be members of CRCNA congregations who plan to pursue their educational goals at Calvin Theological Seminary or any of the colleges affiliated with the CRCNA. They must be interested in training for the ministry of racial reconciliation in church and/or in society. Along with their application, they must submit paragraphs about their personal history and family, Christian faith, and Christian leadership goals. Students who have no prior history with the CRCNA must attend a CRCNA-related college or seminary for a full academic year before they are eligible to apply for this program. Students entering their sophomore year must have earned a GPA of 2.0 or higher as freshmen; students entering their junior year must have earned a GPA of 2.3 or higher as sophomores; students entering their senior year must have earned a GPA of 2.6 or higher as juniors.

Financial data   First-year students receive $500 per semester. Other levels of students may receive up to $2,000 per academic year.

Duration   1 year.

Additional information   This program was first established in 1971 and revised in 1991. Recipients are expected to train to engage actively in the ministry of racial reconciliation in church and in society. They must be able to work in the United States or Canada upon graduating and must consider working for 1 of the agencies of the CRCNA.

Number awarded   Varies each year; recently, 31 students received a total of $21,000 in support.

Deadline   March of each year.

[544]
RADM BENJAMIN HACKER MEMORIAL SCHOLARSHIP

National Naval Officers Association-Washington, D.C.
   Chapter
c/o LCDR Stephen Williams
P.O. Box 30784
Alexandria, VA 22310
(703) 644-2605   Fax: (703) 644-8503
E-mail: Stephen.Williams@navy.mil
Web: www.dcnnoa.org/dcnnoa-scholarship

Summary   To provide financial assistance to African American and other minority high school seniors from the Washington, D.C. area who are interested in attending an Historically Black College or University (HBCU) in any state and enrolling in the Navy Reserve Officers Training Corps (NROTC) program.

Eligibility   This program is open to minority seniors graduating from high schools in the Washington, D.C. metropolitan area who plan to enroll full time at an HBCU in any state that has an NROTC program; they may enroll at another college or university that shares the NROTC unit located at an HBCU. Applicants must have a GPA of 2.5 or higher and be U.S. citizens or permanent residents. Selection is based on academic achievement, community involvement, and financial need.

Financial data   The stipend is $1,000.

Duration   1 year; nonrenewable.

Additional information   This program is sponsored by the Washington D.C. Chapter of the National Naval Officers Association (DCNNOA), an organization of African American naval officers, but all minorities are eligible and recipients are not required to join or affiliate with the military in any way. If the recipient fails to enroll in the NROTC unit, all scholarship funds must be returned.

Number awarded   1 each year.

Deadline   February of each year.

[545]
RAYMOND R. DAVIS SCHOLARSHIP

African Methodist Episcopal Church
Third Episcopal District Lay Organization
c/o Lenora Brogdon-Wyatt, Second Vice President
1113 West Second Street
Xenia, OH 45385
(937) 554-7585   E-mail: lenora.brogdon@yahoo.com
Web: www.ame3.org

Summary   To provide financial assistance to members of African Methodist Episcopal (AME) churches in its Third Episcopal District who are interested in attending college in any state.

Eligibility   This program is open to members of Third Episcopal District AME churches (in Ohio, western Pennsylvania, and West Virginia). Applicants must be high school seniors or students already enrolled in a bachelor's degree program in any field at an accredited college or university in any state. Along with their application, they must submit an essay of 800 to 1,000 words on a theme that changes annually but relates to their personal development. Selection is based on that essay, academic achievement, quality and level of church participation, leadership, extracurricular activities, honors, and letters of recommendation.

Financial data Stipends range from $500 to $1,000.

Duration 1 year.

Number awarded 1 or more each year.

Deadline February of each year.

[546]
RDW GROUP, INC. MINORITY SCHOLARSHIP FOR COMMUNICATIONS

Rhode Island Foundation
Attn: Donor Services Administrator
One Union Station
Providence, RI 02903
(401) 427-4011   Fax: (401) 331-8085
E-mail: rbogert@rifoundation.org
Web: www.rifoundation.org

Summary To provide financial assistance to African American and other undergraduate and graduate students of color in Rhode Island who are interested in preparing for a career in communications at a school in any state.

Eligibility This program is open to undergraduate and graduate students at colleges and universities in any state who are Rhode Island residents of color. Applicants must intend to work on a degree in communications (including computer graphics, art, cinematography, or other fields that would prepare them for a career in advertising). They must be able to demonstrate financial need and a commitment to a career in communications. Along with their application, they must submit an essay (up to 300 words) on the impact they would like to have on the communications field.

Financial data The stipend is approximately $2,000 per year.

Duration 1 year; recipients may reapply.

Additional information This program is sponsored by the RDW Group, Inc.

Number awarded 1 each year.

Deadline April of each year.

[547]
REGION 3 ACADEMIC EXCELLENCE SCHOLARSHIP

National Society of Black Engineers-Region 3
c/o Trejon Spratling, Academic Excellence Chair
Tennessee Technological University
Department of Mechanical Engineering
1 William L. Jones Drive
P.O. Box 5014
Cookeville, TN 38505
(931) 372-3254   E-mail: r3aex@nsbe.org
Web: nsbe.org

Summary To recognize and reward, with scholarships for additional study, undergraduate members of the National Society of Black Engineers (NSBE) in designated states who have demonstrated academic excellence.

Eligibility This award is available to members of the society who are majoring in a field of science, technology, engineering, or mathematics (STEM) at a college or university within NSBE Region 3 (Alabama, Florida, Georgia, Kentucky, Mississippi, and Tennessee). Applicants must have a GPA of 3.0 or higher. Along with their application, they must submit

an essay up to 500 words in length on how NSBE resources have led to their outstanding academic performance. Selection is based on academic performance and NSBE involvement.

Financial data The award is a $1,200 scholarship.

Duration The awards are presented annually.

Number awarded 1 each year.

Deadline March of each year.

[548]
REJESTA V. PERRY SCHOLARSHIP

Sigma Gamma Rho Sorority, Inc.
Attn: National Education Fund
1000 Southhill Drive, Suite 200
Cary, NC 27513
(919) 678-9720   Toll Free: (888) SGR-1922
Fax: (919) 678-9721
E-mail: customerservice@sgrho1922.org
Web: www.sgrho1922.org/nef

Summary To provide financial assistance to African Americans and other undergraduate students working on a degree in education.

Eligibility This program is open to undergraduates working on a degree in education. The sponsor is a traditionally African American sorority, but support is available to males and females of all races. Applicants must have a GPA of 2.0 or higher and be able to demonstrate financial need.

Financial data A stipend is awarded (amount not specified).

Duration 1 year.

Additional information A processing fee of $20 is required.

Number awarded 1 each year.

Deadline April of each year.

[549]
RENAE WASHINGTON-LORINE DUBOSE MEMORIAL SCHOLARSHIPS

Oklahoma CareerTech Foundation
Attn: Oklahoma Association of Minorities in Career and
   Technology Education
c/o Patti Pouncil, Scholarship Committee Chair
3 CT Circle
Drumright, OK 74030
918) 352-2551, ext. 285
Web: www.okcareertech.org

Summary To provide financial assistance to African American and other minority students enrolled at Oklahoma Career and Technology Education (CTE) centers.

Eligibility This program is open to residents of Oklahoma who are members of an ethnic minority group (American Indian/Alaskan, Asian, African American, Hispanic, Native Hawaiian/Pacific Islander). Applicants must be enrolled full time at a CTE center in the state. Along with their application, they must submit a 100-word essay on why they have applied for this scholarship. Financial need is considered in the selection process.

Financial data The stipend is $1,000.

Duration 1 year.

Number awarded 2 each year.
Deadline May of each year.

[550]
RESEARCH AND ENGINEERING APPRENTICESHIP PROGRAM

Academy of Applied Science
Attn: REAP
24 Warren Street
Concord, NH 03301
(603) 228-4530   Fax: (603) 228-4730
E-mail: phampton@aas-world.org
Web: www.usaeop.com/programs/apprenticeships/reap

Summary To provide an opportunity for African American high school students and others from groups historically underrepresented in science, technology, engineering, or mathematics (STEM) to engage in a summer research apprenticeship.

Eligibility This program is open to high school students who meet at least 2 of the following requirements: 1) qualifies for free or reduced lunch; 2) is a member of a group historically underrepresented in STEM, including Blacks/African Americans, Hispanics, Native Americans, Alaskan Natives, Native Hawaiians, or other Pacific Islanders; 3) is a woman in physical science, computer science, mathematics, or engineering; 4) receives special education services; 5) has a disability; 6) speaks English as a second language; or 7) has parents who did not attend college. Applicants must be interested in working as an apprentice on a research project in the laboratory of a mentor scientist at a college or university near their home. Selection is based on demonstrated interests in STEM research and demonstrated potential for a successful career in STEM. They must be at least 16 years of age.

Financial data The stipend is $1,300.

Duration 5 to 8 weeks during the summer.

Additional information The program provides intensive summer training for high school students in the laboratories of scientists. The program, established in 1980, is funded by a grant from the U.S. Army Educational Outreach Program. Students must live at home while they participate in the program and must live in the area of an approved college or university. The program does not exist in every state.

Number awarded Varies; recently, approximately 120 students were funded at more than 50 universities nationwide.

Deadline February of each year.

[551]
RESEARCH EXPERIENCES FOR UNDERGRADUATES PROGRAM IN SOLAR AND SPACE PHYSICS

University of Colorado
Attn: Laboratory for Atmospheric and Space Physics
1234 Innovation Drive
Boulder, CO 80303-7814
(303) 735-2143   E-mail: martin.snow@lasp.colorado.edu
Web: lasp.colorado.edu/home/education/reu

Summary To provide an opportunity for upper-division students, especially African Americans and other underrepresented minorities, to work on research projects related to solar and space physics at laboratories in Boulder, Colorado during the summer.

Eligibility This program is open to students currently enrolled as sophomores and juniors at colleges and universities in any state. Applicants must be interested in participating on a research project related to solar and space physics at a participating laboratory in Boulder, Colorado. They must be U.S. citizens, nationals, or permanent residents. Applications are especially encouraged from underrepresented minorities, persons with disabilities, and women.

Financial data The stipend is $500 per week. Students also receive dormitory housing, a food allowance, and a travel stipend of $500.

Duration 8 weeks, starting in June.

Additional information The participating laboratories are the Laboratory for Atmospheric and Space Physics (LASP) of the University of Colorado, the High Altitude Observatory (HAO) of the National Center for Atmospheric Research (NCAR), the Space Weather Prediction Center (SWPC) of the National Oceanic and Atmospheric Administration (NOAA), the Planetary Science Directorate of the Southwest Research Institute (SwRI), NorthWest Research Associates (NWRA), Atmospheric and Environmental Research (AER), or Atmospheric and Space Technology Research Associates (ASTRA). This program is funded by the National Science Foundation as part of its Research Experiences for Undergraduates (REU) Program.

Number awarded Varies each year; recently, 17 of these internships were awarded.

Deadline February of each year.

[552]
RESEARCH IN SCIENCE AND ENGINEERING PROGRAM

Rutgers University
Attn: Graduate School
25 Bishop Place
New Brunswick, NJ 08901-1181
(848) 932-6584   Fax: (732) 932-7407
E-mail: rise@rci.rutgers.edu
Web: rise.rutgers.edu/index.php

Summary To provide an opportunity for undergraduate students from any state, especially African Americans and members of other underrepresented groups, to work on a summer research project in science, mathematics, or engineering at Rutgers University in New Jersey.

Eligibility This program is open to undergraduates majoring in science (especially the biomedical sciences), mathematics, or engineering at a college or university in any state. Applicants must be interested in participating in a summer research project under the guidance of a faculty member at the graduate school of Rutgers University in New Brunswick. They should have completed at least the sophomore year and have a GPA of 3.0 or higher. Applications are especially encouraged from groups underrepresented in the sciences, math, or engineering; students from economically/educationally disadvantaged backgrounds; first generation to attend college; students attending predominantly undergraduate institutions that do not offer opportunities for independent, cutting-edge research; nontraditional students; and individuals who have faced life challenges. U.S. citizenship or permanent resident status is required.

Financial data The program provides a stipend of up to $5,000, free housing, and up to $500 of reimbursement for travel expenses.

Duration 8 or 10 weeks during the summer.

Additional information This program is administered by the Rutgers University Graduate School. Support is provided by many sponsors, including the National Science Foundation, the Federation of American Societies for Experimental Biology, Merck Research Laboratories, Public Service Electric and Gas, the New Jersey Space Grant Consortium, the New Jersey Commission on Cancer Research, and the McNair Scholars Program.

Number awarded 20 to 25 each year.

Deadline Applications are accepted on a rolling basis; selection begins in January and continues until all places are filled.

[553]
REV. LLOYD ELLIS AND MR. RICHARD CORLEY SCHOLARSHIP

National Naval Officers Association-Washington, D.C.
  Chapter
c/o LCDR Stephen Williams
P.O. Box 30784
Alexandria, VA 22310
(703) 644-2605   Fax: (703) 644-8503
E-mail: Stephen.Williams@navy.mil
Web: www.dcnnoa.org/dcnnoa-scholarship

Summary To provide financial assistance to female African American high school seniors from the Washington, D.C. area who are interested in attending an Historically Black College or University (HBCU) in any state.

Eligibility This program is open to female African American seniors graduating from high schools in the Washington, D.C. metropolitan area who plan to enroll full time at an HBCU in any state. Applicants must have a GPA of 2.5 or higher and be U.S. citizens or permanent residents. Selection is based on academic achievement, community involvement, and financial need.

Financial data The stipend is $1,000.

Duration 1 year; nonrenewable.

Additional information Recipients are not required to join or affiliate with the military in any way.

Number awarded 1 each year.

Deadline February of each year.

[554]
RHO MU OMEGA CHAPTER GENERAL SCHOLARSHIP

Alpha Kappa Alpha Sorority, Inc.-Rho Mu Omega Chapter
Attn: DC Pearls III Foundation
Scholarship Committee
P.O. Box 91191
Washington, DC 20090-1198
(202) 277-8946   E-mail: scholarship@rhomuomega.org
Web: www.rhomuomega.org/scholarship.htm

Summary To provide financial assistance to high school seniors in Washington, D.C. who plan to attend an Historically Black College or University (HBCU) and major in any field.

Eligibility This program is open to seniors graduating from high schools in Washington, D.C. and planning to enroll full time at an HBCU. Applicants may intend to major in any field. They must have a GPA of 2.5 or higher and have taken the ACT or SAT test. Along with their application, they must submit a 2-page personal statement on their most meaningful academic and personal achievement and how that relates to their future goals. Selection is based on academic record, school and community activities, leadership, and financial need. U.S. citizenship or permanent resident status is required.

Financial data The stipend is $2,000 for the freshman year.

Duration 1 year may be enrolled for up to 3 additional years at $1,000 per year, provided the recipient maintains a GPA of 2.5 or higher.

Number awarded 1 each year.

Deadline April of each year.

[555]
RHO MU OMEGA CHAPTER PRESIDENTIAL SCHOLARSHIP

Alpha Kappa Alpha Sorority, Inc.-Rho Mu Omega Chapter
Attn: DC Pearls III Foundation
Scholarship Committee
P.O. Box 91191
Washington, DC 20090-1198
(202) 277-8946   E-mail: scholarship@rhomuomega.org
Web: www.rhomuomega.org/scholarship.htm

Summary To provide financial assistance to high school seniors in Washington, D.C. who have a history of leadership and volunteer service activities and plan to attend an Historically Black College or University (HBCU) to major in any field.

Eligibility This program is open to seniors graduating from high schools in Washington, D.C. and planning to enroll full time at an HBCU. Applicants must have a history of leadership and volunteer service activities, but they may major in any field. They must have a GPA of 2.5 or higher and have taken the ACT or SAT test. Along with their application, they must submit a 2-page personal statement on what leadership means to them with an example of when and how they were an influential leader. Selection is based on academic record, school and community activities, leadership, and financial need. U.S. citizenship or permanent resident status is required.

Financial data The stipend is $2,000 for the freshman year.

Duration 1 year may be enrolled for up to 3 additional years at $1,000 per year, provided the recipient maintains a GPA of 2.5 or higher.

Number awarded 1 each year.

Deadline April of each year.

[556]
RHO MU OMEGA CHAPTER STEM SCHOLARSHIP

Alpha Kappa Alpha Sorority, Inc.-Rho Mu Omega Chapter
Attn: DC Pearls III Foundation
Scholarship Committee
P.O. Box 91191
Washington, DC 20090-1198
(202) 277-8946   E-mail: scholarship@rhomuomega.org
Web: www.rhomuomega.org/scholarship.htm

Summary To provide financial assistance to high school seniors in Washington, D.C. who plan to major in a field of science, technology, engineering, or mathematics (STEM) at an Historically Black College or University (HBCU).

Eligibility This program is open to seniors graduating from high schools in Washington, D.C. and planning to enroll full time at an HBCU. Applicants must intend to major in a field of STEM. They must have a GPA of 2.5 or higher and have taken the ACT or SAT test. Along with their application, they must submit a 2-page personal statement on the importance of STEM fields and how they have developed a seed of interest that could grow into an exciting and rewarding college and STEM career. Selection is based on academic record, school and community activities, leadership, and financial need. U.S. citizenship or permanent resident status is required.

Financial data The stipend is $2,000 for the freshman year.

Duration 1 year may be enrolled for up to 3 additional years at $1,000 per year, provided the recipient maintains a GPA of 2.5 or higher.

Number awarded 1 each year.

Deadline April of each year.

[557]
RICHARD B. FISHER SCHOLARSHIP

Morgan Stanley
Attn: Diversity Recruiting
1585 Broadway
New York, NY 10036
(212) 762-0211   Toll Free: (888) 454-3965
Fax: (212) 507-4972
E-mail: richardbfisherprogram@morganstanley.com
Web: www.morganstanley.com

Summary To provide financial assistance and work experience to African Americans and members of other underrepresented groups who are preparing for a career in technology within the financial services industry.

Eligibility This program is open to African American, Hispanic, Native American and lesbian/gay/bisexual/transgender students who are enrolled in their sophomore or junior year of college (or the third or fourth year of a 5-year program). Applicants must be enrolled full time and have a GPA of 3.4 or higher. They must be willing to commit to a paid summer internship in the Morgan Stanley Information Technology Division. All majors and disciplines are eligible, but preference is given to students preparing for a career in technology within the financial services industry. Along with their application, they must submit 1-page essays on 1) why they are applying for this scholarship and why they should be selected as a recipient; 2) a technical project on which they worked, either through a university course or previous work experience, their role in the project, and how they contributed to the end result; and 3) a software, hardware, or new innovative application of existing technology that they would create if they could and the impact it would have. Financial need is not considered in the selection process.

Financial data The stipend is $7,500 per year.

Duration 1 year (the junior year); may be renewed for the senior year.

Additional information The program, established in 1993, includes a paid summer internship in the Morgan Stan-

ley Information Technology Division in the summer following the time of application.

Number awarded 1 or more each year.

Deadline December of each year.

[558]
RICHARD L. HOLMES COMMUNITY SERVICE AWARD

American Association of Blacks in Energy-Atlanta
  Chapter
Attn: Scholarship Committee
P.O. Box 55216
Atlanta, GA 30308-5216
(404) 506-6756
E-mail: G2AABEATCHAP@southernco.com
Web: www.aabe.org/atlanta

Summary To provide financial assistance to high school seniors who are African Americans or members of other underrepresented minority groups in Georgia and are planning to major in an energy-related field at a college in any state.

Eligibility This program is open to seniors graduating from high schools in Georgia and planning to attend a college or university in any state. Applicants must be African Americans, Hispanics, or Native Americans who have a GPA of 3.0 or higher and who have taken the ACT and/or SAT test. They must be able to demonstrate exceptional responsibility to give back to their community and/or to help others. Their intended major must be business, engineering, technology, mathematics, the physical sciences, or other energy-related field. Along with their application, they must submit a 350-word essay that includes 1) when they discovered their interest in the field of energy and what sparked their interest; and 2) either what excites them about the field of energy or how they expect their education to prepare them for the field of energy. Financial need is not considered in the selection process.

Financial data A stipend is awarded; amount not specified.

Duration 1 year.

Number awarded 1 each year.

Deadline March of each year.

[559]
RICHARD S. SMITH SCHOLARSHIP

United Methodist Church
Attn: General Board of Discipleship
Young People's Ministries
P.O. Box 340003
Nashville, TN 37203-0003
(615) 340-7184   Toll Free: (877) 899-2780, ext. 7184
Fax: (615) 340-7063
E-mail: youngpeople@umcdiscipleship.org
Web: www.umcyoungpeople.org/grants-scholarships

Summary To provide financial assistance to African American and other minority high school seniors who wish to prepare for a Methodist church-related career.

Eligibility This program is open to graduating high school seniors who are members of racial/ethnic minority groups and have been active members of a United Methodist Church for at least 1 year. Applicants must have been admitted to an accredited college or university to prepare for a church-related career. They must have maintained at least a "C" average throughout high school and be able to demonstrate financial need. Along with their application, they must submit brief essays on their participation in church projects and activities, a leadership experience, the role their faith plays in their life, the church-related vocation to which God is calling them, and their extracurricular interests and activities. U.S. citizenship or permanent resident status is required.

Financial data The stipend is $1,000.

Duration 1 year; nonrenewable.

Additional information This program began in 1997. Recipients must enroll full time in their first year of undergraduate study.

Number awarded 2 each year.

Deadline May of each year.

[560]
ROBERT CHAMBERS IV AND GOALS SCHOLARSHIP FUND

POISE Foundation
Two Gateway Center, Suite 1700
603 Stanwix Street
Pittsburgh, PA 15222
(412) 281-4967   Fax: (412) 562-0292
Web: www.poisefoundation.org

Summary To provide financial assistance to African American high school seniors who plan to attend college in any state.

Eligibility This program is open to African American high school seniors planning to enroll at a college, university, or trade school in any state. Students are encouraged to be creative in application presentations.

Financial data The stipend is $1,000.

Duration 1 year.

Additional information This program began in 2011.

Number awarded 5 each year.

Deadline April of each year.

[561]
ROBERT D. LYNCH LEADERSHIP SCHOLARSHIP

Pennsylvania Black Conference on Higher Education
c/o Brenda Sanders Dédé, Scholarship Committee Chair
Clarion University of Pennsylvania
Academic Affairs
115 Carrier
840 Wood Street
Clarion, PA 16214
(814) 393-2223   E-mail: bdede@clarion.edu
Web: www.pbcohe.com/scholarships.html

Summary To provide financial assistance to African American residents of any state who are enrolled as undergraduates at colleges in Pennsylvania and have demonstrated outstanding leadership skills.

Eligibility This program is open to African Americans from any state who have completed at least the first semester as an undergraduate at a college or university in Pennsylvania. Applicants must have a GPA of 3.0 or higher. They must have completed the Robert D. Lynch Student Leadership Development Institute. Along with their application, they must submit an essay, up to 5 pages in length, on why they should receive

this scholarship. Selection is based on leadership skills and academic record.

Financial data The stipend is $1,000.

Duration 1 year.

Number awarded 1 each year.

Deadline January of each year.

[562]
ROBERT P. MADISON SCHOLARSHIP IN ARCHITECTURE

Cleveland Foundation
Attn: Scholarship Processing
1422 Euclid Avenue, Suite 1300
Cleveland, OH 44115-2001
(216) 861-3810   Fax: (216) 861-1729
E-mail: mbaker@clevefdn.org
Web: www.clevelandfoundation.org

Summary To provide financial assistance to African American high school seniors and undergraduates from any state who are interested in studying architecture.

Eligibility This program is open to African American high school seniors and current undergraduates from any state. Applicants must be accepted or enrolled at an accredited college or university that has a degree-granting program in architecture. They must have a GPA of 3.0 or higher and be able to demonstrate financial need. Along with their application, they must submit a brief essay on why they want to be an architect. Selection is based on evidence of commitment to a career as an architect, academic performance, and special skill or talent related to excelling in architectural course work.

Financial data The stipend is $1,000. Funds are paid directly to the recipient's institution to be used for tuition, fees, books, supplies, and/or equipment required for courses.

Duration 1 year; nonrenewable.

Additional information This program began in 2004 by the firm of Robert P. Madison International to honor its founder, the first African American registered to practice architecture in Ohio.

Number awarded Varies each year.

Deadline March of each year.

[563]
ROBERTA BANASZAK GLEITER—ENGINEERING ENDEAVOR SCHOLARSHIP

Society of Women Engineers
Attn: Scholarship Selection Committee
203 North LaSalle Street, Suite 1675
Chicago, IL 60601-1269
(312) 596-5223   Toll Free: (877) SWE-INFO
Fax: (312) 644-8557   E-mail: scholarships@swe.org
Web: societyofwomenengineers.swe.org

Summary To provide financial assistance to members of the Society of Women Engineers (SWE), especially African Americans and other underrepresented students, who will be entering their sophomore or junior year of a program in aeronautical or chemical engineering.

Eligibility This program is open to SWE members who are U.S. citizens entering their sophomore or junior year of full-time study at an ABET-accredited 4-year college or university. Applicants must be studying aeronautical or chemical engineering. Preference is given to members of underrepresented groups, reentry candidates, and students who can demonstrate financial need.

Financial data   The stipend is $1,250 per year.

Duration   1 year; may be renewed, provided the recipient continues to meet eligibility requirements.

Additional information   This program began in 2013.

Number awarded   1 each year.

Deadline   February of each year.

[564]
ROCHON/DAVIS SCHOLARSHIP

National Naval Officers Association-Washington, D.C.
   Chapter
c/o LCDR Stephen Williams
P.O. Box 30784
Alexandria, VA 22310
(703) 644-2605   Fax: (703) 644-8503
E-mail: Stephen.Williams@navy.mil
Web: www.dcnnoa.org/dcnnoa-scholarship

Summary   To provide financial assistance to African American high school seniors from the Washington, D.C. area who are interested in attending an Historically Black College or University (HBCU) in any state.

Eligibility   This program is open to African American seniors graduating from high schools in the Washington, D.C. metropolitan area who plan to enroll full time at an HBCU in any state. Applicants must have a GPA of 3.0 or higher and be U.S. citizens or permanent residents. Selection is based on academic achievement, community involvement, and financial need.

Financial data   The stipend is $1,000.

Duration   1 year; nonrenewable.

Additional information   Recipients are not required to join or affiliate with the military in any way.

Number awarded   1 each year.

Deadline   February of each year.

[565]
RODNEY VERNELL MEMORIAL SCHOLARSHIP

Sigma Gamma Rho Sorority, Inc.
Attn: National Education Fund
1000 Southhill Drive, Suite 200
Cary, NC 27513
(919) 678-9720   Toll Free: (888) SGR-1922
Fax: (919) 678-9721
E-mail: customerservice@sgrho1922.org
Web: www.sgrho1922.org/nef

Summary   To provide financial assistance to undergraduate students, especially African Americans, who are the first generation in their family to attend college and working on a degree in any field.

Eligibility   This program is open to undergraduates working on a degree in any field who are a member of the first generation in their family to attend college. The sponsor is a traditionally African American sorority, but support is available to males and females of all races. Applicants must have a GPA of 2.5 or higher, a record of community service, and demonstrated financial need.

Financial data   A stipend is awarded (amount not specified).

Duration   1 year.

Additional information   A processing fee of $20 is required.

Number awarded   1 each year.

Deadline   April of each year.

[566]
RON BROWN SCHOLAR PROGRAM

CAP Charitable Foundation
Attn: Ron Brown Scholar Program
1160 Pepsi Place, Suite 206
Charlottesville, VA 22901
(434) 964-1588   Fax: (434) 964-1589
E-mail: info@ronbrown.org
Web: www.ronbrown.org

Summary   To provide financial assistance for college to African American high school seniors.

Eligibility   This program is open to academically-talented African American high school seniors who have demonstrated social commitment and leadership potential. They must be interested in attending a 4-year college or university as a full-time student. U.S. citizenship or permanent resident status is required. Finalists are invited to participate in a weekend selection program in Washington, D.C.; their expenses are reimbursed. Final selection is based on academic excellence, leadership, skills, school and community involvement, and financial need.

Financial data   The stipend is $10,000 per year. Funds may be used to cover tuition, fees, books, room, board, and other college-related expenses. Payment is made directly to the recipient's school.

Duration   4 years.

Additional information   Established in 1996, this program honors a former Secretary of Commerce who served during the Clinton administration. During college, recipients are required to pursue 1 or more summer internships devoted to community service (e.g., in education, health, government, politics) and 1 pre-professional internship.

Number awarded   Approximately 20 each year.

Deadline   January of each year.

[567]
RON HERNDON SCHOLARSHIPS

Black United Fund of Oregon
Attn: ACCESS Scholarship Committee
2828 N.E. Alberta
Portland, OR 97211
(503) 282-7973   Fax: (503) 282-3482
E-mail: bufor@bufor.org
Web: www.bufor.org

Summary   To provide financial assistance to African American high school seniors from Oregon and southwestern Washington who plan to attend college in any state.

Eligibility   This program is open to African Americans who are 1) seniors graduating from high schools in Oregon and southwestern Washington; or 2) community college transfer students in that area. Applicants must be planning to attend a 4-year college or university in any state. High school seniors must have a GPA of 2.0 to 3.0 and community college transfer students must have a GPA of 2.5 or higher. Along with their application, they must submit a resume that includes information on extracurricular school activities, paid work experience, volunteer activities outside of school, and awards or honors attained. Financial need is considered in the selection process.

Financial data   The stipend ranges from $1,500 to $2,000.

Duration   1 year; nonrenewable.

Additional information   This program began in 1994.

Number awarded   6 each year.

Deadline   February of each year.

[568]
RONALD E. MCNAIR SCIENTIFIC ACHIEVEMENT AWARD

Omega Psi Phi Fraternity
Attn: Charles R. Drew Memorial Scholarship Commission
3951 Snapfinger Parkway
Decatur, GA 30035-3203
(404) 284-5533   Fax: (404) 284-0333
E-mail: scholarshipchairman@oppf.org
Web: www.oppf.org/scholarship

Summary   To provide financial assistance to undergraduate Omega Psi Phi Fraternity brothers who are majoring in the sciences.

Eligibility   This program is open to fraternity brothers in good standing who are at least sophomores in college and are majoring in a field of science, including (but not limited to) chemistry, physics, biology, engineering, or mathematics. Applicants must be enrolled full time and have a GPA of 3.5 or higher. Along with their application, they must submit a statement of 200 to 250 words on their purpose for applying for this scholarship, how they believe funds from the fraternity can assist them in achieving their career goals, and other circumstances (including financial need) that make it important for them to receive financial assistance.

Financial data   The stipend is $6,000.

Duration   1 year.

Additional information   Omega Psi Phi is a traditionally Black college fraternity. The winner is required to attend the Omega Psi Phi Grand Conclave or Leadership Conference. Up to $1,000 in travel expenses for attendance is provided.

Number awarded   1 or more each year.

Deadline   April of each year.

[569]
ROSA L. PARKS COLLEGE SCHOLARSHIP

Conference of Minority Transportation Officials
Attn: National Scholarship Program
100 M Street, S.E., Suite 917
Washington, DC 20003
(202) 506-2917   E-mail: info@comto.org
Web: www.comto.org/page/scholarships

Summary   To provide financial assistance to African American and other students who have a tie to the Conference of Minority Transportation Officials (COMTO) and are interested in working on an undergraduate or master's degree in transportation.

Eligibility   This program is open to 1) undergraduates who have completed at least 60 semester credit hours in a transportation discipline; and 2) students working on a master's degree in transportation who have completed at least 15 credits. Applicants must be or have a parent, guardian, or

grandparent who has been a COMTO member for at least 1 year. They must have a GPA of 3.0 or higher. Along with their application they must submit a cover letter on their transportation-related career goals and life aspirations. Financial need is not considered in the selection process.

Financial data   The stipend is $4,500. Funds are paid directly to the recipient's college or university.

Duration   1 year.

Number awarded   1 each year.

Deadline   April of each year.

[570]
ROSA L. PARKS HIGH SCHOOL SCHOLARSHIP

Conference of Minority Transportation Officials
Attn: National Scholarship Program
100 M Street, S.E., Suite 917
Washington, DC 20003
(202) 506-2917   E-mail: info@comto.org
Web: www.comto.org/page/scholarships

Summary   To provide financial assistance for college to African American and other children and grandchildren of members of the Conference of Minority Transportation Officials (COMTO) who are interested in studying any field.

Eligibility   This program is open to high school seniors who are members or whose parent, guardian, or grandparent has been a COMTO member for at least 1 year and who have been accepted at an accredited college, university, or vocational/technical institution. Applicants must have a GPA of 3.0 or higher. Along with their application they must submit a cover letter on their transportation-related career goals and life aspirations. Financial need is not considered in the selection process.

Financial data   The stipend is $4,500. Funds are paid directly to the recipient's college or university.

Duration   1 year.

Number awarded   1 each year.

Deadline   April of each year.

[571]
ROSALIND BARNES GRIFFIN ENDOWMENT FUND

Alpha Kappa Alpha Sorority, Inc.
Attn: Educational Advancement Foundation
5656 South Stony Island Avenue
Chicago, IL 60637
(773) 947-0026   Toll Free: (800) 653-6528
Fax: (773) 947-0277   E-mail: akaeaf@akaeaf.net
Web: www.akaeaf.org/fellowships_endowments.htm

Summary   To provide financial assistance to members of Alpha Kappa Alpha Sorority who are seeking additional training in treatment of mental health.

Eligibility   This program is open to members of Alpha Kappa Alpha, a traditionally African American sorority, who are enrolled as sophomores, juniors, seniors, or graduate students at an accredited degree-granting institution in any state. Applicants must be working to obtain additional training in treatment of mental health. Along with their application, they must submit 1) a list of honors, awards, and scholarships received; 2) a list of organizations in which they have memberships, especially minority organizations; and 3) a statement of their personal and career goals, including how this scholarship will enhance their ability to attain those goals.

Financial data   A stipend is awarded (amount not specified).

Duration   1 year.

Number awarded   1 or more each even-numbered year.

Deadline   April of each even-numbered year.

[572]
ROSEWOOD FAMILY SCHOLARSHIP FUND

Florida Department of Education
Attn: Office of Student Financial Assistance
State Scholarship and Grant Programs
325 West Gaines Street, Suite 1314
Tallahassee, FL 32399-0400
(850) 410-5160   Toll Free: (888) 827-2004
Fax: (850) 487-1809   E-mail: osfa@fldoe.org
Web: www.floridastudentfinancialaid.org

Summary   To provide financial assistance for undergraduate education to African American and other needy minority students who wish to study in Florida.

Eligibility   This program is open to residents of any state who wish to enroll full time at a state university, public community college, or public postsecondary vocational/technical school in Florida. Applicants must be a descendant of an African American Rosewood family (whose members were killed by a mob in January 1923). Other minority undergraduate students are considered if funds remain available after awarding Rosewood descendants. Financial need must be demonstrated.

Financial data   Stipends depend on the need of the recipient, to a maximum of $6,100.

Duration   1 year; may be renewed up to 3 additional years, provided the student maintains full-time enrollment and a GPA of 2.0 or higher.

Number awarded   Up to 50 each year.

Deadline   March of each year.

[573]
ROYCE OSBORN MINORITY STUDENT SCHOLARSHIPS

American Society of Radiologic Technologists
Attn: ASRT Foundation
15000 Central Avenue, S.E.
Albuquerque, NM 87123-3909
(505) 298-4500, ext. 1392
Toll Free: (800) 444-2778, ext. 1392
Fax: (505) 298-5063   E-mail: foundation@asrt.org
Web: foundation.asrt.org/what-we-do/scholarships

Summary   To provide financial assistance to African American and other minority students enrolled in entry-level radiologic sciences programs.

Eligibility   This program is open to Blacks or African Americans, American Indians or Alaska Natives, Hispanics or Latinos, Asians, and Native Hawaiians or other Pacific Islanders who are enrolled in an accredited entry-level program in radiography, sonography, magnetic resonance, or nuclear medicine. Applicants must be able to finish their degree or certificate in the year for which they are applying. They must be U.S. citizens, nationals, or permanent residents have a GPA of 3.0 or higher. Along with their application, they must submit

9 essays of 200 words each on assigned topics related to their personal situation and interest in a career in radiologic science. Selection is based on those essays, academic and professional achievements, recommendations, and financial need.

Financial data   The stipend is $4,000. Funds are paid directly to the recipient's institution.

Duration   1 year.

Number awarded   5 each year.

Deadline   January of each year.

[574]
ROYCE R. WATTS SR. SCHOLARSHIP

Watts Charity Association, Inc.
6245 Bristol Parkway, Suite 224
Culver City, CA 90230
(310) 671-0394   Fax: (323) 778-2613
E-mail: wattscharity@yahoo.com
Web: 4watts.tripod.com/id5.html

Summary   To provide financial assistance to upper-division African American college students interested in health, civil rights, or administration.

Eligibility   This program is open to U.S. citizens of African American descent who are enrolled full time as a college or university junior. Applicants must have an interest in health and pre-medicine, community activities and civil rights, or administration. They must have a GPA of 3.0 or higher, be between 17 and 24 years of age, and be able to demonstrate that they intend to continue their education for at least 2 years. Along with their application, they must submit 1) a 1-paragraph statement on why they should be awarded a Watts Charity Association scholarship; and 2) a 1- to 2-page essay on a specific type of cancer, based either on how it has impacted their life or on researched information.

Financial data   A stipend is awarded (amount not specified).

Duration   1 year.

Additional information   Royce R. Watts, Sr. established the Watts Charity Association after he learned he had cancer in 2001.

Number awarded   1 each year.

Deadline   May of each year.

[575]
RUTH M. BATSON SCHOLARSHIPS

Ruth M. Batson Educational Foundation
250 Cambridge Street, Suite 701
Boston, MA 02114
(617) 742-1070   E-mail: dao5753@aol.com

Summary   To provide financial assistance to African American college students who face serious financial need.

Eligibility   This program is open to African American college students who need aid as a supplement to other financial assistance. Emergency grants are also available to students who need assistance to remain in school. Selection is based on academic achievement, character, extracurricular activities, and financial need.

Financial data   Assistance ranges from $500 to $1,500.

Duration   1 year.

Number awarded Varies each year.

Deadline June of each year.

[576]
RUTH WEBB MINORITY SCHOLARSHIP

California Academy of Physician Assistants
2318 South Fairview Street
Santa Ana, CA 92704-4938
(714) 427-0321 Fax: (714) 427-0324
E-mail: capa@capanet.org
Web: www.capanet.org

Summary To provide financial assistance to African American and other minority student members of the California Academy of Physician Assistants (CAPA) enrolled in physician assistant programs in California.

Eligibility This program is open to student members of CAPA enrolled in primary care physician assistant programs in California. Applicants must be members of a minority group (African American, Hispanic, Asian/Pacific Islander, or Native American/Alaskan Native). They must have maintained good academic standing and conducted activities to promote the physician assistant profession. Along with their application, they must submit an essay describing the activities they have performed to promote the physician assistant profession, the importance of representing minorities in their community, and why they should be awarded this scholarship. Financial need is considered in the selection process.

Financial data The stipend is $2,000.

Duration 1 year.

Number awarded 1 each year.

Deadline December of each year.

[577]
S. EVELYN LEWIS MEMORIAL MEDICAL HEALTH SCIENCE SCHOLARSHIP

Zeta Phi Beta Sorority, Inc.
Attn: National Educational Foundation
1734 New Hampshire Avenue, N.W.
Washington, DC 20009
(202) 387-3103 Fax: (202) 232-4593
E-mail: info@zetaphibetasororityhq.org
Web: www.zpbnef1975.org/scholarships-and-descriptions

Summary To provide financial assistance to women, especially African Americans, who are interested in studying medicine or health sciences on the undergraduate or graduate school level.

Eligibility This program is open to women enrolled full time in a program on the undergraduate or graduate school level leading to a degree in medicine or health sciences. Proof of enrollment is required. Applicants need not be members of Zeta Phi Beta Sorority. Along with their application, they must submit a 150-word essay on their educational goals and professional aspirations, how this award will help them to achieve those goals, and why they should receive the award. Financial need is not considered in the selection process.

Financial data The stipend ranges from $500 to $1,000. Funds are paid directly to the college or university.

Duration 1 academic year.

Additional information Zeta Phi Beta is a traditionally African American sorority.

Number awarded 1 or more each year.

Deadline January of each year.

[578]
SACHS FOUNDATION SCHOLARSHIPS

Sachs Foundation
90 South Cascade Avenue, Suite 1410
Colorado Springs, CO 80903-1691
(719) 633-2353
Web: www.sachsfoundation.org

Summary To provide financial assistance to African American high school seniors in Colorado who plan to attend college in any state.

Eligibility This program is open to African American graduating high school seniors who are U.S. citizens and have been residents of Colorado for at least 5 years. Applicants must be planning to attend a college or university in any state. Along with their application, they must submit a 500-word personal biography, transcripts, 3 references, and documentation of financial need. Once accepted as undergraduate scholars, students may later apply for support in graduate school.

Financial data The average annual stipend recently was $6,000 for undergraduates or $7,000 for graduate students. Funds are sent to the financial aid office of the recipient's school.

Duration Normally, undergraduate students receive 4 years of support, provided they maintain full-time enrollment and a current GPA of 2.5 or higher per term. Graduate students receive up to an additional 4 years of support.

Additional information This foundation was established in 1931. Since its founding, it has provided scholarships to more than 5,000 African Americans in Colorado.

Number awarded Approximately 50 each year.

Deadline March of each year.

[579]
SAGINAW BLACK NURSES ASSOCIATION-NELL KELLY SCHOLARSHIP

Saginaw Community Foundation
1 Tuscola, Suite 100
Saginaw, MI 48607
(989) 755-0545 Fax: (989) 755-6524
E-mail: info@saginawfoundation.org
Web: www.saginawfoundation.org

Summary To provide financial assistance to African American and other residents of Michigan who are interested in working on an associate or bachelor's degree in nursing at a school in any state.

Eligibility This program is open to residents of Michigan who are working full or part time on an associate or bachelor's degree in nursing at a college or university in any state. Applicants must have a GPA of 2.5 or higher. Along with their application, they must submit an essay describing their personal and educational goals, including their plans for a major, why they have chosen that field, and what they plan to do with their degree. Selection is based on career goals as demonstrated in that essay (30 points); academic performance (20 points); overall involvement in work, school and community activities (10 points); leadership ability (10 points); community service (10 points); letters of recommendation (10 points); and financial need (10 points).

Financial data A stipend is awarded (amount not specified).

Duration 1 year.

Additional information This program was established in 2010 by the Saginaw Black Nurses Association (SBNA), the local chapter of the National Black Nurses Association. Recipients must agree to become an active member of the SBNA.

Number awarded Varies each year.

Deadline February of each year.

[580]
SANDISK SCHOLARS PROGRAM

SanDisk Foundation
951 SanDisk Drive
Milpitas, CA 97034-7933
(408) 801-1240   Fax: (408) 801-8657
E-mail: Mike.wong@sandisk.com
Web: www.sandisk.com

Summary To provide financial assistance to African American and other high school seniors and lower-division college students who are interested in studying computer science or engineering in college.

Eligibility This program is open to U.S. citizens and legal residents who are high school seniors or college freshmen or sophomores enrolled or planning to enroll full time at a 4-year college or university in the United States, Puerto Rico, the U.S. Virgin Islands, or Guam. Applicants must be interested in majoring in computer science or engineering and have a GPA of 3.0 or higher. Selection is based on academic excellence, demonstrated leadership in extracurricular and/or community activities, a personal statement, and financial need. Some scholarships are reserved for dependents of SanDisk employees, participants in the Center for Talented Youth at Johns Hopkins University, Hispanic students, and African American students.

Financial data The stipend is $2,500 per year.

Duration 1 year; may be renewed up to 3 additional years.

Additional information This program, which began in 2012, is offered in partnership with the United Negro College Fund (UNCF), the Silicon Valley Community Foundation (SVCF), and International Scholarship and Tuition Services (ISTS).

Number awarded 40 each year, including 8 awarded to the general public, 3 to dependents of SanDisk employees, 2 to participants or alumni of the Center for Talented Youth at Johns Hopkins University, 13 to Hispanic students through the Silicon Valley Community Foundation, and 14 to African American students through the United Negro College Fund.

Deadline March of each year.

[581]
SAO REU SUMMER INTERN PROGRAM

Harvard-Smithsonian Center for Astrophysics
Attn: Summer Intern Program
60 Garden Street, Mail Stop 70
Cambridge, MA 02138
(617) 496-7063   E-mail: intern@cfa.harvard.edu
Web: www.cfa.harvard.edu/opportunities/reu//REU.html

Summary To enable undergraduates, especially African Americans and other underrepresented sudents, who are interested in a physical science career or science education to obtain research experience at the Smithsonian Astrophysical Observatory (SAO) at Harvard University.

Eligibility This program is open to U.S. citizens, nationals, and permanent residents enrolled in a program leading to a bachelor's degree. Applicants must be interested in a career in astronomy, astrophysics, physics, or related physical sciences. Along with their application, they must submit an essay of 600 to 800 words describing academic and career goals, scientific interests, relevant work experience, why they would like to be in the program, and why they would be a good candidate. Graduating seniors are not eligible. Applications are especially encouraged from underrepresented minorities, persons with disabilities, and women.

Financial data The stipend is $5,000. Housing and travel expenses are provided.

Duration 10 weeks during the summer.

Additional information Each intern works with a scientist on an individual research project. Potential areas of research include observational and theoretical cosmology, extragalactic and galactic astronomy, interstellar medium and star formation, laboratory astrophysics, supernovae and supernova remnants, planetary science, and solar and stellar astrophysics. Also included in the program are weekly lectures, field trips, and workshops specifically designed for the participants. This program is supported by the National Science Foundation as part of its Research Experiences for Undergraduates (REU) Program.

Number awarded 10 each year.

Deadline January of each year.

[582]
SCHOLARSHIPS FOR RACIAL JUSTICE

Higher Education Consortium for Urban Affairs
Attn: Student Services
2233 University Avenue West, Suite 210
St. Paul, MN 55114-1698
(651) 287-3300   Toll Free: (800) 554-1089
Fax: (651) 659-9421   E-mail: hecua@hecua.org
Web: www.hecua.org

Summary To provide financial assistance to African American and other students of color who are enrolled in programs of the Higher Education Consortium for Urban Affairs (HECUA) at participating colleges and universities and are committed to undoing institutionalized racism.

Eligibility This program is open to students at member colleges and universities who are participating in HECUA programs. Applicants must be a student of color who can demonstrate a commitment to undoing institutionalized racism. Along with their application, they must submit a reflective essay of 550 to 1,700 words on the personal, social, or political influences in their lifetime that have motivated them to work on racial justice issues.

Financial data The stipend is $4,000.

Duration 1 semester.

Additional information This program began in 2012. Consortium members include Augsburg College (Minneapolis, Minnesota), Augustana College (Sioux Falls, South Dakota), Carleton College (Northfield, Minnesota), College of

Saint Scholastica (Duluth, Minnesota), Colorado College (Colorado Springs, Colorado), Denison University (Granville, Ohio), Gustavus Adolphus College (St. Peter, Minnesota), Hamline University (St. Paul, Minnesota), Macalester College (St. Paul, Minnesota), Northland College (Ashland, Wisconsin), Saint Mary's University (Winona, Minnesota), Saint Catherine University (St. Paul, Minnesota), Saint Olaf College (Northfield, Minnesota), Swarthmore College (Swarthmore, Pennsylvania), University of Minnesota (Twin Cities, Duluth, Morris, Crookston, Rochester), and University of Saint Thomas (St. Paul, Minnesota).

Number awarded   Several each year.

Deadline   April of each year for summer and fall programs; November of each year for January and spring programs.

[583]
SCHOLARSHIPS FOR SOCIAL JUSTICE

Higher Education Consortium for Urban Affairs
Attn: Student Services
2233 University Avenue West, Suite 210
St. Paul, MN 55114-1698
(651) 287-3300   Toll Free: (800) 554-1089
Fax: (651) 659-9421   E-mail: hecua@hecua.org
Web: www.hecua.org

Summary   To provide financial assistance to students from African American and other targeted groups who are enrolled in programs of the Higher Education Consortium for Urban Affairs (HECUA) at participating colleges and universities.

Eligibility   This program is open to students at member colleges and universities who are participating in HECUA programs. Applicants must be a first-generation college student, from a low-income family, and/or a student of color. Along with their application, they must submit a reflective essay of 500 to 1,700 words, drawing on their life experiences and their personal and academic goals, on what they believe they can contribute to the mission of HECUA to equip students with the knowledge, experiences, tools, and passion to address issues of social justice and social change. The essay should also explain how the HECUA program will benefit them and the people, issues, and communities they care about.

Financial data   The stipend is $1,500. Funds are applied as a credit to the student's HECUA program fees for the semester.

Duration   1 semester.

Additional information   This program began in 2006. Consortium members include Augsburg College (Minneapolis, Minnesota), Augustana College (Sioux Falls, South Dakota), Carleton College (Northfield, Minnesota), College of Saint Scholastica (Duluth, Minnesota), Colorado College (Colorado Springs, Colorado), Denison University (Granville, Ohio), Gustavus Adolphus College (St. Peter, Minnesota), Hamline University (St. Paul, Minnesota), Macalester College (St. Paul, Minnesota), Northland College (Ashland, Wisconsin), Saint Mary's University (Winona, Minnesota), Saint Catherine University (St. Paul, Minnesota), Saint Olaf College (Northfield, Minnesota), Swarthmore College (Swarthmore, Pennsylvania), University of Minnesota (Twin Cities, Duluth, Morris, Crookston, Rochester), and University of Saint Thomas (St. Paul, Minnesota).

Number awarded   Several each year.

Deadline   April of each year for summer and fall programs; November of each year for January and spring programs.

[584]
SCIENCE AND ENGINEERING APPRENTICE PROGRAM

American Society for Engineering Education
Attn: Army SEAP Help-Desk
1818 N Street, N.W., Suite 600
Washington, DC 20036-2479
Toll Free: (855) 592-3556   E-mail: armyseap@asee.org
Web: www.usaeop.com/programs/apprenticeships/seap

Summary   To provide an opportunity for high school students (especially women, African Americans, and Hispanics) to work during the summer on research projects at selected Department of Defense laboratories.

Eligibility   This program is open to high school students interested in careers in science and engineering. A goal of the program is to encourage women, African Americans, and Hispanics to expand their interest in science and engineering careers. Applicants must submit a 1-page statement on their personal goals and why they want to participate in a research project at a Department of Defense laboratory, 1 or 2 letters of recommendation, and a transcript. Most laboratories require U.S. citizenship, although some accept permanent residents. In a few laboratories, security clearance is required. Selection is based on grades, science and mathematics courses taken, scores on national standardized tests, areas of interest, teacher recommendations, and the personal statement.

Financial data   The stipend is $2,000. Students are responsible for transportation to and from the laboratory site.

Duration   8 weeks during the summer.

Additional information   This program was previously administered by George Washington University. Funding is provided by the U.S. Department of Defense. Participating laboratories include the Army Engineer Research and Development Center, Geospatial Research Laboratory (Alexandria, Virginia); Army Center for Environmental Health Medicine (Fort Detrick, Maryland); Army Medical Research Institute of Chemical Defense (Aberdeen Proving Ground, Maryland); Army Research Institute of Infectious Diseases (Fort Detrick, Maryland); Army Medical Research and Materiel Command, Walter Reed Army Institute of Research (Silver Spring, Maryland); Army Research Laboratory (Aberdeen Proving Ground, Maryland and Adelphi, Maryland); Army Aviation and Missile Research, Development and Engineering Center (Redstone Arsenal, Alabama); Army Engineer Research and Development Center, Construction Engineering Research Laboratory (Champaign, Illinois); Night Vision and Electronic Sensors Directorate (Fort Belvoir, Virginia); and Army Engineer Research and Development Center (Vicksburg, Mississippi).

Number awarded   Varies each year.

Deadline   February of each year.

[585]
SCIENCE AND ENGINEERING PROGRAMS FOR WOMEN AND MINORITIES AT BROOKHAVEN NATIONAL LABORATORY

Brookhaven National Laboratory
Attn: Diversity Office, Human Resources Division
Building 400B
P.O. Box 5000
Upton, New York 11973-5000
(631) 344-2703   Fax: (631) 344-5305
E-mail: palmore@bnl.gov
Web: www.bnl.gov/diversity/programs.asp

Summary   To provide on-the-job training in scientific areas at Brookhaven National Laboratory (BNL) during the summer to African Americans and other underrepresented minority and women students.

Eligibility   This program at BNL is open to women and underrepresented minority (African American/Black, Hispanic, Native American, or Pacific Islander) students who have completed their freshman, sophomore, or junior year of college. Applicants must be U.S. citizens or permanent residents, at least 18 years of age, and majoring in applied mathematics, biology, chemistry, computer science, engineering, high and low energy particle accelerators, nuclear medicine, physics, or scientific writing. Since no transportation or housing allowance is provided, preference is given to students who reside in the BNL area.

Financial data   Participants receive a competitive stipend.

Duration   10 to 12 weeks during the summer.

Additional information   Students work with members of the scientific, technical, and professional staff of BNL in an educational training program developed to give research experience.

Number awarded   Varies each year.

Deadline   April of each year.

[586]
SC-PAAE SCHOLARSHIPS

South Carolina Professional Association for Access and
   Equity
Attn: Financial Secretary
P.O. Box 71297
North Charleston, SC 29415
(843) 670-4890   E-mail: anderson4569@bellsouth.net
Web: www.scpaae.org/#!scholarships/c11tv

Summary   To provide financial assistance to undergraduate students at colleges and universities in South Carolina who are African Americans or other underrepresented minorities on their campus.

Eligibility   This program is open to residents of any state who have completed at least 12 semester hours at a college or university in South Carolina. Applicants must be recognized as an underrepresented ethnic minority on their campus. They must have a GPA of 2.75 or higher. Along with their application, they must submit 1) a personal letter on their academic and career goals, honors and awards, leadership skills and organization participation, community service, and a statement of why they would like to receive this scholarship; and 2) a paragraph defining access and equity and describing how they can assist in achieving access and equity within

South Carolina. Financial need is not considered in the selection process.

Financial data   Stipends are $750 for students at 2-year institutions or $1,000 for students at 4-year institutions.

Duration   1 year.

Number awarded   Varies each year.

Deadline   February of each year.

[587]
SEAN MCNEAL AND BETH POWELL SCHOLARSHIP

Organization of Black Aerospace Professionals, Inc.
Attn: Scholarship Coordinator
One Westbrook Corporate Center, Suite 300
Westchester, IL 60154
(708) 449-7755   Toll Free: (800) JET-OBAP
Fax: (708) 449-7754 E-mail: obapscholarships@obap.org
Web: www.obap.org/sean-mcneal-scholarship

Summary   To provide financial assistance to members of the Organization of Black Aerospace Professionals (OBAP) who are interested in preparing for a career as a professional pilot.

Eligibility   This program is open to OBAP members who are high school seniors or students currently enrolled in an accredited collegiate aerospace program. Applicants must be interested in preparing for a career as a professional pilot. They must have a GPA of 2.5 or higher. Along with their application, they must submit a 300-word essay where they see themselves in 5 years and how they will accomplish their goals.

Financial data   The stipend is $3,000.

Duration   1 year.

Additional information   The OBAP was originally established in 1976 as the Organization of Black Airline Pilots to make certain Blacks and other minorities had a group that would keep them informed about opportunities for advancement within commercial aviation.

Number awarded   1 each year.

Deadline   May of each year.

[588]
SEATTLE CHAPTER AWIS SCHOLARSHIPS

Association for Women in Science-Seattle Chapter
c/o Fran Solomon, Scholarship Committee Chair
5805 16th Avenue, N.E.
Seattle, WA 98105
(206) 522-6441   E-mail: scholarship@seattleawis.org
Web: www.seattleawis.org/award/scholarships

Summary   To provide financial assistance to women undergraduates from any state, especially African Americans and members of other underrepresented groups, who are majoring in science, mathematics, or engineering at colleges and universities in Washington.

Eligibility   This program is open to women from any state entering their junior or senior year at a 4-year college or university in Washington. Applicants must have a declared major in science (e.g., biological sciences, environmental science, biochemistry, chemistry, pharmacy, geology, computer science, physics), mathematics, or engineering. Along with their application, they must submit essays on the events that led to their choice of a major, their current career plans and long-term goals, and their volunteer and community activities. Selection is based on academic excellence, motivation to prepare for a science-based career, record of giving back to their communities, and financial need. At least 1 scholarship is reserved for a woman from a group that is underrepresented in science, mathematics, and engineering careers, including Native American Indians and Alaska Natives, Black/African Americans, Mexican Americans/Chicanas/Latinas, Native Pacific Islanders (Polynesians, Melanesians, and Micronesians), adult learners (returning students), and women with disabilities.

Financial data Stipends range from $1,000 to $5,000.

Duration 1 year.

Additional information This program includes the following named awards: the Virginia Badger Scholarship, the Angela Paez Memorial Scholarship, and the Fran Solomon Scholarship. Support for the program is provided by several sponsors, including the American Chemical Society, Iota Sigma Pi, Rosetta Inpharmatics, and ZymoGenetics, Inc.

Number awarded Varies each year; recently 2 at $5,000, 1 at $1,500, and 1 at $1,000 were awarded.

Deadline March of each year.

[589]
SEATTLE CHAPTER NABA SCHOLARSHIPS

National Association of Black Accountants-Seattle
  Chapter
Attn: Scholarship Committee
P.O. Box 18105
Seattle, WA 98118
E-mail: scholarship@nabaseattle.org
Web: www.nabaseattle.org

Summary To provide financial assistance to members of the National Association of Black Accountants (NABA) from any state who are working on an undergraduate degree in a business-related field at colleges and universities in Washington.

Eligibility This program is open to full-time sophomores, juniors, and seniors working on a degree in accounting, finance, or other business-related field at colleges and universities in Washington. Applicants must be African American or students of African descent and active NABA members. They must have a GPA of 3.0 or higher. Along with their application, they must submit 3 essays of 300 to 400 words each on assigned topics that relate to their background and goals. Financial need is not considered in the selection process.

Financial data Stipends range from $1,000 to $2,000.

Duration 1 year.

Number awarded Varies each year.

Deadline April of each year.

[590]
SELMO BRADLEY SCHOLARSHIP

African Methodist Episcopal Church
Eleventh Episcopal District Lay Organization
c/o Beulah Gregory
712 Bragg Drive
Jacksonville, FL 32305
(850) 574-6596   E-mail: eedlo@eedlo.org
Web: www.eedlo.org/scholarships.html

Summary To provide financial assistance to members of African Methodist Episcopal (AME) churches in Florida who are interested in attending college in any state.

Eligibility This program is open to seniors graduating from public or private high schools in Florida who are members of AME churches. Applicants must be planning to enroll full time at an institution of higher learning in any state: an AME-supported college, a Predominantly Black College or University, or an accredited trade school. They must have a GPA of 2.5 or higher. Along with their application, they must submit a 1-page essay on why a college education is important and a statement regarding their financial need.

Financial data A stipend is awarded (amount not specified).

Duration 1 year.

Number awarded 1 or more each year.

Deadline Students must submit their applications to their local church by January of each year.

[591]
SEO UNDERGRADUATE CAREER PROGRAM

Sponsors for Educational Opportunity
Attn: Career Program
55 Exchange Place
New York, NY 10005
(212) 979-2040   Toll Free: (800) 462-2332
Fax: (646) 706-7113
E-mail: careerprogram@seo-usa.org
Web: www.seocareer.org

Summary To provide undergraduate African Americans and other students of color with an opportunity to gain summer work experience in selected fields.

Eligibility This program is open to students of color at colleges and universities in the United States. Applicants must be interested in a summer internship in 1 of the following fields: asset management, consulting, engineering, finance and accounting, human resources, investment banking, investment research, marketing and sales, nonprofit sector, private equity, sales and trading, technology with banks, technology with global companies, or transaction services. Freshmen are not eligible. Sophomores are eligible for asset management, finance and accounting, investment banking, sales and trading, technology with banks, and transaction services. Juniors are eligible for all fields. Seniors and current graduate students are not eligible. All applicants must have a cumulative GPA of 3.0 or higher. Personal interviews are required.

Financial data Interns receive a competitive stipend of up to $1,300 per week.

Duration 10 weeks during the summer.

Additional information This program began in 1980. Corporate leadership internships are in the New York metro area, New Jersey, Connecticut, Iowa, Massachusetts, North Carolina, Ohio, California, and other areas; banking and private equity internships are in New York City with limited opportunities in New Jersey, Connecticut and possibly Miami or Houston; nonprofit internships are in New York City.

Number awarded Approximately 300 to 400 each year.

Deadline December of each year for sales and trading; January of each year for asset management, consulting, investment banking, investment research, nonprofit sector, private equity, and transaction services; February of each year for engineering, finance and accounting, human resources, marketing and sales, and technology.

[592]
SHARON D. BANKS MEMORIAL UNDERGRADUATE SCHOLARSHIP

Women's Transportation Seminar
Attn: WTS Foundation
1701 K Street, N.W., Suite 800
Washington, DC 20006
(202) 955-5085   Fax: (202) 955-5088
E-mail: wts@wtsinternational.org
Web: www.wtsinternational.org/education/scholarships

Summary To provide financial assistance to undergraduate women, especially African Americans and other minorities, who are interested in a career in transportation.

Eligibility This program is open to women who are working on an undergraduate degree in transportation or a transportation-related field (e.g., transportation engineering, planning, finance, or logistics). Applicants must have a GPA of 3.0 or higher and be interested in a career in transportation. Along with their application, they must submit a 500-word statement about their career goals after graduation and why they think they should receive the scholarship award. Applications must be submitted first to a local chapter; the chapters forward selected applications for consideration on the national level. Minority women are especially encouraged to apply. Selection is based on transportation involvement and goals, job skills, and academic record; financial need is not considered.

Financial data The stipend is $5,000.

Duration 1 year.

Additional information This program began in 1992. Local chapters may also award additional funding to winners in their area.

Number awarded 1 each year.

Deadline Applications must be submitted by November to a local WTS chapter.

[593]
SHELL INCENTIVE FUND SCHOLARSHIPS FOR HIGH SCHOOL SENIORS

Shell Oil Company
Attn: Scholarship Administrator
910 Louisiana, Suite 4476C
Houston, TX 77002
(713) 718-6379
E-mail: SI-Shell-US-Recruitment-Scholarships@shell.
  com
Web: www.shell.us

Summary To provide financial assistance to African American and other minority high school seniors planning to major in specified engineering and geosciences fields in college.

Eligibility This program is open to graduating high school seniors who are members of underrepresented minority groups (Blacks, Hispanic/Latino, American Indian, Alaskan Native) and planning to enroll full time at 22 participating universities. Applicants must be planning to major in engineering (chemical, civil, electrical, geological, geophysical, mechanical, or petroleum) or geosciences (geology, geophysics, or physics). They must be U.S. citizens or authorized to work in the United States. Along with their application, they must sub-

mit a 100-word essay on the kind of work they plan to be doing in 10 years, both in their career and in their community; they should comment specifically on how they could potentially contribute to the petrochemical industry. Financial need is not considered in the selection process.

Financial data The stipend is $2,500.

Duration 1 year; nonrenewable, although recipients may apply for a Shell Incentive Fund Scholarship for Undergraduate Students to cover the remaining years of their undergraduate program.

Additional information This program is managed by International Scholarship and Tuition Services, Inc. The participating institutions are Colorado School of Mines, Cornell University, Florida A&M University, Georgia Institute of Technology, Louisiana State University, Massachusetts Institute of Technology, Michigan State University, North Carolina A&T State University, Ohio State University, Pennsylvania State University, Prairie View A&M University, Purdue University, Rice University, Stanford University, Texas A&M University, University of Colorado at Boulder, University of Houston, University of Illinois at Urbana-Champaign, University of Michigan, University of Oklahoma, University of Texas at Austin, and University of Texas at El Paso.

Number awarded Up to 20 each year.

Deadline February of each year.

[594]
SHELL INCENTIVE FUND SCHOLARSHIPS FOR UNDERGRADUATE STUDENTS

Shell Oil Company
Attn: Scholarship Administrator
910 Louisiana, Suite 4476C
Houston, TX 77002
(713) 718-6379
E-mail: SI-Shell-US-Recruitment-Scholarships@shell.
  com
Web: www.shell.us

Summary To provide financial assistance to African American and other underrepresented minority students majoring in specified engineering and geosciences fields at designated universities.

Eligibility This program is open to students enrolled full time as sophomores, juniors, or seniors at 22 participating universities. Applicants must be U.S. citizens or authorized to work in the United States and members of a race or ethnicity underrepresented in the technical and scientific academic areas (Black, Hispanic/Latino, American Indian, or Alaskan Native). They must have a GPA of 3.2 or higher with a major in engineering (chemical, civil, electrical, geological, geophysical, mechanical, or petroleum) or geosciences (geology, geophysics, or physics). Along with their application, they must submit a 100-word essay on the kind of work they plan to be doing in 10 years, both in their career and in their community. Financial need is not considered in the selection process.

Financial data The stipend is $5,000 per year.

Duration 1 year; may be renewed up to 3 additional years, provided the recipient remains qualified and accepts a Shell Oil Company internship (if offered).

Additional information This program is managed by International Scholarship and Tuition Services Inc. The participating institutions are Colorado School of Mines, Cornell

University, Florida A&M University, Georgia Institute of Technology, Louisiana State University, Massachusetts Institute of Technology, Michigan State University, North Carolina A&T State University, Ohio State University, Pennsylvania State University, Prairie View A&M University, Purdue University, Rice University, Stanford University, Texas A&M University, University of Colorado at Boulder, University of Houston, University of Illinois at Urbana-Champaign, University of Michigan, University of Oklahoma, University of Texas at Austin, and University of Texas at El Paso.

Number awarded Up to 20 each year.

Deadline January of each year.

[595]
SHIRLEY DELIBERO SCHOLARSHIP

American Public Transportation Association
Attn: American Public Transportation Foundation
1666 K Street, N.W., Suite 1100
Washington, DC 20006
(202) 496-4803   Fax: (202) 496-4323
E-mail: pboswell@apta.com
Web: www.aptfd.org/Pages/default.aspx

Summary To provide financial assistance to African American undergraduate and graduate students who are preparing for a career in the public transportation industry.

Eligibility This program is open to African American sophomores, juniors, seniors, and graduate students who are preparing for a career in the transit industry. Any member organization of the American Public Transportation Association (APTA) can nominate and sponsor candidates for this scholarship. Nominees must be enrolled in a fully-accredited institution, have and maintain at least a 3.0 GPA, and be either employed by or demonstrate a strong interest in entering the business administration or management area of the public transportation industry. They must submit a 1,000-word essay on the topic, "In what segment of the public transportation industry will you make a career and why?" Selection is based on demonstrated interest in the transit field as a career, need for financial assistance, academic achievement, essay content and quality, and involvement in extracurricular citizenship and leadership activities.

Financial data The stipend is $2,500.

Duration 1 year; may be renewed.

Number awarded 1 each year.

Deadline June of each year.

[596]
SHPE CHEVRON SCHOLARSHIPS

Society of Hispanic Professional Engineers
Attn: Scholarships
13181 Crossroads Parkway North, Suite 450
City of Industry, CA 91715
(323) 725-3970   Fax: (323) 725-0316
E-mail: scholarships@shpe.org
Web: www.shpe.org/scholarships

Summary To provide financial assistance to African American and other minority undergraduate students who are majoring in designated fields of engineering.

Eligibility This program is open to African American, Latino, and American Indian students who are enrolled full time in an undergraduate engineering program. Applicants must be U.S. citizens or permanent residents and have a GPA of at least 3.0, although preference is given to those with a GPA of 3.3 or higher. Preference is given to, but not limited to, students majoring in computer science or chemical, civil, electrical, or mechanical engineering. Selection is based on academic standing and financial need.

Financial data The stipend is $2,500.

Duration 1 year.

Additional information This program is sponsored by Chevron.

Number awarded 1 or more each year.

Deadline April of each year.

[597]
SIGMA GAMMA RHO SCHOLARSHIPS/ FELLOWSHIPS

Sigma Gamma Rho Sorority, Inc.
Attn: National Education Fund
1000 Southhill Drive, Suite 200
Cary, NC 27513
(919) 678-9720   Toll Free: (888) SGR-1922
Fax: (919) 678-9721
E-mail: customerservice@sgrho1922.org
Web: www.sgrho1922.org/nef

Summary To provide financial assistance for undergraduate or graduate study to applicants who can demonstrate financial need, especially African Americans.

Eligibility This program is open to high school seniors, undergraduates, and graduate students who can demonstrate financial need. The sponsor is a traditionally African American sorority, but support is available to males and females of all races. Applicants must have a GPA of 2.0 or higher.

Financial data A stipend is awarded (amount not specified).

Duration 1 year.

Additional information This program includes the following named awards: the Lorraine A. Williams Scholarship, the Philo Sallie A. Williams Scholarship, the Cleo W. Higgins Scholarship (limited to doctoral students), the Lillie and Carnell VanLandingham Scholarship, the Minnie and William Blakely Book Scholarship, the Inez Colson Memorial Scholarship (limited to students majoring in education or mathematics at Savannah State University), and the Philo Geneva Young Scholarship. A processing fee of $20 is required.

Number awarded Varies each year.

Deadline April of each year.

[598]
SIGNIFICANT OPPORTUNITIES IN ATMOSPHERIC RESEARCH AND SCIENCE (SOARS) PROGRAM

University Corporation for Atmospheric Research
Attn: SOARS Program Manager
3090 Center Green Drive
P.O. Box 3000
Boulder, CO 80307-3000
(303) 497-8622   Fax: (303) 497-8629
E-mail: soars@ucar.edu
Web: www.soars.ucar.edu

Summary To provide summer work experience to undergraduate or graduate students, especially African Americans and those from other underrepresented groups, who are interested in preparing for a career in atmospheric or a related science.

Eligibility This program is open to U.S. citizens or permanent residents who have completed their sophomore year of college and are majoring in atmospheric science or a related field (e.g., biology, chemistry, computer science, earth science, engineering, environmental science, the geosciences, mathematics, meteorology, oceanography, physics, or social science). Applicants must have a GPA of 3.0 or higher and be planning to prepare for a career in the field of atmospheric or a related science. The program especially encourages applications from members of groups that are historically underrepresented in the atmospheric and related sciences, including Blacks/African Americans, Hispanics/Latinos, American Indians/Alaskan Natives, women, first-generation college students, and students with disabilities. It also welcomes applications from students who are gay, lesbian, bisexual, or transgender; have experienced, and worked to overcome, educational or economic disadvantage; or have personal or family circumstances that may complicate their continued progress in research careers.

Financial data Participants receive a competitive stipend and a housing allowance. Round-trip travel between Boulder and any 1 location within the continental United States is also provided. Students who are accepted into a graduate program receive full scholarships (with SOARS and the participating universities each sharing the costs).

Duration 10 weeks during the summer. Students are encouraged to continue for 4 subsequent summers.

Additional information This program began in 1996. Students are assigned positions with a research project. They are exposed to the research facilities at the National Center for Atmospheric Research (NCAR), including computers, libraries, laboratories, and aircraft. NCAR is operated by the University Corporation for Atmospheric Research (a consortium of more than 100 North American universities) with primary support from the National Science Foundation (NSF); other sponsors include the Department of Energy, the Department of Defense, the National Aeronautics and Space Administration (NASA), the Environmental Protection Agency (EPA), the Federal Aviation Administration (FAA), and the National Oceanic and Atmospheric Administration (NOAA). Before completing their senior years, students are encouraged to apply to a master's or doctoral degree program at 1 of the participating universities.

Number awarded Varies each year; recently, 17 were awarded.

Deadline January of each year.

[599]
SINCLAIR BROADCAST DIVERSITY SCHOLARSHIP

Sinclair Broadcast Group, Inc.
10706 Beaver Dam Road
Hunt Valley, MD 21030
(410) 568-1500 E-mail: scholarshipquestions@sbgtv.com
Web: www.sbgi.net/scholarship

Summary To provide financial assistance to college students who are African Americans or members of other underrepresented minority groups and working on a degree in broadcasting, journalism, or marketing.

Eligibility This program is open to students currently enrolled as sophomores or juniors at a 4-year college or university in any state. Applicants must be members of an underrepresented minority group (Asian/Pacific Islander, African American/Black, Hispanic/Latino, or Native American/Alaskan) and taking classes in broadcasting, journalism, or media marketing (although they are not required to be majoring in those fields). They must have a GPA of 3.0 or higher and be able to demonstrate a genuine interest in broadcasting and broadcast journalism. Along with their application, they must submit 1) a 300-word cover letter that explains their personal background, career goals, and financial need; 2) work samples; and 3) a 500-word essay on either the role of journalism in a democracy or why they want a career in broadcasting. In the selection process, consideration is given to academic achievement and work experience, but scholarships are presented only to students who can demonstrate financial need.

Financial data The stipend is $5,000.

Duration 1 year.

Additional information This program began in 2016.

Number awarded Up to 10 each year.

Deadline March of each year.

[600]
SISTER THEA BOWMAN BLACK CATHOLIC EDUCATIONAL FOUNDATION SCHOLARSHIPS

Sister Thea Bowman Black Catholic Educational
  Foundation
c/o Mary Lou Jennings, Executive Director
4870 Woodridge Drive
Hermantown, MN 55811
E-mail: marylouj11@aol.com
Web: www.theabowmanfoundation.org/scholarship.html

Summary To provide financial assistance to African American high school seniors who plan to attend designated Catholic colleges.

Eligibility This program is open to African American seniors graduating from high schools in any state. Applicants must be planning to enroll full time at 1 of the following Catholic colleges and universities: Assumption College (Worcester, Massachusetts), College of Saint Benedict and Saint John's University (Collegeville, Minnesota), College of Saint Mary (Omaha, Nebraska), College of St. Scholastica (Duluth, Minnesota), Duquesne University (Pittsburgh, Pennsylvania), Saint Francis University (Loretto, Pennsylvania), or LaRoche College (Pittsburgh, Pennsylvania). They must have a GPA of 2.5 or higher and be able to demonstrate significant financial need. Along with their application, they must submit a 600-word essay on the impact of the life of Sister Thea Bowman.

Financial data Stipends range from $5,000 to $7,500. Funds are paid directly to the recipient's institution.

Duration 1 year.

Number awarded 1 or more each year.

Deadline March of each year.

[601]
SMILEY SCHOLARS PROGRAM

Tavis Smiley Foundation
Attn: Smiley Scholars
4434 Crenshaw Boulevard
Los Angeles, CA 90043
(323) 290-1888   E-mail: y21@tavistalks.com
Web: www.youthtoleaders.org/smiley_scholars.html

Summary To provide financial assistance for college to high school seniors and college freshmen who have participated in programs of the Tavis Smiley Foundation for African American youth.

Eligibility This program is open to high school seniors and college freshmen who have participated in programs of the Tavis Smiley Foundation (e.g., Youth to Leaders conference series, Youth to Leaders national summit, Tavis Smiley Foundation Leadership Institute, Youth 2 Leaders Ventures of the Talented Tenth High School Tour). Applicants must be enrolled or planning to enroll as full-time students with a GPA of 2.5 or higher. U.S. citizenship is required. Selection is based on academic achievement, evidence of leadership and community service, and participation in foundation programs.

Financial data The stipend is $5,000.

Duration 1 year.

Additional information This program began in 2001.

Number awarded 5 each year.

Deadline October of each year.

[602]
SMITHSONIAN MINORITY AWARDS PROGRAM

Smithsonian Institution
Attn: Office of Fellowships and Internships
470 L'Enfant Plaza, Suite 7102
P.O. Box 37012, MRC 902
Washington, DC 20013-7012
(202) 633-7070   Fax: (202) 633-7069
E-mail: siofi@si.edu
Web: www.smithsonianofi.com

Summary To provide funding to African American and other minority undergraduate and graduate students interested in conducting research at the Smithsonian Institution.

Eligibility This program is open to members of U.S. minority groups underrepresented in the Smithsonian's scholarly programs. Applicants must be undergraduates or beginning graduate students interested in conducting research in the Institution's disciplines and in the museum field. They must be U.S. citizens or permanent residents and have a GPA of 3.0 or higher.

Financial data Students receive a grant of $600 per week.

Duration Up to 10 weeks.

Additional information Recipients must carry out independent research projects in association with the Smithsonian's research staff. Eligible fields of study currently include animal behavior, ecology, and environmental science (including an emphasis on the tropics); anthropology (including archaeology); astrophysics and astronomy; earth sciences and paleobiology; evolutionary and systematic biology; history of science and technology; history of art (especially American, contemporary, African, Asian, and 20th-century art); American crafts and decorative arts; social and cultural history of the United States; and folklife. Students are

required to be in residence at the Smithsonian for the duration of the fellowship.

Number awarded Varies each year; recently, 25 were granted: 2 for fall, 19 for summer, and 4 for spring.

Deadline January of each year for summer and fall residency; September of each year for spring residency.

[603]
SMITHSONIAN MINORITY STUDENT INTERNSHIP

Smithsonian Institution
Attn: Office of Fellowships and Internships
470 L'Enfant, Suite 7102
P.O. Box 37012, MRC 902
Washington, DC 20013-7012
(202) 633-7070   Fax: (202) 633-7069
E-mail: siofi@si.edu
Web: www.smithsonianofi.com/minority-internship-program

Summary To provide African American and other minority undergraduate or graduate students with the opportunity to work on research or museum procedure projects in specific areas of history, art, or science at the Smithsonian Institution.

Eligibility Internships are offered to minority students who are actively engaged in undergraduate or graduate study or have graduated within the past 4 months. Applicants must be U.S. citizens or permanent residents who have an overall GPA of 3.0 or higher. Applicants must be interested in conducting research in any of the following fields of interest to the Smithsonian: animal behavior, ecology, and environmental science (including an emphasis on the tropics); anthropology (including archaeology); astrophysics and astronomy; earth sciences and paleobiology; evolutionary and systematic biology; history of science and technology; history of art (especially American, contemporary, African, Asian, and 20th-century art); American crafts and decorative arts; social and cultural history of the United States; and folklife.

Financial data The program provides a stipend of $600 per week; travel allowances may also be offered.

Duration 10 weeks during the summer or academic year.

Number awarded Varies each year.

Deadline January of each year for summer or fall; September of each year for spring.

[604]
SOUTH EASTERN REGION FELLOWSHIP FOR LIFE-LONG LEARNING

Alpha Kappa Alpha Sorority, Inc.
Attn: Educational Advancement Foundation
5656 South Stony Island Avenue
Chicago, IL 60637
(773) 947-0026   Toll Free: (800) 653-6528
Fax: (773) 947-0277   E-mail: akaeaf@akaeaf.net
Web: www.akaeaf.org/fellowships_endowments.htm

Summary To provide financial assistance to members of Alpha Kappa Alpha (a traditionally African American women's sorority) in southeastern states who are engaged in a program of life-long learning.

Eligibility This program is open to sorority members who are enrolled full time as sophomores or higher in an accredited degree-granting institution and are planning to continue their program of education. Applicants must be residents of

Alabama, Mississippi, or Tennessee and enrolled in a program of life-long learning at a college or university in those states. Along with their application, they must submit 1) a list of honors, awards, and scholarships received; 2) a list of organizations in which they have memberships, especially minority organizations; and 3) a statement of their personal and career goals, including how this scholarship will enhance their ability to attain those goals. The sponsor is a traditionally African American women's sorority.

Financial data A stipend is awarded (amount not specified).

Duration 1 year.

Number awarded 1 each even-numbered year.

Deadline April of each even-numbered year.

[605]
SPHINX COMPETITION AWARDS

Sphinx Organization
Attn: Screening Committee
400 Renaissance Center, Suite 2550
Detroit, MI 48243
(313) 877-9100   Fax: (313) 877-0164
E-mail: Competition@sphinxmusic.org
Web: www.sphinxmusic.org/sphinx-competition

Summary To recognize and reward outstanding junior high, high school, and college-age Black and Latino string instrumentalists.

Eligibility This competition is open to Black and Latino instrumentalists in 2 divisions: junior, for participants who are 17 years of age or younger, and senior, for participants who are between 18 and 30 years of age. All entrants must be current U.S. residents who can compete in the instrumental categories of violin, viola, cello, and double bass. Along with their applications, they must submit a preliminary audition tape that includes all of the required preliminary repertoire for their instrument category. Based on those tapes, qualifiers are invited to participate in the semifinals and finals competitions, held at sites in Detroit and Ann Arbor, Michigan.

Financial data In the senior division, the first-place winner receives the Robert Frederick Smith Prize of $50,000, solo appearances with major orchestras, and a performance with the Sphinx Symphony; the second-place winner receives a $20,000 cash prize and a performance with the Sphinx Symphony; and the third-place winner receives a $10,000 cash prize and a performance with the Sphinx Symphony. In the junior division, the first-place winner receives a $10,000 cash prize, solo appearances with major orchestras, a national radio debut, and performances with the Sphinx Symphony; the second-place winner receives a $5,000 cash prize and a performance with the Sphinx Symphony; the third-place winner receives a $3,000 cash prize and a performance with the Sphinx Symphony. All semifinalists receive scholarships to attend designated summer programs. They also receive full tuition scholarships for their instrumental studies at selected colleges and universities from the Sphinx Music Assistance Fund (MAF) of the League of American Orchestras.

Duration The competition is held annually.

Additional information The sponsoring organization was incorporated in 1996 to hold this competition, first conducted in 1998. The Sphinx Symphony is an all African American and Latino orchestra that performs at Orchestra Hall in Detroit. The MAF program was established by the New York Philharmonic in 1965, transferred to the American Symphony Orchestra League in 1994, and to the League of American Orchestras in 2001. In 2002, it partnered with the Sphinx Organization to provide scholarships to all 18 semifinalists. Applications must be accompanied by a $35 fee. That fee may be waived from both divisions and all instrumental categories if demonstrable need is shown.

Number awarded 18 semifinalists (9 from each age division) are selected each year. Of those, 3 junior and 3 senior competitors win cash prizes.

Deadline November of each year.

[606]
SSRP-AMGEN SCHOLARS PROGRAM

Stanford University
School of Medicine
Attn: Office of Graduate Education
MSOB X1C20
1265 Welch Road
Stanford, CA 94305-5421
(650) 725-8791   Fax: (650) 725-3867
E-mail: ssrpmail@stanford.edu
Web: biosciences.stanford.edu/prospective/diversity/ssrp

Summary To provide African American and other underrepresented minority undergraduate students with a summer research experience at Stanford University in biological and biomedical sciences.

Eligibility This program is open to sophomores, juniors, and non-graduating seniors at 4-year colleges and universities in the United States, Puerto Rico, and U.S. territories. Students from all ethnic backgrounds are eligible, but the program especially encourages applications from African Americans, Latino/Hispanic Americans, Native Americans, Pacific Islanders, and other undergraduates who, by reason of their culture, class, race, ethnicity, background, work and life experiences, skills, and interests would bring diversity to graduate study in the biological and biomedical sciences (biochemistry, bioengineering, biology, biomedical informatics, biophysics, cancer biology, chemical and systems biology, developmental biology, genetics, immunology, microbiology, molecular and cellular physiology, neurosciences, stem cell and regenerative medicine, and structural biology). Applicants must have at least 1 year of undergraduate education remaining before graduation and should be planning to prepare for and enter a Ph.D. program in the biological or biomedical sciences. They must have a GPA of 3.2 or higher. U.S. citizenship or permanent resident status is required.

Financial data The program provides a stipend of $3,500, housing, meals, and transportation to and from the San Francisco Bay area.

Duration 9 weeks during the summer.

Additional information This program encompasses 1) the Stanford component of the Amgen Scholars Program, which operates at 8 other U.S. universities (and the National Institutes of Health) and is funded by the Amgen Foundation; 2) Genetics Department Funding; and 3) Stanford Medicine Dean's Funding.

Number awarded 30 to 35 each year.

Deadline January of each year.

[607]
STATE COUNCIL ON ADAPTED PHYSICAL EDUCATION CULTURAL DIVERSITY STUDENT SCHOLARSHIP

California Association for Health, Physical Education, Recreation and Dance
Attn: State Council on Adapted Physical Education
1501 El Camino Avenue, Suite 3
Sacramento, CA 95815-2748
(916) 922-3596   Toll Free: (800) 499-3596 (within CA)
Fax: (916) 922-0133
E-mail: califstatecouncilape@gmail.com
Web: www.califstatecouncilape.org

Summary To provide financial assistance to African American and other culturally diverse members of the California Association for Health, Physical Education, Recreation and Dance (CAHPERD) who are preparing to become a student teacher in the field of adapted physical education.

Eligibility This program is open to CAHPERD members who are attending a California college or university and specializing in the field of adapted physical education. Applicants must be members of an ethnic or cultural minority group (e.g., African American, American Indian/Native American, Asian American, Filipino, Mexican American, other Latino, Pacific Islander). They must be planning to become a student teacher during the following academic year. Along with their application, they must submit a 300-word statement of their professional goals and philosophy of physical education for individuals with disabilities. Selection is based on academic proficiency; leadership ability; personal qualities; school, community, and professional activities; and experience and interest in working with individuals with disabilities.

Financial data The stipend is $1,000.

Duration 1 year.

Number awarded 1 each year.

Deadline January of each year.

[608]
STEPS TO SUCCESS-THE DOUG PAUL SCHOLARSHIP PROGRAM

Credit Suisse
Attn: Diversity and Inclusion Programs
Eleven Madison Avenue
New York, NY 10010-3629
(212) 325-2000   Fax: (212) 325-6665
E-mail: campus.diversity@credit-suisse.com
Web: www.credit-suisse.com

Summary To provide financial assistance and work experience at Credit Suisse in New York to African American and other underrepresented minority undergraduate students interested in a career in financial services.

Eligibility This program is open to college students entering their junior year who are Black/African American, Hispanic/Latino, or Native American. Applicants must be preparing for a career in financial services by studying such fields as asset management, equity research, finance, investment banking, information technology, operations, and sales and trading. They must be interested in an internship in New York with Credit Suisse. Selection is based on academic excellence, leadership ability, and interest in the financial services industry.

Financial data Students who complete the summer internship receive a stipend of $5,000 for the following year of academic study.

Duration The internship is 10 weeks during the summer, followed by a year of academic study (the junior year) and a possible renewal of the internship the following summer.

Number awarded 1 or more each year.

Deadline June of each year.

[609]
STUDENT OPPORTUNITY SCHOLARSHIPS OF THE PRESBYTERIAN CHURCH (USA)

Presbyterian Church (USA)
Attn: Office of Financial Aid for Service
100 Witherspoon Street
Louisville, KY 40202-1396
(502) 569-5224   Toll Free: (888) 728-7228, ext. 5224
Fax: (502) 569-8766   TDD: (800) 833-5955
E-mail: finaid@pcusa.org
Web: www.presbyterianmission.org

Summary To provide financial assistance to Presbyterian college students, especially African Americans and those of other racial/ethnic minority heritage.

Eligibility This program is open to active members of the Presbyterian Church (USA) who are entering their sophomore, junior, or senior year of college as full-time students in a bachelor's degree program. Preference is given to applicants who are members of racial/ethnic minority groups (African American, Asian American, Hispanic American, Native American, Alaska Native). Applicants must have a GPA of 2.5 or higher and be able to demonstrate financial need.

Financial data Stipends range up to $2,000 per year, depending upon the financial need of the recipient.

Duration 1 year; may be renewed if the recipient continues to need financial assistance and demonstrates satisfactory academic progress.

Number awarded Approximately 80 each year.

Deadline May of each year.

[610]
SUMMER AFFIRMATIVE ACTION INTERNSHIP PROGRAM

Wisconsin Office of State Employment Relations
Attn: Division of Affirmative Action Workforce Planning
101 East Wilson Street, Fourth Floor
P.O. Box 7855
Madison, WI 53707-7855
(608) 266-6475   Fax: (608) 267-1020
E-mail: OSERDAA@wi.gov
Web: oser.state.wi.us/category.asp?linkcatid=342

Summary To provide an opportunity for African Americans and members of other underrepresented groups to gain summer work experience with agencies of the state of Wisconsin.

Eligibility This program is open to women, ethnic/racial minorities (Black or African American, Asian, Native Hawaiian or other Pacific Islander, American Indian or Alaska Native, or Hispanic or Latino), and persons with disabilities. Applicants must be sophomores, juniors, seniors, or graduate students at an accredited 4-year college or university or second-year students in the second year of a 2-year technical or vocational school program. They must be 1) Wisconsin residents enrolled full time at a school in Wisconsin or any other state; or 2) residents of other states who are enrolled full time at a school in Wisconsin.

Financial data Most internships provide a competitive stipend.

Duration Summer months.

Additional information This program began in 1974. Internships are available in criminal justice, engineering, finance/accounting, human resources, information technology, legal research, library science, public administration, recreational leadership, research analyst, social work, vocational/rehabilitation therapy, and various other government jobs.

Number awarded Varies each year. Since the program was established, it has placed more than 3,100 students with more than 30 different agencies and universities throughout the state.

Deadline February of each year.

[611]
SUMMER CLINICAL AND TRANSLATIONAL RESEARCH PROGRAM

Harvard Medical School
Office for Diversity Inclusion and Community Partnership
Attn: Program for Faculty Development and Diversity
  Inclusion
164 Longwood Avenue, Second Floor
Boston, MA 02115-5810
(617) 432-1892   Fax: (617) 432-3834
E-mail: pfdd_dcp@hms.harvard.edu
Web: mfdp.med.harvard.edu

Summary To provide an opportunity for undergraduate students, especially African Americans and other underrepresented minorities, to engage in research at Harvard Medical School during the summer.

Eligibility This program is open to undergraduate sophomores, juniors, and seniors who are preparing for a career in medical research. Priority is given to students at schools that receive funding from the Minority Biomedical Research Support (MBRS) or Minority Access to Research Careers (MARC) programs of the National Institute of Health (NIH), Historically Black Colleges and Universities (HBCUs), Hispanic Serving Institutions (HSIs), or Tribal Colleges and Universities (TCUs). Applicants must be interested in working on a summer research program at Harvard Medical School under the mentorship of a faculty advisor. They must be interested in a research and health-related career, especially in clinical or translational research or research that transforms scientific discoveries arising from laboratory, clinical, or population studies into clinical or population-based applications to improve health. U.S. citizenship, nationality, or permanent resident status is required.

Financial data Participants receive a stipend (amount not specified), housing, and reimbursement of transportation costs to Boston up to $400.

Duration 10 weeks during the summer.

Additional information This program, established in 2008, is funded by the National Center for Research Resources of the NIH. It is a joint enterprise of Harvard University, its 10 schools, its 17 Academic Healthcare Centers, Boston College School of Nursing, MIT, the Cambridge Health Alliance, and other community partners. Interns attend weekly seminars with Harvard faculty focusing on such topics as research methodology, health disparities, ethics, and career paths. They also have the opportunity to participate in offerings of other Harvard Medical School programs, such a career development seminars and networking dinners.

Number awarded Varies each year; recently, 10 college students were admitted to this program.

Deadline December of each year.

[612]
SUMMER HONORS UNDERGRADUATE RESEARCH PROGRAM

Harvard Medical School
Attn: Division of Medical Sciences
Diversity Programs Office
260 Longwood Avenue, T-MEC 335
Boston, MA 02115-5720
(617) 432-4980   Toll Free: (800) 367-9019
Fax: (617) 432-2644   E-mail: shurp@hms.harvard.edu
Web: www.hms.harvard.edu/dms/diversity/shurp

Summary To provide an opportunity for African Americans and other underrepresented minority students to engage in research at Harvard Medical School during the summer.

Eligibility This program at Harvard Medical School is open to undergraduate students belonging to minority groups that are underrepresented in the sciences. Applicants must have had at least 1 summer (or equivalent) of experience in a research laboratory and have taken at least 1 upper-level biology course that includes molecular biology. They should be considering a career in biological or biomedical research. U.S. citizenship or permanent resident status is required.

Financial data The program provides a stipend of $450 per week, dormitory housing, travel costs, a meal card, and health insurance if it is needed.

Duration 10 weeks during the summer.

Number awarded Varies each year.

Deadline January of each year.

[613]
SUMMER INTERNSHIP PROGRAM IN BIOMEDICAL RESEARCH

National Institutes of Health
Attn: Office of Intramural Training and Education
2 Center Drive, Room 2E06
Bethesda, MD 20892-0240
(301) 496-2427   Toll Free: (888) 695-5343
Fax: (301) 594-9606
E-mail: Summer_Postbac_Questions@mail.nih.gov
Web: www.training.nih.gov/programs/sip

Summary To enable students, especially African Americans and other underrepresented minorities, to receive training and participate in ongoing research studies in a variety of laboratory and clinically-related disciplines at the National Institutes of Health (NIH) during the summer.

Eligibility This program is open to graduate, health professions, undergraduate, and high school students who have a strong interest in preparing for a career related to biomedical or behavioral research, including the disciplines of biology, chemistry, physical science, psychology, computer science, biostatistics, mathematics, and biomedical engineering. They must be at least 16 years of age and U.S. citizens, nationals, or permanent residents.

Financial data Salaries depend on the academic level of the recipient, ranging from $1,740 per month for high school students before graduation to $1,940 for high school students after graduation, $2,040 to $2,240 for college students (depending on number of years completed), or $2,340 to $3,160 per month for graduate students (depending on number of years completed).

Duration 8 to 10 weeks, in the summer.

Additional information Most components of the National Institutes of Health participate in this program. Some of them reserve positions for interns who are members of minority groups underrepresented in the biomedical and behavioral sciences (African Americans, Hispanics, Native Americans, and Pacific Islanders). Most laboratories are located in Bethesda, Maryland, but others are in Baltimore, Frederick, and Rockville, Maryland; Detroit, Michigan; Research Triangle Park, North Carolina; Phoenix, Arizona; and Hamilton, Montana.

Number awarded Varies each year; recently, approximately 1,100 interns were selected.

Deadline February of each year.

[614]
SUMMER PROGRAM IN BIOSTATISTICS AND COMPUTATIONAL BIOLOGY

Harvard T.H. Chan School of Public Health
Department of Biostatistics
Attn: Diversity Coordinator
677 Huntington Avenue, SPH2, Fourth Floor
Boston, MA 02115
(617) 432-3175 Fax: (617) 432-5619
E-mail: biostat_diversity@hsph.harvard.edu
Web: www.hsph.harvard.edu

Summary To enable African American and other underrepresented minority or disadvantaged science undergraduates to participate in a summer research internship at Harvard T.H. Chan School of Public Health that focuses on biostatistics, epidemiology, and public health.

Eligibility This program is open to 1) members of ethnic groups underrepresented in graduate education (African Americans, Hispanic/Latinos, Native Americans, Pacific Islanders, biracial/multiracial); 2) first-generation college students; 3) low-income students; or 4) individuals with a disability. Applicants must be current undergraduates interested in participating in a summer program on the use of quantitative methods for biological, environmental, and medical research as preparation for graduate studies in biostatistics or computational biology. They must have a strong GPA, including course work in calculus, and a strong interest in mathematics, statistics, computer science, and other quantitative subjects. U.S. citizenship or permanent resident status is required.

Financial data Funding covers travel, housing, course materials, and a stipend to cover meals and incidentals.

Duration 6 weeks, starting in June.

Additional information Interns take non-credit classes in biostatistics and epidemiology, participate in a collaborative research project, and travel to local laboratories and research centers to observe public health research in action.

Number awarded Normally 12 each year.

Deadline January of each year.

[615]
SUMMER PROGRAM IN EPIDEMIOLOGY

Harvard T.H. Chan School of Public Health
Department of Epidemiology
655 Huntington Avenue
Boston, MA 02115
(617) 432-1050 Fax: (617) 566-7805
E-mail: edigiova@hsph.harvard.edu
Web: www.hsph.harvard.edu

Summary To enable African American and other underrepresented minority or disadvantaged undergraduates to participate in a summer research program in epidemiology at Harvard T.H. Chan School of Public Health.

Eligibility This program is open to undergraduate students who 1) are U.S. citizens, nationals, or permanent residents; 2) have a GPA of 3.0 or higher; 3) have a quantitative science background or have taken several quantitative classes beyond introductory level courses; 4) can demonstrate an interest in public health; and 5) are from at least 1 underrepresented group in biomedical research, including people with disabilities, members of minority racial and ethnic groups (African Americans, Hispanic/Latinos, Native Americans, Pacific Islanders), people of disadvantaged and low socioeconomic status, members of families with annual income below established thresholds, and people from a rural, inner-city, or other environment that has inhibited them from getting the knowledge, skills, and abilities needed for a research career. They must be planning to apply to a graduate program to work on a master's or doctoral degree in epidemiology; students planning to apply to medical school and students already accepted to graduate school are not eligible.

Financial data Interns receive a salary (amount not specified) and support for travel.

Duration 5 weeks, during the summer.

Additional information The program includes introductory course work in epidemiology and biostatistics, formal lectures by faculty at the Harvard T.H. Chan School of Public Health, a group research project, and a Kaplan GRE course.

Number awarded Varies each year; recently, 8 were awarded.

Deadline February of each year.

[616]
SUMMER RESEARCH OPPORTUNITIES PROGRAM (SROP)

Committee on Institutional Cooperation
Attn: Academic and International Programs
1819 South Neil Street, Suite D
Champaign, IL 61820-7271
(217) 333-8475 Fax: (217) 244-7127
E-mail: cic@staff.cic.net
Web: www.cic.net/students/srop/introduction

Summary To provide an opportunity for African American and other diverse undergraduates to gain research experience at member institutions of the Committee on Institutional Cooperation (CIC) during the summer.

Eligibility This program is open to students currently enrolled in a degree-granting program at a college or university who have a GPA of 3.0 or higher and an interest in continuing on to graduate school. Applicants must be interested in conducting a summer research project under the supervision of a faculty mentor at a CIC member institution. The program is designed to increase educational access for students from diverse backgrounds; members of racial and ethnic minority groups and low-income first-generation students are especially encouraged to apply. U.S. citizenship or permanent resident status is required.

Financial data Participants are paid a stipend that depends on the participating CIC member institution, but ranges from $3,000 to $6,000. Faculty mentors receive a $500 research allowance for the cost of materials.

Duration 8 to 10 weeks during the summer.

Additional information Participants work directly with faculty mentors at the institution of their choice and engage in other enrichment activities, such as workshops and social gatherings. In July, all participants come together at 1 of the CIC campuses for the annual SROP conference. The participating CIC member institutions are University of Illinois at Urbana-Champaign, University of Iowa, University of Michigan, University of Minnesota, University of Nebraska at Lincoln, University of Wisconsin at Madison, Michigan State University, Northwestern University, Ohio State University, Pennsylvania State University, Purdue University, and Rutgers University. Students are required to write a paper and an abstract describing their projects and to present the results of their work at a campus symposium.

Number awarded Varies each year.

Deadline February of each year.

[617]
SUMMER RESEARCH PROGRAM IN ECOLOGY

Harvard University
Harvard Forest
324 North Main Street
Petersham, MA 01366
(978) 724-3302　　　　　　　　Fax: (978) 724-3595
E-mail: hfapps@fas.harvard.edu
Web: harvardforest.fas.harvard.edu/other-tags/reu

Summary To provide an opportunity for undergraduate students and recent graduates, especially African Americans and members of other diverse groups, to participate in a summer ecological research project at Harvard Forest in Petersham, Massachusetts.

Eligibility This program is open to undergraduate students and recent graduates interested in participating in a mentored research project at the Forest. The research may relate to the effects of natural and human disturbances on forest ecosystems, including global climate change, hurricanes, forest harvest, changing wildlife dynamics, or invasive species. Investigators come from many disciplines, and specific projects center on population and community ecology, paleoecology, land use history, aquatic ecology, biochemistry, soil science, ecophysiology, and atmosphere-biosphere exchanges. Students from diverse backgrounds are strongly encouraged to apply.

Financial data The stipend is $5,775. Free housing, meals, and travel reimbursement for 1 round trip are also provided.

Duration 11 weeks during the summer.

Additional information Funding for this program is provided by the National Science Foundation (as part of its Research Experience for Undergraduates program).

Number awarded Up to 25 each year.

Deadline February of each year.

[618]
SUMMER TRANSPORTATION INTERNSHIP PROGRAM FOR DIVERSE GROUPS

Department of Transportation
Attn: Summer Transportation Internship Program for
　Diverse Groups
Eighth Floor E81-105
1200 New Jersey Avenue, S.E.
Washington, DC 20590
(202) 366-2907　　　　　　E-mail: Crystal.Taylor@dot.gov
Web: www.fhwa.dot.gov/education/stipdg.cfm

Summary To enable undergraduate, graduate, and law students from African American and other diverse groups to gain work experience during the summer at facilities of the U.S. Department of Transportation (DOT).

Eligibility This program is open to all qualified applicants, but it is designed to provide women, persons with disabilities, and members of diverse social and ethnic groups with summer opportunities in transportation. Applicants must be U.S. citizens currently enrolled in a degree-granting program of study at an accredited institution of higher learning at the undergraduate (community or junior college, university, college, or Tribal College or University) or graduate level. Undergraduates must be entering their junior or senior year; students attending a Tribal or community college must have completed their first year of school; law students must be entering their second or third year of school. Students who will graduate during the spring or summer are not eligible unless they have been accepted for enrollment in graduate school. The program accepts applications from students in all majors who are interested in working on transportation-related topics and issues. Preference is given to students with a GPA of 3.0 or higher. Undergraduates must submit a 1-page essay on their transportation interests and how participation in this program will enhance their educational and career plans and goals. Graduate students must submit a writing sample representing their educational and career plans and goals. Law students must submit a legal writing sample.

Financial data The stipend is $4,000 for undergraduates or $5,000 for graduate and law students. The program also provides housing and reimbursement of travel expenses from interns' homes to their assignment location.

Duration 10 weeks during the summer.

Additional information Assignments are at the DOT headquarters in Washington, D.C., a selected modal administration, or selected field offices around the country.

Number awarded 80 to 100 each year.

Deadline January of each year.

[619]
SUMMER UNDERGRADUATE RESEARCH FELLOW (SURF) INDIVIDUAL AWARDS

American Society for Pharmacology and Experimental
 Therapeutics
9650 Rockville Pike
Bethesda, MD 20814-3995
(301) 634-7060　　　　　　　　　Fax: (301) 634-7061
E-mail: cfry@aspet.org
Web: www.aspet.org/awards/SURF

Summary To provide funding to undergraduate students, especially African Americans and members of other under-represented groups, who are interested in participating in a summer research project at a laboratory affiliated with the American Society for Pharmacology and Experimental Therapeutics (ASPET).

Eligibility This program is open to undergraduate students interested in working during the summer in the laboratory of a society member who must agree to act as a mentor. Fields of study include pharmacology, toxicology, pharmaceutical sciences, and/or biological chemistry. Applications must be submitted jointly by the student and the mentor, and they must include 1) a letter from the mentor with a brief description of the proposed research, a statement of the qualifications of the student, the degree of independence the student will have, a description of enrichment activities available to the student, and a description of how the student will report on the research results; 2) a 500-word statement from the student indicating the nature of their interest in the research project and how participation would contribute to their career goals; 3) a copy of the sponsor's updated curriculum vitae; and 4) copies of all the student's undergraduate transcripts. Selection is based on the nature of the research opportunities provided, student and sponsor qualifications, and the likelihood the student will prepare for a career in pharmacology. Applications from those traditionally underrepresented in the biomedical sciences are particularly encouraged.

Financial data The stipend is $2,800. Funds are paid directly to the institution but may be used only for student stipends.

Duration 10 weeks during the summer.

Additional information Some of these awards are funded through the Glenn E. Ullyot Fund; those recipients are designated as the Ullyot Fellows.

Number awarded Varies each year; recently, 4 were awarded.

Deadline February of each year.

[620]
SUMMER UNDERGRADUATE RESEARCH FELLOWSHIPS IN ORGANIC CHEMISTRY

American Chemical Society
Division of Organic Chemistry
1155 16th Street, N.W.
Washington, DC 20036
(202) 872-4401　　　　Toll Free: (800) 227-5558, ext. 4401
E-mail: division@acs.org
Web: www.organicdivision.org/?nd=p_surf_program

Summary To provide an opportunity for college juniors, especially African Americans and other minorities, to work on a research project in organic chemistry during the summer.

Eligibility This program is open to students who are currently enrolled as juniors at a college or university in the United States and are nominated by their school. Nominees must be interested in conducting a research project in organic chemistry at their home institution during the following summer. The project must be mentored by a member of the Organic Division of the American Chemical Society. Along with their application, students must submit brief statements on the project they propose to undertake, their background that has prepared them to do this work, their proposed methodology, and how a summer research project fits into their long-range plans. U.S. citizenship or permanent resident status is required. Selection is based on demonstrated interest and talent in organic chemistry, merit and feasibility of the research project, commitment of a faculty mentor to support the student, academic record (particularly in organic chemistry and related sciences), and importance of the award in facilitating the personal and career plans of the student. Applications from minorities are especially encouraged.

Financial data Grants range up to $5,000. The program also covers the costs of a trip by all participants to an industrial campus in the fall for a dinner, award session, scientific talks, a tour of the campus, and a poster session where the results of the summer research investigations are presented.

Duration Summer months.

Additional information Current corporate sponsors of this program include Pfizer and Cubist Pharmaceuticals.

Number awarded Up to 12 each year.

Deadline January of each year.

[621]
SURETY AND FIDELITY INDUSTRY SCHOLARSHIP PROGRAM

The Surety Foundation
Attn: Scholarship Program for Minority Students
1101 Connecticut Avenue, N.W., Suite 800
Washington, DC 20036
(202) 463-0600, ext. 638　　　　　Fax: (202) 463-0606
E-mail: scarradine@surety.org
Web: www.thesuretyfoundation.org

Summary To provide financial assistance to African American and other minority undergraduates working on a degree in a field related to insurance.

Eligibility This program is open to full-time undergraduates who are U.S. citizens and members of a minority group (Black, Native American/Alaskan Native, Asian/Pacific Islander, Hispanic). Applicants must have completed at least 30 semester hours of study at an accredited 4-year college or university and have a declared major in insurance/risk management, accounting, business, or finance. They must have a GPA of 3.0 or higher and be able to demonstrate financial need.

Financial data The stipend is $5,000 per year.

Duration 1 year; recipients may reapply.

Additional information This program, established in 2003 by The Surety & Fidelity Association of America, includes the Adrienne Alexander Scholarship and the George W. McClellan Scholarship.

Number awarded Varies each year; recently, 3 were awarded.

Deadline January of each year.

[622]
SYLVIA C. EDGE ENDOWMENT SCHOLARSHIP

New Jersey State Nurses Association
Attn: Institute for Nursing
1479 Pennington Road
Trenton, NJ 08618-2661
(609) 883-5335, ext. 111   Fax: (609) 883-5343
E-mail: sandy@njsna.org
Web: www.njsna.org/?Scholarships

Summary   To provide financial assistance to New Jersey residents of African descent who are preparing for a career as a nurse.

Eligibility   Applicants must be New Jersey residents of African descent currently enrolled in a diploma, associate, or baccalaureate nursing program located in the state. Selection is based on financial need, GPA, and leadership potential.

Financial data   The stipend is $1,000.

Duration   1 year.

Number awarded   1 each year.

Deadline   January of each year.

[623]
SYNOD OF LAKES AND PRAIRIES RACIAL ETHNIC SCHOLARSHIPS

Synod of Lakes and Prairies
Attn: Committee on Racial Ethnic Ministry
2115 Cliff Drive
Eagen, MN 55122-3327
(651) 357-1140   Toll Free: (800) 328-1880, ext. 202
Fax: (651) 357-1141   E-mail: mkes@lakesandprairies.org
Web: www.lakesandprairies.org

Summary   To provide financial assistance to African American and other minority residents of the Presbyterian Church (USA) Synod of Lakes and Prairies who are working on an undergraduate or graduate degree at a college or seminary in any state as preparation for service to the church.

Eligibility   This program is open to members of Presbyterian churches who reside within the Synod of Lakes and Prairies (Iowa, Minnesota, Nebraska, North Dakota, South Dakota, and Wisconsin). Applicants must be members of ethnic minority groups studying at least half time for service in the Presbyterian Church (USA) as a teaching elder, ordained minister, commissioned ruling elder, lay professional, or volunteer. They must be in good academic standing, making progress toward an undergraduate or graduate degree, and able to demonstrate financial need. Along with their application, they must submit essays of 200 to 500 words on 1) what the church needs to do to be faithful to its mission in the world today; and 2) the people, practices, or events that influence their commitment to Christ in ways that renew their fair and strengthen their service.

Financial data   Stipends range from $850 to $3,500.

Duration   1 year.

Number awarded   Varies each year; recently, 9 were awarded.

Deadline   September of each year.

[624]
TABOR 100 CULINARY ARTS SCHOLARSHIPS

Tabor 100
Attn: Scholarships
2330 130th Avenue, N.E., Suite 101
Bellevue, WA 98005
(206) 368-4042   E-mail: education@tabor100.org
Web: www.tabor100.org/EID/spaceneedle.html

Summary   To provide financial assistance to African Americans with ties to the Puget Sound region who are interested in attending college to prepare for a career in culinary arts or the hospitality industry.

Eligibility   This program is open to African Americans who either have a home address or attend college in the Puget Sound region. Applicants must be enrolled or planning to enroll in almost any academic course of study as long as they can demonstrate that their career orientation supports working in green or sustainable energy arenas. They must be able to demonstrate financial need and a record of high academic achievement and/or potential. Along with their application, they must submit a 500-word essay on what they see as their role in serving as an inspiration for high school students of color in the culinary or hospitality industry.

Financial data   The stipend is $2,500 per year.

Duration   1 year; may be renewed 1 additional year.

Additional information   This program consists of the Space Needle Culinary Arts Scholarship and the Chihuly Garden and Glass Culinary Arts Scholarship. It is sponsored by Space Needle LLC.

Number awarded   2 each year.

Deadline   July of each year.

[625]
TABOR 100 GREEN ENERGY SCHOLARSHIPS

Tabor 100
Attn: Scholarships
2330 130th Avenue, N.E., Suite 101
Bellevue, WA 98005
(206) 368-4042   E-mail: education@tabor100.org
Web: www.tabor100.org/EID/pse.html

Summary   To provide financial assistance to African Americans with ties to the Puget Sound region who are interested in attending college to prepare for a career in a field related to green energy.

Eligibility   This program is open to African Americans who either have a home address or attend college in the Puget Sound region. Applicants must be enrolled or planning to enroll in an academic course of study that will prepare them for a career in culinary arts or the hospitality industry. They must be able to demonstrate financial need and a record of high academic achievement and/or potential. Along with their application, they must submit a 500-word essay on how they plan to use their degree knowledge and experience in responding to the demand for green energy solutions.

Financial data   The stipend is $3,500 per year.

Duration   1 year; may be renewed 2 additional years.

Additional information   This program is sponsored by Puget Sound Energy (PSE), Boeing Employees Credit Union (BECU), and Craft3.

Number awarded   3 each year.

Deadline   July of each year.

[626]
THOMAS DARGAN MINORITY SCHOLARSHIP

KATU-TV
Attn: Human Resources
2153 N.E. Sandy Boulevard
P.O. Box 2
Portland, OR 97207-0002
(503) 231-4222
Web: www.katu.com

Summary To provide financial assistance to African American and other minority students from Oregon and Washington who are studying broadcasting or communications in college.

Eligibility This program is open to minority (Black/African American, Asian, Hispanic or Latino, Native Hawaiian or Pacific Islander, American Indian or Alaska Native) U.S. citizens, currently enrolled as a sophomore or higher at a 4-year college or university or an accredited community college in Oregon or Washington. Residents of Oregon or Washington enrolled at a school in any state are also eligible. Applicants must be majoring in broadcasting or communications and have a GPA of 3.0 or higher. Community college students must be enrolled in a broadcast curriculum that is transferable to a 4-year accredited university. Finalists are interviewed. Selection is based on financial need, academic achievement, and an essay on personal and professional goals.

Financial data The stipend is $6,000. Funds are sent directly to the recipient's school.

Duration 1 year; recipients may reapply if they have maintained a GPA of 3.0 or higher.

Additional information Winners are also eligible for a paid internship in selected departments at Fisher Broadcasting/KATU in Portland, Oregon.

Number awarded 1 each year.

Deadline April of each year.

[627]
THOMAS G. NEUSOM SCHOLARSHIPS

Conference of Minority Transportation Officials
Attn: National Scholarship Program
100 M Street, S.E., Suite 917
Washington, DC 20003
(202) 506-2917   E-mail: info@comto.org
Web: www.comto.org/page/scholarships

Summary To provide financial assistance for college or graduate school to African American and other minority members of the Conference of Minority Transportation Officials (COMTO) and their families.

Eligibility This program is open to undergraduate and graduate students who have been members of COMTO or whose parents, guardians, or grandparents have been members for at least 1 year. Applicants must be working (either full or part time) on a degree in a field related to transportation and have a GPA of 2.5 or higher. Along with their application they must submit a cover letter on their transportation-related career goals and life aspirations. Financial need is not considered in the selection process.

Financial data The stipend is $5,500. Funds are paid directly to the recipient's college or university.

Duration 1 year.

Number awarded 1 each year.

Deadline April of each year.

[628]
THOMAS HALBERT SCHOLARSHIP

Community Foundation of the Ozarks
Attn: Scholarship Coordinator
421 East Trafficway
P.O. Box 8960
Springfield, MO 65801-8960
(417) 864-6199   Toll Free: (888) 266-6815
Fax: (417) 864-8344   E-mail: bhersh@cfozarks.org
Web: www.cfozarks.org/scholarships/scholarships/view/174

Summary To provide financial assistance to students, especially African Americans, at nursing schools in Springfield, Missouri who have been admitted to a degree program.

Eligibility This program is open to residents of any state who are attending or entering a nursing school in Springfield, Missouri and who have been accepted to work on a nursing degree. Applicants must submit a high school transcript with cumulative GPA and ACT/SAT scores or a college transcript with cumulative GPA. Preference is given to qualified African American candidates. In the selection process, primary consideration is given to financial need; secondary consideration is given to academic achievement, leadership abilities, and moral character.

Financial data The stipend is $1,250 per year.

Duration 1 year; recipients may reapply.

Number awarded 1 each year.

Deadline March of each year.

[629]
THOMAS R. LEE, JR. SCHOLARSHIPS

Knights of Peter Claver, Inc.
Attn: The Claver Foundation
1825 Orleans Avenue
New Orleans, LA 70116-2894
(504) 821-4225   Fax: (504) 821-4253
E-mail: info@claverfundation.org
Web: www.claverfoundation.org/programs

Summary To provide financial assistance for college to high school seniors with a connection of the Knights of Peter Claver (an organization for Catholic men of color).

Eligibility This program is open to practicing Catholics who are graduating high school seniors planning to attend a college or university. Applicants, or at least 1 of their parents, must be a member of the Knights of Peter Claver or its Ladies Auxiliary. They must rank in the top quarter of their class and have scores of at least 900 on the SAT or 18 on the ACT. U.S. citizenship is required.

Financial data The stipend is $2,000 per year.

Duration 2 years, provided the recipient maintains a GPA of 3.0 or higher during the freshman year of college.

Additional information The Knights of Peter Claver was founded in 1909 at Mobile, Alabama as a Catholic fraternal society for men of color.

Number awarded 2 each year.

Deadline May of each year.

[630]
THOMAS R. PICKERING FOREIGN AFFAIRS FELLOWSHIPS

The Washington Center for Internships
Attn: Foreign Affairs Fellowship Program
1333 16th Street, N.W.
Washington, DC 20036-2205
(202) 238-7900   Fax: (202) 238-7700
E-mail: info@twc.org
Web: www.twc.edu

Summary To provide forgivable loans to undergraduate and graduate students, especially African Americans and members of other underrepresented groups, who are interested in preparing for a career with the Department of State's Foreign Service.

Eligibility This program is open to U.S. citizens who are entering their senior year of undergraduate study or their first year of graduate study. Applicants must be planning to work on a 2-year full-time master's degree program relevant to the work of the U.S. Foreign Service, including public policy, international affairs, public administration, business, economics, political science, sociology, or foreign languages. They must be preparing for a career in the Foreign Service. Applications are especially encouraged from women, members of minority groups historically underrepresented in the Foreign Service, and students with financial need.

Financial data The program pays for tuition, room, board, books, mandatory fees, and 1 round-trip ticket from the fellow's residence to academic institution, to a maximum of $37,500 per academic year.

Duration 2 years: the senior year of undergraduate study and the first year of graduate study for college seniors; the first 2 years of graduate school for entering graduate students.

Additional information This program is funded by the State Department and administered by The Washington Center for Internships. Fellows must commit to a minimum of 5 years of service in an appointment as a Foreign Service Officer following graduation and successful completion of the Foreign Service examination. If they fail to fulfill that commitment, they must refund all money received.

Number awarded Approximately 40 each year: 20 college seniors and 20 entering graduate students.

Deadline January of each year.

[631]
TOM JOYNER FOUNDATION/DENNY'S HUNGRY FOR EDUCATION SCHOLARSHIPS

Tom Joyner Foundation
Attn: Scholarship Committee
P.O. Box 630495
Irving, TX 75063
(972) 789-1058   Fax: (972) 789-1428
Web: www.tomjoynerfoundation.org

Summary To provide financial assistance to students currently enrolled at an Historically Black College or University (HBCU) who have been involved in efforts to fight hunger.

Eligibility This program is open to students who are currently enrolled full time at an HBCU and have a GPA of 2.5 or higher. Applicants must submit a 200-word essay describing their most memorable community service or activity in the past year to combat hunger.

Financial data The stipend is $1,250.

Duration 1 year.

Additional information This program is sponsored by Denny's as 1 of its Hungry for Education scholarship activities.

Number awarded 20 each year.

Deadline December of each year.

[632]
TOM JOYNER FOUNDATION FULL RIDE SCHOLARSHIP

Tom Joyner Foundation
Attn: Scholarship Committee
P.O. Box 630495
Irving, TX 75063
(972) 789-1058   Fax: (972) 789-1428
Web: www.tomjoynerfoundation.org

Summary To provide financial assistance to high school seniors who plan to enroll at an Historically Black College or University (HBCU).

Eligibility This program is open to graduating high school seniors who have a GPA of 3.5 or higher and either an SAT score of 2100 or higher or an ACT score of at least 30. Applicants must be planning to enroll full time at an HBCU. Selection is based on academic accomplishments, an essay on career goals, intellectual and creative distinctions, extracurricular activities, and letters of reference.

Financial data The program provides full payment of tuition and all required fees.

Duration 1 year; may be renewed up to 4 additional years, provided the recipient maintains a GPA of 3.0 or higher and full-time enrollment.

Number awarded 1 each year.

Deadline January of each year.

[633]
TRAILBLAZER SCHOLARSHIP

Conference of Minority Transportation Officials
Attn: National Scholarship Program
100 M Street, S.E., Suite 917
Washington, DC 20003
(202) 506-2917   E-mail: info@comto.org
Web: www.comto.org/page/scholarships

Summary To provide financial assistance for college or graduate school to African American and other minority members of the Conference of Minority Transportation Officials (COMTO) and their families.

Eligibility This program is open to undergraduate and graduate students who have been members of COMTO or whose parents, guardians, or grandparents have been members for at least 1 year. Applicants must be working (either full or part time) on a degree in a field related to transportation and have a GPA of 2.5 or higher. Along with their application they must submit a cover letter on their transportation-related career goals and life aspirations. Financial need is not considered in the selection process.

Financial data The stipend is $2,500. Funds are paid directly to the recipient's college or university.

Duration 1 year.
Number awarded 1 each year.
Deadline April of each year.

[634]
TRANSPORTATION INDUSTRY COLLEGE SCHOLARSHIP

Conference of Minority Transportation Officials-Fort Lauderdale Chapter
Attn: Scholarship Committee
Victor Garcia, South Florida Regional Transportation Authority
801 N.W. 33rd Street
Pompano Beach, FL 33064
(954) 788-7925   Toll Free: (800) GO-SFRTA
Fax: (854) 788-7961   TDD: (800) 273-7545
E-mail: victorgarcia@comtoftlauderdale.org
Web: www.comtoftlauderdale.org/scholarship-program

Summary To provide financial assistance to African American and other minority students working on a transportation-related undergraduate degree at a college in Florida.

Eligibility This program is open to minority students currently enrolled at accredited colleges and universities in Florida. Applicants must be majoring in a transportation-related field and have a GPA of 2.5 or higher. They must be U.S. citizens or permanent residents. Along with their application, they must submit an essay of 500 to 750 words on their transportation-related career goals and life aspirations. Financial need is not considered in the selection process.

Financial data The stipend is $1,500.

Duration 1 year; nonrenewable.

Additional information This program began in 2015.

Number awarded 1 each year.

Deadline April of each year.

[635]
TUSKEGEE AIRMEN SCHOLARSHIPS

Tuskegee Airmen Scholarship Foundation
1816 South Figueroa Street, Suite 4.13
Los Angeles, CA 90015
(213) 742-9541   E-mail: info@taisf.org
Web: www.taisf.org/scholarship-information.html

Summary To provide financial assistance for college to high school seniors and graduates who submit an essay on the history of Tuskegee Airmen, a group of African Americans who served as pilots in World War II.

Eligibility This program is open to students who have graduated or will graduate from high school in the current year with a GPA of 3.0 or higher. Applicants must submit a 1-page essay entitled "The Tuskegee Airmen" that reflects an overview of their history. They must also submit documentation of financial need and a 2-page essay that includes a brief autobiographical sketch, educational aspirations, career goals, and an explanation of why financial assistance is essential. Applications must be submitted to individual chapters of Tuskegee Airmen, Inc. which verify them as appropriate, evaluate them, and forward those considered worthy of further consideration to the national competition. Selection is based on academic achievement, extracurricular and community activities, financial need, recommendations, and both essays.

Financial data The stipend is $1,500.
Duration 1 year; nonrenewable.
Number awarded 40 each year.
Deadline January of each year.

[636]
TYLER J. VINEY MEMORIAL SCHOLARSHIP

Texas Society of Architects
Attn: Texas Architectural Foundation
500 Chicon Street
Austin, TX 78702
(512) 478-7386   Fax: (512) 478-0528
E-mail: foundation@texasarchitect.org
Web: www.texasarchitects.org/v/scholarships

Summary To provide financial assistance to residents of any state, especially African Americans and other minorities, who are entering their fourth or fifth year of study at a school of architecture in Texas.

Eligibility This program is open to residents of any state who are entering their fourth or fifth year of study at 1 of the 8 schools of architecture in Texas. Applicants must submit their application to the office of the dean of their school. Along with their application, they must submit essays on 1) the principal architectural areas or practice categories in which they are most interested, excel, or desire to develop their proficiency; and 2) career plans, short/long-range goals, vision, or other topic about which they are passionate. Selection is based on potential architectural talent, demonstrated interest in photography, and financial need. Priority is given to female and minority students.

Financial data The stipend ranges up to $2,000.
Duration 1 year.
Number awarded 1 each year.
Deadline February of each year.

[637]
UCSD MSTP SUMMER UNDERGRADUATE RESEARCH FELLOWSHIP PROGRAM

University of California at San Diego
Attn: School of Medicine
Medical Scientist Training Program
9500 Gilman Drive, MC 0661
La Jolla, CA 92093-0661
(858) 822-5631   Toll Free: (800) 925-8704
Fax: (858) 822-3067   E-mail: mstp@ucsd.edu
Web: mstp.ucsd.edu/surf/Pages/default.aspx

Summary To provide an opportunity for African American undergraduate students and others from underrepresented groups to work during the summer on a research project in the biomedical sciences at the University of California at San Diego (UCSD).

Eligibility This program is open to undergraduate students at colleges in any state who are members of an underrepresented group (racial and ethnic groups that have been shown to be underrepresented in health-related sciences, individuals with disabilities, or individuals from a disadvantaged background). Applicants must be interested in working on a research project in the laboratory of a UCSD faculty member in the biomedical sciences. They must be U.S. citizens, permanent residents, or nationals. Along with their application, they must submit brief essays on 1) why they consider themselves an individual from a disadvantaged ethnicity or background or are underrepresented in the biomedical sciences; 2) their past research experiences; 3) the areas of research they wish to pursue in the program; 4) their educational and career plans and how this program will advance them towards their goals; and 5) anything else that might help to evaluate their application.

Financial data The program provides a stipend of $1,600 per month, room (but not board), and a $500 travel allowance.

Duration 8 weeks during the summer.

Additional information This program is sponsored by the National Heart, Lung, and Blood Institute (NHLBI) of the National Institutes of Health (NIH).

Number awarded Varies each year; recently, 11 students participated in this program.

Deadline February of each year.

[638]
UNCF GEOGRAPHICALLY-BASED SCHOLARSHIPS

United Negro College Fund
Attn: Scholarships and Grants Department
1805 Seventh Street, N.W.
Washington, DC 20001
(202) 810-0258   Toll Free: (800) 331-2244
E-mail: scholarships@uncf.org
Web: www.scholarships.uncf.org

Summary To provide financial assistance to high school juniors or seniors from designated areas who are interested in attending a member institution of the United Negro College Fund (UNCF).

Eligibility These programs are open to seniors graduating from high schools in designated geographical areas with a GPA of 2.5 or higher. Students who have completed their junior year in high school with a record of distinction may also be considered. Financial need must be demonstrated. Applications should be submitted directly to the UNCF-member institution the student plans to attend.

Financial data The awards are intended to cover tuition and range from a minimum of $500 to a maximum of $7,500 per year.

Duration 1 year; may be renewed.

Additional information Recipients must attend a UNCF-member institution of higher learning. These are: Miles College, Oakwood College, Stillman College, Talladega College, and Tuskegee University in Alabama; Philander Smith College in Arkansas; Bethune-Cookman University, Edward Waters College, and Florida Memorial University in Florida; Clark Atlanta University, Interdenominational Theological Center, Morehouse College, Paine College, and Spelman College in Georgia; Dillard University and Xavier University in Louisiana; Rust College and Tougaloo College in Mississippi; Bennett College, Johnson C. Smith University, Livingstone College, Saint Augustine's University, and Shaw University in North Carolina; Wilberforce University in Ohio; Allen University, Benedict College, Claflin University, Morris College, and Voorhees College in South Carolina; Fisk University, Lane College, and LeMoyne-Owen College in Tennessee; Huston-Tillotson College, Jarvis Christian College, Texas College, and Wiley College in Texas; and Virginia Union University in Virginia.

Number awarded A total of nearly 1,200 UNCF scholarships is awarded each year.

Deadline March of each year.

[639]
UNITED AIRLINES PILOT SCHOLARSHIPS

Organization of Black Aerospace Professionals, Inc.
Attn: Scholarship Coordinator
One Westbrook Corporate Center, Suite 300
Westchester, IL 60154
(708) 449-7755   Toll Free: (800) JET-OBAP
Fax: (708) 449-7754 E-mail: obapscholarships@obap.org
Web: www.obap.org/united-airlines-pilot-scholarship

Summary To provide financial assistance to members of the Organization of Black Aerospace Professionals (OBAP) who are enrolled in a collegiate aviation program.

Eligibility This program is open to OBAP members who have a commercial certificate and instrument rating, preferably for multi-engine. Applicants must be enrolled in an accredited collegiate aviation program. They must have a GPA of 3.0 or higher and a first class medical certificate. Along with their application, they must submit a 500-word essay on their career aspirations and how this award will help advance their aviation career.

Financial data The stipend is $5,000. Funds are paid directly to the college.

Duration 1 year.

Additional information The OBAP was originally established in 1976 as the Organization of Black Airline Pilots to make certain Blacks and other minorities had a group that would keep them informed about opportunities for advancement within commercial aviation. This program is sponsored by United Airlines.

Number awarded 3 each year.

Deadline May of each year.

[640]
UNITED AIRLINES TECH OPS SCHOLARSHIPS

Organization of Black Aerospace Professionals, Inc.
Attn: Scholarship Coordinator
One Westbrook Corporate Center, Suite 300
Westchester, IL 60154
(708) 449-7755   Toll Free: (800) JET-OBAP
Fax: (708) 449-7754 E-mail: obapscholarships@obap.org
Web: www.obap.org/united-airlines-tech-ops-scholarship

Summary To provide financial assistance to members of the Organization of Black Aerospace Professionals (OBAP) who are enrolled in an aeronautical/aerospace engineering or aircraft maintenance program.

Eligibility This program is open to OBAP members who are enrolled in an accredited collegiate program in aeronautical or aerospace engineering or in an aircraft maintenance program. Applicants must have a GPA of 3.0 or higher. Along with their application, they must submit an essay of 500 to 1,000 words on 1) who or what inspired them to prepare for their chosen career; 2) what they consider their strongest characteristic and why; and 3) why are they the most qualified candidate for this scholarship.

Financial data The stipend is $1,500. Funds are paid directly to the college.

Duration 1 year.

Additional information The OBAP was originally established in 1976 as the Organization of Black Airline Pilots to make certain Blacks and other minorities had a group that would keep them informed about opportunities for advancement within commercial aviation. This program is sponsored by United Airlines.

Number awarded 2 each year.

Deadline May of each year.

[641]
UNITED METHODIST FOUNDATION COLLEGE AND UNIVERSITY MERIT SCHOLARS PROGRAM

United Methodist Higher Education Foundation
Attn: Scholarships Administrator
60 Music Square East, Suite 350
P.O. Box 340005
Nashville, TN 37203-0005
(615) 649-3974   Toll Free: (800) 811-8110
Fax: (615) 649-3980
E-mail: umhefscholarships@umhef.org
Web: www.umhef.org

Summary To provide financial assistance to undergraduate students, especially African Americans and other minorities, who are attending colleges and universities affiliated with the United Methodist Church.

Eligibility This program is open to freshmen, sophomores, juniors, and seniors at United Methodist-related 4-year colleges and universities and to freshmen and sophomores at 2-year colleges. Nominees must have been active members of the United Methodist Church for at least 1 year prior to application. They must be planning to enroll full time and have a GPA of 3.0 or higher. Preference is given to ethnic minority and first generation college students. Financial need is considered in the selection process. U.S. citizenship or permanent resident status is required.

Financial data The stipend is $2,000.

Duration 1 year; nonrenewable.

Additional information Students may obtain applications from their school.

Number awarded 420 each year: 1 to a member of each class at each school.

Deadline Nominations from schools must be received by September of each year.

[642]
UNITED PARCEL SERVICE AEROSPACE SCIENCE TECHNOLOGY ENGINEERING AND MATH (STEM) SCHOLARSHIP

Organization of Black Aerospace Professionals, Inc.
Attn: Scholarship Coordinator
One Westbrook Corporate Center, Suite 300
Westchester, IL 60154
(708) 449-7755   Toll Free: (800) JET-OBAP
Fax: (708) 449-7754 E-mail: obapscholarships@obap.org
Web: www.obap.org/ups-stem-scholarship

Summary To provide financial assistance to members of the Organization of Black Aerospace Professionals (OBAP) who are interested in working on a degree in an aerospace-related field of science, technology, engineering, or mathematics (STEM).

Eligibility This program is open to OBAP members who are graduating high school seniors or students enrolled in an accredited collegiate aviation program. Applicants must be majoring in a field of STEM as preparation for a career in aerospace and aviation. They must have a GPA of 3.0 or higher. Along with their application, they must submit a 500-word essay on why STEM is important to our society.

Financial data The stipend is $1,000. Funds are paid directly to the recipient's college.

Duration 1 year.

Additional information The OBAP was originally established in 1976 as the Organization of Black Airline Pilots to make certain Blacks and other minorities had a group that would keep them informed about opportunities for advancement within commercial aviation. This program is sponsored by United Parcel Service (UPS).

Number awarded 2 each year.

Deadline May of each year.

[643]
UNITED PARCEL SERVICE MAINTENANCE AND ENGINEERING SCHOLARSHIP

Organization of Black Aerospace Professionals, Inc.
Attn: Scholarship Coordinator
One Westbrook Corporate Center, Suite 300
Westchester, IL 60154
(708) 449-7755   Toll Free: (800) JET-OBAP
Fax: (708) 449-7754 E-mail: obapscholarships@obap.org
Web: www.obap.org

Summary To provide financial assistance to members of the Organization of Black Aerospace Professionals (OBAP) who are interested in further training as a mechanic to advance their career in the aviation industry.

Eligibility This program is open to OBAP members who are enrolled in or accepted at an aviation mechanic's training school. Applicants must have a GPA of 2.7 or higher. Along with their application, they must submit a 500-word essay on how this award will help advance their aviation career.

Financial data The stipend is $2,500. Funds are paid directly to the training facility.

Duration 1 year.

Additional information The OBAP was originally established in 1976 as the Organization of Black Airline Pilots to make certain Blacks and other minorities had a group that would keep them informed about opportunities for advancement within commercial aviation. This program is sponsored by United Parcel Service (UPS).

Number awarded 1 each year.

Deadline May of each year.

[644]
UNITED PARCEL SERVICE PILOT SCHOLARSHIP

Organization of Black Aerospace Professionals, Inc.
Attn: Scholarship Coordinator
One Westbrook Corporate Center, Suite 300
Westchester, IL 60154
(708) 449-7755   Toll Free: (800) JET-OBAP
Fax: (708) 449-7754 E-mail: obapscholarships@obap.org
Web: www.obap.org/ups-pilot-scholarship

Summary To provide financial assistance to members of the Organization of Black Aerospace Professionals (OBAP) who are interested in further training as a pilot to advance their career in the aviation industry.

Eligibility This program is open to OBAP members who have a commercial instrument rating and are enrolled in an accredited collegiate aviation program. Applicants must have a GPA of 3.0 or higher. Along with their application, they must submit a 500-word essay on how this award will help advance their aviation career and a copy of their first class medical certificate.

Financial data The stipend is $2,000. Funds are paid directly to the recipient's college.

Duration 1 year.

Additional information The OBAP was originally established in 1976 as the Organization of Black Airline Pilots to make certain Blacks and other minorities had a group that would keep them informed about opportunities for advancement within commercial aviation. This program is sponsored by United Parcel Service (UPS).

Number awarded 1 each year.

Deadline May of each year.

[645]
UNITED PARCEL SERVICE SCHOLARSHIP FOR MINORITY STUDENTS

Institute of Industrial and Systems Engineers
Attn: Scholarship Coordinator
3577 Parkway Lane, Suite 200
Norcross, GA 30092
(770) 449-0461, ext. 105　　Toll Free: (800) 494-0460
Fax: (770) 441-3295　　E-mail: bcameron@iisenet.org
Web: www.iienet2.org/Details.aspx?id=857

Summary To provide financial assistance to African American and other minority undergraduates who are studying industrial engineering at a school in the United States, Canada, or Mexico.

Eligibility Eligible to be nominated are minority undergraduate students enrolled at any school in the United States or its territories, Canada, or Mexico, provided the school's engineering program is accredited by an agency recognized by the Institute of Industrial and Systems Engineers (IISE) and the student is pursuing a full-time course of study in industrial engineering with a GPA of at least 3.4. Nominees must have at least 5 full quarters or 3 full semesters remaining until graduation. Students may not apply directly for these awards; they must be nominated by the head of their industrial engineering department. Nominees must be IISE members. Selection is based on scholastic ability, character, leadership, and potential service to the industrial engineering profession.

Financial data The stipend is $4,000.

Duration 1 year.

Additional information Funding for this program is provided by the UPS Foundation.

Number awarded 1 each year.

Deadline Schools must submit nominations by November of each year.

[646]
UNIVERSITY OF CALIFORNIA AT BERKELEY AMGEN SCHOLARS PROGRAM

University of California at Berkeley
Attn: Amgen Scholars Program
158 Barrows Hall
MC 2990
Berkeley, CA 94720-2990
(510) 642-0280　　Fax: (510) 643-6762
E-mail: amgenscholars@berkeley.edu
Web: amgenscholars.berkeley.edu

Summary To provide undergraduate students, especially African Americans and members of other diverse groups, with a summer research experience at the University of California at Berkeley in biological and biomedical sciences.

Eligibility This program is open to sophomores, juniors, and non-graduating seniors at 4-year colleges and universities in the United States, Puerto Rico, and U.S. territories. Applicants must be interested in a summer research experience at UC Berkeley in biochemistry, bioengineering, biophysics, cell and developmental biology, chemical biology, chemical and biomedical engineering, chemistry, computational biology, genetics, genomics and development, immunology, integrative biology, metabolic biology, microbiology, molecular and cell biology, molecular toxicology, neurobiology, neuroscience, pathogenesis, plant and microbial biology, RNA systems biology, structural biology, or synthetic biology. They must have a GPA of 3.2 or higher and an interest in continuing on to a Ph.D. or M.D./Ph.D. (but not M.D.) program. Applications are especially encouraged from students from diverse populations and backgrounds. U.S. citizenship or permanent resident status is required.

Financial data Housing, travel to and from Berkeley, meals, and a stipend of $5,000 are provided.

Duration 10 weeks during the summer.

Additional information This program serves as the UC Berkeley component of the Amgen Scholars Program, which operates at 8 other U.S. universities (and the National Institutes of Health) and is funded by the Amgen Foundation.

Number awarded 25 each year.

Deadline January of each year.

[647]
UNIVERSITY OF CALIFORNIA AT LOS ANGELES AMGEN SCHOLARS PROGRAM

University of California at Los Angeles
Attn: URC-Sciences
2121 Life Sciences Building
621 Charles E. Young Drive
Los Angeles, CA 90095-1606
(310) 206-2182　　Fax: (310) 267-2219
E-mail: amgensch@lifesci.ucla.edu
Web: www.ugresearchsci.ucla.edu/amgenscholars.htm

Summary To provide undergraduate students, especially African Americans and members of other diverse groups, with a summer research experience at the University of California at Los Angeles in biological and biomedical sciences.

Eligibility This program is open to sophomores, juniors, and non-graduating seniors at 4-year colleges and universities in the United States, Puerto Rico, and U.S. territories. Applicants must be interested in a summer research experience at UCLA in biomedical science, chemistry, bioengineering, or chemical engineering. They must have a GPA of 3.2 or higher and an interest in continuing on to a Ph.D. or M.D./Ph.D. (but not M.D.) program. Applications are especially encouraged from students from diverse populations and backgrounds. U.S. citizenship or permanent resident status is required.

Financial data The program provides a stipend of $3,600, on-campus housing, some meals, and a travel allowance for non-UCLA students of $250 for those from California or $500 for students from other states.

Duration 10 weeks during the summer.

Additional information This program serves as the UCLA component of the Amgen Scholars Program, which operates at 8 other U.S. universities (and the National Institutes of Health) and is funded by the Amgen Foundation.

Number awarded 20 each year, including 5 undergraduates from UCLA and 15 from other colleges and universities.

Deadline January of each year.

[648]
UNIVERSITY OF CALIFORNIA AT SAN FRANCISCO SUMMER RESEARCH PROGRAMS

University of California at San Francisco
Office of Graduate Outreach
Attn: Outreach and Student Programs Coordinator
1675 Owens Street, Room 310
Box 0523
San Francisco, CA 94143-0523
(415) 514-3510   Fax: (415) 514-0844
E-mail: julia.clark@ucsf.edu
Web: graduate.ucsf.edu/srtp

Summary To provide undergraduate students, especially African Americans and members of other diverse groups, with a summer research experience at the University of California at San Francisco in biological and biomedical sciences.

Eligibility This activity consists of 5 separate programs, but they operate together and have a common application and requirements. The 5 programs are the Amgen Scholars Program, the Molecular Biosciences Research Experiences for Undergraduates (REU), the Summer Research Training Program (SRTP), the graduate group in biophysics, and the graduate group in pharmaceutical sciences and pharmacogenomics. The activity is open to sophomores, juniors, and non-graduating seniors at 4-year colleges and universities in the United States, Puerto Rico, and U.S. territories. Applicants must be interested in a summer research experience at UC San Francisco in biochemistry, bioengineering, biological and biomedical informatics, biology (molecular, cell, and developmental), biomedical sciences, biophysics, chemical biology, chemistry, epidemiology and translational research, genetics, neuroscience, oral and craniofacial sciences, or pharmaceutical sciences and pharmacogenomics. They must be U.S. citizens or permanent residents. The Amgen Scholars Program requires a GPA of 3.2 or higher but the other 2 components have no minimum GPA requirement; all programs require an interest in continuing on to a Ph.D. or M.D./Ph.D. (but not M.D.) program. Applications are especially encouraged from underrepresented minority, socioeconomically disadvantaged, and first-generation college students and from students with limited access to research laboratories.

Financial data The program provides a stipend of $4,000, a $500 allowance for travel to and from San Francisco, housing in the city, health insurance, and a public transportation pass.

Duration 10 weeks during the summer.

Additional information This program is comprised of 1) the UC San Francisco component of the Amgen Scholars Program, which operates at 8 other U.S. universities (and the National Institutes of Health) and is funded by the Amgen Foundation; 2) the REU program, funded by the National Science Foundation; 3) the SRTP, which is a UCSF program with supplemental funding from Genentech and the Howard Hughes Medical Institute; 4) the graduate group in biophysics, (a component of the SRTP); and 5) the graduate group in pharmaceutical sciences and pharmacogenomics (a component of the SRTP).

Number awarded Approximately 60 each year.

Deadline January of each year.

[649]
UPS/CIC FOUNDATION SCHOLARSHIPS

Wisconsin Association of Independent Colleges and
    Universities
Attn: Senior Vice President for Educational Services
122 West Washington Avenue, Suite 700
Madison, WI 53703-2723
(608) 256-7761, ext. 223   Fax: (608) 256-7065
E-mail: carole.trone@waicu.org
Web: www.waicu.org

Summary To provide financial assistance to students at member institution of the Wisconsin Association of Independent Colleges and Universities (WAICU) who are African Americans or members of other target populations.

Eligibility This program is open to students enrolled full time at WAICU member colleges or universities. The background of applicants must reflect 1 or more of the components of the target population for the UPS Foundation and the First Opportunity Program of the Council of Independent Colleges (CIC): first generation, low-income, minority, or new American students.

Financial data The stipend is $2,600.

Duration 1 year.

Additional information The WAICU member schools are Alverno College, Bellin College, Beloit College, Cardinal Stritch University, Carroll College, Carthage College, Columbia College of Nursing, Concordia University of Wisconsin, Edgewood College, Lakeland College, Lawrence University, Marian College, Marquette University, Medical College of Wisconsin, Milwaukee Institute of Art & Design, Milwaukee School of Engineering, Mount Mary College, Nashotah House Theological Seminary, Northland College, Ripon College, St. Norbert College, Silver Lake College of the Holy Family, Viterbo University, and Wisconsin Lutheran College. This program is supported by the UPS Foundation and administered nationally through CIC.

Number awarded Up to 24 each year: 1 at each of the member schools.

Deadline Each participating college sets its own deadline.

[650]
UPS DIVERSITY SCHOLARSHIPS OF THE AMERICAN SOCIETY OF SAFETY ENGINEERS

American Society of Safety Engineers
Attn: ASSE Foundation
Scholarship Award Program
520 North Northwest Highway
Park Ridge, IL 60068-2538
(847) 699-2929   Fax: (847) 296-3769
E-mail: assefoundation@asse.org
Web: foundation.asse.org/scholarships-and-grants

Summary   To provide financial assistance to African American and other minority upper-division students working on a degree related to occupational safety.

Eligibility   This program is open to students who are U.S. citizens and members of minority ethnic or racial groups. Applicants must be majoring in occupational safety, health, environment, industrial hygiene, occupational health nursing, or a closely-related field (e.g., industrial or environmental engineering). They must be full-time students who have completed at least 60 semester hours and have a GPA of 3.0 or higher. Membership in the American Society of Safety Engineers (ASSE) is not required, but preference is given to members.

Financial data   The stipend is $5,250 per year.

Duration   1 year; recipients may reapply.

Additional information   Funding for this program is provided by the UPS Foundation. Recipients may also be provided with the opportunity to attend a professional development conference related to safety.

Number awarded   3 each year.

Deadline   November of each year.

[651]
UPS FLIGHT DISPATCHER SCHOLARSHIP

Organization of Black Aerospace Professionals, Inc.
Attn: Scholarship Coordinator
One Westbrook Corporate Center, Suite 300
Westchester, IL 60154
(708) 449-7755   Toll Free: (800) JET-OBAP
Fax: (708) 449-7754 E-mail: obapscholarships@obap.org
Web: www.obap.org/ups-flight-dispatcher-scholarship

Summary   To provide financial assistance to members of the Organization of Black Aerospace Professionals (OBAP) who are interested in further training to advance their career in the aviation industry.

Eligibility   This program is open to OBAP members who are graduating high school seniors or students enrolled in an accredited collegiate aviation program. Applicants must have a GPA of 3.0 or higher. Along with their application, they must submit a 500-word essay on how this award will impact their career goals.

Financial data   The stipend is $2,000. Funds are paid directly to the recipient's college.

Duration   1 year.

Additional information   The OBAP was originally established in 1976 as the Organization of Black Airline Pilots to make certain Blacks and other minorities had a group that would keep them informed about opportunities for advancement within commercial aviation. This program is sponsored by United Parcel Service (UPS).

Number awarded   1 each year.

Deadline   May of each year.

[652]
USA FUNDS SUCCESS SCHOLARSHIP OF THE THURGOOD MARSHALL COLLEGE FUND

Thurgood Marshall College Fund
Attn: Senior Manager of Scholarship Programs
901 F Street, N.W., Suite 300
Washington, DC 20004
(202) 507-4851   Fax: (202) 652-2934
E-mail: deshuandra.walker@tmcfund.org
Web: www.tmcf.org

Summary   To provide financial assistance to African American undergraduates at public Historically Black Colleges and Universities (HBCUs) that are members of the Thurgood Marshall College Fund (TMCF).

Eligibility   This program is open to full-time undergraduate students at any of the 47 TMCF member institutions. Applicants may be majoring in any field. They must have a GPA of 3.0 or higher. Selection is based on merit, but students must submit their Student Aid Report from their FAFSA. Along with their application, they must submit a 500-word essay on what inspired them to pursue a degree in their current field of study and their career aspirations. U.S. citizenship or permanent resident status is required.

Financial data   The stipend is $6,200.

Duration   1 year.

Additional information   This program is sponsored by USA Funds.

Number awarded   1 or more each year.

Deadline   April of each year.

[653]
USDA/1890 NATIONAL SCHOLARS PROGRAM

Department of Agriculture
Office of Advocacy and Outreach
Attn: 1890 Programs
1400 Independence Avenue, S.W.
Mail Stop 0170
Washington, DC 20250
(202) 205-4307   Fax: (202) 720-7136
E-mail: 1890init@usda.gov
Web: www.outreach.usda.gov/education/1890/index.htm

Summary   To provide financial assistance to high school seniors and graduates interested in majoring in a field related to agriculture or agribusiness at 1 of the 19 Historically Black 1890 Land Grant Institutions.

Eligibility   This program is open to U.S. citizens who have or will have a high school diploma or GED certificate with a GPA of 3.0 or higher and a verbal/mathematics/written score of at least 1,500 on the SAT or 21 on the ACT. They must be entering their freshman, sophomore, or junior year at 1 of the 19 Historically Black 1890 Land Grant Institutions and study such fields as agriculture, agricultural business/management, agricultural economics, agricultural engineering/mechanics, agricultural production and technology, agronomy or crop science, animal sciences, botany, farm and range management, food sciences/technology, forestry and related services, home economics and nutrition, horticulture, natural resources management, soil conservation/soil science, wildlife management, or other related disciplines. Along with their application, they must submit an essay of 500 to 800 words on their interest in the U.S. Department of Agriculture (USDA), how they envision the scholarship will impact them and their future as a public servant, and their experiences and perceptions about agriculture, food, and natural resource sciences.

Financial data Each award provides annual tuition, employment, employee benefits, use of a laptop computer and software while receiving the scholarship, fees, books, and room and board. Following graduation, scholars are required to perform 1 year of service to the USDA for each year of support received.

Duration 4 years, provided the scholar maintains normal progress toward the bachelor's degree and satisfactory performance.

Additional information The Historically Black 1890 Land Grant institutions are: Alabama A&M University, Alcorn State University, University of Arkansas at Pine Bluff, Central State University of Ohio, Delaware State University, Florida A&M University, Fort Valley State University, Kentucky State University, Langston University, Lincoln University of Missouri, University of Maryland-Eastern Shore, North Carolina A&T State University, Prairie View A&M University, South Carolina State University, Southern University and A&M College, Tennessee State University, Tuskegee University, Virginia State University, and West Virginia State University. Applications must be submitted to the Liaison Officer of the U.S. Department of Agriculture at a participating 1890 institution.

Number awarded 38 or more each year: at least 2 at each of the participating universities.

Deadline April of each year.

[654]
VADM BRUCE AND EMILY GROOMS SCHOLARSHIP

National Naval Officers Association-Washington, D.C.
  Chapter
c/o LCDR Stephen Williams
P.O. Box 30784
Alexandria, VA 22310
(703) 566-3840   Fax: (703) 566-3813
E-mail: Stephen.Williams@Navy.mil
Web: dcnnoa.memberlodge.com/page-309002

Summary To provide financial assistance to African American high school seniors from the Washington, D.C. area who are interested in attending college in any state.

Eligibility This program is open to African American seniors graduating from high schools in the Washington, D.C. metropolitan area who plan to enroll full time at an accredited 2- or 4-year college or university in any state. Applicants must have a GPA of 2.7 or higher and be U.S. citizens or permanent residents. Selection is based on academic achievement, community involvement, and financial need.

Financial data The stipend is $1,000.

Duration 1 year; nonrenewable.

Additional information Recipients are not required to join or affiliate with the military in any way.

Number awarded 1 each year.

Deadline February of each year.

[655]
VADM MICHELLE HOWARD EXCELLENCE IN LEADERSHIP SCHOLARSHIP

National Naval Officers Association-Washington, D.C.
  Chapter
c/o LCDR Stephen Williams
P.O. Box 30784
Alexandria, VA 22310
(703) 644-2605   Fax: (703) 644-8503
E-mail: Stephen.Williams@navy.mil
Web: www.dcnnoa.org/dcnnoa-scholarship

Summary To provide financial assistance to African American high school seniors from the Washington, D.C. area who are interested in attending college in any state.

Eligibility This program is open to African American seniors graduating from high schools in the Washington, D.C. metropolitan area who plan to enroll full time at an accredited 2- or 4-year college or university in any state. Applicants must have a GPA of 2.5 or higher and be U.S. citizens or permanent residents. Selection is based on academic achievement, community involvement, and financial need.

Financial data The stipend is $1,000.

Duration 1 year; nonrenewable.

Additional information Recipients are not required to join or affiliate with the military in any way. In addition to a number of scholarships with additional requirements, this program includes the following named general scholarships: the David and Sheila Garnett Leadership Scholarship, the Pringle & Pringle Higher Education Scholarship, the Rear Admiral Mack and Nancy Gaston Leadership Scholarship, the Rear Admiral Michelle Howard Excellence in Leadership Scholarship, and the William A. Borders Jr. Justice Scholarship.

Number awarded 1 each year.

Deadline February of each year.

[656]
VALERIE RUSSELL SCHOLARSHIP

United Church of Christ
Attn: Associate Director, Grant and Scholarship
  Administration
700 Prospect Avenue East
Cleveland, OH 44115-1100
(216) 736-2166   Toll Free: (866) 822-8224, ext. 2166
Fax: (216) 736-3783   E-mail: scholarships@ucc.org
Web: www.ucc.org/russell_scholarship

Summary To provide financial assistance to African American laywomen who are members of a United Church of Christ (UCC) congregation and working on an undergraduate or graduate degree to advance the justice ministries of the denomination.

Eligibility This program is open to African American laywomen who have a strong theologically-grounded commitment to the justice ministries of the UCC but are not a member in discernment, licensed, commissioned, or ordained. Applicants must be 1) working on an undergraduate or graduate degree in a field that will affirm the values of the UCC and promote its justice commitments; or 2) already professionally engaged in justice work either in the church or in a secular organization and seeking funds for continuing education activities (e.g., classes, workshops, travel) that will assist in personal skill building.

Financial data Stipends range from $1,500 to $2,000 per year. Funds may be used for tuition for undergraduate or graduate study or for continuing education activities.

Duration 1 year; may be renewed.

Additional information This program began in 1997.

Number awarded 1 or more each year.

Deadline February of each year.

[657]
VIRGINIA CHAPTER AABE SCHOLARSHIPS

American Association of Blacks in Energy-Virginia
  Chapter
c/o Teresa Vaughan, Scholarship Committee Chair
701 East Cary Street, Seventh Floor
Richmond, VA 23218
E-mail: Virginia@aabe.org
Web: www.aabe.org

Summary To provide financial assistance to African Americans and members of other underrepresented minority groups who are high school seniors in Virginia and planning to major in an energy-related field at a college in any state.

Eligibility This program is open to seniors graduating from high schools in Virginia and planning to attend a college or university in any state. Applicants must be African Americans, Hispanics, or Native Americans who have a GPA of 3.0 or higher and who have taken the ACT and/or SAT test. Their intended major must be business, engineering, technology, mathematics, the physical sciences, or other energy-related field. Along with their application, they must submit a 350-word essay that includes 1) when they discovered their interest in the field of energy and what sparked their interest; and 2) either what excites them about the field of energy or how they expect their education to prepare them for the field of energy. Financial need is not considered in the selection process.

Financial data Stipends range from $1,000 to $3,000.

Duration 1 year.

Additional information The winner is eligible to compete for regional and national scholarships.

Number awarded 4 each year: 1 at $3,000, 1 at $2,000, and 2 at $1,000.

Deadline March of each year.

[658]
VISUAL TASK FORCE SCHOLARSHIPS

National Association of Black Journalists
Attn: Program Manager
University of Maryland
1100 Knight Hall, Suite 3100
College Park, MD 20742
(301) 405-7520   Fax: (301) 314-1714
E-mail: Sberry@nabj.org
Web: www.nabj.org/?page=ScholarshipsVTF

Summary To provide financial assistance to high school seniors and undergraduate or graduate student members of the National Association of Black Journalists (NABJ) who are interested in a career in visual journalism.

Eligibility This program is open to African American high school seniors and undergraduate and graduate student members of NABJ who are currently enrolled or planning to enroll full time at an accredited 4-year college or university.

Applicants must be interested in working on a degree in a field related to visual journalism (e.g., photojournalism, design and informational graphics, broadcast photojournalism) to prepare for a career in newspaper, magazine, broadcast, or online journalism. They must have a GPA of 2.75 or higher and be able to demonstrate financial need. Along with their application, they must submit samples of their work, an official college transcript, 3 letters of recommendation, a resume, and an essay of 1,000 to 2,000 words on the reasons they wish to prepare for a career in visual journalism and how they use their visual skills to tell a story effectively and creatively.

Financial data The stipend is $1,500. Funds are paid directly to the recipient's college or university.

Duration 1 year; nonrenewable.

Number awarded 2 each year.

Deadline March of each year.

[659]
VIVIAN D. TILLMAN SCHOLARSHIP

Sigma Gamma Rho Sorority, Inc.
Attn: National Education Fund
1000 Southhill Drive, Suite 200
Cary, NC 27513
(919) 678-9720   Toll Free: (888) SGR-1922
Fax: (919) 678-9721
E-mail: customerservice@sgrho1922.org
Web: www.sgrho1922.org/nef

Summary To provide financial assistance to African American and other undergraduate students working on a degree in journalism or communications.

Eligibility This program is open to undergraduates working on a degree in journalism or communications. The sponsor is a traditionally African American sorority, but support is available to males and females of all races. Applicants must have a GPA of 2.0 or higher and be able to demonstrate financial need. Along with their application, they must submit a 500-word essay on how they will use their communication or journalism skills for the betterment of the country.

Financial data A stipend is awarded (amount not specified).

Duration 1 year.

Additional information A processing fee of $20 is required.

Number awarded 1 each year.

Deadline April of each year.

[660]
VSCPA MINORITY ACCOUNTING SCHOLARSHIPS

Virginia Society of Certified Public Accountants
Attn: Educational Foundation
4309 Cox Road
Glen Allen, VA 23060
(804) 612-9417   Toll Free: (800) 733-8272
Fax: (804) 273-1741   E-mail: foundation@vscpa.com
Web: www.vscpa.com

Summary To provide financial assistance to African American and other minority students enrolled in an undergraduate accounting program in Virginia.

Eligibility Applicants must be minority students (African American or Black, Hispanic or Latino, American Indian or Native Alaskan, Asian, Native Hawaiian or other Pacific Islander) currently enrolled in a Virginia college or university undergraduate accounting program. They must be U.S. citizens, be majoring in accounting, have completed at least 3 hours of accounting, be currently registered for 3 more credit hours of accounting, and have a GPA of 3.0 or higher. Selection is based on an essay, transcripts, a current resume, a faculty letter of recommendation, and financial need.

Financial data The stipend is $1,000.

Duration 1 year.

Number awarded Normally 3 each year.

Deadline March of each year.

[661]
W. TERRELL JONES EDUCATIONAL EQUITY SCHOLARSHIP

Pennsylvania Black Conference on Higher Education
c/o Brenda Sanders Dédé, Scholarship Committee Chair
Clarion University of Pennsylvania
Academic Affairs
115 Carrier
840 Wood Street
Clarion, PA 16214
(814) 393-2223   E-mail: bdede@clarion.edu
Web: www.pbcohe.com/scholarships.html

Summary To provide financial assistance to African American residents of any state who are enrolled as undergraduates at colleges in Pennsylvania and have contributed volunteer service in the area of educational equity.

Eligibility This program is open to African Americans from any state who have completed at least the first semester as an undergraduate at a college or university in Pennsylvania. Applicants must have a GPA of 3.0 or higher. They must be able to provide evidence of volunteer service in the area of educational equity. Along with their application, they must submit an essay, up to 5 pages in length, on why they should receive this scholarship. Selection is based on that essay, academics, extracurricular activity participation, leadership qualities, and interpersonal qualities.

Financial data The stipend is $1,000.

Duration 1 year.

Number awarded 1 each year.

Deadline January of each year.

[662]
WALMART FOUNDATION FIRST-GENERATION SCHOLARSHIPS OF THE THURGOOD MARSHALL COLLEGE FUND

Thurgood Marshall College Fund
Attn: Senior Manager of Scholarship Programs
901 F Street, N.W., Suite 300
Washington, DC 20004
(202) 507-4851   Fax: (202) 652-2934
E-mail: deshuandra.walker@tmcfund.org
Web: www.tmcf.org

Summary To provide financial assistance to African American first-generation students entering any of the public Historically Black Colleges and Universities (HBCUs) that are members of the Thurgood Marshall College Fund (TMCF).

Eligibility This program is open to African American high school seniors planning to enroll full time at 1 of the 47 colleges and universities that are TMCF members. Applicants must be the first member of their family to attend college. They must have a GPA of 2.5 or higher and be able to demonstrate financial need. Along with their application, they must submit a 500-word essay on what it means to be the first person in their family to receive a college degree and the impact this scholarship would have on their education. U.S. citizenship is required.

Financial data The stipend is $3,100 per semester ($6,200 per year). Funds are awarded through the institution to be used for tuition, on-campus room and board, and required textbooks.

Duration 1 year.

Additional information This program is sponsored by the Walmart Foundation.

Number awarded Approximately 65 each year.

Deadline April of each year.

[663]
WARNER NORCROSS & JUDD PARALEGAL AND LEGAL SECRETARIAL SCHOLARSHIP

Grand Rapids Community Foundation
Attn: Education Program Officer
185 Oakes Street S.W.
Grand Rapids, MI 49503-4008
(616) 454-1751, ext. 103   Fax: (616) 454-6455
E-mail: rbishop@grfoundation.org
Web: www.grfoundation.org/scholarshipslist

Summary To provide financial assistance to African American and other minority residents of Michigan who are interested in working on a paralegal or legal secretarial studies degree at an institution in the state.

Eligibility This program is open to residents of Michigan who are students of color attending or planning to attend an accredited public or private 2- or 4-year college or university in the state. Applicants must have a declared major in paralegal or legal secretarial studies. They must be U.S. citizens or permanent residents and have a GPA of 2.5 or higher. Financial need is considered in the selection process.

Financial data The stipend is $2,000. Funds are paid directly to the recipient's institution.

Duration 1 year.

Additional information Funding for this program is provided by the law firm Warner Norcross & Judd LLP.

Number awarded 1 each year.

Deadline March of each year.

[664]
WARREN G. MAGNUSON EDUCATIONAL SUPPORT PERSONNEL SCHOLARSHIP GRANT

Washington Education Association
32032 Weyerhaeuser Way South
P.O. Box 9100
Federal Way, WA 98063-9100
(253) 765-7056   Toll Free: (800) 622-3393, ext. 7056
E-mail: Janna.Connor@Washingtonea.org
Web: www.washingtonea.org

Summary To provide funding to Educational Support Personnel (ESP) members of the Washington Education Association (WEA), especially African Americans and other minorities, who are interested in taking classes to obtain an initial teaching certificate.

Eligibility This program is open to WEA/ESP members who are engaged in course work related to obtaining an initial teaching certificate. Applicants must submit a plan for obtaining an initial certificate, a letter describing their passion to become a teacher, evidence of activities and/or leadership in the association, and 3 to 5 letters of reference. Minority members of the association are especially encouraged to apply; 1 of the scholarships is reserved for them.

Financial data The stipend is $1,500.

Duration These are 1-time grants.

Number awarded 3 each year, including 1 reserved for a minority member.

Deadline June of each year.

[665]
WASHINGTON ADMIRAL'S FUND SCHOLARSHIP

National Naval Officers Association-Washington, D.C.
    Chapter
c/o LCDR Stephen Williams
P.O. Box 30784
Alexandria, VA 22310
(703) 644-2605   Fax: (703) 644-8503
E-mail: Stephen.Williams@navy.mil
Web: www.dcnnoa.org/dcnnoa-scholarship

Summary To provide financial assistance to African American and other minority high school seniors from the Washington, D.C. area who are interested in attending a college or university in any state and enrolling in the Navy Reserve Officers Training Corps (NROTC) program.

Eligibility This program is open to minority seniors graduating from high schools in the Washington, D.C. metropolitan area who plan to enroll full time at an accredited 2- or 4-year college or university in any state. Applicants must be planning to enroll in the NROTC program. They must have a GPA of 2.5 or higher and be U.S. citizens or permanent residents. Selection is based on academic achievement, community involvement, and financial need.

Financial data The stipend is $1,000.

Duration 1 year; nonrenewable.

Additional information This program is sponsored by the Washington D.C. Chapter of the National Naval Officers Association (DCNNOA), an organization of African American naval officers, but all minorities are eligible and recipients are not required to join or affiliate with the military in any way. If the recipient fails to enroll in the NROTC unit, all scholarship funds must be returned.

Number awarded 1 each year.

Deadline February of each year.

[666]
WASHINGTON ALLIANCE OF BLACK SCHOOL EDUCATORS SCHOLARSHIPS

Washington Alliance of Black School Educators
Attn: Pamela Lewis-Bridges, President
P.O. Box 39112
Lakewood, WA 98496
(253) 226-4435   E-mail: wabse.info@gmail.com
Web: www.wabse.net

Summary To provide financial assistance to African American high school seniors in Washington who plan to attend college in any state.

Eligibility This program is open to African American seniors graduating from high schools in Washington. Applicants must be planning to attend a 2-year community college or 4-year college or university in any state. They must have completed at least 150 hours of community service and be able to demonstrate financial need. U.S. citizenship is required.

Financial data The stipend is $1,000.

Duration 1 year.

Number awarded 1 or more each year.

Deadline February of each year.

[667]
WASHINGTON DC ALUMNAE CHAPTER SCHOLARSHIPS

Delta Sigma Theta Sorority, Inc.-Washington DC Alumnae
    Chapter
Attn: Scholarship Committee
P.O. Box 90202
Washington, DC 20090-0202
Toll Free: (201) 388-1912
E-mail: scholarship@wdcac.org
Web: www.wdcac.org/scholarship

Summary To provide financial assistance to African American and other high school seniors in Washington, D.C. who plan to attend college in any state.

Eligibility This program is open to seniors graduating from public, charter, parochial, and private high schools in Washington, D.C. and planning to enroll full time at a 2- or 4-year college or university in any state. Applicants must submit an official high school transcript, a copy of their SAT or ACT scores, documentation of financial need, 2 letters of recommendation, and a 1-page autobiographical essay including their academic and career goals, community service involvement, why the scholarship is important, and its expected benefit.

Financial data Stipends range from $1,050 to $2,500 per year.

Duration 1 year; may be renewed.

Additional information The sponsor is the local alumnae chapter of a traditionally African American social sorority.

Number awarded Varies each year.

Deadline March of each year.

[668]
WASHINGTON D.C. AREA SUPPLY OFFICERS SCHOLARSHIP

National Naval Officers Association-Washington, D.C.
    Chapter
c/o LCDR Stephen Williams
P.O. Box 30784
Alexandria, VA 22310
(703) 644-2605   Fax: (703) 644-8503
E-mail: Stephen.Williams@navy.mil
Web: www.dcnnoa.org/dcnnoa-scholarship

Summary To provide financial assistance to African American and other minority high school seniors from the Washington, D.C. area who are interested in attending college in any state.

Eligibility This program is open to minority seniors graduating from high schools in the Washington, D.C. metropolitan area who plan to enroll full time at an accredited 2- or 4-year college or university in any state. Applicants must have a GPA of 3.0 or higher and be U.S. citizens or permanent residents. Selection is based on academic achievement, community involvement, and financial need.

Financial data The stipend is $3,000.

Duration 1 year; nonrenewable.

Additional information This program is sponsored by the Washington D.C. Chapter of the National Naval Officers Association (DCNNOA), an organization of African American naval officers, but all minorities are eligible and recipients are not required to join or affiliate with the military in any way.

Number awarded 1 each year.

Deadline February of each year.

[669]
WASHINGTON DC METROPOLITAN AREA CHAPTER AABE SCHOLARSHIPS

American Association of Blacks in Energy-Washington
  DC Metropolitan Area Chapter
Attn: Scholarship Committee
P.O. Box 77263
Washington, DC 20013
E-mail: aabedc.scholarshipchair@gmail.com
Web: www.aabe.org

Summary To provide financial assistance to members of African American and other underrepresented minority groups who are high school seniors in the Washington, D.C. metropolitan area and planning to major in an energy-related field at a college in any state.

Eligibility This program is open to seniors graduating from high schools in the Washington, D.C. metropolitan area who are planning to work on a bachelor's degree at a college or university in any state. Applicants must be African Americans, Hispanics, or Native Americans who have a GPA of 3.0 or higher and have taken the ACT and/or SAT test. Their intended major must be a field of business, engineering, physical science, mathematics, or technology related to energy. Along with their application, they must submit a 350-word essay that includes 1) when they discovered their interest in the field of energy and what sparked their interest; and 2) either what excites them about the field of energy or how they expect their education to prepare them for the field of energy. Financial need is not considered in the selection process.

Financial data Stipends range from $1,500 to $2,500.

Duration 1 year; nonrenewable.

Additional information Winners are eligible to compete for regional and national scholarships.

Number awarded 3 each year: 1 each at $2,500, $2,000, and $1,500.

Deadline April of each year.

[670]
WASHINGTON SCIENCE TEACHERS ASSOCIATION SCIENCE LEADERSHIP SCHOLARSHIPS

Washington Science Teachers Association
Attn: Andy Boyd, President
2911 88th Street S.E.
Everett, WA 98109
(425) 337-5552   E-mail: boydscience@gmail.com
Web: www.wsta.net/WSTALeadershipScholarship

Summary To provide financial assistance to upper-division students and teachers in Washington, especially African Americans and other minorities, who are interested in training in science education.

Eligibility This program is open to juniors and seniors at colleges and universities in Washington who are working on certification in science education or in elementary education with an emphasis on science. Preference is given to African Americans, Hispanics, Native Americans, Asian and Pacific Islanders, and women.

Financial data The stipend is $2,000.

Duration 1 year; nonrenewable.

Additional information This program began in 2003 as the Peggy Vatter Memorial Scholarships.

Number awarded 1 or more each year.

Deadline June of each year.

[671]
WASHINGTON UNIVERSITY AMGEN SCHOLARS PROGRAM

Washington University
Division of Biology and Biomedical Sciences
Attn: Summer Research Admissions
660 South Euclid Avenue
Campus Box 8226
St. Louis, MO 63110-1093
(314) 362-7963   Toll Free: (800) 852-9074
E-mail: DBBS-summerresearch@wusm.wustl.edu
Web: dbbs.wustl.edu

Summary To provide undergraduate students, especially African Americans and other minorities, with a summer research experience at Washington University in St. Louis in biological and biomedical sciences.

Eligibility This program is open to sophomores, juniors, and non-graduating seniors at 4-year colleges and universities in the United States, Puerto Rico, and U.S. territories. Applicants must be interested in a summer research experience at Washington University in biochemistry, bioengineering, bioinformatics, biology (molecular, cell, and developmental), biopsychology, biotechnology, chemical and biomedical engineering, chemistry, immunology, medical pharmacology, microbiology, molecular genetics, molecular medicine, molecular pharmacology, neurobiology, neuroscience, pathology, physiological psychology, physiological science, statistics, or toxicology. They must have a GPA of 3.2 or higher and an interest in continuing on to a Ph.D. or M.D./Ph.D. (but not M.D.) program. Applications are especially encouraged from students from economically disadvantaged backgrounds, those who attend small liberal arts colleges, and from members of groups traditionally underrepresented in biomedical research (African Americans, Hispanic Americans, Native Americans, Pacific Islanders, women, and people with disabilities). U.S. citizenship or permanent resident status is required.

Financial data Housing, travel to and from St. Louis, meals, and a stipend of $4,000 are provided.

Duration 10 weeks during the summer.

Additional information This program serves as the Washington University component of the Amgen Scholars Program, which operates at 8 other U.S. universities (and the National Institutes of Health) and is funded by the Amgen Foundation.

Number awarded 20 each year.

Deadline January of each year.

[672]
WAVE FELLOWS PROGRAM

California Institute of Technology
Student-Faculty Programs
1200 East California Boulevard
Mail Code 33-087
Pasadena, CA 91125
(626) 395-2885   Fax: (626) 389-5467
E-mail: sfp@caltech.edu
Web: sfp.caltech.edu/programs/wavefellows

Summary To provide an opportunity for African American and other underrepresented college students to work in a research laboratory at California Institute of Technology (Caltech) during the summer.

Eligibility This program is open to underrepresented minorities, women, first-generation college students, geographically underrepresented students, educationally and financially disadvantaged students, and students with disabilities. Applicants must be interested in working during the summer in a modern academic research laboratory at Caltech under the guidance of experienced scientists and engineers. They must be undergraduate sophomores, juniors, or non-graduating seniors who have a GPA of 3.2 or higher and a major in a field of science, technology, engineering, or mathematics (STEM). U.S. citizenship or permanent resident status is required.

Financial data The stipend is $600 per week. A $500 housing allowance is also provided.

Duration 8 to 10 weeks during the summer, beginning in June.

Additional information Support for this program is provided by Edison International and the Genentech Foundation.

Number awarded Varies each year.

Deadline January of each year.

[673]
WAYNE D. CORNILS SCHOLARSHIP

Idaho State Broadcasters Association
1674 Hill Road, Suite 3
Boise, ID 83702
(208) 345-3072   Fax: (208) 343-8046
E-mail: isba@qwestoffice.net
Web: www.idahobroadcasters.org/index.php/scholarships

Summary To provide financial assistance to African Americans and other less advantaged students at Idaho colleges and universities who are preparing for a career in the broadcasting field.

Eligibility This program is open to full-time students at Idaho schools who are preparing for a career in broadcasting, including business administration, sales, journalism, or engineering. Applicants must have a GPA of at least 2.0 for the first 2 years of school or 2.5 for the last 2 years. Along with their application, they must submit a letter of recommendation from the general manager of a broadcasting station that is a member of the Idaho State Broadcasters Association and a 1-page essay describing their career plans and why they want the scholarship. Applications are encouraged from a broad and diverse student population. This scholarship is reserved for a less advantaged applicant.

Financial data The stipend depends on the need of the recipient.

Duration 1 year.

Number awarded 1 each year.

Deadline March of each year.

[674]
WELLS FARGO SCHOLARSHIPS OF THE THURGOOD MARSHALL COLLEGE FUND

Thurgood Marshall College Fund
Attn: Senior Manager of Scholarship Programs
901 F Street, N.W., Suite 300
Washington, DC 20004
(202) 507-4851   Fax: (202) 652-2934
E-mail: deshuandra.walker@tmcfund.org
Web: www.tmcf.org

Summary To provide financial assistance to African American students, especially those majoring in business or finance, at public Historically Black Colleges and Universities (HBCUs) that are members of the Thurgood Marshall College Fund (TMCF).

Eligibility This program is open to full-time sophomores, juniors, and seniors at any of the 47 TMCF member institutions. Applicants may be majoring in any field, but preference is given to those in business or finance. They must have a GPA of 3.0 or higher. Selection is based on merit, but students must submit their Student Aid Report from their FAFSA. Along with their application, they must submit a 500-word essay on the college course that has had the greatest impact of their worldview, personal growth, and/or career plans. U.S. citizenship or permanent resident status is required.

Financial data The stipend is $7,000.

Duration 1 year.

Additional information This program is sponsored by Wells Fargo Bank.

Number awarded 1 or more each year.

Deadline April of each year.

[675]
WESTCHESTER/GREATER CONNECTICUT CHAPTER NBMBAA HIGH SCHOOL SCHOLARSHIP

National Black MBA Association-Westchester/Greater
  Connecticut Chapter
Attn: Scholarship Chair
P.O. Box 3586
Stamford, CT 06905
Toll Free: (866) 966-9942
E-mail: scholarship@nbmbaa-wgc.org
Web: www.nbmbaa-wgc.org/education/scholarship.html

Summary To provide financial assistance to African American and other underrepresented minority high school seniors from Connecticut and Westchester County, New York who plan to study a business-related field at a college in any state.

Eligibility This program is open to seniors graduating from high schools in Connecticut or Westchester County, New York who are members of underrepresented minority groups. Applicants must be planning to enroll full time at an accredited college or university in any state to work on a degree in accounting, business, economics, entrepreneurship, management, marketing, or a related area. They must be U.S. citizens (or in possession of a current student visa) and have a GPA of 3.0 or higher. Along with their application, they must submit a 500-word essay on either of the following topics: 1) why working on a higher education is important to them and their career and educational plans after completion of their undergraduate degree; or 2) how they intend to make an impact in their immediate community, country, and the world through their undergraduate degree. Selection is based on that essay, academic achievement, demonstrated leadership ability, and participation in high school and community activities.

Financial data The stipend is $1,000.

Duration 1 year.

Number awarded 1 or more each year.

Deadline May of each year.

[676]
WESTCHESTER/GREATER CONNECTICUT CHAPTER NBMBAA UNDERGRADUATE SCHOLARSHIP

National Black MBA Association-Westchester/Greater
  Connecticut Chapter
Attn: Scholarship Chair
P.O. Box 3586
Stamford, CT 06905
Toll Free: (866) 966-9942
E-mail: scholarship@nbmbaa-wgc.org
Web: www.nbmbaa-wgc.org/education/scholarship.html

Summary To provide financial assistance to African American and other underrepresented minority residents of Connecticut and Westchester County, New York who are working on a business-related undergraduate degree at a college in any state.

Eligibility This program is open to residents of Connecticut or Westchester County, New York who are members of underrepresented minority groups. Applicants must be enrolled full time at an accredited college or university in any state and working on an undergraduate degree in accounting, business, economics, entrepreneurship, management, marketing, or a related area. They must be U.S. citizens (or in possession of a current student visa) and have a GPA of 3.0 or higher. Along with their application, they must submit a 500-word essay on either of the following topics: 1) why working on a higher education is important to them and their career and educational plans after completion of their undergraduate degree; or 2) how they intend to make an impact in their immediate community, country, and the world through their undergraduate degree. Selection is based on that essay, academic achievement, demonstrated leadership ability, and participation in college and community activities.

Financial data The stipend is $1,000.

Duration 1 year.

Number awarded 1 or more each year.

Deadline December of each year.

[677]
WILLIAM A. BORDERS JR. JUSTICE SCHOLARSHIP

National Naval Officers Association-Washington, D.C.
  Chapter
c/o LCDR Stephen Williams
P.O. Box 30784
Alexandria, VA 22310
(703) 644-2605   Fax: (703) 644-8503
E-mail: Stephen.Williams@navy.mil
Web: www.dcnnoa.org/dcnnoa-scholarship

Summary To provide financial assistance to African American high school seniors from the Washington, D.C. area who are interested in attending college in any state.

Eligibility This program is open to African American seniors graduating from high schools in the Washington, D.C. metropolitan area who plan to enroll full time at an accredited 2- or 4-year college or university in any state. Applicants must have a GPA of 2.5 or higher and be U.S. citizens or permanent residents. Selection is based on academic achievement, community involvement, and financial need.

Financial data The stipend is $1,000.

Duration 1 year; nonrenewable.

Additional information Recipients are not required to join or affiliate with the military in any way. In addition to a number of scholarships with additional requirements, this program includes the following named general scholarships: the David and Sheila Garnett Leadership Scholarship, the Pringle & Pringle Higher Education Scholarship, the Rear Admiral Mack and Nancy Gaston Leadership Scholarship, the Rear Admiral Michelle Howard Excellence in Leadership Scholarship, and the William A. Borders Jr. Justice Scholarship.

Number awarded 1 each year.

Deadline February of each year.

[678]
WILLIAM A. CRAWFORD MINORITY TEACHER SCHOLARSHIP

Indiana Commission for Higher Education
Attn: Financial Aid and Student Support Services
101 West Ohio Street, Suite 300
Indianapolis, IN 46204-4206
(317) 232-1023   Toll Free: (888) 528-4719 (within IN)
Fax: (317) 232-3260   E-mail: Scholars@che.in.gov
Web: www.in.gov/che/4507.htm

Summary To provide scholarship/loans to Black and Hispanic undergraduate students in Indiana interested in preparing for a teaching career at a school in the state.

Eligibility This program is open to Black and Hispanic students seeking certification in order to teach at an accredited elementary or secondary school in Indiana. Applicants must be Indiana residents and U.S. citizens or permanent residents who are enrolled or accepted for enrollment as full-time students at an academic institution in Indiana. Students who are already enrolled in college must have a GPA of 2.0 or higher. Financial need may be considered, but it is not a requirement.

Financial data Minority students demonstrating financial need may receive up to $4,000 per year. They must agree in writing to apply for a teaching position at an accredited school in Indiana following certification and, if hired, to teach for at least 3 years.

Duration 1 year; may be renewed up to 3 additional years if recipients maintain a 2.0 GPA. They may, however, take up to 6 years to complete the program from the start of receiving the first scholarship.

Additional information This program began in 1988 to address the critical shortage of Black and Hispanic teachers in Indiana. It was given its current name in 2016. Participating colleges in Indiana select the recipients. Students must submit their application to the financial aid office of the college they plan to attend.

Number awarded Varies each year.

Deadline September of each year.

[679]
WILLIAM K. SCHUBERT M.D. MINORITY NURSING SCHOLARSHIP

Cincinnati Children's Hospital Medical Center
Attn: Office of Diversity and Inclusion, MLC 9008
3333 Burnet Avenue
Cincinnati, OH 45229-3026
(513) 803-6416   Toll Free: (800) 344-2462
Fax: (513) 636-5643   TDD: (513) 636-4900
E-mail: diversity@cchmc.org
Web: www.cincinnatichildrens.org

Summary To provide financial assistance to African American and members of other underrepresented groups interested in working on a bachelor's or master's degree in nursing to prepare for licensure in Ohio.

Eligibility This program is open to members of groups underrepresented in the nursing profession (Blacks or African Americans, Hispanics or Latinos, American Indians or Alaska Natives, Hawaiian Natives or other Pacific Islanders, Asians, or males). Applicants must be enrolled or accepted in a professional bachelor's or master's registered nurse program at an accredited school of nursing to prepare for initial licensure in Ohio. They must have a GPA of 2.75 or higher. Along with their application, they must submit a 750-word essay that covers 1) their long-range personal, educational, and professional goals; 2) why they chose nursing as a profession; 3) how their experience as a member of an underrepresented group has influenced a major professional and/or personal decision in their life; 4) any unique qualifications, experiences, or special talents that demonstrate their creativity; and 5) how their work experience has contributed to their personal development.

Financial data The stipend is $2,750 per year.

Duration 1 year. May be renewed up to 3 additional years for students working on a bachelor's degree or 1 additional year for students working on a master's degree; renewal requires that students maintain a GPA of 2.75 or higher.

Number awarded 1 or more each year.

Deadline April of each year.

[680]
WILLIAM RANDOLPH HEARST ENDOWMENT SCHOLARSHIPS

National Action Council for Minorities in Engineering
Attn: Director, Scholarships and University Relations
440 Hamilton Avenue, Suite 302
White Plains, NY 10601-1813
(914) 539-4316   Fax: (914) 539-4032
E-mail: scholars@nacme.org
Web: www.nacme.org/scholarships

Summary To provide financial assistance to African American and other underrepresented minority college freshmen or sophomores majoring in engineering or related fields.

Eligibility This program is open to African American, Latino, and American Indian college freshmen and sophomores who have a GPA of 2.8 or higher and have demonstrated academic excellence, leadership skills, and a commitment to science and engineering as a career. Applicants must be enrolled full time at an ABET-accredited engineering program. Fields of study include all areas of engineering as well as computer science, materials science, mathematics, operations research, or physics.

Financial data The stipend is $2,500 per year. Funds are sent directly to the recipient's university.

Duration Up to 4 years.

Additional information This program was established by the William Randolph Hearst Foundation.

Number awarded 2 each year.

Deadline April of each year.

[681]
WILLIAM RUCKER GREENWOOD SCHOLARSHIP

Association for Women Geoscientists-Potomac Chapter
Attn: Scholarships
P.O. Box 6644
Arlington, VA 22206-0644
E-mail: awgpotomacschol@hotmail.com
Web: www.awg.org/members/po_scholarships.htm

Summary To provide financial assistance to African American and other minority women from any state working on an undergraduate or graduate degree in the geosciences at a college in the Potomac Bay region.

Eligibility This program is open to minority women who are residents of any state and currently enrolled as full-time undergraduate or graduate geoscience majors at an accredited, degree-granting college or university in Delaware, the District of Columbia, Maryland, Virginia, or West Virginia. Selection is based on the applicant's 1) participation in geoscience or earth science educational activities; and 2) potential for leadership as a future geoscience professional.

Financial data The stipend is $1,000. The recipient also is granted a 1-year membership in the Association for Women Geoscientists (AWG).

Duration 1 year.

Number awarded 1 each year.

Deadline April of each year.

[682]
WILLIAM SAMBER SR. AVIATION/MATH AND SCIENCE SCHOLARSHIP

African-American/Caribbean Education Association, Inc.
P.O. Box 1224
Valley Stream, NY 11582-1224
(718) 949-6733   E-mail: aaceainc@yahoo.com
Web: www.aaceainc.com/Scholarships.html

Summary To provide financial assistance to high school seniors of African American or Caribbean heritage who plan to study a field related to aviation, mathematics, or science in college.

Eligibility This program is open to graduating high school seniors who are U.S. citizens of African American or Caribbean heritage. Applicants must be planning to attend a college or university and major in a field related to a career in aviation, mathematics, or science. They must have completed 4 years of specified college preparatory courses with a grade of 90 or higher and have an SAT score of at least 1790. They must also have completed at least 200 hours of community service during their 4 years of high school, preferably in the field that they plan to study in college. Financial need is not considered in the selection process. New York residency is not required, but applicants must be available for an interview in the Queens, New York area.

Financial data The stipend ranges from $1,000 to $1,500. Funds are paid directly to the recipient.

Duration 1 year.

Number awarded 2 each year.

Deadline April of each year.

[683]
WILLIE BRADSHAW MEMORIAL ENDOWED SCHOLARSHIPS

North Carolina High School Athletic Association
Attn: Director of Grants and Fundraising
222 Finley Golf Course Road
P.O. Box 3216
Chapel Hill, NC 27515-3216
(919) 240-7371   Fax: (919) 240-7399
E-mail: mary@nchsaa.org
Web: www.nchsaa.org

Summary To provide financial assistance to African American and other minority seniors (males and females considered separately) at high schools in North Carolina who have

participated in lacrosse and plan to attend college in any state.

Eligibility This program is open to African American, Hispanic American, American Indian/Alaska Native, and Asian Pacific Islander American seniors graduating from high schools that are members of the North Carolina High School Athletic Association (NCHSAA). Applicants must be U.S. citizens, nationals, or permanent residents planning to attend college in any state. They must have participated in a sanctioned varsity sport, demonstrate leadership abilities through participation in community service and extracurricular or other activities, have clean school and athletic disciplinary records, and have adjusted gross family income between $30,000 and $75,000 per year. Males and females are considered separately.

Financial data The stipend is $750 for regional winners; state winners receive an additional $1,000.

Duration 1 year; nonrenewable.

Number awarded 16 regional winners (1 male and 1 female in each of 8 regions) are selected each year; from those winners, 1 male and 1 female are selected as state winners.

Deadline February of each year.

[684]
WILLIE J. WILLIAMS MUSIC SCHOLARSHIP

African Methodist Episcopal Church
Eleventh Episcopal District Lay Organization
c/o Beulah Gregory
712 Bragg Drive
Jacksonville, FL 32305
(850) 574-6596   E-mail: eedlo@eedlo.org
Web: www.eedlo.org/scholarships.html

Summary To provide financial assistance to members of African Methodist Episcopal (AME) churches in Florida who are interested in studying music at an Historically Black College or University (HBCU).

Eligibility This program is open to seniors graduating from public or private high schools in Florida who are members of AME churches. Applicants must be planning to enroll at an HBCU and major in music; preference may be given to students at an AME church college or university. Along with their application, they must submit a 1-page essay on why they should be awarded this scholarship and a statement regarding their financial need.

Financial data A stipend is awarded (amount not specified).

Duration 1 year.

Number awarded 1 or more each year.

Deadline Students must submit their applications to their local church by January of each year.

[685]
WILLIE POLK, JR. MEMORIAL SCHOLARSHIPS

Knights of Peter Claver, Inc.
Attn: The Claver Foundation
1825 Orleans Avenue
New Orleans, LA 70116-2894
(504) 821-4225   Fax: (504) 821-4253
E-mail: info@claverfundation.org
Web: www.claverfundation.org/programs

Summary To provide financial assistance for college to high school seniors with a connection of the Knights of Peter Claver (an organization for Catholic men of color).

Eligibility This program is open to practicing Catholics who are graduating high school seniors planning to attend a college or university. Applicants, or at least 1 of their parents, must be a member of the Knights of Peter Claver or its Ladies Auxiliary. They must rank in the top quarter of their class and have scores of at least 900 on the SAT or 18 on the ACT. U.S. citizenship is required.

Financial data The stipend is $1,000.

Duration 1 year; nonrenewable.

Additional information The Knights of Peter Claver was founded in 1909 at Mobile, Alabama as a Catholic fraternal society for men of color.

Number awarded Varies each year.

Deadline May of each year.

[686]
WINGS FINANCIAL SCHOLARSHIPS

Organization of Black Aerospace Professionals, Inc.
Attn: Scholarship Coordinator
One Westbrook Corporate Center, Suite 300
Westchester, IL 60154
(708) 449-7755   Toll Free: (800) JET-OBAP
Fax: (708) 449-7754 E-mail: obapscholarships@obap.org
Web: www.obap.org/wings-financial-scholarship

Summary To provide financial assistance to African American high school seniors and college students who are interested in working on an aerospace degree at a school in any state.

Eligibility This program is open to African American high school seniors and current college students who are enrolled or planning to enroll in an aerospace program at an accredited college or university. Applicants must have a GPA of 2.7 or higher. Along with their application, they must submit a 500-word essay describing how this scholarship would impact their career goals.

Financial data The stipend is $1,000.

Duration 1 year.

Additional information This program is sponsored by Wings Financial Credit Union.

Number awarded 2 each year.

Deadline May of each year.

[687]
WISCONSIN CHAPTER AABE SCHOLARSHIPS

American Association of Blacks in Energy-Wisconsin
   Chapter
Attn: Scholarship Committee
P.O. Box 1907
Milwaukee, WI 53203
E-mail: aabe-wi@we-energies.com
Web: www.aabe.org/index.php?component=pages&id=627

Summary To provide financial assistance to African Americans and members of other underrepresented minority groups who are high school seniors in Wisconsin and planning to major in an energy-related field at a college in any state.

Eligibility This program is open to seniors graduating from high schools in Tennessee and planning to attend a college or university in any state. Applicants must be African Americans, Hispanics, or Native Americans who have a GPA of 3.0 or higher and have taken the ACT and/or SAT test. Their intended major must be business, engineering, technology, mathematics, the physical sciences, or other energy-related field. Along with their application, they must submit a 350-word essay that includes 1) when they discovered their interest in the field of energy and what sparked their interest; and 2) either what excites them about the field of energy or how they expect their education to prepare them for the field of energy. Financial need is not considered in the selection process.

Financial data The stipend is $1,000 for academic scholarships and $250 for book awards.

Duration 1 year.

Additional information Winners are eligible to compete for regional and national scholarships.

Number awarded 1 academic scholarships and 2 book awards are presented each year.

Deadline March of each year.

[688]
WISCONSIN MINORITY TEACHER LOANS

Wisconsin Higher Educational Aids Board
131 West Wilson Street, Suite 902
P.O. Box 7885
Madison, WI 53707-7885
(608) 267-2212   Fax: (608) 267-2808
E-mail: deanna.schulz@wi.gov
Web: www.heab.state.wi.us/programs.html

Summary To provide forgivable loans to African Americans and other minorities in Wisconsin who are interested in teaching at schools in high demand areas of Milwaukee.

Eligibility This program is open to residents of Wisconsin who are African Americans, Hispanic Americans, American Indians, or southeast Asians (students who were admitted to the United States after December 31, 1975 and who are a former citizen of Laos, Vietnam, or Cambodia or whose ancestor was a citizen of 1 of those countries). Applicants must be enrolled at least half time as sophomores, juniors, or seniors at an independent or public institution in the state in a program leading to teaching licensure in a discipline identified as a teacher shortage area and have a GPA of 3.0 or higher. They must agree to teach at a public or private elementary or secondary school in the city of Milwaukee in a high-demand area related to their discipline. Financial need is not considered in the selection process.

Financial data Loans are provided up to $10,000 per year, or a maximum of $30,000. For each year the student teaches in an eligible school and receives a rating of proficient or distinguished on the educator effectiveness system, 25% of the loan is forgiven; if the student does not teach at an eligible school, the loan must be repaid at an interest rate of 5%.

Duration 1 year; may be renewed 2 additional years.

Additional information Eligible students should apply through their school's financial aid office.

Number awarded Varies each year.

Deadline Deadline dates vary by institution; check with your school's financial aid office.

[689]
WISCONSIN MINORITY UNDERGRADUATE RETENTION GRANTS

Wisconsin Higher Educational Aids Board
131 West Wilson Street, Suite 902
P.O. Box 7885
Madison, WI 53707-7885
(608) 267-2212   Fax: (608) 267-2808
E-mail: deanna.schulz@wi.gov
Web: www.heab.state.wi.us/programs.html

Summary To provide financial assistance to African Americans and other minorities in Wisconsin who are currently enrolled at a college in the state.

Eligibility This program is open to residents of Wisconsin who are African Americans, Hispanic Americans, American Indians, or southeast Asians (students who were admitted to the United States after December 31, 1975 and who are a former citizen of Laos, Vietnam, or Cambodia or whose ancestor was a citizen of 1 of those countries). Applicants must be enrolled at least half time as sophomores, juniors, seniors, or fifth-year undergraduates at a Wisconsin technical college, tribal college, or independent college or university in the state. They must be nominated by their institution and be able to demonstrate financial need.

Financial data Stipends range from $250 to $2,500 per year, depending on the need of the recipient.

Duration Up to 4 years.

Additional information The Wisconsin Higher Educational Aids Board administers this program for students at private nonprofit institutions, technical colleges, and tribal colleges. The University of Wisconsin has a similar program for students attending any of the branches of that system. Eligible students should apply through their school's financial aid office.

Number awarded Varies each year.

Deadline Deadline dates vary by institution; check with your school's financial aid office.

[690]
WOMAN WHO MOVES THE NATION SCHOLARSHIP

Conference of Minority Transportation Officials
Attn: National Scholarship Program
100 M Street, S.E., Suite 917
Washington, DC 20003
(202) 506-2917   E-mail: info@comto.org
Web: www.comto.org/page/scholarships

Summary To provide financial assistance to African American and other minority women who are working on an undergraduate or graduate degree in specified fields to prepare for a management career in a transportation-related organization.

Eligibility This program is open to minority women who are working on an undergraduate or graduate degree with intent to lead in some capacity as a supervisor, manager, director, or other position in transit or a transportation-related organization. Applicants may be studying business, entrepreneurship, political science, or other specialized area. They must have a GPA of 3.0 or higher. Along with their application they must submit a cover letter on their transportation-related career goals and life aspirations. Financial need is not considered in the selection process.

Financial data The stipend is $5,000. Funds are paid directly to the recipient's college or university.

Duration 1 year.

Number awarded 1 each year.

Deadline April of each year.

[691]
WOMEN'S TRANSPORTATION SEMINAR JUNIOR COLLEGE SCHOLARSHIP

Women's Transportation Seminar
Attn: WTS Foundation
1701 K Street, N.W., Suite 800
Washington, DC 20006
(202) 955-5085   Fax: (202) 955-5088
E-mail: wts@wtsinternational.org
Web: www.wtsinternational.org/education/scholarships

Summary To provide financial assistance to women, especially African Americans and other minorities, who are enrolled at a community college or trade school to prepare for a career in transportation.

Eligibility This program is open to women who are working on an associate or technical degree in transportation or a transportation-related field (e.g., transportation engineering, planning, finance, or logistics). Applicants must have a GPA of 3.0 or higher. Along with their application, they must submit a 500-word statement about their career goals after graduation and why they think they should receive the scholarship award. Applications must be submitted first to a local chapter; the chapters forward selected applications for consideration on the national level. Minority women are especially encouraged to apply. Selection is based on transportation involvement and goals, job skills, academic record, and leadership potential; financial need is not considered.

Financial data The stipend is $1,000.

Duration 1 year.

Additional information Local chapters may also award additional funding to winners for their area.

Number awarded 1 each year.

Deadline Applications must be submitted by November to a local WTS chapter.

[692]
WOODS HOLE OCEANOGRAPHIC INSTITUTION MINORITY FELLOWSHIPS

Woods Hole Oceanographic Institution
Attn: Academic Programs Office
Clark Laboratory 223, MS 31
360 Woods Hole Road
Woods Hole, MA 02543-1541
(508) 289-2219   Fax: (508) 457-2188
E-mail: education@whoi.edu
Web: www.whoi.edu/page.do?pid=9377

Summary To provide work experience to African American and other minority group members who are interested in preparing for careers in the marine sciences, oceanographic engineering, or marine policy.

Eligibility This program is open to ethnic minority undergraduates enrolled in U.S. colleges or universities who have completed at least 1 year of study and who are interested in the physical or natural sciences, mathematics, engineering, or marine policy. Applicants must be U.S. citizens or permanent residents and African American or Black; Asian American; Chicano, Mexican American, Puerto Rican or other Hispanic; or Native American, Alaska Native, or Native Hawaiian. They must be interested in participating in a program of study and research at Woods Hole Oceanographic Institution. Selection is based on previous academic and scientific achievements and promise as future ocean scientists or ocean engineers.

Financial data   The stipend is $500 per week; trainees also receive free housing and additional support for travel to Woods Hole.

Duration   10 to 12 weeks during the summer or 1 semester during the academic year; renewable.

Additional information   Trainees are assigned advisers who supervise their research programs and supplementary study activities. Some traineeships involve field work or research cruises. This program is conducted as part of the Research Experiences for Undergraduates (REU) Program of the National Science Foundation.

Number awarded   4 to 5 each year.

Deadline   February of each year.

[693]
WOODS HOLE OCEANOGRAPHIC INSTITUTION SUMMER STUDENT FELLOWSHIP PROGRAM

Woods Hole Oceanographic Institution
Attn: Academic Programs Office
Clark Laboratory 223, MS 31
360 Woods Hole Road
Woods Hole, MA 02543-1541
(508) 289-2219   Fax: (508) 457-2188
E-mail: education@whoi.edu
Web: www.whoi.edu/main/ssf/program-overview

Summary   To provide funding to undergraduates, especially African Americans and other underrepresented minorities, who are interested in conducting research at the Woods Hole Oceanographic Institution (WHOI) during the summer.

Eligibility   This program is open to undergraduate students who have completed their junior year at colleges or universities with a major in any science or engineering field, including (but not limited to) biology, chemistry, engineering, geology, geophysics, mathematics, meteorology, physics, oceanography, or marine policy. Applicants must have at least a tentative interest in the ocean sciences, oceanographic engineering, mathematics, or marine policy. They must be interested in conducting an independent research project under the guidance of a member of the WHOI research staff. Along with their application, they must submit a 3-page statement on how a summer of research at WHOI would benefit their education and career plans, the skills they expect to obtain from this research experience, the skills they have that would make them a good researcher, information on previous research projects in which they have been involved, and the areas of marine research in which they are interested and why. Selection is based on previous academic and scientific achievements and promise as future ocean scientists or ocean engineers. The program actively recruits members of groups underrepresented in marine science (African Americans, Hispanic Americans, Native Americans, and Pacific Islanders).

Financial data   The stipend is $585 per week; housing is also provided. Additional support up to $650 may be provided for travel.

Duration   10 to 12 weeks during the summer.

Additional information   Fellows are not required to take any prescribed courses nor are they required to provide any services to the institution in return for the grant. This program is supported by grants from the National Science Foundation's Research Experiences for Undergraduates Program. Fellows are expected to give an oral report on their research.

Number awarded   Between 25 and 30 fellows are selected each year.

Deadline   February of each year.

[694]
WORLDSTUDIO AIGA SCHOLARSHIPS

AIGA, the professional association for design
Attn: Scholarships
233 Broadway, 17th floor
New York, NY 10279
(212) 710-3111   E-mail: scholarship@aiga.org
Web: www.aiga.org/worldstudio-scholarship

Summary   To provide financial assistance to African American and other minority or economically disadvantaged students who are interested in working on an undergraduate or graduate degree in specified fields of the arts.

Eligibility   This program is open to undergraduate and graduate students who are currently enrolled or planning to enroll full time at an accredited college or university and work on a degree in 1 of the following areas: fine art, graphic design (including visual design), illustration (including animation), interactive design (including UI/UX, motion, digital, and web design), or photography. Other fields of the arts, (e.g., industrial design, interior design, film, architecture, landscape design, theater design, fashion design) are not eligible. Although not required, minority status is a significant factor in the selection process. U.S. citizenship or permanent resident status is required. Applicants must have a GPA of 2.0 or higher. Along with their application, they must submit a 600-word statement of purpose that includes a brief autobiography, an explanation of how their experiences have influenced their creative work and/or their career plans, and how they see themselves contributing to the community at large in the future. Selection is based on that statement, the quality of submitted work, financial need, minority status, recommendations, and academic record.

Financial data   Basic stipends range from $2,000 to $3,000, but awards up to $5,000 are also presented at the discretion of the jury. Honorable mentions are $500. Funds are paid directly to the recipient's school.

Duration   1 academic year. Recipients may reapply.

Additional information   This program is offered by AIGA, founded in 1914 as the American Institute of Graphic Arts, in cooperation with the Worldstudio Foundation.

Number awarded   Varies each year; recently, 16 scholarships and 2 honorable mentions were awarded.

Deadline   April of each year.

[695]
WSP/PARSONS BRINCKERHOFF ENGINEERING SCHOLARSHIP

Conference of Minority Transportation Officials
Attn: National Scholarship Program
100 M Street, S.E., Suite 917
Washington, DC 20003
(202) 506-2917   E-mail: info@comto.org
Web: www.comto.org/page/scholarships

Summary To provide financial assistance to African American and other members of the Conference of Minority Transportation Officials (COMTO) and their families who are working on an undergraduate degree in engineering.

Eligibility This program is open to undergraduate students who are members and their parents, guardians, or grandparents who have been members of COMTO for at least 1 year. Applicants must be working on a degree in engineering and have a GPA of 3.0 or higher. Along with their application they must submit a cover letter on their transportation-related career goals and life aspirations. Financial need is not considered in the selection process.

Financial data The stipend is $2,500. Funds are paid directly to the recipient's college or university.

Duration 1 year.

Additional information This program is sponsored by WSP USA, formerly Parsons Brinckerhoff, Inc.

Number awarded 2 each year.

Deadline April of each year.

[696]
WSP/PARSONS BRINCKERHOFF GOLDEN APPLE SCHOLARSHIP

Conference of Minority Transportation Officials
Attn: National Scholarship Program
100 M Street, S.E., Suite 917
Washington, DC 20003
(202) 506-2917   E-mail: info@comto.org
Web: www.comto.org/page/scholarships

Summary To provide financial assistance to African American and other members of the Conference of Minority Transportation Officials (COMTO) and their children who are high school seniors planning to attend college to prepare for a career in transportation.

Eligibility This program is open to graduating high school seniors who are members of COMTO or whose parents are members. Applicants must be planning to attend an accredited college, university, or vocational/technical institution to prepare for a career in transportation. They must have a GPA of 2.0 or higher. Along with their application they must submit a cover letter on their transportation-related career goals and life aspirations. Financial need is not considered in the selection process.

Financial data The stipend is $2,500. Funds are paid directly to the recipient's college or university.

Duration 1 year.

Additional information This program is sponsored by WSP USA, formerly Parsons Brinckerhoff, Inc.

Number awarded 2 each year.

Deadline April of each year.

[697]
WTS TRANSPORTATION YOU HIGH SCHOOL SCHOLARSHIP

Women's Transportation Seminar
Attn: WTS Foundation
1701 K Street, N.W., Suite 800
Washington, DC 20006
(202) 955-5085   Fax: (202) 955-5088
E-mail: wts@wtsinternational.org
Web: www.wtsinternational.org/education/scholarships

Summary To provide financial assistance to female high school seniors, especially African Americans and other minorities, who are studying fields of science, technology, engineering, or mathematics (STEM) and planning to attend college to prepare for a career in transportation.

Eligibility This program is open to women who are high school seniors with a GPA of 3.0 or higher. Applicants must be studying STEM fields in high school and be planning to attend college to prepare for a career in transportation (e.g., civil engineering, city planning, logistics, automotive engineering, truck repair). Along with their application, they must submit a 500-word statement about their career goals after graduation and why they think they should receive the scholarship. Applications must be submitted first to a local chapter; the chapters forward selected applications for consideration on the national level. Minority women are especially encouraged to apply. Selection is based on transportation involvement and goals, job skills, academic record, and leadership potential; financial need is not considered.

Financial data The stipend is $1,000.

Duration 1 year.

Additional information Local chapters may also award additional funding to winners for their area.

Number awarded 1 each year.

Deadline Applications must be submitted by November to a local WTS chapter.

[698]
XEROX TECHNICAL MINORITY SCHOLARSHIP PROGRAM

Xerox Corporation
Attn: Technical Minority Scholarship Program
150 State Street, Fourth Floor
Rochester, NY 14614
Toll Free: (877) 747-3625 E-mail: xtmsp@rballiance.com
Web: www.xerox.com/jobs/minority-scholarships/enus.html

Summary To provide financial assistance to African Americans and other minorities interested in undergraduate or graduate education in the sciences and/or engineering.

Eligibility This program is open to minorities (people of African American, Asian, Pacific Islander, Native American, Native Alaskan, or Hispanic descent) working full time on a bachelor's, master's, or doctoral degree in chemistry, computing and software systems, engineering (chemical, computer, electrical, imaging, manufacturing, mechanical, optical, or software), information management, laser optics, materials science, physics, or printing management science. Applicants must be U.S. citizens or permanent residents with a GPA of 3.0 or higher and attending a 4-year college or university.

Financial data Stipends range from $1,000 to $10,000.

Duration   1 year.

Number awarded   Varies each year, recently, 128 were awarded.

Deadline   September of each year.

[699]
XI PSI OMEGA CHAPTER SCHOLARSHIPS

Alpha Kappa Alpha Sorority, Inc.-Xi Psi Omega Chapter
Attn: President
P.O. Box 140894
Anchorage, AK 99514
(907) 346-3998   E-mail: akaxpo@gmail.com
Web: www.xipsiomega.com/scholarship.html

Summary   To provide financial assistance to high school seniors (especially African American women) from Alaska who plan to attend college in any state.

Eligibility   This program is open to seniors graduating from high schools in Alaska who are planning to attend a 2- or 4-year accredited college or university in any state. Applicants must have a GPA of 2.5 or higher and a record of active participation in school and community activities. Alpha Kappa Alpha (AKA) is currently 1 of the largest social sororities whose membership is predominantly African American women.

Financial data   A stipend is awarded (amount not specified).

Duration   1 year; nonrenewable.

Additional information   The Xi Psi Omega chapter of AKA serves alumnae members in Alaska.

Number awarded   1 or more each year.

Deadline   March of each year.

[700]
XI ZETA OMEGA FELLOWSHIP

Alpha Kappa Alpha Sorority, Inc.
Attn: Educational Advancement Foundation
5656 South Stony Island Avenue
Chicago, IL 60637
(773) 947-0026   Toll Free: (800) 653-6528
Fax: (773) 947-0277   E-mail: akaeaf@akaeaf.net
Web: www.akaeaf.org/fellowships_endowments.htm

Summary   To provide financial assistance to undergraduates from designated states (especially African American women) who are working on a degree in early childhood education.

Eligibility   This program is open to residents of North Atlantic states (Connecticut, Delaware, Maine, Maryland, Massachusetts, New Hampshire, New Jersey, eastern New York, eastern Pennsylvania, Rhode Island, Vermont, and Washington, D.C.) who are enrolled full time as sophomores or higher in an accredited degree-granting institution in any state. Applicants must be majoring in early childhood education. Along with their application, they must submit 1) a list of honors, awards, and scholarships received; 2) a list of organizations in which they have memberships, especially minority organizations; and 3) a statement of their personal and career goals, including how this scholarship will enhance their ability to attain those goals. The sponsor is a traditionally African American women's sorority.

Financial data   A stipend is awarded (amount not specified).

Duration   1 year.

Number awarded   1 or more each even-numbered year.

Deadline   April of each even-numbered year.

[701]
YOUTH PARTNERS ACCESSING CAPITAL SCHOLARSHIPS

Alpha Kappa Alpha Sorority, Inc.
Attn: Educational Advancement Foundation
5656 South Stony Island Avenue
Chicago, IL 60637
(773) 947-0026   Toll Free: (800) 653-6528
Fax: (773) 947-0277   E-mail: akaeaf@akaeaf.net
Web: www.akaeaf.org/undergraduate_scholarships.htm

Summary   To provide financial assistance to undergraduate members of Alpha Kappa Alpha sorority who demonstrate outstanding community service.

Eligibility   This program is open to members of the organization, a traditionally African American women's sorority, who are working at least as sophomores on an undergraduate degree at an accredited degree-granting institution. Applicants must have a GPA of 3.0 or higher and a record of demonstrated participation in leadership, volunteer, civic, or campus activities. They must be able to demonstrate exceptional academic achievement or extreme financial need.

Financial data   Stipends vary; recently, they averaged $1,300.

Duration   1 year.

Number awarded   Varies each year; recently, the sponsor awarded a total of 14 Youth Partners Accessing Capital (P.A.C.) grants.

Deadline   April of each year.

[702]
YOUTH PARTNERS ACCESSING CAPITAL SERVICE AWARDS

Alpha Kappa Alpha Sorority, Inc.
Attn: Educational Advancement Foundation
5656 South Stony Island Avenue
Chicago, IL 60637
(773) 947-0026   Toll Free: (800) 653-6528
Fax: (773) 947-0277   E-mail: akaeaf@akaeaf.net
Web: www.akaeaf.org/undergraduate_scholarships.htm

Summary   To provide funding to undergraduate members of Alpha Kappa Alpha sorority interested in conducting a project to support the platform of the sorority.

Eligibility   This program is open to members of the organization, a traditionally African American women's sorority, who are working at least as sophomores on an undergraduate degree at an accredited degree-granting institution. Applicants must have a GPA of 3.0 or higher and a record of demonstrated participation in leadership, volunteer, civic, or campus activities. They must be proposing to conduct a community service project that will implement 1 of the platforms of the sorority: emerging young leaders, health, global poverty, economic security, social justice and human rights, or internal leadership training for external service. Along with their application, they must submit a personal goal statement on how they promote healing, nurturing, learning, and uplifting of youth by assisting in developing life-long learning skills.

Financial data   Grants range from $500 to $1,000.

Duration 1 year; nonrenewable.

Additional information This program began in 1997.

Number awarded Varies each year; recently, the sponsor awarded a total of 14 Youth Partners Accessing Capital (P.A.C.) grants.

Deadline August of each year.

[703]
ZETA PHI BETA GENERAL UNDERGRADUATE SCHOLARSHIPS

Zeta Phi Beta Sorority, Inc.
Attn: National Educational Foundation
1734 New Hampshire Avenue, N.W.
Washington, DC 20009
(202) 387-3103   Fax: (202) 232-4593
E-mail: info@zetaphibetasororityhq.org
Web: www.zpbnef1975.org/scholarships-and-descriptions

Summary To provide financial assistance to African American and other students interested in postsecondary education.

Eligibility This program is open to high school seniors or college students enrolled or planning to enroll in a postsecondary institution of higher learning in the United States. Applicants must be enrolled or planning to enroll on a full-time basis. Along with their application, they must submit a 150-word essay on their educational goals and professional aspirations, how this award will help them to achieve those goals, and why they should receive the award. Financial need is not considered in the selection process.

Financial data The stipend ranges from $500 to $1,000 per year; funds are paid directly to the recipient's college or university to be applied to tuition or other fees.

Duration 1 academic year; may be renewed.

Additional information Zeta Phi Beta is a traditionally African American sorority.

Number awarded Varies each year.

Deadline January of each year.

Graduate Students

Listed alphabetically by program title and described in detail here are 519 fellowships, forgivable loans, grants, awards, and other sources of "free money" set aside for African Americans who are incoming, continuing, or returning graduate students working on a master's, doctoral, or professional degree. This funding is available to support study, training, research, and/or creative activities in the United States.

[704]
A. GRACE LEE MIMS VOCAL SCHOLARSHIP

Cleveland Foundation
Attn: Scholarship Processing
1422 Euclid Avenue, Suite 1300
Cleveland, OH 44115-2001
(216) 861-3810   Fax: (216) 861-1729
E-mail: mbaker@clevefdn.org
Web: www.clevelandfoundation.org

Summary To provide financial assistance to African Americans who have a connection to Ohio and are interested in working on a master's degree in vocal music or education with an emphasis on Negro spirituals.

Eligibility This program is open to African American graduate students born, reared, or residing in Ohio. Applicants must be working on a master's degree at an institution (college, university, conservatory) in any state in vocal performance or music education with an emphasis on voice. They must have a GPA of 2.0 or higher. Along with their application, they must submit 1) 3 letters of recommendation from voice teachers or music professors attesting to their musical talent, moral character, and dedication to the survival of the Negro spiritual; 2) a personal statement describing their commitment to ensure the preservation of the Negro spiritual through their performance or teaching career; 3) an audio tape or CD of a recent performance (concert or recital); 4) 3 music programs over at least a 2-year span including their performance of Negro spirituals; and 5) a detailed budget for their academic year's educational expenses. U.S. citizenship is required.

Financial data The stipend is $10,000 per year. Funds must be applied to tuition, fees, books, supplies, and equipment required for the program.

Duration 1 year; recipients may reapply.

Number awarded 1 or more each year.

Deadline March of each year.

[705]
ACADEMIC LIBRARY ASSOCIATION OF OHIO DIVERSITY SCHOLARSHIP

Academic Library Association of Ohio
c/o Eileen Theodore-Shusta, Diversity Committee Chair
Ohio University
Library Administrative Services
422 Alden
30 Park Place
Athens, OH 45701
(740) 593-2989   E-mail: theodore@ohio.edu
Web: www.alaoweb.org/procmanual/policies.html#diversity

Summary To provide financial assistance to African American and other residents of Ohio who are working on a master's degree in library science at a school in any state and will contribute to diversity in the profession.

Eligibility This program is open to residents of Ohio who are enrolled or entering an ALA-accredited program for a master's degree in library science, either on campus or via distance education. Applicants must be able to demonstrate how they will contribute to diversity in the profession, including (but not limited to) race or ethnicity, sexual orientation, life experience, physical ability, and a sense of commitment to those and other diversity issues. Along with their application, they must submit 1) a list of participation in honor societies or

professional organizations, awards, scholarships, prizes, honors, or class offices; 2) a list of their community, civic, organizational, or volunteer experiences; and 3) an essay on their understanding of and commitment to diversity in libraries, including how they, as library school students and future professionals, might address the issue.

Financial data The stipend is $1,500.

Duration 1 year.

Number awarded 2 each year.

Deadline March of each year.

[706]
ACADEMY OF NUTRITION AND DIETETICS GRADUATE SCHOLARSHIPS

Academy of Nutrition and Dietetics
Attn: Foundation
120 South Riverside Plaza, Suite 2000
Chicago, IL 60606-6995
(312) 899-4821   Toll Free: (800) 877-1600, ext. 4821
Fax: (312) 899-4796   E-mail: scholarship@eatright.org
Web: www.eatrightacend.org

Summary To provide financial assistance to graduate student members of the Academy of Nutrition and Dietetics, including African Americans and members of other underrepresented groups.

Eligibility This program is open to members of the academy who are enrolled in the second year of a master's or doctoral degree program in dietetics. Applicants who are currently completing a dietetic internship or pre-professional practice program that is combined with a graduate program may also apply. The graduate scholarships are available only to U.S. citizens and permanent residents. Applicants should intend to practice in the field of dietetics. Some scholarships require specific areas of study (e.g., public health nutrition, food service administration) and status as a registered dietitian. Others may require membership in a specific dietetic practice group, residency in a specific state, or underrepresented minority group status. The same application form can be used for all categories.

Financial data Stipends range from $500 to $10,000.

Duration 1 year.

Additional information The Academy of Nutrition and Dietetics was formerly the American Dietetic Association.

Number awarded Approximately 60 each year.

Deadline February of each year.

[707]
ACC GREATER PHILADELPHIA DIVERSITY CORPORATE SUMMER INTERNSHIP

Association of Corporate Counsel-Greater Philadelphia Chapter
c/o Anne Bancroft, Diversity Committee Co-Chair
Exelon Business Services Company
2301 Market Street, Suite 23
Philadelphia, PA 19103
Toll Free: (800) 494-4000
E-mail: anne.bancroft@exeloncorp.com
Web: www.acc.com

Summary To provide an opportunity for law students from African American and other diverse backgrounds to gain summer work experience in corporate law at firms in the Philadelphia area.

Eligibility   This program is open to students who are members of minority groups traditionally underrepresented in the legal profession (African American, Asian/Pacific Islander, Hispanic, American Indian/Alaska Native). Applications are solicited from law schools in the Philadelphia area, but students at all other law schools may be eligible if they are interested in a summer internship in corporate law at a firm in that area. Interested students must submit information about their financial status, a list of extracurricular activities, any relevant legal experience, a legal writing sample, and an essay of 250 to 500 words explaining why they qualify for this internship and what they hope to gain from the experience.

Financial data   The stipend is $7,500.

Duration   Summer months.

Number awarded   Approximately 15 each year.

Deadline   January of each year.

[708]
ACC NATIONAL CAPITAL REGION CORPORATE SCHOLARS PROGRAM

Association of Corporate Counsel-National Capital
  Region
Attn: Executive Director
P.O. Box 2147
Rockville, MD 20847-2147
(301) 881-3018   E-mail: Ilene.Reid-NCR@accglobal.com
Web: m.acc.com/chapters/ncr/scholars.cfm

Summary   To provide an opportunity for summer work experience in the metropolitan Washington, D.C. area to African American and other minority students at law schools in the area who will contribute to the diversity of the profession.

Eligibility   This program is open to students entering their second or third year of part- or full-time study at law schools in the Washington, D.C. metropolitan area (including suburban Maryland and all of Virginia). Applicants must be able to demonstrate how they contribute to diversity in the legal profession, based not only on ideas about gender, race, and ethnicity, but also concepts of socioeconomic background and their individual educational and career path. They must be interested in working during the summer at a sponsoring private corporation and nonprofit organizations in the Washington, D.C. area. Along with their application, they must submit a personal statement of 250 to 500 words explaining why they qualify for this program, a writing sample, their law school transcript, and a resume.

Financial data   The stipend is at least $9,000.

Duration   10 weeks during the summer.

Additional information   The sponsor is the local chapter of the Association of Corporate Counsel (ACC). It established this program in 2004 with support from the Minority Corporate Counsel Association (MCCA).

Number awarded   Varies each year; recently, 13 of these internships were awarded.

Deadline   January of each year.

[709]
ACCESS TO JUSTICE FELLOWSHIPS OF THE OREGON STATE BAR

Oregon State Bar
Attn: Diversity and Inclusion Department
16037 S.W. Upper Boones Ferry Road
P.O. Box 231935
Tigard, OR 97281-1935
(503) 620-0222
Toll Free: (800) 452-8260, ext. 338 (within OR)
Fax: (503) 684-1366   TDD: (503) 684-7416
E-mail: cling@osbar.org
Web: www.osbar.org/diversity/programs.html#access

Summary   To provide summer work experience to African American and other law students in Oregon who have encountered barriers and will help the Oregon State Bar achieve its diversity and inclusion objectives.

Eligibility   This program is open to students at law schools in Oregon who have experienced economic, social, or other barriers; who have a demonstrated commitment to increasing access to justice; who have personally experienced discrimination or oppression; and who will contribute to the Oregon State Bar's diversity and inclusion program, defined to include age, culture, disability, ethnicity, gender and gender identity or expression, geographic location, national origin, race, religion, sex, sexual orientation, and socio-economic status. They must be interested in working for a public employer or nonprofit organization in Oregon during the summer. Preference is given to students who indicate an intention to practice in Oregon. Along with their application, they must submit a 500-word personal statement on either 1) how their status as a person of diversity has influenced their decision to become a lawyer and how will it influence them throughout their legal professional career; or 2) a challenge they have faced, how they met the challenge, and how that experience will affect the decisions they will make as a legal professional. They must also submit a sample of their legal writing. Selection is based on the personal statement (35%), legal writing ability (25%), academic achievement (15%), work experience and honors (10%), and financial need (15%).

Financial data   Fellows receive a stipend of $5,000.

Duration   3 months during the summer.

Number awarded   2 each year.

Deadline   January of each year.

[710]
ACM/IEEE-CS GEORGE MICHAEL MEMORIAL HPC FELLOWSHIPS

Association for Computing Machinery
Attn: Awards Committee Liaison
2 Penn Plaza, Suite 701
New York, NY 10121-0701
(212) 626-0561   Toll Free: (800) 342-6626
Fax: (212) 944-1318   E-mail: acm-awards@acm.org
Web: awards.acm.org/hpcfell/nominations.cfm

Summary   To provide financial assistance to doctoral students, especially African Americans and other underrepresented minorities, who are working on a degree in high performance computing (HPC) and will contribute to diversity in the field.

Eligibility This program is open to students from any country who have completed at least 1 year full-time study in a Ph.D. program in HPC and have at least 1 year remaining before graduating. Applications from women, minorities, international students, and all who contribute to diversity are especially encouraged. Selection is based on overall potential for research excellence, degree to which technical interests align with those of the HPC community, demonstration of current and planned future use of HPC resources, evidence of a plan of student to enhance HPC-related skills, evidence of academic progress to date (including presentations and publications), and recommendation by faculty adviser.

Financial data The stipend is $5,000. Fellows also receive reimbursement of travel expenses to attend the conference of the Association for Computing Machinery (ACM).

Duration 1 year.

Additional information This program, which began in 2007, is sponsored by the IEEE Computer Society.

Number awarded Up to 6 each year.

Deadline April of each year.

[711]
ACM SIGHPC/INTEL COMPUTATIONAL AND DATA SCIENCE FELLOWSHIPS

Association for Computing Machinery
Attn: Special Interest Group on High Performance
  Computing (SIGHPC)
Office of SIG Services
2 Penn Plaza, Suite 701
New York, NY 10121-0701
(212) 626-0606   Toll Free: (800) 342-6626
Fax: (212) 944-1318   E-mail: cappo@hq.acm.org
Web: www.sighpc.org/fellowships

Summary To provide financial assistance to African American and other underrepresented minority graduate students in any country who are working on a degree in computational or data science.

Eligibility This program is open to women and members of racial or ethnic backgrounds that have not traditionally participated in the computing field. Applicants must be enrolled as graduate students at a college or university in any country and working on a graduate degree in computational or data science. They must have completed less than half of their planning program of study; preference is given to students who are still early in their studies. Selection is based on overall potential for excellence in data science and/or computational science, likelihood of successfully completing a graduate degree, and extent to which applicants will increase diversity in the workplace.

Financial data The stipend is $15,000.

Duration 1 year.

Additional information This program was established in 2016 by Intel Corporation.

Number awarded Varies each year; recently, 14 were presented.

Deadline April of each year.

[712]
ACOUSTICAL SOCIETY OF AMERICA MINORITY FELLOWSHIP

Acoustical Society of America
Attn: Office Manager
1305 Walt Whitman Road, Suite 300
Melville, NY 11747-4300
(516) 576-2360   Fax: (631) 923-2875
E-mail: asa@acousticalsociety.org
Web: www.acousticalsociety.org

Summary To provide financial assistance to African American and other underrepresented minorities who are working on a graduate degree involving acoustics.

Eligibility This program is open to U.S. and Canadian citizens and permanent residents who are members of a minority group that is underrepresented in the sciences (African American, Hispanic, or Native American). Applicants must be enrolled in or accepted to a graduate degree program as a full-time student. Their program of study may be in any field of pure or applied science and engineering directly related to acoustics, including acoustical oceanography, architectural acoustics, animal bioacoustics, biomedical ultrasound, bioresponse to vibration, engineering acoustics, musical acoustics, noise, physical acoustics, psychological acoustics, physiological acoustics, signal processing in acoustics, speech communication, structural acoustics and vibration, and underwater acoustics. Along with their application, student must submit a statement on why they are enrolled in their present academic program, including how they intend to use their graduate education to develop a career and how the study of acoustics is relevant to their career objectives.

Financial data The stipend is $20,000 per year. The sponsor strongly encourages the host educational institution to waive all tuition costs and assessed fees. Fellows also receive $1,000 for travel to attend a national meeting of the sponsor.

Duration 1 year; may be renewed for 1 additional year if the recipient is making normal progress toward a degree and is enrolled full time.

Additional information This program began in 1992.

Number awarded 1 each year.

Deadline March of each year.

[713]
ACXIOM DIVERSITY SCHOLARSHIP PROGRAM

Acxiom Corporation
601 East Third Street
P.O. Box 8190
Little Rock, AR 72203-8190
(501) 342-1000   Toll Free: (877) 314-2049
E-mail: Candice.Davis@acxiom.com
Web: www.acxiom.com/about-acxiom/careers

Summary To provide financial assistance and possible work experience to upper-division and graduate students who are Africans or members of other diverse populations that historically have been underrepresented in the information technology work force.

Eligibility This program is open to juniors, seniors, and graduate students who are working full time on a degree in a field of information technology, including computer science, computer information systems, management information systems, information quality, information systems, engineering, mathematics, statistics, or related areas of study. Women, veterans, minorities, and individuals with disabilities are encouraged to apply. Applicants must have a GPA of 3.0 or higher. Along with their application, they must submit a 500-word essay describing how the scholarship will help them achieve their academic, professional, and personal goals. Selection is based on academic achievement, relationship of field of study to information technology, and relationship of areas of professional interest to the sponsor's business needs.

Financial data   The stipend is $5,000 per year.

Duration   1 year; may be renewed 1 additional year, provided the recipient remains enrolled full time, maintains a GPA of 3.0 or higher, and (if offered an internship) continues to meet internship expectations.

Additional information   Recipients may be offered an internship (fall, spring, summer, year-round) at 1 of the sponsor's offices in Austin (Texas), Conway (Arkansas), Downers Grove (Illinois), Little Rock (Arkansas), Nashville (Tennessee), New York (New York), or Redwood City (California).

Number awarded   Up to 5 each year.

Deadline   December of each year.

[714]
ADDIE B. MORRIS SCHOLARSHIP

American Association of Railroad Superintendents
P.O. Box 200
La Fox, IL 60147
(331) 643-3369   E-mail: aars@supt.org
Web: www.railroadsuperintendents.org/Scholarships

Summary   To provide financial assistance to undergraduate and graduate students, especially African Americans and other minorities working on a degree in transportation.

Eligibility   This program is open to full-time undergraduate and graduate students enrolled at accredited colleges and universities in Canada or the United States. Applicants must have completed enough credits to have standing as a sophomore and must have a GPA of 2.75 or higher. Preference is given to minority students enrolled in the transportation field who can demonstrate financial need.

Financial data   The stipend is $1,000. Funds are sent directly to the recipient's institution.

Duration   1 year.

Number awarded   1 or more each year.

Deadline   June of each year.

[715]
ADRIENNE M. AND CHARLES SHELBY ROOKS FELLOWSHIP FOR RACIAL AND ETHNIC THEOLOGICAL STUDENTS

United Church of Christ
Attn: Associate Director, Grant and Scholarship
  Administration
700 Prospect Avenue East
Cleveland, OH 44115-1100
(216) 736-2166   Toll Free: (866) 822-8224, ext. 2166
Fax: (216) 736-3783   E-mail: scholarships@ucc.org
Web: www.ucc.org/ministry_education_scholarships

Summary   To provide financial assistance to African American and other minority students who are either enrolled at an accredited seminary preparing for a career of service in the United Church of Christ (UCC) or working on a doctoral degree in the field of religion.

Eligibility   This program is open to members of underrepresented ethnic groups (African American, Hispanic American, Asian American, Native American Indian, or Pacific Islander) who have been a member of a UCC congregation for at least 1 year. Applicants must be either 1) enrolled in an accredited school of theology in the United States or Canada and working on an M.Div. degree with the intent of becoming a pastor or teacher within the UCC; or 2) doctoral (Ph.D., Th.D., or Ed.D.) students preparing for a scholarly teaching vocation in the field of religion. Seminary students must have a GPA in all postsecondary work of 3.0 or higher and must have begun the in-care process; preference is given to students who have demonstrated leadership (through a history of service to the church) and scholarship (through exceptional academic performance). For doctoral students, preference is given to applicants who have demonstrated academic excellence, teaching effectiveness, and commitment to the UCC and who intend to become professors in colleges, seminaries, or graduate schools.

Financial data   Grants range from $500 to $5,000 per year.

Duration   1 year; may be renewed.

Number awarded   Varies each year; recently, 12 of these scholarships, including 8 for M.Div. students and 4 for doctoral students, were awarded.

Deadline   February of each year.

[716]
AERA-MET DISSERTATION FELLOWSHIP PROGRAM

American Educational Research Association
Attn: Fellowships Program
1430 K Street, N.W., Suite 1200
Washington, DC 20005
(202) 238-3200   Fax: (202) 238-3250
E-mail: fellowships@aera.net
Web: www.aera.net

Summary   To provide funding to doctoral candidates in the field of education, especially African Americans and other underrepresented groups, who are interested in conducting dissertation research using the Measures of Effective Teaching (MET) database.

Eligibility   This program is open to doctoral candidates who are at the dissertation stage of their program in a field of education or related social or behavioral science field (e.g., economics, political science, psychology, sociology). Applicants must be interested in conducting dissertation research utilizing the Measures of Effective Teaching (MET) Longitudinal Database collected by the Inter-university Consortium for Political and Social Research (ICPSR) of the University of Michigan. Selection is based on potential for the study to advance knowledge and understanding with the discipline and/or the education field; what is already known on the issue; appropriateness of the MET database to address the research questions; qualifications of the applicant to carry out the proposed study; and relationship of the methodology to the policy question. Underrepresented racial and ethnic minority researchers and women and strongly encouraged to apply. U.S. citizenship or permanent resident status is required.

Financial data Fellows receive a stipend of $20,000 plus full payment of expenses to attend the fall research conference of the American Educational Research Association (AERA) in Washington, D.C.

Duration 1 year.

Additional information This program is jointly administered by the AERA and the IPCSR with funding provided by the Bill and Melinda Gates Foundation.

Number awarded Several each year.

Deadline May of each year.

[717]
AFPE UNDERREPRESENTED MINORITY PRE-DOCTORAL FELLOWSHIP

American Foundation for Pharmaceutical Education
Attn: Grants Manager
6076 Franconia Road, Suite C
Alexandria, VA 22310-1758
(703) 875-3095   Toll Free: (855) 624-9526
Fax: (703) 875-3098   E-mail: info@afpenet.org
Web: www.afpenet.org

Summary To provide funding for dissertation research to African American and other underrepresented minority graduate students working on a Ph.D. in pharmaceutical science.

Eligibility This program is open to African American/Black, Hispanic/Latino, and Native American students who have completed at least 3 semesters of full-time graduate study and have no more than 3 and a half years remaining to complete a Ph.D. in pharmaceutical science at a U.S. school or college of pharmacy. Students enrolled in joint Pharm.D./Ph.D. programs are eligible if they have completed 3 full semesters of graduate credit toward the Ph.D. and if the Ph.D. degree will be awarded within 3 additional years. Applicants must be U.S. citizens or permanent residents. Selection is based on research plan and experience (50%), academic performance (35%), and leadership and character (15%).

Financial data The grant is $10,000 per year. Funds must be used to enable the students to make progress on their Ph.D. (e.g., student stipend, laboratory supplies, books, materials, travel) but not for indirect costs for the institution.

Duration 1 year; may be renewed 1 additional year.

Number awarded Up to 5 each year.

Deadline December of each year.

[718]
AFRICAN AMERICAN SCHOLARSHIP FUND OF DISCIPLES HOME MISSIONS

Christian Church (Disciples of Christ)
Attn: Disciples Home Missions
130 East Washington Street
P.O. Box 1986
Indianapolis, IN 46206-1986
(317) 713-2652   Toll Free: (888) DHM-2631
Fax: (317) 635-4426   E-mail: mail@dhm.disciples.org
Web: www.discipleshomemissions.org

Summary To provide financial assistance to African Americans interested in preparing for a career in the ministry of the Christian Church (Disciples of Christ).

Eligibility This program is open to African American ministerial students who are members of a Christian Church (Disciples of Christ) congregation in the United States or Canada.

Applicants must plan to prepare for the ordained ministry, be working on an M.Div. or equivalent degree, provide evidence of financial need, be enrolled full time at an accredited school or seminary, provide a transcript of academic work, and be under the care of a regional Commission on the Ministry or in the process of coming under care.

Financial data A stipend is awarded (amount not specified).

Duration 1 year; recipients may reapply.

Additional information This program began in 1939 as the Negro Student Scholarship Fund of the United Christian Missionary Society. Its current name was adopted in 2009.

Number awarded 1 each year.

Deadline March of each year.

[719]
AFRICAN AMERICAN STUDIES FELLOWSHIP

Massachusetts Historical Society
Attn: Short-Term Fellowships
1154 Boylston Street
Boston, MA 02215-3695
(617) 646-0568   Fax: (617) 859-0074
E-mail: fellowships@masshist.org
Web: www.masshist.org/research/fellowships/short-term

Summary To fund research visits to the Massachusetts Historical Society for graduate students and other scholars interested in African American history.

Eligibility This program is open to advanced graduate students, postdoctorates, and independent scholars who are conducting research in African American history and need to use the resources of the Massachusetts Historical Society. Applicants must be U.S. citizens or foreign nationals holding appropriate U.S. government documents. Along with their application, they must submit a curriculum vitae and a proposal describing the project and indicating collections at the society to be consulted. Graduate students must also arrange for a letter of recommendation from a faculty member familiar with their work and with the project being proposed. Preference is given to candidates who live 50 or more miles from Boston.

Financial data The grant is $2,000.

Duration 4 weeks.

Additional information This fellowship was first awarded in 1999.

Number awarded 1 each year.

Deadline February of each year.

[720]
AFRICAN HERITAGE CAUCUS SCHOLARSHIPS

African Heritage Caucus
Attn: Scholarship Chair
2318 Mill Road, Suite 1300
Alexandria, VA 22314-6868
(281) 660-4721   E-mail: aapaahc@gmail.com
Web: www.africanheritagecaucusofaapa.org/190368345

Summary To provide financial assistance to members of the African Heritage Caucus within the American Academy of Physician Assistants (AAPA).

Eligibility This program is open to physician assistant students who are entering their clinical phase of training and are members of both the AAPA and its African Heritage Caucus.

Applicants must submit an essay of 500 to 750 words on 1 of the following topics: 1) their opinion on the impact of universal health care in addressing the issues of racial health care disparities in our country; or 2) the major health care disparities facing the African American community and how they will address those as a practicing physician assistant. Selection is based on academic progress, financial need, community and/or professional activities, and knowledge of health care issues and the physician assistant's role.

Financial data   Stipends range from $500 to $1,000.

Duration   1 year.

Number awarded   Up to 2 each year.

Deadline   May of each year.

[721]
AFRICAN-AMERICAN CHURCH PLANTERS SCHOLARSHIPS

Louisiana Baptist Convention
Attn: Woman's Missionary Union
1250 MacArthur Drive
P.O. Box 311
Alexandria, LA 71309-0311
(318) 448-3402   Toll Free: (800) 622-6549
E-mail: WMM@louisianabaptists.org
Web: www.louisianabaptists.org

Summary   To provide financial assistance to African American Southern Baptists from Louisiana who are enrolled at a seminary in any state to prepare for a career as a missions pastor.

Eligibility   This program is open to African Americans who are endorsed by the director of missions and the pastor of a sponsoring Southern Baptist church in Louisiana. Applicants must be enrolled full time at a Southern Baptist seminary or a satellite campus and working on a master's degree or a Christian education diploma. They must be participating in a missions education organization of the church or on campus and must contribute to offerings of the church and other programs. Along with their application, they must submit evidence of their "devotion to the Lord and their call to ministry."

Financial data   The stipend is $1,200 per year.

Duration   Up to 3 years.

Number awarded   1 or more each year.

Deadline   June of each year.

[722]
AGA INVESTING IN THE FUTURE STUDENT RESEARCH FELLOWSHIPS

American Gastroenterological Association
Attn: AGA Research Foundation
Research Awards Manager
4930 Del Ray Avenue
Bethesda, MD 20814-2512
(301) 222-4012   Fax: (301) 654-5920
E-mail: awards@gastro.org
Web: www.gastro.org

Summary   To provide funding for research on digestive diseases or nutrition to African American and undergraduate and medical students from otherunderrepresented minority groups.

Eligibility   This program is open to undergraduate and medical students at accredited U.S. institutions who are Afri-

can Americans, Hispanic/Latino Americans, Alaska Natives, American Indians, or Natives of the U.S. Pacific Islands. Applicants must be interested in conducting research on digestive diseases or nutrition. They may not hold similar salary support awards from other agencies (e.g., American Liver Foundation, Crohn's and Colitis Foundation). Research must be conducted under the supervision of a preceptor who is a full-time faculty member at an institution in a state other than the student's, directing a research project in a gastroenterology-related area, and a member of the American Gastroenterological Association (AGA).

Financial data   Fellowships provide payment of housing, travel, and a stipend of $5,000.

Duration   8 to 10 weeks. The work may take place at any time during the year.

Additional information   This program is supported by the National Institute of Diabetes and Digestive and Kidney Diseases (NIDDKD) of the U.S. National Institutes of Health (NIH).

Number awarded   12 each year.

Deadline   February of each year.

[723]
AGING RESEARCH DISSERTATION AWARDS TO INCREASE DIVERSITY

National Institute on Aging
Attn: Office of Extramural Affairs
7201 Wisconsin Avenue, Suite 2C-218
Bethesda, MD 20814
(301) 402-4158   Fax: (301) 402-2945
TDD: (301) 451-0088   E-mail: hunterc@nia.nih.gov
Web: www.grants.nih.gov

Summary   To provide financial assistance to doctoral candidates who are African Americans or members of other underrepresented groups who wish to conduct research on aging.

Eligibility   This program is open to doctoral candidates conducting research on a dissertation with an aging-related focus, including the basic biology of aging; chronic, disabling, and degenerative diseases of aging, with a particular focus on Alzheimer's Disease; multiple morbidities; individual behavioral and social changes with aging; caregiving; longevity; and the consequences for society of an aging population. Applicants must be 1) members of an ethnic or racial group underrepresented in biomedical or behavioral research (Blacks or African Americans, Hispanics or Latinos, American Indians, Alaska Natives, Native Hawaiians, and other Pacific Islanders); 2) individuals with disabilities; or 3) individuals from socially, culturally, economically, or educationally disadvantaged backgrounds that have inhibited their ability to prepare for a career in health-related research. They must be U.S. citizens, nationals, or permanent residents.

Financial data   Grants provide $23,376 per year for stipend and up to $20,000 for additional expenses. No funds may be used to pay for tuition or fees associated with completion of doctoral studies. The institution may receive up to 8% of direct costs as facilities and administrative costs per year.

Duration   Up to 2 years.

Number awarded   Up to 5 each year.

Deadline   Applications must be submitted by February, June, or October of each year.

[724]
AGNES JONES JACKSON SCHOLARSHIPS

POISE Foundation
Two Gateway Center, Suite 1700
603 Stanwix Street
Pittsburgh, PA 15222
(412) 281-4967   Fax: (412) 562-0292
Web: www.poisefoundation.org

Summary To provide financial assistance to members of the National Association for the Advancement of Colored People (NAACP) who are attending or planning to attend college or graduate school.

Eligibility This program is open to members of the NAACP who are younger than 25 years of age and full-time undergraduates or full- or part-time graduate students. The minimum GPA is 2.5 for graduating high school seniors and undergraduate students or 3.0 for graduate students. All applicants must be able to demonstrate financial need (family income must be less than $16,755 for a family of 1, ranging up to $58,335 for a family of 8) and U.S. citizenship. Along with their application, they must submit a 1-page essay on their interest in their major and a career, their life's ambition, what they hope to accomplish in their lifetime, and what position they hope to attain.

Financial data The stipend ranges up to $2,000 per year.

Duration 1 year; recipients may apply for renewal.

Additional information This program is managed by POISE Foundation on behalf of the NAACP.

Number awarded Approximately 20 to 40 each year.

Deadline March of each year.

[725]
AHIMA FOUNDATION DIVERSITY SCHOLARSHIPS

American Health Information Management Association
Attn: AHIMA Foundation
233 North Michigan Avenue, 21st Floor
Chicago, IL 60601-5809
(312) 233-1137   Fax: (312) 233-1537
E-mail: info@ahimafoundation.org
Web: www.ahimafoundation.org

Summary To provide financial assistance to African American and other members of the American Health Information Management Association (AHIMA) who are interested in working on an undergraduate or graduate degree in health information management (HIM) or health information technology (HIT) and who will contribute to diversity in the profession.

Eligibility This program is open to AHIMA members who are enrolled at least half time in an accredited program. Applicants must be working on a degree in HIM or HIT at the associate, bachelor's, post-baccalaureate, master's, or doctoral level. They must have a GPA of 3.5 or higher and at least 6 credit hours remaining after the date of the award. To qualify for this support, applicants must demonstrate how they will contribute to diversity in the health information management profession; diversity is defined as differences in race, ethnicity, nationality, gender, sexual orientation, socioeconomic status, age, physical capabilities, or religious beliefs. Along with their application, they must submit essays on assigned topics related to their involvement in the HIM profession. Selection is based on the clarity and completeness of thought in the essays; cumulative GPA; volunteer, work, and/or leadership experience; honors, awards, or recognitions; commitment to the HIM profession; and references.

Financial data Stipends are $1,000 for associate degree students, $1,500 for bachelor's degree or post-baccalaureate certificate students, $2,000 for master's degree students, or $2,500 for doctoral degree students.

Duration 1 year.

Number awarded 1 or more each year.

Deadline September of each year.

[726]
AHRQ GRANTS FOR HEALTH SERVICES RESEARCH DISSERTATIONS

Agency for Healthcare Research and Quality
Attn: Office of Extramural Research, Education and
    Priority Populations
540 Gaither Road
Rockville, MD 20850
(301) 427-1391   Fax: (301) 427-1561
TDD: (301) 451-0088
E-mail: Gregory.Stuppard@ahrq.hhs.gov
Web: www.grants.nih.gov

Summary To provide funding to doctoral candidates, especially African Americans and members of othr underrepresented groups,who are engaged in research for a dissertation that examines an aspect of the health care system.

Eligibility This program is open to citizens, nationals, and permanent residents who are enrolled full time in an accredited research doctoral degree program at an institution in the United States. Applicants must have completed all requirements for the doctoral degree except for the dissertation in such fields as the social or behavioral sciences, mathematics, engineering, health services, nursing, epidemiology, biostatistics, health policy, or health informatics. Their proposed dissertation topic must relate to the strategic goals of the Agency for Healthcare Research and Quality (AHRQ): 1) reducing the risk of harm from health care services by promoting the delivery of appropriate care that achieves the best quality outcomes; 2) achieving wider access to effective health care services and reducing health care costs; and 3) assuring that providers and consumers/patients use beneficial and timely health care information to make informed decisions. Priority is given to proposals that address health services research issues critical to such priority population as individuals living in inner city and rural (including frontier) areas; low-income and minority groups; women, children, and the elderly; and individuals with special health care needs, including those with disabilities and those who need chronic or end-of-life health care. Members of underrepresented racial and ethnic groups, individuals from disadvantaged backgrounds, and individuals with disabilities are especially encouraged to apply.

Financial data This program provides up to $40,000 in direct costs, including $23,376 for the investigator's salary, direct project expenses (travel, data purchasing, data processing, and supplies), and matriculation fees. The institution will receive facilities and administrative costs of 8% of total allowable direct costs, exclusive of tuition and related fees, health insurance, and expenditures for equipment.

Duration 9 to 17 months.

Number awarded   Up to 30 each year.

Deadline   January, April, July, or October of each year.

[727]
AICPA FELLOWSHIPS FOR MINORITY DOCTORAL STUDENTS

American Institute of Certified Public Accountants
Attn: Academic and Career Development Division
220 Leigh Farm Road
Durham, NC 27707-8110
(919) 402-4500   Fax: (919) 402-4505
E-mail: scholarships@aicpa.org
Web: www.aicpa.org

Summary   To provide financial assistance to African American and other underrepresented minority doctoral students who wish to prepare for a career teaching accounting at the college level.

Eligibility   This program is open to underrepresented minority students who have applied to and/or been accepted into a doctoral program with a concentration in accounting. Applicants must have earned a master's degree or completed a minimum of 3 years of full-time work in accounting. They must be attending or planning to attend school full time and agree not to work full time in a paid position, teach more than 1 course as a teaching assistant, or work more than 25% as a research assistant. U.S. citizenship or permanent resident status is required. Preference is given to applicants who have attained a C.P.A. designation and/or are members of the American Institute of Certified Public Accountants (AICPA) and those who perform AICPA committee service. For purposes of this program, the AICPA defines minority students as those whose heritage is Black or African American, Hispanic or Latino, or Native American. Selection is based on academic and professional achievement, commitment to earning an accounting doctoral degree, and financial need.

Financial data   The stipend is $12,000 per year.

Duration   1 year; may be renewed up to 4 additional years.

Number awarded   Varies each year; recently, 25 were awarded.

Deadline   May of each year.

[728]
AICPA SCHOLARSHIPS FOR MINORITY ACCOUNTING STUDENTS

American Institute of Certified Public Accountants
Attn: Academic and Career Development Division
220 Leigh Farm Road
Durham, NC 27707-8110
(919) 402-4500   Fax: (919) 402-4505
E-mail: scholarships@aicpa.org
Web: www.aicpa.org

Summary   To provide financial assistance to African and other minorities interested in studying accounting at the undergraduate or graduate school level.

Eligibility   This program is open to minority undergraduate and graduate students, enrolled full time, who have a GPA of 3.3 or higher (both cumulatively and in their major) and intend to pursue a C.P.A. credential. The program defines minority students as those whose heritage is Black or African American, Hispanic or Latino, Native American, or Asian American. Undergraduates must have completed at least 30 semester

hours, including at least 6 semester hours of a major in accounting. Graduate students must be working on a master's degree in accounting, finance, taxation, or a related program. Applicants must be U.S. citizens or permanent residents and student affiliate members of the American Institute of Certified Public Accountants (AICPA). Along with their application, they must submit 500-word essays on 1) why they want to become a C.P.A. and how attaining that licensure will contribute to their goals; and 2) how they would spread the message about accounting and the C.P.A. profession in their community and school. In the selection process, some consideration is given to financial need.

Financial data   Stipends range up to $5,000 per year. Funds are disbursed directly to the recipient's school.

Duration   1 year; may be renewed up to 3 additional years or until completion of a bachelor's or master's degree, whichever is earlier.

Additional information   This program began in 1969. Additional support is provided by the Accounting Education Foundation of the Texas Society of Certified Public Accountants, the New Jersey Society of Certified Public Accountants, Robert Half International, and the Virgin Islands Society of Certified Public Accountants.

Number awarded   Varies each year; recently, 94 students received funding through this program.

Deadline   March of each year.

[729]
ALBERT W. DENT STUDENT SCHOLARSHIP

American College of Healthcare Executives
Attn: Scholarship Committee
One North Franklin Street, Suite 1700
Chicago, IL 60606-3529
(312) 424-2800   Fax: (312) 424-0023
E-mail: contact@ache.org
Web: www.ache.org

Summary   To provide financial assistance to African American and other minority graduate student members of the American College of Healthcare Executives (ACHE).

Eligibility   This program is open to ACHE student associates entering their final year of classroom work in a health care management master's degree program. Applicants must be minority students, enrolled full time, able to demonstrate financial need, and U.S. or Canadian citizens. Along with their application, they must submit a 1- to 2-page essay describing their leadership abilities and experiences, their community and volunteer involvement, their goals as a health care executive, and how this scholarship can help them achieve their career goals.

Financial data   The stipend is $5,000.

Duration   1 year.

Additional information   The program was established and named in honor of Dr. Albert W. Dent, the foundation's first African American fellow and president emeritus of Dillard University.

Number awarded   Varies each year; the sponsor awards up to 20 scholarships through this and its other scholarship program.

Deadline   March of each year.

[730]
ALCON/NOSA ACADEMIC AWARD SCHOLARSHIP

National Optometric Association
Attn: Student Affairs
1801 North Tryon Street, Suite 315
Charlotte, NC 28206
(704) 918-1809   Toll Free: (877) 394-2020
Fax: (877) NOA-2006
E-mail: noastudentdirector@yahoo.com
Web: www.nationaloptometricassociation.com

Summary To provide financial assistance to African American and other members of the National Optometric Student Association (NOSA) who demonstrate academic achievement.

Eligibility This program is open to NOSA members enrolled in the second, third, or fourth year at a school or college of optometry. Applicants must be able to demonstrate both academic achievement (GPA of 3.0 or higher) and leadership in community service and optometry school. Along with their application, they must submit a 2-page statement on their reasons for applying for this award; their involvement in professional, community, extracurricular activities or events that have displayed their commitment to serving humanity and demonstrated interest in others; and how they hope to impact the profession of optometry positively in the future. Financial need is not considered in the selection process.

Financial data The stipend is $1,000.

Duration 1 year.

Additional information The National Optometric Association was founded in 1969 with the goal of recruiting minority students, especially African Americans, for schools and colleges of optometry. This program is sponsored by the Alcon Foundation.

Number awarded 1 each year.

Deadline May of each year.

[731]
ALCON/NOSA FINANCIAL SUPPORT AWARD SCHOLARSHIP

National Optometric Association
Attn: Student Affairs
1801 North Tryon Street, Suite 315
Charlotte, NC 28206
(704) 918-1809   Toll Free: (877) 394-2020
Fax: (877) NOA-2006
E-mail: noastudentdirector@yahoo.com
Web: www.nationaloptometricassociation.com

Summary To provide financial assistance to African American and other members of the National Optometric Student Association (NOSA) who demonstrate financial need.

Eligibility This program is open to NOSA members enrolled in the second, third, or fourth year at a school or college of optometry. Applicants must have GPA of 2.5 or higher and be able to demonstrate financial need. Along with their application, they must submit a 2-page statement on their reasons for applying for this award, their career goals, community or college involvement, and the impact they have had in affecting positive change that has enhanced minority communities.

Financial data The stipend is $1,000.

Duration 1 year.

Additional information The National Optometric Association was founded in 1969 with the goal of recruiting minority students, especially African Americans, for schools and colleges of optometry. This program is sponsored by the Alcon Foundation.

Number awarded 1 each year.

Deadline May of each year.

[732]
ALCON/NOSA LEADERSHIP AWARD SCHOLARSHIP

National Optometric Association
Attn: Student Affairs
1801 North Tryon Street, Suite 315
Charlotte, NC 28206
(704) 918-1809   Toll Free: (877) 394-2020
Fax: (877) NOA-2006
E-mail: noastudentdirector@yahoo.com
Web: www.nationaloptometricassociation.com

Summary To provide financial assistance to African American and other members of the National Optometric Student Association (NOSA) who demonstrate leadership.

Eligibility This program is open to NOSA members enrolled in the second, third, or fourth year at a school or college of optometry. Applicants must be able to demonstrate leadership in community service and optometry school. They must have a GPA of 2.5 or higher. Along with their application, they must submit a 2-page statement on their reasons for applying for this award; their involvement in professional, community, extracurricular activities or events that have displayed their commitment to serving humanity and demonstrated interest in others; and how they hope to impact the profession of optometry positively in the future. Financial need is not considered in the selection process.

Financial data The stipend is $1,000.

Duration 1 year.

Additional information The National Optometric Association was founded in 1969 with the goal of recruiting minority students, especially African Americans, for schools and colleges of optometry. This program is sponsored by the Alcon Foundation.

Number awarded 1 each year.

Deadline May of each year.

[733]
ALLAN R. BLOOMFIELD DIVERSITY SCHOLARSHIP

Allan R. Bloomfield
118-21 Queens Boulevard, Suite 617
Forest Hills, NY 11375
(718) 544-0500
Web: www.bankruptcyqueens.com/scholarship

Summary To provide financial assistance to African American and members of other ethnic and racial minority groups who are attending law school.

Eligibility This program is open to ethnic and racial minorities who are currently enrolled full time in the first or second year of law school and contributing to the diversity of their student body. Applicants must be U.S. citizens or permanent residents and have a GPA of 3.0 or higher. Along with their application, they must submit a 1-page essay describing how they plan to utilize their law degree.

Financial data　The stipend is $1,000.

Duration　1 year.

Number awarded　1 or more each year.

Deadline　May of each year.

[734]
ALLISON E. FISHER SCHOLARSHIP

National Association of Black Journalists
Attn: Program Manager
University of Maryland
1100 Knight Hall, Suite 3100
College Park, MD 20742
(301) 405-7520　　　　　　　Fax: (301) 314-1714
E-mail: Sberry@nabj.org
Web: www.nabj.org/?page=ScholarshipsFisher

Summary　To provide financial assistance to undergraduate or graduate student members of the National Association of Black Journalists (NABJ) who are majoring in journalism.

Eligibility　This program is open to African American undergraduate or graduate student members of NABJ who are currently enrolled full time at an accredited 4-year college or university. Applicants must be working on a degree in journalism or another communications-related discipline and have a GPA of 3.0 or higher. They must be able to demonstrate financial need. Along with their application, they must submit 5 samples of their work, an official college transcript, 3 letters of recommendation, a resume, and an essay of 1,000 to 2,000 words on the reasons why they are preparing for a career in journalism and what they hope their legacy as a journalist will be.

Financial data　The stipend is $2,500. Funds are paid directly to the recipient's college or university.

Duration　1 year; nonrenewable.

Number awarded　1 each year.

Deadline　February of each year.

[735]
ALMA WELLS GIVENS SCHOLARSHIP

Auxiliary to the National Medical Association
8403 Colesville Road, Suite 820
Silver Spring, MD 20910
(301) 495-3779　　　　　　　Fax: (301) 495-0037
E-mail: anmanationaloffice@earthlink.net
Web: www.anmanet.org

Summary　To provide financial assistance to African American medical students attending selected schools.

Eligibility　This program is open to African American medical school students who have completed their sophomore year at 1 of the following medical schools: Howard University College of Medicine (Washington, D.C.), Meharry Medical College (Nashville, Tennessee), Morehouse School of Medicine (Atlanta, Georgia), or Charles R. Drew University (Los Angeles, California). Selection is based on medical aptitude, academic record, personal record, and need.

Financial data　A stipend is awarded (amount not specified).

Duration　1 year.

Additional information　This program was originally established in 1942. The first scholarships were presented to students at Howard University and Meharry Medical College in 1948-49, at Morehouse College in 1980, and at Charles R. Drew University in 1983.

Number awarded　At least 4 each year (1 at each of the participating medical schools).

Deadline　Deadline not specified.

[736]
ALPHA KAPPA ALPHA ENDOWMENT AWARDS

Alpha Kappa Alpha Sorority, Inc.
Attn: Educational Advancement Foundation
5656 South Stony Island Avenue
Chicago, IL 60637
(773) 947-0026　　　　　　Toll Free: (800) 653-6528
Fax: (773) 947-0277　　　　　E-mail: akaeaf@akaeaf.net
Web: www.akaeaf.org/fellowships_endowments.htm

Summary　To provide financial assistance to undergraduate and graduate students (especially African American women) who meet designated requirements.

Eligibility　This program is open to undergraduate and graduate students who are enrolled full time as sophomores or higher in an accredited degree-granting institution and are planning to continue their program of education. Applicants may apply for scholarships that include specific requirements established by the donor of the endowment that supports it. Along with their application, they must submit 1) a list of honors, awards, and scholarships received; 2) a list of organizations in which they have memberships, especially minority organizations; and 3) a statement of their personal and career goals, including how this scholarship will enhance their ability to attain those goals. The sponsor is a traditionally African American women's sorority.

Financial data　Award amounts are determined by the availability of funds from the particular endowment. Recently, stipends averaged more than $1,700 per year.

Duration　1 year or longer.

Additional information　Each endowment establishes its own requirements. Examples of requirements include residence of the applicant, major field of study, minimum GPA, attendance at an Historically Black College or University (HBCU) or member institution of the United Negro College Fund (UNCF), or other personal feature. For further information on all endowments, contact the sponsor.

Number awarded　Varies each year; recently, 49 were awarded.

Deadline　April of each year.

[737]
ALPHA KAPPA ALPHA GRADUATE SCHOLARSHIPS

Alpha Kappa Alpha Sorority, Inc.
Attn: Educational Advancement Foundation
5656 South Stony Island Avenue
Chicago, IL 60637
(773) 947-0026　　　　　　Toll Free: (800) 653-6528
Fax: (773) 947-0277　　　　　E-mail: akaeaf@akaeaf.net
Web: www.akaeaf.org/graduate_scholarships.htm

Summary　To provide financial assistance for study or research to graduate students (especially African American women).

Eligibility This program is open to students who are working full time on a graduate degree in any state. Applicants may apply either for a scholarship based on merit (requires a GPA of 3.0 or higher) or on financial need (requires a GPA of 2.5 or higher). Along with their application, they must submit 1) a list of honors, awards, and scholarships received; 2) a list of organizations in which they have memberships, especially minority organizations; 3) a description of the project or research on which they are currently working, or (if they are not involved in a project or research) the aspects of their field that interest them; and 4) a statement of their personal and career goals, including how this scholarship will enhance their ability to attain those goals. The sponsor is a traditionally African American women's sorority.

Financial data Stipends range up to $3,000.

Duration 1 year; nonrenewable.

Number awarded Varies each year; recently, 147 were awarded.

Deadline August of each year.

[738]
AMA FOUNDATION MINORITY SCHOLARS AWARDS

American Medical Association
Attn: AMA Foundation
330 North Wabash Avenue, Suite 39300
Chicago, IL 60611-5885
(312) 464-5019   Fax: (312) 464-4142
E-mail: amafoundation@ama-assn.org
Web: www.ama-assn.org

Summary To provide financial assistance to medical school students who are African Americans or members of other underrepresented minority groups.

Eligibility This program is open to first- and second-year medical students who are members of the following traditionally underrepresented groups in the medical profession: African American, American Indian, Native Hawaiian, Alaska Native, or Hispanic. Only nominations are accepted. Each medical school is invited to submit 2 nominees. U.S. citizenship or permanent resident status is required.

Financial data The stipend is $10,000.

Duration 1 year.

Additional information This program is offered by the AMA Foundation of the American Medical Association in collaboration with the Minority Affairs Consortium (MAC) and with support from the Pfizer Medical Humanities Initiative.

Number awarded Varies each year; recently, 20 were awarded.

Deadline March of each year.

[739]
AMAF VALUING DIVERSITY PH.D. SCHOLARSHIPS

American Marketing Association Foundation
Attn: Foundation Manager
311 South Wacker Drive, Suite 5800
Chicago, IL 60606
(312) 542-9015   Fax: (312) 542-9001
E-mail: jschnidman@ama.org
Web: www.themarketingfoundation.org

Summary To provide financial assistance to African Americans and members of other underrepresented minority groups working on a doctoral degree in advertising or marketing.

Eligibility This program is open to African Americans, Hispanics, and Native Americans who have completed at least 1 year of a full-time Ph.D. program in advertising or marketing. Applicants must submit an essay that explains how receiving this scholarship will help them further their research efforts, including information on 1 of the following: 1) how their dissertation research incorporates conceptual, design, or methods issues related to diversity; 2) how their dissertation research contributes to advancing the field of marketing; or 3) how their dissertation research incorporates any innovative theories or advanced, cutting-edge designs, methods, or approaches. They must be U.S. citizens or permanent residents.

Financial data The stipend is $1,000.

Duration 1 year; recipients may reapply.

Additional information This program began in 2003.

Number awarded Varies each year; recently, 5 were awarded.

Deadline April of each year.

[740]
AMELIA KEMP MEMORIAL SCHOLARSHIP

Women of the Evangelical Lutheran Church in America
Attn: Scholarships
8765 West Higgins Road
Chicago, IL 60631-4101
(773) 380-2741   Toll Free: (800) 638-3522, ext. 2741
Fax: (773) 380-2419   E-mail: valora.starr@elca.org
Web: www.womenoftheelca.org

Summary To provide financial assistance to African American and other lay women of color who are members of Evangelical Lutheran Church of America (ELCA) congregations and who wish to study on the undergraduate, graduate, professional, or vocational school level.

Eligibility This program is open to ELCA lay women of color who are at least 21 years of age and have experienced an interruption of at least 2 years in their education since high school. Applicants must have been admitted to an educational institution to prepare for a career in other than ordained ministry. U.S. citizenship is required.

Financial data The maximum stipend is $1,000 per year.

Duration 1 year; recipients may reapply for 1 additional year.

Number awarded 1 or more each year.

Deadline February of each year.

[741]
AMERICAN ANTHROPOLOGICAL ASSOCIATION MINORITY DISSERTATION FELLOWSHIP PROGRAM

American Anthropological Association
Attn: Committee on Minority Issues in Anthropology
2300 Clarendon Boulevard, Suite 1301
Arlington, VA 22201
(703) 528-1902   Fax: (703) 528-3546
E-mail: arussell@aaanet.org
Web: www.aaanet.org/cmtes/minority/Minfellow.cfm

Summary To provide funding to African Americans and other minorities who are working on a Ph.D. dissertation in anthropology.

Eligibility This program is open to Native American, African American, Latino(a), Pacific Islander, and Asian American doctoral students who have been admitted to degree candidacy in anthropology. Applicants must be U.S. citizens, enrolled in a full-time academic program leading to a doctoral degree in anthropology, and members of the American Anthropological Association. They must have a record of outstanding academic success, have had their dissertation proposal approved by their dissertation committee prior to application, be writing a dissertation in an area of anthropological research, and need funding to complete the dissertation. Along with their application, they must submit a cover letter, a research plan summary, a curriculum vitae, a statement regarding employment, a disclosure statement providing information about other sources of available and pending financial support, 3 letters of recommendation, and an official transcript from their doctoral program. Selection is based on the quality of the submitted information and the judged likelihood that the applicant will have a good chance of completing the dissertation.

Financial data The grant is $10,000. Funds are sent in 2 installments (in September and in January) directly to the recipient.

Duration 1 year; nonrenewable.

Number awarded 1 each year.

Deadline February of each year.

[742]
AMERICAN BAR ASSOCIATION LEGAL OPPORTUNITY SCHOLARSHIP

American Bar Association
Attn: Fund for Justice and Education
321 North Clark Street, 21st Floor
Chicago, IL 60654-7598
(312) 988-5927   Fax: (312) 988-6392
E-mail: legalosf@staff.abanet.org
Web: www.americanbar.org

Summary To provide financial assistance to African American and other racial and ethnic minority students who are interested in attending law school.

Eligibility This program is open to racial and ethnic minority college graduates who are interested in attending an ABA-accredited law school. Only students beginning law school may apply; students who have completed 1 or more semesters of law school are not eligible. Applicants must have a cumulative GPA of 2.5 or higher and be citizens or permanent residents of the United States. Along with their application, they must submit a 1,000-word statement describing their personal and family background, community service activities, and other connections to their racial and ethnic minority community. Financial need is also considered in the selection process.

Financial data The stipend is $5,000 per year.

Duration 1 year; may be renewed for 2 additional years if satisfactory performance in law school has been achieved.

Additional information This program began in the 2000-01 academic year.

Number awarded Approximately 20 each year.

Deadline February of each year.

[743]
AMERICAN EDUCATIONAL RESEARCH ASSOCIATION DISSERTATION GRANTS PROGRAM

American Educational Research Association
Attn: Grants Program
1430 K Street, N.W., Suite 1200
Washington, DC 20005
(202) 238-3200   Fax: (202) 238-3250
E-mail: grantsprogram@aera.net
Web: www.aera.net

Summary To provide funding to doctoral students, especially African Americans and other minorities, who are writing their dissertation on educational policy.

Eligibility This program is open to advanced graduate students who are writing their dissertations in such disciplines as (but not limited to) education, sociology, economics, psychology, demography, statistics, or psychometrics. Applicants may be U.S. citizens, U.S. permanent residents, or non-U.S. citizens working at a U.S. institution. Underrepresented ethnic and racial minority researchers are strongly encouraged to apply. Dissertation topics may cover a wide range of policy-related issues, but priority is given to proposals that 1) develop or benefit from new quantitative measures or methodological approaches for addressing education issues; 2) incorporate subject matter expertise, especially when studying science, technology, engineering, or mathematics (STEM) learning; 3) analyze TIMSS, PISA, or other international data resources; or 4) include the integration and analysis of more than 1 data set. The research project must include the analysis of data from at least 1 of the large-scale nationally or internationally representative data sets, such as those of the National Science Foundation (NSF), National Center for Education Statistics (NCES), Department of Labor, Census Bureau, or National Institutes of Health (NIH). Selection is based on the importance of the proposed policy issue, strength of the methodological model and proposed statistical analysis of the study, and relevant experience or research record of the applicant.

Financial data The maximum grant is $20,000 per year. No support is provided for indirect costs to institutions. Funding is linked to approval of the recipient's progress report and final report. Grantees receive one-third of the total award at the beginning of the grant period, one-third upon acceptance of the progress report, and one-third upon acceptance of the final report. Funds can be sent either to the recipients or to their institutions.

Duration 1 year; nonrenewable.

Additional information Funding for this program is provided by the NSF. Grantees must submit a brief (3 to 6 pages) progress report midway through the grant period. A final report must be submitted at the end of the grant period. The final report may be either an article suitable for publication in a scholarly journal or a copy of the dissertation.

Number awarded Approximately 15 each year.

Deadline March or September of each year.

[744]
AMERICAN EDUCATIONAL RESEARCH ASSOCIATION MINORITY FELLOWSHIPS IN EDUCATION RESEARCH

American Educational Research Association
Attn: Fellowships Program
1430 K Street, N.W., Suite 1200
Washington, DC 20005
(202) 238-3200   Fax: (202) 238-3250
E-mail: fellowships@aera.net
Web: www.aera.net

Summary To provide funding to African American and other minority doctoral students writing their dissertation on educational research.

Eligibility This program is open to U.S. citizens and permanent residents who have advanced to candidacy and successfully defended their Ph.D./Ed.D. dissertation research proposal. Applicants must plan to work full time on their dissertation in educational research, the humanities, or social or behavioral science disciplinary or interdisciplinary fields, such as economics, political science, psychology, or sociology. This program is targeted for members of groups historically underrepresented in higher education (African Americans, American Indians, Alaskan Natives, Asian Americans, Native Hawaiian or Pacific Islanders, and Hispanics or Latinos). Selection is based on scholarly achievements and publications, letters of recommendation, quality and significance of the proposed research, and commitment of the applicant's faculty mentor to the goals of the program.

Financial data The grant is $20,000, including up to $1,000 for travel to the sponsor's annual conference.

Duration 1 year; nonrenewable.

Additional information This program began in 1991.

Number awarded Up to 3 each year.

Deadline October of each year.

[745]
AMERICAN EPILEPSY SOCIETY PREDOCTORAL RESEARCH FELLOWSHIPS

American Epilepsy Society
135 South LaSalle Street, Suite 2850
Chicago, IL 60603
(312) 883-3800   Fax: (312) 896-5784
E-mail: info@aesnet.org
Web: www.aesnet.org

Summary To provide funding to doctoral candidates, especially African Americans and members of other underrepresented groups, who are interested in conducting dissertation research related to epilepsy.

Eligibility This program is open full-time doctoral students conducting dissertation research with an epilepsy-related theme under the guidance of a mentor with expertise in epilepsy research. Applicants must have a defined research plan and access to institutional resources to conduct the proposed project. Selection is based on the applicant's potential and commitment to develop as an independent and productive epilepsy researcher, academic record, and research experience; the mentor's research qualifications; the research training plan; and the quality of the research facilities, resources, and training opportunities. Applications are especially encouraged from women, members of minority groups, and people with disabilities. U.S. citizenship is not required, but all research must be conducted in the United States.

Financial data Grants range up $30,000, including $29,000 as stipend and $1,000 for travel support and complimentary registration to attend the sponsor's annual meeting.

Duration 1 year; nonrenewable.

Additional information In addition to the funding provided by the American Epilepsy Society, support is available from the TESS Research Foundation for applications focused on epilepsy due to SLC13A5 mutations; the LGS Foundation for applications focused on Lennox-Gastaut-Syndrome; the PCDH19 Alliance for applications focused on epilepsy due to PCDH19 mutations; the Dravet Syndrome Foundation for applications focused on Dravet Syndrome; Wishes for Elliott for applications focused on epilepsy due to SCN8A mutations; and the TS Alliance for applications focused on epilepsy associated with tuberous sclerosis complex (TSC).

Number awarded Varies each year.

Deadline Letters of intent must be submitted by October of each year; final proposals are due in January.

[746]
AMERICAN GEOGRAPHICAL SOCIETY LIBRARY FELLOWSHIP FOR MSI SCHOLARS

University of Wisconsin at Milwaukee
Attn: Libraries
American Geographical Society Library
2311 East Hartford Avenue
P.O. Box 399,
Milwaukee, WI 53201-0399
(414) 229-6282   Toll Free: (800) 558-8993
Fax: (414) 229-3624   E-mail: agsl@uwm.edu
Web: www.uwm.edu/libraries/agsl/fellowshipdescriptions

Summary To provide funding to pre- and postdoctoral scholars at Minority Serving Institutions (MSIs) interested in conducting research at the American Geographical Society Library (AGSL) of the University of Wisconsin at Milwaukee (UWM) Libraries.

Eligibility This program is open to established scholars and doctoral students who are affiliated with an MSI. Doctoral students must have completed their course work and be writing their dissertations. Individuals with a record of publication relevant to this program and those with government or business ties who could use the library's resources to further policy studies are also eligible. Applicants' research must benefit from extensive use of the AGSL, including (but not limited to) area studies, history of cartography, history of geographic thought, discovery and exploration, historical geography, other geographic themes with a significant historical component, or any topic that has policy, business, or similar applications.

Financial data The grant is $600 per week. Funds must be used to help pay travel and living expenses related to the residency.

Duration Up to 4 weeks.

Additional information Funding for this program is provided by a U.S. Department of Education National Resource Center grant.

Number awarded 1 or more each year.

Deadline November of each year.

[747]
AMERICAN METEOROLOGICAL SOCIETY GRADUATE FELLOWSHIP IN THE HISTORY OF SCIENCE

American Meteorological Society
Attn: Development and Student Program Manager
45 Beacon Street
Boston, MA 02108-3693
(617) 227-2426, ext. 3907   Fax: (617) 742-8718
E-mail: dFernandez@ametsoc.org
Web: www2.ametsoc.org

Summary To provide funding to graduate student members of the American Meteorological Society (AMS), especially African Americans and members of other underrepresented groups, who are interested in conducting dissertation research on the history of meteorology.

Eligibility This program is open to AMS members and student members who are planning to complete a doctoral dissertation on the history of the atmospheric or related oceanic or hydrologic sciences. Applicants must be U.S. citizens or permanent residents and working on a degree at a U.S. institution. Fellowships may be used to support research at a location away from the student's institution, provided the plan is approved by the student's thesis adviser. In such an instance, an effort is made to place the student into a mentoring relationship with a member of the society at an appropriate institution. The sponsor specifically encourages applications from women, minorities, and students with disabilities who are traditionally underrepresented in the atmospheric and related oceanic sciences.

Financial data The stipend is $15,000.

Duration 1 year.

Number awarded 1 each year.

Deadline February of each year.

[748]
AMERICAN MUSEUM OF NATURAL HISTORY GRADUATE STUDENT FELLOWSHIP PROGRAM

American Museum of Natural History
Attn: Richard Gilder Graduate School
Central Park West at 79th Street
New York, NY 10024-5192
(212) 769-5055   E-mail: Fellowships-rggs@amnh.org
Web: www.amnh.org

Summary To provide financial assistance to doctoral students in selected programs at designated universities, especially African Americans and members of other underrepresented groups, who are interested in utilizing the resources of the American Museum of Natural History in their training and research program.

Eligibility This program is open to doctoral students in scientific disciplines practiced at the museum. The applicant's university exercises educational jurisdiction over the program and awards the degree; the museum curator serves as a graduate adviser, co-major professor, or major professor. Both U.S. citizens and noncitizens are eligible to apply. Candidates for a master's degree are not eligible. The museum encourages women, minorities, persons with disabilities, and Vietnam Era and disabled veterans to apply.

Financial data Fellowships provide a stipend and health insurance.

Duration 1 year; may be renewed up to 3 additional years.

Additional information The cooperating universities (and their relevant programs) are Columbia University, in anthropology, vertebrate and invertebrate paleontology, earth and planetary sciences, and evolutionary, ecological, and environmental biology; Cornell University in entomology; the Graduate Center of City University of New York in earth and planetary sciences, paleontology, and evolutionary biology; New York University in molecular biology; and Stony Brook University in astronomy and astrophysics. Students must apply simultaneously to the museum and to 1 of the cooperating universities.

Number awarded Varies each year.

Deadline December of each year.

[749]
AMERICAN NURSES ASSOCIATION MINORITY FELLOWSHIP PROGRAM

American Nurses Association
Attn: SAMHSA Minority Fellowship Programs
8515 Georgia Avenue, Suite 400
Silver Spring, MD 20910-3492
(301) 628-5247   Toll Free: (800) 274-4ANA
Fax: (301) 628-5339   E-mail: janet.jackson@ana.org
Web: www.emfp.org

Summary To provide financial assistance to African American and other minority nurses who are doctoral candidates interested in psychiatric, mental health, and substance abuse issues that impact the lives of ethnic minority people.

Eligibility This program is open to nurses who have a master's degree and are members of an ethnic or racial minority group, including but not limited to Blacks or African Americans, Hispanics or Latinos, American Indians and Alaska Natives, Asians and Asian Americans, and Native Hawaiians and other Pacific Islanders. Applicants must be enrolled full time in an accredited doctoral nursing program. They must be certified as a Mental Health Nurse Practitioner, Mental Health Clinical Nurse Specialist, or Mental Health Nurse. U.S. citizenship or permanent resident status and membership in the American Nurses Association are required. Selection is based on commitment to a career in substance abuse in psychiatric/mental health issues affecting minority populations.

Financial data The program provides an annual stipend of $22,476 and tuition assistance up to $5,000.

Duration 3 to 5 years.

Additional information Funds for this program are provided by the Substance Abuse and Mental Health Services Administration (SAMHSA).

Number awarded 1 or more each year.

Deadline March of each year.

[750]
AMERICAN NURSES ASSOCIATION MINORITY FELLOWSHIP PROGRAM YOUTH

American Nurses Association
Attn: SAMHSA Minority Fellowship Programs
8515 Georgia Avenue, Suite 400
Silver Spring, MD 20910-3492
(301) 628-5247   Toll Free: (800) 274-4ANA
Fax: (301) 628-5339   E-mail: janet.jackson@ana.org
Web: www.emfp.org

Summary To provide financial assistance to African American and other minority nurses who are interested in working on a master's degree in psychiatric/mental health nursing for service to young people.

Eligibility This program is open to nurses who are members of the American Nurses Association and members of an ethnic or racial minority group, including but not limited to Blacks or African Americans, Hispanics or Latinos, American Indians and Alaska Natives, Asians and Asian Americans, and Native Hawaiians and other Pacific Islanders. Applicants must be enrolled full time in an accredited master's degree behavioral health (psychiatric/mental health/substance abuse) nursing program. They must intend to apply for certification to become a Psychiatric Mental Health Nurse Practitioners, a fellowship-approved certification in substance abuse, or another sub-specialty that is associated with behavioral health services for children, adolescents, and youth transitioning into adulthood (ages 16 through 25). U.S. citizenship or permanent resident status is required. Selection is based on commitment to a career that provides behavioral health services to young people.

Financial data The stipend is $11,500 per year. Funds are disbursed directly to the fellow.

Duration 1 year; may be renewed.

Additional information Funds for this program are provided by the Substance Abuse and Mental Health Services Administration (SAMHSA).

Number awarded 1 or more each year.

Deadline March of each year.

[751]
AMERICAN POLITICAL SCIENCE ASSOCIATION MINORITY FELLOWS PROGRAM

American Political Science Association
Attn: Diversity and Inclusion Programs
1527 New Hampshire Avenue, N.W.
Washington, DC 20036-1206
(202) 349-9362   Fax: (202) 483-2657
E-mail: kmealy@apsanet.org
Web: www.apsanet.org/mfp

Summary To provide financial assistance to Africans and other underrepresented minorities interested in working on a doctoral degree in political science.

Eligibility This program is open to African Americans, Asian Pacific Americans, Latino(a)s, and Native Americans who are in their senior year at a college or university or currently enrolled in a master's degree program. Applicants must be planning to enroll in a doctoral program in political science to prepare for a career in teaching and research. They must be U.S. citizens and able to demonstrate financial need. Along with their application, they must submit a 500-word personal statement that includes why they are interested in attending graduate school in political science, what specific fields within the discipline they plan to study, and how they intend to contribute to research within the discipline. Selection is based on interest in teaching and potential for research in political science.

Financial data The stipend is $2,000 per year.

Duration 2 years.

Additional information In addition to the fellows who receive stipends from this program, students who are selected as fellows without stipend are recommended for admission and financial support to every doctoral political science program in the country. This program was established in 1969.

Number awarded Up to 12 fellows receive stipends each year.

Deadline March or October of each year.

[752]
AMERICAN SOCIETY OF HEMATOLOGY MINORITY GRADUATE STUDENT ABSTRACT ACHIEVEMENT AWARD

American Society of Hematology
Attn: Awards Manager
2021 L Street, N.W., Suite 900
Washington, DC 20036
(202) 776-0544   Fax: (202) 776-0545
E-mail: awards@hematology.org
Web: www.hematology.org

Summary To recognize and reward African American and other underrepresented minority graduate students who present outstanding abstracts at the annual meeting of the American Society of Hematology (ASH).

Eligibility This award is available to students who are enrolled in the first 3 years of work on a Ph.D. in the field of hematology and submit an abstract to the annual ASH meeting that is accepted for oral or poster presentation. Applicants must be a member of a racial or ethnic group that has been shown to be underrepresented in health-related sciences in the United States and Canada, including Blacks or African Americans, American Indians, Alaska Natives, Hispanics or Latinos, Native Hawaiians, other Pacific Islanders, African Canadians, Inuit, and First Nation Peoples. They must be working under the direction of an ASH member.

Financial data The award is $1,500.

Duration The award is presented annually.

Number awarded Varies each year; recently, 4 were presented.

Deadline The deadline for applying for these awards is the same as that for submitting abstracts for the annual meeting. Usually, that date is in early August.

[753]
AMERICAN SPEECH-LANGUAGE-HEARING FOUNDATION SCHOLARSHIP FOR MINORITY STUDENTS

American Speech-Language-Hearing Foundation
Attn: Programs Administrator
2200 Research Boulevard
Rockville, MD 20850-3289
(301) 296-8703   Toll Free: (800) 498-2071, ext. 8703
Fax: (301) 296-8567
E-mail: foundationprograms@asha.org
Web: www.ashfoundation.org

Summary To provide financial assistance to African American and other minority graduate students in communication sciences and disorders programs.

Eligibility This program is open to full-time graduate students who are enrolled in communication sciences and disorders programs, with preference given to U.S. citizens who are members of a racial or ethnic minority group. Applicants must submit an essay, up to 5 pages in length, on a topic that relates to the future of leadership in the discipline. Selection is based on academic promise and outstanding academic achievement.

Financial data The stipend is $5,000. Funds must be used for educational support (e.g., tuition, books, school living expenses), not for personal or conference travel.

Duration 1 year.

Number awarded Up to 3 each year.

Deadline May of each year.

[754]
AMERICAN THEOLOGICAL LIBRARY ASSOCIATION DIVERSITY SCHOLARSHIP

American Theological Library Association
Attn: Diversity Committee
300 South Wacker Drive, Suite 2100
Chicago, IL 60606-6701
(312) 454-5100   Toll Free: (888) 665-ATLA
Fax: (312) 454-5505   E-mail: memberrep@atla.com
Web: www.atla.com

Summary To provide funding to library students from African American and other underrepresented groups who are members of the American Theological Library Association (ATLA) interested in working on a master's degree in theological librarianship.

Eligibility This program is open to ATLA members from underrepresented groups (religious, racial, ethnic, or gender) who are enrolled at an ALA-accredited master's degree program in library and information studies. Applicants must submit personal statements on what diversity means to them, why their voice has not yet been heard, how they will increase diversity in their immediate context, and how they plan to increase diversity and participate fully in the ATLA.

Financial data The stipend is $2,400.

Duration 1 year.

Number awarded 1 each year.

Deadline April of each year.

[755]
AMOS T. HALL SCHOLARSHIP FUND

Tulsa Community Foundation
Attn: Scholarships
7030 South Yale Avenue, Suite 600
Tulsa, OK 74136
(918) 494-8823   Fax: (918) 494-9826
E-mail: scholarships@tulsacf.org
Web: www.tulsacf.org/whatwedo/education/scholarships

Summary To provide financial assistance to African American and other minority residents of any state attending law school in Oklahoma.

Eligibility This program is open to minority students from any state enrolled full time at an approved law school in Oklahoma. Selection is based on academic performance, dedication to public service, moral character, and promise for strengthening the legal profession.

Financial data The stipend is $1,000 per year.

Duration 1 year; recipients may reapply.

Additional information This program is sponsored by the Northeastern Oklahoma Black Lawyers Association.

Number awarded 1 or more each year.

Deadline April of each year.

[756]
AMS GRADUATE FELLOWSHIPS

American Meteorological Society
Attn: Development and Student Program Manager
45 Beacon Street
Boston, MA 02108-3693
(617) 227-2426, ext. 3907   Fax: (617) 742-8718
E-mail: dFernandez@ametsoc.org
Web: www2.ametsoc.org

Summary To encourage students entering their first year of graduate school, especially African Americans and members of other underrepresented groups, to work on an advanced degree in the atmospheric and related oceanic and hydrologic sciences.

Eligibility This program is open to students entering their first year of graduate study and planning to work on an advanced degree in the atmospheric or related oceanic or hydrologic sciences. Applicants must be U.S. citizens or permanent residents and have a GPA of 3.25 or higher. Along with their application, they must submit 200-word essays on 1) their most important achievements that qualify them for this scholarship; and 2) their career goals in the atmospheric or related sciences. Selection is based on academic record as an undergraduate. The sponsor specifically encourages applications from women, minorities, and students with disabilities who are traditionally underrepresented in the atmospheric and related sciences.

Financial data The stipend is $25,000 per academic year.

Duration 9 months.

Additional information This program was initiated in 1991. It is funded by high-technology firms and government agencies.

Number awarded Varies each year; recently, 8 were awarded.

Deadline January of each year.

[757]
ANARCHA, BETSY AND LUCY MEMORIAL SCHOLARSHIP AWARD

National Medical Fellowships, Inc.
Attn: Scholarship Program
347 Fifth Avenue, Suite 510
New York, NY 10016
(212) 483-8880   Toll Free: (877) NMF-1DOC
Fax: (212) 483-8897 E-mail: scholarships@nmfonline.org
Web: www.nmfonline.org

Summary To provide financial assistance to African American women who are attending medical school.

Eligibility This program is open to African American women who are enrolled in the first or second year of an accredited medical school in the United States. Applicants must be known descendants of slaves. Selection is based on leadership, commitment to serving medically underserved communities, and financial need.

Financial data The stipend is $5,000.

Duration 1 year; nonrenewable.

Additional information This program is named after 3 slaves who served as subjects of experimentation that helped shape advances in current clinical and surgical knowledge and are recognized as the Mothers of Gynecology.

Number awarded 1 or more each year.

Deadline September of each year.

[758]
ANL LABORATORY–GRADUATE RESEARCH APPOINTMENTS

Argonne National Laboratory
Division of Educational Programs
Attn: Graduate Student Program Office
9700 South Cass Avenue/DEP 223
Argonne, IL 60439-4845
(630) 252-3366   Fax: (630) 252-3193
E-mail: education@anl.gov
Web: www.anl.gov

Summary To offer opportunities for qualified graduate students, especially African Americans and members of other underrepresented groups, to carry out their master's or doctoral thesis research at the Argonne National Laboratory (ANL).

Eligibility Appointments are available for graduate students at U.S. universities who wish to carry out their thesis research under the co-sponsorship of an Argonne National Laboratory staff member and a faculty member. Research may be conducted in the basic physical and life sciences, mathematics, computer science, and engineering, as well as in a variety of applied areas relating to energy, conservation, environmental impact and technology, nanomaterials, and advanced nuclear energy systems. Applicants must be U.S. citizens or permanent residents. The laboratory encourages applications from all qualified persons, especially women and members of underrepresented minority groups.

Financial data Support consists of a stipend, tuition payments up to $5,000 per year, and payment of certain travel expenses. In addition, the student's faculty sponsor may receive payment for limited travel expenses.

Duration 1 year; may be renewed.

Additional information This program, which is also referred to as the Lab–Grad Program, is sponsored by the U.S. Department of Energy. In certain cases, students may be awarded support for pre-thesis studies on campus, provided that they intend to carry out their thesis research at Argonne.

Number awarded Varies each year.

Deadline Applications may be submitted at any time, but a complete application should be submitted at least 2 months prior to the proposed starting date.

[759]
ANTHEM BLUE CROSS BLUE SHIELD OF WISCONSIN NURSING SCHOLARSHIPS

Wisconsin League for Nursing
Attn: Scholarship Chair
P.O. Box 653
Germantown, WI 53022
(414) 454-9561   E-mail: info@wisconsinwln.org
Web: www.wisconsinwln.org/t/Scholarships

Summary To provide financial assistance to residents of Wisconsin, especially African Americans and other minorities, attending a school of nursing in the state.

Eligibility This program is open to residents of Wisconsin who are enrolled at an accredited school of nursing in the state in an L.P.N., A.D.N., B.S.N., M.S.N., D.N.P., or Ph.D. program. Applicants must have completed at least half the credits needed for graduation. Ethnic minority students are especially encouraged to apply. Students must submit their applications to their school, not directly to the sponsor. Each school may nominate 4 graduate students, 6 students in an R.N. program, and 2 L.P.N. students. Selection is based on scholastic ability, professional abilities and/or community service, understanding of the nursing profession, goals upon graduation, and financial need.

Financial data Stipends are $500 for L.P.N. students or $1,000 for all other students.

Duration 1 year.

Additional information This program is sponsored by Anthem Blue Cross Blue Shield of Wisconsin.

Number awarded Varies each year; recently, the program awarded 31 scholarships, including 2 L.P.N. awards, 10 associate degree awards, 16 B.S.N. awards, and 3 graduate awards.

Deadline April of each year.

[760]
APA/DIVISION 39 GRANT

American Psychological Foundation
750 First Street, N.E.
Washington, DC 20002-4242
(202) 336-5843   Fax: (202) 336-5812
E-mail: foundation@apa.org
Web: www.apa.org/apf/funding/division-39.aspx

Summary To provide funding to psychologists who wish to conduct psychoanalytical research related to African Americans and other underserved populations.

Eligibility This program is open to psychologists who have a demonstrated knowledge of psychoanalytical principles. Applicants may be, but are not required to be, practicing psychoanalytic therapists. Preference is given to graduate students involved in dissertation research, early-career professionals, and/or those who demonstrate a long-term interest in research related to underserved populations. The research may be of an empirical, theoretical, or clinical nature. Selection is based on conformance with stated program goals and qualifications; quality and potential impact of both previous and proposed research projects; originality, innovation, and contribution to the field with both previous and proposed research projects; and applicant's demonstrated interest in research related to underserved populations. The sponsor encourages applications from individuals who represent diversity in race, ethnicity, gender, age, disability, and sexual orientation.

Financial data The grant is $4,000.

Duration 1 year.

Additional information This program, which began in 2014, is sponsored by the American Psychological Association's Division 39 (Psychoanalysis).

Number awarded 1 each year.

Deadline July of each year.

[761]
APA MINORITY MEDICAL STUDENT SUMMER MENTORING PROGRAM

American Psychiatric Association
Attn: Division of Diversity and Health Equity
1000 Wilson Boulevard, Suite 1825
Arlington, VA 22209-3901
(703) 907-8653   Toll Free: (888) 35-PSYCH
Fax: (703) 907-7852   E-mail: mking@psych.org
Web: www.psychiatry.org/minority-fellowship

Summary To provide funding to African American and other minority medical students who are interested in working on a summer project with a psychiatrist mentor.

Eligibility This program is open to minority medical students who are interested in psychiatric issues. Minorities include African Americans, American Indians, Alaska Natives, Native Hawaiians, Asian Americans, and Hispanic/Latinos. Applicants must be interested in working with a psychiatrist mentor, primarily on clinical work with underserved minority populations and mental health care disparities. Work settings may be in a research, academic, or clinical environment. Most of them are inner-city or rural and deal with psychiatric subspecialties, particularly substance abuse and geriatrics. Selection is based on interest of the medical student and specialty of the mentor, practice setting, and geographic proximity of the mentor to the student. U.S. citizenship or permanent resident status is required.

Financial data Fellowships provide $1,500 for living and out-of-pocket expenses directly related to the conduct of the fellowship.

Duration Summer months.

Additional information This program is funded by the Substance Abuse and Mental Health Services Administration.

Number awarded Varies each year.

Deadline March of each year.

[762]
APAGS COMMITTEE FOR THE ADVANCEMENT OF RACIAL AND ETHNIC DIVERSITY (CARED) GRANT PROGRAM

American Psychological Association
Attn: American Psychological Association of Graduate
   Students
750 First Street, N.E.
Washington, DC 20002-4242
(202) 336-6014   Fax: (202) 336-5694
E-mail: apags@apa.org
Web: www.apa.org/about/awards/apags-cema.aspx

Summary To provide funding to African American and other graduate student members of the American Psychological Association of Graduate Students (APAGS) who wish to develop a project that increases membership and participation of ethnic minority students within the association.

Eligibility This program is open to members of APAGS who are enrolled at least half time in a master's or doctoral program at an accredited university. Applicants must be interested in developing a project to increase the membership and participation of ethnic minority graduate students within APAGS, advertise education and training opportunities for ethnic minorities, and enhance the recruitment and retention efforts for ethnic minority students in psychology. Examples include, but are not limited to, workshops, conferences, speaker series, mentorship programs, and the development of student organizations with a focus on multiculturalism or ethnic minority concerns.

Financial data The grant is $1,000.

Duration The grant is presented annually.

Additional information This grant was first awarded in 1997.

Number awarded 4 each year.

Deadline November of each year.

[763]
APF GRADUATE STUDENT SCHOLARSHIPS

American Psychological Foundation
750 First Street, N.E.
Washington, DC 20002-4242
(202) 336-5843   Fax: (202) 336-5812
E-mail: foundation@apa.org
Web: www.apa.org/apf/funding/cogdop.aspx

Summary To provide funding for research to graduate students in psychology, especially African Americans and members of other underrepresented groups.

Eligibility Each department of psychology that is a member in good standing of the Council of Graduate Departments of Psychology (COGDOP) may nominate up to 3 candidates for these scholarships. Nominations must include a completed application form, a letter of nomination from the department chair or director of graduate studies, a letter of recommendation from the nominee's graduate research adviser, a transcript of all graduate course work completed by the nominee, a curriculum vitae, and a brief outline of the nominee's thesis or dissertation research project. Selection is based on the context for the research, the clarity and comprehensibility of the research question, the appropriateness of the research design, the general importance of the research, and the use of requested funds. The sponsor encourages applications from individuals who represent diversity in race, ethnicity, gender, age, disability, and sexual orientation.

Financial data Awards range from $1,000 to $5,000 per year. A total of $28,000 is available for these scholarships each year.

Duration 1 year.

Additional information The highest rated nominees receive the Charles and Carol Spielberger Scholarship of $5,000, the Harry and Miriam Levinson Scholarship of $5,000 and the William and Dorothy Bevan Scholarship of $5,000. The next highest rated nominee receives the Ruth G. and Joseph D. Matarazzo Scholarship of $3,000. The next highest rated nominee receives the Clarence J. Rosecrans Scholarship of $2,000. The next highest rated nominees receive the William C. Howell Scholarship, the Dr. Judy Kuriansky Scholarship, and the Peter and Malina James and Dr. Louis P. James Legacy Scholarship of $1,000 each. Another 8 scholarships of $1,000 each, offered by the COGDOP, are also awarded.

Number awarded 16 each year: 3 at $5,000, 1 at $3,000, 1 at $2,000, and 11 at $1,000.

Deadline June of each year.

[764]
ARKANSAS CONFERENCE ETHNIC AND LANGUAGE CONCERNS COMMITTEE SCHOLARSHIPS

United Methodist Church-Arkansas Conference
Attn: Committee on Ethnic and Language Concerns
800 Daisy Bates Drive
Little Rock, AR 72202
(501) 324-8045   Toll Free: (877) 646-1816
Fax: (501) 324-8018   E-mail: mallen@arumc.org
Web: www.arumc.org/docs-and-forms

Summary To provide financial assistance to African American and other ethnic minority Methodist students from Arkansas who are interested in attending college or graduate school in any state.

Eligibility This program is open to ethnic minority undergraduate and graduate students who are active members of local congregations affiliated with the Arkansas Conference of the United Methodist Church (UMC). Applicants must be currently enrolled in an accredited institution of higher education in any state. Along with their application, they must submit an essay explaining how this scholarship will make them a leader in the UMC. Preference is given to students attending a UMC-affiliated college or university.

Financial data The stipend is $500 per semester ($1,000 per year) for undergraduates or $1,000 per semester ($2,000 per year) for graduate students.

Duration 1 year; may be renewed.

Number awarded 5 each year: 1 in each UMC Arkansas district.

Deadline February or September of each year.

[765]
ARL CAREER ENHANCEMENT PROGRAM

Association of Research Libraries
Attn: Director of Diversity Programs
21 Dupont Circle, N.W., Suite 800
Washington, DC 20036
(202) 296-2296   Fax: (202) 872-0884
E-mail: mpuente@arl.org
Web: www.arl.org

Summary To provide an opportunity for African Americans and members of other minority racial and ethnic groups to gain work experience at a library that is a member of the Association of Research Libraries (ARL).

Eligibility This program is open to members of racial and ethnic minority groups that are underrepresented as professionals in academic and research libraries (American Indian or Alaska Native, Asian, Black or African American, Native Hawaiian or other Pacific Islander, or Hispanic or Latino). Applicants must have completed at least 12 credit hours of an M.L.I.S. degree program at an ALA-accredited institution. They must be interested in an internship at 1 of 7 ARL member institutions. Along with their application, they must submit a 500-word essay on what attracts them to an internship opportunity in an ARL library, their professional interests as related to the internship, and their goals for the internship.

Financial data Fellows receive a stipend of $4,800 for the internship, housing reimbursement up to $2,500, relocation assistance up to $1,000, and financial support (approximately $1,400) to attend the annual ARL Leadership Institute.

Duration The internship lasts 6 to 12 weeks (or 240 hours).

Additional information This program is funded by the Institute of Museum and Library Services. Recently, the 7 participating ARL institutions were the University of Arizona, University of California at San Diego, University of Kentucky, University of Michigan, University of Washington, National Library of Medicine, and North Carolina State University.

Number awarded Varies each year; recently, 13 of these fellows were selected.

Deadline October of each year.

[766]
ARL INITIATIVE TO RECRUIT A DIVERSE WORKFORCE

Association of Research Libraries
Attn: Director of Diversity Programs
21 Dupont Circle, N.W., Suite 800
Washington, DC 20036
(202) 296-2296   Fax: (202) 872-0884
E-mail: mpuente@arl.org
Web: www.arl.org

Summary To provide financial assistance to Africans and members of other minority racial and ethnic groups who are interested in preparing for a career as an academic or research librarian.

Eligibility This program is open to members of racial and ethnic minority groups that are underrepresented as professionals in academic and research libraries (Black or African American, American Indian or Alaska Native, Asian, Native Hawaiian or other Pacific Islander, or Hispanic or Latino). Applicants must be interested in working on an M.L.I.S. degree at an ALA-accredited program. They must be citizens or permanent residents of the United States (including Puerto Rico) or Canada.

Financial data The stipend is $5,000 per year.

Duration 2 years.

Additional information This program began in 2000. Funding is currently provided by the Institute of Museum and Library Services and by the contributions of 52 libraries that are members of the Association of Research Libraries (ARL).

Number awarded Varies each year; recently, 15 were awarded.

Deadline April of each year.

[767]
ARL/SAA MOSAIC SCHOLARSHIPS

Society of American Archivists
Attn: Chair, Awards Committee
17 North State Street, Suite 1425
Chicago, IL 60602-4061
(312) 606-0722   Toll Free: (866) 722-7858
Fax: (312) 606-0728   E-mail: info@archivists.org
Web: www2.archivists.org

Summary To provide financial assistance to African American and other minority students who are working on a graduate degree in archival science.

Eligibility This program is open to minority graduate students, defined as those of Black/African American, American Indian/Alaska Native, Asian, Hispanic/Latino, or Native Hawaiian/other Pacific Islander descent. Applicants must be enrolled or planning to enroll full or part time in a master's degree program or a multi-course program in archival science, archival management, digital archives, special collections, or a related program. They may have completed no more than half of the credit requirements for a degree. Along with their application, they must submit a 500-word essay outlining their interests and future goals in the archives profession. U.S. or Canadian citizenship or permanent resident status is required.

Financial data   The stipend is $10,000.

Duration   1 year.

Additional information   This program began in 2009. A second iteration of the program began in 2013 in partnership with the Association of Research Libraries (ARL) and financial support provided by the Institute of Museum and Library Sciences (IMLS).

Number awarded   1 or 2 each year.

Deadline   June of each year.

[768]
ARTTABLE MENTORED INTERNSHIPS FOR DIVERSITY IN THE VISUAL ARTS PROFESSIONS

ArtTable Inc.
1 East 53rd Street, Fifth Floor
New York, NY 10022
(212) 343-1735   Fax: (866) 363-4188
E-mail: info@arttable.org
Web: www.arttable.org/summermentoredinternship

Summary   To provide an opportunity for African American and other women from diverse backgrounds to gain mentored work experience during the summer and to prepare for a career as an art professional.

Eligibility   This program is open to women who are college seniors, recent graduates, or graduate students and interested in preparing for a career as a visual arts professional (including administrative director, art adviser, art appraiser, art critic, art dealer, art librarian, arts funder, arts lawyer, conservator, curator, editor, educator, fundraiser, management consultant, public relations consultant, writer). Applicants must be from a cultural or ethnic background that is underrepresented in the field. They must be interested in working during the summer with a mentor at an art museum or similar facility. U.S. citizenship or permanent resident status is required.

Financial data   The stipend is $3,000. The hosting institution or mentor receives $500 for administrative and other costs.

Duration   8 weeks during the summer.

Additional information   This program began in 2000. Support is provided by the Samuel H. Kress Foundation.

Number awarded   Varies each year; recently, 5 of these internships were awarded.

Deadline   February of each year.

[769]
ASA MINORITY FELLOWSHIP PROGRAM GENERAL FELLOWSHIP

American Sociological Association
Attn: Minority Affairs Program
1430 K Street, N.W., Suite 600
Washington, DC 20005-2504
(202) 383-9005, ext. 322   Fax: (202) 638-0882
TDD: (202) 638-0981 E-mail: minority.affairs@asanet.org
Web: www.asanet.org

Summary   To provide financial assistance to doctoral students in sociology who are African Americans or members of other minority groups.

Eligibility   This program is open to U.S. citizens, permanent residents, and noncitizen nationals who are Blacks/African Americans, Latinos (e.g., Mexican Americans, Puerto Ricans, Cubans), American Indians or Alaskan Natives, Asian Americans (e.g., southeast Asians, Japanese, Chinese, Koreans), or Pacific Islanders (e.g., Filipinos, Samoans, Hawaiians, Guamanians). Applicants must be entering or continuing students in sociology at the doctoral level. Along with their application, they must submit 3-page essays on 1) the reasons why they decided to undertake graduate study in sociology, their primary research interests, and why they hope to do with a Ph.D. in sociology; and 2) what led them to select the doctoral program they attend or hope to attend and how they see that doctoral program preparing them for a professional career in sociology. Selection is based on commitment to research, focus of research experience, academic achievement, writing ability, research potential, and financial need.

Financial data   The stipend is $18,000 per year.

Duration   1 year; may be renewed up to 2 additional years.

Additional information   This program, which began in 1974, is supported by individual members of the American Sociological Association (ASA) and by several affiliated organizations (Alpha Kappa Delta, Sociologists for Women in Society, the Association of Black Sociologists, the Midwest Sociological Society, and the Southwestern Sociological Association).

Number awarded   Varies each year; since the program began, more than 500 of these fellowships have been awarded.

Deadline   January of each year.

[770]
ASCO MEDICAL STUDENT ROTATION FOR UNDERREPRESENTED POPULATIONS

American Society of Clinical Oncology
Attn: Conquer Cancer Foundation of ASCO
2318 Mill Road, Suite 800
Alexandria, VA 22314
(571) 483-1700
E-mail: grants@conquercancerfoundation.org
Web: www.conquercancerfoundation.org

Summary   To provide funding to African Americans and members of other underrepresented groups who are medical students interested in a clinical research oncology rotation.

Eligibility   This program is open to U.S. citizens, nationals, and permanent residents who are currently enrolled at a U.S. medical school. Applicants must be a member of a group currently underrepresented in medicine, defined as American Indian/Alaska Native, Black/African American, Hispanic/Latino, or Native Hawaiian/Pacific Islander. They must be interested in a rotation either in a cancer patient care setting or a cancer clinical research setting; the rotation may take place either at their own school or another institution but must have a faculty member who belongs to the American Society of Clinical Oncology (ASCO) and is willing to serve as a mentor. Selection is based on interest in preparing for a career in oncology; demonstration of leadership, volunteerism and/ or commitment to underserved populations or heath disparities; letters of recommendation; and overall academic record.

Financial data Students receive a stipend of $5,000 plus $1,500 for future travel to the annual meeting of the American Society of Clinical Oncology (ASCO). Their mentor receives a grant of $2,000.

Duration 8 to 10 weeks.

Additional information This program, which began in 2009, is currently sponsored by Lilly and Genentech BioOncology.

Number awarded Varies each year; recently, 4 were awarded.

Deadline January of each year.

[771]
ASME GRADUATE TEACHING FELLOWSHIP

ASME International
Attn: Education Manager
Two Park Avenue, Floor 7
New York, NY 10016-5618
(212) 591-7559   Toll Free: (800) THE-ASME
Fax: (212) 591-7856   E-mail: lawreya@asme.org
Web: www.asme.org

Summary To provide funding to members of the American Society of Mechanical Engineers (ASME), especially African Americans andother minorities, who are working on a doctorate in mechanical engineering.

Eligibility This program is open to U.S. citizens or permanent residents who have an undergraduate degree from an ABET-accredited program, belong to the society as a student member, are currently employed as a teaching assistant with lecture responsibility, and are working on a Ph.D. in mechanical engineering. Along with their application, they must submit a statement about their interest in a faculty career. Applications from women and minorities are particularly encouraged.

Financial data Fellowship stipends are $5,000 per year.

Duration Up to 2 years.

Additional information Recipients must teach at least 1 lecture course.

Number awarded Up to 4 each year.

Deadline February of each year.

[772]
ASP GRADUATE STUDENT VISITOR PROGRAM

National Center for Atmospheric Research
Attn: Advanced Study Program
3090 Center Green Drive
P.O. Box 3000
Boulder, CO 80307-3000
(303) 497-1328   Fax: (303) 497-1646
E-mail: paulad@ucar.edu
Web: www.asp.ucar.edu/graduate/graduate_visitor.php

Summary To provide an opportunity for graduate students, especially African Americans and members of other underrepresented groups, to conduct research at the National Center for Atmospheric Research (NCAR) in Boulder, Colorado under the supervision of a staff member.

Eligibility This program is open to advanced M.S. and Ph.D. students in the atmospheric and related sciences, engineering, and scientific computing. Interdisciplinary studies utilizing the NCAR resources in climate, weather, and related disciplines are also welcome. Applicants should consult with an NCAR staff member who will agree to serve as a host for the research project. Students may not apply directly for this program; the application must be submitted by the NCAR staff member in collaboration with the student's thesis adviser. Selection is based on 1) the programmatic fit and need to visit NCAR as part of the thesis or final project work; and 2) the commitment to student mentoring by the NCAR host and the student's adviser. The program encourages applications from members of groups historically underrepresented in the atmospheric and related sciences, including Blacks or African Americans, Hispanics or Latinos, American Indians and Alaska Natives, women, first-generation college students, LGBT students, and students with disabilities.

Financial data Support is limited to travel expenses for the student and a per diem allowance of $2,000 per month. Travel expenses are also supported for the student's thesis adviser for visits up to 2 weeks. The student's university must provide all support for the student's salary and benefits.

Duration Visits may extend from a few months to a year, but most are 3 to 6 months.

Additional information NCAR is operated by the University Corporation for Atmospheric Research (a consortium of more than 100 North American universities and research institutes) and sponsored by the National Science Foundation. This program was established in 2006.

Number awarded Varies each year; recently, 24 students received support from this program.

Deadline October of each year.

[773]
ASSE DIVERSITY COMMITTEE GRADUATE SCHOLARSHIP

American Society of Safety Engineers
Attn: ASSE Foundation
Scholarship Award Program
520 North Northwest Highway
Park Ridge, IL 60068-2538
(847) 699-2929   Fax: (847) 296-3769
E-mail: assefoundation@asse.org
Web: foundation.asse.org/scholarships-and-grants

Summary To provide financial assistance to graduate students who are African American or members of other diverse groups and working on a degree related to occupational safety.

Eligibility This program is open to students who are working on a graduate degree in occupational safety, health, environment, industrial hygiene, occupational health nursing, or a closely-related field (e.g., industrial or environmental engineering). Applicants must be full- or part-time students who have completed at least 9 semester hours and have a GPA of 3.5 or higher. A goal of this program is to support individuals regardless of race, ethnicity, gender, religion, personal beliefs, age, sexual orientation, physical challenges, geographic location, university, or specific area of study. U.S. citizenship is not required. Membership in the American Society of Safety Engineers (ASSE) is not required, but preference is given to members.

Financial data The stipend is $1,000 per year.

Duration 1 year; recipients may reapply.

Number awarded 1 each year.

Deadline November of each year.

[774]
ASSOCIATION OF BLACK WOMEN LAWYERS OF NEW JERSEY SCHOLARSHIPS

Association of Black Women Lawyers of New Jersey, Inc.
Attn: Scholarship Committee
P.O. Box 22524
Trenton, NJ 08607
E-mail: law860@verizon.net
Web: abwl-nj.org/scholarship-applicationluncheon

Summary To provide financial assistance to African American women from New Jersey attending law school in any state.

Eligibility This program is open to African American women who are 1) residents of New Jersey and currently enrolled in their first, second, or third year at an accredited law school in any state; or 2) residents of other states enrolled at a law school in New Jersey. Applicants must submit either a sample of their legal writing or an essay of 2 to 3 pages on a topic that changes annually; recently, students were asked to write on the use of excessive force in minority and immigrant communities. Selection is based on that writing sample or essay, academic achievement, demonstrated community service and civic involvement, and financial need.

Financial data Stipends range from $1,000 to $2,000.

Duration 1 year.

Number awarded At least 3 each year.

Deadline February of each year.

[775]
ATKINS NORTH AMERICA LEADERSHIP SCHOLARSHIP

Conference of Minority Transportation Officials
Attn: National Scholarship Program
100 M Street, S.E., Suite 917
Washington, DC 20003
(202) 506-2917   E-mail: info@comto.org
Web: www.comto.org/page/scholarships

Summary To provide financial assistance to African American and other minority undergraduate and graduate students interested in working on a degree in transportation or a related field.

Eligibility This program is open to minority 1) undergraduates who have completed at least 12 semester hours of study; and 2) graduate students. Applicants must be studying transportation, engineering, planning, or a related discipline. Along with their application they must submit a cover letter on their transportation-related career goals and life aspirations. Financial need is not considered in the selection process.

Financial data The stipend is $3,000. Funds are paid directly to the recipient's college or university.

Duration 1 year.

Additional information This program is sponsored by Atkins North America.

Number awarded 1 each year.

Deadline April of each year.

[776]
ATLANTA CHAPTER NBMBAA DOCTORAL SCHOLARSHIPS

National Black MBA Association-Atlanta Chapter
Attn: Director, Student Affairs
P.O. Box 54656
Atlanta, GA 30308-0656
E-mail: Scholarship@atlbmba.org
Web: www.atlbmba.org/doctoral-scholarship-application

Summary To provide financial assistance to members of the National Black MBA Association (NBMBAA) from any state working on a doctoral degree in business at a college in the metropolitan Atlanta area of Georgia.

Eligibility This program is open to African American residents of any state who are NBMBAA members and currently enrolled full time at a designated college or university in the Atlanta metropolitan area of Georgia. Applicants must be working on a doctoral degree in accounting, business, finance, management, or a related field. They must have a GPA of 3.0 or higher. Along with their application, they must submit a 750-word essay on a specified topic that changes annually but relates to African Americans and business. Financial need is not considered in the selection process. U.S. citizenship is required.

Financial data The stipend is $2,500.

Duration 1 year.

Additional information The eligible institutions are Clark Atlanta University, Emory University, Clayton State University, Georgia State University, Georgia Institute of Technology, Kennesaw State University, Mercer University, and the University of Georgia. Recipients must agree to attend the annual scholarship awards luncheon and engage in limited public relations activities of the sponsoring organization.

Number awarded 1 or more each year; normally, this sponsor awards $20,000 in scholarships annually.

Deadline September of each year.

[777]
ATLANTA CHAPTER NBMBAA MASTER'S SCHOLARSHIPS

National Black MBA Association-Atlanta Chapter
Attn: Director, Student Affairs
P.O. Box 54656
Atlanta, GA 30308-0656
E-mail: Scholarship@atlbmba.org
Web: www.atlbmba.org/masters-scholarship-application

Summary To provide financial assistance to members of the National Black MBA Association (NBMBAA) from any state working on a master's degree in business at a college in the metropolitan Atlanta area of Georgia.

Eligibility This program is open to African American residents of any state who are NBMBAA members and currently enrolled full time at a designated college or university in the Atlanta metropolitan area of Georgia. Applicants must be working on a master's degree in accounting, business, finance, management, or a related field. They must have a GPA of 3.0 or higher. Along with their application, they must submit a 750-word essay on a specified topic that changes annually but relates to African Americans and business. Financial need is not considered in the selection process. U.S. citizenship is required.

Financial data The stipend is $2,500.

Duration 1 year.

Additional information The eligible institutions are Clark Atlanta University, Clayton State University, Emory University, Georgia Institute of Technology, Georgia State University, Kennesaw State University, Mercer University, and the University of Georgia. Recipients must agree to attend the annual scholarship awards luncheon and engage in limited public relations activities of the sponsoring organization.

Number awarded 1 or more each year; normally, this sponsor awards $20,000 in scholarships annually.

Deadline September of each year.

[778]
AUDRE LORDE SCHOLARSHIP AWARD

ZAMI NOBLA
Attn: Audre Lorde Scholarship Fund
P.O. Box 90986
Atlanta, GA 30364
(404) 647-4754   E-mail: zami@zami.org
Web: www.zami.org/audrelordescholar.html

Summary To provide financial assistance to mature out Black lesbians who are interested in entering or continuing in college or graduate school.

Eligibility This program is open to Black lesbians who are at least 40 years of age and out to themselves and their family, friends, and community. Applicants must be enrolled or planning to enroll full or part time at a technical, undergraduate, or graduate school in any state. They must have a cumulative GPA in high school, college, or technical school of 3.0 or higher. Along with their application, they must submit an essay of 2 to 3 pages on their choice of 2 of 5 assigned topics that relate to their experience as a Black lesbian.

Financial data The stipend is $1,000.

Duration 1 year.

Additional information From 1995 to 2008, the Audre Lorde Scholarship Fund was maintained by an organization named ZAMI: Atlanta's Premiere Organization for Lesbians of African Descent. The fund was reestablished in 2013 by the current sponsor, which stands for ZAMI National Organization of Black Lesbians on Aging.

Number awarded 1 each year.

Deadline April of each year.

[779]
BALFOUR PHI DELTA PHI MINORITY SCHOLARSHIP AWARD

Phi Delta Phi International Legal Fraternity
Attn: Executive Director
P.O. Box 11570
Fort Lauderdale, FL 33339
(202) 223-6801   Toll Free: (800) 368-5606
Fax: (202) 223-6808   E-mail: info@phideltaphi.org
Web: www.phideltaphi.org/?page=BalfourMinorityGuide

Summary To provide financial assistance to African Americans and other minorities who are members of Phi Delta Phi International Legal Fraternity.

Eligibility This program is open to law students who have been members of the legal fraternity for at least 1 year. Applicants must be minorities, defined to include African Americans, Asian/Pacific Islanders, American Indians/Alaskan Natives, Hispanic, or LGBT students. They must affirm that they intend to practice law in inner-cities of the United States, especially in New England. Along with their application, they must submit a 750-word essay on why they consider themselves qualified to serve as role models for minority youth. Priority is given to students at law schools in New England, especially Massachusetts.

Financial data The stipend is $3,000.

Duration 1 year.

Additional information This program began in 1997 with funding from the Lloyd G. Balfour Foundation.

Number awarded 1 each year.

Deadline October of each year.

[780]
BASIC PSYCHOLOGICAL SCIENCE RESEARCH GRANT

American Psychological Association
Attn: American Psychological Association of Graduate Students
750 First Street, N.E.
Washington, DC 20002-4242
(202) 336-6014   E-mail: apags@apa.org
Web: www.apa.org/about/awards/apags-science.aspx

Summary To provide funding to members of the American Psychological Association of Graduate Students (APAGS) who are interested in conducting graduate research in psychological science, including those dealing specifically with diversity issues.

Eligibility This program is open to members of the association who are enrolled at least half time in a psychology or neuroscience graduate program at an accredited university. Applicants must be interested in conducting thesis, dissertation, or other research in psychological science. Along with their application, they must submit a curriculum vitae, letter of recommendation, and 3-page research proposal. The program includes grants specifically reserved for research focused on diversity, defined to include issues of age, sexual orientation, physical disability, socioeconomic status, race/ethnicity, workplace role/position, religious and spiritual orientation, and work/family concerns. Applicants for diversity grants must also submit a 250-word statement that explains 1) how this research applies to one or more areas of diversity; and 2) how the overall merit and broader implications of this study contribute to our psychological understanding of diversity.

Financial data The stipend is $1,000.

Duration 1 year.

Additional information These grants were first awarded in 2009; the diversity component began in 2014.

Number awarded Approximately 12 each year, of which up to 3 are reserved for researchers specifically focusing on diversity issues.

Deadline November of each year.

[781]
BERTHA PITTS CAMPBELL SCHOLARSHIP PROGRAM

Delta Sigma Theta Sorority, Inc.
Attn: Scholarship and Standards Committee Chair
1707 New Hampshire Avenue, N.W.
Washington, DC 20009
(202) 986-2400   Fax: (202) 986-2513
E-mail: dstemail@deltasigmatheta.org
Web: www.deltasigmatheta.org

Summary To provide financial assistance to members of Delta Sigma Theta who are working on an undergraduate or graduate degree in education.

Eligibility This program is open to current undergraduate and graduate students who are working on a degree in education. Applicants must be active, dues-paying members of Delta Sigma Theta. Selection is based on meritorious achievement.

Financial data The stipends range from $1,000 to $2,000. The funds may be used to cover tuition, fees, and living expenses.

Duration 1 year; may be renewed for 1 additional year.

Additional information This sponsor is a traditionally-African American social sorority. The application fee is $20.

Number awarded 1 or more each year.

Deadline March of each year.

[782]
BESLA GENERAL SCHOLARSHIP FUND

Black Entertainment and Sports Lawyers Association
Attn: Scholarships
P.O. Box 230794
New York, NY 10023
E-mail: scholarship@besla.org
Web: www.besla.org/#!scholarship-fund/qe8of

Summary To provide financial assistance to African American and other minority law students who are interested in the fields of entertainment and/or sports law.

Eligibility This program is open to minority students who have completed at least 1 year of full-time study at an accredited law school. Applicants must be able to demonstrate an interest in entertainment or sports law by 2 or more of the following: 1) completed an intellectual property, entertainment,

or sports law related course; 2) completed an internship or clerkship in the entertainment, sports, or related law field; or 3) membership in their school's sports and entertainment club. They must have a GPA of 2.8 or higher. Along with their application, they must submit a 5-page legal memorandum on an issue facing the entertainment or sports industry.

Financial data The stipend is at least $1,500.

Duration 1 year.

Additional information This program, established in 1989, includes the LeBaron and Yvonne M. Taylor Scholarship and the Flash and Bennie Wiley Scholarship.

Number awarded 5 to 7 each year, including at least 1 at each Historically Black Law School (Howard University School of Law, North Carolina Central University School of Law, Southern University Law Center, Florida A&M University School of Law, and Texas Southern University Thurgood Marshall School of Law).

Deadline September of each year.

[783]
BESLA LEGAL WRITING COMPETITION

Black Entertainment and Sports Lawyers Association
Attn: Scholarships
P.O. Box 230794
New York, NY 10023
E-mail: scholarship@besla.org
Web: www.besla.org/#!scholarship/hc901

Summary To recognize and reward law students, especially African Americans, who submit outstanding papers or digital responses on topics related to the fields of entertainment and/or sports law.

Eligibility This program is open to students who have completed at least 1 full year at a law school in the United States or its territories. Applicants must submit a written essay or a digital response (in the form of a video or slide show presentation) on a legal issue facing the entertainment or sports industry. Recently, students were asked to write on either 1) a sports league's practice of collectively selling broadcast rights; or 2) registration of a copyright. Selection is based on focus, organization, critical legal analysis, conclusions and recommendations, originality, voice, and style and mechanics.

Financial data The award is $1,000.

Duration The competition is held annually.

Additional information This program began in 2004.

Number awarded 1 or more each year.

Deadline September of each year.

[784]
BETTY LEA STONE RESEARCH FELLOWSHIP

American Cancer Society-New England Division
30 Speen Street
Framingham, MA 01701
(508) 270-4645   Toll Free: (800) 952-7664, ext. 4645
Fax: (508) 393-8607   E-mail: maureen.morse@cancer.org
Web: www.cancer.org

Summary To provide funding for summer cancer research to medical students in New England, especially African Americans and other minorities.

Eligibility This program is open to first-year students at medical schools in New England. Applicants must be interested in working on a summer research project under the supervision of a faculty sponsor. Minority students and those with American Cancer Society volunteer experience are encouraged to apply.

Financial data The grant is $5,000.

Duration 10 weeks during the summer.

Number awarded 1 or more each year.

Deadline January of each year.

[785]
BILL BERNBACH DIVERSITY SCHOLARSHIPS

American Association of Advertising Agencies
Attn: AAAA Foundation
1065 Avenue of the Americas, 16th Floor
New York, NY 10018
(212) 262-2500   E-mail: bbscholarship@ddb.com
Web: www.aaaa.org

Summary To provide financial assistance to African American and other multicultural students interested in working on an undergraduate or graduate degree in advertising at designated schools.

Eligibility This program is open to African Americans, Asian Americans, Hispanic Americans, and Native Americans (including American Indians, Alaska Natives, Native Hawaiians, and other Pacific Islanders) who are interested in studying the advertising creative arts at designated institutions as a full-time student. Applicants must be working on or have already received an undergraduate degree and be able to demonstrate creative talent and promise. They must be U.S. citizens, nationals, or permanent residents. Along with their application, they must submit 10 samples of creative work in their respective field of expertise.

Financial data The stipend is $5,000.

Duration 1 year.

Additional information This program, which began in 1998, is currently sponsored by DDB Worldwide. The participating schools are the Art Center College of Design (Pasadena, California), Creative Circus (Atlanta, Georgia), Miami Ad School (Miami Beach, Florida), University of Oklahoma (Norman, Oklahoma), University of Texas at Austin, VCU Brandcenter (Richmond, Virginia), Savannah College of Art and Design (Savannah, Georgia), University of Oregon (Eugene), City College of New York, School of Visual Arts (New York, New York), Fashion Institute of Technology (New York, New York), and Howard University (Washington, D.C.).

Number awarded 3 each year.

Deadline May of each year.

[786]
BISHOP THOMAS HOYT, JR. FELLOWSHIP

St. John's University
Attn: Collegeville Institute for Ecumenical and Cultural
  Research
2475 Ecumenical Drive
P.O. Box 2000
Collegeville, MN 56321-2000
(320) 363-3366   Fax: (320) 363-3313
E-mail: staff@CollegevilleInstitute.org
Web: www.collegevilleinstitute.org

Summary To provide funding to African Americans and other students of color who wish to complete their doctoral

dissertation while in residence at the Collegeville Institute for Ecumenical and Cultural Research of St. John's University in Collegeville, Minnesota.

Eligibility This program is open to people of color completing a doctoral dissertation in ecumenical and cultural research. Applicants must be interested in a residency at the Collegeville Institute for Ecumenical and Cultural Research of St. John's University. Along with their application, they must submit a 1,000-word description of the research project they plan to complete while in residence at the Institute.

Financial data The stipend covers the residency fee of $2,500, which includes housing and utilities.

Duration 1 year.

Additional information Residents at the Institute engage in research, publication, and education on the important intersections between faith and culture. They seek to discern and communicate the meaning of Christian identity and unity in a religiously and culturally diverse world.

Number awarded 1 each year.

Deadline January of each year.

[787]
BREAKTHROUGH TO NURSING SCHOLARSHIPS

National Student Nurses' Association
Attn: Foundation
45 Main Street, Suite 606
Brooklyn, NY 11201
(718) 210-0705   Fax: (718) 210-0710
E-mail: nsna@nsna.org
Web: www.nsna.org

Summary To provide financial assistance to African American and other minority undergraduate and graduate students who wish to prepare for careers in nursing.

Eligibility This program is open to students currently enrolled in state-approved schools of nursing or pre-nursing associate degree, baccalaureate, diploma, generic master's, generic doctoral, R.N. to B.S.N., R.N. to M.S.N., or L.P.N./ L.V.N. to R.N. programs. Graduating high school seniors are not eligible. Support for graduate education is provided only for a first degree in nursing. Applicants must be members of a racial or ethnic minority underrepresented among registered nurses (Black or African American, American Indian or Alaska Native, Hispanic or Latino, Native Hawaiian or other Pacific Islander, or Asian). They must be committed to providing quality health care services to underserved populations. Along with their application, they must submit a 200-word description of their professional and educational goals and how this scholarship will help them achieve those goals. Selection is based on academic achievement, financial need, and involvement in student nursing organizations and community health activities. U.S. citizenship or permanent resident status is required.

Financial data Stipends range from $1,000 to $2,000.

Duration 1 year.

Additional information Applications must be accompanied by a $10 processing fee.

Number awarded Varies each year; recently, 13 were awarded: 10 sponsored by the American Association of Critical-Care Nurses and 3 sponsored by the Mayo Clinic.

Deadline January of each year.

[788]
BRONSON T.J. TREMBLAY MEMORIAL SCHOLARSHIP

Colorado Nurses Foundation
Attn: Scholarships
P.O. Box 3406
Englewood, CO 80155
(303) 694-4728   Toll Free: (800) 205-6655
Fax: (303) 200-7099   E-mail: mail@cnfound.org
Web: www.coloradonursesfoundation.com/?page_id=1087

Summary   To provide financial assistance to African American and other non-white male undergraduate and graduate nursing students in Colorado.

Eligibility   This program is open to non-white male Colorado residents who have been accepted as a student in an approved nursing program in the state. Applicants may be 1) second-year students in an associate degree program; 2) junior or senior level B.S.N. undergraduate students; 3) R.N.s enrolled in a baccalaureate or higher degree program in a school of nursing; 4) R.N.s with a master's degree in nursing, currently practicing in Colorado and enrolled in a doctoral program; or 5) students in the second or third year of a Doctorate Nursing Practice (D.N.P.) or Ph.D. program. Undergraduates must have a GPA of 3.25 or higher and graduate students must have a GPA of 3.5 or higher. Selection is based on professional philosophy and goals, dedication to the improvement of patient care in Colorado, demonstrated commitment to nursing, potential for leadership, involvement in community and professional organizations, recommendations, GPA, and financial need.

Financial data   The stipend is $1,000.
Duration   1 year.
Number awarded   1 each year.
Deadline   October of each year.

[789]
BROWN AND CALDWELL MINORITY SCHOLARSHIP

Brown and Caldwell
Attn: HR/Scholarship Program
1527 Cole Boulevard, Suite 300
Lakewood, CO 80401
(303) 239-5400   Fax: (303) 239-5454
E-mail: scholarships@brwncald.com
Web: www.brownandcaldwell.com/Scholarships.asp?id=1

Summary   To provide financial assistance to African American and other minority students working on an undergraduate or graduate degree in an environmental or engineering field.

Eligibility   This program is open to members of minority groups (African Americans, Hispanics, Asians, Pacific Islanders, Native Americans, or Alaska Natives) who are full-time juniors, seniors, or graduate students at an accredited 4-year college or university. Applicants must have a GPA of 3.0 or higher and a declared major in civil, chemical, or environmental engineering or an environmental science (e.g., biology, ecology, geology, hydrogeology). They must be U.S. citizens or permanent residents. Along with their application, they must submit an essay (up to 250 words) on a topic that changes annually but relates to their personal development. Financial need is not considered in the selection process.

Financial data   The stipend is $5,000.
Duration   1 year.
Number awarded   1 each year.
Deadline   May of each year.

[790]
BUCKFIRE & BUCKFIRE MEDICAL SCHOOL DIVERSITY SCHOLARSHIP

Buckfire & Buckfire, P.C.
Attn: Scholarships
25800 Northwestern Highway, Suite 890
Southfield, MI 48075
(248) 569-4646   Toll Free: (800) 606-1717
Fax: (248) 569-6737 E-mail: marketing@buckfirelaw.com
Web: www.buckfirelaw.com/library/general

Summary   To provide financial assistance to medical students who come from a minority background or have a commitment to diversity.

Eligibility   This program is open to U.S. citizens who are members of an ethnic, racial, or other minority or who demonstrate a defined commitment to issues of diversity within their academic career. Applicants must have completed at least 1 semester at an accredited medical school and have a GPA of 3.0 or higher. Selection is based on academic achievement and an essay on how they will utilize their medical degree to promote diversity.

Financial data   The stipend is $2,000.
Duration   1 year.
Additional information   This program began in 2014.
Number awarded   1 each year.
Deadline   May of each year.

[791]
CALIFORNIA BAR FOUNDATION 1L DIVERSITY SCHOLARSHIPS

State Bar of California
Attn: California Bar Foundation
180 Howard Street
San Francisco, CA 94105-1639
(415) 856-0780   Fax: (415) 856-0788
E-mail: scholarships@calbarfoundation.org
Web: www.calbarfoundation.org

Summary   To provide financial assistance to residents of any state who are African Americans or members of other groups historically underrepresented in the legal profession and entering law school in California.

Eligibility   This program to open to residents of any state who are entering their first year at a law school in California. Applicants must be able to contribute to greater diversity in the legal profession. Diversity includes a broad array of backgrounds and life experiences, including students from groups or with skills or attributes that are underrepresented in the legal profession. Students from socially and economically disadvantaged backgrounds are especially encouraged to apply. Along with their application, they must submit a 500-word essay describing their commitment to serving the community and, if applicable, any significant obstacles or hurdles they have overcome to attend law school. Financial need is considered in the selection process.

Financial data   The stipend is $7,500.
Duration   1 year.

Additional information This program began in 2008. Each year, the foundation grants awards named after sponsors that donate funding for the scholarships.

Number awarded Varies each year; recently, 33 were awarded.

Deadline May of each year.

[792]
CALIFORNIA COMMUNITY SERVICE-LEARNING PROGRAM

National Medical Fellowships, Inc.
Attn: Scholarship Program
347 Fifth Avenue, Suite 510
New York, NY 10016
(212) 483-8880   Toll Free: (877) NMF-1DOC
Fax: (212) 483-8897 E-mail: scholarships@nmfonline.org
Web: www.nmfonline.org

Summary To provide funding to African American and other underrepresented medical students in California who wish to participate in a community service program for underserved areas of the state.

Eligibility This program is open to members of underrepresented minority groups (African American, Hispanic/Latino, Native American, Vietnamese, or Cambodian) who are U.S. citizens or DACA certified. Applicants must be currently enrolled in an accredited medical school in California. They must be interested in a self-directed service-learning experience that provides 200 hours of community service in medically-underserved areas of the state. Selection is based on demonstrated leadership early in career and commitment to serving medically underserved communities.

Financial data The stipend is $5,000.

Additional information Funding for this program, which began in 2013 and is administered by National Medical Fellowships (NMF), is provided by the California Wellness Foundation.

Number awarded 10 each year.

Deadline March of each year.

[793]
CALIFORNIA PLANNING FOUNDATION DIVERSITY IN PLANNING SCHOLARSHIP

American Planning Association-California Chapter
Attn: California Planning Foundation
c/o Kelly Main
California Polytechnic State University at San Luis Obispo
City and Regional Planning Department
Office 21-116B
San Luis Obispo, CA 93407-0283
(805) 756-2285   Fax: (805) 756-1340
E-mail: cpfapplications@gmail.com
Web: www.californiaplanningfoundation.org

Summary To provide financial assistance to African American and other undergraduate and graduate students in accredited planning programs at California universities who will increase diversity in the profession.

Eligibility This program is open to students entering their final year for an undergraduate or master's degree in an accredited planning program at a university in California. Applicants must be students who will increase diversity in the planning profession. Along with their application, they must submit 1) a 500-word personal statement explaining why planning is important to them, their potential contribution to the profession of planning in California, and how this scholarship would help them to complete their degree; 2) a 500-word description of their experience in planning (e.g., internships, volunteer experiences, employment); and 3) a 500-word essay on what they consider to be 1 of the greatest planning challenges in California today. Selection is based on academic performance, increasing diversity in the planning profession, commitment to serve the planning profession in California, and financial need.

Financial data The stipend is $3,000. The award includes a 1-year student membership in the American Planning Association (APA) and payment of registration for the APA California Conference.

Duration 1 year.

Additional information The accredited planning programs are at 3 campuses of the California State University system (California State Polytechnic University at Pomona, California Polytechnic State University at San Luis Obispo, and San Jose State University), 3 campuses of the University of California (Berkeley, Irvine, and Los Angeles), and the University of Southern California.

Number awarded 1 each year.

Deadline March of each year.

[794]
CANFIT PROGRAM GRADUATE SCHOLARSHIPS

Communities-Adolescents-Nutrition-Fitness
Attn: Scholarship Program
P.O. Box 3989
Berkeley, CA 94703
(510) 644-1533, ext. 112   Toll Free: (800) 200-3131
Fax: (510) 843-9705   E-mail: info@canfit.org
Web: www.canfit.org/scholarships

Summary To provide financial assistance to African American and other minority graduate students who are working on a degree in nutrition, physical education, or public health in California.

Eligibility This program is open to African Americans, American Indians, Alaska Natives, Asian Americans, Pacific Islanders, and Latinos/Hispanics from California who are enrolled in 1) an approved master's or doctoral program in nutrition, public health, or physical education in the state; or 2) a pre-professional practice program approved by the American Dietetic Association at an accredited university in the state. Applicants must have completed 12 to 15 units of graduate course work and have a cumulative GPA of 3.0 or higher. Along with their application, they must submit 1) documentation of financial need; 2) letters of recommendation from 2 individuals; 3) a 1- to 2-page letter describing their academic goals and involvement in community nutrition and/or physical education activities; and 4) an essay of 500 to 1,000 words on a topic related to healthy foods for youth from low-income communities of color.

Financial data A stipend is awarded (amount not specified).

Number awarded 1 or more each year.

Deadline March of each year.

[795]
CARMEN E. TURNER SCHOLARSHIPS

Conference of Minority Transportation Officials
Attn: National Scholarship Program
100 M Street, S.E., Suite 917
Washington, DC 20003
(202) 506-2917   E-mail: info@comto.org
Web: www.comto.org/page/scholarships

Summary To provide financial assistance for college or graduate school to African American and other members of the Conference of Minority Transportation Officials (COMTO) and their families.

Eligibility This program is open to undergraduate and graduate students who have been members or whose parents, guardians, or grandparents have been members of COMTO for at least 1 year. Applicants must be working on a degree in a field related to transportation and have a GPA of 2.5 or higher. Along with their application they must submit a cover letter on their transportation-related career goals and life aspirations. Financial need is not considered in the selection process.

Financial data The stipend is $3,500. Funds are paid directly to the recipient's college or university.

Duration 1 year.

Number awarded 1 each year.

Deadline April of each year.

[796]
CAROLE SIMPSON NABJ SCHOLARSHIP

National Association of Black Journalists
Attn: Program Manager
University of Maryland
1100 Knight Hall, Suite 3100
College Park, MD 20742
(301) 405-7520   Fax: (301) 314-1714
E-mail: Sberry@nabj.org
Web: www.nabj.org/?page=ScholarshipsSimpson

Summary To provide financial assistance to undergraduate or graduate student members of the National Association of Black Journalists (NABJ) who are working on a degree in broadcast journalism.

Eligibility This program is open to African American undergraduate or graduate student members of NABJ who are currently enrolled full time at an accredited 4-year college or university. Applicants must be studying broadcast journalism as preparation for a career in television news and have a GPA of 2.5 or higher. They must be able to demonstrate financial need. Along with their application, they must submit 5 samples of their work, an official college transcript, 3 letters of recommendation, a resume, and an essay of 1,000 to 2,000 words on how the career of this program's namesake inspired them to prepare for a career in broadcast journalism and what they hope their legacy will be.

Financial data The stipend is $2,500. Funds are paid directly to the recipient's college or university.

Duration 1 year; nonrenewable.

Number awarded 1 each year.

Deadline February of each year.

[797]
CARRINGTON-HSIA-NIEVES SCHOLARSHIP FOR MIDWIVES OF COLOR

American College of Nurse-Midwives
Attn: ACNM Foundation, Inc.
8403 Colesville Road, Suite 1550
Silver Spring, MD 20910-6374
(240) 485-1850   Fax: (240) 485-1818
E-mail: foundation@acnmf.org
Web: www.midwife.org

Summary To provide financial assistance to African American and other midwives of color who are members of the American College of Nurse-Midwives (ACNM) and engaged in doctoral or postdoctoral study.

Eligibility This program is open to ACNM members of color who are certified nurse midwives (CNM) or certified midwives (CM). Applicants must be enrolled in a program of doctoral or postdoctoral education. Along with their application, they must submit brief statements on their 5-year academic career plans, their intended use of the funds, and their intended future participation in the local, regional, and/or national activities of the ACNM and in activities that otherwise contribute substantially to midwifery research, education, or practice.

Financial data The stipend is $5,000.

Duration 1 year.

Number awarded 1 each year.

Deadline October of each year.

[798]
CARTER G. WOODSON INSTITUTE PREDOCTORAL RESIDENTIAL RESEARCH FELLOWSHIP

University of Virginia
Carter G. Woodson Institute for African-American and
  African Studies
Attn: Director of the Fellowship Program
108 Minor Hall
P.O. Box 400162
Charlottesville, VA 22904-4162
(434) 924-3109   Fax: (434) 924-8820
E-mail: woodson@virginia.edu
Web: www.woodson.virginia.edu/fellowship/predoc

Summary To provide funding to doctoral candidates interested in conducting research at the University of Virginia's Woodson Institute in those disciplines of the humanities and social sciences concerned with African American and African studies.

Eligibility This program is open to doctoral candidates who have completed all requirements for the Ph.D. except the dissertation prior to August of the fellowship year. There are no citizenship or residence requirements. Applicants must be working in a field of the humanities or social sciences that focuses on Africa and/or the African Diaspora. Along with their application, they must submit a description of a research project to be conducted during the fellowship period at the Woodson Institute. Selection is based on the significance of the proposed work, the qualifications of the applicant, familiarity with existing relevant research literature, the research design of the project, and the promise of completion within the award period.

Financial data The stipend is $20,000 per year. Health insurance is also provided.

Duration 2 years; nonrenewable.

Additional information Fellows must be in residence at the University of Virginia for the duration of the award period. They are expected to contribute to the intellectual life of the university.

Number awarded 4 each year.

Deadline November of each year.

[799]
CATHY L. BROCK SCHOLARSHIP

Institute for Diversity in Health Management
Attn: Membership and Education Specialist
155 North Wacker Avenue
Chicago, IL 60606
(312) 422-2658   E-mail: cbiddle@aha.org
Web: www.diversityconnection.org

Summary To provide financial assistance to African American and other graduate students in health care management, especially financial operations, who will contribute to ethnic diversity in the profession.

Eligibility This program is open to U.S. citizens who represent ethnically diverse cultural backgrounds. Applicants must be enrolled in the first or second year of a master's degree program in health administration or a comparable program and have a GPA of 3.0 or higher. Along with their application, they must submit 1) a personal statement of 1 to 2 pages on their interest in health care management and their career goals; 2) an essay on what they see as the most challenging issue facing America's hospitals and health systems; and 3) a 500-word essay on their interest and background in health care finance. Selection is based on academic achievement, commitment to a career in health care finance, and financial need.

Financial data The stipend is $1,000.

Duration 1 year.

Number awarded 1 each year.

Deadline January of each year.

[800]
CAVE MEMORIAL AWARD

National Optometric Association
Attn: Student Affairs
1801 North Tryon Street, Suite 315
Charlotte, NC 28206
(704) 918-1809   Toll Free: (877) 394-2020
Fax: (877) NOA-2006
E-mail: noastudentdirector@yahoo.com
Web: www.nationaloptometricassociation.com

Summary To provide financial assistance to African American and other members of the National Optometric Student Association (NOSA) who demonstrate financial need.

Eligibility This program is open to NOSA members enrolled in a school or college of optometry. Applicants must have a GPA of 2.5 or higher and be able to demonstrate community involvement. Along with their application, they must submit a 2-page statement on their reasons for applying for this award, their career goals, community and college involvement, and the impact they have had in affecting positive

change that has enhanced our minority communities. Financial need is considered in the selection process.

Financial data The stipend is $1,000.

Duration 1 year.

Additional information The National Optometric Association was founded in 1969 with the goal of recruiting minority students, especially African Americans, for schools and colleges of optometry.

Number awarded 1 each year.

Deadline May of each year.

[801]
CBCF GENERAL MILLS HEALTH SCHOLARSHIP

Congressional Black Caucus Foundation, Inc.
Attn: Director, Educational Programs
1720 Massachusetts Avenue, N.W.
Washington, DC 20036
(202) 263-2800   Toll Free: (800) 784-2577
Fax: (202) 775-0773   E-mail: scholarships@cbcfinc.org
Web: www.cbcfinc.org/cbcs-cheerios

Summary To provide financial assistance to undergraduate and graduate students who are interested in preparing for a health-related career and who reside in a Congressional district represented by a member of the Congressional Black Caucus (CBC).

Eligibility This program is open to students attending or planning to attend an accredited institution of higher education as a full-time undergraduate or graduate student. Applicants must reside or attend school in a Congressional district represented by a member of the CBC. Preference is given to African Americans. Applicants must be interested in preparing for a career in a medical or other health-related field, including medicine, technology, nutrition, engineering, or other health-related field. They must have a GPA of 2.75 or higher. Along with their application, they must submit transcripts; a 1-page resume listing their extracurricular activities, honors, employment, community service, and special skills; and a personal statement of 500 to 1,000 words on themselves and their interests. They must also be able to demonstrate financial need, leadership ability, and participation in community service activities.

Financial data The stipend is $2,500.

Duration 1 year.

Additional information The program was established in 1998 with support from General Mills, Inc.

Number awarded Up to 46 each year.

Deadline February of each year.

[802]
CENIE "JOMO" WILLIAMS TUITION SCHOLARSHIP

National Association of Black Social Workers
Attn: NABSW Scholarships
2305 Martin Luther King Avenue, S.E.
Washington, DC 20020
(202) 678-4570   Fax: (202) 678-4572
E-mail: office-manager@nabsw.org
Web: www.nabsw.org/?page=ScholarshipsRecipien

Summary To provide financial assistance for college or graduate school to members of the National Association of Black Social Workers (NABSW).

Eligibility This program is open to African American members of NABSW enrolled full time at an accredited social work or social welfare program with a GPA of 2.5 or higher. Applicants must be able to demonstrate community service and a research interest in the Black community. Along with their application, they must submit an essay of 2 to 3 pages on their professional interests, future social work aspirations, previous social work experiences (volunteer and professional), honors and achievements (academic and community service), and research interests within the Black community (for master's and doctoral students). Financial need is considered in the selection process.

Financial data The stipend is $2,000. Funds are sent directly to the recipient's school.

Duration 1 year.

Number awarded 2 each year.

Deadline December of each year.

[803]
CH2M HILL PARTNERSHIP SCHOLARSHIP

Women's Transportation Seminar
Attn: WTS Foundation
1701 K Street, N.W., Suite 800
Washington, DC 20006
(202) 955-5085   Fax: (202) 955-5088
E-mail: wts@wtsinternational.org
Web: www.wtsinternational.org/education/scholarships

Summary To provide financial assistance to women graduate students, especially African Americans and other minorities, who are interested in preparing for a career in transportation.

Eligibility This program is open to women who are enrolled in a graduate degree program in a transportation-related field (e.g., transportation engineering, planning, finance, or logistics). Applicants must have at least a 3.0 GPA and be interested in a career in transportation. Along with their application, they must submit a 750-word statement about their career goals after graduation and why they think they should receive the scholarship award. Applications must be submitted first to a local chapter; the chapters forward selected applications for consideration on the national level. Minority women are particularly encouraged to apply. Selection is based on transportation involvement and goals, job skills, and academic record.

Financial data The stipend is $10,000.

Duration 1 year.

Additional information This program is sponsored by CH2M Hill. Local chapters may also award additional funding to winners in their area.

Number awarded 1 each year.

Deadline Applications must be submitted by November to a local WTS chapter.

[804]
CH2M HILL/WILLIE T. LOUD SCHOLARSHIP

National Forum for Black Public Administrators
Attn: Scholarship Program
777 North Capitol Street, N.E., Suite 807
Washington, DC 20002
(202) 408-9300   Fax: (202) 408-8558
E-mail: vharris@nfbpa.org
Web: www.nfbpa.org/i4a/pages/index.cfm?pageid=4047

Summary To provide financial assistance to African Americans working on a bachelor's or master's degree in public administration.

Eligibility This program is open to African American graduate students preparing for a career in public service. Applicants must be working full time on a bachelor's or master's degree in public administration, urban affairs, or a related field. They must have a GPA of 3.0 or higher, strong interpersonal skills, and excellent writing, analytical, and oral communication abilities. Along with their application, they must submit a 3-page autobiographical essay that includes their academic and career goals and objectives. Selection is based on academic record, leadership ability, participation in school activities, community service, and financial need.

Financial data The stipend is $5,000.

Duration 1 year.

Additional information This program, established in 1997, is sponsored by CH2M Hill. Recipients are required to attend the sponsor's annual conference to receive their scholarship; limited hotel and air accommodations are arranged and provided.

Number awarded 1 each year.

Deadline March of each year.

[805]
CHARLES B. RANGEL GRADUATE FELLOWSHIP PROGRAM

Howard University
Attn: Ralph J. Bunche International Affairs Center
2218 Sixth Street, N.W.
Washington, DC 20059
(202) 806-4367   Toll Free: (877) 633-0002
Fax: (202) 806-5424 E-mail: rangelprogram@howard.edu
Web: www.rangelprogram.org

Summary To provide financial assistance for graduate study in a field related to the work of the Foreign Service, especially to African Americans and members of other underrepresented minority groups.

Eligibility This program is open to U.S. citizens who are either graduating college seniors or recipients of an undergraduate degree. Applicants must be planning to enter graduate school to work on a master's degree in international affairs or other area of interest to the Foreign Service of the U.S. Department of State (e.g., public administration, public policy, business administration, foreign languages, economics, political science, or communications). They must have a GPA of 3.2 or higher. The program encourages applications from members of minority groups historically underrepresented in the Foreign Service and those who can demonstrate financial need.

Financial data The program provides a stipend of $20,000 per year for tuition and fees, $15,000 per year for room, board, books, and other education-related expenses, and a stipend of $10,000 per year for housing, transportation, and related expenses for summer internships.

Duration 2 years.

Additional information This program is offered jointly by Howard University and the U.S. Department of State. Fellows are provided an internship working on international issues for members of Congress during the summer after they are selected and before they begin graduate study. They are provided a second internship at a U.S. embassy overseas during the summer before their second year of graduate study. Fellows who complete the program and Foreign Service entry requirements receive appointments as Foreign Service Officers. Each fellow who obtains a master's degree is committed to at least 5 years of service as a Foreign Service Officer. If recipients do not complete the program successfully or do not fulfill the 3-year service obligation, they may be subject to a reimbursement obligation.

Number awarded 20 each year.

Deadline January of each year.

[806]
CHARLES HAMILTON HOUSTON ESSAY COMPETITION

Washington Bar Association
Attn: Educational Foundation
P.O. Box 56551
Washington, DC 20040
(202) 349-1059   Fax: (202) 659-4082
E-mail: info@washingtonbar.org
Web: www.washingtonbar.org/wbaef/wbaef-scholarships

Summary To recognize and reward African American and other law students in Washington D.C. who submit outstanding essays on legal topics.

Eligibility This program is open first- and second-year full-time law students at schools in Washington, D.C. Applicants must submit essays, up to 7 pages in length, on a topic that changes annually; recently, students were asked to write on the role of social media in police brutality cases. Judging is based on substance and form.

Financial data Prizes are $3,000 for first, $2,000 for second, and $1,000 for third.

Duration The competition is held annually.

Additional information The Washington Bar Association was founded in 1925 by African American attorneys who were denied membership in other bar associations because of their race. It continues to serve the African American legal community of Washington, D.C.

Number awarded 3 each year.

Deadline March of each year.

[807]
CHARLOTTE LEGAL DIVERSITY CLERKSHIP

Mecklenburg County Bar
Attn: Diversity and Inclusion Committee
2850 Zebulon Avenue
Charlotte, NC 28208
(704) 375-8624, ext. 127   Fax: (704) 333-6209
E-mail: adeburst@meckbar.org
Web: www.meckbar.org

Summary To provide summer work experience with a law firm and corporate legal department in Charlotte, North Carolina to African American and other law students from any state who will advance the diversity of the local legal community.

Eligibility This program is open to first-year law students who represent diverse groups. Applicants must be interested in a summer clerkship in Charlotte, North Carolina that includes work with a law firm in the downtown area and with a corporate legal department in the general area. Along with their application, they must submit a 1- to 2-page statement explaining how they would contribute to the goal of creating a more diverse legal community in Charlotte and why they would like to practice in Charlotte.

Financial data Participating law firms pay the same salary as for all of their summer law associates. Participating corporate legal departments jointly determine the compensation for their portion of the program.

Duration 12 weeks during the summer: 6 weeks with a law firm and 6 weeks with a corporate legal department.

Additional information This program began in 2006.

Number awarded 8 each year.

Deadline January of each year.

[808]
CHICAGO CHAPTER NATIONAL BLACK MBA ASSOCIATION SCHOLARSHIP

National Black MBA Association-Chicago Chapter
Attn: Scholarship Chair
P.O. Box 8513
Chicago, IL 60680
(312) 458-9161   E-mail: education@ccnbmbaa.org
Web: www.ccnbmbaa.org/events/mba-scholarship-deadline

Summary To provide financial assistance to African American students working on a master's degree in a business-related field at a university in the Chicago area.

Eligibility This program is open to African American graduate students enrolled at a college or university in the Chicago area. Applicants must be working on a master's degree in finance, human resources, management, marketing, or other business-related field. Along with their application, they must submit a 3-page essay on a topic of current interest that changes annually but relates to African Americans and business. Selection is based on that essay, academic achievement, and community and extracurricular activities.

Financial data A stipend is awarded (amount not specified).

Duration 1 year.

Number awarded Varies each year.

Deadline December of each year.

[809]
CHIPS QUINN SCHOLARS PROGRAM

Newseum Institute
Attn: Chips Quinn Scholars Program
555 Pennsylvania Avenue, N.W.
Washington, DC 20001
(202) 292-6271   Fax: (202) 292-6275
E-mail: kcatone@freedomforum.org
Web: www.newseuminstitute.org

Summary To provide work experience to African American and other minority college students and recent graduates who are majoring in journalism.

Eligibility This program is open to students of color who are college juniors, seniors, graduate students, or recent graduates with journalism majors or career goals in newspapers. Candidates must be nominated or endorsed by journalism faculty, campus media advisers, editors of newspapers, or leaders of minority journalism associations. Along with their application, they must submit a resume, transcripts, 2 letters of recommendation, and an essay of 200 to 400 words on why they want to be a Chips Quinn Scholar. Reporters and copy editors must also submit 6 samples of published articles they have written; photographers must submit 15 to 25 photographs on a DVD; multimedia journalists and graphic designers should submit 6 to 10 samples of their work on a DVD. Applicants must have a car and be available to work as a full-time intern during the spring or summer. U.S. citizenship or permanent resident status is required. Campus newspaper experience is strongly encouraged.

Financial data Students chosen for this program receive a travel stipend to attend a Multimedia training program in Nashville, Tennessee prior to reporting for their internship, a $500 housing allowance from the Freedom Forum, and a competitive salary during their internship.

Duration Internships are for 10 to 12 weeks, in spring or summer.

Additional information This program began in 1991 in memory of the late John D. Quinn Jr., managing editor of the *Poughkeepsie Journal*. Funding is provided by the Freedom Forum, formerly the Gannett Foundation. After graduating from college and obtaining employment with a newspaper, alumni of this program are eligible to apply for fellowship support to attend professional journalism development activities.

Number awarded Approximately 70 each year. Since the program began, more than 1,300 scholars have been selected.

Deadline September of each year.

[810]
CIGNA HEALTHCARE GRADUATE SCHOLARSHIPS

National Forum for Black Public Administrators
Attn: Scholarship Program
777 North Capitol Street, N.E., Suite 807
Washington, DC 20002
(202) 408-9300   Fax: (202) 408-8558
E-mail: vharris@nfbpa.org
Web: www.nfbpa.org/i4a/pages/index.cfm?pageid=4047

Summary To provide financial assistance to African Americans working on a graduate degree in public administration or a related field at an Historically Black College or University (HBCU).

Eligibility This program is open to African American graduate students preparing for a career in public administration. Applicants must be working on a degree in public administration, political science, urban affairs, public policy, or a related field at an HBCU. They must have a GPA of 3.0 or higher, excellent interpersonal and analytical abilities, and strong oral and written communication skills. Along with their application, they must submit a 3-page autobiographical essay that includes their academic and career goals and objectives.

Selection is based on academic record, leadership ability, participation in school activities, community service, and financial need.

Financial data The stipend is $5,000.

Duration 1 year.

Additional information This program is sponsored by CIGNA Healthcare. Recipients are required to attend the sponsor's annual conference to receive their scholarship; limited hotel and air accommodations are arranged and provided.

Number awarded 2 each year.

Deadline March of each year.

[811]
CLA SCHOLARSHIP FOR MINORITY STUDENTS IN MEMORY OF EDNA YELLAND

California Library Association
1055 East Colorado Boulevard, Fifth Floor
Pasadena, CA 91106
(626) 204-4071   E-mail: info@cla-net.org
Web: www.cla-net.org/?page=110

Summary To provide financial assistance to African American and other students of ethnic minority origin in California who are attending graduate school in any state to prepare for a career in library or information science.

Eligibility This program is open to California residents who are members of ethnic minority groups (African American/Black, American Indian/Alaska Native, Latino/Hispanic, Asian American, or Pacific Islander). Applicants must have completed at least 1 course in a master's program at an accredited graduate library school in any state. Evidence of financial need and U.S. citizenship or permanent resident status must be submitted. Finalists are interviewed.

Financial data The stipend is $2,500.

Duration 1 academic year.

Additional information This fellowship is named for the executive secretary of the California Library Association from 1947 to 1963 who worked to promote the goals of the California Library Association and the profession. Until 1985, it was named the Edna Yelland Memorial Scholarship.

Number awarded 3 each year.

Deadline July of each year.

[812]
CLEVELAND NORTHEAST OHIO CHAPTER NBMBAA SCHOLARSHIP PROGRAM

National Black MBA Association-Cleveland Northeast
  Ohio Chapter
Attn: Scholarship Program
P.O. Box 22839
Beachwood, OH 44122-0839
(216) 285-0338
Web: www.nbmbaa-cleveland.org/event-recap-2

Summary To provide financial assistance to African American and other minority students, primarily those at schools in northeast Ohio, working on a graduate degree in business or management.

Eligibility This program is open to minority students working full or part time on a graduate degree in business or management. Applicants may be attending a college or university anywhere in the United States, but they must be available to attend the corporate reception of the Cleveland Northeast Ohio chapter of the National Black MBA Association (NBM-BAA), become a member of the chapter, and participate in its student relations committee. Along with their application, they must submit a 2-page essay on a topic that changes annually but relates to the role of African Americans in business.

Financial data Stipends are $1,500 or $1,000.

Duration 1 year.

Number awarded Varies each year; recently, 4 were awarded: 3 at $1,500 and 1 at $1,000.

Deadline December of each year.

[813]
COMMERCIAL AND FEDERAL LITIGATION SECTION DIVERSITY FELLOWSHIP

The New York Bar Foundation
One Elk Street
Albany, NY 12207
(518) 487-5651 Fax: (518) 487-5699
E-mail: moclair@tnybf.org
Web: www.tnybf.org/fellandschol

Summary To provide an opportunity for residents of any state who are African Americans or member of other diverse groups and attending law school in New York to gain summer work experience in a litigation position in the public sector in the state.

Eligibility This program is open to Black/African American, Latino/a, Native American or Alaskan Native, or Asian/Pacific Islander students from any state who are enrolled in the first year at a law school in New York. Applicants must have demonstrated an interest in commercial and federal litigation. They must be interested in working in a litigation position during the summer in the public sector in New York. Selection is based on content and quality of application materials, demonstrated interest in litigation, work experience, academic record, leadership experience, extracurricular activities, community service, quality of written expression, maturity, integrity, and professionalism.

Financial data The stipend is $6,000.

Duration 10 weeks during the summer.

Additional information This program began in 2007 with support from the Commercial and Federal Litigation Section of the New York State Bar Association. It is administered by The New York Bar Foundation.

Number awarded 1 each year.

Deadline January of each year.

[814]
COMMISSION ON DIETETIC REGISTRATION DIVERSITY SCHOLARSHIPS

Academy of Nutrition and Dietetics
Attn: Foundation
120 South Riverside Plaza, Suite 2000
Chicago, IL 60606-6995
(312) 899-4821 Toll Free: (800) 877-1600, ext. 4821
Fax: (312) 899-4796 E-mail: blabrador@eatright.org
Web: www.eatrightfoundation.org/foundation/scholarships

Summary To provide financial assistance to African Americans and members of other underrepresented minority groups who are enrolled in an undergraduate or graduate program in dietetics.

Eligibility This program is open to students enrolled at a CADE-accredited/approved college or university in the undergraduate coordinated dietetics program, the undergraduate didactic program in dietetics, a dietetic internship program, a dietetic technician program, or a dietetic graduate program. Applicants must be members of underrepresented minority groups (African American, Hispanic, Native American). They must be U.S. citizens or permanent residents and show promise of being a valuable, contributing member of the profession. Membership in the Academy of Nutrition and Dietetics is encouraged but not required.

Financial data The stipend is $5,000.

Duration 1 year.

Number awarded 20 each year.

Deadline March of each year.

[815]
COMMITTEE ON ETHNIC MINORITY RECRUITMENT SCHOLARSHIP

United Methodist Church-California-Pacific Annual Conference
Attn: Board of Ordained Ministry
1720 East Linfield Street
Glendora, CA 91740
(626) 824-2284 E-mail: admin@bom.calpacumc.org
Web: www.calpacumc.org/ordainedministry/scholarships

Summary To provide financial assistance to African Americans and members of other ethnic minority groups in the California-Pacific Annual Conference of the United Methodist Church (UMC) who are attending a seminary in any state to qualify for ordination as an elder or deacon.

Eligibility This program is open to members of ethnic minority groups in the UMC California-Pacific Annual Conference who are enrolled at a seminary in any state approved by the UMC University Senate. Applicants must have been approved as certified candidates by their district committee and be seeking Probationary Deacon or Elder's Orders. They may apply for 1 or more types of assistance: tuition scholarships, grants for books and school supplies (including computers), or emergency living expense grants.

Financial data Tuition stipends are $1,000 per year; books and supplies grants range up to $1,000 per year; emergency living expense grants depend on need and the availability of funds.

Duration 1 year; may be renewed up to 2 additional years.

Additional information The California-Pacific Annual Conference includes churches in southern California, Hawaii, Guam, and Saipan.

Number awarded Varies each year.

Deadline August of each year for fall term; December of each year for spring term.

[816]
CONGRESSIONAL BLACK CAUCUS SPOUSES EDUCATION SCHOLARSHIP

Congressional Black Caucus Foundation, Inc.
Attn: Director, Educational Programs
1720 Massachusetts Avenue, N.W.
Washington, DC 20036
(202) 263-2800   Toll Free: (800) 784-2577
Fax: (202) 775-0773   E-mail: scholarships@cbcfinc.org
Web: www.cbcfinc.org/scholarships.html

Summary   To provide financial assistance to African American and other undergraduate and graduate students, especially those who reside or attend college in a Congressional district represented by a member of the Congressional Black Caucus (CBC).

Eligibility   This program is open to 1) minority and other graduating high school seniors planning to attend an accredited institution of higher education; and 2) currently-enrolled full-time undergraduate, graduate, and doctoral students in good academic standing with a GPA of 2.5 or higher. Preference is given to African Americans who reside or attend school in a Congressional district represented by a member of the CBC. Along with their application, they must a personal statement of 500 to 1,000 words on 1) their future goals, major field of study, and how that field of study will help them to achieve their future career goals; 2) involvement in school activities, community and public service, hobbies, and sports; 3) how receiving this award will affect their current and future plans; and 4) other experiences, skills, or qualifications. They must also be able to demonstrate financial need, leadership ability, and participation in community service activities.

Financial data   A stipend is awarded (amount not specified).

Duration   1 year.

Additional information   The program began in 1988.

Number awarded   Varies each year.

Deadline   May of each year.

[817]
CONSORTIUM FOR GRADUATE STUDY IN MANAGEMENT FELLOWSHIPS

Consortium for Graduate Study in Management
229 Chesterfield Business Parkway
Chesterfield, MO 63005
(636) 681-5553   Fax: (636) 681-5499
E-mail: recruiting@cgsm.org
Web: www.cgsm.org

Summary   To provide financial assistance and work experience to African Americans and other underrepresented racial minorities interested in preparing for a management career in business.

Eligibility   This program is open to African Americans, Hispanic Americans (Chicanos, Cubans, Dominicans, and Puerto Ricans), and Native Americans who have graduated from college and are interested in preparing for a career in business. Other U.S. citizens and permanent residents who can demonstrate a commitment to the sponsor's mission of enhancing diversity in business education are also eligible. An undergraduate degree in business or economics is not required. Applicants must be planning to work on an M.B.A. degree at 1 of the consortium's 18 schools.

Financial data   The fellowship pays full tuition and required fees. Summer internships with the consortium's cooperative sponsors, providing paid practical experience, are also offered.

Duration   Up to 4 semesters.

Additional information   This program began in 1966. The participating schools are Carnegie Mellon University, Cornell University, Dartmouth College, Emory University, Georgetown University, Indiana University, University of Michigan, New York University, University of California at Berkeley, University of California at Los Angeles, University of North Carolina at Chapel Hill, University of Rochester, University of Southern California, University of Texas at Austin, University of Virginia, Washington University, University of Wisconsin at Madison, and Yale University. Fellowships are tenable at member schools only. Application fees are $150 for students applying to 1 or 2 schools, $200 for 3 schools, $240 for 4 schools, $275 for 5 schools, or $300 for 6 schools.

Number awarded   Varies each year; recently, 420 were awarded.

Deadline   January of each year.

[818]
CONSTANGY DIVERSITY SCHOLARS AWARD

Constangy, Brooks, Smith and Prophete LLP
Attn: Chair, Diversity Council
200 West Forsyth Street, Suite 1700
Jacksonville, FL 32202-4317
(904) 356-8900   Fax: (904) 356-8200
E-mail: mzabijaka@constangy.com
Web: www.constangy.com/f-4.html

Summary   To provide financial assistance to African Americans and other students enrolled in law schools in selected states.

Eligibility   This program is open to second-year students enrolled in accredited law schools located in 1 of 3 regions: South (Alabama, Florida, Georgia, South Carolina, Tennessee), Midwest/West Coast (California, Illinois, Kansas, Missouri, Texas, Wisconsin), or East (Massachusetts, New Jersey, North Carolina, Virginia/Washington D.C.). Applicants must submit a personal statement on why diversity is important to them personally and in the legal profession. They must have a GPA of 3.0 or higher. Selection is based on academic achievement, commitment to diversity, and personal achievement in overcoming obstacles.

Financial data   The stipend is $2,500.

Duration   1 year.

Number awarded   1 each year.

Deadline   November of each year.

[819]
CORPORATE PARTNER SCHOLARSHIPS OF THE NATIONAL ASSOCIATION OF BLACK ACCOUNTANTS

National Association of Black Accountants
Attn: National Scholarship Program
7474 Greenway Center Drive, Suite 1120
Greenbelt, MD 20770
(301) 474-NABA   Fax: (301) 474-3114
E-mail: scholarships@nabainc.org
Web: www.nabainc.org/scholarship

Summary To provide financial assistance to student members of the National Association of Black Accountants (NABA) who are working on an undergraduate or graduate degree in a field related to accounting.

Eligibility This program is open to minorities who are NABA members and enrolled full time as 1) an undergraduate freshman, sophomore, junior, or first-semester senior majoring in accounting, business, or finance at a 4-year college or university; or 2) a graduate student working on a master's degree in accounting. High school seniors are not eligible. Applicants must have a GPA of 3.5 or higher in their major and 3.3 or higher overall. Along with their application, they must submit a 500-word personal statement on their involvement in NABA, career objectives, leadership abilities, and community activities. Financial need is not considered in the selection process.

Financial data Stipends range from $1,000 to $10,000.

Duration 1 year.

Number awarded Varies each year.

Deadline January of each year.

[820]
CORRIS BOYD SCHOLARS PROGRAM

Association of University Programs in Health
    Administration
Attn: Prizes, Fellowships and Scholarships
2000 14th Street North, Suite 780
Arlington, VA 22201
(703) 894-0940, ext. 122   Fax: (703) 894-0941
E-mail: lmeckley@aupha.org
Web: www.aupha.org

Summary To provide financial assistance to African Americans and other minority students entering graduate schools affiliated with the Association of University Programs in Health Administration (AUPHA).

Eligibility This program is open to students of color (African Americans, American Indians, Alaska Natives, Asian Americans, Latino/Hispanic, Native Hawaiians, Pacific Islanders) who have been accepted to a master's degree program in health care management at an AUPHA member institution. Applicants must be U.S. citizens or permanent residents and have a GPA of 3.0 or higher. Along with their application, they must submit a personal statement explaining why they are choosing to prepare for a career in health administration. Selection is based on leadership qualities, academic achievement, community involvement, and commitment to health care and health care management as a career path; financial need may be considered if all other factors are equal.

Financial data The stipend is $40,000.

Duration 1 year.

Additional information This program began in 2006.

Number awarded 2 each year.

Deadline April of each year.

[821]
CPS-HR/WALTER VAUGHN EXCELLENCE IN HUMAN RESOURCES SCHOLARSHIP

National Forum for Black Public Administrators
Attn: Scholarship Program
777 North Capitol Street, N.E., Suite 807
Washington, DC 20002
(202) 408-9300   Fax: (202) 408-8558
E-mail: vharris@nfbpa.org
Web: www.nfbpa.org/i4a/pages/index.cfm?pageid=4047

Summary To provide financial assistance to African Americans working on an undergraduate or graduate degree in public administration with an emphasis on human resource management.

Eligibility This program is open to African American undergraduate and graduate students preparing for a career in public service. Applicants must be working full time on a degree in public administration, human resource management, or a related field. They must have a GPA of 3.0 or higher, a record of involvement in extracurricular activities (excluding athletics), excellent interpersonal and leadership abilities, and strong oral and written communication skills. Along with their application, they must submit a 3-page autobiographical essay that includes their academic and career goals and objectives. Selection is based on academic record, leadership ability, participation in school activities, community service, and financial need.

Financial data The stipend is $2,500.

Duration 1 year.

Additional information This program is sponsored by CPS Human Resource Services. Recipients are required to attend the sponsor's annual conference to receive their scholarship; limited hotel and air accommodations are arranged and provided.

Number awarded 1 each year.

Deadline March of each year.

[822]
CREDIT SUISSE MBA FELLOWSHIP

Credit Suisse
Attn: Diversity and Inclusion Programs
Eleven Madison Avenue
New York, NY 10010-3629
(212) 325-2000   Fax: (212) 325-6665
E-mail: campus.diversity@credit-suisse.com
Web: www.credit-suisse.com

Summary To provide financial assistance and work experience at offices of Credit Suisse to African American and other underrepresented minority graduate students working on a master's degree as preparation for a career in investment banking.

Eligibility This program is open to students entering their first year of a full-time M.B.A. program who are female, Black/African American, Hispanic/Latino, or Native American. Applicants must be able to demonstrate a strong interest in a career in investment banking. Selection is based on academic excellence, leadership ability, and interest in the financial services industry.

Financial data The stipend is $15,000 for the first year; for the second year, students may elect to have $30,000 paid directly to their university or to have $15,000 paid to them for tuition and for academic and living expenses.

Duration 1 year (the first year of graduate school), followed by a summer internship at 1 of the offices of Credit Suisse. Students who successfully complete the internship and accept an office of full-time employment with the firm are eligible for a second year of funding.

Additional information Offices of Credit Suisse are located in Chicago, Houston, Los Angeles, New York, and San Francisco.

Number awarded 1 or more each year.

Deadline November of each year.

[823]
CURLS-CARTER GRADUATE STUDENT SCHOLARSHIP

Missouri Legislative Black Caucus Foundation
c/o Representative Gail McCann Beatty
4609 Paseo Boulevard, Suite 102
Kansas City, MO 64110
(573) 761-4166   Toll Free: (877) 63-MLBCF
Fax: (816) 861-2845   E-mail: mail@mlbcf.org
Web: www.mlbcf.org/scholarships/graduate

Summary To provide financial assistance to African American residents of Missouri who are historically underrepresented in higher education and are interested in working on a graduate degree in any field at a school in any state.

Eligibility This program is open to African American residents of Missouri who are enrolled full time in a graduate program at a college or university in any state. Applicants must have a GPA of 3.0 or higher. Along with their application, they must submit a 200-word personal statement on how their education will assist them in achieving their goals. Selection is based on academic performance, community service, leadership skills, and financial need.

Financial data A stipend is awarded (amount not specified).

Duration 1 year; recipients may reapply for up to 3 additional years of support.

Number awarded 1 or more each year.

Deadline May of each year.

[824]
DALMAS A. TAYLOR MEMORIAL SUMMER MINORITY POLICY FELLOWSHIP

Society for the Psychological Study of Social Issues
208 I Street, N.E.
Washington, DC 20002-4340
(202) 675-6956   Toll Free: (877) 310-7778
Fax: (202) 675-6902   E-mail: awards@spssi.org
Web: www.spssi.org

Summary To enable African Americans and other graduate students of color to be involved in the public policy activities of the American Psychological Association (APA) during the summer.

Eligibility This program is open to graduate students who are members of an ethnic minority group (including, but not limited to, African American, Alaskan Native, American Indian, Asian American, Hispanic, and Pacific Islander) and/or have demonstrated a commitment to a career in psychology or a related field with a focus on ethnic minority issues.

Applicants must be interested in spending a summer in Washington, D.C. to work on public policy issues in conjunction with the Minority Fellowship Program of the APA. Their application must indicate why they are interested in the fellowship, their previous and current research experiences, their interest and involvement in ethnic minority psychological issues, and how the fellowship would contribute to their career goals.

Financial data The stipend is $3,000. The sponsor also provides travel expenses and up to $1,500 for living expenses.

Duration 8 to 12 weeks.

Additional information This program began in 2000. The sponsor is Division 9 of the APA.

Number awarded 1 each year.

Deadline February of each year.

[825]
DAVE CALDWELL SCHOLARSHIP

American Water Works Association
Attn: Scholarship Coordinator
6666 West Quincy Avenue
Denver, CO 80235-3098
(303) 794-7771   Toll Free: (800) 926-7337
Fax: (303) 347-0804   E-mail: scholarships@awwa.org
Web: www.awwa.org

Summary To provide financial assistance to outstanding African American and other minority students interested in working on a graduate degree in the field of water supply and treatment.

Eligibility This program is open to minority and female students working on a graduate degree in the field of water supply and treatment at a college or university in Canada, Guam, Mexico, Puerto Rico, or the United States. Students who have been accepted into graduate school but have not yet begun graduate study are encouraged to apply. Applicants must submit a 2-page resume, official transcripts, 3 letters of recommendation, a proposed curriculum of study, a 1-page statement of educational plans and career objectives demonstrating an interest in the drinking water field, and a 3-page proposed plan of research. Selection is based on academic record and potential to provide leadership in applied research and consulting in the drinking water field.

Financial data The stipend is $10,000.

Duration 1 year; nonrenewable.

Additional information Funding for this program comes from the engineering firm Brown and Caldwell.

Number awarded 1 each year.

Deadline January of each year.

[826]
DAVID EATON SCHOLARSHIP

Unitarian Universalist Association
Attn: Ministerial Credentialing Office
24 Farnsworth Street
Boston, MA 02210-1409
(617) 948-6403   Fax: (617) 742-2875
E-mail: mcoadministrator@uua.org
Web: www.uua.org

Summary To provide financial assistance to African American and other minority women preparing for the Unitarian Universalist (UU) ministry.

Eligibility This program is open to women from historically marginalized groups who are currently enrolled or planning to enroll full or at least half time in a UU ministerial training program with aspirant or candidate status. Applicants must be citizens of the United States or Canada. Priority is given first to those who have demonstrated outstanding ministerial ability and secondarily to students with the greatest financial need (especially persons of color).

Financial data The stipend ranges from $1,000 to $15,000 per year.

Duration 1 year.

Number awarded 1 or 2 each year.

Deadline April of each year.

[827]
DAVID SANKEY MINORITY SCHOLARSHIP IN METEOROLOGY

National Weather Association
Attn: Executive Director
3100 Monitor Avenue, Suite 123
Norman, OK 73072
(405) 701-5167 Fax: (405) 701-5227
E-mail: exdir@nwas.org
Web: www.nwas.org

Summary To provide financial assistance to African Americans and members of other underrepresented groups working on an undergraduate or graduate degree in meteorology.

Eligibility This program is open to members of underrepresented ethnic groups who are either entering their sophomore or higher year of undergraduate study or enrolled as graduate students. Applicants must be working on a degree in meteorology. Along with their application, they must submit a 1-page statement explaining why they are applying for this scholarship. Selection is based on that statement, academic achievement, and 2 letters of recommendation.

Financial data The stipend is $1,000.

Duration 1 year.

Additional information This program began in 2002.

Number awarded 1 each year.

Deadline April of each year.

[828]
DCBMBAA CHAPTER GRADUATE SCHOLARSHIP PROGRAM

National Black MBA Association-Washington, DC Chapter
Attn: Scholarship Program
455 Massachusetts Avenue, N.W., Suite 150-331
Washington, DC 20001
(202) 628-0138 E-mail: outreach@dcbmbaa.org
Web: www.dcbmbaa.org/scholarships

Summary To provide financial assistance to African American and other minority students from Washington, D.C., Maryland, or Virginia who are working on a master's degree in business or management at a school in any state.

Eligibility This program is open to minority students who are enrolled full or part time in a graduate business or management program in any state and working on an M.B.A. degree. Applicants must currently reside in Washington, D.C.,

Maryland, or Virginia, either permanently or as a student. Along with their application, they must submit an essay (from 800 to 1,000 words) on a topic that changes annually but focuses on minorities in business. Selection is based on the essay, GPA, extracurricular activity, and community involvement.

Financial data The stipend is $2,500.

Duration 1 year.

Additional information This program began in 2000.

Number awarded 1 each year.

Deadline June of each year.

[829]
DEEP CARBON OBSERVATORY DIVERSITY GRANTS

American Geosciences Institute
Attn: Grant Coordinator
4220 King Street
Alexandria, VA 22302-1502
(703) 379-2480 Fax: (703) 379-7563
E-mail: hrhp@agiweb.org
Web: www.americangeosciences.org

Summary To provide funding to geoscientists who are African Americans or members of other underrepresented ethnic groups and interested in participating in research and other activities of the Deep Carbon Observatory (DCO) project.

Eligibility This program is open to traditionally underrepresented geoscientists (e.g., African Americans, Native Americans, Native Alaskans, Hispanics, Latinos, Latinas, Native Hawaiians, Native Pacific Islanders, Filipinos, of mixed racial/ethnic backgrounds) who are U.S. citizens or permanent residents. Applicants must be interested in participating in the DCO, a global research program focused on understanding carbon in Earth, and must have research interests that are aligned with its mission. They may be doctoral students, postdoctoral researchers, or early-career faculty members or research staff.

Financial data Grants average $5,000.

Duration 1 year.

Additional information This program is funded by the Alfred P. Sloan Foundation.

Number awarded 4 or 5 each year.

Deadline April of each year.

[830]
DELAWARE ATHLETIC TRAINERS' ASSOCIATION ETHNIC DIVERSITY ADVISORY COMMITTEE SCHOLARSHIP

Delaware Athletic Trainers' Association
c/o Education Committee Chair
University of Delaware
159 Fred Rust Ice Arena
Newark, DE 19716
(302) 831-6402 E-mail: kaminski@udel.edu
Web: www.delata.org/scholarship-applications.html

Summary To provide financial assistance to American American and other ethnic minority members of the National Athletic Trainers' Association (NATA) from Delaware who are working on an undergraduate or graduate degree in the field.

Eligibility This program is open to NATA members who are members of ethnic diversity groups and residents of Delaware or attending college in that state. Applicants must be enrolled full time in an undergraduate athletic training education program or a graduate athletic training program and have a GPA of 2.5 or higher. They must intend to prepare for the profession of athletic training. Along with their application, they must submit an 800-word statement on their athletic training background, experience, philosophy, and goals. Selection is based equally on academic performance and athletic training clinical achievement.

Financial data   A stipend is awarded (amount not specified).

Duration   1 year.

Number awarded   1 or more each year.

Deadline   February of each year.

[831]
DELTA SIGMA THETA SORORITY GENERAL SCHOLARSHIPS

Delta Sigma Theta Sorority, Inc.
Attn: Scholarship and Standards Committee Chair
1707 New Hampshire Avenue, N.W.
Washington, DC 20009
(202) 986-2400   Fax: (202) 986-2513
E-mail: dstemail@deltasigmatheta.org
Web: www.deltasigmatheta.org

Summary   To provide financial assistance to members of Delta Sigma Theta who are working on an undergraduate or graduate degree in any field.

Eligibility   This program is open to active, dues-paying members of Delta Sigma Theta who are currently enrolled in college or graduate school. Applicants must submit an essay on their major goals and educational objectives, including realistic steps they foresee as necessary for the fulfillment of their plans. Financial need is considered in the selection process.

Financial data   The stipends range from $1,000 to $2,000. The funds may be used to cover tuition, fees, and living expenses.

Duration   1 year; may be renewed for 1 additional year.

Additional information   This sponsor is a traditionally-African American social sorority. The application fee is $20.

Number awarded   Varies each year.

Deadline   March of each year.

[832]
DETROIT CHAPTER NBMBAA GRADUATE SCHOLARSHIP

National Black MBA Association-Detroit Chapter
Attn: Scholarship Awards
P.O. Box 32960
Detroit, MI 48232-0960
(313) 237-0089   Fax: (313) 237-0093
E-mail: scholarships@detroitblackmba.org
Web: www.detroitblackmba.org

Summary   To provide financial assistance to residents of Michigan and Toledo, Ohio who are members of the Detroit Chapter of the National Black MBA Association (NBMBAA) and working on a master's degree in business at a university in any state.

Eligibility   This program is open to members of the NBMBAA Detroit Chapter who live in Michigan or Toledo, Ohio and

are enrolled as full-time students at a college or university in any state. Applicants must be working on a master's degree in business or management. They must have a GPA of 3.0 or higher. Along with their application, they must submit a 500-word essay on a topic that changes annually but relates to African Americans and business. Selection is based on that essay, transcripts, and a biography.

Financial data   The stipend is $2,000.

Duration   1 year.

Number awarded   1 or more each year.

Deadline   February of each year.

[833]
DIETETIC INTERNSHIP SCHOLARSHIPS

Academy of Nutrition and Dietetics
Attn: Foundation
120 South Riverside Plaza, Suite 2000
Chicago, IL 60606-6995
(312) 899-4821   Toll Free: (800) 877-1600, ext. 4821
Fax: (312) 899-4796   E-mail: scholarship@eatright.org
Web: www.eatrightacend.org

Summary   To provide financial assistance to student members of the Academy of Nutrition and Dietetics, especially African Americans and other underrepresented minorities, who have applied for a dietetic internship.

Eligibility   This program is open to student members who have applied for an accredited dietetic internship. Applicants must be participating in the computer-matching process, be U.S. citizens or permanent residents, and show promise of being a valuable, contributing member of the profession. Some scholarships require membership in a specific dietetic practice group, residency in a specific state, or underrepresented minority group status. The same application form can be used for all categories. Students who are currently completing the internship component of a combined graduate/dietetic internship should apply for the Academy of Nutrition and Dietetics' Graduate Scholarship.

Financial data   Stipends range from $500 to $10,000 but most are for $1,000.

Duration   1 year.

Additional information   The Academy of Nutrition and Dietetics was formerly the American Dietetic Association.

Number awarded   Approximately 40 each year.

Deadline   February of each year.

[834]
DISSERTATION FELLOWSHIPS OF THE CONSORTIUM FOR FACULTY DIVERSITY

Consortium for Faculty Diversity at Liberal Arts Colleges
c/o Gettysburg College
Provost's Office
300 North Washington Street
Campus Box 410
Gettysburg, PA 17325
(717) 337-6796   E-mail: sgockows@gettysburg.edu
Web: www.gettysburg.edu

Summary   To provide an opportunity for African American and other doctoral candidates who will promote diversity to work on their dissertation while in residence at selected liberal arts colleges.

Eligibility This program is open to U.S. citizens and permanent residents who have completed all the requirements for the Ph.D. or M.F.A. except the dissertation. Applicants must be interested in a residency at a member institution of the Consortium for Faculty Diversity at Liberal Arts Colleges during which they will complete their dissertation. They must be able to contribute to diversity at the institution.

Financial data Dissertation fellows receive a stipend based on the average salary paid to instructors at the participating college. Modest funds are made available to finance the fellow's proposed research, subject to the usual institutional procedures.

Duration 1 year.

Additional information The following schools are participating in the program: Allegheny College, Amherst College, Bard College, Bowdoin College, Bryn Mawr College, Bucknell University, Carleton College, Centenary College of Louisiana, Centre College, College of the Holy Cross, Colorado College, Denison University, DePauw University, Dickinson College, Gettysburg College, Grinnell College, Gustavus Adolphus College, Hamilton College, Haverford College, Hobart and William Smith Colleges, Juniata College, Lafayette College, Lawrence University, Luther College, Macalester College, Mount Holyoke College, Muhlenberg College, Oberlin College, Pitzer College, Pomona College, Reed College, Scripps College, Skidmore College, Smith College, Southwestern University, St. Lawrence University, St. Olaf College, Swarthmore College, The College of Wooster, Trinity College, University of Richmond, Vassar College, and Wellesley College. Fellows are expected to teach at least 1 course in each academic term of residency, participate in departmental seminars, and interact with students.

Number awarded Varies each year.

Deadline October of each year.

[835]
DISSERTATION FELLOWSHIPS OF THE FORD FOUNDATION DIVERSITY FELLOWSHIP PROGRAM

The National Academies of Sciences, Engineering, and Medicine
Attn: Fellowships Office
500 Fifth Street, N.W.
Washington, DC 20001
(202) 334-2872   Fax: (202) 334-3419
E-mail: FordApplications@nas.edu
Web: sites.nationalacademies.org

Summary To provide funding for dissertation research to African American and other graduate students whose success will increase the racial and ethnic diversity of U.S. colleges and universities.

Eligibility This program is open to citizens, permanent residents, and nationals of the United States who are Ph.D. or Sc.D. degree candidates committed to a career in teaching and research at the college or university level. Applicants must be completing a degree in 1 of the following fields: American studies, anthropology, archaeology, art and theater history, astronomy, chemistry, communications, computer science, cultural studies, earth sciences, economics, education, engineering, ethnic studies, ethnomusicology, geography, history, international relations, language, life sciences, linguistics, literature, mathematics, performance study, philoso-

phy, physics, political science, psychology, religious studies, sociology, urban planning, and women's studies. Also eligible are interdisciplinary programs such as African American studies, Native American studies, area studies, peace studies, and social justice. Students in practice-oriented areas, terminal master's degrees, other doctoral degrees (e.g., Ed.D., D.F.A., Psy.D.), professional degrees (e.g., medicine, law, public health), or joint degrees (e.g., M.D./Ph.D., J.D./Ph.D., M.F.A./Ph.D.) are not eligible. The following are considered as positive factors in the selection process: evidence of superior academic achievement; promise of continuing achievement as scholars and teachers; membership in a group whose underrepresentation in the American professoriate has been severe and longstanding, including Black/African Americans, Puerto Ricans, Mexican Americans/Chicanos/Chicanas, Native American Indians, Alaska Natives (Eskimos, Aleuts, and other indigenous people of Alaska), and Native Pacific Islanders (Hawaiians, Micronesians, or Polynesians); capacity to respond in pedagogically productive ways to the learning needs of students from diverse backgrounds; sustained personal engagement with communities that are underrepresented in the academy and an ability to bring this asset to learning, teaching, and scholarship at the college and university level; and likelihood of using the diversity of human experience as an educational resource in teaching and scholarship.

Financial data The stipend is $25,000; stipend payments are made through fellowship institutions.

Duration 9 to 12 months.

Additional information The competition for this program is conducted by the National Research Council on behalf of the Ford Foundation. Fellows may not accept remuneration from another fellowship or similar external award while supported by this program; however, supplementation from institutional funds, educational benefits from the Department of Veterans Affairs, or educational incentive funds may be received concurrently with Ford Foundation support. Dissertation fellows are required to submit an interim progress report 6 months after the start of the fellowship and a final report at the end of the 12 month tenure.

Number awarded Approximately 36 each year.

Deadline November of each year.

[836]
DIVERSIFYING HIGHER EDUCATION FACULTY IN ILLINOIS

Illinois Board of Higher Education
Attn: DFI Program
431 East Adams Street, Second Floor
Springfield, IL 62701-1404
(217) 782-2551   Fax: (217) 782-8548
TDD: (888) 261-2881   E-mail: DFI@ibhe.org
Web: www.ibhe.state.il.us/DFI/default.htm

Summary To provide fellowship/loans to African American and other minority students interested in enrolling in graduate school programs in Illinois to prepare for a career in higher education.

Eligibility This program is open to U.S. citizens and permanent residents who 1) are residents of Illinois and have received a baccalaureate degree from an educational institution in the state; or 2) have received a baccalaureate degree from an accredited educational institution in any state and have lived in Illinois for at least the 3 previous years. Applicants must be members of a minority group traditionally underrepresented in graduate school enrollment in Illinois (African Americans, Hispanic Americans, Alaskan Natives, Asian Americans, American Indians, Native Alaskans, Native Hawaiians, or other Pacific Islanders) and have been admitted to a graduate program in the state to work on a doctoral or master's degree and prepare for a career in teaching or administration at an Illinois postsecondary institution or Illinois higher education governing board. They must have a GPA of 2.75 or higher in the last 60 hours of undergraduate work or 3.2 or higher in at least 9 hours of graduate study. Along with their application, they must submit statements on 1) their professional goals (including their intended employment setting, intended position in Illinois higher education, plans for achieving their intended goals, and current and/or past experiences that would be helpful in achieving their intended goals; and 2) their underrepresented status (including how their underrepresented status influenced their personal and academic development and why they should be awarded a fellowship designated specifically for underrepresented groups in higher education). Financial need is considered in the selection process.

Financial data Stipends are $10,000 for new fellows or $13,000 per year for renewal fellows. Some participating institutions also provide a tuition waiver or scholarship. This is a fellowship/loan program. Recipients must agree to accept a position, in teaching or administration, at an Illinois postsecondary educational institution, on an Illinois higher education governing or coordinating board, or at a state agency in an education-related position. Recipients failing to fulfill the conditions of the award are required to repay 20% of the total award.

Duration Up to 2 years for master's degree students; up to 4 years for doctoral students.

Additional information The Illinois General Assembly established this program in 2004 as a successor to 2 earlier programs (both established in 1985); the Illinois Consortium for Educational Opportunity Program (ICEOP) and the Illinois Minority Graduate Incentive Program (IMGIP).

Number awarded Varies each year; recently, 111 new and renewal fellows were receiving support through this program.

Deadline February of each year.

[837]
DIVERSITY SCHOLARSHIP FOR ENTRY-LEVEL ATHLETIC TRAINING STUDENTS

Indiana Athletic Trainers' Association
Attn: Scholarship Committee
125 West Market Street, Suite 300
Indianapolis, IN 46204
(317) 396-0002, ext. 2   Fax: (317) 634-5964
E-mail: jillewing@thecorydongroup.com
Web: www.iata-usa.org/page-1462928

Summary To provide financial assistance to undergraduate and graduate student members of the Indiana Athletic Trainers' Association (IATA) who are African Americans or from another ethnic or social diverse background.

Eligibility This program is open to members of IATA who are from an ethnic or social diverse background and enrolled as full-time juniors, seniors, or graduate students at a college

or university in Indiana. Undergraduates must have been an athletic training student for at least 1 year in a CAATE-accredited program; graduate students must be in the second semester of such a program. All applicants must have a GPA of 3.0 or higher and a sponsor who is a full-time member of the athletic training education program faculty or a full-time member of the athletic training staff. Along with their application, they must submit a brief personal statement on why they chose athletic training as a career and their future plans in the field. Financial need is not considered in the selection process.

Financial data The stipend is $1,000.

Duration 1 year.

Number awarded 1 each year.

Deadline September of each year.

[838]
DIVERSITY SUMMER FELLOWSHIP IN HEALTH LAW

The New York Bar Foundation
One Elk Street
Albany, NY 12207
(518) 487-5651   Fax: (518) 487-5699
E-mail: moclair@tnybf.org
Web: www.tnybf.org/fellandschol

Summary To provide an opportunity for African American and other diverse residents of any state attending law school in New York to gain work experience in health law with an attorney or facility in the state.

Eligibility This program is open to diverse students from any state who are enrolled at a law school in New York. They must be interested in working on health law with a health care attorney or facility in New York. Along with their application, they must submit a writing sample on any topic, preferably health law. Selection is based on content and quality of application materials, demonstrated interest in health law, work experience, academic record, leadership experience, extracurricular activities, community service, quality of written expression, maturity, integrity, and professionalism.

Financial data The stipend is $5,000.

Duration 8 weeks during the summer.

Additional information This program began in 2011 by the Health Law Section of the New York State Bar Association. It is administered by The New York Bar Foundation.

Number awarded 2 each year.

Deadline December of each year.

[839]
DOCTORAL DIVERSITY FELLOWSHIPS IN SCIENCE, TECHNOLOGY, ENGINEERING, AND MATHEMATICS

State University of New York
Attn: Office of Diversity, Equity and Inclusion
State University Plaza, T1000A
353 Broadway
Albany, NY 12246
(518) 320-1189   E-mail: carlos.medina@suny.edu
Web: system.suny.edu/odei/diversity-programs

Summary To provide financial assistance to African American residents of any state who will contribute to the diversity of the student body and are working on a doctoral degree in a field of science, technology, engineering, or mathematics (STEM) at campuses of the State University of New York (SUNY).

Eligibility This program is open to U.S. citizens and permanent residents who are residents of any state and enrolled as doctoral students at any of the participating SUNY institutions. Applicants must be working on a degree in a field of STEM. They must be able to demonstrate how they will contribute to the diversity of the student body, primarily by having overcome a disadvantage or other impediment to success in higher education. Economic disadvantage, although not a requirement, may be the basis for eligibility. Membership in a racial or ethnic group that is underrepresented at the applicant's school or program may serve as a plus factor in making awards, but may not form the sole basis of selection.

Financial data The stipend is $20,000 per year. A grant of $2,000 to support research and professional development is also provided.

Duration 3 years; may be renewed for up to 2 additional years.

Number awarded 2 each year.

Deadline March of each year.

[840]
DOCTORAL/POST-DOCTORAL FELLOWSHIP PROGRAM IN LAW AND SOCIAL SCIENCE

American Bar Foundation
Attn: Administrative Assistant for Academic Affairs and
   Research Administration
750 North Lake Shore Drive
Chicago, IL 60611-4403
(312) 988-6517   Fax: (312) 988-6579
E-mail: aehrhardt@abfn.org
Web: www.americanbarfoundation.org

Summary To provide research funding to scholars, especially African Americans and other minorities, who are completing or have completed doctoral degrees in fields related to law, the legal profession, and legal institutions.

Eligibility This program is open to Ph.D. candidates in the social sciences who have completed all doctoral requirements except the dissertation. Applicants who have completed the dissertation are also eligible. Doctoral and proposed research must be in the general area of sociolegal studies or in social scientific approaches to law, the legal profession, or legal institutions and legal processes. Applications must include 1) a dissertation abstract or proposal with an outline of the substance and methods of the research; 2) 2 letters of recommendation; and 3) a curriculum vitae. Minority candidates are especially encouraged to apply.

Financial data The stipend is $30,000. Fellows may request up to $1,500 to reimburse expenses associated with research, travel to meet with advisers, or travel to conferences at which papers are presented. Relocation expenses of up to $2,500 may be reimbursed on application.

Duration 12 months, beginning in September.

Additional information Fellows are offered access to the computing and word processing facilities of the American Bar Foundation and the libraries of Northwestern University and the University of Chicago. This program was established in 1996. Fellowships must be held in residence at the American Bar Foundation. Appointments to the fellowship are full time; fellows are not permitted to undertake other work.

Number awarded 1 or more each year.

Deadline December of each year.

[841]
DONNA HOKE SCHOLARSHIPS

New York Black Librarians Caucus, Inc.
Attn: Scholarships
Flatbush Station
P.O. Box 260605
Brooklyn, NY 11226
(718) 651-7116   E-mail: scholarship@thenyblc.org
Web: www.thenyblc.org/Scholarship.html

Summary To provide financial assistance to African Americans in New York who wish to pursue a degree in librarianship.

Eligibility This program is open to residents of New York who are of African or African American descent. Applicants must be enrolled in or accepted to an ALA-accredited master's degree program in library science. Selection is based on an essay about their aspirations in librarianship, transcripts, 2 letters of recommendation, and an interview.

Financial data The stipend is $1,000.

Duration 1 year.

Number awarded 2 each year.

Deadline August of each year.

[842]
DOROTHY ATKINSON LEGAL EDUCATION SCHOLARSHIP

National Association of Bench and Bar Spouses, Inc.
Attn: NABBS, Inc. Foundation
2301 West Main Street
Belleville, IL 62226
(618) 741-3589   E-mail: drwillmeanes@yahoo.com
Web: www.nabbsinc.org/Services.html

Summary To provide financial assistance to law students, especially those of interest to an organization of African American spouses of judges and attorneys.

Eligibility This program is open to students enrolled full time in a legal education program at an ABA-accredited law school. Applicants must have a GPA of 2.0 or higher and be able to demonstrate financial need. They must be sponsored by a local chapter of the National Association of Bench and Bar Spouses (NABBS), an organization with historic roots in the African American legal community.

Financial data A stipend is awarded (amount not specified).

Duration 1 year; may be renewed if the recipient maintains a GPA of 2.0 or higher and continues to demonstrate financial need.

Additional information NABBS was founded in 1951 as the National Barristers' Wives, affiliated with the National Bar Association for African American attorneys. In 1987, it adopted its current name and in 1994 it organized the NABBS, Inc. Foundation.

Number awarded 1 or more each year.

Deadline July of each year.

[843]
DR. BESSIE ELIZABETH DELANEY FELLOWSHIP

National Dental Association
Attn: National Dental Association Foundation, Inc.
3517 16th Street, N.W.
Washington, DC 20010
(734) 544-1336   E-mail: admin@ndaonline.org
Web: www.ndafoundation.org

Summary   To provide financial assistance to women who are African Americans or members of other minority groups and interested in working on a postdoctoral degree in fields related to dentistry.

Eligibility   This program is open to female members of minority groups who are working on a postdoctoral degree in an area related to dentistry, such as public health, administration, pediatrics, research, or law. Students working on a master's degree beyond their residency may be considered. Applicants must be members of the National Dental Association (NDA) and U.S. citizens or permanent residents. Along with their application, they must submit a letter explaining why they should be considered for this scholarship, 2 letters of recommendation, a curriculum vitae, a description of the program, nomination by their program director, and documentation of financial need.

Financial data   The stipend is $10,000.

Duration   1 year.

Additional information   This program, established in 1990, is supported by the Colgate-Palmolive Company.

Number awarded   1 each year.

Deadline   May of each year.

[844]
DR. CLIFTON AND LOIS DUMMETT FELLOWSHIP

National Dental Association
Attn: National Dental Association Foundation, Inc.
3517 16th Street, N.W.
Washington, DC 20010
(734) 544-1336   E-mail: admin@ndaonline.org
Web: www.ndafoundation.org/dummett-scholarship.html

Summary   To provide financial assistance to African American and other minority students who are interested in working on a postdoctoral degree in fields related to dentistry.

Eligibility   This program is open to members of minority groups who are working on a postdoctoral degree in an area related to dentistry, such as public health, administration, pediatrics, research, or law. Students working on a master's degree beyond their residency may be considered. Applicants must be members of the National Dental Association (NDA) and U.S. citizens or permanent residents. Along with their application, they must submit a letter explaining why they should be considered for this scholarship, 2 letters of recommendation, a curriculum vitae, a description of the program, nomination by their program director, and documentation of financial need.

Financial data   The stipend is $10,000.

Duration   1 year.

Additional information   This program, established in 1990, is supported by the Colgate-Palmolive Company.

Number awarded   1 each year.

Deadline   May of each year.

[845]
DR. DAVID K. MCDONOUGH SCHOLARSHIP IN OPHTHALMOLOGY/ENT

National Medical Fellowships, Inc.
Attn: Scholarship Program
347 Fifth Avenue, Suite 510
New York, NY 10016
(212) 483-8880   Toll Free: (877) NMF-1DOC
Fax: (212) 483-8897 E-mail: scholarships@nmfonline.org
Web: www.nmfonline.org

Summary   To provide financial assistance to African American and other underrepresented minority students specializing in ophthalmology or ear, nose, and throat (ENT) specialties at medical schools in New York City.

Eligibility   This program is open to African American, Afro-Latino, and Native American medical students enrolled at a school in New York City. Applicants must be preparing for a career in ophthalmology or ENT specialties. They must be U.S. citizens or DACA students. Selection is based on leadership, commitment to serving medically underserved communities, and financial need.

Financial data   The stipend is $5,000.

Duration   1 year.

Number awarded   1 each year.

Deadline   September of each year.

[846]
DR. DAVID MONASH/HARRY LLOYD AND ELIZABETH PAWLETTE MARSHALL MEDICAL STUDENT SERVICE SCHOLARSHIPS

National Medical Fellowships, Inc.
Attn: Scholarship Program
347 Fifth Avenue, Suite 510
New York, NY 10016
(212) 483-8880   Toll Free: (877) NMF-1DOC
Fax: (212) 483-8897 E-mail: scholarships@nmfonline.org
Web: www.nmfonline.org

Summary   To provide funding for a community health project to African American and other underrepresented medical students in Chicago who are committed to remaining in the area and working to reduce health disparities.

Eligibility   This program is open to residents of any state who are currently enrolled in their second through fourth year at a medical school in Chicago. U.S. citizenship is required. Applicants must be interested in conducting a community health project in an underserved community. They must identify as an underrepresented minority student in health care (defined as African American, Hispanic/Latino, American Indian, Alaska Native, Native Hawaiian, Vietnamese, Cambodian, or Pacific Islander) and/or socioeconomically disadvantaged student. Along with their application, they must submit documentation of financial status; a short biography; a resume; 2 letters of recommendation; a personal statement of 500 to 1,000 words on their personal and professional motivation for a medical career, their commitment to primary care and service in a health and/or community setting, their motivation for working to reduce health disparities, and their commitment to improving health care; a personal statement of 500 to 1,000 words on the experiences that are preparing them to practice in an underserved community; and a 150- to 350-word description of their proposed community service project. Selection is based on demonstrated leadership early in career and commitment to serving medically underserved communities in Chicago.

Financial data The stipend is $5,000.

Duration 1 year.

Additional information This program began in 2010 with support from the Chicago Community Trust.

Number awarded 6 each year.

Deadline May of each year.

[847]
DR. DORRI PHIPPS FELLOWSHIPS

Alpha Kappa Alpha Sorority, Inc.
Attn: Educational Advancement Foundation
5656 South Stony Island Avenue
Chicago, IL 60637
(773) 947-0026   Toll Free: (800) 653-6528
Fax: (773) 947-0277   E-mail: akaeaf@akaeaf.net
Web: www.akaeaf.org/fellowships_endowments.htm

Summary To provide financial assistance to students (especially African American women) working on a degree in medicine or conducting research related to lupus.

Eligibility This program is open to students currently enrolled in a medical or related program in any state. Applicants must be working on a degree in medicine or conducting research related to lupus. Along with their application, they must submit 1) a list of honors, awards, and scholarships received; 2) a list of organizations in which they have memberships, especially minority organizations; 3) a description of the project or research on which they are currently working, of (if they are not involved in a project or research) the aspects of their field that interest them; and 4) a statement of their personal and career goals, including how this scholarship will enhance their ability to attain those goals. The sponsor is a traditionally African American women's sorority.

Financial data A stipend is awarded (amount not specified).

Duration 1 year.

Number awarded Varies each even-numbered year; recently, 5 were awarded.

Deadline April of each even-numbered year.

[848]
DR. JOSEPH L. HENRY FIRST YEAR SCHOLARSHIPS

National Dental Association
Attn: National Dental Association Foundation, Inc.
3517 16th Street, N.W.
Washington, DC 20010
(734) 544-1336   E-mail: admin@ndaonline.org
Web: www.ndafoundation.org/henry-scholarship.html

Summary To provide financial assistance to African Americans and other minorities entering their first year of dental school.

Eligibility This program is open to members of minority groups who are entering their first year of dental school as full-time students. Applicants must have an undergraduate GPA of 3.5 or higher. Along with their application, they must submit information on their community service, a letter from their school verifying that they are attending, a letter of recommendation from an undergraduate professor, college transcripts, and documentation of financial need. They must be

U.S. citizens or permanent residents. Selection is based on academic performance in undergraduate school and service to community and/or country.

Financial data The stipend is $2,000 per year.

Duration 1 year; may be renewed up to 3 additional years.

Additional information This program, established in 1990, is supported by the Colgate-Palmolive Company.

Number awarded At least 5 each year.

Deadline May of each year.

[849]
DR. JOYCE BECKETT TUITION SCHOLARSHIP

National Association of Black Social Workers
Attn: NABSW Scholarships
2305 Martin Luther King Avenue, S.E.
Washington, DC 20020
(202) 678-4570   Fax: (202) 678-4572
E-mail: office-manager@nabsw.org
Web: www.nabsw.org/?page=ScholarshipsRecipien

Summary To provide financial assistance to members of the National Association of Black Social Workers (NABSW) who are working on a master's degree.

Eligibility This program is open to African American members of NABSW working full time on a master's degree at an accredited U.S. social work or social welfare program with a GPA of 2.5 or higher. Applicants must be able to demonstrate community service and a research interest in the Black community. Along with their application, they must submit an essay of 2 to 3 pages on their professional interests, future social work aspirations, previous social work experiences (volunteer and professional), honors and achievements (academic and community service), and research interests within the Black community. Financial need is considered in the selection process.

Financial data The stipend is $1,000. Funds are sent directly to the recipient's school.

Duration 1 year.

Number awarded 1 each year.

Deadline December of each year.

[850]
DR. NANCY FOSTER SCHOLARSHIP PROGRAM

National Oceanic and Atmospheric Administration
Attn: Office of National Marine Sanctuaries
1305 East-West Highway
N/ORM 6 SSMC4, Room 11146
Silver Spring, MD 20910
(301) 713-7245   Fax: (301) 713-9465
E-mail: fosterscholars@noaa.gov
Web: fosterscholars.noaa.gov/aboutscholarship.html

Summary To provide financial assistance to graduate students, especially African Americans and other minorities, who are interested in working on a degree in fields related to marine sciences.

Eligibility This program is open to U.S. citizens, particularly women and members of ethnic minority groups, currently working on or intending to work on a master's or doctoral degree in oceanography, marine biology, or maritime archaeology, including all science, engineering, and resource management of ocean and coastal areas. Applicants must submit a description of their academic, research, and career goals, and how their proposed course of study or research will help them to achieve those goals. They must be enrolled full time and have a GPA of 3.3 or higher. As part of their program, they must be interested in participating in a summer research collaboration at a facility of the National Oceanic and Atmospheric Administration (NOAA). Selection is based on academic record and a statement of career goals and objectives (20%); quality of project and applicability to program priorities (30%); recommendations and/or endorsements (15%); additional relevant experience related to diversity of education, extracurricular activities, honors and awards, written and oral communication skills, and interpersonal skills (20%); and financial need (15%).

Financial data The program provides a stipend of $30,000 per academic year, a tuition allowance of up to $12,000 per academic year, and up to $10,000 of support for a 4- to 6-week research collaboration at a NOAA facility is provided.

Duration Master's degree students may receive up to 2 years of stipend and tuition support and 1 research collaboration (for a total of $94,000). Doctoral students may receive up to 4 years of stipend and tuition support and 2 research collaborations (for a total of $188,000).

Additional information This program began in 2001.

Number awarded Varies each year; recently, 3 were awarded.

Deadline December of each year.

[851]
DR. RICHARD ALLEN WILLIAMS AND GENITA EVANGELISTA JOHNSON/ASSOCIATION OF BLACK CARDIOLOGISTS SCHOLARSHIP

American Medical Association
Attn: AMA Foundation
330 North Wabash Avenue, Suite 39300
Chicago, IL 60611-5885
(312) 464-4193   Fax: (312) 464-4142
E-mail: amafoundation@ama-assn.org
Web: www.ama-assn.org

Summary To provide financial assistance to African American medical school students who are interested in cardiology.

Eligibility This program is open to first- and second-year African American medical students who have an interest in cardiology. Only nominations are accepted. Each medical school is invited to submit 1 nominee. U.S. citizenship or permanent resident status is required.

Financial data The stipend is $5,000.

Duration 1 year.

Additional information This program is offered by the AMA Foundation of the American Medical Association as a component of its Minority Scholars Awards. Support is provided by the Association of Black Cardiologists with funding from donor Genita Evangelista Johnson.

Number awarded 1 each year.

Deadline March of each year.

[852]
DR. ROBERT JOHNSON PEDIATRIC/VISION THERAPY AWARD

National Optometric Association
Attn: Student Affairs
1801 North Tryon Street, Suite 315
Charlotte, NC 28206
(704) 918-1809   Toll Free: (877) 394-2020
Fax: (877) NOA-2006
E-mail: noastudentdirector@yahoo.com
Web: www.nationaloptometricassociation.com

Summary To provide financial assistance to African American and other members of the National Optometric Student Association (NOSA) interested in pediatric vision care or binocular vision and vision therapy.

Eligibility This program is open to NOSA members enrolled in the third or fourth year at a school or college of optometry. Applicants must have a GPA of 2.5 or higher and be able to demonstrate community involvement. Along with their application, they must submit a 300-word essay describing their aspirations as an O.D. and commitment to community service related to pediatric vision care or binocular vision/vision therapy. Financial need is not considered in the selection process.

Financial data The stipend is $1,000.

Duration 1 year.

Additional information The National Optometric Association was founded in 1969 with the goal of recruiting minority students, especially African Americans, for schools and colleges of optometry.

Number awarded 1 each year.

Deadline May of each year.

[853]
DR. ROSE M. GREEN THOMAS ACADEMIC MEDICINE SCHOLARSHIP AWARD

Black Women Physicians Educational and Research Foundation
Attn: Scholars Fund
P.O. Box 4502
Gary, IN 46404
(219) 616-3912
Web: www.aacom.org

Summary To provide financial assistance to African and other minority female medical students interested in a career in academic medicine.

Eligibility This program is open to minority women currently enrolled at an accredited medical school in any state. Applicants must submit an essay of 500 to 650 words on their career goals in academic medicine. Selection is based on academic achievement, motivation for a career in academic medicine, leadership activities, and community involvement.

Financial data The stipend is $1,000.

Duration 1 year.

Number awarded 1 each year.

Deadline May of each year.

[854]
DR. SPENCER G. SHAW SCHOLARSHIP

Black Caucus of the American Library Association-
Connecticut Affiliate
Attn: Scholarship Committee
37 Grandview Avenue
Norwalk, CT 06850-3214
Web: www.bcala-ct.org/SCHOLARSHIPS.HTM

Summary To provide financial assistance to African American residents of Connecticut interested in working on a master's degree in librarianship at a school in any state.

Eligibility This program is open to residents of Connecticut who are of African American descent. Applicants must be entering, enrolled, or accepted at an ALA-accredited master's degree program in library and information studies. They must be members of the Connecticut Affiliate of the Black Caucus of the American Library Association (BCALA). Along with their application, they must submit a 1,000-word statement about their future goals, career interests, and commitment to library and information service.

Financial data The stipend is $2,000.

Duration 1 year; recipients may reapply.

Additional information This program began in 2009.

Number awarded 1 each year.

Deadline March of each year.

[855]
DRI LAW STUDENT DIVERSITY SCHOLARSHIP

DRI-The Voice of the Defense Bar
Attn: Deputy Executive Director
55 West Monroe Street, Suite 2000
Chicago, IL 60603
(312) 795-1101   Fax: (312) 795-0747
E-mail: dri@dri.org
Web: www.dri.org/About

Summary To provide financial assistance to African American and other minority law students.

Eligibility This program is open to full-time students entering their second or third year of law school who are African American, Hispanic, Asian, Native American, women, or other students who will come from backgrounds that would add to the cause of diversity, including sexual orientation. Applicants must submit an essay, up to 1,000 words, on a topic that changes annually but relates to the work of defense attorneys. Selection is based on that essay, demonstrated academic excellence, service to the profession, service to the community, and service to the cause of diversity. Students affiliated with the American Association for Justice as members, student members, or employees are not eligible. Finalists are invited to participate in personal interviews.

Financial data The stipend is $10,000.

Duration 1 year.

Additional information This program began in 2004.

Number awarded 2 each year.

Deadline May of each year.

[856]
DRUG ABUSE DISSERTATION RESEARCH

National Institute on Drug Abuse
Attn: Division of Clinical Neuroscience and Behavioral Research
6101 Executive Boulevard, Suite 3154
Bethesda, MD 20892-9593
(301) 443-3207   Fax: (301) 443-6814
E-mail: aklinwm@mail.nih.gov
Web: www.grants.nih.gov

Summary To provide financial assistance to doctoral candidates, especially African Americans and members of other underrepresented groups, who are interested in conducting dissertation research on drug abuse treatment and health services.

Eligibility This program is open to doctoral candidates who are conducting dissertation research in a field of the behavioral, biomedical, or social sciences related to drug abuse treatment, including research in epidemiology, prevention, treatment, services, and women and sex/gender differences. Students working on an M.D., D.O., D.D.S., or similar professional degree are not eligible. Applicants must be U.S. citizens, nationals, or permanent residents and must have completed all requirements for the doctoral degree except the dissertation. Special attention is paid to recruiting members of racial and ethnic groups underrepresented in the biomedical and behavioral sciences (African Americans, Hispanic Americans, Native Americans, Alaskan Natives, and Pacific Islanders), persons with disabilities, and individuals from disadvantaged backgrounds.

Financial data The maximum grant is $50,000 per year, including support for the recipient's salary (up to $21,180 per year), research assistant's salary and direct research project expenses. Funding may not be used for tuition, alterations or renovations, faculty salary, contracting costs, or space rental. The recipient's institution may receive facilities and administrative costs of up to 8% of total direct costs.

Duration Up to 2 years; may be extended for 1 additional year.

Number awarded Varies each year, depending on the availability of funds.

Deadline February, June, or October of each year.

[857]
DWIGHT DAVID EISENHOWER HISTORICALLY BLACK COLLEGES AND UNIVERSITIES TRANSPORTATION FELLOWSHIP PROGRAM

Department of Transportation
Federal Highway Administration
Attn: Universities and Grants Programs
4600 North Fairfax Drive, Suite 800
Arlington, VA 22203-1553
(703) 235-0538   Toll Free: (877) 558-6873
Fax: (703) 235-0593   E-mail: transportationedu@dot.gov
Web: www.fhwa.dot.gov/tpp/ddetfp.htm

Summary To provide financial assistance to undergraduate and graduate students working on a degree in a transportation-related field at a designated Historically Black College or University (HBCU).

Eligibility This program is open to students working on a bachelor's, master's, or doctoral degree at 1 of 18 federally-designated 4-year HBCUs. Applicants must be working on a degree in a transportation-related field (e.g., engineering, business, aviation, architecture, public policy and analysis, urban and regional planning). They must be U.S. citizens or have an I-20 (foreign student) or I-551 (permanent resident) identification card. Undergraduates must be entering at least their junior year and have a GPA of 3.0 or higher. Graduate students must have a GPA of at least 3.25. Selection is based on their proposed plan of study, academic achievement (based on class standing, GPA, and transcripts), transportation work experience, and letters of recommendation.

Financial data Fellows receive payment of full tuition and fees (to a maximum of $10,000) and a monthly stipend of $1,450 for undergraduates, $1,700 for master's students, or $2,000 for doctoral students. They are also provided with a 1-time allowance of up to $1,500 to attend the annual Transportation Research Board (TRB) meeting.

Duration 1 year.

Additional information This program is administered by the participating HBCUs: Alabama A&M University, Benedict College, Florida A&M University, Hampton University, Howard University, Jackson State University, Lincoln University of Pennsylvania, Morgan State University, North Carolina A&T University, Prairie View A&M University, South Carolina State University, Southern University and A&M College, Tuskegee University, Texas Southern University, University of Maryland Eastern Shore, and Virginia State University.

Number awarded Varies each year; recently, 47 were awarded.

Deadline January of each year.

[858]
DWIGHT DAVID EISENHOWER TRANSPORTATION FELLOWSHIP PROGRAM

Department of Transportation
Federal Highway Administration
Attn: Universities and Grants Programs
4600 North Fairfax Drive, Suite 800
Arlington, VA 22203-1553
(703) 235-0538   Toll Free: (877) 558-6873
Fax: (703) 235-0593   E-mail: transportationedu@dot.gov
Web: www.fhwa.dot.gov/tpp/ddetfp.htm

Summary To provide financial assistance to graduate students, especially those at minority-serving institutions, working on a master's or doctoral degree in transportation-related fields.

Eligibility This program is open to students enrolled or planning to enroll full time to work on a master's or doctoral degree in a field of study directly related to transportation. Applicants must be planning to enter the transportation profession after completing their higher-level education. They must be U.S. citizens or have an I-20 (foreign student) or I-551 (permanent resident) identification card. Selection is based on the proposed plan of study, academic records (class standing, GPA, and official transcripts), transportation work experience (including employer's endorsement), and recommendations. Students at Historically Black Colleges and Universities (HBCUs), Hispanic Serving Institutions (HSIs), and Tribal Colleges and Universities (TCUs) are especially encouraged to apply.

Financial data Fellows receive tuition and fees (to a maximum of $10,000 per year), monthly stipends of $1,700 for master's degree students or $2,000 for doctoral students, and

a 1-time allowance of up to $1,500 for travel to an annual meeting of the Transportation Research Board.

Duration For master's degree students, 24 months, and the degree must be completed within 3 years; for doctoral students, 36 months, and the degree must be completed within 5 years.

Number awarded Varies each year; recently, 59 were awarded.

Deadline March of each year.

[859]
E. LORRAINE BAUGH SCHOLARSHIP

New England Regional Black Nurses Association, Inc.
P.O. Box 190690
Roxbury, MA 02119
(617) 524-1951   E-mail: nerbascholarships@gmail.com
Web: nerbna.nursingnetwork.com

Summary To provide financial assistance to residents of New England who are of African descent and interested in working on a graduate degree in nursing at a school in any state.

Eligibility The program is open to African American residents of the New England states who are currently working on a master's or doctoral degree in nursing at a school in any state. Applicants must have a GPA of 3.0 or higher and at least 1 full year of school remaining. They must be members of the New England Regional Black Nurses Association (NERBNA). Along with their application, they must submit a 3-page essay that covers their reasons for furthering their career in nursing; why minority nursing leadership is important; how minority nursing leadership can assist them in furthering their career; why they chose to prepare for a career in nursing; and any financial hardships that may hinder them from completing their education.

Financial data A stipend is awarded (amount not specified).

Duration 1 year.

Number awarded 1 or more each year.

Deadline February of each year.

[860]
EDSA MINORITY SCHOLARSHIP

Landscape Architecture Foundation
Attn: Leadership in Landscape Scholarship Program
1129 20th Street, N.W., Suite 202
Washington, DC 20036
(202) 331-7070   Fax: (202) 331-7079
E-mail: scholarships@lafoundation.org
Web: www.lafoundation.org

Summary To provide financial assistance to African American and other minority college students who are interested in studying landscape architecture.

Eligibility This program is open to African American, Hispanic, Native American, and minority college students of other cultural and ethnic backgrounds. Applicants must be entering their final 2 years of undergraduate study in landscape architecture or working on a graduate degree in that field. Along with their application, they must submit a 500-word essay on a design or research effort they plan to pursue (explaining how it will contribute to the advancement of the profession and to their ethnic heritage), 3 work samples, and

2 letters of recommendation. Selection is based on professional experience, community involvement, extracurricular activities, and financial need.

Financial data The stipend is $5,000.

Additional information This scholarship was formerly designated the Edward D. Stone, Jr. and Associates Minority Scholarship.

Number awarded 1 each year.

Deadline February of each year.

[861]
EDUCATIONAL FOUNDATION OF THE COLORADO SOCIETY OF CERTIFIED PUBLIC ACCOUNTANTS MINORITY SCHOLARSHIPS

Colorado Society of Certified Public Accountants
Attn: Educational Foundation
7887 East Belleview Avenue, Suite 200
Englewood, CO 80111
(303) 773-2877   Toll Free: (800) 523-9082 (within CO)
Fax: (303) 773-6344
Web: www.cocpa.org

Summary To provide financial assistance to African American and other minority upper-division and graduate students in Colorado who are majoring in accounting.

Eligibility This program is open to Colorado minority residents (Black or African American, Hispanic or Latino, Native American, Asian American) who are upper-division or graduate students at colleges and universities in the state and have completed at least 6 semester hours of accounting courses. Applicants must have a GPA of at least 3.0 overall and 3.25 in accounting classes. They must be U.S. citizens or noncitizens legally living and studying in Colorado with a valid visa that enables them to become employed. Financial need is not considered in the selection process.

Financial data The stipend is $2,500. Funds are paid directly to the recipient's school to be used for books, C.P.A. review materials, tuition, fees, and dormitory room and board.

Duration 1 year; recipients may reapply.

Number awarded 1 or more each year.

Deadline May of each year for fall semester or quarter; November of each year for winter quarter or spring semester.

[862]
EDWARD S. ROTH SCHOLARSHIP

Society of Manufacturing Engineers
Attn: SME Education Foundation
One SME Drive
P.O. Box 930
Dearborn, MI 48121-0930
(313) 425-3300   Toll Free: (866) 547-6333
Fax: (313) 425-3411   E-mail: foundation@sme.org
Web: www.smeef.org

Summary To provide financial assistance to students, especially African Americans and other minorities, who are enrolled or planning to work on a bachelor's or master's degree in manufacturing engineering at selected universities.

Eligibility This program is open to U.S. citizens who are graduating high school seniors or currently-enrolled undergraduate or graduate students. Applicants must be enrolled or planning to enroll as a full-time student at 1 of 13 selected 4-year universities to work on a bachelor's or master's degree

in manufacturing engineering. They must have a GPA of 3.0 or higher. Preference is given to 1) students demonstrating financial need; 2) minority students; and 3) students participating in a co-op program. Along with their application, they must submit a brief statement about why they chose their major, their career and educational objectives, and how this scholarship will help them attain those objectives.

Financial data Stipends range from $1,000 to $6,000 and recently averaged approximately $2,000.

Duration 1 year; may be renewed.

Additional information The eligible institutions are California Polytechnic State University at San Luis Obispo, California State Polytechnic State University at Pomona, University of Miami (Florida), Bradley University (Illinois), Central State University (Ohio), Miami University (Ohio), Boston University, Worcester Polytechnic Institute (Massachusetts), University of Massachusetts, St. Cloud State University (Minnesota), University of Texas at Rio Grande Valley, Brigham Young University (Utah), and Utah State University.

Number awarded 2 each year.

Deadline January of each year.

[863]
E.J. JOSEY SCHOLARSHIP AWARD

Black Caucus of the American Library Association
c/o Wanda Kay Brown
Winston-Salem State University
C.G. O'Kelly Library
601 South Martin Luther King Drive
Winston-Salem, NC 27110
(773) 916-6970   E-mail: ejjoseyscholarship@gmail.com
Web: www.bcala.org/2149-2

Summary To provide financial assistance to African Americans interested in working on a graduate degree in librarianship.

Eligibility This program is open to African American citizens of the United States or Canada who are enrolled as graduate students in an accredited library or information science program. Applicants must submit an essay of 1,000 to 1,200 words on a topic that changes annually. Selection is based on the essay's argument development, critical analysis, clear language, conciseness, and creativity.

Financial data The stipend is $2,000.

Duration 1 year.

Number awarded 2 each year.

Deadline December of each year.

[864]
ELLIOTT C. ROBERTS SCHOLARSHIP

Institute for Diversity in Health Management
Attn: Membership and Education Specialist
155 North Wacker Avenue
Chicago, IL 60606
(312) 422-2658   E-mail: cbiddle@aha.org
Web: www.diversityconnection.org

Summary To provide financial assistance to graduate students in health care management who are African Americans or will contribute to ethnic diversity in the profession in other ways.

Eligibility This program is open to U.S. citizens who represent ethnically diverse cultural backgrounds. Applicants must be enrolled in the second year of a master's degree program in health administration or a comparable program and have a GPA of 3.0 or higher. Along with their application, they must submit 1) a personal statement of 1 to 2 pages on their interest in health care management and their career goals; 2) an essay on what they see as the most challenging issue facing America's hospitals and health systems; and 3) a 500-word essay on their interest and background in health care finance. Selection is based on academic achievement, commitment to community service, and financial need.

Financial data The stipend is $1,000.

Duration 1 year.

Number awarded 1 each year.

Deadline January of each year.

[865]
ELLIS INJURY LAW DIVERSITY SCHOLARSHIPS

Ellis Law Corporation
Attn: Scholarship
883 North Douglas Street
El Segundo, CA 90245
Toll Free: (888) 559-7672
E-mail: scholarships@alelaw.com
Web: www.ellisinjurylaw.com/scholarships

Summary To provide financial assistance to pre-law and law students who either are African Americans or members of another ethnic minority group or have been involved in diversity issues.

Eligibility This program is open to students accepted or enrolled at 1) a 4-year college or university with the intention of working on a law degree; and 2) an ABA-accredited law school. Applicants must be either members of an ethnic/racial minority or individuals who have made a demonstrative commitment to diversity within their school and/or community. They must have a GPA of 3.0 or higher. Along with their application, they must submit an essay of 1,500 to 2,000 words answering 3 questions about recent Supreme Court decisions regarding affirmative action. Selection is based on that essay and transcripts.

Financial data The stipend is $1,000.

Duration 1 year.

Additional information This program began in 2014.

Number awarded 3 each year.

Deadline December of each year.

[866]
ELLIS J. BONNER AWARD

National Association of Health Services Executives
Attn: Educational Assistance Program
1050 Connecticut Avenue, N.W., Tenth Floor
Washington, DC 20036
(202) 772-1030   Fax: (202) 772-1072
E-mail: nahsehg@nahse.org
Web: www.nahse.org/student-scholarships.html

Summary To provide financial assistance to African American nontraditional students who are members of the National Association of Health Services Executives (NAHSE) and interested in preparing for a career in health care administration.

Eligibility This program is open to African Americans who are nontraditional students and either enrolled or accepted at an accredited college or university to work on a master's or doctoral degree in health care administration. Applicants must be members of NAHSE and able to demonstrate financial need. They must have a GPA of 2.5 or higher as undergraduates or 3.0 or higher as graduate students. Along with their application, they must submit a 3-page essay that describes themselves and their career goals, commitment and interest in health care management, and financial need.

Financial data The stipend is $2,500. Funds are sent to the recipient's institution.

Duration 1 year.

Number awarded 1 each year.

Deadline May of each year.

[867]
ELSIE MAE WHITE MEMORIAL SCHOLARSHIP FUND

Columbus Foundation
Attn: Scholarship Manager
1234 East Broad Street
Columbus, OH 43205-1453
(614) 251-4000   Fax: (614) 251-4009
E-mail: aszempruch@columbusfoundation.org
Web: tcfapp.org

Summary To provide financial assistance for college or graduate school to African American high school seniors and college students from any state.

Eligibility This program is open to African American high school seniors and college students. High school seniors must rank in the top third of their class; college students must have a GPA of 2.8 or higher. Applicants must be attending or planning to attend an accredited college or university in the United States as a full- or part-time undergraduate or graduate student. Preference is given to students at land grant colleges and universities. Along with their application, they must submit 300-word essays on 1) their educational and career plans and goals, why they have chosen their particular field, and why they think they will be a success; 2) why they feel they need this scholarship, especially as related to financial need; and 3) any other information that will assist the selection committee in making its decision.

Financial data The stipend is $1,000.

Duration 1 year.

Number awarded Varies each year.

Deadline May of each year.

[868]
EMERGING ARCHIVAL SCHOLARS PROGRAM

Archival Education and Research Institute
Center for Information as Evidence
c/o UCLA Graduate School of Education and Information Studies
Office of External Relations
2043 Moore Hall
Los Angeles, CA 90095-1521
(310) 206-0375   Fax: (310) 794-5324
Web: aeri.gseis.ucla.edu/fellowships.htm

Summary To provide an opportunity for African American and other minority undergraduate and graduate students to learn more about the field of archival studies and to be exposed to research in the field.

Eligibility This program is open to undergraduates who have completed their junior year and to students who have completed the first year of a master's degree program. Applicants must be African American, Hispanic/Latino, Asian/Pacific Islander, Native American, Puerto Rican, or any other person who will add diversity to the field of archival studies. They must have a GPA of 3.0 or higher, but they may be working on a degree in any field and are not required to have prior knowledge of or experience in archival studies. U.S. citizenship or permanent resident status is required. Applicants must be interested in attending the week-long Archival Education and Research Institute (AERI), held at a different university each summer, where they are assigned both a faculty research mentor and a Ph.D. student mentor who introduce them to doctoral research and careers in archival studies.

Financial data Grants provide payment of round-trip travel, accommodation, and most meals.

Duration These grants are offered annually.

Additional information This program, first offered in 2009, is supported by the Institute of Museum and Library Services. Scholars who indicate an interest in continuing on to a doctoral program in archival studies after completing the AERI may be invited to participate in a supervised research project that will last up to 1 year and to present results of their research in a poster session at the AERI of the following year.

Number awarded Up to 7 each year.

Deadline April of each year.

[869]
ENVIRONMENT AND NATURAL RESOURCES FELLOWSHIPS

Harvard University
John F. Kennedy School of Government
Belfer Center for Science and International Affairs
Attn: STPP Fellowship Coordinator
79 John F. Kennedy Street, Mailbox 53
Cambridge, MA 02138
(617) 495-1498   Fax: (617) 495-8963
E-mail: patricia_mclaughlin@hks.harvard.edu
Web: belfercenter.ksg.harvard.edu

Summary To provide funding to professionals, postdoctorates, and doctoral students, especially African Americans and members of other underrepresented groups, who are interested in conducting research on environmental and natural resource issues at the Belfer Center for Science and International Affairs at Harvard University in Cambridge, Massachusetts.

Eligibility The postdoctoral fellowship is open to recent recipients of the Ph.D. or equivalent degree, university faculty members, and employees of government, military, international, humanitarian, and private research institutions who have appropriate professional experience. Applicants for predoctoral fellowships must have passed their general examinations. Scholars from a wide range of disciplinary and multi-disciplinary fields and those holding a Ph.D. in engineering or in the natural sciences are strongly encouraged to apply. The program especially encourages applications from women, minorities, and citizens of all countries. All applicants must be interested in conducting research on projects of the Environment and Natural Resources (ENRP) Program. Recently, those included projects on energy technology innovation, sustainable energy development in China, managing the atom, and the geopolitics of energy.

Financial data The stipend is $37,500 for postdoctoral research fellows or $25,000 for predoctoral research fellows. Fellows who renew their grant receive a monthly stipend of $3,750 for postdoctoral fellows or $2,500 for predoctoral fellows. Stipends for advanced research fellows vary. Health insurance is also provided.

Duration 10 months; may be renewed on a month-by-month basis.

Additional information Fellows are expected to devote some portion of their time to collaborative endeavors, as arranged by the appropriate program or project director. Predoctoral fellows are expected to contribute to the program's research activities, as well as work on (and ideally complete) their dissertations. Postdoctoral research fellows are also expected to complete a book, monograph, or other significant publication during their period of residence.

Number awarded A limited number each year.

Deadline January of each year.

[870]
EPISCOPAL BLACK MINISTRIES THEOLOGICAL EDUCATION SCHOLARSHIPS

Episcopal Church Center
Attn: Domestic and Foreign Missionary Society
Scholarship Committee
815 Second Avenue, Fifth Floor
New York, NY 10017-4503
(212) 716-6168   Toll Free: (800) 334-7626
Fax: (212) 867-0395
E-mail: ahercules@episcopalchurch.org
Web: www.episcopalchurch.org

Summary To provide financial assistance to African Americans interested in seeking ordination and serving in a ministry involving African Americans in the Episcopal Church.

Eligibility This program is open to African American students pursuing theological education, including diocesan programs as well as seminary education. Applicants must be a member of an African American constituency in the Episcopal Church and have begun the process of seeking ordination through a local Episcopal diocese. Scholarships are presented both for full- and part-time study.

Financial data The maximum stipend is $10,000 per year.

Duration 1 year; may be renewed up to 3 additional years.

Additional information This program receives support from several funds of the sponsoring agency: the F.K., Jane K., and W.S. Collins Fund (established in 1884), the Richardson Fund (established in 1905), the Dix Memorial Fund (established in 1919), the Hattie Rebecca Anderson Memorial Fund (established in 1948), the Robert W. Patton Memorial Fund (established in 1968), the Mary J. Stroud Fund (established in 1968), the Gertrude M. Davenport Memorial Fund (established in 1972), and the Black Clergy Development Fund (established in 1983).

Number awarded Varies each year; recently, 18 of these scholarships, with a value of $76,897, were awarded.

Deadline April of each year.

[871]
ESTELLE MASSEY OSBORNE SCHOLARSHIP

Nurses Educational Funds, Inc.
Attn: Scholarship Coordinator
137 Montague Street, Suite 144
Brooklyn, NY 11201
(917) 524-8051   E-mail: info@n-e-f.org
Web: www.n-e-f.org/index.php/about/nef-scholarships.html

Summary To provide financial assistance to African American nurses interested in earning a master's degree.

Eligibility This program is open to African American registered nurses who are members of a national professional nursing organization and enrolled full or part time in an accredited master's degree program in nursing. Applicants must have completed at least 12 credits and have a cumulative GPA of 3.6 or higher. They must be U.S. citizens or have declared their official intention of becoming a citizen. Along with their application, they must submit an essay of 750 to 850 words defining their professional goals and assessing their potential for making a contribution to the nursing profession.

Financial data Stipends range from $2,500 to $10,000, depending on the availability of funds.

Duration 1 year; nonrenewable.

Additional information There is a $20 application fee.

Number awarded 1 each year.

Deadline January of each year.

[872]
ESTHER NGAN-LING CHOW AND MAREYJOYCE GREEN SCHOLARSHIP

Sociologists for Women in Society
Attn: Administrative Officer
University of Kansas
Department of Sociology
1415 Jayhawk Boulevard, Room 716
Lawrence, KS 66045
(785) 864-9405   E-mail: swsao@outlook.com
Web: www.socwomen.org

Summary To provide funding to African American and other women of color who are conducting dissertation research in sociology.

Eligibility This program is open to women from a racial/ethnic group that faces discrimination in the United States. Applicants must be in the early stages of writing a doctoral dissertation in sociology on a topic relating to the concerns that women of color face domestically and/or internationally. They must be able to demonstrate financial need. Both domestic and international students are eligible to apply. Along with their application, they must submit a personal statement that details their short- and long-term career and research goals; a resume or curriculum vitae; 2 letters of recommendation; and a 5-page dissertation proposal that includes the purpose of the research, the work to be accomplished through support from this scholarship, and a time line for completion.

Financial data The stipend is $15,000. An additional grant of $500 is provided to enable the recipient to attend the winter meeting of Sociologists for Women in Society (SWS), and travel expenses to attend the summer meeting are reimbursed.

Duration 1 year.

Additional information This program began in 2007 and was originally named the Women of Color Dissertation Scholarship.

Number awarded 1 each year.

Deadline March of each year.

[873]
ETHNIC IN-SERVICE TRAINING FUND FOR CLINICAL PASTORAL EDUCATION (EIST-CPE)

United Methodist Church
Attn: General Board of Higher Education and Ministry
Office of Loans and Scholarships
1001 19th Avenue South
P.O. Box 340007
Nashville, TN 37203-0007
(615) 340-7342   Fax: (615) 340-7367
E-mail: umscholar@gbhem.org
Web: www.gbhem.org

Summary To provide financial assistance to United Methodist Church clergy and candidates for ministry who are African Americans or members of other minority groups interested in preparing for a career as a clinical pastor.

Eligibility This program is open to U.S. citizens and permanent residents who are members of ethnic or racial minority groups and have been active, full members of a United Methodist Church for at least 1 year prior to applying. Applicants must be United Methodist clergy, certified candidates for ministry, or seminary students accepted into an accredited Clinical Pastor Education (CPE) or an accredited American Association of Pastoral Counselors (AAPC) program. They must be preparing for a career as a chaplain, pastoral counselor, or in pastoral care.

Financial data Grants range up to $2,000.

Duration 1 year.

Number awarded 1 each year.

Deadline February of each year.

[874]
EVERETT V. FOX STUDENT CASE COMPETITION

National Association of Health Services Executives
Attn: Case Competition
1050 Connecticut Avenue, N.W., Tenth Floor
Washington, DC 20036
(202) 772-1030   Fax: (202) 772-1072
E-mail: casecompetition@nahse.org
Web: netforum.avectra.com

Summary To recognize and reward teams of master's degree students, including at least 1 African American, who participate in a competition involving a case study in health administration.

Eligibility This competition is open to teams of 1 to 3 students enrolled in a master's degree program in health administration, business administration, or public health. At least 1 member of the team must be African American. Applicants are presented with a case study modeled after real situations faced by actual organizations in the field of health care administration. They have 3 weeks in which to prepare their analysis and recommendations for a 20-minute oral presentation to a panel of judges, followed by a 10-minute question and answer period.

Financial data Awards are $4,000 per member for the first-place team, $3,000 per member for the second-place team, $2,000 per member for the third-place team, $1,000 per member for the fourth-place team, and $500 per member for the fifth-place team.

Duration The competition is held annually.

Additional information This competition was established in 1996. The registration fee is $250 per team member.

Number awarded 5 teams are selected as winners each year.

Deadline August of each year.

[875]
EXTERNSHIP IN ADDICTION PSYCHIATRY

American Psychiatric Association
Attn: Minority Medical Student Awards
1000 Wilson Boulevard, Suite 1825
Arlington, VA 22209-3901
(703) 907-7894   Toll Free: (888) 357-7849
Fax: (703) 907-1087   E-mail: Mfpstudents@psych.org
Web: www.psychiatry.org

Summary To provide an opportunity for African American and other minority medical students to spend an elective residency learning about substance abuse disorders, prevention, and early intervention.

Eligibility This program is open to student members of the American Psychiatric Association (APA) who come from racial/ethnic minorities and are currently enrolled at accredited U.S. medical school. Applicants must be interested in working with a mentor at a designated site to gain exposure to how psychiatrists treat patients with substance abuse disorders and participate in an interactive didactic experiential learning program. Mentors and sites are selected where there is an approved substance abuse training program and a significant number of substance abuse disorder patients from minority and underserved populations. U.S. citizenship or permanent resident status is required.

Financial data The program provides a stipend of $1,500 for living expenses and funding for travel to and from the mentoring site.

Duration 1 month during the summer.

Number awarded 6 each year.

Deadline March of each year.

[876]
FACS GRADUATE FELLOWSHIPS

National Association of Teacher Educators for Family and
    Consumer Sciences
c/o Debra Price, Fellowship Committee Chair
116 East Summit Street
Bolivar, MO 65613
(417) 327-6636   E-mail: debraprice81@gmail.com
Web: www.natefacs.org/Pages/awards.html

Summary To provide financial assistance to graduate students in family and consumer science education, especially African Americans and other minority candidates.

Eligibility This program is open to graduate students working on a master's or doctoral degree in family and consumer sciences education. Applicants must submit an autobiographical sketch (up to 3 pages in length) presenting their professional goals, including information on the institution where they are studying or planning to study, areas or emphases of study, possible research topic, and other pertinent information regarding their plans. Selection is based on likelihood of completing the degree, likelihood of contribution to family and consumer sciences education, previous academic work, professional association involvement, professional experience (including scholarly work), and references. At least 1 fellowship is reserved for a minority (African American, Hispanic American, Native American, or Asian American) candidate.

Financial data Stipends range from $2,000 to $4,000.

Duration 1 year.

Additional information The sponsor is an affiliate of the Family and Consumer Sciences (FACS) Division of the Association for Career and Technical Education (ACTE).

Number awarded Varies each year.

Deadline September of each year.

[877]
FARM CREDIT EAST SCHOLARSHIPS

Farm Credit East
Attn: Scholarship Program
240 South Road
Enfield, CT 06082
(860) 741-4380   Toll Free: (800) 562-2235
Fax: (860) 741-4389
E-mail: specialoffers@famcrediteast.com
Web: www.farmcrediteast.com

Summary To provide financial assistance to residents of designated northeastern states, including African Americans and other minorities, who plan to attend school in any state to work on an undergraduate or graduate degree in a field related to agriculture, forestry, or fishing.

Eligibility This program is open to residents of Connecticut, Maine, Massachusetts, New Jersey, Rhode Island, and portions of New York and New Hampshire. Applicants must be working on or planning to work on an associate, bachelor's, or graduate degree in production agriculture, agribusiness, the forest products industry, or commercial fishing at a college or university in any state. They must submit a 200-word essay on why they wish to prepare for a career in agriculture, forestry, or fishing. Selection is based on the essay, extracurricular activities (especially farm work experience and activities indicative of an interest in preparing for a career in agriculture or agribusiness), and interest in agriculture. The program includes diversity scholarships reserved for members of minority groups (Black or African American, American Indian or Alaska Native, Asian, Native Hawaiian or other Pacific Islander, or Hispanic or Latino).

Financial data The stipend is $1,500. Funds are paid directly to the student to be used for tuition, room and board, books, and other academic charges.

Duration 1 year; nonrenewable.

Additional information Recipients are given priority for an internship with the sponsor in the summer following their junior year. Farm Credit East was formerly named First Pioneer Farm Credit.

Number awarded Varies each year; recently, 32, including several diversity scholarships, were awarded.

Deadline April of each year.

[878]
FAYE AND ROBERT LETT SCHOLARSHIP

American Baptist Churches of Ohio
Attn: Ohio Baptist Education Society
136 Galway Drive North
Granville, OH 43023-9577
(740) 587-0804   Fax: (740) 587-0807
Web: www.abc-ohio.org/index.php/menu-obes

Summary To provide funding to African American upper-division and graduate students from Ohio who are interested in preparing for the Baptist ministry at a college or seminary in any state.

Eligibility This program is open to African American residents of Ohio who have completed at least 2 years of study at an accredited college or university in any state and are interested in continuing their education as an upper-division or seminary student. Applicants must 1) hold active membership in a church affiliated with the American Baptist Churches of Ohio or a church dually-aligned with the American Baptist Churches of Ohio; 2) be in the process of preparing for a professional career in Christian ministry (such as a local church pastor, church education, youth or young adult ministries, church music, specialized ministry, chaplaincy, ministry in higher education, or missionary service); 3) be committed to working professionally within the framework of the American Baptist Churches USA; and 4) acknowledge a personal commitment to the Gospel of Jesus Christ, an understanding of the Christian faith, and a definite call to professional Christian ministry as a life work. Financial need must be demonstrated.

Financial data Stipends generally range from $1,000 to $1,500 a year.

Duration 1 year.

Additional information This program began in 1990.

Number awarded 1 or more each year.

Deadline March of each year.

[879]
FEDERAL EMPLOYEE EDUCATION AND ASSISTANCE (FEEA)-BLACKS IN GOVERNMENT (BIG) SCHOLARSHIP PROGRAM

Blacks in Government
Attn: National Program and Planning Chair
3005 Georgia Avenue, N.W.
Washington, DC 20001-5015
(202) 667-3280   Fax: (202) 667-3705
E-mail: BIGprograms@bignet.org
Web: www.bignet.org

Summary To provide financial assistance for college or graduate school to dependents of members of Blacks in Government (BIG).

Eligibility This program is open to the children, stepchildren, and grandchildren of BIG members. The sponsoring BIG member must have at least 3 years of federal, state, or local government employment and 2 years of membership in BIG. Applicants must be entering or enrolled full time in an accredited 2- or 4-year postsecondary, graduate, or postgraduate program and have a GPA of 3.0 or higher. Along with their application, they must submit a 2-page essay on a topic related to a career in public service with the government, a letter of recommendation, a transcript, a list of extracurricular and community service activities, and verification of govern-

ment employment; high school seniors must also submit a copy of their ACT, SAT, or other examination scores. Financial need is not considered in the selection process.

Financial data The stipend is $1,000 per year.

Duration 1 year; may be renewed.

Additional information This program, established in 2007, is jointly administered by BIG and the Federal Employee Education and Assistance Fund (FEEA).

Number awarded Up to 11 each year: 1 in each BIG region.

Deadline March of each year.

[880]
FELICIA C. BRADY SCHOLARSHIP FUND

Black Nurses' Association of Greater Washington, D.C. Area, Inc.
Attn: Scholarship Committee Chair
P.O. Box 55285
Washington, DC 20040
(202) 291-8866
Web: www.bnaofgwdca.org/scholarships.html

Summary To provide financial assistance to registered nurses from the Washington, D.C. area who are members of the National Black Nurses' Association and its local affiliate, and are interested in working on an advanced degree.

Eligibility This program is open to registered nurses who are currently enrolled in an associate, bachelor's, master's, or doctoral program and have a GPA of 3.0 or higher. Applicants must be residents of Washington, D.C. or adjoining counties in Maryland (Anne Arundel, Calvert, Charles, Howard, Montgomery, and Prince George's). They must be U.S. citizens, members of the National Black Nurses' Association, and members of the Black Nurses' Association of Greater Washington, D.C. Area. Along with their application, they must submit a copy of their nursing license, an official transcript from their nursing program, 2 letters of recommendation, and a written essay that describes their personal goals and objectives, financial need, and contributions to nursing and community service involvement in the greater Washington, D.C. area.

Financial data A stipend is awarded (amount not specified).

Duration 1 year.

Number awarded 1 each year.

Deadline January of each year.

[881]
FELLOWSHIPS FOR DOCTORAL STUDENTS OF AFRICAN DESCENT

Forum for Theological Exploration
Attn: Fellowship Program
160 Clairemont Avenue, Suite 300
Decatur, GA 30030
(678) 369-6755   Fax: (678) 369-6757
E-mail: dhutto@fteleaders.org
Web: www.fteleaders.org

Summary To provide funding to African Americans who are working on a doctoral degree in religious, theological, or biblical studies.

Eligibility This program is open to students of African descent who are U.S. or Canadian citizens or permanent residents working full time on a Ph.D. or Th.D. degree. Applicants must be past the course work stage; they are not required to have been advanced to candidacy, but they must have had their dissertation topic approved and be in a position to devote full time to writing. Students who are working on a Doctor of Ministry (D.Min.) degree are not eligible.

Financial data   The stipend is $25,000.

Duration   1 year.

Additional information   Fellows also receive reimbursement of expenses to attend the sponsor's Christian Leadership Forum. The sponsor was formerly named the The Fund for Theological Education, Inc.

Number awarded   Varies each year; recently, 14 were awarded.

Deadline   January of each year.

[882]
FIRST TRANSIT SCHOLARSHIP

Conference of Minority Transportation Officials
Attn: National Scholarship Program
100 M Street, S.E., Suite 917
Washington, DC 20003
(202) 506-2917   E-mail: info@comto.org
Web: www.comto.org/page/scholarships

Summary   To provide financial assistance to African American and other minority upper-division and graduate students in engineering or other field related to transportation.

Eligibility   This program is open to minority juniors, seniors, and graduate students in transporation, planning, engineering or other technical transportation-related disciplines. Applicants must submit a cover letter on their transportation-related career goals and life aspirations. Financial need is not considered in the selection process.

Financial data   The stipend is $6,000. Funds are paid directly to the recipient's college or university.

Duration   1 year.

Additional information   This program is sponsored by First Transit Inc.

Number awarded   1 each year.

Deadline   April of each year.

[883]
FLORENCE GAYNOR AWARD

National Association of Health Services Executives
Attn: Educational Assistance Program
1050 Connecticut Avenue, N.W., Tenth Floor
Washington, DC 20036
(202) 772-1030   Fax: (202) 772-1072
E-mail: nahsehg@nahse.org
Web: www.nahse.org/student-scholarships.html

Summary   To provide financial assistance to African American women who are members of the National Association of Health Services Executives (NAHSE) and interested in preparing for a career in health care administration.

Eligibility   This program is open to African American women who are either enrolled or accepted at an accredited college or university to work on a master's or doctoral degree in health care administration. Applicants must be members of NAHSE and able to demonstrate financial need. They must have a GPA of 2.5 or higher as undergraduates or 3.0 or higher as graduate students. Along with their application, they

must submit a 3-page essay that describes themselves and their career goals, commitment and interest in health care management, and financial need.

Financial data   The stipend is $2,500. Funds are sent to the recipient's institution.

Duration   1 year.

Number awarded   1 each year.

Deadline   May of each year.

[884]
FLORIDA LIBRARY ASSOCIATION MINORITY SCHOLARSHIPS

Florida Library Association
541 East Tennessee Street, Suite 103
Tallahassee, FL 32308
(850) 270-9205   Fax: (850) 270-9405
E-mail: flaexecutivedirector@comcast.net
Web: www.flalib.org/scholarships.php

Summary   To provide financial assistance to African American and other minority students working on a graduate degree in library and information science in Florida.

Eligibility   This program is open to residents of Florida who are working on a graduate degree in library and information science at schools in the state. Applicants must be members of a minority group: Black/African American, American Indian/Alaska Native, Asian/Pacific Islander, or Hispanic/Latino. They must have some experience in a Florida library, must be a member of the Florida Library Association, and must commit to working in a Florida library for at least 1 year after graduation. Along with their application, they must submit 1) a list of activities, honors, awards, and/or offices held during college and outside college; 2) an essay of 1 to 2 pages on why they are entering librarianship; and 3) an essay of 1 to 2 pages on their career goals with respect to Florida libraries. Financial need is considered in the selection process.

Financial data   The stipend is $2,000.

Duration   1 year.

Number awarded   1 each year.

Deadline   January of each year.

[885]
FRANCIS M. KEVILLE MEMORIAL SCHOLARSHIP

Construction Management Association of America
Attn: CMAA Foundation
7926 Jones Branch Drive, Suite 800
McLean, VA 22101-3303
(703) 677-3361   E-mail: foundation@cmaanet.org
Web: www.cmaafoundation.org

Summary   To provide financial assistance to African American and other minority undergraduate and graduate students working on a degree in construction management.

Eligibility   This program is open to women and members of minority groups who are enrolled as full-time undergraduate or graduate students. Applicants must have completed at least 1 year of study and have at least 1 full year remaining for a bachelor's or master's degree in construction management or a related field. Along with their application, they must submit essays on why they are interested in a career in construction management and why they should be awarded this scholarship. Selection is based on that essay (20%), academic performance (40%), recommendation of the faculty adviser (15%), and extracurricular activities (25%); a bonus of 5% is given to student members of the Construction Management Association of America (CMAA).

Financial data   The stipend is $5,000. Funds are disbursed directly to the student's university.

Duration   1 year.

Number awarded   1 each year.

Deadline   April of each year.

[886]
FRANK/NORRELL SCHOLARSHIP PROGRAM

Southwestern Athletic Conference
Attn: Frank/Norrell Scholarship
2101 Sixth Avenue North, Suite 700
Birmingham, AL 35203
(205) 251-7573   Fax: (205) 297-9820
Web: www.swac.org

Summary   To provide financial assistance to graduate students at member institutions of the Southwestern Athletic Conference (SWAC) who are interested in working on a degree in a field related to physical education.

Eligibility   This program is open to students who currently attend an Historically Black College or University that makes up the SWAC and plan to attend graduate school at a member institution of the conference. Applicants must be interested in working on a degree in health, physical education, recreation, sports administration and management, or a related field. They must have a GPA of 3.0 or higher, a commitment to working full time on a post-baccalaureate professional degree, and a record of participation in athletics that has been a positive influence on their personal and intellectual development.

Financial data   The stipend is $3,000.

Duration   1 year.

Additional information   This program began in 1998 with funding from Dr. Gwen Norrell, former professor and faculty athletics representative at Michigan State University, in honor of Dr. James Frank, long-time commissioner of the SWAC. The members of the SWAC include the following HBCUs: Alabama A&M University (Normal), Alabama State University (Montgomery), Alcorn State University (Alcorn State, Mississippi), University of Arkansas at Pine Bluff, Grambling State University (Grambling, Louisiana), Jackson State University (Jackson, Mississippi), Mississippi Valley State University (Itta Bena, Mississippi), Prairie View A&M University (Prairie View, Texas), Southern University and A&M College (Baton Rouge, Louisiana), and Texas Southern University (Houston).

Number awarded   1 each year.

Deadline   June of each year.

[887]
FRANKLIN C. MCLEAN AWARD

National Medical Fellowships, Inc.
Attn: Scholarship Program
347 Fifth Avenue, Suite 510
New York, NY 10016
(212) 483-8880   Toll Free: (877) NMF-1DOC
Fax: (212) 483-8897 E-mail: scholarships@nmfonline.org
Web: www.nmfonline.org

Summary   To provide financial assistance to African Americans and other underrepresented minority medical students who demonstrate academic achievement.

Eligibility   This program is open to African Americans, Hispanics/Latinos, Native Americans, Vietnamese, Cambodians, and Pacific Islanders who are entering their senior year of medical school. They must be U.S. citizens or DACA students. Selection is based on academic achievement, leadership, and community service.

Financial data   The stipend is $5,000.

Duration   1 year.

Additional information   This program began in 1968.

Number awarded   1 each year.

Deadline   September of each year.

[888]
FREDERICK DOUGLASS INSTITUTE FOR AFRICAN AND AFRICAN-AMERICAN STUDIES PREDOCTORAL DISSERTATION FELLOWSHIP

University of Rochester
Frederick Douglass Institute for African and African-
  American Studies
Attn: Director for Research Fellowships
311 Morey Hall
RC Box 270440
Rochester, NY 14627-0440
(585) 276-5744   Fax: (585) 256-2594
E-mail: FDI@rochester.edu
Web: www.sas.rochester.edu/aas/fellowships/external.html

Summary   To provide funding to doctoral candidates interested in conducting research at the University of Rochester on Africa and its Diaspora.

Eligibility   Graduate students at any university in the United States who are conducting dissertation research on aspects of the African or African American experience are invited to apply if they are interested in spending a year in residence, working on their research, at the University of Rochester. Applicants must have completed their preliminary course work, qualifying exams, and at least 1 chapter of their dissertation.

Financial data   The stipend is $26,000.

Duration   1 academic year.

Additional information   Fellows are given office space within the institute, full access to the facilities of the university, and opportunities for collaboration and discussion. Predoctoral fellows are expected to organize a colloquium, prepare a lecture, and make other contributions to the institute's program. They are expected to be in full-time residence at the institute during the tenure of their award.

Number awarded   1 each year.

Deadline   December of each year.

[889]
FULL CIRCLE COMMUNICATIONS/MAYNARD JACKSON SCHOLARSHIP

National Forum for Black Public Administrators
Attn: Scholarship Program
777 North Capitol Street, N.E., Suite 807
Washington, DC 20002
(202) 408-9300   Fax: (202) 408-8558
E-mail: vharris@nfbpa.org
Web: www.nfbpa.org/i4a/pages/index.cfm?pageid=4047

Summary   To provide financial assistance to African American undergraduate and graduate students preparing for a career in public service or a business field that supports the administration of public service.

Eligibility   This program is open to African American undergraduate and graduate students preparing for a career in public service or a business field that supports the administration of public service. Applicants must be working full time on a degree in public administration, political science, urban affairs, public policy, business administration, or a related field. They must have a GPA of 3.0 or higher, a well-balanced focus of academic excellence and volunteerism/community involvement, and strong leadership and communication (oral and written) skills. Along with their application, they must submit a 3-page autobiographical essay that includes their academic and career goals and objectives. Selection is based on academic record, leadership ability, participation in school activities, community service, and financial need.

Financial data   The stipend is $2,000.

Duration   1 year.

Additional information   This program is sponsored by Full Circle Communications, a media management consulting firm based in Puerto Rico. Recipients are required to attend the sponsor's annual conference to receive their scholarship; limited hotel and air accommodations are arranged and provided.

Number awarded   1 each year.

Deadline   March of each year.

[890]
GABWA FOUNDATION SCHOLARSHIPS

Georgia Association of Black Women Attorneys
Attn: GABWA Foundation
P.O. Box 7381
Atlanta, GA 30309
(678) 825-5675   E-mail: contact@gabwa.org
Web: www.gabwa.org/foundation.php

Summary   To provide financial assistance to Black women from any state enrolled at law schools in Georgia.

Eligibility   This program is open to Black women from any state enrolled in the second or third year at a law school in Georgia. Applicants must be able to demonstrate academic achievement, leadership, and commitment to the profession and their community. Along with their application, they must submit a 300-word personal statement that discusses their experience as a Black woman law student, how they expect their legal career to benefit the community at large, and how this scholarship will benefit their quest for a legal education and future career goals. Financial need is considered in the selection process but is not required.

Financial data   Stipend amounts vary, depending on the availability of funds; recently, they averaged $5,000.

Duration   1 year.

Additional information   This program began in 2002.

Number awarded   Varies each year; recently, 10 were awarded. Since the program was established, it has awarded more than $250,000 to more than 50 African American women law students.

Deadline   October of each year.

[891]
GAIUS CHARLES BOLIN DISSERTATION AND POST-MFA FELLOWSHIPS

Williams College
Attn: Dean of the Faculty
880 Main Street
Hopkins Hall, Third Floor
P.O. Box 141
Williamstown, MA 01267
(413) 597-4351   Fax: (413) 597-3553
E-mail: gburda@williams.edu
Web: faculty.williams.edu

Summary   To provide financial assistance to African Americans and members of other underrepresented groups who are interested in teaching courses at Williams College while working on their doctoral dissertation or building their post-M.F.A. professional portfolio.

Eligibility   This program is open to members of underrepresented groups, including ethnic minorities, first-generation college students, women in predominantly male fields, and scholars with disabilities. Applicants must be 1) doctoral candidates in any field who have completed all work for a Ph.D. except for the dissertation; or 2) artists who completed an M.F.A. degree within the past 2 years and are building their professional portfolio. They must be willing to teach a course at Williams College. Along with their application, they must submit a full curriculum vitae, a graduate school transcript, 3 letters of recommendation, a copy of their dissertation prospectus or samples of their artistic work, and a description of their teaching interests within a department or program at Williams College. U.S. citizenship or permanent resident status is required.

Financial data   Fellows receive $38,000 for the academic year, plus housing assistance, office space, computer and library privileges, and a research allowance of up to $4,000.

Duration   2 years.

Additional information   Bolin fellows are assigned a faculty adviser in the appropriate department. This program was established in 1985. Fellows are expected to teach a 1-semester course each year. They must be in residence at Williams College for the duration of the fellowship.

Number awarded   2 each year.

Deadline   November of each year.

[892]
GEM M.S. ENGINEERING FELLOWSHIP PROGRAM

National Consortium for Graduate Degrees for Minorities in Engineering and Science (GEM)
Attn: Manager, Fellowships Administration
1430 Duke Street
Alexandria, VA 22314
(703) 562-3646　　　　　　　　Fax: (202) 207-3518
E-mail: info@gemfellowship.org
Web: www.gemfellowship.org

Summary To provide financial assistance and summer work experience to African American and other underrepresented minority students interested in working on a master's degree in engineering or computer science.

Eligibility This program is open to U.S. citizens and permanent residents who are members of ethnic groups underrepresented in engineering: Blacks/African Americans, American Indians/Native Americans, or Latinos/Hispanic Americans. Applicants must be a senior or graduate of an ABET-accredited engineering or computer science program and have an academic record that indicates the ability to pursue graduate studies in engineering (including a GPA of 2.8 or higher). They must agree to apply to at least 3 of the 106 GEM member universities that offer a master's degree and to intern during summers with a sponsoring GEM employer.

Financial data Full fellows receive 1) a stipend of $4,000 per semester; 2) full tuition and fees at the GEM member university; and 3) a salary during the summer work assignment as a GEM summer intern. Associate fellows receive the stipend and payment of tuition and fees, but are not offered a summer salary. University fellows receive only payment of tuition from a participating university.

Duration Up to 4 semesters; full fellows also receive summer work internships lasting 10 to 14 weeks for up to 2 summers.

Additional information During the summer internship, each fellow is assigned an engineering project in a research setting. Each project is based on the fellow's interest and background and is carried out under the supervision of an experienced engineer. At the conclusion of the internship, each fellow writes a project report. Recipients must work on a master's degree in the same engineering discipline as their baccalaureate degree.

Number awarded Varies each year; recently, 48 full fellowships, 6 associate fellowships, and 11 university fellowships were awarded.

Deadline November of each year.

[893]
GEM PH.D. ENGINEERING FELLOWSHIP PROGRAM

National Consortium for Graduate Degrees for Minorities in Engineering and Science (GEM)
Attn: Manager, Fellowships Administration
1430 Duke Street
Alexandria, VA 22314
(703) 562-3646　　　　　　　　Fax: (202) 207-3518
E-mail: info@gemfellowship.org
Web: www.gemfellowship.org

Summary To provide financial assistance and summer work experience to African Americans and other underrepresented minority students interested in obtaining a Ph.D. degree in engineering.

Eligibility This program is open to U.S. citizens and permanent residents who are members of ethnic groups underrepresented in engineering: Blacks/African Americans, American Indians/Native Americans, and Latinos/Hispanic Americans. Applicants must be college seniors, master's degree students, or graduates of an ABET-accredited program in engineering and have an academic record that indicates the ability to work on a doctoral degree in engineering (including a GPA of 3.0 or higher). They must agree to apply to at least 3 of the 102 GEM member universities that offer a doctoral degree in engineering and to intern during summer with a sponsoring GEM employer.

Financial data For full fellows, the stipend is $16,000 for the first year; in subsequent years, fellows receive full payment of tuition and fees plus an additional stipend and assistantship from their university that is equivalent to funding received by other doctoral students in their department. They also receive a paid internship during the summer following their first year of study. Associate fellows receive the same first-year stipend and payment of tuition and fees for subsequent years, but the additional stipend paid by the university is optional.

Duration 3 to 5 years for the fellowship; 12 weeks during the summer immediately after sponsorship for the internship.

Additional information This program is valid only at 1 of the 106 participating GEM member universities; contact GEM for a list. The fellowship award is designed to support the student in the first year of the doctoral program without working. Subsequent years may be subsidized by the respective universities and will usually include either a teaching or research assistantship. Recipients must participate in the GEM summer internship; failure to agree to accept the internship cancels the fellowship.

Number awarded Varies each year; recently, 26 full fellowships and 15 associate fellowships were awarded.

Deadline November of each year.

[894]
GEM PH.D. SCIENCE FELLOWSHIP PROGRAM

National Consortium for Graduate Degrees for Minorities in Engineering and Science (GEM)
Attn: Manager, Fellowships Administration
1430 Duke Street
Alexandria, VA 22314
(703) 562-3646　　　　　　　　Fax: (202) 207-3518
E-mail: info@gemfellowship.org
Web: www.gemfellowship.org

Summary To provide financial assistance and summer work experience to African Americans and other underrepresented minority students interested in working on a Ph.D. degree in the life sciences, mathematics, or physical sciences.

Eligibility This program is open to U.S. citizens and permanent residents who are members of ethnic groups underrepresented in the natural sciences: Blacks/African Americans, American Indians/Native Americans, and Latinos/Hispanic Americans. Applicants must be college seniors, master's degree students, or recent graduates in the biological sciences, mathematics, or physical sciences (chemistry, computer science, environmental sciences, and physics) with an academic record that indicates the ability to pursue doctoral studies (including a GPA of 3.0 or higher). They must agree to apply to at least 3 of the 106 GEM member universities that offer a doctoral degree in science and to intern during summer with a sponsoring GEM employer.

Financial data For full fellows, the stipend is $16,000 for the first year; in subsequent years, fellows receive full payment of tuition and fees plus an additional stipend and assistantship from their university that is equivalent to funding received by other doctoral students in their department. They also receive a paid internship during the summer following their first year of study. Associate fellows receive the same first-year stipend and payment of tuition and fees for subsequent years, but the additional stipend paid by the university is optional.

Duration 3 to 5 years for the fellowship; 12 weeks during the summer immediately after sponsorship for the internship.

Additional information This program is valid only at 1 of 106 participating GEM member universities; contact GEM for a list. The fellowship award is designed to support the student in the first year of the doctoral program without working. Subsequent years are subsidized by the respective university and will usually include either a teaching or research assistantship. Recipients must participate in the GEM summer internship; failure to agree to accept the internship cancels the fellowship. Recipients must enroll in the same scientific discipline as their undergraduate major.

Number awarded Varies each year; recently, 28 full fellowships and 14 associate fellowships were awarded.

Deadline November of each year.

[895]
GENERATION GOOGLE SCHOLARSHIPS FOR CURRENT UNIVERSITY STUDENTS

Google Inc.
Attn: Scholarships
1600 Amphitheatre Parkway
Mountain View, CA 94043-8303
(650) 253-0000   Fax: (650) 253-0001
E-mail: generationgoogle@google.com
Web: www.google.com

Summary To provide financial assistance to members of African American and other underrepresented groups enrolled as undergraduate or graduate students in a computer-related field.

Eligibility This program is open to students enrolled as full-time undergraduate or graduate students at a college or university in the United States or Canada. Applicants must be members of a group underrepresented in computer science: African Americans, Hispanics, American Indians, or Filipinos/Native Hawaiians/Pacific Islanders. They must be working on a degree in computer science, computer engineering, or a closely-related field. Selection is based on academic achievement, leadership, and passion for computer science and technology.

Financial data The stipend is $10,000 per year for U.S. students or $C5,000 for Canadian students.

Duration 1 year; may be renewed.

Additional information Recipients are also invited to attend Google's Computer Science Summer Institute at Mountain View, California, Seattle, Washington, or Cambridge, Massachusetts in the summer.

Number awarded Varies each year.

Deadline February of each year.

[896]
GE-NMF PRIMARY CARE LEADERSHIP PROGRAM

National Medical Fellowships, Inc.
Attn: Scholarship Program
347 Fifth Avenue, Suite 510
New York, NY 10016
(212) 483-8880   Toll Free: (877) NMF-1DOC
Fax: (212) 483-8897   E-mail: pclpinfo@nmfonline.org
Web: www.nmfonline.org

Summary To provide funding to African American and other underrepresented medical and nursing students who wish to participate in a summer mentored clinical experience in selected communities.

Eligibility This program is open to members of underrepresented minority groups (African American, Hispanic/Latino, American Indian, Native Hawaiian, Alaska Native, Vietnamese, Cambodian, or Native Pacific Islander) and/or socioeconomically disadvantaged students. U.S. citizenship is required. Applicants must be currently enrolled in an accredited medical school or graduate-level nursing degree program. They must be interested in a mentored clinical service-learning experience that includes a site-specific independent project at a community health center in Atlanta, Boston/Lynn, Chicago, Houston, Los Angeles, Miami, Mound Bayou (Mississippi), New York, Phoenix, Rochester (New York), or Seattle. Along with their application, they must submit documentation of financial status; a short biography; a resume; 2 letters of recommendation; and a 500-word personal statement on their experiences working in or being part of a medically underserved population and how those experiences have impacted their educational path, professional aspirations, and decision to apply to this program.

Financial data The stipend is $5,000. Funds are expected to cover travel, living, and lodging expenses.

Duration Scholars are required to complete 200 clinical service-learning hours within a 6- to 8-week period during the summer following receipt of the award.

Additional information Funding for this program, which began in 2012 and is administered by National Medical Fellowships (NMF), is provided by the GE Foundation.

Number awarded Varies each year, recently, 59 were granted: 2 in Atlanta, 2 in Boston/Lynn, 8 in Chicago, 5 in Houston, 12 in Los Angeles, 8 in Miami, 2 in Bound Bayou, 2 in New York, 8 in Phoenix, 4 in Rochester, and 6 in Seattle.

Deadline March of each year.

[897]
GEOCORPS AMERICA DIVERSITY INTERNSHIPS

Geological Society of America
Attn: Program Officer, GeoCorps America
3300 Penrose Place
P.O. Box 9140
Boulder, CO 80301-9140
(303) 357-1025   Toll Free: (800) 472-1988, ext. 1025
Fax: (303) 357-1070   E-mail: mdawson@geosociety.org
Web: rock.geosociety.org

Summary To provide work experience at national parks to student members of the Geological Society of America (GSA) who are African Americans or members of other underrepresented groups.

Eligibility This program is open to all GSA members, but applications are especially encouraged from groups historically underrepresented in the sciences (African Americans, American Indians, Alaska Natives, Hispanics, Native Hawaiians, other Pacific Islanders, and persons with disabilities). Applicants must be interested in a short-term work experience in facilities of the U.S. government. Geoscience knowledge and skills are a significant requirement for most positions, but students from diverse disciplines (e.g., chemistry, physics, engineering, mathematics, computer science, ecology, hydrology, meteorology, the social sciences, and the humanities) are also invited to apply. Activities involve research; interpretation and education; inventory and monitoring; or mapping, surveying, and GIS. Prior interns are not eligible. U.S. citizenship or possession of a proper visa is required.

Financial data Each internship provides a $2,750 stipend. Also provided are free housing or a housing allowance of $1,500 to $2,000.

Duration 3 months during the spring, summer, fall, or winter.

Additional information This program is offered by the GSA in partnership with the National Park Service, the U.S. Forest Service, and the Bureau of Land Management.

Number awarded Varies each year.

Deadline March of each year for spring or summer positions; June of each year for fall or winter positions.

[898]
GEOLOGICAL SOCIETY OF AMERICA GRADUATE STUDENT RESEARCH GRANTS

Geological Society of America
Attn: Program Officer-Grants, Awards and Recognition
3300 Penrose Place
P.O. Box 9140
Boulder, CO 80301-9140
(303) 357-1060   Toll Free: (888) 443-4472, ext. 1060
Fax: (303) 357-1070   E-mail: awards@geosociety.org
Web: www.geosociety.org/grants/gradgrants.htm

Summary To provide funding to African American and other underrepresented graduate student members of the Geological Society of America (GSA) interested in conducting research at universities in the United States, Canada, Mexico, or Central America.

Eligibility This program is open to GSA members working on a master's or doctoral degree at a university in the United States, Canada, Mexico, or Central America. Applicants must be interested in conducting geological research. Minorities, women, and persons with disabilities are strongly encouraged to apply. Selection is based on the scientific merits of the proposal, the capability of the investigator, and the reasonableness of the budget.

Financial data Grants range up to $2,500 and recently averaged $1,851. Funds can be used for the cost of travel, room and board in the field, services of a technician or field assistant, funding of chemical and isotope analyses, or other expenses directly related to the fulfillment of the research contract. Support is not provided for the purchase of ordinary field equipment, for maintenance of the families of the grantees and their assistants, as reimbursement for work already accomplished, for institutional overhead, for adviser participation, or for tuition costs.

Duration 1 year.

Additional information In addition to general grants, GSA awards a number of specialized grants.

Number awarded Varies each year; recently, the society awarded nearly 400 grants worth more than $723,000 through this and all of its specialized programs.

Deadline January of each year.

[899]
GEORGE A. LOTTIER GOLF FOUNDATION INTERNSHIP AND SCHOLARSHIP AWARD

Atlanta Tribune: The Magazine
Attn: Editor
875 Old Roswell Road, Suite C-100
Roswell, GA 30076-1660
(770) 587-0501, ext. 202   Fax: (770) 642-6501
E-mail: internship@atlantatribune.com
Web: www.atlantatribune.com/extras

Summary To provide financial assistance and summer work experience at the *Atlanta Tribune: The Magazine* to African American and other minority upper-division and graduate students from any state interested in a career in print journalism.

Eligibility This program is open to minority college students from any state entering their junior or senior year of college or enrolled in a graduate program with a GPA of 3.0 or higher. Applicants must be majoring in a field related to print media, including communications, English, graphic design (with an emphasis on publication layout and design), journalism, marketing, or sales. Along with their application, they must submit a 500-word personal essay.

Financial data The program provides a paid internship and a scholarship stipend of $1,500.

Duration 1 year, including 10 weeks during the summer for the internship.

Number awarded Varies each year; recently, 4 of these scholarships and internships were awarded.

Deadline November of each year.

[900]
GEORGE A. STRAIT MINORITY SCHOLARSHIP ENDOWMENT

American Association of Law Libraries
Attn: Chair, Scholarships Committee
105 West Adams Street, Suite 3300
Chicago, IL 60603
(312) 939-4764   Fax: (312) 431-1097
E-mail: scholarships@aall.org
Web: www.aallnet.org

Summary To provide financial assistance to African American or other minority college seniors or college graduates who are interested in becoming law librarians.

Eligibility This program is open to college graduates with meaningful law library experience who are members of minority groups and intend to have a career in law librarianship. Applicants must be degree candidates at an ALA-accredited library school or an ABA-accredited law school.

Along with their application, they must submit a personal statement that discusses their interest in law librarianship, reason for applying for this scholarship, career goals as a law librarian, and any other pertinent information.

Financial data The stipend is $3,500.

Duration 1 year.

Additional information This program, established in 1990, is currently supported by Thomson Reuters.

Number awarded Varies each year; recently, 6 were awarded.

Deadline March of each year.

[901]
GEORGE AND PEARL STRICKLAND SCHOLARSHIP FUND

Community Foundation for Greater Atlanta, Inc.
191 Peachtree Street N.E., Suite 1000
Atlanta, GA 30303
(404) 688-5525   Fax: (404) 688-3060
E-mail: scholarships@cfgreateratlanta.org
Web: www.cfgreateratlanta.org

Summary To provide financial assistance to Georgia residents attending or planning to attend designated Historically Black Colleges and Universities in the Atlanta area.

Eligibility This program is open to residents of Georgia enrolled or accepted for enrollment as undergraduate or graduate students at Clark Atlanta University, Morehouse College, Morehouse School of Medicine, or Spelman College. Applicants must have a GPA of 2.0 or higher and be able to demonstrate financial need, potential for success in their chosen field, and commitment to community service.

Financial data The stipend ranges from $1,000 to $2,000 per year.

Duration 1 year; may be renewed.

Number awarded 20 to 30 each year.

Deadline February of each year.

[902]
GEORGE E. MEARES MEMORIAL SCHOLARSHIP

Omega Psi Phi Fraternity
Attn: Charles R. Drew Memorial Scholarship Commission
3951 Snapfinger Parkway
Decatur, GA 30035-3203
(404) 284-5533   Fax: (404) 284-0333
E-mail: scholarshipchairman@oppf.org
Web: www.oppf.org/scholarship

Summary To provide financial assistance to graduate student members of Omega Psi Phi Fraternity in selected social science fields.

Eligibility This program is open to Omega Psi Phi members who are interested in working on a graduate degree in social work, criminal justice, or social sciences. Applicants must include a statement of 200 to 250 words on their purpose for applying for this scholarship, how they believe funds from the fraternity can assist them in achieving their career goals, and other circumstances (including financial need) that make it important for them to receive financial assistance.

Financial data The stipend is $5,000.

Duration 1 year.

Additional information This program, established in 1977, is named for George E. Meares, who served as Grand Basileus of Omega Psi Phi (an historically Black fraternity) from 1964 to 1967. The winner is required to attend the Omega Psi Phi Grand Conclave or Leadership Conference. Up to $1,000 in travel expenses for attendance is provided.

Number awarded 1 each year.

Deadline April of each year.

[903]
GERBER SCHOLARSHIP IN PEDIATRICS

National Medical Fellowships, Inc.
Attn: Scholarship Program
347 Fifth Avenue, Suite 510
New York, NY 10016
(212) 483-8880   Toll Free: (877) NMF-1DOC
Fax: (212) 483-8897 E-mail: scholarships@nmfonline.org
Web: www.nmfonline.org

Summary To provide financial assistance to African American and other underrepresented minority medical students who are interested in pediatrics.

Eligibility This program is open to African Americans, Hispanics/Latinos, Native Americans, Vietnamese, Cambodians, and Pacific Islanders who are enrolled in medical school. Applicants must be interested in pediatrics with an emphasis on nutrition. They must be U.S. citizens or DACA students. Selection is based on leadership, commitment to serving medically underserved communities, and financial need.

Financial data The stipend is $5,000.

Duration 1 year.

Additional information This program, which began in 1997, is supported by Gerber.

Number awarded 2 each year.

Deadline September of each year.

[904]
GO RED MULTICULTURAL SCHOLARSHIP FUND

American Heart Association
Attn: Go Red for Women
7272 Greenville Avenue
Dallas, TX 75231-4596
Toll Free: (800) AHA-USA1
E-mail: GoRedScholarship@heart.org
Web: www.goredforwomen.org

Summary To provide financial assistance to women who are African Americans or members of other multicultural groups who are preparing for a career in a field of health care.

Eligibility This program is open to women who are currently enrolled at an accredited college, university, health care institution, or program and have a GPA of 3.0 or higher. Applicants must be U.S. citizens or permanent residents of African American, Hispanic, Asian/Pacific Islander, or other minority origin. They must be working on an undergraduate or graduate degree as preparation for a career as a nurse, physician, or allied health care worker. Selection is based on community involvement, a personal essay, transcripts, and 2 letters of recommendation.

Financial data The stipend is $2,500.

Duration 1 year.

Additional information This program, which began in 2012, is supported by Macy's.

Number awarded   16 each year.

Deadline   December of each year.

[905]
GOLDMAN SACHS MBA FELLOWSHIP

Goldman Sachs
Attn: Human Capital Management
200 West Street, 25th Floor
New York, NY 10282
E-mail: Iris.Birungi@gs.com
Web: www.goldmansachs.com

Summary   To provide financial assistance and work experience to African American and other underrepresented minority students interested in working on an M.B.A. degree.

Eligibility   This program is open to graduate students of Black, Hispanic, or Native American descent who are interested in working on an M.B.A. degree. Applicants must be preparing for a career in the financial services industry. Along with their application, they must submit 2 essays of 500 words or less on the following topics: 1) why they are preparing for a career in the financial services industry; and 2) their current involvement with a community-based organization. Selection is based on analytical skills and the ability to identify significant problems, gather facts, and analyze situations in depth; interpersonal skills, including, but not limited to, poise, confidence, and professionalism; academic record; evidence of hard work and commitment; ability to work well with others; and commitment to community involvement.

Financial data   Fellows receive $25,000 toward payment of tuition and living expenses for the first year of business school; an internship at a domestic office of Goldman Sachs during the summer after the first year of business school; and (after successful completion of the summer internship and acceptance of an offer to return to the firm after graduation as a full-time regular employee) either payment of tuition costs for the second year of business school or an additional $25,000 toward tuition and living costs.

Duration   Up to 2 years.

Additional information   This program was initiated in 1997.

Number awarded   1 or more each year.

Deadline   November of each year.

[906]
GOLDSTEIN AND SCHNEIDER SCHOLARSHIPS BY THE MACEY FUND

Society for Industrial and Organizational Psychology Inc.
Attn: SIOP Foundation
440 East Poe Road, Suite 101
Bowling Green, OH 43402
(419) 353-0032   Fax: (419) 352-2645
E-mail: siopfoundation@siop.org
Web: www.siop.org/SIOPAwards/thornton.aspx

Summary   To provide funding to African American and other minority student members of the Society for Industrial and Organizational Psychology (SIOP) who are conducting doctoral research.

Eligibility   This program is open to student affiliate members of SIOP who are enrolled full time in a doctoral program in industrial and organizational (I/O) psychology or a closely-related field at an accredited college or university. Applicants must be members of an ethnic minority group (African/Caribbean American, Native American/Alaskan Native, Asian/Pacific American, or Latino/Hispanic American). They must have an approved dissertation plan that has potential to make significant theoretical and application contributions to the field of I/O psychology.

Financial data   The stipend is $3,000. Students may elect to have the funds paid to them directly or to be deposited into a "professional development" account at their university.

Duration   1 academic year.

Additional information   The SIOP is Division 14 of the American Psychological Association. This program consists of the Benjamin Schneider Scholarship (offered in odd-numbered years) and the Irwin L. Goldstein Scholarship (offered in even-numbered years).

Number awarded   1 each year.

Deadline   October of each year.

[907]
GORDON STAFFORD SCHOLARSHIP IN ARCHITECTURE

Stafford King Wiese Architects
Attn: Scholarship Selection Committee
622 20th Street
Sacramento, CA 95811
(916) 930-5900   Fax: (916) 290-0100
E-mail: info@skwaia.com
Web: www.skwarchitects.com/about/scholarship

Summary   To provide financial assistance to African Americans and members of other minority groups from California interested in studying architecture at a college in any state.

Eligibility   This program is open to California residents currently enrolled at accredited schools of architecture in any state as first-year new or first-year transfer students and working on a bachelor's or 5-year master's degree. Applicants must be able to demonstrate minority status (defined as Black, Hispanic, Native American, Pacific Asian, or Asian Indian). They must submit a 500-word statement expressing their desire to prepare for a career in architecture. Finalists are interviewed and must travel to Sacramento, California at their own expense for the interview.

Financial data   The stipend is $3,000 per year. That includes $1,500 deposited in the recipient's school account and $1,500 paid to the recipient directly.

Duration   1 year; may be renewed up to 4 additional years.

Additional information   This program began in 1995.

Number awarded   Up to 5 each year.

Deadline   June of each year.

[908]
GRADUATE FELLOWSHIP IN THE HISTORY OF SCIENCE

American Geophysical Union
Attn: History of Geophysics
2000 Florida Avenue, N.W.
Washington, DC 20009-1277
(202) 777-7522   Toll Free: (800) 966-2481
Fax: (202) 328-0566
E-mail: HistoryofGeophysics@agu.org
Web: education.agu.org

Summary To provide funding to doctoral candidates, especially African Americans and other underrepresented students, who are conducting dissertation research in the history of geophysics.

Eligibility This program is open to doctoral candidates at U.S. institutions who have passed all preliminary examinations. Applicants must be completing a dissertation in the history of the geophysical sciences, including topics related to atmospheric sciences, biogeosciences, geodesy, geomagnetism and paleomagnetism, hydrology, ocean sciences, planetary sciences, seismology, space physics, aeronomy, tectonophysics, volcanology, geochemistry, and petrology. They must submit a cover letter with a curriculum vitae, undergraduate and graduate transcripts, a 10-page description of the dissertation topic and proposed research plan, and 3 letters of recommendation. U.S. citizenship or permanent resident status is required. Applications are encouraged from women, minorities, and students with disabilities who are traditionally underrepresented in the geophysical sciences.

Financial data The grant is $5,000; funds are to be used to assist with the costs of travel to obtain archival or research materials.

Duration 1 year.

Number awarded 1 each year.

Deadline September of each year.

[909]
GRADUATE RESEARCH FELLOWSHIP PROGRAM OF THE NATIONAL SCIENCE FOUNDATION

National Science Foundation
Directorate for Education and Human Resources
Attn: Division of Graduate Education
4201 Wilson Boulevard, Room 875S
Arlington, VA 22230
(703) 331-3542   Toll Free: (866) NSF-GRFP
Fax: (703) 292-9048   E-mail: info@nsfgrfp.org
Web: www.nsf.gov/funding/pgm_summ.jsp?pims_id=6201

Summary To provide financial assistance to African American and other underrepresented graduate students interested in working on a master's or doctoral degree in fields supported by the National Science Foundation (NSF).

Eligibility This program is open to U.S. citizens, nationals, and permanent residents who wish to work on research-based master's or doctoral degrees in a field of science, technology, engineering, or mathematics (STEM) supported by NSF (including astronomy, chemistry, computer and information sciences and engineering, geosciences, engineering, life sciences, materials research, mathematical sciences, physics, psychology, social sciences, or STEM education and learning). Other work in medical, dental, law, public health, or practice-oriented professional degree programs, or in joint science-professional degree programs, such as M.D./Ph.D. and J.D./Ph.D. programs, is not eligible. Applications normally should be submitted during the senior year in college or in the first year of graduate study; eligibility is limited to those who have completed no more than 12 months of graduate study since completion of a baccalaureate degree. Applicants who have already earned an advanced degree in science, engineering, or medicine (including an M.D., D.D.S., or D.V.M.) are ineligible. Selection is based on 1) intellectual merit of the proposed activity: strength of the academic record, proposed plan of research, previous research experience, references, appropriateness of the choice of institution; and 2) broader impacts of the proposed activity: how well does the activity advance discovery and understanding, how well does it broaden the participation of underrepresented groups (e.g., women, minorities, persons with disabilities, veterans), to what extent will it enhance the infrastructure for research and education, will the results be disseminated broadly to enhance scientific and technological understanding, what may be the benefits of the proposed activity to society).

Financial data The stipend is $32,000 per year; an additional $12,000 cost-of-education allowance is provided to the recipient's institution.

Duration Up to 3 years, usable over a 5-year period.

Number awarded Approximately 2,000 each year.

Deadline October of each year.

[910]
GREAT LAKES SECTION IFT DIVERSITY SCHOLARSHIP

Institute of Food Technologists-Great Lakes Section
c/o Andrea Kirk, Scholarship Chair
Post Foods, LLC
275 Cliff Street
Battle Creek, MI 49014
E-mail: greatlakesift@gmail.com
Web: www.greatlakesift.org/student-scholarships

Summary To provide financial assistance to African American and other minority members of the Great Lakes Section of the Institute of Food Technologists (IFT) from any state who are working on an undergraduate or graduate degree related to food technology at a college in Michigan.

Eligibility This program is open to minority residents of any state who are members of the IFT Great Lakes Section (GLS) and working full time on an undergraduate or graduate degree in food science, nutrition, food engineering, food packaging, or related fields at a college or university in Michigan. Applicants must have a GPA of 3.0 or higher and plans for a career in the food industry. Along with their application, they must submit a 1-page personal statement that covers their academic program, future plans and career goals, extracurricular activities (including involvement in community, university, GLS, or national IFT activities), and work experience. Financial need is not considered in the selection process.

Financial data The stipend is $1,000.

Duration 1 year; nonrenewable.

Number awarded 1 each year.

Deadline February of each year.

[911]
GREATER HARTFORD CHAPTER NABA SCHOLARSHIP ESSAY CONTEST

National Association of Black Accountants-Greater Hartford Chapter
Attn: Ronita Fisher, Scholarship Committee
P.O. Box 0242
Hartford, CT 06141
E-mail: nabaghc@gmail.com
Web: www.nabahartford.org/scholarships.php

Summary To recognize and reward, with scholarships for additional study, undergraduate and graduate accounting students, especially African Americans and other minorities, at colleges and universities in southern and western New England who submit outstanding essays.

Eligibility This competition is open to undergraduate and graduate accounting students enrolled full time at 2- and 4-year colleges and universities in southern and western New England. Graduate students must have entered graduate school immediately after receiving their undergraduate degree. Applicants must submit an essay of 500 to 700 words on their choice of 3 assigned topics that change annually but relate to minorities in accounting. They must also submit a 100-word personal statement describing their involvement in the National Association of Black Accountants (NABA), career objectives, leadership ability, and community activities. In the selection process, consideration is also given to academic excellence, civic responsibility in the community, and need. All students are eligible to apply, but a goal of the sponsoring organization is to address the concerns of minorities entering the accounting profession.

Financial data The award is a $1,000 scholarship.

Duration The competition is held annually.

Additional information This program began in 2008.

Number awarded Up to 10 each year.

Deadline March of each year.

[912]
GREENSPOON MARDER DIVERSITY SCHOLARSHIP PROGRAM FOR LAW STUDENTS

Community Foundation of Sarasota County
Attn: Grants and Scholarships Coordinator
2635 Fruitville Road
P.O. Box 49587
Sarasota, FL 34230-6587
(941) 556-7114   Fax: (941) 952-7115
E-mail: eyoung@cfsarasota.org
Web: www.cfsarasota.org

Summary To provide financial assistance to African American and other minority students from any state attending designated law schools (most of which are in Florida).

Eligibility This program is open to racial and ethnic minority students from any state who are members of groups traditionally underrepresented in the legal profession. Applicants must be entering their second year of full-time study at the University of Florida Levin College of Law, Florida State University College of Law, Stetson University College of Law, Nova Southeastern University Shepard Broad Law Center, St. Thomas University School of Law, Howard University College of Law, Texas Southern University Thurgood Marshall School of Law, Florida Coastal School of Law, or Florida International University College of Law. They must have a GPA of 2.6 or higher. Along with their application, they must submit a 1,000-word personal statement that describes their personal strengths, their contributions through community service, any special or unusual circumstances that may have affected their academic performance, or their personal and family history of educational or socioeconomic disadvantage; it should include aspects of their minority racial or ethnic identity that are relevant to their application. Applicants may also include information about their financial circumstances if they wish to have those considered in the selection process. U.S. citizenship or permanent resident status is required.

Financial data The stipend is $2,500 per semester.

Duration 1 semester (the spring semester of the second year of law school); may be renewed 1 additional semester (the fall semester of the third year).

Additional information This program was established by the Florida law firm Ruden McClosky, which was acquired by the firm Greenspoon Marder in 2011. It is administered by the Community Foundation of Sarasota County, but the law firm selects the recipients.

Number awarded 1 or more each year.

Deadline July of each year.

[913]
H. CARL MOULTRIE I LEGAL SCHOLAR AWARD

Omega Psi Phi Fraternity
Attn: Charles R. Drew Memorial Scholarship Commission
3951 Snapfinger Parkway
Decatur, GA 30035-3203
(404) 284-5533   Fax: (404) 284-0333
E-mail: scholarshipchairman@oppf.org
Web: www.oppf.org/scholarship

Summary To provide financial assistance for law school to members of Omega Psi Phi who have an outstanding academic record.

Eligibility This program is open to members of the fraternity who are currently enrolled full time at an accredited school of law and working on a J.D. or equivalent degree. Applicants must have demonstrated service to the fraternity during the year of application and be in good financial standing at all levels. Along with their application, they must submit a statement of 200 to 250 words on their purpose for applying for this scholarship, how they believe funds from the fraternity can assist them in achieving their career goals, and other circumstances (including financial need) that make it important for them to receive financial assistance. Selection is based on academic excellence.

Financial data The stipend is $5,000.

Duration 1 year.

Additional information The winner is required to attend the Omega Psi Phi Grand Conclave or Leadership Conference. Up to $1,000 in travel expenses for attendance is provided.

Number awarded 1 each year.

Deadline April of each year.

[914]
HARRY R. KENDALL LEADERSHIP DEVELOPMENT SCHOLARSHIPS

United Methodist Church
General Board of Global Ministries
Attn: United Methodist Committee on Relief
Health and Welfare Ministries
475 Riverside Drive, Room 330
New York, NY 10115
(212) 870-3871   Toll Free: (800) UMC-GBGM
E-mail: jyoung@gbgm-umc.org
Web: umc-gbcs.org/conference-connections/grants

Summary To provide financial assistance to African Americans who are Methodists or other Christians and preparing for a career in a health-related field.

Eligibility This program is open to undergraduate and graduate students who are U.S. citizens or permanent residents of African American descent. Applicants must be professed Christians, preferably United Methodists. They must be planning to enter a health care field or already be a practitioner in such a field. Financial need is considered in the selection process.

Financial data The stipend is $2,000.

Duration 1 year.

Additional information This program began in 1980.

Number awarded Varies each year.

Deadline June of each year.

[915]
HARVEY LILLARD SCHOLARSHIP

American Black Chiropractic Association
3915 Cascade Road, Suite 220
Atlanta, GA 30331
(404) 647-BACK   Fax: (404) 699-0988
E-mail: info@abchiro.com
Web: abchiro.com/students/harvey-lillard-scholarship

Summary To provide financial assistance to members of the Student American Black Chiropractic Association (SABCA) who are attending a school of chiropractic.

Eligibility This program is open to SABCA members currently enrolled at an accredited college of chiropractic. Applicants must submit an essay that covers 1) an accomplishment of which they are most proud; 2) any unique challenge or circumstance they face while pursuing their chiropractic or pre-chiropractic education; 3) what they see as challenges and opportunities for the chiropractic profession within the African American community; 4) they vision they see for the chiropractic profession and the American Black Chiropractic Association; and 5) how and why they chose chiropractic.

Financial data A stipend is awarded (amount not specified).

Duration 1 year.

Number awarded Several each year.

Deadline May of each year.

[916]
HAYNES/HETTING AWARD

Philanthrofund Foundation
Attn: Scholarship Committee
1409 Willow Street, Suite 109
Minneapolis, MN 55403-2241
(612) 870-1806   Toll Free: (800) 435-1402
Fax: (612) 871-6587   E-mail: info@PfundOnline.org
Web: www.pfundonline.org/scholarships.html

Summary To provide funds to African American and Native American Minnesota students who have supported gay, lesbian, bisexual, and transgender (GLBT) activities.

Eligibility This program is open to residents of Minnesota and students attending a Minnesota educational institution who are African American or Native American. Applicants must be self-identified as GLBT or from a GLBT family. They may be attending or planning to attend a trade school, technical college, college, or university (as an undergraduate or graduate student). Selection is based on the applicant's 1) affirmation of GLBT or allied identity; 2) evidence of experience and skills in service and leadership; and 3) evidence of service, leading, and working for change in GLBT communi-

ties, including serving as a role model, mentor, and/or adviser.

Financial data The stipend is $5,000. Funds must be used for tuition, books, fees, or dissertation expenses.

Duration 1 year.

Number awarded 1 each year.

Deadline January of each year.

[917]
HAYNES RICE AWARD

National Association of Health Services Executives
Attn: Educational Assistance Program
1050 Connecticut Avenue, N.W., Tenth Floor
Washington, DC 20036
(202) 772-1030   Fax: (202) 772-1072
E-mail: nahsehg@nahse.org
Web: www.nahse.org/student-scholarships.html

Summary To provide financial assistance to African Americans who are members of the National Association of Health Services Executives (NAHSE) and interested in preparing for a career in health care administration.

Eligibility This program is open to African Americans who are either enrolled or accepted at an accredited college or university to work on a master's or doctoral degree in health care administration. Applicants must be members of NAHSE and able to demonstrate financial need. They must have a GPA of 2.5 or higher as undergraduates or 3.0 or higher as graduate students. Along with their application, they must submit a 3-page essay that describes themselves and their career goals, commitment and interest in health care management, and financial need.

Financial data The stipend is $2,500. Funds are sent to the recipient's institution.

Duration 1 year.

Number awarded 1 each year.

Deadline May of each year.

[918]
HEALTH POLICY RESEARCH SCHOLARS

Robert Wood Johnson Foundation
50 College Road East
Princeton, NJ 08540-6614
Toll Free: (877) 843-RWJF   E-mail: mail@rwjf.org
Web: www.rwjf.org

Summary To provide funding to African American and other doctoral students from diverse backgrounds interested in working on a degree related to health policy.

Eligibility This program is open to full-time doctoral students in the first or second year of their program. Applicants must be from underrepresented populations or disadvantaged backgrounds (e.g., first-generation college students, individuals from lower socioeconomic backgrounds, members of racial and ethnic groups underrepresented in doctoral programs, people with disabilities). They must be working on a degree in a field related to health policy, such as urban planning, political science, economics, ethnography, education, social work, or sociology; the program is not intended for students working on a clinical doctorate without a research focus. Prior experience or knowledge in health policy is neither required nor expected.

Financial data The stipend is $30,000 per year. Scholars are also eligible for $10,000 research grants if their dissertation is related to health policy.

Duration Up to 4 years. Participants may continue in the program without the annual stipend for a fifth year or until they complete their doctoral program, whichever occurs first.

Number awarded Up to 50 each year.

Deadline March of each year.

[919]
HEALTH RESEARCH AND EDUCATIONAL TRUST SCHOLARSHIPS

New Jersey Hospital Association
Attn: Health Research and Educational Trust
760 Alexander Road
P.O. Box 1
Princeton, NJ 08543-0001
(609) 275-4224   Fax: (609) 452-8097
E-mail: jhritz@njha.com
Web: www.njha.com/education/scholarships

Summary To provide financial assistance to New Jersey residents, especially African Americans and other minorities, who are working on an undergraduate or graduate degree in a field related to health care administration at a school in any state.

Eligibility This program is open to residents of New Jersey enrolled in an upper-division or graduate program in hospital or health care administration, public administration, nursing, or other allied health profession at a school in any state. Graduate students working on an advanced degree to prepare to teach nursing are also eligible. Applicants must have a GPA of 3.0 or higher and be able to demonstrate financial need. Along with their application, they must submit a 2-page essay (on which 50% of the selection is based) describing their academic plans for the future. Minorities and women are especially encouraged to apply.

Financial data The stipend is $2,000.

Duration 1 year.

Additional information This program began in 1983.

Number awarded Varies each year; recently, 3 were awarded.

Deadline June of each year.

[920]
HELENE M. OVERLY MEMORIAL GRADUATE SCHOLARSHIP

Women's Transportation Seminar
Attn: WTS Foundation
1701 K Street, N.W., Suite 800
Washington, DC 20006
(202) 955-5085   Fax: (202) 955-5088
E-mail: wts@wtsinternational.org
Web: www.wtsinternational.org/education/scholarships

Summary To provide financial assistance to women graduate students, especially African Americans and other minorities, who are interested in preparing for a career in transportation.

Eligibility This program is open to women who are enrolled in a graduate degree program in a transportation-related field (e.g., transportation engineering, planning, finance, or logistics). Applicants must have at least a 3.0 GPA

and be interested in a career in transportation. Along with their application, they must submit a 750-word statement about their career goals after graduation and why they think they should receive the scholarship award. Applications must be submitted first to a local chapter; the chapters forward selected applications for consideration on the national level. Minority women are particularly encouraged to apply. Selection is based on transportation involvement and goals, job skills, and academic record.

Financial data The stipend is $10,000.

Duration 1 year.

Additional information This program began in 1981. Local chapters may also award additional funding to winners in their area.

Number awarded 1 each year.

Deadline Applications must be submitted by November to a local WTS chapter.

[921]
HERBERT W. NICKENS MEDICAL STUDENT SCHOLARSHIPS

Association of American Medical Colleges
Attn: Division of Diversity Policy and Programs
655 K Street, N.W., Suite 100
Washington, DC 20001-2399
(202) 862-6203   Fax: (202) 828-1125
E-mail: nickensawards@aamc.org
Web: www.aamc.org/initiatives/awards/nickens-student

Summary To provide financial assistance to African American and other medical students who have demonstrated efforts to address the health-care needs of minorities.

Eligibility This program is open to U.S. citizens and permanent residents entering their third year of study at a U.S. allopathic medical school. Each medical school may nominate 1 student for these awards. The letter must describe the nominee's 1) academic achievement through the first and second year, including special awards and honors, clerkships or special research projects, and extracurricular activities in which the student has shown leadership abilities; 2) leadership efforts to eliminate inequities in medical education and health care; 3) demonstrated leadership efforts in addressing the educational, societal, and health-care needs of minorities; and 4) awards and honors, special research projects, and extracurricular activities in which the student has shown leadership abilities. Nominees must submit a curriculum vitae and a 2-page essay that discusses their leadership efforts in eliminating inequities in medical education and health care for minorities.

Financial data The stipend is $5,000.

Duration 1 year.

Number awarded 5 each year.

Deadline April of each year.

[922]
HERMAN G. GREEN, PHD MEMORIAL SCHOLARSHIP

South Carolina Professional Association for Access and Equity
Attn: Financial Secretary
P.O. Box 71297
North Charleston, SC 29415
(843) 670-4890   E-mail: anderson4569@bellsouth.net
Web: www.scpaae.org/#!scholarships/c11tv

Summary To provide financial assistance to graduate students at colleges and universities in South Carolina who are African Americans or other underrepresented minorities on their campus.

Eligibility This program is open to residents of any state who have completed at least 9 semester hours of graduate study at a college or university in South Carolina. Applicants must be recognized as an underrepresented ethnic minority on their campus. They must have a GPA of 3.5 or higher. Along with their application, they must submit 1) a personal letter on their public service, academic and career goals, honors and awards, leadership skills and organization participation, community service, and a statement of why they would like to receive this scholarship; and 2) a paragraph defining access and equity and describing how they can assist in achieving access and equity within South Carolina. Financial need is not considered in the selection process.

Financial data The stipend is $1,200.

Duration 1 year.

Number awarded 1 or more each year.

Deadline February of each year.

[923]
HERMAN J. NEAL ACCOUNTING TUITION SCHOLARSHIPS

Illinois CPA Society
Attn: CPA Endowment Fund of Illinois
550 West Jackson, Suite 900
Chicago, Il 60661-5716
(312) 993-0407   Toll Free: (800) 993-0407 (within IL)
Fax: (312) 993-9432
Web: www.icpas.org

Summary To provide financial assistance to African American residents of Illinois enrolled as upper-division or graduate students in accounting at a college or university in the state.

Eligibility This program is open to African American residents of Illinois enrolled as juniors, seniors, or graduate student at a college or university in the state. Applicants must be studying accounting and have a GPA of 3.0 or higher. They must be able to demonstrate a commitment to becoming a C.P.A. and financial need. U.S. citizenship or permanent resident status is required.

Financial data The maximum stipend is $4,000 for payment of tuition and fees.

Duration 1 year.

Additional information The scholarship does not cover the cost of C.P.A. examination review courses. Recipients may not receive a full graduate assistantship, fellowship, or scholarship from a college or university, participate in a full-tuition reimbursement cooperative education or internship program, or participate in an employee full-tuition reimbursement program during the scholarship period.

Number awarded Varies each year; recently, 4 were awarded.

Deadline March of each year.

[924]
HOLLY A. CORNELL SCHOLARSHIP

American Water Works Association
Attn: Scholarship Coordinator
6666 West Quincy Avenue
Denver, CO 80235-3098
(303) 794-7771   Toll Free: (800) 926-7337
Fax: (303) 347-0804   E-mail: scholarships@awwa.org
Web: www.awwa.org

Summary To provide financial assistance to African American and other minority students interested in working on an master's degree in the field of water supply and treatment.

Eligibility This program is open to minority and female students working on a master's degree in the field of water supply and treatment at a college or university in Canada, Guam, Mexico, Puerto Rico, or the United States. Students who have been accepted into graduate school but have not yet begun graduate study are encouraged to apply. Applicants must submit a 2-page resume, official transcripts, 3 letters of recommendation, a proposed curriculum of study, a 1-page statement of educational plans and career objectives demonstrating an interest in the drinking water field, and a 3-page proposed plan of research. Selection is based on academic record and potential to provide leadership in the field of water supply and treatment.

Financial data The stipend is $7,500.

Duration 1 year; nonrenewable.

Additional information Funding for this program, which began in 1990, comes from the consulting firm CH2M Hill.

Number awarded 1 each year.

Deadline January of each year.

[925]
HOUSTON CHAPTER NBMBAA SCHOLARSHIP PROGRAM

National Black MBA Association-Houston Chapter
Attn: Scholarship Program
P.O. Box 56509
Houston, TX 77256
(713) 899-8657
E-mail: scholarships@houstonblackmba.net
Web: nbmbaa.pgmsolutions.com

Summary To provide financial assistance to African American business and management students who have a connection to Houston and are working on an undergraduate or master's degree.

Eligibility This program is open to African American students who are either enrolled at a college or university in the Houston area or natives of Houston enrolled at a college or university in the continental United States. Applicants must be sophomores, juniors, seniors, or master's degree students in a business or management program. Along with their application, they must submit an essay of 650 to 1,000 words identifying 5 critical skills they must obtain while they are completing their degree that will make them the most attractive candidate for internships and full-time employment upon graduation. Financial need is not considered in the selection process.

Financial data A stipend is awarded (amount not specified).

Duration 1 year.

Number awarded Varies each year.

Deadline November of each year.

[926]
HOWARD MAYER BROWN FELLOWSHIP

American Musicological Society
6010 College Station
Brunswick, ME 04011-8451
(207) 798-4243   Toll Free: (877) 679-7648
Fax: (207) 798-4254   E-mail: ams@ams-net.org
Web: www.ams-net.org/fellowships/hmb.php

Summary To provide financial assistance to African American and other minority students who are working on a doctoral degree in the field of musicology.

Eligibility This program is open to members of minority groups historically underrepresented in the field of musicology. In the United States, that includes African Americans, Native Americans, Hispanic Americans, and Asian Americans. In Canada, it refers to aboriginal people and visible minorities. Applicants must have completed at least 1 year of full-time academic work at an institution with a graduate program in musicology and be planning to complete a Ph.D. degree in the field. There are no restrictions on research area, age, or sex. U.S. or Canadian citizenship or permanent resident status is required.

Financial data The stipend is $20,000.

Duration 1 year; nonrenewable.

Additional information This fellowship was first awarded in 1995.

Number awarded 1 each year.

Deadline December of each year.

[927]
HOYA VISION CARE DR. CHARLES COMER COMMUNITY SERVICE SCHOLARSHIP

National Optometric Association
Attn: Student Affairs
1801 North Tryon Street, Suite 315
Charlotte, NC 28206
(704) 918-1809   Toll Free: (877) 394-2020
Fax: (877) NOA-2006
E-mail: noastudentdirector@yahoo.com
Web: www.nationaloptometricassociation.com

Summary To provide financial assistance to African American members of the National Optometric Student Association (NOSA).

Eligibility This program is open to African Americans who have completed at least 1 full year at a school or college of optometry and have at least 1 year remaining. Applicants must be active members of NOSA and willing to complete 3 hours of service at the national convention of the National Optometric Association (NOA). They must be have a GPA of 2.5 or higher and be able to demonstrate excellence in community service. Along with their application, they must submit a 1-page essay describing how their community service has

exemplified the mission of the NOA and the importance of becoming an active NOA member. Financial need is not considered in the selection process.

Financial data The stipend is $1,000.

Duration 1 year.

Additional information The National Optometric Association was founded in 1969 with the goal of recruiting minority students, especially African Americans, for schools and colleges of optometry. This program is sponsored by Hoya Vision Care.

Number awarded 1 each year.

Deadline May of each year.

[928]
HUBERTUS W.V. WILLEMS SCHOLARSHIP FOR MALE STUDENTS

POISE Foundation
Two Gateway Center, Suite 1700
603 Stanwix Street
Pittsburgh, PA 15222
(412) 281-4967   Fax: (412) 562-0292
Web: www.poisefoundation.org

Summary To provide funding to males, particularly male members of the National Association for the Advancement of Colored People (NAACP), who are interested in undergraduate or graduate education in selected scientific fields.

Eligibility This program is open to males who are high school seniors, college students, or graduate students. Applicants must be majoring (or planning to major) in 1 of the following fields: engineering, chemistry, physics, or mathematics. Preference is given to members of the NAACP. The required minimum GPA is 2.5 for graduating high school seniors and undergraduate students or 3.0 for graduate students. Undergraduates must be enrolled full time but graduate students may be full- or part-time students. Applicants must be able to demonstrate financial need, defined as a family income of less than $16,755 for a family of 1 ranging to less than $58,335 for a family of 7. Along with their application, they must submit a 1-page essay on their interest in their major and a career, their life's ambition, what they hope to accomplish in their lifetime, and what position they hope to attain. Full-time enrollment is required for undergraduate students, although graduate students may be enrolled full or part time. U.S. citizenship is required.

Financial data The stipend ranges up to $3,000 per year.

Duration 1 year; may be renewed.

Additional information This program is managed by POISE Foundation on behalf of the NAACP.

Number awarded Approximately 20 to 40 each year.

Deadline March of each year.

[929]
HUGGINS-QUARLES AWARD

Organization of American Historians
Attn: Award and Committee Coordinator
112 North Bryan Street
Bloomington, IN 47408-4141
(812) 855-7311   Fax: (812) 855-0696
E-mail: khamm@oah.org
Web: www.oah.org

Summary To provide funding to African American and other minority graduate students who are completing dissertations in American history.

Eligibility This program is open to graduate students of color (African American, Latino(a), Asian American, Native American) at the dissertation research stage of their Ph.D. programs. Their dissertation must deal with a topic related to American history. Along with their application, they must submit a cover letter that also indicates their progress on the dissertation, a curriculum vitae, a 5-page dissertation proposal (including an explanation of the project's significance and contribution to the field and a description of the most important primary sources) and a 1-page itemized budget explaining travel and research plans.

Financial data The grant is $1,500 (if 1 is presented) or $750 (if 2 are presented). Funds are to be used to assist with costs of travel to collections to complete research on the dissertation.

Additional information This program was established in honor of Benjamin Quarles and the late Nathan Huggins, both outstanding historians of the African American past.

Number awarded 1 or 2 each year.

Deadline November of each year.

[930]
HUGH J. ANDERSEN MEMORIAL SCHOLARSHIPS

National Medical Fellowships, Inc.
Attn: Scholarship Program
347 Fifth Avenue, Suite 510
New York, NY 10016
(212) 483-8880   Toll Free: (877) NMF-1DOC
Fax: (212) 483-8897 E-mail: scholarships@nmfonline.org
Web: www.nmfonline.org

Summary To provide financial assistance to African American and other underrepresented minority medical students at schools in Minnesota.

Eligibility This program is open to African Americans, Hispanics/Latinos, Native Americans, Vietnamese, Cambodians, and Pacific Islanders who are entering the second or third year of medical school. Applicants must be Minnesota residents enrolled at an accredited medical school in Minnesota. They must be U.S. citizens or DACA students. Selection is based on leadership, commitment to serving medically underserved communities, and financial need.

Financial data The stipend is $5,000.

Duration 1 year.

Additional information This program began in 1982.

Number awarded 2 each year.

Deadline September of each year.

[931]
HURSTON/WRIGHT AWARD FOR COLLEGE WRITERS

Zora Neale Hurston/Richard Wright Foundation
Attn: Hurston/Wright Awards
840 First Street, N.E., Third Floor
Washington, DC 20002
(202) 248-5051   E-mail: info@hurstonwright.org
Web: www.hurstonwright.org/programs/college-awards

Summary To recognize and reward the best fiction and poetry written by undergraduate or graduate students of African descent.

Eligibility This program is open to students of African descent who are enrolled full time as undergraduate or graduate students at a college or university in the United States. Applicants should submit a manuscript of fiction (up to 20 pages) or poetry (up to 3 poems). Only 1 entry may be submitted per applicant. Writers who have already published a book (in any genre) are ineligible.

Financial data Cash prizes are awarded (amount not specified).

Duration The prizes are awarded annually.

Additional information There is a $25 processing fee.

Number awarded Varies each year; recently, 3 fiction writers and 1 poet received these awards.

Deadline January of each year.

[932]
IBM PHD FELLOWSHIP PROGRAM

IBM Corporation
Attn: University Relations
1133 Westchester Avenue
White Plains, NY 10604
Toll Free: (800) IBM-4YOU   TDD: (800) IBM-3383
E-mail: phdfellow@us.ibm.com
Web: www.research.ibm.com

Summary To provide funding and work experience to students from any country, especially African Americans and other minorities, who are working on a Ph.D. in a research area of broad interest to IBM.

Eligibility Students nominated for this fellowship should be enrolled full time at an accredited college or university in any country and should have completed at least 1 year of graduate study in computer science or engineering, electrical or mechanical engineering, physical sciences (chemistry, material sciences, physics), mathematical sciences, public sector and business sciences, or service science, management, and engineering (SSME). Focus areas that receive special consideration include technology that creates new business or social value, cognitive computing research, cloud and distributed computing technology and solutions, or fundamental science and technology. Applicants should be planning a career in research. Nominations must be made by a faculty member and endorsed by the department head. The program values diversity, and encourages nominations of women, minorities, and others who contribute to that diversity. Selection is based on the applicants' potential for research excellence, the degree to which their technical interests align with those of IBM, and academic progress to date. Preference is given to students who have had an IBM internship or have closely collaborated with technical or services people from IBM.

Financial data Fellowships pay tuition, fees, and a stipend of $17,500 per year.

Duration 1 year; may be renewed up to 2 additional years, provided the recipient is renominated, interacts with IBM's technical community, and demonstrates continued progress and achievement.

Additional information Recipients are offered an internship at 1 of the IBM Research Division laboratories and are given an IBM computer.

Number awarded Varies each year; recently, 57 were awarded.

Deadline October of each year.

[933]
ILLINOIS JUDICIAL COUNCIL FOUNDATION LAW SCHOOL SCHOLARSHIP

Illinois Judicial Council
Attn: Foundation
20 South Clark Street, Suite 900
Chicago, IL 60603
(312) 726-8775   E-mail: ijcscholarship@gmail.com
Web: www.illinoisjudicialcouncil.org

Summary To provide financial assistance to African American and other students from any state who are enrolled at law schools in Illinois.

Eligibility This program is open to residents of any state who are enrolled full time at law schools in Illinois. Applicants must submit a personal essay describing themselves and their reasons for attending law school. Selection is based on that statement, academic achievement, honors and awards, community activities, extracurricular activities, proven ability to overcome obstacles, an interview, recommendations, and financial need.

Financial data The stipend is $1,500.

Duration 1 year.

Additional information The Illinois Judicial Council was founded in 1983 as an organization of state and federal judges, administrative law judges, and judicial hearing officers of predominantly African American descent.

Number awarded 1 or more each year.

Deadline April of each year.

[934]
ILLINOIS NURSES FOUNDATION CENTENNIAL SCHOLARSHIP

Illinois Nurses Association
Attn: Illinois Nurses Foundation
P.O. Box 636
Manteno, IL 60950
(815) 468-8804   Fax: (773) 304-1419
E-mail: info@ana-illinois.org
Web: www.ana-illinois.org

Summary To provide financial assistance to nursing undergraduate and graduate students who are African American or members of other underrepresented groups.

Eligibility This program is open to students working on an associate, bachelor's, or master's degree at an accredited NLNAC or CCNE school of nursing. Applicants must be members of a group underrepresented in nursing (African Americans, Hispanics, American Indians, Asians, and males). Undergraduates must have earned a passing grade in all nursing courses taken to date and have a GPA of 2.85 or higher. Graduate students must have completed at least 12 semester hours of graduate work and have a GPA of 3.0 or higher. All applicants must be willing to 1) act as a spokesperson to other student groups on the value of the scholarship to continuing their nursing education; and 2) be profiled in any

media or marketing materials developed by the Illinois Nurses Foundation. Along with their application, they must submit a narrative of 250 to 500 words on how they, as nurses, plan to affect policy at either the state or national level that impacts on nursing or health care generally, or how they believe they will impact the nursing profession in general.

Financial data A stipend is awarded (amount not specified).

Duration 1 year.

Number awarded 1 or more each year.

Deadline March of each year.

[935]
INDIANA CLEO FELLOWSHIPS

Indiana Supreme Court
Attn: Division of State Court Administration
30 South Meridian Street, Suite 500
Indianapolis, IN 46204
(317) 232-2542   Toll Free: (800) 452-9963
Fax: (317) 233-6586 E-mail: ashley.rozier@courts.in.gov
Web: www.in.gov/judiciary/cleo/2402.htm

Summary To provide financial assistance to African American and other minority or disadvantaged college seniors from any state interested in attending law school in Indiana.

Eligibility This program is open to residents of Indiana who attend college in the state or attend college out of state and are recommended by the admissions officer at a law school in the state. Applicants must be minority, low income, first-generation college, or limited English proficiency college seniors who have applied to an Indiana law school. Selected applicants are invited to participate in the Indiana Conference for Legal Education Opportunity (Indiana CLEO) Summer Institute, held at a law school in the state. Admission to that program is based on GPA, LSAT scores, 3 letters of recommendation, a resume, a personal statement, and financial need. Students who successfully complete the Institute and are admitted to an Indiana law school receive these fellowships.

Financial data All expenses for the Indiana CLEO Summer Institute are paid. The fellowship stipend is $9,000 per year.

Duration The Indiana CLEO Summer Institute lasts 6 weeks. Fellowships are for 1 year and may be renewed up to 2 additional years.

Additional information The first Summer Institute was held in 1997.

Number awarded 30 students are invited to participate in the summer institute; the number of those selected to receive a fellowship varies each year.

Deadline February of each year.

[936]
INDIANAPOLIS CHAPTER NBMBAA GRADUATE SCHOLARSHIP PROGRAM

National Black MBA Association-Indianapolis Chapter
Attn: Scholarship Program
P.O. Box 2325
Indianapolis, IN 46206-2325
(317) 308-6447   E-mail: scholarship@nbmbaa-indy.org
Web: www.nbmbaa-indy.org/nbmbaa_education.htm

Summary To provide financial assistance to African American students from Indiana working on an M.B.A. degree.

Eligibility This program is open to African American students enrolled full time in a graduate business or management program and working on an M.B.A. degree. Applicants must be Indiana residents or enrolled at an Indiana college or university and have a GPA of 2.0 or higher. They must submit essays on 3 topics that change annually but relate to African Americans and business. U.S. citizenship or permanent resident status is required.

Financial data The stipend is $2,000. A 1-year membership in the National Black MBA Association (NBMBAA) is also provided.

Duration 1 year.

Number awarded 2 each year.

Deadline October of each year.

[937]
INTELLECTUAL PROPERTY LAW SECTION WOMEN AND MINORITY SCHOLARSHIP

State Bar of Texas
Attn: Intellectual Property Law Section
c/o Bhaveeni D. Parmar, Scholarship Selection
  Committee
Law Office of Bhaveeni Parmar PLLC
4447 North Central Expressway, Suite 110-295
Dallas, Texas 75205
E-mail: bhaveeni@parmarlawoffice.com
Web: www.texasbariplaw.org

Summary To provide financial assistance to African American and other minority students at law schools in Texas who plan to practice intellectual property law.

Eligibility This program is open to women and members of minority groups (African Americans, Hispanics, Asian Americans, and Native Americans) from any state who are currently enrolled at an ABA-accredited law school in Texas. Applicants must be planning to practice intellectual property law in Texas. Along with their application, they must submit a 2-page essay explaining why they plan to prepare for a career in intellectual property law in Texas, any qualifications they believe are relevant for their consideration for this scholarship, and (optionally) any issues of financial need they wish to have considered.

Financial data The stipend is $5,000.

Duration 1 year.

Number awarded 2 each year: 1 to a women and 1 to a minority.

Deadline May of each year.

[938]
INTERMOUNTAIN SECTION AWWA DIVERSITY SCHOLARSHIP

American Water Works Association-Intermountain
  Section
Attn: Member Services Coordinator
3430 East Danish Road
Sandy, UT 84093
(801) 712-1619, ext. 2   Fax: (801) 487-6699
E-mail: nicoleb@ims-awwa.org
Web: ims-awwa.site-ym.com/group/StudentPO

Summary To provide financial assistance to African American and other minority undergraduate and graduate students working on a degree in the field of water quality, supply, and treatment at a university in the Intermountain West.

Eligibility This program is open to 1) women; and 2) students who identify as Black or African American, Hispanic or Latino, Native Hawaiian or other Pacific Islander, Asian, or American Indian or Alaska Native. Applicants must be entering or enrolled in an undergraduate or graduate program at a college or university in the Intermountain West (defined to include all or portions of Arizona, Colorado, Idaho, Montana, Nevada, New Mexico, Utah, or Wyoming) that relates to water quality, supply, or treatment. Along with their application, they must submit a 2-page essay on their academic interests and career goals and how those relate to water quality, supply, or treatment. Selection is based on that essay, letters of recommendation, and potential to contribute to the field of water quality, supply, and treatment in the Intermountain West.

Financial data The stipend is $1,000. The winner also receives a 1-year student membership in the Intermountain Section of the American Water Works Association (AWWA).

Duration 1 year; nonrenewable.

Number awarded 1 each year.

Deadline November of each year.

[939]
INTERNATIONAL ASSOCIATION OF BLACK ACTUARIES SCHOLARSHIPS

International Association of Black Actuaries
Attn: IABA Foundation Scholarship Committee
P.O. Box 270701
West Hartford, CT 06127
(860) 906-1286   Fax: (860) 906-1369
E-mail: iaba@blackactuaries.org
Web: www.blackactuaries.org/page/Scholarship

Summary To provide financial assistance to Black upper-division and graduate students preparing for an actuarial career.

Eligibility This program is open to full-time juniors, seniors, and graduate students who are of African descent, originating from the United States, Canada, the Caribbean, or African nations. Applicants must have been admitted to a college or university offering either a program in actuarial science or courses that will prepare them for an actuarial career. They must be citizens or permanent residents of the United States or Canada or eligible to study in those countries under a U.S. student visa or Canadian student authorization. Other requirements include a GPA of 3.0 or higher, a mathematics SAT score of at least 600 or a mathematics ACT score of at least 28, completion of probability and calculus courses, attempting or passing an actuarial examination, completion of Validation by Educational Experience (VEE) requirements, and familiarity with actuarial profession demands. Selection is based on merit and financial need.

Financial data Stipends range from $3,000 to $5,000 per year.

Duration 1 year; may be renewed.

Additional information Support for this program is provided by Allstate, DW Simpson, Ernst & Young, Liberty Mutual, New York Life, Prudential, Travelers, and Willis Towers Watson.

Number awarded Varies each year; recently, 25 of these scholarships, with a total value of $81,000, were awarded.

Deadline May of each year.

[940]
INTERNATIONAL SECURITY AND COOPERATION PREDOCTORAL FELLOWSHIPS

Stanford University
Center for International Security and Cooperation
Attn: Fellowships Coordinator
Encina Hall, Room C206-10
616 Serra Street
Stanford, CA 94305-6165
(650) 723-9625   Fax: (650) 724-5683
E-mail: CISACfellowship@stanford.edu
Web: cisac.fsi.stanford.edu/docs/cisac_fellowship_program

Summary To provide funding to doctoral students, especially African Americans and other minorities, who are interested in working on a dissertation on international security problems at Stanford University's Center for International Security and Cooperation.

Eligibility This program is open to students currently enrolled in doctoral programs at academic institutions in the United States who would benefit from access to the facilities offered by the center. Applicants may be working in any discipline of the social sciences, humanities, natural sciences, law, or engineering that relates to international security problems. Relevant topics include nuclear weapons policy and nonproliferation; nuclear energy; cybersecurity, cyberwarfare, and the future of the Internet; war and civil conflict; global governance, migration and transnational flows, from norms to criminal trafficking; biosecurity and global health; implications of geostrategic shifts; insurgency, terrorism, and homeland security; and consolidating peace after conflict. The sponsor welcomes applications from women, minorities, and citizens of all countries.

Financial data The stipend ranges from $25,000 to $28,000. Medical insurance is available for those who do not have coverage.

Duration 9 to 11 months.

Additional information Fellows are expected to complete dissertation chapters or their dissertation during their fellowship. They should not plan to spend any time conducting research abroad or in other parts of the country.

Number awarded Varies each year; recently, 9 were awarded.

Deadline January of each year.

[941]
IRTS BROADCAST SALES ASSOCIATE PROGRAM

International Radio and Television Society Foundation
Attn: Director, Special Projects
1697 Broadway, 10th Floor
New York, NY 10019
(212) 867-6650   Toll Free: (888) 627-1266
Fax: (212) 867-6653   E-mail: submit@irts.org
Web: 406.144.myftpupload.com

Summary To provide summer work experience to African Nand other minority graduate students interested in working in broadcast sales in the New York City area.

Eligibility This program is open to graduating college seniors and students already enrolled in graduate school who are members of a minority (African American, Hispanic/Latino, Asian/Pacific Islander, American Indian/Alaskan Native) group. Applicants must be interested in working during the summer in a sales training program traditionally reserved for actual station group employees. They must be a communications major or have demonstrated a strong interest in the field through extracurricular activities or other practical experience, but they are not required to have experience in broadcast sales.

Financial data Travel, housing, and a living allowance are provided.

Duration 9 weeks during the summer.

Additional information The program consists of a 1-week orientation to the media and entertainment business, followed by an 8-week internship experience in the sales division of a network stations group.

Number awarded Varies each year.

Deadline February of each year.

[942]
IRTS SUMMER FELLOWSHIP PROGRAM

International Radio and Television Society Foundation
Attn: Director, Special Projects
420 Lexington Avenue, Suite 1601
New York, NY 10170-0101
(212) 867-6650   Toll Free: (888) 627-1266
Fax: (212) 867-6653   E-mail: apply@irts.org
Web: irtsfoundation.org/summer-fellowship-program

Summary To provide summer work experience to upper-division and graduate students, especially African Americans and other minorities, who are interested in working during the summer in broadcasting and related fields in the New York City area.

Eligibility This program is open to juniors, seniors, and graduate students at 4-year colleges and universities. Applicants must either be a communications major or have demonstrated a strong interest in the field through extracurricular activities or other practical experience. Minority (African American, Hispanic/Latino, Asian/Pacific Islander, American Indian/Alaskan Native) students are especially encouraged to apply.

Financial data Travel, housing, and a living allowance are provided.

Duration 9 weeks during the summer.

Additional information The first week consists of a comprehensive orientation to broadcasting, cable, advertising, and new media. Then, the participants are assigned an 8-week fellowship. This full-time "real world" experience in a New York-based corporation allows them to reinforce or redefine specific career goals before settling into a permanent job. Fellows have worked at all 4 major networks, at local New York City radio and television stations, and at national rep firms, advertising agencies, and cable operations. This program includes fellowships reserved for students at designated universities (University of Pennsylvania, Brooklyn College, City College of New York, College of the Holy Cross) and the following named awards: the Thomas S. Murphy Fellowship (sponsored by ABC National Television Sales), the Helen Karas Memorial Fellowship, the Mel Karmazin Fellowship, the Neil Postman Memorial Summer Fellowship, the Ari

Bluman Memorial Summer Fellowship (sponsored by Group M), the Thom Casadonte Memorial Fellowship (sponsored by Bloomberg), the Joanne Mercado Memorial Fellowship (sponsored by Nielsen), the Donald V. West Fellowship (sponsored by the Library of American Broadcasting Foundation), the Leslie Moonves Fellowship (sponsored by CBS Television Station Sales, and the Sumner M. Redstone Fellowship (sponsored by CBS Television Station Sales). Other sponsors include the National Academy of Television Arts & Sciences, Fox Networks, NBCUniversal, and Unilever.

Number awarded Varies; recently, 30 were awarded.

Deadline November of each year.

[943]
ISAAC J. "IKE" CRUMBLY MINORITIES IN ENERGY GRANT

American Association of Petroleum Geologists
 Foundation
Attn: Grants-in-Aid Program
1444 South Boulder Avenue
P.O. Box 979
Tulsa, OK 74101-0979
(918) 560-2644   Toll Free: (855) 302-2743
Fax: (918) 560-2642   E-mail: foundation@aapg.org
Web: foundation.aapg.org

Summary To provide funding to African Amrican and other minority graduate students who are interested in conducting research related to earth science aspects of the petroleum industry.

Eligibility This program is open to women and ethnic minorities (Black, Hispanic, Asian, or Native American, including American Indian, Eskimo, Hawaiian, or Samoan) who are working on a master's or doctoral degree. Applicants must be interested in conducting research related to the search for and development of petroleum and energy-minerals resources and to related environmental geology issues. Selection is based on student's academic and employment history (10 points), scientific merit of proposal (30 points), suitability to program objectives (30 points), financial merit of proposal (20 points), and endorsement by faculty or department adviser (10 points).

Financial data Grants range from $500 to $3,000. Funds are to be applied to research-related expenses (e.g., a summer of field work). They may not be used to purchase capital equipment or to pay salaries, tuition, room, or board.

Duration 1 year. Doctoral candidates may receive a 1-year renewal.

Number awarded 1 each year.

Deadline February of each year.

[944]
ISABEL M. HERSON SCHOLARSHIP IN EDUCATION

Zeta Phi Beta Sorority, Inc.
Attn: National Educational Foundation
1734 New Hampshire Avenue, N.W.
Washington, DC 20009
(202) 387-3103   Fax: (202) 232-4593
E-mail: info@zetaphibetasororityhq.org
Web: www.zpbnef1975.org/scholarships-and-descriptions

Summary To provide financial assistance to undergraduate and graduate students, especiall African American women, interested in preparing for a career in education.

Eligibility This program is open to students enrolled full time in an undergraduate or graduate program leading to a degree in either elementary or secondary education. Proof of enrollment is required. Along with their application, they must submit a 150-word essay on their educational goals and professional aspirations, how this award will help them to achieve those goals, and why they should receive the award. Financial need is not considered in the selection process.

Financial data The stipend ranges from $500 to $1,000.

Duration 1 academic year.

Additional information Zeta Phi Beta is a traditionally African American sorority.

Number awarded 1 or more each year.

Deadline January of each year.

[945]
IVORY MOORE COMMUNITY COLLEGE, UNDERGRADUATE AND GRADUATE SCHOLARSHIPS

Texas Association of Black Personnel in Higher Education
c/o Allison Joubert, Scholarship Committee Chair
St. Philip's College
1801 Martin Luther King Drive
San Antonio, TX 78203
(210) 486-2420   E-mail: ajoubert@mail.accd.edu
Web: www.tabphe.org/Scholarships

Summary To provide financial assistance to African Americans enrolled as community college students, undergraduates, or graduate students at colleges in Texas.

Eligibility This program is open to African American students currently enrolled full time at an accredited community college, 4-year university, or graduate school in Texas. Applicants must have a GPA of 3.0 or higher. Along with their application, they must submit a 500-word essay on the topic, "As an African American student pursuing a degree in the 21st century, how will the Ivory Moore Scholarship assist me in my future career endeavors?"

Financial data Stipends are $500 for community college students or $1,000 for undergraduate and graduate students.

Duration 1 year.

Number awarded 3 each year: 1 each to a community college student, undergraduate, and graduate student.

Deadline January of each year.

[946]
JACK AND SADYE GIBSON SCHOLARSHIP FUND

Black Entertainment and Sports Lawyers Association
Attn: Scholarships
P.O. Box 230794
New York, NY 10023
E-mail: scholarship@besla.org
Web: www.besla.org/#!scholarship-fund/qe8of

Summary To provide financial assistance to members of the National Black Law Students Association (NBLSA) who are interested in the fields of entertainment and/or sports law.

Eligibility This program is open to NBLSA members who have completed at least 1 year of full-time study at an accredited law school. Applicants must be able to demonstrate an interest in entertainment or sports law by 2 or more of the following: 1) completed an intellectual property, entertainment, or sports law related course; 2) completed an internship or clerkship in the entertainment, sports, or related law field; or 3) membership in their school's sports and entertainment club. They must have a GPA of 2.8 or higher. Along with their application, they must submit a 5-page legal memorandum on an issue facing the entertainment or sports industry.

Financial data The stipend is at least $1,500.

Duration 1 year.

Number awarded 1 or more each year.

Deadline September of each year.

[947]
JACK KORALESKI SCHOLARSHIP

Union Pacific Railroad Black Employee Network
c/o Michele Brown
Streamline Company
222 South 15th Street, Suite 402-S
Omaha, NE 68102
Toll Free: (800) 262-2549
Web: www.up.com

Summary To provide financial assistance to African Americans from Nebraska who are attending college or graduate school in that state.

Eligibility This program is open to U.S. citizens who are African American residents of Nebraska. Applicants must be attending a college or university in that state and have completed at least 60 semester credit hours as an undergraduate or 15 semester credit hours of work on a master's degree. They must have a GPA of 3.0 or higher, a record of active involvement in school and community activities, and demonstrated social awareness and involvement. Along with their application, they must submit 5 essays of 200 words each on assigned topics. Selection is based on academic ability, leadership, and community involvement; personal or family financial need may also be considered. Preference is given to applicants majoring in a transportation-related field.

Financial data The stipend is $5,000.

Duration 1 year.

Number awarded 1 or more each year.

Deadline October of each year.

[948]
JACK L. STEPHENS GRADUATE SCHOLARSHIP

Conference of Minority Transportation Officials-Fort
  Lauderdale Chapter
Attn: Scholarship Committee
Victor Garcia, South Florida Regional Transportation
  Authority
801 N.W. 33rd Street
Pompano Beach, FL 33064
(954) 788-7925   Toll Free: (800) GO-SFRTA
Fax: (854) 788-7961   TDD: (800) 273-7545
E-mail: victorgarcia@comtoftlauderdale.org
Web: www.comtoftlauderdale.org/scholarship-program

Summary To provide financial assistance to African American and other minority students working on a transportation-related graduate degree at a college in Florida.

Eligibility This program is open to minority students currently enrolled at accredited colleges and universities in Florida. Applicants must be working on a master's or doctoral degree in a transportation-related field and have a GPA of 2.5 or higher. They must be U.S. citizens or permanent residents. Along with their application, they must submit an essay of 500 to 750 words on their transportation-related career goals and life aspirations. Financial need is not considered in the selection process.

Financial data The stipend is $2,500.

Duration 1 year; nonrenewable.

Additional information This program began in 2015.

Number awarded 1 each year.

Deadline April of each year.

[949]
JACOB WILLIAMS SCHOLARSHIP

United Methodist Foundation of Indiana
8401 Fishers Center Drive
Fishers, IN 46038-2318
(317) 788-7879   Toll Free: (877) 391-8811
Fax: (317) 788-0089
E-mail: foundation@UMFIndiana.org
Web: www.umfindiana.org/endowments

Summary To provide financial assistance to African American and other ethnic minority ministerial students from Indiana who are attending a seminary in any state that is approved by the United Methodist Church (UMC).

Eligibility This program is open to members of ethnic minority groups who are candidates for ordination and certified by a District Committee of the Indiana Conference of the UMC. Applicants must be enrolled full time at an approved seminary in any state. They must be seeking ordination as a deacon or elder. Along with their application, they must submit documentation of financial need and a statement of their vocational goals.

Financial data Stipends are awarded at the rate of $100 per credit hour (per semester) and $200 per projected decade of service remaining (per semester).

Duration 1 year; may be renewed.

Number awarded 1 or more each year.

Deadline May of each year for fall semester; October of each year for spring semester.

[950]
JACQUES AVENT SCHOLARSHIP

Arizona Community Foundation
Attn: Director of Scholarships
2201 East Camelback Road, Suite 405B
Phoenix, AZ 85016
(602) 381-1400   Toll Free: (800) 222-8221
Fax: (602) 381-1575
E-mail: scholarship@azfoundation.org
Web: azfoundation.academicworks.com/opportunities/2468

Summary To provide financial assistance to African American upper-division and graduate students who are preparing for a career in public administration at a college in Arizona.

Eligibility This program is open to African American undergraduates who have completed at least 48 credit hours and full-time graduate students at colleges and universities in Arizona. Applicants must be preparing for a career in public administration by working on a degree in public administration, public affairs, public policy, political science, or urban and metropolitan studies; students in business, criminal justice, education, health care, information technology, and nursing are eligible and encouraged to apply. They must have a GPA of 3.0 or higher. Along with their application, they must submit an essay that covers 1) their educational and career goals; 2) their civic and community involvement; and 3) the challenges facing African American in the field of public administration and how they plan to help strengthen the role of African Americans in public administration.

Financial data The stipend is $5,000.

Duration 1 year.

Additional information This program is supported by the Central Arizona Chapter of the National Forum for Black Public Administrators.

Number awarded 1 or more each year.

Deadline March of each year.

[951]
JAMES B. MORRIS SCHOLARSHIPS

James B. Morris Scholarship Fund
Attn: Scholarship Selection Committee
P.O. Box 12145
Des Moines, IA 50312
(515) 864-0922
Web: www.morrisscholarship.org

Summary To provide financial assistance to African American and other minority undergraduate, graduate, and law students from Iowa.

Eligibility This program is open to minority students (African Americans, Asian/Pacific Islanders, Hispanics, or Native Americans) who are interested in working on an undergraduate or graduate degree. Applicants must be either Iowa residents attending a college or university anywhere in the United States or non-Iowa residents who are attending a college or university in Iowa. Along with their application, they must submit an essay of 250 to 500 words on why they are applying for this scholarship, activities or organizations in which they are involved, and their future plans. Selection is based on the essay, academic achievement (GPA of 2.5 or higher), community service, and financial need. U.S. citizenship is required.

Financial data The stipend ranges from $1,000 to $2,500 per year.

Duration 1 year; may be renewed.

Additional information This fund was established in 1978 in honor of the J.B. Morris family, who founded the Iowa branch of the National Association for the Advancement of Colored People and published the *Iowa Bystander* newspaper. The program includes the Ann Chapman Scholarships, the Vincent Chapman, Sr. Scholarships, the Catherine Williams Scholarships, and the Brittany Hall Memorial Scholarships. Support for additional scholarships is provided by EMC Insurance Group and Wells Fargo Bank.

Number awarded Varies each year; recently, 22 were awarded.

Deadline February of each year.

[952]
JAMES CARLSON MEMORIAL SCHOLARSHIP

Oregon Office of Student Access and Completion
Attn: Scholarship Processing Coordinator
1500 Valley River Drive, Suite 100
Eugene, OR 97401-2146
(541) 687-7422   Toll Free: (800) 452-8807, ext. 7422
Fax: (541) 687-7414   TDD: (800) 735-2900
E-mail: cheryl.a.connolly@state.or.us
Web: app.oregonstudentaid.gov/Catalog/Default.aspx

Summary To provide financial assistance to Oregon residents who are African American or other diverse students majoring in education on the undergraduate or graduate school level at a school in any state.

Eligibility This program is open to residents of Oregon who are U.S. citizens or permanent residents and enrolled at a college or university in any state. Applicants must be either 1) college seniors or fifth-year students majoring in elementary or secondary education; or 2) graduate students working on an elementary or secondary certificate. Full-time enrollment and financial need are required. Priority is given to 1) students who come from diverse environments and submit an essay of 250 to 350 words on their experience living or working in diverse environments; 2) dependents of members of the Oregon Education Association; and 3) applicants committed to teaching autistic children.

Financial data Stipends for scholarships offered by the Oregon Office of Student Access and Completion (OSAC) range from $1,000 to $10,000 but recently averaged $4,368.

Duration 1 year; nonrenewable.

Additional information This program is administered by the OSAC with funds provided by the Oregon Community Foundation.

Number awarded Varies each year; recently, 3 were awarded.

Deadline February of each year.

[953]
JAMES E. WEBB INTERNSHIPS

Smithsonian Institution
Attn: Office of Fellowships and Internships
470 L'Enfant Plaza, Suite 7102
P.O. Box 37012, MRC 902
Washington, DC 20013-7012
(202) 633-7070   Fax: (202) 633-7069
E-mail: siofi@si.edu
Web: www.smithsonianofi.com

Summary To provide internship opportunities throughout the Smithsonian Institution to African American and other minority upper-division and graduate students in business or public administration.

Eligibility This program is open to minorities who are juniors, seniors, or graduate students majoring in areas of business or public administration (finance, human resource management, accounting, or general business administration). Applicants must have a GPA of 3.0 or higher. They must seek placement in offices, museums, and research institutes within the Smithsonian Institution.

Financial data   Interns receive a stipend of $600 per week and a travel allowance.

Duration   10 weeks during the summer, fall, or spring.

Number awarded   Varies each year; recently, 8 of these internships were awarded.

Deadline   January of each year for summer or fall; September of each year for spring.

[954]
JAMES ECHOLS SCHOLARSHIP

California Association for Health, Physical Education,
   Recreation and Dance
Attn: Chair, Scholarship Committee
1501 El Camino Avenue, Suite 3
Sacramento, CA 95815-2748
(916) 922-3596   Toll Free: (800) 499-3596 (within CA)
Fax: (916) 922-0133   E-mail: reception@cahperd.org
Web: www.cahperd.org

Summary   To provide financial assistance to African American and other minority student members of the California Association for Health, Physical Education, Recreation and Dance.

Eligibility   This program is open to California residents who have been members of the association for at least 60 days and are attending a 2- or 4-year college or university in the state. Applicants must be undergraduate or graduate students working on a degree in health education, physical education, recreation, or dance and have completed at least 60 semester hours of college work. Selection is based on scholastic proficiency (a GPA of 3.0 or higher); leadership ability in school, community, and professional activities; and personal qualities of enthusiasm, cooperativeness, responsibility, initiative, and ability to work with others. This scholarship is awarded to the highest-ranked minority (Asian, African American, Latino, or Native American) applicant.

Financial data   The stipend is $1,000.

Duration   1 year.

Number awarded   1 each year.

Deadline   November of each year.

[955]
JAMES W. STOUDT SCHOLARSHIPS

Pennsylvania Bar Association
Attn: Foundation
100 South Street
P.O. Box 186
Harrisburg, PA 17108-0186
(717) 213-2501   Toll Free: (888) 238-3036
Fax: (717) 213-2548   E-mail: info@pabarfoundation.org
Web: www.pabarfoundation.org

Summary   To provide financial assistance to residents of Pennsylvania, especially African Americans and other minorities, who are attending law school in the state.

Eligibility   This program is open to residents of Pennsylvania who are currently enrolled in the second year (or third year of a 4- or 5-year law school program) at a law school in the state. Applicants must be members of the Pennsylvania Bar Association student division. Some of the awards are reserved for students who are members of groups historically underrepresented in the legal profession (African Americans, Hispanic Americans, and Native Americans). Along with their application, they must submit a 500-word essay explaining how they plan to demonstrate their potential for making a contribution to society and the legal profession. Selection is based on that essay, academic achievement, and financial need.

Financial data   The stipend is $3,000.

Duration   1 year.

Number awarded   3 each year, of which 2 are reserved for underrepresented minority students.

Deadline   November of each year.

[956]
JANE C. WALDBAUM ARCHAEOLOGICAL FIELD SCHOOL SCHOLARSHIP

Archaeological Institute of America
c/o Boston University
656 Beacon Street, Sixth Floor
Boston, MA 02215-2006
(617) 358-4184   Fax: (617) 353-6550
E-mail: fellowships@aia.bu.edu
Web: www.archaeological.org/grants/708

Summary   To provide funding to African American and other minority upper-division and graduate students who are interested in participating in an archaeological field project in the United States or any other country.

Eligibility   This program is open to junior and senior undergraduates and first-year graduate students who are currently enrolled at a college or university in the United States or Canada. Minority and disadvantaged students are encouraged to apply. Applicants must be interested in participating in an archaeological excavation or survey project in any country. They may not have previously participated in an archaeological excavation. Students majoring in archaeology or related disciplines are especially encouraged to apply.

Financial data   The grant is $1,000.

Duration   At least 1 month during the summer.

Additional information   These scholarships were first awarded in 2007.

Number awarded   Varies each year; recently, 15 were awarded.

Deadline   February of each year.

[957]
J.D. WILLIAMS SCHOLARSHIP

African Methodist Episcopal Church
Connectional Lay Organization
Attn: Scholarship Chair
P.O. Box 42224
Philadelphia, PA 19101
(215) 941-0344   Fax: (360) 343-0344
Web: www.connectionallay-amec.org

Summary   To provide financial assistance to members of the African Methodist Episcopal (AME) Church who are interested in working on an undergraduate or graduate degree at a college or university affiliated with the denomination.

Eligibility   This program is open to members of AME churches who are working on or planning to work on a bachelor's, M.Div., or D.Min. degree at an AME college, university, or seminary. Applicants must submit a 500-word essay on the importance of a college education in the 21st century. Selection is based on academic record, qualities of leadership, extracurricular activities and accomplishments, reference letters, and financial need.

Financial data The stipend is $5,000. Funds are sent directly to the student.

Duration 1 year.

Number awarded 1 or more each year.

Deadline March of each year.

[958]
JDOS-INTERNATIONAL SCHOLARSHIP

National Forum for Black Public Administrators
Attn: Scholarship Program
777 North Capitol Street, N.E., Suite 807
Washington, DC 20002
(202) 408-9300   Fax: (202) 408-8558
E-mail: vharris@nfbpa.org
Web: www.nfbpa.org/i4a/pages/index.cfm?pageid=4047

Summary To provide financial assistance to African Americans working on an undergraduate or graduate degree in public administration or a related field.

Eligibility This program is open to African American undergraduate and graduate students preparing for a career in public service. Applicants must be working full time on a degree in public administration, political science, urban affairs, public policy, or a related field. They must have excellent interpersonal and analytical abilities and strong oral and written communication skills. Along with their application, they must submit a 3-page autobiographical essay that includes their academic and career goals and objectives. Selection is based on academic record, leadership ability, participation in school activities, community service, and financial need.

Financial data The stipend is $2,000.

Duration 1 year.

Additional information This program is sponsored by the construction management firm JDOS-International of Washington, D.C. Recipients are required to attend the sponsor's annual conference to receive their scholarship; limited hotel and air accommodations are arranged and provided.

Number awarded 1 each year.

Deadline March of each year.

[959]
JEANNE SPURLOCK RESEARCH FELLOWSHIP IN SUBSTANCE ABUSE AND ADDICTION FOR MINORITY MEDICAL STUDENTS

American Academy of Child and Adolescent Psychiatry
Attn: Department of Research, Training, and Education
3615 Wisconsin Avenue, N.W.
Washington, DC 20016-3007
(202) 587-9663   Fax: (202) 966-5894
E-mail: training@aacap.org
Web: www.aacap.org

Summary To provide funding to African American and other minority medical students who are interested in working during the summer on the topics of drug abuse and addiction with a child and adolescent psychiatrist researcher-mentor.

Eligibility This program is open to African American, Asian American, Native American, Alaska Native, Mexican Ameri-

can, Hispanic, and Pacific Islander students in accredited U.S. medical schools. Applicants must present a plan for a program of research training in drug abuse and addiction that involves significant contact with a mentor who is an experienced child and adolescent psychiatrist researcher. The plan should include program planning discussions; instruction in research planning and implementation; regular meetings with the mentor, laboratory director, and research group; and assigned readings. The mentor must be a member of the American Academy of Child and Adolescent Psychiatry (AACAP). Research assignments may include responsibility for part of the observation or evaluation, developing specific aspects of the research mechanisms, conducting interviews or tests, using rating scales, and psychological or cognitive testing of subjects. The training plan also should include discussion of ethical issues in research, such as protocol development, informed consent, collection and storage of raw data, safeguarding data, bias in analyzing data, plagiarism, protection of patients, and ethical treatment of animals. U.S. citizenship or permanent resident status is required.

Financial data The stipend is $4,000. Fellows also receive reimbursement of travel expenses to attend the annual meeting of the American Academy of Child and Adolescent Psychiatry.

Duration 12 weeks during the summer.

Additional information Upon completion of the training program, the student is required to submit a brief paper summarizing the research experience. The fellowship pays expenses for the fellow to attend the academy's annual meeting and present this paper. This program is co-sponsored by the National Institute on Drug Abuse.

Number awarded Up to 5 each year.

Deadline February of each year.

[960]
JESSE B. BARBER, JR., MD MEMORIAL SCHOLARSHIP

Auxiliary to the National Medical Association
8403 Colesville Road, Suite 820
Silver Spring, MD 20910
(301) 495-3779   Fax: (301) 495-0037
E-mail: anmanationaloffice@earthlink.net
Web: www.anmanet.org

Summary To provide financial assistance to African American medical students attending selected schools.

Eligibility This program is open to African American medical school students who are enrolled at 1 of the following medical schools: Howard University College of Medicine (Washington, D.C.), Meharry Medical College (Nashville, Tennessee), Morehouse School of Medicine (Atlanta, Georgia), or Charles R. Drew University (Los Angeles, California). Applicants must have shown an interest in neurosurgery or neurology.

Financial data A stipend is awarded (amount not specified).

Duration 1 year.

Additional information This program was established in 2008.

Number awarded At least 4 each year (1 at each of the participating medical schools).

Deadline Deadline not specified.

[961]
JIM MCKAY SCHOLARSHIP PROGRAM

National Collegiate Athletic Association
Attn: Jim McKay Scholarship Program Staff Liaison
700 West Washington Street
P.O. Box 6222
Indianapolis, IN 46206-6222
(317) 917-6683   Fax: (317) 917-6888
E-mail: lthomas@ncaa.org
Web: www.ncaa.org/jim-mckay-scholarship-program

Summary To provide financial assistance to African American and other minority student-athletes interested in attending graduate school to prepare for a career in sports communications.

Eligibility This program is open to college seniors planning to enroll full time in a graduate degree program and to students already enrolled full time in graduate study at an institution that is a member of the National Collegiate Athletic Association (NCAA). Applicants must have competed in intercollegiate athletics as a member of a varsity team at an NCAA member institution and have an overall undergraduate cumulative GPA of 3.5 or higher. They must be preparing for a career in the sports communications industry. Women and minorities are especially encouraged to apply. Neither financial need nor U.S. citizenship are required. Nominations must be submitted by the faculty athletics representative or chief academic officer at the institution in which the student is or was an undergraduate.

Financial data The stipend is $10,000.

Duration 1 year; nonrenewable.

Additional information This program began in 2008.

Number awarded 2 each year: 1 female and 1 male.

Deadline January of each year.

[962]
JOANN JETER MEMORIAL DIVERSITY SCHOLARSHIP

Associates Foundation
Attn: Claudia Perot, Scholarship Committee Chair
JCD 6
P.O. Box 3621
Portland, OR 97208-3621
(503) 230-3754
Web: www.theassociatesonline.org

Summary To provide financial assistance to African Americans and other students who reflect elements of diversity and are interested in working on an undergraduate or graduate degree in any field.

Eligibility This program is open to students who are enrolled or planning to enroll as a full-time undergraduate or graduate student at an accredited 4-year college or university or a full-time student at a 2-year college enrolled in a program leading to an academic degree. Applicants must be from a diverse background, including first-generation college student, cultural and/or ethnic minority background, low-income, or other clearly articulated aspects of diversity as presented in an essay.

Financial data The stipend ranges from $500 to $1,000.

Duration 1 year.

Number awarded Varies each year; recently, 3 were awarded.

Deadline April of each year.

[963]
JOHN A. MAYES EDAC SCHOLARSHIP

National Athletic Trainers' Association
Attn: Ethnic Diversity Advisory Committee
1620 Valwood Parkway, Suite 115
Carrollton, TX 75006
(214) 637-6282   Toll Free: (800) 879-6282
Fax: (214) 637-2206
Web: www.nata.org

Summary To provide financial aid to African Amrican and other ethnically diverse graduate students who are preparing for a career as an athletic trainer.

Eligibility This program is open to members of ethnically diverse groups who have been accepted into an entry-level master's athletic training degree program or into a doctoral-level athletic training and/or sports medicine degree program. Applicants must be sponsored by a certified athletic trainer who is a member of the National Athletic Trainers' Association (NATA). They must have a cumulative undergraduate GPA of 3.2 or higher. First priority is given to a student working on an entry-level athletic training master's degree; second priority is given to a student entering the second year of an athletic training master's degree program; third priority is given to a student working on a doctoral degree in athletic training or sports medicine. Special consideration is given to applicants who have been members of NATA for at least 2 years.

Financial data The stipend is $2,300.

Duration 1 year.

Additional information This program began in 2009.

Number awarded 1 each year.

Deadline February of each year.

[964]
JOHN AND MURIEL LANDIS SCHOLARSHIPS

American Nuclear Society
Attn: Scholarship Coordinator
555 North Kensington Avenue
La Grange Park, IL 60526-5535
(708) 352-6611   Toll Free: (800) 323-3044
Fax: (708) 352-0499   E-mail: outreach@ans.org
Web: committees.ans.org/need/apply.html

Summary To provide financial assistance to African American and other minority undergraduate or graduate students who are interested in preparing for a career in nuclear-related fields and can demonstrate financial need.

Eligibility This program is open to undergraduate and graduate students at colleges or universities located in the United States who are preparing for, or planning to prepare for, a career in nuclear science, nuclear engineering, or a nuclear-related field. Qualified high school seniors are also eligible. Applicants must have greater than average financial need and have experienced circumstances that render them disadvantaged. Along with their application, they must submit an essay on their academic and professional goals, experiences that have affected those goals, etc. Selection is based on that essay, academic achievement, letters of recommendation, and financial need. Women and members of minority groups are especially urged to apply. U.S. citizenship is not required.

Financial data The stipend is $5,000, to be used to cover tuition, books, fees, room, and board.

Duration 1 year; nonrenewable.

Number awarded Up to 9 each year.

Deadline January of each year.

[965]
JOHN C. DANFORTH CENTER ON RELIGION AND POLITICS DISSERTATION COMPLETION FELLOWSHIP

Washington University
Attn: John C. Danforth Center on Religion and Politics
118 Umrath Hall
Campus Box 1066
One Brookings Drive
St. Louis, MO 63130
(314) 935-9545   Fax: (314) 935-5755
E-mail: rap@wustl.edu
Web: rap.wustl.edu/dissertation-completion-fellowship

Summary To provide financial assistance to African American and other underrepresented graduate students who are interested in completing their dissertation while in residence at the John C. Danforth Center on Religion and Politics of Washington University in St. Louis.

Eligibility This program is open to graduate students currently enrolled in a doctoral program in religion, politics, history, American studies, anthropology, gender and sexuality, or a related field. Applicants must be working on a dissertation that is centrally concerned with historical or contemporary topics in the religious and political experience of the United States. They must have received approval for the dissertation prospectus from their home institutions, satisfied all other requirements for doctoral candidacy, and be prepared to complete their dissertation before the conclusion of the fellowship. Members of underrepresented groups are encouraged to apply.

Financial data Fellows receive a stipend of $28,000 and a limited allowance for relocation expenses.

Duration 1 year; nonrenewable.

Number awarded Up to 2 each year.

Deadline January of each year.

[966]
JOHN HOPE FRANKLIN DISSERTATION FELLOWSHIP

American Philosophical Society
Attn: Director of Grants and Fellowships
104 South Fifth Street
Philadelphia, PA 19106-3387
(215) 440-3429   Fax: (215) 440-3436
E-mail: LMusumeci@amphilsoc.org
Web: amphilsoc.org/grants/johnhopefranklin

Summary To provide funding to African American and other underrepresented minority graduate students conducting research for a doctoral dissertation.

Eligibility This program is open to African American, Hispanic American, and Native American graduate students working on a degree at a Ph.D. granting institution in the United States. Other talented students who have a demonstrated commitment to eradicating racial disparities and enlarging minority representation in academia are also eligible. Applicants must have completed all course work and examinations preliminary to the doctoral dissertation and be able to devote full-time effort, with no teaching obligations, to researching or writing their dissertation. The proposed research should relate to a topic in which the holdings of the Library of the American Philosophical Society (APS) are particularly strong: quantum mechanics, nuclear physics, computer development, the history of genetics and eugenics, the history of medicine, Early American political and cultural history, natural history in the 18th and 19th centuries, the development of cultural anthropology, or American Indian culture and linguistics.

Financial data The grant is $25,000; an additional grant of $5,000 is provided to support the cost of residency in Philadelphia.

Duration 12 months, to begin at the discretion of the grantee.

Additional information This program began in 2005. Recipients are expected to spend a significant amount of time in residence at the APS Library.

Number awarded 1 each year.

Deadline March of each year.

[967]
JOHN L. HOWLETTE AND C. CLAYTON POWELL STUDENT FOUNDERS AWARD

National Optometric Association
Attn: Student Affairs
1801 North Tryon Street, Suite 315
Charlotte, NC 28206
(704) 918-1809   Toll Free: (877) 394-2020
Fax: (877) NOA-2006
E-mail: noastudentdirector@yahoo.com
Web: www.nationaloptometricassociation.com

Summary To provide financial assistance to African American and other members of the National Optometric Student Association (NOSA).

Eligibility This program is open to NOSA members enrolled in the first, second, or third year at a school or college of optometry. Applicants must have a GPA of 3.0 or higher and be able to demonstrate leadership within the profession and community. Along with their application, they must submit a 2-page statement on their reasons for applying for this award; their involvement in professional, community, extracurricular activities or events that have displayed their commitment to serving humanity and demonstrated interest in others; and how they hope to impact the profession of optometry positively in the future. Financial need is not considered in the selection process.

Financial data The stipend is $1,000.

Duration 1 year.

Additional information The National Optometric Association was founded in 1969 with the goal of recruiting minority students, especially African Americans, for schools and colleges of optometry.

Number awarded 1 each year.

Deadline May of each year.

[968]
JOHN M. LANGSTON BAR ASSOCIATION SCHOLARSHIPS

John M. Langston Bar Association
c/o Ibiere Seck, Scholarship Committee
The Cochran Firm
4929 Wilshire Boulevard, Suite 1010
Los Angeles, CA 90010
(323) 435-8205   Toll Free: (800) THE-FIRM
E-mail: iseck@cochranfirm.com
Web: www.langstonbar.org/#!scholarship/c23me

Summary To provide financial assistance to African American students from any state who are attending law schools in California.

Eligibility This program is open to African Americans from any state who are currently enrolled in the first year of a law school in California. Applicants must be able to demonstrate financial need. Along with their application, they must submit essays on 1) what "diversity" means to them and why they think it might be important to have a diverse bar; and 2) a current and prevalent civil rights issue of our time.

Financial data A stipend is awarded (amount not specified).

Duration 1 year.

Additional information The John M. Langston Bar Association, originally named the Langston Law Club, was founded in 1943 by African American attorneys in Los Angeles who were denied membership in other bar associations.

Number awarded 1 or more each year.

Deadline October of each year.

[969]
JOHN MCLENDON MEMORIAL MINORITY POSTGRADUATE SCHOLARSHIP AWARD

National Association of Collegiate Directors of Athletics
Attn: NACDA Foundation
24651 Detroit Road
Westlake, OH 44145
(440) 788-7474   Fax: (440) 892-4007
E-mail: knewman@nacda.com
Web: www.nacda.com/mclendon/scholarship.html

Summary To provide financial assistance to African American and other minority college seniors who are interested in working on a graduate degree in athletics administration.

Eligibility This program is open to minority college students who are seniors, are attending school on a full-time basis, have a GPA of 3.2 or higher, intend to attend graduate school to earn a degree in athletics administration, and are involved in college or community activities. Also eligible are college graduates who have at least 2 years' experience in an athletics administration position. Candidates must be nominated by an official of a member institution of the National Association of Collegiate Directors of Athletics (NACDA) or (for college graduates) a supervisor.

Financial data The stipend is $10,000.

Duration 1 year.

Additional information Recipients must maintain full-time status during the senior year to retain their eligibility. They must attend NACDA-member institutions.

Number awarded 5 each year.

Deadline Nominations must be submitted by April of each year.

[970]
JOHN S. SHROPSHIRE GRADUATE SCHOLARSHIP

Pennsylvania Black Conference on Higher Education
c/o Brenda Sanders Dédé, Scholarship Committee Chair
Clarion University of Pennsylvania
Academic Affairs
115 Carrier
840 Wood Street
Clarion, PA 16214
(814) 393-2223   E-mail: bdede@clarion.edu
Web: www.pbcohe.com/scholarships.html

Summary To provide financial assistance to African American residents of any state who are enrolled as graduate students at universities in Pennsylvania.

Eligibility This program is open to African Americans from any state who have earned at least 6 hours of graduate study at a college or university in Pennsylvania. Applicants must have a GPA of 3.0 or higher. Along with their application, they must submit an essay, up to 5 pages in length, on why they should receive this scholarship. Selection is based on that essay, academics, extracurricular activity participation, leadership qualities, and interpersonal qualities.

Financial data The stipend is $1,000.

Duration 1 year.

Number awarded 1 each year.

Deadline January of each year.

[971]
JOHN STANFORD MEMORIAL WLMA SCHOLARSHIP

Washington Library Association-School Library Division
c/o Susan Kaphammer, Scholarship Chair
521 North 24th Avenue
Yakima, WA 98902
(509) 972-5999   E-mail: scholarships@wlma.org
Web: www.wla.org/school-scholarships

Summary To provide financial assistance to African American and other ethnic minorities in Washington who are interested in attending a school in any state to prepare for a library media career.

Eligibility This program is open to residents of Washington who are working toward a library media endorsement or graduate degree in the field at a school in any state. Applicants must be members of an ethnic minority group. They must be working or planning to work in a school library. Along with their application, they must submit a 3-page letter that includes a description of themselves and their achievements to date, their interest and work in the library field, their personal and professional activities, their goals and plans for further education and professional development, how they expect the studies funded by this award to impact their professional practice and contributions to the Washington school library community, and their financial need.

Financial data The stipend is $1,000.

Duration 1 year.

Additional information The School Library Division of the Washington Library Association was formerly the Washington Library Media Association (WLMA).

Number awarded 1 each year.

Deadline May of each year.

[972]
JOHN W. WORK III MEMORIAL FOUNDATION SCHOLARSHIP

Community Foundation of Middle Tennessee
Attn: Scholarship Coordinator
3833 Cleghorn Avenue, Suite 400
Nashville, TN 37215-2519
(615) 321-4939, ext. 116   Toll Free: (888) 540-5200
Fax: (615) 327-2746   E-mail: pcole@cfmt.org
Web: www.cfmt.org/request/scholarships/allscholarships

Summary To provide financial assistance to upper-division and graduate students from Tennessee, especially African Americans, who are working on a degree in music at a school in any state.

Eligibility This program is open to residents of Tennessee, especially African Americans, enrolled as juniors, seniors, or graduate students at an accredited college, university, or institute in any state. Applicants must be working on a degree in music and have a GPA of 3.0 or higher. Selection is based on demonstrated potential for excellence in music, academic record, standardized test scores, extracurricular activities, work experience, community involvement, recommendations, and financial need.

Financial data Stipends range from $500 to $2,500 per year. Funds are paid to the recipient's school and must be used for tuition, fees, books, supplies, room, board, or miscellaneous expenses.

Duration 1 year.

Additional information This program began in 2002.

Number awarded 1 or more each year.

Deadline March of each year.

[973]
JOHNSON & JOHNSON/AACN MINORITY NURSE FACULTY SCHOLARS PROGRAM

American Association of Colleges of Nursing
One Dupont Circle, N.W., Suite 530
Washington, DC 20036
(202) 463-6930   Fax: (202) 785-8320
E-mail: scholarship@aacn.nche.edu
Web: www.aacn.nche.edu/students/scholarships/minority

Summary To provide fellowship/loans to African American and other minority students who are working on a graduate degree in nursing to prepare for a career as a faculty member.

Eligibility This program is open to members of racial and ethnic minority groups (Black or African American, Alaska Native, American Indian, Native Hawaiian or other Pacific Islander, Hispanic or Latino, or Asian American) who are enrolled full time at a school of nursing. Applicants must be working on 1) a doctoral nursing degree (e.g., Ph.D., D.N.P.); or 2) a clinically-focused master's degree in nursing (e.g., M.S.N., M.S.). They must commit to 1) serve in a teaching capacity at a nursing school for a minimum of 1 year for each year of support they receive; 2) provide 6-month progress reports to the American Association of Colleges of Nursing

(AACN) throughout the entire funding process and during the payback period; 3) agree to work with an assigned mentor throughout the period of the scholarship grant; and 4) attend an annual leadership training conference to connect with their mentor, fellow scholars, and colleagues. Selection is based on ability to contribute to nursing education; leadership potential; development of goals reflecting education, research, and professional involvement; ability to work with a mentor/adviser throughout the award period; proposed research and/or practice projects that are significant and show commitment to improving nursing education and clinical nursing practice in the United States; proposed research and/or clinical education professional development plan that exhibits quality, feasibility, and innovativeness; and evidence of commitment to a career in nursing education and to recruiting, mentoring, and retaining other underrepresented minority nurses. Preference is given to students enrolled in doctoral nursing programs. Applicants must be U.S. citizens, permanent residents, refugees, or qualified immigrants.

Financial data The stipend is $18,000 per year. The award includes $1,500 that is held in escrow to cover the costs for the recipient to attend the leadership training conference. Recipients are required to sign a letter of commitment that they will provide 1 year of service in a teaching capacity at a nursing school in the United States for each year of support received; if they fail to complete that service requirement, they must repay all funds received.

Duration 1 year; may be renewed 1 additional year.

Additional information This program, established in 2007, is sponsored by the Johnson & Johnson Campaign for Nursing's Future.

Number awarded 5 each year.

Deadline April of each year.

[974]
JOSEPHINE FORMAN SCHOLARSHIP

Society of American Archivists
Attn: Chair, Awards Committee
17 North State Street, Suite 1425
Chicago, IL 60602-4061
(312) 606-0722   Toll Free: (866) 722-7858
Fax: (312) 606-0728   E-mail: info@archivists.org
Web: www2.archivists.org

Summary To provide financial assistance to African American and other minority graduate students working on a degree in archival science.

Eligibility This program is open to members of minority groups (Black/African American, American Indian/Alaska Native, Asian, Hispanic/Latino, or Native Hawaiian/other Pacific Islander) currently enrolled in or accepted to a graduate program or a multi-course program in archival administration. The program must offer at least 3 courses in archival science and students may have completed no more than half of the credit requirements toward their graduate degree. Selection is based on potential for scholastic and personal achievement and commitment both to the archives profession and to advancing diversity concerns within it. U.S. citizenship or permanent resident status is required.

Financial data The stipend is $10,000.

Duration 1 year.

Additional information Funding for this program, established in 2011, is provided by the General Commission on Archives and History of the United Methodist Church.

Number awarded 1 each year.

Deadline February of each year.

[975]
JOSIAH MACY JR. FOUNDATION SCHOLARSHIPS

National Medical Fellowships, Inc.
Attn: Scholarship Program
347 Fifth Avenue, Suite 510
New York, NY 10016
(212) 483-8880　　　　　Toll Free: (877) NMF-1DOC
Fax: (212) 483-8897 E-mail: scholarships@nmfonline.org
Web: www.nmfonline.org

Summary To provide financial assistance to African American and other underrepresented minority medical students who demonstrate financial need.

Eligibility This program is open to African Americans, Hispanics/Latinos, Native Americans, Vietnamese, Cambodians, and Pacific Islanders who are entering their second or third year of medical school. They must be U.S. citizens or DACA students. Selection is based on leadership, commitment to serving medically underserved communities, and financial need.

Financial data A stipend is awarded (amount not specified).

Duration 1 year.

Additional information This program is sponsored by the Josiah Macy Jr. Foundation.

Number awarded 4 each year.

Deadline September of each year.

[976]
JOURNEY TOWARD ORDAINED MINISTRY SCHOLARSHIP

United Methodist Church
Attn: General Board of Higher Education and Ministry
Office of Loans and Scholarships
1001 19th Avenue South
P.O. Box 340007
Nashville, TN 37203-0007
(615) 340-7344　　　　　Fax: (615) 340-7367
E-mail: umscholar@gbhem.org
Web: www.gbhem.org

Summary To provide financial assistance to African American and other minority United Methodist students preparing for ministry at a Methodist-related institution.

Eligibility This program is open to members of racial or ethnic minority groups who are 30 years of age or younger and have been active, full members of a United Methodist Church for at least 2 years prior to applying. Applicants must be enrolled as full-time undergraduate or graduate students at a United Methodist-related institution in a program that leads to ordained ministry. Undergraduates must have a GPA of 2.85 or higher and graduate students must have a GPA of 3.0 or higher.

Financial data The stipend is $5,000.

Duration 1 year.

Number awarded 1 or more each year.

Deadline February of each year.

[977]
JTBF SUMMER JUDICIAL INTERNSHIP PROGRAM

Just the Beginning Foundation
c/o Maria Shade Harris, Chief Operating Officer
233 South Wacker Drive, Suite 6600
Chicago, IL 60606
(312) 258-5930　　　　　E-mail: mharris@jtb.org
Web: www.jtb.org/about/our-programs

Summary To provide work experience to African American and other minority or economically disadvantaged law students who plan to seek judicial clerkships after graduation.

Eligibility This program is open to students currently enrolled in their second or third year of law school who are members of minority or economically disadvantaged groups. Applicants must intend to work as a clerk in the federal or state judiciary upon graduation or within 5 years of graduation.

Financial data Program externs receive a summer stipend in an amount determined by the sponsor.

Duration Students must perform at least 35 hours per week of work for at least 8 weeks during the summer.

Additional information This program began in 2005. Law students are matched with federal and state judges across the country who provide assignments to the participants that will enhance their legal research, writing, and analytical skills (e.g., drafting memoranda). Students are expected to complete at least 1 memorandum of law or other key legal document each semester of the externship. Course credit may be offered, but students may not receive academic credit and a stipend simultaneously.

Number awarded Varies each year.

Deadline January of each year.

[978]
JUDGE EUGENE HAMILTON SCHOLARSHIP

Washington Bar Association
Attn: Educational Foundation
P.O. Box 56551
Washington, DC 20040
(202) 349-1059　　　　　Fax: (202) 659-4082
E-mail: info@washingtonbar.org
Web: www.washingtonbar.org/wbaef/wbaef-scholarships

Summary To provide financial assistance to African American and other law students in Washington D.C. who submit outstanding appellate briefs.

Eligibility This program is open first- and second-year full-time law students and second- and third-year part-time law students at schools in Washington, D.C. Applicants must submit an appellate brief on a hypothetical topic that changes annually; recently, students were asked to write on a case involving the Second Amendment. Briefs, up to 13 pages in length, are judged on the basis of substance and form.

Financial data The stipend is $5,000.

Duration 1 year.

Additional information The Washington Bar Association was founded in 1925 by African American attorneys who were denied membership in other bar associations because of their race. It continues to serve the African American legal community of Washington, D.C.

Number awarded 1 each year.

Deadline March of each year.

[979]
JUDICIAL INTERN OPPORTUNITY PROGRAM

American Bar Association
Attn: Section of Litigation
321 North Clark Street
Chicago, IL 60654-7598
(312) 988-6348   Fax: (312) 988-6234
E-mail: Gail.Howard@americanbar.org
Web: www.americanbar.org

Summary To provide an opportunity for African American and other minority or economically disadvantaged law students to gain experience as judicial interns in selected courts during the summer.

Eligibility This program is open to first- and second-year students at ABA-accredited law schools who are 1) members of racial or ethnic groups that are traditionally underrepresented in the legal profession (African Americans, Asians, Hispanics/Latinos, Native Americans); 2) students with disabilities; 3) students who are economically disadvantaged; or 4) students who identify themselves as lesbian, gay, bisexual, or transgender. Applicants must be interested in a judicial internship at courts in selected areas and communities. They may indicate a preference for the area in which they wish to work, but they may not specify a court or a judge. Along with their application, they must submit a current resume, a 10-page legal writing sample, and a 2-page statement of interest that outlines their qualifications for the internship. Screening interviews are conducted by staff of the American Bar Association, either in person or by telephone. Final interviews are conducted by the judges with whom the interns will work. Some spots are reserved for students with an interest in intellectual property law.

Financial data The stipend is $2,000.

Duration 6 weeks during the summer.

Additional information Recently, internships were available in the following locations: Chicago along with surrounding cities and circuits throughout Illinois; Houston, Dallas, and the southern and eastern districts of Texas; Miami, Florida; Phoenix, Arizona; Los Angeles, California; New York City; Philadelphia, Pennsylvania; San Francisco, California; Seattle, Washington; and Washington, D.C. Some internships in Chicago, Los Angeles, Texas, and Washington, D.C. are reserved for students with an interest in intellectual property law.

Number awarded Varies each year; recently, 194 of these internships were awarded, including 31 at courts in Illinois, 17 in Dallas, 14 in Houston, 14 in Miami, 17 in Phoenix, 23 in Los Angeles, 30 in San Francisco, 10 in New York, 12 in Philadelphia, 8 in Seattle, and 18 in Washington, D.C.

Deadline January of each year.

[980]
JUDITH MCMANUS PRICE SCHOLARSHIPS

American Planning Association
Attn: Leadership Affairs Associate
205 North Michigan Avenue, Suite 1200
Chicago, IL 60601
(312) 431-9100   Fax: (312) 786-6700
E-mail: mgroh@planning.org
Web: www.planning.org/scholarships/apa

Summary To provide financial assistance to African American and other underrepresented minority students enrolled in undergraduate or graduate degree programs at recognized planning schools.

Eligibility This program is open to undergraduate and graduate students in urban and regional planning who are women or members of the following minority groups: African American, Hispanic American, or Native American. Applicants must be citizens of the United States and able to document financial need. They must intend to work as practicing planners in the public sector. Along with their application, they must submit a 2-page personal and background statement describing how their education will be applied to career goals and why they chose planning as a career path. Selection is based (in order of importance), on: 1) commitment to planning as reflected in their personal statement and on their resume; 2) academic achievement and/or improvement during the past 2 years; 3) letters of recommendation; 4) financial need; and 5) professional presentation.

Financial data Stipends range from $2,000 to $4,000 per year. The money may be applied to tuition and living expenses only. Payment is made to the recipient's university and divided by terms in the school year.

Duration 1 year; recipients may reapply.

Additional information This program began in 2002.

Number awarded Varies each year; recently, 3 were awarded.

Deadline April of each year.

[981]
JULIA BUMRY JONES SCHOLARSHIP PROGRAM

Delta Sigma Theta Sorority, Inc.
Attn: Scholarship and Standards Committee Chair
1707 New Hampshire Avenue, N.W.
Washington, DC 20009
(202) 986-2400   Fax: (202) 986-2513
E-mail: dstemail@deltasigmatheta.org
Web: www.deltasigmatheta.org

Summary To provide financial assistance to members of Delta Sigma Theta who are interested in working on a graduate degree in journalism or another area of communications.

Eligibility This program is open to graduating college seniors and graduate students who are interested in preparing for a career in journalism or another area of communications. Applicants must be active, dues-paying members of Delta Sigma Theta. Selection is based on meritorious achievement.

Financial data The stipends range from $1,000 to $2,000. The funds may be used to cover tuition, fees, and living expenses.

Duration 1 year; may be renewed for 1 additional year.

Additional information This sponsor is a traditionally-African American social sorority. The application fee is $20.

Number awarded 1 or more each year.

Deadline March of each year.

[982]
JULIE CUNNINGHAM LEGACY SCHOLARSHIP

Conference of Minority Transportation Officials
Attn: National Scholarship Program
100 M Street, S.E., Suite 917
Washington, DC 20003
(202) 506-2917   E-mail: info@comto.org
Web: www.comto.org/page/scholarships

Summary To provide financial assistance to African American and other minority graduate students who are working on a degree in transportation to prepare for a leadership role in that industry.

Eligibility This program is open to minorities who are working on a graduate degree with an interest in leadership in transportation. Applicants must have a GPA of 3.0 or higher. They must be able to demonstrate strong leadership skills, active commitment to community service and diversity, and a commitment to the Conference of Minority Transportation Officials (COMTO) on a local or national level. Along with their application they must submit a cover letter on their transportation-related career goals and life aspirations. Financial need is not considered in the selection process.

Financial data The stipend is $7,500. Funds are paid directly to the recipient's college or university.

Duration 1 year.

Number awarded 1 each year.

Deadline April of each year.

[983]
JULIETTE DERRICOTTE SCHOLARSHIP

Delta Sigma Theta Sorority, Inc.
Attn: Scholarship and Standards Committee Chair
1707 New Hampshire Avenue, N.W.
Washington, DC 20009
(202) 986-2400   Fax: (202) 986-2513
E-mail: dstemail@deltasigmatheta.org
Web: www.deltasigmatheta.org

Summary To provide financial assistance to members of Delta Sigma Theta who are working on a graduate degree in social work.

Eligibility This program is open to graduating college seniors or graduate students who are interested in preparing for a career in social work. Applicants must be active, dues-paying members of Delta Sigma Theta. Selection is based on meritorious achievement.

Financial data The stipends range from $1,000 to $2,000 per year. The funds may be used to cover tuition, school, and living expenses.

Duration 1 year; may be renewed for 1 additional year.

Additional information This sponsor is a traditionally-African American social sorority. The application fee is $20.

Number awarded 1 or more each year.

Deadline March of each year.

[984]
JUNE MULLINS SCHOLARSHIP

Massachusetts Black Librarians' Network
P.O. Box 14
Dorchester, MA 02121
E-mail: massblacklib@gmail.com
Web: www.massblacklib.org/scholarships-and-awards

Summary To provide financial assistance to African Americans in Massachusetts who are interested in preparing for a career in librarianship.

Eligibility This program is open to U.S. citizens of African American descent who are enrolled in or accepted for enrollment in an accredited master's degree program in library and information studies. Applicants must be able to demonstrate a commitment to a career in library work. Along with their application, they must submit a brief essay on what influenced their decision to prepare for a career in library and information studies.

Financial data The stipend is $1,000.

Duration 1 year.

Additional information This program began in 1985 and was given its current name in 1995.

Number awarded 1 each year.

Deadline January of each year.

[985]
JUSTICE JUANITA KIDD STOUT TUITION SCHOLARSHIP

National Bar Association-Women Lawyers Division
Attn: Philadelphia Chapter
c/o Jacqueline Allen, Scholarship Committee Chair
P.O. Box 58004
Philadelphia, PA 19102-8004
(215) 686-7038   E-mail: scholarshipsfdnwldl@gmail.com
Web: www.nbawldphila.org

Summary To provide financial assistance to African American women who are enrolled at designated law schools in the Philadelphia region.

Eligibility This program is open to African American women entering their second or third year at the Thomas R. Kline School of Law at Drexel University, Beasley School of Law at Temple University, Rutgers (Camden) School of Law, University of Pennsylvania School of Law, Villanova School or Law, or Widener University School of Law. Applicants must submit essays on 1) their career aspirations, including how or why they chose a career in the law; and 2) an experience or personal/professional aspiration that would reflect the professional legacy of the scholarship's namesake. Selection is based on academic excellence, commitment to community service, and financial need.

Financial data The stipend is $5,000. Funding is designed to help with the payment of tuition.

Duration 1 year.

Additional information This program began in 2008.

Number awarded 1 each year.

Deadline June of each year.

[986]
KAFI WILFORD CONSTANTINE FELLOWSHIP

Alpha Kappa Alpha Sorority, Inc.
Attn: Educational Advancement Foundation
5656 South Stony Island Avenue
Chicago, IL 60637
(773) 947-0026   Toll Free: (800) 653-6528
Fax: (773) 947-0277   E-mail: akaeaf@akaeaf.net
Web: www.akaeaf.org/fellowships_endowments.htm

Summary To provide financial assistance to members of Alpha Kappa Alpha Sorority who are entering law school.

Eligibility This program is open to members of Alpha Kappa Alpha, a traditionally African American sorority, who are currently completing undergraduate study at a college or university in any state. Applicants must have been accepted into law school. They must submit 1) a list of honors, awards, and scholarships received; 2) a list of organizations in which they have memberships, especially minority organizations; and 3) a statement of their personal and career goals, including how this scholarship will enhance their ability to attain those goals.

Financial data A stipend is awarded (amount not specified).

Duration 1 year.

Number awarded 1 or more each even-numbered year.

Deadline April of each even-numbered year.

[987]
KAISER PERMANENTE COLORADO DIVERSITY SCHOLARSHIP PROGRAM

Kaiser Permanente
Attn: Diversity Development Department
10065 East Harvard Avenue, Suite 400
Denver, CO 80231
Toll Free: (877) 457-4772
E-mail: co-diversitydevelopment@kp.org

Summary To provide financial assistance to Colorado residents who are African Americans or members of other diverse groups and are interested in working on an undergraduate or graduate degree in a health care field at a public college in the state.

Eligibility This program is open to all residents of Colorado, including those who identify as 1 or more of the following: African American, Asian Pacific, Latino, lesbian, gay, bisexual, transgender, intersex, Native American, U.S. veteran, and/or a person with a disability. Applicants must be enrolled or planning to enroll full time at a publicly-funded college, university, or technical school in Colorado as 1) a graduating high school senior with a GPA of 2.7 or higher; 2) a GED recipient with a GED score of 520 or higher; 3) an undergraduate student; or 4) a graduate or doctoral student. They must be preparing for a career in health care (e.g., athletic training, audiology, cardiovascular perfusion technology, clinical medical assisting, cytotechnology, dental assisting, dental hygiene, diagnostic medicine, dietetics, emergency medical technology, medicine, nursing, occupational therapy, pharmacy, phlebotomy, physical therapy, physician assistant, radiology, respiratory therapy, social work, sports medicine, surgical technology). Selection is based on academic achievement, character qualities, community outreach and volunteering, and financial need.

Financial data Stipends range from $1,400 to $2,600 per year.

Duration 1 year; may be renewed.

Number awarded Varies each year; recently, 17 were awarded.

Deadline March of each year.

[988]
KENTUCKY LIBRARY ASSOCIATION SCHOLARSHIP FOR MINORITY STUDENTS

Kentucky Library Association
c/o Executive Director
5932 Timber Ridge Drive, Suite 101
Prospect, KY 40059
(502) 223-5322   Fax: (502) 223-4937
E-mail: info@kylibasn.org
Web: www.klaonline.org/scholarships965.cfm

Summary To provide financial assistance to African Americans and members of other minority groups who are residents of Kentucky or attending school there and are working on an undergraduate or graduate degree in library science.

Eligibility This program is open to members of minority groups (defined as Black, American Indian, Alaskan Native, Hispanic, Pacific Islander, or other ethnic group) who are entering or continuing at a graduate library school accredited by the American Library Association (ALA) or an undergraduate library program accredited by the National Council for Teacher Education (NCATE). Applicants must be residents of Kentucky or a student in a library program in the state. Along with their application, they must submit a statement of their career objectives, why they have chosen librarianship as a career, and their reasons for applying for this scholarship. Selection is based on that statement, cumulative undergraduate and graduate GPA (if applicable), academic merit and potential, and letters of recommendation. U.S. citizenship or permanent resident status is required.

Financial data The stipend is $1,000.

Duration 1 year; nonrenewable.

Number awarded 1 or more each year.

Deadline June of each year.

[989]
KENTUCKY MINORITY EDUCATOR RECRUITMENT AND RETENTION SCHOLARSHIPS

Kentucky Department of Education
Attn: Office of Next-Generation Learners
500 Mero Street, 19th Floor
Frankfort, KY 40601
(502) 564-1479   Fax: (502) 564-4007
TDD: (502) 564-4970
E-mail: jennifer.baker@education.ky.gov
Web: www.education.ky.gov

Summary To provide forgivable loans to African American and other minority undergraduate and graduate students enrolled in Kentucky public institutions who want to become teachers.

Eligibility This program is open to residents of Kentucky who are undergraduate or graduate students pursuing initial teacher certification at a public university or community college in the state. Applicants must have a GPA of 2.75 or higher and either maintain full-time enrollment or be a part-time student within 18 semester hours of receiving a teacher education degree. They must be U.S. citizens and meet the Kentucky definition of a minority student.

Financial data   Stipends are $5,000 per year at the 8 state universities in Kentucky or $2,000 per year at community and technical colleges. This is a scholarship/loan program. Recipients are required to teach 1 semester in Kentucky for each semester or summer term the scholarship is received. If they fail to fulfill that requirement, the scholarship converts to a loan payable at 6% annually.

Duration   1 year; may be renewed up to 3 additional years.

Additional information   The Kentucky General Assembly established this program in 1992.

Number awarded   Varies each year.

Deadline   Each state college of teacher education sets its own deadline.

[990]
KPMG MINORITY ACCOUNTING DOCTORAL SCHOLARSHIPS

KPMG Foundation
Attn: Scholarship Administrator
Three Chestnut Ridge Road
Montvale, NJ 07645-0435
(201) 307-7161   Fax: (201) 624-7763
E-mail: us-kpmgfoundation@kpmg.com
Web: www.kpmgfoundation.org

Summary   To provide funding to African American and other underrepresented minority students working on a doctoral degree in accounting.

Eligibility   Applicants must be African Americans, Hispanic Americans, or Native Americans. They must be U.S. citizens or permanent residents and accepted or enrolled in a full-time accounting doctoral program. Along with their application, they must submit a brief letter explaining their reason for working on a Ph.D. in accounting.

Financial data   The stipend is $10,000 per year.

Duration   1 year; may be renewed up to 4 additional years.

Additional information   These funds are not intended to replace funds normally made available by the recipient's institution. The foundation recommends that the recipient's institution also award, to the recipient, a $5,000 annual stipend, a teaching or research assistantship, and a waiver of tuition and fees.

Number awarded   Approximately 12 each year.

Deadline   April of each year.

[991]
LAGRANT FOUNDATION GRADUATE SCHOLARSHIPS

Lagrant Foundation
Attn: Senior Talent Acquisition and Fundraising Manager
633 West Fifth Street, 48th Floor
Los Angeles, CA 90071
(323) 469-8680, ext. 223   Fax: (323) 469-8683
E-mail: erickainiguez@lagrant.com
Web: www.lagrantfoundation.org

Summary   To provide financial assistance to African American and othr minority graduate students who are working on a degree in advertising, public relations, or marketing.

Eligibility   This program is open to African Americans, Asian American/Pacific Islanders, Hispanics/Latinos, and Native Americans/American Indians who are full-time graduate students at an accredited institution. Applicants must have a GPA of 3.2 or higher and be working on a master's degree in advertising, marketing, or public relations. They must have at least 2 academic semesters remaining to complete their degree. Along with their application, they must submit 1) a 1- to 2-page essay outlining their career goals; why it is important to increase ethnic representation in the fields of advertising, marketing, and public relations; and the role of an advertising, marketing, or public relations practitioner; 2) a paragraph describing the graduate school and/or community activities in which they are involved; 3) a brief paragraph describing any honors and awards they have received; 4) a letter of reference; 5) a resume; and 6) an official transcript. U.S. citizenship or permanent resident status is required.

Financial data   The stipend is $5,000.

Duration   1 year.

Number awarded   Varies each year; recently, 19 were awarded.

Deadline   February of each year.

[992]
LARRY W. CARTER SCHOLARSHIP

Greater Des Moines Community Foundation
Finkbine Mansion
1915 Grand Avenue
Des Moines, IA 50309
(515) 883-2626   Fax: (515) 309-0704
E-mail: trettin@desmoinesfoundation.org
Web:
   www.communityfoundationofgreaterdesmoines.wordpress.com

Summary   To provide financial assistance to African American undergraduate and graduate students in Iowa.

Eligibility   Eligible to apply are African Americans who reside in Iowa and are enrolled in college or graduate school on a full- or part-time basis. Applicants must submit a personal statement that explains why they feel they should be selected to receive this scholarship and describes their personal and educational goals, motivations, and reasons for pursuing higher education. Financial need is considered in the selection process.

Financial data   The stipend is $3,000.

Duration   1 year.

Number awarded   Varies each year; recently, 3 were awarded.

Deadline   May of each year.

[993]
LARRY WHITESIDE SCHOLARSHIP

National Association of Black Journalists
Attn: Program Manager
University of Maryland
1100 Knight Hall, Suite 3100
College Park, MD 20742
(301) 405-7520   Fax: (301) 314-1714
E-mail: Sberry@nabj.org
Web: www.nabj.org/?page=ScholarshipWhiteside

Summary To provide financial assistance to undergraduate or graduate student members of the National Association of Black Journalists (NABJ) who are preparing for a career in sports journalism.

Eligibility This program is open to African American undergraduate or graduate student members of NABJ who are currently enrolled full time at an accredited 4-year college or university. Applicants must be studying journalism as preparing for a career in sports journalism and have a GPA of 2.5 or higher in their major and 2.0 overall. They must be able to demonstrate financial need. Along with their application, they must submit 5 samples of their work, an official college transcript, 3 letters of recommendation, a resume, and an essay of 1,000 to 2,000 words on a sports journalist (living or deceased) whom they admire and why that person has inspired them to prepare for a career in sports journalism.

Financial data The stipend is $3,000. Funds are paid directly to the recipient's college or university.

Duration 1 year; nonrenewable.

Number awarded 1 each year.

Deadline February of each year.

[994]
LAUNCHING LEADERS MBA SCHOLARSHIP

JPMorgan Chase
Campus Recruiting
Attn: Launching Leaders
277 Park Avenue, Second Floor
New York, NY 10172
(212) 270-6000
E-mail: bronwen.x.baumgardner@jpmorgan.com
Web: careers.jpmorgan.com

Summary To provide financial assistance and work experience to Black and other underrepresented minority students enrolled in the first year of an M.B.A. program.

Eligibility This program is open to Black, Hispanic, and Native American students enrolled in the first year of an M.B.A. program. Applicants must have a demonstrated commitment to working in financial services. Along with their application, they must submit essays on 1) a hypothetical proposal on how to use $50 million from a donor to their school to benefit all of its students; and 2) the special background and attributes they would contribute to the sponsor's diversity agenda and their motivation for applying to this scholarship program. They must be interested in a summer associate position in the sponsor's investment banking, sales and trading, or research divisions.

Financial data The stipend is $40,000 for the first year of study; a paid summer associate position is also provided.

Duration 1 year; may be renewed 1 additional year if the recipient successfully completes the 10-week summer associate program.

Number awarded Varies each year.

Deadline October of each year.

[995]
LAURENCE R. FOSTER MEMORIAL SCHOLARSHIPS

Oregon Office of Student Access and Completion
Attn: Scholarship Processing Coordinator
1500 Valley River Drive, Suite 100
Eugene, OR 97401-2146
(541) 687-7422   Toll Free: (800) 452-8807, ext. 7422
Fax: (541) 687-7414   TDD: (800) 735-2900
E-mail: cheryl.a.connolly@state.or.us
Web: app.oregonstudentaid.gov/Catalog/Default.aspx

Summary To provide financial assistance to African American and other residents of Oregon from diverse environments who are enrolled at a college or graduate school in any state to prepare for a public health career.

Eligibility This program is open to residents of Oregon who are enrolled at least half time at a 4-year college or university in any state to prepare for a career in public health (not private practice). Preference is given first to applicants from diverse environments; second to persons employed in, or graduate students working on a degree in, public health; and third to juniors and seniors majoring in a health program (e.g., nursing, medical technology, physician assistant). Applicants must be able to demonstrate financial need. Along with their application, they must submit essays of 250 to 350 words on 1) what public health means to them; 2) the public health aspect they intend to practice and the health and population issues impacted by that aspect; and 3) their experience living or working in diverse environments.

Financial data Stipends for scholarships offered by the Oregon Office of Student Access and Completion (OSAC) range from $1,000 to $10,000 but recently averaged $4,368.

Duration 1 year.

Additional information This program is administered by the OSAC with funds provided by the Oregon Community Foundation.

Number awarded Varies each year; recently, 6 were awarded.

Deadline February of each year.

[996]
LEADERSHIP FOR DIVERSITY SCHOLARSHIP

California School Library Association
Attn: CSL Foundation
6444 East Spring Street, Number 237
Long Beach, CA 90815-1553
Toll Free: (888) 655-8480   Fax: (888) 655-8480
E-mail: info@csla.net
Web: www.csla.net/awards-2/scholarships

Summary To provide financial assistance to African American and other students who reflect the diversity of California's population and are interested in earning a credential as a library media teacher in the state.

Eligibility This program is open to students who are members of a traditionally underrepresented group enrolled in a college or university library media teacher credential program in California. Applicants must intend to work as a library media teacher in a California school library media center for a minimum of 3 years. Along with their application, they must submit a 250-word statement on what they can contribute to

the profession, their commitment to serving the needs of multicultural and multilingual students, and their financial need.
Financial data The stipend is $1,500.
Duration 1 year.
Number awarded 1 each year.
Deadline September of each year.

[997]
LEADERSHIP LEGACY SCHOLARSHIP FOR GRADUATES
Women's Transportation Seminar
Attn: WTS Foundation
1701 K Street, N.W., Suite 800
Washington, DC 20006
(202) 955-5085   Fax: (202) 955-5088
E-mail: wts@wtsinternational.org
Web: www.wtsinternational.org/education/scholarships

Summary To provide financial assistance to graduate women, especially African Americans and other minorities, who are interested in a career in transportation.

Eligibility This program is open to women who are working on a graduate degree in transportation or a transportation-related field (e.g., transportation engineering, planning, business management, finance, or logistics). Applicants must have a GPA of 3.0 or higher and be interested in a career in transportation. Along with their application, they must submit a 1,000-word statement about their vision of how their education will give them the tools to better serve their community's needs and transportation issues. Applications must be submitted first to a local chapter; the chapters forward selected applications for consideration on the national level. Minority women are especially encouraged to apply. Selection is based on transportation involvement and goals, job skills, and academic record; financial need is not considered.

Financial data The stipend is $5,000.
Duration 1 year.
Additional information This program began in 2008. Each year, it focuses on women with a special interest; recently, it was reserved for women who have a specific interest in addressing the impact of transportation on sustainability, land use, environmental impact, security, and quality of life issues internationally.
Number awarded 1 each year.
Deadline Applications must be submitted by November to a local WTS chapter.

[998]
LEON BRADLEY SCHOLARSHIPS
American Association of School Personnel Administrators
Attn: Scholarship Program
11863 West 112th Street, Suite 100
Overland Park, KS 66210
(913) 327-1222   Fax: (913) 327-1223
E-mail: aaspa@aaspa.org
Web: www.aaspa.org/leon-bradley-scholarship

Summary To provide financial assistance to African American and other minority undergraduates, paraprofessionals, and graduate students preparing for a career in teaching and school leadership at colleges in designated southeastern states.

Eligibility This program is open to members of minority groups (Black, American Indian, Alaskan Native, Asian, Pacific Islander, Hispanic, Middle Easterner) currently enrolled full time at a college or university in Alabama, Florida, Georgia, Kentucky, North Carolina, South Carolina, Tennessee, or Virginia. Applicants must be 1) undergraduates in their final year (including student teaching) of an initial teaching certification program; 2) paraprofessional career-changers in their final year (including student teaching) of an initial teaching certification program; or 3) graduate students who have served as a licensed teacher and are working on a school administrator credential. They must have an overall GPA of 3.0 or higher. Priority is given to applicants who 1) can demonstrate work experience that has been applied to college expenses; 2) have received other scholarship or financial aid support; or 3) are seeking initial certification and/or endorsement in a state-identified critical area.

Financial data Stipends are $2,500 for undergraduates in their final year, $1,500 for paraprofessionals in their final year, and $1,500 for graduate students.
Duration 1 year.
Number awarded 4 each year: 1 undergraduate, 1 paraprofessional, and 2 graduate students.
Deadline May of each year.

[999]
LES PAYNE FOUNDER'S SCHOLARSHIP
National Association of Black Journalists
Attn: Program Manager
University of Maryland
1100 Knight Hall, Suite 3100
College Park, MD 20742
(301) 405-7520   Fax: (301) 314-1714
E-mail: Sberry@nabj.org
Web: www.nabj.org/?page=ScholarshipsPayne

Summary To provide financial assistance to undergraduate and graduate student members of the National Association of Black Journalists (NABJ) who are working on a degree in print journalism.

Eligibility This program is open to African American undergraduate or graduate student members of NABJ who are currently enrolled full time at an accredited 4-year college or university. Applicants must be working on a degree in print journalism and have a GPA of 3.0 or higher. They must be able to demonstrate financial need. Along with their application, they must submit 5 samples of their work, an official college transcript, 3 letters of recommendation, a resume, and an essay of 1,000 to 2,000 words describing 3 issues about which they are passionate and which they hope to cover as a professional journalist.

Financial data The stipend is $2,500.
Duration 1 year.
Number awarded 1 each year.
Deadline February of each year.

[1000]
LIBRARY AND INFORMATION TECHNOLOGY ASSOCIATION MINORITY SCHOLARSHIPS

American Library Association
Attn: Library and Information Technology Association
50 East Huron Street
Chicago, IL 60611-2795
(312) 280-4270   Toll Free: (800) 545-2433, ext. 4270
Fax: (312) 280-3257   TDD: (888) 814-7692
E-mail: lita@ala.org
Web: www.ala.org/lita/awards

Summary To provide financial assistance to African American and other minority graduate students interested in preparing for a career in library automation.

Eligibility This program is open to U.S. or Canadian citizens who are interested in working on a master's degree in library/information science and preparing for a career in the field of library and automated systems. Applicants must be a member of 1 of the following ethnic groups: African American, American Indian, Alaskan Native, Asian, Pacific Islander, or Hispanic. They may not have completed more than 12 credit hours of course work for their degree. Selection is based on academic excellence, leadership potential, evidence of a commitment to a career in library automation and information technology, and prior activity and experience in those fields. Financial need is considered when all other factors are equal.

Financial data Stipends are $3,000 or $2,500. Funds are paid directly to the recipient.

Duration 1 year.

Additional information This program includes scholarships funded by Online Computer Library Center (OCLC) and by Library Systems & Services, Inc. (LSSI).

Number awarded 2 each year: 1 at $3,000 (funded by OCLC) and 1 at $2,500 (funded by LSSI).

Deadline February of each year.

[1001]
LIONEL C. BARROW MINORITY DOCTORAL STUDENT SCHOLARSHIP

Association for Education in Journalism and Mass
  Communication
Attn: Communication Theory and Methodology Division
234 Outlet Pointe Boulevard, Suite A
Columbia, SC 29210-5667
(803) 798-0271   Fax: (803) 772-3509
E-mail: aejmc@aejmc.org
Web: www.aejmc.us

Summary To provide financial assistance to African American and other minorities who are interested in working on a doctorate in mass communication.

Eligibility This program is open to minority students enrolled in a Ph.D. program in journalism and/or mass communication. Applicants must submit 2 letters of recommendation, a resume, and a brief letter outlining their research interests and career plans. Membership in the association is not required, but applicants must be U.S. citizens or permanent residents. Selection is based on the likelihood that the applicant's work will contribute to communication theory and/or methodology.

Financial data The stipend is $2,000.

Duration 1 year.

Additional information This program began in 1972.

Number awarded 1 each year.

Deadline May of each year.

[1002]
LORRAINE HANSBERRY PLAYWRITING AWARD

John F. Kennedy Center for the Performing Arts
Education Department
Attn: Kennedy Center American College Theater Festival
2700 F Street, N.W.
Washington, DC 20566
(202) 416-8864   Fax: (202) 416-8860
E-mail: ghenry@kennedy-center.org
Web: web.kennedy-center.org

Summary To recognize and reward student authors of plays on the African American experience in America.

Eligibility Students at any accredited junior or senior college in the United States are eligible to compete, provided their college agrees to participate in the Kennedy Center American College Theater Festival (KCACTF). Undergraduate students must be carrying at least 6 semester hours, graduate students must be enrolled in at least 3 semester hours, and continuing part-time students must be enrolled in a regular degree or certificate program. These awards are presented to the best plays written by students of African or Diasporan descent on the subject of the African American experience.

Financial data The first-place award is $1,000 and the second-place award is $500. Other benefits include appropriate membership in the Dramatists Guild and an all-expense paid professional development opportunity.

Duration The awards are presented annually.

Additional information This program is supported by the Kennedy Center and Dramatic Publishing Company. It honors the first African American playwright to win the New York Drama Critics Award who died in 1965 at the age of 34. First presented in 1977, it is part of the Michael Kanin Playwriting Awards Program. The sponsoring college or university must pay a registration fee of $275 for each production.

Number awarded 2 each year.

Deadline November of each year.

[1003]
LOS ANGELES CHAPTER NBMBAA GRADUATE SCHOLARSHIPS

National Black MBA Association-Los Angeles Chapter
Attn: Director of Student Affairs and Scholarships
P.O. Box 83731
Los Angeles, CA 90083
E-mail: education@labmba.org
Web: www.labmba.org/undergrad-mba-phd

Summary To provide financial assistance to African Americans from Nevada or central or southern California working on a graduate business degree at a college in that area.

Eligibility This program is open to African American residents of Nevada or central or southern California currently enrolled full or part time at an accredited college or university in that area. Applicants must be working on an M.B.A., Ph.D., or D.B.A. degree in business, management, organizational behavior, or other business-related field. Along with their application, they must submit 1) a resume of professional, community, and/or extracurricular activities; 2) a 1-paragraph statement of career objectives; and 3) essays up to 500 words in length on 2 topics that change annually but relate to African Americans and business. Selection is based on the essays, academic achievements, and community and extra-curricular activities. Students who submit outstanding essays are considered for sponsor awards.

Financial data   The stipend is $1,500. Sponsor awards, if available, range from $2,500 to $5,000.

Duration   1 year.

Additional information   Winners also receive a 2-year membership in the National Black MBA Association (NBM-BAA); membership fees are deducted from the award.

Number awarded   1 or more each year.

Deadline   September of each year.

[1004]
LOUISE JANE MOSES/AGNES DAVIS MEMORIAL SCHOLARSHIP

California Librarians Black Caucus-Greater Los Angeles
  Chapter
Attn: Scholarship Committee
P.O. Box 882276
Los Angeles, CA 90009
E-mail: scholarship@clbc.org
Web: www.clbc.org/scholar.html

Summary   To provide financial assistance to African Americans in California who are interested in becoming librarians or library paraprofessionals.

Eligibility   This program is open to African American residents of California who are working on a degree from an accredited library/information science program or an accredited library/information science paraprofessional program in the state. Applicants must submit an essay of 300 to 500 words on their professional goals and their interest in a library or information-related career. Selection is based on demonstrated financial need, scholastic achievement, and commitment to the goals of encouraging and supporting African American library professionals and improving library service to the African American community. Interviews are required.

Financial data   Stipends range from $750 to $1,500.

Duration   1 year.

Number awarded   2 to 3 each year.

Deadline   October of each year.

[1005]
LTK ENGINEERING SCHOLARSHIP

Conference of Minority Transportation Officials
Attn: National Scholarship Program
100 M Street, S.E., Suite 917
Washington, DC 20003
(202) 506-2917   E-mail: info@comto.org
Web: www.comto.org/page/scholarships

Summary   To provide financial assistance to African American and other minority upper-division and graduate students in engineering or other field related to transportation.

Eligibility   This program is open to full-time minority juniors, seniors, and graduate students in engineering or other technical transportation-related disciplines. Applicants must have a GPA of 3.0 or higher. Along with their application they must submit a cover letter on their transportation-related career

goals and life aspirations. Financial need is not considered in the selection process.

Financial data   The stipend is $6,000. Funds are paid directly to the recipient's college or university.

Duration   1 year.

Additional information   This program is sponsored by LTK Engineering Services.

Number awarded   1 each year.

Deadline   April of each year.

[1006]
LTK ENGINEERING TRANSPORTATION PLANNING SCHOLARSHIP

Conference of Minority Transportation Officials
Attn: National Scholarship Program
100 M Street, S.E., Suite 917
Washington, DC 20003
(202) 506-2917   E-mail: info@comto.org
Web: www.comto.org/page/scholarships

Summary   To provide financial assistance to African American and other minority upper-division and graduate students in planning or other field related to transportation.

Eligibility   This program is open to full-time minority juniors, seniors, and graduate students in planning of other technical transportation-related disciplines. Applicants must have a GPA of 3.0 or higher. Along with their application they must submit a cover letter on their transportation-related career goals and life aspirations. Financial need is not considered in the selection process.

Financial data   The stipend is $5,000. Funds are paid directly to the recipient's college or university.

Duration   1 year.

Additional information   This program is sponsored by LTK Engineering Services.

Number awarded   1 each year.

Deadline   April of each year.

[1007]
LUCILLE BLUFORD JOURNALISM SCHOLARSHIP

Missouri Legislative Black Caucus Foundation
c/o Representative Gail McCann Beatty
4609 Paseo Boulevard, Suite 102
Kansas City, MO 64110
(573) 761-4166   Toll Free: (877) 63-MLBCF
Fax: (816) 861-2845   E-mail: mail@mlbcf.org
Web: www.mlbcf.org/scholarships/journalism

Summary   To provide financial assistance to African American residents of Missouri who are interested in working on an undergraduate or graduate degree in journalism at a school in any state.

Eligibility   This program is open to African American residents of Missouri who are enrolled full time in an undergraduate or graduate program in journalism at a college or university in any state. Applicants must have a GPA of 3.0 or higher. Along with their application, they must submit a writing sample and a 200-word personal statement on how their education will assist them in achieving their goals. Selection is based on academic performance, community service, leadership skills, and financial need.

Financial data A stipend is awarded (amount not specified).

Duration 1 year; recipients may reapply for up to 3 additional years of support.

Number awarded 1 or more each year.

Deadline May of each year.

[1008]
LULLELIA W. HARRISON COUNSELING SCHOLARSHIP

Zeta Phi Beta Sorority, Inc.
Attn: National Educational Foundation
1734 New Hampshire Avenue, N.W.
Washington, DC 20009
(202) 387-3103   Fax: (202) 232-4593
E-mail: info@zetaphibetasororityhq.org
Web: www.zpbnef1975.org/scholarships-and-descriptions

Summary To provide financial assistance to undergraduate and graduate students interested in preparing for a career in counseling.

Eligibility This program is open to students enrolled full time in an undergraduate or graduate program leading to a degree in counseling. Proof of enrollment is required. Along with their application, they must submit a 150-word essay on their educational goals and professional aspirations, how this award will help them to achieve those goals, and why they should receive the award. Financial need is not considered in the selection process.

Financial data The stipend ranges from $500 to $1,000.

Duration 1 academic year.

Additional information Zeta Phi Beta is a traditionally African American sorority.

Number awarded 3 or more each year.

Deadline January of each year.

[1009]
M. ELIZABETH CARNEGIE SCHOLARSHIP

Nurses Educational Funds, Inc.
Attn: Scholarship Coordinator
137 Montague Street, Suite 144
Brooklyn, NY 11201
(917) 524-8051   E-mail: info@n-e-f.org
Web: www.n-e-f.org/index.php/about/nef-scholarships.html

Summary To provide financial assistance to African American nurses who wish to work on a doctoral degree.

Eligibility This program is open to African American registered nurses who are members of a national professional nursing organization and enrolled full or part time in a nursing or nursing-related program at the doctoral level. Applicants must have completed at least 12 credits and have a GPA of 3.6 or higher. They must be U.S. citizens or have declared their official intention of becoming a citizen. Along with their application, they must submit an essay of 750 to 850 words defining their professional goals and assessing their potential for making a contribution to the nursing profession.

Financial data Stipends range from $2,500 to $10,000, depending on the availability of funds.

Duration 1 year; nonrenewable.

Additional information There is a $20 application fee.

Number awarded 1 each year.

Deadline January of each year.

[1010]
MADELINE KOUNTZE DUGGER-KELLY SCHOLARSHIP

Black Women in Sport Foundation
Attn: Tina Sloan Green, President/Executive Director
4300 Monument Road
Philadelphia, PA 19131
(215) 877-1925, ext. 320   Fax: (215) 877-1942
E-mail: tinabwsf@temple.edu
Web: www.blackwomeninsport.org/scholarships-1

Summary To provide financial assistance to Black female graduate students who have participated in sports.

Eligibility This program is open to Black women who are currently enrolled full time in an accredited graduate program. Applicants must have participated in athletics during their undergraduate studies and have displayed the qualities of the program's namesake.

Financial data The stipend is $1,000.

Duration 1 year.

Number awarded 1 each year.

Deadline March of each year.

[1011]
MALENA RANCE SCHOLARSHIP FUND

Black Entertainment and Sports Lawyers Association
Attn: Scholarships
P.O. Box 230794
New York, NY 10023
E-mail: scholarship@besla.org
Web: www.besla.org/#!scholarship-fund/qe8of

Summary To provide financial assistance to African American women who are interested in the fields of entertainment and/or sports law.

Eligibility This program is open to African American women who have completed at least 1 year of full-time study at an accredited law school. Applicants must be able to demonstrate an interest in entertainment or sports law by 2 or more of the following: 1) completed an intellectual property, entertainment, or sports law related course; 2) completed an internship or clerkship in the entertainment, sports, or related law field; or 3) membership in their school's sports and entertainment club. They must have a GPA of 3.0 or higher. Along with their application, they must submit a 5-page legal memorandum on an issue facing the entertainment or sports industry.

Financial data The stipend is at least $1,500.

Duration 1 year.

Number awarded 1 or more each year.

Deadline September of each year.

[1012]
MANHATTAN CENTRAL MEDICAL SOCIETY SCHOLARSHIP

National Medical Fellowships, Inc.
Attn: Scholarship Program
347 Fifth Avenue, Suite 510
New York, NY 10016
(212) 483-8880   Toll Free: (877) NMF-1DOC
Fax: (212) 483-8897 E-mail: scholarships@nmfonline.org
Web: www.nmfonline.org

Summary To provide financial assistance to African American students at medical schools in the New York City metropolitan area.

Eligibility This program is open to African Americans who are enrolled at an accredited medical school in the New York City metropolitan area. They must be U.S. citizens or DACA students. Selection is based on leadership, commitment to serving medically underserved communities, and financial need.

Financial data The stipend is $2,000.

Duration 1 year.

Additional information This program began in 2014.

Number awarded 1 each year.

Deadline September of each year.

[1013]
MARILYN A. JACKSON MEMORIAL AWARD

Omaha Presbyterian Seminary Foundation
7101 Mercy Road, Suite 216
Omaha, NE 68106-2616
(402) 397-5138   Toll Free: (888) 244-6714
Fax: (402) 397-4944   E-mail: opsf@opsf-omaha.org
Web: www.omahapresbyterianseminaryfoundation.org

Summary To provide financial assistance to students, especially African Americans and members of other ethnic minority groups, who are enrolled at Presbyterian theological seminaries and willing to serve in designated states.

Eligibility This program is open to members of a Presbyterian Church, under the care of a presbytery as a candidate/inquirer, and accepted or enrolled to work on a master's degree in divinity at 1 of the following 10 Presbyterian theological institutions: Austin Presbyterian Theological Seminary (Austin, Texas); Columbia Theological Seminary (Decatur, Georgia); University of Dubuque Theological Seminary (Dubuque, Iowa); Johnson C. Smith Theological Seminary (Atlanta, Georgia); Louisville Presbyterian Theological Seminary (Louisville, Kentucky); McCormick Theological Seminary (Chicago, Illinois); Pittsburgh Theological Seminary (Pittsburgh, Pennsylvania); Princeton Theological Seminary (Princeton, New Jersey); San Francisco Theological Seminary (San Anselmo, California); or Union Theological Seminary and Presbyterian School of Christian Education (Richmond, Virginia). Applicants must be willing to serve in a small Presbyterian church for 5 years in Colorado, Iowa, Kansas, Minnesota, Missouri, Montana, Nebraska, North Dakota, Oklahoma, South Dakota, Utah, Wisconsin, or Wyoming. Along with their application, they must submit answers to 7 questions about themselves and their commitment to pastoral service. Preference is given to members of ethnic minority groups from the following synods: Lakes and Prairies (Iowa, Minnesota, Nebraska, North Dakota, South Dakota, Wisconsin), Mid-America (Delaware, Maryland, North Carolina, Virginia, Washington, D.C.), Rocky Mountains (Colorado, Montana, Utah, Wyoming), and Sun (Arkansas, Louisiana, Oklahoma, Texas). Financial need is considered in the selection process.

Financial data The stipend is $7,500.

Duration 1 year.

Number awarded 1 each year.

Deadline April of each year.

[1014]
MARJORIE BOWENS-WHEATLEY SCHOLARSHIPS

Unitarian Universalist Association
Attn: UU Women's Federation
258 Harvard Street
Brookline, MA 02446
(617) 838-6989   E-mail: uuwf@uua.org
Web: www.uuwf.org

Summary To provide financial assistance to African American and other women of color who are working on an undergraduate or graduate degree to prepare for Unitarian Universalist ministry or service.

Eligibility This program is open to women of color who are either 1) aspirants or candidates for the Unitarian Universalist ministry; or 2) candidates in the Unitarian Universalist Association's professional religious education or music leadership credentialing programs. Applicants must submit a 1- to 2-page narrative that covers their call to UU ministry, religious education, or music leadership; their passions; how their racial/ethnic/cultural background influences their goals for their calling; and how the work of the program's namesake relates to their dreams and plans for their UU service.

Financial data The stipend is $1,500.

Duration 1 year.

Additional information This program began in 2009.

Number awarded Varies each year; recently, 2 were awarded.

Deadline March of each year.

[1015]
MARK T. BANNER SCHOLARSHIP FOR LAW STUDENTS

Richard Linn American Inn of Court
c/o Amy Ziegler, Scholarship Chair
Green Burns & Crain
300 South Wacker Drive, Suite 2500
Chicago, IL 60606
(312) 987-2926   Fax: (312) 360-9315
E-mail: marktbannerscholarship@linninn.org
Web: www.linninn.org/Pages/scholarship.shtml

Summary To provide financial assistance to law students who are African Americans or members of other groups historically underrepresented in intellectual property law.

Eligibility This program is open to students at ABA-accredited law schools in the United States who are members of groups historically underrepresented (by race, sex, ethnicity, sexual orientation, or disability) in intellectual property law. Applicants must submit a 3-page statement on how ethics, civility, and professionalism have been their focus; how diversity has impacted them; and their commitment to a career in intellectual property law. Selection is based on academic merit; written and oral communication skills; leadership qualities; community involvement; commitment, qualities and actions toward ethics, civility and professionalism; and commitment to a career in IP law.

Financial data The stipend is $5,000.

Duration 1 year.

Number awarded 1 each year.

Deadline November of each year.

[1016]
MARTIN LUTHER KING, JR. MEMORIAL SCHOLARSHIP FUND

California Teachers Association
Attn: CTA Foundation for Teaching and Learning
1705 Murchison Drive
P.O. Box 921
Burlingame, CA 94011-0921
(650) 697-1400   E-mail: scholarships@cta.org
Web: www.cta.org

Summary To provide financial assistance for college or graduate school to African Americans and other racial and ethnic minorities who are members of the California Teachers Association (CTA), children of members, or members of the Student CTA.

Eligibility This program is open to members of racial or ethnic minority groups (African Americans, American Indians/ Alaska Natives, Asians/Pacific Islanders, and Hispanics) who are 1) active CTA members; 2) dependent children of active, retired, or deceased CTA members; or 3) members of Student CTA. Applicants must be interested in preparing for a teaching career in public education or already engaged in such a career.

Financial data Stipends vary each year; recently, they ranged up to $6,000.

Duration 1 year.

Number awarded Varies each year; recently, 24 were awarded: 1 to a CTA member, 10 to children of CTA members, and 13 to Student CTA members.

Deadline February of each year.

[1017]
MARTIN LUTHER KING JR. SCHOLARSHIP AWARDS

American Correctional Association
Attn: Scholarship Award Committee
206 North Washington Street, Suite 200
Alexandria, VA 22314
(703) 224-0000   Toll Free: (800) ACA-JOIN
Fax: (703) 224-0179   E-mail: execoffice@aca.org
Web: www.aca.org

Summary To provide financial assistance for undergraduate or graduate study to African Americans and other minorities interested in a career in the criminal justice field.

Eligibility Members of the American Correctional Association (ACA) may nominate a minority person for these awards. Nominees do not need to be ACA members, but they must have been accepted to or be enrolled in an undergraduate or graduate program in criminal justice at a 4-year college or university. Along with the nomination package, they must submit a 250-word essay describing their reflections on the ideals and philosophies of Dr. Martin Luther King and how they

have attempted to emulate those qualities in their lives. They must provide documentation of financial need, academic achievement, and commitment to the principles of Dr. King.

Financial data A stipend is awarded (amount not specified). Funds are paid directly to the recipient's college or university.

Duration 1 year.

Number awarded 1 each year.

Deadline May of each year.

[1018]
MARY ELIZABETH CARNEGIE SCHOLAR AWARD

American Nurses Foundation
Attn: Nursing Research Grants Program
8515 Georgia Avenue, Suite 400
Silver Spring, MD 20910-3492
(301) 628-5227   Toll Free: (800) 274-4ANA
Fax: (301) 628-5354   E-mail: anf@ana.org
Web: www.anfonline.org

Summary To provide funding to nurses and graduate nursing students who are members of the American Nurses Association and interested in conducting research on African American nurses.

Eligibility This program is open to ANA members who have earned a baccalaureate or higher degree. Applicants may be beginning researchers (have had no more than 3 research-based publications in refereed journals and have received, as a principal investigator, no more than $15,000 in extramural funding) or experienced researchers (those with more than 3 publications and more than $15,000 in research funding). The focus of the research must relate to African American nurses. Proposed research may be for a master's thesis or doctoral dissertation if the project has been approved by the principal investigator's thesis or dissertation committee.

Financial data The grant is $5,000. Funds may not be used as a salary for the principal investigator.

Duration 1 year.

Additional information There is a $100 application fee.

Number awarded 1 each year.

Deadline April of each year.

[1019]
MARY MUNSON RUNGE SCHOLARSHIP

American Pharmacists Association
Attn: APhA Foundation
2215 Constitution Avenue, N.W.
Washington, DC 20037-2985
(202) 429-7503   Toll Free: (800) 237-APhA
Fax: (202) 638-3793   E-mail: bwall@aphanet.org
Web: www.aphafoundation.org

Summary To provide financial assistance to members of the Academy of Student Pharmacists of the American Pharmacists Association (APhA-ASP), especially African Americans and members of other underrepresented minority groups.

Eligibility This program is open to full-time pharmacy students who have been actively involved in their school's APhA-ASP chapter. Applicants must have completed at least 1 year in the professional sequence of courses with a GPA of 2.75 or higher. Preference is given to members of underrepresented minority groups (Blacks or African Americans, American Indians or Alaska Natives, Hispanics or Latinos, Native Hawaiians or other Pacific Islanders). Along with their application, they must submit a 500-word essay on a topic that changes annually but relates to the future of the pharmacy profession, 2 letters of recommendation, a current resume or curriculum vitae, and a list of pharmacy and non-pharmacy related activities. Selection is based on the essay (20 points), academic performance (10 points), pharmacy-related activities (25 points), non-pharmacy/community activities (25 points), and letters of recommendation (20 points).

Financial data The stipend is $1,000.

Duration 1 year; recipients may reapply.

Number awarded 1 each year.

Deadline November of each year.

[1020]
MAX OLIGARIO VISIONARY SCHOLARSHIP

National Black MBA Association-Tampa Bay Chapter
Attn: Scholarship Committee
P.O. Box 173367
Tampa Bay, FL 33672
(813) 476-0242
E-mail: Membership@TampaBayBMBAA.org
Web: www.tampabaybmbaa.org/programs

Summary To provide financial assistance to African American and other minority undergraduate and graduate students at colleges in the Tampa Bay area of Florida working on a degree in business.

Eligibility This program is open to minority students enrolled full time at AACSB-accredited colleges and universities in the Tampa Bay area of Florida. Applicants must be working on an undergraduate or graduate degree in business. Undergraduates must have a GPA of 2.5 or higher. U.S. citizenship is required.

Financial data The stipend is $1,000.

Duration 1 year.

Number awarded 1 each year.

Deadline October of each year.

[1021]
MAXINE V. FENNELL/ROBIN GAINES MEMORIAL SCHOLARSHIP

New England Regional Black Nurses Association, Inc.
P.O. Box 190690
Roxbury, MA 02119
(617) 524-1951　　E-mail: nerbascholarships@gmail.com
Web: nerbna.nursingnetwork.com

Summary To provide financial assistance to registered nurses (R.N.s) from New England who are of African descent and interested in working on a degree in nursing or public health at a school in any state.

Eligibility The program is open to African American residents of the New England states who are R.N.s and currently enrolled in an NLN-accredited bachelor's, master's, or doctoral degree program in nursing or public health at a school in any state. Applicants must have a GPA of 3.0 or higher and at least 1 full year of school remaining. They must be members of the New England Regional Black Nurses Association (NERBNA). Along with their application, they must submit a 3-page essay that covers their reasons for furthering their

career in nursing; why minority nursing leadership is important; how minority nursing leadership can assist them in furthering their career; why they chose to prepare for a career in nursing; and any financial hardships that may hinder them from completing their education.

Financial data A stipend is awarded (amount not specified).

Duration 1 year.

Number awarded 1 or more each year.

Deadline February of each year.

[1022]
MCKINNEY FAMILY FUND SCHOLARSHIP

Cleveland Foundation
Attn: Scholarship Processing
1422 Euclid Avenue, Suite 1300
Cleveland, OH 44115-2001
(216) 861-3810　　　　　　　　Fax: (216) 861-1729
E-mail: mbaker@clevefdn.org
Web: www.clevelandfoundation.org

Summary To provide financial assistance to residents of Ohio, especially African Americans and members of other minority groups, who are interested in attending college or graduate school in any state.

Eligibility This program is open to U.S. citizens who have been residents of Ohio for at least 2 years. Applicants must be high school seniors or graduate students and interested in working full or part time on an associate, bachelor's, master's, or doctoral degree at an accredited college or university in any state. They must have a GPA of 2.5 or higher. Preference is given to applicants of minority descent. Selection is based on evidence of sincerity toward obtaining an academic credential. Financial need may be used as a tiebreaker.

Financial data The stipend is $2,000 per year. Funds are paid directly to the school and must be applied to tuition, fees, books, supplies, and equipment required for course work.

Duration 1 year; may be renewed up to 3 additional.

Number awarded 1 or more each year.

Deadline March of each year.

[1023]
MCKNIGHT DOCTORAL FELLOWSHIP PROGRAM

Florida Education Fund
201 East Kennedy Boulevard, Suite 1525
Tampa, FL 33602
(813) 272-2772　　　　　　　　Fax: (813) 272-2784
E-mail: mdf@fefonline.org
Web: www.fefonline.org/mdf.html

Summary To provide financial assistance to African American and Hispanic doctoral students from any state who are working on a degree in designated fields at selected universities in Florida and preparing for an academic career in that state.

Eligibility This program is open to African Americans and Hispanics from any state who are working on a Ph.D. degree at 1 of 9 universities in Florida. Fellowships may be given in any discipline in the arts and sciences, business, engineering, health sciences, nursing, or the visual and performing arts; preference is given to the following fields of study: agriculture, biology, business administration, chemistry, computer science, engineering, marine biology, mathematics, physics, or psychology. Academic programs that lead to professional degrees (such as the M.D., D.B.A., D.D.S., J.D., or D.V.M.) are not covered by the fellowship. Graduate study in education, whether leading to an Ed.D. or a Ph.D., is generally not supported. Because this program is intended to increase African American and Hispanic graduate enrollment at the 9 participating universities, currently-enrolled doctoral students at those universities are not eligible to apply. U.S. citizenship is required.

Financial data Each award provides annual tuition up to $5,000 and an annual stipend of $12,000. Recipients are also eligible for the Fellows Travel Fund, which supports recipients who wish to attend and present papers at professional conferences.

Duration 3 years; an additional 2 years of support may be provided by the university if the recipient maintains satisfactory performance and normal progress toward the Ph.D. degree.

Additional information This program began in 1984. The participating universities are Florida Agricultural and Mechanical University, Florida Atlantic University, Florida Institute of Technology, Florida International University, Florida State University, University of Central Florida, University of Florida, University of Miami, and University of South Florida.

Number awarded Up to 50 each year.

Deadline January of each year.

[1024]
MEDICAL RESEARCH FELLOWS PROGRAM

Howard Hughes Medical Institute
Attn: Department of Science Education
4000 Jones Bridge Road
Chevy Chase, MD 20815-6789
(301) 951-6708   Toll Free: (800) 448-4882, ext. 8889
Fax: (301) 215-8888   E-mail: medfellows@hhmi.org
Web: www.hhmi.org

Summary To provide financial assistance to medical, dental, and veterinary students, especially African Americans and other underrepresented groups, who are interested in pursuing research training.

Eligibility Applicants must be enrolled in a medical, dental, or veterinary school in the United States, although they may be citizens of any country with a visa authorizing them to work in this country. They must describe a proposed research project to be conducted at an academic or nonprofit research institution in the United States (other than a facility of the National Institutes of Health or other federal agency) or at the sponsor's Janelia Research Campus in Ashburn, Virginia. Research proposals should reflect the interests of the Howard Hughes Medical Institute (HHMI), especially in biochemistry, bioinformatics, biomedical engineering, biophysics, biostatistics, cell biology, developmental biology, epidemiology, genetics, immunology, mathematical and computational biology, microbiology, molecular biology, neuroscience, pharmacology, physiology, structural biology, or virology. Applications from women and minorities underrepresented in the sciences (Blacks or African Americans, Hispanics, American Indians, Native Alaskans, and Native Pacific Islanders) are especially encouraged. Students enrolled in M.D./Ph.D., Ph.D., or Sc.D. programs and those who have completed a Ph.D. or Sc.D. in a laboratory-based science are not eligible. Selection is based on the applicant's ability and promise for a research career as a physician-scientist and the quality of training that will be provided.

Financial data Fellows receive a stipend of $33,000 per year, an allowance of $5,500 for research-related enrichment activities, and an allowance of $5,500 for health, dental, and vision insurance and education and moving expenses.

Duration 12 months, beginning any time between June and August.

Additional information HHMI has entered into partnership agreements with designated sponsors to support fellows in certain areas; those include the Burroughs Wellcome Fund for veterinary students, the Foundation Fighting Blindness for ophthalmology research (particularly in the area of inherited retinal degenerative diseases), the Duchenne Research Fund for research in a field related to Duchenne Muscular Dystrophy, Citizens United for Research in Epilepsy for epilepsy research, the American Society of Human Genetics for genetics research, the Orthopaedic Research and Education Foundation for orthopaedic research, the Parkinson's Disease Foundation for Parkinson's Disease research, and the Society of Interventional Radiology Foundation for preclinical research in interventional radiology.

Number awarded Up to 60 each year.

Deadline January of each year.

[1025]
MEDICAL STUDENT ELECTIVE IN HIV PSYCHIATRY

American Psychiatric Association
Attn: Office of HIV Psychiatry
1000 Wilson Boulevard, Suite 1825
Arlington, VA 22209-3901
(703) 907-8668   Toll Free: (888) 357-7849
Fax: (703) 907-1087   E-mail: aids@psych.org
Web: www.psychiatry.org

Summary To provide an opportunity for African American and other minority medical students to spend an elective residency learning about HIV psychiatry.

Eligibility This program is open to medical students entering their fourth year at an accredited M.D. or D.O. degree-granting institution. Preference is given to minority candidates and those who have primary interests in services related to HIV/AIDS and substance abuse and its relationship to the mental health or the psychological well-being of ethnic minorities. Applicants should be interested in a psychiatry, internal medicine, pediatrics, or research career. They must be interested in participating in a program that includes intense training in HIV mental health (including neuropsychiatry), a clinical and/or research experience working with a mentor, and participation in the Committee on AIDS of the American Psychiatric Association (APA). U.S. citizenship is required.

Financial data A small stipend is provided (amount not specified).

Duration 1 month.

Additional information The heart of the program is in establishing a mentor relationship at 1 of several sites, becoming involved with a cohort of medical students interested in HIV medicine/psychiatry, participating in an interactive didactic/experimental learning program, and developing expertise in areas related to ethnic minority mental health research or psychiatric services. Students selected for the program who are not APA members automatically receive membership.

Number awarded Varies each year.

Deadline March of each year.

[1026]
MENTAL HEALTH AND SUBSTANCE ABUSE FELLOWSHIP PROGRAM

Council on Social Work Education
Attn: Minority Fellowship Program
1701 Duke Street, Suite 200
Alexandria, VA 22314-3457
(703) 683-2050   Fax: (703) 683-8099
E-mail: mfpy@cswe.org
Web: www.cswe.org

Summary To provide financial assistance to African Americans and other racial minority members interested in preparing for a clinical career in the mental health fields.

Eligibility This program is open to U.S. citizens, noncitizen nationals, and permanent residents who have been underrepresented in the field of social work. These include but are not limited to the following groups: Blacks, American Indians/Alaskan Natives, Asian/Pacific Islanders (e.g., Chinese, East Indians, South Asians, Filipinos, Hawaiians, Japanese, Koreans, and Samoans), and Hispanics (e.g., Mexicans/Chicanos, Puerto Ricans, Cubans, Central or South Americans). Applicants must be interested in and committed to a career in mental health and/or substance abuse with specialization in the delivery of services of ethnic and racial minority groups. They must have a degree in social work and be accepted to or enrolled in a full-time master's or doctoral degree program. Selection is based on evidence of strong fit with and commitment to behavioral health services for underserved racial/ethnic populations; life experiences relevant to and/or volunteer or work experience with racial/ethnic populations; high quality scholarly writing showing ability to think and write at the doctoral level; academic evidence of ability to achieve timely degree completion; and fit of the sponsor's mission with the applicant's behavioral health services or research agenda.

Financial data The program provides a monthly stipend (amount not specified), specialized training, and support for professional development.

Duration 1 academic year; renewable for 2 additional years if funds are available and the recipient makes satisfactory progress toward the degree objectives.

Additional information The program has been funded since 1978 by the Center for Mental Health Services (CMHS), the Center for Substance Abuse Prevention (CSAP), and the Center for Substance Abuse Treatment (CSAT) within the Substance Abuse and Mental Health Services Administration. The master's degree program was added in 2014.

Number awarded Varies each year; recently, 40 master's degree students, 12 new doctoral fellows and 12 returning doctoral fellows were appointed.

Deadline February of each year.

[1027]
MENTAL HEALTH RESEARCH DISSERTATION GRANT TO INCREASE WORKFORCE DIVERSITY

National Institute of Mental Health
Attn: Division of Extramural Activities
6001 Executive Boulevard, Room 6138
Bethesda, MD 20892-9609
(301) 443-3534   Fax: (301) 443-4720
TDD: (301) 451-0088   E-mail: armstrda@mail.nih.gov
Web: www.grants.nih.gov

Summary To provide research funding to African Ameican and other doctoral candidates from underrepresented groups planning to prepare for a research career in any area relevant to mental health and/or mental disorders.

Eligibility This program is open to doctoral candidates conducting dissertation research in a field related to mental health and/or mental disorders at a university, college, or professional school with an accredited doctoral degree granting program. Applicants must be 1) members of an ethnic or racial group that has been determined by the National Science Foundation to be underrepresented in health-related sciences (i.e., African Americans, Hispanic Americans, Alaska Natives, American Indians, Native Hawaiians, and other Pacific Islanders); 2) individuals with disabilities; or 3) individuals from socially, culturally, economically, or educationally disadvantaged backgrounds that have inhibited their ability to prepare for a career in health-related research. They must be U.S. citizens, nationals, or permanent residents.

Financial data The stipend is $23,376. An additional grant up to $15,000 is provided for additional research expenses, fringe benefits (including health insurance), travel to scientific meetings, and research costs of the dissertation. Facilities and administrative costs are limited to 8% of modified total direct costs.

Duration Up to 2 years; nonrenewable.

Number awarded Varies each year.

Deadline Applications must be submitted by February, June, or October of each year.

[1028]
METRO DC CHAPTER NABA SCHOLARSHIP

National Association of Black Accountants-Metro
  Washington DC Chapter
Attn: Student Member Services Directors
P.O. Box 18602
Washington, DC 20036-8602
(202) 455-LIFT
E-mail: studentservices@nabametrodc.org
Web: www.nabametrodc.org

Summary To provide financial assistance to members of the Metro Washington DC chapter of the National Association of Black Accountants (NABA) who are working on an undergraduate or graduate degree in accounting, business, or finance.

Eligibility This program is open to NABA members who live or attend school in the Metropolitan Washington D.C. area (Maryland, northern Virginia, and the District of Columbia). Applicants must be 1) full-time freshmen, sophomores, juniors, or first-year seniors majoring in accounting, business, or finance; or 2) graduate students enrolled in a C.P.A. review program. They must have an overall GPA of 3.0 or higher. Along with their application, they must submit an essay of 500 to 750 words on a topic that changes annually but relates to minorities in finance. Financial need is not considered in the selection process.

Financial data A stipend is awarded (amount not specified).

Duration 1 year.

Number awarded 1 or more each year.

Deadline February of each year.

[1029]
METRO NEW YORK CHAPTER NBMBAA SCHOLARSHIPS

National Black MBA Association-Metro New York Chapter
Attn: Scholarship Committee
P.O. Box 8135
New York, NY 10116
(212) 202-7544
E-mail: studentrelations@nyblackmba.org
Web: www.nyblackmba.org/learn/scholarship-application-2

Summary To provide financial assistance to African American and other minority students from any state working on an undergraduate or graduate degree at a school in the New York metropolitan area.

Eligibility This program is open to minority students who may be residents of any state but must be enrolled full or part time in an accredited New York metropolitan area graduate business or management program working toward an undergraduate or graduate degree. Applicants must have a record of at least 5 hours of community service or extracurricular activities each semester. Along with their application, they must submit 1,000-word essays on 1) how they are involved in improving the African American or minority community; and 2) their leadership style. Financial need is not considered in the selection process.

Financial data A stipend is awarded (amount not specified).

Duration 1 year.

Number awarded Varies each year.

Deadline November of each year.

[1030]
MIAMI CHAPTER BLACK NURSES' ASSOCIATION GRADUATE SCHOLARSHIP

Black Nurses' Association, Inc.-Miami Chapter
Attn: Scholarship Committee
P.O. Box 472826
Miami, FL 33147-2826
(305) 754-2280   E-mail: miamibna@gmail.com
Web: www.bna-miami.org/annual-scholarship—1.html

Summary To provide financial assistance to members of the National Black Nurses' Association (NBNA) from Florida who are working on a degree in nursing at a school in any state.

Eligibility This program is open to residents of Florida who are NBNA members and enrolled in a nursing program (doctoral, M.S.N., B.S.N., A.S.N., L.P.N.) at a school in any state. Applicants must have a GPA of 2.5 or higher and be able to demonstrate financial need. Along with their application, they must submit a brief statement about themselves, their future goals in nursing, and how they will be an asset to the sponsor

and its community. U.S. citizenship or permanent resident status is required.

Financial data The stipend is $1,000.

Duration 1 year.

Number awarded 3 to 4 each year.

Deadline April of each year.

[1031]
MICHAEL A. ANDERSON, SR. MEMORIAL SCHOLARSHIP

United Methodist Church-Indiana Conference
Attn: Commission on the Status and Role of Women
301 Pennsylvania Parkway, Suite 300
Indianapolis, IN 46280
(317) 564-3250   Fax: (317) 735-4228
E-mail: questions@inumc.org
Web: www.inumc.org/cosrow

Summary To provide financial assistance to African American Methodist women from Indiana who are attending a seminary in any state.

Eligibility This program is open to female African American seminarians who are preparing for the ordained ministry in the Indiana Conference of the United Methodist Church (UMC) at a seminary in any state. Applicants must submit 1) a 1-page autobiography; 2) a 1-page summary of their understanding of their call to ministry and the impact that has on their professional goals; and 3) a financial statement. Selection is based on financial need (50%), clarity of call (20%), recommendations (20%), and academic honors and awards (10%).

Financial data A stipend is awarded (amount not specified). Funds are sent directly to the seminary attended by the recipient.

Duration 1 year.

Number awarded 1 each year.

Deadline April of each year.

[1032]
MICHELLE JACKSON SCHOLARSHIP FUND

Christian Church (Disciples of Christ)
Attn: Disciples Home Missions
130 East Washington Street
P.O. Box 1986
Indianapolis, IN 46206-1986
(317) 713-2652   Toll Free: (888) DHM-2631
Fax: (317) 635-4426   E-mail: mail@dhm.disciples.org
Web: www.discipleshomemissions.org

Summary To provide financial assistance to African American women interested in preparing for a career in the ministry of the Christian Church (Disciples of Christ).

Eligibility This program is open to female African American ministerial students who are members of a Christian Church (Disciples of Christ) congregation in the United States or Canada. Applicants must plan to prepare for the ordained ministry, be working on an M.Div. or equivalent degree, provide evidence of financial need, be enrolled full time in an accredited school or seminary, provide a transcript of academic work, and be under the care of a regional Commission on the Ministry or in the process of coming under care.

Financial data A stipend is awarded (amount not specified).

Duration 1 year; recipients may reapply.
Number awarded 1 each year.
Deadline March of each year.

[1033]
MICHIGAN AUTO LAW DIVERSITY SCHOLARSHIP

Michigan Auto Law
Attn: Natalie Lombardo
30101 Northwestern Highway
Farmington Hills, MI 48334
(248) 353-7575   Fax: (248) 353-4504
E-mail: bwarner@ michiganautolaw.com
Web: www.michiganautolaw.com

Summary To provide financial assistance to African American or othr law students who will contribute to diversity of their school's student body.

Eligibility This program is open to students entering their first, second, or third year at an accredited law school in the United States. Applicants must be a member of an ethnic or racial minority or demonstrate a defined commitment to issues of diversity within their academic career. They must be U.S. citizens and have a GPA of 3.0 or higher. Selection is based on transcripts and an essay describing their efforts to encourage greater racial or ethnic diversity within the student body of their law school and/or undergraduate program.

Financial data The stipend is $2,000.
Duration 1 year.
Number awarded 1 each year.
Deadline April of each year.

[1034]
MICKEY LELAND ENERGY FELLOWSHIPS

Oak Ridge Institute for Science and Education
Attn: MLEF Fellowship Program
1299 Bethel Valley Road, Building SC-200
P.O. Box 117, MS 36
Oak Ridge, TN 37831-0117
(865) 574-6440   Fax: (865) 576-0734
E-mail: barbara.dunkin@orau.org
Web: orise.orau.gov/mlef/index.html

Summary To provide summer work experience at fossil energy sites of the Department of Energy (DOE) to African American and other underrepresented minority students or postdoctorates.

Eligibility This program is open to U.S. citizens currently enrolled full time at an accredited college or university. Applicants must be undergraduate, graduate, or postdoctoral students in fields of science, technology (IT), engineering, or mathematics (STEM) and have a GPA of 3.0 or higher. They must be interested in a summer work experience at a DOE fossil energy research facility. Along with their application, they must submit a 100-word statement on why they want to participate in this program. A goal of the program is to recruit women and underrepresented minorities into careers related to fossil energy, although all qualified students are encouraged to apply.

Financial data Weekly stipends are $600 for undergraduates, $750 for master's degree students, or $850 for doctoral and postdoctoral students. Travel costs for a round trip to and

from the site and for a trip to a designated place for technical presentations are also paid.

Duration 10 weeks during the summer.

Additional information This program began as 3 separate activities: the Historically Black Colleges and Universities Internship Program established in 1995, the Hispanic Internship Program established in 1998, and the Tribal Colleges and Universities Internship Program, established in 2000. Those 3 programs were merged into the Fossil Energy Minority Education Initiative, renamed the Mickey Leland Energy Fellowship Program in 2000. Sites to which interns may be assigned include the National Energy Technology Laboratory (Morgantown, West Virginia, Albany, Oregon and Pittsburgh, Pennsylvania), Pacific Northwest National Laboratory (Richland, Washington), Sandia National Laboratory (Livermore, California), Lawrence Berkeley National Laboratory (Berkeley, California), Los Alamos National Laboratory (Los Alamos, New Mexico), Strategic Petroleum Reserve Project Management Office (New Orleans, Louisiana), or U.S. Department of Energy Headquarters (Washington, D.C.).

Number awarded Varies each year; recently, 30 students participated in this program.

Deadline December of each year.

[1035]
MIDWIVES OF COLOR-WATSON MIDWIFERY STUDENT SCHOLARSHIP

American College of Nurse-Midwives
Attn: ACNM Foundation, Inc.
8403 Colesville Road, Suite 1550
Silver Spring, MD 20910-6374
(240) 485-1850   Fax: (240) 485-1818
E-mail: foundation@acnmf.org
Web: www.midwife.org

Summary To provide financial assistance for midwifery education to African American and other students of color who belong to the American College of Nurse-Midwives (ACNM).

Eligibility This program is open to ACNM members of color who are currently enrolled in an accredited basic midwife education program and have successfully completed 1 academic or clinical semester/quarter or clinical module. Applicants must submit they must submit a 150-word essay on their 5-year midwifery career plans; a 150-word essay on their intended future participation in the local, regional, and/or national activities of the ACNM; a 150-word essay on their need for financial assistance; and a 100-word statement on how they would use the funds if they receive the scholarship. Selection is based on academic excellence, leadership potential, and financial need.

Financial data The stipend is $3,000.
Duration 1 year.
Number awarded Varies each year; recently, 3 were awarded.
Deadline February of each year.

[1036]
MILDRED CARTER BRADHAM SOCIAL WORK FELLOWSHIP

Zeta Phi Beta Sorority, Inc.
Attn: National Educational Foundation
1734 New Hampshire Avenue, N.W.
Washington, DC 20009
(202) 387-3103   Fax: (202) 232-4593
E-mail: info@zetaphibetasororityhq.org
Web: www.zpbnef1975.org/scholarships-and-descriptions

Summary To provide financial assistance to members of Zeta Phi Beta Sorority who are interested in studying social work on the graduate level.

Eligibility This program is open to members of Zeta Phi Beta who are interested in working full time on a graduate or professional degree in social work. Applicants must have shown scholarly distinction or unusual ability in their chosen field. Along with their application, they must submit a 150-word essay on their educational goals and professional aspirations, how this award will help them to achieve those goals, and why they should receive the award. Financial need is not considered in the selection process.

Financial data The stipend ranges from $500 to $1,000 per year; funds are paid directly to the college or university.

Duration 1 academic year; may be renewed.

Additional information Zeta Phi Beta is a traditionally African American sorority.

Number awarded 1 each year.

Deadline January of each year.

[1037]
MILLER JOHNSON WEST MICHIGAN DIVERSITY LAW SCHOOL SCHOLARSHIP

Grand Rapids Community Foundation
Attn: Education Program Officer
185 Oakes Street S.W.
Grand Rapids, MI 49503-4008
(616) 454-1751, ext. 103   Fax: (616) 454-6455
E-mail: rbishop@grfoundation.org
Web: www.grfoundation.org/scholarshipslist

Summary To provide financial assistance to African Americans and other minorities from Michigan who are attending law school in any state.

Eligibility This program is open to U.S. citizens who are students of color (African American, Asian, Hispanic, Native American, Pacific Islander) and residents of Michigan. Applicants must be attending an accredited law school in any state. They must have a GPA of 3.0 or higher and be able to demonstrate financial need.

Financial data The stipend is $5,000. Funds are paid directly to the recipient's institution.

Duration 1 year.

Number awarded 1 each year.

Deadline March of each year.

[1038]
MINORITIES IN GOVERNMENT FINANCE SCHOLARSHIP

Government Finance Officers Association
Attn: Scholarship Committee
203 North LaSalle Street, Suite 2700
Chicago, IL 60601-1210
(312) 977-9700   Fax: (312) 977-4806
Web: www.gfoa.org

Summary To provide financial assistance to African American and other minority upper-division and graduate students who are preparing for a career in state and local government finance.

Eligibility This program is open to upper-division and graduate students who are preparing for a career in public finance by working on a degree in public administration, accounting, finance, political science, economics, or business administration (with a specific focus on government or nonprofit management). Applicants must be members of a minority group, citizens or permanent residents of the United States or Canada, and able to provide a letter of recommendation from a representative of their school. Selection is based on career plans, academic record, plan of study, letters of recommendation, and GPA. Financial need is not considered.

Financial data The stipend is $6,000.

Duration 1 year.

Additional information This program defines minorities as Blacks or African Americans, American Indians or Alaskan Natives, Hispanics or Latinos, Native Hawaiians or other Pacific Islanders, or Asians.

Number awarded 1 each year.

Deadline February of each year.

[1039]
MINORITY AND UNDERREPRESENTED ENVIRONMENTAL LITERACY PROGRAM

Missouri Department of Higher Education
Attn: Student Financial Assistance
205 Jefferson Street
P.O. Box 1469
Jefferson City, MO 65102-1469
(573) 751-2361   Toll Free: (800) 473-6757
Fax: (573) 751-6635   E-mail: info@dhe.mo.gov
Web: www.dhe.mo.gov/ppc/grants/muelp_0310_final.php

Summary To provide financial assistance to African American and other underrepresented students from Missouri who are or will be working on a bachelor's or master's degree in an environmental field.

Eligibility This program is open to residents of Missouri who are high school seniors or current undergraduate or graduate students enrolled or planning to enroll full time at a college or university in the state. Priority is given to members of the following underrepresented minority ethnic groups: African Americans, Hispanic or Latino Americans, Native Americans and Alaska Natives, and Native Hawaiians and Pacific Islanders. Applicants must be working on or planning to work on a bachelor's or master's degree in 1) engineering (civil, chemical, environmental, mechanical, or agricultural); 2) environmental studies (geology, biology, wildlife management, natural resource planning, natural resources, or a closely-related course of study); 3) environmental chemistry;

or 4) environmental law enforcement. They must be U.S. citizens or permanent residents or otherwise lawfully present in the United States. Graduating high school seniors must have a GPA of 3.0 or higher; students currently enrolled in college or graduate school must have a GPA of 2.5 or higher. Along with their application, they must submit a 1-page essay on why they are applying for this scholarship, 3 letters of recommendation, a resume of school and community activities, and transcripts that include SAT or ACT scores. Financial need is not considered in the selection process.

Financial data Stipends vary each year; recently, they averaged approximately $3,045 per year.

Duration 1 year; may be renewed if the recipient maintains a GPA of 2.5 or higher and full-time enrollment.

Additional information This program was established by the Missouri Department of Natural Resources but transferred to the Department of Higher Education in 2009.

Number awarded Varies each year.

Deadline May of each year.

[1040]
MINORITY FACULTY DEVELOPMENT SCHOLARSHIP AWARD IN PHYSICAL THERAPY

American Physical Therapy Association
Attn: Honors and Awards Program
1111 North Fairfax Street
Alexandria, VA 22314-1488
(703) 684-APTA   Toll Free: (800) 999-APTA, ext. 8082
Fax: (703) 684-7343   TDD: (703) 683-6748
E-mail: honorsandawards@apta.org
Web: www.apta.org

Summary To provide financial assistance to African American and other minority faculty members in physical therapy who are interested in working on a post-professional doctoral degree.

Eligibility This program is open to U.S. citizens and permanent residents who are members of the following minority groups: African American or Black, Asian, Native Hawaiian or other Pacific Islander, American Indian or Alaska Native, or Hispanic/Latino. Applicants must be full-time faculty members, teaching in an accredited or developing professional physical therapist education program, who will have completed the equivalent of 2 full semesters of post-professional doctoral course work. They must possess a license to practice physical therapy in a U.S. jurisdiction and be enrolled as a student in an accredited post-professional doctoral program whose content has a demonstrated relationship to physical therapy. Along with their application, they must submit a personal essay on their professional goals, including their plans to contribute to the profession and minority services. Selection is based on contributions in the area of minority affairs and services and contributions to the profession of physical therapy. Preference is given to members of the American Physical Therapy Association (APTA).

Financial data A stipend is awarded (amount not specified).

Duration 1 year.

Additional information This program began in 1999.

Number awarded 1 or more each year.

Deadline November of each year.

[1041]
MINORITY FELLOWSHIPS IN ENVIRONMENTAL LAW

New York State Bar Association
Attn: Environmental Law Section
One Elk Street
Albany, NY 12207
(518) 463-3200   Fax: (518) 487-5517
E-mail: lbataille@nysba.org
Web: www.nysba.org

Summary To provide an opportunity for African American and other minority law students from New York to gain summer work experience in environmental law.

Eligibility This program is open to law students who are African American, Latino, Native American, Alaskan Native, Asian, or Pacific Islander. Applicants must be residents of New York or attending law school in that state. They must be interested in a summer internship working on legal matters for a government environmental agency or public interest environmental organization in New York State. Selection is based on interest in environmental issues, academic record (undergraduate and/or law school), personal qualities, leadership abilities, and financial need.

Financial data The stipend is $6,000.

Duration At least 10 weeks during the summer.

Additional information This program began in 1992.

Number awarded 1 each year.

Deadline December of each year.

[1042]
MINORITY MEDICAL STUDENT AWARD PROGRAM OF THE AMERICAN SOCIETY OF HEMATOLOGY

American Society of Hematology
Attn: Awards Manager
2021 L Street, N.W., Suite 900
Washington, DC 20036
(202) 776-0544   Fax: (202) 776-0545
E-mail: awards@hematology.org
Web: www.hematology.org

Summary To provide an opportunity for African American and other underrepresented minority medical students to conduct a research project in hematology.

Eligibility This program is open to medical students enrolled in D.O., M.D., or M.D./Ph.D. programs in the United States or Canada who are members of minority groups. For purposes of this program, minority is defined as a member of a racial or ethnic group that has been shown to be underrepresented in health-related sciences in the United States and Canada, including Blacks or African Americans, American Indians, Alaska Natives, Hispanics or Latinos, Native Hawaiians, other Pacific Islanders, African Canadians, Inuit, and First Nation Peoples. Applicants must be interested in conducting a research project in hematology at their home institution or at another institution that has agreed to host them. They must work with 2 mentors who are members of the American Society of Hematology (ASH): a research mentor who oversees the participant's work and progress and a career development mentor (who is from the same minority group as the student) who participates for the duration of the program. U.S. or Canadian citizenship or permanent resident status is required.

Financial data The grant includes $5,000 for research support, an additional $1,000 to support travel to the annual meeting of the ASH, and another $1,000 for making a short presentation about the research experience at a special reception at the ASH annual meeting. Research mentors receive an allowance of $2,000 for supplies and $1,000 for attendance at the ASH annual meeting. Career development mentors receives $1,000 as a travel allowance each time they accompany the student to an ASH annual meeting during their remaining years of medical school and residency.

Duration 8 to 12 weeks.

Additional information This program is supported by Amgen, Celgene Corporation, Cephalon Oncology, and Genentech BioOncology.

Number awarded Up to 10 each year.

Deadline March of each year.

[1043]
MINORITY MEDICAL STUDENT SUMMER EXTERNSHIP IN ADDICTION PSYCHIATRY

American Psychiatric Association
Attn: Division of Diversity and Health Equity
1000 Wilson Boulevard, Suite 1825
Arlington, VA 22209-3901
(703) 907-8653   Toll Free: (888) 35-PSYCH
Fax: (703) 907-7852   E-mail: mking@psych.org
Web: www.psychiatry.org/minority-fellowship

Summary To provide funding to African American and other minority medical students who are interested in working on a research externship during the summer with a mentor who specializes in addiction psychiatry.

Eligibility This program is open to minority medical students who have a specific interest in services related to substance abuse treatment and prevention. Minorities include African Americans, American Indians, Alaska Natives, Native Hawaiians, Asian Americans, and Hispanics/Latinos. Applicants must be interested in working with a mentor who specializes in addiction psychiatry. Work settings provide an emphasis on working clinically with or studying underserved minority populations and issues of co-occurring disorders, substance abuse treatment, and mental health disparity. Most of them are in inner-city or rural settings.

Financial data Externships provide $1,500 for travel expenses to go to the work setting of the mentor and up to another $1,500 for out-of-pocket expenses directly related to the conduct of the externship.

Duration 1 month during the summer.

Additional information Funding for this program is provided by the Substance Abuse and Mental Health Services Administration (SAMHSA).

Number awarded 10 each year.

Deadline March of each year.

[1044]
MINORITY TEACHERS OF ILLINOIS SCHOLARSHIP PROGRAM

Illinois Student Assistance Commission
Attn: Scholarship and Grant Services
1755 Lake Cook Road
Deerfield, IL 60015-5209
(847) 948-8550   Toll Free: (800) 899-ISAC
Fax: (847) 831-8549   TDD: (800) 526-0844
E-mail: isac.studentservices@isac.illinois.gov
Web: www.isac.org

Summary To provide scholarship/loans to African Americans and other minority students in Illinois who plan to become teachers at the preschool, elementary, or secondary level.

Eligibility Applicants must be Illinois residents, U.S. citizens or eligible noncitizens, members of a minority group (African American/Black, Hispanic American, Asian American, or Native American), and high school graduates or holders of a General Educational Development (GED) certificate. They must be enrolled at least half time as an undergraduate or graduate student, have a GPA of 2.5 or higher, not be in default on any student loan, and be enrolled or accepted for enrollment in a teacher education program.

Financial data Grants up to $5,000 per year are awarded. This is a scholarship/loan program. Recipients must agree to teach full time 1 year for each year of support received. The teaching agreement may be fulfilled at a public, private, or parochial preschool, elementary school, or secondary school in Illinois; at least 30% of the student body at those schools must be minority. It must be fulfilled within the 5-year period following the completion of the undergraduate program for which the scholarship was awarded. The time period may be extended if the recipient serves in the U.S. armed forces, enrolls full time in a graduate program related to teaching, becomes temporarily disabled, is unable to find employment as a teacher at a qualifying school, or takes additional courses on at least a half-time basis to obtain certification as a teacher in Illinois. Recipients who fail to honor this work obligation must repay the award with 5% interest.

Duration 1 year; may be renewed for a total of 8 semesters or 12 quarters.

Number awarded Varies each year.

Deadline Priority consideration is given to applications received by February of each year.

[1045]
MLA/NLM SPECTRUM SCHOLARSHIPS

Medical Library Association
Attn: Grants Coordinator
65 East Wacker Place, Suite 1900
Chicago, IL 60601-7246
(312) 419-9094, ext. 15   Fax: (312) 419-8950
E-mail: awards@mail.mlahq.org
Web: www.mlanet.org/p/cm/ld/fid=449

Summary To provide financial assistance to African Americans and members of other minority groups interested in preparing for a career as a medical librarian.

Eligibility This program is open to members of minority groups (African Americans, Hispanics, Asians, Native Americans, and Pacific Islanders) who are attending library schools accredited by the American Library Association (ALA). Applicants must be interested in preparing for a career as a health sciences information professional.

Financial data The stipend is $3,250.

Duration 1 year.

Additional information This program, established in 2001, is jointly sponsored by the Medical Library Association (MLA) and the National Library of Medicine (NLM) of the U.S. National Institutes of Health (NIH). It operates as a component of the Spectrum Initiative Scholarship program of the ALA.

Number awarded 2 each year.

Deadline February of each year.

[1046]
MLA SCHOLARSHIP FOR MINORITY STUDENTS

Medical Library Association
Attn: Grants Coordinator
65 East Wacker Place, Suite 1900
Chicago, IL 60601-7246
(312) 419-9094, ext. 15   Fax: (312) 419-8950
E-mail: awards@mail.mlahq.org
Web: www.mlanet.org/p/cm/ld/fid=304

Summary To assist African American and other minority students interested in preparing for a career in medical librarianship.

Eligibility This program is open to racial minority students (Blacks or African Americans, Asians, Hispanics or Latinos, Aboriginals, North American Indians or Alaskan Natives, Native Hawaiians, or other Pacific Islanders) who are entering an ALA-accredited graduate program in librarianship or who have completed less than half of their academic requirements for a master's degree in library science. They must be interested in preparing for a career in medical librarianship. Selection is based on academic record, letters of reference, professional potential, and the applicant's statement of career objectives. U.S. or Canadian citizenship or permanent resident status is required.

Financial data The stipend is $5,000.

Duration 1 year.

Additional information This program began in 1973.

Number awarded 1 each year.

Deadline November of each year.

[1047]
MORGAN STANLEY MBA FELLOWSHIP

Morgan Stanley
Attn: Diversity Recruiting
1585 Broadway
New York, NY 10036
(212) 762-0211   Toll Free: (888) 454-3965
Fax: (212) 507-4972
E-mail: mbafellowship@morganstanley.com
Web: www.morganstanley.com

Summary To provide financial assistance and work experience to African Americans and members of other underrepresented groups who are working on an M.B.A. degree.

Eligibility This program is open to full-time M.B.A. students who are women, African Americans, Hispanics, Native Americans, or lesbian/gay/bisexual/transgender. Selection is based on assigned essays, academic achievement, recom-

mendations, extracurricular activities, leadership qualities, and on-site interviews.

Financial data The program provides full payment of tuition and fees and a paid summer internship.

Duration 1 year; may be renewed for a second year, providing the student remains enrolled full time in good academic standing and completes the summer internship following the first year.

Additional information The paid summer internship is offered within Morgan Stanley institutional securities (equity research, fixed income, institutional equity, investment banking), investment management, or private wealth management. This program was established in 1999.

Number awarded 1 or more each year.

Deadline December of each year.

[1048]
MOSS ADAMS FOUNDATION SCHOLARSHIP

Educational Foundation for Women in Accounting
Attn: Foundation Administrator
136 South Keowee Street
Dayton, OH 45402
(937) 424-3391   Fax: (937) 222-5749
E-mail: info@efwa.org
Web: www.efwa.org/scholarships_graduate.php

Summary To provide financial support to women, including African American and other minority women, who are working on an accounting degree.

Eligibility This program is open to women who are enrolled in an accounting degree program at an accredited college or university. Applicants must meet 1 of the following criteria: 1) women pursuing a fifth-year requirement either through general studies or within a graduate program; 2) women returning to school as current or reentry juniors or seniors; or 3) minority women. Selection is based on aptitude for accounting and business, commitment to the goal of working on a degree in accounting (including evidence of continued commitment after receiving this award), clear evidence that the candidate has established goals and a plan for achieving those goals (both personal and professional), financial need, and a demonstration of how the scholarship will impact her life. U.S. citizenship is required.

Financial data The stipend is $1,000.

Duration 1 year.

Additional information This program was established by Rowling, Dold & Associates LLP, a woman-owned C.P.A. firm based in San Diego. It was renamed when that firm merged with Moss Adams LLP.

Number awarded 2 each year: 1 to an undergraduate and 1 to a graduate student.

Deadline April of each year.

[1049]
MSCPA MINORITY SCHOLARSHIPS

Missouri Society of Certified Public Accountants
Attn: MSCPA Educational Foundation
540 Maryville Centre Drive, Suite 200
P.O. Box 958868
St. Louis, MO 63195-8868
(314) 997-7966   Toll Free: (800) 264-7966 (within MO)
Fax: (314) 997-2592   E-mail: dhull@mocpa.org
Web: www.mocpa.org/students/scholarships

Summary To provide financial assistance to African American and other minority residents of Missouri who are working on an undergraduate or graduate degree in accounting at a university in the state.

Eligibility This program is open to members of minority groups underrepresented in the accounting profession (Black/African American, Hispanic/Latino, Native American, Asian American) who are currently working full time on an undergraduate or graduate degree in accounting at a college or university in Missouri. Applicants must either be residents of Missouri or the children of members of the Missouri Society of Certified Public Accountants (MSCPA). They must be U.S. citizens, have completed at least 30 semester hours of college work, have a GPA of 3.3 or higher, and be student members of the MSCPA. Selection is based on the GPA, involvement in MSCPA, educator recommendations, and leadership potential. Financial need is not considered.

Financial data The stipend is $1,250 per year.

Duration 1 year; may be renewed.

Number awarded Varies each year; recently, 3 were awarded.

Deadline February of each year.

[1050]
MSCPA/NABA SCHOLARSHIPS

Massachusetts Society of Certified Public Accountants
Attn: MSCPA Educational Foundation
105 Chauncy Street, Tenth Floor
Boston, MA 02111
(617) 556-4000   Toll Free: (800) 392-6145
Fax: (617) 556-4126   E-mail: info@mscpaonline.org
Web: www.cpatrack.com/scholarships

Summary To provide financial assistance to members of the National Association of Black Accountants (NABA) from Massachusetts working on an undergraduate or graduate degree in accounting at a college or university in the state.

Eligibility This program is open to African American students from Massachusetts who are members of the Boston Metropolitan Chapter of NABA and enrolled at a college or university in the state. Applicants must be undergraduates who have completed at least the first semester of their sophomore year or graduate students. They must be able to demonstrate financial need, academic excellence, and an intention to prepare for a career as a Certified Public Accountant (C.P.A.) at a firm in Massachusetts.

Financial data The stipend is $2,500.

Duration 1 year.

Additional information This program is sponsored by the Boston Metropolitan Chapter of NABA and the Massachusetts Society of Certified Public Accountants (MSCPA).

Number awarded 2 each year.

Deadline March of each year.

[1051]
MSIPP INTERNSHIPS

Department of Energy
Office of Environmental Management
Savannah River National Laboratory
Attn: MSIPP Program Manager
Building 773-41A, 232
Aiken, SC 29808
(803) 725-9032   E-mail: connie.yung@srnl.doe.gov
Web: srnl.doe.gov/msipp/internships.htm

Summary To provide an opportunity for undergraduate and graduate students at Minority Serving Institutions (MSIs) to work on a summer research project at designated National Laboratories of the U.S. Department of Energy (DOE).

Eligibility This program is open to full-time undergraduate and graduate students enrolled at an accredited MSI. Applicants must be interested in working during the summer on a research project at a participating DOE National Laboratory. They must be working on a degree in a field of science, technology, engineering, or mathematics (STEM); the specific field depends on the particular project on which they wish to work. Their GPA must be 3.0 or higher. U.S. citizenship is required.

Financial data The stipend depends on the cost of living at the location of the host laboratory.

Duration 10 weeks during the summer.

Additional information This program is administered at the Savannah River National Laboratory (SRNL) in Aiken, South Carolina, which serves as the National Laboratory for the DOE Office of Environmental Management. The other participating National Laboratories are Argonne National Laboratory (ANL) in Argonne, Illinois, Idaho National Laboratory (INL) in Idaho Falls, Idaho, Los Alamos National Laboratory (LANL) in Los Alamos, New Mexico, Oak Ridge National Laboratory (ORNL) in Oak Ridge, Tennessee, and Pacific Northwest National Laboratory (PNNL) in Richland, Washington. The program began in 2016.

Number awarded Varies each year. Recently, the program offered 11 research projects at SRNL, 12 at ANL, 1 at INL, 7 at LANL, 4 at ORNL, and 7 at PNNL.

Deadline March of each year.

[1052]
MULTICULTURAL AUDIENCE DEVELOPMENT INITIATIVE INTERNSHIPS

Metropolitan Museum of Art
Attn: Internship Programs
1000 Fifth Avenue
New York, NY 10028-0198
(212) 570-3710   Fax: (212) 570-3782
E-mail: mmainterns@metmuseum.org
Web: www.metmuseum.org

Summary To provide summer work experience at the Metropolitan Museum of Art to college undergraduates, graduate students, and recent graduates who are African Americans or members of diverse groups.

Eligibility This program is open to members of diverse groups who are undergraduate juniors and seniors, students currently working on a master's degree, or individuals who completed a bachelor's or master's degree within the past year. Ph.D. students may be eligible to apply during the first 12 months of their program, provided they have not yet achieved candidacy. Students from various academic backgrounds are encouraged to apply, but they must be interested in preparing for a career in the arts and museum fields. Freshmen and sophomores are not eligible.

Financial data The stipend is $3,750.

Duration 10 weeks, beginning in June.

Additional information Interns are assigned to departmental projects (curatorial, administration, or education) at the Metropolitan Museum of Art; other assignments may include giving gallery talks and working at the Visitor Information Center. The assignment is for 35 hours a week. The internships are funded by the Multicultural Audience Initiative at the museum.

Number awarded 1 or more each year.

Deadline January of each year.

[1053]
MYRA DAVIS HEMMINGS SCHOLARSHIP

Delta Sigma Theta Sorority, Inc.
Attn: Scholarship and Standards Committee Chair
1707 New Hampshire Avenue, N.W.
Washington, DC 20009
(202) 986-2400   Fax: (202) 986-2513
E-mail: dstemail@deltasigmatheta.org
Web: www.deltasigmatheta.org

Summary To provide financial assistance to members of Delta Sigma Theta who are interested in working on a graduate degree in the performing or creative arts.

Eligibility This program is open to graduating college seniors and graduate students who are interested in preparing for a career in the performing or creative arts. Applicants must be active, dues-paying members of Delta Sigma Theta. Selection is based on meritorious achievement.

Financial data The stipends range from $1,000 to $2,000 per year. The funds may be used to cover tuition and living expenses.

Duration 1 year; may be renewed for 1 additional year.

Additional information This sponsor is a traditionally-African American social sorority. The application fee is $20.

Number awarded 1 or more each year.

Deadline March of each year.

[1054]
NABA ATLANTA CHAPTER SCHOLARSHIPS

National Association of Black Accountants-Atlanta
   Chapter
Attn: Student Member Services
P.O. Box 92811
Atlanta, GA 30314
E-mail: students@nabaatl.org
Web: thiswaytocpa.com

Summary To provide financial assistance to members of the National Association of Black Accountants (NABA) from Georgia who are working on an undergraduate or master's degree in an accounting-related field.

Eligibility This program is open to NABA members who are working full time on an undergraduate or master's degree

in accounting, business, or finance. Applicants must be residents of Georgia or residents of other states attending a college or university in that state. They must have completed at least 3 hours of accounting classes but have at least 1 semester remaining before completion of their degree. Selection is based on academic excellence and extracurricular involvement.

Financial data Stipends range from $500 to $5,000.

Duration 1 year.

Number awarded 8 each year.

Deadline March of each year.

[1055]
NABA MEMBER SCHOLARSHIP AWARDS

National Association of Black Accountants
Attn: National Scholarship Program
7474 Greenway Center Drive, Suite 1120
Greenbelt, MD 20770
(301) 474-NABA   Fax: (301) 474-3114
E-mail: scholarships@nabainc.org
Web: www.nabainc.org/scholarship

Summary To provide financial assistance to student members of the National Association of Black Accountants (NABA) who are working on an undergraduate or graduate degree in a field related to accounting.

Eligibility This program is open to minorities who are NABA members and enrolled full time as 1) an undergraduate freshman, sophomore, junior, or first-semester senior majoring in accounting, business, or finance at a 4-year college or university; or 2) a graduate student working on a master's degree in accounting. High school seniors are not eligible. Applicants must have a GPA of 3.5 or higher in their major and 3.3 or higher overall. Along with their application, they must submit a 500-word personal statement on their involvement in NABA, career objectives, leadership abilities, and community activities. Financial need is not considered in the selection process.

Financial data The stipend ranges from $1,000 to $3,000.

Duration 1 year.

Additional information This program includes named scholarships that vary from time to time. Recently, those included the Ralph and Valerie Thomas Scholarship, the TDC Scholarship, the Crimson and Cream Scholarship (sponsored by Delta Sigma Theta Sorority), the Lloyd Trotter/GEAAF Scholarship, the Chuck Burch Scholarship, the Eddie Nesby Memorial Scholarship, the Les Netter Scholarship, the William L. Jackson, Jr. Memorial Scholarship, and the Claudette Griffin Memorial Scholarship.

Number awarded Varies each year.

Deadline January of each year.

[1056]
NABA NATIONAL SCHOLARSHIP

National Association of Black Accountants
Attn: National Scholarship Program
7474 Greenway Center Drive, Suite 1120
Greenbelt, MD 20770
(301) 474-NABA   Fax: (301) 474-3114
E-mail: scholarships@nabainc.org
Web: www.nabainc.org

Summary   To provide financial assistance to student members of the National Association of Black Accountants (NABA) who are working on an undergraduate or graduate degree in a field related to accounting.

Eligibility   This program is open to minorities who are NABA members and enrolled full time as 1) an undergraduate freshman, sophomore, junior, or first-semester senior majoring in accounting, business, or finance at a 4-year college or university; or 2) a graduate student working on a master's degree in accounting. High school seniors are not eligible. Applicants must have a GPA of 3.5 or higher in their major and 3.3 or higher overall. Along with their application, they must submit a 500-word personal statement on their involvement in NABA, career objectives, leadership abilities, and community activities. Financial need is not considered in the selection process.

Financial data   The stipend is $1,500.

Duration   1 year.

Number awarded   1 each year.

Deadline   January of each year.

[1057]
NABJ SCHOLARSHIP

National Association of Black Journalists
Attn: Program Manager
University of Maryland
1100 Knight Hall, Suite 3100
College Park, MD 20742
(301) 405-7520   Fax: (301) 314-1714
E-mail: Sberry@nabj.org
Web: www.nabj.org/?page=ScholarshipsNABJ

Summary   To provide financial assistance to undergraduate or graduate student members of the National Association of Black Journalists (NABJ) who are working on a degree in a field related to journalism.

Eligibility   This program is open to African American undergraduate or graduate student members of NABJ who are currently enrolled full time at an accredited 4-year college or university. Applicants must be working on a degree in journalism or other communications-related field and have a GPA of 2.5 or higher. They must be able to demonstrate financial need and a record of community service. Along with their application, they must submit 5 samples of their work, an official college transcript, 3 letters of recommendation, a resume, and an essay of 1,000 to 2,000 words on how they see themselves as a journalist and what they would improve about the media business.

Financial data   The stipend is $2,500. Funds are paid directly to the recipient's college or university.

Duration   1 year; nonrenewable.

Number awarded   1 each year.

Deadline   February of each year.

[1058]
NABNA-FEEA SCHOLARSHIP PROGRAM

National Association of Black Narcotic Agents
c/o Federal Employee Education and Assistance Fund
Attn: Scholarship Program
3333 South Wadsworth Boulevard, Suite 300
Lakewood, CO 80227
(303) 933-7580   Toll Free: (800) 323-4140
Fax: (303) 933-7587   E-mail: admin@feea.org
Web: www.feea.org

Summary   To provide financial assistance for college or graduate school to members of the National Association of Black Narcotic Agents (NABNA) and their dependents.

Eligibility   This program is open to federal employees who are NABNA members and their dependent spouses and children entering or enrolled in an accredited 2- or 4-year undergraduate, graduate, or postgraduate program. Dependents must be full-time students; federal employees may be part-time students. Applicants or their sponsoring federal employee must have at least 3 years of civilian federal service. Along with their application, they must submit a 2-page essay on a topic related to a career in public service with the federal government, a letter of recommendation, a transcript with a GPA of 3.0 or higher, and a copy of their federal "Notice of Personnel Action;" high school seniors must also submit a copy of their ACT, SAT, or other examination scores. Financial need is not considered in the selection process.

Financial data   The stipend is $1,000 per year.

Duration   1 year; may be renewed.

Additional information   This program is jointly administered by NABNA and the Federal Employee Education and Assistance Fund (FEEA).

Number awarded   1 or more each year.

Deadline   March of each year.

[1059]
NANCY B. WOOLRIDGE MCGEE GRADUATE FELLOWSHIP

Zeta Phi Beta Sorority, Inc.
Attn: National Educational Foundation
1734 New Hampshire Avenue, N.W.
Washington, DC 20009
(202) 387-3103   Fax: (202) 232-4593
E-mail: info@zetaphibetasororityhq.org
Web: www.zpbnef1975.org/scholarships-and-descriptions

Summary   To provide financial assistance for graduate school to members of Zeta Phi Beta Sorority.

Eligibility   This program is open to members of Zeta Phi Beta Sorority who are working on or are interested in working full time on a graduate or professional degree. Applicants must have shown scholarly distinction or unusual ability in their chosen profession. Along with their application, they must submit a 150-word essay on their educational goals and professional aspirations, how this award will help them to achieve those goals, and why they should receive the award. Financial need is not considered in the selection process.

Financial data   The stipend ranges from $500 to $1,000 per year; funds are paid to the college or university.

Duration   1 academic year; may be renewed.

Additional information   Zeta Phi Beta is a traditionally African American sorority.

Number awarded 1 each year.

Deadline January of each year.

[1060]
NASA EDUCATION AERONAUTICS SCHOLARSHIP AND ADVANCED STEM TRAINING AND RESEARCH FELLOWSHIP

National Aeronautics and Space Administration
Attn: National Scholarship Deputy Program Manager
Office of Education and Public Outreach
Ames Research Center
Moffett Field, CA 94035
(650) 604-6958   E-mail: elizabeth.a.cartier@nasa.gov
Web: nspires.nasaprs.com

Summary To provide financial assistance to African Americans and members of other underrepresented groups interested in working on a graduate degree in fields of science, technology, engineering, and mathematics (STEM) of interest to the U.S. National Aeronautics and Space Administration (NASA).

Eligibility This program (identified as AS&ASTAR) is open to students who have a bachelor's degree and have historically been underrepresented in NASA-related fields (women, minorities, persons with disabilities, and veterans). Applicants must be working on a research-based master's or doctoral degree in a NASA-related field of STEM, including chemistry, computer and information science and engineering, geosciences (e.g., geophysics, hydrology, oceanography, paleontology, planetary science), engineering (e.g., aeronautical, aerospace, biomedical, chemical, civil, computer, electrical, electronic, environmental, industrial, materials, mechanical, nuclear, ocean, optical, systems), life sciences (e.g., biochemistry, cell biology, environmental biology, genetics, neurosciences, physiology), materials research, mathematical sciences, or physics and astronomy). They must arrange with a researcher at a NASA Center to serve as a technical adviser in collaboration with the student's faculty adviser. Research must be conducted at a NASA Center as a team project involving the student, the faculty adviser, and the NASA technical adviser. In the selection process, consideration is given to the proposed use of NASA facilities, content, and people. Applications must include a plan for a Center-Based Research Experience (CBRE) to be conducted during the summer at the NASA facility. Students must be U.S. citizens and have a GPA of 3.0 or higher.

Financial data Grants provide a stipend of $25,000 for master's degree students or $30,000 for doctoral candidates, $10,000 for tuition offset and fees, $8,000 as a CBRE allowance, $1,000 as a health insurance allowance, $4,500 as a faculty adviser allowance, and $1,500 as a fellow professional development allowance.

Duration 1 year; may be renewed up to 2 additional years.

Additional information The participating NASA facilities are Ames Research Center (Moffett Field, California), Armstrong Flight Research Center (Edwards, California), Glenn Research Center (Cleveland, Ohio), Goddard Space Flight Center (Greenbelt, Maryland), Jet Propulsion Laboratory (Pasadena, California), Johnson Space Center (Houston, Texas), Kennedy Space Center (Kennedy Space Center, Florida), Langley Research Center (Hampton, Virginia), Marshall Space Flight Center (Marshall Space Flight Center, Alabama), and Stennis Space Center (Stennis Space Center, Mississippi).

Number awarded At least 13 each year.

Deadline June of each year.

[1061]
NASP-ERT MINORITY SCHOLARSHIP PROGRAM

National Association of School Psychologists
Attn: Education and Research Trust
4340 East-West Highway, Suite 402
Bethesda, MD 20814
(301) 657-0270   Toll Free: (866) 331-NASP
Fax: (301) 657-0275   TDD: (301) 657-4155
E-mail: kbritton@naspweb.org
Web: www.nasponline.org

Summary To provide financial assistance to African American and other minority graduate students who are members of the National Association of School Psychologists (NASP) and enrolled in a school psychology program.

Eligibility This program is open to minority students who are NASP members enrolled full or part time in a regionally-accredited school psychology program in the United States. Applicants must have a GPA of 3.0 or higher. Doctoral candidates are not eligible. Applications must be accompanied by 1) a resume that includes undergraduate and/or graduate schools attended, awards and honors, student and professional activities, work and volunteer experiences, research and publications, workshops or other presentations, and any special skills, training, or experience, such as bilingualism, teaching experience, or mental health experience; and 2) a statement, up to 1,000 words, of professional goals. Selection is based on adherence to instructions; completeness of the application; applicant's experience, interests and growth as reflected on their resume; applicant's professional goals statement; recommendations; financial standing; and degree of scholarship. U.S. citizenship is required.

Financial data The stipend is $5,000 per year.

Duration 1 year; may be renewed up to 2 additional years.

Additional information This program, which began in 1995, includes the Deborah Peek Crockett Minority Scholarship Award, the Wayne Gressett Memorial Minority Scholarship Award, and the Pearson Minority Scholarship Award.

Number awarded Varies each year; recently, 4 were awarded.

Deadline November of each year.

[1062]
NATIONAL ASSOCIATION OF NEGRO MUSICIANS SCHOLARSHIP CONTEST

National Association of Negro Musicians, Inc.
Attn: Treasurer
P.O. Box 51669
Durham, NC 27717
E-mail: nanm@nanm.org
Web: www.nanm.org/scholar-main

Summary To recognize and reward (with scholarships for additional study) young musicians who are sponsored by a branch of the National Association of Negro Musicians.

Eligibility This competition is open to musicians between 18 and 30 years of age. Contestants must be sponsored by a branch in good standing, although they do not need to be a member of a local branch or the national organization. For each category of the competition, they must select 2 compositions from assigned lists to perform, of which 1 list consists of works by African American composers. People ineligible to compete include former first-place winners of this competition; full-time public school teachers and college faculty (although graduate students holding teaching assistantships are still eligible if they receive less than 50% of their employment from that appointment); vocalists who have contracts as full-time solo performers in operatic, oratorio, or other types of professional singing organizations; instrumentalists with contractual full-time orchestral or ensemble jobs; and professional performers under management. Local branches nominate competitors for regional competitions. Regional winners advance to the national competition. The category of the competition rotates on a 5-year schedule as follows: 2018: organ; 2019: winds and percussion; 2020: piano; 2021: voice; 2022: strings.

Financial data In the national competition, awards are at least $3,000 for first place, $2,000 for second, $1,000 for third, and $250 for each honorable mention. All funds are paid directly to the winner's teacher/coach or institution.

Duration The competition is held annually.

Additional information The application fee is $50.

Number awarded 5 each year.

Deadline February of each year.

[1063]
NATIONAL ASSOCIATION OF UNIVERSITY WOMEN FELLOWSHIPS

National Association of University Women
Attn: Fellowship Chair
1001 E Street, S.E.
Washington, DC 20003
(202) 547-3967　　　　　　Fax: (202) 547-5226
E-mail: info@nauw1910.org
Web: www.nauw1910.org

Summary To provide financial assistance to African American and other members of the National Association of University Women (NAUW) and other women who are working on a doctoral degree.

Eligibility This program is open to women who already have a master's degree and are enrolled in a program leading to a doctoral degree. They should be close to completing their degree. Along with their application, they must submit an outline of their proposed study with reasons for their choice and a developmental outline of their future educational plan. Preference is given to members of NAUW, an organization that historically has served African American women.

Financial data The stipend is $3,000.

Duration 1 year; nonrenewable.

Number awarded 2 each year: 1 to a member of NAUW and 1 to a non-member.

Deadline April of each year.

[1064]
NATIONAL BAR INSTITUTE LAW STUDENT FELLOWSHIP PROGRAM

National Bar Institute
1225 11th Street, N.W.
Washington, DC 20001-4217
(202) 842-3900　　　　　　Fax: (202) 315-3051
E-mail: nbischolarship@outlook.com
Web: www.nationalbar.org/NBA/NBI/NBA/NBI.aspx

Summary To provide financial assistance to African American students working on a law degree.

Eligibility This program is open to African Americans who have completed 2 years of full-time study at a U.S. law school. Applicants must have demonstrated a commitment to social justice and an intention of practicing law in an historically underserved community once their legal training is completed. U.S. citizenship or permanent resident status and membership in the National Bar Association (NBA) are required. Selection is based on the applicant's academic qualifications, potential to make a significant contribution to the field of law, commitment to African American issues in the field of study and/or community, and financial need.

Financial data Stipends range from $1,000 to $10,000, but most are approximately $2,500.

Duration 1 year.

Additional information The National Bar Institute was established in 1982 as the philanthropic arm of the National Bar Association, an organization of African American lawyers.

Number awarded Up to 3 each year.

Deadline May of each year.

[1065]
NATIONAL BLACK ASSOCIATION FOR SPEECH-LANGUAGE AND HEARING STUDENT RESEARCH AWARD

National Black Association for Speech-Language and Hearing
Attn: Awards and Scholarship Committee
700 McKnight Park Drive, Suite 708
Pittsburgh, PA 15237
(855) 727-2836　　　　　　Fax: (888) 729-3489
E-mail: nbaslh@nbaslh.org
Web: www.nbaslh.org/scholarships/scholarship-main.html

Summary To recognize and reward outstanding research papers on communication sciences or disorders written by undergraduate or graduate student members of the National Black Association for Speech-Language and Hearing (NBASLH).

Eligibility This competition is open to African American students who are NBASLH members and enrolled full time in an ASHA-accredited undergraduate, master's, or doctoral degree program in speech-language pathology, audiology, or the speech-language-hearing sciences. Applicants must submit a paper of scientific or scholarly merit that deals with issues relevant to communication sciences and disorders. The research should focus on culturally and linguistically diverse populations. It may address 1 of the following: 1) an empirical investigation that requires data gathering and analysis; 2) an issue paper that aims to redefine, evaluate, and synthesize existing knowledge in ways that offer a new conceptual framework or approach for conducting research or engaging in clinical practice; or 3) a description of a clinical case study that has implications for future research and/or clinical practice. The manuscript should not exceed 8 typed pages (2,000 words). Selection is based on completeness, appropriateness, manuscript quality, and significance.

Financial data The award is $1,000. In addition, the winner receives a $100 travel allowance to attend the association's convention (and read the paper there).

Duration The award is presented annually.

Number awarded 2 each year.

Deadline February of each year.

[1066]
NATIONAL BLACK MBA ASSOCIATION GRADUATE SCHOLARSHIP PROGRAM

National Black MBA Association
Attn: Scholarship Program
400 West Peachtree Street N.W., Suite 203
Atlanta, GA 30308
(404) 260-5444   E-mail: scholarship@nbmbaa.org
Web: www.nbmbaa.org

Summary To provide financial assistance to members of the National Black MBA Association (NBMBAA) interested in working on a master's degree in a field related to business.

Eligibility This program is open to NBMBAA members who are entering or continuing in a full- or part-time master's degree program in business, management, or related field in the United States or Canada. Applicants must submit a 300-word essay on an assigned topic that relates to minorities in business. They must have a GPA of 3.0 or higher. Selection is based on the quality of the paper, academic excellence, leadership potential, communication skills, and involvement in local communities through service to others. U.S. or Canadian citizenship is required.

Financial data Stipends range up to $10,000.

Duration 1 year.

Number awarded Varies each year; recently, the sponsor awarded 18 undergraduate and graduate scholarships.

Deadline June of each year.

[1067]
NATIONAL DEFENSE SCIENCE AND ENGINEERING GRADUATE FELLOWSHIP PROGRAM

American Society for Engineering Education
Attn: NDSEG Fellowship Program
1818 N Street, N.W., Suite 600
Washington, DC 20036-2479
(202) 649-3831   Fax: (202) 265-8504
E-mail: ndseg@asee.org
Web: ndseg.asee.org/about_ndseg

Summary To provide financial assistance to doctoral students, especially African Americans and members of other underrepresented groups, in areas of science and engineering that are of potential military importance.

Eligibility This program is open to U.S. citizens and nationals entering or enrolled in the early stages of a doctoral program in aeronautical and astronautical engineering; biosciences, including toxicology; chemical engineering; chemistry; civil engineering; cognitive, neural, and behavioral sciences;

computer and computational sciences; electrical engineering; geosciences, including terrain, water, and air; materials science and engineering; mathematics; mechanical engineering; naval architecture and ocean engineering; oceanography; or physics, including optics. Applicants must be enrolled or planning to enroll as full-time students. Applications are particularly encouraged from women, members of ethnic minority groups (American Indians, African Americans, Hispanics or Latinos, Native Hawaiians and other Pacific Islanders, Alaska Natives, and Asians), and persons with disabilities. Selection is based on all available evidence of ability, including academic records, letters of recommendation, and GRE scores.

Financial data The annual stipend is $30,500 for the first year, $31,000 for the second year; and $31,500 for the third year; the program also pays the recipient's institution full tuition and required fees (not to include room and board). Medical insurance is covered up to $1,000 per year.

Duration 3 years, as long as satisfactory academic progress is maintained.

Additional information This program is sponsored by the High Performance Computing Modernization Program within the Department of Defense, the Army Research Office, the Air Force Office of Scientific Research, and the Office of Naval Research. Recipients do not incur any military or other service obligation.

Number awarded Approximately 200 each year.

Deadline December of each year.

[1068]
NATIONAL MEDICAL FELLOWSHIPS EMERGENCY SCHOLARSHIP FUND

National Medical Fellowships, Inc.
Attn: Scholarship Program
347 Fifth Avenue, Suite 510
New York, NY 10016
(212) 483-8880   Toll Free: (877) NMF-1DOC
Fax: (212) 483-8897 E-mail: scholarships@nmfonline.org
Web: www.nmfonline.org

Summary To provide financial assistance to African American and other minority medical students who are facing financial emergencies.

Eligibility This program is open to U.S. citizens who are enrolled in the third or fourth year of an accredited M.D. or D.O. degree-granting program in the United States and are facing extreme financial difficulties because of unforeseen training-related expenses. The emergency must be sudden, unexpected, and unbudgeted. Applicants must be African Americans, Latinos, Native Hawaiians, Alaska Natives, American Indians, Pacific Islanders, Vietnamese, or Cambodians who permanently reside in the United States. They must be interested in primary care practice in underserved communities.

Financial data Assistance ranges up to $5,000.

Duration 1 year; nonrenewable.

Additional information This program began in 2008.

Number awarded Varies each year; recently, 3 were awarded.

Deadline Applications may be submitted at any time.

[1069]
NATIONAL PHYSICAL SCIENCE CONSORTIUM GRADUATE FELLOWSHIPS

National Physical Science Consortium
c/o University of Southern California
3716 South Hope Street, Suite 348
Los Angeles, CA 90007-4344
(213) 821-2409   Toll Free: (800) 854-NPSC
Fax: (213) 821-6329   E-mail: npsc@npsc.org
Web: www.npsc.org

Summary To provide financial assistance and summer work experience to African Americans and other underrepresented minorities interested in working on a Ph.D. in designated science and engineering fields.

Eligibility This program is open to U.S. citizens who are seniors graduating from college with a GPA of 3.0 or higher, enrolled in the first year of a doctoral program, completing a terminal master's degree, or returning from the workforce and holding no more than a master's degree. Students currently in the third or subsequent year of a Ph.D. program or who already have a doctoral degree in any field (Ph.D., M.D., J.D., Ed.D.) are ineligible. Applicants must be interested in working on a Ph.D. in fields that vary but emphasize astronomy, chemistry, computer science, engineering (chemical, computer, electrical, environmental, or mechanical), geology, materials science, mathematical sciences, or physics. The program welcomes applications from all qualified students and continues to emphasize the recruitment of underrepresented minority (African American, Hispanic, Native American Indian, Eskimo, Aleut, and Pacific Islander) and women physical science and engineering students. Fellowships are provided to students at more than 100 universities that are members of the consortium. Selection is based on academic standing (GPA), course work taken in preparation for graduate school, university and/or industry research experience, letters of recommendation, and GRE scores.

Financial data The fellowship pays tuition and fees plus an annual stipend of $20,000. It also provides on-site paid summer employment to enhance technical experience. The exact value of the fellowship depends on academic standing, summer employment, and graduate school attended; the total amount generally exceeds $200,000.

Duration Support is initially provided for 2 or 3 years, depending on the employer-sponsor. If the fellow makes satisfactory progress and continues to meet the conditions of the award, support may continue for a total of up to 6 years or completion of the Ph.D., whichever comes first.

Additional information This program began in 1989. Tuition and fees are provided by the participating universities. Stipends and summer internships are provided by sponsoring organizations. Students must submit separate applications for internships, which may have additional eligibility requirements. Internships are currently available at Lawrence Livermore National Laboratory in Livermore, California (astronomy, chemistry, computer science, geology, materials science, mathematics, and physics); National Institute of Standards and Technology in Gaithersburg, Maryland (various fields of STEM); National Security Agency in Fort Meade, Maryland (astronomy, chemistry, computer science, geology, materials science, mathematics, and physics); Sandia National Laboratory in Livermore, California (biology, chemistry, computer science, environmental science, geology, materials science, mathematics, and physics); and Sandia National Laboratory in Albuquerque, New Mexico (chemical engineering, chemistry, computer science, materials science, mathematics, mechanical engineering, and physics). Fellows must submit a separate application for dissertation support in the year prior to the beginning of their dissertation research program, but not until they can describe their intended research in general terms.

Number awarded Varies each year; recently, 11 were awarded.

Deadline November of each year.

[1070]
NATIONAL SPACE GRANT COLLEGE AND FELLOWSHIP PROGRAM

National Aeronautics and Space Administration
Attn: Office of Education
300 E Street, S.W.
Mail Suite 6M35
Washington, DC 20546-0001
(202) 358-1069   Fax: (202) 358-7097
E-mail: aleksandra.korobov@nasa.gov
Web: www.nasa.gov

Summary To provide financial assistance to undergraduate and graduate students, especially African Americans and other underrepresented minorities, interested in preparing for a career in a space-related field.

Eligibility This program is open to undergraduate and graduate students at colleges and universities that participate in the National Space Grant program of the U.S. National Aeronautics and Space Administration (NASA) through their state consortium. Applicants must be interested in a program of study and/or research in a field of science, technology, engineering, or mathematics (STEM) related to space. A specific goal of the program is to recruit and train U.S. citizens, especially underrepresented minorities, women, and persons with disabilities, for careers in aerospace science and technology. Financial need is not considered in the selection process.

Financial data Each consortium establishes the terms of the fellowship program in its state.

Additional information NASA established the Space Grant program in 1989. It operates through 52 consortia in each state, the District of Columbia, and Puerto Rico. Each consortium includes selected colleges and universities in that state as well as other affiliates from industry, museums, science centers, and state and local agencies.

Number awarded Varies each year.

Deadline Each consortium sets its own deadlines.

[1071]
NATIONAL VISION PRIMARY EYE CARE ESSAY GRANTS

National Optometric Association
Attn: Student Affairs
1801 North Tryon Street, Suite 315
Charlotte, NC 28206
(704) 918-1809   Toll Free: (877) 394-2020
Fax: (877) NOA-2006
E-mail: noastudentdirector@yahoo.com
Web: www.nationaloptometricassociation.com

Summary To recognize and reward, with grants for continuing study, African Americans and other members of the National Optometric Student Association (NOSA) who submit essays on primary eye care.

Eligibility This program is open to NOSA members enrolled in any year at a school or college of optometry. Applicants must submit 1) a 1-page resume highlighting their community service and involvement in optometric organizations; and 2) a 500-word essay on "The Importance of Primary Care Optometry in a Changing Health Care Environment: Addressing the Need for Affordable Eyecare."

Financial data Awards, in the form of academic grants, are $4,000 for first place, $2,000 for second, and $1,000 for third.

Duration Awards are presented annually.

Additional information The National Optometric Association was founded in 1969 with the goal of recruiting minority students, especially African Americans, for schools and colleges of optometry. This program is sponsored by National Vision, Inc.

Number awarded 3 each year.

Deadline June of each year.

[1072]
NAVAL RESEARCH LABORATORY SUMMER RESEARCH PROGRAM FOR HBCU/MI UNDERGRADUATES AND GRADUATES

Naval Research Laboratory
Attn: Personnel Operations Branch
4555 Overlook Avenue, S.W.
Washington, DC 20375-5320
(202) 767-8313
Web: www.nrl.navy.mil/hbcu/description

Summary To provide research experience at the Naval Research Laboratory (NRL) to undergraduate and graduate students in fields of science, technology, engineering, and mathematics (STEM) at minority institutions.

Eligibility This program is open to undergraduate and graduate students who have completed at least 1 year of study at an Historically Black College or University (HBCU), Minority Institution (MI), or Tribal College or University (TCU). Applicants must be working on a degree in a field of STEM and have a cumulative GPA of 3.0 or higher. They must be interested in participating in a research program at NRL under the mentorship of a senior staff scientist. U.S. citizenship or permanent resident status is required.

Financial data The stipend is $810 per week for undergraduates or $1,050 per week for graduate students. Subsidized housing is provided at a motel in the area.

Duration 10 weeks during the summer.

Additional information This program is conducted in accordance with a planned schedule and a working agreement between NRL, the educational institution, and the student.

Number awarded Varies each year.

Deadline February of each year.

[1073]
NBCC MINORITY FELLOWSHIP PROGRAM

National Board for Certified Counselors
Attn: NBCC Foundation
3 Terrace Way
Greensboro, NC 27403
(336) 232-0376   Fax: (336) 232-0010
E-mail: foundation@nbcc.org
Web: nbccf-mfpdr.applicantstack.com/x/detail/a2b3qvixcgjm

Summary To provide financial assistance to doctoral candidates, especially African Americans and members of other racially and ethnically diverse populations, and who are interested in working on a degree in mental health and/or substance abuse counseling.

Eligibility This program is open to U.S. citizens and permanent residents who are enrolled full time in an accredited doctoral degree mental health and/or substance abuse and addictions counseling program. Applicants must have a National Certified Counselor or equivalent credential. They must commit to provide mental health and substance abuse services to racially and ethnically diverse populations. African Americans, Alaska Natives, American Indians, Asian Americans, Hispanics/Latinos, Native Hawaiians, and Pacific Islanders are especially encouraged to apply. Applicants must be able to commit to providing substance abuse and addictions counseling services to underserved minority populations for at least 2 years after graduation.

Financial data The stipend is $20,000.

Duration 1 year.

Additional information This program began in 2012 with support from the Substance Abuse and Mental Health Services Administration.

Number awarded 23 each year.

Deadline June of each year.

[1074]
NBCC MINORITY FELLOWSHIP PROGRAM (MASTER'S ADDICTIONS)

National Board for Certified Counselors
Attn: NBCC Foundation
3 Terrace Way
Greensboro, NC 27403
(336) 232-0376   Fax: (336) 232-0010
E-mail: foundation@nbcc.org
Web: nbccf-mfp.applicantstack.com/x/detail/a2hlw8mozup7

Summary To provide financial assistance to students, especially African Americans and members of other racially and ethnically diverse populations, who are interested in working on a master's degree in substance abuse and addictions counseling.

Eligibility This program is open to U.S. citizens and permanent residents who are enrolled full time in an accredited master's degree substance abuse and addictions counseling program. Applicants must demonstrate knowledge of and experience with racially and ethnically diverse populations. They must be able to commit to applying for the National Certified Counselor credential prior to graduation and to providing substance abuse and addictions counseling services to underserved minority transition-age youth populations (16-25 years of age) for at least 2 years after graduation. African Americans, Alaska Natives, American Indians, Asian Americans, Hispanics/Latinos, Native Hawaiians, and Pacific Islanders are especially encouraged to apply.

Financial data The stipend is $11,000.

Duration 1 year.

Additional information This program began in 2012 with support from the Substance Abuse and Mental Health Services Administration.

Number awarded 40 each year.

Deadline June of each year.

[1075]
NBCC MINORITY FELLOWSHIP PROGRAM (MASTER'S MENTAL HEALTH)

National Board for Certified Counselors
Attn: NBCC Foundation
3 Terrace Way
Greensboro, NC 27403
(336) 232-0376 Fax: (336) 232-0010
E-mail: foundation@nbcc.org
Web: nbccf-mfp.applicantstack.com/x/detail/a2hlw8m1394v

Summary To provide financial assistance to African American and other students who have knowledge of and experience with racially and ethnically diverse populations and are interested in working on a master's degree in mental health counseling.

Eligibility This program is open to U.S. citizens and permanent residents who are enrolled full time in an accredited master's degree mental health counseling program. Applicants must demonstrate knowledge of and experience with racially and ethnically diverse populations. They must be able to commit to applying for the National Certified Counselor credential prior to graduation and to providing mental health counseling services to underserved minority transition-age youth populations (16-25 years of age) for at least 2 years after graduation. African Americans, Alaska Natives, American Indians, Asian Americans, Hispanics/Latinos, Native Hawaiians, and Pacific Islanders are especially encouraged to apply.

Financial data The stipend is $5,000.

Duration 1 year.

Additional information This program is supported by the Substance Abuse and Mental Health Services Administration.

Number awarded 40 each year.

Deadline June of each year.

[1076]
NBLSA OUTSTANDING STUDENT LEADER SCHOLARSHIP

National Black Law Students Association
Attn: Director of Education and Career Development
1225 11th Street, N.W.
Washington, DC 20001-4217
(202) 618-2572 E-mail: educationcareer@nblsa.org
Web: www.nblsa.org/education-career

Summary To provide financial assistance for law school to members of the National Black Law Students Association (NBLSA) who have been active in the association.

Eligibility This program is open to members of the association who are currently enrolled in the first, second, or third year of law school. Applicants must rank in the top 30% of

their class and have a record of activity in their NBLSA chapter and community. Along with their application, they must submit an essay, up to 500 words in length, on a topic that changes annually. Recently, students were invited to define their ideal leader and discuss how they have exhibited leadership among their colleagues. Selection is based on that essay, class rank, a letter of recommendation from a professional or faculty member, and a letter from a NBLSA officer or board member discussing their contributions to the association.

Financial data The stipend is $2,500.

Duration 1 year.

Number awarded 1 each year.

Deadline January of each year.

[1077]
NBNA SCHOLARSHIP PROGRAM

National Black Nurses Association, Inc.
Attn: Scholarship Committee
8630 Fenton Street, Suite 330
Silver Spring, MD 20910-3803
(301) 589-3200 Fax: (301) 589-3223
E-mail: gbelizaire@nbna.org
Web: www.nbna.org/content.asp?contentid=82

Summary To provide financial assistance for undergraduate or graduate nursing education to members of the National Black Nurses Association (NBNA).

Eligibility This program is open to members of the association who are currently enrolled in a B.S.N., A.D., diploma, L.P.N./L.V.N., master's, or doctoral program with at least 1 full year of school remaining. Along with their application, they must submit a 2-page essay 1) describing their extracurricular activities and community involvement (including local chapter activities, community-based projects, school level projects, organizational efforts, state-level student nurse activities, and other activities impacting on the health and social condition of African Americans and other culturally diverse groups); 2) presenting their ideas of what they can do as an individual nurse to improve the health status and/or social condition of African Americans; and 3) stating their future goals in nursing.

Financial data The stipend ranges from $1,000 to $6,000 per year.

Duration 1 year; may be renewed.

Additional information This program includes the following named scholarships: the Dr. Lauranne Sams Scholarship, the Martha R. Dudley Scholarship, the Maria Dudley Advanced Scholarship, the NBNA Board of Directors Scholarship, the Rita E. Miller Scholarship, the Dr. Martha A. Dawson Genesis Scholarship, the Margaret Pemberton Scholarship, the Lynne Edwards Research Scholarship, the Dr. Hilda Richards Scholarship, the Children's Mercy Hospitals and Clinics Scholarship, and the George Freeman Memorial Scholarship.

Number awarded Varies each year.

Deadline April of each year.

[1078]
NCAA ETHNIC MINORITY ENHANCEMENT POSTGRADUATE SCHOLARSHIP FOR CAREERS IN ATHLETICS

National Collegiate Athletic Association
Attn: Office for Diversity and Inclusion
700 West Washington Street
P.O. Box 6222
Indianapolis, IN 46206-6222
(317) 917-6683   Fax: (317) 917-6888
E-mail: lthomas@ncaa.org
Web: www.ncaa.org

Summary To provide funding to African American and other ethnic minority graduate students who are interested in preparing for a career in intercollegiate athletics.

Eligibility This program is open to members of minority groups who have been accepted into a program at a National Collegiate Athletic Association (NCAA) member institution that will prepare them for a career in intercollegiate athletics (athletics administrator, coach, athletic trainer, or other career that provides a direct service to intercollegiate athletics). Applicants must be U.S. citizens, have performed with distinction as a student body member at their respective undergraduate institution, have a cumulative undergraduate GPA of 3.2 or higher, and be entering the first semester or term of full-time postgraduate study. Selection is based on the applicant's involvement in extracurricular activities, course work, commitment to preparing for a career in intercollegiate athletics, and promise for success in that career. Financial need is not considered.

Financial data The stipend is $7,500; funds are paid to the college or university of the recipient's choice.

Duration 1 year; nonrenewable.

Number awarded 13 each year.

Deadline February of each year.

[1079]
NEIGHBORHOOD DIABETES EDUCATION PROGRAM

National Medical Fellowships, Inc.
Attn: Scholarship Program
347 Fifth Avenue, Suite 510
New York, NY 10016
(212) 483-8880   Toll Free: (877) NMF-1DOC
Fax: (212) 483-8897 E-mail: scholarships@nmfonline.org
Web: www.nmfonline.org

Summary To provide funding to African American and other underrepresented medical and nursing students who wish to participate in a neighborhood diabetes education project in New York City.

Eligibility This program is open to members of underrepresented minority groups (African American, Hispanic/Latino, Native American, Vietnamese, or Cambodian) who are U.S. citizens. Applicants must be currently enrolled in an accredited medical school or graduate-level nursing degree program in Connecticut, New Jersey, New York, or Pennsylvania. They must be interested in a mentored service-learning experience that provides 200 hours of proactive diabetes education at a variety of community sites and health care settings in New York City. Selection is based on demonstrated leadership early in career and commitment to serving medically underserved communities.

Financial data The stipend is $5,000.

Additional information Funding for this program, which began in 2015 and is administered by National Medical Fellowships (NMF), is provided by the Empire BlueCross BlueShield Foundation.

Number awarded 10 each year.

Deadline March of each year.

[1080]
NELLIE STONE JOHNSON SCHOLARSHIP

Nellie Stone Johnson Scholarship Program
P.O. Box 40309
St. Paul, MN 55104
(651) 738-1404   Toll Free: (866) 738-5238
E-mail: info@nelliestone.org
Web: www.nelliestone.org/scholarship-program

Summary To provide financial assistance to African American and other racial minority union members and their families who are interested in working on an undergraduate or graduate degree in any field at a Minnesota state college or university.

Eligibility This program is open to students in undergraduate and graduate programs at a 2- or 4-year institution that is a component of Minnesota State Colleges and Universities (MnSCU). Applicants must be a minority (Asian, American Indian, Alaska Native, Black/African American, Chicano(a) or Latino(a), Native Hawaiian, or Pacific Islander) and a union member or the child, grandchild, or spouse of a minority union member. They must submit a 2-page essay about their background, educational goals, career goals, and commitment to the causes of human or civil rights. Undergraduates must have a GPA of 2.0 or higher; graduate students must have a GPA of 3.0 or higher. Preference is given to Minnesota residents. Selection is based on the essay, commitment to human or civil rights, extracurricular activities, volunteer activities, community involvement, academic standing, and union verification.

Financial data Stipends are $1,200 per year for full-time students or $500 per year for part-time students.

Duration 1 year; may be renewed up to 3 additional years for students working on a bachelor's degree, 1 additional year for students working on a master's degree, or 1 additional year for students in a community or technical college program.

Number awarded Varies each year; recently, 18 were awarded.

Deadline May of each year.

[1081]
NEW YORK COMMUNITY TRUST/NMF MEDICAL EDUCATION AND POLICY SCHOLARSHIP

National Medical Fellowships, Inc.
Attn: Scholarship Program
347 Fifth Avenue, Suite 510
New York, NY 10016
(212) 483-8880   Toll Free: (877) NMF-1DOC
Fax: (212) 483-8897 E-mail: scholarships@nmfonline.org
Web: www.nmfonline.org

Summary To provide funding for medical education or health policy research to African American and other underrepresented minority students at designated medical schools in New York City.

Eligibility This program is open to African Americans, Hispanics/Latinos, Native Americans, Vietnamese, Cambodians, and Pacific Islanders who are enrolled at Montefiore Medical Center, Icahn School of Medicine at Mount Sinai, or Columbia University's College of Physicians and Surgeons. Applicants must be interested in conducting medical education or health policy research. They must be U.S. citizens or DACA students. Selection is based on leadership, commitment to serving medically underserved communities, and financial need.

Financial data The stipend is $6,000.

Duration 1 year.

Additional information This program is sponsored by the New York Community Trust.

Number awarded 1 each year.

Deadline September of each year.

[1082]
NEW YORK COMMUNITY TRUST/NMF MEDICAL RESEARCH SCHOLARSHIPS

National Medical Fellowships, Inc.
Attn: Scholarship Program
347 Fifth Avenue, Suite 510
New York, NY 10016
(212) 483-8880   Toll Free: (877) NMF-1DOC
Fax: (212) 483-8897 E-mail: scholarships@nmfonline.org
Web: www.nmfonline.org

Summary To provide funding for community health research to African American and other underrepresented minority students at medical schools in New York City.

Eligibility This program is open to African Americans, Hispanics/Latinos, Native Americans, Vietnamese, Cambodians, and Pacific Islanders who are entering their second through fourth year at a medical school in New York City. Applicants must be interested in conducting community health research that addresses health inequities in the city. They must be U.S. citizens or DACA students. Selection is based on leadership, commitment to serving medically underserved communities, and financial need.

Financial data The stipend is $6,000.

Duration 1 year.

Additional information This program was established by the New York Community Trust in 2013.

Number awarded 2 each year.

Deadline September of each year.

[1083]
NEW YORK EXCEPTIONAL UNDERGRADUATE/ GRADUATE STUDENT SCHOLARSHIP

Conference of Minority Transportation Officials
Attn: National Scholarship Program
100 M Street, S.E., Suite 917
Washington, DC 20003
(202) 506-2917   E-mail: info@comto.org
Web: www.comto.org/page/scholarships

Summary To provide financial assistance to African American and other minority students who are members or relatives of members of the Conference of Minority Transportation Officials (COMTO) in New York and working on an undergraduate or graduate degree in transportation.

Eligibility This program is open to minorities who have been members or relatives of members of COMTO in New York for at least 1 year. Applicants must be enrolled full time at an accredited college, university, or vocational/technical institute and working on an undergraduate or graduate degree in a transportation-related discipline. They must have a GPA of 3.5 or higher. Along with their application they must submit a cover letter on their transportation-related career goals and life aspirations. Financial need is not considered in the selection process.

Financial data The stipend is $5,000. Funds are paid directly to the recipient's college or university.

Duration 1 year.

Number awarded 1 each year.

Deadline April of each year.

[1084]
NMF NATIONAL ALUMNI COUNCIL SCHOLARSHIP PROGRAM

National Medical Fellowships, Inc.
Attn: Scholarship Program
347 Fifth Avenue, Suite 510
New York, NY 10016
(212) 483-8880   Toll Free: (877) NMF-1DOC
Fax: (212) 483-8897 E-mail: scholarships@nmfonline.org
Web: www.nmfonline.org

Summary To provide financial assistance to African American and other underrepresented minority medical students who are committed to the health of underserved communities.

Eligibility This program is open to African Americans, Hispanics/Latinos, Native Americans, Vietnamese, Cambodians, and Pacific Islanders who are entering their fourth year of medical school. Applicants must have demonstrated commitment to the health of underserved communities through community service and leadership potential at an early stage in their professional careers. They must be U.S. citizens or DACA students. Financial need is considered in the selection process.

Financial data The stipend is $5,000.

Duration 1 year.

Number awarded 8 each year.

Deadline September of each year.

[1085]
NOA FUTURE CONTACT LENS LEADER SCHOLARSHIPS

National Optometric Association
Attn: Student Affairs
1801 North Tryon Street, Suite 315
Charlotte, NC 28206
(704) 918-1809   Toll Free: (877) 394-2020
Fax: (877) NOA-2006
E-mail: noastudentdirector@yahoo.com
Web: www.nationaloptometricassociation.com

Summary To provide financial assistance to African American and other members of the National Optometric Student Association (NOSA) who are interested in contact lenses.

Eligibility This program is open to NOSA members who are either entering their final year at a school or college of optometry or are currently enrolled in their final year of study and planning to enter a contact lens residency. Applicants must be able to demonstrate a high interest in contact lenses. Along with their application, they must submit a 350-word essay describing an experience with a patient, family member, friend, or themselves that heightened their interest in contact lenses. Financial need is not considered in the selection process.

Financial data The stipend is $1,000.

Duration 1 year.

Additional information The National Optometric Association was founded in 1969 with the goal of recruiting minority students, especially African Americans, for schools and colleges of optometry. This program is sponsored by the National Optometric Association (NOA) with support from CooperVision.

Number awarded 3 each year.

Deadline April of each year.

[1086]
NOAA EDUCATIONAL PARTNERSHIP PROGRAM WITH MINORITY SERVING INSTITUTIONS GRADUATE RESEARCH AND TRAINING SCHOLARSHIP PROGRAM

National Oceanic and Atmospheric Administration
Attn: Office of Education
1315 East-West Highway
SSMC3, Room 10600
Silver Spring, MD 20910-6233
(301) 628-2900   E-mail: gsp@noaa.gov
Web: www.noaa.gov/office-education/epp-msi/grtsp

Summary To provide financial assistance and summer research experience to graduate students at Minority Serving Institutions who are majoring in scientific fields of interest to the National Oceanic and Atmospheric Administration (NOAA).

Eligibility This program is open to full-time graduate students working on master's or doctoral degrees at Minority Serving Institutions, including Alaska Native Serving Institutions (ANSIs), Hispanic Serving Institutions (HSIs), Historically Black Colleges and Universities (HBCUs), Native Hawaiian Serving Institutions (NHSIs), and Tribal Colleges and Universities (TCUs). Applicants must be working on a degree in biology, chemistry, computer science, economics, engineering, environmental law, geography, geology, mathematics, physical science, physics, or social science. They must have a GPA of 3.5 or higher. The program includes a training program during the summer at a NOAA research facility. Selection is based on academic records, a statement of career interests and goals, and compatibility of applicant's background with the interests of NOAA. U.S. citizenship is required.

Financial data Doctoral candidates receive a stipend of $45,000 to support tuition and fees and up to $10,000 to support research travel and to present findings at conferences; master's degree candidates receive $36,000 to support tuition and fees and up to $7,000 to support research travel and to present findings at conferences.

Duration 1 year; may be renewed 1 additional year for doctoral students, provided the recipient maintains a GPA of 3.5 or higher.

Number awarded Varies each year; recently, 9 were awarded.

Deadline January of each year.

[1087]
NORTH TEXAS EXCEPTIONAL UNDERGRADUATE/GRADUATE STUDENT SCHOLARSHIP

Conference of Minority Transportation Officials
Attn: National Scholarship Program
100 M Street, S.E., Suite 917
Washington, DC 20003
(202) 506-2917   E-mail: info@comto.org
Web: www.comto.org/page/scholarships

Summary To provide financial assistance to African American and other minority residents of Texas who are working on an undergraduate or graduate degree in transportation.

Eligibility This program is open to minorities who are residents of Texas enrolled at an accredited college, university, or vocational/technical institute and working on an undergraduate or graduate degree in a transportation-related discipline. Applicants must have a GPA of 2.5 or higher. Along with their application they must submit a cover letter on their transportation-related career goals and life aspirations. Financial need is not considered in the selection process. Membership in the Conference of Minority Transportation Officials (COMTO) is considered a plus but is not required.

Financial data The stipend is $4,500. Funds are paid directly to the recipient's college or university.

Duration 1 year.

Number awarded 1 each year.

Deadline April of each year.

[1088]
NOTRE DAME INSTITUTE FOR ADVANCED STUDY GRADUATE STUDENT FELLOWSHIPS

University of Notre Dame
Institute for Advanced Study
Attn: Programs Administrator
1124 Flanner Hall
Notre Dame, IN 46556
(574) 631-1305   Fax: (574) 631-8997
E-mail: csherman@nd.edu
Web: ndias.nd.edu/fellowships/graduate-student

Summary To provide funding to African American and other underrepresented graduate students who are interested in conducting research on topics of interest to the Notre Dame Institute for Advanced Study (NDIAS) while in residence at the institute.

Eligibility This program is open to graduate students in all disciplines, including the arts, engineering, the humanities, law, and the natural, social, and physical sciences. Applicants must be interested in conducting research that furthers the work of the NDIAS, defined as cultivating "the contemplative ideal that is an essential factor in the Catholic intellectual tradition and vital for the progression of scholarship." They must be able to demonstrate excellent records of scholarly, artistic, or research accomplishment in their field; ability to interact with other fellows and to engage in collegial discussions of research presentations; a willingness to contribute to a cooperative community of scholars; and projects that touch on normative, integrative, or ultimate questions, especially as they involve the Catholic intellectual tradition. Applications are especially encouraged from traditionally underrepresented groups. There are no citizenship requirements; non-U.S. nationals are welcome to apply.

Financial data The grant is $25,000, including a $1,000 research account, office facilities, a computer and printer, access to libraries and other facilities, and twice-weekly institute seminars and events.

Duration 1 academic year.

Number awarded Varies each year; recently, 2 were awarded.

Deadline October of each year.

[1089]
NSCA MINORITY SCHOLARSHIPS

National Strength and Conditioning Association
Attn: NSCA Foundation
1885 Bob Johnson Drive
Colorado Springs, CO 80906-4000
(719) 632-6722, ext. 152   Toll Free: (800) 815-6826
Fax: (719) 632-6367   E-mail: foundation@nsca.org
Web: www.nsca.com/foundation/nsca-scholarships

Summary To provide financial assistance to African American and other minorities who are interested in working on an undergraduate or graduate degree in strength training and conditioning.

Eligibility This program is open to Blacks, Hispanics, Asian Americans, and Native Americans who are 17 years of age and older. Applicants must have been accepted into an accredited postsecondary institution to work on an undergraduate or graduate degree in the strength and conditioning field. Along with their application, they must submit a 500-word essay on their personal and professional goals and how receiving this scholarship will assist them in achieving those goals. Selection is based on that essay, academic achievement, strength and conditioning experience, honors and awards, community involvement, letters of recommendation, and involvement in the National Strength and Conditioning Association (NSCA).

Financial data The stipend is $1,500.

Duration 1 year.

Additional information The NSCA is a nonprofit organization of strength and conditioning professionals, including coaches, athletic trainers, physical therapists, educators, researchers, and physicians. This program was first offered in 2003.

Number awarded Varies each year; recently, 5 were awarded.

Deadline March of each year.

[1090]
OACTA LAW STUDENT DIVERSITY SCHOLARSHIPS

Ohio Association of Civil Trial Attorneys
17 South High Street, Suite 200
Columbus, OH 43215
(614) 228-4727   E-mail: oacta@assnoffices.com
Web: www.oacta.org/About/diversity_scholarship.aspx

Summary To provide financial assistance to African American and other minorities who are enrolled at law schools in Ohio.

Eligibility This program is open to students entering their second or third year at a law school in Ohio. Applicants must be women or members of minority ethnic or racial groups (African American, Hispanic, Asian, Pan Asian, or Native American). Along with their application, they must submit a law school transcript and a cover letter that addresses their academic, personal, and professional accomplishments and why they should be selected as a recipient of this scholarship. Selection is based on academic achievement in law school, professional interest in civil defense practice, service to community, and service to the cause of diversity.

Financial data The stipend is $1,250.

Duration 1 year.

Number awarded Up to 3 each year.

Deadline April of each year.

[1091]
OHIO SOCIETY OF CPAS COLLEGE SCHOLARSHIP PROGRAM

Ohio Society of CPAs
Attn: Ohio CPA Foundation
535 Metro Place South
P.O. Box 1810
Dublin, OH 43017-7810
(614) 764-2727, ext. 344
Toll Free: (800) 686-2727, ext. 344
Fax: (614) 764-5880   E-mail: oscpa@ohio-cpa.com
Web: www.ohiocpa.com

Summary To provide financial assistance to undergraduate and graduate student members of the Ohio Society of CPAs, especially African Americans and members of other underrepresented groups, who are working on a degree in accounting at colleges and universities in the state.

Eligibility This program is open to U.S. citizens who are Ohio residents working on undergraduate or graduate degrees in accounting at colleges and universities in the state in order to complete the 150 hours required for the C.P.A. examination. Applicants must have completed at least 30 hours of college credit and have a GPA of 3.0 or higher. Awards are available to 3 categories of students: 1) 2-year awards, for students at community colleges or other 2-year institutions; 2) 4-year awards, for students at 4-year colleges and universities; and 3) diversity awards, for students from underrepresented ethnic, racial, or cultural groups.

Financial data The stipend is $2,000.

Duration 1 year; nonrenewable.

Number awarded Varies each year; recently, 20 were awarded.

Deadline November of each year.

[1092]
OKLAHOMA CAREERTECH FOUNDATION TEACHER RECRUITMENT/RETENTION SCHOLARSHIP FOR TEACHERS

Oklahoma CareerTech Foundation
Attn: Administrator
1500 West Seventh Avenue
Stillwater, OK 74074-4364
(405) 743-5453   Fax: (405) 743-5541
E-mail: leden@careertech.ok.gov
Web: www.okcareertech.org

Summary   To provide financial assistance to African American and other residents of Oklahoma who reflect the diversity of the state and are interested in attending a college or university in the state to earn a credential or certification for a career in the Oklahoma CareerTech system.

Eligibility   This program is open to residents of Oklahoma who are incumbent CareerTech teachers working toward a CareerTech credential or certification at an institution of higher education in the state. Applicants must reflect the ethnic diversity of the state. Along with their application, they must submit brief statements on their interest and commitment to the CareerTech teaching profession and their financial need.

Financial data   The stipend ranges from $500 per semester to $1,500 per year.

Duration   1 semester; may be renewed, provided the recipient maintains a GPA of 2.5 or higher.

Number awarded   1 or more each year.

Deadline   May of each year.

[1093]
OLIVER GOLDSMITH, M.D. SCHOLARSHIP

Kaiser Permanente Southern California
Attn: Residency Administration and Recruitment
393 East Walnut Street, Fifth Floor
Pasadena, CA 91188
Toll Free: (877) 574-0002   Fax: (626) 405-6581
E-mail: socal.residency@kp.org
Web: residency-scal-kaiserpermanente.org

Summary   To provide financial assistance to African American and other medical students who will help bring diversity to the profession.

Eligibility   This program is open to students entering their third or fourth year of allopathic or osteopathic medical school. Members of all ethnic and racial groups are encouraged to apply, but applicants must have demonstrated their commitment to diversity through community service, clinical volunteering, or research. They may be attending medical school in any state, but they must intend to practice in southern California and they must be available to participate in a mentoring program and a clerkship at a Kaiser Permanente facility in that region.

Financial data   The stipend is $5,000.

Duration   1 year.

Additional information   This program began in 2004.

Number awarded   12 each year.

Deadline   January of each year.

[1094]
OMEGA PSI PHI FOUNDERS' MEMORIAL SCHOLARSHIPS

Omega Psi Phi Fraternity
Attn: Charles R. Drew Memorial Scholarship Commission
3951 Snapfinger Parkway
Decatur, GA 30035-3203
(404) 284-5533   Fax: (404) 284-0333
E-mail: scholarshipchairman@oppf.org
Web: www.oppf.org/scholarship

Summary   To provide financial assistance to outstanding undergraduate and graduate members of Omega Psi Phi fraternity.

Eligibility   This program is open to members of the fraternity who are enrolled full time as sophomores, juniors, or graduate students and have a GPA of 3.0 or higher. Each chapter may nominate 1 undergraduate and 1 graduate member to the district. Candidates must submit a statement of 200 to 250 words on their purpose for applying for this scholarship, how they believe funds from the fraternity can assist them in achieving their career goals, and other circumstances (including financial need) that make it important for them to receive financial assistance. Selection is based on academic achievement, extracurricular activities, and community and campus involvement.

Financial data   The stipend is $5,000.

Duration   The scholarships are offered annually.

Additional information   Omega Psi Phi is a traditionally Black college fraternity. The winners are required to attend the Omega Psi Phi Grand Conclave or Leadership Conference. Up to $1,000 in travel expenses for attendance is provided.

Number awarded   4 each year: 3 to undergraduates and 1 to a graduate student.

Deadline   Applications must be submitted to the district scholarship committee chair by January of each year.

[1095]
OMEGA PSI PHI GRAND BASILEUS AWARD

Omega Psi Phi Fraternity
Attn: Charles R. Drew Memorial Scholarship Commission
3951 Snapfinger Parkway
Decatur, GA 30035-3203
(404) 284-5533   Fax: (404) 284-0333
E-mail: scholarshipchairman@oppf.org
Web: www.oppf.org/scholarship

Summary   To provide financial assistance for graduate or professional education to members of Omega Psi Phi who have an outstanding academic record.

Eligibility   This program is open to members of the fraternity who are graduating college seniors planning to continue on to graduate or professional school. Applicants must be enrolled full time at a 4-year college or university and have a GPA of 3.3 or higher. Along with their application, they must submit a statement of 200 to 250 words on their purpose for applying for this scholarship, how they believe funds from the fraternity can assist them in achieving their career goals, and other circumstances (including financial need) that make it important for them to receive financial assistance.

Financial data   The stipend is $5,000.

Duration   1 year.

Additional information Omega Psi Phi is a traditionally Black college fraternity. The winner is required to attend the Omega Psi Phi Grand Conclave or Leadership Conference. Up to $1,000 in travel expenses for attendance is provided.

Number awarded 1 each year.

Deadline April of each year.

[1096]
OMEGA PSI PHI UNDERGRADUATE AND GRADUATE SCHOLARSHIPS

Omega Psi Phi Fraternity
Attn: Charles R. Drew Memorial Scholarship Commission
3951 Snapfinger Parkway
Decatur, GA 30035-3203
(404) 284-5533   Fax: (404) 284-0333
E-mail: scholarshipchairman@oppf.org
Web: www.oppf.org/scholarship

Summary To provide financial assistance for undergraduate, graduate, or professional education to members of Omega Psi Phi who have an outstanding academic record.

Eligibility This program is open to members of the fraternity who are either 1) a sophomore, junior, or senior planning to continue on to graduate or professional school; or 2) currently attending graduate or professional school. Applicants must be enrolled full time at a 4-year college or university and have a GPA of 3.0 or higher. Along with their application, they must submit a statement of 200 to 250 words on their purpose for applying for this scholarship, how they believe funds from the fraternity can assist them in achieving their career goals, and other circumstances (including financial need) that make it important for them to receive financial assistance.

Financial data The stipend is $4,000.

Duration 1 year.

Additional information Omega Psi Phi is a traditionally Black college fraternity. The winners are required to attend the Omega Psi Phi Grand Conclave or Leadership Conference. Up to $1,000 in travel expenses for attendance is provided.

Number awarded 2 each year: 1 to an undergraduate and 1 to a graduate student.

Deadline April of each year.

[1097]
OPERATION JUMP START III SCHOLARSHIPS

American Association of Advertising Agencies
Attn: AAAA Foundation
1065 Avenue of the Americas, 16th Floor
New York, NY 10018
(212) 262-2500   E-mail: ameadows@aaaa.org
Web: www.aaaa.org

Summary To provide financial assistance to African American andother multicultural art directors and copywriters interested in working on an undergraduate or graduate degree in advertising.

Eligibility This program is open to African Americans, Asian Americans, Hispanic Americans, and Native Americans who are U.S. citizens or permanent residents. Applicants must be incoming graduate students at 1 of 6 designated portfolio schools or full-time juniors at 1 of 2 designated colleges. They must be able to demonstrate extreme financial need, creative talent, and promise. Along with their applica-

tion, they must submit 10 samples of creative work in their respective field of expertise.

Financial data The stipend is $5,000 per year.

Duration Most awards are for 2 years.

Additional information Operation Jump Start began in 1997 and was followed by Operation Jump Start II in 2002. The current program began in 2006. The 6 designated portfolio schools are the AdCenter at Virginia Commonwealth University, the Creative Circus in Atlanta, the Portfolio Center in Atlanta, the Miami Ad School, the University of Texas at Austin, and Pratt Institute. The 2 designated colleges are the Minneapolis College of Art and Design and the Art Center College of Design at Pasadena, California.

Number awarded 20 each year.

Deadline Deadline not specified.

[1098]
OREGON STATE BAR SCHOLARSHIPS

Oregon State Bar
Attn: Diversity and Inclusion Department
16037 S.W. Upper Boones Ferry Road
P.O. Box 231935
Tigard, OR 97281-1935
(503) 620-0222
Toll Free: (800) 452-8260, ext. 338 (within OR)
Fax: (503) 684-1366   TDD: (503) 684-7416
E-mail: cling@osbar.org
Web: www.osbar.org/diversity/programs.html#scholar

Summary To provide financial assistance to entering and continuing students from any state enrolled at law schools in Oregon, especially African Americans and others who will help the Oregon State Bar achieve its diversity and inclusion objectives.

Eligibility This program is open to students entering or continuing at 1 of the law schools in Oregon (Willamette, University of Oregon, and Lewis and Clark). Preference is given to students who will contribute to the Oregon State Bar's diversity and inclusion program, defined to include age, culture, disability, ethnicity, gender and gender identity or expression, geographic location, national origin, race, religion, sex, sexual orientation, and socio-economic status. Along with their application, they must submit a 500-word personal statement on either 1) how their status as a person of diversity has influenced their decision to become a lawyer and how will it influence them throughout their legal professional career; or 2) a challenge they have faced, how they met the challenge, and how that experience will affect the decisions they will make as a legal professional. They must also submit a sample of their legal writing. Selection is based on the personal statement (35%), legal writing ability (25%), academic achievement (15%), work experience and honors (10%), and financial need (15%).

Financial data The stipend is $2,000 per year. Funds are credited to the recipient's law school tuition account.

Duration 1 year; recipients may reapply.

Number awarded 10 each year.

Deadline March of each year.

[1099]
ORGANIC CHEMISTRY GRADUATE STUDENT FELLOWSHIPS

American Chemical Society
Division of Organic Chemistry
1155 16th Street, N.W.
Washington, DC 20036
(202) 872-4401　　　Toll Free: (800) 227-5558, ext. 4401
E-mail: division@acs.org
Web: www.organicdivision.org/?nd=graduate_fellowship

Summary　To provide funding for research to members of the Division of Organic Chemistry of the American Chemical Society (ACS), especially African Americans and other minorities, who are working on a doctoral degree in organic chemistry.

Eligibility　This program is open to members of the division who are entering the third or fourth year of a Ph.D. program in organic chemistry. Applicants must submit 3 letters of recommendation, a resume, and a short essay on a research area of their choice. U.S. citizenship or permanent resident status is required. Selection is based primarily on evidence of research accomplishment. Applications from women and minorities are especially encouraged.

Financial data　The stipend is $26,000; that includes $750 for travel support to present a poster of their work at the National Organic Symposium.

Duration　1 year.

Additional information　This program began in 1982. It includes the Emmanuil Troyansky Fellowship. Current corporate sponsors include Organic Syntheses, Boehringer Ingelheim, and Amgen.

Number awarded　Varies each year; recently, 5 were awarded.

Deadline　May of each year.

[1100]
OSA LEADERSHIP TUITION SCHOLARSHIP

National Association of Black Social Workers
Attn: NABSW Scholarships
2305 Martin Luther King Avenue, S.E.
Washington, DC 20020
(202) 678-4570　　　Fax: (202) 678-4572
E-mail: office-manager@nabsw.org
Web: www.nabsw.org/?page=ScholarshipsRecipien

Summary　To provide financial assistance to members of the National Association of Black Social Workers (NABSW) who have provided outstanding community service and are working on an undergraduate or graduate degree.

Eligibility　This program is open to African American members of NABSW who are enrolled at least half time at an accredited U.S. institution. Applicants must be working on an associate, bachelor's, master's, or Ph.D. degree in social work, sociology, or other field of human services. They must have a GPA of 3.0 or higher and a record of volunteer service to the African American community. Along with their application, they must submit a letter of recommendation from a prestigious community leader that highlights their volunteer work and leadership efforts within the African American community. Financial need is considered in the selection process.

Financial data　The stipend is $1,000. Funds are sent directly to the recipient's school.

Duration　1 year.

Number awarded　1 each year.

Deadline　December of each year.

[1101]
PA STUDENT SCHOLARSHIPS

American Academy of Physician Assistants
Attn: Physician Assistant Foundation
2318 Mill Road, Suite 1300
Alexandria, VA 22314-6868
(703) 836-2272　　　　　　Fax: (703) 684-1924
E-mail: pafoundation@aapa.org
Web: www.pa-foundation.org

Summary　To provide financial assistance to student members of the American Academy of Physician Assistants (AAPA) who are African Americans, otherunderrepresented minorities, or economically and/or educationally disadvantaged.

Eligibility　This program is open to AAPA student members attending a physician assistant program accredited by the Commission on Accreditation of Allied Health Education Programs. Applicants must qualify as 1) an underrepresented minority (Black or African American, Alaska Native, American Indian, Hispanic or Latino, Native Hawaiian or other Pacific Islander, or Asian other than Chinese, Filipino, Japanese, Korean, Asian Indian, or Thai); 2) economically disadvantaged (with income below a specified level); or 3) educationally disadvantaged (from a high school with low SAT scores, from a school district in which less than half of graduates go on to college, has a diagnosed physical or mental impairment, English is not their primary language, the first member of their family to attend college). They must have completed at least 1 semester of PA studies.

Financial data　Stipends are $2,500, $2,000, or $1,000.

Duration　1 year; nonrenewable.

Additional information　This program includes the AAPA Past Presidents Scholarship, the Bristol-Myers Squibb Endowed Scholarship, the National Commission on Certification of Physician Assistants Endowed Scholarships, the Procter & Gamble Endowed Scholarship, and the PA Foundation Scholarships.

Number awarded　Varies each year; recently, 32 were awarded: 3 at $2,500, 27 at $2,000, and 2 at $1,000.

Deadline　January of each year.

[1102]
PATRICIA G. ARCHBOLD PREDOCTORAL SCHOLAR AWARD

National Hartford Center of Gerontological Nursing Excellence
Attn: Hartford Institute for Geriatric Nursing
NYU Rory Myers College of Nursing
433 First Avenue, Fifth Floor
New York, NY 10010
(202) 779-1439　　　　　E-mail: nhcgne@nyu.edu
Web: www.nhcgne.org

Summary　To provide funding to African American and other underrepresented minority nurses who are interested in working on a doctoral degree in gerontological nursing.

Eligibility　This program is open to registered nurses who are members of underrepresented minority groups (American

Indians, Alaska Natives, Asians, Blacks or African Americans, Hispanics or Latinos/Latinas, Native Hawaiians or other Pacific Islanders) and have been admitted to a doctoral program as a full-time student. The institution they plan to attend must be a member of the National Hartford Center of Gerontological Nursing Excellence (NHCGNE). Applicants must plan an academic research career in geriatric nursing. They must identify a mentor/adviser with whom they will work and whose program of research in geriatric nursing is a good match with their own research interest area. Selection is based on potential for substantial long-term contributions to the knowledge base in geriatric nursing; leadership potential; evidence of commitment to a career in academic geriatric nursing; and evidence of involvement in educational, research, and professional activities. U.S. citizenship or permanent resident status is required.

Financial data The stipend is $50,000 per year. An additional stipend of $5,000 is available to fellows whose research includes the study of pain in the elderly.

Duration 2 years.

Additional information This program began in 2001 with funding from the John A. Hartford Foundation. In 2004, the Mayday Fund added support to scholars who focus on the study of pain in the elderly. Until 2013 it was known as the Building Academic Geriatric Nursing Capacity Program.

Number awarded 1 or more each year.

Deadline January of each year.

[1103]
PATRICIA M. LOWRIE DIVERSITY LEADERSHIP SCHOLARSHIP

Association of American Veterinary Medical Colleges
Attn: Diversity Committee
1101 Vermont Avenue, N.W., Suite 301
Washington, DC 20005-3536
(202) 371-9195, ext. 147   Toll Free: (877) 862-2740
Fax: (202) 842-0773   E-mail: lgreenhill@aavmc.org
Web: www.aavmc.org

Summary To provide financial assistance to veterinary students who are African Americans or have promoted diversity in the profession in other ways.

Eligibility This program is open to second-, third-, and fourth-year students at veterinary colleges in the United States. Applicants must have a demonstrated record of contributing to enhancing diversity and inclusion through course projects, co-curricular activities, outreach, domestic and community engagement, research, and/or an early reputation for influencing others to be inclusive. Along with their application, they must submit a 3-page personal statement that describes 1) why diversity and inclusion are important to them personally and professionally; 2) how they intend to continue contributing to diversity and inclusion efforts in the veterinary profession after graduation; and 3) what it might mean to be honored as a recipient of this scholarship. They must also indicate how they express their race and/or ethnicity (Black or African American, American Indian or Alaskan, Asian, Hispanic, Native Hawaiian or Pacific Islander, or White) and how they express their gender (male, female, transgender spectrum, or other). Selection is based primarily on documentation of a demonstrated commitment to promoting diversity in academic veterinary medicine; consideration is also given to academic achievement, the student's broader community service record, and financial need.

Financial data The stipend is $6,000.

Duration 1 year; nonrenewable.

Additional information This program began in 2013.

Number awarded 1 each odd-numbered year.

Deadline October of each even-numbered year.

[1104]
PEGGY PETERMAN SCHOLARSHIP

Tampa Bay Times
Attn: Director of Corporate Giving
490 First Avenue South
St. Petersburg, FL 33701
(727) 893-8780   Toll Free: (800) 333-7505, ext. 8780
Fax: (727) 892-2257   E-mail: waclawek@tampabay.com
Web: www.tampabay.com

Summary To provide financial assistance to African American and other minority undergraduate and graduate students who are interested in preparing for a career in the newspaper industry and who accept an internship at the *Tampa Bay Times*.

Eligibility This program is open to minority college sophomores, juniors, seniors, and graduate students from any state who are interested in preparing for a career in the newspaper industry. Applicants must be interested in an internship at the *Tampa Bay Times* and must apply for that at the same time as they apply for this scholarship. They should have experience working on a college publication and at least 1 professional internship.

Financial data The stipend is $5,000.

Duration Internships are for 12 weeks during the summer. Scholarships are for 1 year.

Number awarded 1 each year.

Deadline October of each year.

[1105]
PFATS-NFL CHARITIES MINORITY SCHOLARSHIPS

Professional Football Athletic Trainers Society
c/o Britt Brown, ATC, Associate Athletic Trainer
Dallas Cowboys
One Cowboys Parkway
Irving, TX 75063
(972) 497-4992   E-mail: bbrown@dallascowboys.net
Web: www.pfats.com/about/scholarships

Summary To provide financial assistance to African American and other ethnic minority undergraduate and graduate students working on a degree in athletic training.

Eligibility This program is open to ethnic minority students who are working on an undergraduate or graduate degree in athletic training. Applicants must have a GPA of 2.5 or higher. Along with their application, they must submit a cover letter, a curriculum vitae, and a letter of recommendation from their supervising athletic trainer. Female athletic training students are encouraged to apply.

Financial data A stipend is awarded (amount not specified).

Duration 1 year.

Additional information Recipients also have an opportunity to work at summer training camp of a National Football League (NFL) team. Support for this program, which began in 1993, is provided by NFL Charities.

Number awarded 1 or more each year.

Deadline March of each year.

[1106]
PHILADELPHIA CHAPTER NBMBAA GRADUATE SCHOLARSHIP

National Black MBA Association-Philadelphia Chapter
Attn: Scholarship Ad Hoc Committee
P.O. Box 1384
Philadelphia, PA 19105
(215) 472-BMBA
E-mail: studentaffairs@nbmbaa-philly.org
Web: www.nbmbaa-philly.org/scholarships.html

Summary To provide financial assistance to African American residents of the greater Philadelphia metropolitan area working on a graduate degree in business in any state.

Eligibility This program is open to African American residents of the greater Philadelphia metropolitan area (Delaware, southern New Jersey, and the Pennsylvania counties of Berks, Bucks, Chester, Delaware, Lehigh, Montgomery, and Philadelphia). Applicants must be entering or currently enrolled full time at an AACSB-accredited college or university in any state and working on a master's or doctoral degree in a business-related or management field. Along with their application, they must submit a 2-page essay on a topic that changes annually but relates to African Americans and business. Selection is based on that essay, academic achievement, community service and involvement, verbal communication skills, a resume, and reference letters.

Financial data The stipend ranges from $500 to $2,500. Funds are disbursed directly to the college or university.

Duration 1 year; nonrenewable.

Number awarded Varies each year.

Deadline September of each year.

[1107]
PHILLIPS EXETER ACADEMY DISSERTATION YEAR FELLOWSHIP

Phillips Exeter Academy
Attn: Dean of Multicultural Affairs
20 Main Street
Exeter, NH 03833-2460
(603) 772-4311   Fax: (603) 777-4393
E-mail: teaching_opportunities@exeter.edu
Web: www.exeter.edu

Summary To provide an opportunity for African American and other diverse doctoral candidates to work on their dissertation during a residency at Phillips Exeter Academy in Exeter, New Hampshire.

Eligibility This program is open to Ph.D. candidates in any discipline who are in the completion stage of their dissertation. Applicants must be prepared to devote full time to their writing during a residency at the academy. Along with their application, they must submit a curriculum vitae, 2 letters of reference, a 2- to 3-page synopsis of the dissertation, and a 500-word statement of purpose testifying to the appropriateness of the fellowship. Candidates who are interested in

potentially teaching in an independent school setting and who are underrepresented in higher education are particularly encouraged to apply.

Financial data This program provides a stipend ($14,310), research and travel funds up to $1,000, room and board, benefits, access to facilities and resources of the school, and professional development opportunities.

Duration 1 academic year.

Additional information Fellows do not have any regular or prescribed duties. During the tenure of the program, fellows may not have any other full- or part-time job.

Number awarded 1 each year.

Deadline March of each year.

[1108]
PITTSBURGH CHAPTER NBMBAA GRADUATE SCHOLARSHIP

National Black MBA Association-Pittsburgh Chapter
Attn: Education Director
P.O. Box 3502
Pittsburgh, PA 15230-3502
(724) 382-3063   E-mail: education@nbmbaapgh.org
Web: www.nbmbaa-pittsburgh.org/?page_id=4661

Summary To provide financial assistance to African American graduate students working on a master's degree in business at colleges in southwestern Pennsylvania.

Eligibility This program is open to African Americans enrolled full or part time at a college or university in southwestern Pennsylvania. Applicants must be in the first or second year of a master's degree program in business or management. Along with their application, they must submit an essay of 2 to 3 pages on a topic that changes annually; recently, students were asked to describe the recommendations they would give to business schools that want to design their recruitment strategies to attract minority candidates.

Financial data The stipend is $3,000.

Duration 1 year.

Number awarded Multiple scholarships are awarded.

Deadline July of each year.

[1109]
PORTER PHYSIOLOGY DEVELOPMENT AWARDS

American Physiological Society
Attn: Education Office
9650 Rockville Pike, Room 3111
Bethesda, MD 20814-3991
(301) 634-7132   Fax: (301) 634-7098
E-mail: education@the-aps.org
Web: www.the-aps.org

Summary To provide financial assistance to African Americans and other minorities who are members of the American Physiological Society (APS) interested in working on a doctoral degree in physiology.

Eligibility This program is open to U.S. citizens and permanent residents who are members of racial or ethnic minority groups (Black or African American, Hispanic or Latino, American Indian or Alaska Native, Asian, or Native Hawaiian or other Pacific Islander). Applicants must be currently enrolled in or accepted to a doctoral program in physiology at a university as full-time students. They must be APS members and have actively participated in its work. Selection is based on the applicant's potential for success (academic record, statement of interest, previous awards and experiences, letters of recommendation); applicant's proposed training environment (including quality of preceptor); and applicant's research and training plan (clarity and quality).

Financial data   The stipend is $28,300 per year. No provision is made for a dependency allowance or tuition and fees.

Duration   1 year; may be renewed for 1 additional year and, in exceptional cases, for a third year.

Additional information   This program is supported by the William Townsend Porter Foundation (formerly the Harvard Apparatus Foundation). The first Porter Fellowship was awarded in 1920. In 1966 and 1967, the American Physiological Society established the Porter Physiology Development Committee to award fellowships to minority students engaged in graduate study in physiology. The highest ranked applicant for these fellowships is designated the Eleanor Ison Franklin Fellow.

Number awarded   Varies each year; recently, 6 were awarded.

Deadline   January of each year.

[1110]
POST-BACCALAUREATE INTERNSHIP PROGRAM IN BIOSTATISTICS AND COMPUTATIONAL BIOLOGY

Harvard T.H. Chan School of Public Health
Department of Biostatistics
Attn: Diversity Coordinator
677 Huntington Avenue, SPH2, Fourth Floor
Boston, MA 02115
(617) 432-3175   Fax: (617) 432-5619
E-mail: biostat_diversity@hsph.harvard.edu
Web: www.hsph.harvard.edu

Summary   To enable African American and other underrepresented minority or disadvantaged science post-baccalaureates to participate in a summer research internship at Harvard T.H. Chan School of Public Health that focuses on biostatistics and epidemiology.

Eligibility   This program is open to students who have received a bachelor's degree and are interested in or planning to attend a graduate degree program in biostatistics or epidemiology. Applicants must be U.S. citizens or permanent residents who are 1) members of ethnic groups underrepresented in graduate education (African Americans, Hispanic/Latinos, Native Americans, Pacific Islanders, biracial/multiracial); 2) first-generation college students; 3) low-income students; or 4) individuals with a disability. They must have a strong GPA, including course work in calculus, and a strong interest in mathematics, statistics, computer science, and other quantitative subjects.

Financial data   Interns receive a salary (amount not specified) and support for travel.

Duration   2 to 3 months, starting in June.

Additional information   Interns conduct biostatistical or epidemiologic research alongside a Harvard faculty mentor and graduate student mentor, participate in collaborative research projects, attend regular seminars, and receive directed mentoring and support for graduate school applications and selection.

Number awarded   2 each year.
Deadline   January of each year.

[1111]
PREDOCTORAL FELLOWSHIPS OF THE FORD FOUNDATION DIVERSITY FELLOWSHIP PROGRAM

The National Academies of Sciences, Engineering, and Medicine
Attn: Fellowships Office
500 Fifth Street, N.W.
Washington, DC 20001
(202) 334-2872   Fax: (202) 334-3419
E-mail: FordApplications@nas.edu
Web: sites.nationalacademies.org

Summary   To provide financial assistance for graduate school to African American and other students whose success will increase the racial and ethnic diversity of U.S. colleges and universities.

Eligibility   This program is open to citizens, permanent residents, and nationals of the United States who are enrolled or planning to enroll full time in a Ph.D. or Sc.D. degree program and are committed to a career in teaching and research at the college or university level. Applicants may be undergraduates in their senior year, individuals who have completed undergraduate study or some graduate study, or current Ph.D. or Sc.D. students who can demonstrate that they can fully utilize a 3-year fellowship award. They must be working on or planning to work on a degree in 1 of the following fields: American studies, anthropology, archaeology, art and theater history, astronomy, chemistry, communications, computer science, cultural studies, earth sciences, economics, education, engineering, ethnic studies, ethnomusicology, geography, history, international relations, language, life sciences, linguistics, literature, mathematics, performance study, philosophy, physics, political science, psychology, religious studies, sociology, urban planning, and women's studies. Also eligible are interdisciplinary programs such as African American studies, Native American studies, area studies, peace studies, and social justice. Students in practice-oriented areas, terminal master's degrees, other doctoral degrees (e.g., Ed.D., D.F.A., Psy.D.), professional degrees (e.g., medicine, law, public health), or joint degrees (e.g., M.D./Ph.D., J.D./Ph.D., M.F.A./Ph.D.) are not eligible. The following are considered as positive factors in the selection process: evidence of superior academic achievement; promise of continuing achievement as scholars and teachers; membership in a group whose underrepresentation in the American professoriate has been severe and longstanding, including Black/African Americans, Puerto Ricans, Mexican Americans/Chicanos/Chicanas, Native American Indians, Alaska Natives (Eskimos, Aleuts, and other indigenous people of Alaska), and Native Pacific Islanders (Hawaiians, Micronesians, or Polynesians); capacity to respond in pedagogically productive ways to the learning needs of students from diverse backgrounds; sustained personal engagement with communities that are underrepresented in the academy and an ability to bring this asset to learning, teaching, and scholarship at the college and university level; and likelihood of using the diversity of human experience as an educational resource in teaching and scholarship.

Financial data The program provides a stipend to the student of $24,000 per year and an award to the host institution of $2,000 per year in lieu of tuition and fees.

Duration 3 years of support is provided, to be used within a 5-year period.

Additional information The competition for this program is conducted by the National Research Council on behalf of the Ford Foundation. Applicants who merit receiving the fellowship but to whom awards cannot be made because of insufficient funds are given Honorable Mentions; this recognition does not carry with it a monetary award but honors applicants who have demonstrated substantial academic achievement. The National Research Council publishes a list of those Honorable Mentions who wish their names publicized. Fellows may not accept remuneration from another fellowship or similar external award while on this program; however, supplementation from institutional funds, educational benefits from the Department of Veterans Affairs, or educational incentive funds may be received concurrently with Ford Foundation support. Predoctoral fellows are required to submit an interim progress report 6 months after the start of the fellowship and a final report at the end of the 12 month tenure.

Number awarded Approximately 60 each year.

Deadline November of each year.

[1112]
PRE-DOCTORAL SCHOLARSHIPS FOR 2ND/3RD/4TH YEAR DENTAL STUDENTS

National Dental Association
Attn: National Dental Association Foundation, Inc.
3517 16th Street, N.W.
Washington, DC 20010
(734) 544-1336   E-mail: admin@ndaonline.org
Web: www.ndafoundation.org/pre-doctoral-scholarship.html

Summary To provide financial assistance to African American and other minority dental students.

Eligibility This program is open to members of minority groups who are entering their second, third, or fourth year of dental school. Applicants must be members of the Student National Dental Association (SNDA) and U.S. citizens or permanent residents. Along with their application, they must submit a letter explaining why they should be considered for this scholarship, 2 letters of recommendation, and documentation of financial need. Selection is based on academic performance and service to community and/or country.

Financial data The stipend is $1,000 per year.

Duration 1 year. Recipients may reapply.

Additional information This program, established in 1990, is supported by the Colgate-Palmolive Company.

Number awarded Varies each year; recently, 65 were awarded.

Deadline May of each year.

[1113]
PRESBYTERIAN WOMEN OF COLOR GRANTS

Presbyterian Church (USA)
Attn: Office of Financial Aid for Service
100 Witherspoon Street
Louisville, KY 40202-1396
(502) 569-5224   Toll Free: (888) 728-7228, ext. 5224
Fax: (502) 569-8766   TDD: (800) 833-5955
E-mail: finaid@pcusa.org
Web: www.presbyterianmission.org

Summary To provide financial assistance to graduate students who are African Americans or other women of color and Presbyterian Church (USA) members interested in preparing for church occupations.

Eligibility This program is open to women of color who are full-time graduate students at a PCUSA seminary or accredited theological institution approved by their Committee on Preparation for Ministry. Applicants must be working on 1) an M.Div. degree and enrolled as an inquirer or candidate by a PCUSA presbytery; or 2) an M.A.C.E. degree and preparing for a church occupation. They must be PCUSA members, U.S. citizens or permanent residents, able to demonstrate financial need, and recommended by the financial aid officer at their theological institution. Along with their application, they must submit a 1,000-word essay on what they believe God is calling them to do in ministry.

Financial data Stipends range from $1,000 to $3,000 per year. Funds are intended as supplements to students who have been awarded a Presbyterian Study Grant but still demonstrate remaining financial need.

Duration 1 year; may be renewed up to 2 additional years.

Number awarded Varies each year; the sponsor awards approximately 130 grants for this and 3 related programs each year.

Deadline June of each year.

[1114]
PRISCILLA GREEN SCHOLARSHIP AWARD

George W. Crawford Black Bar Association
c/o Thamar Esperance, Scholarship Committee Co-Chair
Greater Hartford Legal Aid
999 Asylum Avenue, Third Floor
Hartford, CT 06105-2465
(860) 541-5000   Fax: (860) 511-5050
E-mail: TEsperance@ghla.org
Web: www.georgecrawfordblackbar.org/links/law-students

Summary To provide financial assistance to African American and other minority law students who are committed to practicing in Connecticut.

Eligibility This program is open to minority students currently enrolled in law school who can demonstrate a commitment to practicing law in Connecticut and furthering the mission of the George W. Crawford Black Bar Association: working for the enhancement of the role of Black people in the legal profession, increasing their numbers in the state of Connecticut, focusing on legal issues that affect members of the Black community, providing a vehicle for interaction of Black organizations and individuals in Connecticut, and establishing lines of communication with other legal organizations. Selection is based on academic and extracurricular achievement plus an essay of 1,000 words on how their background matches the goals of the sponsoring organization.

Financial data   The stipend is $1,000.

Duration   1 year; nonrenewable.

Number awarded   1 or more each year.

Deadline   March of each year.

[1115]
PROGRAM IN AFRICAN AMERICAN HISTORY MELLON SCHOLAR DISSERTATION FELLOWSHIP

Library Company of Philadelphia
Attn: Program in African American History
1314 Locust Street
Philadelphia, PA 19107-5698
(215) 546-3181   Fax: (215) 546-5167
E-mail: era@udel.edu
Web: www.librarycompany.org/fellowships/dissertation.htm

Summary   To provide funding to doctoral candidates who are African Amerians or from other underrepresented backgrounds who are interested in conducting research on African American history at the Library Company of Philadelphia.

Eligibility   This program is open to doctoral candidates from underrepresented backgrounds who are in the later stages of research or writing a dissertation and interested in conducting research in Philadelphia at the Library Company. The proposed research must relate to African American history prior to 1900.

Financial data   The grant is $25,000 for an academic year or $12,500 for a semester.

Duration   1 academic year or 1 semester.

Additional information   The Library Company of Philadelphia established its Program in African American History in 2013 with support from the Andrew W. Mellon Foundation.

Number awarded   Either 1 fellowship for a year or 2 for a semester are supported each year.

Deadline   February of each year.

[1116]
PROGRAM IN AFRICAN AMERICAN HISTORY SHORT-TERM MELLON SCHOLARS FELLOWSHIPS

Library Company of Philadelphia
Attn: Program in African American History
1314 Locust Street
Philadelphia, PA 19107-5698
(215) 546-3181   Fax: (215) 546-5167
E-mail: era@udel.edu
Web: www.librarycompany.org/fellowships/shortterm.htm

Summary   To provide funding to pre- and postdoctorates who are African Americans or from other underrepresented backgrounds and interested in conducting short-term research on African American history at the Library Company of Philadelphia.

Eligibility   This program is open to doctoral candidates and senior scholars from underrepresented backgrounds who are interested in conducting research in Philadelphia at the Library Company. The proposed research must relate to African American history prior to 1900.

Financial data   The stipend is $2,500.

Duration   1 month.

Additional information   The Library Company of Philadelphia established its Program in African American History in 2013 with support from the Andrew W. Mellon Foundation.

Number awarded   4 each year.

Deadline   February of each year.

[1117]
PUBLIC HONORS FELLOWSHIPS OF THE OREGON STATE BAR

Oregon State Bar
Attn: Diversity and Inclusion Department
16037 S.W. Upper Boones Ferry Road
P.O. Box 231935
Tigard, OR 97281-1935
(503) 620-0222
Toll Free: (800) 452-8260, ext. 338 (within OR)
Fax: (503) 684-1366   TDD: (503) 684-7416
E-mail: cling@osbar.org
Web: www.osbar.org/diversity/programs.html#honors

Summary   To provide law students in Oregon with summer work experience in public interest law, especially African Americans or others who will help the Oregon State Bar achieve its diversity and inclusion objectives.

Eligibility   This program is open to students at law schools in Oregon who are not in the first or final year of study. Each school may nominate up to 5 students. Nominees must have demonstrated a career goal in public interest or public sector law. Preference is given to students who will contribute to the Oregon State Bar's diversity and inclusion program, defined to include age, culture, disability, ethnicity, gender and gender identity or expression, geographic location, national origin, race, religion, sex, sexual orientation, and socio-economic status. They must be interested in working in a law office during the summer; the employment should be in Oregon, although exceptions will be made if the job offers the student special experience not available within the state. Along with their application, they must submit a 500-word personal statement on either 1) how their status as a person of diversity has influenced their decision to become a lawyer and how will it influence them throughout their legal professional career; or 2) a challenge they have faced, how they met the challenge, and how that experience will affect the decisions they will make as a legal professional. They must also submit a sample of their legal writing. Selection is based on the personal statement (35%), legal writing ability (25%), academic achievement (15%), work experience and honors (10%), and financial need (15%). The information on those students is forwarded to prospective employers in Oregon and they arrange to interview the selectees.

Financial data   Fellows receive a stipend of $5,000.

Duration   3 months during the summer.

Additional information   There is no guarantee that all students selected by the sponsoring organization will receive fellowships at Oregon law firms.

Number awarded   6 each year: 2 from each of the law schools.

Deadline   Each law school sets its own deadline.

[1118]
PUBLIC POLICY AND INTERNATIONAL AFFAIRS FELLOWSHIPS

Public Policy and International Affairs Fellowship Program
c/o University of Minnesota
Humphrey School of Public Affairs
130 Humphrey School
301 19th Avenue South
Minneapolis, MN 55455
Toll Free: (877) 774-2001   E-mail: hadd0029@umn.edu
Web: www.ppiaprogram.org/ppia

Summary   To provide financial assistance to African Americans and students from other underrepresented groups who have completed a specified summer institute and are interested in preparing for graduate study in the fields of public policy and/or international affairs.

Eligibility   This program is open to people of color historically underrepresented in public policy and international affairs. Applicants must be U.S. citizens or permanent residents interested in a summer institute in public policy and international affairs. They must first apply directly to the summer institute. Following participation in that institute, they apply for graduate study in fields of their choice at 41 designated universities. For a list of participating institutions, contact the sponsor.

Financial data   The participating programs in public policy and/or international affairs have agreed to waive application fees and grant fellowships of at least $5,000 to students who have participated in the summer institutes.

Duration   1 summer and 1 academic year.

Additional information   This program was established in 1981 when the Alfred P. Sloan Foundation provided a grant to the Association for Public Policy Analysis and Management (APPAM). From 1981 through 1988, participants were known as Sloan Fellows. From 1889 through 1995, the program was supported by the Ford Foundation and administered by the Woodrow Wilson National Fellowship Administration, so participants were known as Woodrow Wilson Fellows in Public Policy and International Affairs. Beginning in 1995, the program's name was shortened to the Public Policy and International Affairs Fellowship Program (PPIA) and the Association of Professional Schools of International Affairs (APSIA) also became an institutional sponsor. In 1999, the Ford Foundation ended its support for PPIA effective with the student cohort that participated in summer institutes in 1999. The APPAM and APSIA incorporated PPIA as an independent organization and have continued to sponsor it. Since summer of 2001, summer institutes have been held at 5 universities: the Summer Program in Public Policy and International Affairs at the Gerald R. Ford School of Public Policy at the University of Michigan, the Humphrey School Junior Institute at the Humphrey School of Public Affairs at the University of Minnesota (which serves as host of the program), the UCP-PIA Junior Summer Institute at the Richard and Rhoda Goldman School of Public Policy at the University of California at Berkeley, the PPIA Junior Summer Institute at the Woodrow Wilson School of Public and International Affairs at Princeton University, and the PPIA Junior Summer Institute at the Heinz School of Public Policy and Management at Carnegie Mellon University. For information on those institutes, contact the respective school. Additional support is currently provided by the Foundation for Child Development and the William T. Grant Foundation.

Number awarded   Varies each year.

Deadline   Each of the 5 participating universities that offer summer institutes and each of the 41 universities that accept students for graduate study sets its own deadline.

[1119]
RACE RELATIONS MULTIRACIAL STUDENT SCHOLARSHIP

Christian Reformed Church
Attn: Office of Race Relations
1700 28th Street, S.E.
Grand Rapids, MI 49508
(616) 224-5883   Toll Free: (877) 864-3977
Fax: (616) 224-0834   E-mail: elugo@crcna.org
Web: www.crcna.org/race/scholarships

Summary   To provide financial assistance to undergraduate and graduate African Americans and other minority students interested in attending colleges related to the Christian Reformed Church in North America (CRCNA).

Eligibility   This program is open to students of color in the United States and Canada. Normally, applicants are expected to be members of CRCNA congregations who plan to pursue their educational goals at Calvin Theological Seminary or any of the colleges affiliated with the CRCNA. They must be interested in training for the ministry of racial reconciliation in church and/or in society. Along with their application, they must submit paragraphs about their personal history and family, Christian faith, and Christian leadership goals. Students who have no prior history with the CRCNA must attend a CRCNA-related college or seminary for a full academic year before they are eligible to apply for this program. Students entering their sophomore year must have earned a GPA of 2.0 or higher as freshmen; students entering their junior year must have earned a GPA of 2.3 or higher as sophomores; students entering their senior year must have earned a GPA of 2.6 or higher as juniors.

Financial data   First-year students receive $500 per semester. Other levels of students may receive up to $2,000 per academic year.

Duration   1 year.

Additional information   This program was first established in 1971 and revised in 1991. Recipients are expected to train to engage actively in the ministry of racial reconciliation in church and in society. They must be able to work in the United States or Canada upon graduating and must consider working for 1 of the agencies of the CRCNA.

Number awarded   Varies each year; recently, 31 students received a total of $21,000 in support.

Deadline   March of each year.

[1120]
RACIAL ETHNIC PASTORAL LEADERSHIP PROGRAM

Synod of Southern California and Hawaii
Attn: Racial Ethnic Pastoral Leadership Program
14225 Roscoe Boulevard
Panorama, CA 91402
(213) 483-3840, ext. 112   Fax: (818) 891-0212
E-mail: ntucker@synod.org
Web: www.synod.org/#repl

Summary To provide financial assistance to African Americans and members of racial minority groups in the Presbyterian Church (USA) Synod of Southern California and Hawaii who are preparing for a career as a pastor or other church vocation.

Eligibility Applicants must be under care of their church's Session and enrolled with a Presbytery within the Synod of Southern California and Hawaii. They must be members of racial ethnic groups interested in becoming a Presbyterian pastor or other church worker (e.g., commissioned ruling elder, certified Christian educator) and serving in a racial ethnic ministry within the PCUSA. Racial ethnic persons who already have an M.Div. degree, are from another denomination in correspondence with the PCUSA, and are seeking to meet PCUSA requirements for ordination or transfer may also be eligible if they plan to serve in a racial ethnic congregation or an approved specialized ministry. Applicants must submit documentation of financial need, recommendations from the appropriate presbytery committee or session, a current transcript, and essays on their goals and objectives. They must be enrolled full or part time in a PCUSA seminary or other seminary approved by the Committee on Preparation for Ministry of their Presbytery.

Financial data The stipend is $5,000 per year.

Duration 1 year; may be renewed.

Additional information This program began in 1984.

Number awarded Varies each year; recently, 5 students were receiving support from this program. Since the program began, it has awarded $372,375 to approximately 335 seminarians.

Deadline April of each year.

[1121]
RACIAL ETHNIC SUPPLEMENTAL GRANTS

Presbyterian Church (USA)
Attn: Office of Financial Aid for Service
100 Witherspoon Street
Louisville, KY 40202-1396
(502) 569-5224   Toll Free: (888) 728-7228, ext. 5224
Fax: (502) 569-8766   TDD: (800) 833-5955
E-mail: finaid@pcusa.org
Web: www.presbyterianmission.org

Summary To provide financial assistance to African American and other minority graduate students who are Presbyterian Church (USA) members interested in preparing for church occupations.

Eligibility This program is open to racial/ethnic graduate students (Asian American, African American, Hispanic American, Native American, or Alaska Native) who are enrolled full time at a PCUSA seminary or accredited theological institution approved by their Committee on Preparation for Ministry.

Applicants must be working on 1) an M.Div. degree and enrolled as an inquirer or candidate by a PCUSA presbytery; or 2) an M.A.C.E. degree and preparing for a church occupation. They must be PCUSA members, U.S. citizens or permanent residents, able to demonstrate financial need, and recommended by the financial aid officer at their theological institution. Along with their application, they must submit a 1,000-word essay on what they believe God is calling them to do in ministry.

Financial data Stipends range from $500 to $1,000 per year. Funds are intended as supplements to students who have been awarded a Presbyterian Study Grant but still demonstrate remaining financial need.

Duration 1 year; may be renewed up to 2 additional years.

Number awarded Varies each year; the sponsor awards approximately 130 grants for this and 3 related programs each year.

Deadline June of each year.

[1122]
RAFAEL DODD GRADUATE SCHOLARSHIP

National Black MBA Association-Memphis Chapter
Attn: Leadership Team
P.O. Box 770907
Memphis, TN 38117
(901) 347-8786   E-mail: Memphis_nbmbaa@yahoo.com
Web: www.nbmbaamemphis.org/programs

Summary To provide financial assistance to African American and other minority residents of any state working on a graduate degree in business at a university in the Memphis region.

Eligibility This program is open to minority students currently enrolled at a college or university in Memphis and its surrounding counties (Fayette, Shelby, and Tipton in Tennessee, DeSoto and Marshall in Mississippi, and Crittenden in Arkansas). Applicants must be working on a graduate degree (e.g., M.B.A., M.P.H., Ph.D., Ed.D., D.B.A.) in business or management. Along with their application, they must submit a 3-page essay on a topic that changes annually; recently, students were asked to write on "Rational intelligence-The future competitive advantage for leaders." Selection is based on that essay, academic achievement, a resume, community service, references, and verbal skills in an interview.

Financial data The stipend is $1,000.

Duration 1 year.

Number awarded 1 or more each year.

Deadline March of each year.

[1123]
RALPH PHILLIPS SCHOLARSHIP

Southern New England Association of Technical Professionals
Attn: Scholarships
P.O. Box 280303
East Hartford, CT 06128-0115
E-mail: sneatp@gmail.com
Web: www.sneatp.org

Summary To provide financial assistance to members of the National Society of Black Engineers (NSBE) at colleges in Connecticut or western Massachusetts who are working on a graduate degree in a field of science, technology, engineering, or mathematics (STEM).

Eligibility   This program is open to residents of any state enrolled at ABET-accredited colleges and universities in Connecticut and western Massachusetts who are actively involved in NSBE. Applicants must be working on a graduate degree in a STEM field of study. They must have a GPA of 2.8 or higher. Along with their application, they must submit a 500-word essay on what the NSBE should be doing to impact the community positively and how they are positively impacting their local community.

Financial data   The stipend is $1,000.

Duration   1 year.

Number awarded   1 each year.

Deadline   June of each year.

[1124]
RALPH W. SHRADER GRADUATE DIVERSITY SCHOLARSHIP

Armed Forces Communications and Electronics
  Association
Attn: AFCEA Educational Foundation
4400 Fair Lakes Court
Fairfax, VA 22033-3899
(703) 631-6147   Toll Free: (800) 336-4583, ext. 6147
Fax: (703) 631-4693   E-mail: edfoundation@afcea.org
Web: www.afcea.org

Summary   To provide financial assistance to African Americans and other minorities working on a master's degree students in fields related to communications and electronics.

Eligibility   This program is open to women and minorities working full time on a graduate degree at an accredited college or university in the United States. Applicants must be studying biometrics, computer science, cybersecurity, engineering (computer, electrical, electronics, network, robotics, telecommunications), geospatial science, information technology, information resources management, mathematics, network security, operations research, physics, robotics, statistics, strategic intelligence, or telecommunications. They must have a GPA of 3.5 or higher. U.S. citizenship is required.

Financial data   The stipend is $3,000. Funds are paid directly to the recipient.

Duration   1 year.

Additional information   This program is sponsored by Booz Allen Hamilton.

Number awarded   1 or more each year.

Deadline   April of each year.

[1125]
RAMSEY COUNTY BAR FOUNDATION LAW STUDENT SCHOLARSHIP

Ramsey County Bar Foundation
Attn: Diversity Committee
E-1401 First National Bank Building
332 Minnesota Street
St. Paul, MN 55101
(651) 222-0846   Fax: (651) 223-8344
E-mail: Cheryl@ramseybar.org
Web: www.ramseybar.org/news/law-student-scholarship

Summary   To provide financial assistance to African Americans and members of other groups traditionally underrepresented in the legal profession who are attending law school in Minnesota.

Eligibility   This program is open to residents of any state who are currently enrolled at a Minnesota law school. Applicants must be a member of a group traditionally underrepresented in the legal profession, including race, sex, ethnicity, sexual orientation, or disability. They must contribute meaningfully to diversity in their community, have a record of academic or professional achievement, and display leadership qualities through past work experience, community involvement, or student activities.

Financial data   The stipend ranges up to $6,000.

Duration   1 year.

Number awarded   1 each year.

Deadline   February of each year.

[1126]
RDW GROUP, INC. MINORITY SCHOLARSHIP FOR COMMUNICATIONS

Rhode Island Foundation
Attn: Donor Services Administrator
One Union Station
Providence, RI 02903
(401) 427-4011   Fax: (401) 331-8085
E-mail: rbogert@rifoundation.org
Web: www.rifoundation.org

Summary   To provide financial assistance to African American and other undergraduate and graduate students of color in Rhode Island who are interested in preparing for a career in communications at a school in any state.

Eligibility   This program is open to undergraduate and graduate students at colleges and universities in any state who are Rhode Island residents of color. Applicants must intend to work on a degree in communications (including computer graphics, art, cinematography, or other fields that would prepare them for a career in advertising). They must be able to demonstrate financial need and a commitment to a career in communications. Along with their application, they must submit an essay (up to 300 words) on the impact they would like to have on the communications field.

Financial data   The stipend is approximately $2,000 per year.

Duration   1 year; recipients may reapply.

Additional information   This program is sponsored by the RDW Group, Inc.

Number awarded   1 each year.

Deadline   April of each year.

[1127]
RETAIL REAL ESTATE DIVERSITY SCHOLARSHIP

International Council of Shopping Centers
Attn: ICSC Foundation
1221 Avenue of the Americas, 41st Floor
New York, NY 10020-1099
(646) 728-3628   Fax: (732) 694-1690
E-mail: foundation@icsc.org
Web: www.icsc.org

Summary   To provide financial assistance to African American and other minority graduate students who are members of the International Council of Shopping Centers (ICSC) and preparing for a career as a retail real estate professional.

Eligibility This program is open to U.S. citizens who are graduate student members of ICSC and working on a degree related to the retail real estate profession. Applicants must be a member of an underrepresented ethnic minority group (African American, American Indian or Alaskan Native, Asian or Pacific Islander, Hispanic, Caribbean). They must have a GPA of 3.0 or higher and be enrolled full time or enrolled part time while working.

Financial data The stipend is $2,500.

Duration 1 year.

Number awarded 1 or more each year.

Deadline January of each year.

[1128]
REUBEN BUSSEY, ESQUIRE LAW SCHOLARSHIP

Sigma Gamma Rho Sorority, Inc.
Attn: National Education Fund
1000 Southhill Drive, Suite 200
Cary, NC 27513
(919) 678-9720   Toll Free: (888) SGR-1922
Fax: (919) 678-9721
E-mail: customerservice@sgrho1922.org
Web: www.sgrho1922.org/nef

Summary To provide financial assistance to law students. especially African Americans.

Eligibility This program is open to students working on a law degree. The sponsor is a traditionally African American sorority, but support is available to males and females of all races. Applicants must have a GPA of 2.0 or higher and be able to demonstrate financial need.

Financial data A stipend is awarded (amount not specified).

Duration 1 year.

Additional information A processing fee of $20 is required.

Number awarded 1 each year.

Deadline April of each year.

[1129]
RICHARD D. HAILEY SCHOLARSHIP

American Association for Justice
Attn: AAJ Education
777 Sixth Street, N.W., Suite 200
Washington, DC 20001
(202) 684-9563   Toll Free: (800) 424-2725
Fax: (202) 965-0355   E-mail: education@justice.org
Web: www.justice.org

Summary To provide financial assistance for law school to African American and other minority student members of the American Association for Justice (AAJ).

Eligibility This program is open to African American, Hispanic, Asian American, Native American, and biracial members of the association who are entering the first, second, or third year of law school. Applicants must submit a 500-word essay on how they meet the selection criteria: commitment to the association, involvement in student chapter and minority caucus activities, desire to represent victims, interest and proficiency of skills in trial advocacy, and financial need.

Financial data The stipend is $1,000.

Duration 1 year.

Additional information The American Association for Justice was formerly the Association of Trial Lawyers of America.

Number awarded Up to 6 each year.

Deadline May of each year.

[1130]
ROBERT A. CATLIN/DAVID W. LONG MEMORIAL SCHOLARSHIP

American Planning Association
Attn: Planning and the Black Community Division
205 North Michigan Avenue, Suite 1200
Chicago, IL 60601
(312) 431-9100   Fax: (312) 786-6700
E-mail: planningandtheblackcommunity@gmail.com
Web: www.planning.org

Summary To provide financial assistance to African Americans interested in working on a graduate degree in planning or a related field.

Eligibility This program is open to African Americans who are 1) undergraduate students applying to or accepted into an urban planning program for graduate students; or 2) graduate students already working on a degree in urban planning or a related field (e.g., geography, environmental studies, urban studies, urban policy). Applicants must submit 1) a 1-page personal statement on what interests them about the field of planning and their professional goals; and 2) a 3-page essay explaining the positive role that planning could play in developing and supporting Black communities. Financial need is not considered in the selection process.

Financial data The stipend is $1,500.

Duration 1 year; nonrenewable.

Number awarded 1 each year.

Deadline March of each year.

[1131]
ROBERT D. WATKINS GRADUATE RESEARCH FELLOWSHIP

American Society for Microbiology
Attn: Education Board
1752 N Street, N.W.
Washington, DC 20036-2904
(202) 942-9283   Fax: (202) 942-9329
E-mail: fellowships@asmusa.org
Web: www.asm.org

Summary To provide funding for research in microbiology to African American and other underrepresented minority doctoral students who are members of the American Society for Microbiology (ASM).

Eligibility This program is open to African Americans, Hispanics, Native Americans, Alaskan Natives, and Pacific Islanders enrolled as full-time graduate students who have completed their first year of doctoral study and who are members of the society. Applicants must propose a joint research plan in collaboration with a society member scientist. They must have completed all graduate course work requirements for the doctoral degree by the date of the activation of the fellowship. U.S. citizenship or permanent resident status is required. Selection is based on academic achievement, evidence of a successful research plan developed in collaboration with a research adviser/mentor, relevant career goals in the microbiological sciences, and involvement in activities that serve the needs of underrepresented groups.

Financial data Students receive $21,000 per year as a stipend; funds may not be used for tuition or fees.

Duration 3 years.

Number awarded Varies each year.

Deadline April of each year.

[1132]
ROBERT TOIGO FOUNDATION FELLOWSHIPS

Robert Toigo Foundation
Attn: Fellowship Program Administrator
180 Grand Avenue, Suite 450
Oakland, CA 94612
(510) 763-5771   Fax: (510) 763-5778
E-mail: info@toigofoundation.org
Web: www.toigofoundation.org

Summary To provide financial assistance to African American and other minority students working on a master's degree in business administration or a related field.

Eligibility This program is open to members of minority groups (African American, Hispanic/Latino, Native American/ Alaskan Native, South Asian American, or Asian American/ Pacific Islander) who are entering or enrolled in a program for an M.B.A., J.D./M.B.A., master's in real estate, or master's in finance. Applicants must be preparing for a career in finance, including (but not limited to) investment management, investment banking, corporate finance, real estate, private equity, venture capital, business development, pension fund investment, or financial services consulting. U.S. citizenship or permanent resident status is required.

Financial data The stipend is $2,500 per year.

Duration Up to 2 years.

Additional information The application fee is $50.

Number awarded Approximately 50 to 60 each year.

Deadline March of each year.

[1133]
RODNEY PULLIAM MEMORIAL SCHOLARSHIP

National Black Law Students Association
Attn: Director of Education and Career Development
1225 11th Street, N.W.
Washington, DC 20001-4217
(202) 618-2572   E-mail: educationcareer@nblsa.org
Web: www.nblsa.org/education-career

Summary To provide financial assistance to members of the National Black Law Students Association (NBLSA) who are preparing for a career in public interest.

Eligibility This program is open to members of the association who are third- or fourth-year law students. Applicants must be interested in public interest law. Along with their application, they must submit an essay, up to 500 words in length, on a topic that changes annually. Recently, students were asked to present their ideas on a recent opinion of the American Bar Association regarding pro bono service by attorneys.

Financial data The stipend is $1,250.

Duration Grants are awarded annually.

Number awarded 2 each year.

Deadline January of each year.

[1134]
RONALD M. DAVIS SCHOLARSHIP

American Medical Association
Attn: AMA Foundation
330 North Wabash Avenue, Suite 39300
Chicago, IL 60611-5885
(312) 464-4193   Fax: (312) 464-4142
E-mail: amafoundation@ama-assn.org
Web: www.ama-assn.org

Summary To provide financial assistance to medical school students who are African Americans or members of other underrepresented minority groups and are planning to become a primary care physician.

Eligibility This program is open to first- and second-year medical students who are members of the following minority groups: African American/Black, American Indian, Native Hawaiian, Alaska Native, or Hispanic/Latino. Candidates must have an interest in becoming a primary care physician. Only nominations are accepted. Each medical school is invited to submit 2 nominees. U.S. citizenship or permanent resident status is required.

Financial data The stipend is $10,000.

Duration 1 year.

Additional information This program is offered by the AMA Foundation of the American Medical Association as a component of its Minority Scholars Awards. Support is provided by the National Business Group on Health.

Number awarded 1 each year.

Deadline March of each year.

[1135]
ROSA L. PARKS COLLEGE SCHOLARSHIP

Conference of Minority Transportation Officials
Attn: National Scholarship Program
100 M Street, S.E., Suite 917
Washington, DC 20003
(202) 506-2917   E-mail: info@comto.org
Web: www.comto.org/page/scholarships

Summary To provide financial assistance to African American and other students who have a tie to the Conference of Minority Transportation Officials (COMTO) and are interested in working on an undergraduate or master's degree in transportation.

Eligibility This program is open to 1) undergraduates who have completed at least 60 semester credit hours in a transportation discipline; and 2) students working on a master's degree in transportation who have completed at least 15 credits. Applicants must be or have a parent, guardian, or grandparent who has been a COMTO member for at least 1 year. They must have a GPA of 3.0 or higher. Along with their application they must submit a cover letter on their transportation-related career goals and life aspirations. Financial need is not considered in the selection process.

Financial data The stipend is $4,500. Funds are paid directly to the recipient's college or university.

Duration 1 year.

Number awarded 1 each year.

Deadline April of each year.

[1136]
ROSALIND BARNES GRIFFIN ENDOWMENT FUND

Alpha Kappa Alpha Sorority, Inc.
Attn: Educational Advancement Foundation
5656 South Stony Island Avenue
Chicago, IL 60637
(773) 947-0026   Toll Free: (800) 653-6528
Fax: (773) 947-0277   E-mail: akaeaf@akaeaf.net
Web: www.akaeaf.org/fellowships_endowments.htm

Summary To provide financial assistance to members of Alpha Kappa Alpha Sorority who are seeking additional training in treatment of mental health.

Eligibility This program is open to members of Alpha Kappa Alpha, a traditionally African American sorority, who are enrolled as sophomores, juniors, seniors, or graduate students at an accredited degree-granting institution in any state. Applicants must be working to obtain additional training in treatment of mental health. Along with their application, they must submit 1) a list of honors, awards, and scholarships received; 2) a list of organizations in which they have memberships, especially minority organizations; and 3) a statement of their personal and career goals, including how this scholarship will enhance their ability to attain those goals.

Financial data A stipend is awarded (amount not specified).

Duration 1 year.

Number awarded 1 or more each even-numbered year.

Deadline April of each even-numbered year.

[1137]
RURAL OPPORTUNITY FELLOWSHIPS OF THE OREGON STATE BAR

Oregon State Bar
Attn: Diversity and Inclusion Department
16037 S.W. Upper Boones Ferry Road
P.O. Box 231935
Tigard, OR 97281-1935
(503) 620-0222
Toll Free: (800) 452-8260, ext. 338 (within OR)
Fax: (503) 684-1366   TDD: (503) 684-7416
E-mail: cling@osbar.org
Web: www.osbar.org/diversity/programs.html#rural

Summary To provide summer work experience in rural areas to AFrican American and other law students in Oregon who will help the Oregon State Bar achieve its diversity and inclusion objectives.

Eligibility This program is open to students at law schools in Oregon who are interested in working for a public employer or nonprofit organization in rural areas of the state during the summer. The program defines rural areas as anywhere along the Oregon coast, anywhere east of the Cascade Mountains, or anywhere south of Roseburg. Applicants must contribute to the Oregon State Bar's diversity and inclusion program, defined to include age, culture, disability, ethnicity, gender and gender identity or expression, geographic location, national origin, race, religion, sex, sexual orientation, and socio-economic status. They must be planning to practice in Oregon. Along with their application, they must submit a 500-word personal statement on either 1) how their status as a person of diversity has influenced their decision to become a

lawyer and how will it influence them throughout their legal professional career; or 2) a challenge they have faced, how they met the challenge, and how that experience will affect the decisions they will make as a legal professional. They must also submit a sample of their legal writing. Selection is based on the personal statement (35%), legal writing ability (25%), academic achievement (15%), work experience and honors (10%), and financial need (15%).

Financial data Fellows receive a stipend of $8,360.

Duration 3 months during the summer.

Number awarded 2 each year.

Deadline January of each year.

[1138]
RUTH D. PETERSON FELLOWSHIPS FOR RACIAL AND ETHNIC DIVERSITY

American Society of Criminology
Attn: Awards Committee
1314 Kinnear Road, Suite 212
Columbus, OH 43212-1156
(614) 292-9207   Fax: (614) 292-6767
E-mail: asc@asc41.com
Web: www.asc41.com

Summary To provide financial assistance to African Americans and other ethnic minority doctoral students in criminology and criminal justice.

Eligibility This program is open to students of color, especially members of ethnic groups underrepresented in the field of criminology and criminal justice, including (but not limited to) Blacks, Asians, Indigenous peoples, and Latina/os. Applicants must have been accepted into a doctoral program in the field. Along with their application, they must submit an up-to-date curriculum vitae; a personal statement on their race or ethnicity; copies of undergraduate and graduate transcripts; a statement of need and prospects for other financial assistance; a letter describing career plans, salient experiences, and nature of interest in criminology and criminal justice; and 3 letters of reference.

Financial data The stipend is $6,000.

Duration 1 year.

Additional information This program began in 1988 as the American Society of Criminology Graduate Fellowships for Ethnic Minorities. Its current name was adopted in 2016.

Number awarded 3 each year.

Deadline February of each year.

[1139]
RUTH L. KIRSCHSTEIN NATIONAL RESEARCH SERVICE AWARDS FOR INDIVIDUAL PREDOCTORAL FELLOWSHIPS TO PROMOTE DIVERSITY IN HEALTH-RELATED RESEARCH

National Institutes of Health
Office of Extramural Research
Attn: Grants Information
6705 Rockledge Drive, Suite 4090
Bethesda, MD 20892-7983
(301) 435-0714   Fax: (301) 480-0525
TDD: (301) 451-5936   E-mail: grantsinfo@nih.gov
Web: www.grants.nih.gov

Summary To provide financial assistance to African Americans and students from other underrepresented groups who are interested in working on a doctoral degree and preparing for a career in biomedical and behavioral research.

Eligibility This program is open to students enrolled or accepted for enrollment in a Ph.D. or equivalent research degree program; a formally combined M.D./Ph.D. program; or other combined professional doctoral/research Ph.D. program in the biomedical, behavioral, or clinical sciences. Students in health professional degree programs (e.g., M.D., D.O., D.D.S., D.V.M.) are not eligible. Applicants must be 1) members of an ethnic or racial group underrepresented in biomedical or behavioral research; 2) individuals with disabilities; or 3) individuals from socially, culturally, economically, or educationally disadvantaged backgrounds that have inhibited their ability to prepare for a career in health-related research. They must be U.S. citizens, nationals, or permanent residents.

Financial data The fellowship provides an annual stipend of $23,376, a tuition and fee allowance (60% of costs up to $16,000 or 60% of costs up to $21,000 for dual degrees), and an institutional allowance of $4,200 ($3,100 at for-profit and federal institutions) for travel to scientific meetings, health insurance, and laboratory and other training expenses.

Duration Up to 5 years for Ph.D. students or up to 6 years for M.D./Ph.D. or other combined research degree programs.

Additional information These fellowships are offered by most components of the National Institutes of Health (NIH). Contact the NIH for a list of names and telephone numbers of responsible officers at each component.

Number awarded Varies each year.

Deadline April, August, or December of each year.

[1140]
RUTH WEBB MINORITY SCHOLARSHIP

California Academy of Physician Assistants
2318 South Fairview Street
Santa Ana, CA 92704-4938
(714) 427-0321   Fax: (714) 427-0324
E-mail: capa@capanet.org
Web: www.capanet.org

Summary To provide financial assistance to African American and other minority student members of the California Academy of Physician Assistants (CAPA) enrolled in physician assistant programs in California.

Eligibility This program is open to student members of CAPA enrolled in primary care physician assistant programs in California. Applicants must be members of a minority group (African American, Hispanic, Asian/Pacific Islander, or Native American/Alaskan Native). They must have maintained good academic standing and conducted activities to promote the physician assistant profession. Along with their application, they must submit an essay describing the activities they have performed to promote the physician assistant profession, the importance of representing minorities in their community, and why they should be awarded this scholarship. Financial need is considered in the selection process.

Financial data The stipend is $2,000.

Duration 1 year.

Number awarded 1 each year.

Deadline December of each year.

[1141]
RUTH WHITEHEAD WHALEY SCHOLARSHIP

Association of Black Women Attorneys, Inc.
Attn: Scholarship Committee Chair
1001 Avenue of the Americas, Eleventh Floor
New York, NY 10018
E-mail: info@abwanewyork.org
Web: www.abwanewyork.org/scholarships

Summary To provide financial assistance to African American and other minority students at law schools in Connecticut, New Jersey, and New York who are interested in public interest or civil rights law.

Eligibility This program is open to minority students from any state who are currently enrolled at accredited law schools in Connecticut, New Jersey, or New York. Applicants must be able to demonstrate financial need and an interest in public interest or civil rights law. Along with their application, they must submit a 200-word essay on their professional goals, especially community service activities or events in areas where they have been employed or volunteered. In the selection process, academic performance is not the deciding factor.

Financial data A stipend is awarded (amount not specified).

Duration 1 year.

Additional information This program began in 1995 to honor the first African American woman admitted to the North Carolina Bar.

Number awarded Varies each year; since the program was established, it has awarded more than $30,000 in scholarships.

Deadline February of each year.

[1142]
S. EVELYN LEWIS MEMORIAL MEDICAL HEALTH SCIENCE SCHOLARSHIP

Zeta Phi Beta Sorority, Inc.
Attn: National Educational Foundation
1734 New Hampshire Avenue, N.W.
Washington, DC 20009
(202) 387-3103   Fax: (202) 232-4593
E-mail: info@zetaphibetasororityhq.org
Web: www.zpbnef1975.org/scholarships-and-descriptions

Summary To provide financial assistance to women, especially African Americans, who are interested in studying medicine or health sciences on the undergraduate or graduate school level.

Eligibility This program is open to women enrolled full time in a program on the undergraduate or graduate school level leading to a degree in medicine or health sciences. Proof of enrollment is required. Applicants need not be members of Zeta Phi Beta Sorority. Along with their application, they must submit a 150-word essay on their educational goals and professional aspirations, how this award will help them to achieve those goals, and why they should receive the award. Financial need is not considered in the selection process.

Financial data The stipend ranges from $500 to $1,000. Funds are paid directly to the college or university.

Duration 1 academic year.

Additional information Zeta Phi Beta is a traditionally African American sorority.

Number awarded 1 or more each year.

Deadline January of each year.

[1143]
SADANAND SINGH MEMORIAL SCHOLARSHIP

American Academy of Audiology Foundation
Attn: Director of Operations and Development
11480 Commerce Park Drive, Suite 220
Reston, VA 20191
(703) 226-1049   Fax: (703) 476-5157
E-mail: kculver@audiology.org
Web: www.audiologyfoundation.org

Summary To provide financial assistance to African American and other minority students working on a doctoral degree in audiology.

Eligibility This program is open to full-time minority and international students in at least the second year of an Au.D., Ph.D., or Au.D./Ph.D. program. Applicants must be able to demonstrate exceptional promise as a clinical audiologist. They must submit a personal statement on their personal career goals in audiology and how those are being accomplished through their current clinical training, research training, and service-related activities.

Financial data The stipend is $1,000.

Duration 1 year; nonrenewable, although recipients may apply later for a different scholarship offered by this foundation.

Additional information This program is supported by Plural Publishing.

Number awarded 1 each year.

Deadline April of each year.

[1144]
SADIE T.M. ALEXANDER BOOK SCHOLARSHIPS

National Bar Association-Women Lawyers Division
Attn: Philadelphia Chapter
c/o Jacqueline Allen, Scholarship Committee Chair
P.O. Box 58004
Philadelphia, PA 19102-8004
(215) 686-7038   E-mail: scholarshipsfdnwldl@gmail.com
Web: www.nbawldphila.org

Summary To provide financial assistance to African American women who are enrolled at designated law schools in the Philadelphia region.

Eligibility This program is open to African American women entering their second or third year at the Thomas R. Kline School of Law at Drexel University, Beasley School of Law at Temple University, Rutgers (Camden) School of Law, University of Pennsylvania School of Law, Villanova School or Law, or Widener University School of Law. Applicants must submit essays on 1) their career aspirations, including how or why they chose a career in the law; and 2) an experience or personal/professional aspiration that would reflect the professional legacy of the scholarship's namesake. Selection is based on academic excellence, commitment to community service, and financial need.

Financial data The stipend ranges from $500 to $1,000. Funding is designed to help with the purchase of books.

Duration 1 year.

Number awarded Up to 6 each year.

Deadline June of each year.

[1145]
SADIE T.M. ALEXANDER SCHOLARSHIP

Delta Sigma Theta Sorority, Inc.
Attn: Scholarship and Standards Committee Chair
1707 New Hampshire Avenue, N.W.
Washington, DC 20009
(202) 986-2400   Fax: (202) 986-2513
E-mail: dstemail@deltasigmatheta.org
Web: www.deltasigmatheta.org

Summary To provide financial assistance to members of Delta Sigma Theta who are interested in preparing for a career in law.

Eligibility This program is open to graduating college seniors and students who are currently enrolled in law school. Applicants must be active, dues-paying members of Delta Sigma Theta. Selection is based on meritorious achievement.

Financial data The stipends range from $1,000 to $2,000 per year. The funds may be used to cover tuition and living expenses.

Duration 1 year; may be renewed for 1 additional year.

Additional information This sponsor is a traditionally African American social sorority. The application fee is $20.

Number awarded 1 or more each year.

Deadline March of each year.

[1146]
SANDY BROWN MEMORIAL SCHOLARSHIPS

National Black Law Students Association
Attn: Director of Education and Career Development
1225 11th Street, N.W.
Washington, DC 20001-4217
(202) 618-2572   E-mail: educationcareer@nblsa.org
Web: www.nblsa.org/education-career

Summary To provide financial assistance for law school to members of the National Black Law Students Association (NBLSA).

Eligibility This program is open to members of the association who are currently enrolled in the first or second year of law school. Along with their application, they must submit an essay, up to 1,500 words in length, on a topic that changes annually. Recently, students were invited to write on some of the legal issues that involve discrimination in housing.

Financial data The stipend is $1,250.

Duration 1 year.

Number awarded 1 each year.

Deadline January of each year.

[1147]
SARASOTA COUNTY BAR ASSOCIATION DIVERSITY SCHOLARSHIP

Community Foundation of Sarasota County
Attn: Grants and Scholarships Coordinator
2635 Fruitville Road
P.O. Box 49587
Sarasota, FL 34230-6587
(941) 556-7114   Fax: (941) 952-7115
E-mail: eyoung@cfsarasota.org
Web: www.cfsarasota.org

Summary To provide financial assistance and work experience in Sarasota County, Florida to law students from any state who are African Americans or will add to the diversity of the legal profession in other ways.

Eligibility   This program is open to first- through third-year law students of traditionally underrepresented backgrounds (e.g., race, color, religion, national origin, ethnicity, age, gender, sexual orientation, physical disability, socioeconomic background). Applicants must be interested in practicing law after graduation and in obtaining summer placement in private law firms or government agencies in Sarasota County. They may be attending law school in any state but they should have or have had family, school, or community ties to the county. Along with their application, they must submit a 250-word essay describing how their particular background would help the Sarasota County Bar Association achieve its goal of making the local legal community more diverse.

Financial data   Students receive a salary for their summer employment and a stipend of $5,000, sent directly to their law school, upon completion of their employment.

Duration   1 summer for employment and 1 year for law school enrollment.

Additional information   This program, also known as the Richard R. Garland Diversity Scholarship, is sponsored by the Sarasota County Bar Association.

Number awarded   1 or more each year.

Deadline   February of each year.

[1148]
SASP ADVANCED STUDENT DIVERSITY SCHOLARSHIPS

American Psychological Association
Attn: Division 16 (School Psychology)
750 First Street, N.E.
Washington, DC 20002-4242
(202) 336-6165   Fax: (202) 218-3599
TDD: (202) 336-6123   E-mail: cchambers@apa.org
Web: www.apadivisions.org/division-16/awards/sasp.aspx

Summary   To provide financial assistance to continuing graduate student members of the Student Affiliates in School Psychology (SASP) of Division 16 (School Psychology) of the American Psychological Association (APA) who are African Americans or from other underrepresented cultural backgrounds.

Eligibility   This program is open to SASP members who come from underrepresented cultural backgrounds. Applicants must be working on a graduate degree to prepare for a career as a school psychologist. They must be entering their third, fourth, or fifth year of graduate study.

Financial data   The stipend is $1,000.

Duration   1 year; nonrenewable.

Number awarded   1 each year.

Deadline   April of each year.

[1149]
SATARIE THELMA EDWARDS MINORITY MEDICAL SCHOLARSHIP

Student National Medical Association
Attn: Scholarship
5113 Georgia Avenue, N.W.
Washington, DC 20011
(202) 882-2881   Fax: (202) 882-2886
E-mail: execdir@snma.org
Web: snma.site-ym.com

Summary   To provide financial assistance for medical school to African American and other members of the Student National Medical Association (SNMA).

Eligibility   This program is open to SNMA members who are enrolled in their first or second year of study at a school of medicine. Applicants must be interested in a career in oncology and be willing to complete a clinical rotation at the Moffitt Cancer Center in Tampa, Florida. Along with their application, they must submit a 1,000-word essay on how they and/or their family overcame adversity, if they are the first in their family to attend medical school, why they are interested in a career in oncology, and other information they consider important. Selection is based on that essay; demonstration of leadership skills and/or interest in aspects of medicine, the educational, societal, and health care needs of racial and ethnic minorities; participation in extracurricular activities such as SNMA or MAPS; letters of recommendation; and past or current research projects and/or publications.

Financial data   A stipend is awarded (amount not specified).

Duration   1 year.

Additional information   The SNMA is the student affiliate of the National Medical Association, an historically African American association of medical doctors.

Number awarded   2 to 5 each year.

Deadline   November of each year.

[1150]
SCHOLARSHIP FOR A THEOLOGICAL LIBRARIANSHIP COURSE

American Theological Library Association
Attn: Diversity Committee
300 South Wacker Drive, Suite 2100
Chicago, IL 60606-6701
(312) 454-5100   Toll Free: (888) 665-ATLA
Fax: (312) 454-5505   E-mail: memberrep@atla.com
Web: www.atla.com

Summary   To provide funding to African American library students and those from other underrepresented groups who are members of the American Theological Library Association (ATLA) interested in taking a course in theological librarianship.

Eligibility   This program is open to ATLA members from underrepresented groups (religious, racial, ethnic, or gender) who wish to attend a theological librarianship course at an ALA-accredited master's program in library and information studies. Applicants must submit personal statements on what diversity means to them, why their voice has not yet been heard, how their voice will add diversity to the theological librarianship course, how they will increase diversity in their immediate context, and how they plan to increase diversity and participate fully in the ATLA.

Financial data The stipend is $1,200.

Duration Up to 1 year.

Number awarded 1 each year.

Deadline April of each year.

[1151]
SCOVEL RICHARDSON SCHOLARSHIPS

Mound City Bar Association
c/o Kathy A. Surratt-States, Scholarship Committee
111 South 10th Street, Fourth Floor
St. Louis, MO 63102
(314) 244-4541
E-mail: Kathy_Surratt-States@moeb.uscourts.gov
Web: www.moundcitybar.com

Summary To provide financial assistance to African American and other minority law students who have limited financial resources.

Eligibility This program is open to minority students entering the second or third year of law school. Applicants must be able to demonstrate financial need and a record of community service and leadership. Along with their application, they must submit a short autobiographical sketch, including the individuals and/or events that have helped to shape their life, their short- and long-term career goals, and the contributions they would like to make to create a better community. Special consideration is given to students who plan to live and work in the greater St. Louis metropolitan area.

Financial data Recently, stipends averaged $3,000.

Duration 1 year.

Additional information The Mound City Bar Association was established in 1922 as the St. Louis Negro Bar Association. It established this program is help create a judiciary that is more responsive and accountable to African Americans and other minorities.

Number awarded Varies each year; recently, 6 were awarded.

Deadline May of each year.

[1152]
SECTION OF BUSINESS LAW DIVERSITY CLERKSHIP PROGRAM

American Bar Association
Attn: Section of Business Law
321 North Clark Street
Chicago, IL 60654-7598
(312) 988-5588   Fax: (312) 988-5578
E-mail: businesslaw@americanbar.org
Web: www.americanbar.org

Summary To provide summer work experience in business law to student members of the American Bar Association (ABA) and its Section of Business Law who are African Americans or will help the section to fulfill its goal of promoting diversity in other ways.

Eligibility This program is open to first- and second-year students at ABA-accredited law schools who are interested in a summer business court clerkship. Applicants must 1) be a member of an underrepresented group (student of color, woman, student with disabilities, gay, lesbian, bisexual, or transgender); or 2) have overcome social or economic disadvantages, such as a physical disability, financial constraints, or cultural impediments to becoming a law student. They must be able to demonstrate financial need. Along with their application, they must submit a 500-word essay that covers why they are interested in this clerkship program, what they would gain from the program, how it would positively influence their future professional goals as a business lawyer, and how they meet the program's criteria. Membership in the ABA and its Section of Business Law are required.

Financial data The stipend is $6,000.

Duration Summer months.

Additional information This program began in 2008. Assignments vary, but have included business courts in Delaware, Illinois, Maryland, Pennsylvania, and South Carolina.

Number awarded 9 each year.

Deadline January of each year.

[1153]
SELECTED PROFESSIONS FELLOWSHIPS FOR WOMEN OF COLOR

American Association of University Women
Attn: AAUW Educational Foundation
1111 16th Street, N.W.
Washington, DC 20036-4873
(202) 785-7700   Toll Free: (800) 326-AAUW
Fax: (202) 872-1425   TDD: (202) 785-7777
E-mail: aauw@applyists.com
Web: www.aauw.org

Summary To aid African Americans and other women of color who are in their final year of graduate training in the fields of business administration, law, or medicine.

Eligibility This program is open to women who are working full time on a degree in fields in which women of color have been historically underrepresented: business administration (M.B.A.), law (J.D.), or medicine (M.D., D.O.). They must be African Americans, Mexican Americans, Puerto Ricans and other Hispanics, Native Americans, Alaska Natives, Asian Americans, or Pacific Islanders. U.S. citizenship or permanent resident status is required. Applicants in business administration must be entering their second year of study; applicants in law must be entering their third year of study; applicants in medicine may be entering their third or fourth year of study. Special consideration is given to applicants who 1) demonstrate their intent to enter professional practice in disciplines in which women are underrepresented, to serve underserved populations and communities, or to pursue public interest areas; and 2) are nontraditional students. Selection is based on professional promise and personal attributes (50%), academic excellence and related academic success indicators (40%), and financial need (10%).

Financial data Stipends range from $5,000 to $18,000.

Duration 1 year, beginning in July.

Additional information The filing fee is $35.

Number awarded Varies each year; recently, a total of 25 Selected Professions Fellowships were awarded.

Deadline January of each year.

[1154]
SEMICONDUCTOR RESEARCH CORPORATION MASTER'S SCHOLARSHIP PROGRAM

Semiconductor Research Corporation
Attn: Global Research Collaboration
1101 Slater Road, Suite 120
P.O. Box 12053
Research Triangle Park, NC 27709-2053
(919) 941-9400   Fax: (919) 941-9450
E-mail: students@src.org
Web: www.src.org/student-center/fellowship/#tab2

Summary   To provide financial assistance to African Americans and other minorities interested in working on a master's degree in a field of microelectronics relevant to the interests of the Semiconductor Research Corporation (SRC).

Eligibility   This program is open to women and members of underrepresented minority groups (African Americans, Hispanics, and Native Americans). Applicants must be U.S. citizens or have permanent resident, refugee, or political asylum status in the United States. They must be admitted to an SRC participating university to work on a master's degree in a field relevant to microelectronics under the guidance of an SRC-sponsored faculty member and under an SRC-funded contract. Selection is based on academic achievement.

Financial data   The fellowship provides full tuition and fee support, a competitive stipend (recently, $2,536 per month), an annual grant of $2,000 to the university department with which the student recipient is associated, and travel expenses to the Graduate Fellowship Program Annual Conference.

Duration   Up to 2 years.

Additional information   This program began in 1997 for underrepresented minorities and expanded to include women in 1999.

Number awarded   Approximately 12 each year.

Deadline   January of each year.

[1155]
SEO CAREER LAW PROGRAM

Sponsors for Educational Opportunity
Attn: Career Program
55 Exchange Place
New York, NY 10005
(212) 979-2040   Toll Free: (800) 462-2332
Fax: (646) 706-7113
E-mail: careerprogram@seo-usa.org
Web: www.seo-usa.org/Career/Corporate_Law

Summary   To provide summer work experience to African Americans and other students of color interested in studying law.

Eligibility   This program is open to students of color who are college seniors or recent graduates planning to attend law school in the United States. Applicants must be interested in a summer internship at a participating law firm that specializes in corporate law, including initial public offerings of stock, mergers and acquisitions, joint ventures, corporate reorganizations, cross-border financing, including securities, tax, bankruptcy, antitrust, real estate and white-collar crime. They must have a cumulative GPA of 3.0 or higher. Personal interviews are required.

Financial data   Interns receive a competitive stipend of up to $1,300 per week.

Duration   10 weeks during the summer.

Additional information   This program began in 1980. Internships are available in New York City, Washington, D.C., Houston, Los Angeles, San Francisco, Menlo Park, Palo Alto, or Atlanta.

Number awarded   Varies each year.

Deadline   February of each year.

[1156]
SERVICES FOR TRANSITION AGE YOUTH FELLOWSHIP

American Psychological Association
Attn: Minority Fellowship Program
750 First Street, N.E.
Washington, DC 20002-4242
(202) 336-6127   Fax: (202) 336-6012
TDD: (202) 336-6123   E-mail: mfp@apa.org
Web: www.apa.org/pi/mfp/psychology/stay/index.aspx

Summary   To provide financial assistance to master's degree students committed to providing mental health services to African American and other ethnic minority youth.

Eligibility   Applicants must be U.S. citizens, nationals, or permanent residents, enrolled full time in a terminal master's degree program that will prepare them to provide mental health services to ethnic minority transition age youth (16 through 25 years of age) and their families. Their program must be housed in the same department as an APA-accredited doctoral program. They are not required to identify as ethnic minorities, but members of such groups (African Americans, Hispanics/Latinos, American Indians, Alaskan Natives, Asian Americans, Native Hawaiians, and other Pacific Islanders) are especially encouraged to apply. Along with their application, they must submit a 2-page essay on their interests and career goals in psychology. Students enrolled in counseling, marriage and family therapy, and addiction programs are not eligible.

Financial data   The stipend is $6,000.

Duration   1 year.

Additional information   Funding is provided by the U.S. Substance Abuse and Mental Health Services Administration.

Number awarded   Varies each year; recently, 24 were awarded.

Deadline   January of each year.

[1157]
SHERRY R. ARNSTEIN MINORITY STUDENT SCHOLARSHIP

American Association of Colleges of Osteopathic
  Medicine
Attn: Scholarships
5550 Friendship Boulevard, Suite 310
Chevy Chase, MD 20815-7231
(301) 968-4142   Fax: (301) 968-4101
E-mail: jshepperd@aacom.org
Web: www.aacom.org

Summary   To provide financial assistance to African American and other underrepresented minority students entering or enrolled in osteopathic medical school.

Eligibility This program is open to African American, mainland Puerto Rican, Hispanic, Native American, Native Hawaiian, and Alaska Native students who are entering or currently enrolled in good standing in their first, second, or third year of osteopathic medical school. Applicants must submit a 4-page essay on what osteopathic medical schools can do to recruit and retain more underrepresented minority students, what they personally plan to do as a student and as a future D.O. to help increase minority student enrollment at a college of osteopathic medicine, and how and why they were drawn to osteopathic medicine.

Financial data The stipend is $2,500.

Duration 1 year; nonrenewable.

Number awarded 2 each year: 1 entering and 1 continuing student.

Deadline March of each year.

[1158]
SHIRLEY DELIBERO SCHOLARSHIP

American Public Transportation Association
Attn: American Public Transportation Foundation
1666 K Street, N.W., Suite 1100
Washington, DC 20006
(202) 496-4803   Fax: (202) 496-4323
E-mail: pboswell@apta.com
Web: www.aptfd.org/Pages/default.aspx

Summary To provide financial assistance to African American undergraduate and graduate students who are preparing for a career in the public transportation industry.

Eligibility This program is open to African American sophomores, juniors, seniors, and graduate students who are preparing for a career in the transit industry. Any member organization of the American Public Transportation Association (APTA) can nominate and sponsor candidates for this scholarship. Nominees must be enrolled in a fully-accredited institution, have and maintain at least a 3.0 GPA, and be either employed by or demonstrate a strong interest in entering the business administration or management area of the public transportation industry. They must submit a 1,000-word essay on the topic, "In what segment of the public transportation industry will you make a career and why?" Selection is based on demonstrated interest in the transit field as a career, need for financial assistance, academic achievement, essay content and quality, and involvement in extracurricular citizenship and leadership activities.

Financial data The stipend is $2,500.

Duration 1 year; may be renewed.

Number awarded 1 each year.

Deadline June of each year.

[1159]
SIDNEY B. WILLIAMS, JR. INTELLECTUAL PROPERTY LAW SCHOOL SCHOLARSHIPS

Thurgood Marshall College Fund
Attn: Senior Manager of Scholarship Programs
1770 St. James Place, Suite 414
Houston, TX 77056
(713) 955-1073   Fax: (202) 448-1017
E-mail: deshuandra.walker@tmcf.org
Web: tmcf.org

Summary To provide financial assistance to African American and other underrepresented minority law school students who are interested in preparing for a career in intellectual property law.

Eligibility This program is open to members of underrepresented minority groups currently enrolled in or accepted to an ABA-accredited law school. Applicants must be U.S. citizens with a demonstrated intent to engage in the full-time practice of intellectual property law. Along with their application, they must submit a 250-word essay on how this scholarship will make a difference to them in meeting their goal of engaging in the full-time practice of intellectual property law and why they intend to do so. Selection is based on 1) demonstrated commitment to developing a career in intellectual property law; 2) academic performance at the undergraduate, graduate, and law school levels (as applicable); 3) general factors, such as leadership skills, community activities, or special accomplishments; and 4) financial need.

Financial data The stipend is $10,000 per year. Funds may be used for tuition, fees, books, supplies, room, board, and a patent bar review course.

Duration 1 year; may be renewed up to 2 additional years if the recipient maintains a GPA of 2.0 or higher.

Additional information This program, which began in 2002, is administered by the Thurgood Marshall College Fund with support from the American Intellectual Property Law Education Foundation.

Number awarded Varies each year; recently, 12 were awarded.

Deadline March of each year.

[1160]
SIGMA GAMMA RHO SCHOLARSHIPS/ FELLOWSHIPS

Sigma Gamma Rho Sorority, Inc.
Attn: National Education Fund
1000 Southhill Drive, Suite 200
Cary, NC 27513
(919) 678-9720   Toll Free: (888) SGR-1922
Fax: (919) 678-9721
E-mail: customerservice@sgrho1922.org
Web: www.sgrho1922.org/nef

Summary To provide financial assistance for undergraduate or graduate study to applicants who can demonstrate financial need, especially African Americans.

Eligibility This program is open to high school seniors, undergraduates, and graduate students who can demonstrate financial need. The sponsor is a traditionally African American sorority, but support is available to males and females of all races. Applicants must have a GPA of 2.0 or higher.

Financial data A stipend is awarded (amount not specified).

Duration 1 year.

Additional information This program includes the following named awards: the Lorraine A. Williams Scholarship, the Philo Sallie A. Williams Scholarship, the Cleo W. Higgins Scholarship (limited to doctoral students), the Lillie and Carnell VanLandingham Scholarship, the Minnie and William Blakely Book Scholarship, the Inez Colson Memorial Scholarship (limited to students majoring in education or mathematics at Savannah State University), and the Philo Geneva Young Scholarship. A processing fee of $20 is required.

Number awarded Varies each year.

Deadline April of each year.

[1161]
SLA NEW ENGLAND DIVERSITY LEADERSHIP DEVELOPMENT SCHOLARSHIP

SLA New England
c/o Khalilah Gambrell, Diversity Chair
EBSCO Information Services
10 Estes Street
Ipswich, MA 01938
(978) 356-6500   Toll Free: (800) 653-2726
Fax: (978) 356-6565   E-mail: gambrell9899@gmail.com
Web: newengland.sla.org/member-benefits/stipends

Summary To provide financial assistance for library science tuition or attendance at the annual conference of the Special Libraries Association (SLA) to members of SLA New England who are African Americans or represent another diverse population.

Eligibility This program is open to SLA New England members who are of Black (African American), Hispanic, Asian American, Pacific Islander American, Native Alaskan, or Native Hawaiian heritage. Applicants must be seeking funding for SLA annual meeting attendance, tuition reimbursement for a library science program, or tuition reimbursement for a course directly related to the library and information science field. Along with their application, they must submit a 500-word essay on how they will encourage and celebrate diversity within the SLA New England community.

Financial data The award covers actual expenses up to $1,500.

Duration This is a 1-time award.

Number awarded 1 each year.

Deadline April of each year.

[1162]
SMITHSONIAN MINORITY AWARDS PROGRAM

Smithsonian Institution
Attn: Office of Fellowships and Internships
470 L'Enfant Plaza, Suite 7102
P.O. Box 37012, MRC 902
Washington, DC 20013-7012
(202) 633-7070   Fax: (202) 633-7069
E-mail: siofi@si.edu
Web: www.smithsonianofi.com

Summary To provide funding to African American and other minority undergraduate and graduate students interested in conducting research at the Smithsonian Institution.

Eligibility This program is open to members of U.S. minority groups underrepresented in the Smithsonian's scholarly programs. Applicants must be undergraduates or beginning graduate students interested in conducting research in the Institution's disciplines and in the museum field. They must be U.S. citizens or permanent residents and have a GPA of 3.0 or higher.

Financial data Students receive a grant of $600 per week.

Duration Up to 10 weeks.

Additional information Recipients must carry out independent research projects in association with the Smithson-

ian's research staff. Eligible fields of study currently include animal behavior, ecology, and environmental science (including an emphasis on the tropics); anthropology (including archaeology); astrophysics and astronomy; earth sciences and paleobiology; evolutionary and systematic biology; history of science and technology; history of art (especially American, contemporary, African, Asian, and 20th-century art); American crafts and decorative arts; social and cultural history of the United States; and folklife. Students are required to be in residence at the Smithsonian for the duration of the fellowship.

Number awarded Varies each year; recently, 25 were granted: 2 for fall, 19 for summer, and 4 for spring.

Deadline January of each year for summer and fall residency; September of each year for spring residency.

[1163]
SMITHSONIAN MINORITY STUDENT INTERNSHIP

Smithsonian Institution
Attn: Office of Fellowships and Internships
470 L'Enfant, Suite 7102
P.O. Box 37012, MRC 902
Washington, DC 20013-7012
(202) 633-7070   Fax: (202) 633-7069
E-mail: siofi@si.edu
Web: www.smithsonianofi.com/minority-internship-program

Summary To provide African American and other minority undergraduate or graduate students with the opportunity to work on research or museum procedure projects in specific areas of history, art, or science at the Smithsonian Institution.

Eligibility Internships are offered to minority students who are actively engaged in undergraduate or graduate study or have graduated within the past 4 months. Applicants must be U.S. citizens or permanent residents who have an overall GPA of 3.0 or higher. Applicants must be interested in conducting research in any of the following fields of interest to the Smithsonian: animal behavior, ecology, and environmental science (including an emphasis on the tropics); anthropology (including archaeology); astrophysics and astronomy; earth sciences and paleobiology; evolutionary and systematic biology; history of science and technology; history of art (especially American, contemporary, African, Asian, and 20th-century art); American crafts and decorative arts; social and cultural history of the United States; and folklife.

Financial data The program provides a stipend of $600 per week; travel allowances may also be offered.

Duration 10 weeks during the summer or academic year.

Number awarded Varies each year.

Deadline January of each year for summer or fall; September of each year for spring.

[1164]
SOCIETY FOR THE STUDY OF SOCIAL PROBLEMS RACIAL/ETHNIC MINORITY GRADUATE SCHOLARSHIP

Society for the Study of Social Problems
Attn: Executive Officer
University of Tennessee
901 McClung Tower
Knoxville, TN 37996-0490
(865) 689-1531   Fax: (865) 689-1534
E-mail: sssp@utk.edu
Web: www.sssp1.org

Summary To provide funding to African American and other ethnic and racial minority members of the Society for the Study of Social Problems (SSSP) who are interested in conducting research for their doctoral dissertation.

Eligibility This program is open to SSSP members who are Black or African American, Hispanic or Latino, Asian or Asian American, Native Hawaiian or other Pacific Islander, or American Indian or Alaska Native. Applicants must have completed all requirements for a Ph.D. (course work, examinations, and approval of a dissertation prospectus) except the dissertation. They must have a GPA of 3.25 or higher and be able to demonstrate financial need. Their field of study may be any of the social and/or behavioral sciences that will enable them to expand their perspectives in the investigation into social problems. U.S. citizenship or permanent resident status is required.

Financial data The stipend is $15,000. Additional grants provide $500 for the recipient to 1) attend the SSSP annual meeting prior to the year of the work to receive the award; and 2) attend the meeting after the year of the award to present a report on the work completed.

Duration 1 year.

Number awarded 1 each year.

Deadline January of each year.

[1165]
SOUTHERN REGIONAL EDUCATION BOARD DISSERTATION AWARDS

Southern Regional Education Board
Attn: Coordinator, Institute and Scholar Services
592 Tenth Street N.W.
Atlanta, GA 30318-5776
(404) 879-5516   Fax: (404) 872-1477
E-mail: tammy.wright@sreb.org
Web: www.sreb.org/types-awards

Summary To provide funding to African American and other minority students who wish to complete a Ph.D. dissertation, especially in fields of science, technology, engineering, or mathematics (STEM), while in residence at a university in the southern states.

Eligibility This program is open to U.S. citizens and permanent residents who are members of racial/ethnic minority groups (Native Americans, Hispanic Americans, Asian Americans, and African Americans) and have completed all requirements for a Ph.D. except the dissertation. Applicants must be enrolled at a designated college or university in the following 11 states: Alabama, Arkansas, Georgia, Kentucky, Louisiana, Maryland, Mississippi, South Carolina, Tennessee, Virginia, or West Virginia. Enrollment at a graduate

school in 5 of those states (Georgia, Mississippi, South Carolina, Tennessee, and Virginia) is available only to residents of those states. Residents of any state in the country may attend a university in the other 5 states. Preference is given to students in STEM disciplines with particularly low minority representation, although all academic fields are eligible. Applicants must be in a position to write full time and must expect to complete their dissertation within the year of the fellowship. Eligibility is limited to individuals who plan to become full-time faculty members at a college or university upon completion of their doctoral degree. The program is not open to students working on other doctoral degrees (e.g., M.D., D.B.A., D.D.S., J.D., D.V.M., Ed.D., Pharm.D., D.N.P., D.P.T.).

Financial data Fellows receive waiver of tuition and fees (in or out of state), a stipend of $20,000, a $500 research allowance, and reimbursement of expenses for attending the Compact for Faculty Diversity's annual Institute on Teaching and Mentoring.

Duration 1 year; nonrenewable.

Additional information This program began in 1993 as part of the Compact for Faculty Diversity, supported by the Pew Charitable Trusts and the Ford Foundation. It currently operates at universities in 10 of the member states of the Southern Regional Education Board (SREB): Alabama, Arkansas, Georgia, Kentucky, Louisiana, Mississippi, South Carolina, Tennessee, Virginia, and West Virginia; the other 6 member states (Delaware, Florida, Maryland, North Carolina, Oklahoma, and Texas) do not participate.

Number awarded Varies each year.

Deadline March of each year.

[1166]
SPECTRUM SCHOLARSHIP PROGRAM

American Library Association
Attn: Office for Diversity
50 East Huron Street
Chicago, IL 60611-2795
(312) 280-5048   Toll Free: (800) 545-2433, ext. 5048
Fax: (312) 280-3256   TDD: (888) 814-7692
E-mail: spectrum@ala.org
Web: www.ala.org/offices/diversity/spectrum

Summary To provide financial assistance to African American and other minority students interested in working on a degree in librarianship.

Eligibility This program is open to ethnic minority students (African American or Black, Asian, Native Hawaiian or other Pacific Islander, Latino or Hispanic, and American Indian or Alaska Native). Applicants must be U.S. or Canadian citizens or permanent residents who have completed no more than a third of the requirements for a master's or school library media degree. They must be enrolled full or part time at an ALA-accredited school of library and information studies or an ALA-recognized NCATE school library media program. Selection is based on academic leadership, outstanding service, commitment to a career in librarianship, statements indicating the nature of the applicant's library and other work experience, letters of reference, and personal presentation.

Financial data The stipend is $5,000.

Duration 1 year; nonrenewable.

Additional information This program began in 1998. It is administered by a joint committee of the American Library Association (ALA).

Number awarded Varies each year; recently, 69 were awarded.

Deadline February of each year.

[1167]
SREB DOCTORAL AWARDS

Southern Regional Education Board
Attn: Coordinator, Institute and Scholar Services
592 Tenth Street N.W.
Atlanta, GA 30318-5776
(404) 879-5516   Fax: (404) 872-1477
E-mail: tammy.wright@sreb.org
Web: www.sreb.org/types-awards

Summary To provide financial assistance to African American and other minority students who wish to work on a doctoral degree, especially in fields of science, technology, engineering, or mathematics (STEM), at designated universities in the southern states.

Eligibility This program is open to U.S. citizens and permanent residents who are members of racial/ethnic minority groups (African Americans, Native Americans, Hispanic Americans, and Asian Americans) and have or will receive a bachelor's or master's degree. Applicants must be entering or enrolled in the first year of a Ph.D. program at a designated college or university in the following 11 states: Alabama, Arkansas, Georgia, Kentucky, Louisiana, Maryland, Mississippi, South Carolina, Tennessee, Virginia, West Virginia. Enrollment at a graduate school in 5 of those states (Georgia, Mississippi, South Carolina, Tennessee, and Virginia) is available only to residents of those states. Residents of any state in the country may attend a university in the other 5 states. Applicants must indicate an interest in becoming a full-time college or university professor. The program does not support students working on other doctoral degrees (e.g., M.D., D.B.A., D.D.S., J.D., D.V.M., Ed.D., Pharm.D., D.N.P., D.P.T.). Preference is given to applicants in STEM disciplines with particularly low minority representation, although all academic fields are eligible.

Financial data Scholars receive a waiver of tuition and fees (in or out of state) for up to 5 years, an annual stipend of $20,000 for 3 years, an annual allowance of $500 for research and professional development activities, and reimbursement of travel expenses to attend the Compact for Faculty Diversity's annual Institute on Teaching and Mentoring.

Duration Up to 5 years.

Additional information This program began in 1993 as part of the Compact for Faculty Diversity, supported by the Pew Charitable Trusts and the Ford Foundation.

Number awarded Varies each year; recently, the program was supporting more than 300 scholars.

Deadline March of each year.

[1168]
STANLEY J. TARVER MEMORIAL SCHOLARSHIP FUND

Community Foundations of the Hudson Valley
Attn: Scholarship Committee
80 Washington Street, Suite 201
Poughkeepsie, NY 12601
(845) 452-3077   Fax: (845) 452-3083
E-mail: cfhv@cfhvny.org
Web: cfhvny.org/Receive/Scholarships

Summary To provide financial assistance to students of African descent who are working on a graduate degree in African history and/or culture.

Eligibility This program is open to graduate students of African descent, including African Americans and Black people of other nationalities. Applicants must be working on a master's or doctorate degree in African history and/or culture and have completed at least 1 year of graduate study at a college or university in the United States. Along with their application, they must submit a 500-word essay on their interest, project, and activities in African history and/or culture.

Financial data The stipend ranges from $1,000 to $2,000.

Duration 1 year; nonrenewable.

Additional information This program began in 1994.

Number awarded 1 each year.

Deadline March of each year.

[1169]
STANTON NUCLEAR SECURITY FELLOWSHIP

Stanford University
Center for International Security and Cooperation
Attn: Fellowships Coordinator
Encina Hall, Room C206-10
616 Serra Street
Stanford, CA 94305-6165
(650) 723-9625   Fax: (650) 724-5683
E-mail: CISACfellowship@stanford.edu
Web: cisac.fsi.stanford.edu/docs/cisac_fellowship_program

Summary To provide funding to doctoral candidates and junior scholars, especially African Americans and members of other underrepresented groups, who are interested in conducting research on nuclear security issues at Stanford University's Center for International Security and Cooperation.

Eligibility This program is open to doctoral candidates, recent postdoctorates, and junior faculty. Applicants must be interested in conducting research on nuclear security issues while in residence at the center. The sponsor welcomes applications from women, minorities, and citizens of all countries.

Financial data The stipend ranges from $25,000 to $28,000 for doctoral candidates or from $48,000 to $66,000 for postdoctorates, depending on experience. Medical insurance is available for those who do not have coverage.

Duration 9 to 11 months.

Additional information Fellows are expected to write a dissertation chapter or chapters, publishable article or articles, and/or make significant progress on turning a thesis into a book manuscript. They should not plan to spend any time conducting research abroad or in other parts of the country.

Number awarded Varies each year; recently, 3 were awarded: 1 doctoral candidate, 1 recent postdoctorate, and 1 junior faculty member.

Deadline January of each year.

[1170]
STAR SUPPORTER SCHOLARSHIP/LOAN

Christian Church (Disciples of Christ)
Attn: Disciples Home Missions
130 East Washington Street
P.O. Box 1986
Indianapolis, IN 46206-1986
(317) 713-2652 Toll Free: (888) DHM-2631
Fax: (317) 635-4426 E-mail: mail@dhm.disciples.org
Web: www.discipleshomemissions.org

Summary To provide scholarship/loans to African Americans interested in preparing for a career in the ministry of the Christian Church (Disciples of Christ).

Eligibility This program is open to African American seminary students who are members of a Christian Church (Disciples of Christ) congregation in the United States or Canada. Applicants must plan to prepare for the ordained ministry, be working on an M.Div. or equivalent degree, provide evidence of financial need, be enrolled full time in an accredited school or seminary, provide a transcript of academic work, and be under the care of a regional Commission on the Ministry or in the process of coming under care.

Financial data Recipients are awarded funds in the form of a scholarship/loan, with 2 methods of repayment: 1) the amount of the scholarship/loan must be repaid in cash (with 6% interest, beginning 3 months after leaving school) if the recipient does not enter the ministry; or 2) the amount of the scholarship/loan is reduced by one-third for each year of full-time professional ministry performed by the recipient, so that 3 years of service cancels the entire amount.

Duration 1 year; may be renewed.

Additional information Recipients must sign a promissory note.

Number awarded Varies each year.

Deadline March of each year.

[1171]
SUMMER AFFIRMATIVE ACTION INTERNSHIP PROGRAM

Wisconsin Office of State Employment Relations
Attn: Division of Affirmative Action Workforce Planning
101 East Wilson Street, Fourth Floor
P.O. Box 7855
Madison, WI 53707-7855
(608) 266-6475 Fax: (608) 267-1020
E-mail: OSERDAA@wi.gov
Web: oser.state.wi.us/category.asp?linkcatid=342

Summary To provide an opportunity for African Americans and members of other underrepresented groups to gain summer work experience with agencies of the state of Wisconsin.

Eligibility This program is open to women, ethnic/racial minorities (Black or African American, Asian, Native Hawaiian or other Pacific Islander, American Indian or Alaska Native, or Hispanic or Latino), and persons with disabilities. Applicants must be sophomores, juniors, seniors, or graduate students at an accredited 4-year college or university or second-year

students in the second year of a 2-year technical or vocational school program. They must be 1) Wisconsin residents enrolled full time at a school in Wisconsin or any other state; or 2) residents of other states who are enrolled full time at a school in Wisconsin.

Financial data Most internships provide a competitive stipend.

Duration Summer months.

Additional information This program began in 1974. Internships are available in criminal justice, engineering, finance/accounting, human resources, information technology, legal research, library science, public administration, recreational leadership, research analyst, social work, vocational/rehabilitation therapy, and various other government jobs.

Number awarded Varies each year. Since the program was established, it has placed more than 3,100 students with more than 30 different agencies and universities throughout the state.

Deadline February of each year.

[1172]
SUMMER INTERNSHIP PROGRAM IN BIOMEDICAL RESEARCH

National Institutes of Health
Attn: Office of Intramural Training and Education
2 Center Drive, Room 2E06
Bethesda, MD 20892-0240
(301) 496-2427 Toll Free: (888) 695-5343
Fax: (301) 594-9606
E-mail: Summer_Postbac_Questions@mail.nih.gov
Web: www.training.nih.gov/programs/sip

Summary To enable students, especially African Americans and other underrepresented minorities, to receive training and participate in ongoing research studies in a variety of laboratory and clinically-related disciplines at the National Institutes of Health (NIH) during the summer.

Eligibility This program is open to graduate, health professions, undergraduate, and high school students who have a strong interest in preparing for a career related to biomedical or behavioral research, including the disciplines of biology, chemistry, physical science, psychology, computer science, biostatistics, mathematics, and biomedical engineering. They must be at least 16 years of age and U.S. citizens, nationals, or permanent residents.

Financial data Salaries depend on the academic level of the recipient, ranging from $1,740 per month for high school students before graduation to $1,940 for high school students after graduation, $2,040 to $2,240 for college students (depending on number of years completed), or $2,340 to $3,160 per month for graduate students (depending on number of years completed).

Duration 8 to 10 weeks, in the summer.

Additional information Most components of the National Institutes of Health participate in this program. Some of them reserve positions for interns who are members of minority groups underrepresented in the biomedical and behavioral sciences (African Americans, Hispanics, Native Americans, and Pacific Islanders). Most laboratories are located in Bethesda, Maryland, but others are in Baltimore, Frederick, and Rockville, Maryland; Detroit, Michigan; Research Triangle Park, North Carolina; Phoenix, Arizona; and Hamilton, Montana.

Number awarded Varies each year; recently, approximately 1,100 interns were selected.

Deadline February of each year.

[1173]
SUMMER INTERNSHIPS IN NUCLEAR FORENSICS AND ENVIRONMENTAL RADIOCHEMISTRY

Lawrence Livermore National Laboratory
Physical and Life Sciences Directorate
Attn: Director of Student Programs
7000 East Avenue, L-452
Livermore, CA 94550
(925) 422-6351   E-mail: kulp2@llnl.gov
Web: www-pls.llnl.gov

Summary To provide an opportunity for graduate students, especially African Americans and other minorities, to work on summer research projects on nuclear forensics and environmental radiochemistry at Lawrence Livermore National Laboratory (LLNL).

Eligibility This program is open to full-time master's and doctoral students who are interested in working on research projects at LLNL involving nuclear forensics, nuclear chemistry, and environmental radiochemistry. Applicants must be U.S. citizens. Selection is based on academic record, aptitude, research interests, and recommendations of instructors. Strong preference is given to students with exceptional academic records and potential for making outstanding contributions to applied science. Women and minorities are encouraged to apply.

Financial data The stipend ranges from $4,100 to $4,900 per month, depending on number of school years completed. Living accommodations and arrangements are the responsibility of the intern.

Duration 8 weeks, during the summer.

Number awarded 10 to 15 each year.

Deadline February of each year.

[1174]
SUMMER RESEARCH OPPORTUNITY PROGRAM IN PATHOLOGY

American Society for Investigative Pathology
Attn: Executive Officer
9650 Rockville Pike, Suite E133
Bethesda, MD 20814-3993
(301) 634-7130   Fax: (301) 634-7990
E-mail: asip@asip.org
Web: www.asip.org/awards/sropp.cfm

Summary To provide an opportunity for African Americans and other underrepresented minorities to participate in a summer research program in pathology.

Eligibility This program is open to students who are members of underrepresented minority groups. Applicants must be interested in visiting prominent research laboratories and institutions during the summer to learn and participate in new research in the mechanisms of disease.

Financial data The program provides housing at the host laboratory and a grant of $2,800 to cover travel costs to and from the site, living expenses, and a stipend.

Duration 10 weeks during the summer.

Additional information This program operates in partnership with the Intersociety Council for Pathology Information.

Number awarded Varies each year; recently, 2 laboratories were selected and 1 student was assigned to each.

Deadline March of each year.

[1175]
SUMMER TRANSPORTATION INTERNSHIP PROGRAM FOR DIVERSE GROUPS

Department of Transportation
Attn: Summer Transportation Internship Program for
   Diverse Groups
Eighth Floor E81-105
1200 New Jersey Avenue, S.E.
Washington, DC 20590
(202) 366-2907   E-mail: Crystal.Taylor@dot.gov
Web: www.fhwa.dot.gov/education/stipdg.cfm

Summary To enable undergraduate, graduate, and law students from African American and other diverse groups to gain work experience during the summer at facilities of the U.S. Department of Transportation (DOT).

Eligibility This program is open to all qualified applicants, but it is designed to provide women, persons with disabilities, and members of diverse social and ethnic groups with summer opportunities in transportation. Applicants must be U.S. citizens currently enrolled in a degree-granting program of study at an accredited institution of higher learning at the undergraduate (community or junior college, university, college, or Tribal College or University) or graduate level. Undergraduates must be entering their junior or senior year; students attending a Tribal or community college must have completed their first year of school; law students must be entering their second or third year of school. Students who will graduate during the spring or summer are not eligible unless they have been accepted for enrollment in graduate school. The program accepts applications from students in all majors who are interested in working on transportation-related topics and issues. Preference is given to students with a GPA of 3.0 or higher. Undergraduates must submit a 1-page essay on their transportation interests and how participation in this program will enhance their educational and career plans and goals. Graduate students must submit a writing sample representing their educational and career plans and goals. Law students must submit a legal writing sample.

Financial data The stipend is $4,000 for undergraduates or $5,000 for graduate and law students. The program also provides housing and reimbursement of travel expenses from interns' homes to their assignment location.

Duration 10 weeks during the summer.

Additional information Assignments are at the DOT headquarters in Washington, D.C., a selected modal administration, or selected field offices around the country.

Number awarded 80 to 100 each year.

Deadline January of each year.

[1176]
SUNY GRADUATE DIVERSITY FELLOWSHIP PROGRAM

State University of New York
Attn: Office of Diversity, Equity and Inclusion
State University Plaza, T1000A
353 Broadway
Albany, NY 12246
(518) 320-1189   E-mail: carlos.medina@suny.edu
Web: system.suny.edu/odei/diversity-programs

Summary   To provide financial assistance to graduate students at campuses of the State University of New York (SUNY) who are African Americans or will contribute to the diversity of the student body in other ways.

Eligibility   This program is open to U.S. citizens and permanent residents who are entering or enrolled full-time graduate or professional students at any of the participating SUNY colleges. Applicants must be able to demonstrate how they will contribute to the diversity of the student body for the program for which they are applying, including having overcome a disadvantage or other impediment to success in higher education. Economic disadvantage, although not a requirement, may be the basis for eligibility. Membership in a racial or ethnic group that is underrepresented in the graduate or professional program involved may serve as a plus factor in making awards, but may not form the sole basis of selection. Awards are granted in the following priority order: 1) new graduate students who are being recruited but have not yet accepted admission to a graduate program; 2) Graduate Opportunity Waiver Program students who can be awarded a stipend to supplement their waiver to tuition; 3) currently-enrolled doctoral candidates who have completed all degree requirements except the dissertation; and 4) graduate assistants and teaching assistants who can receive a supplement to their current stipends to enhance their retention in graduate studies.

Financial data   Stipends range from $7,500 to $10,000.

Duration   1 year; renewable.

Number awarded   Varies each year; recently, this program awarded nearly $6 million in fellowships to 511 graduate students on 24 SUNY campuses. Of the recipients 32% were Latinos, 34% African Americans, 17% Whites, 5% Asians, and 5% Native Americans.

Deadline   Deadline not specified.

[1177]
SYNOD OF LAKES AND PRAIRIES RACIAL ETHNIC SCHOLARSHIPS

Synod of Lakes and Prairies
Attn: Committee on Racial Ethnic Ministry
2115 Cliff Drive
Eagen, MN 55122-3327
(651) 357-1140   Toll Free: (800) 328-1880, ext. 202
Fax: (651) 357-1141   E-mail: mkes@lakesandprairies.org
Web: www.lakesandprairies.org

Summary   To provide financial assistance to African American and other minority residents of the Presbyterian Church (USA) Synod of Lakes and Prairies who are working on an undergraduate or graduate degree at a college or seminary in any state as preparation for service to the church.

Eligibility   This program is open to members of Presbyterian churches who reside within the Synod of Lakes and Prai-

ries (Iowa, Minnesota, Nebraska, North Dakota, South Dakota, and Wisconsin). Applicants must be members of ethnic minority groups studying at least half time for service in the Presbyterian Church (USA) as a teaching elder, ordained minister, commissioned ruling elder, lay professional, or volunteer. They must be in good academic standing, making progress toward an undergraduate or graduate degree, and able to demonstrate financial need. Along with their application, they must submit essays of 200 to 500 words on 1) what the church needs to do to be faithful to its mission in the world today; and 2) the people, practices, or events that influence their commitment to Christ in ways that renew their fair and strengthen their service.

Financial data   Stipends range from $850 to $3,500.

Duration   1 year.

Number awarded   Varies each year; recently, 9 were awarded.

Deadline   September of each year.

[1178]
TEXAS MEDICAL ASSOCIATION MINORITY SCHOLARSHIP PROGRAM

Texas Medical Association
Attn: Director, Educational Loans, Scholarships and
   Awards
401 West 15th Street, Suite 100
Austin, TX 78701-1680
(512) 370-1600   Toll Free: (800) 880-1300, ext. 1600
Fax: (512) 370-1693
E-mail: gail.schatte@tmaloanfunds.com
Web: www.tmaloanfunds.com/Content/Template.aspx?id=9

Summary   To provide financial assistance to African Americans and members of other underrepresented minority groups from any state who are entering medical school in Texas.

Eligibility   This program is open to members of minority groups that are underrepresented in the medical profession (African American, Mexican American, Native American). Applicants must have been accepted at a medical school in Texas; students currently enrolled are not eligible. Along with their application, they must submit a 750-word essay on how they, as a physician, would improve the health of all Texans.

Financial data   The stipend is $2,500 per year.

Duration   4 years.

Additional information   This program began in 1999.

Number awarded   12 each year: 1 at each of the medical schools in Texas.

Deadline   February of each year.

[1179]
TEXAS YOUNG LAWYERS ASSOCIATION DIVERSITY SCHOLARSHIP PROGRAM

Texas Young Lawyers Association
Attn: Diversity Committee
1414 Colorado, Fourth Floor
P.O. Box 12487
Austin, TX 78711-2487
(512) 427-1529   Toll Free: (800) 204-2222, ext. 1529
Fax: (512) 427-4117   E-mail: btrevino@texasbar.com
Web: www.tyla.org

Summary To provide financial assistance to residents of any state who are African Americans or members of other diverse groups attending law school in Texas.
Eligibility This program is open to members of recognized diverse groups, including diversity based on gender, national origin, race, ethnicity, sexual orientation, gender identity, disability, socioeconomic status, and geography. Applicants must be attending an ABA-accredited law school in Texas. Along with their application, they must submit a brief essay on 1) why they believe diversity is important to the practice of law; and 2) what the Texas Young Lawyers Association and the State Bar of Texas can do to promote and support diversity in the legal profession. Selection is based on those essays, academic performance, demonstrated commitment to diversity, letters of recommendation, and financial need.
Financial data The stipend is $1,000.
Duration 1 year.
Number awarded At least 9 each year: at least 1 at each accredited law school in Texas.
Deadline October of each year.

[1180]
THE LEADERSHIP INSTITUTE SCHOLARSHIPS

The Leadership Institute for Women of Color Attorneys, Inc.
Attn: Scholarship Chair
1266 West Paces Ferry Road, N.W., Suite 263
Atlanta, GA 30327
(404) 443-5715   E-mail: hhorton@mcquirewoods.com
Web: www.leadingwomenofcolor.org

Summary To provide financial assistance to African Americans and other women of color who are attending law school.
Eligibility This program is open to women of color who have completed at least 1 year at an accredited law school and have a GPA of 3.0 or higher. Applicants must be U.S. citizens who can demonstrate a commitment to the legal profession. Along with their application, they must submit brief statements on their work experience, extracurricular activities, why they think it is important for women of color to serve in the legal profession, what they believe is necessary for success in the legal profession, and what they plan to do with their law degree.
Financial data The stipend is $3,000.
Duration 1 year.
Number awarded 5 each year.
Deadline December of each year.

[1181]
THE REV. DR. JOSEPH H. EVANS PASTORAL SCHOLARSHIP

United Church of Christ
Attn: Associate Director, Grant and Scholarship Administration
700 Prospect Avenue East
Cleveland, OH 44115-1100
(216) 736-2166   Toll Free: (866) 822-8224, ext. 2166
Fax: (216) 736-3783   E-mail: scholarships@ucc.org
Web: www.ucc.org/evans_fund

Summary To provide financial assistance to African American members of United Church of Christ (UCC) congregations and currently enrolled at a seminary.
Eligibility This program is open to African Americans who have been members of a UCC congregation for at least 1 year. Applicants must be enrolled full or part time in the second or third year of an ATS-accredited seminary and have a GPA of 3.0 or higher.
Financial data A stipend is awarded (amount not specified).
Duration 1 year.
Additional information This scholarship was established in 2009 and first awarded in 2014.
Number awarded 1 or more each year.
Deadline February of each year.

[1182]
THOMAS G. NEUSOM SCHOLARSHIPS

Conference of Minority Transportation Officials
Attn: National Scholarship Program
100 M Street, S.E., Suite 917
Washington, DC 20003
(202) 506-2917   E-mail: info@comto.org
Web: www.comto.org/page/scholarships

Summary To provide financial assistance for college or graduate school to African American and other minority members of the Conference of Minority Transportation Officials (COMTO) and their families.
Eligibility This program is open to undergraduate and graduate students who have been members of COMTO or whose parents, guardians, or grandparents have been members for at least 1 year. Applicants must be working (either full or part time) on a degree in a field related to transportation and have a GPA of 2.5 or higher. Along with their application they must submit a cover letter on their transportation-related career goals and life aspirations. Financial need is not considered in the selection process.
Financial data The stipend is $5,500. Funds are paid directly to the recipient's college or university.
Duration 1 year.
Number awarded 1 each year.
Deadline April of each year.

[1183]
THOMAS R. PICKERING FOREIGN AFFAIRS FELLOWSHIPS

The Washington Center for Internships
Attn: Foreign Affairs Fellowship Program
1333 16th Street, N.W.
Washington, DC 20036-2205
(202) 238-7900   Fax: (202) 238-7700
E-mail: info@twc.org
Web: www.twc.edu

Summary To provide forgivable loans to undergraduate and graduate students, especially African Americans and members of other underrepresented groups, who are interested in preparing for a career with the Department of State's Foreign Service.
Eligibility This program is open to U.S. citizens who are entering their senior year of undergraduate study or their first year of graduate study. Applicants must be planning to work on a 2-year full-time master's degree program relevant to the work of the U.S. Foreign Service, including public policy, international affairs, public administration, business, economics,

political science, sociology, or foreign languages. They must be preparing for a career in the Foreign Service. Applications are especially encouraged from women, members of minority groups historically underrepresented in the Foreign Service, and students with financial need.

Financial data The program pays for tuition, room, board, books, mandatory fees, and 1 round-trip ticket from the fellow's residence to academic institution, to a maximum of $37,500 per academic year.

Duration 2 years: the senior year of undergraduate study and the first year of graduate study for college seniors; the first 2 years of graduate school for entering graduate students.

Additional information This program is funded by the State Department and administered by The Washington Center for Internships. Fellows must commit to a minimum of 5 years of service in an appointment as a Foreign Service Officer following graduation and successful completion of the Foreign Service examination. If they fail to fulfill that commitment, they must refund all money received.

Number awarded Approximately 40 each year: 20 college seniors and 20 entering graduate students.

Deadline January of each year.

[1184]
THURGOOD MARSHALL DISSERTATION FELLOWSHIP FOR AFRICAN-AMERICAN SCHOLARS

Dartmouth College
Attn: Office of Graduate Studies
37 Dewey Field Road
6062 Wentworth Hall, Room 304
Hanover, NH 03755-1419
(603) 646-2106   Fax: (603) 646-8762
Web: graduate.dartmouth.edu

Summary To provide funding to African American and other doctoral students who are interested in working on their dissertation at Dartmouth College.

Eligibility This program is open to doctoral candidates who have completed all requirements for the Ph.D. except the dissertation and are planning a career in higher education. Applicants must be African Americans or other graduate students with a demonstrated commitment and ability to advance educational diversity. They must be interested in working on their dissertation at Dartmouth College. All academic fields that are taught in the Dartmouth undergraduate Arts and Sciences curriculum are eligible. Selection is based on academic achievement and promise; demonstrated commitment to increasing opportunities for underrepresented minorities and increasing cross-racial understanding; and potential for serving as an advocate and mentor for minority undergraduate and graduate students.

Financial data The stipend is $36,000. In addition, fellows receive office space, library privileges, and a $2,500 research allowance.

Duration 1 year, beginning in September.

Additional information The fellows are affiliated with a department or program at Dartmouth College. Fellows are expected to be in residence at Dartmouth College for the duration of the program and to complete their dissertation during that time. They are also expected to teach a course, either as the primary instructor or as part of a team.

Number awarded 1 each year.
Deadline January of each year.

[1185]
TRAILBLAZER SCHOLARSHIP

Conference of Minority Transportation Officials
Attn: National Scholarship Program
100 M Street, S.E., Suite 917
Washington, DC 20003
(202) 506-2917   E-mail: info@comto.org
Web: www.comto.org/page/scholarships

Summary To provide financial assistance for college or graduate school to African American and other minority members of the Conference of Minority Transportation Officials (COMTO) and their families.

Eligibility This program is open to undergraduate and graduate students who have been members of COMTO or whose parents, guardians, or grandparents have been members for at least 1 year. Applicants must be working (either full or part time) on a degree in a field related to transportation and have a GPA of 2.5 or higher. Along with their application they must submit a cover letter on their transportation-related career goals and life aspirations. Financial need is not considered in the selection process.

Financial data The stipend is $2,500. Funds are paid directly to the recipient's college or university.

Duration 1 year.

Number awarded 1 each year.

Deadline April of each year.

[1186]
TRANSAMERICA RETIREMENT SOLUTIONS LEADERS IN HEALTH CARE SCHOLARSHIP

Institute for Diversity in Health Management
Attn: Membership and Education Specialist
155 North Wacker Avenue
Chicago, IL 60606
(312) 422-2658   E-mail: cbiddle@aha.org
Web: www.diversityconnection.org

Summary To provide financial assistance to graduate students in health care management who are African Americans or will contribute to ethnic diversity in the profession in other ways.

Eligibility This program is open to U.S. citizens who represent ethnically diverse cultural backgrounds. Applicants must be enrolled in the second year of a master's degree program in health administration or a comparable program and have a GPA of 3.0 or higher. Along with their application, they must submit 1) a personal statement of 1 to 2 pages on their interest in health care management and their career goals; 2) an essay on what they see as the most challenging issue facing America's hospitals and health systems; and 3) a 500-word essay on their interest and background in health care finance. Selection is based on academic achievement, commitment to community service, and financial need.

Financial data The stipend is $5,000.

Duration 1 year.

Additional information This program began in 2007 as the Diversified Investment Advisors Leaders in Healthcare Scholarship. Its current name became effective in 2013 when Transamerica Retirement Solutions assumed sponsorship.

Number awarded   2 each year.
Deadline   January of each year.

[1187]
UCSB BLACK STUDIES DISSERTATION FELLOWSHIPS

University of California at Santa Barbara
Attn: Department of Black Studies
South Hall, Room 3702
Santa Barbara, CA 93106-3150
(805) 893-8045   Fax: (805) 893-3597
E-mail: mgalicia@blackstudies.ucsb.edu
Web: www.blackstudies.ucsb.edu

Summary   To enable doctoral candidates in African, Caribbean, and African American studies to complete their dissertations while teaching at the University of California at Santa Barbara (UCSB).

Eligibility   This program is open to students currently enrolled in a doctoral program at an accredited university who have completed all requirements for the Ph.D. except the dissertation. Applicants should be conducting research that focuses on intersections of race, class, gender, and sexuality in African, Caribbean, African American, or Diasporic studies. They must be interested in working on their dissertation at UCSB.

Financial data   The fellowship provides a stipend of $27,000, office space, and library privileges.

Duration   9 months.

Additional information   Fellows are expected to work on their dissertation, teach 1 undergraduate course in their specified area of research, and present 1 public lecture during the fellowship period. Recipients must be in residence at UCSB for the entire fellowship period.

Number awarded   2 each year.
Deadline   February of each year.

[1188]
UNCF ACHIEVEMENT CAPSTONE SCHOLARSHIPS

United Negro College Fund
Attn: Scholarships and Grants Department
1805 Seventh Street, N.W.
Washington, DC 20001
(202) 810-0258   Toll Free: (800) 331-2244
E-mail: scholarships@uncf.org
Web: www.uncf.org

Summary   To provide funding for retirement of educational costs or continuing education to African American seniors at Historically Black Colleges and Universities (HBCUs) or other predominantly black institutions.

Eligibility   This program is open to African American seniors graduating from 4-year HBCUs or other predominantly black institutions. Students must be nominated by their institution. Nominees must be seeking funding for retirement of undergraduate educational costs or to pay for future educational expenses. They must submit, along with the letter nominating them, a letter that addresses 1) the ways in which their undergraduate career and plans for the future reflect the legacy of the 1964 Civil Rights Act; and 2) their service to the campus and wider communities.

Financial data   Stipends range from $2,500 to $5,000.

Duration   These are 1-time awards.

Additional information   This program began in 2016 when the National Merit Scholarship Corporation (NMSC) transferred the assets of its National Achievement Scholarship Program to the UNCF. The NMSC had established that program in 1965, following the passage of the Civil Rights Act of 1964, in order to provide an opportunity for talented African American students to obtain higher education.

Number awarded   Varies each year.
Deadline   Deadline not specified.

[1189]
UNDERREPRESENTED MINORITY DENTAL STUDENT SCHOLARSHIP

American Dental Association
Attn: ADA Foundation
211 East Chicago Avenue
Chicago, IL 60611
(312) 440-2547   Fax: (312) 440-3526
E-mail: adaf@ada.org
Web: www.adafoundation.org/en/how-to-apply/education

Summary   To provide financial assistance to African Americans and other underrepresented minorities who wish to enter the field of dentistry.

Eligibility   This program is open to U.S. citizens from a minority group that is currently underrepresented in the dental profession: Native American, African American, or Hispanic. Applicants must have a GPA of 3.25 or higher and be entering their second year of full-time study at a dental school in the United States accredited by the Commission on Dental Accreditation. Selection is based upon academic achievement, a written summary of personal and professional goals, letters of reference, and demonstrated financial need.

Financial data   The maximum stipend is $2,500. Funds are sent directly to the student's financial aid office to be used to cover tuition, fees, books, supplies, and living expenses.

Duration   1 year.

Additional information   This program, established in 1991, is supported by the Harry J. Bosworth Company, Colgate-Palmolive, Sunstar Americas, and Procter & Gamble Company. Students receiving a full scholarship from any other source are ineligible to receive this scholarship.

Number awarded   Approximately 25 each year.
Deadline   November of each year.

[1190]
UNITED HEALTH FOUNDATION/NMF DIVERSE MEDICAL SCHOLARS PROGRAM

National Medical Fellowships, Inc.
Attn: Scholarship Program
347 Fifth Avenue, Suite 510
New York, NY 10016
(212) 483-8880   Toll Free: (877) NMF-1DOC
Fax: (212) 483-8897 E-mail: scholarships@nmfonline.org
Web: www.nmfonline.org

Summary   To provide financial assistance to African American and other underrepresented minority students at medical schools in designated areas who are interested in conducting a community health project.

Eligibility   This program is open to African Americans, Hispanics/Latinos, Native Americans, Vietnamese, Cambodians, and Pacific Islanders who are currently enrolled at an accredited medical school in the greater New York City metropolitan area (including Connecticut, New Jersey, New York, and Pennsylvania), Florida (Orlando, Tampa, and greater Miami), Arizona (Phoenix), New Mexico (Albuquerque), Tennessee (Nashville), Texas (San Antonio), Wisconsin (Milwaukee), or Georgia (Atlanta). Applicants must have demonstrated leadership and a commitment to serving medically underserved communities. They must be interested in conducting a self-directed health project of 200 hours at a site of choice in an underserved community in the same area as their medical school. U.S. citizenship or DACA status is required.

Financial data The grant is $7,000.

Duration 1 year; recipients may apply for a second year of funding.

Additional information This program, sponsored by United Health Foundation, began in 2007.

Number awarded 30 each year.

Deadline October of each year.

[1191]
UNITED HEALTHCARE/LAWYERS COLLABORATIVE FOR DIVERSITY CLERKSHIP

Lawyers Collaborative for Diversity
Attn: Program Coordinator
P.O. Box 230637
Hartford, CT 06123-0637
(860) 275-0668
E-mail: kdavis@lawyerscollaborativefordiversity.org
Web: www.lcdiversity.com/scholarships.htm

Summary To provide summer work experience at United Healthcare Services in Hartford, Connecticut to African Americans and other underrepresented students at law schools in Connecticut and western Massachusetts.

Eligibility This program is open to women and students of color in their first year at law schools in Connecticut or western Massachusetts. Applicants must be interested in a summer internship at United Healthcare Services in Harford, Connecticut. Along with their application, they must submit 500-word essays on 1) why they should be selected for this opportunity; and 2) their thoughts about diversity in Connecticut's legal community.

Financial data The stipend is $5,000.

Duration 8 weeks during the summer.

Additional information This program is sponsored by United HealthCare Services, Inc.

Number awarded 1 each year.

Deadline February of each year.

[1192]
UNITED METHODIST FOUNDATION THEOLOGICAL AND PROFESSIONAL SCHOOL MERIT SCHOLARS PROGRAM

United Methodist Higher Education Foundation
Attn: Scholarships Administrator
60 Music Square East, Suite 350
P.O. Box 340005
Nashville, TN 37203-0005
(615) 649-3974   Toll Free: (800) 811-8110
Fax: (615) 649-3980
E-mail: umhefscholarships@umhef.org
Web: www.umhef.org

Summary To provide financial assistance to African American and other minority students who are preparing for ordination at seminaries affiliated with the United Methodist Church.

Eligibility This program is open to first- through third-year students working on a master's degree at the 14 United Methodist-related theological and professional schools. Applicants must be U.S. citizens or permanent residents and active members of the United Methodist Church for at least 1 year prior to application. They must be planning to enroll full time and have a GPA of 3.0 or higher. Preference is given to ethnic minority and first generation college students. Financial need is considered in the selection process.

Financial data The stipend is $3,000.

Duration 1 year; nonrenewable.

Additional information Students may obtain applications from their school.

Number awarded 42 each year: 1 to a member of each class at each school.

Deadline Nominations from schools must be received by September of each year.

[1193]
UNITED METHODIST WOMEN OF COLOR SCHOLARS PROGRAM

United Methodist Church
Attn: General Board of Higher Education and Ministry
Office of Loans and Scholarships
1001 19th Avenue South
P.O. Box 340007
Nashville, TN 37203-0007
(615) 340-7342   Fax: (615) 340-7367
E-mail: umscholar@gbhem.org
Web: www.gbhem.org

Summary To provide financial assistance to Methodist women of color who are working on a doctoral degree to prepare for a career as an educator at a United Methodist seminary.

Eligibility This program is open to women of color (have at least 1 parent who is African American, African, Hispanic, Asian, Native American, Alaska Native, or Pacific Islander) who have an M.Div. degree. Applicants must have been active, full members of a United Methodist Church for at least 3 years prior to applying. They must be enrolled full time in a degree program at the Ph.D. or Th.D. level to prepare for a career teaching at a United Methodist seminary.

Financial data The maximum stipend is $10,000 per year.

Duration 1 year; may be renewed up to 3 additional years.

Number awarded Varies each year; recently, 10 were awarded.

Deadline January of each year.

[1194]
UTC/LCD DIVERSITY SCHOLARS PROGRAM

Lawyers Collaborative for Diversity
Attn: Program Coordinator
P.O. Box 230637
Hartford, CT 06123-0637
(860) 275-0668
E-mail: kdavis@lawyerscollaborativefordiversity.org
Web: www.lcdiversity.com/scholarships.htm

Summary To provide financial assistance and summer work experience to African Americans and other underrepresented students at law schools in Connecticut and western Massachusetts.

Eligibility This program is open to women and people of color from any state who are currently enrolled in the first year at a law school in Connecticut or western Massachusetts. Applicants must be available to work as an intern during the summer following their first year. Along with their application, they must submit 500-word essays on 1) why diversity is important to them and how the Connecticut legal community can improve diversity in the legal profession; and 2) why they should be selected for this program.

Financial data The program provides a stipend of $2,000 per year for the second and third years of law school, a paid internship during the summer after the first year at a member firm of the Lawyers Collaborative for Diversity (LCD), and an unpaid internship with a legal department of United Technologies Corporation during that same summer.

Duration The scholarship is for 2 years; the paid internship is for 5 weeks during the summer; the unpaid internship is for 3 weeks during the summer.

Additional information This program is sponsored by United Technologies Corporation (UTC).

Number awarded 2 each year.

Deadline January of each year.

[1195]
VALERIE RUSSELL SCHOLARSHIP

United Church of Christ
Attn: Associate Director, Grant and Scholarship
  Administration
700 Prospect Avenue East
Cleveland, OH 44115-1100
(216) 736-2166   Toll Free: (866) 822-8224, ext. 2166
Fax: (216) 736-3783   E-mail: scholarships@ucc.org
Web: www.ucc.org/russell_scholarship

Summary To provide financial assistance to African American laywomen who are members of a United Church of Christ (UCC) congregation and working on an undergraduate or graduate degree to advance the justice ministries of the denomination.

Eligibility This program is open to African American laywomen who have a strong theologically-grounded commitment to the justice ministries of the UCC but are not a member in discernment, licensed, commissioned, or ordained. Applicants must be 1) working on an undergraduate or graduate degree in a field that will affirm the values of the UCC

and promote its justice commitments; or 2) already professionally engaged in justice work either in the church or in a secular organization and seeking funds for continuing education activities (e.g., classes, workshops, travel) that will assist in personal skill building.

Financial data Stipends range from $1,500 to $2,000 per year. Funds may be used for tuition for undergraduate or graduate study or for continuing education activities.

Duration 1 year; may be renewed.

Additional information This program began in 1997.

Number awarded 1 or more each year.

Deadline February of each year.

[1196]
VASHTI TURLEY MURPHY SCHOLARSHIP PROGRAM

Delta Sigma Theta Sorority, Inc.
Attn: Scholarship and Standards Committee Chair
1707 New Hampshire Avenue, N.W.
Washington, DC 20009
(202) 986-2400   Fax: (202) 986-2513
E-mail: dstemail@deltasigmatheta.org
Web: www.deltasigmatheta.org

Summary To provide financial assistance to members of Delta Sigma Theta who are interested in working on a graduate degree to prepare for a career in ministry.

Eligibility This program is open to graduating college seniors and graduate students who are interested in working on a master's or doctoral degree to prepare for a career in ministry. Applicants must be active, dues-paying members of Delta Sigma Theta. Selection is based on meritorious achievement.

Financial data The stipends range from $1,000 to $2,000. The funds may be used to cover tuition, fees, and living expenses.

Duration 1 year; may be renewed for 1 additional year.

Additional information This sponsor is a traditionally-African American social sorority. The application fee is $20.

Number awarded 1 or more each year.

Deadline March of each year.

[1197]
VERNE LAMARR LYONS MEMORIAL SCHOLARSHIP

National Association of Social Workers
Attn: NASW Foundation
750 First Street, N.E., Suite 800
Washington, DC 20002-4241
(202) 408-8600, ext. 298   Fax: (202) 336-8292
E-mail: naswfoundation@naswdc.org
Web: www.naswfoundation.org/fellowships.asp

Summary To provide financial assistance to African American and other students interested in working on a master's degree in social work.

Eligibility This program is open to members of the National Association of Social Workers (NASW) who have applied to or been accepted into an accredited M.S.W. program. Applicants must have demonstrated a commitment to working with African American communities and have an interest and/or demonstrated ability in health/mental health practice. They must have the potential for completing an M.S.W. program and have a GPA of 3.0 or higher.

Financial data The program provides a stipend of $4,000 disbursed directly to the recipient's university and up to $1,500 for professional development and travel to conferences.

Duration 1 year.

Additional information Effective in 2016, this program became part of the Social Work HEALS Project, a collaborative program of NASW and CSWE funded by the Robert and Ellen Popper Scholarship Fund of the New York Community Trust.

Number awarded 4 each year.

Deadline February of each year.

[1198]
VICTOR GRIFOLS ROURA SCHOLARSHIP

National Medical Fellowships, Inc.
Attn: Scholarship Program
347 Fifth Avenue, Suite 510
New York, NY 10016
(212) 483-8880   Toll Free: (877) NMF-1DOC
Fax: (212) 483-8897 E-mail: scholarships@nmfonline.org
Web: www.nmfonline.org

Summary To provide financial assistance to African American and other underrepresented minority students at medical schools in the Los Angeles metropolitan area.

Eligibility This program is open to African Americans, Hispanics/Latinos, Native Americans, Vietnamese, Cambodians, and Pacific Islanders who are entering their second or third year at a medical school in the Los Angeles metropolitan area. Applicants must demonstrate an interest in hematology (diseases of the blood). They must be U.S. citizens or DACA students. Selection is based on leadership, commitment to serving medically underserved communities, and financial need.

Financial data The stipend is $7,500.

Duration 1 year.

Additional information This program began in 2013.

Number awarded 1 each year.

Deadline September of each year.

[1199]
VISION COUNCIL OPPORTUNITY SCHOLARSHIPS

National Optometric Association
Attn: Student Affairs
1801 North Tryon Street, Suite 315
Charlotte, NC 28206
(704) 918-1809   Toll Free: (877) 394-2020
Fax: (877) NOA-2006
E-mail: noastudentdirector@yahoo.com
Web: www.nationaloptometricassociation.com

Summary To provide financial assistance to African American members of the National Optometric Student Association (NOSA) who express an interest in working with underserved populations.

Eligibility This program is open to NOSA members entering their final year at a school or college of optometry. Applicants must be able to demonstrate an interest in working with underserved populations, financial need, and a GPA of 2.5 or higher. They must participate in optometric community service. Along with their application, they must submit a 1-page essay describing any extenuating financial circumstances, interest and history of serving with underserved populations, experience with community service, and plan to promote growth of the optometric industry.

Financial data The stipend is $1,000.

Duration 1 year.

Additional information The National Optometric Association was founded in 1969 with the goal of recruiting minority students, especially African Americans, for schools and colleges of optometry. This program is sponsored by The Vision Council, formerly the Optical Industry Association.

Number awarded 19 each year: 1 at each school of optometry with a NOSA chapter.

Deadline May of each year.

[1200]
VISITING RESEARCH INTERNSHIP PROGRAM

Harvard Medical School
Office for Diversity Inclusion and Community Partnership
Attn: Program for Faculty Development and Diversity
  Inclusion
164 Longwood Avenue, Second Floor
Boston, MA 02115-5810
(617) 432-1892   Fax: (617) 432-3834
E-mail: pfdd_dcp@hms.harvard.edu
Web: mfdp.med.harvard.edu

Summary To provide an opportunity for medical students, especially African Americans and other underrepresented minorities, to conduct a mentored research project at Harvard Medical School during the summer.

Eligibility This program is open to first- and second-year medical students, particularly underrepresented minority and/or disadvantaged individuals, in good standing at accredited U.S. medical schools. Applicants must be interested in conducting a summer research project at Harvard Medical School under the mentorship of a faculty advisor. They must be interested in a research and health-related career, especially in clinical or translational research or research that transforms scientific discoveries arising from laboratory, clinical, or population studies into clinical or population-based applications to improve health. U.S. citizenship, nationality, or permanent resident status is required.

Financial data Participants receive a stipend (amount not specified), housing, and reimbursement of transportation costs to Boston up to $400.

Duration 8 weeks during the summer.

Additional information This program, established in 2008, is funded by the National Center for Research Resources of the National Institutes of Health NIH). It is a joint enterprise of Harvard University, its 10 schools, its 17 Academic Healthcare Centers, Boston College School of Nursing, MIT, the Cambridge Health Alliance, and other community partners. Interns attend weekly seminars with Harvard faculty focusing on such topics as research methodology, health disparities, ethics, and career paths. They also have the opportunity to participate in offerings of other Harvard Medical School programs, such a career development seminars and networking dinners.

Number awarded Varies each year; recently, 6 medical students were admitted to this program.

Deadline December of each year.

[1201]
VISUAL TASK FORCE SCHOLARSHIPS

National Association of Black Journalists
Attn: Program Manager
University of Maryland
1100 Knight Hall, Suite 3100
College Park, MD 20742
(301) 405-7520   Fax: (301) 314-1714
E-mail: Sberry@nabj.org
Web: www.nabj.org/?page=ScholarshipsVTF

Summary To provide financial assistance to high school seniors and undergraduate or graduate student members of the National Association of Black Journalists (NABJ) who are interested in a career in visual journalism.

Eligibility This program is open to African American high school seniors and undergraduate and graduate student members of NABJ who are currently enrolled or planning to enroll full time at an accredited 4-year college or university. Applicants must be interested in working on a degree in a field related to visual journalism (e.g., photojournalism, design and informational graphics, broadcast photojournalism) to prepare for a career in newspaper, magazine, broadcast, or online journalism. They must have a GPA of 2.75 or higher and be able to demonstrate financial need. Along with their application, they must submit samples of their work, an official college transcript, 3 letters of recommendation, a resume, and an essay of 1,000 to 2,000 words on the reasons they wish to prepare for a career in visual journalism and how they use their visual skills to tell a story effectively and creatively.

Financial data The stipend is $1,500. Funds are paid directly to the recipient's college or university.

Duration 1 year; nonrenewable.

Number awarded 2 each year.

Deadline March of each year.

[1202]
W. MONTAGUE COBB MEDICAL SCHOLAR AWARD

Omega Psi Phi Fraternity
Attn: Charles R. Drew Memorial Scholarship Commission
3951 Snapfinger Parkway
Decatur, GA 30035-3203
(404) 284-5533   Fax: (404) 284-0333
E-mail: scholarshipchairman@oppf.org
Web: www.oppf.org/scholarship

Summary To provide financial assistance for medical school to members of Omega Psi Phi who have an outstanding academic record.

Eligibility This program is open to members of the fraternity who are currently enrolled full time at an accredited school of medicine and working on a doctoral degree (not a residency). Applicants must have demonstrated service to the fraternity during the year of application and be in good financial standing at all levels. Along with their application, they must submit a statement of 200 to 250 words on their purpose for applying for this scholarship, how they believe funds

from the fraternity can assist them in achieving their career goals, and other circumstances (including financial need) that make it important for them to receive financial assistance. Selection is based on academic excellence.

Financial data The stipend is $5,000.

Duration 1 year.

Additional information Omega Psi Phi is a traditionally Black college fraternity. The winner is required to attend the Omega Psi Phi Grand Conclave or Leadership Conference. Up to $1,000 in travel expenses for attendance is provided.

Number awarded 1 each year.

Deadline April of each year.

[1203]
WALMART AND SAM'S CLUB HEALTH AND WELLNESS/NOSA ACADEMIC SCHOLARSHIP

National Optometric Association
Attn: Student Affairs
1801 North Tryon Street, Suite 315
Charlotte, NC 28206
(704) 918-1809   Toll Free: (877) 394-2020
Fax: (877) NOA-2006
E-mail: noastudentdirector@yahoo.com
Web: www.nationaloptometricassociation.com

Summary To provide financial assistance to African American and other members of the National Optometric Student Association (NOSA) who demonstrate academic achievement.

Eligibility This program is open to NOSA members enrolled in the second, third, or fourth year at a school or college of optometry. Applicants must be able to demonstrate both academic achievement (GPA of 3.0 or higher) and leadership in community service and optometry school. Along with their application, they must submit a 2-page statement on their reasons for applying for this award; their involvement in professional, community, extracurricular activities or events that have displayed their commitment to serving humanity and demonstrated interest in others; and how they hope to impact the profession of optometry positively in the future. Financial need is not considered in the selection process.

Financial data The stipend is $1,000.

Duration 1 year.

Additional information The National Optometric Association was founded in 1969 with the goal of recruiting minority students, especially African Americans, for schools and colleges of optometry. This program is sponsored by Walmart.

Number awarded 1 each year.

Deadline May of each year.

[1204]
WALMART AND SAM'S CLUB HEALTH AND WELLNESS/NOSA LEADERSHIP SCHOLARSHIP

National Optometric Association
Attn: Student Affairs
1801 North Tryon Street, Suite 315
Charlotte, NC 28206
(704) 918-1809   Toll Free: (877) 394-2020
Fax: (877) NOA-2006
E-mail: noastudentdirector@yahoo.com
Web: www.nationaloptometricassociation.com

Summary To provide financial assistance to African American and other members of the National Optometric Student Association (NOSA) who demonstrate leadership.

Eligibility This program is open to NOSA members enrolled in the second, third, or fourth year at a school or college of optometry. Applicants must be able to demonstrate leadership in community service and optometry school. They must have a GPA of 2.5 or higher. Along with their application, they must submit a 2-page statement on their reasons for applying for this award; their involvement in professional, community, extracurricular activities or events that have displayed their commitment to serving humanity and demonstrated interest in others; and how they hope to impact the profession of optometry positively in the future. Financial need is not considered in the selection process.

Financial data The stipend is $1,000.

Duration 1 year.

Additional information The National Optometric Association was founded in 1969 with the goal of recruiting minority students, especially African Americans, for schools and colleges of optometry. This program is sponsored by Walmart.

Number awarded 2 each year.

Deadline May of each year.

[1205]
WARNER NORCROSS & JUDD LAW SCHOOL SCHOLARSHIP

Grand Rapids Community Foundation
Attn: Education Program Officer
185 Oakes Street S.W.
Grand Rapids, MI 49503-4008
(616) 454-1751, ext. 103   Fax: (616) 454-6455
E-mail: rbishop@grfoundation.org
Web: www.grfoundation.org/scholarshipslist

Summary To provide financial assistance to African Americans and other minorities from Michigan who are attending law school.

Eligibility This program is open to students of color who are attending or planning to attend an accredited law school. Applicants must be residents of Michigan or attending law school in the state. They must be U.S. citizens or permanent residents and have a GPA of 2.5 or higher. Financial need is considered in the selection process.

Financial data The stipend is $5,000. Funds are paid directly to the recipient's institution.

Duration 1 year.

Additional information Funding for this program is provided by the law firm Warner Norcross & Judd LLP.

Number awarded 1 each year.

Deadline March of each year.

[1206]
WAYNE ANTHONY BUTTS SCHOLARSHIP

National Medical Fellowships, Inc.
Attn: Scholarship Program
347 Fifth Avenue, Suite 510
New York, NY 10016
(212) 483-8880   Toll Free: (877) NMF-1DOC
Fax: (212) 483-8897 E-mail: scholarships@nmfonline.org
Web: www.nmfonline.org

Summary To provide financial assistance to African American and other underrepresented minority students at medical schools in the New York City metropolitan area.

Eligibility This program is open to African Americans, Hispanics/Latinos, Native Americans, Vietnamese, Cambodians, and Pacific Islanders who are entering their first or second year of medical school. Applicants must be enrolled at a school in the New York City metropolitan area. They must be U.S. citizens or DACA students. Selection is based on leadership, commitment to serving medically underserved communities, and financial need.

Financial data The stipend is $3,000.

Duration 1 year.

Additional information This program began in 2013.

Number awarded 1 each year.

Deadline September of each year.

[1207]
WESTCHESTER/GREATER CONNECTICUT CHAPTER NBMBAA GRADUATE SCHOLARSHIP

National Black MBA Association-Westchester/Greater
  Connecticut Chapter
Attn: Scholarship Chair
P.O. Box 3586
Stamford, CT 06905
Toll Free: (866) 966-9942
E-mail: scholarship@nbmbaa-wgc.org
Web: www.nbmbaa-wgc.org/education/scholarship.html

Summary To provide financial assistance to African American and other underrepresented minority residents of Connecticut and Westchester County, New York who are working on a business-related graduate degree at a college in any state.

Eligibility This program is open to residents of Connecticut or Westchester County, New York who are members of underrepresented minority groups. Applicants must be enrolled full time at an accredited college or university in any state and working on a graduate degree in accounting, business, economics, entrepreneurship, management, marketing, or a related area. They must be U.S. citizens (or in possession of a current student visa) and have a GPA of 3.0 or higher. Along with their application, they must submit a 500-word essay on either of the following topics: 1) why they have chosen their advanced degree area of focus and they societal impact they hope to create; or 2) their anticipation that an advanced degree will increase or decrease in value. Selection is based on that essay, academic achievement, demonstrated leadership ability, and participation in college and community activities.

Financial data The stipend is $2,000.

Duration 1 year.

Number awarded 1 or more each year.

Deadline December of each year.

[1208]
WIDEX AUDIOLOGY SCHOLARSHIP

National Black Association for Speech-Language and Hearing
Attn: Awards and Scholarship Committee
700 McKnight Park Drive, Suite 708
Pittsburgh, PA 15237
(855) 727-2836　　　　　　　　Fax: (888) 729-3489
E-mail: nbaslh@nbaslh.org
Web: www.nbaslh.org/scholarships/scholarship-main.html

Summary　To recognize and reward, with a scholarship, members of the National Black Association for Speech-Language and Hearing (NBASLH) who submit outstanding papers at its annual convention.

Eligibility　This award is available to NBASLH members who submit research papers at the organization's annual convention. The research study must be in the area of audiology, which may include research related to hearing screening, communication strategies, auditory and visual speech perception and training, hearing aids, cochlear implants, counseling, tinnitus management, or underrepresented minorities. Selection is based on theoretical and scientific rationale, professional relevance, originality and innovation, strength of the study design and data analysis, interpretation and discussion of results, and overall clarity.

Financial data　The award is a $1,000 scholarship.

Duration　1 year.

Additional information　This program, which began in 2016, is supported by Widex.

Number awarded　1 each year.

Deadline　February of each year.

[1209]
WILEY W. MANUEL LAW FOUNDATION SCHOLARSHIPS

Wiley W. Manuel Law Foundation
c/o Law Offices of George Holland
1970 Broadway, Suite 1030
Oakland, CA 94612
(510) 465-4100
Web: www.wileymanuel.org/forms.html

Summary　To provide financial assistance to African American and other minority students from any state enrolled at law schools in northern California.

Eligibility　This program is open to minority students entering their third year at law schools in northern California. Applicants should exemplify the qualities of the late Justice Wiley Manuel, the first African American to serve on the California Supreme Court. Along with their application, they must submit a 250-word essay on why they should be awarded this scholarship. Financial need is also considered in the selection process.

Financial data　The stipend is approximately $1,500.

Duration　1 year.

Number awarded　Varies each year; recently, 12 were awarded.

Deadline　August of each year.

[1210]
WILLIAM AND CHARLOTTE CADBURY AWARD

National Medical Fellowships, Inc.
Attn: Scholarship Program
347 Fifth Avenue, Suite 510
New York, NY 10016
(212) 483-8880　　　　　　Toll Free: (877) NMF-1DOC
Fax: (212) 483-8897　E-mail: scholarships@nmfonline.org
Web: www.nmfonline.org

Summary　To provide financial assistance to African American and other underrepresented minority medical students who demonstrate academic achievement.

Eligibility　This program is open to African Americans, Hispanics/Latinos, Native Americans, Vietnamese, Cambodians, and Pacific Islanders who are entering their senior year of medical school. They must be U.S. citizens or DACA students. Selection is based on academic achievement, leadership, and community service.

Financial data　The stipend is $5,000.

Duration　1 year.

Additional information　This program began in 1977.

Number awarded　1 each year.

Deadline　September of each year.

[1211]
WILLIAM G. ANDERSON, D.O. MINORITY SCHOLARSHIP

American Osteopathic Foundation
Attn: Director, Internal and External Affairs
142 East Ontario Street
Chicago, IL 60611-2864
(312) 202-8235　　　　　　Toll Free: (866) 455-9383
Fax: (312) 202-8216　　E-mail: ehart@aof-foundation.org
Web: www.aof.org

Summary　To provide financial assistance to African American and other minority students enrolled at colleges of osteopathic medicine.

Eligibility　This program is open to minority (African American, Native American, Asian American, Pacific Islander, or Hispanic) students entering their second, third, or fourth year at an accredited college of osteopathic medicine. Applicants must demonstrate 1) interest in osteopathic medicine, its philosophy, and its principles; 2) academic achievement; 3) leadership efforts in addressing the educational, societal, and health needs of minorities; 4) leadership efforts in addressing inequities in medical education and health care; 5) accomplishments, awards and honors, special projects, and extracurricular activities that demonstrate the applicant's ability to be a leader.

Financial data　The stipend is $7,500.

Duration　1 year.

Additional information　This program began in 1998.

Number awarded　1 each year.

Deadline　April of each year.

[1212]
WILLIAM K. SCHUBERT M.D. MINORITY NURSING SCHOLARSHIP

Cincinnati Children's Hospital Medical Center
Attn: Office of Diversity and Inclusion, MLC 9008
3333 Burnet Avenue
Cincinnati, OH 45229-3026
(513) 803-6416   Toll Free: (800) 344-2462
Fax: (513) 636-5643   TDD: (513) 636-4900
E-mail: diversity@cchmc.org
Web: www.cincinnatichildrens.org

Summary To provide financial assistance to African American and members of other underrepresented groups interested in working on a bachelor's or master's degree in nursing to prepare for licensure in Ohio.

Eligibility This program is open to members of groups underrepresented in the nursing profession (Blacks or African Americans, Hispanics or Latinos, American Indians or Alaska Natives, Hawaiian Natives or other Pacific Islanders, Asians, or males). Applicants must be enrolled or accepted in a professional bachelor's or master's registered nurse program at an accredited school of nursing to prepare for initial licensure in Ohio. They must have a GPA of 2.75 or higher. Along with their application, they must submit a 750-word essay that covers 1) their long-range personal, educational, and professional goals; 2) why they chose nursing as a profession; 3) how their experience as a member of an underrepresented group has influenced a major professional and/or personal decision in their life; 4) any unique qualifications, experiences, or special talents that demonstrate their creativity; and 5) how their work experience has contributed to their personal development.

Financial data The stipend is $2,750 per year.

Duration 1 year. May be renewed up to 3 additional years for students working on a bachelor's degree or 1 additional year for students working on a master's degree; renewal requires that students maintain a GPA of 2.75 or higher.

Number awarded 1 or more each year.

Deadline April of each year.

[1213]
WILLIAM RUCKER GREENWOOD SCHOLARSHIP

Association for Women Geoscientists-Potomac Chapter
Attn: Scholarships
P.O. Box 6644
Arlington, VA 22206-0644
E-mail: awgpotomacschol@hotmail.com
Web: www.awg.org/members/po_scholarships.htm

Summary To provide financial assistance to African American and other minority women from any state working on an undergraduate or graduate degree in the geosciences at a college in the Potomac Bay region.

Eligibility This program is open to minority women who are residents of any state and currently enrolled as full-time undergraduate or graduate geoscience majors at an accredited, degree-granting college or university in Delaware, the District of Columbia, Maryland, Virginia, or West Virginia. Selection is based on the applicant's 1) participation in geoscience or earth science educational activities; and 2) potential for leadership as a future geoscience professional.

Financial data The stipend is $1,000. The recipient also is granted a 1-year membership in the Association for Women Geoscientists (AWG).

Duration 1 year.

Number awarded 1 each year.

Deadline April of each year.

[1214]
WOMAN WHO MOVES THE NATION SCHOLARSHIP

Conference of Minority Transportation Officials
Attn: National Scholarship Program
100 M Street, S.E., Suite 917
Washington, DC 20003
(202) 506-2917   E-mail: info@comto.org
Web: www.comto.org/page/scholarships

Summary To provide financial assistance to African American and other minority women who are working on an undergraduate or graduate degree in specified fields to prepare for a management career in a transportation-related organization.

Eligibility This program is open to minority women who are working on an undergraduate or graduate degree with intent to lead in some capacity as a supervisor, manager, director, or other position in transit or a transportation-related organization. Applicants may be studying business, entrepreneurship, political science, or other specialized area. They must have a GPA of 3.0 or higher. Along with their application they must submit a cover letter on their transportation-related career goals and life aspirations. Financial need is not considered in the selection process.

Financial data The stipend is $5,000. Funds are paid directly to the recipient's college or university.

Duration 1 year.

Number awarded 1 each year.

Deadline April of each year.

[1215]
WORLD COMMUNION NATIONAL SCHOLARSHIPS

United Methodist Church
General Board of Global Ministries
Attn: Scholarship/Leadership Development Office
475 Riverside Drive, Room 1479
New York, NY 10115
(212) 870-3787   Toll Free: (800) UMC-GBGM
Fax: (212) 870-3654   E-mail: scholars@umcmission.org
Web: www.umcor.org/explore-our-work/Scholarships

Summary To provide financial assistance to African Americans and other U.S. students of color who are interested in attending graduate school to prepare for leadership in promoting the mission goals of the United Methodist Church.

Eligibility This program is open to U.S. citizens and permanent residents who are members of a community of color. Applicants must have applied to or been admitted to a master's, doctoral, or professional program at an institution of higher education in the United States. They must indicate a willingness to provide 5 years of Christian service after graduation in the areas of elimination of poverty, expansion of global health, leadership development, or congregational development. High priority is given to members of the United

Methodist Church. Financial need is considered in the selection process.

Financial data The stipend ranges from $1,000 to $12,500, depending on the recipient's related needs and school expenses.

Duration 1 year.

Additional information These awards are funded by the World Communion Offering received in United Methodist Churches on the first Sunday in October.

Number awarded 5 to 10 each year.

Deadline November of each year.

[1216]
WORLDSTUDIO AIGA SCHOLARSHIPS

AIGA, the professional association for design
Attn: Scholarships
233 Broadway, 17th floor
New York, NY 10279
(212) 710-3111   E-mail: scholarship@aiga.org
Web: www.aiga.org/worldstudio-scholarship

Summary To provide financial assistance to African American and other minority or economically disadvantaged students who are interested in working on an undergraduate or graduate degree in specified fields of the arts.

Eligibility This program is open to undergraduate and graduate students who are currently enrolled or planning to enroll full time at an accredited college or university and work on a degree in 1 of the following areas: fine art, graphic design (including visual design), illustration (including animation), interactive design (including UI/UX, motion, digital, and web design), or photography. Other fields of the arts, (e.g., industrial design, interior design, film, architecture, landscape design, theater design, fashion design) are not eligible. Although not required, minority status is a significant factor in the selection process. U.S. citizenship or permanent resident status is required. Applicants must have a GPA of 2.0 or higher. Along with their application, they must submit a 600-word statement of purpose that includes a brief autobiography, an explanation of how their experiences have influenced their creative work and/or their career plans, and how they see themselves contributing to the community at large in the future. Selection is based on that statement, the quality of submitted work, financial need, minority status, recommendations, and academic record.

Financial data Basic stipends range from $2,000 to $3,000, but awards up to $5,000 are also presented at the discretion of the jury. Honorable mentions are $500. Funds are paid directly to the recipient's school.

Duration 1 academic year. Recipients may reapply.

Additional information This program is offered by AIGA, founded in 1914 as the American Institute of Graphic Arts, in cooperation with the Worldstudio Foundation.

Number awarded Varies each year; recently, 16 scholarships and 2 honorable mentions were awarded.

Deadline April of each year.

[1217]
WRITING COMPETITION TO PROMOTE DIVERSITY IN LAW SCHOOLS AND IN THE LEGAL PROFESSION

Law School Admission Council
Attn: Office of Diversity Initiatives
662 Penn Street
P.O. Box 40
Newtown, PA 18940-0040
(215) 968-1338   TDD: (215) 968-1169
E-mail: DiversityOffice@lsac.org
Web: www.lsac.org

Summary To recognize and reward law students who submit outstanding essays on what law schools can do to promote diversity.

Eligibility This competition is open to J.D. candidates in each year of study at law schools in the United States and Canada that are members of the Law School Admission Council (LSAC). Applicants must submit articles, up to 20 pages in length, on the techniques, resources and strategies law schools can utilize to recruit and retain students of color, students living with a disability, LGBTQ students, and other students who are from groups underrepresented in law schools and the legal profession. Selection is based on research and use of relevant sources and authorities; quality and clarity of legal analysis, persuasion, and writing; understanding, interpretations, and conclusions regarding diversity and the implications of diversity in this context; and compliance with all competition procedures.

Financial data The prize is $5,000.

Duration The prize is awarded annually.

Number awarded 3 each year: 1 to a student in each year of law school.

Deadline April of each year.

[1218]
WSP/PARSONS BRINCKERHOFF WOMEN IN LEADERSHIP SCHOLARSHIP

Conference of Minority Transportation Officials
Attn: National Scholarship Program
100 M Street, S.E., Suite 917
Washington, DC 20003
(202) 506-2917   E-mail: info@comto.org
Web: www.comto.org/page/scholarships

Summary To provide financial assistance to African American and other minority women who are working on a master's degree in civil engineering or other transportation-related field.

Eligibility This program is open to minority women who are working full time on a master's degree in civil engineering with intent to prepare for a leadership role in transportation. They must have a GPA of 3.0 or higher. Along with their application they must submit a cover letter on their transportation-related career goals and life aspirations. Financial need is not considered in the selection process.

Financial data The stipend is $3,000. Funds are paid directly to the recipient's college or university.

Duration 1 year.

Additional information This program is sponsored by WSP USA, formerly Parsons Brinckerhoff, Inc.

Number awarded 1 each year.

Deadline April of each year.

[1219]
XEROX TECHNICAL MINORITY SCHOLARSHIP PROGRAM

Xerox Corporation
Attn: Technical Minority Scholarship Program
150 State Street, Fourth Floor
Rochester, NY 14614
Toll Free: (877) 747-3625 E-mail: xtmsp@rballiance.com
Web: www.xerox.com/jobs/minority-scholarships/enus.html

Summary To provide financial assistance to African Americans and other minorities interested in undergraduate or graduate education in the sciences and/or engineering.

Eligibility This program is open to minorities (people of African American, Asian, Pacific Islander, Native American, Native Alaskan, or Hispanic descent) working full time on a bachelor's, master's, or doctoral degree in chemistry, computing and software systems, engineering (chemical, computer, electrical, imaging, manufacturing, mechanical, optical, or software), information management, laser optics, materials science, physics, or printing management science. Applicants must be U.S. citizens or permanent residents with a GPA of 3.0 or higher and attending a 4-year college or university.

Financial data Stipends range from $1,000 to $10,000.

Duration 1 year.

Number awarded Varies each year, recently, 128 were awarded.

Deadline September of each year.

[1220]
ZETA PHI BETA GENERAL GRADUATE FELLOWSHIPS

Zeta Phi Beta Sorority, Inc.
Attn: National Educational Foundation
1734 New Hampshire Avenue, N.W.
Washington, DC 20009
(202) 387-3103   Fax: (202) 232-4593
E-mail: info@zetaphibetasororityhq.org
Web: www.zpbnef1975.org/scholarships-and-descriptions

Summary To provide financial assistance to African American and other women who are working on a professional degree, master's degree, doctorate, or postdoctorate.

Eligibility Women graduate or postdoctoral students are eligible to apply if they have achieved distinction or shown promise of distinction in their chosen fields. Applicants need not be members of Zeta Phi Beta. They must be enrolled full time in a professional, graduate, or postdoctoral program. Along with their application, they must submit a 150-word essay on their educational goals and professional aspirations, how this award will help them to achieve those goals, and why they should receive the award. Financial need is not considered in the selection process.

Financial data The stipend ranges up to $2,500, paid directly to the recipient.

Duration 1 academic year; may be renewed.

Additional information Zeta Phi Beta is a traditionally African American sorority.

Number awarded 1 or more each year.

Deadline January of each year.

[1221]
ZOETIS/AAVMC VETERINARY STUDENT SCHOLARSHIP PROGRAM

Association of American Veterinary Medical Colleges
Attn: Associate Executive Director for Academic and
  Research Affairs
1101 Vermont Avenue, N.W., Suite 301
Washington, DC 20005-3536
(202) 371-9195, ext. 118   Toll Free: (877) 862-2740
Fax: (202) 842-0773   E-mail: tmashima@aavmc.org
Web: www.aavmc.org

Summary To provide financial assistance to veterinary students in all areas of professional interest, especially African Americans and other minorities.

Eligibility This program is open to second- and third-year students at veterinary colleges in the United States. Applicants may have a professional interest in any area, including food animal medicine, small animal clinical medicine, research, government services, public health, or organized veterinary medicine. Along with their application, they must submit a 3-page personal statement that describes 1) why diversity and inclusion are important to them personally and professionally; 2) how they intend to continue contributing to diversity and inclusion efforts in the veterinary profession after graduation; and 3) what it might mean to be honored as a recipient of this scholarship. They must also indicate how they express their race and/or ethnicity (Black or African American, Hispanic, American Indian or Alaskan, Asian, Native Hawaiian or Pacific Islander, or White) and how they express their gender (male, female, transgender spectrum, or other). Selection is based primarily on documentation of a demonstrated commitment to promoting diversity in academic veterinary medicine; consideration is also given to academic achievement, the student's broader community service record, and financial need.

Financial data The stipend is $2,000.

Duration 1 year; nonrenewable.

Additional information This program was established by Zoetis in 2010. That firm partnered with the Association of American Veterinary Medical Colleges (AAVMC) in 2014 to administer the program.

Number awarded Varies each year; recently, 452 were awarded.

Deadline November of each year.

[1222]
ZORA NEALE HURSTON SCHOLARSHIP

Zeta Phi Beta Sorority, Inc.
Attn: National Educational Foundation
1734 New Hampshire Avenue, N.W.
Washington, DC 20009
(202) 387-3103   Fax: (202) 232-4593
E-mail: info@zetaphibetasororityhq.org
Web: www.zpbnef1975.org/scholarships-and-descriptions

Summary To provide financial assistance to African American and other graduate students working on a degree in anthropology or related fields.

Eligibility   This program is open to full-time graduate students in anthropology or related fields. Applicants need not be members of Zeta Phi Beta. Along with their application, they must submit a 150-word essay on their educational goals and professional aspirations, how this award will help them to achieve those goals, and why they should receive the award. Financial need is not considered in the selection process.

Financial data   The stipend ranges from $500 to $1,000.

Duration   1 academic year; may be renewed.

Additional information   Zeta Phi Beta is a traditionally African American sorority.

Number awarded   1 each year.

Deadline   January of each year.

Professionals/
Postdoctorates

Listed alphabetically by program title and described in detail here are 155 grants, awards, educational support programs, residencies, and other sources of "free money" available to African American professionals and postdoctorates. This funding is available to support research, creative activities, professional projects, training courses, and/or residencies in the United States.

[1223]
A. PHILLIP RANDOLPH MESSENGER AWARDS

National Newspaper Publishers Association
Attn: NNPA Foundation
1816 12th Street, N.W.
Washington, DC 20009
(202) 588-8764   Fax: (202) 588-5302
E-mail: nnpafoundation@nnpa.org
Web: www.nnpa.org/nnpa-foundation

Summary To recognize and reward journalists, especially African Americans, at newspapers that are members of the National Newspaper Publishers Association (NNPA) who submit outstanding articles in designated categories.

Eligibility This program is open to journalists at newspapers that are members of NNPA. Applicants must submit articles (news stories, editorials, or commentary) in the following categories: 1) breaking news; 2) economic empowerment (workforce development and jobs); 3) sustainability and environment (green stories); 4) feature; or 5) commentary. Entries may be submitted by a single reporter or a team; they must be factual coverage of current events and should have local, regional, national, or international significance.

Financial data The awards are $5,000 for the winner and $500 for each finalist.

Duration The awards are presented annually.

Additional information The NNPA, also known as the Black Press of America, is a federation of more than 200 Black community newspapers from across the United States. It offers these awards in cooperation with MillerCoors (formerly Miller Brewing Company).

Number awarded 15 each year: 1 winner and 2 finalists in each category.

Deadline May of each year.

[1224]
ABC 4TH YEAR FELLOWSHIP AWARD IN CARDIAC ELECTROPHYSIOLOGY

Association of Black Cardiologists, Inc.
Attn: Membership Committee
122 East 42nd Street, 18th Floor
New York, NY 10068
Toll Free: (800) 753-9222   Fax: (888) 281-3574
E-mail: membershipservices@abcardio.org
Web: www.abcardio.org

Summary To provide funding to members of the Association of Black Cardiologists (ABC) interested in training in clinical electrophysiology (EP).

Eligibility This program is open to underrepresented minorities enrolled in accredited cardiology academic training programs and active in the ABC Cardiologists-in-Training (CIT) program. Applicants must submit brief statements on their career goals and their relationship, membership status, and interests in the ABC.

Financial data The grant is $40,000 per year. Funds may be used for salary, fringe benefits, and overhead costs.

Duration 1 year; may be renewed.

Number awarded 1 each year.

Deadline May of each year.

[1225]
ACADEMY OF NUTRITION AND DIETETICS GRADUATE SCHOLARSHIPS

Academy of Nutrition and Dietetics
Attn: Foundation
120 South Riverside Plaza, Suite 2000
Chicago, IL 60606-6995
(312) 899-4821   Toll Free: (800) 877-1600, ext. 4821
Fax: (312) 899-4796   E-mail: scholarship@eatright.org
Web: www.eatrightacend.org

Summary To provide financial assistance to graduate student members of the Academy of Nutrition and Dietetics, including African Americans and members of other underrepresented groups.

Eligibility This program is open to members of the academy who are enrolled in the second year of a master's or doctoral degree program in dietetics. Applicants who are currently completing a dietetic internship or pre-professional practice program that is combined with a graduate program may also apply. The graduate scholarships are available only to U.S. citizens and permanent residents. Applicants should intend to practice in the field of dietetics. Some scholarships require specific areas of study (e.g., public health nutrition, food service administration) and status as a registered dietitian. Others may require membership in a specific dietetic practice group, residency in a specific state, or underrepresented minority group status. The same application form can be used for all categories.

Financial data Stipends range from $500 to $10,000.

Duration 1 year.

Additional information The Academy of Nutrition and Dietetics was formerly the American Dietetic Association.

Number awarded Approximately 60 each year.

Deadline February of each year.

[1226]
ADVANCED POSTDOCTORAL FELLOWSHIPS IN DIABETES RESEARCH

Juvenile Diabetes Research Foundation International
Attn: Senior Director, Research Administration
26 Broadway, 14th Floor
New York, NY 10004
(212) 479-7519   Toll Free: (800) 533-CURE
Fax: (212) 785-9595   E-mail: emilligan@jdrf.org
Web: grantcenter.jdrf.org

Summary To provide advanced research training to scientists, especially African Americans and members of other underrepresented groups, who are beginning their professional careers and are interested in conducting research in the United States or abroad on the causes, treatment, prevention, or cure of diabetes or its complications.

Eligibility This program is open to postdoctorates who show extraordinary promise for a career in diabetes research. Applicants must have received their first doctoral degree (M.D., Ph.D., D.M.D., or D.V.M.) within the past 5 years and should have completed 1 to 3 years of postdoctoral training. They may not have a faculty appointment. There are no citizenship requirements. Applications are encouraged from women, members of minority groups underrepresented in the sciences, and people with disabilities. The proposed research training may be conducted at foreign or domestic, for-profit or nonprofit, or public or private institutions, including universities, colleges, hospitals, laboratories, units of state or local government, or eligible agencies of the federal government. Selection is based on the applicant's previous experience and academic record; the caliber of the proposed research; the quality of the mentor, training program, and environment; and the applicant's potential to obtain an independent research position in the future. Fellows who obtain a faculty position at any time during the term of the fellowship may apply for a transition award for support during their first year as a faculty member.

Financial data The total grant is $90,000 per year, including salary that depends on number of years of experience, ranging from $42,840 for zero up to $56,376 for 7 or more years of experience. In the first year only, funds in excess of the grant may be used for travel to scientific meetings (up to $2,000), journal subscriptions, books, training courses, laboratory supplies, equipment, or purchase of a personal computer (up to $2,000). Indirect costs are not allowed. Fellows who receive a faculty position are granted a transition award of up to $110,000 for 1 year, including up to 10% in indirect costs.

Duration Up to 3 years.

Number awarded 1 each year.

Deadline July of each year.

[1227]
AERA FELLOWSHIP PROGRAM ON THE STUDY OF DEEPER LEARNING

American Educational Research Association
Attn: Fellowships Program
1430 K Street, N.W., Suite 1200
Washington, DC 20005
(202) 238-3200   Fax: (202) 238-3250
E-mail: fellowships@aera.net
Web: www.aera.net

Summary To provide an opportunity for early-career scholars, especially African Americans and members of other underrepresented groups in the field of education, to conduct research using the Deeper Learning dataset.

Eligibility This program is open to scholars who received a Ph.D. or Ed.D. degree within the past 7 years in a field of education or related social or behavioral science field (e.g., economics, political science, psychology, psychometrics, sociology). Applicants must be proposing a program of research utilizing the Study of Deeper Learning (SDL) dataset collected by the American Institutes for Research (AIR). Selection is based on potential for the study to advance knowledge and understanding with the discipline and/or the education field; what is already known on the issue; appropriateness of the SDL dataset to address the research questions; qualifications of the applicant to carry out the proposed study; and alignment of the research procedures, methods, and approaches with the study objectives. Underrepresented racial and ethnic minority researchers and women and strongly encouraged to apply. U.S. citizenship or permanent resident status is required.

Financial data Fellows receive a stipend of $20,000 plus full payment of expenses to attend a study overview and data training session in Washington, D.C. at the beginning of the fellowship and the fall research conference of the American Educational Research Association (AERA), also in Washington, D.C.

Duration 1 year.

Additional information This program is jointly administered by the AERA and the AIR with funding provided by the William and Flora Hewlett Foundation.

Number awarded Up to 8 each year.

Deadline June of each year.

[1228]
AES RESEARCH AND TRAINING FELLOWSHIP FOR CLINICIANS

American Epilepsy Society
135 South LaSalle Street, Suite 2850
Chicago, IL 60603
(312) 883-3800   Fax: (312) 896-5784
E-mail: info@aesnet.org
Web: www.aesnet.org

Summary To provide funding to African American and other minority clinicians who are interested in conducting research related to epilepsy.

Eligibility This program is open to clinical fellows, postdoctoral fellows, and newly appointed clinical faculty members who have an M.D., Ph.D., Sc.D., Pharm.D., R.N., or equivalent degree. Applicants must be interested in conducting research with an epilepsy-related theme under the guidance of a mentor with expertise in epilepsy research. They must have a defined research plan and access to institutional resources to conduct the proposed project with at least 50% of their time devoted to the fellowship. Physicians whose research will involve direct patient care or direct involvement with patients must have completed all residency training and be licensed to practice medicine at their institution. Selection is based on the applicant's potential and commitment to develop as an independent and productive epilepsy researcher, academic record, and research experience; the mentor's research qualifications; the research training plan; and the quality of the research facilities, resources, and training opportunities. Applications are especially encouraged from women, members of minority groups, and people with disabilities. U.S. citizenship is not required, but all research must be conducted in the United States.

Financial data Grants range up $50,000, including $49,000 as stipend and $1,000 for travel support and complimentary registration to attend the sponsor's annual meeting.

Duration 1 year; nonrenewable.

Additional information In addition to the funding provided by the American Epilepsy Society, support is available from the TESS Research Foundation for applications focused on epilepsy due to SLC13A5 mutations; the LGS Foundation for applications focused on Lennox-Gastaut-Syndrome; the PCDH19 Alliance for applications focused on epilepsy due to PCDH19 mutations; the Dravet Syndrome Foundation for applications focused on Dravet Syndrome; Wishes for Elliott for applications focused on epilepsy due to SCN8A mutations; and the TS Alliance for applications focused on epilepsy associated with tuberous sclerosis complex (TSC).

Number awarded Varies each year.

Deadline Letters of intent must be submitted by October of each year; final proposals are due in January.

[1229]
AFRICAN AMERICAN STUDIES FELLOWSHIP

Massachusetts Historical Society
Attn: Short-Term Fellowships
1154 Boylston Street
Boston, MA 02215-3695
(617) 646-0568   Fax: (617) 859-0074
E-mail: fellowships@masshist.org
Web: www.masshist.org/research/fellowships/short-term

Summary To fund research visits to the Massachusetts Historical Society for graduate students and other scholars interested in African American history.

Eligibility This program is open to advanced graduate students, postdoctorates, and independent scholars who are conducting research in African American history and need to use the resources of the Massachusetts Historical Society. Applicants must be U.S. citizens or foreign nationals holding appropriate U.S. government documents. Along with their application, they must submit a curriculum vitae and a proposal describing the project and indicating collections at the society to be consulted. Graduate students must also arrange for a letter of recommendation from a faculty member familiar with their work and with the project being proposed. Preference is given to candidates who live 50 or more miles from Boston.

Financial data The grant is $2,000.

Duration 4 weeks.

Additional information This fellowship was first awarded in 1999.

Number awarded 1 each year.

Deadline February of each year.

[1230]
AFRICAN AMERICAN STUDIES PROGRAM VISITING SCHOLARS

University of Houston
African American Studies Program
Attn: Visiting Scholars Program
629 Agnes Arnold Hall
Houston, TX 77204-3047
(713) 743-2811   Fax: (713) 743-2818
E-mail: jconyers@uh.edu
Web: www.uh.edu

Summary To provide support to junior scholars who are interested in conducting research on the African American community while affiliated with the University of Houston's African American Studies Program.

Eligibility Applications are sought from junior scholars in social sciences, humanities, or African American studies who completed their Ph.D. within the past 6 years. They must be interested in conducting research on the African American community while affiliated with the University of Houston's African American Studies Program and in assuming a tenured or tenure-track position there after their residency as a Visiting Scholar is completed. They must be available for consultation with students and professional colleagues, make at least 2 formal presentations based on their research project, and contribute generally to the intellectual discourse in the discipline of African Studies/Africology. Along with their application, they must submit a current curriculum vitae, a 2-page description of the proposed research, 3 letters of recommen-

dation, and a syllabus of the undergraduate course to be taught. Minorities, women, veterans, and persons with disabilities are specifically encouraged to apply.

Financial data Visiting Scholars receive a salary appropriate to their rank.

Duration 1 academic year.

Additional information Visiting Scholars are assigned a research assistant, if needed, and are provided administrative support. Recipients must teach 1 class related to African American studies. They are required to be in residence at the university for the entire academic year and must make 2 presentations on their research. In addition, they must acknowledge the sponsor's support in any publication that results from their tenure at the university.

Number awarded At least 2 each year.

Deadline Applications are accepted until the positions are filled.

[1231]
AFRICAN AMERICAN STUDIES VISITING SCHOLAR AND VISITING RESEARCHER PROGRAM

University of California at Los Angeles
Institute of American Cultures
Attn: Bunche Center for African American Studies
160 Haines Hall
P.O. Box 951545
Los Angeles, CA 90095-1545
(310) 825-7403   Fax: (310) 206-3421
E-mail: acramon@bunche.ucla.edu
Web: www.iac.ucla.edu/fellowships_visitingscholar.html

Summary To provide funding to scholars interested in conducting research in African American studies at UCLA's Bunche Center for African American Studies.

Eligibility Applicants must have completed a doctoral degree in African American or related studies. They must be interested in teaching or conducting research at UCLA's Bunche Center for African American Studies. Visiting Scholar appointments are available to people who currently hold permanent academic appointments; Visiting Researcher appointments are available to postdoctorates who recently received their degree. UCLA faculty, students, and staff are not eligible. U.S. citizenship or permanent resident status is required.

Financial data Fellows receive a stipend of $35,000, health benefits, and up to $4,000 in research support. Visiting Scholars are paid through their home institution; Visiting Researchers receive their funds directly from UCLA.

Duration 9 months, beginning in October.

Additional information Fellows must teach or do research in the programs of the center. The award is offered in conjunction with UCLA's Institute of American Cultures (IAC).

Number awarded 1 each year.

Deadline January of each year.

[1232]
AGA MICROBIOME JUNIOR INVESTIGATOR AWARD

American Gastroenterological Association
Attn: AGA Research Foundation
Research Awards Manager
4930 Del Ray Avenue
Bethesda, MD 20814-2512
(301) 222-4012   Fax: (301) 654-5920
E-mail: awards@gastro.org
Web: www.gastro.org

Summary   To provide funding to young investigators, especially African Americans and other underrepresented minorities, who are interested in conducting research related to the gut microbiome.

Eligibility   This program is open to investigators interested in conducting research into relationships between the gut microbiome and functioning of the digestive system in health and disease. Applicants must have an M.D. or Ph.D. degree and a full-time faculty position at a North American educational institution. They should be early in their careers: clinicians who completed clinical training and investigators who received their final research degree no more than 7 years previously. Membership in the American Gastroenterological Association (AGA) is required. Selection is based on significance of the proposed research and its implication for preventing or treating disease, innovation, scientific approach, institutional environment and support, and applicant potential and commitment. Women and members of underrepresented minority groups are strongly encouraged to apply.

Financial data   The grant is $30,000 per year. Funds are to be used for project costs, including salary, supplies, and equipment but excluding travel. Indirect costs are not allowed.

Duration   2 years.

Number awarded   1 each year.

Deadline   June of each year.

[1233]
ALFRED P. SLOAN FOUNDATION RESEARCH FELLOWSHIPS

Alfred P. Sloan Foundation
630 Fifth Avenue, Suite 2200
New York, NY 10111-0242
(212) 649-1632   Fax: (212) 757-5117
E-mail: researchfellows@sloan.org
Web: www.sloan.org

Summary   To provide funding for research in selected fields of science to recent doctorates, especially African Americans and members of other underrepresented groups.

Eligibility   This program is open to scholars who are no more than 6 years from completion of the most recent Ph.D. or equivalent in chemistry, computational and evolutionary molecular biology, computer science, economics, mathematics, neuroscience, ocean sciences (including marine biology), physics, or a related interdisciplinary field. Applicants must have a tenure track position at a college or university in the United States or Canada. Direct applications are not accepted; candidates must be nominated by department heads or other senior scholars. Although fellows must be at an early stage of their research careers, they should give strong evidence of independent research accomplishments and creativity. The sponsor strongly encourages the participation of women and members of underrepresented minority groups.

Financial data   The stipend is $30,000 per year. Funds are paid directly to the fellow's institution to be used by the fellow for equipment, technical assistance, professional travel, trainee support, or any other research-related expense; they may not be used to augment an existing full-time salary.

Duration   2 years; may be extended if unexpended funds still remain.

Additional information   This program began in 1955, when it awarded $235,000 to 22 chemists, physicists, and pure mathematicians. Neuroscience was added in 1972, economics and applied mathematics in 1980, computer science in 1993, computational and evolutionary molecular biology in 2002, and ocean sciences in 2012. Currently, the program awards more than $5.5 million in grants annually.

Number awarded   126 each year: 23 in chemistry, 12 in computational and evolutionary molecular biology, 16 in computer science, 8 in economics, 20 in mathematics, 16 in neuroscience, 8 in ocean sciences, and 23 in physics.

Deadline   September of each year.

[1234]
ALONZO DAVIS FELLOWSHIP

Virginia Center for the Creative Arts
Attn: Admissions Committee
154 San Angelo Drive
Amherst, VA 24521
(434) 946-7236   Fax: (434) 946-7239
E-mail: vcca@vcca.com
Web: www.vcca.com

Summary   To provide support to writers, visual artists, and composers who are of African or Latino descent and interested in a residency at the Virginia Center for the Creative Arts in Sweet Briar, Virginia.

Eligibility   This program is open to writers, visual artists, and composers who are interested in a residency at the center so they can concentrate solely on their creative work. Applicants must be U.S citizens of African or Latino descent. They must submit samples of their work completed within the past 4 years.

Financial data   The fellowship provides payment of all residency costs, including a private bedroom, separate studio, and 3 prepared meals a day.

Duration   Up to 1 month.

Additional information   This fellowship was established in 2004. The application fee is $40.

Number awarded   1 each year.

Deadline   January of each year for June to September residencies; May of each year for October to January residencies; September of each year for February to May residencies.

[1235]
ALZHEIMER'S ASSOCIATION CLINICAL FELLOWSHIPS TO PROMOTE DIVERSITY

Alzheimer's Association
Attn: Medical and Scientific Affairs
225 North Michigan Avenue, 17th Floor
Chicago, IL 60601-7633
(312) 335-5747   Toll Free: (800) 272-3900
Fax: (866) 699-1246   TDD: (312) 335-5886
E-mail: grantsapp@alz.org
Web: www.alz.org

Summary To provide funding for clinical research training on Alzheimer's Disease to recent postdoctorates who are African Americans or will contribute to diversity in the field.

Eligibility This program is open to junior faculty members at recognized academic institutions who completed residency for an M.D. or D.O. or a postdoctoral fellowship (Ph.D.) or both within the past 5 years. Applicants must be proposing to conduct clinical research training in Alzheimer's and related dementias. Proposals are strongly encouraged from individuals training with a focus on dementia or cognitive disorders in behavioral neurology and neuropathy, geriatrics, geriatric psychiatry, or neuropsychology. Eligibility is restricted to investigators who will contribute to diversity in the field of biomedical research, including 1) members of underrepresented racial and ethnic minority groups (African Americans, Hispanic Americans, American Indians, Alaska Natives, Native Hawaiians, and Pacific Islanders); 2) individuals with disabilities; and 3) individuals from disadvantaged backgrounds. Selection is based on applicant's ability and promise as a clinician scientist (30%), quality and nature of the training to be provided and the institutional, departmental, and mentor-specific training environment (30%), and quality and originality of the research plan (40%).

Financial data Grants up to $60,000 per year, including direct expenses and up to 10% for overhead costs, are available. The total award for the life of the grant may not exceed $175,000, including $155,000 for costs related to the proposed research, $10,000 to the fellow upon successful completion of the program, and $10,000 to the primary mentor upon successful completion of the program.

Duration 2 to 3 years.

Number awarded 1 or 2 each year.

Deadline Letters of intent must be submitted by the end of September of each year. Final applications are due in November.

[1236]
ALZHEIMER'S ASSOCIATION RESEARCH FELLOWSHIPS TO PROMOTE DIVERSITY

Alzheimer's Association
Attn: Medical and Scientific Affairs
225 North Michigan Avenue, 17th Floor
Chicago, IL 60601-7633
(312) 335-5747   Toll Free: (800) 272-3900
Fax: (866) 699-1246   TDD: (312) 335-5886
E-mail: grantsapp@alz.org
Web: www.alz.org

Summary To provide funding for research training on Alzheimer's Disease to postdoctoral fellows who are African Americans or will contribute to diversity in the field in other ways.

Eligibility This program is open to postdoctoral fellows who have not received their first independent faculty position. Applicants must be proposing to conduct research related to Alzheimer's Disease. They must identify a mentor who is experienced in conducting Alzheimer's and related dementia research and in mentoring junior investigators. Eligibility is restricted to investigators who will contribute to diversity in the field of biomedical research, including 1) members of underrepresented racial and ethnic minority groups (African Americans, Hispanic Americans, American Indians, Alaska Natives, Native Hawaiians, and Pacific Islanders); 2) individuals with disabilities; and 3) individuals from disadvantaged backgrounds. Selection is based on quality and nature of the training to be provided and the institutional, departmental, and mentor-specific training environment (30%), quality and emphasis of the applicant and originality of the research plan (40%), and significance of the question being studied, quality of the work plan, and impact-risk of the proposal (30%).

Financial data Grants up to $60,000 per year, including direct expenses and up to 10% for overhead costs, are available. The total award for the life of the grant may not exceed $175,000, including $155,000 for costs related to the proposed research, $10,000 to the fellow upon successful completion of the program, and $10,000 to the mentor upon successful completion of the program.

Duration Up to 3 years.

Number awarded 1 or 2 each year.

Deadline Letters of intent must be submitted by the end of September of each year. Final applications are due in November.

[1237]
ALZHEIMER'S ASSOCIATION RESEARCH GRANTS TO PROMOTE DIVERSITY

Alzheimer's Association
Attn: Medical and Scientific Affairs
225 North Michigan Avenue, 17th Floor
Chicago, IL 60601-7633
(312) 335-5747   Toll Free: (800) 272-3900
Fax: (866) 699-1246   TDD: (312) 335-5886
E-mail: grantsapp@alz.org
Web: www.alz.org

Summary To provide funding for preliminary research on Alzheimer's Disease to junior investigators who are African Americans or will contribute to diversity in the field in other ways.

Eligibility This program is open to investigators who are less than 10 years past their doctoral or post-residency (M.D. or D.O.) or who are new to Alzheimer's and related dementia research. Applicants must be seeking funding that will allow them to develop preliminary or pilot data, to test procedures, and to develop hypotheses that will lay the groundwork for future grant applications to major governmental or private funding agencies. Eligibility is restricted to investigators who will contribute to diversity in the field of biomedical research, including 1) members of underrepresented racial and ethnic minority groups (African Americans, Hispanic Americans, American Indians, Alaska Natives, Native Hawaiians, and Pacific Islanders); 2) individuals with disabilities; and 3) individuals from disadvantaged backgrounds.

Financial data Grants up to $60,000 per year, including direct expenses and up to 10% for overhead costs, are available. The total award for the life of the grant may not exceed $150,000.

Duration   2 or 3 years.

Number awarded   1 or 2 each year.

Deadline   Letters of intent must be submitted by the end of September of each year. Final applications are due in November.

[1238]
AMERICAN ASSOCIATION OF OBSTETRICIANS AND GYNECOLOGISTS FOUNDATION RESEARCH AND TRAINING SCHOLARSHIPS

American Association of Obstetricians and Gynecologists
   Foundation
9 Newport Drive, Suite 200
Forest Hill, MD 21050
(443) 640-1051   Fax: (443) 640-1031
E-mail: info@aaogf.org
Web: www.aaogf.org/scholarship.asp

Summary   To provide funding to physicians, especially African Americans and other minorities, who are interested in a program of research training in obstetrics and gynecology.

Eligibility   Applicants must have an M.D. degree and be eligible for the certification process of the American Board of Obstetrics and Gynecology (ABOG). They must be interested in participating in research training conducted by 1 or more faculty mentors at an academic department of obstetrics and gynecology in the United States or Canada. The research training may be either laboratory-based or clinical, and should focus on fundamental biology, disease mechanisms, interventions or diagnostics, epidemiology, or translational research. Applicants for the scholarship co-sponsored by the Society for Maternal-Fetal Medicine (SMFM) must also be members or associate members of the SMFM. Women and minority candidates are strongly encouraged to apply. Selection is based on the scholarly, clinical, and research qualifications of the candidate; evidence of the candidate's commitment to an investigative career in academic obstetrics and gynecology in the United States or Canada; qualifications of the sponsoring department and mentor; overall quality of the mentoring plan; and quality of the research project.

Financial data   The grant is $120,000 per year. Sufficient funds to support travel to the annual fellows' retreat must be set aside. The balance of the funds may be used for salary, technical support, and supplies.

Duration   1 year; may be renewed for 2 additional years, based on satisfactory progress of the scholar.

Additional information   Scholars must devote at least 75% of their effort to the program of research training.

Number awarded   2 each year: 1 co-sponsored by ABOG and 1 co-sponsored by SMFM.

Deadline   June of each year.

[1239]
AMERICAN EDUCATIONAL RESEARCH ASSOCIATION RESEARCH GRANTS PROGRAM

American Educational Research Association
Attn: Grants Program
1430 K Street, N.W., Suite 1200
Washington, DC 20005
(202) 238-3200   Fax: (202) 238-3250
E-mail: grantsprogram@aera.net
Web: www.aera.net

Summary   To provide funding to faculty members and other postdoctorates, especially African Americans and other minorities, who are interested in conducting research on educational policy.

Eligibility   This program is open to scholars who have completed a doctoral degree in such disciplines as (but not limited to) education, sociology, economics, psychology, demography, statistics, or psychometrics. Applicants may be U.S. citizens, U.S. permanent residents, or non-U.S. citizens working at a U.S. institution. Underrepresented ethnic and racial minority researchers are strongly encouraged to apply. Research topics may cover a wide range of policy-related issues, but priority is given to proposals that 1) develop or benefit from new quantitative measures or methodological approaches for addressing education issues; 2) include interdisciplinary teams with subject matter expertise, especially when studying science, technology, engineering, or mathematics (STEM) learning; 3) analyze TIMSS, PISA, or other international data resources; or 4) include the integration and analysis of more than 1 data set. Research projects must include the analysis of data from at least 1 of the large-scale, nationally or internationally representative data sets, such as those of the National Science Foundation (NSF), National Center for Education Statistics (NCES), or other federal agencies. Selection is based on the importance of the proposed policy issue, the strength of the methodological model and proposed statistical analysis of the study, and relevant experience or research record.

Financial data   Grants up to $20,000 for 1 year or $35,000 for 2 years are available. Funding is linked to the approval of the recipient's progress report and final report. Grantees receive one-third of the total award at the beginning of the grant period, one-third upon acceptance of the progress report, and one-third upon acceptance of the final report.

Duration   1 or 2 years.

Additional information   Funding for this program is provided by the NSF. Grantees must submit a brief (3 to 6 pages) progress report midway through the grant period. A final report must be submitted at the end of the grant period.

Number awarded   Approximately 15 each year.

Deadline   March or September of each year.

[1240]
AMERICAN EPILEPSY SOCIETY JUNIOR INVESTIGATOR RESEARCH AWARD

American Epilepsy Society
135 South LaSalle Street, Suite 2850
Chicago, IL 60603
(312) 883-3800   Fax: (312) 896-5784
E-mail: info@aesnet.org
Web: www.aesnet.org

Summary To provide funding to junior investigators, especially African Americans and members of other underrepresented groups, who are interested in conducting research related to epilepsy.

Eligibility This program is open to recently independent investigators who have an M.D., Ph.D., Pharm.D., R.N., or equivalent degree and an academic appointment at the level of assistant professor or equivalent. Applicants must be interested in conducting basic, translational, or clinical epilepsy research, including studies of disease mechanisms or treatments, epidemiological or behavioral studies, the development of new technologies, or health services and outcomes research. Applications are especially encouraged from women, members of minority groups, and people with disabilities. U.S. citizenship is not required, but all research must be conducted in the United States.

Financial data The grant is $50,000 per year for direct costs of research.

Duration 1 year; nonrenewable.

Additional information In addition to the funding provided by the American Epilepsy Society, support is available from the TESS Research Foundation for applications focused on epilepsy due to SLC13A5 mutations; the LGS Foundation for applications focused on Lennox-Gastaut-Syndrome; the PCDH19 Alliance for applications focused on epilepsy due to PCDH19 mutations; the Dravet Syndrome Foundation for applications focused on Dravet Syndrome; Wishes for Elliott for applications focused on epilepsy due to SCN8A mutations; and the TS Alliance for applications focused on epilepsy associated with tuberous sclerosis complex (TSC).

Number awarded Varies each year.

Deadline Letters of intent must be submitted by October of each year; final proposals are due in January.

[1241]
AMERICAN EPILEPSY SOCIETY
POSTDOCTORAL RESEARCH FELLOWSHIPS

American Epilepsy Society
135 South LaSalle Street, Suite 2850
Chicago, IL 60603
(312) 883-3800   Fax: (312) 896-5784
E-mail: info@aesnet.org
Web: www.aesnet.org

Summary To provide funding to postdoctoral fellows, especially African Americans and members of other underrepresented groups, who are interested in conducting mentored research related to epilepsy.

Eligibility This program is open to postdoctoral fellows who have an M.D., Ph.D., Sc.D., Pharm.D., R.N., or equivalent degree. Applicants must be interested in conducting research with an epilepsy-related theme under the guidance of a mentor with expertise in epilepsy research. They must have a defined research plan and access to institutional resources to conduct the proposed project. Selection is based on the applicant's potential and commitment to develop as an independent and productive epilepsy researcher, academic record, and research experience; the mentor's research qualifications; the research training plan; and the quality of the research facilities, resources, and training opportunities. Applications are especially encouraged from women, members of minority groups, and people with disabilities. U.S. citizenship is not required, but all research must be conducted in the United States.

Financial data Grants range up $45,000, including $44,000 as stipend and $1,000 for travel support and complimentary registration to attend the sponsor's annual meeting.

Duration 1 year; nonrenewable.

Additional information In addition to the funding provided by the American Epilepsy Society, support is available from the TESS Research Foundation for applications focused on epilepsy due to SLC13A5 mutations; the LGS Foundation for applications focused on Lennox-Gastaut-Syndrome; the PCDH19 Alliance for applications focused on epilepsy due to PCDH19 mutations; the Dravet Syndrome Foundation for applications focused on Dravet Syndrome; Wishes for Elliott for applications focused on epilepsy due to SCN8A mutations; and the TS Alliance for applications focused on epilepsy associated with tuberous sclerosis complex (TSC).

Number awarded Varies each year.

Deadline Letters of intent must be submitted by October of each year; final proposals are due in January.

[1242]
AMERICAN GEOGRAPHICAL SOCIETY LIBRARY
FELLOWSHIP FOR MSI SCHOLARS

University of Wisconsin at Milwaukee
Attn: Libraries
American Geographical Society Library
2311 East Hartford Avenue
P.O. Box 399,
Milwaukee, WI 53201-0399
(414) 229-6282   Toll Free: (800) 558-8993
Fax: (414) 229-3624   E-mail: agsl@uwm.edu
Web: www.uwm.edu/libraries/agsl/fellowshipdescriptions

Summary To provide funding to pre- and postdoctoral scholars at Minority Serving Institutions (MSIs) interested in conducting research at the American Geographical Society Library (AGSL) of the University of Wisconsin at Milwaukee (UWM) Libraries.

Eligibility This program is open to established scholars and doctoral students who are affiliated with an MSI. Doctoral students must have completed their course work and be writing their dissertations. Individuals with a record of publication relevant to this program and those with government or business ties who could use the library's resources to further policy studies are also eligible. Applicants' research must benefit from extensive use of the AGSL, including (but not limited to) area studies, history of cartography, history of geographic thought, discovery and exploration, historical geography, other geographic themes with a significant historical component, or any topic that has policy, business, or similar applications.

Financial data The grant is $600 per week. Funds must be used to help pay travel and living expenses related to the residency.

Duration Up to 4 weeks.

Additional information Funding for this program is provided by a U.S. Department of Education National Resource Center grant.

Number awarded 1 or more each year.

Deadline November of each year.

[1243]
AMERICAN NURSES ASSOCIATION MINORITY FELLOWSHIP PROGRAM

American Nurses Association
Attn: SAMHSA Minority Fellowship Programs
8515 Georgia Avenue, Suite 400
Silver Spring, MD 20910-3492
(301) 628-5247   Toll Free: (800) 274-4ANA
Fax: (301) 628-5339   E-mail: janet.jackson@ana.org
Web: www.emfp.org

Summary To provide financial assistance to African American and other minority nurses who are doctoral candidates interested in psychiatric, mental health, and substance abuse issues that impact the lives of ethnic minority people.

Eligibility This program is open to nurses who have a master's degree and are members of an ethnic or racial minority group, including but not limited to Blacks or African Americans, Hispanics or Latinos, American Indians and Alaska Natives, Asians and Asian Americans, and Native Hawaiians and other Pacific Islanders. Applicants must be enrolled full time in an accredited doctoral nursing program. They must be certified as a Mental Health Nurse Practitioner, Mental Health Clinical Nurse Specialist, or Mental Health Nurse. U.S. citizenship or permanent resident status and membership in the American Nurses Association are required. Selection is based on commitment to a career in substance abuse in psychiatric/mental health issues affecting minority populations.

Financial data The program provides an annual stipend of $22,476 and tuition assistance up to $5,000.

Duration 3 to 5 years.

Additional information Funds for this program are provided by the Substance Abuse and Mental Health Services Administration (SAMHSA).

Number awarded 1 or more each year.

Deadline March of each year.

[1244]
AMERICAN SOCIETY FOR CELL BIOLOGY MINORITIES AFFAIRS COMMITTEE VISITING PROFESSOR AWARDS

American Society for Cell Biology
Attn: Minority Affairs Committee
8120 Woodmont Avenue, Suite 750
Bethesda, MD 20814-2762
(301) 347-9323   Fax: (301) 347-9310
E-mail: dmccall@ascb.org
Web: ascb.org/mac-visiting-professorship-awards

Summary To provide funding for summer research to faculty members at primarily teaching institutions that serve minority students and scientists, especially African Americans and other minorities.

Eligibility Eligible to apply for this support are professors at primarily teaching institutions. They must be interested in working in the laboratories of members of the American Society for Cell Biology during the summer. Hosts and visitor scientists are asked to submit their applications together as a proposed team. Minority professors and professors at Minority Serving Institutions are especially encouraged to apply for this award. Minorities are defined as U.S. citizens of Black, Native American, Chicano/Hispanic, or Pacific Islands background.

Financial data The stipend for the summer is $13,500 plus $700 for travel expenses and $4,000 to the host institution for supplies.

Duration From 8 to 10 weeks during the summer.

Additional information Funds for this program, established in 1997, are provided by the Minorities Access to Research Careers (MARC) program of the National Institutes of Health.

Number awarded Varies each year; recently, 3 were awarded.

Deadline March of each year.

[1245]
ANAC STUDENT DIVERSITY MENTORSHIP SCHOLARSHIP

Association of Nurses in AIDS Care
Attn: Awards Committee
3538 Ridgewood Road
Akron, OH 44333-3122
(330) 670-0101   Toll Free: (800) 260-6780
Fax: (330) 670-0109   E-mail: anac@anacnet.org
Web: www.nursesinaidscare.org

Summary To provide financial assistance to student nurses from African American and other minority groups who are interested in HIV/AIDS nursing and in attending the national conference of the Association of Nurses in AIDS Care (ANAC).

Eligibility This program is open to student nurses from a diverse racial or ethnic background, defined to include African Americans, Hispanics/Latinos, Asians/Pacific Islanders, and American Indians/Alaskan Natives. Candidates must have a genuine interest in HIV/AIDS nursing, be interested in attending the ANAC national conference, and desire to develop a mentorship relationship with a member of the ANAC Diversity Specialty Committee. They may be 1) pre-licensure students enrolled in an initial R.N. or L.P.N./L.V.N. program (i.e. L.P.N./L.V.N., A.D.N., diploma, B.S./B.S.N.); or 2) current licensed R.N. students with an associate or diploma degree who are enrolled in a bachelor's degree program. Nominees may be recommended by themselves, nursing faculty members, or ANAC members, but their nomination must be supported by an ANAC member. Along with their nomination form, they must submit a 2,000-character essay describing their interest or experience in HIV/AIDS care and why they want to attend the ANAC conference.

Financial data Recipients are awarded a $1,000 scholarship (paid directly to the school), up to $599 in reimbursement of travel expenses to attend the ANAC annual conference, free conference registration, an award plaque, a free ticket to the awards ceremony at the conference, and a 2-year ANAC membership.

Duration 1 year.

Additional information The mentor will be assigned at the conference and will maintain contact during the period of study.

Number awarded 1 each year.

Deadline August of each year.

[1246]
ANISFIELD-WOLF BOOK AWARDS

Cleveland Foundation
1422 Euclid Avenue, Suite 1300
Cleveland, OH 44115-2001
(216) 861-3810 Fax: (216) 861-1729
E-mail: Hello@anisfield-wolf.org
Web: www.anisfield-wolf.org

Summary To recognize and reward recent books that have contributed to an understanding of racism or appreciation of the rich diversity of human cultures.

Eligibility Works published in English during the preceding year that "contribute to our understanding of racism or our appreciation of the rich diversity of human cultures" are eligible to be considered. Entries may be either scholarly or imaginative (fiction, poetry, memoir). Plays and screenplays are not eligible, nor are works in progress. Manuscripts and self-published works are not eligible, and no grants are made for completing or publishing manuscripts.

Financial data The prize is $10,000. If more than 1 author is chosen in a given year, the prize is divided equally among the winning books.

Duration The award is presented annually.

Additional information This program began in 1936.

Number awarded 2 each year: 1 for fiction or poetry and 1 for nonfiction, biography, or scholarly research.

Deadline December of each year.

[1247]
APA/DIVISION 39 GRANT

American Psychological Foundation
750 First Street, N.E.
Washington, DC 20002-4242
(202) 336-5843 Fax: (202) 336-5812
E-mail: foundation@apa.org
Web: www.apa.org/apf/funding/division-39.aspx

Summary To provide funding to psychologists who wish to conduct psychoanalytical research related to African Americans and other underserved populations.

Eligibility This program is open to psychologists who have a demonstrated knowledge of psychoanalytical principles. Applicants may be, but are not required to be, practicing psychoanalytic therapists. Preference is given to graduate students involved in dissertation research, early-career professionals, and/or those who demonstrate a long-term interest in research related to underserved populations. The research may be of an empirical, theoretical, or clinical nature. Selection is based on conformance with stated program goals and qualifications; quality and potential impact of both previous and proposed research projects; originality, innovation, and contribution to the field with both previous and proposed research projects; and applicant's demonstrated interest in research related to underserved populations. The sponsor encourages applications from individuals who represent diversity in race, ethnicity, gender, age, disability, and sexual orientation.

Financial data The grant is $4,000.

Duration 1 year.

Additional information This program, which began in 2014, is sponsored by the American Psychological Association's Division 39 (Psychoanalysis).

Number awarded 1 each year.

Deadline July of each year.

[1248]
APA/SAMHSA MINORITY FELLOWSHIP PROGRAM

American Psychiatric Association
Attn: Division of Diversity and Health Equity
1000 Wilson Boulevard, Suite 1825
Arlington, VA 22209-3901
(703) 907-8653 Toll Free: (888) 35-PSYCH
Fax: (703) 907-7852 E-mail: mking@psych.org
Web: www.psychiatry.org/minority-fellowship

Summary To provide educational enrichment to psychiatrists-in-training, especialy African Americans and other minorities, who are interested in providing quality and effective services to minorities and the underserved.

Eligibility This program is open to residents who are in at least their second year of psychiatric training, members of the American Psychiatric Association (APA), and U.S. citizens or permanent residents. A goal of the program is to develop leadership to improve the quality of mental health care for members of ethnic minority groups (African Americans, American Indians, Native Alaskans, Asian Americans, Native Hawaiians, Native Pacific Islanders, and Hispanics/Latinos). Applicants must be interested in working with a component of the APA that is of interest to them and relevant to their career goals. Along with their application, they must submit a 2-page essay on how the fellowship would be utilized to alter their present training and ultimately assist them in achieving their career goals. Selection is based on commitment to serve ethnic minority populations, demonstrated leadership abilities, awareness of the importance of culture in mental health, and interest in the interrelationship between mental health/illness and transcultural factors.

Financial data Fellows receive a monthly stipend (amount not specified) and reimbursement of transportation, lodging, meals, and incidentals in connection with attendance at program-related activities. They are expected to use the funds to enhance their own professional development, improve training in cultural competence at their training institution, improve awareness of culturally relevant issues in psychiatry at their institution, expand research in areas relevant to minorities and underserved populations, enhance the current treatment modalities for minority patients and underserved individuals at their institution, and improve awareness in the surrounding community about mental health issues (particularly with regard to minority populations).

Duration 1 year; may be renewed 1 additional year.

Additional information Funding for this program is provided by the Substance Abuse and Mental Health Services Administration (SAMHSA). As part of their assignment to an APA component, fellows must attend the fall component meetings in September and the APA annual meeting in May. At those meeting, they can share their experiences as residents and minorities and discuss issues that impact on minority populations. This program is an outgrowth of the fellowships that were established in 1974 under a grant from the National Institute of Mental Health in answer to concerns about the underrepresentation of minorities in psychiatry.

Number awarded Varies each year; recently, 21 were awarded.

Deadline January of each year.

[1249]
ARTTABLE MENTORED INTERNSHIPS FOR DIVERSITY IN THE VISUAL ARTS PROFESSIONS

ArtTable Inc.
1 East 53rd Street, Fifth Floor
New York, NY 10022
(212) 343-1735   Fax: (866) 363-4188
E-mail: info@arttable.org
Web: www.arttable.org/summermentoredinternship

Summary To provide an opportunity for African American and other women from diverse backgrounds to gain mentored work experience during the summer and to prepare for a career as an art professional.

Eligibility This program is open to women who are college seniors, recent graduates, or graduate students and interested in preparing for a career as a visual arts professional (including administrative director, art adviser, art appraiser, art critic, art dealer, art librarian, arts funder, arts lawyer, conservator, curator, editor, educator, fundraiser, management consultant, public relations consultant, writer). Applicants must be from a cultural or ethnic background that is underrepresented in the field. They must be interested in working during the summer with a mentor at an art museum or similar facility. U.S. citizenship or permanent resident status is required.

Financial data The stipend is $3,000. The hosting institution or mentor receives $500 for administrative and other costs.

Duration 8 weeks during the summer.

Additional information This program began in 2000. Support is provided by the Samuel H. Kress Foundation.

Number awarded Varies each year; recently, 5 of these internships were awarded.

Deadline February of each year.

[1250]
ASH-AMFDP AWARDS

American Society of Hematology
Attn: Awards Manager
2021 L Street, N.W., Suite 900
Washington, DC 20036
(202) 776-0544   Fax: (202) 776-0545
E-mail: awards@hematology.org
Web: www.hematology.org

Summary To provide an opportunity for African American and other historically disadvantaged postdoctoral physicians to conduct a research project in hematology.

Eligibility This program is open to postdoctoral physicians who are members of historically disadvantaged groups, defined as individuals who face challenges because of their race, ethnicity, socioeconomic status, or other similar factors. Applicants must be committed to a career in academic medicine in hematology and to serving as a role model for students and faculty of similar backgrounds. They must identify a mentor at their institution to work with them and give them research and career guidance. Selection is based on excellence in educational career; willingness to devote 4 consecu-

tive years to research; and commitment to an academic career, improving the health status of the underserved, and decreasing health disparities. U.S. citizenship or permanent resident status is required.

Financial data The grant includes a stipend of up to $75,000 per year, a grant of $30,000 per year for support of research activities, complimentary membership in the American Society of Hematology (ASH), and travel support to attend the ASH annual meeting.

Duration 4 years.

Additional information This program, first offered in 2006, is a partnership between the ASH and the Robert Wood Johnson Foundation, whose Minority Medical Faculty Development Program (MMFDP) was renamed the Harold Amos Medical Faculty Development Program (AMFDP) in honor of the first African American to chair a department at the Harvard Medical School. Scholars must spend at least 70% of their time in research activities.

Number awarded At least 1 each year.

Deadline March of each year.

[1251]
AWARDS FOR FACULTY AT HISTORICALLY BLACK COLLEGES AND UNIVERSITIES

National Endowment for the Humanities
Attn: Division of Research Programs
400 Seventh Street, S.W.
Washington, DC 20506
(202) 606-8200   Toll Free: (800) NEH-1121
Fax: (202) 606-8204   TDD: (866) 372-2930
E-mail: FacultyAwards@neh.gov
Web: www.neh.gov

Summary To provide funding for research to faculty at Historically Black Colleges and Universities (HBCUs).

Eligibility This program is open to faculty members at HBCUs who are interested in conducting research of value to humanities scholars, students, or general audiences. Eligible projects include conducting research in primary and secondary sources; producing articles, monographs, books, digital materials, archaeological site reports, translations, editions, or other scholarly resources; or conducting basic research leading to the improvement of an existing undergraduate course or the achievement or institutional or community research goals. Applicants must be U.S. citizens or foreign nationals who have lived in the United States for at least 3 years. They are not required to have advanced degrees, but individuals enrolled in a degree-granting program are ineligible.

Financial data The grant is $4,200 per month, to a maximum of $50,400 for 12 months.

Duration 2 to 12 months.

Number awarded Approximately 3 each year.

Deadline April of each year.

[1252]
BRONSON T.J. TREMBLAY MEMORIAL SCHOLARSHIP

Colorado Nurses Foundation
Attn: Scholarships
P.O. Box 3406
Englewood, CO 80155
(303) 694-4728   Toll Free: (800) 205-6655
Fax: (303) 200-7099   E-mail: mail@cnfound.org
Web: www.coloradonursesfoundation.com/?page_id=1087

Summary To provide financial assistance to African American and other non-white male undergraduate and graduate nursing students in Colorado.

Eligibility This program is open to non-white male Colorado residents who have been accepted as a student in an approved nursing program in the state. Applicants may be 1) second-year students in an associate degree program; 2) junior or senior level B.S.N. undergraduate students; 3) R.N.s enrolled in a baccalaureate or higher degree program in a school of nursing; 4) R.N.s with a master's degree in nursing, currently practicing in Colorado and enrolled in a doctoral program; or 5) students in the second or third year of a Doctorate Nursing Practice (D.N.P.) or Ph.D. program. Undergraduates must have a GPA of 3.25 or higher and graduate students must have a GPA of 3.5 or higher. Selection is based on professional philosophy and goals, dedication to the improvement of patient care in Colorado, demonstrated commitment to nursing, potential for leadership, involvement in community and professional organizations, recommendations, GPA, and financial need.

Financial data The stipend is $1,000.

Duration 1 year.

Number awarded 1 each year.

Deadline October of each year.

[1253]
BYRD FELLOWSHIP PROGRAM

Ohio State University
Byrd Polar and Climate Research Center
Attn: Fellowship Committee
Scott Hall Room 108
1090 Carmack Road
Columbus, OH 43210-1002
(614) 292-6531   Fax: (614) 292-4697
E-mail: contact@bpcrc.osu.edu
Web: bpcrc.osu.edu/byrdfellow

Summary To provide funding to postdoctorates, especially African Americans and members of other underrepresented groups, who are interested in conducting research on the Arctic or Antarctic areas at Ohio State University.

Eligibility This program is open to postdoctorates of superior academic background who are interested in conducting advanced research on either Arctic or Antarctic problems at the Byrd Polar and Climate Research Center at Ohio State University. Applicants must have received their doctorates within the past 5 years. Along with their application, they must submit a description of the specific research to be conducted during the fellowship and a curriculum vitae. Women, minorities, Vietnam-era veterans, disabled veterans, and individuals with disabilities are particularly encouraged to apply.

Financial data The stipend is $44,000 per year; an allowance of $5,000 for research and travel is also provided.

Duration 18 months.

Additional information This program was established by a major gift from the Byrd Foundation in memory of Rear Admiral Richard Evelyn Byrd and Marie Ames Byrd, his wife. Except for field work or other research activities requiring absence from campus, fellows are expected to be in residence at the university for the duration of the program.

Number awarded 1 each year.

Deadline March of each year.

[1254]
CAREER DEVELOPMENT AWARDS IN DIABETES RESEARCH

Juvenile Diabetes Research Foundation International
Attn: Senior Director, Research Administration
26 Broadway, 14th Floor
New York, NY 10004
(212) 479-7519   Toll Free: (800) 533-CURE
Fax: (212) 785-9595   E-mail: emilligan@jdrf.org
Web: grantcenter.jdrf.org

Summary To assist young scientists, especially African Americans and members of other underrepresented groups, to develop into independent investigators in diabetes-related research.

Eligibility This program is open to postdoctorates early in their faculty careers who show promise as diabetes researchers. Applicants must have received their first doctoral (M.D., Ph.D., D.M.D., D.V.M., or equivalent) degree at least 3 but not more than 7 years previously. They may not have an academic position at the associate professor, professor, or equivalent level, but they must be a faculty member (instructor or assistant professor) at a university, health science center, or comparable institution with strong, well-established research and training programs. The proposed research must relate to Type 1 diabetes, but it may be basic or clinical. There are no citizenship requirements. Applications are encouraged from women, members of minority groups underrepresented in the sciences, and people with disabilities. The proposed research may be conducted at foreign or domestic, for-profit or non-profit, or public or private institutions, including universities, colleges, hospitals, laboratories, units of state or local government, or eligible agencies of the federal government. Selection is based on the applicant's perceived ability and potential for a career in Type 1 diabetes research, the caliber of the proposed research, and the quality and commitment of the host institution.

Financial data The total award may be up to $150,000 each year. Indirect costs cannot exceed 10%.

Duration Up to 5 years.

Additional information Fellows must spend up to 75% of their time in research.

Number awarded Varies each year; recently, 2 were awarded.

Deadline July of each year.

[1255]
CAROLINE CRAIG AUGUSTYN AND DAMIAN AUGUSTYN AWARD IN DIGESTIVE CANCER

American Gastroenterological Association
Attn: AGA Research Foundation
Research Awards Manager
4930 Del Ray Avenue
Bethesda, MD 20814-2512
(301) 222-4012   Fax: (301) 654-5920
E-mail: awards@gastro.org
Web: www.gastro.org

Summary To provide funding to junior investigators, especially African Americans and other underrepresented minorities, who are interested in conducting research related to digestive cancer.

Eligibility Applicants must have an M.D., Ph.D., or equivalent degree and a full-time faculty position at an accredited North American institution. They must have received an NIH K series or other federal or non-federal career development award of at least 4 years duration, but may not have received an R01 or equivalent award. For M.D. applicants, no more than 7 years may have elapsed following the completion of clinical training, and for Ph.D. applicants no more than 7 years may have elapsed since the completion of their degree. Individual membership in the American Gastroenterology Association (AGA) is required. The proposal must relate to the pathogenesis, prevention, diagnosis, or treatment of digestive cancer. Women and underrepresented minority investigators are strongly encouraged to apply. Selection is based on the qualifications of the candidate; the novelty, feasibility, and significance of their research; and their potential for an independent research career.

Financial data The grant is $40,000. Funds may be used for salary, supplies, or equipment. Indirect costs are not allowed.

Duration 1 year.

Number awarded 1 each year.

Deadline January of each year.

[1256]
CARRINGTON-HSIA-NIEVES SCHOLARSHIP FOR MIDWIVES OF COLOR

American College of Nurse-Midwives
Attn: ACNM Foundation, Inc.
8403 Colesville Road, Suite 1550
Silver Spring, MD 20910-6374
(240) 485-1850   Fax: (240) 485-1818
E-mail: foundation@acnmf.org
Web: www.midwife.org

Summary To provide financial assistance to African American and other midwives of color who are members of the American College of Nurse-Midwives (ACNM) and engaged in doctoral or postdoctoral study.

Eligibility This program is open to ACNM members of color who are certified nurse midwives (CNM) or certified midwives (CM). Applicants must be enrolled in a program of doctoral or postdoctoral education. Along with their application, they must submit brief statements on their 5-year academic career plans, their intended use of the funds, and their intended future participation in the local, regional, and/or national activities of the ACNM and in activities that otherwise contribute substantially to midwifery research, education, or practice.

Financial data The stipend is $5,000.

Duration 1 year.

Number awarded 1 each year.

Deadline October of each year.

[1257]
CARTER G. WOODSON INSTITUTE POSTDOCTORAL RESIDENTIAL RESEARCH AND TEACHING FELLOWSHIP

University of Virginia
Carter G. Woodson Institute for African-American and
  African Studies
Attn: Director of the Fellowship Program
108 Minor Hall
P.O. Box 400162
Charlottesville, VA 22904-4162
(434) 924-3109   Fax: (434) 924-8820
E-mail: woodson@virginia.edu
Web: www.woodson.virginia.edu/fellowship/postdoc

Summary To support postdoctoral research at the University of Virginia's Woodson Institute in those disciplines of the humanities and social sciences concerned with African American and African studies.

Eligibility Applicants for postdoctoral fellowships must have completed their Ph.D. by the time of application or furnish proof of its receipt before July of the fellowship year. They must be interested in conducting research in the fields of African American studies, African studies, or Afro-Caribbean studies, and in those disciplines within the humanities and social sciences traditionally related to those fields. Preference is given to applicants whose work 1) advances theories on the construction of race and race in relation to other social identities (class, gender, sexuality, nationality, disability) as well as that which focuses on refining methods of interdisciplinary scholarship on race; 2) engages the professions (law, medicine, social work, public policy, education, architecture, planning) in innovative ways; or 3) can be readily adapted for the creation of courses and pedagogies directly related to the institute's curriculum in African American and Diasporic Studies. Selection is based on the significance of the proposed work, the qualifications of the applicant, familiarity with existing relevant research literature, the research design of the project, and the promise of completion within the award period. Awards are granted without restriction on citizenship or current residence.

Financial data The grant is $45,000 per year.

Duration 2 years.

Additional information Fellows must be in residence at the University of Virginia for the duration of the award period. They are expected to contribute to the intellectual life of the university.

Number awarded 1 or 2 each year.

Deadline November of each year.

[1258]
CAVE CANEM FELLOWSHIP

Vermont Studio Center
80 Pearl Street
P.O. Box 613
Johnson, VT 05656
(802) 635-2727　　　　　　　　Fax: (802) 635-2730
E-mail: info@vermontstudiocenter.org
Web: www.vermontstudiocenter.org

Summary To provide funding to African American poets who are interested in a residency at the Vermont Studio Center in Johnson, Vermont.

Eligibility This program is open to African American poets who are interested in a residency at the center in Johnson, Vermont. Applicants must submit up to 10 pages of their work. Selection is based on artistic merit.

Financial data The award pays $3,950, which covers all residency fees.

Duration 4 weeks.

Additional information This fellowship, first awarded in 2009, is sponsored by Cave Canem, an organization of African American poets founded in 1996.

Number awarded 1 each year.

Deadline June of each year.

[1259]
CENTER FOR ADVANCED STUDY IN THE BEHAVIORAL SCIENCES FELLOWSHIPS

Center for Advanced Study in the Behavioral Sciences
Attn: Secretary and Program Coordinator
75 Alta Road
Stanford, CA 94305-8090
(650) 736-0100　　　　　　　　Fax: (650) 736-0221
E-mail: casbs-info@casbs.org
Web: casbs.stanford.edu/fellowships

Summary To provide funding to behavioral scientists, especially African Americans and members of other underrepresented groups, who are interested in conducting research at Stanford University's Center for Advanced Study in the Behavioral Sciences.

Eligibility Eligible to be nominated for this fellowship are scientists and scholars from this country or abroad who show exceptional accomplishment or promise in the core social and behavioral disciplines: anthropology, economics, history, political science, psychology, or sociology; applications are also accepted from scholars in a wide range of humanistic disciplines, communications, education, linguistics, and the biological, computer, health, and natural sciences. Selection is based on standing in the field rather than on the merit of a particular project under way at a given time. A special effort is made to promote diversity among the scholars by encouraging participation from groups that often have been overlooked in academia: women, minorities, international scholars, and scholars from a wide variety of colleges and universities.

Financial data The stipend is based on the fellow's regular salary for the preceding year, with a cap of $73,000. In most cases, the fellow contributes to the cost of the stipend with support from sabbatical or other funding source.

Duration From 9 to 11 months.

Additional information This program partners with the Berggruen Institute to select fellows whose work focuses on understanding technological, social, and cultural changes that may radically transform humanity; the American Council of Learned Societies to participate in the Frederick Burkhardt Residential Fellowship Program; the William T. Grant Foundation to select scholars whose work emphasizes reducing inequality; the Mindset Scholars Network which hosts a fellow who is interested in interdisciplinary scholarship on mindsets and serving in a leadership role in the Mindset research community; the Presence-CASBS Fellowship that addresses focus areas of harnessing technology for the human experience in medicine, studying and advocating for the patient-physician relationship, and reducing medical errors; the Stanford Cyber Initiative which selects a fellow who will be engaged in producing policy-relevant research on the integration of cyber technologies in our ways of life and informing debate about urgent cyber issues; and the National Applied Research Laboratories of Taiwan which selects a fellow in the behavioral and social sciences from Taiwan. Fellows must be in residence in a community within 10 miles of the center for the duration of the program (that requirement excludes San Francisco, Berkeley, and San Jose, for example).

Number awarded Approximately 45 each year.

Deadline November of each year.

[1260]
CHEST DIVERSITY COMMITTEE MINORITY INVESTIGATOR RESEARCH GRANT

American College of Chest Physicians
Attn: The CHEST Foundation
2595 Patriot Boulevard
Glenview, IL 60026
(224) 521-9527　　　　　　　　Toll Free: (800) 343-2227
Fax: (224) 521-9801　　　　　　E-mail: grants@chestnet.org
Web: www.chestnet.org

Summary To provide funding to African American and other minority physicians who are interested in conducting clinical or translational research on topics of interest to the American College of Chest Physicians (ACCP).

Eligibility This program is open to members of the ACCP who are members of an underrepresented group (African American, Latin American, Hispanic American, Asian/Pacific Island American, Native American, women). Applicants must be interested in conducting a clinical or translational research project that contributes to the understanding of the pathophysiology or treatment of conditions or diseases related to pulmonary, cardiovascular, critical care, or sleep medicine. They may be at later career stages, but special consideration is given to those within 5 years of completing an advanced training program.

Financial data The grant is $25,000.

Duration 1 year, beginning in July.

Additional information This program is supported in part by AstraZeneca.

Number awarded 1 each year.

Deadline April of each year.

[1261]
CHIPS QUINN SCHOLARS PROGRAM

Newseum Institute
Attn: Chips Quinn Scholars Program
555 Pennsylvania Avenue, N.W.
Washington, DC 20001
(202) 292-6271   Fax: (202) 292-6275
E-mail: kcatone@freedomforum.org
Web: www.newseuminstitute.org

Summary To provide work experience to African American and other minority college students and recent graduates who are majoring in journalism.

Eligibility This program is open to students of color who are college juniors, seniors, graduate students, or recent graduates with journalism majors or career goals in newspapers. Candidates must be nominated or endorsed by journalism faculty, campus media advisers, editors of newspapers, or leaders of minority journalism associations. Along with their application, they must submit a resume, transcripts, 2 letters of recommendation, and an essay of 200 to 400 words on why they want to be a Chips Quinn Scholar. Reporters and copy editors must also submit 6 samples of published articles they have written; photographers must submit 15 to 25 photographs on a DVD; multimedia journalists and graphic designers should submit 6 to 10 samples of their work on a DVD. Applicants must have a car and be available to work as a fulltime intern during the spring or summer. U.S. citizenship or permanent resident status is required. Campus newspaper experience is strongly encouraged.

Financial data Students chosen for this program receive a travel stipend to attend a Multimedia training program in Nashville, Tennessee prior to reporting for their internship, a $500 housing allowance from the Freedom Forum, and a competitive salary during their internship.

Duration Internships are for 10 to 12 weeks, in spring or summer.

Additional information This program began in 1991 in memory of the late John D. Quinn Jr., managing editor of the *Poughkeepsie Journal*. Funding is provided by the Freedom Forum, formerly the Gannett Foundation. After graduating from college and obtaining employment with a newspaper, alumni of this program are eligible to apply for fellowship support to attend professional journalism development activities.

Number awarded Approximately 70 each year. Since the program began, more than 1,300 scholars have been selected.

Deadline September of each year.

[1262]
CIVIL SOCIETY INSTITUTE FELLOWSHIPS

Vermont Studio Center
80 Pearl Street
P.O. Box 613
Johnson, VT 05656
(802) 635-2727   Fax: (802) 635-2730
E-mail: info@vermontstudiocenter.org
Web: www.vermontstudiocenter.org/fellowships

Summary To provide funding to African American and other minority artists from the East Coast who are interested in a residency at the Vermont Studio Center in Johnson, Vermont.

Eligibility Eligible to apply for this support are painters, sculptors, printmakers, new and mixed-media artists, photographers who are members of a minority group and residents of the East Coast. Preference is given to applicants from New Haven (Connecticut), Jersey City (New Jersey), or Baltimore (Maryland). Applicants must be interested in a residency at the center in Johnson, Vermont. Visual artists must submit up to 20 slides or visual images of their work, poets must submit up to 10 pages, and other writers must submit 10 to 15 pages. Selection is based on artistic merit and financial need.

Financial data The residency fee of $3,950 covers studio space, room, board, lectures, and studio visits. The fellowship pays all residency fees plus a $500 travel stipend.

Duration 4 weeks.

Additional information This program is sponsored by the Institute for Civil Society.

Number awarded 3 each year (1 for each term).

Deadline February, June, or September of each year.

[1263]
CONGRESSIONAL BLACK CAUCUS FOUNDATION CONGRESSIONAL FELLOWS PROGRAM

Congressional Black Caucus Foundation, Inc.
Attn: Leadership Institute for Public Service
1720 Massachusetts Avenue, N.W.
Washington, DC 20036
(202) 263-2800   Toll Free: (800) 784-2577
Fax: (202) 775-0773   E-mail: internships@cbcfinc.org
Web: www.cbcfinc.org

Summary To provide African Americans with the opportunity to work directly with members of Congress on their committees or as personal staff.

Eligibility This program is open to African Americans who have a master's or professional degree and familiarity with the federal legislative process, Congress, the Congressional Black Caucus (CBC), and its members. Applicants must be interested in working in Washington, D.C. on the staff or committee of a member of the CBC. They must be able to demonstrate an interest in public policy, a record of academic and professional achievement, evidence of leadership skills, potential for further growth, and U.S. citizenship or permit to work in the United States. Preference is given to applicants with expertise in areas that support policy agendas of CBC members.

Financial data The stipend is $40,000; fellows are responsible for their own travel, housing, and other expenses.

Duration 20 months, beginning in September.

Additional information This program began in 1976 as a graduate intern program and was expanded to its present form in 1982.

Number awarded 6 to 9 each year.

Deadline March of each year.

[1264]
COVIDIEN RESEARCH AND DEVELOPMENT PILOT AWARD IN TECHNOLOGY

American Gastroenterological Association
Attn: AGA Research Foundation
Research Awards Manager
4930 Del Ray Avenue
Bethesda, MD 20814-2512
(301) 222-4012   Fax: (301) 654-5920
E-mail: awards@gastro.org
Web: www.gastro.org

Summary To provide funding to investigators, especially African Americans and other minorities, who are interested in conducting research and development of devices or technologies that may impact the diagnosis or treatment of digestive disease.

Eligibility This program is open to investigators interested in researching and developing new devices, designing and testing a significant improvement to an existing technology, developing a new diagnostic, developing a novel research method technology, and/or investigating the application of nanotechnology or methodologies such as computational biology to the field of gastroenterology. Applicants must have an M.D. or Ph.D. degree and a full-time faculty position at a North American educational institution. Membership in the American Gastroenterological Association (AGA) is required. Selection is based primarily on the potential impact of the study on diagnosing or treating digestive disease. Women and minorities are strongly encouraged to apply.

Financial data The grant is $30,000. Funds are to be used for project costs, including salary, supplies, and equipment but excluding travel. Indirect costs are not allowed. An additional $1,000 is provided as a travel stipend to attend the AGA Technology Summit.

Duration 1 year.

Number awarded 1 each year.

Deadline January of each year.

[1265]
DARLENE CLARK HINE AWARD

Organization of American Historians
Attn: Award and Committee Coordinator
112 North Bryan Street
Bloomington, IN 47408-4141
(812) 855-7311   Fax: (812) 855-0696
E-mail: khamm@oah.org
Web: www.oah.org

Summary To recognize and reward authors of outstanding books dealing with African American women's and gender history.

Eligibility This award is presented to the author of the outstanding book in African American women's and gender history. Entries must have been published during the current calendar year.

Financial data The award is $1,000.

Duration The award is presented annually.

Additional information This award was first presented in 2010.

Number awarded 1 each year.

Deadline September of each year.

[1266]
DEEP CARBON OBSERVATORY DIVERSITY GRANTS

American Geosciences Institute
Attn: Grant Coordinator
4220 King Street
Alexandria, VA 22302-1502
(703) 379-2480   Fax: (703) 379-7563
E-mail: hrhp@agiweb.org
Web: www.americangeosciences.org

Summary To provide funding to geoscientists who are African Americans or members of other underrepresented ethnic groups and interested in participating in research and other activities of the Deep Carbon Observatory (DCO) project.

Eligibility This program is open to traditionally underrepresented geoscientists (e.g., African Americans, Native Americans, Native Alaskans, Hispanics, Latinos, Latinas, Native Hawaiians, Native Pacific Islanders, Filipinos, of mixed racial/ethnic backgrounds) who are U.S. citizens or permanent residents. Applicants must be interested in participating in the DCO, a global research program focused on understanding carbon in Earth, and must have research interests that are aligned with its mission. They may be doctoral students, postdoctoral researchers, or early-career faculty members or research staff.

Financial data Grants average $5,000.

Duration 1 year.

Additional information This program is funded by the Alfred P. Sloan Foundation.

Number awarded 4 or 5 each year.

Deadline April of each year.

[1267]
DIETETIC INTERNSHIP SCHOLARSHIPS

Academy of Nutrition and Dietetics
Attn: Foundation
120 South Riverside Plaza, Suite 2000
Chicago, IL 60606-6995
(312) 899-4821   Toll Free: (800) 877-1600, ext. 4821
Fax: (312) 899-4796   E-mail: scholarship@eatright.org
Web: www.eatrightacend.org

Summary To provide financial assistance to student members of the Academy of Nutrition and Dietetics, especially African Americans and other underrepresented minorities, who have applied for a dietetic internship.

Eligibility This program is open to student members who have applied for an accredited dietetic internship. Applicants must be participating in the computer-matching process, be U.S. citizens or permanent residents, and show promise of being a valuable, contributing member of the profession. Some scholarships require membership in a specific dietetic practice group, residency in a specific state, or underrepresented minority group status. The same application form can be used for all categories. Students who are currently completing the internship component of a combined graduate/dietetic internship should apply for the Academy of Nutrition and Dietetics' Graduate Scholarship.

Financial data Stipends range from $500 to $10,000 but most are for $1,000.

Duration 1 year.

Additional information The Academy of Nutrition and Dietetics was formerly the American Dietetic Association.

Number awarded Approximately 40 each year.

Deadline February of each year.

[1268]
DOCTORAL/POST-DOCTORAL FELLOWSHIP PROGRAM IN LAW AND SOCIAL SCIENCE

American Bar Foundation
Attn: Administrative Assistant for Academic Affairs and
   Research Administration
750 North Lake Shore Drive
Chicago, IL 60611-4403
(312) 988-6517   Fax: (312) 988-6579
E-mail: aehrhardt@abfn.org
Web: www.americanbarfoundation.org

Summary To provide research funding to scholars, especially African Americans and other minorities, who are completing or have completed doctoral degrees in fields related to law, the legal profession, and legal institutions.

Eligibility This program is open to Ph.D. candidates in the social sciences who have completed all doctoral requirements except the dissertation. Applicants who have completed the dissertation are also eligible. Doctoral and proposed research must be in the general area of sociolegal studies or in social scientific approaches to law, the legal profession, or legal institutions and legal processes. Applications must include 1) a dissertation abstract or proposal with an outline of the substance and methods of the research; 2) 2 letters of recommendation; and 3) a curriculum vitae. Minority candidates are especially encouraged to apply.

Financial data The stipend is $30,000. Fellows may request up to $1,500 to reimburse expenses associated with research, travel to meet with advisers, or travel to conferences at which papers are presented. Relocation expenses of up to $2,500 may be reimbursed on application.

Duration 12 months, beginning in September.

Additional information Fellows are offered access to the computing and word processing facilities of the American Bar Foundation and the libraries of Northwestern University and the University of Chicago. This program was established in 1996. Fellowships must be held in residence at the American Bar Foundation. Appointments to the fellowship are full time; fellows are not permitted to undertake other work.

Number awarded 1 or more each year.

Deadline December of each year.

[1269]
DONALD M. PAYNE FOREIGN POLICY FELLOWS PROGRAM

Congressional Black Caucus Foundation, Inc.
Attn: Leadership Institute for Public Service
1720 Massachusetts Avenue, N.W.
Washington, DC 20036
(202) 263-2800   Toll Free: (800) 784-2577
Fax: (202) 775-0773   E-mail: internships@cbcfinc.org
Web: www.cbcfinc.org

Summary To provide an opportunity for young professionals to work on a program of training in foreign policy issues in collaboration with the Congressional Black Caucus (CBC).

Eligibility This program is open to professionals who have a graduate or professional degree in a foreign policy-related field and familiarity with the federal legislative process, Congress, and the CBC. Applicants must be interested in working in Washington, D.C. on foreign policy-related issues, especially how those policies affect African Americans and other minorities, as a member of the staff or committee of a member of the CBC. They must be able to demonstrate an interest in public policy, commitment to creating and implementing policy to improve the living conditions for underserved and underrepresented individuals, a record of academic and professional achievement, evidence of leadership skills, the potential for further growth, and U.S. citizenship or permit to work in the United States.

Financial data Fellows receive a stipend of $40,000 per year and benefits.

Duration 20 months, beginning in September.

Additional information This program began in 2012. Fellows are assigned to Congressional offices or committees and work on issues related to foreign policy.

Number awarded 1 or more each year.

Deadline March of each year.

[1270]
DOROTHY BRACY/JANICE JOSEPH MINORITY AND WOMEN NEW SCHOLAR AWARD

Academy of Criminal Justice Sciences
7339A Hanover Parkway
P.O. Box 960
Greenbelt, MD 20768-0960
(301) 446-6300   Toll Free: (800) 757-ACJS
Fax: (301) 446-2819   E-mail: info@acjs.org
Web: www.acjs.org/Awards

Summary To recognize and reward african American and other minority junior scholars who have made outstanding contributions to the field of criminal justice.

Eligibility This award is available to members of the Academy of Criminal Justice Sciences (ACJS) who are members of a group that has experienced historical discrimination, including ethnic minorities and women. Applicants must have obtained a Ph.D. in a field of criminal justice within the past 7 years and be able to demonstrate a strong record as a new scholar in the areas of research, teaching, and service.

Financial data The award is $1,000.

Duration The award is presented annually.

Number awarded 1 each year.

Deadline October of each year.

[1271]
DR. BESSIE ELIZABETH DELANEY FELLOWSHIP

National Dental Association
Attn: National Dental Association Foundation, Inc.
3517 16th Street, N.W.
Washington, DC 20010
(734) 544-1336   E-mail: admin@ndaonline.org
Web: www.ndafoundation.org

Summary To provide financial assistance to women who are African Americans or members of other minority groups and interested in working on a postdoctoral degree in fields related to dentistry.

Eligibility This program is open to female members of minority groups who are working on a postdoctoral degree in an area related to dentistry, such as public health, administration, pediatrics, research, or law. Students working on a master's degree beyond their residency may be considered. Applicants must be members of the National Dental Association (NDA) and U.S. citizens or permanent residents. Along with their application, they must submit a letter explaining why they should be considered for this scholarship, 2 letters of recommendation, a curriculum vitae, a description of the program, nomination by their program director, and documentation of financial need.

Financial data The stipend is $10,000.

Duration 1 year.

Additional information This program, established in 1990, is supported by the Colgate-Palmolive Company.

Number awarded 1 each year.

Deadline May of each year.

[1272]
DR. CLIFTON AND LOIS DUMMETT FELLOWSHIP

National Dental Association
Attn: National Dental Association Foundation, Inc.
3517 16th Street, N.W.
Washington, DC 20010
(734) 544-1336   E-mail: admin@ndaonline.org
Web: www.ndafoundation.org/dummett-scholarship.html

Summary To provide financial assistance to African American and other minority students who are interested in working on a postdoctoral degree in fields related to dentistry.

Eligibility This program is open to members of minority groups who are working on a postdoctoral degree in an area related to dentistry, such as public health, administration, pediatrics, research, or law. Students working on a master's degree beyond their residency may be considered. Applicants must be members of the National Dental Association (NDA) and U.S. citizens or permanent residents. Along with their application, they must submit a letter explaining why they should be considered for this scholarship, 2 letters of recommendation, a curriculum vitae, a description of the program, nomination by their program director, and documentation of financial need.

Financial data The stipend is $10,000.

Duration 1 year.

Additional information This program, established in 1990, is supported by the Colgate-Palmolive Company.

Number awarded 1 each year.

Deadline May of each year.

[1273]
DR. DANIEL D. SAVAGE MEMORIAL SERVICE AWARD

Association of Black Cardiologists, Inc.
Attn: Membership Committee
122 East 42nd Street, 18th Floor
New York, NY 10068
Toll Free: (800) 753-9222   Fax: (888) 281-3574
E-mail: membershipservices@abcardio.org
Web: www.abcardio.org

Summary To recognize and reward scientific achievement in the areas of cardiovascular disease and research by members of the Association of Black Cardiologists.

Eligibility This award is available to scientists and researchers who have made major contributions to the advancement of scientific knowledge in the field of cardiovascular medicine. Nominees must be members of the Association of Black Cardiologists. Self-nominations are accepted.

Financial data The award is $2,000.

Duration The award is presented annually.

Additional information This award was first presented in 1990.

Number awarded 1 each year.

Deadline Nominations must be submitted by May of each year.

[1274]
DR. DAVID MONASH/HARRY LLOYD AND ELIZABETH PAWLETTE MARSHALL RESIDENCY SCHOLARSHIPS

National Medical Fellowships, Inc.
Attn: Scholarship Program
347 Fifth Avenue, Suite 510
New York, NY 10016
(212) 483-8880   Toll Free: (877) NMF-1DOC
Fax: (212) 483-8897 E-mail: scholarships@nmfonline.org
Web: www.nmfonline.org

Summary To provide funding for repayment of student loans and other expenses to African Amrican and other underrepresented medical residents in Chicago who are committed to remaining in the area and working to reduce health disparities.

Eligibility This program is open to residents of any state who graduated from a medical school in Chicago and are currently engaged in a clinical residency program in the area in primary care, community/family medicine, or a related field. U.S. citizenship is required. Applicants must be seeking funding for repayment of student loans and other residency-related expenses. They must identify as an underrepresented minority student in health care (defined as African American, Hispanic/Latino, American Indian, Alaska Native, Native Hawaiian, Vietnamese, Cambodian, or Pacific Islander) and/or socioeconomically disadvantaged student. Along with their application, they must submit documentation of financial status; a short biography; a resume; 2 letters of recommendation; a personal statement of 500 to 1,000 words on their personal and professional motivation for a medical career, their commitment to primary care and service in a health and/or community setting, their motivation for working to reduce health disparities, and their commitment to improving health care; a personal statement of 500 to 1,000 words on the experiences that are preparing them to practice in an underserved community; and a copy of a residency contract from a Chicago clinical residency program. Selection is based on demonstrated leadership early in career and commitment to serving medically underserved communities in Chicago.

Financial data The grant is $25,000, of which 80% must be used to decrease medical school debt.

Duration 1 year.

Additional information This program began in 2010 with support from the Chicago Community Trust.

Number awarded   4 each year.

Deadline   May of each year.

[1275]
DR. JAY BROWN BEST ABSTRACT AWARD

Association of Black Cardiologists, Inc.
Attn: Membership Committee
122 East 42nd Street, 18th Floor
New York, NY 10068
Toll Free: (800) 753-9222   Fax: (888) 281-3574
E-mail: membershipservices@abcardio.org
Web: www.abcardio.org/articles/abstractform.html

Summary   To recognize and reward cardiology residents and fellows who are members of the Association of Black Cardiologists (ABC) and submit outstanding abstracts.

Eligibility   This award is available to ABC members who are currently in a residency or cardiology fellowship training program. Applicants must submit an abstract for presentation at the ABC Annual Scientific Sessions that relates to cardiovascular disease; the research may be clinical, basic, or population science. They must also submit a 3-page essay that including their research interests and experiences, publications, career goals, and involvement in ABC.

Financial data   The winner receives an award of $1,000. The winner and honorable mentions receive up to $1,000 to attend the ABC Annual Scientific Sessions, where the winner presents the research paper.

Duration   The award is presented annually.

Number awarded   1 winner and 3 honorable mentions are selected each year.

Deadline   February of each year.

[1276]
DUBOIS-MANDELA-RODNEY FELLOWSHIP PROGRAM

University of Michigan
Attn: Department of Afroamerican and African Studies
4700 Haven Hall
505 South State Street
Ann Arbor, MI 48109-1045
(734) 764-5513   Fax: (734) 763-0543
E-mail: daas-info@umich.edu
Web: lsa.umich.edu

Summary   To provide funding to scholars who are interested in conducting research on African American, African, and Caribbean experiences at the University of Michigan's Department of Afroamerican and African Studies.

Eligibility   Applicants must have a Ph.D. in hand but be no more than 5 years beyond completion of their degree. They should be interested in conducting research on Africa or the African Diaspora at the center. Consideration is given to all disciplines, including, but not limited to, the humanities, social sciences, physical sciences, and professional schools. Scholars from or who study the Gullah speaking Sea islands, Cape Verde islands, the Anglophone Caribbean, the Canary Islands, Madagascar, and/or other less studied areas are especially encouraged to apply.

Financial data   The program provides a stipend of $42,000, health insurance, $1,000 for research, and up to $2,000 for travel expenses.

Duration   1 academic year, beginning in September of each even-numbered year.

Additional information   Fellows must spend their fellowship year at the University of Michigan's Center for Afroamerican and African Studies. They must conduct at least 1 seminar.

Number awarded   1 each even-numbered year.

Deadline   November of each odd-numbered year.

[1277]
DUPONT MINORITIES IN ENGINEERING AWARD

American Society for Engineering Education
Attn: Awards Administration
1818 N Street, N.W., Suite 600
Washington, DC 20036-2479
(202) 331-3550   Fax: (202) 265-8504
E-mail: board@asee.org
Web: www.asee.org

Summary   To recognize and reward outstanding achievements by engineering educators to increase diversity by ethnicity and gender in science, engineering, and technology.

Eligibility   Eligible for nomination are engineering or engineering technology educators who, as part of their educational activity, either assume or are charged with the responsibility of motivating underrepresented students to enter and continue in engineering or engineering technology curricula at the college or university level, graduate or undergraduate. Nominees must demonstrate leadership in the conception, organization, and operation of pre-college and college activities designed to increase participation by underrepresented students in engineering and engineering technology.

Financial data   The award consists of $1,500, a certificate, and a grant of $500 for travel expenses to the ASEE annual conference.

Duration   The award is granted annually.

Additional information   Funding for this award is provided by DuPont. It was originally established in 1956 as the Vincent Bendix Minorities in Engineering Award.

Number awarded   1 each year.

Deadline   January of each year.

[1278]
EARLY CAREER PATIENT-ORIENTED DIABETES RESEARCH AWARD

Juvenile Diabetes Research Foundation International
Attn: Senior Director, Research Administration
26 Broadway, 14th Floor
New York, NY 10004
(212) 479-7519   Toll Free: (800) 533-CURE
Fax: (212) 785-9595   E-mail: emilligan@jdrf.org
Web: grantcenter.jdrf.org

Summary   To provide funding to physician scientists (particularly women, African Americans and other minorities, and persons with disabilities) who are interested in pursuing a program of clinical diabetes-related research training.

Eligibility   This program is open to investigators in diabetes-related research who have an M.D. or M.D./Ph.D. degree and a faculty appointment at the late training or assistant professor level. Applicants must be sponsored by an investigator who is affiliated full time with an accredited institution, who pursues patient-oriented clinical research, and who agrees to supervise the applicant's training. There are no citizenship requirements. Applications are encouraged from women, members of minority groups underrepresented in the sciences, and people with disabilities. Areas of relevant research can include: mechanisms of human disease, therapeutic interventions, clinical trials, and the development of new technologies. The proposed research may be conducted at foreign or domestic, for-profit or nonprofit, or public or private institutions, including universities, colleges, hospitals, laboratories, units of state or local government, or eligible agencies of the federal government.

Financial data The total award may be up to $150,000 each year, up to $75,000 of which may be requested for research (including a technician, supplies, equipment, and travel). The salary request must be consistent with the established salary structure of the applicant's institution. Equipment purchases in years other than the first must be strongly justified. Indirect costs may not exceed 10%.

Duration The award is for 5 years and is generally nonrenewable.

Number awarded Varies each year.

Deadline July of each year.

[1279]
EDWARD A. BOUCHET AWARD

American Physical Society
Attn: Honors Program
One Physics Ellipse
College Park, MD 20740-3844
(301) 209-3268   Fax: (301) 209-0865
E-mail: honors@aps.org
Web: www.aps.org/programs/honors/awards/bouchet.cfm

Summary To recognize and reward outstanding research in physics by African Americans or members of other underrepresented minority group.

Eligibility Nominees for this award must be African Americans, Hispanic Americans, or Native Americans who have made significant contributions to physics research and are effective communicators.

Financial data The award consists of a grant of $3,500 to the recipient, a travel allowance for the recipient to visit 3 academic institutions to deliver lectures, and an allowance for travel expenses to the meeting of the American Physical Society (APS) at which the prize is presented.

Duration The award is presented annually.

Additional information This award was established in 1994 by a grant from the Research Corporation and is currently funded by institutional and individual donations. As part of the award, the recipient visits 3 academic institutions where the impact of the visit on minority students will be significant. The purpose of those visits is to deliver technical lectures on the recipient's field of specialization, to visit classrooms where appropriate, to assist the institution with precollege outreach efforts where appropriate, and to talk informally with faculty and students about research and teaching careers in physics.

Number awarded 1 each year.

Deadline June of each year.

[1280]
E.E. JUST ENDOWED RESEARCH FELLOWSHIP FUND

Marine Biological Laboratory
Attn: Division of Research
7 MBL Street
Woods Hole, MA 02543-1015
(508) 289-7173   Fax: (508) 457-1924
E-mail: research@mbl.edu
Web: www.mbl.edu/research/whitman-awards

Summary To provide funding to African American and other minority scientists who wish to conduct summer research at the Marine Biological Laboratory (MBL) in Woods Hole, Massachusetts.

Eligibility This program is open to minority faculty members who are interested in conducting summer research at the MBL. Applicants must submit a statement of the potential impact of this award on their career development. The program encourages applications focused on 1) evolutionary, genetic, and genomic approaches in developmental biology with an emphasis on novel marine organisms; and 2) integrated imaging and computational approaches to illuminate cellular function and biology emerging from the study of marine and other organisms.

Financial data Grants range from $5,000 to $25,000, typically to cover laboratory rental and/or housing costs. Awardees are responsible for other costs, such as supplies, shared resource usage, affiliated staff who accompany them, or travel.

Duration 4 to 10 weeks during the summer.

Number awarded 1 each year.

Deadline December of each year.

[1281]
ELSEVIER GUT MICROBIOME PILOT RESEARCH AWARD

American Gastroenterological Association
Attn: AGA Research Foundation
Research Awards Manager
4930 Del Ray Avenue
Bethesda, MD 20814-2512
(301) 222-4012   Fax: (301) 654-5920
E-mail: awards@gastro.org
Web: www.gastro.org

Summary To provide funding to new or established gastroenterologists, especially African Americans and other minorities, for pilot research projects in areas related to the gut microbiome.

Eligibility Applicants must have an M.D., Ph.D., or equivalent degree and a full-time faculty position at an accredited North American institution. They may not hold grants for projects on a similar topic from other agencies. Individual membership in the American Gastroenterology Association (AGA) is required. The proposal must enable investigators to obtain new data on the relationships of the gut microbiota to digestive health and disease that can ultimately lead to subsequent grant applications for more substantial funding and duration. Women and minority investigators are strongly encouraged to apply. Selection is based on novelty, importance, feasibility, environment, and overall likelihood that the project will lead to more substantial grants in gut microbiome research.

Financial data The grant is $25,000. Funds may be used for salary, supplies, or equipment. Indirect costs are not allowed.

Duration 1 year.

Additional information This award is sponsored by Elsevier Science.

Number awarded 1 each year.

Deadline January of each year.

[1282]
ELSEVIER PILOT RESEARCH AWARDS

American Gastroenterological Association
Attn: AGA Research Foundation
Research Awards Manager
4930 Del Ray Avenue
Bethesda, MD 20814-2512
(301) 222-4012　　　　　　　　Fax: (301) 654-5920
E-mail: awards@gastro.org
Web: www.gastro.org

Summary To provide funding to new or established investigators, especially African Americans and other minorities, for pilot research projects in areas related to gastroenterology or hepatology.

Eligibility Applicants must have an M.D., Ph.D., or equivalent degree and a full-time faculty position at an accredited North American institution. They may not hold grants for projects on a similar topic from other agencies. Individual membership in the American Gastroenterology Association (AGA) is required. The proposal must involve obtaining new data that can ultimately provide the basis for subsequent grant applications for more substantial funding and duration in gastroenterology- or hepatology-related areas. Women and minority investigators are strongly encouraged to apply. Selection is based on novelty, importance, feasibility, environment, institutional commitment, and overall likelihood that the project will lead to more substantial grants.

Financial data The grant is $25,000. Funds may be used for salary, supplies, or equipment. Indirect costs are not allowed.

Duration 1 year.

Additional information This award is sponsored by Elsevier Science.

Number awarded 2 each year.

Deadline January of each year.

[1283]
ENVIRONMENT AND NATURAL RESOURCES FELLOWSHIPS

Harvard University
John F. Kennedy School of Government
Belfer Center for Science and International Affairs
Attn: STPP Fellowship Coordinator
79 John F. Kennedy Street, Mailbox 53
Cambridge, MA 02138
(617) 495-1498　　　　　　　　Fax: (617) 495-8963
E-mail: patricia_mclaughlin@hks.harvard.edu
Web: belfercenter.ksg.harvard.edu

Summary To provide funding to professionals, postdoctorates, and doctoral students, especially African Americans and members of other underrepresented groups, who are interested in conducting research on environmental and nat-

ural resource issues at the Belfer Center for Science and International Affairs at Harvard University in Cambridge, Massachusetts.

Eligibility The postdoctoral fellowship is open to recent recipients of the Ph.D. or equivalent degree, university faculty members, and employees of government, military, international, humanitarian, and private research institutions who have appropriate professional experience. Applicants for predoctoral fellowships must have passed their general examinations. Scholars from a wide range of disciplinary and multi-disciplinary fields and those holding a Ph.D. in engineering or in the natural sciences are strongly encouraged to apply. The program especially encourages applications from women, minorities, and citizens of all countries. All applicants must be interested in conducting research on projects of the Environment and Natural Resources (ENRP) Program. Recently, those included projects on energy technology innovation, sustainable energy development in China, managing the atom, and the geopolitics of energy.

Financial data The stipend is $37,500 for postdoctoral research fellows or $25,000 for predoctoral research fellows. Fellows who renew their grant receive a monthly stipend of $3,750 for postdoctoral fellows or $2,500 for predoctoral fellows. Stipends for advanced research fellows vary. Health insurance is also provided.

Duration 10 months; may be renewed on a month-by-month basis.

Additional information Fellows are expected to devote some portion of their time to collaborative endeavors, as arranged by the appropriate program or project director. Predoctoral fellows are expected to contribute to the program's research activities, as well as work on (and ideally complete) their dissertations. Postdoctoral research fellows are also expected to complete a book, monograph, or other significant publication during their period of residence.

Number awarded A limited number each year.

Deadline January of each year.

[1284]
EPILEPSY FOUNDATION CLINICAL RESEARCH APPRENTICESHIP

American Epilepsy Society
135 South LaSalle Street, Suite 2850
Chicago, IL 60603
(312) 883-3800　　　　　　　　Fax: (312) 896-5784
E-mail: info@aesnet.org
Web: www.aesnet.org

Summary To provide funding to clinical health care professionals, especially African Americans and members of other underrepresented groups, who are interested in a mentored clinical research training apprenticeship.

Eligibility This program is open to clinicians who have a doctoral degree and have been accepted into an epilepsy fellowship at a level 3 or 4 epilepsy center in the United States. Applicants must identify a mentor at the center who will agree to work with them and be able to identify their role in the project that will leader to a publication or independent scholarship related to the project. The individualized training program may consist of both didactic training and a supervised research experience that is designed to develop the necessary knowledge and skills in the chosen area of research and foster their career goals. Selection is based on the quality of the proposed research training program, the applicant's qualifications, the preceptor's qualifications, and the adequacy of clinical training, research facilities, and other epilepsy-related programs at the institution. Applications are especially encouraged from women, members of minority groups, and people with disabilities. U.S. citizenship is not required, but all research must be conducted in the United States.

Financial data The grant provides $25,000 per year for salary plus $10,000 per year for class work and travel to appropriate meetings.

Duration 1 year, either the first or second year of fellowship.

Additional information Support for this program is provided by the Epilepsy Foundation.

Number awarded 2 each year.

Deadline Letters of intent must be submitted by October of each year; final proposals are due in January.

[1285]
ESTELLE MASSEY OSBORNE SCHOLARSHIP

Nurses Educational Funds, Inc.
Attn: Scholarship Coordinator
137 Montague Street, Suite 144
Brooklyn, NY 11201
(917) 524-8051   E-mail: info@n-e-f.org
Web: www.n-e-f.org/index.php/about/nef-scholarships.html

Summary To provide financial assistance to African American nurses interested in earning a master's degree.

Eligibility This program is open to African American registered nurses who are members of a national professional nursing organization and enrolled full or part time in an accredited master's degree program in nursing. Applicants must have completed at least 12 credits and have a cumulative GPA of 3.6 or higher. They must be U.S. citizens or have declared their official intention of becoming a citizen. Along with their application, they must submit an essay of 750 to 850 words defining their professional goals and assessing their potential for making a contribution to the nursing profession.

Financial data Stipends range from $2,500 to $10,000, depending on the availability of funds.

Duration 1 year; nonrenewable.

Additional information There is a $20 application fee.

Number awarded 1 each year.

Deadline January of each year.

[1286]
ETHNIC IN-SERVICE TRAINING FUND FOR CLINICAL PASTORAL EDUCATION (EIST-CPE)

United Methodist Church
Attn: General Board of Higher Education and Ministry
Office of Loans and Scholarships
1001 19th Avenue South
P.O. Box 340007
Nashville, TN 37203-0007
(615) 340-7342   Fax: (615) 340-7367
E-mail: umscholar@gbhem.org
Web: www.gbhem.org

Summary To provide financial assistance to United Methodist Church clergy and candidates for ministry who are Afri-

can Americans or members of other minority groups interested in preparing for a career as a clinical pastor.

Eligibility This program is open to U.S. citizens and permanent residents who are members of ethnic or racial minority groups and have been active, full members of a United Methodist Church for at least 1 year prior to applying. Applicants must be United Methodist clergy, certified candidates for ministry, or seminary students accepted into an accredited Clinical Pastor Education (CPE) or an accredited American Association of Pastoral Counselors (AAPC) program. They must be preparing for a career as a chaplain, pastoral counselor, or in pastoral care.

Financial data Grants range up to $2,000.

Duration 1 year.

Number awarded 1 each year.

Deadline February of each year.

[1287]
FELICIA C. BRADY SCHOLARSHIP FUND

Black Nurses' Association of Greater Washington, D.C. Area, Inc.
Attn: Scholarship Committee Chair
P.O. Box 55285
Washington, DC 20040
(202) 291-8866
Web: www.bnaofgwdca.org/scholarships.html

Summary To provide financial assistance to registered nurses from the Washington, D.C. area who are members of the National Black Nurses' Association and its local affiliate, and are interested in working on an advanced degree.

Eligibility This program is open to registered nurses who are currently enrolled in an associate, bachelor's, master's, or doctoral program and have a GPA of 3.0 or higher. Applicants must be residents of Washington, D.C. or adjoining counties in Maryland (Anne Arundel, Calvert, Charles, Howard, Montgomery, and Prince George's). They must be U.S. citizens, members of the National Black Nurses' Association, and members of the Black Nurses' Association of Greater Washington, D.C. Area. Along with their application, they must submit a copy of their nursing license, an official transcript from their nursing program, 2 letters of recommendation, and a written essay that describes their personal goals and objectives, financial need, and contributions to nursing and community service involvement in the greater Washington, D.C. area.

Financial data A stipend is awarded (amount not specified).

Duration 1 year.

Number awarded 1 each year.

Deadline January of each year.

[1288]
FIRST BOOK GRANT PROGRAM FOR MINORITY SCHOLARS

Louisville Institute
Attn: Executive Director
1044 Alta Vista Road
Louisville, KY 40205-1798
(502) 992-5432   Fax: (502) 894-2286
E-mail: info@louisville-institute.org
Web: www.louisville-institute.org

Summary To provide funding to African American and other scholars of color interested in completing a major research and book project that focuses on an aspect of Christianity in North America.

Eligibility This program is open to members of racial/ethnic minority groups (African Americans, Hispanics, Native Americans, Asian Americans, Arab Americans, and Pacific Islanders) who have an earned doctoral degree (normally the Ph.D. or Th.D.). Applicants must be a non-tenured faculty member in a full-time, tenure-track position at an accredited institution of higher education (college, university, or seminary) in North America. They must be able to negotiate a full academic year free from teaching and committee responsibilities in order to engage in a scholarly research project leading to the publication of their first (or second) book focusing on an aspect of Christianity in North America. Selection is based on the intellectual quality of the research and writing project, its potential to contribute to scholarship in religion, and the potential contribution of the research to the vitality of North American Christianity.

Financial data The grant is $40,000. Awards are intended to make possible a full academic year of sabbatical research and writing by providing up to half of the grantee's salary and benefits for that year. Funds are paid directly to the grantee's institution, but no indirect costs are allowed.

Duration 1 academic year; nonrenewable.

Additional information The Louisville Institute is located at Louisville Presbyterian Theological Seminary and is supported by the Lilly Endowment. These grants were first awarded in 2003. Grantees may not accept other awards that provide a stipend during the tenure of this award, and they must be released from all teaching and committee responsibilities during the award year.

Number awarded Varies each year; recently, 3 were awarded.

Deadline January of each year.

[1289]
FREDERICK DOUGLASS INSTITUTE FOR AFRICAN AND AFRICAN-AMERICAN STUDIES POSTDOCTORAL FELLOWSHIP

University of Rochester
Frederick Douglass Institute for African and African-
  American Studies
Attn: Director for Research Fellowships
311 Morey Hall
RC Box 270440
Rochester, NY 14627-0440
(585) 276-5744   Fax: (585) 256-2594
E-mail: FDI@rochester.edu
Web: www.sas.rochester.edu/aas/fellowships/internal.html

Summary To support postdoctoral research on African and African American studies at the University of Rochester.

Eligibility This program is open to scholars who have a Ph.D. degree in a field related to the African and African American experience. Applicants must be interested in completing a research project at the Frederick Douglass Institute at the University of Rochester. Along with their application, they must submit a curriculum vitae, a 3- to 5-page description of the project, a sample of published or unpublished writing on a topic related to the proposal, and 3 letters of recommendation.

Financial data The program provides a stipend of $40,000 and a $3,000 fund for research-related activities.

Duration 1 year; nonrenewable.

Additional information This is a residential fellowship. All fellows are given office space within the institute, full access to the facilities of the university, and opportunities for collaboration and discussion there. Fellows are expected to teach 2 courses (1 each semester) during the fellowship year. Fellows must be in full-time residence at the institution during the tenure of the award.

Number awarded 1 each year.

Deadline December of each year.

[1290]
GAIUS CHARLES BOLIN DISSERTATION AND POST-MFA FELLOWSHIPS

Williams College
Attn: Dean of the Faculty
880 Main Street
Hopkins Hall, Third Floor
P.O. Box 141
Williamstown, MA 01267
(413) 597-4351   Fax: (413) 597-3553
E-mail: gburda@williams.edu
Web: faculty.williams.edu

Summary To provide financial assistance to African Americans and members of other underrepresented groups who are interested in teaching courses at Williams College while working on their doctoral dissertation or building their post-M.F.A. professional portfolio.

Eligibility This program is open to members of underrepresented groups, including ethnic minorities, first-generation college students, women in predominantly male fields, and scholars with disabilities. Applicants must be 1) doctoral candidates in any field who have completed all work for a Ph.D. except for the dissertation; or 2) artists who completed an M.F.A. degree within the past 2 years and are building their professional portfolio. They must be willing to teach a course at Williams College. Along with their application, they must submit a full curriculum vitae, a graduate school transcript, 3 letters of recommendation, a copy of their dissertation prospectus or samples of their artistic work, and a description of their teaching interests within a department or program at Williams College. U.S. citizenship or permanent resident status is required.

Financial data Fellows receive $38,000 for the academic year, plus housing assistance, office space, computer and library privileges, and a research allowance of up to $4,000.

Duration 2 years.

Additional information Bolin fellows are assigned a faculty adviser in the appropriate department. This program was established in 1985. Fellows are expected to teach a 1-semester course each year. They must be in residence at Williams College for the duration of the fellowship.

Number awarded 2 each year.

Deadline November of each year.

[1291]
GEORGE A. STRAIT MINORITY SCHOLARSHIP ENDOWMENT

American Association of Law Libraries
Attn: Chair, Scholarships Committee
105 West Adams Street, Suite 3300
Chicago, IL 60603
(312) 939-4764   Fax: (312) 431-1097
E-mail: scholarships@aall.org
Web: www.aallnet.org

Summary To provide financial assistance to African American or other minority college seniors or college graduates who are interested in becoming law librarians.

Eligibility This program is open to college graduates with meaningful law library experience who are members of minority groups and intend to have a career in law librarianship. Applicants must be degree candidates at an ALA-accredited library school or an ABA-accredited law school. Along with their application, they must submit a personal statement that discusses their interest in law librarianship, reason for applying for this scholarship, career goals as a law librarian, and any other pertinent information.

Financial data The stipend is $3,500.

Duration 1 year.

Additional information This program, established in 1990, is currently supported by Thomson Reuters.

Number awarded Varies each year; recently, 6 were awarded.

Deadline March of each year.

[1292]
GERALD OSHITA MEMORIAL FELLOWSHIP

Djerassi Resident Artists Program
Attn: Admissions
2325 Bear Gulch Road
Woodside, CA 94062-4405
(650) 747-1250   Fax: (650) 747-0105
E-mail: drap@djerassi.org
Web: www.djerassi.org/oshita.html

Summary To provide an opportunity for African American and other composers of color to participate in the Djerassi Resident Artists Program.

Eligibility This program is open to composers of African, Asian, Latino, or Native American ethnic background. Applicants must be interested in utilizing a residency to compose, study, rehearse, and otherwise advance their own creative projects.

Financial data The fellow is offered housing, meals, studio space, and a stipend of $2,500.

Duration 1 month, from late March through mid-November.

Additional information This fellowship was established in 1994. The program is located in northern California, 45 miles south of San Francisco, on 600 acres of rangeland, redwood forests, and hiking trails. There is a $45 non-refundable application fee.

Number awarded 1 each year.

Deadline February of each year.

[1293]
GLORIA E. ANZALDUA BOOK PRIZE

National Women's Studies Association
Attn: Book Prizes
11 East Mount Royal Avenue, Suite 100
Baltimore, MD 21202
(410) 528-0355   Fax: (410) 528-0357
E-mail: awards@nwsa.org
Web: www.nwsa.org

Summary To recognize and reward members of the National Women's Studies Association (NWSA) who have written outstanding books on women of color and transnational issues.

Eligibility This award is available to NWSA members who submit a book that was published during the preceding year. Entries must present groundbreaking scholarship in women's studies and make a significant multicultural feminist contribution to women of color and/or transnational studies.

Financial data The award provides an honorarium of $1,000 and lifetime membership in NWSA.

Duration The award is presented annually.

Additional information This award was first presented in 2008.

Number awarded 1 each year.

Deadline April of each year.

[1294]
GO ON GIRL UNPUBLISHED WRITER AWARD

Go On Girl! Book Club, Inc.
P.O. Box 3368
New York, NY 10185
E-mail: writingawards@goongirl.org
Web: www.goongirl.org/scholarships/index.php

Summary To recognize and reward unpublished works of fiction by people of African descent.

Eligibility This award is presented to U.S. citizens of African descent. Applicants must submit 4 copies of an original, unpublished work of fiction (short story or novel excerpt) up to 2,000 words. A cover sheet must include a 250-word autobiographical sketch with their writing goals and current status.

Financial data The award is $1,000.

Duration 1 year.

Additional information Go On Girl! Book Club was founded in 1991 and is currently the largest reading group for Black women in the country. It first presented this award in 2000.

Number awarded 1 each year.

Deadline March of each year.

[1295]
HARRY R. KENDALL LEADERSHIP DEVELOPMENT SCHOLARSHIPS

United Methodist Church
General Board of Global Ministries
Attn: United Methodist Committee on Relief
Health and Welfare Ministries
475 Riverside Drive, Room 330
New York, NY 10115
(212) 870-3871   Toll Free: (800) UMC-GBGM
E-mail: jyoung@gbgm-umc.org
Web: umc-gbcs.org/conference-connections/grants

Summary To provide financial assistance to African Americans who are Methodists or other Christians and preparing for a career in a health-related field.

Eligibility This program is open to undergraduate and graduate students who are U.S. citizens or permanent residents of African American descent. Applicants must be professed Christians, preferably United Methodists. They must be planning to enter a health care field or already be a practitioner in such a field. Financial need is considered in the selection process.

Financial data The stipend is $2,000.

Duration 1 year.

Additional information This program began in 1980.

Number awarded Varies each year.

Deadline June of each year.

[1296]
HISTORICALLY BLACK COLLEGES AND UNIVERSITIES (HBCUS) GRANT PROGRAM

Centers for Medicare & Medicaid Services
Attn: Center for Medicare and Medicaid Innovation
Mail Stop WB-06-05
7500 Security Boulevard
Baltimore, MD 21244-1850
(410) 786-7250   Toll Free: (877) 267-2323
TDD: (877) 486-2048
E-mail: Richard.Bragg@cms.hhs.gov
Web: www.cms.gov

Summary To provide funding to faculty at Historically Black Colleges and Universities (HBCUs) interested in carrying out health services research activities.

Eligibility This program is open to faculty at HBCUs that meet 1 of the following requirements: 1) offers a Ph.D. or master's degree in 1 or more of the following disciplines: allied health, gerontology, health care administration, nursing, pharmacology, public health, or social work; 2) has a school of medicine; or 3) is a member of the National HBCU Network for Health Services and Health Disparities. Applicants must be interested in conducting small research projects that relate to health care delivery and health financing issues affecting African American communities, including issues of access to health care, utilization of health care services, health outcomes, quality of services, cost of care, health disparities, socio-economic differences, cultural barriers, managed care systems, and activities related to health screening, prevention, outreach, and education.

Financial data Grants range up to $100,000 per year.

Duration Up to 2 years.

Additional information This program began in 1997. Until 2001, the Centers for Medicare & Medicaid Services was known as the Health Care Financing Administration.

Number awarded 1 each year.

Deadline Letters of intent must be submitted in June of each year. Final applications are due in July.

[1297]
HURSTON/WRIGHT LEGACY AWARD

Zora Neale Hurston/Richard Wright Foundation
Attn: Hurston/Wright Awards
840 First Street, N.E., Third Floor
Washington, DC 20002
(202) 248-5051   E-mail: info@hurstonwright.org
Web: www.hurstonwright.org/legacy-awards

Summary To recognize and reward the best fiction, nonfiction, and poetry written by authors of African descent.

Eligibility This award is available to writers of African descent from any area of the Diaspora. Publishers may submit (with permission of the author) books in 4 categories: fiction (novel, novella, or short story collection); debut fiction (first works of fiction); nonfiction (autobiography, memoir, biography, history, social issues, or literary criticism); or poetry (books in verse, prose poetry, formal verse, experimental verse). Paperback originals, self-published authors, and English translations of books originally written in another language are eligible, but reprints of a book published in a previous year, poetry books with less than 50 pages, and books written by more than 1 author are not considered. Entries must have been published in the preceding calendar year in the United States or be U.S. editions of foreign books published for the first time in the United States.

Financial data Cash prizes are awarded.

Duration The prizes are awarded annually.

Additional information This program began in 2002. There is a $40 entry fee for each title.

Number awarded The number of awards varies each year; recently, 2 were presented.

Deadline November of each year.

[1298]
INTERNATIONAL SECURITY AND COOPERATION POSTDOCTORAL FELLOWSHIPS

Stanford University
Center for International Security and Cooperation
Attn: Fellowships Coordinator
Encina Hall, Room C206-10
616 Serra Street
Stanford, CA 94305-6165
(650) 723-9625   Fax: (650) 724-5683
E-mail: CISACfellowship@stanford.edu
Web: cisac.fsi.stanford.edu/docs/cisac_fellowship_program

Summary To provide funding to postdoctorates, especially African Americans and members of other underrepresented groups, who are interested in conducting research on international security problems at Stanford University's Center for International Security and Cooperation.

Eligibility This program is open to scholars who have a Ph.D. or equivalent degree from the United States or abroad and would benefit from using the resources of the center. Applicants may be working in any discipline of the social sciences, humanities, natural sciences, law, or engineering that relates to international security problems. Relevant topics include nuclear weapons policy and nonproliferation; nuclear energy; cybersecurity, cyberwarfare, and the future of the Internet; war and civil conflict; global governance, migration and transnational flows, from norms to criminal trafficking; biosecurity and global health; implications of geostrategic shifts; insurgency, terrorism, and homeland security; and consolidating peace after conflict. The sponsor welcomes applications from women, minorities, and citizens of all countries.

Financial data The stipend ranges from $48,000 to $66,000, depending on experience. Medical insurance is available for those who do not have coverage.

Duration 9 to 11 months.

Additional information Fellows are expected to write a publishable article or articles and/or make significant progress on turning a thesis into a book manuscript. They should not plan to spend any time conducting research abroad or in other parts of the country.

Number awarded Varies each year; recently, 7 were awarded.

Deadline January of each year.

[1299]
INTERNATIONAL SECURITY AND COOPERATION PROFESSIONAL FELLOWSHIPS

Stanford University
Center for International Security and Cooperation
Attn: Fellowships Coordinator
Encina Hall, Room C206-10
616 Serra Street
Stanford, CA 94305-6165
(650) 723-9625   Fax: (650) 724-5683
E-mail: CISACfellowship@stanford.edu
Web: cisac.fsi.stanford.edu/docs/cisac_fellowship_program

Summary To provide funding to professionals, especially African Americans and members of other underrepresented groups, who are interested in conducting research in residence on topics of interest to Stanford University's Center for International Security and Cooperation.

Eligibility This program is open to mid-career professionals in journalism, law, the military, government, or international organizations, either from the United States or abroad. Applicants must be interested in conducting research in any discipline of the social sciences, humanities, natural sciences, law, or engineering that relates to international security problems. Relevant topics include nuclear weapons policy and nonproliferation; nuclear energy; cybersecurity, cyberwarfare, and the future of the Internet; war and civil conflict; global governance, migration and transnational flows, from norms to criminal trafficking; biosecurity and global health; implications of geostrategic shifts; insurgency, terrorism, and homeland security; and consolidating peace after conflict. The sponsor welcomes applications from women, minorities, and citizens of all countries.

Financial data The stipend depends on experience and is determined on a case-by-case basis. Additional funds may be available for dependents and travel.

Duration 9 to 11 months.

Additional information Fellows are expected to write a publishable article during their fellowship. They should not

plan to spend any time conducting research abroad or in other parts of the country.

Number awarded Varies each year; recently, 2 were awarded.

Deadline January of each year.

[1300]
J. ROBERT GLADDEN ORTHOPAEDIC SOCIETY BASIC RESEARCH GRANTS

J. Robert Gladden Orthopaedic Society
Attn: Scientific Committee
9400 West Higgins Road, Suite 500
Rosemont, IL 60018
(847) 698-1633   Fax: (847) 823-4921
E-mail: jrgos@aaos.org
Web: www.gladdensociety.org

Summary To provide funding to African American and other underrepresented minority members of the J. Robert Gladden Orthopaedic Society (JRGOS) who are interested in conducting a basic research project.

Eligibility This program is open to members of underrepresented minority groups who are JRGOS members and interested in conducting a basic research project. Applicants must be affiliated with a research institution that provides laboratory space and basic facilities. They must be able to demonstrate the compatibility of their project's clinical relevance with the mission and goals of the society. Preference is given to applicants planning to work with a senior JRGOS member.

Financial data The grant is $25,000.

Duration 1 year.

Additional information This program is sponsored by DePuy/Johnson & Johnson.

Number awarded 1 or more each year.

Deadline September of each year.

[1301]
J. ROBERT GLADDEN ORTHOPAEDIC SOCIETY RESEARCH GRANTS

J. Robert Gladden Orthopaedic Society
Attn: Scientific Committee
9400 West Higgins Road, Suite 500
Rosemont, IL 60018
(847) 698-1633   Fax: (847) 823-4921
E-mail: jrgos@aaos.org
Web: www.gladdensociety.org

Summary To provide funding to African American and other underrepresented minority members of the J. Robert Gladden Orthopaedic Society (JRGOS) who are interested in conducting a clinical research project in areas where funding is difficult to obtain.

Eligibility This program is open to members of underrepresented minority groups who are new or experienced JRGOS members and interested in conducting a research project in clinical areas where funding is difficult to obtain. Applicants must be seeking seed money to initiate studies to obtain background data with the goal of obtaining future funding from other sources. They must be able to demonstrate the compatibility of their project's clinical problems with the mission and goals of the society. Preference is given to applicants planning to work with a senior JRGOS member.

Financial data The grant is $30,000 per year.

Duration 1 year; may be renewed 1 additional year.

Additional information This program is sponsored by Smith & Nephew.

Number awarded 1 or more each year.

Deadline September of each year.

[1302]
J. ROBERT GLADDEN ORTHOPAEDIC SOCIETY RESIDENT RESEARCH GRANTS

J. Robert Gladden Orthopaedic Society
Attn: Scientific Committee
9400 West Higgins Road, Suite 500
Rosemont, IL 60018
(847) 698-1633   Fax: (847) 823-4921
E-mail: jrgos@aaos.org
Web: www.gladdensociety.org

Summary To provide funding to African American and other underrepresented minority members of the J. Robert Gladden Orthopaedic Society (JRGOS) who are medical residents and interested in conducting a research project.

Eligibility This program is open to members of underrepresented minority groups who are medical residents and JRGOS members. Applicants must be seeking funding to conduct a research project with a measurable outcome that can be achieved at the end of the grant cycle. They must be able to demonstrate that their proposed project correlates with the mission and goals of the society. Preference is given to applicants planning to work with a senior JRGOS member.

Financial data The grant is $10,000.

Duration 1 year.

Additional information This program is sponsored by DePuy/Johnson & Johnson.

Number awarded 1 or more each year.

Deadline September of each year.

[1303]
JAMES A. RAWLEY PRIZE

Organization of American Historians
Attn: Award and Committee Coordinator
112 North Bryan Street
Bloomington, IN 47408-4141
(812) 855-7311   Fax: (812) 855-0696
E-mail: khamm@oah.org
Web: www.oah.org

Summary To recognize and reward authors of outstanding books dealing with race relations in the United States.

Eligibility This award is presented to the author of the outstanding book on the history of race relations in America. Entries must have been published during the current calendar year.

Financial data The award is $1,000 and a certificate.

Duration The award is presented annually.

Additional information This award was established in 1990.

Number awarded 1 each year.

Deadline September of each year.

[1304]
JESSICA M. BLANDING MEMORIAL SCHOLARSHIP

New England Regional Black Nurses Association, Inc.
P.O. Box 190690
Roxbury, MA 02119
(617) 524-1951   E-mail: nerbascholarships@gmail.com
Web: nerbna.nursingnetwork.com

Summary To provide financial assistance to licensed practical nurses from New England who are of African descent and interested in working on a degree.

Eligibility The program is open to African American residents of the New England states who are licensed practical nurses working on an associate or bachelor's degree in nursing at a school in any state. Applicants must have a GPA of 3.0 or higher and at least 1 full year of school remaining. They must be members of the New England Regional Black Nurses Association (NERBNA). Along with their application, they must submit a 3-page essay that covers their reasons for furthering their career in nursing; why minority nursing leadership is important; how minority nursing leadership can assist them in furthering their career; why they chose to prepare for a career in nursing; and any financial hardships that may hinder them from completing their education.

Financial data A stipend is awarded (amount not specified).

Duration 1 year.

Number awarded 1 or more each year.

Deadline February of each year.

[1305]
JOHN MCLENDON MEMORIAL MINORITY POSTGRADUATE SCHOLARSHIP AWARD

National Association of Collegiate Directors of Athletics
Attn: NACDA Foundation
24651 Detroit Road
Westlake, OH 44145
(440) 788-7474   Fax: (440) 892-4007
E-mail: knewman@nacda.com
Web: www.nacda.com/mclendon/scholarship.html

Summary To provide financial assistance to African American and other minority college seniors who are interested in working on a graduate degree in athletics administration.

Eligibility This program is open to minority college students who are seniors, are attending school on a full-time basis, have a GPA of 3.2 or higher, intend to attend graduate school to earn a degree in athletics administration, and are involved in college or community activities. Also eligible are college graduates who have at least 2 years' experience in an athletics administration position. Candidates must be nominated by an official of a member institution of the National Association of Collegiate Directors of Athletics (NACDA) or (for college graduates) a supervisor.

Financial data The stipend is $10,000.

Duration 1 year.

Additional information Recipients must maintain full-time status during the senior year to retain their eligibility. They must attend NACDA-member institutions.

Number awarded 5 each year.

Deadline Nominations must be submitted by April of each year.

[1306]
JOHN W. BLASSINGAME AWARD

Southern Historical Association
c/o Stephen Berry, Secretary-Treasurer
University of Georgia
Department of History
LeConte Hall, Room 111
Athens, GA 30602-1602
(706) 542-8848   E-mail: berrys@thesha.org
Web: sha.uga.edu/awards/blassingame.htm

Summary To recognize and reward faculty members who have contributed outstanding scholarship and mentorship in African American studies.

Eligibility This award is available to members of all areas of the academic community, including community and junior colleges, Historically Black Colleges and Universities, and large research universities. Nominations may be submitted by members of the Southern Historical Association, based on distinguished careers as mentors of African American students, personal scholarly accomplishments, or some combination of both. For nominations involving a primary role of mentoring African American students, letters from students (undergraduate or graduate) are particularly welcome.

Financial data The award is $1,000.

Duration The award is presented triennially (2018, 2021, etc.).

Additional information This award was first presented in 2004.

Number awarded 1 every third year.

Deadline May of the year of the award.

[1307]
JUVENILE DIABETES RESEARCH FOUNDATION INNOVATIVE GRANTS

Juvenile Diabetes Research Foundation International
Attn: Senior Director, Research Administration
26 Broadway, 14th Floor
New York, NY 10004
(212) 479-7519   Toll Free: (800) 533-CURE
Fax: (212) 785-9595   E-mail: emilligan@jdrf.org
Web: grantcenter.jdrf.org

Summary To provide funding to scientists, especially African Americans and members of other underrepresented groups, who are interested in conducting innovative diabetes-related research.

Eligibility Applicants must have an M.D., D.M.D., D.V.M., Ph.D., or equivalent degree and have a full-time faculty position or equivalent at a college, university, medical school, or other research facility. They must be seeking "seed" money for investigative work based on a sound hypothesis for which preliminary data are insufficient for a regular research grant but that are likely to lead to important results for the treatment of diabetes and its complications. Applicants must specifically explain how the proposal is innovative. Selection is based on 1) innovation, potential impact, and relevance to the goals of the sponsor; 2) feasibility of experimental approach and completion in 1 year; 3) clarity of proposed objectives; 4) qualifications and research experience of the principal investigators and collaborators; 5) availability of resources and facilities necessary for the project; and 6) appropriateness of the proposed budget in relation to the proposed research. There are no citizenship requirements. Applications are encouraged from women, members of minority groups underrepresented in the sciences, and people with disabilities. The proposed research may be conducted at foreign or domestic, for-profit or nonprofit, or public or private institutions, including universities, colleges, hospitals, laboratories, units of state or local government, or eligible agencies of the federal government.

Financial data Awards are limited to $100,000 plus 10% indirect costs.

Duration 1 year; nonrenewable.

Number awarded Varies each year; recently, 5 were awarded.

Deadline July of each year.

[1308]
JUVENILE DIABETES RESEARCH FOUNDATION STRATEGIC RESEARCH AGREEMENTS

Juvenile Diabetes Research Foundation International
Attn: Senior Director, Research Administration
26 Broadway, 14th Floor
New York, NY 10004
(212) 479-7519   Toll Free: (800) 533-CURE
Fax: (212) 785-9595   E-mail: emilligan@jdrf.org
Web: grantcenter.jdrf.org

Summary To provide funding to scientists, especially African Americans and members of other underrepresented groups, who are interested in conducting diabetes-related research that addresses critical gaps and challenges.

Eligibility Applicants must have an M.D., D.M.D., D.V.M., Ph.D., or equivalent degree and have a full-time faculty position or equivalent at a college, university, medical school, or other research facility. They must be seeking funding to address critical gaps and challenges and potential breakthroughs in Type 1 diabetes research. Selection is based on potential to prove principle of new approaches to unsolved problems of Type 1 diabetes; relevance to the objectives of the sponsor; scientific, technical, or medical significant of the research proposal; innovative quality of the proposed study; soundness of the clinical study design; availability of sufficient pre-clinical data to justify the proposed clinical study; qualifications and research experience of the principal investigators and collaborators; potential benefits and risks to patients who will be involved in the research, plans to limit risks, and other ethical considerations; availability of resources and facilities necessary for the study; and appropriateness of the proposed budget in relation to the proposed research. There are no citizenship requirements. Applications are encouraged from women, members of minority groups underrepresented in the sciences, and people with disabilities. The proposed research may be conducted at foreign or domestic, for-profit or nonprofit, or public or private institutions, including universities, colleges, hospitals, laboratories, units of state or local government, or eligible agencies of the federal government.

Financial data Awards depend on the availability of funds.

Duration Up to 3 years.

Number awarded Varies each year.

Deadline February, August, or November of each year.

[1309]
KING-CHAVEZ-PARKS VISITING PROFESSORS PROGRAM

University of Michigan
Attn: Office of the Provost and Executive Vice President
  for Academic Affairs
503 Thompson Street
3084 Fleming Administration Building
Ann Arbor, MI 48109-1340
(734) 764-3982   Fax: (734) 764-4546
E-mail: provost@umich.edu
Web: www.provost.umich.edu

Summary   To provide an opportunity for African American and other minority scholars to visit and teach at the University of Michigan.

Eligibility   Outstanding minority (African American, Asian/Pacific American, Latino/a-Hispanic American, and Native American) scholars, performers, or practitioners are eligible to be nominated by University of Michigan faculty members to visit and lecture there. Nominations that include collaborations with other educational institutions in Michigan are of high priority.

Financial data   Visiting Professors receive round-trip transportation and an appropriate honorarium.

Duration   Visits range from 1 to 5 days.

Additional information   This program was established in 1986. Visiting Professors are expected to lecture or teach at the university, offer at least 1 event open to the general public, and meet with minority campus/community groups, including local K-12 schools.

Number awarded   Varies each year.

Deadline   Nominations may be submitted at any time, but they must be received at least 30 days before a funding decision is required.

[1310]
LAURENCE R. FOSTER MEMORIAL SCHOLARSHIPS

Oregon Office of Student Access and Completion
Attn: Scholarship Processing Coordinator
1500 Valley River Drive, Suite 100
Eugene, OR 97401-2146
(541) 687-7422   Toll Free: (800) 452-8807, ext. 7422
Fax: (541) 687-7414   TDD: (800) 735-2900
E-mail: cheryl.a.connolly@state.or.us
Web: app.oregonstudentaid.gov/Catalog/Default.aspx

Summary   To provide financial assistance to African American and other residents of Oregon from diverse environments who are enrolled at a college or graduate school in any state to prepare for a public health career.

Eligibility   This program is open to residents of Oregon who are enrolled at least half time at a 4-year college or university in any state to prepare for a career in public health (not private practice). Preference is given first to applicants from diverse environments; second to persons employed in, or graduate students working on a degree in, public health; and third to juniors and seniors majoring in a health program (e.g., nursing, medical technology, physician assistant). Applicants must be able to demonstrate financial need. Along with their application, they must submit essays of 250 to 350 words on 1) what public health means to them; 2) the public health

aspect they intend to practice and the health and population issues impacted by that aspect; and 3) their experience living or working in diverse environments.

Financial data   Stipends for scholarships offered by the Oregon Office of Student Access and Completion (OSAC) range from $1,000 to $10,000 but recently averaged $4,368.

Duration   1 year.

Additional information   This program is administered by the OSAC with funds provided by the Oregon Community Foundation.

Number awarded   Varies each year; recently, 6 were awarded.

Deadline   February of each year.

[1311]
LEON BRADLEY SCHOLARSHIPS

American Association of School Personnel Administrators
Attn: Scholarship Program
11863 West 112th Street, Suite 100
Overland Park, KS 66210
(913) 327-1222   Fax: (913) 327-1223
E-mail: aaspa@aaspa.org
Web: www.aaspa.org/leon-bradley-scholarship

Summary   To provide financial assistance to African American and other minority undergraduates, paraprofessionals, and graduate students preparing for a career in teaching and school leadership at colleges in designated southeastern states.

Eligibility   This program is open to members of minority groups (Black, American Indian, Alaskan Native, Asian, Pacific Islander, Hispanic, Middle Easterner) currently enrolled full time at a college or university in Alabama, Florida, Georgia, Kentucky, North Carolina, South Carolina, Tennessee, or Virginia. Applicants must be 1) undergraduates in their final year (including student teaching) of an initial teaching certification program; 2) paraprofessional career-changers in their final year (including student teaching) of an initial teaching certification program; or 3) graduate students who have served as a licensed teacher and are working on a school administrator credential. They must have an overall GPA of 3.0 or higher. Priority is given to applicants who 1) can demonstrate work experience that has been applied to college expenses; 2) have received other scholarship or financial aid support; or 3) are seeking initial certification and/or endorsement in a state-identified critical area.

Financial data   Stipends are $2,500 for undergraduates in their final year, $1,500 for paraprofessionals in their final year, and $1,500 for graduate students.

Duration   1 year.

Number awarded   4 each year: 1 undergraduate, 1 paraprofessional, and 2 graduate students.

Deadline   May of each year.

[1312]
LOUIS STOKES URBAN HEALTH PUBLIC POLICY FELLOWS PROGRAM

Congressional Black Caucus Foundation, Inc.
Attn: Leadership Institute for Public Service
1720 Massachusetts Avenue, N.W.
Washington, DC 20036
(202) 263-2800   Toll Free: (800) 784-2577
Fax: (202) 775-0773   E-mail: internships@cbcfinc.org
Web: www.cbcfinc.org

Summary To provide an opportunity for health policy professionals to work on a program of original research, advanced legislative training, and health policy analysis in collaboration with the Congressional Black Caucus (CBC).

Eligibility This program is open to professionals who have a graduate or professional degree in a health-related field (behavioral sciences, social sciences, biological sciences, and health professions) and familiarity with the federal legislative process, Congress, and the CBC. Applicants must be interested in working in Washington, D.C. on health-related issues, especially how health policies affect African Americans and other minorities, as a member of the staff or committee of a member of the CBC. They must be able to demonstrate an interest in public health policy, a record of academic and professional achievement, evidence of leadership skills, the potential for further growth, and U.S. citizenship or permit to work in the United States.

Financial data Fellows receive a stipend of $40,000 per year and benefits.

Duration 20 months, beginning in September.

Additional information This program began in 2003. Fellows are assigned to Congressional offices or committees and work on issues related to minority health.

Number awarded 2 each year.

Deadline March of each year.

[1313]
LYMAN T. JOHNSON POSTDOCTORAL FELLOWSHIP

University of Kentucky
Attn: Vice President for Research
311 Main Building, 0032
Lexington, KY 40506-0032
(859) 257-5090   Fax: (859) 323-2800
E-mail: vprgrants@uky.edu
Web: www.research.uky.edu

Summary To provide an opportunity for recent postdoctorates, especially African Americans and other minorities, to conduct research at the University of Kentucky (U.K.).

Eligibility This program is open to U.S. citizens and permanent residents who have completed a doctoral degree within the past 2 years. Applicants must be interested in conducting an individualized research program under the mentorship of a U.K. professor. They should indicate, in their letter of application, how their participation in this program would contribute to the compelling interest of diversity at U.K. Race, ethnicity, and national origin are among the factors that contribute to diversity. Selection is based on evidence of scholarship with competitive potential for a tenure-track faculty appointment at a research university, compatibility of specific research interests with those in doctorate-granting units at

U.K., quality of the research proposal, support from mentor and references, and effect of the appointment on the educational benefit of diversity within the research or professional area.

Financial data The fellowship provides a stipend of $35,000 plus $5,000 for support of research activities.

Duration Up to 2 years.

Additional information In addition to conducting an individualized research program under the mentorship of a U.K. professor, fellows actively participate in research, teaching, and service to the university, their profession, and the community. This program began in 1992.

Number awarded 2 each year.

Deadline October of each year.

[1314]
M. ELIZABETH CARNEGIE SCHOLARSHIP

Nurses Educational Funds, Inc.
Attn: Scholarship Coordinator
137 Montague Street, Suite 144
Brooklyn, NY 11201
(917) 524-8051   E-mail: info@n-e-f.org
Web: www.n-e-f.org/index.php/about/nef-scholarships.html

Summary To provide financial assistance to African American nurses who wish to work on a doctoral degree.

Eligibility This program is open to African American registered nurses who are members of a national professional nursing organization and enrolled full or part time in a nursing or nursing-related program at the doctoral level. Applicants must have completed at least 12 credits and have a GPA of 3.6 or higher. They must be U.S. citizens or have declared their official intention of becoming a citizen. Along with their application, they must submit an essay of 750 to 850 words defining their professional goals and assessing their potential for making a contribution to the nursing profession.

Financial data Stipends range from $2,500 to $10,000, depending on the availability of funds.

Duration 1 year; nonrenewable.

Additional information There is a $20 application fee.

Number awarded 1 each year.

Deadline January of each year.

[1315]
MANY VOICES FELLOWSHIPS

Playwrights' Center
Attn: Artistic Programs Administrator
2301 East Franklin Avenue
Minneapolis, MN 55406-1024
(612) 332-7481, ext. 115   Fax: (612) 332-6037
E-mail: julia@pwcenter.org
Web: www.pwcenter.org/programs/many-voices-fellowships

Summary To provide funding to African American and other playwrights of color from Minnesota and other states so they can spend a year in residence at the Playwrights' Center in Minneapolis.

Eligibility This program is open to playwrights of color who are citizens or permanent residents of the United States; residents of Minnesota and of other states are eligible. Applicants must be interested in playwriting and creating theater in a supportive artist community at the Playwrights' Center.

Financial data Fellows receive a $10,000 stipend, $2,500 for living expenses, and $1,500 in play development funds.

Duration 9 months, beginning in October.

Additional information This program, which began in 1994, is funded by the Jerome Foundation. Fellows must be in residence at the Playwrights' Center for the duration of the program.

Number awarded 2 each year: 1 to a resident of Minnesota and 1 to a resident of any state.

Deadline November of each year.

[1316]
MARTIN LUTHER KING, JR. MEMORIAL SCHOLARSHIP FUND

California Teachers Association
Attn: CTA Foundation for Teaching and Learning
1705 Murchison Drive
P.O. Box 921
Burlingame, CA 94011-0921
(650) 697-1400   E-mail: scholarships@cta.org
Web: www.cta.org

Summary To provide financial assistance for college or graduate school to African Americans and other racial and ethnic minorities who are members of the California Teachers Association (CTA), children of members, or members of the Student CTA.

Eligibility This program is open to members of racial or ethnic minority groups (African Americans, American Indians/ Alaska Natives, Asians/Pacific Islanders, and Hispanics) who are 1) active CTA members; 2) dependent children of active, retired, or deceased CTA members; or 3) members of Student CTA. Applicants must be interested in preparing for a teaching career in public education or already engaged in such a career.

Financial data Stipends vary each year; recently, they ranged up to $6,000.

Duration 1 year.

Number awarded Varies each year; recently, 24 were awarded: 1 to a CTA member, 10 to children of CTA members, and 13 to Student CTA members.

Deadline February of each year.

[1317]
MARY ELIZABETH CARNEGIE SCHOLAR AWARD

American Nurses Foundation
Attn: Nursing Research Grants Program
8515 Georgia Avenue, Suite 400
Silver Spring, MD 20910-3492
(301) 628-5227   Toll Free: (800) 274-4ANA
Fax: (301) 628-5354   E-mail: anf@ana.org
Web: www.anfonline.org

Summary To provide funding to nurses and graduate nursing students who are members of the American Nurses Association and interested in conducting research on African American nurses.

Eligibility This program is open to ANA members who have earned a baccalaureate or higher degree. Applicants may be beginning researchers (have had no more than 3 research-based publications in refereed journals and have received, as a principal investigator, no more than $15,000 in extramural funding) or experienced researchers (those with

more than 3 publications and more than $15,000 in research funding). The focus of the research must relate to African American nurses. Proposed research may be for a master's thesis or doctoral dissertation if the project has been approved by the principal investigator's thesis or dissertation committee.

Financial data The grant is $5,000. Funds may not be used as a salary for the principal investigator.

Duration 1 year.

Additional information There is a $100 application fee.

Number awarded 1 each year.

Deadline April of each year.

[1318]
MAXINE V. FENNELL/ROBIN GAINES MEMORIAL SCHOLARSHIP

New England Regional Black Nurses Association, Inc.
P.O. Box 190690
Roxbury, MA 02119
(617) 524-1951   E-mail: nerbascholarships@gmail.com
Web: nerbna.nursingnetwork.com

Summary To provide financial assistance to registered nurses (R.N.s) from New England who are of African descent and interested in working on a degree in nursing or public health at a school in any state.

Eligibility The program is open to African American residents of the New England states who are R.N.s and currently enrolled in an NLN-accredited bachelor's, master's, or doctoral degree program in nursing or public health at a school in any state. Applicants must have a GPA of 3.0 or higher and at least 1 full year of school remaining. They must be members of the New England Regional Black Nurses Association (NERBNA). Along with their application, they must submit a 3-page essay that covers their reasons for furthering their career in nursing; why minority nursing leadership is important; how minority nursing leadership can assist them in furthering their career; why they chose to prepare for a career in nursing; and any financial hardships that may hinder them from completing their education.

Financial data A stipend is awarded (amount not specified).

Duration 1 year.

Number awarded 1 or more each year.

Deadline February of each year.

[1319]
MICKEY LELAND ENERGY FELLOWSHIPS

Oak Ridge Institute for Science and Education
Attn: MLEF Fellowship Program
1299 Bethel Valley Road, Building SC-200
P.O. Box 117, MS 36
Oak Ridge, TN 37831-0117
(865) 574-6440   Fax: (865) 576-0734
E-mail: barbara.dunkin@orau.org
Web: orise.orau.gov/mlef/index.html

Summary To provide summer work experience at fossil energy sites of the Department of Energy (DOE) to African American and other underrepresented minority students or postdoctorates.

Eligibility This program is open to U.S. citizens currently enrolled full time at an accredited college or university. Applicants must be undergraduate, graduate, or postdoctoral students in fields of science, technology (IT), engineering, or mathematics (STEM) and have a GPA of 3.0 or higher. They must be interested in a summer work experience at a DOE fossil energy research facility. Along with their application, they must submit a 100-word statement on why they want to participate in this program. A goal of the program is to recruit women and underrepresented minorities into careers related to fossil energy, although all qualified students are encouraged to apply.

Financial data Weekly stipends are $600 for undergraduates, $750 for master's degree students, or $850 for doctoral and postdoctoral students. Travel costs for a round trip to and from the site and for a trip to a designated place for technical presentations are also paid.

Duration 10 weeks during the summer.

Additional information This program began as 3 separate activities: the Historically Black Colleges and Universities Internship Program established in 1995, the Hispanic Internship Program established in 1998, and the Tribal Colleges and Universities Internship Program, established in 2000. Those 3 programs were merged into the Fossil Energy Minority Education Initiative, renamed the Mickey Leland Energy Fellowship Program in 2000. Sites to which interns may be assigned include the National Energy Technology Laboratory (Morgantown, West Virginia, Albany, Oregon and Pittsburgh, Pennsylvania), Pacific Northwest National Laboratory (Richland, Washington), Sandia National Laboratory (Livermore, California), Lawrence Berkeley National Laboratory (Berkeley, California), Los Alamos National Laboratory (Los Alamos, New Mexico), Strategic Petroleum Reserve Project Management Office (New Orleans, Louisiana), or U.S. Department of Energy Headquarters (Washington, D.C.).

Number awarded Varies each year; recently, 30 students participated in this program.

Deadline December of each year.

[1320]
MILDRED BARRY GARVIN PRIZE

New Jersey Historical Commission
Attn: Grants and Prizes
225 West State Street
P.O. Box 305
Trenton, NJ 08625-0305
(609) 292-6062   Fax: (609) 633-8168
E-mail: Feedback@sos.state.nj.us
Web: www.state.nj.us/state/historical/dos_his_grants.html

Summary To recognize and reward New Jersey educators for outstanding teaching of Black American history.

Eligibility This program is open to teachers, guidance counselors, and school librarians in New Jersey. Nominees must have demonstrated outstanding teaching of Black American history in kindergarten through high school or outstanding performance in a related activity, such as developing curriculum materials. Self-nominations are accepted.

Financial data The award is $1,500.

Duration The award is presented annually.

Number awarded 1 each year.

Deadline October of each year.

[1321]
MINORITY FACULTY DEVELOPMENT SCHOLARSHIP AWARD IN PHYSICAL THERAPY

American Physical Therapy Association
Attn: Honors and Awards Program
1111 North Fairfax Street
Alexandria, VA 22314-1488
(703) 684-APTA   Toll Free: (800) 999-APTA, ext. 8082
Fax: (703) 684-7343   TDD: (703) 683-6748
E-mail: honorsandawards@apta.org
Web: www.apta.org

Summary To provide financial assistance to African American and other minority faculty members in physical therapy who are interested in working on a post-professional doctoral degree.

Eligibility This program is open to U.S. citizens and permanent residents who are members of the following minority groups: African American or Black, Asian, Native Hawaiian or other Pacific Islander, American Indian or Alaska Native, or Hispanic/Latino. Applicants must be full-time faculty members, teaching in an accredited or developing professional physical therapist education program, who will have completed the equivalent of 2 full semesters of post-professional doctoral course work. They must possess a license to practice physical therapy in a U.S. jurisdiction and be enrolled as a student in an accredited post-professional doctoral program whose content has a demonstrated relationship to physical therapy. Along with their application, they must submit a personal essay on their professional goals, including their plans to contribute to the profession and minority services. Selection is based on contributions in the area of minority affairs and services and contributions to the profession of physical therapy. Preference is given to members of the American Physical Therapy Association (APTA).

Financial data A stipend is awarded (amount not specified).

Duration 1 year.

Additional information This program began in 1999.

Number awarded 1 or more each year.

Deadline November of each year.

[1322]
MINORITY POSTDOCTORAL FELLOWSHIP AWARDS IN DIABETES

American Diabetes Association
Attn: Research Programs
1701 North Beauregard Street
Alexandria, VA 22311
(703) 549-1500, ext. 2362   Toll Free: (800) DIABETES
Fax: (703) 549-1715
E-mail: grantquestions@diabetes.org
Web: professional.diabetes.org

Summary To provide financial assistance to African American and other minority postdoctoral fellows for additional research training in diabetes.

Eligibility This program is open to members of underrepresented minority groups (African American, Hispanic or Latino, American Indian or Alaskan Native, Native Hawaiian or Pacific Islander) who have an M.D., Ph.D., D.O., D.P.M., or Pharm.D. degree and less than 10 years of postdoctoral experience. Applicants must be authorized to work in the

United States or its territories. They must be interested in a program of research (basic, clinical, or translational) training related to diabetes under the supervision of a mentor. Selection is based on the potential of the project and investigator to significantly impact the field of diabetes research and/or advance the prevention, cure or treatment of diabetes; applicant's scientific potential and potential for establishing a successful and independent career in diabetes-related research; quality and originality of the research proposal and experimental approach, and its relevance to diabetes; tangible evidence of the applicant's performance in research in the form of peer-reviewed scientific publications or equivalent; and evidence of a strong commitment from the mentor toward providing quality training and support in preparation for an independent career in diabetes research.

Financial data The investigator's stipend ranges from $42,000 to $55,272 per year, depending on the number of years of postdoctoral experience. Other support includes a $5,000 training allowance (travel to diabetes-related scientific meetings, computer, books, publication costs, equipment, training courses/workshops, reagents, laboratory supplies) and a $5,000 fringe benefits allowance. Indirect costs are not covered.

Duration Up to 3 years.

Number awarded Varies each year.

Deadline April of each year.

[1323]
MULTICULTURAL AUDIENCE DEVELOPMENT INITIATIVE INTERNSHIPS

Metropolitan Museum of Art
Attn: Internship Programs
1000 Fifth Avenue
New York, NY 10028-0198
(212) 570-3710   Fax: (212) 570-3782
E-mail: mmainterns@metmuseum.org
Web: www.metmuseum.org

Summary To provide summer work experience at the Metropolitan Museum of Art to college undergraduates, graduate students, and recent graduates who are African Americans or members of diverse groups.

Eligibility This program is open to members of diverse groups who are undergraduate juniors and seniors, students currently working on a master's degree, or individuals who completed a bachelor's or master's degree within the past year. Ph.D. students may be eligible to apply during the first 12 months of their program, provided they have not yet achieved candidacy. Students from various academic backgrounds are encouraged to apply, but they must be interested in preparing for a career in the arts and museum fields. Freshmen and sophomores are not eligible.

Financial data The stipend is $3,750.

Duration 10 weeks, beginning in June.

Additional information Interns are assigned to departmental projects (curatorial, administration, or education) at the Metropolitan Museum of Art; other assignments may include giving gallery talks and working at the Visitor Information Center. The assignment is for 35 hours a week. The internships are funded by the Multicultural Audience Initiative at the museum.

Number awarded 1 or more each year.

Deadline January of each year.

[1324]
NATIONAL ASSOCIATION OF NEGRO MUSICIANS SCHOLARSHIP CONTEST

National Association of Negro Musicians, Inc.
Attn: Treasurer
P.O. Box 51669
Durham, NC 27717
E-mail: nanm@nanm.org
Web: www.nanm.org/scholar-main

Summary To recognize and reward (with scholarships for additional study) young musicians who are sponsored by a branch of the National Association of Negro Musicians.

Eligibility This competition is open to musicians between 18 and 30 years of age. Contestants must be sponsored by a branch in good standing, although they do not need to be a member of a local branch or the national organization. For each category of the competition, they must select 2 compositions from assigned lists to perform, of which 1 list consists of works by African American composers. People ineligible to compete include former first-place winners of this competition; full-time public school teachers and college faculty (although graduate students holding teaching assistantships are still eligible if they receive less than 50% of their employment from that appointment); vocalists who have contracts as full-time solo performers in operatic, oratorio, or other types of professional singing organizations; instrumentalists with contractual full-time orchestral or ensemble jobs; and professional performers under management. Local branches nominate competitors for regional competitions. Regional winners advance to the national competition. The category of the competition rotates on a 5-year schedule as follows: 2018: organ; 2019: winds and percussion; 2020: piano; 2021: voice; 2022: strings.

Financial data In the national competition, awards are at least $3,000 for first place, $2,000 for second, $1,000 for third, and $250 for each honorable mention. All funds are paid directly to the winner's teacher/coach or institution.

Duration The competition is held annually.

Additional information The application fee is $50.

Number awarded 5 each year.

Deadline February of each year.

[1325]
NATIONAL BLACK PROGRAMMING CONSORTIUM 360 INCUBATOR AND FUND

National Black Programming Consortium
Attn: Grants Manager
68 East 131st Street, Seventh Floor
New York, NY 10037
(212) 234-8200   Fax: (212) 234-7032
E-mail: info@nbpc.tv
Web: www.blackpublicmedia.org/nbpc-360

Summary To provide funding to producers of African American and African Diaspora films and videos.

Eligibility This program is open to producers and directors who are creating film and video work about the African American and African Diaspora experience. Grants are available for nonfiction multi-part projects for broadcast, webisodic stories, and interactive transmedia about the Black experience. Applicants have wide creative latitude and a range of artistic styles about travel, current affairs, contemporary stories on social issues of importance to African American, lifestyle or DIY, and other subjects with specific points of view. Ineligible projects include student films or thesis projects, industrial or promotional projects, music videos, programs where public television broadcast rights are unavailable, and international projects without a U.S. citizen as the producer or director. Selection is based on appropriateness for a national public television broadcast, strength of the storytelling, experience and ability of crew, likelihood of project completion within 2 years, a realistic budget, and the strength of the distribution or outreach plan.

Financial data Grants range from $50,000 to $150,000.

Duration Pilot projects must be completed within 6 months of funding. All pilots that receive series funding must be completed within 18 months.

Additional information Funding for this program, which began in 2015, is provided by the Corporation for Public Broadcasting.

Number awarded Varies each year; recently, 7 were awarded.

Deadline March of each year.

[1326]
NBCC MINORITY FELLOWSHIP PROGRAM

National Board for Certified Counselors
Attn: NBCC Foundation
3 Terrace Way
Greensboro, NC 27403
(336) 232-0376   Fax: (336) 232-0010
E-mail: foundation@nbcc.org
Web: nbccf-mfpdr.applicantstack.com/x/detail/a2b3qvixcgjm

Summary To provide financial assistance to doctoral candidates, especially African Americans and members of other racially and ethnically diverse populations, and who are interested in working on a degree in mental health and/or substance abuse counseling.

Eligibility This program is open to U.S. citizens and permanent residents who are enrolled full time in an accredited doctoral degree mental health and/or substance abuse and addictions counseling program. Applicants must have a National Certified Counselor or equivalent credential. They must commit to provide mental health and substance abuse services to racially and ethnically diverse populations. African Americans, Alaska Natives, American Indians, Asian Americans, Hispanics/Latinos, Native Hawaiians, and Pacific Islanders are especially encouraged to apply. Applicants must be able to commit to providing substance abuse and addictions counseling services to underserved minority populations for at least 2 years after graduation.

Financial data The stipend is $20,000.

Duration 1 year.

Additional information This program began in 2012 with support from the Substance Abuse and Mental Health Services Administration.

Number awarded 23 each year.

Deadline June of each year.

[1327]
NSF STANDARD AND CONTINUING GRANTS

National Science Foundation
4201 Wilson Boulevard
Arlington, VA 22230
(703) 292-5111   TDD: (800) 281-8749
E-mail: info@nsf.gov
Web: www.nsf.gov/funding/aboutfunding.jsp

Summary To provide financial support to students, engineers, and educators, especially African Americans and members of other underrepresened groups, for research in broad areas of science and engineering.

Eligibility The National Science Foundation (NSF) supports research through its Directorates of Biological Sciences; Computer and Information Science and Engineering; Education and Human Resources; Engineering; Geosciences; Mathematical and Physical Sciences; and Social, Behavioral, and Economic Sciences. Within those general areas of science and engineering, NSF awards 2 types of grants: 1) standard grants, in which NSF agrees to provide a specific level of support for a specified period of time with no statement of NSF intent to provide additional future support without submission of another proposal; and 2) continuing grants, in which NSF agrees to provide a specific level of support for an initial specified period of time with a statement of intent to provide additional support of the project for additional periods, provided funds are available and the results achieved warrant further support. Although NSF often solicits proposals for support of targeted areas through issuance of specific program solicitations, it also accepts unsolicited proposals. Scientists, engineers, and educators usually act as the principal investigator and initiate proposals that are officially submitted by their employing organization. Most employing organizations are universities, colleges, and non-profit non-academic organizations (such as museums, observatories, research laboratories, and professional societies). Certain programs are open to for-profit organizations, state and local governments, or unaffiliated individuals. Principal investigators usually must be U.S. citizens, nationals, or permanent residents. In the selection process, consideration is given to the achievement of societally relevant outcomes, including full participation of women, persons with disabilities, and underrepresented minorities.

Financial data Funding levels vary, depending on the nature of the project and the availability of funds. Awards resulting from unsolicited research proposals are subject to statutory cost-sharing.

Duration Standard grants specify the period of time, usually up to 1 year; continuing grants normally specify 1 year as the initial period of time, with support to continue for additional periods.

Additional information Researchers interested in support from NSF should contact the address above to obtain further information on areas of support and programs operating within the respective directorates. They should consult with a program officer before submitting an application. Information on programs is available on the NSF home page. NSF does not normally support technical assistance, pilot plant efforts, research requiring security classification, the development of products for commercial marketing, or market research for a particular project or invention. Bioscience research with disease-related goals, including work on the etiology, diagnosis, or treatment of physical or mental disease, abnormality, or malfunction in human beings or animals, is normally not supported.

Number awarded Approximately 11,000 new grants are awarded each year.

Deadline Many programs accept proposals at any time. Other programs establish target dates or deadlines; those target dates and deadlines are published in the *NSF Bulletin* and in specific program announcements/solicitations.

[1328]
OKLAHOMA CAREERTECH FOUNDATION TEACHER RECRUITMENT/RETENTION SCHOLARSHIP FOR TEACHERS

Oklahoma CareerTech Foundation
Attn: Administrator
1500 West Seventh Avenue
Stillwater, OK 74074-4364
(405) 743-5453   Fax: (405) 743-5541
E-mail: leden@careertech.ok.gov
Web: www.okcareertech.org

Summary To provide financial assistance to African American and other residents of Oklahoma who reflect the diversity of the state and are interested in attending a college or university in the state to earn a credential or certification for a career in the Oklahoma CareerTech system.

Eligibility This program is open to residents of Oklahoma who are incumbent CareerTech teachers working toward a CareerTech credential or certification at an institution of higher education in the state. Applicants must reflect the ethnic diversity of the state. Along with their application, they must submit brief statements on their interest and commitment to the CareerTech teaching profession and their financial need.

Financial data The stipend ranges from $500 per semester to $1,500 per year.

Duration 1 semester; may be renewed, provided the recipient maintains a GPA of 2.5 or higher.

Number awarded 1 or more each year.

Deadline May of each year.

[1329]
OMOHUNDRO INSTITUTE NEH POSTDOCTORAL FELLOWSHIP

Omohundro Institute of Early American History and
   Culture
1 Landrum Drive
P.O. Box 8781
Williamsburg, VA 23187-8781
(757) 221-1115   Fax: (757) 221-1047
E-mail: oieahc@wm.edu
Web: oieahc.wm.edu/fellowship/submission/index.cfm

Summary To provide funding to scholars in American studies, especially African Americans and members of other underrepresented groups, who wish to revise their dissertation or other manuscript in residence at the Omohundro Institute of Early American History and Culture in Williamsburg, Virginia.

Eligibility Applicants must have completed a Ph.D. in a field that encompasses all aspects of the lives of North America's indigenous and immigrant peoples during the colonial,

Revolutionary, and early national periods of the United States and the related histories of Canada, the Caribbean, Latin America, the British Isles, Europe, and Africa, from the 16th century to approximately 1820. They must be U.S. citizens or have lived in the United States for the 3 previous years. The proposed fellowship project must not be under contract to another publisher. The revisions must be made at the Omohundro Institute. Applicants may not have previously published a book or have entered into a contract for the publication of a scholarly monograph. Selection is based on the potential of the candidate's dissertation or other manuscript to make a distinguished, book-length contribution to scholarship. The Institute encourages applications from women, minorities, protected veterans, and individuals with disabilities.

Financial data The fellowship includes a stipend of $50,400 per year, funds for travel to conferences and research centers, and access to office, research, and computer facilities at the institute.

Duration 2 years.

Additional information Funding for this program is provided by the National Endowment for the Humanities (NEH) for the first year and by the Omohundro Institute for the second year. Fellows have an option to teach at the College of William and Mary during the second year.

Number awarded 1 each year.

Deadline October of each year.

[1330]
PATRICIA M. LOWRIE DIVERSITY LEADERSHIP SCHOLARSHIP

Association of American Veterinary Medical Colleges
Attn: Diversity Committee
1101 Vermont Avenue, N.W., Suite 301
Washington, DC 20005-3536
(202) 371-9195, ext. 147   Toll Free: (877) 862-2740
Fax: (202) 842-0773   E-mail: lgreenhill@aavmc.org
Web: www.aavmc.org

Summary To provide financial assistance to veterinary students who are African Americans or have promoted diversity in the profession in other ways.

Eligibility This program is open to second-, third-, and fourth-year students at veterinary colleges in the United States. Applicants must have a demonstrated record of contributing to enhancing diversity and inclusion through course projects, co-curricular activities, outreach, domestic and community engagement, research, and/or an early reputation for influencing others to be inclusive. Along with their application, they must submit a 3-page personal statement that describes 1) why diversity and inclusion are important to them personally and professionally; 2) how they intend to continue contributing to diversity and inclusion efforts in the veterinary profession after graduation; and 3) what it might mean to be honored as a recipient of this scholarship. They must also indicate how they express their race and/or ethnicity (Black or African American, American Indian or Alaskan, Asian, Hispanic, Native Hawaiian or Pacific Islander, or White) and how they express their gender (male, female, transgender spectrum, or other). Selection is based primarily on documentation of a demonstrated commitment to promoting diversity in academic veterinary medicine; consideration is also given to academic achievement, the student's broader community service record, and financial need.

Financial data The stipend is $6,000.

Duration 1 year; nonrenewable.

Additional information This program began in 2013.

Number awarded 1 each odd-numbered year.

Deadline October of each even-numbered year.

[1331]
PAULA DE MERIEUX RHEUMATOLOGY FELLOWSHIP AWARD

American College of Rheumatology
Attn: Rheumatology Research Foundation
2200 Lake Boulevard N.E.
Atlanta, GA 30319
(404) 633-3777   Fax: (404) 633-1870
E-mail: foundation@rheumatology.org
Web: rheumresearch.org/Awards/Education_Training

Summary To provide funding to African Americans and other underrepresented minorities interested in a program of training for a career providing clinical care to people affected by rheumatic diseases.

Eligibility This program is open to trainees at ACGME-accredited institutions. Applications must be submitted by the training program director at the institution who is responsible for selection and appointment of trainees. The program must train and prepare fellows to provide clinical care to those affected by rheumatic diseases. Trainees must be women or members of underrepresented minority groups, defined as Black Americans, Hispanics, and Native Americans (Native Hawaiians, Alaska Natives, and American Indians). They must be U.S. citizens, nationals, or permanent residents. Selection is based on the institution's pass rate of rheumatology fellows, publication history of staff and previous fellows, current positions of previous fellows, and status of clinical faculty.

Financial data The grant is $50,000, to be used as salary for the trainee. Other trainee costs (e.g., fees, health insurance, travel, attendance at scientific meetings) are to be incurred by the recipient's institutional program. Supplemental or additional support to offset the cost of living may be provided by the grantee institution.

Duration Up to 1 year.

Additional information This fellowship was first awarded in 2005.

Number awarded 1 each year.

Deadline July of each year.

[1332]
PEN OPEN BOOK AWARD

PEN American Center
Attn: Literary Awards Associate
588 Broadway, Suite 303
New York, NY 10012
(212) 334-1660, ext. 4813   Fax: (212) 334-2181
E-mail: awards@pen.org
Web: www.pen.org/content/pen-open-book-award-5000

Summary To recognize and reward outstanding African American and other authors of color from any country.

Eligibility This award is presented to an author of color (African, Arab, Asian, Caribbean, Latino, and Native Ameri-

can) whose book-length writings were published in the United States during the current calendar year. Works of fiction, literary nonfiction, biography/memoir, poetry, and other works of literary character are strongly preferred. U.S. citizenship or residency is not required. Nominations must be submitted by publishers or literary agents. Self-published books are not eligible.

Financial data The prize is $5,000.

Duration The prizes are awarded annually.

Additional information This prize was formerly known as the Beyond Margins Award. The entry fee is $75.

Number awarded 1 or 2 each year.

Deadline August of each year.

[1333]
POSTDOCTORAL FELLOWSHIPS IN DIABETES RESEARCH

Juvenile Diabetes Research Foundation International
Attn: Senior Director, Research Administration
26 Broadway, 14th Floor
New York, NY 10004
(212) 479-7519   Toll Free: (800) 533-CURE
Fax: (212) 785 9595   E-mail: emilligan@jdrf.org
Web: grantcenter.jdrf.org

Summary To provide research training to scientists, especially African Americans and members of other underrepresented groups, who are beginning their professional careers and are interested in participating in research training on the causes, treatment, prevention, or cure of diabetes or its complications.

Eligibility This program is open to postdoctorates who are interested in a career in Type 1 diabetes-relevant research. Applicants must have received their first doctoral degree (M.D., Ph.D., D.M.D., or D.V.M.) within the past 5 years and may not have a faculty appointment. There are no citizenship requirements. Applications are encouraged from women, members of minority groups underrepresented in the sciences, and people with disabilities. The proposed research training may be conducted at foreign or domestic, for-profit or nonprofit, or public or private institutions, including universities, colleges, hospitals, laboratories, units of state or local government, or eligible agencies of the federal government. Applicants must be sponsored by an investigator who is affiliated full time with an accredited institution and who agrees to supervise the applicant's training. Selection is based on the applicant's previous experience and academic record; the caliber of the proposed research; and the quality of the mentor, training program, and environment.

Financial data Stipends range from $42,840 to $56,376 per year (depending upon years of experience). In any case, the award may not exceed the salary the recipient is currently earning. Fellows also receive a research allowance of $5,500 per year.

Duration 3 years.

Additional information Fellows must devote 100% of their effort to the fellowship project.

Number awarded Varies each year; recently, 8 were awarded.

Deadline July of each year.

[1334]

POSTDOCTORAL FELLOWSHIPS OF THE CONSORTIUM FOR FACULTY DIVERSITY

Consortium for Faculty Diversity at Liberal Arts Colleges
c/o Gettysburg College
Provost's Office
300 North Washington Street
Campus Box 410
Gettysburg, PA 17325
(717) 337-6796   E-mail: sgockows@gettysburg.edu
Web: www.gettysburg.edu

Summary To make available the facilities of liberal arts colleges to scholars who recently received their doctoral/advanced degree and are African Americans or will otherwise enhance diversity at their college.

Eligibility This program is open to scholars in the liberal arts and engineering who are U.S. citizens or permanent residents and received the Ph.D. or M.F.A. degree within the past 5 years. Applicants must be interested in a residency at a participating institution that is part of the Consortium for Faculty Diversity at Liberal Arts Colleges. They must be able to enhance diversity at the institution.

Financial data Fellows receive a stipend equivalent to the average salary paid by the host college to beginning assistant professors. Modest funds are made available to finance the fellow's proposed research, subject to the usual institutional procedures.

Duration 1 year.

Additional information The following schools are participating in the program: Allegheny College, Amherst College, Bard College, Bowdoin College, Bryn Mawr College, Bucknell University, Carleton College, Centenary College of Louisiana, Centre College, College of the Holy Cross, Colorado College, Denison University, DePauw University, Dickinson College, Gettysburg College, Grinnell College, Gustavus Adolphus College, Hamilton College, Haverford College, Hobart and William Smith Colleges, Juniata College, Lafayette College, Lawrence University, Luther College, Macalester College, Mount Holyoke College, Muhlenberg College, Oberlin College, Pitzer College, Pomona College, Reed College, Scripps College, Skidmore College, Smith College, Southwestern University, St. Lawrence University, St. Olaf College, Swarthmore College, The College of Wooster, Trinity College, University of Richmond, Vassar College, and Wellesley College. Fellows are expected to teach at least 60% of a regular full-time faculty member's load, participate in departmental seminars, and interact with students.

Number awarded Varies each year; recently, 23 of the 43 member institutions made a total of 51 appointments through this program.

Deadline October of each year.

[1335]

POSTDOCTORAL FELLOWSHIPS OF THE FORD FOUNDATION DIVERSITY FELLOWSHIP PROGRAM

The National Academies of Sciences, Engineering, and Medicine
Attn: Fellowships Office
500 Fifth Street, N.W.
Washington, DC 20001
(202) 334-2872   Fax: (202) 334-3419
E-mail: FordApplications@nas.edu
Web: sites.nationalacademies.org

Summary To provide funding for postdoctoral research to be conducted in the United States or any other country to African American or other scholars whose success will increase the racial and ethnic diversity of U.S. colleges and universities.

Eligibility This program is open to U.S. citizens, permanent residents, and nationals who earned a Ph.D. or Sc.D. degree within the past 7 years and are committed to a career in teaching and research at the college or university level. The following are considered as positive factors in the selection process: evidence of superior academic achievement; promise of continuing achievement as scholars and teachers; membership in a group whose underrepresentation in the American professoriate has been severe and longstanding, including Black/African Americans, Puerto Ricans, Mexican Americans/Chicanos/Chicanas, Native American Indians, Alaska Natives (Eskimos, Aleuts, and other indigenous people of Alaska), and Native Pacific Islanders (Hawaiians, Micronesians, or Polynesians); capacity to respond in pedagogically productive ways to the learning needs of students from diverse backgrounds; sustained personal engagement with communities that are underrepresented in the academy and an ability to bring this asset to learning, teaching, and scholarship at the college and university level; and likelihood of using the diversity of human experience as an educational resource in teaching and scholarship. Eligible areas of study include American studies, anthropology, archaeology, art and theater history, astronomy, chemistry, communications, computer science, cultural studies, earth sciences, economics, education, engineering, ethnic studies, ethnomusicology, geography, history, international relations, language, life sciences, linguistics, literature, mathematics, performance study, philosophy, physics, political science, psychology, religious studies, sociology, urban planning, and women's studies. Also eligible are interdisciplinary programs such as African American studies, Native American studies, area studies, peace studies, and social justice. Awards are not available for practice-oriented programs or professional programs such as medicine, law, or public health. Research may be conducted at an appropriate institution of higher education in the United States (normally) or abroad, including universities, museums, libraries, government or national laboratories, privately sponsored nonprofit institutes, government chartered nonprofit research organizations, or centers for advanced study. Applicants should designate a faculty member or other scholar to serve as host at the proposed fellowship institution. They are encouraged to choose a host institution other than that where they are affiliated at the time of application.

Financial data The stipend is $45,000. Funds may be supplemented by sabbatical leave pay or other sources of support that do not carry with them teaching or other responsibilities. The employing institution receives an allowance of $1,500, paid after fellowship tenure is completed; the employing institution is expected to match the grant and to use the allowance and the match to assist with the fellow's continuing research expenditures.

Duration 9 to 12 months.

Additional information Fellows may not accept another major fellowship while they are being supported by this program.

Number awarded Approximately 24 each year.

Deadline November of each year.

[1336]
PROGRAM IN AFRICAN AMERICAN HISTORY MELLON SCHOLAR POSTDOCTORAL FELLOWSHIPS

Library Company of Philadelphia
Attn: Program in African American History
1314 Locust Street
Philadelphia, PA 19107-5698
(215) 546-3181   Fax: (215) 546-5167
E-mail: era@udel.edu
Web: www.librarycompany.org/fellowships/postdoc.htm

Summary To provide funding to postdoctorates who are African Americans or from other underrepresented backgrounds and interested in conducting research on African American history at the Library Company of Philadelphia.

Eligibility This program is open to scholars from underrepresented backgrounds who have completed a Ph.D. and are interested in conducting research in Philadelphia at the Library Company. The proposed research must relate to African American history prior to 1900.

Financial data The grant is $50,000 for an academic year or $25,000 for a semester.

Duration 1 academic year or 1 semester.

Additional information The Library Company of Philadelphia established its Program in African American History in 2013 with support from the Andrew W. Mellon Foundation.

Number awarded Either 1 fellowship for a year or 2 for a semester are supported each year.

Deadline February of each year.

[1337]
PROGRAM IN AFRICAN AMERICAN HISTORY SHORT-TERM MELLON SCHOLARS FELLOWSHIPS

Library Company of Philadelphia
Attn: Program in African American History
1314 Locust Street
Philadelphia, PA 19107-5698
(215) 546-3181   Fax: (215) 546-5167
E-mail: era@udel.edu
Web: www.librarycompany.org/fellowships/shortterm.htm

Summary To provide funding to pre- and postdoctorates who are African Americans or from other underrepresented backgrounds and interested in conducting short-term research on African American history at the Library Company of Philadelphia.

Eligibility This program is open to doctoral candidates and senior scholars from underrepresented backgrounds who are interested in conducting research in Philadelphia at the

Library Company. The proposed research must relate to African American history prior to 1900.

Financial data The stipend is $2,500.

Duration 1 month.

Additional information The Library Company of Philadelphia established its Program in African American History in 2013 with support from the Andrew W. Mellon Foundation.

Number awarded 4 each year.

Deadline February of each year.

[1338]
R. ROBERT & SALLY FUNDERBURG RESEARCH AWARD IN GASTRIC CANCER

American Gastroenterological Association
Attn: AGA Research Foundation
Research Awards Manager
4930 Del Ray Avenue
Bethesda, MD 20814-2512
(301) 222-4012   Fax: (301) 654-5920
E-mail: awards@gastro.org
Web: www.gastro.org

Summary To provide funding to established investigators, especially African Americans and other minorities, who are working on research that enhances fundamental understanding of gastric cancer pathobiology.

Eligibility This program is open to faculty at accredited North American institutions who have established themselves as independent investigators in the field of gastric biology, pursuing novel approaches to gastric mucosal cell biology, including the fields of gastric mucosal cell biology, regeneration and regulation of cell growth, inflammation as precancerous lesions, genetics of gastric carcinoma, oncogenes in gastric epithelial malignancies, epidemiology of gastric cancer, etiology of gastric epithelial malignancies, or clinical research in diagnosis or treatment of gastric carcinoma. Applicants must be individual members of the American Gastroenterological Association (AGA). Women and minority investigators are strongly encouraged to apply. Selection is based on the novelty, feasibility, and significance of the proposal. Preference is given to novel approaches.

Financial data The grant is $50,000 per year. Funds are to be used for the salary of the investigator. Indirect costs are not allowed.

Duration 2 years.

Number awarded 1 each year.

Deadline August of each year.

[1339]
REGINALD F. LEWIS FELLOWSHIP FOR LAW TEACHING

Harvard Law School
Attn: Lewis Committee
Griswold Two South
1525 Massachusetts Avenue
Cambridge, MA 02138
(617) 495-3109
E-mail: LewisFellowship@law.harvard.edu
Web: hls.harvard.edu

Summary To provide funding to law school graduates, especially African Americans and others of color, who are preparing for a career in law teaching and are interested in a program of research and training at Harvard Law School.

Eligibility This program is open to recent graduates of law school who have demonstrated an interest in law scholarship and teaching. Applicants must be interested in spending time in residence at Harvard Law School where they will audit courses, attend workshops, and follow a schedule of research under the sponsorship of the committee. The program encourages the training of prospective law teachers who will enhance the diversity of the profession and especially encourages applications from candidates of color.

Financial data The stipend is $50,000 per year.

Duration 2 years.

Number awarded 1 each year.

Deadline January of each year.

[1340]
RESEARCH AND TRAINING PROGRAM ON POVERTY AND PUBLIC POLICY POSTDOCTORAL FELLOWSHIPS

University of Michigan
Gerald R. Ford School of Public Policy
Attn: National Poverty Center
Joan and Sanford Weill Hall
735 South State Street, Room 5100
Ann Arbor, MI 48109-3091
(734) 764-3490   Fax: (734) 763-9181
E-mail: npcinfo@umich.edu
Web: npc.umich.edu/opportunities/visiting

Summary To provide funding to African American and other minority postdoctorates interested in conducting research and pursuing intensive training on poverty-related public policy issues at the University of Michigan.

Eligibility This program is open to U.S. citizens and permanent residents who are African Americans or members of other minority groups that are underrepresented in the social sciences. Applicants must have received the Ph.D. degree within the past 5 years and be engaged in research on poverty and public policy. Along with their application, they must submit a research proposal that represents either a significant extension upon previous work or a new poverty research project; a 1- to 2-page statement that specifies the ways in which residence at the University of Michigan will foster their career development and research goals and provides information about how their racial/ethnic/regional/economic background qualifies them as a members of a group that is underrepresented in the social sciences; a curriculum vitae; and a sample of their scholarly writing. Preference is given to proposals that would benefit from resources available at the University of Michigan and from interactions with affiliated faculty.

Financial data The stipend is $50,000 per calendar year.

Duration 1 or 2 years.

Additional information This program is funded by the Ford Foundation. Fellows spend the year participating in a seminar on poverty and public policy and conducting their own research. Topics currently pursued include the effects of the recession and the American Recovery and Reinvestment Act of 2009 on workers, families, and children; evolution of the social safety net; longitudinal analyses of youth development; family formation and healthy marriages; immigration and poverty; investing in low-income families: the accumula-

tion of financial assets and human capital; and qualitative and mixed-methods research on poverty. Fellows must be in residence at the University of Michigan for the duration of the program.

Number awarded 1 or more each year.

Deadline January of each year.

[1341]
RESEARCH SCHOLAR AWARDS OF THE AMERICAN GASTROENTEROLOGICAL ASSOCIATION

American Gastroenterological Association
Attn: AGA Research Foundation
Research Awards Manager
4930 Del Ray Avenue
Bethesda, MD 20814-2512
(301) 222-4012   Fax: (301) 654-5920
E-mail: awards@gastro.org
Web: www.gastro.org/grants/research-scholar-award-rsa

Summary To provide research funding to young investigators, especially African Americans and other minorities, who are developing an independent career in an area of gastroenterology, hepatology, or related fields.

Eligibility Applicants must hold full-time faculty positions at North American universities or professional institutes at the time of application. They should be early in their careers (fellows and established investigators are not appropriate candidates). Candidates with an M.D. degree must have completed clinical training within the past 7 years and those with a Ph.D. must have completed their degree within the past 7 years. Membership in the American Gastroenterological Association (AGA) is required. Selection is based on significance, investigator, innovation, approach, environment, relevance to AGA mission, and evidence of institutional commitment. Women, minorities, and physician/scientist investigators are strongly encouraged to apply.

Financial data The grant is $90,000 per year. Funds are to be used for project costs, including salary, supplies, and equipment but excluding travel. Indirect costs are not allowed.

Duration 3 years.

Additional information At least 70% of the recipient's research effort should relate to the gastrointestinal tract or liver.

Number awarded Varies each year; recently, 5 were awarded.

Deadline August of each year.

[1342]
ROBERT WOOD JOHNSON HEALTH POLICY FELLOWSHIPS

National Academy of Medicine
Attn: Health Policy Fellowships Program
500 Fifth Street, N.W.
Washington, DC 20001
(202) 334-1506   Fax: (202) 334-3862
E-mail: info@healthpolicyfellows.org
Web: www.healthpolicyfellows.org/apply

Summary To provide an opportunity to health professionals and behavioral and social scientists, especially African Americans and members of other underrepresented groups who have an interest in health, to participate in the formulation of national health policies while in residence at the National Academy of Medicine (NAM) in Washington, D.C.

Eligibility This program is open to mid-career professionals from academic faculties and nonprofit health care organizations who are interested in experiencing health policy processes at the federal level. Applicants must have a background in allied health professions, biomedical sciences, dentistry, economics or other social sciences, health services organization and administration, medicine, nursing, public health, social and behavioral health, or health law. They must be sponsored by the chief executive officer of an eligible nonprofit health care organization or academic institution. Selection is based on potential for leadership in health policy, potential for future growth and career advancement, professional achievements, interpersonal and communication skills, potential for significant contributions to building a Culture of Health, and individual plans for incorporating the fellowship experience into specific career goals. U.S. citizenship or permanent resident status is required. Applications are especially encouraged from candidates with diverse backgrounds of race, ethnicity, gender, age, disability, and socioeconomic status.

Financial data Total support for the Washington stay and continuing activities may not exceed $165,000. Grant funds may cover salary support at a level of up to $104,000 plus fringe benefits. Fellows are reimbursed for relocation expenses to and from Washington, D.C. No indirect costs are paid.

Duration The program lasts 1 year and includes an orientation in September and October; meetings in November and December with members of Congress, journalists, policy analysts, and other experts on the national political and governmental process; and working assignments from January through August. Fellows then return to their home institutions, but they receive up to 2 years of continued support for further development of health policy leadership skills.

Additional information This program, initiated in 1973, is funded by the Robert Wood Johnson Foundation.

Number awarded Up to 6 each year.

Deadline November of each year.

[1343]
ROME FOUNDATION FUNCTIONAL GI AND MOTILITY DISORDERS PILOT RESEARCH AWARD

American Gastroenterological Association
Attn: AGA Research Foundation
Research Awards Manager
4930 Del Ray Avenue
Bethesda, MD 20814-2512
(301) 222-4012   Fax: (301) 654-5920
E-mail: awards@gastro.org
Web: www.gastro.org

Summary To provide funding to investigators at all levels, especially African Americans and other minorities, who are interested in conducting pilot research related to functional gastrointestinal and motility disorders.

Eligibility This program is open to early stage and established investigators, postdoctoral research fellows, and combined research and clinical fellows. Applicants must be interested in conducting pilot research on the pathophysiology, diagnosis, and/or treatment of functional gastrointestinal or

motility disorders. They must have an M.D. or Ph.D. degree and a full-time faculty position at a North American educational institution. Membership in the American Gastroenterological Association (AGA) is required. Selection is based on novelty, importance, feasibility, environment, and the overall likelihood that the project will lead to subsequent, more substantial grants in the areas of functional gastrointestinal and motility disorders research. Women and minorities are strongly encouraged to apply.

Financial data The grant is $50,000. Funds are to be used for project costs, including salary, supplies, and equipment but excluding travel. Indirect costs are not allowed.

Duration 1 year.

Additional information This program is sponsored by the Rome Foundation.

Number awarded Varies each year; recently, 2 were awarded.

Deadline January of each year.

[1344]
SCHOLARLY EDITIONS AND TRANSLATIONS GRANTS

National Endowment for the Humanities
Attn: Division of Research Programs
400 Seventh Street, S.W.
Washington, DC 20506
(202) 606-8200   Toll Free: (800) NEH-1121
Fax: (202) 606-8204   TDD: (866) 372-2930
E-mail: editions@neh.gov
Web: www.neh.gov

Summary To provide funding to scholars, especially those from minority-serving institutions, who are interested in preparing texts and documents in the humanities.

Eligibility This program is open to 1) U.S. citizens and foreign nationals who have been living in the United States or its jurisdictions for at least 3 years; 2) state and local governmental agencies; and 3) nonprofit, tax-exempt institutions and organizations in the United States. It supports the preparation of editions and translations of pre-existing texts and documents of value to the humanities that are currently inaccessible or available in inadequate editions. Projects must be undertaken by a team of at least 1 editor or translator and 1 other staff member. Grants typically support editions and translations of significant literary, philosophical, and historical materials, but other types of work, such as the editing of musical notation, are also eligible. Selection is based on 1) the intellectual significance of the project, including its potential contribution to scholarship in the humanities, the likelihood that it will stimulate new research, its relationship to larger themes in the humanities, and the significance of the material on which the project is based; 2) the appropriateness of the research methods, critical apparatus, and editorial policies; the appropriateness of selection criteria; the thoroughness and feasibility of the work plan; and the quality of the samples; 3) the qualifications, expertise, and levels of commitment of the project director and key project staff or contributors, and the appropriateness of the staff to the goals of the project; 4) the promise of quality, usefulness, and impact on scholarship of any resulting publication or other product; and 5) the potential for success, including the likelihood that the project will be successfully completed within the projected time frame. The program encourages submission of applications from faculty at Historically Black Colleges and Universities, Hispanic Serving Institutions, and Tribal Colleges and Universities.

Financial data Grants range from $50,000 to $100,000 per year. The use of federal matching funds in encouraged. Normally, support does not exceed 80% of total costs.

Duration 1 to 3 years.

Number awarded Approximately 26 each year.

Deadline December of each year.

[1345]
SCHOMBURG CENTER SCHOLARS-IN-RESIDENCE PROGRAM

New York Public Library
Attn: Schomburg Center for Research in Black Culture
515 Malcolm X Boulevard
New York, NY 10037-1801
(212) 491-2218   Fax: (212) 491-6760
Web: www.nypl.org

Summary To provide financial support for research and writing on the history, literature, and cultures of the peoples of Africa and the African Diaspora at the Schomburg Center of the New York Public Library.

Eligibility This program is open to 1) scholars studying the history, literature, and culture of the peoples of African descent from a humanistic perspective; and 2) professionals in fields related to the sponsor's collections and program activities. Projects in the social sciences, psychology, science and technology, education, and religion are eligible if they utilize a humanistic approach and contribute to humanistic knowledge. Applicants must be U.S. citizens or foreign nationals who have resided in the United States for at least 3 years. Selection is based on qualifications of the applicant, quality and feasibility of the project plan, importance of the proposed project to the applicant's field and to the humanities, relationship of the project to the humanities, relationship of the project to the resources of the Schomburg Center, likelihood that the project will be completed successfully, and provisions for making the results of the project available to scholars and to the public at large.

Financial data The stipend is $30,000.

Duration 6 months.

Additional information This program is made possible by grants from the National Endowment for the Humanities, the Andrew W. Mellon Foundation, the Ford Foundation, and the Samuel I. Newhouse Foundation. Participants in the program must be in residence at the Schomburg Center of the New York Public Library on a full-time basis. They may not hold other major fellowships/grants or be employed during the residency. No support is available to students conducting research leading to a degree.

Number awarded Up to 8 each year.

Deadline December of each year.

[1346]
SLA NEW ENGLAND DIVERSITY LEADERSHIP DEVELOPMENT SCHOLARSHIP

SLA New England
c/o Khalilah Gambrell, Diversity Chair
EBSCO Information Services
10 Estes Street
Ipswich, MA 01938
(978) 356-6500   Toll Free: (800) 653-2726
Fax: (978) 356-6565   E-mail: gambrell9899@gmail.com
Web: newengland.sla.org/member-benefits/stipends

Summary To provide financial assistance for library science tuition or attendance at the annual conference of the Special Libraries Association (SLA) to members of SLA New England who are African Americans or represent another diverse population.

Eligibility This program is open to SLA New England members who are of Black (African American), Hispanic, Asian American, Pacific Islander American, Native Alaskan, or Native Hawaiian heritage. Applicants must be seeking funding for SLA annual meeting attendance, tuition reimbursement for a library science program, or tuition reimbursement for a course directly related to the library and information science field. Along with their application, they must submit a 500-word essay on how they will encourage and celebrate diversity within the SLA New England community.

Financial data The award covers actual expenses up to $1,500.

Duration This is a 1-time award.

Number awarded 1 each year.

Deadline April of each year.

[1347]
SMITHSONIAN MINORITY STUDENT INTERNSHIP

Smithsonian Institution
Attn: Office of Fellowships and Internships
470 L'Enfant, Suite 7102
P.O. Box 37012, MRC 902
Washington, DC 20013-7012
(202) 633-7070   Fax: (202) 633-7069
E-mail: siofi@si.edu
Web: www.smithsonianofi.com/minority-internship-program

Summary To provide African American and other minority undergraduate or graduate students with the opportunity to work on research or museum procedure projects in specific areas of history, art, or science at the Smithsonian Institution.

Eligibility Internships are offered to minority students who are actively engaged in undergraduate or graduate study or have graduated within the past 4 months. Applicants must be U.S. citizens or permanent residents who have an overall GPA of 3.0 or higher. Applicants must be interested in conducting research in any of the following fields of interest to the Smithsonian: animal behavior, ecology, and environmental science (including an emphasis on the tropics); anthropology (including archaeology); astrophysics and astronomy; earth sciences and paleobiology; evolutionary and systematic biology; history of science and technology; history of art (especially American, contemporary, African, Asian, and 20th-century art); American crafts and decorative arts; social and cultural history of the United States; and folklife.

Financial data The program provides a stipend of $600 per week; travel allowances may also be offered.

Duration 10 weeks during the summer or academic year.

Number awarded Varies each year.

Deadline January of each year for summer or fall; September of each year for spring.

[1348]
STANFORD HUMANITIES CENTER EXTERNAL FACULTY FELLOWSHIPS

Stanford Humanities Center
Attn: Fellowship Administrator
424 Santa Teresa Street
Stanford, CA 94305-4015
(650) 723-3054   Fax: (650) 723-1895
E-mail: pterraza@stanford.edu
Web: shc.stanford.edu/fellowships/non-stanford-faculty

Summary To offer scholars in the humanities, especially African Americans and members of other underrepresented groups, an opportunity to conduct research and teach at Stanford University.

Eligibility External fellowships at Stanford University fall into 2 categories: 1) senior fellowships for scholars who are more than 10 years beyond receipt of the Ph.D.; and 2) junior fellowships for scholars who at the time of application are at least 3 but normally no more than 10 years beyond receipt of the Ph.D. The fields of study should be the humanities as defined in the act that established the National Foundation for the Arts and Humanities. There are no citizenship requirements; non-U.S. nationals are eligible. Scholars who are members of traditionally underrepresented groups are encouraged to apply. Applications are judged on 1) the promise of the specific research project being proposed; 2) the originality and intellectual distinction of the candidate's previous work; 3) the research project's potential interest to scholars in different fields of the humanities; and 4) the applicant's ability to engage in collegial interaction and to contribute to the discussion of presentations.

Financial data The annual stipend is up to $70,000. In addition, a housing/travel subsidy of up to $30,000, depending on size of family, is offered.

Duration 1 academic year.

Additional information Fellows are expected to make an intellectual contribution not only within the center but to humanistic studies in general at Stanford. Normally, this requirement is fulfilled by teaching an undergraduate or graduate course or seminar for 1 quarter within a particular department or program. Fellows should live within 10 miles of Stanford University. Regular attendance at center events is expected and fellows are expected to be present during the fall, winter, and spring quarters and to attend weekday lunches on a regular basis.

Number awarded 6 to 8 each year.

Deadline October of each year.

[1349]
STANTON NUCLEAR SECURITY FELLOWSHIP

Stanford University
Center for International Security and Cooperation
Attn: Fellowships Coordinator
Encina Hall, Room C206-10
616 Serra Street
Stanford, CA 94305-6165
(650) 723-9625   Fax: (650) 724-5683
E-mail: CISACfellowship@stanford.edu
Web: cisac.fsi.stanford.edu/docs/cisac_fellowship_program

Summary To provide funding to doctoral candidates and junior scholars, especially African Americans and members of other underrepresented groups, who are interested in conducting research on nuclear security issues at Stanford University's Center for International Security and Cooperation.

Eligibility This program is open to doctoral candidates, recent postdoctorates, and junior faculty. Applicants must be interested in conducting research on nuclear security issues while in residence at the center. The sponsor welcomes applications from women, minorities, and citizens of all countries.

Financial data The stipend ranges from $25,000 to $28,000 for doctoral candidates or from $48,000 to $66,000 for postdoctorates, depending on experience. Medical insurance is available for those who do not have coverage.

Duration 9 to 11 months.

Additional information Fellows are expected to write a dissertation chapter or chapters, publishable article or articles, and/or make significant progress on turning a thesis into a book manuscript. They should not plan to spend any time conducting research abroad or in other parts of the country.

Number awarded Varies each year; recently, 3 were awarded: 1 doctoral candidate, 1 recent postdoctorate, and 1 junior faculty member.

Deadline January of each year.

[1350]
STUDIO MUSEUM IN HARLEM ARTIST-IN-RESIDENCE PROGRAM

Studio Museum in Harlem
Attn: Education and Public Programs Department
144 West 125th Street
New York, NY 10027
(212) 864-4500, ext. 230   Fax: (212) 864-4800
Web: www.studiomuseum.org/learn/artist-in-residence

Summary To support visual artists of African and Latino descent who are interested in a residency at the Studio Museum in Harlem.

Eligibility This program is open to artists of African and Latino descent locally, nationally, or internationally. Applicants may be working in sculpture, painting, photography, printmaking, film and video, digital art, or mixed media. They must be professional artists with at least 3 years of professional commitment and currently engaged in studio work; high school, college, and graduate students are not considered. Selection is based on quality of the work, a record of exhibition and critical review, demonstration of a serious and consistent dedication to the professional practice of fine arts, evidence that the applicant is at a critical juncture in development that will be advanced by a residency, and letters of recommendation.

Financial data This fellowship provides non-residential studio space, a stipend of $20,000, and a $1,000 material grant.

Duration 11 months.

Additional information Support for this program is provided by the Robert Lehman Foundation, the Jerome Foundation, and the Milton and Sally Avery Arts Foundation. Additional support is provided by the Andrew W. Mellon Foundation, New York City Department of Cultural Affairs, New York State Council on the Arts, and the New York City Council. Artists must spend at least 20 hours per week in their studios, exhibit their works in the museum, and conduct 2 public presentations/workshops.

Number awarded 3 each year.

Deadline March of each year.

[1351]
SUBSTANCE ABUSE FELLOWSHIP PROGRAM

American Psychiatric Association
Attn: Division of Diversity and Health Equity
1000 Wilson Boulevard, Suite 1825
Arlington, VA 22209-3901
(703) 907-8653　　　　Toll Free: (888) 35-PSYCH
Fax: (703) 907-7852　　　　E-mail: mking@psych.org
Web: www.psychiatry.org/minority-fellowship

Summary To provide educational enrichment to African American and other minority psychiatrists-in-training and stimulate their interest in providing quality and effective services related to substance abuse to minorities and the underserved.

Eligibility This program is open to psychiatric residents who are members of the American Psychiatric Association (APA) and U.S. citizens or permanent residents. A goal of the program is to develop leadership to improve the quality of mental health care for members of ethnic minority groups (African Americans, Native Alaskans, American Indians, Asian Americans, Native Hawaiians, Native Pacific Islanders, and Hispanics/Latinos). Applicants must be in at least their fifth year of a substance abuse training program approved by an affiliated medical school or agency where a significant number of substance abuse patients are from minority and underserved groups. They must also be interested in working with a component of the APA that is of interest to them and relevant to their career goals. Along with their application, they must submit a 2-page essay on how the fellowship would be utilized to alter their present training and ultimately assist them in achieving their career goals. Selection is based on commitment to serve ethnic minority populations, demonstrated leadership abilities, awareness of the importance of culture in mental health, and interest in the interrelationship between mental health/illness and transcultural factors.

Financial data Fellows receive a monthly stipend (amount not specified) and reimbursement of transportation, lodging, meals, and incidentals in connection with attendance at program-related activities. They are expected to use the funds to enhance their own professional development, improve training in cultural competence at their training institution, improve awareness of culturally relevant issues in psychiatry at their institution, expand research in areas relevant to minorities and underserved populations, enhance the current treatment modalities for minority patients and underserved individuals at their institution, and improve awareness in the surrounding community about mental health issues (particularly with regard to minority populations).

Duration 1 year; may be renewed 1 additional year.

Additional information Funding for this program is provided by the Substance Abuse and Mental Health Services Administration (SAMHSA). As part of their assignment to an APA component, fellows must attend the fall component meetings in September and the APA annual meeting in May. At those meeting, they can share their experiences as residents and minorities and discuss issues that impact minority populations. This program is an outgrowth of the fellowships that were established in 1974 under a grant from the National Institute of Mental Health in answer to concerns about the underrepresentation of minorities in psychiatry.

Number awarded Varies each year; recently, 3 were awarded.

Deadline January of each year.

[1352]
SUMMER RESEARCH PROGRAM IN ECOLOGY

Harvard University
Harvard Forest
324 North Main Street
Petersham, MA 01366
(978) 724-3302　　　　Fax: (978) 724-3595
E-mail: hfapps@fas.harvard.edu
Web: harvardforest.fas.harvard.edu/other-tags/reu

Summary To provide an opportunity for undergraduate students and recent graduates, especially African Americans and members of other diverse groups, to participate in a summer ecological research project at Harvard Forest in Petersham, Massachusetts.

Eligibility This program is open to undergraduate students and recent graduates interested in participating in a mentored research project at the Forest. The research may relate to the effects of natural and human disturbances on forest ecosystems, including global climate change, hurricanes, forest harvest, changing wildlife dynamics, or invasive species. Investigators come from many disciplines, and specific projects center on population and community ecology, paleoecology, land use history, aquatic ecology, biochemistry, soil science, ecophysiology, and atmosphere-biosphere exchanges. Students from diverse backgrounds are strongly encouraged to apply.

Financial data The stipend is $5,775. Free housing, meals, and travel reimbursement for 1 round trip are also provided.

Duration 11 weeks during the summer.

Additional information Funding for this program is provided by the National Science Foundation (as part of its Research Experience for Undergraduates program).

Number awarded Up to 25 each year.

Deadline February of each year.

[1353]
TOXICOLOGISTS OF AFRICAN ORIGIN DISTINGUISHED SCIENTIFIC PRESENTATION AWARD

Society of Toxicology
Attn: Toxicologists of African Origin Special Interest Group
1821 Michael Faraday Drive, Suite 300
Reston, VA 20190-5348
(703) 438-3115   Fax: (703) 438-3113
E-mail: sothq@toxicology.org
Web: www.toxicology.org/ai/af/awards_details.aspx?id=222

Summary To recognize and reward research presentations by postdoctoral fellows and junior faculty who are members of the Society of Toxicology (SOT) and its Toxicologists of African Origin (TAO) Special Interest Group.

Eligibility This award is presented to members of the SOT and TAO who are postdoctoral fellows or junior tenure-track faculty members at colleges and universities. Applicants must have an accepted abstract for presentation to the next SOT annual meeting. The award is presented for work that substantially advances understanding of toxicology.

Financial data A monetary award is presented.

Duration The award is presented annually.

Number awarded 1 each year.

Deadline January of each year.

[1354]
UC BERKELEY'S CHANCELLOR'S POSTDOCTORAL FELLOWSHIP PROGRAM FOR ACADEMIC DIVERSITY

University of California at Berkeley
Attn: Division of Equity and Inclusion
402 Sproul Hall
Berkeley, CA 94720-5920
(510) 643-8235   E-mail: ppfpinfo@berkeley.edu
Web: diversity.berkeley.edu

Summary To provide an opportunity for recent postdoctorates who will increase diversity at the University of California at Berkeley to conduct research on the campus.

Eligibility This program is open to U.S. citizens and permanent residents who received a doctorate within 3 years of the start of the fellowship. The program solicits applications from scholars whose research, teaching, and service will contribute to diversity and equal opportunity at the university. The contributions to diversity may include public service towards increasing equitable access in fields where women and minorities are underrepresented or research focusing on underserved populations or understanding inequalities related to race, gender, disability, or LGBT issues. Applicants should have the potential to bring to their academic and research careers the perspective that comes from their non-traditional educational background or understanding of the experiences of members of groups historically underrepresented in higher education.

Financial data The stipend is $44,500 per year (11 months, plus 1 month vacation). The award also includes health insurance, vision and dental benefits, and up to $5,000 for research-related and program travel expenses.

Duration 1 year; may be renewed 1 additional year.

Additional information This program operates in addition to the University of California President's Postdoctoral Fellow-ship Program for Academic Diversity. Interested candidates may apply to either program.

Number awarded Varies each year; recently, 3 were awarded.

Deadline October of each year.

[1355]
UC DAVIS CHANCELLOR'S POSTDOCTORAL FELLOWSHIP PROGRAM

University of California at Davis
Attn: Office of Graduate Studies
250 Mrak Hall
One Shields Avenue
Davis, CA 95616
(530) 752-0650   Fax: (530) 752-6222
E-mail: gradservices@ucdavis.edu
Web: gradstudies.ucdavis.edu

Summary To provide an opportunity for recent postdoctorates who will increase diversity at the University of California at Davis to conduct research at the university.

Eligibility This program is open to scholars who have a Ph.D. in any field from an accredited university. Applicants must be interested in conducting research at UC Davis under the mentorship of an established scholar in their field. The program particularly solicits applications from scholars whose research, teaching, and service will contribute to the diversity and equal opportunity at the university. Those contributions may include public service addressing the needs of our increasingly diverse society, efforts to improve equitable access to higher education, or research focusing on underserved populations or understanding inequities related to race, gender, disability, or LGBT status. They must be able to demonstrate that they are legally authorized to work in the United States without restrictions or limitations; individuals granted deferred action status under the Deferred Action for Childhood Arrivals (DACA) program are encouraged to apply. Selection is based on academic accomplishments, strength of research proposal, and potential for faculty careers that will contribute to diversity through their teaching, research, and service.

Financial data The stipend is at least $44,500 per year (11 months, plus 1 month vacation). The award also includes health insurance, vision and dental benefits, and up to $5,000 for research-related and program travel expenses.

Duration 1 year; may be renewed 1 additional year.

Additional information This program, which began in 2012, operates in addition to the University of California President's Postdoctoral Fellowship Program for Academic Diversity. Interested candidates may apply to either program.

Number awarded Varies each year; recently, 7 were appointed.

Deadline October of each year.

[1356]
UC SAN DIEGO CHANCELLOR'S POSTDOCTORAL FELLOWSHIP PROGRAM FOR ACADEMIC DIVERSITY

University of California at San Diego
Attn: Office of the Vice Chancellor for Equity, Diversity and Inclusion
302 University Center, Room 102
La Jolla, CA 92093-0029
(858) 246-1923   E-mail: mcg005@ucsd.edu
Web: facultyexcellence.ucsd.edu/funding/cpfp1/index.html

Summary   To provide an opportunity for recent postdoctorates who will increase diversity at the University of California at San Diego to conduct research at the university.

Eligibility   This program is open to U.S. citizens and permanent residents who received a doctorate within 3 years of the start of the fellowship and are interested in conducting research at UCSD. The program particularly solicits applications from scholars whose research, teaching, and service will contribute to the diversity and equal opportunity at the university. Those contributions may include public service towards increasing equitable access in fields where women and minorities are under-represented. In some fields, the contributions may include research focusing on underserved populations or understanding inequalities related to race, gender, disability, or LGBT. The program is seeking applicants with the potential to bring to their academic and research careers the critical perspective that comes from their nontraditional educational background or understanding of the experiences of members of groups historically under-represented in higher education in the United States.

Financial data   The stipend is $44,500 per year (11 months, plus 1 month vacation). The award also includes health insurance, vision and dental benefits, and up to $5,000 for research-related and program travel expenses.

Duration   1 year; may be renewed 1 additional year.

Additional information   This program operates in addition to the University of California President's Postdoctoral Fellowship Program for Academic Diversity. Interested candidates may apply to either program.

Number awarded   2 each year.

Deadline   October of each year.

[1357]
UCAR VISITING SCIENTIST PROGRAMS

University Corporation for Atmospheric Research
Attn: Visiting Scientist Programs
3090 Center Green Drive
P.O. Box 3000
Boulder, CO 80307-3000
(303) 497-1605   Fax: (303) 497-8668
E-mail: vspapply@ucar.edu
Web: www.vsp.ucar.edu

Summary   To provide funding to recent postdoctorates in atmospheric sciences, especially African Americans and other minorities, who wish to participate in designated research programs.

Eligibility   This program is open to postdoctorates (preferably those who received their Ph.D. within the preceding 3 years) who wish to conduct research with experienced scientists at designated facilities. Applicants must submit a cover letter stating the name of the program, potential host and institution, and where they learned of this opportunity; their curriculum vitae; names and addresses of at least 4 professional references; an abstract of their Ph.D. dissertation; and a description of the research they wish to conduct at the relevant facility. Women and minorities are encouraged to apply. U.S. citizenship is not required, although the research must be conducted at a U.S. institution.

Financial data   The salary is $60,000 for the first year and $62,000 for the second year. A moving allowance of $750, an allowance of $5,000 per year for scientific travel, and a $3,000 publication allowance for the term of the award are also provided. Benefits include health and dental insurance, sick and annual leave, paid holidays, participation in a retirement fund, and life insurance.

Duration   2 years.

Additional information   Recently, positions were available through 3 programs: 1) the NOAA Climate and Global Change Postdoctoral Fellowship Program (sponsored by the National Oceanic and Atmospheric Administration; 2) the Postdocs Applying Climate Expertise (PACE) Fellowship Program; and 3) the Jack Eddy Postdoctoral Program in heliophysics (defined as all science common to the field of Sun-Earth connections).

Number awarded   Recently, 8 fellowships for the NOAA Climate and Global Change Postdoctoral Fellowship Program, 2 for the PACE Fellowship Program, and 4 for the Jack Eddy Postdoctoral Program were awarded.

Deadline   January of each year for the NOAA Climate and Global Change Postdoctoral Fellowship Program and the Jack Eddy Postdoctoral Program; May of each year for the PACE Fellowship Program.

[1358]
UCLA CHANCELLOR'S POSTDOCTORAL FELLOWSHIP PROGRAM

University of California at Los Angeles
Attn: Office for Diversity and Faculty Development
3109 Murphy Hall
P.O. Box 951407
Los Angeles, CA 90095-1407
(310) 206-7411   Fax: (310) 206-8427
E-mail: facdiversity@conet.ucla.edu
Web: faculty.diversity.ucla.edu

Summary   To provide an opportunity for recent postdoctorates who will increase diversity at the University of California at Los Angeles to conduct research at the university.

Eligibility   This program is open to U.S. citizens and permanent residents who received a doctorate within 3 years of the start of the fellowship. Applicants must be interested in conducting research at UCLA. The program particularly solicits applications from scholars whose research, teaching, and service will contribute to the diversity and equal opportunity at the university. Those contributions may include public service addressing the needs of our increasingly diverse society, efforts to improve equitable access to higher education, or research focusing on underserved populations or understanding inequities related to race, gender, disability, or LGBT status.

Financial data   The stipend is at least $44,500 per year (11 months, plus 1 month vacation). The award also includes health insurance, vision and dental benefits, and up to $5,000 for research-related and program travel expenses.

Duration 1 year; may be renewed 1 additional year.

Additional information This program operates in addition to the University of California President's Postdoctoral Fellowship Program for Academic Diversity. Interested candidates may apply to either program.

Number awarded 2 each year.

Deadline October of each year.

[1359]
UNCF ACHIEVEMENT CAPSTONE SCHOLARSHIPS

United Negro College Fund
Attn: Scholarships and Grants Department
1805 Seventh Street, N.W.
Washington, DC 20001
(202) 810-0258   Toll Free: (800) 331-2244
E-mail: scholarships@uncf.org
Web: www.uncf.org

Summary To provide funding for retirement of educational costs or continuing education to African American seniors at Historically Black Colleges and Universities (HBCUs) or other predominantly black institutions.

Eligibility This program is open to African American seniors graduating from 4-year HBCUs or other predominantly black institutions. Students must be nominated by their institution. Nominees must be seeking funding for retirement of undergraduate educational costs or to pay for future educational expenses. They must submit, along with the letter nominating them, a letter that addresses 1) the ways in which their undergraduate career and plans for the future reflect the legacy of the 1964 Civil Rights Act; and 2) their service to the campus and wider communities.

Financial data Stipends range from $2,500 to $5,000.

Duration These are 1-time awards.

Additional information This program began in 2016 when the National Merit Scholarship Corporation (NMSC) transferred the assets of its National Achievement Scholarship Program to the UNCF. The NMSC had established that program in 1965, following the passage of the Civil Rights Act of 1964, in order to provide an opportunity for talented African American students to obtain higher education.

Number awarded Varies each year.

Deadline Deadline not specified.

[1360]
UNITED AIRLINES PILOT SCHOLARSHIPS

Organization of Black Aerospace Professionals, Inc.
Attn: Scholarship Coordinator
One Westbrook Corporate Center, Suite 300
Westchester, IL 60154
(708) 449-7755   Toll Free: (800) JET-OBAP
Fax: (708) 449-7754 E-mail: obapscholarships@obap.org
Web: www.obap.org/united-airlines-pilot-scholarship

Summary To provide financial assistance to members of the Organization of Black Aerospace Professionals (OBAP) who are enrolled in a collegiate aviation program.

Eligibility This program is open to OBAP members who have a commercial certificate and instrument rating, preferably for multi-engine. Applicants must be enrolled in an accred-

ited collegiate aviation program. They must have a GPA of 3.0 or higher and a first class medical certificate. Along with their application, they must submit a 500-word essay on their career aspirations and how this award will help advance their aviation career.

Financial data The stipend is $5,000. Funds are paid directly to the college.

Duration 1 year.

Additional information The OBAP was originally established in 1976 as the Organization of Black Airline Pilots to make certain Blacks and other minorities had a group that would keep them informed about opportunities for advancement within commercial aviation. This program is sponsored by United Airlines.

Number awarded 3 each year.

Deadline May of each year.

[1361]
UNIVERSITY OF CALIFORNIA PRESIDENT'S POSTDOCTORAL FELLOWSHIP PROGRAM FOR ACADEMIC DIVERSITY

University of California at Berkeley
Attn: Office of Equity and Inclusion
402 Sproul Hall
Berkeley, CA 94720-5920
(510) 643-8235   E-mail: ppfpinfo@berkeley.edu
Web: ppfp.ucop.edu/info

Summary To provide an opportunity to conduct research at campuses of the University of California to recent postdoctorates who are committed to careers in university teaching and research and who will contribute to diversity.

Eligibility This program is open to U.S. citizens or permanent residents who have a Ph.D. from an accredited university. Applicants must be proposing to conduct research at a branch of the university under the mentorship of a faculty or laboratory sponsor. They must have the potential to contribute to higher education through their understanding of the barriers facing women, domestic minorities, LGBTQ individuals, students with disabilities, and other domestic groups in fields where they are underrepresented. Along with their application, they must submit an Education Background Statement that includes their potential to contribute to higher education through their understanding of the barriers facing members of groups underrepresented in higher education careers as evidenced by their life experiences and educational background.

Financial data The stipend is $44,500 or higher, depending on the field and level of experience. The program also offers health benefits and up to $5,000 for supplemental and research-related expenses.

Duration Appointments are for 1 academic year, with possible renewal for a second year.

Additional information Research may be conducted at any of the University of California's 10 campuses (Berkeley, Davis, Irvine, Los Angeles, Merced, Riverside, San Diego, San Francisco, Santa Barbara, or Santa Cruz). The program provides mentoring and guidance in preparing for an academic career. This program was established in 1984 to encourage applications from minority and women scholars in fields where they were severely underrepresented; it is now open to all qualified candidates whose research, teaching, and service will contribute to diversity and equal opportunity at the University of California. In addition to this program for UC campuses in general, the Universities of California at Berkeley, Davis, Irvine, Los Angeles, Merced, Riverside, and San Diego offer separate Chancellor's Postdoctoral Fellowship programs for their institutions. Interested candidates may apply to those programs and/or this system-wide program.

Number awarded Varies each year; recently, 33 were selected.

Deadline October of each year.

[1362]
UNIVERSITY OF NORTH CAROLINA POSTDOCTORAL PROGRAM FOR FACULTY DIVERSITY

University of North Carolina at Chapel Hill
Attn: Office of Postdoctoral Affairs
301 Bynum Hall, CB 4100
Chapel Hill, NC 27599-4100
(919) 843-4793   Fax: (919) 962-6769
E-mail: jennifer_pruitt@unc.edu
Web: www.research.unc.edu/carolina-postdocs/applicants

Summary To support African American and other minority scholars who are interested in teaching and conducting research at the University of North Carolina (UNC).

Eligibility This program is open to scholars, especially members of underrepresented groups (African Americans, Native Americans, and Hispanic Americans) who have completed their doctoral degree within the past 5 years. Applicants must be interested in teaching and conducting research at UNC. Preference is given to U.S. citizens and permanent residents. Selection is based on the evidence of scholarship potential and ability to compete for tenure-track appointments at UNC and other research universities.

Financial data Fellows receive $47,476 per year, plus an allowance of $2,000 for research and travel. Health benefits are also available.

Duration Up to 2 years.

Additional information Fellows must be in residence at the Chapel Hill campus for the duration of the program. They teach 1 course per year and spend the rest of the time in research. This program began in 1983.

Number awarded 4 or 5 each year.

Deadline November of each year.

[1363]
VALERIE RUSSELL SCHOLARSHIP

United Church of Christ
Attn: Associate Director, Grant and Scholarship
  Administration
700 Prospect Avenue East
Cleveland, OH 44115-1100
(216) 736-2166   Toll Free: (866) 822-8224, ext. 2166
Fax: (216) 736-3783   E-mail: scholarships@ucc.org
Web: www.ucc.org/russell_scholarship

Summary To provide financial assistance to African American laywomen who are members of a United Church of Christ (UCC) congregation and working on an undergraduate or graduate degree to advance the justice ministries of the denomination.

Eligibility This program is open to African American laywomen who have a strong theologically-grounded commitment to the justice ministries of the UCC but are not a member in discernment, licensed, commissioned, or ordained. Applicants must be 1) working on an undergraduate or graduate degree in a field that will affirm the values of the UCC and promote its justice commitments; or 2) already professionally engaged in justice work either in the church or in a secular organization and seeking funds for continuing education activities (e.g., classes, workshops, travel) that will assist in personal skill building.

Financial data Stipends range from $1,500 to $2,000 per year. Funds may be used for tuition for undergraduate or graduate study or for continuing education activities.

Duration 1 year; may be renewed.

Additional information This program began in 1997.

Number awarded 1 or more each year.

Deadline February of each year.

[1364]
WARREN G. MAGNUSON EDUCATIONAL SUPPORT PERSONNEL SCHOLARSHIP GRANT

Washington Education Association
32032 Weyerhaeuser Way South
P.O. Box 9100
Federal Way, WA 98063-9100
(253) 765-7056   Toll Free: (800) 622-3393, ext. 7056
E-mail: Janna.Connor@Washingtonea.org
Web: www.washingtonea.org

Summary To provide funding to Educational Support Personnel (ESP) members of the Washington Education Association (WEA), especially African Americans and other minorities, who are interested in taking classes to obtain an initial teaching certificate.

Eligibility This program is open to WEA/ESP members who are engaged in course work related to obtaining an initial teaching certificate. Applicants must submit a plan for obtaining an initial certificate, a letter describing their passion to become a teacher, evidence of activities and/or leadership in the association, and 3 to 5 letters of reference. Minority members of the association are especially encouraged to apply; 1 of the scholarships is reserved for them.

Financial data The stipend is $1,500.

Duration These are 1-time grants.

Number awarded 3 each year, including 1 reserved for a minority member.

Deadline June of each year.

[1365]
W.E.B. DUBOIS FELLOWSHIP FOR RESEARCH ON RACE AND CRIME

Department of Justice
National Institute of Justice
Attn: W.E.B. DuBois Fellowship Program
810 Seventh Street, N.W.
Washington, DC 20531
Toll Free: (800) 851-3420   Fax: (301) 240-5830
TDD: (301) 240-6310   E-mail: grants@ncjrs.gov
Web: www.nij.gov

Summary To provide funding to junior investigators, especially African Americans and other minorities, who are interested in conducting research on "crime, justice, and culture in various societal contexts."

Eligibility This program is open to investigators who have a Ph.D. or other doctoral-level degree (including a legal degree of J.D. or higher). Applicants should be early in their careers and not have been awarded tenure. They must be interested in conducting research that relates to specific areas that change annually but relate to criminal justice policy and practice in the United States. The sponsor strongly encourages applications from women and minorities. Selection is based on understanding of the problem and its importance (10%); quality and technical merit (40%); potential for a significant scientific or technical advance that will improve criminal/juvenile justice in the United states (20%); capabilities, demonstrated productivity, and experience of the principal investigator and the institution (15%); and dissemination strategy to broader audiences (15%).

Financial data Grants range up to $100,000 for fellows who propose to conduct secondary data analysis or up to $150,000 for fellows who proposed to conduct primary data collection. Funds may be used for salary, fringe benefits, reasonable costs of relocation, travel essential to the project, and office expenses not provided by the sponsor. Indirect costs are limited to 20%.

Duration Up to 24 months; residency at the National Institute of Justice (NIJ) is not required but it is available.

Number awarded Up to 3 each year.

Deadline May of each year.

[1366]
W.E.B. DUBOIS SCHOLARS

Department of Justice
National Institute of Justice
Attn: W.E.B. DuBois Fellowship Program
810 Seventh Street, N.W.
Washington, DC 20531
Toll Free: (800) 851-3420   Fax: (301) 240-5830
TDD: (301) 240-6310   E-mail: grants@ncjrs.gov
Web: www.nij.gov

Summary To provide funding to advanced investigators, especially African Ameicans and other minorities, who are interested in conducting research on "crime, justice, and culture in various societal contexts."

Eligibility This program is open to investigators who received their terminal degree in their field more than 5 years previously. Applicants must be interested in conducting primary research that relates to specific areas that change annually but relate to criminal justice policy and practice in the United States. The sponsor strongly encourages applications from women and minorities. Selection is based on understanding of the problem and its importance (10%); quality and technical merit (40%); potential for a significant scientific or technical advance that will improve criminal/juvenile justice in the United states (20%); capabilities, demonstrated productivity, and experience of the principal investigator and the institution (15%); and dissemination strategy to broader audiences (15%).

Financial data Grants range up to $500,000. Funds may be used for salary, fringe benefits, reasonable costs of relocation, travel essential to the project, and office expenses not provided by the sponsor.

Duration Up to 36 months; residency at the National Institute of Justice (NIJ) is not required but it is available.

Number awarded Up to 4 each year.

Deadline May of each year.

[1367]
WESLEY-LOGAN PRIZE IN AFRICAN DIASPORA HISTORY

American Historical Association
Attn: Book Prize Administrator
400 A Street, S.E.
Washington, DC 20003-3889
(202) 544-2422   Fax: (202) 544-8307
E-mail: awards@historians.org
Web: www.historians.org

Summary To recognize and reward outstanding work in African Diaspora history.

Eligibility The prize is awarded to the best book on some aspect of the history of the dispersion, settlement, adjustment, or return of peoples originally from Africa. Books in any chronological period and any geographical location are eligible. Only works of high scholarly and literary merit are considered.

Financial data The prize is $1,000.

Duration The award is granted annually.

Additional information This prize was established in 1992 to honor 2 early pioneers in the field, Charles H. Wesley and Rayford W. Logan. It is jointly sponsored by the American Historical Association and the Association for the Study of African American Life and History.

Number awarded 1 each year.

Deadline May of each year.

[1368]
WILLIAM J. PERRY FELLOWSHIP IN INTERNATIONAL SECURITY

Stanford University
Center for International Security and Cooperation
Attn: Fellowships Coordinator
Encina Hall, Room C206-10
616 Serra Street
Stanford, CA 94305-6165
(650) 723-9625   Fax: (650) 724-5683
E-mail: perryfellows@stanford.edu
Web: cisac.fsi.stanford.edu/fellowships/perry_fellowship

Summary To provide funding to professionals, especially African Americans and members of other underrepresented groups, who are interested in conducting policy-relevant research on international security issues while in residence at Stanford University's Center for International Security and Cooperation.

Eligibility This program is open to early and mid-career professionals from academia, the public and private sectors, national laboratories, and the military, either from the United States or abroad. Applicants must have a record of outstanding work in natural science, engineering, or mathematics and a genuine interest in and dedication to solving international security problems. Their proposed research may involve interlapping issues of nuclear weapons policy and nuclear proliferation, regional tensions, biosecurity, homeland security, and effective global engagement. The sponsor welcomes applications from women, minorities, and citizens of all countries.

Financial data The stipend depends on experience and is determined on a case-by-case basis. Health care and other benefits are also provided.

Duration 9 to 11 months.

Additional information Fellows are expected to produce a publishable manuscript based on their research. They should not plan to spend any time conducting research abroad or in other parts of the country.

Number awarded Varies each year; recently, 3 of these fellows were in residence.

Deadline January of each year.

[1369]
WILLIAM L. FISHER CONGRESSIONAL GEOSCIENCE FELLOWSHIP

American Geosciences Institute
Attn: Government Affairs Program
4220 King Street
Alexandria, VA 22302-1502
(703) 379-2480   Fax: (703) 379-7563
E-mail: govt@agiweb.org
Web: www.americangeosciences.org

Summary To provide members of an American Geosciences Institute (AGI) component society, especially African Americans and other minorities, with an opportunity to gain professional experience in the office of a member of Congress or a Congressional committee.

Eligibility This program is open to members of 1 of AGI's 51 member societies who have a master's degree in engineering and at least 3 years of post-degree engineering experience or a Ph.D. Applicants should have a broad geoscience background and excellent written and oral communications skills. They must be interested in working with Congress. Although prior experience in public policy is not required, a demonstrated interest in applying science to the solution of public problems is desirable. Applications from women and minorities are especially encouraged. U.S. citizenship or permanent resident status is required.

Financial data Fellows receive a stipend of up to $68,000 plus allowances for health insurance, relocation, and travel.

Duration 12 months, beginning in September.

Additional information This program is 1 of more than 20 Congressional Science Fellowships operating in affiliation with the American Association for the Advancement of Science (AAAS), which provides a 2-week orientation on Congressional and executive branch operations.

Number awarded 1 each year.

Deadline January of each year.

[1370]
WILLIAM SANDERS SCARBOROUGH PRIZE

Modern Language Association of America
Attn: Office of Programs
85 Broad Street, Suite 500
New York, NY 10004-2434
(646) 576-5141   Fax: (646) 458-0030
E-mail: awards@mla.org
Web: www.mla.org

Summary To recognize and reward authors of outstanding books on African American literature.

Eligibility This award is presented to authors of outstanding scholarly studies of African American literature or culture published the previous year. Books that are primarily translations are not eligible. Authors need not be members of the Modern Language Association.

Financial data The prize is $1,000 and a certificate.

Duration The prize is awarded annually.

Additional information This prize was first awarded in 2001.

Number awarded 1 each year.

Deadline April of each year.

[1371]
WILLIAM W. GRIMES AWARD FOR EXCELLENCE IN CHEMICAL ENGINEERING

American Institute of Chemical Engineers
Attn: Minority Affairs Committee
120 Wall Street, FL 23
New York, NY 10005-4020
Toll Free: (800) 242-4363   Fax: (203) 775-5177
E-mail: awards@aiche.org
Web: www.aiche.org

Summary To recognize and reward chemical engineers who serve as a role model for African American students.

Eligibility Members of the American Institute of Chemical Engineers (AIChE) may nominate any individual who serves as a role model for African Americans in chemical engineering. Nominees must be chemical engineers who have demonstrated outstanding technical, business, or related achievements and have voluntarily given time and effort to help increase the interest and/or performance of members of underrepresented minority groups in science, mathematics, engineering, and related areas in either an educational or business environment.

Financial data The award consists of a plaque and $1,000, plus a $500 travel allowance to attend the AIChE annual meeting where the award is presented.

Duration The award is presented annually.

Additional information The Minority Affairs Committee has presented this award in honor of William W. Grimes, the first African American Fellow of AIChE, since 1995.

Number awarded 1 each year.

Deadline Nominations must be submitted by June of each year.

[1372]
WOODS HOLE OCEANOGRAPHIC INSTITUTION SUMMER STUDENT FELLOWSHIP PROGRAM

Woods Hole Oceanographic Institution
Attn: Academic Programs Office
Clark Laboratory 223, MS 31
360 Woods Hole Road
Woods Hole, MA 02543-1541
(508) 289-2219   Fax: (508) 457-2188
E-mail: education@whoi.edu
Web: www.whoi.edu/main/ssf/program-overview

Summary To provide funding to undergraduates, especially African Americans and other underrepresented minorities, who are interested in conducting research at the Woods Hole Oceanographic Institution (WHOI) during the summer.

Eligibility This program is open to undergraduate students who have completed their junior year at colleges or universities with a major in any science or engineering field, including (but not limited to) biology, chemistry, engineering, geology, geophysics, mathematics, meteorology, physics, oceanography, or marine policy. Applicants must have at least a tentative interest in the ocean sciences, oceanographic engineering, mathematics, or marine policy. They must be interested in conducting an independent research project under the guidance of a member of the WHOI research staff. Along with their application, they must submit a 3-page statement on how a summer of research at WHOI would benefit their education and career plans, the skills they expect to obtain from this research experience, the skills they have that would make them a good researcher, information on previous research projects in which they have been involved, and the areas of marine research in which they are interested and why. Selection is based on previous academic and scientific achievements and promise as future ocean scientists or ocean engineers. The program actively recruits members of groups underrepresented in marine science (African Americans, Hispanic Americans, Native Americans, and Pacific Islanders).

Financial data The stipend is $585 per week; housing is also provided. Additional support up to $650 may be provided for travel.

Duration 10 to 12 weeks during the summer.

Additional information Fellows are not required to take any prescribed courses nor are they required to provide any services to the institution in return for the grant. This program is supported by grants from the National Science Foundation's Research Experiences for Undergraduates Program. Fellows are expected to give an oral report on their research.

Number awarded Between 25 and 30 fellows are selected each year.

Deadline February of each year.

[1373]
WRITERS OF COLOR FELLOWSHIPS OF OREGON LITERARY FELLOWSHIPS

Literary Arts, Inc.
Attn: Oregon Book Awards and Fellowships Program
  Coordinator
925 S.W. Washington Street
Portland, OR 97205
(503) 227-2583   Fax: (503) 243-1167
E-mail: susan@literary-arts.org
Web: www.literary-arts.org

Summary To provide funding to African Americans or other writers of color in Oregon interested in working on a literary project.

Eligibility This program is open to writers of color who have been residents of Oregon for at least 1 year and are interested in initiating, developing, or completing a literary project in the areas of poetry, fiction, literary nonfiction, drama, or young readers' literature. Priority is given to writers whose work promotes perspectives from a variety of cultural, ethnic, and racial backgrounds. Writers in the early stages of their careers are especially encouraged to apply. Selection is based primarily on literary merit.

Financial data Grants are at least $2,500.
Duration The grants are presented annually.
Additional information This program began in 2016.
Number awarded 1 each year.
Deadline June of each year.

[1374]
YERBY POSTDOCTORAL FELLOWSHIP PROGRAM

Harvard T.H. Chan School of Public Health
Attn: Office of Faculty Affairs
90 Smith Street, First Floor
Boston, MA 02120
(617) 432-1047   Fax: (617) 432-4711
E-mail: cburkot@hsph.harvard.edu
Web: www.hsph.harvard.edu

Summary To provide postdoctorates who are African Americans or will contribute to diversity in other ways with an opportunity to pursue a program of research training at Harvard School of Public Health.

Eligibility This program is open to postdoctorates who are interested in preparing for a career in public health. The program emphasizes applicants who will contribute to academic diversity, meaning 1) members of minority groups underrepresented in public health (American Indians or Alaska Natives, Blacks or African Americans, Hispanics or Latinos, and Native Hawaiians or other Pacific Islanders); and 2) individuals with disabilities.

Financial data Fellows receive a competitive salary.
Duration 1 year; may be renewed 1 additional year.
Number awarded Up to 5 each year.
Deadline November of each year.

[1375]
ZENITH FELLOWS AWARD PROGRAM

Alzheimer's Association
Attn: Medical and Scientific Affairs
225 North Michigan Avenue, 17th Floor
Chicago, IL 60601-7633
(312) 335-5747   Toll Free: (800) 272-3900
Fax: (866) 699-1246   TDD: (312) 335-5886
E-mail: grantsapp@alz.org
Web: www.alz.org

Summary To provide funding to African American and other underrepresented established investigators interested in conducting advanced research on Alzheimer's Disease.

Eligibility Eligible are scientists who have already contributed significantly to the field of Alzheimer's Disease research and are likely to continue to make significant contributions for many years to come. The proposed research must be "on the cutting edge" of basic, biomedical research and may not fit current conventional scientific wisdom or may challenge the prevailing orthodoxy. It should address fundamental problems related to early detection, etiology, pathogenesis, treatment, and/or prevention of Alzheimer's Disease. Scientists from underrepresented groups are especially encouraged to apply.

Financial data Grants up to $250,000 per year, including direct expenses and up to 10% for overhead costs, are available. The total award for the life of the grant may not exceed $450,000.

Duration 2 or 3 years.

Additional information This program began in 1991.

Number awarded Up to 4 each year.

Deadline Letters of intent must be submitted by the end of March of each year. Final applications are due in May.

[1376]
ZETA PHI BETA GENERAL GRADUATE FELLOWSHIPS

Zeta Phi Beta Sorority, Inc.
Attn: National Educational Foundation
1734 New Hampshire Avenue, N.W.
Washington, DC 20009
(202) 387-3103   Fax: (202) 232-4593
E-mail: info@zetaphibetasororityhq.org
Web: www.zpbnef1975.org/scholarships-and-descriptions

Summary To provide financial assistance to African American and other women who are working on a professional degree, master's degree, doctorate, or postdoctorate.

Eligibility Women graduate or postdoctoral students are eligible to apply if they have achieved distinction or shown promise of distinction in their chosen fields. Applicants need not be members of Zeta Phi Beta. They must be enrolled full time in a professional, graduate, or postdoctoral program. Along with their application, they must submit a 150-word essay on their educational goals and professional aspirations, how this award will help them to achieve those goals, and why they should receive the award. Financial need is not considered in the selection process.

Financial data The stipend ranges up to $2,500, paid directly to the recipient.

Duration 1 academic year; may be renewed.

Additional information Zeta Phi Beta is a traditionally African American sorority.

Number awarded 1 or more each year.

Deadline January of each year.

[1377]
ZORA NEALE HURSTON AWARD

American Library Association
Attn: Reference and User Services Association
50 East Huron Street
Chicago, IL 60611-2795
(312) 280-4398   Toll Free: (800) 545-2433, ext. 4398
Fax: (312) 280-5273   TDD: (888) 814-7692
E-mail: rusa@ala.org
Web: www.ala.org/rusa/awards/znh

Summary To recognize and reward members of the American Library Association (ALA) who have demonstrated leadership in promoting African American literature.

Eligibility This award is available to ALA members who have developed a project to promote African American literature. Project examples include, but are not limited to, a program, display, collection building efforts, special readers' advisory focus, or innovation in service. Selection is based on the quality and contribution of the project, the extent the project promotes African American literature and highlights its rich history and diversity, the extent to which the project serves as a model for others, its innovativeness, and the extent to which it advances service in this area.

Financial data The award includes an honorarium of $1,250 to help fund travel expenses to the ALA annual conference, 2 tickets to the United for Libraries author events, 2 complete sets of Zora Neale Hurston's books and audiobooks, and a personalized plaque.

Duration The award is presented annually.

Additional information This award was established in 2008.

Number awarded 1 each year.

Deadline December of each year.

Indexes

Program Title Index ●

Sponsoring Organization Index ●

Residency Index ●

Tenability Index ●

Subject Index ●

Calendar Index ●

Program Title Index

If you know the name of a particular funding program open to African Americans and want to find out where it is covered in the directory, use the Program Title Index. Here, program titles are arranged alphabetically, word by word. To assist you in your search, every program is listed by all its known names or abbreviations. In addition, we've used an alphabetical code (within parentheses) to help you determine if the program is aimed at you: U = Undergraduates;   G = Graduate Students;   P = Professionals/Postdoctorates. Here's how the code works: if a program is followed by (U) 241, the program is described in the Undergraduates chapter, in entry 241. If the same program title is followed by another entry number—for example, (P) 1101—the program is also described in the Professionals/Postdoctorates chapter, in entry 1101. Remember: the numbers cited here refer to program entry numbers, not to page numbers in the book.

U–Undergraduates   **G–Graduate Students**   **P–Professionals/Postdoctorates**

U–Undergraduates   **G–Graduate Students**   **P–Professionals/Postdoctorates**

U–Undergraduates **G–Graduate Students** **P–Professionals/Postdoctorates**

U–Undergraduates   **G–Graduate Students**   **P–Professionals/Postdoctorates**

U–Undergraduates   **G–Graduate Students**   **P–Professionals/Postdoctorates**

U–Undergraduates   **G–Graduate Students**   **P–Professionals/Postdoctorates**

U–Undergraduates **G–Graduate Students** **P–Professionals/Postdoctorates**

U–Undergraduates   **G–Graduate Students**   **P–Professionals/Postdoctorates**

Lynne Edwards Research Scholarship. *See* NBNA Scholarship Program, entries (U) 484, (G) 1077

Lyons Memorial Scholarship. *See* Verne LaMarr Lyons Memorial Scholarship, entry (G) 1197

M

M. Elizabeth Carnegie Scholarship, (G) 1009, (P) 1314

Mabel Smith Memorial Scholarship, (U) 396

Macri Scholarship. *See* CAPT Cynthia I. Macri Scholarship, entry (U) 116

Macy Jr. Foundation Scholarships. *See* Josiah Macy Jr. Foundation Scholarships, entry (G) 975

Madeline Kountze Dugger-Kelly Scholarship, (G) 1010

Madison Scholarship in Architecture. *See* Robert P. Madison Scholarship in Architecture, entry (U) 562

Mae Dell Young Scholarship. *See* Coy and Mae Dell Young Scholarship, entry (U) 166

Magnuson Educational Support Personnel Scholarship Grant. *See* Warren G. Magnuson Educational Support Personnel Scholarship Grant, entries (U) 664, (P) 1364

Mahlon Martin Fellowships, (U) 397

Mahogany and Blues Babe Foundation Scholarship Program, (U) 398

Mahoney Scholarship. *See* Mary Eliza Mahoney Scholarship, entry (U) 408

Maine Section ASCE High School Scholarship, (U) 399

Malena Rance Scholarship Fund, (G) 1011

Malina James and Dr. Louis P. James Legacy Scholarship. *See* APF Graduate Student Scholarships, entry (G) 763

Malveaux Scholarship. *See* Dr. Julianne Malveaux Scholarship, entry (U) 199

Mandela-Rodney Fellowship Program. *See* DuBois-Mandela-Rodney Fellowship Program, entry (P) 1276

Manhattan Central Medical Society Scholarship, (G) 1012

Mann Memorial Scholarship. *See* Kathy Mann Memorial Scholarship, entry (U) 357

Manuel Law Foundation Scholarships. *See* Wiley W. Manuel Law Foundation Scholarships, entry (G) 1209

Many Voices Fellowships, (P) 1315

Marcia Silverman Minority Student Award, (U) 400

Mareyjoyce Green Scholarship. *See* Esther Ngan-ling Chow and Mareyjoyce Green Scholarship, entry (G) 872

Margaret A. Pemberton Scholarship Fund, (U) 401

Margaret Pemberton Scholarship. *See* NBNA Scholarship Program, entries (U) 484, (G) 1077

Maria Dudley Advanced Scholarship. *See* NBNA Scholarship Program, entries (U) 484, (G) 1077

Marilyn A. Jackson Memorial Award, (G) 1013

Marjorie Bowens-Wheatley Scholarships, (U) 402, (G) 1014

Mark T. Banner Scholarship for Law Students, (G) 1015

Marriott Scholarship Fund. *See* Alice S. Marriott Scholarship Fund, entry (U) 29

Marshall Dissertation Fellowship for African-American Scholars. *See* Thurgood Marshall Dissertation Fellowship for African-American Scholars, entry (G) 1184

Marshall Medical Student Service Scholarships. *See* Dr. David Monash/Harry Lloyd and Elizabeth Pawlette Marshall Medical Student Service Scholarships, entry (G) 846

Marshall Residency Scholarships. *See* Dr. David Monash/Harry Lloyd and Elizabeth Pawlette Marshall Residency Scholarships, entry (P) 1274

Martha A. Dawson Genesis Scholarship. *See* NBNA Scholarship Program, entries (U) 484, (G) 1077

Martha R. Dudley Scholarship. *See* NBNA Scholarship Program, entries (U) 484, (G) 1077

Martin Fellowships. *See* Mahlon Martin Fellowships, entry (U) 397

Martin Luther King, Jr. Drum Major for Justice Advocacy Competition. *See* Dr. Martin Luther King, Jr. Drum Major for Justice Advocacy Competition, entry (U) 200

Martin Luther King, Jr. Memorial Scholarship Fund, (U) 403, (G) 1016, (P) 1316

Martin Luther King, Jr. Scholarship. *See* Dr. Martin Luther King, Jr. Scholarship, entry (U) 201

Martin Luther King Jr. Scholarship Awards, (U) 404, (G) 1017

Martins Scholarship. *See* Alvaro L. Martins Scholarship, entry (U) 38

Mary A. McDowell Fellowship, (U) 405

Mary E. Border Scholarship, (U) 406

Mary E. Wood Scholarship, (U) 407

Mary Eliza Mahoney Scholarship, (U) 408

Mary Elizabeth Carnegie Scholar Award, (G) 1018, (P) 1317

Mary Hill Davis Ethnic/Minority Scholarship Program, (U) 409

Mary Ida Vandross Scholarships. *See* Luther and Mary Ida Vandross Scholarships, entry (U) 394

Mary McLeod Bethune Scholarships, (U) 410

Mary Munson Runge Scholarship, (G) 1019

Maryland Sea Grant Research Experiences for Undergraduates Program, (U) 411

Mason/Maude Bisson Scholarship. *See* Omega Mason/Maude Bisson Scholarship, entry (U) 511

Massachusetts Society of Certified Public Accountants/National Association of Black Accountants Scholarships. *See* MSCPA/NABA Scholarships, entries (U) 458, (G) 1050

MassMutual Scholars Program, (U) 412

Matarazzo Scholarship. *See* APF Graduate Student Scholarships, entry (G) 763

Maude Bisson Scholarship. *See* Omega Mason/Maude Bisson Scholarship, entry (U) 511

Maude Davis/Joseph C. McKinney Scholarship, (U) 413

Maureen L. and Howard N. Blitman, P.E. Scholarship to Promote Diversity in Engineering, (U) 414

Max Oligario Visionary Scholarship, (U) 415, (G) 1020

Maxine V. Fennell/Robin Gaines Memorial Scholarship, (U) 416, (G) 1021, (P) 1318

Mayes EDAC Scholarship. *See* John A. Mayes EDAC Scholarship, entry (G) 963

Maynard Jackson Scholarship. *See* Full Circle Communications/Maynard Jackson Scholarship, entries (U) 251, (G) 889

McClellan Scholarship. *See* Surety and Fidelity Industry Scholarship Program, entry (U) 621

McDonough Scholarship in Ophthalmology/ENT. *See* Dr. David K. McDonough Scholarship in Ophthalmology/ENT, entry (G) 845

McDowell Fellowship. *See* Mary A. McDowell Fellowship, entry (U) 405

McGee Graduate Fellowship. *See* Nancy B. Woolridge McGee Graduate Fellowship, entry (G) 1059

McKay Scholarship Program. *See* Jim McKay Scholarship Program, entry (G) 961

McKinney Family Fund Scholarship, (U) 417, (G) 1022

McKinney Scholarship. *See* Joseph C. McKinney Scholarship, entry (U) 344

McKnight Doctoral Fellowship Program, (G) 1023

McLean Award. *See* Franklin C. McLean Award, entry (G) 887

McLendon Minority Postgraduate Scholarship Program. *See* John McLendon Memorial Minority Postgraduate Scholarship Award, entries (G) 969, (P) 1305

McNair Scientific Achievement Award. *See* Ronald E. McNair Scientific Achievement Award, entry (U) 568

McNeal and Beth Powell Scholarship. *See* Sean McNeal and Beth Powell Scholarship, entry (U) 587

McSween (New York Life) Scholarship. *See* Cirilo McSween (New York Life) Scholarship, entry (U) 141

Meares Memorial Scholarship. *See* George E. Meares Memorial Scholarship, entry (G) 902

Measures of Effective Teaching Dissertation Fellowship Program. *See* AERA-MET Dissertation Fellowship Program, entry (G) 716

Media General Minority Scholarship and Training Program, (U) 418

Medical Library Association/National Library of Medicine Spectrum Scholarships. *See* MLA/NLM Spectrum Scholarships, entry (G) 1045

Medical Library Association Scholarship for Minority Students. *See* MLA Scholarship for Minority Students, entry (G) 1046

Medical Research Fellows Program, (G) 1024

Medical Student Elective in HIV Psychiatry, (G) 1025

Meekins Scholarship. *See* Phyllis G. Meekins Scholarship, entry (U) 532

Mel Karmazin Fellowship. *See* IRTS Summer Fellowship Program, entries (U) 314, (G) 942

Mellon Undergraduate Curatorial Fellowship Program, (U) 419

Mcloid Algood Tuition Scholarship. *See* Emma and Meloid Algood Tuition Scholarship, entry (U) 221

Mental Health and Substance Abuse Fellowship Program, (G) 1026

Mental Health Research Dissertation Grant to Increase Workforce Diversity, (G) 1027

Mercado Memorial Fellowship. *See* IRTS Summer Fellowship Program, entries (U) 314, (G) 942

Mercer Scholarship. *See* Carmen Mercer Scholarship, entry (U) 120

Merchant Excellence and Leadership and Excellence HBCU Scholarship, (U) 420

MET Dissertation Fellowship Program. *See* AERA-MET Dissertation Fellowship Program, entry (G) 716

Metro DC Chapter NABA Scholarship, (U) 421, (G) 1028

Metro New York Chapter NBMBAA Scholarships, (U) 422, (G) 1029

Miami Chapter Black Nurses' Association Graduate Scholarship, (U) 423, (G) 1030

Miami Chapter Black Nurses' Association Undergraduate Scholarships, (U) 424

Michael A. Anderson, Sr. Memorial Scholarship, (G) 1031

Michael Baker Scholarship for Diversity in Engineering, (U) 425

Michael Files Eagle Scout Leadership Scholarship. *See* LCDR Michael Files Eagle Scout Leadership Scholarship, entry (U) 371

Michael Memorial HPC Fellowships. *See* ACM/IEEE-CS George Michael Memorial HPC Fellowships, entry (G) 710

Michael P. Johnson Scholarship. *See* Cuba Wadlington, Jr. and Michael P. Johnson Scholarship, entry (U) 168

Michelle Howard Excellence in Leadership Scholarship. *See* VADM Michelle Howard Excellence in Leadership Scholarship, entry (U) 655

Michelle Jackson Scholarship Fund, (G) 1032

Michigan Auto Law Diversity Scholarship, (G) 1033

Michigan Chapter AABE Scholarships, (U) 426

Michigan Chapter COMTO Scholarships, (U) 427

Mickey Leland Energy Fellowships, (U) 428, (G) 1034, (P) 1319

Mickey Williams Minority Scholarships. *See* PDEF Mickey Williams Minority Scholarships, entry (U) 522

Microbiome Junior Investigator Award. *See* AGA Microbiome Junior Investigator Award, entry (P) 1232

Midwives of Color-Watson Midwifery Student Scholarship, (U) 429, (G) 1035

Mildred Barry Garvin Prize, (P) 1320

Mildred Carter Bradham Social Work Fellowship, (G) 1036

Mildred Collins Nursing/Health Science/Medicine Scholarship, (U) 430

Miller Johnson West Michigan Diversity Law School Scholarship, (G) 1037

Miller Scholarship. *See* NBNA Scholarship Program, entries (U) 484, (G) 1077

MillerCoors Scholarships of the Thurgood Marshall College Fund, (U) 431

Mims Vocal Scholarship. *See* A. Grace Lee Mims Vocal Scholarship, entry (G) 704

Minnesota Association of Counselors of Color Student of Color Scholarship. *See* MnACC Student of Color Scholarship, entry (U) 447

Minnesota Social Service Association Diversity Scholarship, (U) 432

Minnie and William Blakely Book Scholarship. *See* Sigma Gamma Rho Scholarships/Fellowships, entries (U) 597, (G) 1160

Minorities in Government Finance Scholarship, (U) 433, (G) 1038

Minority Affairs Committee's Award for Outstanding Scholastic Achievement, (U) 434

Minority and Underrepresented Environmental Literacy Program, (U) 435, (G) 1039

Minority Faculty Development Scholarship Award in Physical Therapy, (G) 1040, (P) 1321

Minority Fellowships in Environmental Law, (G) 1041

Minority Medical Student Award Program of the American Society of Hematology, (G) 1042

Minority Medical Student Summer Externship in Addiction Psychiatry, (G) 1043

Minority Nurse Faculty Scholars Program. *See* Johnson & Johnson/AACN Minority Nurse Faculty Scholars Program, entry (G) 973

Minority Postdoctoral Fellowship Awards in Diabetes, (P) 1322

Minority Scholarship Award for Academic Excellence in Physical Therapy, (U) 436

Minority Scholarship Awards for College Students in Chemical Engineering, (U) 437

Minority Scholarship Awards for Incoming College Freshmen in Chemical Engineering, (U) 438

Minority Scholarship in Classics and Classical Archaeology, (U) 439

Minority Serving Institution Scholarship Program, (U) 440

Minority Serving Institutions Partnership Program Internships. *See* MSIPP Internships, entries (U) 459, (G) 1051

Minority Teacher Education Scholarships, (U) 441

Minority Teachers of Illinois Scholarship Program, (U) 442, (G) 1044

Minority Teaching Fellows Program of Tennessee, (U) 443

Minority University Research and Education Project (MUREP) Scholarships. *See* NASA Scholarship and Research Opportunities (SRO) Minority University Research and Education Project (MUREP) Scholarships, entry (U) 471

Miranda Access Scholarship. *See* Freddy Miranda Access Scholarship, entry (U) 248

U–Undergraduates   **G–Graduate Students**   **P–Professionals/Postdoctorates**

U–Undergraduates   **G–Graduate Students**   **P–Professionals/Postdoctorates**

U–Undergraduates   **G–Graduate Students**   **P–Professionals/Postdoctorates**

U–Undergraduates　　　**G–Graduate Students**　　　**P–Professionals/Postdoctorates**

U–Undergraduates   **G–Graduate Students**   **P–Professionals/Postdoctorates**

U–Undergraduates **G–Graduate Students** **P–Professionals/Postdoctorates**

U–Undergraduates G–Graduate Students P–Professionals/Postdoctorates

U–Undergraduates   **G–Graduate Students**   **P–Professionals/Postdoctorates**

Sponsoring Organization Index

The Sponsoring Organization Index makes it easy to identify agencies that offer financial aid to African Americans. In this index, the sponsoring organizations are listed alphabetically, word by word. In addition, we've used an alphabetical code (within parentheses) to help you identify the intended recipients of the funding offered by the organizations: U = Undergraduates; G = Graduate Students; P = Professionals/Postdoctorates. For example, if the name of a sponsoring organization is followed by (U) 241, a program sponsored by that organization is described in the Undergraduate chapter, in entry 241. If that sponsoring organization's name is followed by another entry number—for example, (P) 1101—the same or a different program sponsored by that organization is described in the Professionals/Postdoctorates chapter, in entry 1101. Remember: the numbers cited here refer to program entry numbers, not to page numbers in the book.

A

ABC National Television Sales, (U) 314, (G) 942

Academic Library Association of Ohio, (G) 705

Academy of Applied Science, (U) 550

Academy of Criminal Justice Sciences, (P) 1270

Academy of Nutrition and Dietetics, (U) 5, 154, 184, (G) 706, 814, 833, (P) 1225, 1267

Accountancy Board of Ohio, (U) 8

Accounting and Financial Women's Alliance, (U) 373

Acoustical Society of America, (G) 712

Act Six, (U) 9

Actuarial Foundation, (U) 10

Acxiom Corporation, (U) 11, (G) 713

Advanced Laboratory Physics Association, (U) 3

African American Network-Carolinas, (U) 16

African Heritage Caucus, (U) 17, (G) 720

African Methodist Episcopal Church, (U) 40, 93, 247, 275, 330, 332, 344, 362, 413, 461, 545, 590, 684, (G) 957

African-American/Caribbean Education Association, Inc., (U) 292, 430, 682

AIGA, the professional association for design, (U) 694, (G) 1216

Airport Minority Advisory Council, (U) 39, 76

Alabama Society of Certified Public Accountants, (U) 64

Alcon Foundation, (G) 730-732

Alfred P. Sloan Foundation, (G) 829, (P) 1233, 1266

Allan R. Bloomfield, (G) 733

Allina Health System, (U) 226

Allstate Insurance Company, (U) 310, (G) 939

Alpha Kappa Alpha Sorority, Inc., (U) 29, 33-34, 55, 77, 135, 348, 358, 364, 405, 451, 571, 604, 700-702, (G) 736-737, 847, 986, 1136

Alpha Kappa Alpha Sorority, Inc. Rho Mu Omega Chapter, (U) 53, 554-556

Alpha Kappa Alpha Sorority, Inc. Theta Omega Omega Chapter, (U) 318

Alpha Kappa Alpha Sorority, Inc. Xi Psi Omega Chapter, (U) 699

Alpha Kappa Delta, (G) 769

Alpha Phi Alpha Fraternity, Inc. Xi Alpha Lambda Chapter, (U) 312

Altria Group, (U) 36

Alzheimer's Association, (P) 1235-1237, 1375

American Academy of Audiology Foundation, (G) 1143

American Academy of Child and Adolescent Psychiatry, (G) 959

American Academy of Physician Assistants, (U) 519, (G) 1101

American Advertising Federation. Louisville, (U) 2

American Airlines, (U) 42

American Anthropological Association, (G) 741

American Association for Justice, (G) 1129

American Association for Respiratory Care, (U) 336

American Association of Advertising Agencies, (U) 51, 90, 185, 515, (G) 785, 1097

American Association of Blacks in Energy, (U) 43

American Association of Blacks in Energy. Atlanta Chapter, (U) 72, 558

American Association of Blacks in Energy. Baltimore Chapter, (U) 81

American Association of Blacks in Energy. Birmingham Chapter, (U) 92

American Association of Blacks in Energy. Connecticut Chapter, (U) 160

American Association of Blacks in Energy. Denver Area Chapter, (U) 144

American Association of Blacks in Energy. East Tennessee Chapter, (U) 208, 687

American Association of Blacks in Energy. Florida Chapter, (U) 240

American Association of Blacks in Energy. Houston Chapter, (U) 294

American Association of Blacks in Energy. Indiana Chapter, (U) 304

U–Undergraduates   **G–Graduate Students**   **P–Professionals/Postdoctorates**

American Society for Pharmacology and Experimental Therapeutics, (U) 619

American Society of Civil Engineers. Maine Section, (U) 399

American Society of Clinical Oncology, (G) 770

American Society of Criminology, (G) 1138

American Society of Hematology, (G) 752, 1042, (P) 1250

American Society of Human Genetics, (G) 1024

American Society of Landscape Architects, (U) 65

American Society of Radiologic Technologists, (U) 573

American Society of Safety Engineers, (U) 66, 96, 650, (G) 773

American Sociological Association. Minority Affairs Program, (G) 769

American Speech-Language-Hearing Foundation, (G) 753

American Theological Library Association, (G) 754, 1150

American Water Works Association, (G) 825, 924

American Water Works Association. Intermountain Section, (U) 309, (G) 938

American Welding Society, (U) 341

American Welding Society. Fox Valley Section, (U) 79

American Welding Society. Tidewater Section, (U) 80

Amgen Foundation, (U) 48, 111, 153, 278, 446, 606, 646-648, 671

Amgen Inc., (G) 1042, 1099

Andrew W. Mellon Foundation, (U) 419, (G) 1115-1116, (P) 1336-1337, 1345, 1350

Anheuser-Busch Companies, Inc., (U) 91

Anthem Blue Cross Blue Shield of Wisconsin, (U) 57, (G) 759

Apple Inc., (U) 58

Appraisal Institute, (U) 27

ArcelorMittal, (U) 60

Archaeological Institute of America, (U) 331, (G) 956

Archival Education and Research Institute, (U) 219, (G) 868

Argonne National Laboratory, (G) 758

Arizona Community Foundation, (U) 323, (G) 950

Arkansas Department of Higher Education, (U) 397

Armed Forces Communications and Electronics Association, (G) 1124

Art Institute of Chicago, (U) 419

ArtTable Inc., (U) 63, (G) 768, (P) 1249

Asian American Journalists Association. Seattle Chapter, (U) 501

Asian & Pacific Islander American Scholarship Fund, (U) 253

ASME International, (G) 771

Associated Food and Petroleum Dealers, (U) 67

Associates Foundation, (U) 337, (G) 962

Association for Computing Machinery, (U) 533, (G) 710

Association for Computing Machinery. Special Interest Group on High Performance Computing, (G) 711

Association for Education in Journalism and Mass Communication, (G) 1001

Association for Public Policy Analysis and Management, (G) 1118

Association for the Study of African American Life and History, (P) 1367

Association for Women Geoscientists, (U) 68

Association for Women Geoscientists. Potomac Chapter, (U) 681, (G) 1213

Association for Women in Science. Seattle Chapter, (U) 588

Association of American Medical Colleges, (G) 921

Association of American Veterinary Medical Colleges, (G) 1103, 1221, (P) 1330

Association of Black Cardiologists, Inc., (G) 851, (P) 1224, 1273, 1275

Association of Black Sociologists, (G) 769

Association of Black Women Attorneys, Inc., (G) 1141

Association of Black Women Lawyers of New Jersey, Inc., (G) 774

Association of Corporate Counsel. Greater Philadelphia Chapter, (G) 707

Association of Corporate Counsel. National Capital Region, (G) 708

Association of Independent Colleges and Universities of Pennsylvania, (U) 425

Association of National Advertisers, (U) 51

Association of Nurses in AIDS Care, (U) 52, (P) 1245

Association of Professional Schools of International Affairs, (G) 1118

Association of Research Libraries, (G) 765-767

Association of University Programs in Health Administration, (G) 820

AstraZeneca Pharmaceuticals, L.P., (P) 1260

Atkins North America, Inc., (U) 69-71, (G) 775

Atlanta Jamaican Association, (U) 74

Atlanta Tribune: The Magazine, (U) 261, (G) 899

Auxiliary to the National Medical Association, (U) 374, 511, (G) 735, 960

B

Back Bay Staffing Group, (U) 493

Baptist Communicators Association, (U) 28

Baptist General Convention of Texas, (U) 409

Bayer Corporation, (U) 83

BECA, Incorporated, (U) 211

Bechtel Group Foundation, (U) 87

Berggruen Institute, (P) 1259

Bill and Melinda Gates Foundation, (U) 253, (G) 716

Billy Rose Foundation, (U) 460, (G) 1052, (P) 1323

Black Data Processing Associates, (U) 84-85, 98, 196, 216, 448

Black Entertainment and Sports Lawyers Association, (G) 782-783, 946, 1011

Black Journalists Association of Seattle, (U) 501

Black Nurses' Association, Inc. Miami Chapter, (U) 423-424, (G) 1030

Black Nurses' Association of Greater Washington, D.C. Area, Inc., (U) 94, 198, 238, 401, (G) 880, (P) 1287

Black United Fund of Oregon, (U) 567

Black Women in Sport Foundation, (G) 1010

Black Women Physicians Educational and Research Foundation, (G) 853

Blacks in Government, (U) 237, (G) 879

Blacks in Government. Department of Health and Human Services/College Park Complex Chapter, (U) 286

Blacks in Government. National Oceanic and Atmospheric Administration Chapter, (U) 82

Bloomberg, (U) 314, (G) 942

BlueCross and BlueShield of Illinois, (U) 98

BlueCross and BlueShield of Montana, (U) 98

BlueCross and BlueShield of New Mexico, (U) 98

BlueCross and BlueShield of Oklahoma, (U) 98

BlueCross and BlueShield of Texas, (U) 98

BlueCross BlueShield of Tennessee, (U) 99

Blues Babe Foundation, (U) 398

BNSF Railway Foundation, (U) 517

Boehringer Ingelheim Pharmaceuticals, Inc., (G) 1099

Boeing Employees Credit Union, (U) 625

Booz Allen Hamilton, (G) 1124

U–Undergraduates **G–Graduate Students** **P–Professionals/Postdoctorates**

U–Undergraduates   **G–Graduate Students**   **P–Professionals/Postdoctorates**

National Dental Association, (G) 843-844, 848, 1112, (P) 1271-1272

National Forum for Black Public Administrators, (U) 132, 139, 167, 251, 333, (G) 804, 810, 821, 889, 958

National Forum for Black Public Administrators. Central Arizona Chapter, (U) 323, (G) 950

National Hook-Up of Black Women, Inc., (U) 194

National Medical Fellowships, Inc., (G) 757, 792, 845-846, 887, 896, 903, 930, 975, 1012, 1068, 1079, 1081-1082, 1084, 1190, 1198, 1206, 1210, (P) 1274

National Merit Scholarship Corporation, (G) 1188, (P) 1359

National Minority Junior Golf Scholarship Association, (U) 91

National Naval Officers Association. Washington, D.C. Chapter, (U) 116, 148, 166, 173, 225, 255, 369-371, 395, 420, 453, 456, 536, 544, 553, 564, 654-655, 665, 668, 677

National Newspaper Publishers Association, (P) 1223

National Optometric Association, (G) 730-732, 800, 852, 927, 967, 1071, 1085, 1199, 1203-1204

National Organization of Black County Officials, (U) 276

National Organization of Black Law Enforcement Executives, (U) 88, 133, 313

National Organization of Professional Black Natural Resources Conservation Service Employees, (U) 455

National Physical Science Consortium, (G) 1069

National Press Club, (U) 479

National Science Foundation, (U) 97, 108, 124, 130, 150, 163, 186, 189, 388, 411, 551-552, 581, 598, 617, 648, 692-693, (G) 743, 772, (P) 1239, 1327, 1352, 1372

National Science Foundation. Directorate for Education and Human Resources, (G) 909

National Society of Black Engineers, (U) 136, 233, 502

National Society of Black Engineers. Region 3, (U) 547

National Society of Professional Engineers, (U) 414

National Sorority of Phi Delta Kappa, Inc., (U) 480

National Sorority of Phi Delta Kappa, Inc. Delta Beta Chapter, (U) 120

National Strength and Conditioning Association, (U) 503, (G) 1089

National Student Nurses' Association, (U) 102, (G) 787

National Vision, Inc., (G) 1071

National Weather Association, (U) 172, (G) 827

National Women's Studies Association, (P) 1293

Native American Journalists Association. Seattle Chapter, (U) 501

NBCUniversal, (U) 314, (G) 942

Nellie Stone Johnson Scholarship Program, (U) 485, (G) 1080

Nelson-Atkins Museum of Art, (U) 419

New England Regional Black Nurses Association, Inc., (U) 243, 335, 408, 416, (G) 859, 1021, (P) 1304, 1318

New Jersey Commission on Cancer Research, (U) 552

New Jersey Historical Commission, (P) 1320

New Jersey Hospital Association, (U) 282, (G) 919

New Jersey Society of Certified Public Accountants, (U) 26, (G) 728

New Jersey Space Grant Consortium, (U) 552

New Jersey State Nurses Association, (U) 622

New Jersey Utilities Association, (U) 491

The New York Bar Foundation, (G) 813, 838

New York Black Librarians Caucus, Inc., (G) 841

New York City Department of Cultural Affairs, (P) 1350

New York Community Trust, (G) 1081-1082, 1197

New York Life Insurance Company, (U) 141, 310, (G) 939

New York Public Library. Schomburg Center for Research in Black Culture, (P) 1345

New York State Association for College Admission Counseling, (U) 504

New York State Bar Association. Commercial and Federal Litigation Section, (G) 813

New York State Bar Association. Environmental Law Section, (G) 1041

New York State Bar Association. Health Law Section, (G) 838

New York State Council on the Arts, (P) 1350

New York Women in Communications, Inc., (U) 311

Newseum Institute, (U) 137, (G) 809, (P) 1261

NFL Charities, (U) 525, (G) 1105

Nielsen Company, (U) 314, (G) 942

Nokia Bell Laboratories, (U) 492

North Carolina Association of Certified Public Accountants, (U) 495

North Carolina Association of Educators, Inc., (U) 201

North Carolina Foundation for Public School Children, (U) 201

North Carolina High School Athletic Association, (U) 683

Northeast Human Resources Association, (U) 493, 537

Northeastern Oklahoma Black Lawyers Association, (G) 755

Northwest Farm Credit Services, (U) 500

Northwest Journalists of Color, (U) 501

NorthWest Research Associates, (U) 551

Nurses Educational Funds, Inc., (G) 871, 1009, (P) 1285, 1314

NW Natural, (U) 517

O

Oak Ridge Institute for Science and Education, (U) 428, (G) 1034, (P) 1319

Ohio Association for College Admission Counseling, (U) 134

Ohio Association of Civil Trial Attorneys, (G) 1090

Ohio High School Athletic Association, (U) 505

Ohio Newspaper Association, (U) 506

Ohio Nurses Association, (U) 507

Ohio Society of CPAs, (U) 508, (G) 1091

Ohio State University. Byrd Polar and Climate Research Center, (P) 1253

Oklahoma Association of Minorities in Career and Technology Education, (U) 549

Oklahoma CareerTech Foundation, (U) 509, 549, (G) 1092, (P) 1328

Omaha Presbyterian Seminary Foundation, (G) 1013

Omega Psi Phi Fraternity, (U) 284, 512-514, 568, (G) 902, 913, 1094-1096, 1202

Omohundro Institute of Early American History and Culture, (P) 1329

Online Computer Library Center, (G) 1000

Oracle Corporation, (U) 85

Oregon Alliance of Independent Colleges and Universities, (U) 517

Oregon Community Foundation, (U) 325, 368, (G) 952, 995, (P) 1310

Oregon State Bar, (G) 709, 1098, 1117, 1137

Oregon Student Access Commission, (U) 325, 368, (G) 952, 995, (P) 1310

Organic Syntheses, Inc., (G) 1099

Organization of American Historians, (G) 929, (P) 1265, 1303

Organization of Black Aerospace Professionals, Inc., (U) 42, 101, 117, 204, 587, 639-640, 642-644, 651, 686, (P) 1360

Orthopaedic Research and Education Foundation, (G) 1024

U–Undergraduates **G–Graduate Students** **P–Professionals/Postdoctorates**

U–Undergraduates   **G–Graduate Students**   **P–Professionals/Postdoctorates**

Residency Index

Some programs listed in this book are set aside for African Americans who are residents of a particular state or region. Others are open to applicants wherever they may live. The Residency Index will help you pinpoint programs available in your area as well as programs that have no residency restrictions at all (these are listed under the term "United States"). To use this index, look up the geographic areas that apply to you (always check the listings under "United States"), jot down the entry numbers listed for the educational level that applies to you (Undergraduates, Graduate Students, or Professionals/Postdoctorates), and use those numbers to find the program descriptions in the directory. To help you in your search, we've provided some "see" and "see also" references in the index entries. Remember: the numbers cited here refer to program entry numbers, not to page numbers in the book.

A

Alabama: **Undergraduates,** 92, 228, 604. *See also* United States

Alaska: **Undergraduates,** 93, 247, 699. *See also* United States

Alexandria, Virginia: **Undergraduates,** 286. *See also* Virginia

Anne Arundel County, Maryland: **Undergraduates,** 94, 198, 238, 401; **Graduate Students,** 880; **Professionals/ Postdoctorates,** 1287. *See also* Maryland

Arizona: **Undergraduates,** 62, 93, 247, 291. *See also* United States

Arkansas: **Undergraduates,** 61, 296, 334; **Graduate Students,** 764, 1013. *See also* United States

Arlington County, Virginia: **Undergraduates,** 286. *See also* Virginia

B

Baltimore, Maryland: **Professionals/Postdoctorates,** 1262. *See also* Maryland

Berks County, Pennsylvania: **Undergraduates,** 530; **Graduate Students,** 1106. *See also* Pennsylvania

Bucks County, Pennsylvania: **Undergraduates,** 528, 530; **Graduate Students,** 1106. *See also* Pennsylvania

Burnett County, Wisconsin: **Undergraduates,** 226. *See also* Wisconsin

C

California: **Undergraduates,** 62, 93, 109-110, 114-115, 138, 142, 146, 247, 270, 291, 327, 334, 372, 383, 403, 576, 607; **Graduate Students,** 793-794, 811, 907, 954, 996, 1004, 1016, 1140; **Professionals/Postdoctorates,** 1316. *See also* United States

California, central: **Graduate Students,** 1003. *See also* California

California, southern: **Graduate Students,** 815, 1003, 1120. *See also* California

Calvert County, Maryland: **Undergraduates,** 94, 198, 238, 401; **Graduate Students,** 880; **Professionals/Postdoctorates,** 1287. *See also* Maryland

Campbellsville, Kentucky. *See* Kentucky

Charles County, Maryland: **Undergraduates,** 94, 198, 238, 286, 401; **Graduate Students,** 880; **Professionals/ Postdoctorates,** 1287. *See also* Maryland

Chester County, Pennsylvania: **Undergraduates,** 528, 530; **Graduate Students,** 1106. *See also* Pennsylvania

Clark County, Indiana: **Undergraduates,** 2. *See also* Indiana

Colorado: **Undergraduates,** 93, 104, 107, 129, 144, 152, 157, 213, 247, 352, 578; **Graduate Students,** 788, 861, 987, 1013; **Professionals/Postdoctorates,** 1252. *See also* United States

Connecticut: **Undergraduates,** 32, 160-161, 234, 265, 311, 538, 675-676, 700; **Graduate Students,** 854, 877, 1207. *See also* New England states; Northeastern states; United States

D

Delaware: **Undergraduates,** 142, 175, 394, 528-530, 700; **Graduate Students,** 830, 1013, 1106. *See also* Northeastern states; Southeastern states; United States

Delaware County, Pennsylvania: **Undergraduates,** 528, 530; **Graduate Students,** 1106. *See also* Pennsylvania

District of Columbia. *See* Washington, D.C.

F

Fairfax County, Virginia: **Undergraduates,** 286. *See also* Virginia

Fairfax, Virginia: **Undergraduates,** 286. *See also* Virginia

Falls Church, Virginia: **Undergraduates,** 286. *See also* Virginia

Florida: **Undergraduates,** 142, 145, 228, 240, 291, 329, 358, 410, 423-424, 441, 590, 684; **Graduate Students,** 884, 1030. *See also* Southeastern states; United States

Floyd County, Indiana: **Undergraduates,** 2. *See also* Indiana

G

Georgia: **Undergraduates,** 72, 142, 228, 262, 264, 358, 465, 558; **Graduate Students,** 901, 1054. *See also* Southeastern states; United States

Tenability Index

Some programs listed in this book can be used only in specific cities, counties, states, or regions. Others may be used anywhere in the United States (or even abroad). The Tenability Index will help you locate funding that is restricted to a specific area as well as funding that has no tenability restrictions (these are listed under the term "United States"). To use this index, look up the geographic areas where you'd like to go (always check the listings under "United States"), jot down the entry numbers listed for the recipient group that represents you (Undergraduates, Graduate Students, Professionals/Postdoctorates), and use those numbers to find the program descriptions in the directory. To help you in your search, we've provided some "see" and "see also" references in the index entries. Remember: the numbers cited here refer to program entry numbers, not to page numbers in the book.

Y

Subject Index

There are hundreds of specific subject fields covered in this directory. Use the Subject Index to identify this focus, as well as the recipient level supported (Undergraduates, Graduate Students, or Professionals/Postdoctorates) by the available funding programs. To help you pinpoint your search, we've included many "see" and "see also" references. Since a large number of programs are not restricted by subject, be sure to check the references listed under the "General programs" heading in the subject index (in addition to the specific terms that directly relate to your interest areas); hundreds of funding opportunities are listed there that can be used to support activities in any subject area—although the programs may be restricted in other ways. Remember: the numbers cited in this index refer to program entry numbers, not to page numbers in the book.

A

Academic librarianship. *See* Libraries and librarianship, academic

Accounting: **Undergraduates,** 8, 16, 26, 36, 39, 64, 73, 76, 145, 164, 168, 213, 240, 272, 283, 308, 326, 329, 373, 379, 421, 433, 452, 457-458, 465-468, 495, 498, 500, 508, 589, 591, 610, 621, 660, 675-676; **Graduate Students,** 727-728, 776-777, 819, 861, 911, 923, 953, 990, 1028, 1038, 1048-1050, 1054-1056, 1091, 1171, 1207. *See also* Finance; General programs

Acoustical engineering. *See* Engineering, acoustical

Acoustics: **Graduate Students,** 712. *See also* General programs; Physics

Acquired Immunodeficiency Syndrome. *See* AIDS

Acting. *See* Performing arts

Actuarial sciences: **Undergraduates,** 10, 310, 412, 462, 621; **Graduate Students,** 939. *See also* General programs; Statistics

Addiction. *See* Alcohol use and abuse; Drug use and abuse

Administration. *See* Business administration; Education, administration; Management; Nurses and nursing, administration; Personnel administration; Public administration

Adolescents: **Graduate Students,** 959. *See also* Child development; General programs

Advertising: **Undergraduates,** 2, 51, 90, 155, 185, 311, 363, 506, 515, 546; **Graduate Students,** 739, 785, 991, 1097, 1126. *See also* Communications; General programs; Marketing; Public relations

Aeronautical engineering. *See* Engineering, aeronautical

Aeronautics: **Graduate Students,** 1060. *See also* Aviation; Engineering, aeronautical; General programs; Physical sciences

Aerospace engineering. *See* Engineering, aerospace

Aerospace sciences. *See* Space sciences

Affirmative action: **Undergraduates,** 305. *See also* Equal opportunity; General programs

African American affairs: **Professionals/Postdoctorates,** 1325. *See also* General programs; Minority affairs

African American studies: **Undergraduates,** 381; **Graduate Students,** 719, 798, 835, 888, 1002, 1111, 1115-1116, 1187; **Professionals/Postdoctorates,** 1229-1231, 1257, 1265, 1276, 1289, 1306, 1320, 1335-1337, 1345, 1367, 1370, 1377. *See also* African American affairs; General programs; Minority studies

African history. *See* History, African

African studies: **Graduate Students,** 798, 888, 1168, 1187; **Professionals/Postdoctorates,** 1257, 1276, 1289, 1345, 1367. *See also* General programs; Humanities

Aged and aging: **Graduate Students,** 723; **Professionals/Postdoctorates,** 1296. *See also* General programs; Social sciences

Agribusiness: **Undergraduates,** 234, 455, 500, 653; **Graduate Students,** 877. *See also* Agriculture and agricultural sciences; Business administration; General programs

Agricultural economics. *See* Economics, agricultural

Agricultural engineering. *See* Engineering, agricultural

Agricultural technology: **Undergraduates,** 653. *See also* Agriculture and agricultural sciences; General programs; Technology

Agriculture and agricultural sciences: **Undergraduates,** 234, 455, 653; **Graduate Students,** 877, 1023. *See also* Biological sciences; General programs

Agrimarketing and sales. *See* Agribusiness

Agronomy: **Undergraduates,** 455, 653. *See also* Agriculture and agricultural sciences; General programs

AIDS: **Undergraduates,** 52, 279; **Graduate Students,** 1025; **Professionals/Postdoctorates,** 1245. *See also* Disabilities; General programs; Immunology; Medical sciences

Air conditioning industry. *See* Cooling industry

Alcohol use and abuse: **Graduate Students,** 875, 1026, 1074; **Professionals/Postdoctorates,** 1351. *See also* Drug use and abuse; General programs; Health and health care

Alzheimer's Disease: **Graduate Students,** 723; **Professionals/Postdoctorates,** 1235-1237, 1375. *See also* Aged and aging; Disabilities; General programs; Medical sciences

American history. *See* History, American

Calendar Index

Since most funding programs have specific deadline dates, some may have already closed by the time you begin to look for money. You can use the Calendar Index to identify which programs are still open. To do that, go to the recipient category (Undergraduates, Graduate Students, or Professionals/ Postdoctorates) that interests you, think about when you'll be able to complete your application forms, go to the appropriate months, jot down the entry numbers listed there, and use those numbers to find the program descriptions in the directory. Keep in mind that the numbers cited here refer to program entry numbers, not to page numbers in the book.

Undergraduates:

January: 6, 15, 30, 37, 48, 102, 108, 113, 120, 134, 149, 153, 155, 164, 188-189, 198, 201, 205, 210, 214, 224, 238, 249-250, 253-254, 260, 278-279, 281, 298, 300, 305, 311, 315, 317, 326, 339, 351, 353, 385, 393, 399, 406, 418, 440, 446, 460, 466-467, 472, 480, 507, 513, 519, 533, 535, 552, 561, 566, 573, 577, 581, 590, 594, 598, 602-603, 606-607, 612, 614, 618, 620-622, 630, 632, 635, 646-648, 661, 671-672, 684, 703

February: 5, 16, 21-22, 31, 41, 44, 46-47, 49-50, 56, 59-61, 63, 65, 79, 83, 95, 97, 111, 116, 121, 124, 127, 130, 140, 144, 148, 158, 163, 166, 169-170, 173, 175, 179-180, 183-184, 186, 191, 194-195, 199, 206, 212, 225, 228, 243, 245, 255-257, 262, 271, 290-291, 296, 316, 318, 320, 324-325, 331, 335, 338, 341, 350, 357, 363, 366, 368-371, 379-380, 382, 388, 395, 403, 408, 411, 414, 416, 419-421, 429, 433, 442, 450, 453, 456-457, 468-469, 473-475, 478-479, 482, 490, 493, 495, 498, 500, 512, 536-537, 539-540, 544-545, 550-551, 553, 563-564, 567, 579, 584, 586, 593, 610, 613, 615-617, 619, 636-637, 654-656, 665-666, 668, 677, 683, 692-693

March: 1, 4, 12, 23, 26, 28, 38, 43, 54, 64, 67, 72, 78, 81, 86, 89, 92, 99, 110, 114-115, 129, 132, 136, 139, 143, 154, 157, 167, 177, 197, 200, 215, 227, 235-237, 240, 242, 248, 251, 259, 267, 272-273, 275, 283, 286, 294, 297, 301, 303-304, 308, 323, 329-330, 332-334, 343-344, 346, 352, 355-356, 376, 402, 412, 417, 426, 444, 447, 458-459, 465, 470-471, 477, 486, 494, 499, 503, 506, 517, 521, 525, 529, 534, 538, 543, 547, 558, 562, 572, 578, 580, 588, 599-600, 628, 638, 657-658, 660, 663, 667, 673, 687, 699

April: 2, 10, 14, 18, 25, 27, 29, 33-34, 36, 40, 45, 53, 55, 57-58, 62, 69-71, 75, 77, 80, 87-88, 94, 118-119, 125-126, 131, 133, 135, 141, 147, 152, 160-161, 165, 171-172, 176, 178, 193, 202-203, 208, 211, 219, 234, 239, 241, 244, 252, 263-264, 266, 274, 284-285, 288, 292, 299, 307, 312-313, 321-322, 337, 345, 348-349, 354, 358, 361, 364, 386, 390-391, 394, 401, 405, 409, 423-425, 427, 430-431, 443, 451-452, 463-464, 484, 488-489, 491, 496-497, 501, 505, 511, 514, 516, 520, 524, 527-528, 531, 546, 548, 554-556, 560, 565, 568-571, 585, 589, 596-597, 604, 626-627, 633-634, 652-653, 659, 662, 669, 674, 679-682, 690, 694-696, 700-701

May: 17, 35, 39, 42, 74, 76, 90-91, 93, 101, 105, 112, 117, 122, 138, 142, 145, 150, 159, 182, 190, 192, 204, 209, 218, 226, 231-233, 246-247, 280, 293, 310, 347, 365, 374-375, 377, 392, 396, 404, 407, 432, 434-435, 445, 461, 483, 485, 504, 509, 532, 541, 549, 559, 574, 587, 609, 629, 639-640, 642-644, 651, 675, 685-686

June: 13, 19, 68, 82, 107, 146, 156, 168, 174, 181, 220, 229-230, 265, 270, 276-277, 282, 328, 336, 359, 378, 400, 413, 437-438, 441, 476, 502, 510, 575, 595, 608, 664, 670

July: 85, 98, 109, 185, 216, 362, 448, 487, 624-625

August: 3, 52, 702

September: 24, 73, 137, 151, 187, 372-373, 454, 530, 623, 641, 678, 698

October: 32, 84, 100, 104, 162, 207, 306, 319, 340, 367, 383, 397-398, 415, 455, 462, 523, 601

November: 7, 9, 20, 66, 96, 213, 261, 295, 309, 314, 327, 381, 384, 422, 436, 492, 508, 542, 582-583, 592, 605, 645, 650, 691, 697

December: 11, 103, 128, 217, 221, 258, 268-269, 289, 387, 389, 428, 439, 518, 522, 557, 576, 591, 611, 631, 676

Any time: 8, 222

Deadline not specified: 51, 106, 123, 196, 223, 287, 302, 342, 360, 410, 449, 481, 515, 526, 649, 688-689

Graduate Students:

January: 707-709, 756, 769-770, 784, 786-787, 799, 805, 807, 813, 817, 819, 825, 857, 862, 864, 869, 871, 880-881, 884, 898, 916, 924, 931, 940, 944-945, 953, 961, 964-965, 970, 977, 979, 984, 1008-1009, 1023-1024, 1036, 1052, 1055-1056, 1059, 1076, 1086, 1093-1094, 1101-1102, 1109-1110, 1127, 1133, 1137, 1142, 1146, 1152-1154, 1156, 1162-1164, 1169, 1175, 1183-1184, 1186, 1193-1194, 1220, 1222

February: 706, 715, 719, 722-723, 734, 740-742, 747, 764, 768, 771, 774, 796, 801, 824, 830, 832-833, 836, 856, 859-860, 873, 895, 901, 910, 922, 935, 941, 943, 951-952, 956, 959, 963, 974, 976, 991, 993, 995, 999-1000, 1016, 1021, 1026, 1028, 1035, 1038, 1044-1045, 1049, 1057, 1062, 1065, 1072, 1078, 1115-1116, 1125, 1138, 1141, 1147, 1155, 1166, 1171-1173, 1178, 1181, 1187, 1191, 1195, 1197, 1208